The Encyclopedia *of* Psychological Trauma

The Encyclopedia *of* Psychological Trauma

Edited

by

Gilbert Reyes
Jon D. Elhai
Julian D. Ford

WILEY

John Wiley & Sons, Inc.

Copyright © 2008 by John Wiley & Sons, Inc. All rights reserved.

Published by John Wiley & Sons, Inc., Hoboken, New Jersey.
Published simultaneously in Canada.

For general information on our other products and services please contact our Customer Care Department within the United States at (800) 762-2974, outside the United States at (317) 572-3993 or fax (317) 572-4002.

Wiley also publishes its books in a variety of electronic formats. Some content that appears in print may not be available in electronic books. For more information about Wiley products, visit our website at www.wiley.com.

Library of Congress Cataloging-in-Publication Data:

The encyclopedia of psychological trauma / edited by Gilbert Reyes, Jon D. Elhai, Julian D. Ford.
    p. ; cm.
  Includes bibliographical references and index.
  ISBN 978-0-470-11006-5 (cloth : alk. paper)
 1. Post-traumatic stress disorder—Encyclopedias. I. Reyes, Gilbert. II. Elhai, Jon D. III. Ford, Julian D., 1951-
  [DNLM: 1. Stress Disorders, Traumatic—Encyclopedias—English. WM 13 E567 2008]
  RC552.P67E53 2008
  616.85'21003—dc22
                                            2008019016

ISBN 978-0-470-11006-5

Printed in the United States of America

10 9 8 7 6 5 4 3 2 1

FOR:

April Howell Reyes

Adrienne Fricker-Elhai

Judith Gay Ford

PREFACE

Psychological trauma is among the most discussed, debated, and researched topics in the history of psychology and psychiatry. More than most topics in the mental health disciplines, psychological trauma and its emotional effects have captured the attention and interest of the mainstream culture and worked their way into daily conversations, the arts, and the news and entertainment media. Psychological trauma has also become an important component of the forensic and legal disciplines and regularly influences criminal and civil court decisions. The emotional toll of psychological trauma is a particularly distressing aspect of the suffering caused by global terrorism, genocide, and war. Psychological trauma also affects millions of people who have survived mass disasters such as hurricanes, cyclones, tsunamis, tornadoes, floods, industrial explosions, and epidemic illnesses, and perhaps tens of millions more people who suffer "private disasters" due to deaths, devastating injuries, or threats to them and their loved ones' lives and safety as a result of life-threatening accidents or illnesses, childhood or elder abuse and neglect, or violence in their families or communities.

From its historical beginnings in psychoanalysis to its adoption by the popular culture, and most recently the production of scientific findings illuminating the genetic and neurobiological aspects of the psychological response to traumatic stress, the investigation of psychological trauma has spawned a plethora of related concepts, terminology, and findings that often are poorly understood even by scientists and professionals working with psychological trauma survivors. Many excellent articles and books have been published that capture important aspects of this topic, but no definitive reference work covering the entire field has ever been published. Thus, an encyclopedic reference on psychological trauma and post-traumatic stress disorder (PTSD) is needed and now is available. The need for such a volume is demonstrated by the rapid growth in the past decade of citations in electronic bibliographic databases (e.g., Medline and PsycInfo), research and clinical journals, and books on psychological trauma and PTSD. Every major health-care, social and behavioral science, medical and neuroscience, education, and human and social service discipline and subspecialty now includes psychological trauma and PTSD as key topics for researchers, educators and trainees, and clinical practitioners.

Public interest among ordinary people from all walks of life, as well as in government and politics, and the media, business, and even the entertainment industries, also has increased dramatically in the past decade, particularly in the wake of the September 11, 2001, terrorist attacks, the Iraq War, and Hurricane Katrina in the United States, the earthquake in China, and natural cataclysms, human-made disasters, terrorism, and political violence internationally. This public interest has culminated in the growing frequency of popular commercial media articles or stories referring to psychological trauma and PTSD. Thus, authoritative factual information about psychological trauma is urgently needed to inform media reports, fictional representations, public opinion, political and governmental laws and policies, and the educational system for people across the life span, and in scientific and professional efforts to assist trauma survivors.

MEETING THE NEED: CREATION OF AN ENCYCLOPEDIA OF PSYCHOLOGICAL TRAUMA

This *Encyclopedia* presents the best available scientific evidence, clinical practice guidelines, and social policies and initiatives from experts on psychological trauma and PTSD in those fields. The *Encyclopedia* is intended to be a reference for academic researchers, educators, and students, for traumatic stress clinical specialists from a wide range of disciplines (including psychology, psychiatry, social work, nursing, marriage and family therapy, counseling, criminal justice, and human services), as well as for students, scientists, educators, professionals, administrators, consultants, and informed consumers concerned with issues related to psychological trauma and traumatic stress. The *Encyclopedia* provides entries that describe the most up-to-date evidence about how psychological trauma plays a role in, and can be dealt with, when people are exposed to violence, disaster, war, occupational stress, serious health problems, parenting and child development, and social issues such as racial, cultural, and socioeconomic disparities and conflicts.

The *Encyclopedia* was conceived and assembled by the senior editors, but at every step along the way there has been invaluable input from a diverse collection of colleagues who bring a remarkable range of expertise to this final product. At the outset, the senior editors sought the counsel of a distinguished group of associate editors who formed the editorial board for this *Encyclopedia*. The associate editors who compose this board are internationally recognized experts in 10 broad domains of knowledge regarding psychological trauma: *Adjustment and Sequelae, Adult Interventions and Services, Assessment and Diagnosis, Biological Processes, Cognitive and Emotional Processes, Cultural and International Aspects, Developmental Aspects and Child Interventions, Psychological Trauma as a Discipline, Risk and Resilience Factors,* and *Social and Community Aspects.*

With the guidance of the associate editors, a comprehensive set of topics was selected using the definitive bibliographic reference source in the field of psychological trauma, the Published International Literature on Traumatic Stress (PILOTS) database that has been created and rigorously updated by Frederick Lerner under the auspices of the U.S. Department of Veterans Affairs' National Center for PTSD (www.ncptsd.org). The senior and associate editors identified the leading expert(s) on each topic, and over a 2-year period these experts authored the *Encyclopedia* entries with detailed editorial input on each entry from the senior editors. The authors were charged with providing concise, thorough, scientifically and clinically grounded summaries of their topics, as well as recommended references that readers could peruse for additional background information or more detailed descriptions of scientific findings, historical and cultural developments, clinical practices, or political and policy implications and initiatives. The editors and readers of the *Encyclopedia* share a debt of gratitude to the score of expert authors for their lucid, informative, and interesting coverage of each topic.

OVERVIEW: ANSWERS TO KEY QUESTIONS ABOUT PSYCHOLOGICAL TRAUMA

This *Encyclopedia* is a comprehensive reference source for laypersons, policy makers, and students, as well as researchers, clinicians, educators, administrators, and advocates, who have questions about psychological trauma. The *Encyclopedia* provides concise, cutting edge expert summaries of the scientific, clinical, and sociopolitical knowledge addressing such questions as:

- *The nature of psychological trauma:* What is psychological trauma, how is it defined and studied historically, and how has it been represented in the arts and popular media? How reliable are recollections of traumatic experiences, and can false memories of trauma be implanted? How universal is this concept of psychological trauma given that culture influences the way people come to understand and react to their experiences?

- *The after-effects (i.e., sequelae) of psychological trauma:* How does psychological trauma affect the body, mind, relationships, spirituality, and entire communities and societies? Does psychological trauma cause permanent and irreversible harm to people and societies? Is Gulf War syndrome a valid after-effect of trauma exposure in soldiers? Does dissociative identity disorder represent an after-effect of trauma exposure? Does exposure to trauma predispose the victim to violence, suicide, or medical illness?

- *Posttraumatic stress disorder (PTSD):* How is PTSD defined, assessed, and diagnosed? Why do some people develop PTSD and others do not? Who is at risk and who is likely to be resilient in the wake of psychological trauma? Can it be heritable based on genetics? How and why does gender play a role in PTSD? Is PTSD a mental illness? Can it first develop many years after the traumatic stressor was first experienced? Is PTSD a permanent and chronically deteriorating condition, or is it curable? Can people who are suffering from PTSD have normal healthy relationships, careers, and lives? Are there certain mental disorders or medical illnesses that commonly accompany PTSD?

- *Prevention and treatment of PTSD:* Can PTSD be prevented, and if so, how? How do professionals treat PTSD, with psychological or medication therapies? What treatments are scientifically proven to be effective for PTSD? Do controversial treatments such as debriefing and eye movement desensitization and reprocessing work? What should clients and professionals know to ensure that trauma survivors get the best possible PTSD treatment? When should treatment be provided for PTSD? What happens if treatment is provided too early or delayed too long? Are there treatments that can help trauma survivors with other psychiatric or medical disorders ("comorbidities") that accompany PTSD?

- *Research on psychological trauma and PTSD:* How do scientists study psychological trauma and PTSD, with animals as well as with humans? What features distinguish between strong and weak scientific methodology in research on psychological trauma and PTSD? What are the newest breakthroughs in the scientific study of psychological trauma and PTSD, and what future discoveries are researchers working on in this field? How are treatments for PTSD established as evidence-based practices by research?

- *Professional organizations and training in the field of psychological trauma:* What organizations nationally and internationally represent research, clinical, and educational professionals whose work focuses on psychological trauma and PTSD? What training curricula and codes of practice and ethics are necessary in order to prepare professionals to become experts in psychological trauma research and treatment?

- *Governmental and nongovernmental organizations and policies addressing psychological trauma:* What organizations represent the interests of trauma-affected persons, families, communities, and societies nationally and internationally? What policies and laws address the effects, treatment, and prevention of psychological trauma and PTSD?

- *Cross-cultural aspects of psychological trauma and PTSD:* Does psychological trauma differ in how it occurs and how it affects survivors and their communities depending on the culture and nationality in which they live? Are there both culture-specific and also universal or transcultural forms of PTSD and related traumatic stress and dissociative disorders? How do culture, ethnicity, and socioeconomic status affect the incidence, experience, and aftereffects of psychological trauma and PTSD?

While detailed concise answers to these and many other related questions about psychological trauma can be found among the entries in this *Encyclopedia,* we use this set of eight questions as a framework for providing a brief synopsis to highlight the key issues and facts addressed by this *Encyclopedia*'s entries.

Defining Psychological Trauma

Many definitions have been proposed to characterize psychological trauma (*see:* **Trauma, Definition**). A common feature of past and current definitions of psychological trauma is that it represents events that are emotionally shocking or horrifying, which threaten or actually involve death(s) or a violation of bodily integrity (such as sexual violation or torture) or that render the affected person(s) helpless to prevent or stop the resultant psychological and physical harm. Psychological trauma may involve physical traumas such as severe wounds, injury, illness, or invasive or otherwise painful medical procedures, but most psychologically traumatic events involve only the imminent threat of severe physical trauma, or being an observer or witness to physical traumas experienced by other persons. For example, although war combat is likely to be psychologically traumatic for military personnel or civilian victims, most of these people are never actually severely physically harmed themselves; instead the trauma is psychological in nature because they witness the death or suffering of other persons (and sometimes entire communities), or experience the shock of losing family, friends, or other important persons to tragic deaths, or are threatened with death or horrific devastation to themselves that never actually happen. Thus, it is important to understand that psychological trauma indeed involves a psychological component of terrible or horrifying events, something that occurs independently of the actual physical damage or harm. The psychological experience of trauma is related to the objective nature or impact of traumatic events, but also is an independent unique aspect of trauma beyond the merely physical.

Impact and Aftereffects of Psychological Trauma

To understand the impact that psychological trauma can have on affected persons, communities, organizations, societies, and cultures, it is necessary to learn how people are changed psychologically when they are confronted with death or extreme physical and spiritual violation and suffering, or to an imminent threat to themselves or their loved ones of death or bodily violation. Paradoxically, to understand the psychological impact of trauma, it is important to begin with the biological changes that occur when an individual is faced with the psychological shock of trauma. Research with animals as well as humans has begun to describe the incredibly complex physiological and neurological changes in the brain and body that are produced by traumatic stressors. Relatively automatic shifts occur in how the brain and body respond to stress when survival is threatened or severe bodily violation or pain occurs. These changes in the brain and body's stress reaction system are adaptive in the crisis—that is, they are essential to survive the danger or harm involved in traumatic events. However, these neurobiological changes that occur in response to traumatic stressors may also lead to alterations in the brain's systems for processing perceptions, cognitions (thoughts, beliefs, plans, decisions), and emotions that can fundamentally alter a person's psychological outlook, coping, and adjustment. Traumatic stress-related changes in the brain/body's stress reaction system also can alter the body's systems for protecting against pathogens that may cause illness (the immune system), for providing oxygen to every area of the body (the cardiopulmonary system), and for motivation and the seeking of chemical agents such as drugs (the reward system).

Posttraumatic Stress Disorder (PTSD)

Most people have heard of the term PTSD and know that it represents a serious problem that can occur when a person experiences psychological trauma. However, most people do not know that PTSD is a controversial concept that historically was viewed with suspicion by scientists and professionals, and only accepted as a scientifically valid phenomenon when it was included as a diagnosis in 1980 in the Third Edition of the American Psychiatric Association's

Diagnostic and Statistical Manual for Mental Disorders. Only a fraction—perhaps 15% to 20%—of persons who experience psychological trauma will develop PTSD, and most people who develop PTSD do not receive any specialized treatment but nevertheless recover fully or partially within 6 months. There is no definite way to determine in advance if a person affected by psychological trauma will develop PTSD, but there are both risk and protective factors that, respectively, predispose toward or against developing PTSD. Both women and men, girls and boys, may develop PTSD, but research consistently shows that females are almost twice as likely as males to develop PTSD following psychological trauma. The reason for this gender difference is not firmly established (although it has been vigorously researched; *see:* **Gender; Women and Trauma**). The difference may be due in part to genetic and sex role socialization: females are more likely than males to develop a number of anxiety and depressive disorders. However, gender differences in the risk of exposure to different types of psychological trauma— females more often experience sexual assault and abuse, males more often are subjected to war and physical assault trauma—also may contribute to gender differences in PTSD.

PTSD involves four general types of symptoms that include unwanted memories (or reminders) of past traumatic experiences, attempts to avoid those memories or reminders, a reduction in the ability to feel positive emotions, and an increase in physical tension, sleeplessness, watchfulness for danger, and negative emotions (particularly anger, frustration, and anxiety).

The PTSD symptoms appear to involve changes in the brain and body's stress and mood regulation systems that have been identified in scientific neuroimaging research and that may have a genetic basis. PTSD often also involves serious problems with other forms of anxiety (such as panic or phobias), depression, anger and impulse management, and stress-related medical illness (or somatic complaints that cannot be medically diagnosed). Some forms of psychological trauma, particularly those that occur in childhood and that tend to be harmful to the child's psychological development, and to the

relationships the child depends on for security, have been described as "betrayal trauma" (such as child abuse or neglect or family violence; *see:* **Betrayal Trauma**). Betrayal traumas appear to lead to PTSD more often than do other forms of psychological trauma (in as many as 50% to 75% of affected persons), and may result in complex forms of PTSD (*see:* **Complex Posttraumatic Stress Disorder**).

Prevention and Treatment of PTSD

Psychological trauma is very difficult to prevent, requiring large-scale initiatives aimed at increasing public safety, public health, child care, industrial safety, international relations, and peacekeeping as well as decreasing poverty and sociocultural inequities, epidemic illness, family and community violence, child abuse and neglect, transportation fatalities, terrorism, genocide, war, and climate change. However, none of these vital efforts have, or ever could, completely eradicate psychological trauma. Programs that prepare people to undertake hazardous jobs (such as military personnel, law enforcement or firefighters, emergency medical professionals, disaster responders, journalists who work in dangerous circumstances), or that assist them or survivors of traumatic events immediately afterwards (early interventions such as psychological first aid) may reduce psychological trauma's adverse impact, but have not been conclusively shown to prevent PTSD.

When psychological trauma has initially occurred and stress reactivity problems are temporarily debilitating (which has been designated as acute stress disorder) or persist for 1 month or more (which is the minimum time period required for a diagnosis of PTSD), treatment has been shown to help many affected persons to manage and overcome these symptoms. The treatment approach that has the strongest scientific evidence base for acute stress disorder and for PTSD is cognitive behavior therapy (CBT). There are several different approaches to CBT for adults, and these also have been adapted for children and adolescents. Still other psychotherapy models have been shown to be effective with very young trauma-exposed children and their parents. Medication (pharmacotherapy) has shown evidence of reducing some PTSD symptoms for adults, as well as the potential to help adults, children, and adolescents with some emotional and behavioral problems that are associated with PTSD. With all age groups, psychotherapy models (including psychodynamic, interpersonal, emotion-focused, group, family, and marital/couple approaches to psychotherapy as well as CBT) have shown a greater ability to produce sustained, long-lasting improvement in PTSD than pharmacotherapy. Pharmacotherapy for PTSD may be indicated if critical symptoms or problems (such as depression or suicidality) require immediate reduction, or when psychotherapy does not result in improvement in specific PTSD or related symptoms.

Research on Psychological Trauma and PTSD

Although much has been learned about psychological trauma and PTSD, many questions remain to be answered by research. Whether there are specific genetic combinations or variations and features of the brain's structure or activity that may not only predispose a person to develop PTSD, but also that may influence which forms of treatment will be most effective in preventing or facilitating recovery from PTSD, are questions that PTSD neuroscience and treatment scientists are actively investigating. Researchers also are studying differences in how psychological trauma and PTSD affect people at all ages across the life span, from infancy to older adulthood. Factors that determine who is at risk and who is protected from developing not only PTSD, but also a wide range of psychiatric, behavioral, educational/vocational, interpersonal, and physical health problems that are known to often accompany (i.e., to be comorbid with) PTSD, and how those factors lead to different sequences or trajectories (pathways) of posttraumatic problems (as well as positive adaptations such as resilience or recovery) are another vital research area. To better measure and treat (or prevent) PTSD, research is ongoing to identify the specific psychological factors (emotion, cognition, learning, personality, motivation, integration) that are involved in PTSD's development and maintenance and that could serve as specific targets for PTSD interventions. Also, clinical research is ongoing internationally to develop and test reliable and valid psychological measures (psychometric and psychophysiological) for the assessment of PTSD and associated posttraumatic changes (including the controversial outcome of posttraumatic growth), and to develop and test effectiveness of psychotherapies and medications for the treatment of children and adults with PTSD (including complex forms of PTSD).

Professional Organizations and Training

A number of professional organizations exist nationally and internationally to help professionals, scientists, educators, students, and laypersons who are interested in becoming involved in studying, treating, or teaching about psychological trauma and PTSD, or in getting up-to-date and accurate facts about PTSD research, assessment, or treatment, or in finding a qualified clinical professional for help for themselves or their family due to having experienced psychological trauma or PTSD. These organizations, such as the International Society for Traumatic Stress Studies (www.istss.org), the International Society for the Study of Trauma and Dissociation (www.isstd.org), and the National Child Traumatic Stress Network (www.nctsnet.org), provide information via the Internet, annual conventions, publications, specialized trainings, and special interest groups. Along with the large national and international professional organizations representing the mental health, social and behavioral sciences, and social and human services professions (which have designated Sections, Divisions, Task Forces, Work Groups, and Committees to address psychological trauma and PTSD), these professional organizations have developed practice standards, practice guidelines, and ethical principles to guide clinicians, researchers, and educators in studying and treating psychological trauma and PTSD within the accepted standards for human rights, scientific rigor, and professionalism.

Professional organizations also sponsor thorough scholarly investigations into key social and political issues such as racial, cultural, gender, and age-based disparities in services and scientific knowledge, the controversial question of how to determine the truth or validity of memories of psychological trauma and claims (including for legal/forensic purposes) of PTSD, how to prevent the institutionalization of traumatic practices such as torture or terrorism by ethnic or racial factions or entire governments, and the challenge of delivering evidence-based treatments to vast numbers of people who may benefit from psychosocial intervention, but who have limited or no access to those services.

Governmental and Nongovernmental Organizations and Initiatives

Given the tragic fact that psychological trauma is pervasive worldwide, and particularly prevalent in communities and nations affected by poverty and ethnic strife, governments have increasingly directed attention toward programs designed to prevent or reduce the adverse impact of psychological trauma on high-risk communities and groups. Government sponsored laws, regulations, and initiatives address a variety of forms of psychological trauma including disaster, violence, child maltreatment, and terrorism. Many other organizations operating internationally with nongovernmental funding (such as the Red Cross or Red Crescent, United Nations, World Health Organization, or Interagency Standing Committee) provide humanitarian aid to traumatized communities and societies on a large scale and set standards for governments to use in enhancing the safety, health, and economic and educational opportunities that are known to mitigate against the occurrence of psychological trauma and PTSD and to be vital resources for people, communities, and nations that are recovering from the adverse effects of past or ongoing psychological trauma and both individual PTSD and collective forms of posttraumatic distress. Immigrants from war-torn or violence-infested countries and communities, who are seeking to escape and recover from the effects of their and their families' exposure to psychological trauma, including those who are formally seeking political asylum, face special challenges that often require the resources of nongovernmental humanitarian organizations.

Culture and Psychological Trauma

Unfortunately, psychological trauma occurs in every part of the world and across all cultures. However, the types of traumatic events and the nature of their impact in terms of traumatic stress problems may differ depending on geography, climate, language, nationality, and cultural norms, values, and practices. Life-threatening and personally violating experiences ubiquitously are followed by traumatic stress reactions, but the extent to which people interpret events as dangerous or harmful, and the specific symptoms that result from traumatic stress reactions, may differ substantially based on culture and associated factors such as language and socioeconomic resources. In some cultures, psychological distress tends to be expressed through medical symptoms or communal or spiritual suffering more than as emotional distress. In some cultures and societies, psychological trauma may have more deleterious effects because access to technological knowledge and economic resources is limited, while in others the social bonds that are essential to recovering from psychological trauma and traumatic stress have been weakened by modernity or traditionally have not been highly valued. Approaches to prevention, diagnosis, and treatment of traumatic stress disorders thus may differ profoundly depending upon the culture in which psychological trauma occurs.

CONCLUSION

There are several excellent sourcebooks for information about psychological trauma and PTSD, including several comprehensive handbooks published in the past 10 years. However, none of these books is organized to enable readers to rapidly access information that is presented in a concise manner about specific topics related to psychological trauma. Therefore, the *Encyclopedia of Psychological Trauma* is a unique resource for academic university faculty, librarians, and undergraduate and graduate students, administrators, policy makers and advocates, and practicing clinicians not only within the mental health and social/behavioral sciences but also in medicine, nursing, social work, public health, law, sociology, anthropology, history, political science, the biological sciences, and business.

GUIDE FOR READERS

The *Encyclopedia of Psychological Trauma* is organized alphabetically by topic and the topic labels were chosen based on the most commonly employed terminology among academic and clinical professionals. Some topics are not covered in a distinct entry and are instead covered in the context of a broader topic. In such cases, readers will find only the title for a topic that has no entry of its own, accompanied by an instruction (*See:...*) suggesting attention to one or more other topics that might prove relevant to the reader's interests. Also, because every topic relates to several others, each entry is followed by a list of one or more related topics preceded by the words *See also.* In addition to these *see* and *see also* suggestions, this *Encyclopedia* provides an extensive index of the topics covered across all entries (*see:* **Subject Index**) and an index of authors who contributed entries or who were prominently named in one or more entries (*see:* **Author Index**). Readers are also encouraged to use the references and recommended readings provided at the end of an entry for the purpose of learning more than what was covered in this *Encyclopedia.*

The editors of *The Encyclopedia of Psychological Trauma* invite the feedback and input of readers. Readers who detect errors or who have suggestions for improving the quality of the next edition of *The Encyclopedia of Psychological Trauma* are invited to write to us at ept.reader.feedback@gmail.com. Input from readers will influence our editorial decisions as future editions of this *Encyclopedia* are produced.

ACKNOWLEDGMENTS

The editors gratefully acknowledge the invaluable assistance provided by the Associate Editors who served as the Editorial Board for this *Encyclopedia*. We also appreciate the diligent efforts of Ariel Del Gaizo and Elizabeth Hunziker, the Editorial Assistants who handled much of the communication and organizational tasks necessary for managing the flow of documents and messages among editors and authors. It is difficult to adequately express our debt of gratitude to the contributing authors, who brought to this project the wealth of experience and expertise necessary for producing an authoritative reference work on the complex topic of psychological trauma. At John Wiley & Sons, we were fortunate to work with Executive Editor Patricia Rossi, Editor Isabel Pratt, Editorial Assistant Katie DeChants, and Senior Production Editor Kim A. Nir, all of whom proved to be exceptionally talented, professional, and gracious with their assistance. Finally, the editors wish to acknowledge the groundwork for this volume laid by the international community of scientists, scholars, and practitioners who have developed the field of psychological trauma and traumatic stress over the past several decades. We are particularly grateful to organizations such as the International Society for Traumatic Stress Studies, the International Society for the Study of Trauma and Dissociation, the National Center for Posttraumatic Stress Disorder, and the National Child Traumatic Stress Network, whose leadership in the field of psychological trauma and traumatic stress has benefited thousands of scientists and providers and countless persons who are courageously recovering from psychological trauma.

EDITORIAL BOARD

Nancy Kassam-Adams, PhD
Associate Director for Behavioral Research
Center for Injury Research & Prevention
Children's Hospital of Philadelphia

Effects on Communities
Krzysztof Kaniasty, PhD
Professor of Psychology
Indiana University of Pennsylvania

Fran H. Norris, PhD
Research Professor
Dartmouth Medical School

Psychological Trauma as a Discipline
Christine A. Courtois, PhD
Psychologist in Private Practice
Washington, DC

Risk and Resilience Factors
Brett T. Litz, PhD
Professor
Boston University School of Medicine
National Center for PTSD—Boston

Alexander C. McFarlane, MD
Head of the University of Adelaide Node of
* the Center of Military and Veterans Health*
Professor of Psychiatry
University of Adelaide

ADVISORY BOARD

EDITORIAL ASSISTANTS

CONTRIBUTORS

Jon G. Allen, PhD
Baylor College of Medicine

Rashed A. Al-Sahel, PhD
Kuwait University

Julie A. Alvarez, PhD
Tulane University

Ananda B. Amstadter, PhD
Medical University of South Carolina

Susan L. Andersen, PhD
Harvard Medical School

Majed Ashy, PhD
Harvard Medical School

Gordon J. G. Asmundson, PhD
University of Regina

Deborah Augenbraun, PsyD
University of Connecticut School of Medicine

Seth R. Axelrod, PhD
Yale University School of Medicine

Ellen L. Bassuk, MD
National Center on Family Homelessness

Andrew Baum, PhD
University of Pittsburgh

Chiara Baxt, PhD
Children's Hospital of Philadelphia

Randal Beaton, PhD, EMT
University of Washington

Carolyn Black Becker, PhD
Trinity University

Jean C. Beckham, PhD
Duke University Medical Center

Michele Bedard-Gilligan, MS
University of Washington

David M. Benedek, MD
Uniformed Services University of the Health Sciences

Charles C. Benight, PhD
University of Colorado, Colorado Springs

Quinn M. Biggs, MPH
Uniformed Services University of the Health Sciences

Joyce N. Bittinger, MS
University of Washington

Jessica M. Boarts, MA
Kent State University

George A. Bonanno, PhD
Columbia University

Cameo F. Borntrager, PhD
University of Hawaii, Manoa

H. Stefan Bracha, MD
National Center for Posttraumatic Stress Disorder

Benjamin Bregman, MD
Tel Aviv University

J. Douglas Bremner, MD
Emory University School of Medicine

Chris R. Brewin, PhD
University College

John Briere, PhD
University of Southern California

Richard A. Bryant, PhD
University of New South Wales

Thema Bryant-Davis, PhD
Pepperdine University

Melissa J. Brymer, PhD, PsyD
National Center for Child Traumatic Stress, UCLA

Lisa D. Butler, PhD
Stanford University School of Medicine

Patrick S. Calhoun, PhD
Duke University Medical Center

Etzel Cardeña, PhD
Lund University

Eve B. Carlson, PhD
National Center for Posttraumatic Stress Disorder

Shelley H. Carson, PhD
National Center for Posttraumatic Stress Disorder

Alexander L. Chapman, PhD, RPsych
Simon Fraser University

Michelle Tsang Mui Chung, BA
University of Hawaii

George A. Clum, PhD
Virginia Polytechnic Institute

Sara B. Cohen, BA
University of Pennsylvania School of Medicine

Daniel F. Connor, MD
University of Connecticut School of Medicine

Joan M. Cook, PhD
Yale University School of Medicine

Matthew Cordova, PhD
Pacific Graduate School of Psychology

Christine A. Courtois, PhD
Private Practice, Washington, DC

Mark Creamer, PhD
University of Melbourne

Constance Dalenberg, PhD
Alliant International University

Priscilla Dass-Brailsford, EdD
Lesley University

Joanne L. Davis, PhD
University of Tulsa

Eve H. Davison, PhD
Veterans Affairs Boston Healthcare System

Janet de Merode, PhD
Fielding Graduate University

Eric Dedert, PhD
Durham Veterans Affairs Medical Center

Douglas L. Delahanty, PhD
Kent State University

Rani A. Desai, PhD, MPH
Yale University School of Medicine

Ben Dickstein, MA
National Center for Posttraumatic Stress Disorder

Daniel Dodgen, PhD
U.S. Department of Health and Human Services

Angela Liegey Dougall, PhD
University of Texas

Kent D. Drescher, PhD
National Center for Posttraumatic Stress Disorder

Donald G. Dutton, PhD
University of British Columbia

Mary Ann Dutton, PhD
Georgetown University Medical Center

Marisa Edelberg, MS
Institute of Living

Jon D. Elhai, PhD
University of South Dakota

Cynthia B. Eriksson, PhD
Fuller Theological Seminary

John A. Fairbank, PhD
National Center for Child Traumatic Stress at Duke University

Roger D. Fallot, PhD
Community Connections

Sherry A. Falsetti, PhD
University of Illinois College of Medicine at Rockford

Candice Feiring, PhD
The College of New Jersey

Janina Fisher, PhD
Sensorimotor Psychotherapy Institute

Philip A. Fisher, PhD
Oregon Social Learning Center

Courtney Landau Fleisher, PhD
La Rabida Children's Hospital

Kenneth E. Fletcher, PhD
University of Massachusetts Medical School

Victoria M. Follette, PhD
University of Nevada

Alan Fontana, PhD
Veterans Affairs Northeast Program Evaluation Center

David Forbes, PhD
University of Melbourne

Julian D. Ford, PhD
University of Connecticut School of Medicine

David W. Foy, PhD
Pepperdine University

Lisa A. Fraleigh, DO
University of Connecticut School of Medicine

Paul A. Frewen, PhD
University of Western Ontario

Jennifer J. Freyd, PhD
University of Oregon

Matthew J. Friedman, MD, PhD
National Center for Posttraumatic Stress Disorder

Carol S. Fullerton, PhD
Uniformed Services University of the Health Sciences

Sandro Galea, MD, DRPH
University of Michigan

Robert W. Garlan, PhD
Stanford University School of Medicine

Steven N. Gold, PhD
Nova Southeastern University

Emily Goldmann, MPH
University of Michigan

Julia Golier, MD
*Mount Sinai School of Medicine,
    New York*

Kim L. Gratz, PhD
University of Maryland, College Park

Matt J. Gray, PhD
University of Wyoming

Neil Greenberg, MRC Psych, MD
King's College London

Michelle S. Grennan, MA
Long Island University

Anouk L. Grubaugh, PhD
Medical University of South Carolina

Robin H. Gurwitch, PhD
*University of Oklahoma Health Sciences
    Center*

Brian J. Hall, MA
Kent State University

Susan Hamilton, PhD
Private Practice, Sterling, VA

Kathryn Handwerger, MS
Tufts University

Rochelle F. Hanson, PhD
Medical University of South Carolina

Melanie S. Harned, PhD
University of Washington

Maxine Harris, PhD
Community Connections

Christina M. Hassija, MS
University of Wyoming

Patricia L. Haynes, PhD
University of Arizona

Christine Heim, PhD
Emory University School of Medicine

Julia R. Heiman, PhD
*Kinsey Institute for Research in Sex, Gender
    and Reproduction*

Steph J. Hellawell, PhD
Fleming Nuffield Unit

Elizabeth A. Hembree, PhD
*University of Pennsylvania School of
    Medicine*

Judith L. Herman, MD
Harvard Medical School

Stevan E. Hobfoll, PhD
Kent State University

Hans-Georg Hofer, Dr. Phil.
University of Bonn

Annie Hogh, PhD
*National Research Center for the Working
    Environment*

Mardi Horowitz, MD
*University of California,
    San Francisco*

Grace S. Hubel, BA
Medical University of South Carolina

Amy C. Hudnall, MA
Appalachian State University

Chandra Ghosh Ippen, PhD
*University of California,
    San Francisco*

Anne K. Jacobs, PhD
University of Kansas

Matthew Jakupcak, PhD
Puget Sound Health Care System

James Jaranson, MD, MPH
International Rehabilitation Council for Torture Victims

Jeremy S. Joseph, MS
University of Wyoming

Stephen Joseph, PhD
University of Nottingham

Danny G. Kaloupek, PhD
Veterans Affairs Boston Healthcare System

Jayesh Kamath, MD, PhD
University of Connecticut School of Medicine

Debra Kaminer, PhD
University of Cape Town

Krzysztof Kaniasty, PhD
Indiana University of Pennsylvania

Nancy Kassam-Adams, PhD
Children's Hospital of Philadelphia

Terence M. Keane, PhD
National Center for Posttraumatic Stress Disorder

Kathleen Kendra, MA
National Center for Posttraumatic Stress Disorder

Rachel Kimerling, PhD
National Center for Posttraumatic Stress Disorder

Daniel W. King, PhD
Veterans Affairs Boston Healthcare System

Lynda A. King, PhD
Veterans Affairs Boston Healthcare System

Karestan C. Koenen, PhD
Harvard School of Public Health

Barry Krakow, MD
Sleep and Human Health Institute

Janice L. Krupnick, PhD
Georgetown University School of Medicine

Harold Kudler, MD
Duke University Medical Center

Eric Kuhn, PhD
Veterans Affairs Palo Alto Health Care System

Elisabeth Kunzle, MA
University of Windsor

Jason M. Lang, PhD
University of Connecticut School of Medicine

Ruth A. Lanius, MD, PhD
London Health Sciences Center

Cheryl Lanktree, PhD
Miller Children's Hospital

Nathaniel Laor, MD, PhD
Tel Aviv University

Joseph LeDoux, PhD
New York University

Stacy M. Lenze, BA
Hawaii Pacific University

Jane Leserman, PhD
University of North Carolina

Alicia F. Lieberman, PhD
University of California, San Francisco

Katie M. Lindblom, MS
University of Wyoming

P. Alex Linley, PhD
*Center for Applied Positive
    Psychology*

Brett Litz, PhD
*National Center for Posttraumatic Stress
    Disorder*

Richard J. Loewenstein, MD
Sheppard Pratt Health Systems

Mary E. Long, MS, MA, PhD
Medical University of South Carolina

Chalsa M. Loo, PhD
*National Center for Posttraumatic Stress
    Disorder*

Katelyn P. Mack, BSc
*National Center for Posttraumatic Stress
    Disorder*

Caitlin E. Macy, BA
Hawaii Pacific University

Andreas Maercker, MD, PhD
University of Zurich

Gina Magnea, MD
London Health Sciences Center

Anthony D. Mancini, PhD
Columbia University

Jody Todd Manly, PhD
University of Rochester

James Marinchak, BA
*University of Pennsylvania School of
    Medicine*

John C. Markowitz, MD
*New York State Psychiatric
    Institute*

Anthony Marsella, PhD
University of Hawaii, Manoa

Randall D. Marshall, MD
Columbia University

Christina Maslach, PhD
University of California, Berkeley

James E. McCarroll, PhD, MPH
*Uniformed Services University of the Health
    Sciences*

Alexander C. McFarlane, MD
University of Adelaide

Kelly McKinney, PhD
McGill University

Richard J. McNally, PhD
Harvard University

Lauren B. McSweeney, BA
*National Center for Posttraumatic Stress
    Disorder*

Jessica Meed, MS
U.S. Public Health Service

Michaela Mendelsohn, PhD
Cambridge Health Alliance

Patricia L. Metzger, MS
University of Wyoming

Mark W. Miller, PhD
*National Center for Posttraumatic Stress
    Disorder*

Joshua Moses, MA
City University of New York

Kim T. Mueser, PhD
Dartmouth Medical School

Luma Muhtadie, BSc, BA
Palo Alto Institute for Research and Education

Lisa M. Najavits, PhD
National Center for Posttraumatic Stress Disorder

Carryl P. Navalta, PhD
Harvard Medical School

Charles B. Nemeroff, MD, PhD
Emory University School of Medicine

Yuval Neria, PhD
Columbia University

Elana Newman, PhD
University of Tulsa

Ellert R. S. Nijenhuis, PhD
Mental Health Care Drenthe, Assen, The Netherlands

Michael A. Norman, BS
University of Washington School of Medicine

Fran H. Norris, PhD
National Center for Posttraumatic Stress Disorder

Raymond W. Novaco, PhD
University of California, Irvine

Nicole R. Nugent, PhD
Kent State University

Casey O'Donnell, PsyD
La Salle University

Meaghan O'Donnell, PhD
University of Melbourne

Frank Ochberg, MD
Dart Center for Journalism and Trauma

Lewis A. Opler, MD, PhD
Columbia University College of Physicians and Surgeons

Paige Ouimette, PhD
State University of New York, Upstate Medical University

Sandra C. Paivio, PhD
University of Windsor

Anthony Papa, PhD
National Center for Posttraumatic Stress Disorder

Ruth Pat-Horenczyk, PhD
Hebrew University of Jerusalem

Zoë D. Peterson, PhD
University of Missouri

Nnamdi Pole, PhD
University of Michigan

Stefan Priebe, Dr. MED. HABIL.
University of London

Holly Prigerson, PhD
Harvard Medical School

Annabel Prins, PhD
San Jose State University

Katharine M. Putman, PsyD
Fuller Theological Seminary

Robert S. Pynoos, MD
National Center for Child Traumatic Stress at UCLA

Jose Quiroga, MD
Program for Torture Victims, Los Angeles

Moataz M. Ragheb, MD
Brown University, Alpert Medical School

Anne M. Rakip, EdD
Durham Veterans Affairs Medical Center

Aparna Rao, MA
Fielding Graduate University

Jennifer P. Read, PhD
State University of New York

David J. Ready, PhD
*Emory University School of
Medicine*

Annemarie F. Reardon, PhD
*National Center for Posttraumatic Stress
Disorder*

Phillip Resnick, MD
Case Western Reserve University

Gilbert Reyes, PhD
Fielding Graduate University

Elspeth Cameron Ritchie, MD, MPH
*Uniformed Services University of the Health
Sciences*

Shireen L. Rizv, PhD
New School for Social Research

Patrick J. Ronan, PhD
*University of South Dakota School of
Medicine*

Stanley D. Rosenberg, PhD
Dartmouth Medical School

Robert Rosenheck, MD
*Veterans Affairs Northeast Program
Evaluation Center*

Barbara O. Rothbaum, PhD
*Emory University School
of Medicine*

Allen Rubin, PhD
University of Texas, Austin

Simon Shimshon Rubin, PhD
University of Haifa

Kenneth J. Ruggiero, PhD
Medical University of South Carolina

Josef I. Ruzek, PhD
*National Center for Posttraumatic Stress
Disorder*

Kristalyn Salters-Pedneault, PhD
*National Center for Posttraumatic Stress
Disorder*

Genelle Sawyer, PhD
Medical University of South Carolina

Stephanie Schneider, MS
Children's Hospital of Philadelphia

Paula P. Schnurr, PhD
*National Center for Posttraumatic Stress
Disorder*

M. Tracie Shea, PhD
Brown University

Jessica M. Shelton, BA
University of Hawaii

Heather Shibley, MD
Medical University of South Carolina

Lisa M. Shin, PhD
Tufts University

Regana Cortini Sisson, MD
Medical University of South Carolina

Martina Smit, PhD
University of California, San Francisco

Dana K. Smith, PhD
Oregon Social Learning Center

Sherif Soliman, MD
Case Western Reserve University

Marion F. Solomon, PhD
Life Span Learning Institute

Zahava Solomon, PhD
Tel Aviv University

Kathy Steele, MN, CS
Metropolitan Counseling Services, Atlanta, GA

Maria Steenkamp, MA
Boston University

Murray B. Stein, MD, MPH
University of California, San Diego

Alan M. Steinberg, PhD
National Center for Child Traumatic Stress at UCLA

Bradley C. Stolbach, PhD
La Rabida Children's Hospital

Eun Jung Suh, PhD
Columbia University

Cliff H. Summers, PhD
University of South Dakota School of Medicine

Lynn S. Taska, PhD
The College of New Jersey

Steven Taylor, PhD
University of British Columbia

Martin H. Teicher, MD, PhD
Harvard Medical School

Steven R. Thorp, PhD
Veterans Affairs Healthcare System, San Diego

Shaquita Tillman, MA
Pepperdine University

David F. Tolin, PhD
Institute of Living

Mary Tramontin, PsyD
Bronx Veterans Affairs Medical Center

Elisa Triffleman, MD
Private Practice, Port Washington, NY

Stuart Turner, MD
The Trauma Clinic, London, UK

Sarah E. Ullman, PhD
University of Illinois

Robert J. Ursano, MD
Uniformed Services University of the Health Sciences

Onno van der Hart, PhD
Utrecht University

Patricia Van Horn, PhD
University of California, San Francisco

Mark van Ommeren, PhD
World Health Organization

Edward M. Varra, PhD
Veterans Affairs Puget Sound Health Care System

Jennifer J. Vasterling, PhD
National Center for Posttraumatic Stress Disorder

Eric M. Vernberg, PhD
University of Kansas

Aditi Vijay, EdM
University of Nevada

Vera Vine, BA
National Center for Posttraumatic Stress Disorder

Lynn C. Waelde, PhD
Pacific Graduate School of Psychology

Amy W. Wagner, PhD
Portland Veterans Affairs Medical Center

Eddie Waldrep, BA
University of Colorado, Colorado Springs

Kristen H. Walter, MA
Kent State University

Patricia J. Watson, PhD
*National Center for Posttraumatic Stress
    Disorder*

Frank W. Weathers, PhD
Auburn University

Stevan M. Weine, MD
University of Illinois College of Medicine

Daniel S. Weiss, PhD
University of California, San Francisco

Michael Wessells, PhD
Columbia University

Cathy Spatz Widom, PhD
City University of New York

John P. Wilson, PhD
Cleveland State University

Andrew Winokur, MD, PhD
University of Connecticut School of Medicine

Hadas Wiseman, PhD
University of Haifa

Leo Wolmer, MA
Tel Aviv University

Douglas F. Zatzick, MD
University of Washington School of Medicine

Claudia Zayfert, PhD
*National Center for Posttraumatic Stress
    Disorder*

Mark Zimmerman, MD
Brown University Alpert Medical School

Lori A. Zoellner, PhD
University of Washington

ABUSE, CHILD PHYSICAL

A 1962 article by Kempe and his colleagues (Kempe, Silverman, Steele, Droegemueller, & Silver, 1962) called attention to the clinical condition of child physical abuse in its title "The Battered Child Syndrome" and propelled the problem of child abuse into national attention. In 1974, the first U.S. federal statute (Pub. L. 93-247) was passed outlining the responsibilities of the states to develop standards for defining abuse, to establish mandatory reporting of suspicions of maltreatment, and to identify state agencies responsible for investigating abuse allegations (Child Abuse Prevention and Treatment Act of 1974 [CAPTA]). Most recent statistics from the Administration on Children, Youth, and Families indicate that an estimated 3.6 million children in the United States were investigated and 899,000 determined to be victims of abuse or neglect in 2005 (U.S. Department of Health and Human Services, Administration on Children, Youth, and Families, 2007). Physical child abuse accounted for 16.6% of these cases and almost a quarter (24.1%) of fatalities associated with child maltreatment in 2005.

Definition of Physical Child Abuse

Physical abuse of children is generally defined as an act or acts of commission by a parent, guardian, or caretaker resulting in actual or potential harm or injury. The Federal Child Abuse Prevention and Treatment Act (CAPTA; 42 USCA §5106g), as amended by the Keeping Children and Families Safe Act of 2003, provides a foundation for states by identifying a minimum set of acts or behaviors that define child abuse. CAPTA does not provide definitions for specific types of child abuse. Legal definitions of child physical abuse vary by state, but generally include physical injury (ranging from minor bruises to severe fractures or death) as a result of punching, beating, kicking, biting, shaking, throwing, stabbing, choking, hitting (with a hand, stick, strap, or other object), burning, or otherwise harming a child. Injurious consequences can range from red marks that persist for a matter of hours to bruises, other soft tissue injuries, or fractures. A "child" under this definition generally means a person who is under the age of 18 or who is not an emancipated minor. For research purposes, operational definitions of physical abuse vary, reflecting local statutes, regulations, or policies and/or methodological or theoretical positions of researchers; there is no gold standard against which definitions of physical abuse can be judged.

Short- and Long-Term Consequences

Immediate consequences may involve physical injuries that can have lasting effects on the subsequent development of the child. For example, some forms of physical abuse (e.g., battering) may lead to developmental retardation that, in turn, may affect school performance and behaviors. A child does not need to be struck on the head to sustain brain injuries, since infants may be shaken so forcefully that they suffer intracranial and intraocular bleeding with no signs of external trauma. Furthermore, the emotional and developmental scars that physically abused children receive may persist into adolescence and adulthood.

Physical abuse may affect multiple domains of functioning. Neurological and medical consequences range from minor physical injuries to severe brain damage and even death. Studies with physically abused children have documented significant neuropsychological handicaps, including growth retardation, central nervous system damage, mental retardation, learning and speech disorders, and poor school performance. Deficiencies in reading ability and academic performance have been documented in physically abused children followed up into adolescence and young adulthood. Physically abused children also manifest behavioral and social problems, including reports of being physically assaultive toward peers and aggressive in school settings at young ages and at risk for conduct disorder, school problems, delinquency, crime, and violence in adolescence and young adulthood. Psychologically and emotionally, physical abuse takes a toll on the development of children. Physically abused children are at increased risk for posttraumatic stress disorder (PTSD; Widom, 1999) and major depressive disorder (Widom, DuMont, & Czaja, 2007) as well as self-destructive behaviors (suicide attempts and self-mutilation) and revictimization.

Consequences of Physical Abuse

A variety of theories have been offered to explain consequences associated with childhood physical abuse, although most have focused on the externalizing or aggressive and violent behavioral consequences. From a social learning perspective, physical aggression between family members provides a likely model for the learning of aggressive behavior as well as for the appropriateness of such behavior within the family (Bandura, 1973). Children learn behavior, at least in part, by imitating someone else's behavior, and this modeling of behavior is particularly potent when the model observed is someone of high status (such as a parent).

Bowlby's (1951) attachment theory (*see:* **Attachment**) has also influenced explanations of the developmental outcomes of abused children. The assumption is that infants develop an "internal working model" of the world that functions as a framework for further interaction with the interpersonal environment and involves expectations about the way the world functions. Abusive parenting is thought to lead to the development of an insecure-avoidant child,

likely to interpret neutral or even friendly behavior as hostile, and to show inappropriate aggressive behavior.

Other writers have speculated that physical abuse may alter a child's self-concept, attitudes, or attributional styles, which, in turn, may influence his or her response to later situations. Experiences of childhood physical abuse may lead to physiological changes in the child that, in turn, relate to the development of antisocial and aggressive behaviors. For example, as a result of being beaten continually, or as a result of the severe stress associated with intermittent physical abuse, a child might become "desensitized" to future painful or anxiety-provoking experiences. Such desensitization might result in a diminished physiological response to the needs of others and manifest traits such as callousness, lack of empathy, and lack of remorse or guilt. Relatedly, physical abuse may cause stress that, if occurring during critical periods in development, may alter normal brain chemistry leading to aggressive *or* withdrawn behaviors. Increasingly scholars are conducting research with nonhuman infants (rats or monkeys) using laboratory analogs to assess the effects of physical abuse on development. It is also possible that violent behavior is a genetic predisposition that is passed on from generation to generation (DiLalla & Gottesman, 1991).

Physically abused children may adopt maladaptive styles of coping. For example, characteristics such as a lack of realistic long-term goals, being conniving or manipulative, pathological lying, or glibness or superficial charm might begin as a means of coping with an abusive home environment. They may also withdraw or disengage from activities and relationships as a means of coping with anxiety, shame, or grief. Adaptations or coping styles that may be functional at one point in development (e.g., running away, avoiding an abusive parent, fighting to protect oneself or one's friends or family, using alcohol or drugs, or desensitizing oneself against feelings), may later compromise the person's ability to draw on and respond to the environment in an adaptive and flexible way.

Critical Questions

Important questions remain that challenge investigators and clinicians in the field:

What are the mechanisms whereby physical child abuse leads to short and long-term consequences?

What might account for the fact that not all physically abused children manifest negative consequences and, according to some studies, appear rather resilient?

To what extent does physical child abuse reflect a traumatic experience?

Or to what extent does physical abuse represent the extreme end of a continuum of physical discipline?

How do subcultural differences in normative standards of physical child abuse affect consequences for children?

Given that much research and clinical practice is based on a person's (client's) report of his or her childhood experiences, to what extent does the person's cognitive appraisal of the child's experience or experience with the events influence outcomes?

To what extent does the long-term impact of childhood physical abuse depend on characteristics of the community or practices of the community and justice and social service systems in which the child lived at the time of the abuse?

All of these questions require answers and those answers will inform interventions with parents to prevent child abuse from occurring and direct the treatment of child victims.

REFERENCES

Bandura, A. (1973). *Aggression: A social learning analysis.* Englewood Cliffs, NJ: Prentice-Hall.

Bowlby, J. (1951). *Maternal care and mental health.* Geneva, Switzerland: World Health Organization.

Child Abuse Prevention and Treatment Act of 1974, Pub. L. No. 93-247, § 88, Stat 4, codified as amended by Keeping Children and Families Safe Act of 2003, Pub. L. No. 108-36, § 1(a), 117 Stat 800 (2003).

DiLalla, L. F., & Gottesman, I. I. (1991). Biological and genetic contributors to violence: Widom's untold tale. *Psychological Bulletin, 109,* 125–129.

Kempe, C. H., Silverman, F. N., Steele, B. F., Droegemueller, W., & Silver, H. K. (1962). The battered-child syndrome. *Journal of the American Medical Association, 181,* 17–24.

U.S. Department of Health and Human Services, Administration on Children, Youth, and Families. (2007). *Child maltreatment 2005.* Washington, DC: U.S. Government Printing Office.

Widom, C. S. (1999). Posttraumatic stress disorder in abused and neglected children grown up. *American Journal of Psychiatry, 156,* 1223–1229.

Widom, C. S., DuMont, K. A., & Czaja, S. J. (2007). A prospective investigation of major depression disorder and comorbidity in abused and neglected children grown up. *Archives of General Psychiatry, 64,* 49–56.

RECOMMENDED READINGS

Belsky, J. (1993). Etiology of child maltreatment: A developmental-ecological analysis. *Psychological Bulletin, 114,* 415–434.

Widom, C. S. (2000). Understanding the consequences of child abuse and neglect. In R. M. Reece (Ed.), *Treatment of child abuse* (pp. 339–361). Baltimore: Johns Hopkins University Press.

CATHY SPATZ WIDOM
City University of New York

See also: Abuse, Child Sexual; Child Maltreatment

ABUSE, CHILD SEXUAL

Child sexual abuse (CSA) is a particularly repugnant and pernicious form of child maltreatment and can result in multiple types of psychological and social harm, including psychological trauma. Once considered to be rare, the scope of the problem is now understood to be vast, with global estimates of 150 million girls and 73 million boys under the age of 18 being forced into sexual intercourse or other forms of sexual exploitation (World Health Organization, 2006). Varying degrees of awareness and acknowledgment of CSA and its ramifications in terms of psychological trauma, both within and between nations, have made the assessment of its international public health importance and the response to its clinically pertinent consequences particularly difficult to mobilize and coordinate.

Clinical and Legal Frameworks

Although the task of defining CSA has sometimes proven elusive and controversial, there is reasonable consensus among clinicians and researchers that CSA can be thought of as having two distinct components that may potentially overlap. Those are "(a) forced or coerced sexual behavior imposed on a child, and (b) sexual activity between a child and a much older person, whether or not obvious coercion is involved" (Browne & Finkelhor, 1986, p. 66). A commonly used standard in the United States for defining "much older" is an age difference of 5 or more years, implying that the perpetrator may be an adult or an older child. Types of sexual activity involved can range from exposure and display (e.g., child pornography, lewd exposure by the perpetrator) to various forms of sexualized bodily contact, which might include genital or anal penetration.

Clinicians have found it useful to analyze the phenomenon of sexual abuse within a framework that differentiates the degrees to which sexual actions are abusive. Such a framework identifies differences between the offender to the victim, in terms of three factors: (1) a power differential (i.e., the extent to which the offender controls/or has more power than the victim); (2) a knowledge differential (i.e., the extent to which the offender has a more sophisticated understanding of the act or is developmentally more advanced than the victim); and (3) a gratification differential (i.e., the extent to which the primary purpose is sexual gratification of the offender versus mutual gratification of both persons). The severity of sexual abuse increases as the extent to which the potentially abusive sexual acts involve the offender having greater power, knowledge, and gratification than the victim (Faller, 1993).

In addition to clinical frameworks, an equally relevant but distinguishable and informative perspective is the legal framework for defining CSA that has been developed in some countries. While the age of consent for sexual involvement may vary with and between countries, sexual relations with a child below the age of consent are illegal in the United States and in most of the Western industrialized nations. Most, if not all, nations and cultures set limits on sexual contact with children, though these may not always take the form of clearly defined legal statutes. In the United States, legal principles for determining the legality of sexual activity with children can be found in both civil and criminal law, namely the legal statutes that define the conditions required for child protection or welfare, and the legal statutes that prohibit criminal behavior, respectively. Violation of these laws can result in substantial penalties, depending on the age of child, the level of physical force or harm involved in sexually abusive acts, the relationship between victim and offender, and the type of sexual act (Faller, 1993).

CSA and Psychological Trauma

Psychological trauma by definition represents the overwhelming or flooding of an individual's capacity to cope with the emotions, thoughts, and somatic experiences associated with a event(s) that involve either the threat of death or a violation of the person's bodily integrity (American Psychiatric Association, 2000), can be particularly debilitating during childhood because this is a developmental period in which psychological and physiological defenses are rapidly developing and relatively immature. Given the dynamic and sensitive nature of child development, a combination of intrinsic (e.g., individual child characteristics) and extrinsic (e.g., different types of stressful events; social support) factors influence the extent to which a particular event or circumstance is experienced by the child as psychologically traumatic. The severity of psychological trauma caused by CSA therefore depends on factors such as the power and knowledge differentials described above, but also on other factors including (Cicchetti, 2004):

- Whether the CSA involved a single sexual act or series of sexual acts or encounters
- The child's age (with younger children generally more vulnerable than older children; although this is a matter of degree, and sexual acts or encounters that involve a power, knowledge, and gratification differential almost invariably are considered to be psychologically traumatic for children of all ages)
- The presence of an attachment relationship between the child and the perpetrator (most notably in the case of incest by a parent or primary guardian) that therefore compromises the child's ability to develop a secure sense of attachment and trust in caring relationships (*see*: **Attachment; Betrayal Trauma; Complex Posttraumatic Stress Disorder**)
- The frequency and chronicity (length of time over which they occurred) of the abusive acts, with greater frequency and chronicity usually more traumatic
- The severity of bodily violation

The psychological impact of CSA can include symptoms that are generally associated with posttraumatic stress disorder (PTSD). However, CSA also may lead to a wide range of other behavioral and emotional problems or symptoms that have been described as the result of the "traumagenic dynamics" of CSA. These problems include excessively sexualized behavior, a profound sense of powerlessness and stigma that can cause or exacerbate affective or anxiety disorders, and a sense of betrayal that can compromise the child's ability to develop safe and trusting relationships (Finkelhor, 1990). Some experts contend that CSA is not so much an event as it is a chronic situation, referring to the observation that CSA is often a recurring process subsumed in a familiar relationship with a caregiver or family member or responsible adult (Finkelhor, 1990). Particular to CSA, the notion of *complex*

PTSD (*see*: **Complex Posttraumatic Stress Disorder**) has been put forth to more fully capture the nature of CSA-associated problems of emotional arousal and regulation, somatization (i.e., stress-related breakdowns in bodily health and functioning), changes in perception of self (such as viewing oneself as permanently damaged), changes in relationship patterns (such as avoidance or excessive seeking of intimacy, and extreme degrees of conflict), and a loss of sustaining beliefs or spiritual faith (Herman, 1997).

Various dimensions of psychological trauma associated with CSA have been conceptualized and highlighted over the past 2 decades, beginning with Finkelhor and Browne's traumagenic dynamics model (1985). This model continues to be one of the widely used frameworks for describing the harmful effects of CSA, and has fueled multiple programs of research and clinical applications (Banyard et al., 2001). The model outlines four core dimensions of trauma experienced by the CSA victim, namely (1) traumatic sexualization, (2) betrayal, (3) stigmatization, and (4) powerlessness. *Traumatic sexualization* associated with CSA has been found to impact a child's sexuality either through hypersexual behaviors (i.e., an extremely early age of onset and excessive involvement in sexual behavior) or through avoidance and negative sexual encounters (Meston, Rellini, & Heiman, 2006). *Betrayal* trauma may have a profound traumatic effect because it signifies a breakdown of trust in caretaking relationships and has been shown to be linked to anger and acting out behaviors, and significant difficulties in relationships (*see*: **Betrayal Trauma**). *Stigmatization,* also referred in the literature as "damaged goods syndrome" (Jennings, 2003), is manifested in feelings of guilt and beliefs centered on self-blame or the assumption that other persons would blame the victim for the abuse and for the consequences of disclosure (such as for legal charges being brought against a perpetrator of CSA, or shame and embarrassment experienced by the family, or for the child her- or himself or siblings being taken from the family by child protective services agencies).

These beliefs and feelings related to betrayal and stigma may be expressed or coped with through behaviors that are self-destructive or risk-taking, such as self-mutilation, suicidal attempts, substance abuse, and other provocative behaviors that elicit punishment.

The fourth traumagenic dynamic, namely *powerlessness,* is characterized by feelings of vulnerability and helplessness, balanced against aggressive impulses to gain control of the situation. Feelings of acute helplessness, as a result of the belief that one is powerless to stop powerful other persons from inflicting violation and harm, can lead to avoidant and dissociative behaviors, such as phobias, eating disorders, and revictimization. A sense of powerlessness also can lead the CSA survivor to develop a pervasive desire to control others and to prevail in any event or experience that is perceived as a personal threat or challenge, which can lead to identification with the aggressor (i.e., admiring or attempting to model oneself after the perpetrator of abuse or other supposedly powerful persons), and in some cases to engaging in acts that involve the exploitation of others. Although some perpetrators of CSA have themselves been victims of CSA in their childhoods, most CSA survivors do not ever become perpetrators of CSA. They may however struggle emotionally with thoughts and feelings that involve a wish to be able to turn the tables and be the "powerful" person in control in relationships, which can lead to many conflicts and difficulties in important relationships such as marriage or parenting.

Another approach to examining the relationship between psychological trauma and CSA has been to focus on various aspects of the CSA experience. Examples of these aspects of the abuse include the type of abusive act, circumstances surrounding the abuse, the duration of the abusive pattern, the age of the child when the abuse began (onset) and when it ended (offset), characteristics of the perpetrator (e.g., age, relationship to the victim, the number of perpetrators), and characteristics of the victim (e.g., age while abuse was occurring, gender, education level and intellectual abilities, extent and type of social support during and after the abuse), and to relate these dimensions to various trauma-related outcomes (Manly, Kim, Rogosch, & Cicchetti, 2001). Such models have sought to explain how the characteristics of the abuse, the perpetrator, and the victim together influence the type, magnitude, and persistence or patterns of traumatic stress problems in the time since the abuse began. In general, rather than any one dimension standing out in predicting traumatic impact, research suggests that CSA may best be viewed as a multidimensional construct. Depending on the specific nature of the abuse and the characteristics and relationships of the perpetrator(s) and victim, CSA can have a range of differential effects on the victim's emotional and behavioral functioning and on developmental outcomes such as the child's ability to achieve expectable physical, psychological, educational, and social milestones (*see:* **Adolescence; Child Development**).

Aftereffects of CSA during Childhood

Great strides have been made in our understanding of CSA since the 1970s, when acknowledgment and awareness of the issue in the United States and a few other Western industrialized nations began to fuel research and clinical knowledge in this domain. The first 2 decades largely involved retrospective studies of adults abused as children, culminating in the landmark report of the Adverse Childhood Experiences Study (ACES; Felitti et al., 1998) in which more than 20,000 adults in a U.S. health-care organization were surveyed concerning their stressful and traumatic childhood experiences and their current psychological and medical health. Exposure to adversity in childhood, including CSA, was found to be associated with as much as a 20-fold increase in the risk of serious psychological and medical disorders.

More recent research in the past decade has included prospective longitudinal studies (*see:* **Research Methodology**) of sexually abused children who were surveyed over the course of their childhoods into adolescence and adulthood (Putnam, 2003). These and other recent studies have focused on children at different ages and their ecological contexts, thus enabling a developmental lens to be applied to the issue (Murthi & Espelage, 2005). The recent developmental focus has shed light on the initial or short-term effects in the aftermath of CSA, typically defined as within 2 years of the termination of the abuse. These effects can take the form of internalizing or externalizing problems. Internalizing problems include sleep disturbances, eating disorders, severe anxiety and phobias, depression and suicidality, dissociative disorders, guilt, and shame. Externalizing problems include extreme degrees of, or difficulty in managing, anger, hostility, impulsiveness, risk-taking, and distractibility, which may take the form of oppositional defiant disorder, conduct disorder, substance use disorders, or serious problems with the law, social isolation, educational and work failure, and residential instability and homelessness. CSA is not clearly the cause of these problems, but has been shown to contribute to the person's risk of developing these significant difficulties and the severity of the symptoms or problems.

Research has shown that some sequelae (i.e., aftereffects) of CSA are more prevalent at certain ages than others. Of note, internalizing symptoms are particularly stark for preschoolers, which may be explained in part by the concept of imminent justice, whereby very young children may be particularly likely to view CSA as the negative outcome of their own misbehavior (Quas, Goodman, & Jones, 2003). Other internalizing problems commonly associated with CSA among preschoolers have been anxiety, nightmares, and inappropriate sexual behaviors (Kendall-Tackett, Williams, & Finkelhor, 1993). Although young children who are victims of CSA may show problems with anger, aggression, difficulties with attention and impulsivity, these externalizing problems are particularly likely to occur among school-age children, problems of hyperactivity, regressive behaviors, and learning difficulties often are observed in the wake of CSA (Bromberg & Johnson, 2001). Social stigmatization associated with CSA can result in withdrawal, aggression, and negative self-perceptions. Adolescents who have experienced CSA are at risk for developing PTSD, depression, suicidal or self-injurious behaviors, substance abuse, running away, school problems, and legal problems (Putnam, 2003).

Aftereffects of CSA during Adulthood

For a variety of reasons, including that CSA often goes undetected and undisclosed during childhood, retrospective studies of adults who were abused as children are far more common than prospective studies that begin in childhood. Long-term sequelae of CSA in adulthood include developmental disabilities, depression, alexithymia, PTSD, sexual dysfunction, eating disorders, substance abuse, homelessness, problems in interpersonal relationships, promiscuity, and avoidance of physical intimacy (Kendler et al., 2000; Murthi & Espelage, 2005). In addition, there has been recent interest on the phenomenon of revictimization among adult survivors of CSA (Messman-Moore, Long, & Siegfried, 2000). It has been found that childhood psychological trauma, especially CSA, may make the adult survivor particularly vulnerable for further victimization, setting off traumatic "chain reactions" across the life span (Banyard et al., 2001). Results from empirical studies point to the importance of understanding the interconnectedness between these multiple victimizations in assessing the overall impact of CSA on adult survivors. Thus, when children who have been victimized by sexual abuse encounter other psychological traumas in childhood, adolescence, or adulthood, this revictimization appears to have a "cumulative" adverse effect in terms of making them more likely to experience a wide range of more severe and persistent psychological and medical problems than other persons who experienced no additional psychological trauma beyond CSA or who did not suffer CSA but have experienced other psychological traumas (Ford, Stockton, Kaltman, & Green, 2006) (*see:* **Retraumatization**).

There is no definitive answer to the question of why CSA victims are at risk for further psychological trauma, but the research does not support the idea that CSA victims "cause" or "seek" additional traumatic experiences. Instead, it seems more likely that the adversities that often (but not always) co-occur with CSA, including family problems, social isolation, and living with limited socioeconomic resources, may lead to the increased likelihood of retraumatization rather than any characteristic of the CSA victim per se or of the experience of being victimized by CSA. It should also be noted that, while CSA is associated with an array of psychopathological consequences, a considerable proportion of sexually abused children demonstrate adaptive outcomes as they mature, albeit with potentially different affective-cognitive configurations or psychological adaptations than nonabused children.

Treatment Considerations

While treatment goals vary in accordance with the client's clinical presentation and the treatment modality being employed, there are certain therapeutic goals that are consistently acknowledged as salient to the successful treatment of the aftereffects of CSA. In the immediate aftermath of CSA, short-term goals for the sexually abused child include providing safety and containment within the therapeutic relationship, along with helping the child to distinguish between healthy and destructive coping mechanisms (*see:* **Child Abuse, Cognitive Behavior Therapy**). Another often cited goal is to clearly identify for the victim that the perpetrator is responsible for the sexual abuse, in order to help the child understand that she or he is not to blame and to begin to therapeutically address the "traumagenic" beliefs that may result from CSA (Finkelhor, 1990).

Effectiveness of treatments for children who were victimized by CSA, above and beyond therapist characteristics and competencies, has been shown to hinge on the therapist helping the child to develop a solid grasp of how and why sexual abuse occurred, accompanied by a thorough assessment of the potential mediating or moderating roles played by individual, environmental, and CSA-event related factors (Hetzel-Riggin, Brausch, & Montgomery, 2007). Additionally, the heterogeneity of internalizing and externalizing problems associated with CSA complicate treatment selection and outcome measurement. Controversies surrounding treatment referrals, such as whether it is appropriate to therapeutically treat apparently asymptomatic children, can be partly attributed to the nature of child sexual abuse, which is an experience rather than a syndrome or a disorder, and partly due to a noticeable dearth of CSA studies involving the systematic identification of what constitute clinically significant symptoms, and the empirical validation of treatment methods. Current best practice is to provide thorough ongoing screening or assessment of the asymptomatic child and family's functioning, and education for the child and family about the expectable aftereffects of CSA in a manner that provides them with hope for a positive recovery but awareness of signs of problems that might warrant therapeutic treatment (Ford & Cloitre, in press).

During adulthood, CSA victims may struggle with difficulties in intimate relationships. It has been found that sexually abused adult patients in therapy are several times more likely than nonabused patients to refuse sexual activity at one extreme, or to show promiscuity at the other (Linden & Zehner, 2007). An important therapeutic goal is to help the adult CSA survivor reestablish appropriate interpersonal boundaries, including the clarification and adherence to therapeutic boundaries between the client and the therapist. Another central goal in adult therapy for CSA survivors is for the individual to recognize herself or himself as a survivor (rather than only a victim) of abuse, and to overcome negative and potentially self-destructive behaviors. This is critical given empirical data from meta-analytic studies that adults who have been CSA survivors display a threefold increase in attempted suicidal behavior, citing reasons of despair, guilt, and self-blame (Linden & Zehner, 2007). The presence of other potential long-term sequelae of CSA, such as substance abuse, eating disorders, and revictimization, make it necessary to design treatments and evaluate the efficacy of treatments for adult CSA survivors with careful consideration of the full range of potential problems that may need to be addressed in order to help the individual recover fully.

In addition to formal psychotherapy (and medication therapy for PTSD, depression, and other associated problems; *see:* **Pharmacotherapy, Child**), there are other options that have been used to combat the enduring negative consequences of CSA. Many adult survivors turn to self-help books, manualized programs, and support or educational groups aimed at cultivating self-validating behaviors and healthy coping skills. With the rise of the Internet, virtual communities comprised of adult survivors of sexual abuse have become increasingly popular as they foster the sharing of individual stories while still retaining the anonymity of the individual members. Spiritual healing is yet another manner in which adult survivors have sought to rebuild shattered trust through the power of faith and communal support. No matter what the modality, relief from the negative repercussions of CSA has typically involved a delicate balance between disclosure and expression of the horrific experience(s) with the maintenance of the emotional distance from those troubling memories that is needed in order to reestablish a sense of personal safety, to rebuild trust through positive relationship experiences, and to engage in self-affirming behaviors (Harvey, 1996).

Prevalence, Culture, and Attitudes

In several communities around the world, culture and attitudes have been found to play a key role in the extent to which CSA is understood, acknowledged, and addressed. In the United States during 2005, 9% of the 899,000 substantiated cases of child maltreatment were cases of child sexual abuse. Many researchers have argued that these statistics are subject to underreporting, given that CSA cases are often well-hidden within the family context due to shame, stigmatization, fear of prosecution,

fear of loss of close relationships, and victims' unfounded but common beliefs implicating themselves as having been at least partially responsible for their own abuse. Global estimates of sexual violence against children point to the perpetrator as typically a member of the child's family circle. Similarly, in the United States, a majority of perpetrators in substantiated CSA cases are parents or other relatives. Nevertheless, CSA also may be perpetrated by other trusted adults (e.g., religious leaders, teachers, coaches, members of the extended family) or by strangers.

Accepted cultural practices may serve to increase the risk of CSA in many countries. To uncover these cultural nuances and to more fully comprehend the extent of violence against children, the United Nations recently commissioned an overarching study that involved the participation of 133 governments, several hundred organizations, and the unprecedented and substantive participation of children around the world expressing their views on violence as experienced by them (Pinheiro, 2006). The study found that the absence of legally established minimum ages for sexual consent and marriage practices can expose children to substantial partner violence, while harmful traditional practices such as female genital mutilation, violent initiation rites, and dowry-related violence in many cultures may affect children disproportionately, due to their dependent and powerless status. These practices, even if not considered sexual abuse within specific cultural contexts, are likely to be psychologically traumatic. Thus, while the definition of CSA must take into account not only a scientific/clinical perspective but also the beliefs and practices of specific cultures, the traumatic impact of sexual harm to children is a universal clinically/scientifically documented phenomenon.

Many communities around the world currently find themselves battling with the spiraling societal consequences of denial or inadequate attention to the problem of CSA. Results from a participatory action research project conducted by a leading child service agency in Northern Tanzania found linkages between rampant sexual abuse and primary school dropouts, truancy, and migration to the streets (Mkombozi Center for Street Children, 2006). In the latter study, perpetrators of CSA included older students, parents, and local community members. Further, the study pointed to widespread denial of the issue among government officials, school authorities, and parents. Despite considerable school-based efforts in some regions of the world, cultural sensitivity on the part of the child's family can greatly hinder the appropriate design and effectiveness of psychoeducational services. In a study conducted across seven elementary schools in China, nearly half of all parents surveyed expressed concern that CSA preventive education might result in their children knowing "too much about sex" (Chen, Dunne, & Han, 2007). Moreover, many parents themselves were found to lack knowledge about CSA, especially about the psychological consequences of CSA, the possibility of sexual abuse of boys, and about perpetrator characteristics. Hence, there is considerable variability in CSA knowledge worldwide, due to differing contextual and cultural factors that can substantially influence reporting, prevention, and intervention efforts.

Conclusion

The sexual abuse of children is a well-established risk factor that is associated with a host of psychosocial problems, including symptoms associated with psychological trauma and PTSD. While some children are remarkably resilient to this form of exploitation, most are likely to suffer substantial distress and some will develop clinically significant symptoms of psychiatric disorders. The ways in which children adapt to experiencing sexual abuse in childhood may include interruptions and derailing of normal development that negatively affect their sense of personal identity and their relationships. Because there are culturally diverse perspectives on the sexual roles that are or are not permissible for children and concerning what is acceptable with regard to educating children and families about sexuality and

its place in normal social development, there is also disagreement on what constitutes sexual abuse in distinction to local variations in sexual customs and familial practices. Prevention of sexual abuse is the most ideal form of intervention, but because of the privacy and intimacy of human sexuality, inappropriate and illegal sexual relationships can be readily hidden, especially if those involved in the sexual conduct are motivated to prevent disclosure due to shame, guilt, self-reproach, or the threat of prosecution or violence.

Relief from the enduring negative consequences of sexual abuse can take many forms, including personally resilient adaptation, spiritual forms of healing, self-help groups, and psychotherapy. There are a variety of models for therapeutic treatment of children who have been sexually abused, and the effectiveness of these treatments is greatly influenced by the extent to which due consideration is given to the heterogeneity of the secondary problems associated with CSA as well as the potential mediating and moderating roles played by the unique risk and protective factors associated with a particular child.

Many people who were sexually abused in childhood do not seek treatment until sometime in adulthood, and there are also various approaches to providing therapy for this population. The effectiveness of therapy in adulthood for the aftereffects of CSA may be complicated by the presence of other long-term problems (*see:* **Complex Posttraumatic Stress Disorder**). It is also noteworthy that a considerable number of adult survivors of CSA demonstrate strongly positive psychological adaptations. Thus, it appears that more research is needed to clarify the heterogeneity of presentations, identification of clinically significant symptoms, the effectiveness of various treatment elements and the differential outcomes associated with CSA. What is clear is that without a move toward more widespread public awareness, acknowledgment, and psychoeducation regarding the issue worldwide, CSA will remain a clandestine issue that negatively impacts millions of children worldwide.

REFERENCES

American Psychiatric Association. (2000). *Diagnostic and statistical manual of mental disorders* (4th ed., text rev.). Washington, DC: Author.

Banyard, V., Williams, L., & Siegel, J. (2001). The long-term mental health consequences of child sexual abuse: An exploratory study of the impact of multiple traumas in a sample of women. *Journal of Traumatic Stress, 14,* 697–715.

Bromberg, D., & Johnson, B. (2001). Sexual interest in children, child sexual abuse, and psychological sequelae for children. *Psychology in the Schools, 38,* 343–355.

Browne, A., & Finkelhor, D. (1986). Impact of child sexual abuse: A review of the research. *Psychological Bulletin, 99,* 66–77.

Chen, J., Dunne, M. P., & Han, P. (2007). Prevention of child sexual abuse in China: Knowledge, attitudes, and communication practices of parents of elementary school children. *Child Abuse and Neglect, 31,* 747–755.

Cicchetti, D. (2004). An odyssey of discovery: Lessons learned through three decades of research on child maltreatment. *American Psychologist, 59,* 731–741.

Faller, K. C. (1993). *Child sexual abuse: Intervention and treatment issues.* McLean, VA: U.S. Department of Health and Human Services, Circle Solutions.

Felitti, V., Anda, R., Nordenberg, D., Williamson, D., Spitz, A., Edwards, V., et al. (1998). Relationship of childhood abuse and household dysfunction to many of the leading causes of death in adults. *American Journal of Preventive Medicine, 14,* 245–258.

Finkelhor, D. (1990). Early and long-term effects of child sexual abuse: An update. *Professional Psychology: Research and Practice, 21,* 325–330.

Finkelhor, D., & Browne, A. (1985). The traumatic impact of child sexual abuse: A conceptualization. *Journal of Orthopsychiatry, 55,* 530–541.

Ford, J. D., & Cloitre, M. (in press). Psychotherapy for children and adolescents with complex traumatic stress disorders: Overview and provisional practice principles. In C. Courtois & J. D. Ford (Eds.), *Complex traumatic stress disorders: An evidence based clinician's guide* (Chapter 2). New York: Guilford Press.

Ford, J. D., Stockton, P., Kaltman, S., & Green, B. L. (2006). Disorders of extreme stress (DESNOS) symptoms are associated with interpersonal trauma exposure in a sample of healthy young women. *Journal of Interpersonal Violence, 21,* 1399–1416.

Harvey, M. (1996). An ecological view of psychological trauma and trauma recovery. *Journal of Traumatic Stress, 9,* 3–23.

Herman, J. (1997). *Trauma and recovery.* New York: Basic Books.

Hetzel-Riggin, M., Brausch, A., & Montgomery, B. (2007). A meta-analytic investigation of therapy modality outcomes for sexually abused children and adolescents: An exploratory study. *Child Abuse and Neglect, 31,* 125–141.

Jennings, L. P. (2003). *Damaged goods: Once molested, then a predator.* Bloomington, IN: Authorhouse.

Kendall-Tackett, K., Williams, L., & Finkelhor, D. (1993). Impact of sexual abuse on children: A review and synthesis of recent empirical studies. *Psychological Bulletin, 113,* 164–180.

Kendler, K., Bulik, C., Silberg, J., Hettema, J., Myers, J. P., & Prescott, C. A. (2000). Childhood sexual abuse and adult psychiatric and substance abused disorders in women. *Archives of General Psychiatry, 57,* 953–959.

Linden, M., & Zehner, A. (2007). The role of childhood sexual abuse (CSA) in adult cognitive behavior therapy. *Behavioral and Cognitive Psychotherapy, 35,* 447–456.

Manly, J. T., Kim, J. E., Rogosch, F. A., & Cicchetti, D. (2001). Dimensions of child maltreatment and children's adjustment: Contributions of developmental timing and subtype. *Development and Psychopathology, 13,* 759–782.

Messman-Moore, T., Long, P., & Siegfried, N. (2000). The revictimization of child sexual abuse survivors: An examination of the adjustment of college women with child sexual abuse, adult sexual assault, and adult physical abuse. *Child Maltreatment, 5,* 18–27.

Meston, C., Rellini, A., & Heiman, J. (2006). Women's history of sexual abuse, their sexuality, and sexual self-schemas. *Journal of Consulting and Clinical Psychology, 74,* 229–236.

Mkombozi Center for Street Children. (2006). *Culture and attitude play a key role in child sexual abuse.* Retrieved December 7, 2007, from www.mkombozi.org/publications/press_release/2006_08_23_press_release_sexual_abuse.pdf.

Murthi, M., & Espelage, D. L. (2005). Childhood sexual abuse, social support, and psychological outcomes: A loss framework. *Child Abuse and Neglect, 29,* 1215–1231.

Pinheiro, P. S. (2006). *United Nations study on violence against children: Report of an independent expert.* New York: United Nations.

Putnam, F. (2003). Ten year research update review: Child sexual abuse. *Journal of the American Academy of Child and Adolescent Psychiatry, 42,* 269–278.

Quas, J., Goodman, G., & Jones, D. (2003). Predictors of attributions of self-blame and internalizing behavior problems in sexually abused children. *Journal of Child Psychology and Psychiatry, 44,* 723–736.

World Health Organization. (2006). *Global estimates of health consequences due to violence against children.* Geneva, Switzerland: Author.

APARNA RAO
Fielding Graduate University

GILBERT REYES
Fielding Graduate University

JULIAN D. FORD
University of Connecticut School of Medicine

See also: **Abuse, Child Physical; Child Maltreatment**

ACCEPTANCE AND COMMITMENT TREATMENTS

See: Meditation

ACCIDENT TRAUMA

See: Motor Vehicle Collisions

ACUTE STRESS DISORDER

Acute stress disorder (ASD) is a relatively recent diagnosis that was introduced in *DSM-IV* in 1994 (American Psychiatric Association, 1994). This diagnosis was introduced to describe posttraumatic stress reactions that occur in the initial month after a traumatic event (for a review, see Bryant & Harvey, 2000). It was also intended to identify people shortly after the trauma who are

likely to subsequently develop chronic posttraumatic stress disorder (PTSD). The disorder is present when a person has a fearful response to experiencing or witnessing a threatening event, displays at least three dissociative symptoms, one reexperiencing symptom, marked avoidance, marked anxiety or increased arousal, has significant distress or impairment, and lasts for at least 2 days and a maximum of 4 weeks, after which time a diagnosis of PTSD may be considered.

Aside from ASD's shorter symptom duration, the major difference between the ASD and PTSD criteria is the former's emphasis on acute dissociation. Specifically, the ASD diagnosis requires that people display at least three of the following dissociative symptoms: (a) a subjective sense of numbing or detachment, (b) reduced awareness of their surroundings, (c) derealization, (d) depersonalization, or (e) dissociative amnesia. This requirement was introduced because of a theoretical model that proposes that acute dissociation results in fragmented memories and affect being encoded at the time of trauma, and that these responses impede subsequent processing of traumatic memories and adaptation of traumatic stress.

Does Acute Stress Disorder Predict Posttraumatic Stress Disorder?

There is overwhelming evidence that whereas the majority of trauma survivors will be distressed in the initial weeks after trauma exposure, the majority of people will adapt in the following 3 to 6 months. This pattern poses a challenge for the ASD diagnosis because it intends to discern between those trauma survivors who are experiencing a transient stress reaction from those who will develop PTSD.

Since the introduction of the ASD diagnosis, there has been a series of prospective studies that have assessed ASD in adults and children in the initial month after trauma, and subsequently assessed participants for PTSD at increased variable time periods after the trauma. A significant proportion of studies indicate that approximately three-quarters of trauma survivors who display ASD subsequently develop PTSD. Although this pattern appears to show promising predictive power of the ASD diagnosis, there is a less encouraging pattern in terms of the people who develop PTSD and who do not initially meet ASD criteria. In terms of people who eventually developed PTSD, approximately half of those met criteria for ASD in the initial month.

This convergence across studies suggests that whereas the majority of people who develop ASD are at high risk for developing subsequent PTSD, there are also many other people who will develop PTSD who do not initially meet ASD criteria. It seems that the major reason for people who are high risk for PTSD not meeting ASD criteria is the requirement that dissociative symptoms be displayed. It is possible that there are multiple pathways for developing PTSD, and that the initial course may not involve dissociative responses.

Treatment of Acute Stress Disorder

The psychological treatment of choice for ASD is cognitive behavior therapy (CBT), and typically comprises psychoeducation, anxiety management, cognitive restructuring, imaginal and *in vivo* exposure, and relapse prevention. Psychoeducation provides information about common symptoms following a traumatic event, legitimizes the trauma reactions, and establishes a rationale for treatment. Anxiety management techniques provide individuals with coping skills to assist them to gain a sense of mastery over their fear, to reduce arousal levels, and to assist the individual when engaging in exposure to the traumatic memories. Anxiety management approaches often include breathing retraining, relaxation skills, and positive self-talk. Prolonged imaginal exposure requires the individual to vividly imagine the trauma for prolonged periods—typically occurring for at least 50 minutes—and is usually supplemented by daily homework exercises. Most exposure treatments supplement imaginal exposure with *in vivo* exposure that involves live graded exposure to the feared trauma-related stimuli (e.g., gradually confronting the feared stimuli associated with the trauma, such as returning to a physical scene similar to where the trauma occurred). Cognitive restructuring, which is based on the premise that maladaptive appraisals underpinning the maintenance of PTSD involves teaching patients to identify and evaluate the evidence for negative automatic thoughts, as well as helping patients to evaluate their beliefs about the trauma, the self, the world, and the future in an evidence-based manner. The duration of CBT for ASD is typically five sessions. There are numerous controlled trials that attest to the efficacy of CBT for treating PTSD, and approximately 80% of people who complete treatment do not develop PTSD.

Future of Acute Stress Disorder

It is likely that ASD will not survive in the publication of *DSM-V*. The diagnosis can be criticized because (a) the primary role of the ASD diagnosis is to predict another diagnosis, (b) distinguishing between two diagnoses that have similar symptoms primarily on the basis of the duration of the symptoms is not justified, and (c) there is insufficient evidence to support its role as a reliable predictor of subsequent PTSD. More accurate prediction of PTSD will come from a broader range of acute reactions, including biological and cognitive responses, rather than a diagnostic category. Despite the limitations of the ASD diagnosis, the introduction of a diagnostic category has stimulated much research and increased our understanding of acute stress reactions. Most importantly, it has raised the possibility of secondary prevention of PTSD by providing early interventions to those who are at high risk for developing PTSD. Through more rigorous prospective study of acute and chronic reactions to trauma, improved formulae can be developed to identify those people who are most likely to need early intervention after trauma.

REFERENCES

American Psychiatric Association. (1994). *Diagnostic and statistical manual of mental disorders* (4th ed.). Washington, DC: Author.

Bryant, R. A., & Harvey, A. G. (2000). *Acute stress disorder: A handbook of theory, assessment, and treatment.* Washington, DC: American Psychological Association.

Harvey, A. G., & Bryant, R. A. (2002). Acute stress disorder: A synthesis and critique. *Psychological Bulletin, 128,* 886–902.

RICHARD A. BRYANT
University of New South Wales

See also: Anxiety Management Training; Cognitive Behavior Therapy, Adult; Early Intervention; Exposure Therapy, Adult; Exposure Therapy, Child; Posttraumatic Stress Disorder

ADJUSTMENT DISORDERS

An adjustment disorder (AdjD) is a maladaptive reaction to identifiable stressors or to changes in life circumstances and is thus similar in some respects to posttraumatic stress disorder (PTSD), which is also a reaction to stressful life experiences. The symptoms of AdjD emerge within 3 months of the stressor's onset, and should not persist for more than an additional 6 months. Symptoms may include a wide variety of impairments in social or occupational functioning, as well as maladaptive extremes of anxiety and depression, and impulse control problems. If the symptoms would also satisfy the diagnostic criteria for another clinical (Axis I) disorder, then the other diagnosis should supersede that of AdjD and AdjD should not be diagnosed. There are various subtypes of AdjD, including types with depressed mood, disturbance of conduct, mixed disturbance of emotions and conduct, and an unspecified subtype.

Diagnosing AdjD has been controversial because it is loosely defined, has inadequate support for its validity, and has been neglected by academic scholars and researchers, with only little attention in psychiatry textbooks and very few empirical studies (Strain & Diefenbacher, 2008). However, the AdjD diagnosis is retained because of its usefulness as a clinical concept. In the general population, roughly 1 out of 200 people (0.5%) would qualify for a diagnosis of AdjD, whereas 12% to 20% of patients in medical settings receive this diagnosis.

Researchers proposed grouping AdjD into the (new) category of "Reactions to Severe Stress" that also includes acute stress disorder, posttraumatic stress disorder, and prolonged grief disorder (Maercker, Einsle, & Kollner, 2007). Based on this categorization, AdjD is a consequence of a stressful life event that differs from a traumatic event by its extent of threat to life or physical integrity. Individual predisposition or vulnerability seem to play an important role in the risk of occurrence and manifestation although systematic research is still lacking.

Primary treatment goals for AdjD are to relieve symptoms and re-achieve a level of adaptation by a broad range of psychological (i.e., crisis intervention) or psychosocial (i.e., workload reduction or restructuring) interventions. Treatments include individual psychotherapy and short-term medication led by best practice standards due to the lack of formal treatment guidelines.

REFERENCES

Maercker, A., Einsle, F., & Kollner, V. (2007). Adjustment disorders as stress response syndromes. *Psychopathology, 40,* 135–146.

Strain, J. J., & Diefenbacher, A. (2008). The adjustment disorders: The conundrums of the diagnoses. *Comprehensive Psychiatry, 49,* 121–130.

ANDREAS MAERCKER
University of Zurich

See also: Acute Stress Disorder; Posttraumatic Stress Disorder

ADOLESCENCE

Adolescence, the age period approximately from 12 to 18 years old, is a time of rapid change and growth biologically, psychologically, and socially for children. Adolescence often is a time of physical and emotional turmoil, yet is also a period in which critical accomplishments that can shape the individual's adult life can either occur or be thwarted, including: personality development, identity consolidation, peer group formation and social role definition, emergence of sexuality in the form of interest and exploratory activities, and consolidation of knowledge, skills, and goals in education, work, and avocational/recreational life pursuits. If psychological trauma has occurred earlier in an adolescent's life and has left the imprint of problems with traumatic stress reactions (such as posttraumatic stress disorder or PTSD, or symptoms of other anxiety disorders, depression, or dissociative conduct, eating, or substance use disorders), the normal adolescent emotional/relational turmoil is greatly amplified and those crucial developmental attainments may be hindered, interrupted, altered, or blocked. If psychological trauma occurs during adolescence, the youth is likely to experience stress reactions that also may interfere with the complicated psychosocial, educational/vocational, and self-identity development tasks of adolescence. Following a brief overview of the biological and psychosocial changes that occur normally in adolescence, this entry describes how psychological trauma impacts adolescents.

Adolescent Biological and Psychosocial Development

Although brain development occurs most intensively and rapidly prenatally and in early childhood, the central nervous system (CNS) continues to grow and reshape itself throughout childhood, with a second peak of growth and reorganization in late childhood and early adolescence (Anderson, 2003). CNS areas grow and change at different rates (Anderson, 2003), with deeper (e.g., brainstem, hippocampus) more posterior (e.g., occipital cortex) structures maturing earliest, and the outer front-most area, the prefrontal portion of the frontal cortex (PFC), peaking in growth in early adolescence (Giedd et al., 1999; Kanemura, Aihara, Aoki, Araki, & Nakazawa, 2003). From childhood into adolescence, areas of the brain cortex that are responsible for sensory and perceptual processes appear to shrink and become more efficient (Sowell, Thompson, Tessner, & Toga, 2001), while the brain cortex areas activated by rewarding experiences (particularly the middle and lower portions of the PFC, the medial

and orbital PFC; May et al., 2004) appear to grow in size and complexity (Giedd et al., 1999; Kanemura et al., 2003). These brain changes are consistent with the shift from early to later childhood away from impulsiveness and self-protectiveness toward ego control or inhibition control (Eisenberg et al., 1995). Specific areas in the medial PFC that are required for such mature self-control include the anterior portion of the cingulate cortex, which appears to monitor potential problems with positive or negative outcomes (e.g., conflict, errors) and to signal the upper and side areas of the PFC (dorsolateral PFC) to become engaged when a discrepancy between intended and actual outcomes requires conscious evaluation and effortful correction of behavior (Eisenberger, Lieberman, & Williams, 2003, p. 291). Neural pathways from the orbital PFC reduce reactivity by inhibiting neural activation in the locus coeruleus, amygdala, and hippocampus. The dorsolateral PFC seems to exert preemptive control (i.e., resulting in reactive responding; Matsumoto, Suzuki, & Tanaka, 2004), while the orbital PFC appears to give rise to self-awareness of meaningful and adaptively useful connections between emotions, goals, and behavioral options.

In these areas of the brain's cortex and limbic system, another transitional period occurs late in preadolescence and early in adolescence, in which neuronal growth and shaping in these areas of the brain accompanied by an increase in the creation of the protective covering for neural connections (the myelin sheath) is put into place rapidly in brain areas that are involved in higher-order symbolic thought and memory (e.g., hippocampus; Benes, Turtle, Khan, & Farol, 1994). This "paving over" of the formerly rudimentary pathways connecting crucial areas within and across the cortical and limbic centers of the brain is consistent with the fact that adolescence is a developmental period that is associated with rigidity and inflexibility (e.g., moral and intellectual egocentrism and entitlement) as well as with psychosocial chaos and fluctuation (e.g., emotional and spiritual questioning and confusion). As these areas of the brain become progressively more complex and reliably interconnected (e.g., the myelination process), the adolescent is increasingly able to not only think in more complex and abstract terms with an expanded base of knowledge, but moreover to think before (re)acting.

Adolescence also tends to involve a shift in relational focus away from bonding and affiliation with family and caregivers and toward peer relationships, which require greater independence of thought and action. Yet, as adolescents acquire increased autonomy, consistent ongoing primary (family) relationships continue to be essential (El-Sheikh, 2001) for sustaining sufficient emotional security to permit the youth to venture into the world of events and ideas and develop increasingly autonomous ways of living. In addition, a stable relational base helps the adolescent to cope with the rapid changes in brain development that occur during this transitional developmental period. With this stability, adolescents are more likely to succeed in coping effectively with the turmoil in their lives, which occurs because "behaviors become unmoored from their entrenched habits, [and] a variety of new forms proliferate for a while" (Lewis, 2005, p. 255). When adolescents are able to successfully handle these transitional challenges, a "subset of these [behavioral patterns] stabilizes, providing new habits for the next stage of development" (p. 256).

Impact of Psychological Trauma on Adolescent Development and Functioning

In adolescence, the aftereffects of psychological traumas experienced earlier in childhood may include problems in the very areas of biopsychosocial functioning that are most crucially and rapidly developing during this transitional period between childhood and adulthood. Adolescents who experienced abuse or domestic violence earlier in childhood are at risk for PTSD and problems with regulating their emotions (e.g., internalizing disorders such as major depressive disorder or dysthymic disorder, agoraphobia/panic or social anxiety disorders, phobias, dissociative disorders) and behavior (e.g., sleep disorders; Noll, Trickett, Susman, & Putnam, 2006); externalizing disorders, such

as oppositional defiant or conduct disorder, attentional or impulse control disorders, or substance use disorders, as well as eating and sexual and gender identity disorders (Cook et al., 2005). Impaired regulation of emotions and behavioral impulses in adolescence may take the form of exacerbated forms of these psychiatric disorders as well as traits that, if continued in adulthood, could constitute personality disorders.

Adolescents who experienced physical abuse before age 5 were more likely to be arrested for violent, nonviolent, and status offenses. Those who had been physically abused also less often graduated from high school and more often were fired from a job, were a teen parent, or had been pregnant or impregnated someone while being unmarried (Lansford et al., 2007). Childhood abuse or domestic violence also is associated with problems among adolescents involved in the juvenile justice system, including truancy, teen pregnancy, gang involvement, and suicidality (Ford, Hartman, Hawke, & Chapman, 2008).

Although neuroimaging studies have not been reported with adolescents who are diagnosed with PTSD (except in mixed samples that include children and adolescents), children with psychiatric disorders or a family history of addiction have been found to have greater difficulties in focusing attention as they traverse adolescence, consistent with findings of reduced volumes of the area in the brain's limbic system that is associated with fear and anxiety, the amygdala (primarily in the brain's right hemisphere; Hill & Shen, 2002). Adolescents who experienced psychological trauma in childhood and were depressed showed less evidence of problems with autobiographical memory ("over general memory retrieval") than depressed adolescents with no reported psychological trauma (Kuyken, Howell, & Dalgleish, 2006). PTSD has a stronger relationship to problems with autobiographical memory in adulthood than exposure to psychological trauma per se, but PTSD was not reported as a potential factor in this study. However, the study's findings suggest that psychological trauma may increase depressed adolescents' focus on self-relevant memories (compared to the reduction in this which occurs among depressed adolescents generally), and therefore treatments that help depressed adolescents restore or develop autobiographical memory capacities may be more readily undertaken if the adolescent has had traumatic past experiences. Whether adolescents who are depressed and have experienced psychological trauma are good candidates for either trauma memory-focused therapies such as trauma-focused cognitive behavior therapy or personal narrative memory reconstruction therapies (e.g., Cloitre et al., 2006), remains to be tested in psychotherapy research with traumatized adolescents.

When psychological trauma occurs during adolescence, the youth is at risk for PTSD and anxiety, mood, and substance use disorders and problems with risky sexual behavior, suicidal thoughts, and aggression that may persist into adulthood or emerge for the first time later in adulthood (Green et al., 2005). Even a single incident of interpersonal psychological trauma (i.e., sexual assault) in adolescence was found to be associated with an increased likelihood of PTSD and risky sexual behavior among college women (Green et al., 2005). Research with adolescents from a wider range of backgrounds, and with boys as well as girls, is needed to document the effects of psychological trauma exposure before and during adolescence on the posttraumatic stress-related problems that adolescents experience as teens and later in their lives as adults. The likelihood that many adolescent trauma survivors underreport their extent of traumatic stress symptoms (e.g., one in six in a study of emergency department-treated adolescents; McCart et al., 2005) must be considered when estimates are made of the prevalence or severity of posttraumatic stress problems among adolescents.

Interventions for Adolescents Who Are Experiencing Posttraumatic Stress Problems

Developmental transitional periods such as adolescence can be an opportune time for therapeutic and prevention interventions precisely because the developing brain and personality are in such flux at those times that any stabilizing or informative inputs may help the youth to gain a clearer and more positive direction for the future. Key protective factors that increase the likelihood of positive developmental outcomes for traumatized youths (Collishaw et al., 2007; Dumont, Widom, & Czaja, 2007) and adaptive function by traumatized adults (Schnurr, Lunney, & Sengupta, 2004) include primarily a strong, caring, and reliable social support system (e.g., responsive caregivers in childhood; mentoring, access to socioeconomic and educational resources and a cohesive peer group and family system in adolescence and adulthood) and secondarily personal attributes that enhance psychological hardiness. Interventions are being developed to enable adolescents and their families and communities to build these psychosocial resources, and have shown promise in clinical research studies (e.g., Cloitre, Cohen, & Koenen, 2006; DeRosa & Pelcovitz, in press). Group therapy for sexually abused girls also has shown promise in clinical research, with interpersonal/emotion-focused models (psychodrama) potentially reducing depression symptom severity and cognitive behavior therapy models potentially reducing PTSD symptom severity (Avinger & Jones, 2006). Adolescents have been shown to benefit from family therapy when they have problems such as aggressive behavior, depression, and substance use problems (Diamond & Josephson, 2005), but only one pilot study has evaluated the effectiveness of family therapy, with promising results in terms of reducing the distress reported by adolescents recovering from cancer and their parents (Kazak et al., 2004).

REFERENCES

Andersen, S. (2003). Trajectories of brain development. *Neuroscience and Biobehavioral Reviews, 27,* 3–18.

Avinger, K., & Jones, R. (2006). Group treatment of sexually abused adolescent girls: A review of outcome studies. *American Journal of Family Therapy, 35,* 315–326.

Benes, F., Turtle, M., Khan, Y., & Farol, P. (1994). Myelination of a key relay zone in the hippocampal formation occurs in the human brain during childhood, adolescence, and adulthood. *Archives of General Psychiatry, 51,* 477–484.

Cloitre, M., Cohen, L., & Koenen, K. (2006). *Treating survivors of childhood abuse: Psychotherapy for the interrupted life.* New York: Guilford Press.

Collishaw, S., Pickles, A., Messer, J., Rutter, M., Shearer, C., & Maughan, B. (2007). Resilience to adult psychopathology following childhood maltreatment: Evidence from a community sample. *Child Abuse and Neglect, 31,* 211–229.

Cook, A., Spinazzola, J., Ford, J. D., Lanktree, C., Blaustein, M., Cloitre, M., et al. (2005). Complex trauma in children and adolescents. *Psychiatric Annals, 35,* 390–398.

DeRosa, R., & Pelcovitz, D. (in press). Group treatment for chronically traumatized adolescents: Igniting SPARCS of change. In D. Brom, R. Pat-Horenczyk, & J. D. Ford (Eds.), *Treating traumatized children: Risk, resilience, and recovery.* London: Routledge.

Diamond, G., & Josephson, A. (2005). Family-based treatment research: A 10-year update. *Journal of the American Academy of Child and Adolescent Psychiatry, 44,* 872–887.

Dumont, K., Widom, C. S., & Czaja, S. (2007). Predictors of resilience in abused and neglected children grown-up. *Child Abuse and Neglect, 31,* 255–274.

Eisenberg, N., Fabes, R. A., Murphy, B., Maszk, P., Smith, M., & Karbon, M. (1995). The role of emotionality and regulation in children's social functioning. *Child Development, 66,* 1360–1384.

Eisenberger, N., Lieberman, M., & Williams, K. (2003). Does rejection hurt? *Science, 302,* 290–292.

El-Sheikh, M. (2001). Parental drinking problems and children's adjustment: Vagal regulation and emotional reactivity as pathways and moderators of risk. *Journal of Abnormal Psychology, 110,* 499–515.

Ford, J. D., Hartman, J. K., Hawke, J., & Chapman, J. (2008). Traumatic victimization, posttraumatic stress disorder, suicidal ideation, and substance abuse risk among juvenile justice-involved youths. *Journal of Child and Adolescent Trauma, I,* 75–92.

Giedd, J., Blumenthal, J., Jeffries, N., Castellanos, F., Liu, H., Zijdenbos, A., et al. (1999). Brain development during childhood and adolescence: A longitudinal MRI study. *Nature Neuroscience, 2*(10) 861–863.

Green, B., Krupnick, J., Stockton, P., Goodman, L., Corcoran, C., & Petty, R. (2005). Effects of adolescent trauma exposure on risky behavior in college women. *Psychiatry, 68,* 363–378.

Hill, S. Y., & Shen, S. (2002). Patterns of visual P3b in association with familial risk and childhood diagnosis. *Biological Psychiatry, 51,* 621–631.

Kanemura, H., Aihara, M., Aoki, S., Araki, T., & Nakazawa, S. (2003). Development of the prefrontal lobe in infants and children. *Brain and Development, 25,* 195–199.

Kazak, A. E., Alderfer, M. A., Streisand, R., Simms, S., Rourke, M. T., Barakat, L. P., et al. (2004). Treatment of posttraumatic stress symptoms in adolescent survivors of childhood cancer and their families. *Journal of Family Psychology, 18,* 493–504.

Kuyken, W., Howell, R., & Dalgleish, T. (2006). Overgeneral autobiographical memory in depressed adolescents with, versus without, a reported history of trauma. *Journal of Abnormal Psychology, 115,* 387–396.

Lansford, J., Miller-Johnson, S., Berlin, L., Dodge, K., Bates, J., & Petit, G. (2007). Early physical abuse and later violent delinquency: A prospective longitudinal study. *Child Maltreatment, 12,* 233–245.

Lewis, M. D. (2005). Self-organizing individual differences in brain development. *Developmental Review, 25,* 252–277.

Matsumoto, K., Suzuki, W., & Tanaka, K. (2003). Neuronal correlates of goal-based motor selection in the prefrontal cortex. *Science, 301,* 229–232.

May, J. C., Delgado, M., Dahl, R., Stenger, A., Ryan, N., Fiez, J., et al. (2004). Event-related magnetic resonance imaging of reward-related brain circuitry in children and adolescents. *Biological Psychiatry, 55,* 359–366.

McCart, M., Davies, W. H., Harris, R., Wincek, J., Calhoun, A., & Melzer-Lange, M. (2005). Assessment of trauma symptoms among adolescent assault victims. *Journal of Adolescent Health, 36*(1), 70.e7–70.e13.

Noll, J., Trickett, P., Susman, E., & Putnam, F. (2006). Sleep disturbances and childhood sexual abuse. *Journal of Pediatric Psychology, 31,* 469–480.

Schnurr, P. P., Lunney, C., & Sengupta, A. (2004). Risk factors for the development versus maintenance of posttraumatic stress disorder. *Journal of Traumatic Stress, 17,* 85–95.

Sowell, E., Thompson, P., Tessner, K., & Toga, A. (2001). Mapping continued brain growth and gray matter density reduction in dorsal frontal cortex. *Journal of Neuroscience, 21,* 8819–8829.

JULIAN D. FORD
University of Connecticut School of Medicine

See also: Amygdala; Biology, Brain Structure, and Function, Child; Child Development; Cognitive Behavior Therapy, Child Abuse; Family Systems; Hippocampus; Memories of Traumatic Experiences

AGGRESSION

Aggression is a heterogeneous and very broad category of behavior with diverse causes and consequences. Aggression often is defined as hostile, destructive, and/or injurious activity that has the potential and/or intention of inflicting damage to an inanimate object or harm to a living being. Terms such as aggressive, violent, conduct disordered, oppositional, psychopathic, under-aroused, delinquent, and antisocial have all been used to describe persons with persistent and frequent aggressive behavior. Overt aggression involves a direct confrontation with the environment including verbal threats of violence, impulsive episodes of property destruction, self-injurious behaviors, and physical assault. Covert aggression includes hidden and furtive behaviors such as lying, shoplifting, vandalism, and fire setting (Frick et al., 1993). Proactive, instrumental, or predatory aggression is motivated by reward. Reactive, affective, defensive, or impulsive aggression is motivated by reaction to threat or frustration in goal-directed behavior. Aggression can be adaptive or maladaptive based on its appropriateness to the context and its consequences for the person and others.

Although trauma does not cause aggression, traumatized individuals are at increased risk for both expressing aggression and/or being exposed to aggression by others. This may occur through several mechanisms. First, aggression is an associated symptom of diverse disorders such as depression, bipolar disorder, posttraumatic stress disorder (PTSD), psychosis, attention deficit/hyperactivity disorder, and/or anxiety disorders (Connor & McLaughlin, 2006). Traumatized individuals meeting criteria for PTSD frequently meet diagnostic criteria for other psychiatric disorders that may have aggression as an associated symptom. Additionally, many of these associated diagnoses include symptoms of diminished impulse control that may lead traumatized individuals into environmental situations where they may be exposed to aggression by others. Second, the hyperarousal symptoms of PTSD such as problems with anger or irritability may lead to aggressive behavior or cause the individual to be aggressed upon by others. Third, acute, sudden, life-threatening stress activates many alarm systems in the central nervous system that are designed to perceive and evaluate threat, and to organize an adaptive response that will increase the individual's chances of survival and avoidance of injury. If the threat is too intense, too uncontrollable, too inescapable, or too chronic, these neurobiological mechanisms can become disorganized and are no longer adaptive (Adamec, Blundell, & Burton, 2006; Charney, 2003). Diminished inhibition may then result in the release of explosive moods and behaviors. Even when the acute trauma has resolved, increased rage, hostility, irritability, and aggression in the face of memories or reminders of the traumatic event may then occur, particularly if the past trauma involved being aggressed against and the individual now also is experiencing problems with depression (O'Donnell, Cook, Thompson, Riley, & Neria, 2006).

REFERENCES

Adamec, R. E., Blundell, J., & Burton, P. (2006). Relationship of the predatory attack experience to neural plasticity, pCREB expression and neuroendocrine response. *Neuroscience and Biobehavioral Reviews, 30*(3), 356–375.

Charney, D. S. (2003). Neuroanatomical circuits modulating fear and anxiety behaviors. *Acta Psychiatrica Scandinavica Supplementum, 417,* 38–50.

Connor, D. F., & McLaughlin, T. J. (2006). Aggression and diagnosis in psychiatrically referred children.

Child Psychiatry and Human Development, 37(1), 1–14.

Frick, P. J., Lahey, B. B., Loeber, R., Tannenbaum, L., Van Horn, Y., Christ, M. A. G., et al. (1993). Oppositional defiant disorder and conduct disorder: A meta-analytic review of factor analyses and cross-validation in a clinical sample. *Clinical Psychology Review, 13,* 319–340.

O'Donnell, C., Cook, J. M., Thompson, R., Riley, K., & Neria, Y. (2006). Verbal and physical aggression in World War II former prisoners of war: Role of posttraumatic stress disorder and depression. *Journal of Traumatic Stress, 19*(6), 859–866.

Daniel F. Connor
University of Connecticut School of Medicine

See also: Anger; Antisocial Behavior; Domestic Violence

ALCOHOL USE DISORDERS

People with posttraumatic stress disorder (PTSD) often qualify for diagnoses related to substance use, one of which is alcohol use disorder (AUD). In epidemiological research, lifetime PTSD signals an increased risk for lifetime AUD and prior PTSD predicts the onset of AUDs. Studies of patients with substance use disorders (SUD; i.e., *DSM-IV*-defined substance dependence, substance abuse) find current rates of PTSD to be much higher than those found in the general population, and range from 25–55%; patients seeking PTSD treatment have SUD rates ranging from 65–80% (as reviewed in Ouimette & Brown, 2003). Thus, the co-occurrence of SUD and PTSD is commonly found in community and clinical samples, and across a range of treatment settings.

The prognostic implications for patients with both SUD and PTSD are decidedly negative. Longitudinal studies suggest that over time, patients with both SUDs and PTSD consume more alcohol, relapse more quickly, have less social support, are more likely to be unemployed, and have treatment readmission rates that are higher than those for SUD patients without PTSD. SUD patients with comorbid PTSD incur an estimated $3,000 more annually in SUD treatment costs than those without PTSD. Substance abuse also has negative implications for patients seeking PTSD treatment because patients who continue to use substances have poorer PTSD outcomes than those who abstain from using (Ouimette & Brown, 2003).

Models

A number of hypotheses regarding associations between PTSD and AUD have been proposed. Among the most popular of these is the self-medication model, which is based on the premise that substance abuse constitutes an effort to cope with the distressing affect associated with a traumatic event in a manner that is analogous to the use of medication to alleviate symptoms of an illness. According to this model, persons with PTSD use mind-altering substances to mute emotional arousal or to lessen the disturbing effects of traumatic memories. Conversely, it also has been proposed that alcohol use contributes to the occurrence of trauma and PTSD (i.e., the High Risk Hypothesis; see Ouimette & Brown, 2003, for chapters reviewing models). For example, heavy drinkers may put themselves at risk for accidents, violence, or other potentially traumatic events. Additionally, substance use may trigger or exacerbate PTSD symptoms (Saladin, Brady, Dansky, & Kilpatrick, 1995).

A social learning perspective (SLT; Maisto, Carey, & Bradizza, 1999) also can be applied to the PTSD-SUD co-occurrence. According to this conceptualization, the desire to regulate learned emotional responses (fear, arousal, depression) to trauma motivates substance use. A component of SLT is *reciprocal determinism,* which describes dynamic associations among environmental and individual variables and behavior over time. Here, trauma exposure and posttraumatic stress symptoms could be both causes and effects of substance use. Cognitions related to the interpretation of trauma-related cues, the individual's ability to manage emotional cue responses, and beliefs about the palliative effects of substances also play a central role.

Changes in brain structure and chemistry may also explain PTSD-SUD associations. As noted by Brady and Sinha (2005), these underlying biological changes (1) may be shared by PTSD and SUD and/or (2) may be the result of prolonged substance use, which then in turn leads to the development of PTSD. Examples of such structural changes in the brain include, but are not limited to, alterations in the way the amygdala (the brain's emotion processing center; *see:* **Amygdala**) works, alterations in dopamine in the brain's reward pathways, and problems in regulating noradrenergic and neuroendocrine functioning, both of which are associated with the body's reaction to stressful stimuli.

Nonbiological, shared vulnerability mechanisms also have been implicated in PTSD-SUD co-occurrence. Among these are trait-level constructs such as anxiety sensitivity, negative emotionality, and behavioral undercontrol. Each of these personality variables has been suggested to contribute to increased risk for substance use as well as poor adaptation to trauma (i.e., posttraumatic stress), and thus potentially account for the frequent co-occurrence of the two disorders.

Importantly, although many models of PTSD-AUD associations consider which disorder develops first, the complexity of an individual's trauma history and the challenges of determining substance use and problem onset often make temporal delineation difficult. Thus, though an understanding of the primacy of one disorder may provide useful clinical information, establishing such primacy may prove challenging to ascertain in a clinical setting.

Treatments

While it is generally accepted in academic communities that integrated AUD-PTSD treatment is considered best practice and patients would prefer such concurrent therapy, most clinics do not treat both disorders simultaneously. Clinical researchers have developed integrated AUD-PTSD treatments with or without exposure therapy elements. Debate has ensued about the inclusion of an exposure component, which is a recommended evidence-based practice for PTSD alone. Concern includes the potential for alcohol relapse, although preliminary data counter such concern. Concurrent treatment of PTSD and cocaine dependence combines coping skills training with exposure therapy for PTSD. Retention rates in this protocol were similar to those in treatments without exposure components, suggesting that exposure did not negatively affect patients' participation.

The most researched integrated treatment to date is called *Seeking Safety,* a present-focused coping skills therapy. Some key elements include: a focus on safety, working concurrently on PTSD and AUD, and coping skills work. Several studies support its effectiveness across several treatment populations. One study randomly assigned women to Seeking Safety or Relapse Prevention with a nonrandomized treatment-as-usual comparison group, and outcomes for Seeking Safety were comparable to Relapse Prevention and better than treatment as usual (see Ouimette & Brown, 2003 for chapters reviewing these interventions).

Conclusion

Further explication of the underlying mechanisms —psychological and biological—of PTSD-SUD comorbidity is needed. Identification of patient subgroups, including gender-specific types would be helpful in improving treatment effectiveness. Treatments need to be further evaluated for efficacy and cost-effectiveness relative to standard care and other programs. Given the popularity and practical utility of self-help approaches in the United States, an investigation of whether self-help can provide a helpful adjunct to integrated treatment would be useful, particularly for adult populations. Last, a preventative approach would be helpful, possibly addressing trauma-related symptoms and alcohol abuse before the development of full-fledged disorders, looking toward other settings such as primary care to identify at-risk individuals.

REFERENCES

Brady, K. T., & Sinha, R. (2005). Co-occurring mental and substance use disorders: The neurobiological effects of chronic stress. *American Journal of Psychiatry, 162,* 1483–1493.

Maisto, S. A., Carey, K. B., & Bradizza, C. M. (1999). Social learning theory. In K. E. Leonard & H. T. Blane (Eds.), *Psychological theories of drinking and alcoholism* (2nd ed., pp. 106–163). New York: Guilford Press.

Ouimette, P., & Brown, P. J. (2003). *Trauma and substance abuse: Causes, consequences, and treatment of comorbid disorders.* Washington, DC: American Psychological Association.

Saladin, M. E., Brady, K. T., Dansky, B. S., & Kilpatrick, D. G. (1995). Understanding comorbidity between PTSD and substance use disorders: Two preliminary investigations. *Addictive Behaviors, 20,* 643–655.

RECOMMENDED READING

Coffey, S. F., Read, J. P., & Norberg, M. M. (2008). Posttraumatic stress disorder and substance use disorder: Neuroimaging, neuroendocrine, and physiological findings. In S. H. Stewart & P. J. Conrod (Eds.), *Anxiety and substance abuse disorders: The vicious cycle of comorbidity.* New York: Springer.

PAIGE OUIMETTE
State University of New York

JENNIFER P. READ
State University of New York

See also: Substance Use Disorders

ALEXITHYMIA

The term *alexithymia* literally means "no words for feelings" and is characterized by deficits in the ability to identify and label, as well as communicate affective experience. Alexithymia thus is considered an affect regulation disturbance (Taylor, Bagby, & Parker, 1997). Although alexithymic individuals are able to experience emotions, when asked to describe their internal experience they are able only to give vague, unelaborated descriptions of feelings (e.g., "upset"), or may report somatic or cognitive aspects of their experience. Additionally, alexithymia is an externally oriented thinking style, characterized by communication that is lacking in personal involvement and devoid of references to personal feelings, thoughts, reactions, or attitudes about the event.

Measurement

Although a number of measures have been developed to assess specific aspects of alexithymia, such as emotional awareness, the Toronto Alexithymia Scale (TAS-20; Bagby, Parker, & Taylor, 1994a, 1994b) is widely accepted as the most comprehensive, reliable, and valid across populations and languages. This 20-item, self-report questionnaire asks individuals to rate, on a five-point Likert-type scale, the degree to which they agree with test items. Subscale items assess the three components of alexithymia described previously. Research (Bagby et al., 1994a) also has established cut-off scores on the TAS-20 used for identifying clinical levels of alexithymia. Prevalence rates, using this TAS-20 criterion, have been estimated as ranging between 13% and 24% in community and undergraduate college samples (Mason, Tyson, Jones, & Potts, 2005; Paivio & McCullough, 2003), and between 17% and 59% in clinical samples (Honkalampi et al., 2004; Muller, Buhner, & Ellgring, 2003).

Associated Psychological Disturbances

Alexithymia has important implications for functioning. Emotions provide vital information about self and relationships that guide perceptions and behavior so that limited awareness of feelings leaves the person disoriented (Damasio, 1999). Individuals without the capacity to identify and communicate feelings are more likely to experience negative emotions as confusing and express distress through somatic symptoms or through physical means, including violence to self or others (Paivio & McCullough, 2003; van der Kolk, Perry, & Herman, 1991). Alexithymia also has been associated with difficulty recognizing emotions in others, interpersonal problems, and limited social support (Turner & Paivio, 2002), and with a number of psychological disturbances (for a review, see Taylor et al., 1997). These include posttraumatic stress disorder (PTSD), depression, anxiety, eating disorders, substance abuse, somatoform disorders, borderline personality, dissociative experiences, and self-injurious behaviors. Finally, alexithymia has been associated with development of weaker therapeutic alliances (Mallinckrodt, King, & Coble, 1998) and thus can interfere with an individual's capacity to benefit from psychotherapy.

Etiology

Developmental and social learning theories currently are the most commonly accepted explanations for alexithymia. These perspectives (e.g., Gottman, 1997) suggest that alexithymia develops when children learn that communicating emotion is inappropriate or ineffective in getting needs met. Gender role socialization, for example, explains the higher prevalence of alexithymia in males who frequently are taught to suppress normal emotional expressivity. As well, social learning effects are intensified in environments in which children learn that expression of feelings is not only meaningless but dangerous. There is considerable evidence supporting an association between alexithymia and a history of childhood maltreatment (e.g., Paivio & McCullough, 2003; Taylor et al., 1997; Turner & Paivio, 2002; Zlotnick, Mattia, & Zimmerman, 2001). Abused children can learn to ignore or avoid emotional experience as a strategy for coping with overwhelming negative affect and instead learn to rely on external cues and events to guide behavior.

Treatment

There are few psychological treatments specifically for alexithymia although a number of treatments for particular disorders (e.g., borderline personality, complex PTSD, eating disorders) address problems with emotion awareness and modulation. These approaches typically focus on increasing emotion awareness and labeling capacities through skills training. Research supports the efficacy of these approaches (e.g., Becker-Stoll & Gerlinghoff, 2004; Kennedy & Franklin, 2002; Linehan, 1993). Results of a recent study (Ralston, 2006) indicated significant reductions in alexithymia over the course of emotion focused therapy for child abuse trauma (EFTT; Paivio, Chagigiorgis, Hall, Jarry, & Ralston, 2007). EFTT relies on promoting client experiencing (exploration of feelings and meanings) rather than skills training. This suggests that alexithymia may be more related to problems with complex affective meaning rather than emotion word vocabulary, per se, and treatments focusing on affective meaning construction may be effective options.

REFERENCES

Bagby, M., Parker, J., & Taylor, G. (1994a). The twenty-item Toronto Alexithymia Scale I: Item selection and cross-validation of the factor structure. *Journal of Psychosomatic Research, 38,* 23–32.

Bagby, M., Parker, J., & Taylor, G. (1994b). The twenty-item Toronto Alexithymia Scale II: Convergent, discriminant, and concurrent validity. *Journal of Psychosomatic Research, 38,* 33–40.

Becker-Stoll, F., & Gerlinghoff, M. (2004). Impact of a four month day treatment programme on alexithymia in eating disorders. *European Eating Disorders Review, 12,* 159–163.

Damasio, A. R. (1999). *The feeling of what happens: Body and emotion in the making of consciousness.* New York: Harcourt Brace.

Gottman, K. M. (1997). *The heart of parenting: Raising an emotionally intelligent child.* New York: Simon & Schuster.

Honkalampi, K., Koiivumaa-Honkanen, H., Antikainen, R., Haatiinen, K., Hintikka, J., & Viitamaki, H. (2004). Relationships among alexithymia, adverse childhood experiences, sociodemographic variables, and actual mood disorder: A 2-year clinical follow-up study of patients with major depressive disorder. *Psychosomatics, 45,* 197–204.

Kennedy, M., & Franklin, J. (2002). Skills based treatment for alexithymia: An exploratory case series. *Behavior Change, 19,* 158–171.

Linehan, M. M. (1993). *Cognitive-behavioral treatment for borderline personality disorder.* New York: Guilford Press.

Mallinckrodt, B., King, J. L., & Coble, H. M. (1998). Family dysfunction, alexithymia, and client attachment to therapist. *Journal of Counseling Psychology, 45,* 497–504.

Mason, O., Tyson, M., Jones, C., & Potts, S. (2005). Alexithymia: Its prevalence and correlates in a British undergraduate sample. *Psychology and Psychotherapy: Theory, Research, and Practice, 78,* 113–125.

Muller, J., Buhner, M., & Ellgring, H. (2003). Is there a reliable factor structure in the 20 item Toronto Alexithymia Scale? A comparison of factor models in clinical and normative adult samples. *Journal of Psychosomatic Research, 55,* 561–568.

Paivio, S. C., Chagigiorgis, H., Hall, I., Jarry, J., & Ralston M. (2007). *Comparative efficacy of two versions of emotion focused therapy for child abuse trauma: A dismantling study.* Manuscript submitted for publication.

Paivio, S. C., & McCullough, C. R. (2003). Alexithymia as a mediator between childhood trauma and self-injurious behaviours. *Child Abuse and Neglect, 28,* 339–354.

Ralston, M. B. (2006). *Imaginal confrontation versus evocative empathy in emotion focused trauma therapy.* Unpublished doctoral dissertation, University of Windsor, Windsor, Ontario, Canada.

Taylor, G., Bagby, M., & Parker, J. (1997). *Disorders of affect regulation: Alexithymia in medical and psychiatric illness.* Cambridge: Cambridge University Press.

Turner A., & Paivio, S. (2002, August). *Relations among childhood trauma, alexithymia, social anxiety, and social support.* Poster presented at the annual meeting of the American Psychological Association, Chicago.

Van der Kolk, B., Perry, C., & Herman, J. (1991). Childhood origins of self-destructive behavior. *American Journal of Psychiatry, 148,* 1665–1670.

Zlotnick, C., Mattia, J. I., & Zimmerman, M. (2001). The relationship between posttraumatic stress disorder, childhood trauma, and alexithymia in an outpatient sample. *Journal of Traumatic Stress, 14,* 177–188.

ELISABETH KUNZLE
University of Windsor

SANDRA C. PAIVIO
University of Windsor

See also: **Dissociation; Emotional Numbing**

ALIENATION AND TRAUMA

Alienation is a psychological concept consisting of some positive and mostly negative feelings. Such positive feelings may involve feeling that the individual is unique emotionally, but negative feelings involve feeling that he or she is aliened, isolated, and withdrawn from reality (Al-Sahel & Hanoora, 2001). Brown, Higgins, and Paulsen (2003) defined alienation "as the negative sense of fragmentation, estrangement, and separation." Moreover, there are many other definitions of alienation as a psychological concept, however, the main common elements between them is that alienation denotes feelings of estrangement, being lost, loneliness or isolation from others, feeling helpless, and feeling as if one is losing relationships with others (Dimen, 2003; Florence & Bernard, 1967; Hanoora, 1998; Reber, 1995; Seeman, 1959).

Little has been written about the relationship between trauma and the deep-seated sense of guilt and shame of trauma's victims, in which the alienation from others is the main expression of these feelings. In addition, Ebert and Dyck (2004) indicated that exposure to extreme interpersonal stress can lead to alienation from others, shame and guilt, and a sense of being permanently damaged. Psychologically, most of the victims of trauma try to appear normal/healthy when they are still emotionally suffering from the traumatic event, but they do not want others to see that suffering. For example, it was found that most combat veterans remain alienated when they appear to be normal because just under the surface are the unintegrated personality fragments that cannot grieve, feel fear, and express anger without something self-destructive happening (Brende & McDonald, 1989).

Studies show that alienation could be recognized when the traumatic event victim avoids people, activities, or places, which arouse recollections of the original trauma (which is a symptom of PTSD; Forbes et al., 2002; Morison, 2002). In addition, Brende and McDonald (1989) found that severe and intractable symptoms of PTSD in Vietnam combat veterans were related to entrenched guilt and shame. These symptoms include changes in self-identity, destructive, and self-destructive behavior. It was also found that trauma victims indicated an overall feeling of alienation from self and others (Ehlers et al., 1998; Evans & Stinnett, 2006).

REFERENCES

Al-Sahel, R. A., & Hanoora, M. A. (2001). Level of feeling of trauma and its relationship with personality values, alienation, and psychological disorders among youth. *Journal of Social Sciences: The Academic Publication Council, Kuwait University, 29,* 55–80.

Brende, J., & McDonald, E. (1989). Posttraumatic spiritual alienation and recovery in Vietnam combat veterans. *Spirituality Today, 3,* 319–340.

Brown, M. R., Higgins, K., & Paulsen, K. (2003). Adolescent alienation: What is it and what can educators do about it? *Intervention in School and Clinic, 39,* 3–9.

Dimen, M. (2003). Keep on keepin' on: Alienation and trauma commentary on Ruth Fallenbaum's paper. *Studies in Gender and Sexuality, 4,* 93–103.

Ebert, A., & Dyck, M. (2004). The experience of mental death: The core feature of complex posttraumatic stress disorder. *Clinical Psychology Review, 24,* 617–636.

Ehlers, A., Clark, D. M., Dunmore, E., Jaycox, L., Meadows, E., & Foa, E. B. (1998). Prediction response to exposure treatment in PTSD: The role of mental defeat and alienation. *Journal of Traumatic Stress, 11,* 457–471.

Evans, L. G., & Stinnett, J. O. (2006). Structure and prevalence of PTSD symptomology in children who have experienced a severe tornado. *Psychology in the School, 43,* 283–295.

Florence, R., & Bernard, K. (1967). Alienation and family crisis. *Sociological Quarterly, 8,* 397–405.

Forbes, D., Creamer, M., Allen, N., McHugh, T., Debenham, P., & Hopwood, M. (2002). MMPI-2 as predictor of change in PTSD symptoms. *Journal of Personality Assessment, 8,* 183–186.

Hanoora, M. (1998). *Personality and mental health.* Cairo, Egypt: Anglo Press.

Morison, J. (2002). PTSD in victims of sexual molestation: Its incidence, characteristics, and treatment strategies. *Behaviour Research and Therapy, 4,* 439–457.

Reber, A. (1995). *The Penguin dictionary of psychology* (2nd ed.). London: Penguin Books.

Seeman, M. (1959). On the meaning of alienation. *American Sociological Review, 24,* 783–791.

RECOMMENDED READINGS

Ehlers, A., Clark, D. M., Dunmore, E., Jaycox, L., Meadows, E., & Foa, E. B. (1998). Prediction response to exposure treatment in PTSD: The role of mental defeat and alienation. *Journal of Traumatic Stress, 11,* 457–471.

Lieb, R., Wittchen, H., & Van Os, J. (2006). Impact of psychological trauma on the development of psychotic symptoms: Relationship with psychosis proneness. *British Journal of Psychiatry, 188,* 527–533.

RASHED A. AL-SAHEL
Kuwait University

See also: Avoidance; Social Support

AMYGDALA

The *amygdala* is a complex brain structure involved in a variety of normal brain functions and psychiatric conditions. The existence of the amygdala was first recognized in the early nineteenth century. The name, derived from the Greek language, was meant to denote the almond-like shape of this region in the medial temporal lobe. It is traditionally thought to consist of an evolutionarily primitive division associated with the olfactory (i.e., smell) system (the cortico-medial region) and an evolutionarily newer division associated with the neocortex (the basolateral region).

Each nucleus has unique connections. For example, the lateral amygdala is a major site receiving convergent inputs from visual, auditory, somatosensory (including pain) systems. The central nucleus connects with brainstem areas that control the expression of innate behaviors and associated physiological responses. And the medial nucleus of the amygdala is strongly connected with the olfactory system.

In the late 1930s, researchers observed that damage to the temporal lobe resulted in profound changes in fear reactivity, feeding, and sexual behavior that came to be called the Kluver-Bucy syndrome. Around mid-century, it was determined that damage to the amygdala accounted for these changes in emotional processing. Numerous studies subsequently attempted to understand the role of the amygdala in emotional functions, especially fear. Studies in rodents have mapped the inputs to and outputs of amygdala nuclei that are involved in fear conditioning. In particular, it is widely accepted that when an animal is repeatedly exposed to a painful stimulus (an unconditioned stimulus) and a neutral stimulus (a conditioned stimulus), this leads to change in the neurons (synaptic plasticity) in the lateral amygdala. When the conditioned stimulus then occurs alone later, neural activation flows through these potentiated synapses to the other amygdala targets and ultimately to the central nucleus, outputs of which control conditioned fear responses. Specific cellular and molecular mechanisms within lateral amygdala cells have been shown to underlie these changes in brain activation associated with learned fear.

Although fear is the emotion best understood in terms of brain mechanisms, the amygdala has also been implicated in a variety of other emotional functions. A relatively large body of research has focused on the role of the amygdala in processing rewards and the use of rewards to motivate and reinforce behavior. As with aversive conditioning, the lateral, basal, and central amygdala have been implicated in different aspects of reward learning and motivation. The amygdala has also been implicated in emotional states associated with aggressive, maternal, sexual, and ingestive (eating and drinking) behaviors. Less is known about the detailed circuitry involved in these emotional states than is known about the brain activity involved in fear.

Because the amygdala is altered by and stores information about emotional events, it is said to participate in *emotional memory*. Emotional memory is viewed as an implicit or unconscious form of memory and contrasts with explicit or declarative memory mediated by the hippocampus.

In addition to its role in emotion and unconscious emotional memory, the amygdala is also involved in the regulation or modulation of a variety of cognitive functions, such as attention, perception, and explicit memory. It is generally thought that these cognitive functions are modulated by the amygdala's processing of the emotional significance of external stimuli. Outputs of the amygdala then lead to the release of hormones and/or neuromodulators in the brain that alter cognitive processing in cortical areas. For example, via amygdala outputs that ultimately affect the hippocampus, explicit memories about emotional situations are enhanced.

Over the past decade, interest in the human amygdala has grown considerably, spurred on by the progress in animal studies and by the development of functional imaging techniques. As in the animal brain, damage to the human amygdala interferes with fear conditioning and functional activity changes in the human amygdala in response to fear conditioning. Further, exposure to emotional faces potently activates the human amygdala. Both conditioned stimuli and emotional faces produce strong amygdala activation when presented unconsciously, emphasizing the importance of the amygdala as an implicit information processor and its role in unconscious memory. Findings regarding the human amygdala are mainly at the level of the whole region rather than nuclei.

Structural and/or functional changes in the amygdala are associated with a wide variety of psychiatric conditions, including anxiety disorders such as PTSD, phobias, and panic disorder, depression, schizophrenia, and autism. This does not mean that the amygdala causes these disorders. It simply means that in people who have these disorders, alterations occur in the amygdala. Because each of these disorders involves fear and anxiety to some extent, the involvement of the amygdala in some of these disorders may be related to increased anxiety in these patients.

RECOMMENDED READINGS

Cardinal, R. N., Parkinson, J. A., Hall, J., & Everitt, B. J. (2002). Emotion and motivation: The role of the amygdala, ventral striatum, and prefrontal cortex. *Neuroscience and Biobehavior Review, 26,* 321–352.

Charney, D. S. (2003). Neuroanatomical circuits modulating fear and anxiety behaviors. *Acta Psychiatrica Scandinavica* (Suppl.), 38–50.

LeDoux, J. E. (1996). *The emotional brain.* New York: Simon & Schuster.

McGaugh, J. L. (2003). *Memory and emotion: The making of lasting memories.* London: Orion.

Phelps, E. A. (2006). Emotion and cognition: Insights from studies of the human amygdala. *Annual Review of Psychology, 57,* 27–53.

Shinnick-Gallagher, P., Pitkanen, A., Shekhar, A., & Cahill, L. (Eds.). (2003). *The amygdala in brain function: Basic and clinical approaches.* New York: New York Academy of Sciences.

JOSEPH LEDOUX
New York University

See also: Biology, Animal Models; Biology, Brain Structure, and Function, Adult; Biology, Brain Structure, and Function, Child; Biology, Neurochemistry; Conditioned Fear; Hippocampus; Limbic System

ANGER

Anger is a negatively toned emotion, subjectively experienced as an aroused state of antagonism toward someone or something perceived to be the source of an aversive event. It is triggered or provoked situationally by events that are perceived to constitute deliberate harm-doing by an instigator toward oneself or toward those to whom one is endeared. Provocations usually take the form of insults, unfair treatments, or thwartings appraised as intended. Anger is prototypically experienced as a justified response to a perceived "wrong." While anger is situationally triggered by acute, proximal occurrences, it is shaped and facilitated contextually by conditions affecting the cognitive, arousal, and behavioral systems that comprise anger reactions. Anger activation is centrally linked to threat perceptions and survival responding, and thus it has intrinsic relevance for understanding trauma.

As a normal human emotion, anger has considerable adaptive value, although there are sociocultural variations in the acceptability of its expression and the form that such expression

takes. In the face of adversity, it can mobilize psychological resources, energize behaviors for corrective action, and facilitate perseverance. Anger serves as a guardian to self-esteem, operates as a means of communicating negative sentiment, potentiates the ability to redress grievances, and boosts determination to overcome obstacles to our happiness and aspirations. Akin to aggressive behavior, anger has functional value for survival. Anger, an emotion, should be distinguished from hostility, which is an attitudinal disposition, and from aggression, which is behavior intended to do harm.

Despite having multiple adaptive functions, anger also has maladaptive effects on personal and social well-being. Generally, strong physiological arousal impairs the processing of information and lessens cognitive control of behavior. Because heightened physiological arousal is a core component of anger, people are not cognitively proficient when they become angry. Also, because the activation of anger is accompanied by aggressive impulses, anger can motivate harm toward other people, which in turn can produce undesirable consequences for the angered person, either from direct retaliation, loss of supportive relationships, or social censure. An angry person is not optimally alert, thoughtful, empathic, prudent, or physically healthy. Being a turbulent emotion ubiquitous in everyday life, anger is now known to be substantially associated with various stress-related disorders, such as cardiovascular disorders, in addition to its relevance for trauma and for posttraumatic stress disorder (PTSD).

Trauma and Anger Dysregulation

Anger, since at least 1942, has been identified as a component of traumatic reactions in clinical and field studies. Anger is a recognized feature of a range of clinical disorders that may result from psychological trauma exposure, such as dissociative amnesia, dissociative identity disorder, borderline personality disorder, head-trauma dementia, major depressive disorder, and especially PTSD. "Irritability/outburst of anger" is one of five symptoms in the hyperarousal cluster for PTSD diagnosis (since *DSM-III-R*'s publication). Although typically viewed as merely a symptom of PTSD, anger can alternatively be seen as a dynamic factor bearing on the course of traumatic stress and its treatment. While anger or irritability is a PTSD diagnostic symptom, PTSD diagnostic criteria can be met in the absence of anger or irritability.

The meta-analysis by Orth and Wieland (2006), who reviewed 39 studies between 1985 and 2003, demonstrated that anger is substantially associated with PTSD in trauma-exposed adults, with the largest effect size being obtained for those having military war experience. As well, they found other trauma sources, such as technological disaster, crime victimization, and motor vehicle accidents to have medium to large effects for anger and hostility's association with PTSD.

Beyond this associative linkage, anger has been found to be predictive of PTSD chronicity, severity, and treatment response with various trauma populations. Studies with noncombat populations show anger to be a key long-term symptom resulting from trauma, as found with sexual assault survivors, motor vehicle accident victims, violence-exposed adolescents, domestic violence victims, political prisoners, refugees, and general samples of psychiatric patients. A growing body of research indicates that the relevance of anger is more than that of a mere symptom or diagnostic marker. Multiple studies point to anger's importance for the course of PTSD and for treatment efficacy, including longitudinal studies of Vietnam veterans, adult victims of violent crime, and motor vehicle accident victims. Anger assessed at early stages of trauma has been found to be predictive of later PTSD severity and response to treatment after statistically controlling for initial PTSD and various background and psychosocial factors.

As a result of trauma, anger occurs as part of a dyscontrol syndrome activated by sensing a threat in one's environment. The engagement of anger in PTSD involves hostile appraisal, heightened arousal, and antagonistic behavior as survival responding in contextually inappropriate conditions, such that the person becomes dysregulated in reacting to the demands of the environment. While anger is situationally triggered by acute, proximal occurrences, it can be primed by trauma-related stimuli and contexts. Threat perception and anger schemas are reciprocally influenced.

Because of the survival function of the threat-sensing aspects of anger schemas, the detection of threat carries urgent priority and rapidly engages anger. Linking anger to survival needs allows for understanding its activation in PTSD and increasing violence risk: (1) its onset carries a coping response urgency that preempts alternative appraisals of the triggering event and considerations of alternative action plans; (2) it engages cognitive processes and behavior that further bias the system toward confirmation of the expectation of threat; (3) the strong arousal and the peremptory nature of the threat schemas suppress inhibitory controls of aggressive behavior; and (4) threat-anger responses are organized as a positive feedback loop—the more threat is perceived, the more anger and aggression are engaged; and, conversely, the more anger and aggression, the greater is the readiness to perceive threat. The cognitive distortions linked to threat perceptions and highly automatized anger have powerful immediacy and validity, and anger is infused with themes of justification.

Why does anger dysregulation occur in the context of trauma? One possibility is that anger serves to suppress both fear and pain in conjunction with activating approach or attack behaviors. Anger counters "loss of control," providing an antidote to the debilitating sense of vulnerability or uncontrollability. Anger keeps the adversary in mind (maintaining attentional focus on that which threatens survival), and it may prolong PTSD because it entails rumination, entraining the reexperiencing of one's trauma through a cognitive network of associations. Anger also causes alarm and has symbolic links to madness and badness. Long after trauma exposure, heightened arousal from everyday provocations might overwhelm self-regulatory capacity and reevoke the trauma experience.

Treatment of Anger in Trauma-Related Disorders

Essential to reinstituting regulatory controls for anger and aggression is treating the patient's self-monitoring deficits. This entails helping the person to (1) monitor cognitions during anger episodes; (2) identifying signs of arousal, as well as its intensity, duration, and lability in response to the perception of danger; (3) recognizing how anger reactions can escalate the threat potential of a situation; and (4) distinguishing impulsive actions from more controlled responses. Anger's cognitive, arousal, and behavioral domains are thus segmented for self-monitoring. In the treatment of anger disorders, cognitive behavioral therapy (CBT) approaches have been found to be effective with a wide range of clinical populations, including combat veterans with severe anger and severe PTSD (Chemtob, Novaco, Hamada, & Gross, 1997).

The CBT psychotherapeutic procedure is an adjunctive treatment involving cognitive restructuring, somatic arousal reduction, and behavioral coping skills enhancement. To facilitate anger regulation, the therapist strives to disconnect anger from the threat system, first through provision of safety, patience, and psychological space for reflection, exploration, and choice. The client's view of anger is normalized, to obviate worries about being a "bad" or unworthy person. The therapist acknowledges the legitimacy of the client's feelings, affirming his or her self-worth. Building trust in the therapeutic relationship is pivotal. As self-regulation hinges on knowledge, education about anger and discovery of the client's personal anger patterns or "anger signature" is facilitated. Much is done to augment self-monitoring and to encourage the moderation of anger intensity. Because tension or strain may surface in the course of treatment, the therapist models and reinforces nonanger alternative responding so as to build replacements for the automatized angry reactions that had been the client's default coping style.

In the CBT stress inoculation approach to anger treatment, provocation is simulated by therapeutically paced exposure to anger incidents created in imaginal visualization and in role-play. The progressively graduated exposure, directed by the therapist, involves a hierarchy of anger incidents produced by the collaborative work of client and therapist. This graduated, hierarchical exposure, done in conjunction with the teaching of stress coping skills, is the basis for the inoculation metaphor. Anger-control coping skills are rehearsed with the therapist and practiced while visualizing and role-playing progressively more intense anger-arousing scenes from the personal hierarchies. See Novaco and Chemtob (1998) for more detailed discussion.

REFERENCES

Chemtob, C. M., Novaco, R. W., Hamada, R. S., & Gross, D. M. (1997). Cognitive-behavioral treatment for severe anger in post-traumatic stress disorder. *Journal of Consulting and Clinical Psychology, 65,* 184–189.

Novaco, R. W., & Chemtob, C. M. (1998). Anger and trauma: Conceptualization, assessment, and treatment. In V. M. Follette, J. I. Rusek, & F. R. Abueg (Eds.), *Cognitive behavioral therapies for trauma* (pp. 162–190). New York: Guilford Press.

Orth, U., & Wieland, E. (2006). Anger, hostility, and posttraumatic stress disorder in trauma-exposed adults: A meta-analysis. *Journal of Consulting and Clinical Psychology, 74,* 698–706.

RAYMOND W. NOVACO
University of California, Irvine

See also: Aggression; Cognitive Behavior Therapy, Adult; Social Cognitive Theory

ANHEDONIA

See: Depression; Emotional Numbing

ANNIVERSARY REACTIONS

Stimuli that reactivate traumatic memories (i.e., "triggers") often include significant dates or times of the year that are associated with unresolved traumatic experiences. These stimuli can induce particular time-related responses called *anniversary reactions* that range from mild and transient, to severe and prolonged. Anniversary reactions are typically understood as annual phenomena, but belong to a broader category of reactions that include more frequent time-related triggers, such as months, weeks, days, or even time of day.

Unresolved experiences associated with anniversary reactions include traumatic birth and deaths (Bowlby, 1980), abortions (Franco et al., 1989), abuse, accidents, natural disasters, or war experiences (Morgan, Hill, Fox, Kingham, & Southwick, 1999). Anniversary reactions involve symptoms and features of posttraumatic stress and complicated grief: flashbacks, nightmares, sleep disorders, fear and anxiety, rage, sadness, guilt, shame, suicidality, depression, or manic episodes (Beratis, Gourzis, & Gabriel, 1996), and brief reactive psychoses. Avoidance, numbing, and detachment symptoms may be prominent around the anniversary date, including efforts to avoid any reminders of the event, narrowed focus of attention, reduction in awareness of surroundings, derealization, depersonalization, and obsessive compulsive behaviors that serve to contain anxiety.

One patient reported taking heavy doses of sleeping pills in order to sleep through the entire 24-hour period that triggered her. Significant somatic symptoms associated with the traumatic experience may occur (Cavenar, Nash, & Maltbie, 1978). For example, a woman who as a child was tied up and raped during Christmas holidays had nausea, intense vaginal pain, and numbing in her hands every December.

Symptoms of anniversary reactions may last several days or weeks, and in rare instances they may last months. Many individuals are not consciously aware of the connection between their current distress and the original event. Since the inclusion of posttraumatic stress disorder in *DSM-III* in 1980 (American Psychiatric Association, 1980), anniversary reactions are considered to be a special feature of this disorder. These specific experiences were subsumed under the more general category of posttraumatic triggers, resulting in fewer studies on anniversary reactions in the literature since the mid-1980s. The most widely studied anniversary reactions pertain to the anniversary of the death of a loved one that was experienced as traumatic and has not been sufficiently mourned and integrated (Bowlby, 1980; Volkan, 1989).

Hilgard (1953; see also Volkan, 1989) distinguished a particular form of anniversary reactions. Parents may experience symptoms when their child reaches the age at which they themselves experienced a traumatic event. She described a man who developed severe headaches and psychosis, and made a suicide attempt when his son was 4 years old. When he had been the same age as his son, the man's father had unexpectedly died and his mother had to return to work, precipitating severe unresolved feelings of abandonment. Conversely, children of parents who died or were traumatized at a certain age may experience anniversary reactions when they reach the same age as the parent. For example, a patient developed severe panic, phobia of bathrooms, and suicidality when she reached the same age as her mother at the time of her suicide. The daughter, a child at the time of her mother's death, had found her mother dead in the bathtub, and had been instructed by the family never to speak of it.

Some religious and cultural traditions have recognized that anniversary reactions involve unresolved mourning and have designated special commemorations of anniversaries of painful or traumatic events (Lamm, 1969). Such observances are helpful in resolving traumatic experiences. There are several essential aspects to commemorations that parallel psychotherapy of anniversary reactions: (1) evocation and narration of a conscious memory of the event, which is an exposure technique; (2) social support, which has shown to be an essential part of overcoming traumatic reactions; and (3) setting aside a specific time for mourning and other emotions, with gradual support to move back to normal life. Psychotherapy also includes reworking maladaptive or incorrect beliefs that maintain overwhelming negative emotions. For example, patients often inappropriately blame themselves for accidents, their own abuse, or the death of a loved one. Final resolution of anniversary reactions occurs when the individual is able to fully realize and integrate the traumatic experience.

REFERENCES

American Psychiatric Association. (1980). *Diagnostic and statistical manual of mental disorders* (3rd ed.). Washington, DC: Author.

Beratis, S., Gourzis, P., & Gabriel, J. (1996). Psychological factors in the development of mood disorders with a seasonal pattern. *Psychopathology, 29,* 331–339.

Bowlby, J. (1980). *Loss: Sadness and depression.* London: Hogarth Press.

Cavenar, J. O., Nash, J. L., & Maltbie, A. A. (1978). Anniversary reactions presenting as physical complaints. *Journal of Clinical Psychiatry, 39,* 369–374.

Franco, K., Campbell, N., Tamburrino, M., Jurs, S., Pentz, J., & Evans, C. (1989). Anniversary reactions and due date responses following abortion. *Psychotherapy and Psychosomatics, 52,* 151–154.

Hilgard, J. R. (1953). Anniversary reactions in parents precipitated by children. *Psychiatry, 16,* 73–80.

Lamm, M. (1969). *The Jewish way in death and mourning.* Middle Village, NY: Jonathan David.

Morgan III, C. A., Hill, S., Fox, P., Kingham, P., & Southwick, S. M. (1999). Anniversary reactions in Gulf War veterans: A follow-up inquiry 6 years after the war. *American Journal of Psychiatry, 156,* 1075–1079.

Volkan, G. H. (1989). *The mourning-liberation process* (Vols. 1 & 2). Madison, CT: International Universities Press.

ONNO VAN DER HART
Utrecht University

KATHY STEELE
Metropolitan Counseling Services

See also: Acute Stress Disorder; Memories of Traumatic Experiences; Posttraumatic Stress Disorder

ANTERIOR CINGULATE CORTEX

Basic Anatomy and Function

The anterior cingulate cortex (ACC) is a medial prefrontal structure located anterior to (in front of) the genu of the corpus callosum (see Figure 1). The ACC differs from other subregions of the cingulate gyrus in its cytoarchitecture, connectivity with other structures,

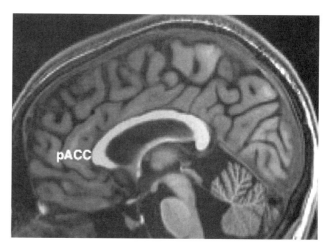

Figure 1. This magnetic resonance image shows the midsagittal (middle) surface of the human brain. Perigenual anterior singulate cortex (pACC) lies anterior to (in front of) the genu of the corpus callosum.

and function (Bush, Luu, & Posner, 2000; Vogt, Berger, & Derbyshire, 2003). Specifically, the perigenual (front portion of the) ACC is reciprocally connected to the amygdala (*see:* **Amygdala**), sends projections to autonomic centers in the brainstem, and appears to be involved in the processing of emotional information and the regulation of emotional responses. The ventral (lower portion of the) ACC and other ventral medial prefrontal regions appear to play an important role in the retention of fear extinction after fear conditioning.

In contrast, the portion of the cingulate that is dorsal to (behind) the ACC (i.e., the anterior midcingulate cortex [aMCC]) has fewer connections to the amygdala and more connections to parietal and motor areas, and is involved in executive functions including response selection and monitoring of conflict and errors.

The nomenclature used to describe the boundaries and subdivisions of the ACC has evolved over the years. The nomenclature used in this entry reflects the most recent research of Vogt and colleagues (Vogt, in press; Vogt et al., 2003).

ACC Function in Posttraumatic Stress Disorder

The results of many recent functional neuroimaging studies suggest diminished function of the perigenual ACC and surrounding medial frontal cortex in posttraumatic stress disorder (PTSD) relative to individuals without PTSD (Shin, Rauch, & Pitman, 2006). This finding has been reported when participants view traumatic reminders, recall and imagine their own traumatic events, view fearful facial expressions, recall emotional words, perform emotional Stroop interference tasks, and undergo extinction after fear conditioning. Although a small number of studies have yielded discrepant results, the majority of studies have provided evidence for diminished perigenual ACC function in PTSD. Notably, several studies have reported that the degree of ACC activation is inversely related to symptom severity, such that individuals with lower ACC activation have more severe symptoms. Two treatment studies have reported a relationship between symptomatic response to serotonin reuptake inhibitors and increased activation of medial prefrontal cortical regions. Preliminary data suggests that the function of more dorsal portions of the ACC may not be diminished in PTSD.

According to current neurocircuitry models of PTSD, perigenual ACC and adjacent medial prefrontal regions are less responsive than normal and fail to inhibit an over-responsive amygdala (Shin et al., 2006). There is indeed evidence that the amygdala is overly responsive to reminders of trauma and to emotional, trauma-unrelated stimuli in PTSD. Four studies have reported a functional relationship between ACC and amygdala in PTSD, although the direction of this relationship is not yet clear.

Structural magnetic resonance imaging (MRI) studies have revealed that ACC volumes are smaller in PTSD patients compared to trauma-exposed control participants, even when controlling for alcohol use and total brain volume. Additionally, two studies have found ACC volume to be inversely correlated with severity of PTSD symptoms. One study has found shape differences in the ACC in PTSD.

Complementing the structural MRI studies, a magnetic resonance spectroscopy study has reported diminished N-acetyl aspartate (NAA)/creatine ratios (which is thought to reflect a loss of functional nerve cells) in the pregenual

ACC in PTSD. However, another study failed to replicate this finding. Thus while the exact mechanisms are unclear, PTSD appears to involve a compromise to the pregenual ACC's neural structure. This may be related to diminished function of the ACC and reduced inhibition of the amygdala in PTSD.

Although a wealth of data suggests diminished perigenual ACC function and volumes in PTSD, whether these abnormalities are a concomitant of the disorder or whether they represent a preexisting vulnerability is currently unknown.

REFERENCES

Bush, G., Luu, P., & Posner, M. I. (2000). Cognitive and emotional influence in anterior cingulate cortex. *Trends in Cognitive Sciences, 4*, 215–222.

Shin, L. M., Rauch, S. L., & Pitman, R. K. (2006). Amygdala, medial prefrontal cortex, and hippocampal function in PTSD. *Annals of the New York Academy of Sciences, 1071*, 67–79.

Vogt, B. A. (Ed.). (in press). *Cingulate neurobiology and disease: Vol. 1. Infrastructure, diagnosis, and treatment.* New York: Oxford University Press.

Vogt, B. A., Berger, G. R., & Derbyshire, S. W. (2003). Structural and functional dichotomy of human midcingulate cortex. *European Journal of Neuroscience, 18*, 3134–3144.

LISA M. SHIN
Tufts University

KATHRYN HANDWERGER
Tufts University

See also: **Biology, Brain Structure, and Function, Adult; Biology, Brain Structure, and Function, Child; Biology, Neurochemistry; Frontal Cortex; Hippocampus; Limbic System**

ANTHROPOLOGICAL PERSPECTIVES

There has long been a dialogue between anthropologists and psychologists interested in trauma, dating back at least to the work of physician/anthropologist W.H.R. Rivers in the 1920s. Rivers early on recognized trauma as a legitimate way for soldiers to suffer from combat experiences. Abraham Kardiner, another key figure in early trauma studies, who wrote an important volume on combat stress (Shepherd, 2001), had an association with one of the titans of American anthropology, Franz Boas, and his influential student Ruth Benedict at Columbia University in New York City.

Even before the term "culture bound syndrome" (Yap, 1951) was coined to describe "exotic" disorders found in the non-Western world, such as the much-debated Indonesian *Latah* (Winzeler, 1995), anthropologists have questioned the universality of Western diagnostic categories. For many years, anthropologists were concerned with seemingly bizarre disorders in non-Western contexts, largely ignoring the cultural nature of Western diagnostics. Recently, as many anthropologists have moved from a focus on culture bound syndromes to seeing all "idioms of distress" (Nichter, 1981) as culture bound, students of psychological trauma have increasingly been interested in the interactions between PTSD and globalization. This has lead to an emphasis on social suffering, structural violence, and collective memory rather than solely intrapsychic distress (Kleinman, Das, & Lock, 1997).

Anthropological versus Psychological Perspectives

The key difference between anthropology and psychology is one of emphasis—culture or biology. Clifford Geertz famously wrote (2000) that people often see biology as the cake and culture as the icing. Anthropologists argue that culture is also the cake. Thus, while psychology has typically been concerned with discovering universal aspects of human behavior, anthropology has focused on the culturally imbedded nature of human experience. Diagnostic categories have often been criticized by anthropologists for their bias toward Western perspectives, and successive generations of anthropologists have tried to develop ways to describe distress within the context of locally distinct cultures. Cultural anthropology tends to either dismiss biological knowledge as reductionistic (Good, 1992; Kirmayer, 2007), avoiding challenges researchers face in acquiring expertise in biological sciences,

and the complexity involved in developing models accounting for both biological and sociocultural processes relating to trauma.

Current Perspectives on Trauma

It was not until the 1990s that anthropology began to approach trauma as an object of study. Several lines of inquiry have developed: (1) analyses of the *social construction* of and *biomedical discourses* on trauma and PTSD; (2) *critiques of the mass-trauma paradigm* used to justify humanitarian disaster interventions; and (3) *ethnographies* of collective violence, cultural trauma, identity, and memory.

In the first category (*social construction*), Allan Young's work on the social construction of PTSD and its antecedents has become foundational and widely cited in both anthropological and psychiatric literature. His research locates and identifies the historical emergence, evolution, and logic of this psychiatric category within specific social practices and institutions, including the science of epidemiology, clinical settings, and legal and bureaucratic sites (e.g., Young, 1995). A group of researchers in England (e.g., Kilshaw, 2006) has examined the changing face of trauma for war veterans within shifting contexts of compensation, and related literature in this category has criticized the assumption that PTSD is a timeless and universal psychiatric illness by examining its historical and cultural-specificity (e.g., Bracken, Giller, & Summerfield, 1995). This work also links with the second category (*critiques of the mass-trauma paradigm*), and stems from a concern for the implications of exporting the PTSD model and associated psychosocial interventions to resource-poor countries during humanitarian emergencies. These critiques have focused on the medicalization and de-politicization of suffering, the cultural economy of victimhood, and the construction of new forms of sovereignty and governance as aspects of humanitarian aid (e.g., Breslau, 2004; Pupavac, 2004).

Research in the third category (*ethnographies*) has been the most wide-ranging. The bulk of this third line of literature examines the politics of collective memory and idioms of distress in conflict and postconflict societies. Two notable contributions include one edited volume dedicated to the intersection between psychology and anthropology in regard to historical trauma (Robben & Suárez-Orozco, 2000) and another volume that focuses on culture, trauma, memory-making, and identity (Antze & Lambek, 1996).

Conclusion

Recently, efforts have been made to integrate the findings of neuroscience and other biological sciences with the social and cultural experiences of trauma and its aftermath (e.g., Kirmayer, Lemelson, & Barad, 2007). This promising direction takes into account anthropological critiques of diagnostic categories while maintaining the importance of biological factors.

REFERENCES

Antze, P., & Lambek, M. (Eds.). (1996). *Tense past: Cultural essays in trauma and memory.* New York: Routledge.

Bracken, P., Giller, J., & Summerfield, D. (1995). Psychological responses to war and atrocity: The limitations of current concepts. *Social Science and Medicine, 40,* 1073–1082.

Breslau, J. (2004). Cultures of trauma: Anthropological views of posttraumatic stress disorder in international health. *Culture, Medicine, and Psychiatry, 28,* 113–126, 211–220.

Geertz, C. (2000). *Available light: Anthropological reflections on philosophical topics.* Princeton, NJ: Princeton University Press.

Good, B. (1992). Culture and psychopathology: Directions for psychiatric anthropology. In T. Schwartz, G. M. White, & C. A. Lutz (Eds.), *New directions in psychological anthropology* (pp. 181–206). Cambridge: Cambridge University Press.

Kilshaw, S. (2006). On being a gulf veteran: An anthropological perspective. *Philosophical Transactions of the Royal Society of London. Series B, Biological Sciences, 361,* 697–706.

Kirmayer, L., Lemelson, R., & Barad, M. (2007). *Understanding trauma: Integrating biological, clinical and cultural perspectives.* Cambridge: Cambridge University Press.

Kleinman, A., Das, V., & Lock, M. (Eds.). (1997). *Social suffering.* Berkeley: University of California Press.

Nichter, M. (1981). Idioms of distress, alternatives in the expression of psychosocial distress: A case study from South India. *Culture, Medicine and Psychiatry, 5,* 379–408.

Pupavac, V. (2004). International therapeutic peace and justice in Bosnia. *Social and Legal Studies, 13,* 377–401.

Robben, A. C. G. M., & Suárez-Orozco, M. M. (Eds.). (2000). *Cultures under siege: Collective violence and trauma.* Cambridge: Cambridge University Press.

Shephard, B. (2001). *A war of nerves: Soldiers and psychiatrists in the twentieth century, 1914–1994.* Cambridge, MA: Harvard University Press.

Winzeler, R. L. (1995). *Latah in Southeast Asia: The ethnography and history of a culture-bound syndrome.* Cambridge: Cambridge University Press.

Yap, P. M. (1951). Mental diseases peculiar to certain cultures: A survey of comparative psychiatry. *Journal of Mental Science, 97,* 313–327.

Young, A. (1995). *The harmony of illusions: Inventing posttraumatic stress disorder.* Princeton, NJ: Princeton University Press.

JOSHUA MOSES
City University of New York

KELLY MCKINNEY
McGill University

See also: **Culture and Trauma; Culture-Bound Syndromes**

ANTISOCIAL BEHAVIOR

High rates of both childhood trauma exposure (including physical and sexual abuse) and posttraumatic stress disorder (PTSD) have been observed among individuals who are incarcerated or who engage in antisocial behaviors such as drug and alcohol abuse, interpersonal aggression, and domestic violence. Indeed, childhood trauma and PTSD are two of the most robust and frequently examined risk factors for later antisocial behavior, and have been found to be associated with increased risk for these behaviors among both male and female samples. However, the causal link between trauma/PTSD and later antisocial behavior remains controversial.

In addition to traumatic experiences such as physical and sexual abuse, however, other aspects of the family environment during childhood may also increase the risk for later antisocial behaviors. In particular, evidence suggests that parental neglect or rejection, inconsistent patterns of discipline, family instability (e.g., divorce or death of a parent), disruptions in the attachment relationship, and family dysfunction in general are predictive of adult perpetration of antisocial behavior. These developmental, contextual factors are thought to contribute to an intergenerational cycle of violence.

In addition to these environmental and interpersonal risk factors, individual (i.e., intrapersonal) risk factors have also been implicated in the development of antisocial behavior, including genetics, biological factors (e.g., reduced serotonin levels), and personality traits (e.g., impulsivity, affective instability, and insecure attachment). Further, recent research suggests that emotion dysregulation and distress intolerance may underlie antisocial behaviors, with these behaviors (in particular, intimate partner abuse perpetration, aggressive behaviors, and substance abuse) functioning to escape, avoid, or otherwise regulate unwanted feelings and emotional distress. In fact, research suggests that emotion dysregulation may mediate the relationship between childhood trauma and other distressing experiences and later antisocial behaviors.

Much attention has been paid to PTSD and antisocial behavior among returning combat veterans reintegrating into society. Pre-military factors (e.g., family environment, childhood conduct disorder, the presence of personality disorders [especially borderline and antisocial]) have demonstrated a direct association with postwar antisocial behaviors and represent the best predictors of interpersonal aggression following combat service. However, factors such as war zone combat exposure or negative homecoming experiences also may be related to antisocial behaviors through their relationship with PTSD, with PTSD serving as a mediating variable.

RECOMMENDED READINGS

Bushman, B. J., Baumeister, R. F., & Phillips, C. M. (2001). Do people aggress to improve their mood? Catharsis beliefs, affect regulation opportunity, and aggressive responding. *Journal of Personality and Social Psychology, 81,* 17–32.

Dixon, A., Howie, P., & Franzcp, J. S. (2005). Trauma exposure, posttraumatic stress, and psychiatric comorbidity in female juvenile offenders. *Journal of the American Academy of Child and Adolescent Psychiatry, 44,* 798–806.

Dutton, D. G. (1995). Trauma symptoms and PTSD-like profiles in perpetrators of intimate abuse. *Journal of Traumatic Stress, 8,* 299–316.

Egeland, B., Jacobvitz, J., & Paptola, K. (1989). Intergenerational continuity of abuse. In J. Lancaster & R. Gelles (Eds.), *Biosocial aspects of child abuse* (pp. 255–266). New York: Jossey-Bass.

Fontana, A., & Rosenheck, R. (2005). The role of war-zone trauma and PTSD in the etiology of antisocial behavior. *Journal of Nervous and Mental Disease, 193,* 203–209.

Heim, A., & Westen, D. (2005). Theories of personality and personality disorders. In J. M. Oldham, A. E. Skodol, & D. E. Bender (Eds.), *Textbook of personality disorders* (pp. 17–33). Washington, DC: American Psychiatric Publishing.

Jang, K. L., Stein, M. B., Taylor, S., Asmundson, G. J., & Livesley, W. J. (2003). Exposure to traumatic events and experiences: Aetiological relationships with personality function. *Psychiatry Research, 120,* 61–69.

Paris, J. (1997). Antisocial and borderline personality disorders: Two separate diagnoses or two aspects of the same psychopathology? *Comprehensive Psychiatry, 38,* 237–242.

Stuart, G. L., Moore, T. M., Coop Gordon, K., Ramsey, S. E., & Kahler, C. W. (2006). Psychopathology in women arrested for domestic violence. *Journal of Interpersonal Violence, 21,* 376–389.

MATTHEW JAKUPCAK
Puget Sound Health Care System

KIM L. GRATZ
University of Maryland

See also: Aggression; Anger; Disruptive Behavior Disorders

ANXIETY DISORDERS

Anxiety disorders include posttraumatic stress disorder (PTSD), panic disorder (PD), generalized anxiety disorder (GAD), social anxiety disorder (SAD; or social phobia), obsessive compulsive disorder (OCD) and specific phobias (*DSM-IV;* American Psychiatric Association, 1994). This entry reviews the potential relationship of traumatic event exposure to anxiety disorders. Although many people who have anxiety disorders may have had traumatic event exposure, the causal relationships may vary by disorder.

Traumatic event exposure may serve as a primary cause, a predisposing cause, a precipitating cause, or a reinforcing cause in the development of an anxiety disorder. *Primary causes* are the conditions necessary for the disorder to occur. It is a necessary, but not always sufficient factor in the development of a disorder. *Predisposing causes* are conditions that occur prior to the onset of a disorder, which pave the way for the disorder to occur under certain conditions. These are often referred to as vulnerability factors. *Precipitating causes* are conditions that overwhelm the individual's resources to cope and trigger the disorder; and a *reinforcing cause* is a condition that maintains the disorder once it develops. These differing levels of causality will be considered.

The assessment of traumatic event exposure in people with anxiety disorders other than PTSD has not always been considered important or even relevant in prior literature. As a result, it has only been within the past 15 years that traumatic event exposure has been studied in any depth in relationship to anxiety disorders other than PTSD, which by definition includes the experience of a traumatic event. Because of this, the types of traumatic stressors that have been assessed have varied greatly from study to study and the instruments used to assess trauma have also varied widely. Some studies have used only brief questionnaires, whereas others have used well-validated instruments. The type of sample assessed has also greatly affected results. Some studies have assessed the anxiety of college students, while others have assessed specific anxiety disorders in patient populations. Other studies have been epidemiological or have investigated large samples after mass traumas such as the September 11, 2001, terrorist attacks or major natural disasters. Still others have examined veterans returning from war.

The original National Comorbidity Survey Study (NCS) indicated that 50% to 60% of the U.S. population, ages 15 to 54, has experienced a traumatic event within their lifetime (Kessler, Sonnega, Bromet, Hughes, & Nelson, 1995). Rates of anxiety disorders in the U.S. population are also quite high, with a lifetime prevalence of 29% (Kessler, Chiu, Demler, & Walters, 2005) and a 12-month prevalence of 18% for any anxiety disorder (Kessler, Berglund, et al., 2005).

It is estimated that approximately 4% of the population suffers from PTSD, 3% from PD, 3% from GAD, 7% from SAD, 1% from OCD, and 9% with specific phobias within a 12-month period (Kessler, Berglund, et al., 2005). Lifetime prevalence rates are considerably higher, with estimates of 7% for PTSD, 5% for PD, 6% GAD, 12% SAD, 2% from OCD, and 13% for specific phobias (Kessler, Chiu, et al., 2005). The relationship between traumatic event exposure and each anxiety disorder is explored next.

Posttraumatic Stress Disorder

A diagnosis of PTSD requires the presence of a traumatic stressor. Traumatic event exposure is a primary cause of PTSD by definition. Several types of stressors have been found to be most associated with PTSD, with military combat and rape having the highest probability of resulting in a PTSD diagnosis (Kessler et al., 1995). Studies have indicated that women are more likely to develop PTSD following trauma than men are, and that the more traumatic events that a person experiences, the more likely that they are to develop PTSD. It has been found that approximately 32% of women who have experienced rape, 38% of physical assault victims, 22% of those who have had a loved one murdered (Resnick, Kilpatrick, Dansky, Saunders, & Best, 1993), and 30% of male and 27% of female veterans suffer from lifetime PTSD (Kulka, Schlenger, Fairbank, Hough, & Jordan, 1990).

Several pre-traumatic event, peri-event, and postevent characteristics have been found to influence the development of PTSD. These include factors such as previous psychiatric history, perceived life threat during the event, physical injury resulting from the event, and social support after the event (Brewin, Andrews, & Valentine, 2000).

Individuals with PTSD often present with a variety of comorbid psychiatric conditions including substance abuse, major depression, obsessive compulsive disorder, dysthymic disorder, bipolar disorder, and panic disorder (Back et al., 2000; Falsetti & Resnick, 1997; Hamner et al., 2000; Kessler, 2000; Kilpatrick et al., 2000). In fact, psychiatric comorbidity is between 2 to 6 times more likely to occur in adults with PTSD compared to adults without PTSD. PTSD when comorbid with other disorders may also negatively influence treatment response (Green et al., 2006). Data strongly support that traumatic event exposure is a primary cause of PTSD.

Panic Disorder

Traumatic event exposure is quite high in PD samples and is often comorbid with PTSD. Resnick, Falsetti, Kilpatrick, and Foy (1994) found that 90% of rape victims assessed within 72 hours post-assault met full criteria for panic attacks during that time frame. Similarly, Bryant and Panasetis (2001) found that 53% of civilian trauma survivors reportedly met criteria for panic attacks during traumatic event exposure. Reported panic symptoms during the traumatic event were significantly positively correlated with measures of acute stress disorder and panic assessed between 2 and 28 days post-event.

Data from a random sample of 1,008 residents of Manhattan at the time of the September 11 terrorists attacks indicated that a relatively large percentage of those near the disaster reportedly experienced panic attacks during the

terrorist attacks or soon after learning of the them; in fact 12% reported panic attacks acutely following the event (Galea, Ahern, Resnick, Kilpatrick, & Bucuvalas, 2002). Importantly, report of a peri-event panic attack was a significant predictor of current PTSD diagnosis in the 5 to 8 weeks following the attacks. Estimated prevalence of PTSD in that study was 8%, while 10% of the sample reported symptoms consistent with a diagnosis of current major depression. Further, those reporting a panic attack during the terror attacks were eight times more likely than those without panic to later have a PTSD diagnosis, after controlling for race, prior stressors in the previous 12 months, loss of possessions due to the attacks, and residence below or within close proximity to the World Trade Center. Report of a peri-event panic attack was also a significant predictor of current depression, after controlling for other predictors (Galea et al., 2002). Finally, these data were corroborated by Pfefferbaum, Stuber, Galea, and Fairbrother (2006), who reported similar associations of PTSD and peri-event panic attacks in adolescents. Based on research conducted thus far, it appears that trauma may be a predisposing cause of PD.

Employing Barlow's concept that panic reactions are triggered by alarms, Falsetti, Resnick, Dansky, Lydiard, and Kilpatrick (1995) proposed that for many people, a "true alarm," such as a physical assault or rape, may trigger the first panic attack. Subsequently, the panic attack is signaled by both external and internal stimuli associated with the traumatic event. Examples of external cues include places, situations, objects, smells, and sounds associated with the trauma, while internal cues include emotions, the physiological arousal experienced during traumatic events, as well as cognitions about dying or going crazy. Over time, these cues elicit a conditioned response (i.e., panic attack) that in effect becomes a "learned alarm."

Similar to Foa and Kozak's (1986) theory, Falsetti et al. (1995) proposed that external cues associated with the event, and internal cues, such as physiological arousal, thoughts, and emotions experienced at the time of the event, comprise a fear network in one's cognitions. Activation of any component in the network may lead to an anxiety response, including panic attacks. Given that panic attacks may be triggered by internal cues, this accounts for why panic symptoms may seem to come from "out of the blue," since individuals may not perceive the symptoms as directly connected to any particular event. Thus, panic may not only develop directly from a past traumatic experience, but may be a consequence of the chronic hyperarousal noted in PTSD, which can increase vulnerability to panic by decreasing the amount of further arousal needed to reach the threshold for a panic attack to occur.

Falsetti et al. (1995) also proposed that although individuals may possess a biological predisposition for anxiety, this is not considered to be a necessary condition for development of either a conditioned emotional response or avoidance symptoms. Finally, the avoidance symptoms are hypothesized to further strengthen the associational network of conditioned ·cues and responses through escape-avoidance learning and lack of extinction, thereby maintaining a cycle of chronic hyperarousal and panic attacks.

Because there may be no actual physical danger at the time of these future attacks, it is also possible that when such physiological symptoms do occur when the individual becomes frightened and focuses on the arousal symptoms, thinking he or she is having a heart attack, going crazy, or dying (Barlow, 1988). In fact, evidence suggests that many people with PD demonstrate a specific hypervigilance to signs of threat (Mathews & McLeod, 1986) and are excessively preoccupied with fears of physical danger (Hibbert, 1984). In addition, Litz and Keane (1989) found that anxious subjects have an attentional bias toward threat cues. If such a theory is applied to the understanding of panic in individuals with a traumatic event history, then it would be expected that physiological cues would be considered part of that fear network and vigilance toward such cues would further increase the likelihood of future panic attacks. Falsetti and Resnick developed a treatment specifically for comorbid PTSD and panic attacks called multiple channel exposure therapy (Falsetti, Resnick, & Davis, 2005, in press; Falsetti, Resnick, & Gibbs, 2001).

Generalized Anxiety Disorder

Research on the relationship of traumatic event exposure and GAD is sparse. Most studies that have assessed stressful life events in relation to GAD have included life events that would not meet Criterion A for PTSD in terms of traumatic event exposure. Few studies were found that examined traumatic event exposure. One study (Smith, North, McCool, & Shea, 1990) conducted with hotel workers who survived a jet plane crash into a hotel where they worked found that more than half the sample met criteria for a psychiatric disorder 4 to 6 weeks following the crash. Of the employees who were on site at the time of the crash, 29% were diagnosed with PTSD, 12% with alcohol abuse/dependence, 41% with depression, and 29% with GAD. Diagnoses for employees who were offsite at the time of the crash included 17% with PTSD, 14% with alcohol abuse/dependence, 41% with depression, and 14% with GAD. However, two-thirds of these disorders were predicted by prior psychiatric history, making it unclear to what extent the stressor contributed to the development or reemergence of these disorders.

Another study (Roemer, Molina, Litz, & Borkovec, 1997) examined 94 patients with a principal diagnosis of GAD and compared these patients to 48 nonanxious participants. They found that patients were significantly more likely to report a past potentially traumatic event than nonpatients. However, the types of events that were experienced were not reported.

In another study, the types and rates of traumatic event exposure and differences in symptom endorsement in a clinical sample of patients diagnosed with GAD were reported (Brawman-Mintzer, Monnier, Wolitzky, & Falsetti, 2005). Results indicated that 95% of the GAD sample reported a traumatic event. The most common events were natural disaster (64%), serious accident (29%), childhood sexual assault (26%), and adulthood sexual assault (21%). Trauma exposure preceded onset of GAD in 65% of patients.

At this time, given the limited data, the extent of causality of traumatic event exposure in the development of GAD is unclear.

Social Anxiety Disorder, Obsessive Compulsive Disorder, and Specific Phobias

It has long been believed that people who suffer from social anxiety disorder may have suffered from early social experiences that were traumatic (Wolpe, 1958) or aversive (Trower, Bryant, & Argyle, 1978). Despite this belief, there have been very few studies conducted that have examined traumatic event exposure in patients who suffer from social anxiety. David, Giron, and Mellman (1995) assessed childhood traumatic event histories of 51 patients with PD with agoraphobia and/or social phobia and a nonclinical comparison group of 51 participants. They found that 63% of the patient group was positive for childhood trauma compared to 3% of the nonclinical comparison group. Fifty percent of the social phobia group had a history of physical or sexual abuse compared to 2% of the patients without social phobia. The social phobia fear and avoidance subscale ratings were higher in patients with physical/sexual abuse than in patients without. The authors hypothesized that trauma exposure may interact with a genetic vulnerability and other factors to influence how phobic symptoms are expressed. This study did not assess for PTSD, so it is unknown as to how many patients may have also had comorbid PTSD.

A study of early traumatic events, parental rearing styles, family history of mental disorders, and birth risk factors in patients with social anxiety disorder found higher rates of traumatic childhood experiences in patients with social anxiety (88%) compared to health controls (48%; Bandelow et al., 2004). When the other factors assessed were statistically adjusted though, there was only a trend toward a significant contribution of childhood sexual abuse.

Social phobia does appear to be highly comorbid with PTSD when PTSD is the principal diagnosis. Zayfert, DeViva, and Hofman (2005) reported that in a sample of 443 patients seeking treatment of PTSD, SP, or both, that 43% of those with a principal diagnosis of PTSD had SP. In comparison in those patients with a primary diagnosis of SP, only 7% had a comorbid diagnosis of PTSD. Another study compared traumatic event histories of patients with OCD and SAD (Fontenelle et al., 2007). They found that patients with OCD reported significantly lower rates of exposure to traumatic events compared to patients with SAD.

Finally, a twin study that evaluated the stress-diathesis model in the development of phobias did not find trauma to be associated with higher risk of developing phobias (Kendler, Myers, & Prescott, 2002). There is insufficient evidence at this time to determine a causal role of trauma in the development of social anxiety disorder, OCD, and specific phobias.

REFERENCES

American Psychiatric Association. (1994). *Diagnostic and statistical manual of mental disorders* (4th ed.). Washington, DC: Author.

Back, S., Dansky, B. S., Coffey, S. F., Saladin, M. E., Sonne, S., & Brady, K. T. (2000). Cocaine dependence with and without posttraumatic stress disorder: A comparison of substance use, trauma history and psychiatric comorbidity. *American Journal on Addictions, 9,* 51–62.

Bandelow, B., Torrente, A. C., Wedekind, D., Broocks, A., Hajak, G., & Ruther, E. (2004). Early traumatic life events, parental rearing styles, family history of mental disorders, and birth risk factors in patients with social anxiety disorder. *European Archives of Psychiatry Clinical Neuroscience, 254,* 397–405.

Barlow, D. H. (1988). *Anxiety and its disorders.* New York: Guilford Press.

Brawman-Mintzer, O., Monnier, J., Wolitzky, K. B., & Falsetti, S. A. (2005). Patients with generalized anxiety disorder and a history of trauma: Somatic symptom endorsement. *Journal of Psychiatric Practice,* 212–215.

Brewin, C. R., Andrews, B., & Valentine, J. D. (2000). Meta-analysis of risk factors for posttraumatic stress disorder in trauma-exposed adults. *Journal of Consulting and Clinical Psychology, 68,* 748–766.

Bryant, R. A., & Panasetis, P. (2001). Panic symptoms during trauma and acute stress disorder. *Behavior Research and Therapy, 39,* 961–969.

David, D., Giron, A., & Mellman, T. A. (1995). Panic-phobic patients and developmental trauma. *Journal of Clinical Psychiatry, 56,* 113–124.

Falsetti, S. A., & Resnick, H. S. (1997). Frequency and severity of panic attack symptoms in a treatment seeking sample of trauma victims. *Journal of Traumatic Stress, 10*(4), 683–689.

Falsetti, S. A., Resnick, H. S., Dansky, B. S., Lydiard, R. B., & Kilpatrick, D. G. (1995). The relationship of stress to panic disorder: Cause or effect. In C. M. Mazure (Ed.), *Does stress cause psychiatric illness?* (pp. 111–147). Washington, DC: American Psychiatric Press.

Falsetti, S. A., Resnick, H. S., & Davis, J. L. (2005). Multiple channel exposure therapy: Combining cognitive behavioral therapies for the treatment of posttraumatic stress disorder with panic attacks. *Behavior Modification, 29,* 70–94.

Falsetti, S. A., Resnick, H. S., Davis J. (in press). An investigation of the long-term effectiveness of multiple channel exposure therapy for the treatment of PTSD with comorbid panic attacks. *Depression and Anxiety.*

Falsetti, S. A., Resnick, H. S., & Gibbs, N. A. (2001). Treatment of PTSD with panic attacks combining cognitive processing therapy with panic control treatment techniques. *Group Dynamics: Theory, Research and Practice, 5,* 252–260.

Foa, E. B., & Kozak, M. J. (1986). Emotional processing of fear: Exposure to corrective information. *Psychological Bulletin, 99,* 20–35.

Fontenelle, L. F., Domingues, A. M., Souza, W. F., Mendlowicz, M. V., de Menezes, G. B., & Figueira, I. L. (2007). History of trauma and dissociative symptoms among patients with obsessive-compulsive disorder and social anxiety disorder. *Psychiatric Quarterly, 78,* 241–250.

Galea, S., Ahern, J., Resnick, H., Kilpatrick, D., & Bucuvalas, M. (2002). Psychological sequelae of the September 11 terrorist attacks in New York City. *New England Journal of Medicine, 346,* 982–987.

Green, B. L., Krupnick, J. L., Chung, J., Siddique, J., Krause, E. D., Revicki, D., et al. (2006). Impact of PTSD comorbidity on one-year outcomes in a depression trial. *Journal of Clinical Psychology, 62,* 815–835.

Hamner, M. B., Frueh, B. C., Ulmer, H. G., Huber, M. G., Twomey, T. J., Tyson, C., et al. (2000).

Psychotic features in chronic posttraumatic stress disorder and schizophrenia: Comparative severity. *Journal of Nervous and Mental Disease, 188,* 217–221.

Hibbert, G. A. (1984). Ideational components of anxiety: Their origin and content. *British Journal of Psychiatry, 144,* 618–624.

Kendler, K. S., Myers, J., & Prescott, C. A. (2002). The etiology of phobias: An evaluation of the stress-diathesis model. *Archives of General Psychiatry, 59,* 242–248.

Kessler, R. C. (2000). The epidemiology of pure and comorbid generalized anxiety disorder: A review and evaluation of recent research. *Acta Psychiatric Scandinavia Supplement, 406,* 7–13.

Kessler, R. C., Berglund, P., Demler, O., Jin, R., Merikangas, K. R., & Walters, E. E. (2005). Lifetime prevalence and age-of-onset distributions of DSM-IV disorders in the National Comorbidity Survey Replication. *Archives of General Psychiatry, 62,* 593–602.

Kessler, R. C., Chiu, W. T., Demler, O., & Walters, E. E. (2005). Prevalence, severity, and comorbidity of 12-month DSM-IV disorders in the National Comorbidity Survey Replication. *Archives of General Psychiatry, 62,* 617–709.

Kessler, R. C., Sonnega, A., Bromet, E., Hughes, M., & Nelson, C. B. (1995). Posttraumatic stress disorder in the National Comorbidity Survey. *Archives of General Psychiatry, 52,* 1048–1060.

Kilpatrick, D. G., Acierno, R., Saunders, B., Resnick, H. S., Best, C. L., & Schnurr, P. P. (2000). Risk factors for adolescent substance abuse and dependence: Data from a national sample. *Journal of Consulting and Clinical Psychology, 68,* 19–30.

Kulka, R. A., Schlenger, W. E., Fairbank, J. A., Hough, R. L., & Jordan, B. K. (1990). *Trauma and the Vietnam war generation: Report of findings from the National Vietnam Veterans Readjustment Study.* New York: Brunner/Mazel.

Litz, B. T., & Keane, T. M. (1989). Information processing in anxiety disorders: Application to the understanding of post-traumatic stress disorder. *Clinical Psychology Review, 9,* 243–257.

Mathews, A. M., & MacLeod, C. (1986). Discrimination of threat cues without awareness in anxiety states. *Journal of Abnormal Psychology, 95,* 131–138.

Pfefferbaum, B., Stuber, J., Galea, S., & Fairbrother, G. (2006). Panic reactions to terrorist attacks and probable posttraumatic stress disorder in adolescents. *Journal of Traumatic Stress, 19,* 217–228.

Resnick, H. S., Falsetti, S. A., Kilpatrick, D. G., & Foy, D. W. (1994, November). *Associations between panic attacks during rape assaults and follow-up PTSD or panic attack outcomes.* Paper presented at the 10th annual meeting of the International Society for Traumatic Stress, Chicago.

Resnick, H. S., Kilpatrick, D. G., Dansky, B. S., Saunders, B. E., & Best, C. L. (1993). Prevalence of civilian trauma and posttraumatic stress disorder in a representative national sample of women. *Journal of Consulting and Clinical Psychology, 61,* 984–991.

Roemer, L., Molina, S., Litz, B. T., & Borkovec, T. D. (1997). Preliminary investigation of the role of previous exposure to potentially traumatizing events in generalized anxiety disorder. *Depression and Anxiety, 4,* 134–138.

Smith, E. M., North, C. S., McCool, R. E., & Shea, J. M. (1990). Acute postdisaster psychiatric disorders: Identification of persons at risk. *American Journal of Psychiatry, 147,* 202–218.

Trower, P., Bryant, B. M., & Argyle, M. (1978). *Social skills and mental health.* London: Methuen.

Wolpe, J. (1958). *Psychotherapy and reciprocal inhibition.* Stanford, CA: Stanford University Press.

Zayfert, C., DeViva, J. C., & Hofman, S. G. (2005). Comorbid PTSD and social phobia in a treatment seeking population. *Journal of Nervous and Mental Disease, 193,* 93–101.

SHERRY A. FALSETTI
University of Illinois College of Medicine at Rockford

See also: Anxiety Management Training; Comorbidity; Posttraumatic Stress Disorder

ANXIETY MANAGEMENT TRAINING

The conceptual framework underlying anxiety management training is rooted in theories of stress and coping. In this model, stress is neither an environmental event nor the person's emotional and behavioral response to the environment. Rather, stress results from the *interaction* of the person and the environment when events are experienced as exceeding or taxing one's coping resources and thus causing a threat to one's welfare. In this transactional view, stress is also seen as an inevitable aspect of life that cannot be eliminated. Anxiety is a normal response to stress and is often useful in motivating coping behavior. However, anxiety can become excessive and disruptive, as is the case for people who have developed persistent posttraumatic stress symptoms.

Anxiety management training is a set of cognitive-behavioral interventions that have been applied with psychological trauma survivors for several decades (Rothbaum, Meadows, Resick, & Foy, 2000). Its use increased significantly when posttraumatic stress disorder (PTSD) was formally codified as an anxiety disorder by the American Psychiatric Association in 1980. At that time, some cognitive behavioral researchers and clinicians viewed PTSD as a complex phobia with extensive generalization (i.e., in which fear responses spread, or "generalized" to stimuli or circumstances beyond the original stressful experiences), and thus applied interventions that were known to be effective for pathological anxiety. These included exposure therapy procedures (*see:* **Exposure Therapy, Adult**) that had been found successful in the treatment of phobias, and anxiety management procedures, known to be successful for those with generalized anxiety. Participants in anxiety management programs were often female survivors of assault or military combat veterans.

One such program that has been commonly employed in the past 30 years is stress inoculation training (SIT; Meichenbaum, 1975, 1985). SIT, which provides techniques or skills that the person can use to manage and reduce anxiety, is a relatively well-researched program that was used in early studies of treatments for female rape and crime victims. The goal of stress inoculation treatment is to teach the person to understand the dynamics of stress and to develop or improve intrapersonal and interpersonal skills for managing stress reactions. These coping skills, which typically include breathing and relaxation training, cognitive restructuring, guided (task-enhancing) self-dialogue, assertiveness training, role-playing, and covert modeling, help the person to manage her reactions to trauma-related cues or situations. Treatment usually begins with discussing the person's stress and anxiety from the transactional perspective, and the rationale or conceptual groundwork for the skills training is laid down. The next phase includes training and practice of coping skills. The core skills of SIT are central to most other anxiety management programs, and are briefly described next.

Breathing Training

The therapist gives specific instructions for reducing tension by slowing the rate of respiration and pairing breathing with a cue for calming and relaxing the mind (e.g., silently and slowly drawing out the word "calm" or "relax" while exhaling very slowly). Typically, the therapist models this slow breathing pattern, and then observes the person practice and provides appropriate feedback. Sometimes a tape recording is made of the therapist guiding the person through a number of respiratory cycles for the person to practice at home. Homework is given to practice the skill several times daily in order to develop its usefulness in reducing tension and managing anxiety.

Relaxation Training

There are many methods of relaxation, but the one that is utilized in SIT and was commonly used in early programs for trauma survivors is progressive muscle relaxation (PMR). During PMR training the person is taught to systematically tense and then relax specific muscle groups throughout the body, while focusing attention on the contrast, or how these muscles feel when tense and when relaxed. The goal is to learn to identify excess muscular tension and to eliminate it when detected. The therapist typically records the relaxation training instructions for the client's use in daily practice at home.

Cognitive Restructuring

Cognitive restructuring is based on cognitive theory, which hypothesizes that it is the *interpretation* of events, rather than events themselves, which leads to specific emotional responses such as anxiety. Using an example that is commonly experienced by psychological trauma survivors, when "safe" or harmless events are viewed as threatening, unrealistic or excessive anxiety results. The aim of cognitive restructuring is to help the client to understand the role of his or her beliefs and interpretations in influencing emotional reactions, to identify the ways that the traumatic event or experience has influenced his or her beliefs and expectations (especially those that trigger excessive negative emotions such as fear, anger, and shame), and to learn to challenge and modify these beliefs and expectations in a rational, evidence-based manner.

Guided Self-Dialogue

The way we think and messages that we give ourselves can help or hinder our management of stressful situations. Guided self-dialogue teaches the person to focus on her or his internal dialogue, or on what he or she "is saying" to her/himself, with the objective of replacing irrational, self-critical, or negative dialogue with rational, facilitative, and task-enhancing dialogue. The therapist and client focus on coping with stressful events in a series of steps: (1) preparation, (2) confrontation and management, (3) coping with feelings of being overwhelmed, and (4) reinforcement. For each step, the patient and therapist generate a series of questions and/or statements which encourage the patient to: (1) assess the actual probability of a negative event happening, (2) manage overwhelming avoidance behavior, (3) control self-criticism and self-devaluation, (4) engage in a feared behavior, and (5) reinforce her/himself for attempting the behavior and for following the plan.

Behavioral Rehearsal

Behavioral rehearsal is a means of learning new or developing existing behaviors to replace old (less effective) ways of responding to stressful situations, and provides a chance to practice the new behaviors before the "real-life" event occurs. The client and therapist act out scenes (either in imagination or in role-play) in which the client confronts a difficult or stressful situation. The premise is that repeated practice of a behavior reduces anxiety and makes it more likely that a new behavior will be used when it is called for.

Covert modeling is a behavioral rehearsal technique that permits practice of the desired behaviors or coping response via imagination (i.e., covert). First the therapist and client select a stressful or difficult situation to work on. Often the therapist will then model successful coping: closing her or his eyes and describing aloud what he or she is visualizing, the therapist explains how he or she is utilizing anxiety management skills during the difficult situation and successfully works through it. The client then takes a turn and visualizes her/himself coping successfully with the situation, describing aloud her/his imaginal use of the skills. If suitable, scenes used for covert modeling are sometimes those later utilized for role-play practice in session.

Role-play involves the acting out of behaviors, and rehearsal of responses, while pretending to be in a particular situation. During role-play, as in covert modeling, it is common for the therapist to first play the client's role and model appropriate social skills. Next roles are reversed with the client playing himself. Each role-play is discussed and the client is encouraged to point out positive aspects of his performance as well as areas that can be improved. Role-plays are repeated with the goal of shaping desired behavior and developing better skill through practice.

Empirical Research on Anxiety Management Training

Randomized controlled research studies comparing various forms of cognitive behavior therapy (CBT) for psychological trauma survivors with PTSD have shown that stress inoculation training is efficacious at reducing PTSD as well as other trauma-related symptoms (e.g., depression), particularly among women who have survived sexual assault (Foa et al., 1999; Foa, Rothbaum, Riggs, & Murdock, 1991). These studies have found stress inoculation training to be fairly comparable to exposure

therapy and more effective than control conditions such as waitlist and supportive counseling. In two studies conducted with veterans, stress inoculation training was not as strongly supported, because one study found that veterans treated with stress management in group format did not improve in terms of reductions in PTSD (and neither did the trauma-focused group in that study; Monson, Rodriguez, & Warner, 2005) although the other study found stress management (focused heavily on anger management) more effective than routine clinical care in reduction of anger and PTSD intrusive reexperiencing symptoms (Chemtob, Novaco, Harnada, & Gross, 1997). Several other studies have used single anxiety management skills such as relaxation training, biofeedback, and assertion training as comparison conditions, but failed to find them efficacious. For example, three randomized trial research studies have found relaxation training to be less efficacious than exposure therapy, cognitive therapy, and their combination.

Conclusion

Research studies have generally found that anxiety management skills training is effective at reducing psychological trauma-related pathology in female assault survivors but perhaps less effective when used with male military veterans. Stress inoculation training has been studied less extensively than other forms of CBT, however, and most studies involving SIT were conducted in the 1980s and 1990s. This may be in part due to a shift from earlier, heavily behavioral conceptualizations of PTSD to formulations that emphasize the role of cognition in explaining the development and maintenance of chronic traumatic stress-related disorders.

Thus, while anxiety management approaches showed early promise at reducing traumatic stress-related symptoms, most psychological trauma researchers moved on to investigating treatments that address the factors that are thought to maintain posttraumatic symptoms and difficulties, and thus may offer deeper or longer-lasting change in traumatic stress-related symptoms. These treatments—exposure therapy (*see:* **Exposure Therapy, Adult**) and cognitive therapy (*see:* **Cognitive Behavior Therapy, Adult**)—are designed to help the survivor to emotionally process his or her memories of traumatic experiences and to modify the unhelpful or inaccurate beliefs about the world and the self that may be maintaining traumatic stress-related fears and other symptoms.

REFERENCES

Chemtob, C. M., Novaco, R. W., Harnada, R. S., & Gross, D. M. (1997). Cognitive-behavioral treatment for severe anger in PTSD. *Journal of Consulting and Clinical Psychology, 65*(1), 184–189.

Foa, E. B., Dancu, C. V., Hembree, E., Jaycox, L. H., Meadows, E. A., & Street, G. P. (1999). The efficacy of exposure therapy, stress inoculation training and their combination in ameliorating PTSD for female victims of assault. *Journal of Consulting and Clinical Psychology, 67,* 194–200.

Foa, E. B., Rothbaum, B. O., Riggs, D., & Murdock, T. (1991). Treatment of PTSD in rape victims: A comparison between cognitive-behavioral procedures and counseling. *Journal of Consulting and Clinical Psychology, 59,* 715–723.

Meichenbaum, D. (1975). Self-instructional methods. In F. H. Kanfer & A. P. Goldstein (Eds.), *Helping people change* (pp. 357–391). New York: Pergamon Press.

Meichenbaum, D. (1985). *Stress inoculation training.* New York: Pergamon Press.

Monson, C. M., Rodriguez, B. F., & Warner, R. (2005). Cognitive-behavioral therapy for PTSD in the real world: Do interpersonal relationships make a real difference? *Journal of Clinical Psychology, 61,* 751–761.

Rothbaum, B. O., Meadows, E. A., Resick, P., & Foy, D. W. (2000). Cognitive-behavioral therapy. In E. Foa, T. Keane, & M. Friedman (Eds.), *Effective treatments for PTSD: Practice guidelines from the International Society for Traumatic Stress Studies* (pp. 320–325). New York: Guilford Press.

Elizabeth A. Hembree
University of Pennsylvania

See also: Anxiety Disorders; Cognitive Behavior Therapy, Adult; Cognitive Behavior Therapy, Child Abuse; Coping Skills Training; Exposure Therapy, Adult; Exposure Therapy, Child; Psychoeducation

ARTISTIC DEPICTIONS OF PSYCHOLOGICAL TRAUMA

The human experience of psychological trauma finds expression in many forms. The very symptoms of posttraumatic stress disorder (PTSD) themselves are often described as a form of expression because they are understood by some to communicate the complexities of the traumatic experience in ways that are physical, behavioral, emotional, and cognitive. The verbal expression of the traumatic experience can be terribly difficult and frustrating to accomplish. Because of the intensely disturbing and degrading aspects of traumatic events, and the intimately personal nature of some of the concomitant violations, verbally expressing traumatic experiences may require finding words for the ineffable and speaking the unspeakable (*see:* **Literary Depictions of Psychological Trauma**). Nonverbal artistic forms of creative expression therefore have been an important set of media for depictions of the nature and effects of psychological trauma.

Dating back to the earliest cave paintings, art has stood as a means for capturing and expressing the human experience with a power beyond words. Artistic depictions of events display more than a setting and scene. They convey emotions and layers of meaning in a manner that is both veridical and symbolic, while avoiding some of the confusions, clichés, and reductions to which words are so vulnerable. This is not to demean all written and verbal depictions of psychological trauma, but rather to admire the courage and skill of those who find with words and phrases a means of expressing to others what is so deeply painful and so painfully necessary to convey. But among the most powerful characteristics of the visual arts is their ability to convey the depths of the human experience beyond the limits of words and the impediments of language. The prehistoric paintings preserved in France on the cavernous walls beneath Lascaux have long outlived whatever languages may have been spoke by their creators and demonstrate the profound capacity for artistic depictions of the human experience to transcend time, language, and culture.

When portraying psychological trauma, artists and photographers work at the intersection of mind and emotion to visually represent what is by definition an unimaginable and unbearable shock. The visual artist applies paint, line, color, a lens, or a blend of media to the subject, expressing either a personal traumatic experience, or attempting to depict the traumatic experiences or reactions of others. These artistic depictions have the latitude for conveying the psychologically traumatic experience from any angle of view and within any imaginable frame of reference. The depicted scene may be broad in scope, or narrowed to a very fine point. Viewers may be drawn into small details and variations of texture, or cast back to vantage points where the scene's entirety can be viewed in full. Moreover, the psychological impact of the trauma on a previously organized perspective can be conveyed through varying degrees of distortion, as is evident in the works of the Cubists and Surrealists.

To whom does the artist address this visual depiction of psychological trauma? Victims? Perpetrators? Bystanders? Few artists reveal their explicit purpose in bringing to the public eye a work that is ultimately about personal horror. And many people consider psychological trauma a private matter owned only by the victims, as for instance in cases of child abuse, rape, or domestic violence. These subjects are found less often in art galleries than in very personal works meant more often for expressing than for sharing. But Plutarch's tale of the public abduction of conquered women by Romans seeking wives, *The Rape of the Sabine Women,* was rendered in Giambologna's sixteenth-century writhing sculpture and painted in classically stylized scenes of chaotic frenzy a century later by Poussin and Rubens, and in the eighteenth century by David. Much later, in the early 1960s, Pablo Picasso took inspiration from David's vision of this event, which he transformed by stripping away its classic patina to reveal a scene of crushing violence and domination. Working in a related vein in the twenty-first century, Chinese artist Li Hu created the *Rape of Nanking; The Forgotten Holocaust* (2005), a large and powerful exhibition of his artwork depicting the horrors that ensued for the Chinese people when the Imperial Japanese Army laid siege to the city in 1937.

Art across time and cultures shows a long fascination with psychological trauma. From depictions of inhuman evil forces in early allegorical paintings of demons and devils, to the real blood and gore of the battlefield, artists and photographers have recorded what is most feared and most vicious. American photographer and writer Susan Sontag pointed out in her essay *Regarding the Pain of Others* (2003) that in the art of trauma, the primary focus is on the gruesome abuses humans inflict on each other, rather than on the miseries of the human condition itself—such as illness, poverty, or natural disasters. "In each instance, the gruesome invites us to be spectators or cowards, unable to look" (p. 42), Sontag wrote, emphasizing the classical role of torment as spectacle in art, where often onlookers depicted in the painting itself are either horrified or impervious to the scene. While the "evil that men do" may be the most recurrent theme in artistic depictions of psychological trauma, they also include portrayals of traumatic events that are the result of larger forces such as natural disasters. For example, English painter J. M. W. Turner's graphic *Slavers Throwing Overboard the Dead and Dying, Typhoon Coming On* (1840), shows the torment of drowning slaves abandoned to a raging sea. Traumatic art and photography objectify, bringing a grand scale event to within the imagination of an individual viewer, condensing all that has transpired in the event to a single, instantaneous shock.

This is made strikingly evident in Picasso's *Guernica,* a massive painting commissioned by the Spanish government for its Pavilion at the 1937 World's Fair. Picasso (1881–1973), distressed by personal problems and the ugly civil war in his native Spain, was appalled by a vicious air attack on the village of Guernica that murdered or wounded some 1,600 civilians. He began work the day he learned of the bombing. The seven-meter wide, horizontal painting is executed only in black and white in an angular, modernist style, with central images of a bull, wounded horse, and harsh light bulb over wounded and dying people in agony. Sympathizers exhibited the piece widely to call attention to the Fascist conspiracy that massacred the people of Guernica. Both as an artistic wonder and as a political instrument, the piece became an icon of twentieth century art as protest.

Picasso was certainly influenced by his countryman and predecessor Francisco Goya (1746–1828), who chronicled in excruciating realism humanity gone mad during the Napoleonic invasion of Spain. Torn between the morality of liberating Spain from a despotic monarchy and the brutalities with which it was done, he painted and etched a prolific number of works, as if to empty his own mind of emotions in turmoil. His disturbingly graphic series entitled *Disasters of War,* begun in 1810, numbers over 100 prints and drawings. Goya produced it after the conflict was long over and throughout a decade, as if his memory of the savagery would not stop churning out new evidence. His painting, *The Third of May 1808* (1814), stands among the greatest works of art in its depiction of a lantern-lit scene where rebels stand helpless as soldiers execute them by firing squad in the dark of night.

Working without the restrictions that the state and church imposed on early painters, Fernando Botero (b. 1932), a Columbian artist, tackled the highly controversial incident of prisoner torture in his 2005 series *Abu Ghraib*. Botero's unique neo-figurative style typically presents bulbous high-society people in prettified contexts, a presumed commentary on the excesses of the moneyed class. In *Abu Ghraib*, Botero carries his overfed characters into prison, with wrenching scenes he built from newspaper photographs and accounts of actual abuse inflicted by American troops on Iraqi prisoners. Beware, he seems to say, this can happen to any of us if we let it.

Using experiential art forms, many contemporary artists have moved from simply depicting traumatic scenes to actually placing the viewer in them, a shift Australian Professor Jill Bennett (2005) describes as a move from communicative to transactive art fostering "empathic vision." In part, this answers the

development of the photographic image and subsequent ascension of live television as recorded truth in the matters of war and violence rather than artistic imagination. The camera lens installs the viewer in the scene, or brings it home, so to speak. This artistic trend grew in parallel to the recognition of traumatic stress disorders such as PTSD by the mental health and medical fields as a diagnosis of incapacitating mental anguish. In art as well as psychology, the notion of "secondary or vicarious trauma" (*see:* **Vicarious Traumatization**) appeared, recognizing that bystanders and viewers, too, could be affected by the force of the images of psychological trauma.

The American artist Jasper Johns (b. 1930) produced a series of paintings and mixed media works in the 1950s featuring prominent, ringed targets that exemplify the beginning of this trend. Art critic Robert Hughes (1997) points out that this was the era of the Cold War, when the threat of nuclear apocalypse haunted the world, and particularly Americans, toward whom—they were relentlessly reminded by the press and politicians—the Soviet Union pointed its missiles. In *Target with Four Faces* (1955), half-hidden plaster faces peer out from tight boxes with hinged doors above a large bulls-eye, evoking collective fear and a sense of being trapped and inevitably doomed. But it is the viewer who stands in the position of aiming the weapon at the target, becoming the aggressor, inflicting the fear on the hiding faces.

A similar message of a public and private conscience for mass traumatic loss infuses visitors to the Vietnam veterans memorial, known as The Wall, in Washington, DC. It is a prime example of a *countermonument*—a term coined by American Professor James Young to describe a memorial in structural form that is marked by its context, a feeling of absence completed by the viewer's participation and thus constant redefinition. Maya Lin, a Chinese-American artist, was 21 years old at the time she submitted her drawings in a blind competition for the memorial design. In antithesis of many towering war monuments, the memorial is cut into the earth and simply carries on its wall of tablets the carved names of the 58,000 U.S.

soldiers lost in the protracted conflict. As a visitor descends the pathway to walk alongside The Wall, the black polished marble reflects his or her own face rippling across the names, thus uniting witness and victim, and drawing strong emotions in the process.

The personalization of psychological trauma in art is a process enveloping many artists in their own work. In a struggle to live with their own suffering, or the pain of their loved ones or community, they are both witness and portrayer as they commit to an image. Joerg Bose (2005), in discussing the disturbing self-portraits of Mexican painter Frida Kahlo (1917–1954), refers to this intrapsychic duality. He believes that for a painter such as Kahlo, who suffered immeasurable physical and emotional pain in her life, her ability to paint her pain into images to express the horror of her existence may have supported her ability to survive. She often painted dual images in her self-portraits, such as in *The Two Fridas* (1939). The painting depicts her two selves dressed beautifully, seated formally side-by-side and holding hands, turned toward the viewer without expression. The power of the painting comes from the juxtaposition of this emotionless gaze with the two figures' hearts depicted anatomically on their chests as if surgically removed and placed there, with veins intertwined and one Frida holding scissors that sever the end of a vein which is bleeding onto her white dress. It is a painting that captures not only the overpowering presence of psychological trauma but also the emotional emptiness that is often left behind in its wake, a common PTSD symptom. Translating this psychic void into a work of art gives form and substance to the feelings of loss in two ways, both of which can ease suffering, according to psychoanalysts Dori Laub and Daniel Podell (1995). It allows the individual to shift from being consumed by the memories of the traumatic experience to entering into an internal dialogue with the experience as represented. The representation of the lived experience can also become a shared burden with others as witnesses, as much of the art of the Holocaust has served to do, in enhancing the *knowing* of psychological trauma.

Tanzanian artist and writer Everlyn Nicodemus (b. 1954) finds ways large and small to bring the subject of cultural trauma into this knowing. In her *Reference Scroll on Genocide, Massacre and Ethnic Cleansing* (2004), she draws on I. W. Charny's *Encyclopedia of Genocide* (1999) to meticulously record on a seemingly unending scroll the atrocities rained down upon peoples of vulnerable ethnic, social and cultural communities. The force of the work originates in the choice of a scroll's form, suggesting a religious inscription and thus a deeply held and timeless human value. Nicodemus also addresses her personal knowing of one person's trauma, represented hauntingly in *Birthmask,* a work in mixed media showing a frozen scream of horror on a traditionally dressed doll figure. The doll is flattened, with outstretched arms bound by a taut mesh web barring escape. Below the doll's waist, a large round hole gapes with only slightly torn edges, as if punched out methodically. While the meaning of the work is indeterminate because of its entirely nonverbal presentation, Nicodemus clearly conveys a sense of both psychic and physical entrapment and damage that is consistent with the impact of psychological trauma.

Around the world, the processing of strong emotion underlies the use of art to give voice to traumatized individuals and communities. In South Africa, women of the impoverished Mapula region embroider quilts with scenes of domestic violence, child abuse, and AIDS, challenging the taboos of public discussion (Schmahmann, 2005). Polish artist and architect Krzysztof Wodiczko films interviews with survivors of rape, police brutality, and the nuclear holocaust of World War II and projects the faces large-scale onto public monuments, where they demand attention. In the Philippines, an exhibit by Asian women artists entitled "Trauma, Interrupted" (Manila, 2007) displays art drawing attention to forced sexual slavery of some 200,000 Asian women during World War II.

In a very different style, two contemporary artists have used the form of graphic novels, or drawn stories similar to cartoons, to depict psychological trauma in a way that blends visual images with verbal expressions of satire and irony to traumatic experiences of the Holocaust and political upheaval in Iran. Art Spiegelman (b. 1948), the American son of a Holocaust survivor, won the 1992 Pulitzer Prize with his *Maus: A Survivor's Tale* (1986), which used cartoon animals to symbolize the Germans, Jews, Russians, Americans, and other historical participants in the Holocaust. The tale recounts his father's struggles, but his own as well, as a generation once removed but still very much impacted by the Holocaust. Marjane Satrapi (b. 1969), an Iranian woman who lived through the violent revolution from the end of the Shah's regime to Islamic fundamentalists, has also drawn her memories into an autobiographical cartoon in *Persepolis: The Story of a Childhood* (2003), which was later animated for a film. In both cases, the subject matter is deeply experienced trauma, but the injection of humorous affect holds it at arm's length, as if to better examine it, manipulate it with symbols to attenuate the shock, and see what can be understood when the overwhelming emotional burden is temporarily relieved.

When the artist gives us a visual language for psychological trauma, a point of view is involved. Similarly, a photographer may crop a photo, or otherwise frame a point of view. Botero painted his *Abu Ghraib* series to show the point of view of the prisoner and his agony, contrary to the newspaper photos that concentrated on the soldiers delivering the abuse. Spiegelman and Satrapi give us new ways of seeing old pain, and Johns and Lin compel us to participate in the scene. Thus, through creative application of image, tonality, texture, and light, artists render personal and historic horrors that illuminate humanity's darkest recesses, with a power to pierce the hidden depths of our vulnerability.

REFERENCES

Bennett, J. (2005). *Empathic vision: Affect, trauma, and contemporary art.* Stanford, CA: Stanford University Press.

Bose, J. (2005, Spring). Images of trauma: Pain, recognition, and disavowal in the works of Frida Kahlo and Francis Bacon. *Journal of the American Academy of Psychoanalysis and Dynamic Psychiatry, 33*(1), 51–70.

Charny, I. W. (Ed.). (1999). *Encyclopedia of genocide* (Vols. 1 & 2). Santa Barbara, CA: Abc-Clio.

Hughes, R. (1997). *American visions: The epic history of art in America.* New York: Random House.

Laub, D., & Podell, D. (1995). Art and trauma. *International Journal of Psychoanalysis, 76,* 995–1005.

Satrapi, M. (2003). *Persepolis: The story of a childhood.* New York: Pantheon Books.

Schmahmann, B. (2005, Autumn). Stitches as sutures: Trauma and recovery in works by women in the Mapula embroidery project. *African Arts, 38*(33), 52–65.

Sontag, S. (2003). *Regarding the pain of others.* New York: Picador.

Spiegelman, A. (1986). *Maus: A survivor's tale.* New York: Pantheon Books.

JANET DE MERODE
Fielding Graduate University

GILBERT REYES
Fielding Graduate University

See also: Literary Depictions of Psychological Trauma; Movie Depictions of Psychological Trauma; Vicarious Traumatization

ASSESSMENT, PSYCHOMETRIC, ADULT

The use of standardized, psychometrically sound self-report measures and structured interviews is the foundation of the evidence-based assessment of trauma exposure and posttraumatic stress disorder (PTSD). Such measures provide an efficient, cost-effective means for collecting essential information regarding an individual's unique responses to catastrophic life events, and are administered routinely to accomplish a wide range of clinical and research assessment tasks, including screening for trauma exposure and PTSD, establishing a PTSD diagnosis, quantifying PTSD symptom severity, evaluating comorbid emotional problems, evaluating response bias, and gathering information relevant for case conceptualization and treatment planning.

The development and empirical evaluation of psychometric measures has been one of the most active and productive areas in the field of traumatic stress. Dozens of checklists, questionnaires, and interviews are now available, a growing number of which have been extensively validated in diverse settings and trauma populations. Recent reviews of the various measures and guidelines for their application are available in Briere (2004) and Wilson and Keane (2004). Also of interest, Elhai, Gray, Kashdan, and Franklin (2005) recently reported the prevalence of use of the various measures among trauma professionals. In the next two sections, several of the most widely used interviews and self-report measures of PTSD and trauma exposure are briefly described. In the last section, recommendations for conducting evidence-based assessments of PTSD are provided.

Assessment of PTSD

PTSD measures vary substantially in format, most notably with respect to method of administration (interview versus self-report), number of items, item content, response dimension (e.g., symptom frequency, subjective distress), number of response or rating options, time frame (e.g., past week, past month), and whether symptoms are linked explicitly to a specific traumatic event. A key difference among measures is the extent to which they correspond to the diagnostic criteria for PTSD in the *DSM-IV-TR* (American Psychiatric Association, 2000). All of the interviews and many of the self-report measures are *DSM-IV*-correspondent (American Psychiatric Association, 1994), with items conforming to the 17 *DSM-IV* (American Psychiatric Association, 1994) symptoms of PTSD, but several self-report measures are not, although they tap trauma-relevant symptoms.

The choice of a PTSD measure for a given application depends primarily on the purpose of the assessment. Structured interviews, particularly those that yield both a diagnosis and a continuous measure of symptom severity, are essential whenever PTSD is the major focus of a study or clinical assessment and

whenever a formal PTSD diagnosis is required. A structured interview administered by an experienced clinician is considered the "gold standard" or most widely accepted criterion measure for PTSD assessment. When an interview is not feasible, *DSM-IV* correspondent (American Psychiatric Association, 1994) self-report measures can be substituted, and are particularly useful for screening, large-scale surveys, and ongoing monitoring of symptom severity, as in treatment outcome research. PTSD-focused but non-*DSM-IV*-correspondent (American Psychiatric Association, 1994) self-report measures can be useful supplements as part of a battery of measures, but whenever possible should be used in conjunction with interviews and *DSM-IV*-correspondent (American Psychiatric Association, 1994) self-report measures.

Structured Interviews

There are several widely used, well-validated structured interviews for PTSD. They vary in format, administration, and scoring, as well as in the nature of the assessment information they yield. Valid administration and scoring of these interviews requires a strong background in psychopathology, proficiency in diagnostic interviewing and differential diagnosis, and a thorough understanding of psychological trauma and the clinical phenomenology of PTSD. Therefore, an adequate description of an interview, or explicit operational definition of its use in a given context, must include not only the features of the interview per se, but also the qualifications of the interviewer.

Structured Clinical Interview for DSM-IV

The Structured Clinical Interview for *DSM-IV* (SCID; First, Spitzer, Gibbon, & Williams, 1996; *see:* **Structured Clinical Interview for DSM-IV—Posttraumatic Stress Disorder Module**) is a comprehensive structured interview that assesses all the major *DSM-IV* (American Psychiatric Association, 1994) disorders. Its PTSD module can be administered in the context of a complete administration of the

SCID, but is often administered as a stand-alone module. As with other SCID modules, the PTSD module directly assesses each of the *DSM-IV-TR* (American Psychiatric Association, 2000) diagnostic criteria. The module begins with a brief screening question that evaluates possible exposure to traumatic life events. This screening is followed by two questions that identify an index event for symptom inquiry and determine whether that event meets the definition of a trauma according to *DSM-IV* (American Psychiatric Association, 1994) PTSD's Criterion A. Next is the symptom inquiry section, which consists of single prompt questions for each of the 17 PTSD symptoms, although interviewers are encouraged to generate additional spontaneous prompts as needed to clarify responses. If clinically significant symptoms are present, the module concludes with questions regarding their onset, course, and severity. Following SCID conventions, symptoms are rated as *? = Inadequate information, 1 = Absent, 2 = Subthreshold,* or *3 = Threshold,* and symptom cluster criteria and the PTSD diagnosis are rated dichotomously as *1 = Absent* or *3 = Threshold.*

The advantages of the SCID PTSD module are that it is relatively brief, it follows the well-established, user-friendly structure of the SCID, and it appears to have adequate psychometric properties (*see:* **Structured Clinical Interview for *DSM-IV*—Posttraumatic Stress Disorder Module**). However, there are two main disadvantages. First, the trauma screening question is brief and likely insufficient for assessing lifetime trauma exposure. Second, it yields essentially dichotomous ratings for individual symptoms and for a PTSD diagnosis. It does not yield a continuous measure of PTSD symptom severity, which significantly limits its utility.

PTSD Symptom Scale-Interview

The PTSD Symptom Scale-Interview (PSS-I; Foa, Riggs, Dancu, & Rothbaum, 1993; *see:* **Posttraumatic Stress Disorder Symptom Scale**) consists of 17 questions corresponding to the symptom criteria for PTSD. The severity of each symptom over the past 2 weeks is rated on a 4-point scale. In the original version the rating scale anchors were 0 = Not at all, 1 = A little bit, 2 = Somewhat, and 3 = Very much. In the current version the anchors include combined frequency and severity ratings, for example, 1 = Once per week or less/A little and 3 = 5 or more times per week/Very much, which allows the interviewer to apply whichever dimension, frequency or severity, is more appropriate for a given symptom (Foa & Tolin, 2000). The PSS-I thus yields a severity score for each of three PTSD symptom clusters as well as a total PTSD severity score. It also yields a dichotomous PTSD diagnosis, which is derived by means of a rationally derived scoring rule whereby items are counted as symptoms toward a diagnosis if they are rated at least as 1 = Once per week or less/A little or higher.

The advantages of the PSS-I are that it is relatively brief, it yields continuous severity scores for the three symptom clusters and the full syndrome as well as a dichotomous PTSD diagnosis, and it has excellent psychometric properties. One disadvantage is that the diagnostic scoring rule, which was rationally rather than empirically derived, may be too lenient in that it yields substantially higher PTSD prevalence rates than even the most lenient diagnostic rule for the Clinician-Administered PTSD Scale (Foa & Tolin, 2000).

Clinician-Administered PTSD Scale

The Clinician-Administered PTSD Scale (CAPS; Blake et al., 1990, 1995; *see:* **Clinician-Administered PTSD Scale**) is a 30-item structured interview for PTSD that assesses all of the *DSM-IV-TR* (American Psychiatric Association, 2000) criteria for PTSD, including trauma exposure, the 17 core symptoms, onset and duration, and degree of subjective distress and functional impairment. The CAPS also assesses five associated symptoms, including trauma-related guilt and dissociation, as well overall response validity, symptom severity, and symptom improvement. The Life Events Checklist component of the CAPS is used to first screen for exposure to traumatic events, and a trauma inquiry section is administered to evaluate both parts of Criterion A and identify an index event for symptom inquiry.

The CAPS differs from other PTSD interviews in several important ways. First, the CAPS assesses the frequency and intensity of each of the core and associated symptoms on separate 5-point (0 to 4) rating scales. Second, CAPS items include initial prompt questions as well a number of standardized follow-up prompts. Third, CAPS prompts and rating scale anchors contain explicit behavioral referents to increase the reliability of the inquiry and ratings. Fourth, for the numbing and hyperarousal symptoms the CAPS requires interviewers to assess the link between symptoms and the index event and make an explicit "trauma-related" rating. Fifth, the CAPS provides explicit guidelines for assessing lifetime PTSD diagnostic status. Finally, a number of rationally and empirically derived scoring rules have been developed for generating a dichotomous PTSD diagnosis from CAPS frequency and intensity scores (Weathers, Ruscio, & Keane, 1999).

The advantages of the CAPS are that it provides a comprehensive evaluation of PTSD and associated features, it yields continuous measures of symptom severity as well as a dichotomous PTSD diagnosis, and it has excellent psychometric properties (Weathers, Keane, & Davidson, 2001). The CAPS has been studied extensively and has become the most widely PTSD interview. The main disadvantages of the CAPS are that relative to other PTSD interviews it typically takes longer to administer and requires more extensive training.

Self-Report Measures

DSM-Correspondent Measures

PTSD Checklist The PTSD Checklist (PCL; Weathers et al., 1993; *see:* **Posttraumatic Stress Disorder Checklist**) is a 17-item self-report measure of PTSD. The PCL is directly *DSM-IV*-correspondent (American Psychiatric Association, 1994) in that the 17 items reflect the 17 *DSM-IV* (American Psychiatric Association, 1994) symptoms of PTSD. PCL

ratings are based on the response dimension of subjective distress. Respondents indicate how much they were bothered by each symptom over the past month using a five-point scale ranging from 1 = Not at all to 5 = Extremely. There are three versions of the PCL, which differ only in the description of the index event in the first eight items (i.e., the five reexperiencing symptoms, two effortful avoidance symptoms, and amnesia). The civilian version (PCL-C), which refers to "a stressful experience from the past," and the military version (PCL-M), which refers to "a stressful military experience," are appropriate when a specific stressor has not been identified. In contrast, the specific version (PCL-S) is appropriate when a specific stressor has been identified. On the PCL-S respondents are instructed to write in a brief label for their target stressor and indicate the date it occurred, then answer all items with reference to this stressor.

The PCL yields a continuous measure of PTSD symptom severity for each of the three PTSD symptoms clusters and for the whole syndrome. It also yields a dichotomous PTSD diagnosis, which is obtained by considering items rated 3 = Moderately or higher as a symptom and following the *DSM-IV-TR* (American Psychiatric Association, 2000) diagnostic rule. The PCL is one of the most widely used self-report measures of PTSD. It has been evaluated extensively and has excellent psychometric properties across a wide variety of trauma populations. One disadvantage is that the PCL only measures the 17 symptoms of PTSD and does measure trauma exposure, course and duration, or functional impairment.

Posttraumatic Stress Diagnostic Scale The Posttraumatic Stress Diagnostic Scale (PDS; Foa, 1995; Foa, Cashman, Jaycox, & Perry, 1997) is a 49-item self-report measure of PTSD that assesses all of the *DSM-IV-TR* (American Psychiatric Association, 2000) criteria for PTSD. The PDS consists of four sections. The first two sections assess PTSD's Criterion A and identify an index event for symptom inquiry, the third section assesses the frequency of the 17 PTSD symptoms over the past month, and the last section assesses functional impairment associated with the symptoms. Respondents rate symptoms on a 4-point frequency scale, with 0 = Not at all or only one time, 1 = Once a week or less/once in a while, 2 = 2 to 4 times a week/half the time, and 3 = 5 or more times a week/almost always. The PDS yields a continuous measure of symptom severity for each of the three symptom clusters, as well as a total severity score which ranges from 0 to 51 and is classified into one of four severity categories: mild (10 or lower), moderate (11 to 20), moderate to severe (21 to 35), and severe (36 or higher). The PDS also yields a dichotomous PTSD diagnosis, which is obtained by considering items rated at least 1 = Once a week or less/once in a while as symptoms and following the *DSM-IV-TR* (American Psychiatric Association, 2000) diagnostic rules.

The advantages of the PDS are that it assesses all the PTSD diagnostic criteria, it yields both a continuous measure of symptom severity and a PTSD diagnosis, and it has good psychometric properties. The PDS has been widely adopted in a variety of settings and has been translated into a number of languages for use in cross-cultural trauma research. One disadvantage is that the PTSD diagnosis it yields is based on a single, rationally derived scoring rule, and other rules have not been proposed or empirically evaluated.

Detailed Assessment of Posttraumatic Stress The Detailed Assessment of Posttraumatic Stress (DAPS; Briere, 2001) is a 104-item, comprehensive self-report measure of trauma and PTSD. Like the PDS, the DAPS assesses all *DSM-IV-TR* (American Psychiatric Association, 2000) criteria for PTSD, including trauma exposure, the 17 PTSD symptoms, and the degree of functional impairment. However, the DAPS also includes scales assessing peri-traumatic distress and dissociation, trauma-specific dissociation, substance abuse, and suicidality. In addition, the DAPS is one of the only dedicated PTSD measures to include scales assessing response bias. DAPS scales are reported as T scores derived from a normative sample of approximately 400

trauma-exposed adults. On the clinical scales, T score elevations of 65 and above are considered clinically significant. In addition, the DAPS provides decision rules that yield a probable diagnosis for PTSD and acute stress disorder.

The DAPS is a very promising newer measure of PTSD. It has a number of advantages including the assessment of response validity, the assessment of all PTSD diagnostic criteria, the assessment of peri-traumatic responses and associated features of PTSD, and the use of norms to generate T scores. A potential disadvantage is that it is longer than other self-report PTSD measures. Also, it is a relatively new instrument and to date little psychometric work beyond that presented in the manual has appeared in the literature.

PTSD-Focused Measures

Impact of Event Scale The Impact of Event Scale (IES; Horowitz, Wilner, & Alvarez, 1979) is one of the most widely used self-report measures in the field of traumatic stress and is routinely included in clinical and research assessment batteries. Based on Horowitz's biphasic model of stress response, the IES consists of 15 items, 7 of which assess intrusive symptoms and 8 of which assess avoidance. Respondents rate the frequency of each symptom over the past week on a 4-point scale ranging from 0 = Not at all, 1 = Rarely, 3 = Sometimes, and 5 = Often. The IES has been extensively evaluated and has excellent psychometric properties (Sundin & Horowitz, 2002).

However, because the IES does not assess hyperarousal symptoms, it does not provide complete coverage of the PTSD symptom criteria. To address this limitation and to refashion the rating scale to bring it more in line with a typical Likert format, Weiss and Marmar (1997) developed a 22-item revised version of the IES (IES-R; *see:* **Impact of Event Scale—Revised**). They added six hyperarousal items and one dissociative item and substantially modified the rating scale, changing the response dimension from frequency to subjective distress, expanding it to a five-point scale, and relabeling the anchors such that 0 = Not at all, 1 = A little bit, 2 = Moderately, 3 = Quite a bit, and 4 = Extremely. Even with these changes, though, the IES-R is still not completely *DSM-IV* correspondent (American Psychiatric Association, 1994). Some *DSM-IV* (American Psychiatric Association, 1994) PTSD symptoms are not assessed at all (diminished interest, estrangement, foreshortened future), and others are assessed somewhat ambiguously (amnesia, restricted range of affect). Nonetheless, the IES-R is a valuable measure and its use has grown steadily since its introduction. Also, as Sundin and Horowitz (2002) have noted, the introduction of IES-R did not render the IES obsolete, and both measures continue to be used effectively.

Mississippi Scale for Combat-Related PTSD
The Mississippi Scale for Combat-Related PTSD (Mississippi Scale; Keane, Caddell, & Taylor, 1988; *see:* **Mississippi Combat PTSD Scale**) is a 35-item self-report measure of PTSD symptoms and associated features. Items are rated on a 5-point scale with anchors that vary according to item content (e.g., 1 = Never to 5 = Very Frequently; 1 = Never True to 5 = Always True). The Mississippi Scale is the most widely used measure of combat-related PTSD. It has been extensively investigated and has excellent psychometric properties. Although it is not directly *DSM-IV* correspondent (American Psychiatric Association, 1994) it assesses many core and associated symptoms of PTSD and is a valuable component of a multimethod approach to PTSD assessment.

Because of the success of the Mississippi Scale, a civilian version (CMS) was developed (*see:* **Mississippi Civilian Scale for PTSD— Revised**). The most important modifications involved revising items that referred to the military, and adding four items to provide better coverage of the PTSD diagnostic criteria. Despite additional modifications involving item content and rating scale format (e.g., Inkelas, Loux, Bourque, Widawski, & Nguyen, 2000; Norris & Perilla, 1996) the CMS has not performed as well as the original combat version.

Multiscale Personality Inventories

Multiscale inventories such as the Minnesota Multiphasic Personality Inventory—2nd edition (MMPI-2; Butcher et al., 2001; *see:* **Minnesota Multiphasic Personality Inventory-2**) and the Personality Assessment Inventory (PAI; Morey, 1991) are valuable additions to a PTSD assessment battery. They complement dedicated PTSD interviews and self-report measures by providing crucial information regarding response validity, comorbidity, clinical management issues, and general personality factors, all of which can greatly facilitate differential diagnosis, case conceptualization, and treatment planning. These instruments also include specialized PTSD scales, which, although they are not *DSM-IV*-correspondent (American Psychiatric Association, 1994), provide useful converging evidence as part of a multimethod approach to assessing PTSD.

Minnesota Multiphasic Personality Inventory
The Minnesota Multiphasic Personality Inventory MMPI/MMPI-2 (Butcher et al., 2001; *see:* **Minnesota Multiphasic Personality Inventory-2**) is one of the oldest and most popular measures of personality and psychopathology and has been used extensively in the assessment of PTSD (Penk, Rierdan, Losardo, & Robinowitz, 2006). The original investigations of the MMPI in male combat veterans identified a mean *F-2-8* PTSD profile and led to the development of a specialized PTSD scale, the Keane PTSD scale (*PK* scale; Fairbank, Keane, & Malloy, 1983; Keane, Malloy, & Fairbank, 1984). Mean elevations on F, 2, and 8 have generally been replicated in other PTSD samples, although other scales often are elevated and there appears to be considerable heterogeneity in mean profile and prevalence of individual profiles across studies (e.g., Glenn, Beckham, & Sampson, 2002; Wise, 1996).

Similarly, the utility of the *PK* scale for discriminating individuals with and without PTSD has generally been replicated, although performance has varied across studies and optimal cutoff scores have generally been lower than originally reported (e.g., Cannon, Bell, Andrews, & Finkelstein, 1987; Watson, Kucala, & Manifold, 1986). The PK scale has also been used to assess PTSD in civilian trauma samples (e.g., Koretzky & Peck, 1990), although there is some evidence that it may function more as a measure of general distress than as a measure of PTSD specifically (Scheibe, Bagby, Miller, & Dorian, 2001). The PK scale has also been evaluated as a stand-alone measure and appears to perform equally well in this format (Herman, Weathers, Litz, & Keane, 1996; Lyons & Scotti, 1994).

In addition to PTSD-specific information, the MMPI-2 provides information regarding two other vital domains, comorbidity and response bias. The MMPI-2 includes a number of empirically and conceptually derived scales that assess a wide variety of conditions commonly comorbid with PTSD, and thus contributes to a richly detailed assessment of the full clinical presentation in trauma survivors. In addition, the MMPI-2 includes an extensive set of response validity indicators. Given the concerns regarding malingering in the PTSD literature (e.g., Rosen, 2004), the MMPI-2 scales that detect a fake-bad response style, especially F, Fp, and Ds (Rogers, Sewell, Martin, & Vitaco, 2003), are particularly relevant. Beyond these general indicators of malingering, a new scale specific to detecting feigned PTSD, $Fptsd$, was recently developed and found to outperform existing MMPI-2 scales (Elhai, Ruggiero, Frueh, Beckham, & Gold, 2002). However, Marshall and Bagby (2006) recently questioned the incremental validity of $Fptsd$, so additional studies are needed to clarify the relative performance of these scales.

Personality Assessment Inventory Developed in 1991, the Personality Assessment Inventory (PAI; Morey, 1991) is a newer multiscale inventory designed to address some of the limitations of previous instruments. The PAI was developed in a construct validation framework that emphasized conceptual explication of the constructs to be assessed, the importance of content validity in generating items, and the use of multiple empirical parameters for evaluating items and retaining them for the final scale. The PAI consists of 344 items, which are rated on a 4-point scale with anchors of False, Not At All True; Slightly True; Mainly True; and Very True. There are 22 primary scales, including four response validity scales, 11 clinical scales, five treatment scales, and two interpersonal scales. In addition, nine clinical scales and one treatment scale have subscales to assess specific components of the parent scale. The response validity scales detect random responding and overly positive and overly negative self-presentation. The clinical scales assess well-established clinical syndromes, the treatment scales assess several areas relevant to clinical management, and the interpersonal scales assess key aspects of normal personality.

Although relatively few studies have been conducted to date, the PAI appears to have considerable promise for the assessment of PTSD and represents a viable alternative to the MMPI-2. The PAI includes an 8-item specialized PTSD scale, the Traumatic Stress Scale of the Anxiety-Related Disorders Scale (*ARD-T*), which assesses reexperiencing, effortful avoidance, loss of interest in usual activities, and guilt. Although it does not provide full coverage of the *DSM-IV* (American Psychiatric Association, 1994) PTSD symptom criteria, *ARD-T* does assess many of the distinctive aspects of PTSD and typically is the most elevated PAI scale in PTSD profiles. In addition, recent studies have found that several other PAI scales differentiate those with and without PTSD, including scales measuring depression, anxiety, somatic complaints, and borderline features (McDevitt-Murphy, Weathers, Adkins, & Daniels, 2005; McDevitt-Murphy, Weathers, Flood, Eakin, & Benson, 2007). Further, in one recent study the PAI outperformed the MMPI-2 in discriminating PTSD from depressive disorders (McDevitt-Murphy et al., 2007).

Assessment of Trauma Exposure

In contrast to the remarkable progress that has been made in the development of psychometrically sound measures of PTSD, considerably less progress has been made in the development of measures of trauma exposure (see Weathers & Keane, 2007 for a full discussion of issues regarding the definition and measurement of trauma). Numerous trauma exposure measures have been developed but few have been adequately investigated or widely adopted. This is due in large part to the fact that trauma is difficult to define, both in a broad conceptual sense with respect to delineating traumatic stressors from ordinary stressors, and in a more specific, practical sense of considering key aspects of trauma exposure such as event type (e.g., combat, sexual assault, natural disaster), dimensions of stressor severity and burden (e.g., life threat, physical harm, interpersonal loss, frequency, duration), and exposure level (e.g., directly experienced, witnessed, learned about).

Trauma measures vary considerably in scope and format in accordance with the assessment questions they are intended to address (see Norris & Hamblen, 2004 for a recent review of trauma exposure measures). Often the main purpose of the trauma assessment is to determine if an individual has experienced at least one event that would meet both parts of the definition of a trauma in Criterion A of the *DSM-IV-TR* (American Psychiatric Association, 2000) PTSD criteria. Some measures, such as the Criterion A component of the SCID PTSD module, consist of a few questions that screen for exposure to possible traumatic stressors, identify an index event for symptom inquiry, and determine if the event satisfies Criterion A. Others, such as the Criterion A section of the PDS and DAPS, provide a list of traumatic event types and direct respondents to check all that apply, then select the worst event and write a brief narrative. The Life Events Checklist (LEC), the trauma assessment component of the CAPS, combines a self-report screener with an interview-based inquiry. The screener consists of a list of 17 event categories with five response options to indicate exposure level, including "happened to me," "witnessed it," "learned about it," "not sure if it happened," and "did not happen." The interview component identifies up to three events for symptom inquiry, then determines if the events meet both parts of Criterion A. The LEC may also be used in conjunction with self-report measures of PTSD. In our own research, for example, we often administer an extended form of the LEC along with the PCL.

In addition to identifying an index event for PTSD symptom inquiry, measures have also been developed to quantify the severity of trauma exposure within a single domain of exposure and to quantify trauma exposure across the life span. An example of a domain-specific measure is the Combat Exposure Scale (CES; Keane et al., 1989), a widely used, 7-item self-report measure that quantifies the severity of exposure to war-zone stress. Examples of carefully constructed measures that are useful for evaluating trauma across the life span include the Traumatic Life Events Questionnaire (TLEQ; Kubany et al., 2000), Life Stressor Checklist—Revised (McHugo et al., 2005), and Evaluation of Lifetime Stressors (ELS; Krinsley, Gallagher, Weathers, Kutter, & Kaloupek, 2003).

Conclusion

Considerable progress has been in the development and evaluation of standardized measures of trauma exposure PTSD, and such measures are essential for the evidence-based assessment of PTSD. There are a number of issues that need to be addressed when selecting measures for a given clinical or research application. First, the goals for the assessment must be clearly established. Self-report measures are appropriate for screening and quantifying symptom severity, but structured interview are best for establishing a PTSD diagnosis and should be administered whenever possible. Second, the overall size and scope of the assessment battery must be determined. A comprehensive assessment would include a thorough evaluation of lifetime trauma exposure, a structured interview, one or more self-report measures, and a multiscale inventory. Such a battery would provide information regarding PTSD diagnostic status, PTSD symptom severity, comorbidity and differential diagnosis, clinical management concerns, and response validity. When resources are limited a smaller battery could suffice for some applications. However, adding additional measures would in many cases unnecessarily increase respondent burden and raise the issue of incremental validity.

Third, the target population must be taken into account. Measures should be selected only if they have been shown to be valid for the intended purpose in the specific population in which they are to be used. When a relevant empirical literature does not yet exist, measures should be used and interpreted with caution. Last, given the controversy surrounding trauma and PTSD and the potential for malingering it is crucial to formally evaluate response bias whenever possible. This can be accomplished with the use of multiscale inventories such as the MMPI-2 or PAI, or through the use of specialized measures of malingering such as the Structured Interview of Reported Symptoms (SIRS; Rogers, Bagby, & Dickens, 1992).

REFERENCES

American Psychiatric Association. (1994). *Diagnostic and statistical manual of mental disorders* (4th ed.). Washington, DC: Author.

American Psychiatric Association. (2000). *Diagnostic and statistical manual of mental disorders* (4th ed., text rev.). Washington, DC: Author.

Blake, D. D., Weathers, F. W., Nagy, L. M., Kaloupek, D. G., Gusman, F. D., Charney, D. S., et al. (1995). The development of a clinician-administered PTSD scale. *Journal of Traumatic Stress, 8,* 75–90.

Blake, D. D., Weathers, F. W., Nagy, L. M., Kaloupek, D. G., Klauminser, G., Charney, D. S., et al. (1990). A clinician rating scale for assessing current and lifetime PTSD: The CAPS-1. *Behavior Therapist, 18,* 187–188.

Briere, J. (2001). *Detailed Assessment of Posttraumatic Stress (DAPS).* Odessa, FL: Psychological Assessment Resources.

Briere, J. (2004). *Psychological assessment of adult posttraumatic states: Phenomenology, diagnosis, and measurement* (2nd ed.). Washington, DC: American Psychological Association.

Butcher, J. N., Graham, J. R., Ben-Porath, Y. S., Tellegen, A. M., Dahlstrom, W. G., & Kaemmer, B. (2001). *Minnesota Multiphasic Personality Inventory-2: Manual for administration, scoring, and interpretation* (Rev. ed.). Minneapolis: University of Minnesota Press.

Cannon, D. S., Bell, W. E., Andrews, R. H., & Finkelstein, A. S. (1987). Correspondence between MMPI PTSD measures and clinical diagnosis. *Journal of Personality Assessment, 51,* 517–521.

Elhai, J. D., Gray, M. J., Kashdan, T. B., & Franklin, C. L. (2005). Which instruments are most commonly used to assess traumatic event exposure and posttraumatic effects?: A survey of traumatic stress professionals. *Journal of Traumatic Stress, 18,* 541–545.

Elhai, J. D., Ruggiero, K. J., Frueh, B. C., Beckham, J. C., & Gold, P. B. (2002). The Infrequency-Posttraumatic Stress Disorder Scale (Fptsd) for the MMPI-2: Development and initial validation with veterans presenting with combat-related PTSD. *Journal of Personality Assessment, 79,* 531–549.

Fairbank, J. A., Keane, T. M., & Malloy, P. F. (1983). Some preliminary data on the psychological characteristics of Vietnam veterans with posttraumatic stress disorders. *Journal of Consulting and Clinical Psychology, 51,* 912–919.

First, M. B., Spitzer, R. L., Gibbon, M., & Williams, J. B. W. (1996). *Structured Clinical Interview for DSM-IV Axis I Disorders, Clinician Version* (SCID-CV). Washington, DC: American Psychiatric Press.

Foa, E. B. (1995). *Posttraumatic Stress Diagnostic Scale* [Manual]. Minneapolis, MN: National Computer Systems.

Foa, E. B., Cashman, L., Jaycox, L., & Perry, K. (1997). The validation of a self-report measure of posttraumatic stress disorder: The Posttraumatic Diagnostic Scale. *Psychological Assessment, 9,* 445–451.

Foa, E. B., Riggs, D. S., Dancu, C. V., & Rothbaum, B. O. (1993). Reliability and validity of a brief instrument for assessing post-traumatic stress disorder. *Journal of Traumatic Stress, 6,* 459–473.

Foa, E. B., & Tolin, D. F. (2000). Comparison of the PTSD Symptom Scale-Interview version and the Clinician-Administered PTSD Scale. *Journal of Traumatic Stress, 13,* 181–191.

Glenn, D. M., Beckham, J. C., & Sampson, W. S. (2002). MMPI-2 profiles of Gulf and Vietnam combat veterans with chronic posttraumatic stress disorder. *Journal of Clinical Psychology, 58,* 371–381.

Herman, D. S., Weathers, F. W., Litz, B. T., & Keane, T. M. (1996). Psychometric properties of the embedded and stand-alone versions of the MMPI-2 Keane PTSD Scale. *Assessment, 3,* 437–442.

Horowitz, M. J., Wilner, N., & Alvarez, W. (1979). Impact of Event Scale: A measure of subjective stress. *Psychosomatic Medicine, 41,* 209–218.

Inkelas, M., Loux, L. A., Bourque, L. B., Widawski, M., & Nguyen, L. H. (2000). Dimensionality and reliability of the Civilian Mississippi Scale for PTSD in a postearthquake community. *Journal of Traumatic Stress, 13,* 149–167.

Keane, T. M., Caddell, J. M., & Taylor, K. L. (1988). Mississippi Scale for combat-related posttraumatic stress disorder: Three studies in reliability and validity. *Journal of Consulting and Clinical Psychology, 56,* 85–90.

Keane, T. M., Fairbank, J. A., Caddell, J. M., Zimering, R. T., Taylor, K. L., & Mora, C. A. (1989). Clinical evaluation of a measure to assess combat exposure. *Psychological Assessment, 1,* 53–55.

Keane, T. M., Malloy, P. F., & Fairbank, J. A. (1984). Empirical development of an MMPI subscale for the assessment of combat-related posttraumatic stress disorder. *Journal of Consulting and Clinical Psychology, 52,* 888–891.

Koretzky, M. B., & Peck, A. H. (1990). Validation and cross-validation of the PTSD Subscale of the MMPI with civilian trauma victims. *Journal of Clinical Psychology, 46,* 296–300.

Krinsley, K. E., Gallagher, J. G., Weathers, F. W., Kutter, C. J., & Kaloupek, D. G. (2003). Consistency of retrospective reporting about exposure to traumatic events. *Journal of Traumatic Stress, 16,* 399–409.

Kubany, E. S., Haynes, S. N., Leisen, M. B., Owens, J. A., Kaplan, A. S., Watson, S. B., et al. (2000). Development and preliminary validation of a brief broad-spectrum measure of trauma exposure: The Traumatic Life Events Questionnaire. *Psychological Assessment, 12,* 210–224.

Lyons, J. A., & Scotti, J. R. (1994). Comparability of two administration formats of the Keane Posttraumatic Stress Disorder Scale. *Psychological Assessment, 6,* 209–211.

Marshall, M. B., & Bagby, R. M. (2006). The incremental validity and clinical utility of the MMPI-2 Infrequency Posttraumatic Stress Disorder Scale. *Assessment, 13,* 417–429.

McDevitt-Murphy, M. E., Weathers, F. W., Adkins, J. W., & Daniels, J. B. (2005). Use of the Personality Assessment Inventory in assessment of posttraumatic stress disorder in women. *Journal of Psychopathology and Behavioral Assessment, 27,* 57–65.

McDevitt-Murphy, M. E., Weathers, F. W., Flood, A. M., Benson, T., & Eakin, D. E. (2007). A comparison of the MMPI-2 and PAI for discriminating PTSD from depression and social phobia. *Assessment, 14,* 181–195.

McHugo, G. J., Caspi, Y. Y., Kammerer, N., Mazelis, R., Jackson, E. W., Russell, L., et al. (2005). The assessment of trauma history in women with co-occurring substance abuse and mental disorders and a history of interpersonal violence. *Journal of Behavioral Health Services and Research, 32,* 113–127.

Morey, L. C. (1991). *Personality Assessment Inventory: Professional manual.* Lutz, FL: Psychological Assessment Resources.

Norris, F. H., & Hamblen, J. L. (2004). Standardized self-report measures of civilian trauma and PTSD. In J. P. Wilson & T. M. Keane (Eds.), *Assessing psychological trauma and PTSD* (2nd ed., pp. 63–102). New York: Guilford Press.

Norris, F. H., & Perilla, J. L. (1996). The revised Civilian Mississippi Scale for PTSD: Reliability, validity, and cross-language stability. *Journal of Traumatic Stress, 9,* 285–298.

Penk, W. E., Rierdan, J., Losardo, M., & Robinowitz, R. (2006). The MMPI-2 and assessment of posttraumatic stress disorder (PTSD). In J. N. Butcher (Ed.), *MMPI-2: A practitioner's guide* (pp. 121–139). Washington, DC: American Psychological Association.

Rogers, R., Bagby, R. M., & Dickens, S. E. (1992). *Structured Interview of Reported Symptoms (SIRS) and professional manual.* Odessa, FL: Psychological Assessment Resources.

Rogers, R., Sewell, K. W., Martin, M. A., & Vitacco, M. J. (2003). Detection of feigned mental disorders: A meta-analysis of the MMPI-2 and malingering. *Assessment, 10,* 160–177.

Rosen, G. M. (2004). Malingering and the PTSD data base. In G. M. Rosen (Ed.), *Posttraumatic stress disorder: Issues and controversies* (pp. 85–99). Hoboken, NJ: Wiley.

Scheibe, S., Bagby, R. M., Miller, L. S., & Dorian, B. J. (2001). Assessing posttraumatic stress disorder with the MMPI-2 in a sample of workplace accident victims. *Psychological Assessment, 13,* 369–374.

Sundin, E. C., & Horowitz, M. J. (2002). Impact of Event Scale: Psychometric properties. *British Journal of Psychiatry, 180,* 205–209.

Watson, C. G., Kucala, T., & Manifold, V. (1986). A cross-validation of the Keane and Penk MMPI

Scales as measures of post-traumatic stress disorder. *Journal of Clinical Psychology, 42,* 727–732.

Weathers, F. W., & Keane, T. M. (2007). The Criterion A problem revisited: Controversies and challenges in defining and measuring psychological trauma. *Journal of Traumatic Stress, 20,* 107–121.

Weathers, F. W., Keane, T. M., & Davidson, J. R. (2001). Clinician-Administered PTSD Scale: A review of the first ten years of research. *Depression and Anxiety, 13,* 132–156.

Weathers, F. W., Litz, B. T., Herman, D. S., Huska, J. A., & Keane, T. M. (1993, October). *The PTSD Checklist (PCL): Reliability, validity, and diagnostic utility.* Paper presented at the annual meeting of the International Society for Traumatic Stress Studies, San Antonio, TX.

Weathers, F. W., Ruscio, A. M., & Keane, T. M. (1999). Psychometric properties of nine scoring rules for the Clinician-Administered Posttraumatic Stress Disorder Scale. *Psychological Assessment, 11,* 124–133.

Weiss, D. S., & Marmar, C. R. (1997). The Impact of Event Scale—Revised. In J. P. Wilson & T. M. Keane (Eds.), *Assessing psychological trauma and PTSD* (pp. 399–411). New York: Guilford Press.

Wilson, J. P., & Keane, T. M. (Eds.). (2004). *Assessing psychological trauma and PTSD* (2nd ed.). New York: Guilford Press.

Wise, E. A. (1996). Diagnosing posttraumatic stress disorder with the MMPI clinical scales: A review of the literature. *Journal of Psychopathology and Behavioral Assessment, 18,* 71–82.

FRANK W. WEATHERS
Auburn University

TERENCE M. KEANE
National Center for Posttraumatic Stress Disorder

See also: Clinician-Administered PTSD Scale; Diagnosis of Traumatic Stress Disorders (*DSM & ICD*); Impact of Event Scale—Revised; Minnesota Multiphasic Personality Inventory-2; Mississippi Civilian Scale for PTSD—Revised; Mississippi Combat PTSD Scale; Posttraumatic Stress Disorder Checklist; Posttraumatic Stress Disorder, Diagnosis of; Posttraumatic Stress Disorder Symptom Scale; Structured Clinical Interview for *DSM-IV*—Posttraumatic Stress Disorder Module; Trauma, Definition

ASSESSMENT, PSYCHOMETRIC, CHILD

A thorough clinical assessment is crucial to effective treatment interventions for traumatized children and adolescents. Comprehensive evaluation of psychological trauma and its effects typically includes information from a number of sources, including the child's or adolescent's self-report, caretaker reports of the child's functioning, and collateral reports from other providers. The primary targets of assessment are the child's trauma exposure history and current emotional symptoms. However, information may also be collected on caretaker and family functioning, the child's developmental history, primary attachment relationships, child protective services involvement and placement history, current school functioning, history of losses, medical status, coping skills, and environmental stressors such as community violence. Once consent for release of information is provided, the clinician can gather more complete background information from agencies interacting with the child and family, such as child protective services, law enforcement, and other mental health agencies.

Evaluation of Trauma Exposure History

The most common types of traumatic events evaluated are child abuse (physical, sexual, and psychological), emotional neglect, assaults by peers (both physical and sexual), community violence, witnessing violence done to others, traumatic loss, exposure to accidents (e.g., motor vehicle accidents) and disasters, and serious medical illness or injury. Assessment typically involves determining not only the nature of these various traumas, but also their frequency, type, and age of onset.

Unfortunately, the child or adolescent may not report all significant instances of trauma exposure during the initial assessment session or early in treatment. Instead, important historical events may be disclosed later in treatment, as the child engages more fully with the therapist and experiences a greater sense of trust and safety. The manner in which children and adolescents, as well as caretakers, are questioned regarding trauma exposure will also determine the extent to which a more complete account is provided (Lanktree, Briere, & Zaidi, 1991). Clinical sensitivity is often required regarding particularly difficult, embarrassing, traumatic, or shame-inducing experiences. If a child or caretaker has fears regarding the repercussions of the disclosure (e.g., removal of the child from the home), this may also further limit the accuracy of abuse or violence-related disclosures. Finally, the child's or adolescent's tendency to avoid thinking about and disclosing distressing material may decrease his or her participation in the assessment, thereby leading to underreporting of trauma exposure (Elliott & Briere, 1994).

The context in which the assessment is conducted also can affect the extent of trauma-related information that is disclosed by the child and/or family, whether by interview or on psychological tests. For example, in school settings, the child may not feel as free to divulge information due to concerns about confidentiality, including fear that his or her trauma history or symptoms will be shared with school personnel or other students. In hospital settings, where a child may be assessed for psychological trauma following a serious medical illness or condition (e.g., HIV infection, cancer, surgeries) or traumatic injury (e.g., an automobile accident), the child's and family's need to cope with urgent or chronic medical issues may lead them to overlook or suppress information regarding prior (or current) abuse or violence.

In forensic settings, issues of blame, punishment, and authority may cause the child to fear (a) retribution from those he or she implicates in a crime by virtue of disclosing the trauma, or (b) maltreatment, loss, or family disruption as a result of criminal justice and child welfare system involvement in his or her life—each of which may motivate underreporting of traumatic experiences. On the other hand, if a child has been able to disclose abuse or violence-related exposures in a forensic interview, he or she may be able to more easily express symptoms and discuss traumatic exposure during the psychological assessment, especially if all

services are delivered at the same center. This assessment should be conducted separately in a clinical environment that is not part of the forensic investigation, with ongoing consideration of the current safety of the child or adolescent (e.g., possible ongoing exposure to child abuse, domestic violence, or risk related to gang-related community violence).

Because the words used to label traumatic events may confuse or intimidate children (e.g., asking about "rape" or "abuse"), evaluation of trauma exposure is often more effective when behavioral descriptions of these events are employed. This is often best accomplished by using a structured measure or interview that assesses exposure to the major types of traumatic events in a standardized and behaviorally specific way. Trauma exposure measures on which either the child or a caretaker can report about traumatic experiences include the KID-SAVE (Flowers, Hastings, & Kelley, 2000), Traumatic Events Screening Inventory (TESI; Ford et al., 2000), and Violence Exposure Scale for Children—Revised (VEX-R; Fox & Leavitt, 1995). These and similar measures facilitate a relatively complete review of the child's lifetime trauma exposure, and typically have been evaluated psychometrically to determine their effectiveness and validity.

Evaluation of Trauma-Relevant Symptoms

An optimal assessment of children's trauma-related symptomatology includes evaluation of immediate safety issues, such as suicidality, substance abuse, and involvement in high-risk behaviors, as well as a preliminary estimation of current emotional functioning and potential targets for treatment. The results of such assessment, in turn, will determine whether an immediate clinical response is indicated (e.g., crisis intervention, hospitalization, harm reduction activities), as well as which specific treatment modalities (e.g., play therapy, cognitive interventions, therapeutic exposure, family therapy) might be most helpful. Further, when the same tests are administered on multiple occasions (e.g., every 2 or 3 months), the ongoing effects of clinical intervention can be ascertained, allowing the clinician to make mid-course corrections in strategy or focus when specific symptoms are seen to decrease or exacerbate.

For some children and adolescents, multiple trauma exposures such as abuse, neglect, family and community violence, relational losses, and injuries or illnesses may occur concomitantly, resulting in a more complex clinical picture. For example, a child with early, sustained, and multiple traumatic experiences may evidence significant disturbances in emotional, behavioral, developmental, cognitive, and relational domains, as well as presenting with significant posttraumatic stress (Briere & Spinazzola, 2005; Cook et al., 2005). In addition, gender-related, developmental, and cultural factors may affect how any given symptom manifests. For this reason, it is usually preferable to administer multiple tests tapping a variety of different symptoms, rather than a single measure, and to take mediating demographic, social, and cultural issues into account.

As is true in other areas of assessment, standardized assessment measures of trauma-related symptomatology are almost always preferable to those without norms or validation studies. Such measures may be either generic (i.e., tapping symptoms that occur in both traumatized and nontraumatized children, such as anxiety, depression, or aggression) or trauma-specific (i.e., evaluating symptoms that are more commonly associated with trauma exposure, such as posttraumatic stress, dissociation, or reactive sexual behavior).

These tests commonly involve either caretaker reports of the child's symptoms and behaviors or child self-reports of their own distress and/or behavioral disturbance. The choice of whether to use child or caretaker reports of child symptoms can be difficult, since each approach has its own potential benefits and weaknesses.

Child self-report measures allow the child to directly disclose his or her internal experience or problems, as opposed to the clinician relying on "second-hand" reports of a parent or caretaker. However, the child's report may be affected by his or her fears of disclosure, denial of emotional distress, or—especially in younger children—inability to report on complex internal

states (Friedrich, 2002). Caretaker report of the child's symptomatology has the potential benefit of providing a more objective report of the child's symptoms and behaviors, yet may be compromised by parental denial, guilt, or preoccupation with the child's trauma, as well as parental/caretaker difficulties in accurately assessing the child's internal experience, especially if the child avoids describing those experiences to the caretaker (Lanktree et al., in press; Reid, Kavanaugh, & Baldwin, 1987). For these reasons, it is recommended that the assessment of traumatized children use *both* child- and caretaker-report measures, so that the advantages of each methodology can be maximized, and the child's actual clinical status can be triangulated by virtue of multiple sources of information (Lanktree et al., in press; Nader, 2004).

Just as effective assessment often involves both caretaker and child reports, it is also important to use both generic and trauma-specific tests when evaluating traumatized children. Reliance on solely generic tests (e.g., of depression or behavior problems) may result in inadequate information on more trauma-specific responses (e.g., posttraumatic stress or dissociation). In contrast, solely administering trauma-specific measures can easily lead to an underestimation of important, yet less trauma-specific, clinical conditions (e.g., severe depression in a sexually abused child or adolescent).

Perhaps the most commonly used generic measure in the assessment of traumatized children and youth is the Child Behavior Checklist (CBCL; Achenbach, 1991), which has separate Parent Report, Teacher Report, and Youth Self-Report versions. This test evaluates the extent of internalizing (e.g., anxiety or depression) and externalizing (e.g., behavior problems) symptomatology, as well as measuring some resilience or adaptive functions. General emotional functioning can also be evaluated using measures such as the Child Depression Inventory (CDI; Kovacs, 1992).

Trauma-specific measures, completed by a child or adolescent, include the UCLA PTSD Index for *DSM-IV* (UPID; Pynoos, Rodriguez, Steinberg, Stuber, & Frederick, 1998; *see:* **UCLA PTSD Reaction Index**), Child Dissociative

Checklist (CDC; Putnam, Helmers, & Trickett, 1993), and the Trauma Symptom Checklist for Children (TSCC; Briere, 1996; *see:* **Trauma Symptom Checklist for Children**). Trauma-specific measures completed by the primary caretaker on behalf of the child include the Child Sexual Behavior Inventory (CSBI; Friedrich, 1998) and Trauma Symptom Checklist for Young Children (TSCYC; Briere, 2005).

A carefully selected psychological test battery can help determine the extent of the child's trauma-related symptomatology, as well as any other emotional difficulties (e.g., depression) that also may be present. This insight into the child's internal emotional experience and behavioral responses, in turn, can help the clinician devise an effective treatment regimen that is relevant to the child's specific clinical presentation and needs.

When assessment is repeated over time, psychometric evaluation can also signal the need to change or augment the treatment focus as necessary. For example, ongoing assessment may suggest a shift in therapeutic focus when post-traumatic stress symptoms begin to respond to treatment but other symptoms continue relatively unabated (e.g., Briere, 2001; Lanktree & Briere, 1995). Finally, repeated administration of measures can increase accountability and quality control, and can add to the clinical knowledge-base regarding the effectiveness of various trauma-related psychotherapies. When administered at the end of psychotherapy (and, potentially, several months later, at follow-up), such pre-post data can help the clinician or agency determine the effectiveness of a given treatment for a given child or group of children. Generally, we suggest a test-retest interval of at least 2 or 3 months, in order to avoid possible biasing or sensitizing effects of repeated testing over shorter periods of time.

Conclusion

Psychological assessment is an important component of effective treatment for traumatized children. An initial assessment should ideally include both child self-reports and caretaker reports on the child, and should address history of trauma exposure and subsequent trauma-related emotional symptoms. At the same time, less trauma-related (i.e., more generic) symptoms also should be evaluated, since they, too, may require clinical intervention. Because of the breadth of symptoms potentially associated with childhood trauma exposure, effective psychometric assessment often will include a number of different tests that tap a range of potential symptoms and problems. Repeated assessment is recommended for those children undergoing trauma-focused therapy, so that changes in symptomatology over time can be detected and the focus of therapy can be adjusted accordingly. Repeat assessment also increases accountability and quality control, since the effectiveness of treatment can be tracked within and across child clients.

REFERENCES

Achenbach, T. M. (1991). *Manual for the Child Behavior Checklist/4-18 and 1991 Profile.* Burlington: University of Vermont, Department of Psychiatry.

Briere, J. (1996). *Trauma Symptom Checklist for Children (TSCC).* Odessa, FL: Psychological Assessment Resources.

Briere, J. (2001). Evaluating treatment outcome. In M. Winterstein & S. R. Scribner (Eds.), *Mental healthcare for child crime victims: Standards of care task force guidelines.* Sacramento: California Victims Compensation and Government Claims Board, Victims of Crime Program, State of California.

Briere, J. (2005). *Trauma Symptom Checklist for Young Children (TSCYC).* Odessa, FL: Psychological Assessment Resources.

Briere, J., & Spinazzola, J. (2005). Phenomenology and psychological assessment of complex post-traumatic states. *Journal of Traumatic Stress, 18,* 401–412.

Cook, A., Spinazzola, J., Ford, J., Lanktree, C., Blaustein, M., Cloitre, M., et al. (2005). Complex trauma in children and adolescents. *Psychiatric Annals, 35,* 390–398.

Elliott, D. M., & Briere, J. (1994). Forensic sexual abuse evaluations of older children: Disclosures and symptomatology. *Behavioral Sciences and the Law, 12,* 261–277.

Flowers, A. L., Hastings, T. L., & Kelley, M. L. (2000). Development of a screening instrument for exposure to violence in children: The KID-SAVE. *Journal of Psychopathology and Behavioral Assessment, 22*(1), 91–104.

Ford, J. D., Racusin, R., Ellis, C., Daviss, W. B., Reiser, J., Fleischer, A., et al. (2000). Child maltreatment, other trauma exposure, and posttraumatic symptomatology among children with oppositional defiant and attention deficit hyperactivity disorders. *Child Maltreatment, 5,* 205–217.

Fox, N. A., & Leavitt, L. A. (1995). *The Violence Exposure Scale for Children-VEX-R.* College Park: University of Maryland, Department of Human Development.

Friedrich, W. N. (1998). *The Child Sexual Behavior Inventory professional manual.* Odessa, FL: Psychological Assessment Resources.

Friedrich, W. N. (2002). *Psychological assessment of sexually abused children and their families.* Thousand Oaks, CA: Sage.

Kovacs, M. (1992). *Children's Depression Inventory.* New York: Multi-Health Systems.

Lanktree, C. B., & Briere, J. (1995). Outcome of therapy for sexually abused children: A repeated measures study. *Child Abuse and Neglect, 19,* 1145–1155.

Lanktree, C. B., Briere, J., & Zaidi, L. Y. (1991). Incidence and impacts of sexual abuse in a child outpatient sample: The role of direct inquiry. *Child Abuse and Neglect, 15,* 447–453.

Lanktree, C. B., Gilbert, A. M., Briere, J., Taylor, N., Chen, K., Maida, C. A., et al. (in press). Multi-informant assessment of maltreated children: Convergent and discriminant validity of the TSCC and TSCYC. *Child Abuse and Neglect.*

Nader, K. O. (2004). Assessing traumatic experiences in children and adolescents: Self-reports of DSM PTSD criteria B-D symptoms. In J. P. Wilson & T. M. Keane (Eds.), *Assessing psychological trauma and PTSD* (2nd ed., pp. 513–537). New York: Guilford Press.

Putnam, F. W., Helmers, K., & Trickett, P. K. (1993). Development, reliability, and validity of a child dissociation scale. *Child Abuse and Neglect, 17,* 731–741.

Pynoos, R., Rodriguez, N., Steinberg, A., Stuber, M., & Frederick, C. (1998). *The UCLA PTSD Index for DSM-IV.* Los Angeles: UCLA Trauma Psychiatry Program.

Reid, J. B., Kavanagh, K. A., & Baldwin, D. V. (1987). Abusive parents' perceptions of child problem behaviors: An example of parental bias. *Journal of Abnormal Child Psychology, 15,* 457–466.

CHERYL LANKTREE
Miller Children's Hospital

JOHN BRIERE
University of Southern California

See also: Child Development; Diagnosis of Traumatic Stress Disorders (*DSM & ICD*); Posttraumatic Stress Disorder, Diagnosis of; Trauma, Definition; Trauma Symptom Checklist for Children; UCLA PTSD Reaction Index

ASSESSMENT, PSYCHOPHYSIOLOGICAL

Psychophysiological assessment (PA) is a generic term often substituted for psychological challenge testing or (emotion) provocation testing. Psychophysiological procedures involve monitoring biological systems that are reactive to psychologically meaningful events, in contrast to physiological measurement that is concerned with biological state per se. It is common for PA to include nonphysiological measures as well.

Measurement for PA occurs during controlled presentation of stimulus material that has known impact on psychological state. One format of PA examines differences between measures recorded during a target state (e.g., fear) and the same measures recorded during a reference state (e.g., engagement in a nonfearful task). This approach assumes that differences reflect the degree to which the state of interest has been evoked, and the magnitude of differences can be used as one source of evidence regarding the severity of a condition or disorder. Another format of PA examines differences in reactions to the same stimulus material on two or more occasions in order to evaluate change. This approach can be used to demonstrate the effect of treatment (e.g., reduction in fear after therapy)

Rationale

Trauma-related PA is conceptually tied to the fight or flight response. It involves presentation of an evocative cue—a trauma-related reminder—that is expected to trigger a negative emotional state. The ability of the cue to evoke emotion is commonly attributed to classical conditioning, a learning process believed to occur during the traumatic experience. The negative emotion is expected to involve reactions in at least three domains: (1) biological mobilization, (2) subjective distress, and (3) behavioral withdrawal.

The biological component most often involves measures of bodily systems that are activated by the sympathetic nervous system in preparation for self-protective behavior. For example, increases in heart rate and blood pressure provide more blood as muscles are readied to power escape, and increases in sweating on the palms (the basis for skin conductance measurement) may reduce the risk of skin abrasion and blood loss during attack or self-defense.

It is common to measure the subjective component of PA on a simple rating scale with endpoints indicating high and low distress. Subjective ratings are sometimes obtained on two dimensions thought to be primary constituents of global distress: valence (positive-negative) and arousal (quiescent-activated).

While PA procedures generally limit opportunity for measuring overt escape behavior (e.g., due to electrode attachments), a person may still disengage from the task by behavior such as turning away from a video monitor displaying the trauma reminder. Self-report of behavioral intentions (e.g., the strength of desire to escape from the situation) is another potential index. Measures in this domain have received less attention in the published PA literature than have physiological and subjective measures.

History and Evidence

Trauma-related PA can be traced to two lines of research in the mid-twentieth century. One began in the 1940s and examined physiological reactions of combat-exposed military veterans when they were presented reminders of war. Individuals conducting this work included Abraham Kardiner and M. A. Wenger. The second line began in the 1960s and examined psychophysiological reactions of phobic individuals when presented their self-identified feared object (e.g., a snake). Peter Lang provided both theoretical impetus and methodological innovation

for these efforts (e.g., Lang, Melamed, & Hart, 1970).

Contemporary PA with traumatized populations began in the early 1980s after the PTSD diagnosis was adopted. Studies variously used auditory, audiovisual, and imaginal formats to present reminders of the war zone to groups of combat-exposed military veterans, comparing reactions between those who did and did not meet criteria for PTSD. Typically, these studies demonstrated greater physiological reactivity and distress for the individuals with PTSD.

Since then, numerous traumatized populations have been tested using PA methods and have replicated the essential findings. Examples include individuals who experienced motor vehicle accidents, sexual assault, childhood sexual abuse, and occupational trauma (e.g., police; firefighters), as well as additional military veterans. Other studies using PA with various PTSD populations also have demonstrated that successful trauma-related treatment leads to reductions in physiological and subjective distress reactions.

REFERENCE

Lang, P. J., Melamed, B. G., & Hart, J. (1970). A psychophysiological analysis of fear modification using an automated desensitization procedure. *Journal of Abnormal Psychology, 76,* 220–234.

RECOMMENDED READINGS

Keane, T. M., Kolb, L. C., Kaloupek, D. G., Orr, S. P., Blanchard, E. B., Thomas, R. G., et al. (1998). Utility of psychophysiological measurement in the diagnosis of post-traumatic stress disorder: Results from a Department of Veterans Affairs Cooperative Study. *Journal of Consulting and Clinical Psychology, 66,* 914–923.

Orr, S. P., Metzger, L. J., Miller, M. W., & Kaloupek, D. G. (2004). Psychophysiological assessment of posttraumatic stress disorder. In J. P. Wilson & T. M. Keane (Eds.), *Assessing psychological trauma and PTSD: A handbook for practitioners* (2nd ed., pp. 289–343). New York: Guilford Press.

Danny G. Kaloupek
Veterans Affairs Boston Healthcare System

See also: **Biofeedback; Biology, Physiology**

ASYLUM SEEKERS

Refugees, applying for protection in a foreign country, are called asylum seekers. The 1951 UN Refugee Convention still provides the central legal framework across most of the world and asserts that, "No Contracting State shall expel or return (*"refouler"*) a refugee in any manner whatsoever to the frontiers of territories where his life or freedom would be threatened on account of his race, religion, nationality, membership of a particular social group or political opinion." This is intended to provide an important safeguard for refugees who may fear imprisonment, torture, or death if they are captured by their state authorities. These protections may also be supplemented by other local frameworks such as the European Convention on Human Rights.

Asylum seekers who are not recognized as refugees may still have fled civil war or violent oppression, and thus are likely to have high trauma exposure and an elevated rate of physical and psychiatric morbidity. In addition to dealing with their past histories, asylum seekers face the challenges and difficulties of dealing with different cultural expectations as they transition into an alien world. Moreover, they must often accomplish this alone without the benefits of family and other social ties. They may feel adrift from a former political activism, isolated from their friends, colleagues, and communities.

It is a testimony to human resilience that many asylum seekers and refugees successfully adapt to their new circumstances, without developing persistent psychiatric disorder. There is a debate about the degree to which there is an elevation of psychiatric illness in asylum seekers. Different methodologies have been used to survey different populations of refugees with different cultural backgrounds and different experiences (Turner, 2004). However, the general conclusion is that there is a greater likelihood of psychiatric disorder in refugees and asylum seekers. In one study (Steel, Silove, Phan, & Bauman, 2002), evidence was found that this effect is still detectable many years later; although by then the absolute prevalence figures for psychiatric disorder had fallen. Significantly, trauma exposure was found to be the most important predictor of mental health status in these refugees.

REFERENCES

Steel, Z., Silove, D. M., Phan, T., & Bauman, A. (2002). Long-term effects of psychological trauma on the mental health of Vietnamese refugees resettled in Australia: A population-based study. *Lancet, 360,* 1056–1062.

Turner, S. W. (2004). Emotional reactions to torture and organized state violence. *PTSD Research Quarterly, 15*(2), 1–7.

STUART TURNER
The Trauma Clinic, London, UK

See also: Laws, Legislation, and Policy; Refugees; Torture

ATTACHMENT

According to attachment theory (Bowlby, 1969), humans and other primates are biologically inclined to establish close affiliative bonds—that is, emotional attachments—beginning soon after birth. The most fundamental attachment relationship is formed between the biological mother and child, though there are various other pairings that qualify as primary attachments, both in early childhood and at various stages across the lifespan. Attachment theory is rooted in the premise from evolutionary theory that natural selection conferred an adaptive advantage to parents and infants who maintained close physical proximity to each other, which helped both to decrease infant mortality by reducing the risks of accidents and predation and to support the social maturation of the infant. Thus, attachment is thought to provide increased objective security and support for psychosocial development in the developing child. Therefore, the best types of attachments are those that reliably provide protection while also encouraging the child to engage in behaviors that foster learning and the development of skills for relating to other people (e.g., exploration and mastery of environments, active interaction with the primary caregiver and other persons, and increasingly autonomous functioning).

While infants are biologically inclined to form attachment relationships with parents and other *attachment figures* (that is, persons who provide emotional and physical caregiving to the infant), the quality of these attachments varies depending on how caregivers interact with the infant. When caregivers are able to consistently ensure the physical safety and comfort of the infant, and also interact verbally and nonverbally in ways that are loving and responsive to the infant's biological and psychological needs, the emotional attachment tends to be beneficial to the infant's physical and psychosocial development. It is important to note that the caregiver need not be "perfect" in protecting and facilitating the infant's comfort and growth, but simply "good enough" to enable the infant to be and feel safe, cared for, and encouraged to explore the world (Winnicott, 1971).

The most commonly observed variations in infants' responses to adult caregiving are labeled *attachment styles,* which have been classified into typologies describing relational dispositions (that is, patterns of behavior by the infant in interacting with the caregiver) and working models (that is, beliefs and expectations that the infant develops about relationships). Attachment styles are first seen in early childhood, but tend to extend throughout childhood and adulthood in the person's primary family and peer relationships and intimate (e.g., marital, parenting) and friendship adult relationships. Thus, measures have been developed to assess both infants' and children's attachments styles, and also adolescent and adult attachment styles.

Developmental psychologist Mary Ainsworth and her coworkers (1978) developed an observational protocol known as the *Strange Situation Test*, the first and foremost method for assessing and classifying infants' and toddlers' attachment styles. The test involves a series of apparently simple, but theoretically and relationally powerful, activities that challenge the infant's ability to *tolerate separation* from a primary caregiver (e.g., the caregiver first plays with the infant and then leaves the infant with another adult whom the infant does not know [the "stranger," who actually is a well-trained researcher who interacts pleasantly with the infant]). Most infants, particularly around the age of 12 to 18 months old, become distressed when their primary caregiver leaves, but the extent of their distress differs and provides an indication of their ability to tolerate the separation. Equally important, the test assesses the infant's capacity to *emotionally accept reunion* with the caregiver (i.e., the caregiver returns to the room and begins to console and play with the infant again). Attachment style has as much or more to do with the infant's ability to regain a calm and happy emotional state, and the caregiver's ability to "soothe" the child so as to facilitate that emotional regrouping, as it does with distress during separation. This line of research produced ample evidence of attachment behaviors and patterns that were consistent with and supportive of Bowlby's theoretical framework.

The most frequently occurring and advantageous attachment style is labeled as *secure attachment* because the child appears to feel a sense of emotional security before and after the separation, by demonstrating a balance between seeking and maintaining adequate proximity to the attachment figure (e.g., getting the caregiver's attention, moving closer to the caregiver) and engaging in developmentally appropriate exploratory behavior (e.g., leaving the caregiver's immediate area to play with toys) without showing signs of undue distress. When circumstances trigger increased activation of the attachment behavioral repertoire (such as after playing autonomously for a short time, or when the caregiver leaves the room), the child physically seeks contact with the attachment figure and will protest and resist separation. Upon reunion with the attachment figure, the securely attached child's distress can be readily soothed by sensitive and responsive behavior on the part of the attachment figure. Thus, a secure attachment style provides a reliable and responsive base both in the infant-caregiver relationship and in the child's inner sense of confidence in both self and the relationship that enables the infant to develop trust and security both in relationships and in her or himself. The responsive and facilitative caregiver thus provides effective protection for the infant without inhibiting the infant's maturation as an autonomous individual.

Three variations on *insecure attachment*—a pattern of attachment characterized by fearfulness and distress rather than security and trust—have also been identified. An *ambivalent* attachment style describes a relationship in which the child shows distress upon separation from the attachment figure, but signs of ambivalence upon their reunion (e.g., anger, resistance to being soothed). An *avoidant* attachment style describes a relationship in which the child shows little or no response to separation from the attachment figure and little if any response upon reunion. A more recently identified attachment style is characterized as being *disorganized* (Main & Solomon, 1986) because the child appears not to have any consistent strategy for coping with separation from attachment figure and upon reunion may demonstrate combinations of freezing, avoidance, disorientation, anger, depression, and a variety of apparently odd behaviors (such as alternately clinging to or ignoring both the caregiver and the stranger). This disorganized attachment style is often observed among children who have been maltreated or whose parents have a psychiatric disorder (Main, 1995), and it is associated with significant psychosocial problems (such as chronic dissociation) decades later in adulthood (Lyons-Ruth et al., 2006). Disorganized attachment thus has special significance in relation to psychological trauma, as will be discussed later.

While these attachment styles are evident and classifiable in early childhood, and appear to remain relatively stable across time, they are also malleable and may change as the child or adult adapts to changing environments, relationships, and experiences. Bowlby (1969) hypothesized that attachments in infancy produce *internal working models* that are the person's fundamental (and typically unquestioned) assumptions guiding her or his lifelong expectations and behavior regarding close personal relationships. These internal working models combine durability with plasticity—that is, they are relatively enduring yet can be modified—and serve to influence and limit subsequent relational behavior while undergoing persistent elaboration in the face of actual relational transactions. Attachment is thus considered to be an important aspect of personality across the life span with implications for social and relational functioning in a wide range of contexts (Bohlin, Hagekull, & Rydell, 2000; Hazan & Shaver, 1994).

Attachment and Psychological Trauma

Studies of attachment across the life span indicate that attachment styles are related to a variety of important aspects of social and psychological functioning. Among these are findings indicating that attachment styles predict symptoms of various mental disorders (e.g., Atkinson & Zucker, 1997; Greenberg, 1999; Pianta, Egeland, & Adam, 1996), with insecure and disorganized styles of attachment demonstrating significant linkages to psychological trauma.

Attachment theory provides an explanatory framework for those linkages because of the significant role that attachment relationships play in helping the child to cope with or recover from threats to optimal development. By definition, potentially traumatic events constitute major threats to physical and psychological integrity and development. Thus, when children experience psychological trauma, this may affect their style or working models of attachment in several ways. Moreover, the child's attachment style may affect how the child responds to the traumatic events. First, the traumatic events may alter formative attachment (bonding) experiences, such as by interfering with or preventing caregivers from protecting and providing responsive care to the child. Thus, traumatic events may influence the child's development of internal working models of attachment, potentially leading the child to adopt more insecure, ambivalent, or disorganized attachment styles.

Second, traumatic events also test the adaptive effectiveness of attachment models and behaviors that the child previously has developed, potentially shifting a child from secure toward insecure attachment styles and working models.

Third, the child's preexisting attachment working models may reduce the adverse impact of traumatic stressors if the working models are predominantly secure, and this may "buffer" or protect the child from developing severe or persistent posttraumatic stress symptoms. However, if a child's attachment experiences and working models were primarily insecure or disorganized prior to exposure to potentially traumatic events, the child may be more likely to develop traumatic stress symptoms that are severe or persistent (as well as potentially shifting toward more insecure attachment styles) than a child who was securely attached.

Thus, while secure attachment may confer substantial resilience for children in the face of traumatic stress, and insecure attachment appears to constitute a risk factor for undesirable posttraumatic outcomes, the child's attachment style and working models also are vulnerable to the pernicious effects of acute and chronic exposure to traumatic stressors. Traumatic stressors experienced in early childhood place the individual at risk for problems with basic forms of self-regulation (such as difficulties in regulating emotions or managing physical injury or pain) and cognitive development (such as impairments in memory or judgment) which may be, in part, related to the disruption of secure attachment (Ford, 2005). Early life experiences with caregivers that promote the development of a secure style and working models of attachment teach children not only how to feel safe and trusting in relationships, but also how to develop skills for self-regulation and cognitive processing that the child needs in order to explore the world and achieve autonomy.

Secure attachment develops through experiences that have been labeled "co-regulation" (Schore, 2001; Siegel, 2001), in which the infant learns to regulate her or his emotions, thinking, and body by experiencing the caregiver's own self-regulation. The caregiver thus "jump starts" the child's self-regulatory abilities by using her or his ability to reduce or increase physical arousal level to directly alter the infant's arousal and affective states. The infant thus learns to self-regulate when the caregiver takes the lead and helps the infant to intuitively adopting similar self-regulatory strategies. For example, as a caregiver soothes a distressed infant, the infant learns experientially (that is, simply by experiencing the changes) how to use certain comforting forms of physical contact, tones of voice, and facial expressions to soothe her or himself.

When traumatic stressors occur in the life of a child or caregiver, this often makes it more difficult either for the caregiver to provide the intimate modeling of self-regulation that is needed or for the infant to attend to and "take in" the experience of co-regulating. The result in either case is that the caregiver has difficulty in protecting and being responsive to the child, which leads the child to have difficulty both in developing a secure sense of attachment and to learn how to self-regulate physically (Sethre-Hofstad, Stansbury, & Rice, 2002) and emotionally. The result can be a long-term impairment in the infant's relational and self-regulatory functioning that can undermine the child's effective use of social support, which is often cited as an essential aspect of resilience to traumatic stress. Thus, when exposure to traumatic stressors in early childhood disrupt the development of secure attachment, the child is less likely to be able to cope with traumatic stress reactions because she or he is likely to have difficulties with both self-regulation (that is, adjusting her or his bodily and emotion state) and getting help from others (that is, seeking and utilizing helpful social support).

Attachment and Treatment of Traumatic Stress Disorders

Attachment relationships and internal working models of attachment are promising targets for interventions with adults and children who exhibit signs of posttraumatic stress reactions. The purpose of attachment-oriented therapeutic interventions is to bolster resilience by improving existing relationships while increasing the potential for developing additional relationships that can support the child's or adult's psychosocial functioning. Relational interventions informed by attachment theory may be conducted at any stage of life, beginning with traumatized young children and their caregivers (Van Horn & Lieberman, in press), but also including traumatized adolescents and adults (Cloitre, Cohen, & Koenen, 2006; Lamagna & Gleiser, 2007; Ogden, Minton, & Pain, 2006). Parents and others who provide care for infants and toddlers exposed to potentially traumatic events, even when these same caregivers may have been involved in abusing or neglecting the child, may improve their caregiving and relational skills with the benefit of careful training and feedback (*see:* **Parent-Child Intervention**). Attachment-based dyadic (parent-child) interventions are designed to prevent further harm to the child while supporting the development of more effective attachment relationships with additional positive effects of the internal working models of children and their caregivers.

Attachment-based psychotherapies for adolescents and adults focus on providing a trustworthy and responsive therapeutic relationship (*see:* **Psychotherapeutic Processes**) and assisting the client(s) in developing increased recognition of and ability to regulate bodily reactions (Ogden et al., 2006), emotions (Lamagna & Gleiser, 2007), and beliefs (or *schemas*) about oneself and the world (Cloitre et al., 2006). Through the combination of experiencing security in the therapeutic relationship—which includes knowing that the therapist both cares about but also will not be excessively or intrusively involved with oneself—and learning by example and practice to develop self-regulation and interpersonal effectiveness skills, the attachment-based approaches to psychotherapy seek to help the client to develop a sense of internal security that was interrupted (Cloitre et al., 2006) or prevented by prior experiences of psychological trauma. An attachment approach to psychotherapy thus is consistent with all models of PTSD psychotherapy, and may be particularly important with clients who suffered early life betrayal traumas (*see:* **Betrayal Trauma**) in the form of childhood maltreatment or family violence (*see:* **Complex Posttraumatic Stress Disorder**).

Conclusion

Attachment theory has received strong research support and gained widespread acceptance as an explanatory framework for understanding close relationships across the span of human development. A critical function of attachment is to support survival and adaptive development in situations ranging from optimal conditions to those of extreme adversity, with more secure attachment styles being predictive of more resilient adaptations. Thus, in the face of potentially traumatic experiences, attachment activation is likely and may provide a degree of protection against the impact of traumatic stress. In turn, since attachment styles reflect relational experiences, exposure to some types of traumatic stressors (e.g., intimate abuse, emotional betrayal) may influence the development of internal working models of attachment in ways that generally undermine relational functioning and decrease resilience to potentially traumatic events. Interventions informed by attachment theory show promise for strengthening attachment bonds with traumatized young and older children and adults, and of improving relational quality in ways that could improve resilience to stressful life events and assist in resolving the residual effects of prior exposure to traumatic stress.

REFERENCES

Ainsworth, M. D. S., Blehar, M. C., Waters, E., & Wall, S. N. (1978). *Patterns of attachment: A psychological study of the strange situation.* Hillsdale, NJ: Erlbaum.

Atkinson, L., & Zucker, K. J. (Eds.). (1997). *Attachment and psychopathology.* New York: Guilford Press.

Bohlin, G., Hagekull, B., & Rydell, A-M. (2000). Attachment and social functioning: A longitudinal study from infancy to middle childhood. *Social Development, 9,* 24–39.

Bowlby, J. (1969). *Attachment and loss: Attachment* (Vol. 1). New York: Basic Books.

Cloitre, M., Cohen, L., & Koenen, K. (2006). *Treating survivors of childhood abuse: Psychotherapy for the interrupted life.* New York: Guilford Press.

Ford, J. D. (2005). Treatment implications of altered neurobiology, affect regulation and information processing following child maltreatment. *Psychiatric Annals, 35,* 410–419.

Greenberg, M. T. (1999). Attachment and psychopathology in childhood. In J. Cassidy & P. R. Shaver (Eds.), *Handbook of attachment: Theory, research, and clinical applications* (pp. 469–496). New York: Guilford Press.

Hazan, C. & Shaver, P. R. (1994). Attachment as an organizational framework for research on close relationships. *Psychological Inquiry, 5,* 1–22.

Lamagna, J., & Gleiser, K. (2007). Building a secure internal attachment: An intra-relational approach to ego strengthening and emotional processing with chronically traumatized clients. *Journal of Trauma and Dissociation, 8,* 25–52.

Lyons-Ruth, K., Dutra, L., Schuder, M., & Bianchi, I. (2006). From infant attachment disorganization to adult dissociation: Relational adaptations or traumatic experiences? *Psychiatric Clinics of North America, 29,* 63–86.

Main, M. (1995). Attachment: Overview, with selected implications for clinical work. In S. Goldberg, R. Muir, & J. Kerr (Eds.), *Attachment theory: Social, developmental, and clinical perspectives* (pp. 407–474). Hillsdale, NJ: Analytic Press.

Main, M., & Solomon, J. (1986). Discovery of an insecure disorganized/disoriented attachment pattern: Procedures, findings and implications for classification of behavior. In M. W. Yogman & T. B. Brazelton (Eds.), *Affective development in infancy* (pp. 95–124). Norwood, NJ: Ablex.

Ogden, P., Minton, K., & Pain, C. (2006). *Trauma and the body: A sensorimotor approach to psychotherapy.* New York: Norton.

Pianta, R. C., Egeland, B., & Adam, E. K. (1996). Adult attachment classification and self-reported psychiatric symptomatology as assessed by the Minnesota Multiphasic Personality Inventory-2. *Journal of Consulting and Clinical Psychology, 64,* 273–281.

Schore, A. (2001). Effects of a secure attachment relationship on right brain development, affect regulation, and infant mental health. *Infant Mental Health Journal, 22,* 7–66.

Sethre-Hofstad, L., Stansbury, K., & Rice, M. (2002). Attunement of maternal and child adrenocortical response to child challenge. *Psychoneuroendocrinology, 27,* 731–747.

Siegel, D. (2001). Toward an interpersonal neurobiology of the developing mind. *Infant Mental Health Journal, 22,* 67–94.

Van Horn, P., & Lieberman, A. (in press). Using dyadic therapies to treat traumatized children. In D. Brom, R. Pat-Horenczyk, & J. D. Ford (Eds.), *Treating traumatized children: Risk, resilience, and recovery.* London: Routledge.

Winnicott, D. W. (1971). *Playing and reality.* London: Routledge.

GILBERT REYES
Fielding Graduate University

JULIAN D. FORD
University of Connecticut School of Medicine

See also: Betrayal Trauma; Child Development; Child Maltreatment; Complex Posttraumatic Stress Disorder; Family Systems; Parent-Child Intervention; Psychodynamic Psychotherapy, Child; Psychotherapeutic Processes

ATTENTION

See: Cognitive Impairments; Information Processing

ATTRIBUTIONS

Attribution theorists contend that individuals who experience unexpected, unwanted, or otherwise unusual events are motivated to create explanations that lend meaning to those events. Further, the explanations they construct (i.e., attributions) may have implications for subsequent adjustment.

Attributions have generally been considered with reference to four dimensions—locus, stability, controllability, and generalizability. Locus refers to assigning causality to either oneself (internal attribution) or to other persons or environmental factors (external attributions). The dimension of stability refers to whether the cited cause of an event is enduring and unremitting, or whether it is transient in nature. By way of example, attributing a motor vehicle accident to a malfunctioning traffic signal would be relatively unstable, whereas attributing an accident to a perceived increase in bad drivers would be a much more stable attribution. Generalizability (also referred to in the literature as globality) involves the degree to which the individual attributes the event to factors that pervade many aspects of their life (e.g., personality, intellect) or very few. The dimension of controllability relates to whether the causal factors culminating in an event are deemed by the individual to be personally modifiable. Clearly, this dimension is not independent of locus and some have suggested that controllability is an aggregate of locus and stability.

The role of causal attributions has been examined within the area of posttraumatic stress disorder (PTSD) and it has been proposed that the type of causal explanations an individual creates to explain the occurrence of an event may serve as a risk factor for developing the disorder. Evidence from the literature has supported the hypothesis that certain attributional styles may be more adaptive than others. An attributional style refers to habitual or dispositional tendencies to invoke certain types of causal explanations for varied life events. For example, a pessimistic attributional style, comprised of internal, global, and stable attributions, has been shown to be associated with more severe PTSD symptoms. Recent research indicates that certain attributional tendencies may differ in adaptiveness depending on the type of trauma experienced. For example, there is general consensus in the literature that internal attributions (i.e., self-blame) for trauma are associated with poorer adjustment among sexual assault survivors. Among combat survivors and motor vehicle accident victims, however, some studies have documented poorer adjustment when an external attributional style (i.e., other blame) is maintained.

As is often the case, apparently discordant findings in the literature may result from methodological discrepancies as opposed to modest or unstable associations among the variables of interest. By way of example, some studies purporting to evaluate attributional tendencies as they relate to posttraumatic distress have utilized third parties to corroborate responsibility for the event (e.g., motor vehicle accident). In so doing, these studies inadvertently focus on true causality that is less relevant from an attributional perspective. There are many maladaptive posttraumatic attributions (e.g., self-blame following a sexual assault) that are objectively erroneous but nevertheless have significant implications for subsequent adjustment.

In terms of other methodological considerations, most studies to date have been cross-sectional in nature, which renders causal statements premature at this time. Also, dispositional attributional style and event-specific attributions have typically not been examined concurrently with known risk factors for PTSD. Accordingly, the relative importance of causal attributions as a posttraumatic risk factor is largely unknown. For a more detailed review of the role of causal attributions in PTSD, the reader is referred to Massad and Hulsey's (2006) examination of attributions and their implications for clinical research and practice.

REFERENCE

Massad, P. M., & Hulsey, T. L. (2006). Causal attributions in posttraumatic stress disorder: Implications for clinical research and practice. *Psychotherapy: Theory, research, practice, training, 43*(2), 201–215.

Christina M. Hassija
University of Wyoming

Matt J. Gray
University of Wyoming

See also: Cognitive Behavior Therapy, Adult; Cognitive Behavior Therapy, Child Abuse; Cognitive Behavior Therapy, Childhood Traumatic Grief; Social Cognitive Theory

AVOIDANCE

Avoidance is commonly observed among people with elevated anxiety and is even more pronounced among people with anxiety disorders.

Avoiding situations that are reminiscent of a traumatic event is a diagnostic feature of post-traumatic stress disorder (PTSD). Avoidance can be more or less apparent, because some forms of avoidance include avoiding thoughts or feeling that are associated with traumatic experiences.

The current diagnostic criteria for PTSD classify emotional numbing into the avoidance symptom cluster, although it is questionable that numbing is a form of avoidance. Recent research, moreover, suggests that avoidance and numbing are better explained as separate factors that differ in their clinical correlates, prognostic significance, and response to treatment (Asmundson, Stapleton, & Taylor, 2004). These findings are consistent with theories suggesting that numbing arises from a biological mechanism associated with a response called *conditioned analgesia,* which dampens arousal. In contrast, avoidance appears to be a more conscious and intentional strategy for regulating distressing emotional states.

Some forms of avoidance are obvious, such as when a survivor of a serious motor vehicle accident goes to considerable effort to avoid passing by the site of the accident, or when a combat veteran avoids watching news pertaining to war. Other forms of avoidance are not so obvious. For example, a physically abused child might refrain from making eye contact with the abusive parent in an effort to avert provocation of another beating. Likewise, to circumvent anxiety-related bodily sensations (e.g., palpitations, pain) that can serve as reminders of traumatic events, a person may refrain from physical exertion, such as household chores. Perhaps most subtle of all, some people try to avoid trauma-related thoughts by deliberately suppressing these thoughts by means of distraction.

Avoidance can be an effective strategy for managing fear or distress and, in some cases, can be adaptive. An example of adaptive avoidance might include staying away from parts of the city where violent crimes are known to be high. But avoidance in people with PTSD is generally not adaptive because, while it does alleviate distress in the short-term, it may also prevent the person from experiencing the corrective information necessary for learning how to distinguish between safe and risky situations. Deliberate attempts at thought suppression can also have the paradoxical effect of increasing trauma-related thoughts, which in turn may increase the severity and frequency of re-experiencing symptoms. Therefore, avoidance is more likely to exacerbate and perpetuate PTSD symptoms than promote adaptive behavior.

A potent alternative to avoiding trauma-related stimuli is to intentionally expose oneself to safe but distressing reminders under controlled conditions. Studies have demonstrated that the most effective means of treating avoidance is through the application of one or more forms of exposure therapy (Taylor, 2006). These include imaginal, interoceptive (i.e., to fear-evoking but harmless bodily sensations), and situational exposure. Each form of exposure is designed to allow the traumatized person to re-establish the capacity for distinguishing between situations that are reasonably safe and those that pose real danger. This in turn allows patients to resume activities consistent with their pre-trauma level of functioning and promotes more adaptive and progressive improvements in functioning.

REFERENCES

Asmundson, G. J. G., Stapleton, J. A., & Taylor, S. (2004). Avoidance and numbing are distinct PTSD symptom clusters. *Journal of Traumatic Stress, 17,* 467–475.

Taylor, S. (2006). *Clinician's guide to PTSD: A cognitive-behavioral approach.* New York: Guilford Press.

Gordon J. G. Asmundson
University of Regina

Steven Taylor
University of British Columbia

See also: Conditioned Fear; Emotional Numbing; Exposure Therapy, Adult; Exposure Therapy, Child; Posttraumatic Stress Disorder

B

BEHAVIOR THERAPY

See: Anxiety Management Training; Cognitive Behavior Therapy, Adult; Cognitive Behavior Therapy, Child Abuse; Cognitive Behavior Therapy, Childhood Traumatic Grief; Exposure Therapy, Adult; Exposure Therapy, Child

BEHAVIORAL HEALTH

See: Alcohol Use Disorders; Medical Illness; Somatic Complaints; Substance Abuse

BEREAVEMENT

Bereavement refers to the state of grief associated with the death of someone of personal significance. Generally, the bereaved individual is responding to the loss of a close family member such as a parent, spouse, sibling, or child, but loss of other relationships can trigger the bereavement response. The terms *grief* and *mourning* are also used to describe reactions to interpersonal loss. Grief typically refers to the cognitive-emotional response to loss whereas mourning may refer to the ritual and cultural practices associated with bereavement. Religious and cultural mourning practices are quite varied, but share the potential to offer emotional and social support and a framework to assist the bereaved person in understanding the loss.

Trauma and bereavement are closely related because traumatic events may include the loss of someone of close personal significance. The term *traumatic bereavement* denotes bereavement occurring under traumatic conditions, while the *traumatic of bereavement* refers to the psychosocial disruption that accompanies significant loss. But while both psychological trauma and bereavement stimulate life change and the need for coping, there are significant differences as illustrated in the Two-Track Model of Bereavement (Rubin, 1999). According to this model, adjustment occurs in two general domains: general biopsychosocial functioning (encompassing affective, cognitive, somatic, social, psychotraumatic response, and meaning systems) and the cognitive-emotional relationship to the deceased (including the nature, extent, and quality of that ongoing relationship). The model advocates assessment of both domains to determine response to loss. Changes in functioning accompany both exposure to psychological trauma and the experience of loss and bereavement.

Bereavement involves a focus on the lost person or relationship, which is not always present in psychological trauma. A variety of changes in cognitive, somatic, affective, and behavioral patterns are common to both trauma and bereavement, but a number of the manifestations of traumatic stress disorders that involve attempts to anticipate severe danger (such as hypervigilance) and to ward off distressing memories of severe danger are not commonly seen in response to bereavement. Bereavement has long been a focus of modern scientific and medical interest. Freud's article, "Mourning and Melancholia" (Freud, 1957/1917), has been particularly influential. It described mourning as a normal process that involves "grave departures" from everyday living, but needed no interference as the "work of mourning" would accomplish the withdrawal of emotional investment in the deceased for use in alternative relationships and the tasks of living. The psychoanalytic emphasis on emotional detachment from the deceased person or lost relationship exerted a major influence in the field until it lost favor due to the rise of empirically based approaches to bereavement.

Current perspectives on bereavement emphasize that a continuing bond with the deceased is normal and healthy following loss. Attitudes toward bereavement are shaped by a variety of influences, including cultural, societal, professional, and lay perspectives on loss, as well as by advances in theory and research. For example, parents who lose children may learn from self-help groups, the media, and/or from scientific reports directly, that many bereaved parents indicate that it takes years to come to terms with such a loss. The course of bereavement is neither uniform nor invariable. Age, gender, kinship relationship, emotional dependency and intimacy, time since loss, social support, psychological resilience, and circumstances of the death are among the variables that moderate response to loss. Deaths that were anticipated and were preceded by caretaking may reduce some of the pain of loss while losses associated with sudden, violent, and malevolent death tend to exacerbate the pain of loss. Adult bereavement often involves feelings of shock; anxiety; disbelief; sadness and depression; yearning for the deceased; and somatic changes in appetite, sleep, and sexuality.

Stage theories of grief have been advanced to chart the responses of the bereaved. Bowlby (1980) described stages: shock and numbness (the initial response), searching and yearning (attempt at reunion), disorganization (depressive and ineffective responses), and reorganization (achievement of readiness to meet the demands of reality). Kubler-Ross (1969), working with ill and dying patients, postulated a five-stage process of accommodating to terminal illness: Denial and disbelief, anger, bargaining, depression, and acceptance. The simplistic application of stage theories implying that people must progress along a predetermined sequence of stages is problematic. Kubler-Ross's stage theory was recently tested and received mixed support (Maciejewski,

Zhang, Block, & Prigerson, 2007). In the study reported, each indicator of the five stages peaked in the exact sequence postulated by the theory within 6 months after the loss. However, acceptance and yearning for the deceased were the most frequently reported thoughts and feelings throughout the study observation period. Moreover, other stage indicators such as depressed mood were never more frequent than either acceptance or yearning.

The duration of bereavement is variable. The responses to loss can be profound and varied, including biological, psychological, and social domains of impact. This reflects the broad range of challenges triggered by a profoundly personal and social loss. Examples include changes in the nature and availability of social support and economic security. A wide range of instrumental roles previously filled by the deceased require the bereaved to adapt and compensate for the loss of what was previously available. Adjustment and accommodation to these changes unfold over time, and with varying degrees of success. In contrast, the emotional connection to the deceased and its impact on the bereaved can persist long after adjustment to the loss itself and the changes it engendered have been successfully negotiated.

Bereavement is a stressful life event that can trigger a variety of medical and psychological difficulties. Strong and painful emotions as well as major changes in living characterize normal grief and mourning, and generally resolve without professional attention. In addition to the social support that is provided by friends and relatives, self-help groups composed of individuals who share the experience of bereavement have eased the isolation and provided support for bereaved individuals.

An estimated 10% to 20% of bereaved persons require mental health intervention. A proposal to classify a specific bereavement disorder as a formal psychiatric diagnosis is in development (Prigerson, Vanderwerker, & Maciejewski, in press). Previously labeled pathological grief, or complicated grief, the current proposal describes a prolonged grief disorder that interferes significantly with the bereaved's functioning. Among the defining characteristics associated with the proposed diagnosis are difficulty accepting the loss, longing, confusion about one's role in life or a diminished sense of self, bitterness over the loss, feeling emotionally numb or detached from others, significant dysfunction in management of life tasks, and persistence of these symptoms for a period of 6 months.

Research that has compared symptoms and diagnoses of prolonged grief disorder in samples surviving psychological trauma (e.g., disaster, fatal accidents, murder) with samples surviving natural deaths (e.g., cancer) has failed to demonstrate substantial differences in symptomatology or rates of diagnosis (Boelen & Van Den Bout, 2007; Prigerson et al., 2002). However, a study of bereaved college students found that failure to find meaning in a loss was a crucial pathway to prolonged grief disorder (Currier, Holland, & Neimeyer, 2006), suggesting that the extent to which the traumatic loss makes it more difficult for the bereaved survivor to process the loss and/ or the relationship to the deceased would be expected to exacerbate prolonged grief disorder symptomatology. A more systematic comparison of prolonged grief disorder symptoms following traumatic and nontraumatic deaths is warranted.

Other mental disorders (e.g., anxiety, depression, PTSD) may coexist with bereavement difficulties and may have been present prior to the loss or as a result of it. Research and clinical evidence suggest that, where the need for professional intervention is indicated, it is particularly efficacious to target specific aspects of the problematic responses to loss such as anxiety, depression, or PTSD. At the same time, it has been shown that interventions with a focus on reworking the bereaved person's relationship to the deceased are important to include together with the other targeted interventions (Malkinson & Rubin, 2007). The uniquely interpersonal aspects of bereavement are emerging as significant elements in both adaptive and maladaptive response to loss.

REFERENCES

Boelen, P. A., & Van Den Bout, J. (2007). Examination of proposed criteria for complicated grief in people confronted with violent or nonviolent loss. *Death Studies, 31* (2),155–164.

Bowlby, J. (1980). *Attachment and loss: Vol. 3. Loss.* New York: Basic Books.

Currier, J., Holland, J., & Neimeyer, R. (2006). Sense-making, grief, and the experience of violent loss: Toward a mediational model. *Death Studies, 30* (5), 403–428.

Freud, S. (1957). Mourning and melancholia. In J. Strachey (Ed.), *The standard edition of the complete psychological works of Sigmund Freud* (Vol. 14, pp. 237–258). London: Hogarth Press. (Original work published 1917)

Kubler-Ross, E. (1969). *On death and dying.* New York: Macmillan.

Maciejewski, P. K., Zhang, B., Block, S. D., & Prigerson, H. G. (2007). An empirical examination of the state theory of grief resolution. *Journal of the American Medical Association, 297,* 716–723.

Malkinson, R., & Rubin, S. (2007). The two-track model of bereavement: A balanced model. In R. Malkinson (Ed.), *Cognitive grief therapy: Constructing a rational meaning to life following loss* (pp. 23–43). New York: Norton.

Prigerson, H. G., Ahmed, I., Silverman, G. K., Saxena, A. K., Maciejewski, P. K., Jacobs, S. C., et al. (2002). Rates and risks of complicated grief among psychiatric clinic patients in Karachi, Pakistan. *Death Studies, 26* (10), 781–792.

Prigerson, H. G., Vanderwerker, L. C., & Maciejewski, P. K. (in press). Prolonged grief disorder: A case for inclusion in DSM-V. In M. S. Stroebe, R. Hansson, W. Stroebe, & H. Schut (Eds.), *Handbook of bereavement research and practice: 21st century perspectives.* Washington, DC: American Psychological Association.

Rubin, S. (1999). The two-track model of bereavement: Overview, retrospect and prospect. *Death Studies, 23* (8), 681–714.

SIMON SHIMSHON RUBIN
University of Haifa

HOLLY PRIGERSON
Harvard Medical School

See also: Attachment; Cognitive Behavior Therapy, Childhood Traumatic Grief; Freud, Sigmund

BETRAYAL TRAUMA

Betrayal trauma refers to a social dimension of psychological trauma, independent of posttraumatic stress reactions (Freyd, 1996). Betrayal trauma occurs when the people or institutions on which a person depends for survival significantly violate that person's trust or well-being: Childhood physical, emotional, or sexual abuse perpetrated by a caregiver are examples of betrayal trauma. When psychological trauma involves betrayal, the victim may be less aware or less able to recall the traumatic experience because to do so will likely lead to confrontation or withdrawal by the betraying caregiver, threatening a necessary attachment relationship and thus the victim's survival. Research findings indicate that adults are less likely to fully recall childhood abuse by caregivers or close others than by strangers (Freyd, DePrince, & Gleaves, 2007). In addition, betrayal trauma may be associated with other problems such as physical illness, alexithymia, depression, and anxiety (Freyd, Klest, & Allard, 2005). Females, compared with males, report greater exposure to traumas high in betrayal; the reverse is true for traumas low in betrayal (Goldberg & Freyd, 2006). Betrayal trauma theory highlights the importance of safe and trustworthy attachment relationships in understanding posttraumatic outcomes.

REFERENCES

Freyd, J. J. (1996). *Betrayal trauma: The logic of forgetting childhood abuse.* Cambridge, MA: Harvard University Press.

Freyd, J. J., DePrince, A. P., & Gleaves, D. (2007). The state of betrayal trauma theory: Reply to McNally (2007)—Conceptual issues and future directions. *Memory, 15,* 295–311.

Freyd, J. J., Klest, B., & Allard, C. B. (2005). Betrayal trauma: Relationship to physical health, psychological distress, and a written disclosure intervention. *Journal of Trauma and Dissociation, 6* (3), 83–104.

Goldberg, L. R., & Freyd, J. J. (2006). Self-reports of potentially traumatic experiences in an adult community sample: Gender differences and test-retest stabilities of the items in a Brief Betrayal-Trauma Survey. *Journal of Trauma and Dissociation, 7* (3), 39–63.

JENNIFER J. FREYD
University of Oregon

See also: Abuse, Child Physical; Abuse, Child Sexual; Child Maltreatment

BIOFEEDBACK

Biofeedback techniques have been adapted clinically and scientifically tested for the treatment of posttraumatic stress disorder (PTSD). Feedback as a treatment intervention for PTSD involves providing information to an individual about some aspect of his or her behavior that occurs in response to experiencing stimuli associated with the past psychological trauma. Biofeedback specifically involves providing feedback about bodily reactions, hence the addition of the prefix *bio* to the generic term *feedback*.

Feedback appropriate to individuals experiencing PTSD may be provided via a variety of modalities that impart information about the individual's response to the presentation/experience of trauma-related stimuli, the individual's progress toward an identified goal such as being able to experience trauma-related stimuli without the extreme or debilitating psychological or biological reactions that characterize PTSD, or information about some aspect of behavior that is thought to help the individual control or reduce the experience of PTSD symptoms (such as the person's success in using relaxation skills to reduce bodily arousal).

Theoretical Underpinnings

The use of biofeedback in the change process for individuals with PTSD is anchored in self-regulation theory. Self-regulation refers to those processes that mediate goal-directed behavior. For example, an individual whose goal was to reduce hyper-responsiveness to trauma-related stimuli might set a subgoal of becoming more relaxed. Because low levels of muscle tension are associated with relaxation, the individual would utilize a biofeedback apparatus to monitor muscle tension via electromyographic (EMG) recording of the frontalis muscle in the forehead. Reductions in muscle tension would signal that improvement is occurring and that the individual was becoming more relaxed. This relaxation, in turn, would reduce the individual's hyper-responsiveness to threatening stimuli and thus reduce this particular symptom of PTSD. Goal-directed behavior can be viewed as being regulated in a process in which individuals identify goals, initiate a set of behaviors to attain those goals, monitor their progress toward their goals, compare their level of accomplishment to their goals, and determine whether their behavior should be adjusted in order to meet their goals. Biofeedback is a process wherein biological correlates of the individual's behavior are monitored and a feedback loop automatically and continuously supplies information to the individual about the success of his or her efforts. The monitored outcome of the individual's behavior can then be used as a source of information for the individual to modify his or her behavior to better produce he desired change in the correlates of his or her behavior. This modification takes the form of increasing or decreasing behaviors intended to help reach the goal or by identifying new strategies to help attain the objective.

Goal-directed behavior that includes biofeedback involves the production by the individual of an increase/decrease in biological responses associated with a decrease in PTSD symptoms. For example, individuals with PTSD would set a goal of decreasing their heart rate when presented with stimuli that reminded them of their traumatic events. They would then utilize strategies to reduce their heart rate, receive feedback about their success, alter their responses accordingly, with a goal of experiencing reduced symptoms of PTSD.

Assessment of PTSD-Relevant Targets for Biofeedback

To identify which behaviors to target during the biofeedback process, biological correlates of PTSD must be identified. This can be accomplished formally by comparing persons diagnosed with PTSD against individuals without the disorder, or by hypothesizing suspected correlates. Increased levels of anxiety/tension are a likely chronic state in individuals with PTSD and are often targeted in studies of biofeedback treatments for PTSD. Physiological, neuromuscular or neurocortical measures that increase when individuals with PTSD, relative to controls, are presented with visual, auditory, or imagined stimuli provide the basis for what to target in the biofeedback process. Heart rate, skin resistance, and blood pressure are frequently used to provide feedback about physiologic responses. Electromyographic recordings are used to provide feedback about muscular tension and alpha brain waves are used to provide feedback about general arousal. These correlates are monitored during exposure to trauma-related stimuli and feedback supplied to the individual regarding their change. In a typical experiment, individuals with and without PTSD are presented with stimuli associated with their traumatic event. Physiological, neuromuscular and/or neurocortical substrates are evaluated, with those that display differences between individuals in the two groups identified as central to the PTSD experience.

In a series of studies that compared individuals with PTSD and those without, increased autonomic nervous system (ANS) responding was found among those with PTSD in response to trauma-related stimuli that included either auditory stimuli and/or audiovisual stimuli (*see:* **Biology, Physiology**). Heart rate, skin resistance, and systolic blood pressure were all elevated when combat trauma stimuli were presented to individuals with PTSD relative to individuals without PTSD. In addition to changes in ANS activity during the presentation of trauma stimuli, changes in muscle tension, especially in the facial muscles, have been elevated in individuals with PTSD. Muscle tension, as reflected in increased responsivity of the frontalis (forehead), zygomaticus, and corrugator muscles of the face have been found to correlate with presentations of trauma stimuli. These latter findings have also been found for combat-related visual slides that did not include auditory stimuli. Changes in facial muscle tension during presentation of trauma stimuli may be specific to emotions associated with trauma, as opposed to changes in ANS measures that likely reflect general increased autonomic arousal.

However, when individuals with PTSD are compared to individuals without PTSD who have experienced similar traumatic experiences, differences in ANS responding to trauma stimuli are not always found. This was the case in a study (Jones-Alexander, Blanchard, & Hickling, 2005) that compared children and adolescents who had been in a motor vehicle accident (MVA) and who had PTSD or subsyndromal PTSD to MVA victims without PTSD and non-MVA controls. No group differences were found to auditory and imaginal (i.e., thought about) cues of a MVA. Further, individuals with subsyndromal PTSD or who have been in less severe motor vehicle accidents, are less likely to respond to trauma stimuli with increased heart rate (Veazy, Blanchard, Hickling, & Buckley, 2004). A substantial minority of trauma victims with PTSD do not respond with increased physiological activity when presented with trauma cues, while a minority of individuals without a history of exposure to psychological trauma or PTSD does respond to trauma cues with elevated physiological activity. The differences between these two groups are reliable enough, however, to recommend using ANS-mediated physiological changes to track changes in PTSD when treatments are applied.

Symptom Response as a Measure of PTSD Treatment Outcome

Psychological trauma victims' physiological and neuromuscular responses to trauma stimuli have been used to track improvement during treatment. Changes on a heart rate measure during cognitive behavioral treatment (CBT), provided to individuals who had been in motor vehicle accidents, paralleled improvement in PTSD symptoms (Rabe, Dorfel, Zollner,

Maercker, & Karl, 2006). This finding supports the contention that changes in correlates of PTSD symptoms can be expected to coincide with changes in the PTSD symptoms themselves. Therefore, an intervention such as biofeedback, which is designed to help individuals to modify ANS and other bodily responses, may be an approach to reducing PTSD severity.

How Biofeedback Treatments Are Conducted

In the typical study examining the effectiveness of biofeedback approaches to the treatment of PTSD, participants go through four phases: (1) a baseline phase in which individuals accommodate to being connected to the physiological measurement apparatus while recordings are made of the physiological, neuromuscular, or other measure that serves as feedback; (2) Phase 2, where recordings on the dependent measures such as heart rate, skin conductance, or muscle tension are made while the person responds to trauma-related stimuli, delivered via visual, auditory or imagined modalities (e.g., watching a film depicting war combat, or listening to a script describing a personal experience of psychological trauma); (3) a treatment phase, during which the individual is instructed to reduce his or her response to the trauma-related stimuli using biofeedback from the dependent measure (scores on the dependent measure during the treatment phase are compared to changes during Phase 2, with decreases reflective of therapeutic improvement); and (4) a resolution or second baseline phase during which no stimuli are presented and the individual is allowed to return to baseline (i.e., to regain a state of reduced arousal). When individuals serve as their own control subjects, each participant's scores during Phase 3 are compared to scores during Phase 2. When a control group is used, responses of some persons who receive the full biofeedback procedure are compared to responses of other persons who do not receive some or all of the procedure, and reductions between the two phases are compared between the treated and untreated groups. Additionally, when there is a control group, individuals in the biofeedback group may be compared to individuals in the control group on measures not directly targeted during the feedback sessions, such as self-report or interview-based measures of PTSD symptoms.

Effectiveness of Biofeedback in the Treatment of PTSD

Three different biofeedback approaches have been used to treat individuals with PTSD: (1) feedback used to produce relaxation, (2) relaxation instructions enhanced by feedback, and (3) feedback of brain waves associated with PTSD. In almost all of the treatment studies, combat veterans with combat-related PTSD have been studied. Six combat veterans with PTSD were given relaxation/EMG feedback over a period of 8 to 26 weeks. Improvements were found in EMG recordings, clinical scales of the Minnesota Multiphasic Personality Inventory (MMPI), and clinical ratings. The effectiveness of EMG-assisted desensitization was assessed in a study of 16 combat veterans with PTSD. Individuals were assigned to either the EMG feedback or a control condition. Muscle tension in the frontalis region was used to provide feedback. Individuals in the treated group improved on muscle tension, nightmares, and flashbacks, while individuals in the control group did not improve. In another study, alpha-theta brainwave neuro-feedback was compared to traditional medical treatment in a sample of Vietnam combat veterans. Individuals with increased alpha could be expected to experience higher levels of relaxation compared to individuals without such feedback. Individuals who received the neuro-feedback scored lower on clinical scales of the Minnesota Multiphasic Personality Inventory when compared to those receiving standard medical treatment, an effect that continued over a 30-month follow-up period. Taken together, these three studies provide some beginning support for the effectiveness of feedback-assisted relaxation in the treatment of individuals with PTSD.

A second question relates to whether biofeedback-assisted relaxation is more effective

than other forms of relaxation training for individuals with PTSD. To answer this question, a group of 100 male combat veterans with PTSD were placed in treatments involving Eye Movement Desensitization and Reprocessing (EMDR), relaxation training (RT) or biofeedback (BF). EMDR was the most effective treatment, followed by RT and BF (Silver, Brooks, & Oberchain, 1995). A second study compared the effectiveness of relaxation instructions (RI), RI plus deep breathing instructions (RI + DB) and RI + DB + thermal biofeedback in a group of 90 male combat veterans with PTSD. No single treatment was more effective than any other, indicating that simple instructions to relax are as effective in reducing PTSD symptoms as biofeedback-enhanced relaxation (Carlson, Singelis, & Chemtob, 1997). In the only study to use individuals with other than combat-related PTSD a group of 12 individuals with headaches secondary to motor vehicle accidents were studied. All individuals received relaxation training with supportive psychotherapy, with seven also receiving biofeedback training. Eight of the 12 experienced clinically significant improvement, though it could not be determined if the addition of biofeedback enhanced treatment outcome. These studies indicate that biofeedback does not enhance effective treatments for PTSD. Rothbaum, Meadows, Resick, and Foy (2000) compared biofeedback training to other forms of treatments for PTSD and arrived at a similar conclusion.

Conclusion

Biofeedback can be used either adjunctively, in combination with other treatments, or as a stand-alone treatment for PTSD. Feedback in a variety of different systems has been effectively used to reduce both symptoms of PTSD and correlates of PTSD. These systems include ANS correlates, especially heart rate; muscle tension, especially involving facial muscles; and brain waves, especially, alpha-theta waves. Evidence exists that improvements are stable over moderately long follow-up periods. When stand-alone biofeedback is compared to other standard treatments for PTSD or to other approaches for teaching relaxation, no incremental effect has been shown for biofeedback techniques.

REFERENCES

Carlson, J. G., Singelis, T. M., & Chemtob, C. M. (1997). Facial EMG responses to combat-related visual stimuli in veterans with and without post-traumatic stress disorder. *Applied Psychophysiology and Biofeedback, 22,* 247–259.

Jones-Alexander, J., Blanchard, E. B., & Hickling, E. J. (2005). Psychophysiological assessment of youthful motor vehicle accident survivors. *Applied Psychophysiology and Biofeedback, 30,* 115–123.

Rabe, S., Dorfel, D., Zollner, T., Maercker, A., & Karl, A. (2006). Cardiovascular correlates of motor vehicle accident related posttraumatic stress disorder and its successful treatment. *Applied Psychophysiology and Biofeedback, 31,* 315–330.

Rothbaum, B. O., Meadows, E. A., Resick, P., & Foy, D. W. (2000). Cognitive-behavioral therapy. In E. B. Foa, T. M. Keane, & M. J. Friedman (Eds.), *Effective treatments for PTSD: Practice guidelines for the International Society for Traumatic Stress Studies* (pp. 60–83). New York: Guilford Press.

Silver, S. M., Brooks, A., & Obenchain, J. (1995). Treatment of Vietnam war veterans with PTSD: A comparison of eye movement desensitization and reprocessing, biofeedback, and relaxation training. *Journal of Traumatic Stress, 8,* 337–342.

Veazey, C. H., Blanchard, E. B., Hickling, E. J., & Buckley, T. C. (2004). Physiological Responsiveness of motor vehicle accident survivors with chronic posttraumatic stress disorder. *Applied Psychophysiology and Biofeedback, 29,* 51–62.

GEORGE A. CLUM
Virginia Polytechnic Institute and State University

See also: Assessment, Psychophysiological; Biology, Physiology; Cognitive Behavior Therapy, Adult; Exposure Therapy, Adult

BIOLOGY, ANIMAL MODELS

The need to model traumatic stress and post-traumatic stress disorder (PTSD) is critical to understanding the neural substrates involved in the etiology and maintenance of this disorder as well as in developing and testing treatment strategies. Though many animal models of stress are claimed to be models of PTSD, relatively few actually mimic aspects of the human condition. It is impossible in an animal paradigm to fully model the complexities of PTSD. This is not the goal of animal research. Using animal models, we can mimic certain aspects of traumatic stress-induced disorders and gain insight into the mechanisms underlying both adaptive as well as maladaptive brain responses to stress and coping. Technological advances with human brain imaging have provided much insight into the functional neuroanatomy of PTSD (*see:* **Biology, Brain Structure, and Function, Adult; Biology, Brain Structure, and Function, Child**). However, only with animal models is it possible to readily obtain brain tissue to more precisely identify the molecular mechanisms underlying this disorder. Additionally, treatment strategies can be first tested in animal models. Already some of these animal models have yielded information that is now being used to test treatments in human PTSD patients.

The earliest animal models of traumatic stress relied on a very quantitative and repeatable stressor—namely electrical shock. Many questions, both ethical as well as scientific, are raised by these models. Aside from our moral obligation to minimize any pain and distress in research animals, the question arises of whether shock is even an appropriate stressor to model "traumatic" stress in a rodent? Does shock model the "emotional" component of a traumatic stress? Do the physical effects of the shock confound interpretation of findings? As a result, of these concerns, researchers are taking a fresh look at alternative animal models. Many new models are being developed that take the natural history of the organism (generally the rat) into account.

Stressors that are more "ecologically relevant" (i.e., comparable to animals' natural environments and experiences) such as exposure to predator cues or aggressive species may actually be more effective in modeling PTSD. Here we provide a brief overview of some of the more widely used or interesting models and then discuss the importance of ecologically relevant models. This is by no means a comprehensive review of this topic and readers are encouraged to see Steckler, Kalin, and Reul's (2004) recent textbook for a more detailed review of the topic.

Certain criteria are used to evaluate the overall validity of animal models of human disorders. These criteria consist of face validity (i.e., does the paradigm mimic the etiology and symptoms of the disorder?), predictive validity (i.e., do recognized treatments ameliorate symptoms in the animal model?), and construct validity (are the physiological and neurobiological mechanisms consistent with what is known about the disorder?). Most animal models of PTSD rely almost exclusively on face validity since there are few accepted treatments and little is known about the underlying molecular mechanisms. An excellent article is available detailing proposed criteria for prospective animal models of PTSD (Siegmund & Wotjak, 2006).

One established animal model that has considerable face validity for traumatic stress and PTSD is learned helplessness (LH). This model is often referred to as "inescapable stress-induced behavioral depression" and has been proposed as a model of both depression as well as PTSD (Petty, Kramer, Wu, & Davis, 1997; Ronan, Steciuk, Kramer, Kram, & Petty, 2000). In this paradigm, first developed by Seligman and Maier (1967), animals are exposed to an inescapable stressor (in rodents this could be a tail- or footshock) and subsequently display behavioral depression when given the opportunity to escape. One interesting and important aspect of this model is that not all rats exposed to the traumatic stressor develop PTSD-like symptoms. Approximately half of the animals exposed to the "learned helplessness" stressor develop behavioral depression (deficits in "escape" behavior). The others ("nonhelpless") are behaviorally indistinguishable from controls and readily learn an escape response. This is much like the human PTSD response in which two individuals may be exposed to the exact same traumatic stressor but only one develops PTSD. Most models of PTSD do not take individual variability of response to a stressor into account. This is an important point because in certain animal models of stress, even among a genetically matched population, individual variations can mask real molecular or behavioral responses. Not all individuals exposed to a traumatic stressor develop PTSD. Models like the learned helplessness paradigm may also help identify key molecular mechanisms of risk factors or resilience to traumatic stress and thus provide hints for treatment strategies.

The predator stress model is another model that takes variation of individual stress vulnerability into account. Rather than shock, rodents are briefly exposed to a predator stimulus (such as cat or urine odor). Seven days later, rats are tested on behavioral measures of PTSD-like symptoms, including avoidance, anxiety-like behavior or startle response. Indicative of strong face validity, rodents have much variance and clustering of their responses. Cohen and Zohar (2004) propose using diagnostic inclusion/exclusion criteria like those used in clinical studies to separate the rats into two populations based on their responses. The predator stress model, like the learned helplessness model, allows researchers to study mechanisms of both maladaptive as well as adaptive coping responses.

Other nonshock models include the social defeat or resident-intruder model. There are many variations to this model. In general, rats are exposed to a larger, more aggressive rat in that rat's home-cage. The aggressive rat is territorial and initiates a physical conflict. This is often repeated for a number of days or, after the initial fight, the experimental rat is placed in proximity to the aggressive rat such that visual, auditory and olfactory cues are experienced. Socially defeated rats display a number of behaviors that mimic those found in PTSD. These behaviors include increased drug self-administration, social withdrawal, anxiety-like behavior, acoustic startle, and decreased motivation (Huhman, 2006).

A hypersensitive or enhanced glucocorticoid negative feedback is another feature of PTSD (*see:* **Biology, Neurochemistry**). This abnormality in the stress-related chemicals and receptors of the hypothalamic, pituitary, adrenal axis is modeled by the single prolonged stress (SPS) paradigm (Liberzon, Krstov, & Young, 1997). In this model, rats are exposed to a single session of prolonged stress consisting of restraint stress followed by a forced swim in 24°C water and exposure to ether vapors. SPS-induced neuroendocrine effects are only evident if the rats are left undisturbed for 7 days following the stressors.

It is well-accepted that associative memory processes play a role in the development of PTSD (see: **Information Processing; Memory**). Pavlovian fear conditioning may provide one of the best rodent models of stress-induced anxiety disorders, including PTSD. In Pavlovian conditioning fear conditioning models, rodents are trained with the pairing of a conditioned stimulus (light or tone) and unconditioned stimulus (footshock). Subsequent behavioral responses (conditioned response) can then be quantified (e.g., enhanced freezing). One benefit of these models, aside from robust behavioral effects, is that they have been established with mice as well as rats. This cross-species generalization allows for a range of genetic manipulations to better understand the receptors and mechanisms underlying contextual fear conditioning. Studies examining fear conditioning in rodents whelp elucidate basic mechanisms of fear memory and the development of treatments. Recently, these models have provided breakthrough treatment strategies that are now being proposed to be taken to clinical trials for the treatment of PTSD (Cai, Blundell, Han, Greene, & Powell, 2006; Davis, Ressler, Rothbaum, & Richardson, 2006).

Many animal models of psychological trauma or psychosocial stress neglect the important aspect of context. While footshock presents a significant aversive stressor, and can be used to induce maladaptive behavioral responses such as learned helplessness, it is not as a potent a stressor as aggressive social interaction is (Koolhaas, de Boer, De Rutter, Meerlo, & Sgoifo, 1997). The potency of social stress derives partly from the natural temporal progression that yields an uncontrollable and unpredictable result (Summers et al., 2005),

but also because this social stressor and its unpredictability are well-understood parts of the natural history and life experience of any animal or human. Contextually relevant elements of life experience are reliable activators of the reward pathways in the central nervous system, which react to salient aversive stimuli as well as to positive rewards. As the mesolimbic reward/salience pathways (see: **Limbic System**) and the cortical/hippocampal (see: **Frontal Cortex; Hippocampus**) pathways that modify them are powerfully influenced by stress steroids and peptides, everyday contextual elements influence the psychobiological impact of stressful conditions. That is to say, social aggression models of PTSD, anxiety, depression, and other psychological problems are more likely to accurately reflect the nature and course of traumatic stress disorders in humans than models that rely on contextually irrelevant stressors, such as foot shock. These social aggression models are dependent on the structural elements of life history (such as recognizable social opponents/allies and spatial reference to territorial resources and dangers), which influence the individual's interpretation of adaptation to traumatic stressors as stress-coping strategies rather than as purely pathological reactions (Koolhaas, de Boer, Buwalda, & van Reenen, 2007; Korzan & Summers, 2007; Øverli et al., 2007). Choice of stress-coping strategies that provide an adaptive recourse to traumatic events has been demonstrated to be influenced by classical Pavlovian conditioning (Potegal, Huhman, Moore, & Meyerhoff, 1993; Summers, Carpenter, & Arendt, 2007). This learning produces immediate submission in the conditioned defeat model in hamsters (Huhman et al., 2003).

In a newly developed model for fish and rodents, the fear conditioning model depends on social aggression as the unconditioned stimulus, but the behavioral output is not fixed, and a choice of escape or social submission is available and recognized as a part of the model (Carpenter & Summers, 2006; Summers et al., 2007). As choice of adaptive strategies is difficult for patients with PTSD, anxiety and depression, this is a potentially informative model for these trauma-related disorders. In this escape-submit model there is a dichotomy between two distinct types of learning, fear conditioning (for submission) and spatial learning (for escaping), evident in animals choosing the alternative stress coping strategies, which may elucidate the mechanisms that control decision making during traumatic events.

REFERENCES

Cai, W. H., Blundell, J., Han, J., Greene, R. W., & Powell, C. M. (2006). Postreactivation glucocorticoids impair recall of established fear memory. *Journal of Neuroscience, 26,* 9560–9566.

Carpenter, R. E., & Summers, C. H. (2006). Escapé! Socially mediated fear learning in rainbow trout. *Brain Behavior and Evolution, 68,* 110.

Cohen, H., & Zohar, J. (2004). An animal model of posttraumatic stress disorder: The use of cut-off behavioral criteria. *Annals of the New York Academy of Science, 1032,* 167–178.

Davis, M., Ressler, K., Rothbaum, B. O., & Richardson, R. (2006). Effects of D-cycloserine on extinction: Translation from preclinical to clinical work. *Biological Psychiatry, 60,* 369–375.

Huhman, K. L. (2006). Social conflict models: Can they inform us about human psychopathology? *Hormones and Behavior, 50,* 640–646.

Huhman, K. L., Solomon, M. B., Janicki, M., Harmon, A. C., Lin, S. M., Israel, J., et al. (2003). Conditioned defeat in male and female Syrian hamsters. *Hormones and Behavior, 44,* 293–299.

Koolhaas, J. M., de Boer, S. F., Buwalda, B., & van Reenen, K. (2007). Individual variation in coping with stress: A multidimensional approach of ultimate and proximate mechanisms. *Brain Behavior and Evolution, 70,* 218–226.

Koolhaas, J. M., de Boer, S. F., De Rutter, A. J., Meerlo, P., & Sgoifo, A. (1997). Social stress in rats and mice. *Acta Physiological Scandinavica, 640,* (Suppl.), 69–72.

Korzan, W. J., & Summers, C. H. (2007). Behavioral diversity and neurochemical plasticity: Selection of stress coping strategies that define social status. *Brain Behavior and Evolution, 70,* 257–266.

Liberzon, I., Krstov, M., & Young, E. A. (1997). Stress-restress: Effects on ACTH and fast feedback. *Psychoneuroendocrinology, 22,* 443–453.

Øverli, Ø., Sørensen, C., Pulman, K. G., Pottinger, T. G., Korzan, W., Summers, C. H., et al. (2007). Evolutionary background for stress-coping styles: Relationships between physiological, behavioral, and cognitive traits in non-mammalian vertebrates. *Neuroscience and Biobehavioral Reviews, 31,* 396–412.

Petty, F., Kramer, G. L., Wu, J., & Davis, L. L. (1997). Posttraumatic stress and depression: A neurochemical anatomy of the learned helplessness animal model. *Annals of the New York Academy of Science, 821,* 529–532.

Potegal, M., Huhman, K., Moore, T., & Meyerhoff, J. (1993). Conditioned defeat in the Syrian golden hamster (*Mesocricetus auratus*). *Behavioral and Neural Biology, 60,* 93–102.

Ronan, P. J., Steciuk, M., Kramer, G. L., Kram, M., & Petty, F. (2000). Increased septal 5-HIAA efflux in rats that do not develop learned helplessness after inescapable stress. *Journal of Neuroscience Research, 61,* 101–106.

Seligman, M. E., & Maier, S. F. (1967). Failure to escape traumatic shock. *Journal of Experimental Psychology, 74,* 1–9.

Siegmund, A., & Wotjak, C. T. (2006). Toward an animal model of posttraumatic stress disorder. *Annals of the New York Academy of Science, 1071,* 324–334.

Steckler, T., Kalin, N. H., & Reul, J. M. H. M. (2004). *Handbook on stress and the brain.* Amsterdam: Elsevier.

Summers, C. H., Carpenter, R. E., & Arendt, D. H. (2007). A new model of fear learning. *Social Neurosciences Abstracts, 33,* 529.1.

Summers, C. H., Forster, G. L., Korzan, W. J., Watt, M. J., Larson, E. T., Overli, O., et al. (2005). Dynamics and mechanics of social rank reversal. *Journal of Comparative Physiology, A-Neuroethology, Sensory, Neural, and Behavioral Physiology, 191,* 241–252.

PATRICK J. RONAN
University of South Dakota School of Medicine

CLIFF H. SUMMERS
University of South Dakota School of Medicine

See also: **Biology, Brain Structure, and Function, Adult; Biology, Brain Structure, and Function, Child; Biology, Neurochemistry; Conditioned Fear; Frontal Cortex; Hippocampus; Information Processing; Learned Helplessness; Limbic System; Memories of Traumatic Experiences; Memory**

BIOLOGY, BRAIN STRUCTURE, AND FUNCTION, ADULT

Psychological stress can vary according to the severity, duration of exposure, and type of stressor, ultimately having wide ranging effects on individuals. According to the *Diagnostic and Statistical Manual* (*DSM-IV-TR;* American Psychiatric Association, 2000), the definition of traumatic stressors refers to the most severe range of the stressor spectrum, such as experiencing or witnessing an event that involved threatened death, serious injury, or physical integrity of self or others that is experienced with intense fear, helplessness, or horror. While it is estimated that more than 75% of persons living in the United States are exposed to at least one traumatic event in their lives (Breslau & Kessler, 2001) only 6.8% of them develop PTSD (Kessler, Chiu, Demler, Merikangas, & Walters, 2005). Studies of war veterans show short-term PTSD in about a third of individuals, while 15% develop chronic PTSD (Bremner, 2006).

Still, the question remains of whom of all the people exposed to psychological trauma is going to develop PTSD. Several predictors have been noted. These factors can be divided into pre-traumatic (sex, race, level of education, personality style, socioeconomic status, previous psychiatric disorder or previous psychological trauma, family history of psychopathology), peritraumatic (severity and perceived life threat of trauma, dissociation and emotional responses during and immediately after), and posttraumatic (social support, life stressors), with peritraumatic dissociation and responses being the strongest predictor of all (Bisson, 2007; Ozer, Best, Lipsey, & Weiss, 2003). However, the development and pathophysiology of stress and PTSD, remains a complex process, whose understanding requires an integration of the neurochemical, neurophysiological, and neuroendocrinological findings with neuroanatomical and functional studies (Liberzon & Martis, 2006).

Biology

From a neurohormonal point of view, it is and experiencing stress reactions are associated with the activation of the hypothalamic-pituitary-adrenal (HPA) axis and the noradrenergic (norepinephrine-related) system (*see:* **Biology, Neurochemistry**). Under severe stress, the hypothalamus responds by releasing corticotrophin-releasing factor (CRF), which subsequently stimulates the release of adrenocorticotropin hormone (ACTH) from the pituitary gland. In turn, this results in cortisol release from the adrenal gland whose effect on pituitary and other central brain sites initiates negative feedback on the HPA axis (Bremner, 2006). Since 1980 when PTSD was finally recognized as a distinct clinical entity, the understanding of the biology of this condition has evolved markedly showing that PTSD represents a specific type of adaptation to psychological trauma. Trauma survivors with PTSD often show evidence of a highly sensitized HPA axis, leading to increased negative feedback regulation and decreased basal cortisol levels (Yehuda, 2001). Other studies have shown that blood or urinary cortisol levels in PTSD patients can be either increased (Cicchetti & Rogosch, 2001; Gunnar, Bruce, & Hickman, 2001; Pico-Alfonso, Garcia-Linares, Celda-Navarro, Herbert, & Martinez, 2004), no different than controls (Mason et al., 2002; Young & Breslau, 2004), or low (Glover & Poland, 2002; Kanter et al., 2001; Oquendo et al., 2003; Yehuda, Giller, Southwick, Lowy, & Mason, 1991; Yehuda, Teicher, Trestman, Levengood, & Siever, 1996).

Some authors have argued that cortisol levels in subjects with PTSD can be abnormally elevated when anticipating stress or during stressor exposure, returning to normal levels or even to levels lower than controls in the poststress phase (Elzinga, Schmahl, Vermetten, van Dyck, & Bremner, 2003). Also, Bremner, Vermetten, and Kelley (2007) have shown that women with a history of childhood abuse and current PTSD have lower levels of cortisol in the afternoon (12–8~P.M.) compared to the other women with PTSD without childhood abuse, suggesting that resting hypocortisolemia in the afternoon hours and increased fluctuations in cortisol levels are associated with childhood abuse-related PTSD in women (Bremner et al., 2007). This hyperregulation of HPA axis has been hypothesized to be related to the finding that lymphocyte glucocorticoid receptors are higher and more sensitive in PTSD patients than in nontraumatized subjects leading to a strong negative feedback despite low levels of cortisol (Yehuda, 1997; Yehuda, Boisoneau, Lowy, & Giller, 1995).

Still, the role of HPA axis alterations in PTSD remains controversial to date, given frequent normal or negative results, confounding premorbid alterations and also the fact that HPA axis is a fundamentally dynamic system, with transient increases and hyper-responsivity to various environmental conditions (Yehuda, 2006).

Research also seems to support the fact that PTSD is associated with an increased activity in the sympathetic nervous system. Exposure to stressors will activate the locus coeruleus, resulting in release of norepinephrine throughout the brain (Abercrombie & Jacobs, 1987). Studies with patients with PTSD have shown increased levels of norepinephrine either at baseline or after exposure to traumatic cues (Bremner et al., 1997; De Bellis et al., 1999). Moreover, promoting release of norepinephrine in the brain by administration of yohimbine (a noradrenergic receptor agonist) is followed by increased PTSD symptoms, while decreased yohimbine facilitates hippocampal and frontal function (Bremner et al., 1997).

Brain Structure after Psychological Trauma

The main brain regions that seem to be consistently involved in the pathophysiology of PTSD are the hippocampus, amygdala, and the medial prefrontal cortex (Shin, Rauch, & Pitman, 2006). A recent meta-analysis of structural brain abnormalities after exposure to psychological trauma included 50 imaging studies (23 hippocampal studies and 27 studies of other brain areas). The results showed smaller bilaterally hippocampal volume in trauma exposed subjects either with or without PTSD when compared with controls. Moreover, in the case of samples with severe PTSD, the subjects exhibited significantly smaller hippocampal volumes when compared with trauma-exposed controls without PTSD. The same review also showed that when compared to trauma-exposed controls, adults with PTSD

demonstrated significantly smaller anterior cingulate cortex and amygdala volumes bilaterally (Karl et al., 2006). The relationship between PTSD and smaller hippocampal size is unclear, given that lower hippocampal size can predispose to PTSD (thus possibly representing a confounding factor rather than a result or complication of PTSD; Gilbertson et al., 2002).

It has been theorized that the decrease in hippocampal size following exposure to psychological trauma is due to the effect of raised levels of corticoids on neuronal proliferation (Tanapat, Hastings, Rydel, Galea, & Gould, 2001). The effects of corticosteroids secreted after stress seem to be mediated by mineralocorticoid receptors (MR) and glucocorticoid receptors (GR), which are amply expressed in limbic structures (Joels, Karst, Derijk, & de Kloet, 2008; *see:* **Limbic System**). Moreover, human carriers of mineralocorticoid receptor gene variant (MR180V) can have amplified neuroendocrine and sympathetic activity after a stressful experience, due to a low-affinity membrane version of the mineralocorticoid receptor (DeRijk et al., 2006). This low-affinity MR seems to contribute to the enhanced initial phase, while the glucocorticoid receptor complements and terminates the stress reaction (Joels et al., 2008). Some studies have shown that that activation of MR and GR in the brain by using receptor agonists (aldosterone, RU362) negatively reduces neurogenesis (the formation of new neurons), while antagonists of MR and GR (spironolactone or mifepristone, respectively) can increase proliferation of progenitor neurons (i.e., the formation of new neurons; Wong & Herbert, 2005). More recently, it has been suggested that in contrast with antidepressants that require lengthy administration, glucocorticoid receptor blockade with mifepristone can rapidly normalize the effects of chronic stress on neurogenesis after only a few days of treatment, being particularly potent in a high stress environment (Mayer et al., 2006; Oomen, Mayer, de Kloet, Joels, & Lucassen, 2007).

Brain Function after Psychological Trauma

Reviewing the recent published evidence of cognitive impairment in PTSD (*see:* **Cognitive**

Impairments), Garofeanu, Thorpe, and Lanius (2007) found 23 studies published between 1993 and 2007 describing an association between PTSD and cognitive impairment while 8 studies failed to show such an association. The most common cognitive impairment seemed to be memory deficit (18 studies), followed by attention difficulties (11 studies), and executive dysfunction (6 studies).

The hippocampus is involved in explicit memory processes and the acquisition, contextual encoding, and context-dependent retrieval of fear conditioning (Corcoran, Desmond, Frey, & Maren, 2005) as well as emotion regulation and regulation of stress (Jacobson & Sapolsky, 1991). The medial prefrontal cortex (*see:* **Frontal Cortex**) includes the anterior cingulate cortex, subcallosal cortex and medial frontal gyrus (Shin et al., 2006). The role of medial prefrontal cortex in the pathophysiology of PTSD is suggested by studies that show that lesions or impairment in this area seem to be related to impairment in the extinction of fear conditioning and the consolidation of extinction learning (Milad & Quirk, 2002; Quirk, Russo, Barron, & Lebron, 2000). PTSD is associated with reduced activation and performance of the medial prefrontal cortex, consistent with the problems with chronic unwanted memories (intrusive reexperiencing symptoms) in PTSD (see next). The prefrontal cortex also seems to be involved in executive functions that control attention, working memory, and discriminate relevant information, while the hippocampus is involved in emotional regulation and explicit memory (Weber & Reynolds, 2004). As a result, the previously noted cognitive deficits in PTSD are consistent with dysfunction in these brain areas.

Functional Neuroimaging Studies

Functional neuroimaging studies have shown great variety of brain activation in response to different types of laboratory tests in which participants are reminded of past experiences of psychological trauma. Most of the published evidence to date seems to support the observation that PTSD is associated with heightened responsivity of the amygdala, diminished responsivity of the medial prefrontal cortex, as well as impaired hippocampal function (Shin et al., 2006). The amygdala is involved in the assessment of threat-related stimuli and is necessary for the process of fear conditioning (Davis & Whalen, 2001). Functional neuroimaging studies of PTSD have provided evidence in support of heightened amygdala responsivity to both traumatic reminders and more general affective stimuli (Francati, Vermetten, & Bremner, 2007; Shin et al., 2006). Moreover, several studies have consistently reported a positive relationship between PTSD symptom severity and amygdala activation (Shin et al., 2006). Another common finding is that of hypoactivation (i.e., reduced levels of activation) of the medial prefrontal cortex (mPFC) in patients with PTSD (Francati et al., 2007). This finding seems to be consistent across studies irrespective of the type paradigm used (Bremner, 1999; Bremner et al., 2003; Francati et al., 2007; Lanius et al., 2001). Several studies have also suggested a relationship or direct functional link between the amygdala and the mPFC (Francati et al., 2007). The concomitant decrease in mPFC activation and hyperactivation of the amygdala, is noted by some studies supporting the theory that this relationship provides a system of negative feedback to the amygdala, regulating its activation during emotional conditions (Francati et al., 2007). However, the debate remains open, since other studies have noted parallel activation of both amygdala and mPFC or no activation at all (Lanius et al., 2001, 2002).

With respect to hippocampus, apart from the noted volume reduction, an altered hippocampal function has been reported as well. The hippocampus plays a critical role in the consolidation of novel memories of facts and events. Most of the studies have shown failure or reduced activation on memory-related tasks such as declarative memory tasks or script-driven imagery or word-stem completion tasks (Bremner, 1999, 2003; Shin et al., 2004). Interestingly, the studies using tasks with emotional content have reported inconsistent results (Shin et al., 2001). Several studies have suggested an interregional brain activation that seems to be different in PTSD patients than in controls (Lanius et al., 2002, 2004, 2005). A recent extensive review of neuroimaging studies in PTSD patients has proposed that the heterogeneity of response seen in the multitude of functional studies might be due to the existence of two major subtypes of traumatic stress response, one characterized predominantly by hyperarousal and the other primarily by dissociation. Moreover, these different responses might therefore reflect different experiential, psychophysiological, and neurobiological patterns of traumatic symptom provocation (Lanius et al., 2005). For instance, the hyperarousal response, often referred to as "primary dissociation" (van der Kolk et al., 1996), which in the majority of cases occurs together with autonomic changes indicative of arousal, tends to involve certain regions of the brain, including the anterior cingulate cortex, mPFC, thalamus, and amygdala (Lanius et al., 2005). PTSD patients who reported dissociative responses to the laboratory tests that involve recalling or being reminded of past psychological traumas described experiences such as depersonalization, derealization, or "zoning out," phenomena termed "secondary dissociation" (van der Kolk et al., 1996), which generally fail to be associated with autonomic changes such as increase in heart rate, although this may vary (Lanius et al., 2002). Interestingly, these patients show a different pattern of brain activation, consistent with findings of higher levels of brain activation in the superior and middle temporal gyri, the inferior frontal gyrus, the occipital lobe, the parietal lobe, the medial frontal gyrus, the medial prefrontal cortex, and the anterior cingulate gyrus (Lanius et al., 2002, 2005). Less frequently, a state of mixed response, both dissociative and hyperaroused, can also coexist, combining features of the two states on all levels, clinical, physiologic, and brain activation (Lanius et al., 2005).

Conclusion

Several physiological stress response systems and brain areas associated with the processing of emotions, memories, and other forms of information crucial to adjusting the body's level of arousal and maintaining conscious self-awareness appear to be altered in persons with PTSD. These findings concerning the biology of the body and brain are consistent with the problems with unwanted memories, hyperarousal, and dissociation that commonly are experienced when PTSD occurs.

REFERENCES

Abercrombie, E. D., & Jacobs, B. L. (1987). Single-unit response of noradrenergic neurons in the locus coeruleus of freely moving cats: Pt. II. Adaptation to chronically presented stressful stimuli. *Journal of Neuroscience, 7,* 2844–2848.

American Psychiatric Association. (2000). *Diagnostic and statistical manual of mental disorders* (4th ed., text rev.). Washington, DC: Author.

Bisson, J. I. (2007). Posttraumatic stress disorder. *British Medical Journal (Clinical research ed.), 334* (7597), 789–793.

Bremner, J. D. (1999). Alterations in brain structure and function associated with posttraumatic stress disorder. *Seminars in Clinical Neuropsychiatry, 4,* 249–255.

Bremner, J. D. (2003). Long-term effects of childhood abuse on brain and neurobiology. *Child and Adolescent Psychiatric Clinics of North America, 12,* 271–292.

Bremner, J. D. (2006). Stress and brain atrophy. *Central Nervous System and Neurological Disorders Drug Targets, 5,* 503–512.

Bremner, J. D., Innis, R. B., Ng, C. K., Staib, L. H., Salomon, R. M., Bronen, R. A., et al. (1997). Positron emission tomography measurement of cerebral metabolic correlates of yohimbine administration in combat-related posttraumatic stress disorder. *Archives of General Psychiatry, 54,* 246–254.

Bremner, J. D., Vermetten, E., & Kelley, M. E. (2007). Cortisol, dehydroepiandrosterone, and estradiol measured over 24 hours in women with childhood sexual abuse-related posttraumatic stress disorder. *Journal of Nervous and Mental Disease, 195,* 919–927.

Bremner, J. D., Vythilingam, M., Vermetten, E., Southwick, S. M., McGlashan, T., Staib, L. H., et al. (2003). Neural correlates of declarative memory for emotionally valenced words in women with posttraumatic stress disorder related to early childhood sexual abuse. *Biological Psychiatry, 53*(10), 879–889.

Breslau, N., & Kessler, R. C. (2001). The stressor criterion in DSM-IV posttraumatic stress disorder: An empirical investigation. *Biological Psychiatry, 50,* 699–704.

Cicchetti, D., & Rogosch, F. A. (2001). Diverse patterns of neuroendocrine activity in maltreated children. *Development and Psychopathology, 13,* 677–693.

Corcoran, K. A., Desmond, T. J., Frey, K. A., & Maren, S. (2005). Hippocampal inactivation disrupts the acquisition and contextual encoding of fear extinction. *Journal of Neuroscience, 25,* 8978–8987.

Davis, M., & Whalen, P. J. (2001). The amygdala: Vigilance and emotion. *Molecular Psychiatry, 6,* 13–34.

De Bellis, M. D., Baum, A. S., Birmaher, B., Keshavan, M. S., Eccard, C. H., Boring, A. M., et al. (1999). Biological stress systems. *Biological Psychiatry, 45,* 1259–1270.

DeRijk, R. H., Wust, S., Meijer, O. C., Zennaro, M. C., Federenko, I. S., Hellhammer, D. H., et al. (2006). A common polymorphism in the mineralocorticoid receptor modulates stress responsiveness. *Journal of Clinical Endocrinology and Metabolism, 91,* 5083–5089.

Elzinga, B. M., Schmahl, C. G., Vermetten, E., van Dyck, R., & Bremner, J. D. (2003). Higher cortisol levels following exposure to traumatic reminders in abuse-related PTSD. *Neuropsychopharmacology, 28,* 1656–1665.

Francati, V., Vermetten, E., & Bremner, J. D. (2007). Functional neuroimaging studies in posttraumatic stress disorder: Review of current methods and findings. *Depression and Anxiety, 24,* 202–218.

Garofeanu, G. C., Thorpe, L., & Lanius, R. (2007). *PTSD and cognitive impairment: A systematic review of the published evidence.* Unpublished manuscript.

Gilbertson, M. W., Shenton, M. E., Ciszewski, A., Kasai, K., Lasko, N. B., Orr, S. P., et al. (2002). Smaller hippocampal volume predicts pathologic vulnerability to psychological trauma. *Nature Neuroscience, 5,* 1242–1247.

Glover, D. A., & Poland, R. E. (2002). Urinary cortisol and catecholamines in mothers of child cancer survivors with and without PTSD. *Psychoneuroendocrinology, 27,* 805–819.

Gunnar, M. R., Bruce, J., & Hickman, S. E. (2001). Salivary cortisol response to stress in children. *Advances in Psychosomatic Medicine, 22,* 52–60.

Jacobson, L., & Sapolsky, R. (1991). The role of the hippocampus in feedback regulation of the hypothalamic-pituitary-adrenocortical axis. *Endocrine Reviews, 12,* 118–134.

Joels, M., Karst, H., Derijk, R., & de Kloet, E. R. (2008). The coming out of the brain mineralocorticoid receptor. *Trends in Neurosciences, 31,* 1–7.

Kanter, E. D., Wilkinson, C. W., Radant, A. D., Petrie, E. C., Dobie, D. J., McFall, M. E., et al. (2001). Glucocorticoid feedback sensitivity and adrenocortical responsiveness in posttraumatic stress disorder. *Biological Psychiatry, 50,* 238–245.

Karl, A., Schaefer, M., Malta, L. S., Dorfel, D., Rohleder, N., & Werner, A. (2006). A meta-analysis of structural brain abnormalities in PTSD. *Neuroscience and Biobehavioral Reviews, 30,* 1004–1031.

Kessler, R. C., Chiu, W. T., Demler, O., Merikangas, K. R., & Walters, E. E. (2005). Prevalence, severity, and comorbidity of 12-month DSM-IV disorders in the national comorbidity survey replication. *Archives of General Psychiatry, 62,* 617–627.

Lanius, R. A., Williamson, P. C., Bluhm, R. L., Densmore, M., Boksman, K., Neufeld, R. W., et al. (2005). Functional connectivity of dissociative responses in posttraumatic stress disorder: A functional magnetic resonance imaging investigation. *Biological Psychiatry, 57,* 873–884.

Lanius, R. A., Williamson, P. C., Boksman, K., Densmore, M., Gupta, M., Neufeld, R. W., et al. (2002). Brain activation during script-driven imagery induced dissociative responses in PTSD: A functional magnetic resonance imaging investigation. *Biological Psychiatry, 52,* 305–311.

Lanius, R. A., Williamson, P. C., Densmore, M., Boksman, K., Gupta, M. A., Neufeld, R. W., et al. (2001). Neural correlates of traumatic memories in posttraumatic stress disorder: A functional MRI investigation. *American Journal of Psychiatry, 158,* 1920–1922.

Lanius, R. A., Williamson, P. C., Densmore, M., Boksman, K., Neufeld, R. W., Gati, J. S., et al. (2004). The nature of traumatic memories: A 4-T FMRI functional connectivity analysis. *American Journal of Psychiatry, 161,* 36–44.

Liberzon, I., & Martis, B. (2006). Neuroimaging studies of emotional responses in PTSD. *Annals of the New York Academy of Sciences, 1071,* 87–109.

Mason, J. W., Wang, S., Yehuda, R., Lubin, H., Johnson, D., Bremner, J. D., et al. (2002). Marked lability in urinary cortisol levels in subgroups of combat veterans with posttraumatic stress disorder during an intensive exposure treatment program. *Psychosomatic Medicine, 64*, 238–246.

Mayer, J. L., Klumpers, L., Maslam, S., de Kloet, E. R., Joels, M., & Lucassen, P. J. (2006). Brief treatment with the glucocorticoid receptor antagonist mifepristone normalises the corticosterone-induced reduction of adult hippocampal neurogenesis. *Journal of Neuroendocrinology, 18*, 629–631.

Milad, M. R., & Quirk, G. J. (2002). Neurons in medial prefrontal cortex signal memory for fear extinction. *Nature, 420*(6911), 70–74.

Oomen, C. A., Mayer, J. L., de Kloet, E. R., Joels, M., & Lucassen, P. J. (2007). Brief treatment with the glucocorticoid receptor antagonist mifepristone normalizes the reduction in neurogenesis after chronic stress. *European Journal of Neuroscience, 26*, 3395–3401.

Oquendo, M. A., Echavarria, G., Galfalvy, H. C., Grunebaum, M. F., Burke, A., Barrera, A., et al. (2003). Lower cortisol levels in depressed patients with comorbid posttraumatic stress disorder. *Neuropsychopharmacology, 28*, 591–598.

Ozer, E. J., Best, S. R., Lipsey, T. L., & Weiss, D. S. (2003). Predictors of posttraumatic stress disorder and symptoms in adults: A meta-analysis. *Psychological Bulletin, 129*, 52–73.

Pico-Alfonso, M. A., Garcia-Linares, M. I., Celda-Navarro, N., Herbert, J., & Martinez, M. (2004). Changes in cortisol and dehydroepiandrosterone in women victims of physical and psychological intimate partner violence. *Biological Psychiatry, 56*, 233–240.

Quirk, G. J., Russo, G. K., Barron, J. L., & Lebron, K. (2000). The role of ventromedial prefrontal cortex in the recovery of extinguished fear. *Journal of Neuroscience, 20*, 6225–6231.

Shin, L. M., Rauch, S. L., & Pitman, R. K. (2006). Amygdala, medial prefrontal cortex, and hippocampal function in PTSD. *Annals of the New York Academy of Sciences, 1071*, 67–79.

Shin, L. M., Shin, P. S., Heckers, S., Krangel, T. S., Macklin, M. L., Orr, S. P., et al. (2004). Hippocampal function in posttraumatic stress disorder. *Hippocampus, 14*, 292–300.

Shin, L. M., Whalen, P. J., Pitman, R. K., Bush, G., Macklin, M. L., Lasko, N. B., et al. (2001). An fMRI study of anterior cingulate function in posttraumatic stress disorder. *Biological Psychiatry, 50*, 932–942.

Tanapat, P., Hastings, N. B., Rydel, T. A., Galea, L. A., & Gould, E. (2001). Exposure to fox odor inhibits cell proliferation in the hippocampus of adult rats via an adrenal hormone-dependent mechanism. *Journal of Comparative Neurology, 437*, 496–504.

van der Kolk, B. A., Pelcovitz, D., Roth, S., Mandel, F. S., McFarlane, A., & Herman, J. L. (1996). Dissociation, somatization, and affect dysregulation: The complexity of adaptation of trauma. *American Journal of Psychiatry, 153* (Suppl. 7), 83–93.

Weber, D. A., & Reynolds, C. R. (2004). Clinical perspectives on neurobiological effects of psychological trauma. *Neuropsychology Review, 14*, 115–129.

Wong, E. Y., & Herbert, J. (2005). Roles of mineralocorticoid and glucocorticoid receptors in the regulation of progenitor proliferation in the adult hippocampus. *European Journal of Neuroscience, 22*, 785–792.

Yehuda, R. (1997). Sensitization of the hypothalamic-pituitary-adrenal axis in posttraumatic stress disorder. *Annals of the New York Academy of Sciences, 821*, 57–75.

Yehuda, R. (2001). Biology of posttraumatic stress disorder. *Journal of Clinical Psychiatry, 62* (Suppl. 17), 41–46.

Yehuda, R. (2006). Advances in understanding neuroendocrine alterations in PTSD and their therapeutic implications. *Annals of the New York Academy of Sciences, 1071*, 137–166.

Yehuda, R., Boisoneau, D., Lowy, M. T., & Giller, E. L., Jr. (1995). Dose-response changes in plasma cortisol and lymphocyte glucocorticoid receptors following dexamethasone administration in combat veterans with and without posttraumatic stress disorder. *Archives of General Psychiatry, 52*, 583–593.

Yehuda, R., Giller, E. L., Southwick, S. M., Lowy, M. T., & Mason, J. W. (1991). Hypothalamic-pituitary-adrenal dysfunction in posttraumatic stress disorder. *Biological Psychiatry, 30*, 1031–1048.

Yehuda, R., Teicher, M. H., Trestman, R. L., Levengood, R. A., & Siever, L. J. (1996). Cortisol regulation in posttraumatic stress disorder and major depression: A chronobiological analysis. *Biological Psychiatry, 40*, 79–88.

Young, E. A., & Breslau, N. (2004). Cortisol and catecholamines in posttraumatic stress disorder: An epidemiologic community study. *Archives of General Psychiatry, 61*, 394–401.

Gina Magnea
London Health Sciences Center

Ruth A. Lanius
London Health Sciences Center

See also: Amygdala; Anterior Cingulate Cortex; Biology, Brain Structure, and Function, Child; Biology, Neurochemistry; Cognitive Impairments; Frontal Cortex; Hippocampus; Limbic System

BIOLOGY, BRAIN STRUCTURE, AND FUNCTION, CHILD

The brain is programmed by genetics, but sculpted by experience. Brain development proceeds along a sequenced process, including neurogenesis (the birth of new brain cells, or neurons); neuronal migration (the movement of neurons to different parts of the brain) and differentiation (the development of more complexly formed neurons); synapse formation and remodeling (the creation and modification of connections among neurons in which chemical messages are sent from one neuron to another); development of glia, myelination, and vascularization (the development of protective and support systems for neurons); and neurodegeneration (the aging and death of neurons). Although genetics largely guides these progressions, experiential factors play an important role in this process.

Specific windows are present during a child's development when brain regions are especially susceptible to formative experiences. One window is known as a *critical period* when appropriate stimulation is required for normal development. A second type of window is known as a *sensitive period* when stimuli (e.g., stressors) exert a maximal influence. However, stimuli at other times than these "windows" also can influence brain development, just to a lesser degree. The responsiveness of brain structures to experience serves to fine-tune the brain to match the needs of the environment. For example, exposure to stressors early in life during a specific developmental stage may alter the brain and neuroendocrine system's structure or functioning in ways that lead the child to overreact to subsequent stressors.

Puberty has often been found to signal the end of an important sensitive period. This point was brought to light most clearly by Hubel and Wiesel who discovered that experience played a critical role in shaping the development of the visual cortex prior to the onset of puberty, but not after. Similarly, subcortical dopamine systems are modified to a greater extent by prepubertal than postpubertal exposure to stressors. Because sensory systems, neurotransmitters, and stress-response circuits appear to be modified by experience during specific times in early development, we have hypothesized that the impact of exposure to child abuse (CA) on neurobehavioral development is quite time-dependent. A compelling illustration of this timing issue is found in a recent preclinical (animal model) research study. Young rats were exposed to stress by repeatedly being separated from their female parents (maternal separation, which is a species-relevant stressor). Other similar rats were not separated from their female parents. No discernible effect of these stressful experiences on the density of synapses in the hippocampus was apparent as the rats grew and entered puberty. However, a marked difference emerged between stressed and nonstressed rats as they entered adulthood. These findings suggest that exposure to stressors in childhood can exert delayed effects that impact the trajectory of brain development, which only become manifest at a much later time.

This view, that childhood exposure to traumatic stressors during windows of vulnerability has particularly pronounced effects on brain development over time, fits well with clinical research evidence, including: (a) the recent clinical observation that the trajectory of hippocampal development is attenuated in adolescents with histories of CA who have clinical symptoms as well as high levels of stress hormones, compared to adolescents with histories of CA who are not symptomatic and have lower hormone levels; and (b) preliminary evidence from a new study of young women exposed to childhood sexual abuse (CSA) indicating that the hippocampus is most sensitive to CSA that occurs between 3 to 5 or 11 to 13 years of age.

Moreover, the corpus callosum seems especially susceptible to stressor effects between 9 to 10 years of age. Brain imaging studies showing evidence that children have a smaller and less fully protected (white matter myelination) corpus callosum than adolescents under normal conditions suggest that rapid maturation of this brain area may occur between these developmental stages, which is indicative of a sensitive period.

The protracted development of some brain regions is also likely related to a sensitive period for stress effects. The prefrontal cortex, which includes the anterior cingulate cortex, is a late-maturing brain structure. This region undergoes significant increases in innervation (neuronal connectedness), myelination (formation of a protective cover or sheath), and expression (activation) of glucocorticoid (GC) receptors that peak during adolescence. These developmental factors, most likely in combination, contribute to a later sensitive period to CA and other stressors during adolescence. Animal studies show that exposure to stressors reduces synaptic density (interconnectedness among neurons) in the prefrontal cortex when it occurs during adolescence, but not prior to puberty.

As a traumatic stressor, CA unleashes an outburst of neurobiological processes that underlie the mammalian stress response. Specifically, two systems govern this responding: (1) sympathetic-adrenomedullary system; and (2) hypothalamic-pituitary-adrenocortical (HPA) system (*see:* **Biology, Neurochemistry; Stress**). The former system releases epinephrine (adrenaline) necessary for the fight/flight response whereas the latter system regulates production of GCs (stress hormones, specifically cortisol in humans). The immature brain may be particularly vulnerable to high levels of GCs. For example, the hippocampus contains a high density of GC receptors that make this area highly susceptible to the effects of exposure to stressors. Preclinical studies have found that exposure to stressors can shrink the dendritic tree of pyramidal cells (large neurons in the hippocampus that provide primary connections to other brain regions), and if sufficiently severe, can even result in their deaths. Further, stress exposure suppresses the postnatal neurogenesis of granule cells, which are small local neurons in the hippocampus involved in information processing.

Early life exposure to stressors is presumed to modify brain development through a cascade of biochemical effects. The first step in the cascade begins with exposure to stressors early in life, which activates stress response systems and fundamentally alters their molecular organization to modify their sensitivity and response bias to subsequent stressors.

The second stage of the cascade centers on the effects of increased activation of the stress hormone systems on the developing brain. Stress hormones either directly, or indirectly, through effects on monoamine (dopamine, serotonin, and norepinephrine) and excitatory neurotransmitters (e.g., glutamate), modulate the development of synapses and the myelin sheath. This sheath is produced by glial cells and wraps around nerve fibers to greatly facilitate the propagation of nerve impulses.

The third component of the cascade is the differential sensitivity to stress across brain regions, which depends in part upon genetics, sex, timing, rate of development, density of GC receptors, and the extent to which stress enhances regional corticotropin releasing hormone levels.

The fourth step in the cascade is the impact of regional changes on systemwide neurobiology. For example, stress-related effects on corpus callosum myelination may lead to a diminished degree of integration and communication between left and right hemispheres. On another level, stress-induced alterations in the subunit structure of the gamma aminobutyric acid A (GABA-A) receptor may lead to a diminished degree of inhibitory neurotransmission, which in turn can result in excessive electrical activity and abnormal EEG signals from susceptible brain regions.

Finally, the fifth component of the cascade is the clinical consequences of these effects. Changes in neuroanatomy and function ultimately impact behavioral, emotional, and cognitive development.

Several neurobiological factors have been identified that make a given region of the developing brain uniquely vulnerable to the effects of exposure to stressors. First, the timing of vulnerability to stressor exposure may be partially controlled by the expression of GC receptors themselves. These receptors, for example, are expressed early in life in the hippocampus and maintain a relatively higher rate of expression throughout life. In contrast, GC receptors are not highly expressed in the prefrontal cortex until adolescence. Prior to this period, the prefrontal cortex is thus relatively immune from GC exposure. Aside from the general effects of corticosteroids, stress produces a progression of other effects that can modulate brain development. The release of cortisol and other stress hormones has been hypothesized to enhance the turnover of neurotransmitters (e.g., dopamine, serotonin, norepinephrine) in key brain regions.

Child Abuse and Brain Development

Indirect support for the deleterious effects of stress on neurotransmitter systems comes from research demonstrating increased concentrations of urinary dopamine, norepinephrine, and epinephrine as well as urinary-free cortisol in children with CA-related PTSD. Additionally, these neurotransmitters have trophic effects on the developing brain by altering the form and function of neurons and neural networks through processes such as myelination, synaptogenesis, and neurogenesis, thereby further contributing to the effects of stress exposure on brain development. Major shifts have occurred throughout history in our beliefs regarding the relative importance of nature versus nurture in shaping human behavior. Studies on the impact of childhood abuse on brain development reveal the complexity and sophistication of the interplay between a child's inborn characteristics and the child's life experiences. We now understand that genes ("nature") and experience ("nurture") interact to determine each person's unique physical and psychological characteristics, but the magnitude and direction of their interaction are critically dependent on the person's developmental stage. Hence, the consequences of exposure to CA depend on the person's genetic endowment and the timing of the exposure to abuse in childhood that can maximally interfere with the development of specific brain regions.

Documentation of associations between CA and anomalies of the brain began to emerge in the scientific literature in the 1990s. To date, five published studies of adults exposed to CA who had current diagnoses of PTSD, major depression, dissociative identity disorder, or borderline personality disorder have demonstrated reductions of hippocampal volume (particularly on the left side of the brain). Clinical observations of diminished anterior cingulate volume and function have also been observed in adults with CA-related PTSD. In contrast to the adult evidence, findings in three studies of children with PTSD secondary to CA showed no reduction in hippocampal volume during childhood or early adolescence. On the other hand, clinically significant EEG abnormalities (which are described technically as spike waves, sharp waves, and paroxysmal slowing), reductions in the midsaggital area of the corpus callosum, changes in frontal lobe activation patterns across the brain's two hemispheres (which are described technically as an attenuation in frontal lobe asymmetry), as well as smaller total brain and cerebral volumes have been documented in children and adolescents with CA histories. The frontal lobe is typically uneven between the left and right hemispheres in both structure and function; and the changes associated with CA include a reduction ("attenuation") in this unevenness ("asymmetry"). Together, these studies suggest that the effects of CA alter normal changes in brain development that occur during childhood (which technically is described as an alteration in neurodevelopmental trajectories).

Last, exposure to traumatic stressors in the form of CA can be influenced by genetic factors that, in turn, affect whether detrimental psychosocial effects occur (*see:* **Genetics**). Recent research has demonstrated, for example, that polymorphisms of the monoamine oxidase A gene and the corticotropin-releasing hormone type 1 receptor gene moderate the development of antisocial behavior and depression, respectively, after exposure to CA. Such findings suggest that the outcomes of exposure to CA reflect interactions among the stress responses of the sympathetic and neuroendocrine systems, the time frames within neurodevelopment when the exposures occur, and genetic programming that differs for each individual child. While drawing any firm conclusions is premature, evidence from animal and human studies indicate that different brain regions possess disparate sensitive periods when exposure to traumatic stressors such as CA can have particularly deleterious effects on brain development and on the development of associated psychological and behavioral competencies that are important for learning, personality development, and resilience to stress.

RECOMMENDED READINGS

De Bellis, M. D., & Van Dillen, T. (2005). Childhood post-traumatic stress disorder: An overview. *Child and Adolescent Psychiatric Clinics of North America, 14,* 745–772.

Gunnar, M., & Quevedo, K. (2007). The neurobiology of stress and development. *Annual Review of Psychology, 58,* 145–173.

Kaufman, J., Plotsky, P. M., Nemeroff, C. B., & Charney, D. S. (2000). Effects of early adverse experiences on brain structure and function: Clinical implications. *Biological Psychiatry, 48,* 778–790.

Teicher, M. H., Andersen, S. L., Polcari, A., Anderson, C. M., Navalta, C. P., & Kim, D. M. (2003). The neurobiological consequences of early stress and childhood maltreatment. *Neuroscience and Biobehavioral Reviews, 27,* 33–44.

Teicher, M. H., Tomoda, A., & Andersen, S. L. (2006). Neurobiological consequences of early stress and childhood maltreatment: Are results from human and animal studies comparable. In R. Yehuda (Ed.), *Psychobiology of posttraumatic stress disorders: A decade of progress* (Vol. 1071, pp. 313–323). Malden, MA: Blackwell.

Carryl P. Navalta
Harvard Medical School

Susan L. Andersen
Harvard Medical School

Martin H. Teicher
Harvard Medical School

See also: **Abuse, Child Physical; Abuse, Child Sexual; Amygdala; Anterior Cingulate Cortex; Biology, Brain Structure, and Function, Adult; Biology, Neurochemistry; Child Development; Child Maltreatment; Cognitive Impairments; Frontal Cortex; Genetics; Hippocampus; Limbic System**

BIOLOGY, NEUROCHEMISTRY

Our society faces surprisingly high rates of exposure to traumatic stressors. Childhood abuse, accidents, terrorism, combat, rape, assault, and a wide variety of other severe psychological traumas all are associated with potentially lasting effects on the individual (*see:* **Epidemiology**). A traumatic event is defined as an experience that is threatening to oneself or a close person, accompanied by intense fear, horror, or helplessness (*see:* **Trauma, Definition**). Exposure to a traumatic event, defined in this way, is required for the diagnosis of posttraumatic stress disorder (PTSD), making PTSD one of the only mental disorders that by definition is related to and occurs as a consequence of a stressful or traumatic event. There are three defined clusters of symptoms that occur as a response to the traumatic event in PTSD (*see:* **Posttraumatic Stress Disorder**), including reexperiencing of the event, avoidance of reminders of the event, and hyperarousal.

While initial theories proposed that PTSD represents a normative response to exposure to extreme stressors, only a minority of individuals who experience a traumatic event actually develop the disorder. Thus, while most individuals are able to cope with the stressor and maintain or regain homeostasis, others fail to recover and exhibit prolonged and abnormal, behavioral and physiological responses to the traumatic experience, as manifested in the symptoms of PTSD. The symptoms of PTSD are believed to reflect stress-induced changes in neurobiological systems and/or an inadequate adaptation of neurobiological systems to exposure to severe stressors. Consequently, much research has been focused on elucidating alterations in stress-regulating neurobiological systems in patients with PTSD. Neurobiological systems that have been implicated in the pathophysiology of PTSD include the hypothalamic-pituitary-adrenal (HPA) axis as well as various neurotransmitters and neuropeptides that act in a connected network of brain regions to regulate fear and stress responses, including the prefrontal cortex, hippocampus, amygdala, and brainstem nuclei.

Identified neurobiological changes can be linked to specific features that constitute PTSD, such as altered mechanisms of learning and extinction (*see:* **Extinction; Learning Theory**), sensitization to stressor exposure, and arousal. More recently, there is increasing consideration of genetic variability (*see:* **Genetics**) in neurobiological systems that may determine individual vulnerability versus resilience in developing PTSD in response to trauma. On the basis of such neurobiological findings, important hypotheses for developing novel strategies to prevent or treat PTSD have been derived. The current entry summarizes core neurobiological findings in PTSD, with a focus on HPA axis and neurotransmitter alterations.

Hypothalamic-Pituitary-Adrenal Axis

The HPA axis, which constitutes the organism's major neuroendocrine stress response system, has been closely scrutinized in patients with PTSD. On exposure to stress, neurons in the hypothalamic paraventricular nucleus (PVN) secrete corticotropin-releasing hormone (CRH) from the median eminence into the hypothalamo-hypophyseal portal circulation, which stimulates the production and release of adrenocorticotropin (ACTH) from the anterior pituitary. ACTH in turn stimulates the release of glucocorticoids from the adrenal cortex. Glucocorticoids affect metabolism, immune function, and the brain, adjusting physiological functions and behavior to the stressor. Several brain pathways modulate HPA axis activity. The hippocampus and prefrontal cortex (PFC) inhibit the HPA axis, whereas the amygdala and monoaminergic input

from the brainstem stimulate PVN CRF neurons. Glucocorticoids exert negative feedback control of the HPA axis by regulating hippocampal and hypothalamic PVN neurons through binding to glucocorticoid receptors (GR). Sustained glucocorticoid exposure has been shown in laboratory studies with animals to have adverse effects on hippocampal neurons, including reduction in dendritic branching (the development of additional branches in the portion of the neuron known as the dendrite), loss of dendritic spines, and impairment of neurogenesis (the birth of new neurons).

Although acute exposure to stressors or pharmacologically induced states of stress activate the HPA axis, leading to increased secretion of cortisol, initial studies in combat veterans with PTSD revealed paradoxical decreases in cortisol concentrations, measured in urine or blood, compared to healthy controls and other diagnostic groups. This counterintuitive finding has been replicated in Holocaust survivors, refugees, and abused persons with PTSD, although findings are not uniformly consistent across studies. Differences in type and timing of the psychological trauma, symptom patterns, comorbidity, and personality and genetic dispositions, among other factors, may contribute to this inconsistency.

Studies using low-dose dexamethasone suppression and metyrapone testing (two pharmacological agents that alter the effect of stress hormones exerting feedback on the HPA axis) revealed that hypocortisolism (i.e., unusually low levels of cortisol) in PTSD occurs in the context of increased sensitivity of the HPA axis to negative glucocorticoid feedback. Cortisol is involved in a "negative feedback" loop at multiple levels of control, including the hippocampus, hypothalamus, and pituitary, in which it actually signals the system to reduce the production of stress hormones—and in PTSD it appears that lesser amounts of cortisol are necessary than usual in order to have this down-regulation effect. Findings of increased GR binding and function (i.e., increased sensitivity of GR to cortisol, as measured in lymphocytes) support the assumption of increased negative feedback sensitivity of the HPA axis in PTSD. At the central nervous system (CNS) level, marked and sustained increases of CRH concentrations have been measured in cerebrospinal fluid (CSF) of patients with PTSD, supporting the hypothesis that PTSD involves an excess in production of this neuroendocrine regulator. Evidence of blunted ACTH responses to CRH stimulation in PTSD further support the hypothesis that PTSD involves elevated levels of hypothalamic CRH activity and corresponding attempts by the "downstream" organs in the HPA axis, in this case the pituitary gland, to compensate for the hypothalamus's overproduction of CRH by down-regulating receptors. In addition, reduced volume of the hippocampus, the major brain region inhibiting the HPA axis, is a cardinal feature of PTSD, potentially reflecting a preexisting disposition, toxic effects of increased glucocorticoid exposure at the time of the trauma and/or increased glucocorticoid sensitivity of hippocampal GR (see: **Hippocampus**). Taken together, the specific constellation of neuroendocrine findings reflects sensitization of the HPA axis to exposure to stressors. Accordingly increased HPA axis responses have been observed in response to traumatic reminders in PTSD patients. This neuroendocrine pattern distinguishes PTSD from major depression, a frequently comorbid but distinct disorder (for review, see Yehuda, 2006).

Studies have shown that low cortisol levels at the time of exposure to psychological trauma predict the development of PTSD, suggesting that hypocortisolism might be a preexisting risk factor that is associated with maladaptive stress responses such as PTSD. Consequently, administration of hydrocortisone directly after exposure to psychological trauma has been shown to effectively prevent PTSD in humans in several studies. In addition, it was recently demonstrated that hydrocortisone treatment, simulating normal circadian cortisol rhythm, is effective in the treatment of PTSD. Indeed, decreased availability of cortisol may have permissive effects toward the sustained activation of neural systems involved in stress reactivity and fear, including the CRH and norepinephrine systems—that is, hypocortisolism may actually facilitate CNS changes that are implicated in the development of PTSD, as discussed next (Yehuda & LeDoux, 2007).

Corticotropin-Releasing Hormone (CRH)

CRH neurons integrate information relevant to stress not only at the hypothalamic PVN, serving as the central component of the HPA axis, but are also found in a widespread circuitry throughout the brain, including the prefrontal and cingulate cortices, central nucleus of the amygdala, bed nucleus of the stria terminalis, nucleus accumbens, periaqueductal gray, as well as the norepinephrine-containing locus ceruleus (LC), and the serotonin nuclei in the dorsal and median raphé. Direct injection of CRH into the brain of laboratory animals produces physiological stress responses and anxiety-like behavior, including neophobia (fear of new things), enhanced startle reactivity, and facilitated fear conditioning. Anxiety-like behaviors have been specifically linked with increased activity of CRF-containing neurons connecting the amygdala with the LC. Of note, glucocorticoids (cortisol in humans, corticosteerone in rodents) inhibit CRH-induced activation of LC noradrenergic neurons, providing a potential mechanism by which low cortisol may facilitate sustained central stress and fear responses, as noted earlier.

The effects of CRH are mediated through two types of CRH receptors, CRH_1 and CRH_2. CRH_1 receptor antagonists (i.e., pharmacologic agents that block or reduce the action of these receptors) or CRH_1 receptor knockouts (i.e., animals that have had genetic modifications that block or reduce the action of these receptors) exhibit attenuated stress responses and reduced anxiety. Thus, CRH_1 receptors appear to be involved in facilitating stress responses and anxiety. By contrast, CRH_2 deficient mice demonstrate stress sensitization and increased anxiety, suggesting a role of the CRH_2 receptor in reducing the body's stress reactivity.

As noted, increased concentrations of CRH have been measured in CSF of patients with PTSD, both in single lumbar puncture and serial sampling studies. Sustained elevations in CRH concentrations have been measured in the context of comparably low cortisol secretion. Although the source of CRH peptide measured in CSF is not discernable, CSF CRH concentrations are believed to reflect CRH activity at extra-hypothalamic sites—that is, the production of CRH in other areas of the brain than the hypothalamus. Increased CNS CRH activity may promote cardinal features of PTSD (i.e. conditioned fear responses, increased startle reactivity, sensitization to exposure to stressors, and hyperarousal). These results suggest that CRH_1 receptor antagonists might have important therapeutic potential in the treatment of PTSD (see Newport & Nemeroff, 2000).

Catecholamines

The catecholamines comprise a family of neurotransmitters derived from the amino acid tyrosine. The rate-limiting factor in the synthesis of catecholamines is tyrosine hydroxylase, an enzyme that converts tyrosine into DOPA, which subsequently is converted into dopamine (DA). Another enzyme, dopamine ß-hydroxylase, converts DA into norepinephrine (NE). NE is one of the principal mediators of the central and autonomic stress responses. The majority of CNS NE is derived from neurons of the LC that project to various brain regions involved in the stress responses, including the prefrontal cortex, amygdala, hippocampus, hypothalamus, periaqueductal gray, and thalamus. There is evidence for a feed-forward circuit connecting the amygdala and the hypothalamus with the LC, in which CRH and NE interact to increase fear conditioning and encoding of emotional memories, enhance arousal and vigilance, and integrate endocrine and autonomic responses to stress. Glucocorticoids such as cortisol inhibit this cascade. In the periphery (other areas of the body outside the CNS), sympathoadrenal (i.e., a combination of sympathetic nervous system and adrenal gland) activation during exposure to stressors results in the release of NE and epinephrine from the adrenal medulla, increased release of NE from the sympathetic nerve endings, and changes in blood flow to a variety of organs, reflecting an alarm reaction that mobilizes the body to allow for optimal coping. The effects of NE are mediated via postsynaptic α_1, $ß_1$ and $ß_2$ receptors (three types of neural and peripheral receptors that are activated by NE),

whereas another NE-activated receptor, the α_2 receptor, serves as a presynaptic autoreceptor inhibiting NE release. Because of its multiple roles in regulating arousal and autonomic stress responses, as well as promoting the encoding of emotional memories, NE has been a central candidate in studying the pathophysiology of PTSD over the past 20 years.

A cardinal feature of patients with PTSD is sustained hyperactivity of the sympathetic branch of the autonomic nervous system, as evidenced by heart rate, blood pressure, skin conductance level, and other psychophysiological measures. Accordingly, increased urinary excretion of NE and epinephrine, and their metabolites, has been documented in combat veterans, abused women, and children with PTSD. In addition, patients with PTSD exhibit increased heart rate, blood pressure, and NE responses to challenge, such as traumatic reminders (*see:* **Assessment, Psychophysiological; Biology, Physiology**). Decreased platelet α_2 receptor binding (i.e., reduced ability of these receptors to activate in response to NE) further suggests NE hyperactivity in PTSD. There is also evidence for a role of altered CNS NE function in PTSD. Administration of the α_2 receptor antagonist yohimbine, which increases NE release, induces symptoms of flashbacks and increased autonomic responses in patients with PTSD. Serial sampling revealed sustained increases in CSF NE concentrations and increased CSF NE responses to psychological stressors in PTSD. Taken together, increased CNS NE (re)activity plausibly contributes to features of PTSD, including hyperarousal, increased startle, and encoded fear memories (see Strawn & Geracioti, 2008).

Studies have shown that increased heart rate and peripheral epinephrine excretion at the time of (or soon after) exposure to psychological trauma predict subsequent development of PTSD. Remarkably, administration of the centrally acting ß adrenergic blocker propranolol shortly after exposure to psychological trauma has been shown to reduce reactivity to reminders of the traumatic event (when these reminders were initiated by having the patients vividly recall the traumatic event several months later). Although this did not prevent the development of PTSD, it may have blocked traumatic memory consolidation and therefore may reduce the severity or chronicity of PTSD. Various anti-adrenergic agents have been tested for their therapeutic efficiency in the treatment of PTSD in open label trials, though there is a paucity of controlled trials (see Strawn & Geracioti, 2008; *see:* **Pharmacotherapy, Adult; Pharmacotherapy, Child**).

It should be mentioned that increased urinary excretion of DA and its metabolite has been reported for patients with PTSD. At the CNS level, mesolimbic (i.e., in portions of the limbic system) dopamine plays a role in the processing of rewards. DA has also been implicated in fear conditioning. There is evidence in humans that exposure to stressors induces mesolimbic DA release, which in turn is related to HPA axis responses. Whether the CNS DA system is altered in PTSD remains obscure, although the genetic variations in the DA system have been implicated in moderating risk for PTSD (see next section).

Serotonin

Serotonin, also known as 5-hydroxytryptamine (5HT), is a monoamine neurotransmitter synthesized from the amino acid tryptophan. Neurons comprising 5HT originate in the dorsal and medial nuclei raphé (areas in the brainstem) and project to multiple forebrain regions, including the amygdala, bed nucleus of the stria terminalis, hippocampus and prefrontal cortex. 5HT has roles in regulating sleep, appetite, sexual behavior, aggression/impulsivity, motor function, analgesia, and neuroendocrine control. 5HT also has been implicated in the modulation of affective and stress responses. The direction of the modulatory effects of 5HT on affective and stress responses depends on stressor intensity, brain region, and receptor type. It is believed that 5HT neurons of the dorsal raphé projecting to the amygdala and hippocampus mediate anxiogenic (stress-increasing) effects via $5HT_2$ receptors, whereas 5HT neurons from the median raphé have anxiolytic effects, facilitate extinction and suppress encoding of learned

associations via $5HT_{1A}$ receptors. Chronic exposure to stressors induces upregulation of $5HT_2$ and downregulation of $5HT_{1A}$ receptors in animal models. $5HT_{1A}$ knockouts exhibit increased stress responses. The 5HT system interacts with the CRH and NE systems in coordinating affective and stress responses.

Indirect evidence suggests a role of 5HT in the pathophysiology of PTSD, including symptoms of impulsivity, hostility, and aggression, depression, suicidality, and, most importantly, the therapeutic efficiency of selective serotonin reuptake inhibitors (SSRI; *see:* **Pharmacotherapy, Adult; Pharmacotherapy, Child**). Other evidence for altered 5HT neurotransmission in PTSD includes decreased serum (peripheral blood level) concentrations of 5HT, decreased density of platelet 5HT uptake sites, and altered responsiveness to CNS serotonergic challenge (i.e., the administration of chemical agents that affect serotonin production or activity, such as fenfluramine testing; see Ressler & Nemeroff, 2000; Vermetten & Bremner, 2002). However, no differences in CNS $5HT_{1A}$ receptor binding were detected in patients with PTSD compared to controls using PET scan imaging (Bonne et al., 2005). Variation in the serotonin transporter gene determines risk versus resilience to develop PTSD in response to psychological trauma (see next). Taken together, altered 5HT transmission may contribute to symptoms of PTSD such as hypervigilance, increased startle, impulsivity, and intrusive memories, although its role in PTSD remains somewhat uncertain.

GABA/Benzodiazepine Receptor System

Gamma-aminobutyric acid (GABA) is the principal inhibitory neurotransmitter in the brain. GABA has profound anxiolytic effects and dampens behavioral and physiological responses to exposure to stressors by inhibiting the CRH/NE circuits involved in mediating fear and stress responses. GABA's effects are achieved by binding to $GABA_A$ receptors, which are co-localized with benzodiazepine receptors that potentiate the inhibitory effects of GABA on the postsynaptic neuron. Uncontrollable stress leads to alterations in the $GABA_A$/benzodiazepine receptor complex. Treatment with benzodiazepines, GABA agonists (pharmacologic agents that enhance GABA's effects) or GABA reuptake inhibitors decreases symptoms of anxiety in PTSD, suggesting that the GABA/benzodiazepine system may be involved in the pathophysiology of PTSD. Patients with PTSD also exhibit decreased peripheral benzodiazepine binding sites. SPECT and PET scan imaging studies revealed decreased binding of radio-labeled benzodiazepine receptor ligands in the cortex, hippocampus and thalamus of patients with PTSD, suggesting decreased density or affinity of the benzodiazepine receptors may play a role in PTSD. However, treatment with benzodiazepines after exposure to psychological trauma does not prevent PTSD. Taken together, while there are multiple studies implicating the GABA/benzodiazepine receptor system in anxiety disorders, studies in PTSD are sparse (see Vermetten & Bremner, 2002).

Glutamate/NMDA Receptor System

Glutamate is the primary excitatory neurotransmitter in the brain—that is, it stimulates heightened levels of activity in several brain systems. Exposure to stressors and the release or administration of glucocorticoids activate glutamate release in the brain. Glutamate binds to N-methyl D-aspartate (NMDA) receptors that are localized throughout the brain. The glutamate/NMDA receptor system has been implicated in synaptic plasticity (i.e., change in the synapses connecting brain neurons), learning, and memory, including the phenomenon of long-term potentiation. Long-term potentiation refers to extended excitation of interconnected groups of brain cells (neurons), leading to long-lasting enhancement in communication between neurons that are stimulated simultaneously. This process is believed to underlie the process of conditioning and memory consolidation. Long-term potentiation plausibly contributes to consolidation of trauma memories in PTSD. Of note, the partial NMDA-receptor antagonist (i.e., a pharmacologic agent that partially blocks or

reduces NMDA receptor activity) D-cycloserine has been shown to improve the extinction of fear in rodents and in phobic patients undergoing exposure therapy. Whether or not D-cycloserine is effective in enhancing the outcome of exposure therapy in PTSD remains to be studied (see Davis, Ressler, Rothbaum, & Richardson, 2006). In addition to its role in learning and memory, overexposure to glutamate is associated with excitotoxicity (i.e., excessive levels of neural activity that may be damaging to brain cells and may lead to neuronal death), and may contribute to a loss of neurons in the hippocampus and prefrontal cortex in PTSD. Interestingly, elevated glucocorticoids increase the expression and/or sensitivity of NMDA receptors, which may sensitize the brain to excitoxic insults.

Neuropeptide Y

Neuropeptide Y (NPY) is a protective neuropeptide that has anxiolytic and stress-buffering properties. NPY has been shown to inhibit CRH/NE circuits involved in stress and fear responses and reduces the release of NE from sympathetic nerve cells. A lack of NPY may promote maladaptive stress responses and contribute to the development of PTSD. Indeed, patients with PTSD exhibit decreased basal plasma NPY concentrations and blunted NPY responses to yohimbine challenge/administration compared to controls, suggesting that decreased NPY activity may contribute to noradrenergic hyperactivity in PTSD (see, e.g., Yehuda, Flory, Southwick, & Charney, 2006).

Endogenous Opiates

Endogenous opiates such as the endorphins or enkephalins are chemicals produced by the brain (hence, the term *endogenous*) that operate on receptors that are activated by exogenous opioid chemicals such as morphine or heroin. Alterations in endogenous opiates may be involved in symptoms of numbing, stress-induced analgesia, and dissociation in PTSD.

Endogenous opiates further exert inhibitory influences on the HPA axis. Naloxone, an opiate antagonist, increases HPA axis activation by blocking an inhibitory opioidergic tone on hypothalamic CRH secretion (i.e., the ability of opioids to inhibit the production of CRH by the hypothalamus), and patients with PTSD exhibit an exaggerated HPA axis response to naloxone. Naloxone also has been shown to reverse analgesic reactions in PTSD patients when they are exposed to traumatic reminders. Finally, PTSD patients exhibit increased b-endorphin levels in cerebrospinal fluid, suggesting increased activation of the endogenous opioid system. The nonselective opiate receptor antagonist, naltrexone, appears to be effective in treating symptoms of dissociation and flashbacks in traumatized persons (see Newport & Nemeroff, 2000; Vermetten & Bremner, 2002).

Gene-Environment Interactions in the Neurobiology of PTSD

Evidence from family and twin studies has long suggested a heritable contribution to the development of PTSD (*see:* **Genetics**). In addition, there is evidence for heritable contributions to some of the neurobiological endophenotypes of PTSD, such as decreased hippocampal volume. Although it is beyond the scope of this entry to comprehensively discuss the genetics of PTSD, it should be noted that there is an exciting literature emerging on genetic variations in neurobiological systems that determine responses to trauma and, consequently, risk versus resilience to develop PTSD. For example, one study has linked a polymorphism in the DA transporter gene to PTSD risk, inasmuch as there was an excess of the SLC6A3 9 repeat allele in those with PTSD. These findings suggest that genetically determined changes in DA reactivity may contribute to PTSD among trauma survivors.

Several studies have investigated polymorphisms in the D_2 receptor in relation to PTSD risk, although results have not been consistent (see Broekman, Olff, & Boer, 2007). Finally, there is considerable evidence linking a low-expression

variant of the serotonin transporter to stress responsiveness and risk for developing depression in relation to exposure to life stressors. The same variant has now been associated with risk for developing PTSD, particularly in the presence of low social support (Kilpatrick et al., 2007). It should be noted that, in addition to genetic dispositions, previous experience can moderate risk to develop PTSD in response to psychological trauma, particularly when experienced early in life. There is a burgeoning literature documenting that early adverse experience has profound and long-lasting effects on neurobiological systems and stress responsiveness (see Nemeroff, 2004). Studies are needed that consider interactions between genetic and early life factors in determining neurobiological risk versus resilience to develop PTSD.

Conclusion

Some of the core features of PTSD include low cortisol secretion and enhanced negative feedback control of the HPA axis, increased autonomic responsiveness, increased central CRH and NE activity, and alterations in serotonergic, GABA-ergic, glutamatergic, NPY, and opioidergic systems. These neuroendocrine and neurochemical changes reflect functional changes in a connected network of brain regions that is involved in the regulation and integration of fear and stress responses. Several of the neurobiological changes (i.e., low cortisol and increased autonomic response at the time of exposure to psychological trauma) predict the development of subsequent PTSD. Such studies have allowed for testing preventive interventions to reduce PTSD risk after exposure to psychological trauma (*see:* **Early Intervention; Prevention, Adult; Prevention, Child**). Important new insights are currently gained from studies assessing gene-environment interactions in determining neurobiological responses to psychological trauma and hence risk for PTSD. Such studies, taken together, have the potential to uncover novel brain targets to prevent or treat PTSD.

REFERENCES

Bonne, O., Bain, E., Neumeister, A., Nugent, A. C., Vythilingam, M., Carson, R. E., et al. (2005). No change in serotonin type 1A receptor binding in patients with posttraumatic stress disorder. *American Journal of Psychiatry, 162,* 383–385.

Broekman, B. F., Olff, M., & Boer, F. (2007). The genetic background to PTSD. *Neuroscience and Biobehavioral Reviews, 3,* 348–362.

Davis, M., Ressler, K., Rothbaum, B. O., & Richardson, R. (2006). Effects of D-cycloserine on extinction: Translation from preclinical to clinical work. *Biological Psychiatry, 60,* 369–375.

Kilpatrick, D. G., Koenen, K. C., Ruggiero, K. J., Acierno, R., Galea, S., Resnick, H. S., et al. (2007). The serotonin transporter genotype and social support and moderation of posttraumatic stress disorder and depression in hurricane-exposed adults. *American Journal of Psychiatry, 164,* 1693–1699.

Nemeroff, C. B. (2004). Neurobiological consequences of childhood trauma. *Journal of Clinical Psychiatry, 65,* 18–28.

Newport, D. J., & Nemeroff, C. B. (2000). Neurobiology of posttraumatic stress disorder. *Current Opinions in Neurobiology, 10,* 211–218.

Ressler, K. J., & Nemeroff, C. B. (2000). Role of serotonergic and noradrenergic systems in the pathophysiology of depression and anxiety disorders. *Depression and Anxiety, 12,* 2–19.

Strawn, J. R., & Geracioti, T. D., Jr. (2008). Noradrenergic dysfunction and the psychopharmacology of posttraumatic stress disorder. *Depression and Anxiety, 25,* 260–271.

Vermetten, E., & Bremner, J. D. (2002). Circuits and systems in stress: Pt. II. Applications to neurobiology and treatment in posttraumatic stress disorder. *Depression and Anxiety, 16,* 14–38.

Yehuda, R. (2006). Advances in understanding neuroendocrine alterations in PTSD and their therapeutic implications. *Annals of the New York Academy of Sciences, 1071,* 137–166.

Yehuda, R., Flory, J. D., Southwick, S., & Charney, D. S. (2006). Developing an agenda for translational studies of resilience and vulnerability following trauma exposure. *Annals of the New York Academy of Sciences, 1071,* 379–396.

Yehuda, R., & LeDoux, J. (2007). Response variation following trauma: A translational neuroscience approach to understanding PTSD. *Neuron, 56,* 19–32.

CHRISTINE HEIM
Emory University School of Medicine

CHARLES B. NEMEROFF
Emory University School of Medicine

See also: Amygdala; Anterior Cingulate Cortex; Assessment, Psychophysiological; Biology, Brain Structure, and Function, Adult; Biology, Brain Structure, and Function, Child; Biology, Physiology; Frontal Cortex; Genetics; Hippocampus

BIOLOGY, PHYSIOLOGY

Biology of Psychological Trauma

Most research examining the biological correlates of trauma exposure and posttraumatic stress has focused on examining abnormalities of the primary stress pathways (e.g., the sympathetic nervous system [SNS] and the hypothalamic-pituitary-adrenal [HPA] axis). These studies have largely focused on elucidating abnormalities associated with posttraumatic stress disorder (PTSD), and biological risk and resiliency factors associated with the development of PTSD. Findings of these studies are being used to facilitate effective screening of high-risk individuals and to guide the development of early interventions designed to prevent or buffer the development of PTSD.

Initial research into the biology of PTSD focused on examining alterations present in adults with chronic PTSD such as combat military veterans. The most consistently observed biological abnormality in chronic PTSD was SNS hyper-reactivity to trauma-reminiscent and nontrauma-reminiscent stimuli (i.e., exaggerated startle responses). These findings were further supported by relatively consistent reports of elevated 24-hour urinary catecholamine levels in PTSD. In contrast, studies examining alterations in HPA axis activity have produced variable findings. Initial studies were relatively consistent and somewhat surprising in that they found lower 24-hour urinary cortisol excretion in patients with PTSD relative to patents without PTSD and normal controls (see Yehuda, 2002 for a review). Findings of greater numbers of lymphocyte glucocorticoid receptors in PTSD further suggested hypofunctioning of the HPA axis in PTSD. However, more recently, contradictory findings have been reported, with some studies finding higher 24-hour urinary cortisol levels in PTSD, and some finding no differences in cortisol output between patients with PTSD and controls. A number of possible explanations for these discrepant findings have been posited (see Rasmusson, Vythilingam, & Morgan, 2003). Of note, studies reporting higher levels of cortisol in PTSD have typically included samples consisting primarily of premenopausal women, suggesting that inconsistent findings may reflect differences in gender and/or menopausal status between studies. Finally, failure to consider the presence of diagnoses comorbid with PTSD, such as major depressive disorder (which typically is associated with elevated cortisol levels), may also contribute to the discrepant findings.

Based on findings in chronic PTSD patients and basic research on the impact of stress on memory formation, researchers hypothesized that abnormalities observed in chronic PTSD, if present during and soon after trauma exposure, would lead to increased risk for the development of PTSD. Heart rate (HR) levels routinely assessed at varying times following hospital admission have been positively associated with increased risk for subsequent PTSD. Similarly, studies of rape and motor vehicle accident (MVA) victims have found lower levels of cortisol within hours post-trauma to be associated with greater risk for the development of PTSD at follow-up. Additional evidence for the role of initial biological responses to trauma serving as risk factors for PTSD has been provided by intervention studies that pharmacologically alter biological levels in an attempt to decrease posttraumatic stress symptoms (PTSS). These secondary interventions involve administering pharmacological agents soon after trauma in an attempt to prevent or reduce the development of subsequent PTSS. Preliminary research examining the administration of propranolol (a beta-blocker that reduces arousal) or hydrocortisone (cortisol) soon after trauma

has demonstrated promising results with respect to decreasing psychophysiological reactivity to trauma memories (but less consistently with respect to reducing PTSS) at later time points, underscoring the role of initial biological reactions to trauma as possible mechanisms through which trauma could lead to PTSD in some at-risk individuals (Pitman & Delahanty, 2005).

As only a minority of trauma victims typically develops PTSD, researchers have attempted to identify variables that might be associated with abnormal biological responses to trauma and subsequent increased risk for PTSD. Prior trauma history (especially when experienced during childhood) is one of the most consistent predictors of PTSD following a subsequent trauma, and researchers have hypothesized that prior trauma experiences could disrupt SNS and HPA axis functioning, leading to increased risk for PTSD. This hypothesis has been supported by a number of studies finding that trauma history is associated with altered stress hormone levels following trauma (typically lower cortisol levels) and increased risk for developing PTSD.

Research into biological alterations of the primary stress pathways in traumatized children has shed light on how childhood trauma may be associated with increased risk for PTSD following adult trauma. Similar to findings in the adult literature, chronic PTSD in children appears to be associated with increased catecholamine levels. Research examining HPA axis alterations in children has also produced mixed results, with studies assessing cortisol levels within a few years of the trauma typically reporting higher cortisol levels in children with PTSD. However, studies examining children 5+ years posttrauma often report lower levels of cortisol in children with PTSD.

Few studies have explored acute biological predictors of PTSD in children. Consistent with the adult literature, elevated HR soon after trauma is associated with increased risk for the development of PTSD in child trauma victims. Initial hormonal predictors of PTSS in child trauma victims have also been examined. In contrast to the adult literature, in traumatized children with no trauma history, *higher* levels of in-hospital urinary cortisol and epinephrine predicted higher PTSS 6-weeks posttrauma (Delahanty, Nugent, Christopher, & Walsh, 2005). It should be noted that these findings were driven by significant findings in boys, but not in girls. These results suggest a developmental model of PTSD whereby at-risk children respond with overactivity of SNS and HPA axis hormones. Over time (probably years) high levels of cortisol may sensitize the HPA axis, resulting in lower circulating cortisol levels in adults with prior trauma and increased risk for PTSD (De Bellis et al., 1999).

Although the vast majority of research into the biology of PTSD has focused on abnormalities of the SNS and HPA axis, more recent research has suggested additional biological variables that may act as risk or resilience factors. For instance, preliminary evidence suggests that neuropeptide Y (NPY) and dehydroepiandrosterone (DHEA) and its sulfated metabolite (DHEAS) may serve as biological resilience factors for PTSD. NPY has been found to be altered in trauma-exposed individuals, and influences HPA axis activity, while DHEA may attenuate the possible deleterious impact of elevated cortisol. However, more research is needed in a wider range of trauma victims of differing ages to increase confidence in these findings.

Conclusion

PTSD appears to be associated with alterations of the SNS and HPA axis, although the direction of the relationship may differ due to a variety of variables. The impact of trauma history and chronicity of PTSS are just beginning to be examined, and the impact of person-variables such as age, gender, and sex hormone influences are important covariates to consider. A better understanding of how these alterations impact the development of PTSD is needed to efficiently and effectively identify high-risk patients and to guide the development of novel pharmacological interventions that may prevent the development of PTSS.

REFERENCES

De Bellis, M. D., Baum, A. S., Birmaher, B., Keshavan, M. S., Eccard, C. H., Boring, A. M., et al. (1999). Developmental traumatology: Pt. I. Biological stress systems. *Biological Psychiatry, 45*, 1259–1270.

Delahanty, D. L., Nugent, N. R., Christopher, N. C., & Walsh, M. (2005). Initial urinary epinephrine and cortisol levels predict acute PTSD symptoms in child trauma victims. *Journal of Psychoneuroendocrinology, 30*, 121–128.

Pitman, R. K., & Delehanty, D. L. (2005). Conceptually driven pharmacologic approaches to acute trauma. *CNS Spectrums, 10*, 99–106.

Rasmusson, A. M., Vythilingam, M., & Morgan, C. A. (2003). The neuroendocrinology of posttraumatic stress disorder: New directions. *CNS Spectrum, 8*, 651–656, 665–667.

Yehuda, R. (2002). Posttraumatic stress disorder. *New England Journal of Medicine, 346*, 108–114.

Young, E. A., Tolman, R., Witkowski, K., & Kaplan, G. A. (2004, March). Salivary cortisol and posttraumatic stress disorder in a low-income community sample of women. *Biological Psychiatry, 55*(6), 621–626.

RECOMMENDED READINGS

Rasmusson, A. M., Vythilingam, M., & Morgan, C. A. (2003). The neuroendocrinology of posttraumatic stress disorder: New directions. *CNS Spectrum, 8*, 651–656, 665–667.

Yehuda, R. (Ed.). (2006). *Psychobiology of posttraumatic stress disorder: A decade of progress.* Boston: Blackwell.

Douglas L. Delahanty
Kent State University

Jessica M. Boarts
Kent State University

See also: Assessment, Psychophysiological; Biofeedback; Biology, Neurochemistry; Biology, Brain Structure, and Function, Adult; Biology, Brain Structure, and Function, Child; Conditioned Fear

BORDERLINE PERSONALITY DISORDER

See: Personality Disorders

BRAIN

See: Amygdala; Anterior Cingulate Cortex; Biology, Animal Models; Biology, Brain Structure, and Function, Adult; Biology, Brain Structure, and Function, Child; Biology, Neurochemistry; Biology, Physiology; Frontal Cortex; Hippocampus; Limbic System; Loecus Coeruleus; Psychoneuroimmunology

BURNOUT

Burnout is a psychological syndrome of exhaustion, cynicism, and inefficacy in the workplace. It is an individual stress experience embedded in a context of complex social relationships, and it involves the person's conception of both self and others on the job. *Exhaustion* refers to feelings of being overextended, and depleted of one's emotional and physical resources. Workers feel drained and used up, and lack enough energy to face another day or another person in need. *Cynicism* refers to a negative, hostile, or excessively detached response to the job, which often includes a loss of idealism. It may develop in response to the overload of exhaustion and is self-protective at first—an emotional buffer of "detached concern"—but the risk is that the detachment can turn into dehumanization. *Inefficacy* refers to a decline in feelings of competence and productivity at work. People experience a growing sense of inadequacy about their ability to do the job well, and this may result in a self-imposed verdict of failure. Much research, in many countries, has been conducted on burnout over the past 30 years (see reviews by Maslach & Leiter, 2005; Schaufeli & Enzmann, 1998). The principal measure of burnout across all occupations is the Maslach Burnout Inventory (MBI; Maslach & Jackson, 1981), which provides an assessment of each of the three dimensions of burnout.

Unlike acute stress reactions that develop in response to specific critical incidents, burnout is a cumulative stress reaction to ongoing occupational stressors. With burnout, the emphasis has been more on the *process of psychological erosion,* and the psychological and social outcomes of this chronic exposure, rather than just the physical ones. Because burnout is a prolonged response to chronic interpersonal stressors on the job, it tends to be fairly stable over time. It is an important mediator of the causal link between various job stressors and individual stress outcomes.

Burnout can affect workers in all kinds of jobs and in all professions; however, some professions, professional settings, and the demands and exposure that they require may hold a higher potential for burnout. In this entry, we discuss the development of burnout in human service professionals who work with and treat individuals who have been exposed to psychological trauma and/or who have posttraumatic stress disorder (PTSD; e.g., first responders, emergency medical technicians, police, medical personnel, psychotherapists, refugee workers, shelter workers). Figley (1995) has used the label *compassion fatigue* and Stamm (1995) used the term *secondary traumatic stress* to describe a special species of clinical burnout—including but not limited to helping-induced trauma—that is associated with work with the trauma-exposed. McCann and Pearlman (1990) described *vicarious traumatization* (VT; *see:* **Vicarious Traumatization**) as the process of transformation of the helper who works with traumatized clients, including shifts in core beliefs and assumptions about self, others, and the world. VT is not burnout per se but is a process that, if unrecognized and unaddressed, might result in burnout.

Clients exposed to psychological trauma pose special risks to helpers in a number of ways. Direct exposure to their injuries and their traumatic circumstance (e.g., in the case of accidents, disasters, war, refugee camps) and their stories of victimization (especially at the hands of others) may be extremely graphic and difficult for helpers to see and to listen to; moreover, they might exhibit what has been called "traumatic transference" to the helper (*see:* **Countertransference**). Trauma-exposed individuals may be mistrustful, suspicious, hostile, and demanding, or alternately they may be overly trusting and exceedingly dependent, grateful, compliant, and needy, or they may show a confusing and sometimes exasperating mixture of the two alternative presentations (Wilson & Lindy, 1994). Helpers (especially, but not limited to, novices and those who have not received training in working with traumatized clients) may be hard pressed to know what to do and may end up feeling de-skilled and frustrated to the point of hostility and disengagement. Miller (1998) described the challenges in psychotherapy with such clients in succinct and graphic terms: "Doing trauma psychotherapy is not for everyone. It's tough, grimy, demanding work that can take an exhausting toll on its practitioners" (p. 137). Miller further describes one more risk, that of being traumatized directly by interactions with or by assaults by disturbed or violent patients, or by agencies that are not responsive when such an assault has occurred. Although not all trauma-exposed clients pose challenges such as these, when they do there is a high potential for burnout among trauma helpers.

The effects of burnout can be widespread and problematic; hence, there is relevance and even urgency in identifying its antecedents and addressing them before the worker reaches a stage of cynicism and disengagement. As noted, a primary effect is on individual helpers who may have started their human services jobs and careers as optimists dedicated to helping others and who, over time, become pessimistic to the point of cynicism, indifference and disengagement, and hostility.

Burnout has been associated with various forms of job withdrawal—absenteeism, intention to leave the job, and actual turnover; furthermore, it is linked to poorer quality of work, as people shift to doing the bare minimum, rather than performing at their best. They may make more errors, become less thorough, and have less creativity for solving problems.

There is also some evidence that burnout has a negative spillover effect on people's home life. Research and clinical observations on secondary traumatic stress and vicarious traumatization attest to this effect (*see:* **Vicarious Traumatization**). Helpers who are affected to the point of burnout often withdraw at home as well as on the job. They may sleep more,

turn to food or alcohol to cope, exhibit signs of anxiety and depression (including in extreme cases becoming suicidal), and be minimally interactive with family and friends. They may also be irritable and quick to anger, and in extreme cases may engage in domestic abuse, hurting and alienating those who are potential sources of support and sustenance. As is true of other stress experiences, the helper experiencing burnout may begin to display a variety of somatic and medical concerns.

Burnout diminishes opportunities for satisfying experiences at work, and it is associated with decreased job satisfaction and a reduced commitment to the job, the organization, its mission, and the clientele. In the worst case, burnout may be associated with helper behavior that emotionally harms and revictimizes trauma-exposed clients, causing what has been called the "second injury" where the person turned to for help does not help, and instead, adds to the distress. Second injury unfortunately has been reported by a number of traumatized clients; burnout associated with VT may be a contributing factor (see Miller, 1998; Saakvitne & Pearlman, 1996; Wilson & Lindy, 1994). Additionally, helpers who experience burnout can have a profoundly negative impact not only on their clients but also on their colleagues and their work settings resulting in interpersonal conflict and disruption of job tasks. Thus, burnout can be "contagious" and may perpetuate itself through negativity and conflicted interactions on the job.

Situational and Personal Factors

Inherent to the fundamental concept of stress is the problematic relationship between the individual and the situation. Thus, prior research has tried to identify both the key personal and job characteristics that put individuals at risk for burnout. In general, far more evidence has been found for the impact of job variables than for personal ones. These job factors fall into six key domains within the workplace: workload, control, reward, community, fairness, and values.

Workload

Both qualitative and quantitative work over-load contribute to burnout by depleting the capacity of people to meet the demands of the job. When this kind of overload is a chronic job condition, there is little opportunity to rest, recover, and restore balance. A sustainable workload, in contrast, provides opportunities to use and refine existing skills as well as to become effective in new areas of activity. In recent years, human service professionals have faced increasing caseloads due to a number of factors, including greater numbers of referrals of severely impaired or traumatized clients at the same time that clients' ability to pay, insurance plans' provisions for payment, and public and private funding for human service organizations have decreased and restrictions imposed by managed care or other administrative policies have increased. Thus, in the human services and behavioral health fields, helping professionals and staff who work with trauma-exposed clients are subject to caseload and fiscal pressures that may compound the difficulties of simply providing services to troubled and often disadvantaged clients, thus placing these helpers at risk for burnout.

Control

Research has identified a clear link between a lack of control and high levels of stress and burnout. However, when people have the perceived capacity to influence decisions that affect their work, to exercise professional autonomy, and to gain access to the resources necessary to do an effective job, they are more likely to experience job engagement. A recent study of psychologists (Rupert & Kent, 2007) suggested that work in agency settings may result in less control and more propensity to burnout than work in private practice settings. This may be especially the case with helpers who serve traumatized clients or those whose jobs require ongoing exposure to traumatic circumstances (e.g., emergency medical personnel, police, emergency room personnel).

Reward

Insufficient recognition and reward (whether financial, institutional, or social) increases people's vulnerability to burnout, because it devalues both the work and the workers and is closely associated with feelings of inefficacy. In contrast, consistency in the reward dimension between the person and the job means that there are both material rewards and opportunities for intrinsic satisfaction. Many services for trauma-exposed clients are notoriously underfunded and/or funding may fluctuate according to political or governmental agendas that do not correspond to the helpers' and helping organization's mission or need. In such circumstances, helpers may feel insecure in their job status and unrecognized (financially or otherwise) for the work that they do.

Community

Community has to do with the ongoing relationships that workers have with other people on the job. When these relationships are characterized by a lack of support and trust, and by unresolved conflict, then there is a greater risk of burnout. However, when these job-related relationships are working well, there is a great deal of social support, people have effective means of working out disagreements, and they are more likely to experience job engagement. Support is a major moderator of the emotional effects of trauma exposure and applies to helpers who are feeling the effects of working with such clients on a sustained basis. Managers and coworkers who anticipate and understand reactions and who take steps to support the helper and other staff can help offset factors leading to burnout.

Fairness

Fairness is the extent to which decisions at work are perceived as being fair and equitable. People use the quality of the procedures, and their own treatment during the decision-making process, as an index of their place in the community. Cynicism, anger, and hostility are likely to arise when people feel they are not being treated with the respect that comes from being treated fairly. Human service professionals who treat trauma-exposed clients often feel misunderstood. They may face questions from colleagues or family and friends such as, "Why would you want to do *that kind of work?* Don't you get depressed? Don't these clients bother you with their demands, depression, and whining?" Alternatively, some helpers who work with traumatized clients are highly respected in their communities and by their clients, and this well-deserved respect and recognition may be an important buffer against burnout.

Values

Values are the ideals and motivations that originally attracted people to their job, and thus they are the motivating connection between the worker and the workplace, which goes beyond the utilitarian exchange of time for money or advancement. When there is a values conflict on the job, and thus a gap between individual and organizational values, helpers will find themselves making a trade-off between work they want to do and work they have to do, and this can lead to greater burnout. In agencies, it is not unusual for helpers who specialize in treating traumatized clients to be seen as and treated as "less than" (i.e., as if they are not as valued as other agency staff or clinicians) while being assigned large caseloads of such clients because "they're good at working with those difficult clients." Over time, this combination of high demand/low regard can take a high toll on the helper, leading to exhaustion and burnout (Saakvitne & Pearlman, 1996).

Although job variables and the organizational context are the prime predictors of burnout and engagement, a few personality variables have shown some consistent correlational patterns. In general, burnout scores are higher for people who have a less "hardy" personality, who have a more external locus of control, and who score as "neurotic" on the Five-Factor Model of personality. Individuals who are more passive/avoidant or confronting in coping style and thus likely to have a lower sense of personal control may be more prone to burnout in human service positions (Brown & O'Brien, 1998; Jenaro, Flores, & Arias, 2007; Rupert & Kent, 2007). There is also some evidence that people who exhibit Type-A behavior

(which tends to predict coronary heart disease) are more prone to the exhaustion dimension of burnout, possibly due to a stance of over-responsibility. There are few consistent relationships of burnout with demographic characteristics, such as gender or age. These weak demographic relationships are congruent with the view that the work environment is of greater significance than personal characteristics in the development of burnout; yet, as more data are accumulated on personal characteristics of helpers serving traumatized clients, other factors might emerge. For example, Shapiro, Dorman, Burkey, and Welker (1999) found greater job satisfaction in professionals working with child abuse who themselves had a personal history of childhood sexual abuse or neglect. Young, inexperienced therapists tend to report higher levels of burnout than older, more seasoned therapists (Pearlman & MacIan, 1995), even though the older therapists report higher levels of emotional exhaustion (Rupert & Kent, 2007).

However, recent theorizing has argued that both personal and job characteristics need to be considered jointly within the context of the organizational environment. The degree of fit, or match, between the person and the job within the six areas of work life, will determine the extent to which the person experiences engagement or burnout, which in turn will determine various outcomes, such as personal health and emotional well-being, job satisfaction, work behaviors, and organizational measures. In other words, the burnout-engagement continuum (with its three dimensions) mediates the impact of the six areas of work-life on important individual and situational outcomes.

Interventions

The personal and organizational costs of burnout have led to the development of various intervention strategies. Some approaches are designed to treat burnout after it has occurred, while others focus on how to reduce the risk of burnout. A more recent approach has been to prevent burnout by emphasizing the need for self-care as a psychotherapist (or other type of human service worker) due to stresses that are inherent in the work (Norcross & Guy, 2007), especially in work with traumatized clients (Figley, 1995; McCann & Pearlman, 1990; Wilson & Lindy, 1994), and building engagement and support among helpers and in organizations (Brown & O'Brien, 1998; Shapiro et al., 1999). Interventions may occur on the level of the individual, workgroup, or an entire organization (Saakvitne & Pearlman, 1996). It is recommended that all interventions should be ongoing and should be multimodal. Interventions to prevent burnout address the existential/spiritual and relational as well as practical aspects of burnout, and may include recreational and wellness-focused activities to increase worker's range of rejuvenating activities outside work. At each level, the number of people affected by an intervention and the potential for enduring change increases. However, in line with research findings, any progress in dealing with burnout will depend on the development of strategies that focus on the job context and its impact on the individuals who work within it.

Recently, attention has been given to the opposite of burnout, namely job engagement. Engagement in work is a productive and fulfilling state, and is defined in terms of the same three dimensions as burnout, but the positive end of those dimensions rather than the negative. Thus, engagement consists of a state of high energy (rather than exhaustion), strong involvement (rather than cynicism and withdrawal), and a sense of efficacy (rather than inefficacy). Personal, collegial, and organizational strategies that stress support and appreciation and increase engagement, involvement, and a sense of efficacy all have great utility in working against burnout in general but more specifically in helpers who work with trauma-exposed clients.

REFERENCES

Brown, C., & O'Brien, K. M. (1998). Understanding stress and burnout in shelter workers. *Professional Psychology: Research and Practice, 29,* 383–385.

Figley, C. R. (1995). *Compassion fatigue: Coping with secondary traumatic stress disorder in those who treat the traumatized.* New York: Brunner/Mazel.

Jenaro, C., Flores, N., & Arias, B. (2007). Burnout and coping in human service practitioners. *Professional Psychology: Research and Practice, 38,* 80–87.

Maslach, C., & Jackson, S. E. (1981). *Maslach Burnout Inventory* [Manual]. Palo Alto, CA: Consulting Psychologists Press.

Maslach, C., & Leiter, M. P. (2005). Stress and burnout: The critical research. In C. L. Cooper (Ed.), *Handbook of stress medicine and health* (2nd ed., pp. 153–170). Boca Raton, FL: CRC Press.

McCann, L. L., & Pearlman, L. A. (1990). Vicarious traumatization: A framework for understanding the psychological effects of working with victims. *Journal of Traumatic Stress, 3,* 131–149.

Miller, L. (1998). Our own medicine: Traumatized psychotherapists and the stresses of doing therapy. *Psychotherapy: Theory, Research and Practice, 35,* 137–146.

Norcross, J., & Guy, J. (2007). *Leaving it at the office: A guide to psychotherapist self-care.* New York: Guilford Press.

Pearlman, L. A., & MacIan, P. S. (1995). Vicarious traumatization: An empirical study of the effects of trauma work on trauma therapists. *Professional Psychology: Research and Practice, 26,* 558–565.

Rupert, P. A., & Kent, J. S. (2007). Gender and work setting differences in career-sustaining behaviors and burnout among professional psychologists. *Professional Psychology: Research and Practice, 38,* 88–96.

Saakvitne, K. W., & Pearlman, L. A. (1996). *Transforming the pain: A workbook on vicarious traumatization.* New York: Norton.

Schaufeli, W. B., & Enzmann, D. (1998). *The burnout companion to study and practice: A critical analysis.* London: Taylor & Francis.

Shapiro, J. P., Dorman, R. L., Burkey, W. M., & Welker, C. J. (1999). Predictors of job satisfaction and burnout in child abuse professionals: Coping, cognition, and victimization history. *Journal of Child Sexual Abuse, 7*(4), 23–42.

Stamm, B. H. (Ed.). (1995). *Secondary traumatic stress: Self-care issues for clinicians, researchers, and educators.* Lutherville, MD: Sidran Press.

Wilson, J. P., & Lindy, J. D. (Eds.). (1994). *Countertransference in the treatment of PTSD.* New York: Guilford Press.

CHRISTINA MASLACH
University of California, Berkeley

CHRISTINE A. COURTOIS
Private Practice, Washington, DC

See also: Vicarious Traumatization

BURNS

Burns are among the most painful injuries one can experience, and, until recently, were often fatal. Burn severity is measured by two dimensions: the depth of the injury, or how many layers of the skin are affected; and the size of the injury, or how much of the total body surface area (TBSA) has been burned. In the mid-1970s, individuals with burns covering more than 20% of their TBSA rarely lived. Currently, due to advancements in medical and surgical care, people can survive with burns covering as much as 90% of their TBSA, although permanent impairment is often present (National Institutes of Health [NIH], 2006).

The study of burns as potentially traumatic events has informed the general conceptualization and understanding of traumatic stress reactions. Burns were among the first types of events identified to result in traumatic stress reactions. Furthermore, early research on burns contributed to the original classification of PTSD in the *DSM-III* (American Psychiatric Association, 1980; Andreasen, 1974; Andreasen, Hartford, Knott, & Canter, 1977; Andreasen, Noyes, & Hartford, 1972). Events that result in burn injuries often involve characteristics that induce intense fear, helplessness, or horror. People who have experienced burns may also have lost loved ones in a fire or explosion or may have seen them endure severe injury. Additionally, as noted, severe pain from the initial injuries, postsurgical sites, debridement (cleaning of the wounds), and dressing changes are associated with burn injuries. Furthermore, significant disfigurement and scarring can occur as a consequence of burns. For children, separation from caregivers during or in the immediate aftermath of the burn event may be particularly traumatic.

In their review of the literature, McKibben and colleagues (McKibben, Bresnick, Weichman Askay, & Fauerbach, 2008) noted that PTSD prevalence rates in patients with burns range from 23% to 33% during the 3 to 6 months immediately after the injury, and from 15% to 45% of patients after 1 year has passed. A major focus of research with this population has been identifying predictors of PTSD for the purpose of guiding the development of preventive interventions. In adult samples, chronic PTSD is best predicted by the severity of early traumatic stress symptoms (Bryant, 1996; Difede & Barocas, 1999; Difede et al., 2002; Ehde, Patterson, Weichman, & Wilson, 2000; McKibben et al., 2008). While the early appearance of symptoms in the avoidance, hyperarousal, and reexperiencing categories consistently predicts subsequent PTSD, research findings on peritraumatic dissociation as a predictor of later trauma symptoms have been inconclusive (Bryant, 1996; Difede et al., 2002; Saxe et al., 2005; Van Loey, Maas, Faber, & Taal, 2003).

Burn-related variables such as TBSA, location of the burn, and pain are inconsistent predictors of PTSD in both adult and child samples (Bryant, 1996; Drake et al., 2006; Ehde et al., 2000; Saxe et al., 2005; Van Loey, et al., 2003). In children 4 years of age and younger, PTSD is associated with having burns that cover more of the child's TBSA, more dressing changes, and with a more rapid heart rate (Drake et al., 2006). Stolbach and colleagues (Stolbach et al., 2007) found that children's burn-related posttraumatic symptoms were related solely to prior exposure to other traumatic stressors. Saxe and colleagues (2005) found that the relationship between burn-related variables and PTSD was mediated by separation anxiety and dissociation in the acute aftermath of the burn. Parents' acute traumatic stress symptoms have also been found to be associated with children's ratings of acute traumatic stress symptoms (Saxe et al., 2005; Stoddard et al., 2006). The impact of another person's response to the event is a finding unique to pediatric patients, yet consistent with the notion that caregivers help young people assess fear-inducing situations and assist in soothing children in the face of extreme adversity.

In addition to those experiencing diagnostic levels of PTSD, many patients with burns experience significant levels of traumatic stress reactions that do not meet the criteria for a diagnosis of PTSD. Because patients with burns come into the emergency and medical systems immediately following the traumatic event (i.e., in the peritraumatic period), a unique opportunity exists to ensure that a trauma-informed system of care is in place to minimize further trauma exposure in the course of treatment and to offer universal and targeted interventions to address traumatic stress symptoms (Kazak et al., 2006; Saxe, Ellis, & Kaplow, 2007). As has been suggested in a recent article highlighting research priorities to improve the psychological health and function of burn survivors (Fauerbach, Pruzinsky, & Saxe, 2007), there is an urgent need to develop and test preventive and rehabilitative interventions for PTSD in survivors of burns.

Although it does not specifically target PTSD symptoms, social skills training geared toward the challenges specific to burn patients (Blakeney et al., 2005) has been found to be an effective intervention for burned adolescents. Numerous resources also exist for burn survivor support, including the Phoenix Society, which organizes the World Burn Congress and offers programs that target school reentry, enhanced body image functioning, feelings of self-efficacy, as well as overall quality of life. Moreover, many Burn Camp summer programs provide opportunities for children and adolescents to interact, build friendships, and learn skills with others who have been burned.

Conclusion

Burn injuries represent potentially traumatic events that lead to PTSD in a substantial proportion of pediatric and adult patients. Factors that may be associated with the development of posttraumatic symptoms in burn survivors include TBSA, burn location, pain, peritraumatic heart rate and reactions, prior trauma exposure, and, in children, separation anxiety and parents' peritraumatic reactions. Despite the fact that the study of burns as potential traumatic stressors has greatly informed the general understanding of traumatic stress and PTSD, routine care of burn patients, which necessarily focuses on physical survival and medical procedures, in many settings includes little attention to trauma-related emotional responses and rarely includes routine psychological care. Opportunities exist for trauma-informed screening and psychological intervention in burn care

settings that have the potential to reduce the likelihood that burn patients will develop lasting posttraumatic symptoms and thereby reduce the prevalence of PTSD among burn survivors.

REFERENCES

American Psychiatric Association. (1980). *Diagnostic and statistical manual of mental disorders* (3rd ed.). Washington, DC: Author.

Andreasen, N. J. (1974). Neuropsychiatric complications in burn patients. *International Journal of Psychiatry in Medicine, 5,* 161–171.

Andreasen, N. J., Hartford, C. E., Knott, J. R., & Canter, A. (1977). EEG changes associated with burn delirium. *Diseases of the Nervous System, 38,* 27–31.

Andreasen, N. J., Noyes, R. R., Jr., & Hartford, C. E. (1972). Factors influencing adjustment of burn patients during hospitalization. *Psychosomatic Medicine, 34,* 517–525.

Blakeney, P., Thomas, C., Holzer III, C., Rose, M., Berniger, F., & Meyer III, W. J. (2005). Efficacy of a short-term, intensive social skills training program for burned adolescents. *Journal of Burn Care and Rehabilitation, 26,* 546–555.

Bryant, A. (1996). Predictors of posttraumatic stress disorder following burns injury. *Burns, 22,* 89–92.

Difede, J., & Barocas, D. (1999). Acute intrusive and avoidant PTSD symptoms as predictors of chronic PTSD following burn injury. *Journal of Traumatic Stress, 12,* 363–369.

Difede, J., Ptacek, J. T., Roberts, J., Barocas, D., Rives, W., Apfeldorf, W., et al. (2002). Acute stress disorder after burn injury: A predictor of posttraumatic stress disorder? *Psychosomatic Medicine, 64,* 826–834.

Drake, J. E., Stoddard, F. J., Jr., Murphy, J. M., Ronfeldt, H., Snidman, N., Kagan, J., et al. (2006). Trauma severity influences acute stress in young burned children. *Journal of Burn Care and Research, 27,* 174–182.

Ehde, D. M., Patterson, D. R., Wiechman, S. A., & Wilson, L. G. (2000). Posttraumatic stress symptoms and distress 1 year after burn injury. *Journal of Burn Care and Rehabilitation, 21,* 105–111.

Fauerbach, J. A., Pruzinsky, T., & Saxe, G. N. (2007). Psychological health and function after burn injury: Setting research priorities. *Journal of Burn Care and Research, 28,* 587–592.

Kazak, A. E., Kassam-Adams, N., Schneider, S., Zelnikofsky, N., Alderfer, M. A., & Rourke, M.

(2006). An integrative model of pediatric medical traumatic stress. *Journal of Pediatric Psychology, 31,* 343–355.

McKibben, J. B., Bresnick, M. G., Weichman Askay, S. A., & Fauerbach, J. A. (2008). Acute stress disorder and posttraumatic stress disorder: A prospective study of prevalence, course, and predictors in a sample with major burn injuries. *Journal of Burn Care and Research, 29,* 22–35.

National Institutes of Health. (2006). *Burns and traumatic injury* [Brochure]. Washington, DC: Author.

Saxe, G. N., Ellis, B. H., & Kaplow, J. B. (2007). *Collaborative treatment of traumatized children and teens: The trauma systems therapy approach.* New York: Guilford Press.

Saxe, G. N., Stoddard, F., Hall, E., Chawla, N., Lopez, C., Sheridan, R., et al. (2005). Pathways to PTSD: Pt. I. Children with burns. *American Journal of Psychiatry, 162,* 1299–1304.

Stoddard, F. J., Ronfeldt, H., Kagan, J., Drake, J. E., Snidman, N., Murphy, J. M., et al. (2006). Young burned children: The course of acute stress and physiological and behavioral responses. *American Journal of Psychiatry, 163,* 1084–1090.

Stolbach, B. C., Fleisher, C. L., Gazibara, T., Gottlieb, L., Mintzer, L. L., & West, M. (2007, November). *Relationship of prior trauma exposure and posttraumatic stress symptoms in pediatric burn patients.* Poster presented at the 23rd annual meeting of the International Society for Traumatic Stress Studies, Baltimore.

Van Loey, N. E., Maas, C. J. M., Faber, A. W., & Taal, L. A. (2003). Predictors of chronic posttraumatic stress symptoms following burn injury: Results of a longitudinal study. *Journal of Traumatic Stress, 16,* 361–369.

Courtney Landau Fleisher
La Rabida Children's Hospital

Bradley C. Stolbach
La Rabida Children's Hospital

See also: Acute Stress Disorder; Medical Illness, Adult; Medical Illness, Child

C

CAT SCAN

See: Biology, Brain Structure, and Function, Adult; Biology, Brain Structure, and Function, Child

CHARCOT, JEAN-MARTIN (1825–1893)

Admired, feared, and vilified, Charcot was the most influential neurologist in nineteenth-century Europe. He transformed one of the most backward wards of the Salpêtrière asylum in Paris into a modern teaching department of neurology. Patients on this ward were women suffering from convulsions, and Charcot sought to find the distinguishing features between patients with epileptic seizures and those with pseudo-epileptic seizures who were diagnosed with hysteria (Trillat, 1986) (*see:* **Hysteria**). Subsequently, he studied various other symptoms including more complex hysterical attacks. Although these attacks in his female patients often involved reexperiences of sexual abuse, as exemplified in his patient Augustine, he ignored the etiological role of such early trauma in the development of the disorder. In his growing interest in male hysterical patients, however, he did acknowledge the contribution of traumatic experience in victims of work-related accidents and train disasters. Still, he maintained the customary French view that hysteria basically involved hereditary weakness or degeneration. Charcot regarded traumatizing events merely as an *agent provocateur* (Micale, 2001) that evoked a "great psychical shaking up," in *traumatic hysteria.* Charcot noted that fear played a dominant role in this psychical upheaval. When a psychologically traumatic event also involved physical damage, he did not consider the physical trauma a necessary element in the development of a posttraumatic emotional disorder. Thus, Charcot believed that constitutional weakness was the primary etiology of hysteria, whether it was trauma-related or not. In contrast, Auguste Voisin, Charcot's colleague at the Salpêtrière, observed during the Franco-Prussian War that "perfectly healthy" individuals could also be traumatized and develop serious mental disorders.

Charcot noted the role of traumatization in male patients, but did not acknowledge the potential of chronic childhood trauma, including sexual abuse, as a precipitant of hysteria as manifested in female patients. This may have been due to a gender bias because most hysterical patients were female and women historically have been viewed as constitutionally "weaker" than men. It also may reflect a bias toward emphasizing only the effects of acute psychological trauma, and overlooking the impact of early life exposure to psychological trauma or chronic trauma. Freud subsequently, for a short period of time, considered childhood sexual abuse as the main cause of hysteria in his female patients, thereby overlooking other forms of childhood trauma (*see:* **Freud, Sigmund**). During World War I, many French and British military physicians relied on Charcot's writings and regarded so-called shell shock cases as similar to his *traumatic hysteria,* that is, as the product of a constitutional weakness in the soldier that was worsened—but not caused—by exposure to war traumatizing events and the vehement emotions they evoked.

In 1886, Charcot acknowledged that trauma's emotional effects involved a "dissociation of the mental unity of the ego," in which certain "psychological centers" of the individual operate without the awareness or control of other "centers" (*see:* **Dissociation**). At the same time, Pierre Janet developed this dissociation theory in much greater detail (*see:* **Janet, Pierre**).

REFERENCES

Micale, M. S. (2001). Jean-Martin Charcot and *les névroses traumatiques:* From medicine to culture in French trauma theory of the late 19th century. In M. S. Micale & P. Lerner (Eds.), *Traumatic pasts* (pp. 115–139). Cambridge: Cambridge University Press.

Trillat, E. (1986). *Histoire de l'hystérie.* Paris: Seghers.

RECOMMENDED READING

Charcot, J.-M. (1991). *Clinical lectures on diseases of the nervous system* (edited with an introduction by Ruth Harris). London: Routledge. (Original work published 1887)

ONNO VAN DER HART
Utrecht University

See also: Dissociation; Freud, Sigmund; History of Psychological Trauma; Hysteria; Janet, Pierre

CHILD DEVELOPMENT

Children have historically occupied a disproportionately small place in the psychological trauma literature despite the commonality of childhood trauma as seen, for example, in studies from the United States that show that two-thirds of children have experienced at least one traumatic event. Of these traumatized children, 13% develop some posttraumatic stress disorder (PTSD) symptoms (Copeland, Keeler, Angold, & Costello, 2007). The data from other less-developed countries and cultures reflect an even more dramatic situation, with substantially higher prevalence of both exposure to psychological trauma and PTSD (e.g., Seedat, Nyamai, Nienga, Vythilingum, & Stein, 2005). Nevertheless, in the past, there has been denial and disbelief regarding childhood psychological trauma and its effects as well as professional skepticism with respect to the development of PTSD-type symptoms in healthy, trauma-exposed children. These attitudes have mostly changed, and currently interest in and research on psychological trauma and its effects on child development, while still in its infancy compared to studies with traumatized adults, are flourishing.

What Is Childhood Psychological Trauma?

A traumatic event for young children has been defined as any direct or witnessed event that threatened his or her own and/or his or her caregiver's physical and/or emotional integrity. However, even though many children encounter potentially traumatic events, most children are resilient. The level of personal distress that a child feels after a potentially traumatic event is determined by a number of factors, including the influence of the parents or the caregivers, the child's personal characteristics and the contextual and environmental factors.

Only a small number of children who are exposed to traumatic events develop more than a few generally transient PTSD-related symptoms (Copeland et al., 2007). However, children exposed to psychological trauma have almost twice the rate of mental disorders as those not exposed—particularly anxiety, depression, and behavioral disorders and, in adolescence, substance abuse disorders and risk-taking behaviors (Pat-Horenczyk et al., 2007).

Prognosis is generally favorable after a single incident of childhood psychological trauma; however, children experiencing multiple traumatic events have an increased probability of adverse posttraumatic reactions. In addition, an overview of epidemiological studies points to the differential rates of posttraumatic distress after different types of traumatic experiences. Natural disasters, traffic accidents, and medical illness are unfortunately relatively common in the lives of children, but do not often lead to severe or persistent PTSD or psychiatric disorders, while the less common experience of being exposed directly to war, life-threatening domestic or community violence, or maltreatment and neglect are more likely to result in PTSD or other psychiatric or behavioral disorders. Sexual abuse, especially within the family, results in the highest rates of PTSD (Gabbay, Oatis, Silva, & Hirsch, 2004).

Clinical Diagnosis of Childhood PTSD

The diagnosis of childhood PTSD was only recently recognized as differing from adult PTSD. In fact it was not until the publication of the *DSM-III-R* (American Psychiatric Association, 1987) that features of PTSD specific to children were included in order to account for the unique characteristics of children and adolescents and their developmental differences. The revised criteria for childhood PTSD include the occurrence of a traumatic event, along with manifestation of symptoms from each of the following categories: (a) Reexperiencing, with symptoms of either repetitive posttraumatic play, distress with reminders of the trauma, or dissociation episodes; (b) Numbing of responsiveness or interference with developmental momentum, with symptoms of either social withdrawal, restricted affect, or loss of skills; and (c) Increased arousal, with symptoms of either sleep disorder, short attention span, hypervigilance, or startle response.

Further attempts to adapt the PTSD diagnosis for young children have been suggested by Scheeringa, Zeanah, Myers, and Putnam (2003), who added an additional "developmental" cluster of PTSD symptoms for preschool children. Such symptoms include loss of developmental skills, new aggression, new separation anxiety, and unrelated fears.

Difficulties in diagnosing PTSD in children and adolescents can also be attributed to the parents', caregivers', teachers', and clinicians' failure to notice the extent of a child's response to a traumatic event. Parents or caregivers themselves may be dealing with the repercussions of the traumatic event that may make it difficult for them to fully recognize or accurately interpret changes in their children's emotions or behaviors following traumatic experiences. Teachers and clinicians only observe a sample of a child's emotional, social, and academic functioning which, although valuable when PTSD symptoms do show up in the school or clinic context, may not reflect the child's symptomatic difficulties in other settings and relationships. Thus, a cardinal rule for assessment and diagnosis of childhood PTSD is the collection of data from as many different adults who interact with the child (or did so in the past) as possible, in order to assemble the best picture of the child's prior development and the changes in behavior and functioning in multiple settings that may reflect PTSD.

Development and Trauma

Developmental issues revolving around age, experience, and cognitive ability also are important to consider when assessing or diagnosing PTSD in children and adolescents. The developmental stage of a child plays a crucial role in the way a child or adolescent perceives and responds to a given traumatic event. This knowledge has allowed professionals to realize that children of all ages respond to traumatic events, though perhaps in a way different from that of adults. Children normally have differing types and levels of age-appropriate fears, which have been seen to correlate with the variety of responses to specific stressors seen in infants, school-aged children, and adolescents. For instance, verbal descriptions appear to be difficult for young children to express and therefore traumatized young children may present more behavioral and developmental problems such as fears, separation anxiety, sleep disturbances, and posttraumatic play (i.e., playing out scenarios in which they repeat themes of traumatic events).

There is also controversy surrounding the developmental stages at which exposure to a traumatic event is most critical. There is an effort to establish a working definition of a new childhood psychiatric diagnosis, developmental trauma disorder (DTD) (van der Kolk, 2005) that is being spearheaded by the National Child Traumatic Stress Network (NCTSN; www. nctsnet.org). As provisionally formulated, DTD specifically requires that a child is exposed to "developmentally adverse interpersonal trauma" (Ford, 2005), that is, to traumatic events that not only threaten a child's or caregiver's life or physical integrity but that also involve the disruption of relationships that are essential to the child's healthy development. DTD also requires that the child not simply experience fear or anxiety as in PTSD, but also (or instead) manifest serious problems in the two fundamental benchmarks of healthy child psychological development—the ability to adapt psychologically and biologically to changing life circumstances (self-regulation; Ford, 2005), and the acquisition of expectations that enable the child to seek and find healthy relationships and activities with optimism and self-esteem. Thus, DTD represents a novel attempt to identify how psychological trauma can severely disrupt healthy child development.

Early Childhood

Until recently, the pervading scientific opinion was that infants do not understand or remember the significance of danger, and therefore cannot develop symptoms of PTSD. More recent studies based on literature reviews have asserted that: (a) infants may have the ability to perceive and remember traumatic events and develop symptoms that are similar to those exhibited by older children and adults with PTSD, and (b) the developmental skills of the infant affect the phenomenology of the infant's reactions as well as the extent to which events become traumatic (Scheeringa & Zeanah, 2001). PTSD-like reactions have been reported through clinical observations of preschoolers following traumatic events such as a car accident, witnessing a parent being murdered, experiencing physical or sexual abuse, being exposed to terrorist attacks, or natural disasters.

Mid-Childhood and Adolescence

The reactions of older children and adolescents are often different from those of young children because the former have acquired self-regulation abilities and healthy expectations, which have not yet emerged fully in early childhood. It is also not uncommon for older children to exhibit delayed onset of PTSD many years after a traumatic event. Additionally, older children and adolescents may develop PTSD without being directly exposed to the traumatic event; for example, media coverage and indirect exposure (such as the death of a close relative or friend, even if not directly witnessed) may be enough to prompt the onset of PTSD (Pfefferbaum, Pfefferbaum, North, & Neas, 2002). In addition, adolescents may show signs of depression and psychological withdrawal, and may engage in more acting-out and risk-taking behaviors. Adolescents and older children also may be stimulated by psychological trauma to seek revenge, engage in defiant or even violent behaviors, or to seek an escape from traumatic stress symptoms, through social withdrawal, substance abuse, or self-harm. These posttraumatic reactions occur in younger children, but far less commonly than in older children or adolescents.

Risk and Protective Factors

Researchers are now not only focusing on risk factors leading to PTSD, but also on identifying the protective and resiliency factors that may enable children to be relatively immune to or to rapidly recover from the shock and distress caused by psychological trauma. Child and adolescent research has suggested that, in addition to the severity and immediacy of the traumatic experiences themselves, risk factors and protective factors such as age, gender, level of development at the time of exposure to traumatic events, personal characteristics, family and social support, and cultural characteristics all appear to have an effect on the extent and severity of PTSD symptoms displayed by children and adolescents (Pat-Horenczyk, Rabinowitz, Rice, & Tucker-Levin, in press). Research suggests that children and adolescents with easy-going temperaments, high intellectual ability, a positive family environment, internal locus of control, socioeconomic advantage, and supportive relationships with peers, family members, and other adults are at less risk than other children of developing PTSD symptoms. Trust, optimism, and lack of guilt are positive characteristics that also may be linked to resilience against the development of PTSD symptoms. On the contrary, feelings of guilt, helplessness, and pessimism among children and adolescents may act as risk factors that increase the likelihood of the occurrence of PTSD symptoms.

Children are less likely than adults to experience a potentially traumatic event in the context of otherwise normal or noncorrosive circumstances. Unlike adults who are more often affected by a single occurrence of a traumatic event, traumatic events that affect children are more frequently ongoing events, such as ongoing physical or sexual abuse. Ongoing traumatic experiences tend to lead the person to have both high levels of physical proximity and emotional proximity (which is greatest in events that involve having a loved one cause or suffer from the traumatic events, or die or be lost to the child as a result). Physical and emotional proximity have been shown to play an important role in increasing the likelihood that PTSD will occur; thus, children often are at higher risk for PTSD than adults, not because children are less resilient but because they often are subject to a greater traumatic shock than are many of the adults who experience psychological trauma.

The role of ethnicity is difficult to study because definitions of race and ethnicity vary and because there are many confounding variables, such as socioeconomic status. Regardless, research has suggested that culture and ethnicity may serve as either a risk factor or as a protective factor when children are exposed to psychological trauma. Ethnic and cultural differences in beliefs about how to handle emotional disturbances can influence the way in which children and their family, friends, and clinicians react to traumatic stressors and interpret traumatic stress reactions.

Individual characteristics have also been shown to play a large role in the development of PTSD in children and adolescents. A child's trauma history can be an important

determinant of their response to trauma. Like adults, children who have previously been exposed to a traumatic event are at greater risk of developing PTSD upon being exposed to trauma again. Intelligence and self-efficacy also appear to be protective against the development of PTSD. Higher intelligence among youths appears to enhance their coping strategies, resilience, and adjustment processes against developing PTSD symptoms. Self-efficacy is the belief in one's ability to deal effectively with a specific situation. Adolescents with PTSD, have significantly lower self-efficacy than more resilient adolescents who do not show signs of PTSD.

Age and developmental level have also been perceived to greatly affect a child's resiliency and vulnerability to developing PTSD. Studies suggest that older children, who have the cognitive ability to truly recognize the significance and meaning of a trauma, are ultimately at a higher risk for developing PTSD. However, while some studies imply that adolescents are at higher risk, others indicate that younger children are at higher risk. Thus, it appears that age is not an independent risk factor, but interacts with other factors in determining the risk of PTSD, such as familial variables and the nature of the psychological trauma.

In regard to gender, child and adolescent research has shown that gender affects symptom development. Studies have found that girls have a higher propensity to develop PTSD than boys, which may be related to coping style differences between male and females. However, both boys and girls may be affected by traumatic stressors, but in different ways. For example, after a natural disaster or sexual abuse, girls tend to manifest more symptoms related to emotional processing (depression, anxiety) while boys experience symptoms related to cognitive or behavior factors (aggression, antisocial behavior). The types of psychological trauma children and adolescents are exposed to also appear to differ between genders. For example, sexual abuse is more common for females, while physical abuse appears more prevalent for males.

Children's Relationships and the Impact of Psychological Trauma

Parents and Attachment

It is quite clear that parents and the nature of the parent-child relationship are the most crucial risk or protective factor for children exposed to traumatic events. Attachment serves as the mechanism through which parents affect their children's sense of "felt security" when they feel threatened, vulnerable, or distressed. It is through the attachment relationship with a primary caregiver (usually the mother) that a child learns to organize and regulate his or her emotional experiences— an ability shown to be an important factor in healthy psychological development. Of great help in this process is the caregiver's skill in reflecting the infant's emotions and in representing them symbolically. Many researchers believe that the attachment relationship is so important that its role should be explicitly incorporated into conceptualizations of PTSD in young children (Ford, 2005).

The power of parental attachment and bonding may be seen in light of the role it may play in strengthening resilience and countering the negative effects of problems in the family and/ or community. Specifically, it has been suggested that a warm, nurturing, and supportive relationship with at least one parent, may protect against, or mitigate, the effects of family adversity in general, and psychological trauma specifically. This in turn has been shown to be a predictor of self-acceptance and a relationship with a trusted confidant as a teen (Bifulco, in press). Parents who are emotionally available teach their children emotion regulation and coping skills. Children of parents who are supportive are less likely to experience negative emotions or negative behavior with peers. It is also through this relationship that children learn to organize and regulate their emotional experiences.

The importance of the parental relationship can also be seen in instances in which parents' exhibit health problems. Mental illness in parents is highly correlated with various developmental problems in childhood. A possible explanation for this phenomenon is that parental psychopathology is likely to endanger the quality of parent-child attachment, and parents with difficulties in providing their children with secure attachment tend to have children who are at risk for psychopathology in preschool, middle childhood, and adolescence. It has also been well established that maternal PTSD symptoms have a significant effect on infants' behavior and their ability to develop secure attachments. Conversely, parental social competence is thought to be an important protective factor for children, buffering them from stressors and helping to prevent serious emotional and behavior problems in the child's later life.

Parents and children exposed to the same traumatic event show a significant correlation between the intrusive thoughts and avoidance symptoms of the mothers and the severity of PTSD in young children. This relationship does not persist in older children, suggesting that younger children are more vulnerable because they are more dependent on parental protective factors. School-aged children and adolescents are more advanced in their ability to cognitively process events and regulate affect. There is a significant correlation between the severity of the parent's distress and symptoms and the severity of the child's distress and symptoms when there is a concurrent exposure of parents and children to a traumatic event.

Other Protective Relationships

Parents are not the only ones who can offer a protective relationship to children. First responders, such as police officers, emergency management teams, or firefighters, and other significant adults such as child-care providers, are effective as adult attachment figures. These first responders, who reach out to young children in distress, may take on the role of "angels," providing an alternate response to that of an ineffective parent. They may help children internalize a positive working model of self, building a sense that there may be other people in their lives whom they can trust to be available at difficult times. Another possible explanation for the effectiveness of first responders is that encounters with first responders may bring to mind the more positive experiences young children have had with primary attachment figures earlier in their lives. The most important protective resource is a strong relationship with a competent, caring, positive adult, who is most often a parent but can also be another trusted person.

Transgenerational Effects of Trauma

Significant evidence has pointed to the transgenerational effects of PTSD in the parent on the child. Most knowledge concerning this is taken from clinical reports and research on families of Holocaust survivors and Vietnam veterans. Several mechanisms have been proposed to explain the relationship between the symptoms of a trauma-exposed parent and those of a child lacking direct trauma experience. One mechanism, called the "conspiracy of silence," occurs when the child senses the parent's vulnerability and makes every effort to avoid providing any stimulus that will hurt or remind the parent of the trauma. At the same time, the parent might be afraid to burden the child with his harsh stories. In this way, the silence becomes a barrier between parent and child and prevents the child from receiving help or consolation from the parent. A second possible mechanism is emotional flooding, which occurs when parents reveal too much and explain their experiences in detail to their children, who become overwhelmed by their inability to handle the information. A third mechanism is called identification, which occurs when the child is repeatedly exposed to the parents' posttraumatic behavior and comes to identify with the parental role as victim and to mimic the parents' traumatic stress-related behaviors.

In addition to these possible psychological explanations, a biological one called *epigenesis* has been proposed. Epigenesis refers to changes in how genes affect a person's physical and psychological attributes as the person grows older. Epigenetic changes result from physical maturation and life experiences: they are a product of the person's genetic inheritance ("nature") and environment ("nurture"). Thus, epigenetic changes are heritable, that is, can be passed from one generation to the next, both based on the genes a child is born with and the child's life experiences. Epigenetic changes affect the person's physical and emotional health (called the "phenotype"), but occur without a change in the sequence of building blocks (DNA) that make up the person's genes (called the "genotype"). With respect to PTSD, recent studies have shown evidence of transgenerational transmission of a risk factor for PTSD—reduced resting cortisol levels—in the babies of mothers with PTSD due to the September 11, 2001, terrorist incidents and in the adult offspring of Holocaust survivors with PTSD (Yehuda & Bierer, 2007). The fact that this alteration in the body's stress response system was observed not only in adulthood, but also as early as the first year of life in babies, suggests that it may be at least in part genetically transferred. While the possibility that PTSD may be transmitted genetically across generations either by the altered gene functioning or by learned experiences is intriguing, it is important to recall that none of these hypothesized mechanisms of intergenerational effects of PTSD have conclusive empirical support.

In the case of psychological mechanisms, the proposals are not intended to place blame on parents as the "cause" of their children's difficulties with PTSD. Instead, they reflect researchers' and clinicians' observations that in spite of parents' best intents and efforts, when parents face the challenge of PTSD, their children may be adversely affected. In most cases, the child is *not* traumatized by the parent, unless the parent is directly abusive or severely neglectful of the child. Rather, the child learns to adapt to the parent's stress reactions. This can be disruptive to the child's development because the child must focus on managing stress reactions rather than focusing on the ordinary challenges that face all children as they grow up. Although these children often are adept at handling stressful situations in life, their biological and emotional stress response systems can become depleted, leaving them susceptible to PTSD should they experience psychological traumas of their own in childhood or adulthood.

Conclusion

General interest in the traumatic stress field has burgeoned, but studies of how children cope with and recover from psychological trauma are just beginning to gain momentum. The development of specific interventions for traumatized children has not received the major attention it deserves. The emphasis has been on extrapolating from clinical experience and research on adults exposed to psychological trauma. This is not a sound basis for drawing conclusions about trauma and child development. Instead, both research and clinical practice—including assessment, diagnosis, and treatment of traumatic stress-related disorders in childhood—must be done directly with children and must take into account normal developmental stages, as well as individual risk and protective factors.

In such research, the age and developmental level of the child at the time of exposure to traumatic stressors must be considered as well as the nature of family functioning and the quality of attachment relationships provided by the child's caregivers. The effect of trauma exposure, particularly ongoing psychological trauma and traumatic stress reactions (such as occurs when child abuse or domestic, community, or war violence continue for months or years) on development from infancy through adolescence, and into adulthood as well, must be explored. The requirements for diagnosing PTSD and other traumatic stress disorders, and the tools used to clinically assess these conditions, must be adapted to fit the developmental achievements and challenges facing children at different points from infancy through adolescence. Risk factors that increase the probability of a pathological response and protective factors that decrease this probability need to be identified and their underlying processes understood specifically for children. Finally, systematic research is needed to elucidate how children not only cope but grow and thrive after exposure to psychological trauma.

REFERENCES

American Psychiatric Association. (1987). *Diagnostic and statistical manual of mental disorders* (3rd ed., rev.). Washington, DC: Author.

Bifulco, A. (in press). Risk and resilience in young Londoners. In D. Brom, R. Pat-Horenczyk, & J. D. Ford (Eds.), *Treating traumatized children: Risk, resilience and recovery*. Oxford, England: Routledge.

Copeland, W. E., Keeler, G., Angold, A., & Costello, E. J. (2007). Traumatic events and posttraumatic stress in childhood. *Archives of General Psychiatry, 64,* 577–584.

Ford, J. D. (2005). Treatment implications of altered neurobiology, affect regulation and information processing following child maltreatment. *Psychiatric Annals, 35,* 410–419.

Gabbay, V., Oatis, M. D., Silva, R. R., & Hirsch, G. S. (2004). Epidemiological aspects of PTSD in children and adolescents. In R. R. Silva (Ed.), *Posttraumatic stress disorders in children and adolescents* (pp. 1–17). New York: Norton.

Pat-Horenczyk, R., Peled, O., Miron, T., Villa, Y., Brom, D., & Chemtob, C. M. (2007). Risk-taking behaviors among Israeli adolescents exposed to recurrent terrorism. *American Journal of Psychiatry, 164*(1), 66–72.

Pat-Horenczyk, R., Rabinowitz, R., Rice, A., & Tucker-Levin, A. (in press). The search for risk and protective factors in childhood PTSD: From variables to processes. In D. Brom, R. Pat-Horenczyk, & J. D. Ford (Eds.), *Treating traumatized children: Risk, resilience and recovery*. Oxford, England: Routledge.

Pfefferbaum, B., Pfefferbaum, R. L., North, C. S., & Neas, B. R. (2002). Does television viewing satisfy criteria for exposure in posttraumatic stress disorder? *Psychiatry, 65,* 306–309.

Scheeringa, M. S., & Zeanah, C. H. (2001). A relational perspective on PTSD in infancy. *Journal of Traumatic Stress, 14,* 799–815.

Scheeringa, M. S., Zeanah, C. H., Myers, L., & Putnam, F. W. (2003). New findings on alternative criteria for PTSD in preschool children. *Journal of the American Academy of Child and Adolescent Psychiatry, 42,* 561–570.

Seedat, S., Nyamai, C., Nienga, F., Vythilingum, B., & Stein, B. (2005). Trauma exposure and post-traumatic stress symptoms in urban African schools: Survey in Cape Town and Nairobi. *British Journal of Psychiatry, 184,* 169–175.

van der Kolk, B. (2005). Developmental trauma disorder. *Psychiatric Annals, 35,* 439–448.

Yehuda, R., & Bierer, L. M. (2007). Transgenerational transmission of cortisol and PTSD risk. *Progress in Brain Research, 1*(167), 121–135.

Ruth Pat-Horenczyk
Hebrew University of Jerusalem

See also: Adolescence; Attachment; Epidemiology; Etiology; Family Systems; Gender; Resilience

CHILD MALTREATMENT

Child maltreatment is the broad term for the phenomena of child abuse and neglect. The U.S. Child Abuse Prevention and Treatment Act (CAPTA; Pub. L. 93-247) in 1974 established child maltreatment as a national public policy issue. Since that time, its reauthorization as the Keeping Children and Families Safe Act of 2003 (Pub. L. 108-36) provides federal funding to U.S. states and established minimum standards and record keeping systems to track child maltreatment nationally. The federal standards include "at a minimum, any recent act or failure to act on the part of a parent or caretaker, which results in death, serious physical or emotional harm, sexual abuse or exploitation, or an act or failure to act which presents an imminent risk of serious harm" (Pub. L. 108-36; 42 U.S.C.A., 5106g). All 50 states have laws that require suspected child abuse and neglect be reported to Child Protective Services (CPS). Each state has its own interpretation of this federal definition, however, and the policies and legal criteria that have been developed across states are inconsistent.

Developing definitional criteria for child maltreatment has involved complex issues. Cultural factors play a role in determining whether particular practices are considered to be maltreatment. One approach to defining child abuse and neglect is to view parenting behaviors on a continuum ranging from effective and nurturing parenting to inappropriate parenting practices, with maltreating behaviors as the extreme end of the inappropriate portion of the continuum. Parenting behaviors may be difficult to quantify, however, and thresholds for distinguishing between effective and inappropriate parenting, or between mildly to moderately inappropriate parenting and maltreatment, are difficult to determine.

Subtypes of Maltreatment

Although definitions vary, four types of maltreatment are generally recognized. Multiple subtype occurrence is frequent. *Physical Abuse* generally refers to nonaccidental physical injuries. *Sexual abuse* includes sexual contact between a child and an adult or someone at least several years older.

Whereas abuse is thought of as acts of commission (i.e., actions that are directly harmful), *Physical neglect* can include many different acts of omission (i.e., failures to take necessary actions). Failing to meet children's physical needs may include absence of food, clothing, shelter, adequate hygiene, medical, dental, education, or mental health care. Often neglect is difficult to differentiate from the effects of poverty, however. Inadequate supervision, such as leaving young children home alone, is frequently reported, but no clear standards exist regarding what constitutes appropriate supervision, and supervision requirements vary by children's age or developmental level and behavior.

Although all types of maltreatment have psychological implications, emotional or psychological maltreatment includes acts that specifically involve psychological harm by a persistent or extreme thwarting of children's basic emotional needs, including needs for psychological safety and security, acceptance and positive self-concept, and age-appropriate autonomy. It is often difficult to differentiate poor parenting or family dysfunction from emotional abuse.

Examples of emotional maltreatment include persistent and severe belittling, humiliating, exposure to violence and chaotic environments, threatening, exploiting, or lack of emotional responsiveness.

Classification of Maltreatment

Other dimensions of maltreatment also are important to consider. Age of onset, duration, frequency, and chronicity affect the impact that maltreatment has on children's development. For example, early onset and chronic maltreatment (e.g., physical abuse beginning in infancy and continuing through late childhood) have been linked with more maladaptive outcomes. Severity may influence children's responses, although even milder forms of abuse and neglect are likely to have detrimental consequences.

Additional dimensions of maltreatment include the relationship of the child to the perpetrator, separations such as foster care resulting from the incident, and treatment or response to the incident. For example, degree of familiarity with the perpetrator and number of perpetrators have been associated with rates of psychological symptomatology for sexual abuse victims. While foster placement may be necessary to ensure child safety, children in foster care often have high rates of physical and mental health problems. Although many maltreated children do not receive services to address their traumatic stress-related needs, supportive responses by caring adults and availability of treatment to ameliorate symptomatology can result in positive outcomes for child victims.

Significance of the Problem

The U.S. Congress mandated National Incidence Studies (NIS) to examine the scope of the problem of child maltreatment. Definitions included two levels of severity: a "Harm Standard" and an "Endangerment Standard." The Harm Standard included more stringent criteria requiring demonstrable harm to the child, whereas the Endangerment Standard was more inclusive of abuse or neglect that placed children at risk of harm. The NIS-3 (Sedlak & Broadhurst, 1996) found that 1.5 million children were maltreated according to the Harm Standard (an incidence rate of 23.1 per 1,000), and 2.8 million were classified according to the Endangerment Standard (41.9/1,000). Other findings were that children of single parents, those from large families, and those from low-income families were at greater risk. These families tend to experience more stressors (e.g., divorce, losses, unemployment, stigma) and have fewer or more strained resources (e.g., poverty, reduced availability of parent[s] to their children, less social support) than more conventional dual parent families with fewer children to care for and higher incomes. Thus, it is not clear that family structure or size per se places children at risk for maltreatment as opposed to the stressors or resource limitations that face some families (see following discussion).

National data from CPS are compiled annually in the National Child Abuse and Neglect Data System (NCANDS; USDHHS, 2007). In 2005, 3.3 million CPS referrals were received on alleged maltreatment of 6.0 million children (48.3/1,000). Of these, 899,000 children were substantiated as victims of maltreatment. The most common form was neglect (62.8%), followed by physical abuse (16.6%), sexual abuse (9.3%), and emotional maltreatment (7.1%). The highest victimization rate and the majority of fatalities occurred for children under age four. Only a small percentage of maltreatment was perpetrated by someone outside of the family (79.4% of maltreatment cases involved parents and 6.8% other family members). Because these statistics are derived from incidents in the child welfare system, they likely underestimate the extent of maltreatment that occurs nationally.

Etiology of Maltreatment

Early perspectives on the causes of child maltreatment focused on unidimensional factors, such as parental psychopathology or poverty. Current theories underscore a complex interplay among multiple levels of risk and protective factors that contribute to the etiology of child maltreatment. At the broadest macrocultural level, risk factors include societal acceptance of violence, high poverty rates for children, and absence of sufficient familial supports. Within neighborhoods and communities, unemployment and violence impact families via exposure to multiple stressors that erode the resources needed to support children. In high poverty areas, difficulty in obtaining resources for children's basic needs may increase rates of neglect. Cultural attitudes toward child-rearing practices, such as acceptance of corporal punishment, may influence the likelihood of maltreatment.

At the level of family dynamics, domestic violence, social isolation, and parenting difficulties heighten risk for maltreatment. In contrast, support from extended family members, positive parent-child relationships, and marital harmony protect against maltreatment. Parental history of maltreatment, psychopathology, substance abuse, and parenting deficits increase risk for maltreatment. The balance of risk and protective factors that impinge on families influences the likelihood that maltreatment will occur.

Consequences of Child Maltreatment

Child abuse and neglect impact children's abilities to master stage-salient tasks in the unfolding process of their development. Children who have experienced maltreatment in one development period may have fewer resources to address subsequent developmental challenges or additional stressors. Research has demonstrated negative consequences of maltreatment across numerous areas of development, but there are many different pathways of adaptation, and maltreated children display a range of functioning.

Emotional Development

Even early in infancy, maltreated children demonstrate differences in their expression of negative emotions. Maltreated children have difficulty accurately identifying, verbalizing, and regulating their emotions. For example, maltreated children may be hypersensitive to anger cues. Physically abused children are more reactive to anger that they observe in others, and they may respond with heightened fear, distractibility, aggressive behaviors, and emotional insecurity. Attentional processes, such as poor concentration and overactivity, often are demonstrated by maltreated children, and these difficulties may interact with forms of maladaptive social information processing, such as a heightened sensitivity to anger, to increase the risk of reactive aggressive behavior by maltreated children.

Social and Self-Development

Maltreatment exerts a negative impact on the interpersonal development of maltreated children. In the first year of life, the development of a secure attachment relationship with a primary caregiver is an essential developmental task that sets the stage for the many other important skills in future relationships and in exploration of the environment necessary for cognitive development. Maltreated children frequently form insecure attachment relationships. Although attachment security can change over time, the insecure attachment relationships of maltreated children often persist. These stable, highly dysfunctional relationships place maltreated children at extreme disadvantage in other areas. For example, insecure attachment relationships are associated with self-development, such that children who do not feel loved may view themselves as unlovable. Maltreatment may disrupt self-system processes, such as the development of independent functioning, identification and expression of internal states, self-knowledge, and positive self-concept. Maltreated children have been found to exhibit low self-esteem and higher rates of problems with self-integration such as dissociation (*see:* **Cognitive Integration, Biopsychosocial; Dissociation**).

Maltreated children also have difficulty in nonfamilial social relationships, including lower social competence and less acceptance by peers. Maltreated children's peer relationships are characterized by increased rates of aggression and withdrawn behavior. Maltreated children often learn roles of both victim and victimizer and exhibit increased bullying behavior and are victimized more frequently. Maltreated and neglected children's behavior problems also contribute to difficulty in school, and they are more likely to receive suspensions and disciplinary referrals. Additionally, they demonstrate poor academic performance, receive lower grades, perform more poorly on standardized tests, and more frequently are retained in grade. Problematic relationships are also often evident when maltreated children interact with teachers.

Psychopathology

Child maltreatment has been linked with increased rates of psychopathology over time. Individuals maltreated as children have higher rates of affective symptomatology, attention deficit hyperactivity disorder, oppositional defiant disorder, posttraumatic stress disorder, juvenile delinquency, personality disorders, substance abuse, anxiety disorders, and a greater number of lifetime stressors.

Physiological Processes

Maltreatment can disrupt physiological processes related to optimal physical and mental health. Burgeoning research on biological processes and brain development has begun to examine the physiological consequences of chronic stress associated with maltreatment, but much remains to be explained. Neuroimaging studies have found differences in the brain development and functioning of maltreated children, including deviations in volume, blood flow, hemispheric symmetry, and activation of specific brain areas. However, not all maltreated children evidence the same patterns of neurobiological structure and function. The timing of maltreatment likely plays a role in how abuse and neglect affect brain development. While evidence is still emerging, existing research suggests that

early onset and longer duration of maltreatment have the most negative effects on the developing brain (DeBellis et al., 1999). Abuse or neglect may alter the development of the brain's neurons, the differentiation of these cells, mechanisms by which the brain processes information, and regulatory systems for managing stress. Maltreatment at one point in development may begin a cascading process, affecting the structures and maturation in the brain that then impacts other processes in arousal, attention, emotion regulation, and stress management.

Brain activation in response to emotional stimuli has been found to differ for maltreated and nonmaltreated children. Exposure to psychological trauma may impact how the brain processes information, how memories are stored, deeply held beliefs that contribute to shaping personality development and relationships, and how children understand emotions in subsequent situations.

In response to maltreatment, stress reactions can alter activation of physiological systems, such as those in the brain's hypothalamic-pituitary-adrenal (HPA) axis, but maltreatment does not affect development uniformly. Several factors determine responses to stress, including genetics, early experiences, physical and mental health, and ongoing life circumstances. Changes in hormones levels, such as cortisol, as found in maltreated children, reflect disruptions in regulatory processes associated with chronic stress. Maltreatment experiences in combination with symptoms of PTSD or depression are associated with greater changes in the biological stress response systems than those seen in nonmaltreated children or in maltreated children without mental health symptomatology.

Genetic variations also may interact with maltreatment to influence individual differences. Stressful life events may be more likely to result in psychopathology in individuals with certain genetic characteristics. The combination of maltreatment and gene variations may result in maladaptive behavior patterns. Genes regulating brain neurotransmitters may be activated in stressful circumstances, such that maltreated individuals with certain gene variations appear to be more likely to develop conduct disorder, antisocial personality disorder, or depression in later life. Social support can function as an environmental protective factor. Thus, even for individuals who experience maltreatment and have higher genetic risk, protective processes and supports can promote resilient functioning and positive outcomes.

Costs Associated with Maltreatment

The negative consequences of maltreatment across multiple domains of functioning result in considerable cost, not only to victimized individuals, but also to society as a whole. In 2001, Prevent Child Abuse America estimated that $94 billion is spent annually in the United States on direct and indirect expenses associated with child maltreatment. Direct costs include child welfare and law enforcement expenses and costs associated with increased medical and mental health needs of abused and neglected children. Indirect costs are associated with longer-term outcomes such as increases in special education, health care, and juvenile delinquency services over time, as well as the lost productivity of victims. Despite these high costs of victimization, the amount of federal money allocated to child maltreatment nationally amounts to only about $10 per affected individual, a number dwarfed by much larger investments in other public health issues.

Resilience

Although substantial research documents extreme adversity and chronic stress for maltreated children across multiple developmental domains, not all affected individuals demonstrate maladaptive outcomes. Resilience, as defined by the capacity to function competently despite this adversity, although uncommon, has been demonstrated, especially for maltreated children with at least average intellectual performance and with positive relationships with at least one caring adult. Self-reliance, including protective effects of high self-esteem, internal locus of control for good events, ego-resiliency, and ego-overcontrol,

was more predictive of resilience for maltreated than for nonmaltreated children. This may be because maltreatment requires children to cope with extreme stressors or the absence of parental or familial caring and support, such that resilience is necessary not only to develop in a healthy manner but simply to survive physically and emotionally. This is different than the common belief that adversity strengthens or inoculates children against later difficulties because maltreatment does not appear to make children stronger or less susceptible to problems. Instead, maltreated children who have internal or external resources that enable them to be resilient must rely more heavily on those resources than children who are not maltreated.

Intervention and Prevention

Home visitation programs have shown promise in preventing child maltreatment. Nurse home visitation with young, low-income, first-time mothers from pregnancy through age two resulted in several positive outcomes, including fewer repeat pregnancies and increased self-sufficiency. Evaluation results when children were 15 years old revealed that maltreatment rates were significantly lower for the intervention group (Olds et al., 1997). Parents as Teachers (PAT) also has demonstrated reductions in maltreatment rates for participants (Behrman, 1999). Other home visitation programs have demonstrated varying rates of success in reducing child maltreatment.

Because of limitations in parenting skills in maltreating families, many intervention approaches have focused on teaching parenting skills. One such approach (Parent-Child Interaction Therapy, PCIT) utilizes a bug-in-the-ear tool to give feedback to parents during interactions with their children. Evaluation of PCIT yielded lower rates of subsequent reports to CPS (Chaffin et al., 2004). Other parenting skills training programs have been found to be effective in increasing positive parenting behavior, but many have not been evaluated specifically with respect to maltreatment outcomes.

Other approaches to child maltreatment prevention have focused on improving parent-child attachment relationships. Interventions derived from attachment theory, such as child-parent psychotherapy, have shown promise in improving relationship security that may promote more positive functioning. Some therapeutic approaches have focused on ameliorating the functioning of child victims. Cognitive-behavioral approaches for trauma and abuse victims have demonstrated improvements in children's functioning.

Because maltreated children's lives take a variety of courses that are influenced by many complex risk and resilience factors, multiple approaches to intervention and prevention may be necessary to decrease incidence and prevalence of child maltreatment. These approaches need to integrate risk and protective factors occurring at multiple levels of functioning to have a significant impact. However, simple approaches, such as training on "stranger danger," appear to be of limited benefit, in part because most maltreatment is perpetrated by adults who are known to the child.

Conclusion

Maltreatment affects a large number of children and can result in long-term consequences across multiple areas of functioning. Cost estimates underscore the necessity of prevention and early intervention approaches to reduce negative sequelae and promote resilient functioning for affected individuals. Research and clinical advances hold promise for yielding additional avenues for addressing this complex and significant phenomenon.

REFERENCES

Behrman, R. E. (Ed.). (1999). Home visiting: Recent program evaluations. *Future of Children, 9* (1).

Chaffin, M., Silovsky, J. F., Funderburk, B., Valle, L. A., Brestan, E. V., Balachova, T., et al. (2004). Parent-child interaction therapy with physically abusive parents: Efficacy for reducing future abuse reports. *Journal of Consulting and Clinical Psychology, 72,* 500–510.

Child Abuse Prevention and Treatment Act (CAPTA), PL. 93-247, U.S.C. Title 42, Chapter 67 (1974).

DeBellis, M. D., Keshavan, M., Clark, D., Casey, B. J., Giedd, J., Boring, A., et al. (1999). Developmental traumatology: Pt. II. Brain development. *Biological Psychiatry, 45,* 1271–1284.

Keeping Children and Families Safe Act, PL. 108-36, U.S.C. Title 42, 5106 (2003).

Olds, D. L., Eckenrode, J., Henderson, C. R., Kitzman, H., Powers, J., Cole, R., et al. (1997). Long-term effects of home visitation on maternal life course and child abuse and neglect: 15-year follow-up of a randomized trial. *Journal of the American Medical Association, 278,* 637–643.

Sedlak, A. J., & Broadhurst, D. D. (1996). *Third annual incidence study of child abuse and neglect: Final report.* Washington, DC: U.S. Department of Health and Human Services.

U.S. Department of Health and Human Services, Administration on Children, Youth, and Families. (2007). *Child maltreatment, 2005.* Washington, DC: U.S. Government Printing Office.

RECOMMENDED READING

Cicchetti, D., & Valentino, K. (2006). An ecological transactional perspective on child maltreatment: Failure of the average expectable environment and its influence upon child development. In D. Cicchetti & D. J. Cohen (Eds.), *Developmental psychopathology: Vol. 3. Risk, disorder, and adaptation* (2nd ed., pp. 129–201). Hoboken, NJ: Wiley.

JODY TODD MANLY
University of Rochester

See also: **Abuse, Child Physical; Abuse, Child Sexual; Biology, Brain Structure, and Function, Child; Biology, Neurochemistry; Domestic Violence; Genetics; Law Legislation, and Policy; Prevention, Child; Resilience**

CLASSIFICATION

See: **Diagnosis of Traumatic Stress Disorders (*DSM & ICD*); Posttraumatic Stress Disorder, Diagnosis of; Typology of Traumatic Stress Disorders**

CLINICIAN-ADMINISTERED PTSD SCALE

The Clinician-Administered PTSD Scale (CAPS; Blake et al., 1990, 1995) is a comprehensive structured interview for PTSD developed in 1989 at the National Center for PTSD. The CAPS was designed to address some of the limitations of existing interviews and to serve as a standard criterion measure for diagnosing PTSD and quantifying PTSD symptom severity.

The CAPS incorporates a number of features intended to enhance the reliability and validity of PTSD assessment. First, the CAPS assesses trauma exposure (using a checklist of potentially traumatic events, the Life Events Checklist; Gray, Litz, Wang, & Lombardo, 2004) and the 17 symptoms of PTSD, as well as four associated symptoms—response validity, overall symptom severity, degree of functional impairment, and degree of improvement since a previous evaluation.

Second, the CAPS assesses the frequency and intensity of each symptom on separate five-point rating scales, yielding continuous and dichotomous scores for individual symptoms, for the three symptom clusters, and for the full syndrome.

Third, CAPS items include behaviorally anchored prompt questions and rating scales to standardize the inquiry across interviewers and increase the reliability of severity ratings.

Fourth, the CAPS assesses current and lifetime endorsements of PTSD, providing specific guidelines for lifetime PTSD to ensure that the symptoms occurred as a syndrome during the same period lasting at least 1 month.

Fifth, for symptoms that are not inherently linked to a specific trauma (i.e., the emotional numbing and hyperarousal symptoms in the core PTSD syndrome, as well as the three dissociative symptoms in the associated features) the CAPS provides an explicit trauma-related inquiry and three-point rating scale to determine if they are attributable to the index trauma.

Finally, a number of rationally and empirically derived scoring rules have been developed and evaluated for converting continuous CAPS frequency and intensity scores into a dichotomous PTSD diagnosis (Weathers, Ruscio, & Keane, 1999).

The format of the CAPS has evolved substantially since it was first developed, both to keep pace with changes to the PTSD criteria and to incorporate user feedback (see Weathers, Keane, & Davidson, 2001 for a full discussion). The original CAPS was based on *DSM-III-R* (American Psychiatric Association, 1987) PTSD criteria. Following the *DSM-IV* (American Psychiatric Association, 1994) revision to the PTSD criteria in 1994, the CAPS was modified extensively. Key changes included adding a protocol for assessing trauma exposure (using the Life Events Checklist to assess Criterion A; see Gray, Litz, Wang, & Lombardo [2004] for an examination of its psychometric properties), rewording some of the intensity scale anchors, adding the trauma-related inquiry and rating scale, and replacing six of the eight original associated features.

Three more recent modifications are also of note. The first modification involves the elimination of the two versions of the CAPS and the creation of a single CAPS that can be used to rate symptoms over the past week or past month for current PTSD, or worst month since the trauma for lifetime PTSD. Originally there were two versions of the CAPS: (1) the CAPS-1 or CAPS-DX, which assessed symptoms over a 1-month interval, and (2) the CAPS-2 or CAPS-SX, which assessed symptoms over the past week and was intended for monitoring symptom status over brief intervals in treatment outcome trials. However, because of the different time referent, the frequency scores on the two versions were not directly comparable, making it difficult to compare or combine data across the two forms when both were used in the same study. Therefore, the versions were combined and the scoring procedure was modified so that the current combined version may be used to assess 1-month or 1-week intervals and yields comparable scores for either application.

The second modification involves the development and evaluation of the various CAPS diagnostic scoring rules noted earlier. The third modification involves the development of rationally derived severity score ranges for interpreting CAPS total severity scores. There are five specific categories and descriptors that can be used to characterize the clinical significance of a given CAPS total severity score: 0–19 = asymptomatic/few symptoms, 20–39 = mild PTSD/subthreshold, 40–59 = moderate PTSD/threshold, 60–79 = severe PTSD symptomatology, ≥80 = extreme PTSD symptomatology. In addition, a 15-point change in CAPS total severity score has been proposed as a marker of clinically significant change. At this point, the severity score ranges and 15-point marker are preliminary and await empirically evaluation, but they provide reasonable guidelines for interpreting CAPS severity scores and using the CAPS to measure change in PTSD symptom status.

As Weathers et al. (2001) have discussed in detail, the CAPS has been studied extensively and has excellent psychometric properties. It has proven useful for a wide range of clinical and research assessment tasks in a variety of trauma-exposed populations, and has become the most widely used structured interview for PTSD. The limitations of the CAPS are that it typically takes longer than other interviews to administer, and it requires more extensive training to become proficient in standard administration and scoring. The CAPS is available in a published version, which includes the interview booklet, an interviewer's guide, and a technical manual (Weathers et al., 2004). Qualified investigators may obtain a research version of the CAPS and an abbreviated manual from the National Center for PTSD.

REFERENCES

American Psychiatric Association. (1987). *Diagnostic and statistical manual of mental disorders* (3rd ed., rev.). Washington, DC: Author.

American Psychiatric Association. (1994). *Diagnostic and statistical manual of mental disorders* (4th ed.). Washington, DC: Author.

Blake, D. D., Weathers, F. W., Nagy, L. M., Kaloupek, D. G., Gusman, F. D., Charney, D. S., et al. (1995). The development of a clinician-administered PTSD scale. *Journal of Traumatic Stress, 8,* 75–90.

Blake, D. D., Weathers, F. W., Nagy, L. M., Kaloupek, D. G., Klauminzer, G., Charney, D. S., et al. (1990). A clinician rating scale for assessing current and lifetime PTSD: The CAPS-1. *Behavior Therapist, 13,* 187–188.

Gray, M. J., Litz, B. T., Wang, J., & Lombardo, T. W. (2004). Psychometric properties of the Life Events Checklist. *Assessment, 11,* 330–341.

Weathers, F. W., Keane, T. M., & Davidson, J. R. T. (2001). The Clinician-Administered PTSD Scale: A review of the first ten years of research. *Depression and Anxiety, 13,* 132–156.

Weathers, F. W., Newman, E., Blake, D. D., Nagy, L. M., Schnurr, P. P., Kaloupek, D. G., et al. (2004). *Clinician-Administered PTSD Scale (CAPS): Interviewer's guide.* Los Angeles: Western Psychological Services.

Weathers, F. W., Ruscio, A. M., & Keane, T. M. (1999). Psychometric properties of nine scoring rules for the Clinician-Administered Posttraumatic Stress Disorder Scale. *Psychological Assessment, 11,* 124–133.

FRANK W. WEATHERS
Auburn University

See also: Assessment, Psychometric, Adult; Diagnosis of Traumatic Stress Disorders (*DSM & ICD*); Posttraumatic Stress Disorder, Diagnosis of

COGNITIVE BEHAVIOR THERAPY, ADULT

The idea that to recover from a traumatic experience the survivor must face the memory of the psychological trauma and deal with the emotions and thoughts that are connected to it has long existed. The influence of this concept on treatment of trauma-related mental health disorders is evident in early analytic schools of psychotherapy as well as more contemporary therapy approaches. Cognitive behavior therapy (CBT) is an approach that directly addresses the thoughts and beliefs that are often associated with posttrauma fear and other negative emotions. It also addresses the avoidance of trauma-related thoughts, feelings, and situations that is often extensive following a psychological trauma. The general goal of the CBT approach is to help the survivor process and integrate the traumatic event and attain a realistic perspective on it, and to help him or her return to former life and activity by reducing or eliminating the avoidance behaviors.

Use of CBT to treat psychological trauma survivors with chronic symptoms and problems such as posttraumatic stress disorder (PTSD) began to grow in the early 1980s, when cognitive behavioral researchers and therapists began studying treatment programs designed to facilitate recovery from psychological trauma. The early treatment research programs conducted in the United States were aimed at two main groups of trauma survivors: combat veterans, particularly those of the Vietnam War, and women who survived the trauma of rape or other forms of assault. In the past two decades, the focus of treatment research has expanded to include people who are exposed to traumas including motor vehicle accidents, childhood abuse, aggravated assault, natural disasters, acts of terrorism, and others. Most of these programs have focused on treatment of trauma survivors with PTSD; much of what is known about CBT interventions is actually about their efficacy in the treatment of PTSD (*see:* **Posttraumatic Stress Disorder**).

In order to understand how CBT treatments facilitate recovery from trauma, it is helpful to first consider what maintains trauma-related symptoms long after the traumatic event itself has ended.

Why Do Symptoms Persist?

Traumatic experiences are by definition events that are extremely distressing or terrifying and often have lingering impact on the survivor's thoughts, feelings, and behavior. They can dramatically alter the way that the person views the world, other people, or the self. Specifically, traumatic experiences can leave the survivor with the view that the world is very dangerous and that terrible things can happen suddenly that are unpredictable and uncontrollable, that other people cannot be trusted, or that the person him- or herself is weak and incompetent.

Just thinking about a psychological trauma or being confronted with reminders of the event(s) can elicit distressing images and strong feelings of fear and anxiety or other negative emotions such as guilt, shame, grief, and anger.

One very natural response to these distressing thoughts and feelings is to begin to avoid the situations, places, and activities or people that remind the survivor of the trauma or that feel unsafe or risky. In addition, the memory of the psychological trauma itself and thoughts or discussion about what happened are avoided because of the painful feelings they bring up. Indeed, these forms of avoidance are two of the specific symptoms of PTSD. Avoidance may bring about a good bit of relief by temporarily reducing discomfort and anxiety. However, this may become a habitual way of responding to stressful trauma reminders, which can lead to restrictions in activity that actually increase rather than reduce the person's feelings of anxiety and distress. Avoidance also prevents the person from having experiences that might help him or her to put the traumatic event in perspective and to learn that the anxiety triggered by thinking and talking about the trauma or encountering other reminders actually is manageable and does not last forever.

These patterns of negative thinking and extensive avoidance associated with PTSD are frequently disruptive to the person's life. But equally important, they are factors that serve to maintain the fear and anxiety that are associated with the memory of the traumatic experience and the worry that something else bad will happen. Fortunately, they are also problems that are very amenable to cognitive behavioral interventions.

Cognitive Behavior Therapy

The CBT interventions most commonly employed for trauma-related disorders like PTSD include exposure therapy, anxiety management training, cognitive therapy, eye movement desensitization and reprocessing (EMDR), and combinations of these approaches. Each of these is discussed in detail elsewhere in this volume, and will be briefly described here.

Exposure Therapy

Exposure therapy has a very long history in the treatment of excessive or pathological anxiety, and is highly efficacious in the treatment of phobias and other anxiety disorders. Exposure therapy is also the most extensively studied form of CBT for PTSD. While in early studies exposure was seen as reducing trauma-induced anxiety via purely behavioral mechanisms, it has increasingly been seen as a means of promoting modification of the cognitive structure that underlies trauma-related disorders. The aim of exposure therapy is to help survivors to safely confront the trauma memory and trauma-related situations in order to reduce excessive or unrealistic anxiety and to modify trauma-related unrealistic beliefs and expectations. Two types of exposure are typically utilized in CBT for PTSD: *imaginal exposure* and *in vivo exposure.*

Imaginal exposure involves repeatedly revisiting the trauma memory in imagination. Imaginal exposure is designed to help the survivor to emotionally process her or his experience of the traumatic event(s) by vividly imagining the traumatic event(s) as if the event(s) were happening right at the current moment—while also being fully aware that the event(s) are not actually happening. This is typically done with eyes closed and describing the event(s) aloud, including the thoughts, emotions, and physical sensations that were experienced during the event(s). This imaginal revisiting of the traumatic event(s) is typically repeated over and over throughout treatment or until the trauma memory ceases to elicit intense anxiety or distress.

In vivo exposure entails repeatedly facing safe but avoided situations, places, activities, or objects that evoke unrealistic anxiety because of their association with the trauma memory. *In vivo* exposure further enhances the processing of the traumatic experiences by asking the person to confront and remain in these planned situations until anxiety decreases or habituates significantly. Such therapeutic exposure provides powerful learning experiences that help the person to feel safer and attain more realistic views of the world.

Exposure therapy for PTSD may utilize either or both of these forms of exposure— imaginal or *in vivo.* Or, the client may repeatedly write the narrative of the traumatic event(s) rather than verbalize it out loud. Exposure therapy has also been conducted in group format as well as in individual therapy (*see:* **Group Therapy**), where participants may take turns describing their traumatic experiences. Whatever the variation, the goal is to confront the trauma memories and related reminders in order to process and integrate the memory and reduce the associated anxiety.

One of the most extensively studied exposure therapy programs for PTSD is prolonged exposure (PE; Foa, Hembree, & Rothbaum, 2007). PE is an individual therapy that is typically conducted in 9 to 12 weekly or biweekly sessions averaging 90 minutes in length, although depending on rate of symptom reduction the number of sessions can either be reduced or increased. The first three sessions of PE focus on providing the client with a good rationale for treatment in the form of education about what maintains trauma-related symptoms and problems and how *in vivo* and imaginal exposure will address and reduce these symptoms. *In vivo* exposure is initiated in Session 2 with the construction of a list of avoided situations that will be confronted over the course of therapy. The items on the list are organized in a hierarchy according to the level of discomfort that the client anticipates she or he will feel when confronting them. Most *in vivo* exposure in PE is done by the client between therapy sessions. The first *in vivo* homework exposures are begun with exercises that are relatively low on the hierarchy (i.e., less anxiety-arousing). The client works up to the more challenging situations as treatment progresses.

Imaginal exposure is introduced in Session 3, and is conducted during each therapy session until the termination of treatment. Each session thereafter begins with homework review, moves to 30 to 45 minutes of imaginal exposure followed by 15 to 20 minutes of discussion of the imaginal experience, and ends with assignment of homework for the following week. In the final session, as in most CBT approaches, progress is reviewed and plans are made for the client's continued use of the tools that were learned in treatment.

Anxiety Management Training

This form of CBT focuses on the development of skills for managing and reducing excessive anxiety (*see:* **Anxiety Management Training**). Stress inoculation training or SIT (Meichenbaum, 1975) is a specific anxiety management program that was one of the first cognitive behavioral treatments applied for PTSD, and was primarily used in early research on female survivors of assault (e.g., Foa et al., 1999). This approach is based on the idea that stress, an inevitable aspect of life, occurs when the person experiences the environment as exceeding or overwhelming his or her coping resources, resulting in a sense of threatened welfare. Anxiety is a normal response to stressful experiences, but can reach an intensity or frequency that is excessive and disruptive, as in the case of PTSD. As used in these early programs, anxiety management interventions were designed to help the person to understand the dynamics of stress and anxiety and to teach them coping skills for managing their trauma-related anxiety. Clients were taught a variety of skills and encouraged to practice these for homework.

Anxiety management training typically includes skills that address the physiological, cognitive, and behavioral "channels" or ways in which anxiety is experienced. The skills include controlled breathing and progressive muscle relaxation training, guided self-dialogue or learning to use task-enhancing self-talk when preparing for and handling stressful events, cognitive restructuring (that is, identifying thoughts or beliefs [cognitions] that elicit excessive anxiety or other negative emotions and replacing them with more reasonable or rational responses), assertiveness training, and behavioral rehearsal (that is, practicing new behaviors) via role-playing with the therapist and via imaginal rehearsal of successful coping. Clients learn the skills in treatment sessions and are encouraged to repeatedly practice

them as homework to manage "normal" anxiety as well as fear and anxiety brought on by trauma-related cues or situations. As originally intended in stress inoculation training, in some PTSD treatment programs, after learning and practicing the skills clients were encouraged to implement them during *in vivo* exposure exercises.

Cognitive Therapy

The study of cognitive therapy as a treatment for PTSD followed the early studies utilizing exposure therapy and anxiety management training. This is in part because the early conceptualizations of PTSD that were purely behavioral and emphasized the modification of conditioned anxiety responses gave way to conceptualizations that emphasized the role of cognitive factors in explaining the development and persistence of trauma-related disorder. This naturally led to an interest in using and investigating the efficacy of cognitive therapy as a treatment for PTSD.

In cognitive theory (Beck, 1976), it is the interpretation of events, rather than events themselves, which leads to specific emotional responses. These interpretations can be realistic and accurate, as when a person sees a speeding car heading toward him and has the immediate thought, "He's going to hit me!" accompanied by intense fear and running to safety. Interpretations of events may also be unrealistic, as when "safe" or harmless events are viewed as threatening or dangerous. In these latter instances, the inaccurate interpretation leads to unrealistic or excessive anxiety. Moreover, according to cognitive theory, individuals may be characterized by the particular ways in which they think about the world, other people, and themselves. Because psychological trauma survivors sometimes view the world as dangerous and themselves as weak or incompetent, this may lead to a tendency to interpret harmless events as dangerous and threatening. Indeed, Ehlers and Clark (2000) suggested in their adaptation of cognitive theory to the treatment of PTSD that the core cognitive distortion underlying PTSD is the interpretation of PTSD reexperiencing symptoms (that is, distressing and intrusive recollections, images, flashbacks, and thoughts of the traumatic event) as threatening when they are actually unpleasant but harmless memories.

Cognitive therapy for adults with trauma-related disorders typically begins with explaining to the client that traumatic events often affect the way people think and how they view the world and themselves. The therapist helps the client to identify how traumatic experiences have affected his or her beliefs and thoughts. The client learns to identify trauma-related thinking that triggers avoidance or excessive negative emotions, and to challenge these beliefs and expectations in a rational, evidence-based way. This may involve examining the evidence for and against a particular way of thinking, or considering alternative ways of looking at something. First in therapy sessions, and then as homework between sessions, the client practices identifying thoughts and interpretations that lead to excessive negative emotions and challenging them by reviewing evidence, considering alternative explanations, and generating rational responses. Sometimes the solution also includes practicing different ways of behaving in response to situations that elicit anxiety or other negative emotions.

Cognitive processing therapy (CPT; Resick, Nishith, Weaver, Astin, & Feuer, 2002) is a treatment developed specifically for use with psychological trauma survivors that utilizes cognitive restructuring. CPT also includes an exposure component in the form of repeatedly writing about the traumatic experience(s) and rereading the narrative. This writing exposure is used to help the client to identify the ways that the traumatic events have affected his or her life and to activate thoughts and feelings that are further processed with the cognitive therapy.

Eye Movement Desensitization and Reprocessing

Beginning in the early 1990s, eye movement desensitization and reprocessing (EMDR; Shapiro, 1995; *see:* **Eye Movement Desensitization and Reprocessing**) has been used quite extensively as a treatment for trauma-related problems including PTSD. The major characteristic that distinguishes EMDR from other forms of CBT for PTSD is that the therapist provides or uses some form of bilateral sensory stimulation during exposure therapy in order to enhance trauma memory processing. Originally, this occurred by asking the client to generate images of the trauma or focus on trauma-related thoughts, feelings, and/or sensations, while the therapist elicited rapid saccadic (side to side) eye movements by having the client visually track a finger rapidly waved back and forth in front of his or her face. Other forms of laterally alternating stimuli (e.g., finger tapping, flashing lights, beating drum) are sometimes used now rather than the original finger tracking. The bilateral stimulation is woven throughout a session in which the client is asked to evaluate the thoughts and feelings associated with their images and sensations, and to generate alternative cognitive appraisals of the traumatic event(s) or their behavior during traumatic experiences.

Brief Summary of Major Findings of CBT Studies

Numerous, well-controlled scientific studies of CBT interventions for adults with trauma-related disorders have been conducted by researchers in the United States and in other countries. The type of psychological traumas suffered by participants in these studies include combat, rape, physical assault, childhood sexual abuse, domestic violence, motor vehicle accidents, and disasters. For thorough reviews of the treatment outcome literature, see Rothbaum, Meadows, Resick, and Foy (2000); Harvey, Bryant, and Tarrier (2003); and the most recent findings on treatment of PTSD published by the Institute of Medicine (2008).

In general, many studies have found CBT approaches highly effective in reducing trauma-related symptoms. The evidence clearly points to CBT as the most empirically supported approach among the psychosocial treatments for adults with PTSD. Comparative treatment studies have been conducted that randomly assigned survivors of psychological trauma (who typically are suffering from PTSD) to treatments including exposure therapies such as PE, cognitive therapies such as CPT, EMDR, anxiety management approaches such as SIT, or combinations of these interventions. Results have generally shown that adults treated with exposure therapy, SIT, cognitive therapy, combinations of these three (e.g., exposure therapy with SIT or with cognitive therapy), or EMDR, achieve comparable and highly significant reductions in trauma-related symptoms including PTSD, depression, and anxiety (e.g., Foa et al., 1999, 2005; Marks, Lovell, Noshirvani, Livanou, & Thrasher, 1998; Resick et al., 2002; Rothbaum, Astin, & Marsteller, 2005). CBT interventions are also quite efficient; treatment is usually completed in 12 sessions or less. Follow-up evaluations of up to one year generally indicate excellent maintenance of treatment gains. There is increasing focus on dissemination of these highly effective CBT treatments to community settings and community treatment providers, so that they may be more widely available to survivors of traumatic events.

REFERENCES

Beck, A. T. (1976). *Cognitive therapy and the emotional disorders.* New York: International University Press.

Ehlers, A., & Clark, D. M. (2000). A cognitive model of persistent posttraumatic stress disorder. *Behaviour Research and Therapy, 38,* 319–345.

Foa, E. B., Dancu, C. V., Hembree, E. A., Jaycox, L. H., Meadows, E. A., & Street, G. P. (1999). A comparison of exposure therapy, stress inoculation training, and their combination for reducing posttraumatic stress disorder in female assault victims. *Journal of Consulting and Clinical Psychology, 67,* 194–200.

Foa, E. B., Hembree, E. A., Cahill, S. P., Rauch, S. A. M., Riggs, D. S., Feeny, N. C., et al. (2005). Randomized trail of prolonged exposure for post-traumatic stress disorder with and without cognitive restructuring: Outcome at academic and community clinics. *Journal of Consulting and Clinical Psychology, 73,* 953–964.

Foa, E. B., Hembree, E. A., & Rothbaum, B. O. (2007). *Prolonged exposure therapy for PTSD: Emotional processing of traumatic experiences.* New York: Oxford University Press.

Harvey, A. G., Bryant, R. A., & Tarrier, N. (2003). Cognitive behaviour therapy for posttraumatic stress disorder. *Clinical Psychology Review, 3,* 501–522.

Institute of Medicine. (2008). *Treatment of posttraumatic stress disorder: An assessment of the evidence.* Washington, DC: National Academies Press.

Marks, I., Lovell, K., Noshirvani, H., Livanou, M., & Thrasher, S. (1998). Treatment of post-traumatic stress disorder by exposure and/or cognitive restructuring. *Archives of General Psychiatry, 55,* 317–325.

Meichenbaum, D. (1975). Self-instructional methods. In F. H. Kanfer & A. P. Goldstein (Eds.), *Helping people change* (pp. 357–391). New York: Pergamon Press.

Resick, P. A., Nishith, P., Weaver, T., Astin, M. C., & Feuer, C. A. (2002). A comparison of cognitive processing therapy, prolonged exposure, and a waiting condition for the treatment of posttraumatic stress disorder in female rape victims. *Journal of Consulting and Clinical Psychology, 70,* 867–879.

Rothbaum, B. O., Astin, M. C., & Marsteller, F. (2005). Prolonged exposure versus eye movement desensitization and reprocessing (EMDR) for PTSD rape victims. *Journal of Traumatic Stress, 18,* 607–616.

Rothbaum, B. O., Meadows, E. A., Resick, P., & Foy, D. (2000). Cognitive-behavioral therapy. In E. B. Foa, T. M. Keane, & M. J. Friedman (Eds.), *Effective treatments for PTSD: Practice guidelines from the International Society for Traumatic Stress Studies* (pp. 320–325). New York: Guilford Press.

Shapiro, F. (1995). *Eye movement desensitization and reprocessing: Basic principles, protocols, and procedures.* New York, Guilford Press.

ELIZABETH A. HEMBREE
University of Pennsylvania School of Medicine

JAMES MARINCHAK
University of Pennsylvania School of Medicine

See also: **Anxiety Management Training; Coping Skills Training; Exposure Therapy, Adult; Eye Movement Desensitization and Reprocessing; Group Therapy; Prevention, Adult; Psychoeducation**

COGNITIVE BEHAVIOR THERAPY, CHILD ABUSE

Child sexual and physical abuse affects children of all ethnic, racial, and socioeconomic backgrounds. The prevalence of abuse in children and its emotional and psychological consequences has prompted the development of therapeutic interventions to reduce symptomatology and mitigate subsequent effects.

A cognitive behavioral therapy (CBT) approach has been modified to address symptoms most commonly seen in children who have experienced physical or sexual abuse (Cohen, Mannarino, & Deblinger, 2006; Deblinger & Heflin, 1996). Usually a short- to moderate-term treatment model (around 10 to 20 sessions), research has shown that CBT can provide significant benefits in terms of PTSD and depression symptom reduction for children, ranging in age from 3 to 13. CBT has also been effective in reducing nonoffending caregiver's symptoms of distress related to the abuse and enhancing their sense of competence (Cohen, Deblinger, Mannarino, & Steer, 2004; Deblinger & Heflin, 1996; Deblinger, Steer, & Lippmann, 1999).

The most important prerequisites of CBT for sexually or physically abused children are that that the child is safe (i.e., not exposed to further abuse or other psychological trauma); and that crisis issues, such as suicidal or psychotic behavior, have been stabilized. In addition, it is suggested that the allegations of abuse be substantiated, or at least deemed as credible, through a Child Protective Services' investigation or some other type of forensic evaluation. However, what is most important is that the child is experiencing symptoms related to the alleged abuse, including having at least one clear memory of the abuse that causes distress. Furthermore, this treatment model emphasizes the involvement of a nonoffending caregiver who can provide the child needed support and can also learn skills to cope with the abuse and its effects.

This model is based on the central idea that cognitions, emotions, and behaviors are interdependent. CBT is adjusted to the child's developmental level (i.e., differing for toddlers, early school-age, school-age, and early adolescent children) in order to help the child to experience memories, thoughts, and stimuli related to the abuse without feeling overwhelmed by or unable to cope with the associated negative emotions.

One of the first goals of CBT treatment is to help the child to manage the physiological manifestations of fear and anxiety by teaching and practicing relaxation and anxiety management skills. Diaphragmatic (deep) breathing, progressive muscle relaxation, and guided imagery are taught to the child to increase his or her ability to recognize and manage bodily arousal. These skills help prepare the child to recall and discuss memories of the abuse, and to feel in control when confronted with reminders of the abuse.

CBT also teaches children skills for identifying and expressing their emotions. First, it is important to help the child develop a vocabulary for emotions and be able to express them with words. Often abused children experience a wide range of emotions and find it difficult to label them verbally. In treatment, they learn to recognize and identify other people's emotions, through facial or postural clues. "Look, listen, ask" is an easy phrase that can remind the child to look at the person's face, listen to what the person is saying, and, if it is not clear, ask that person how she or he is feeling. Coping strategies to express strong emotions, such as anger, can be taught using role-play or puppets. The process of learning to express emotions should move gradually toward a discussion of emotions related to the abuse and identification of "safe" people in the child's life, those who can be trusted and to whom the child can go, when feeling confused or overwhelmed.

CBT also teaches children cognitive coping skills by explaining how thoughts, feelings, and behaviors influence each other and by using examples familiar to the child. The goal is to help the child understand that different thoughts result in different emotions and that negative thoughts can be disputed and examined from a variety of perspectives (the "best friend" role-play is very useful). Practice and developmentally appropriate examples are important in learning this skill. Correcting myths and cognitive distortions, such as thoughts of self-blame, guilt, or extreme distrust toward others are an important part of CBT. Both the child and the caregiver are guided in recognizing and disputing dysfunctional and overly pessimistic interpretations and thoughts about the abuse and its emotional and physical consequences. Cognitive restructuring (i.e., trying out new thoughts that help the child feel better or more in control), thought stopping (i.e., saying "stop" silently when negative thoughts occur), and guided self-dialogue can be used to challenge abuse-related beliefs, and role-plays of these techniques can take place in the session. The caregiver also learns ways to use thinking to cope more effectively.

Psychoeducation is also an important component of treatment and should include information in a form that is appropriate to the child's age about physical and sexual abuse, healthy sexuality, and risk reduction. The main goal of psychoeducation is to clarify misinformation and incorrect knowledge of sexuality, body parts, and health-related issues. The child is encouraged to develop a safety plan, learn to say "no," and know the difference between "okay" and "not okay" touches. Caregivers are provided with similar education in adult terms.

As the child progresses through CBT treatment and learns to cope with difficult emotions and thoughts, he or she is becoming equipped to handle the next treatment component: *gradual exposure.*

The goal of gradual exposure is to help the child confront his or her fears and anxieties related to the abuse and to prevent avoidance (of discussing/being reminded of the trauma) and its negative psychological consequences. This approach combines two types of well-documented interventions: prolonged exposure and systematic desensitization. The child is encouraged to face the fear-producing stimuli, beginning with the ones that provoke lower anxiety responses and gradually achieving the ability to discuss the most anxiety-provoking memories. These memories are carefully reviewed in a manner and at a pace that the child can tolerate, until they no longer evoke fear, anxiety, and avoidance. The gradual exposure should be sensitive to the child's developmental level and ability to express feelings and emotions. Because abuse and trauma-related memories are distressing, it is important for caregivers, teachers, and therapists to understand that children may make active attempts to avoid exposure sessions. They may refuse to attend treatment or their symptoms may initially worsen. Caregivers need to be aware of this possible outcome so that they can be prepared to help the child during this component of treatment. As the child becomes more comfortable talking about the abuse, often because of the application of previously learned coping skills and relaxation techniques, the child can recall and describe bad memories without feeling overwhelmed. The therapist also helps the child (and the caregiver) correct any misconceptions related to the event(s). It is important to highlight that most children realize that they are capable of gaining control over these anxiety-producing emotions and memories if they learn the skills to deal with them.

Several different gradual exposure methods are used by CBT therapists, including: (1) reenactment with dolls or puppets; (2) visualization of past events in imagination; (3) recalling sensory details of the abuse experience; (4) drawing, painting, or writing about thoughts and experiences; and (5) *in vivo* exposure (doing activities or going places that are reminders of abuse experiences). The use of a narrative approach in the form of a book containing drawings, poems, pictures, and written memories of the abuse seems very helpful in maintaining focus and continuity during treatment of young children. The specific method will vary depending on the age or developmental level of the child. Importantly, the therapist should engage in a variety of methods to meet the needs of the individual child.

Structuring gradual exposure sessions is central to achieve the goal of trauma-focused treatment and to prevent avoidance or dissociative coping mechanisms by the child victim. Each exposure session should have some sense of closure, a review of the progress made and an assessment of the degree to which the child's anxiety has decreased. It is important to praise the child for the difficult work accomplished and to point out to her or him that the fears related to the abuse will diminish over time.

In vivo exposure, in which the child confronts specific anxiety-producing situations or stimuli, is a technique that is very useful in the later phase of the exposure process. It is important to be certain that the *in vivo* exposure will not place the child in any real danger. Once this is assured, it is helpful to involve the nonoffending caregiver, so that *in vivo* sessions can be conducted outside of the therapy setting. For example, if the child is afraid of the dark because of their abuse, an *in vivo* exposure exercise would be to have the child and caregiver develop a series of small steps aimed at helping the child ultimately sleep in a dark room at home. The therapist instructs the nonoffending caregiver and encourages the use of support and praise for the child's efforts.

The final part of CBT treatment focuses on preparing the child to go back into his or her social environment feeling strong and equipped with the necessary tools to be safe. Education regarding personal safety skills should be reviewed and discussed before the end of treatment. This can include information about healthy sexuality, body ownership, the right to say no, awareness of high risk situations, identifying safe people and places, the ability to communicate effectively, and how to ask for help if needed. As mentioned, the nonoffending caregiver should be involved in the treatment because the caregiver's ability to deal with her own distress and provide emotional support to her child appears to be one of the most critical factors influencing the child's post-abuse psychological adjustment. Throughout treatment, the nonoffending caregiver is engaged in parallel sessions addressing the same core components: psychoeducation, anxiety management, emotion identification and processing,

cognitive coping skills training, gradual exposure, and personal safety skills. In addition, caregivers are taught behavioral management skills to help them with disciplining and setting limits with their child. In the latter stages of therapy, the nonoffending caregiver and the child discuss the child's memories of the abuse in conjoint caregiver-child sessions. With the support and guidance of the therapist, they are encouraged to continue this open communication about any additional feelings, thoughts, or memories related to the abuse, and about other current-day matters that are important to them, at home.

REFERENCES

Cohen, J. A., Deblinger, E., Mannarino, T., & Steer, R. A. (2004). A multisite randomized controlled trial for sexually abused children with posttraumatic stress disorder symptoms. *Journal of the Academy of Child and Adolescent Psychiatry, 43,* 393–402.

Cohen, J. A., Mannarino, A. P., & Deblinger, E. (2006). *Treating trauma and traumatic grief in children and adolescents.* New York: Guilford Press.

Deblinger, E., & Heflin, A. H. (1996). *Treating sexually abused children and their nonoffending parents: A cognitive behavioral approach.* Thousand Oaks, CA: Sage.

Deblinger, E., Steer, R., & Lippmann, J. (1999). Two-year follow-up study of cognitive behavioral therapy for sexually abused children suffering posttraumatic stress symptoms. *Child Abuse and Neglect, 23,* 1371–1378.

ROCHELLE F. HANSON
Medical University of South Carolina

REGANA CORTINI SISSON
Medical University of South Carolina

See also: **Anxiety Management Training; Bereavement; Cognitive Behavior Therapy, Childhood Traumatic Grief; Coping Skills Training; Exposure Therapy, Child; Eye Movement Desensitization and Reprocessing; Group Therapy; Prevention, Child; Psychoeducation**

COGNITIVE BEHAVIOR THERAPY, CHILDHOOD TRAUMATIC GRIEF

Childhood grief (CTG) is a condition where the process by which a child grieves the death of a loved one is impaired and overwhelmed by traumatic stress reactions triggered by reminders of the loved one's death. Characteristics of CTG were originally described by Eth and Pynoos (1985) based on observations that children who witnessed their parents' murder often had posttraumatic stress disorder (PTSD) symptoms while grieving. Recently, CTG has been described as a combination of unresolved grief and PTSD symptoms (often accompanied by depressive symptoms) in children who witness the death of a loved one or experience a loved one's death as traumatic (e.g., sudden, unexpected, and/or horrifying; Cohen, Mannarino, & Deblinger, 2006). CTG differs from typical grief or bereavement in that the child suffers from unresolved grief symptoms (e.g., yearning for the deceased, difficulty accepting the death) and symptoms of posttraumatic stress (e.g., intrusive thoughts, reexperiencing the death, avoidance of stimuli associated with the deceased, emotional detachment). CTG grief symptoms are similar to those found in adults suffering from complicated grief. However, a specialized form of psychotherapy was developed to treat children with this constellation of symptoms: cognitive behavioral therapy for childhood traumatic grief (CBT-CTG; Cohen, Mannarino, & Deblinger, 2006).

CBT-CTG addresses the following tasks that are thought to be part of the typical grieving process for children of all ages and backgrounds: experiencing the pain of the loss; accepting the permanence of the loss; reminiscing about and remembering the loved one as he or she was; shifting the relationship with the loved one from interaction to memory; internalizing qualities of the loved one; and continued development of healthy relationships. CBT-CTG also treats PTSD symptoms that interfere with this typical grieving process, which may include reexperiencing the traumatic death (e.g., through flashbacks, nightmares, or intrusive thoughts), avoidance of trauma reminders (e.g., pictures, thoughts, and other reminders of the deceased or the traumatic death), or hyperarousal (e.g., excessive anger or bitterness about the death).

Prior to the development of CBT-CTG, Pynoos (1992) described three types of reminders that can trigger children's PTSD symptoms and complicate their grieving: trauma-related reminders (e.g., places, people, or sensory cues that remind the child of the traumatic death), loss reminders (e.g., places, people, objects, or thoughts that remind the child of the deceased), and change reminders (e.g., people, places, or objects that remind the child of the changes in living situation that occurred following the death). When reminders consistently activate PTSD symptoms and cause distress, children may attempt to avoid thinking about, talking about, having feelings about, or doing things that remind them of the deceased. The avoidance response may be negatively reinforced by a reduction in anxiety. However, avoidance of reminders can impair important tasks of the typical grieving process (e.g., accepting the loss, reminiscing about the deceased, internalizing the deceased's qualities). As Pynoos (1992) writes, "It is difficult for a child to reminisce . . . when an image of . . . mutilation is what first comes to mind" (p. 7). CBT-CTG was developed to help children remember the lost loved one and the traumatic experience(s) surrounding the death in a therapeutic manner that can enable them to overcome their sense of fear and resume (or begin) the process of grieving and recovery.

Research on treatments for CTG is just beginning to emerge. Initial approaches (prior to CBT-CTG's development) were manualized school-based group interventions that showed some success at reducing PTSD, depression, and anxiety symptoms (see Cohen & Mannarino, 2004, for a brief review). Cohen and Mannarino built therapy (TF-CBT) is an evidence-based short-term treatment for trauma-exposed children (Cohen, Mannarino, & Deblinger, 2006).

CBT-CTG is a 12- to 16-session intervention developed for children and adolescents from

6 to 17 years old (Cohen & Mannarino, 2004). A phase-based treatment is used, with trauma-focused components generally comprising the initial eight sessions, and grief-focused components the last four to eight sessions. CBT-CTG also includes significant involvement with a supportive parent or other caregiver in every session. For most sessions, the time is split between seeing the child and caregiver individually. Four conjoint sessions (i.e., the therapist meets with the child and caregiver[s] together) are also provided for the child to share his or her trauma narrative with the caregiver and to begin processing grief associated with the loss.

In the first CBT-CTG session, the child and caregiver are introduced to the treatment model, rationale, and time line. Psychoeducation is provided about the concepts of psychological trauma, traumatic stress, grief, and CTG in developmentally appropriate terms. Early sessions also include activities to help the child identify and express feelings. Children learn to identify a range of feelings, particularly difficult feelings like sadness, fear, anger, and guilt, and to rate the magnitude of each of these feelings. Depending on the child's age, activities to promote the expression of feelings might include using feelings faces, drawing what feelings look like in their body, using puppets or dolls to discuss feelings, or playing games such as Emotional Bingo. In the separate parallel session, the caregiver discusses his or her feelings about the deceased and is introduced to behavior management techniques (e.g., praise, time out, use of consequences).

Subsequent sessions involve teaching the child relaxation skills that can be used to reduce anxiety, stress, and hyperarousal symptoms (e.g., insomnia). The techniques selected will depend on the child's age and interest, but might include deep breathing exercises, positive imagery, or progressive muscle relaxation. Some children, and particularly adolescents, prefer to utilize familiar activities such as exercising, playing a sport, reading, or listening to music. The caregiver sessions involve educating the caregiver about relaxation skills that will be helpful to the child as well as continued discussion of behavior management

techniques to modify any child behaviors that are problematic (such as fighting or breaking family rules).

The concept of the cognitive triangle (interrelationships between thoughts, feelings, and behaviors) is introduced at approximately the third session. Children learn to identify and monitor their thoughts, and learn how thoughts are related to emotions and behaviors. The goal is to learn how negative or unhelpful thoughts may contribute to difficult feelings, negative social situations, and behavior problems. Techniques for modifying unhelpful thinking are taught through role-plays and other activities (Cohen & Mannarino, 2004). These techniques are initially practiced with everyday events, but will subsequently be used to help the child make sense of the traumatic death in the next phase of CBT-CTG.

The middle portion of treatment (roughly, sessions four through eight) involves creating a trauma narrative, imaginal and gradual exposure to upsetting trauma reminders by reviewing the narrative repeatedly, and then sharing the trauma narrative with the caregiver in conjoint sessions (Cohen & Mannarino, 2004). First, the therapist helps the child prepare for temporarily increased feelings of anxiety or hyperarousal with coping skills that have been taught in earlier sessions. A medical analogy that may be used is that the pain caused by upsetting memories of a loved one's death is akin to a seriously infected wound. For the wound to heal, it is necessary to open and clean it, despite the significant, but temporary, increase in pain. Similarly, it is important to be able to open up and talk about memories, thoughts, and feelings related to the loved one's death to reduce the stress reactions caused by trauma reminders and to facilitate mourning. The trauma narrative is developed to "tell the story" of the most difficult experience(s) associated with the traumatic death, and to help the child express feelings and make sense of what happened. The form of the narrative is flexible, and it might be, for example, a story, a poem, a book, a song, or a puppet show. The narrative includes details of the child's thoughts and feelings about what happened, and is repeated multiple times to help the child modify unhelpful thoughts and feel prepared to manage upsetting feelings associated with the traumatic death. Parallel sessions are used to read the narrative to the caregiver separately from the child and to prepare the caregiver for conjoint sessions with the child. In the conjoint sessions, the child shares the trauma narrative with the caregiver and has the opportunity to ask questions of the caregiver. The family also identifies potentially troubling trauma reminders that might occur in the future, as well as appropriate coping strategies for managing these reminders.

Children generally show improvement in PTSD symptoms following this trauma-focused phase of treatment (Cohen, Mannarino, & Staron, 2006). A reduction in hyperarousal and avoidance when faced with trauma, loss, or change reminders then enables the child to begin the grieving process.

The grief-focused phase, which encompasses the last four to eight sessions of CBT-CTG, begins with psychoeducation about grief and death. The child's understanding about death and grief is assessed, and information and responses to the child's questions are presented in a truthful, developmentally appropriate way. The tremendous loss and pain associated with the death must be acknowledged and mourned, including the loss of the interactive relationship and of any future interactions with the deceased (Cohen & Mannarino, 2004). It is often helpful for the child and therapist to make lists of "Things I Miss" about the deceased, along with methods of coping with each. This activity models that having painful feelings about death is normal and appropriate, that expression of these feelings is healthy, and that the pain will gradually diminish over time (Cohen, Mannarino, & Deblinger, 2006). In parallel sessions, the therapist separately shares the child's stated losses with the caregiver and also encourages the caregiver to share his or her own feelings and thoughts about the loss. The therapist works with the caregiver to understand and reduce the impact on the child and the family of any secondary losses that may occur following a death, such as loss of the

home or changing schools (Cohen & Mannarino, 2004).

In addition to discussing "Things I Miss," children are encouraged to address any ambivalent feelings about the deceased (e.g., unresolved past conflicts, anger at the deceased's choices). This is particularly important for potentially stigmatizing deaths, such as suicide or a drug overdose, where anger and shame are common. To facilitate discussion of these feelings, children can make a second list of "Things I Do NOT Miss" or can write a letter to the deceased and a letter the deceased might write back to him/her (Cohen, Mannarino, & Deblinger, 2006). The goal is for the child to begin developing an integrated and accurate representation of the deceased, including both positive and negative memories.

The child can then work toward preserving positive memories of the deceased, which Cohen and Mannarino (2004) describe as a necessary step before the child can recommit to current and new relationships. Based on the child's preferences, preserving positive memories might entail creating a scrapbook or picture album, making a memorial, writing a poem, drawing pictures, and collecting keepsakes. The goal is for the child to remember the joy he or she shared with the deceased, that the deceased will not be forgotten, and that memories of the deceased can produce happiness (as well as negative emotions). Some children might also wish to plan and hold their own memorial service for the deceased, particularly if they were not involved in the funeral (Cohen & Mannarino, 2004). The child's (and caregiver's) relationship with the deceased is then redefined to one of memory rather than interaction. In the separate parallel sessions, the therapist shares the child's work with the caregiver and also discusses the caregiver's feelings about preserving memories of the deceased.

The final phase of CBT-CTG involves helping the child make meaning of the loss, recommit to healthy relationships, and to bring some closure to therapy with a conjoint session. The therapist helps the child integrate the experiences of loss, mourning, and treatment into his or her worldview so the child recognizes not only how difficult and painful the process has been but also how much he or she has grown and matured because of it. The therapist might help the child answer questions such as "How has this experience changed you?" or "What would you tell another child who just had a traumatic loss?" (Cohen & Mannarino, 2004). Some children find it helpful and empowering to advocate or reach out to others in similar situations (e.g., speak to peers about the dangers of drug abuse or community violence).

The final conjoint caregiver-child session(s) of CBT-CTG allow the family to jointly discuss the loss and their feelings, reminisce about the deceased, and share their methods of coping with difficult emotions (Cohen & Mannarino, 2004). The family discusses how far they have come in therapy since the traumatic death and identifies potentially difficult reminders that might occur in the future (e.g., anniversary of the death, holidays, the deceased's birthday), along with methods of coping with the sad feelings that will likely persist. The therapist encourages open communication about the traumatic loss between the child and caregiver, with the expectation that the caregiver will be the most important support for the child in the future. While therapy might be completed (and CTG symptoms improved) in 12 to 16 sessions, it is important to acknowledge that mourning is likely to continue much longer. However, CBT-CTG gives the child and caregiver the knowledge and skills to facilitate this lengthy process.

Although CBT-CTG is a relatively recent innovation, a growing evidence base supporting the efficacy of CBT-CTG is emerging. In pilot studies of the 16-session model with 22 children (Cohen, Mannarino, & Knudsen, 2004) and of the 12-session model with 39 children (Cohen, Mannarino, & Staron, 2006), significant improvements were observed in children's CTG, PTSD, depression, anxiety, and behavior problems as well as parents' own PTSD symptoms. To date, no randomized controlled treatment studies of CBT-CTG that compare it against a no-treatment condition have been published.

REFERENCES

Cohen, J. A., & Mannarino, A. P. (2004). Treatment of childhood traumatic grief. *Journal of Clinical Child and Adolescent Psychology, 33,* 819–831.

Cohen, J. A., Mannarino, A. P., & Deblinger, E. (2006). *Treating trauma and traumatic grief in children and adolescents.* New York: Guilford Press.

Cohen, J. A., Mannarino, A. P., & Knudsen, K. (2004). Treating childhood traumatic grief: A pilot study. *Journal of the American Academy of Child and Adolescent Psychiatry, 43,* 1225–1233.

Cohen, J. A., Mannarino, A. P., & Staron, V. R. (2006). A pilot study of modified cognitive-behavioral therapy for childhood traumatic grief (CBT-CTG). *Journal of the American Academy of Child Psychiatry, 45,* 1465–1473.

Eth, S., & Pynoos, R. S. (1985). Interaction of trauma and grief in childhood. In S. Eth & R. S. Pynoos (Eds.), *Posttraumatic stress disorder in children* (pp. 171–186). Washington, DC: American Psychiatric Association.

Pynoos, R. S. (1992). Grief and trauma in children and adolescents. *Bereavement Care, 11,* 2–10.

Jason M. Lang
University of Connecticut School of Medicine

Julian D. Ford
University of Connecticut School of Medicine

See also: Anxiety Management Training; Bereavement; Cognitive Behavior Therapy, Child Abuse; Coping Skills Training; Exposure Therapy, Child; Eye Movement Desensitization and Reprocessing; Group Therapy; Prevention, Child; Psychoeducation

COGNITIVE IMPAIRMENTS

Paralleling the vast gains in knowledge informing the neurobiological basis of PTSD, a growing empirical literature has focused on behavioral manifestation of brain abnormalities (i.e., cognitive dysfunction) associated with PTSD. Current knowledge draws from clinical neuropsychological tasks and experimental information processing tasks. Several conclusions emerge from these approaches.

First, PTSD is associated with cognitive compromise, particularly in attention and learning. This may be explained in part by a "cognitive draw" to threat-relevant (i.e., trauma-related) information. That is, information that is perceived to be associated with a person's traumatic experience captures the individual's attention and memory, leading to them having less capacity to attend to and remember other information that is not as emotional in content. Second, cognitive findings converge with those from the neurobiological, electrophysiological, and neuroimaging literatures, suggesting dysfunction of an integrated brain circuit involving regions associated with emotions and control of emotions (prefrontal cortical regions, the amygdala, and hippocampus). This entry summarizes current knowledge regarding the neurocognitive correlates of PTSD, emphasizing evidence from information-processing and neuropsychological approaches.

Information Processing

People with PTSD are more apt to process threat-relevant information in a biased manner. The most well-documented biases include *attentional* and *memory* biases (*see:* **Information Processing**). There also is preliminary evidence that individuals with PTSD are biased to interpret emotionally ambiguous information as threatening under certain conditions. All of this is consistent with the hypervigilance aspect of PTSD, which describes an elevated sensitivity toward environmental cues of potential threats. The tendency among people with PTSD to attend to threat-relevant information has been particularly robust when tested with the emotional Stroop test, which involves performing a perceptual task (i.e., naming the color of ink in which a word is printed) in the face of potentially distracting semantic content varied according to its emotional and trauma relevance. Individuals with PTSD are typically slower at naming the color of trauma-related words than they are when the colored words are emotionally neutral or irrelevant to trauma.

Although not as extensively studied, there also is evidence of memory biases in individuals with PTSD. The disorder has been associated with enhanced recall of trauma-related, as compared to nontrauma-related, words, although the evidence is weaker when recognition formats are used. On autobiographical memory tasks, PTSD diagnosis has been associated with production of "overgeneral" memories (i.e., recall reflects only broad categories of events rather than specific, detailed accounts of life events).

Neuropsychological Functioning

Learning and Memory

Memory is perhaps the most frequently examined cognitive domain within the PTSD literature, with many (but not all) memory studies revealing that individuals with PTSD perform less proficiently than those without PTSD. As a first step in the process of learning and remembering information, the initial acquisition stage of new learning, especially for verbal information, appears to be particularly vulnerable. PTSD also is associated with heightened sensitivity to proactive and retroactive interference. Specifically, previously learned information interferes with learning additional information (proactive interference) and new information interferes with recall of previously learned information (retroactive interference). However, the evidence for PTSD-related forgetting of newly learned information over delayed intervals is less conclusive. Because forgetting is linked closely to the brain region known as the hippocampus, (*see:* **Hippocampus**) mixed evidence regarding how well people with PTSD remember information over time calls into question the extent to which hippocampal dysfunction drives memory impairment for nonemotional information in PTSD.

Attention, Executive, and Prefrontal Functioning

While concentration difficulties are a core diagnostic feature of PTSD, they do not appear generalized but rather reflect a more specific pattern of attentional/executive deficits. Working memory deficits in PTSD have been documented repeatedly, including in studies using associated electrophysiological and functioning neuroimaging methods. In addition, PTSD has been associated with *cognitive disinhibition* and *commission errors* across attention and memory tasks, a pattern collectively suggestive of prefrontal cortical dysfunction and consistent with contemporary neuroanatomical conceptualizations of PTSD, implicating dysfunction of the prefrontal cortex, especially regarding its inhibitory functions.

Intellectual and Other Neuropsychological Functions

Compared to trauma-exposed individuals with PTSD, those without PTSD tend to perform better on intelligence (IQ) tests, especially verbal tasks. Little research has been conducted examining basic language, visuospatial, and motor functions in PTSD. However, studies examining these functional domains generally have failed to reveal PTSD-related deficits, except for tasks involving a strong executive component (e.g., complex figural copying, word list generation, and motor sequencing); such tasks have demonstrated PTSD-related deficits.

Remaining Questions

There are a number of questions remaining regarding the relationship of PTSD to cognitive functioning. Among the most central of these questions are: (1) whether neuropsychological abnormalities are predispositional and/or consequential (i.e., does cognitive functioning alter PTSD following trauma exposure, does trauma exposure and PTSD lead to cognitive decline, or both?); (2) the degree to which complicating clinical factors such as comorbid psychiatric disorders, associated health problems, and pharmacological treatment affect cognitive functioning in PTSD; (3) whether neuropsychological functioning is yoked to PTSD symptom presentation or persists independently of any natural recovery of emotional symptoms;

and (4) whether there are interactions among developmental stage (e.g., childhood, aging), PTSD, and cognitive functioning.

RECOMMENDED READINGS

McNally, R. J. (2006). Cognitive abnormalities in posttraumatic stress disorder. *Trends in Cognitive Science, 10,* 271–277.

Vasterling, J. J., & Brewin, C. R. (Eds.). (2005). *The neuropsychology of PTSD: Biological, cognitive, and clinical perspectives.* New York: Guilford Press.

JENNIFER J. VASTERLING
National Center for Posttraumatic Stress Disorder

JULIE A. ALVAREZ
Tulane University

See also: Hippocampus; Information Processessing; Memory

COGNITIVE INTEGRATION, BIOPSYCHOSOCIAL

Integrating an adverse or (extremely) stressful event constitutes a major biopsychosocial challenge for anyone. However, what counts as an extremely stressful event and what is "traumatic" can only be defined in relation to a living individual as a biopsychosocial system, and, eventually, to his or her response pattern to the situation of concern (Van der Hart, Nijenhuis, & Steele, 2006). Consistent with this perspective, empirical findings show that events usually described as *traumatic* in the traumatic stress literature (assault, combat exposure, disaster, etc.) do not cause or trigger psychopathology in all individuals who have been exposed to them. Whereas not everyone becomes injured in a biopsychosocial sense when exposed to such events (the term *trauma* literally means wound or injury), chronic exposure to them will probably leave no one unharmed: We all have our breaking point (Ross, 1941). Generally speaking, a particular event (or a particular series of events) is *a necessary but insufficient factor* in the development of an individual's psychopathology related to that event. Considering that (very) stressful events are not inherently traumatic, we believe they are better described as *potentially traumatizing* rather than as *traumatic.* We acknowledge that our term "traumatizing event" is not in common use in the traumatic stress literature, more typically referred to as a "traumatic event" or "potentially traumatic event."

A *potentially* traumatizing event becomes an *actual* traumatizing event for an individual when he or she is unable to integrate the experience of being exposed to the event into his or her personality. In this case, we say that the individual has been *traumatized.* Whereas, thus, per definition all traumatized individuals have failed to integrate traumatic experiences or components thereof, most of them also have difficulty integrating ongoing stressful and benevolent events in part or in full. Integrating experiences involves a set of difficult mental and behavioral actions that can be subsumed under the subordinate terms *synthesis* and *realization* (Van der Hart et al., 2006).

Synthesis

Our experiences involve ongoing personal constructions of what happens. Synthesis entails binding together a range of different mental actions such as sensing the body and perceiving the environment, and behavioral actions. Thus, in synthesis, a mental action in itself, we bind our various actual bodily sensations, perceptions, thoughts, affect, and behavioral actions together into a coherent, experiential whole (Hurley, 1998; Revonsuo & Newman, 1999; Van der Hart et al., 2006). Synthesis also includes connecting this whole with our idea of self in the present moment. Binding various components into experiential wholes must go along with an ability to differentiate these components from each other. In synthesis, we bind and at the same time differentiate what we see, hear, feel, and do. Synthesis also entails binding and differentiating what we experience as self and other ("I feel very close to my daughter, but appreciate that she is a different person"; "This is my room, not my friend's"), and as internal and external ("My

memory of the event may be different from the actual event or your memory of it"; "You cannot hear my thoughts"). On a broader scale, we bind and differentiate various experiences, and in this fashion generate our personal history. Providing the basic foundation of our normal unity of consciousness, synthesis is indispensable for adaptation.

In trauma survivors, synthesis of traumatic experiences, and of their personality as a whole, is deficient. This deficiency manifests in psychopathological symptoms. For example, such individuals may not adequately synthesize particular bodily feelings, thoughts, or movements into their personality as a whole. Apart from dissociative symptoms (*see:* **Dissociation**), they may experience maladaptive alterations of consciousness such as disturbances of attention, changes in time perception, or depersonalization.

Realization

Realization entails that we have (1) developed full conscious awareness of what happened and that it happened to us personally, (2) accepted the experiences and facts, and (3) adapted our subsequent mental and behavioral actions accordingly. The term *realization* thus captures a set of related complex actions that include more than merely knowing what took place and how we experienced it at the time. Whereas knowing something is a cognitive action, realization additionally includes strong affective and behavioral components. The core problems of traumatized individuals (defined previously, and not to be confused with individuals who have been merely exposed to potentially traumatizing events and consequently adapted to them) are that they are not fully aware of the dread that struck them, how it has affected and still affects their lives, how they might best adapt to the present, and who they were then and are now. From this perspective, trauma-related mental disorders are primarily syndromes of nonrealization (Janet, 1935).

Realization has two major components, as Janet concluded a century ago (cf., Van der Hart et al., 2006). One is *presentification,* which involves knowing and experiencing that we live in the present moment, which is related to but different from past and expected future events. Presentification also includes knowing and experiencing that past events really happened ("My parents neglected me"), and that there will be a future (e.g., "Avoiding intimacy will affect my relations with other people"). Presentification thus entails binding and differentiating the past, the present, and the future, while knowing, accepting, and adapting to the fact that it is only possible to act in the present and that, in this sense, the present is more *real* than the past and the future. Presentification also includes a conscious awareness that the near past and future are experienced as more real than the distant past and future. A higher experienced degree of reality of proximate events pertains to the fact that consideration of these near events is often more relevant to our current adaptive concerns than consideration of remote events. For example, it is usually more important for us to appreciate what we and significant others are about to do in the next couples of minutes and hours, than to focus on a wish for the distant future. However, our focus on the present moment and the near past and future should be embedded in a solid orientation to the more remote past and future: We must know where we come from and where we are headed. The other component of realization is the challenge to personify experiences. *Personification* (the second component of Realization) is a mental action in which we combine an experience or fact with an explicit sense of ownership, so that we can say: "That experience is *mine;* The event happened to *me.*"

Survivors may fail to meet these integrative challenges in part or in full. This becomes evident, for example, when their traumatic memories have been reactivated. These are hallucinatory, solitary, and involuntary experiences that consist of visual images, vehement emotions, sensations, thoughts such as "I am going to die," and physical actions such as measures to protect the body from harm. Traumatic memories can occupy the entire perceptual field for some time to the expense of an adaptive orientation toward the present situation. They lack condensation in the sense that they do not function as symbolized summary descriptions of previous experiences (i.e., as narratives). And they are terrifying to the individual who believes that the traumatizing event is a present happening rather than an event of the past. To develop an integrated autobiographical memory of a traumatizing event, survivors must transform their traumatic memories into narratives, and personify and presentify them.

Self-Models

Synthesis and personification require a subjective idea of self. What we experience as our self (i.e., our "I," "me," and "myself") can, like our other experiences, be understood as a personal construction (Metzinger, 2003; Nijenhuis, 2008). In this perspective, our self is not, as Cartesians contend, a substance, unchangeable essence, or thing, but rather a continuously updated *model*. Particular portions of the complete biopsychosocial system that we construct are the basics of our self-model (Damasio, 1999; Edelman & Tononi, 2000). Dreamless sleep aside, the involved integrative mental actions are ongoing.

We do not experience our basic self-model as a model but as given. This is because the portions of the system that construct the basic self-model do not represent and integrate into this model how this construction is achieved and what portions of the system engage in this construction. However, at higher levels of mental action, we may become aware of such constructions. For example, this happens when a traumatized individual eventually personifies a traumatic experience ("How awful! It happened to *me, I* was abused").

Integrating traumatic experiences into one coherent self-model is a major challenge. Traumatized individuals have not managed to initiate or complete this action, which is a primary reason for the dissociation of their personality (*see:* **Dissociation**).

Action Systems

Adaptive functioning requires ongoing integration of particular sensations, perceptions, affects, cognitions, and behavioral actions (Gibbs, 2005). It is currently believed that this integration is mediated by evolutionary derived, teleological (i.e., functional and goal-oriented) *emotional operating systems* (Panksepp, 1998), also described as *action systems* (Van der Hart et al., 2006). As Hurley (1998) emphasizes, this view differs from the traditional perspective that holds that individuals encompass separate perceptual, emotional, cognitive, and motor systems.

Personality is based on two major groups of action systems: (1) one group for approaching attractive stimuli (e.g., exploration, caretaking, sexuality/reproduction), and (2) another for avoiding or escaping from aversive stimuli (e.g., the mammalian defense system with subsystems such as freeze and flight; for a review, Nijenhuis & Den Boer, in press). Each action system includes values that guide what sensations, perceptions, affect, cognitions, and behavioral actions are to be synthesized in a given episode. For example, the action system of energy management involves approaching and consuming food as values, and the action system of mammalian defense physical distancing from a threatening individual or object.

Adaptive functioning is dependent on the integration of the different action systems we encompass. In the context of traumatization, this integration of action systems is insufficient. The basic type of dissociation of the personality in traumatized individuals pertains to a lack of integration among action systems of daily life and mammalian defense (*see*: **Dissociation**). Synthesis and realization of very stressful experiences, and the associated integration of action systems for approaching attractive cues and for avoidance of aversive cues are among the most difficult human actions. This is particularly the case when potentially or actually traumatizing events are ongoing, when they are committed by caretakers, when the survivor is a child, and when social support is lacking.

REFERENCES

Damasio, A. (1999). *The feeling of what happens: Body and emotion in the making of consciousness.* Orlando, FL: Harcourt Brace Jovanovich.

Edelman, G. M., & Tononi, G. (2000). *A universe of consciousness: How matter becomes imagination.* New York: Basic Books.

Gibbs, R. W. (2005). *Embodiment and cognitive science.* New York: Cambridge University Press.

Hurley, S. (1998). *Consciousness in action.* Cambridge, MA: Harvard University Press.

Janet, P. (1935). Réalisation et interprétation [Realization and interpretation]. *Annales Médico-Psychologiques, 93,* 329–366.

Metzinger, T. (2003). *Being no one: The self-model theory of subjectivity.* Cambridge, MA: MIT Press.

Nijenhuis, E. R. S. (2008). Bewustzijn en zelfbewustzijn in dissociatieve stoornissen [Consciousness and self-consciousness in dissociative disorders]. In J. A. den Boer, G. Glas, & A. Mooij (Eds.), *Kernproblemen van de psychiatrie [Kernal problems of psychiatry].* Meppel, The Netherlands: Boom.

Nijenhuis, E. R. S., & Den Boer, J. A. (in press). Psychobiology of traumatization and trauma-related structural dissociation of the personality. In P. Dell & J. O'Neil (Eds.), *Dissociation and the dissociative disorders: DSM-V and beyond.* Oxford, England: Routledge.

Panksepp, J. (1998). *Affective neuroscience: The foundations of human and animal emotions.* New York: Oxford University Press.

Revonsuo, A., & Newman, J. (1999). Binding and consciousness. *Consciousness and Cognition, 8,* 123–127.

Ross, T. A. (1941). *Lectures on war neuroses.* Baltimore: Williams & Wilkins.

Van der Hart, O., Nijenhuis, E. R. S., & Steele, K. (2006). *The haunted self: Structural dissociation and the treatment of chronic traumatization.* New York: Norton.

RECOMMENDED READINGS

Siegel, D. J. (1999). *The developing mind: Toward a neurobiology of interpersonal experience.* New York: Guilford Press.

Van der Hart, O., Nijenhuis, E. R. S., & Steele, K. (2006). *The haunted self: Structural dissociation and the treatment of chronic traumatization.* New York: Norton.

Ellert R. S. Nijenhuis
Mental Health Care Drenthe, Assen, The Netherlands

Onno van der Hart
Utrecht University

See also: **Dissociation; Janet, Pierre; Social Cognitive Theory**

COGNITIVE PROCESSES

See: Cognitive Impairments; Information Processing; Memory; Social Cognitive Theory

COGNITIVE PROCESSING THEORY

See: Information Processing; Social Cognitive Theory

COGNITIVE PROCESSING THERAPY

See: Cognitive Behavior Therapy, Adult; Exposure Therapy, Adult

COMBAT STRESS REACTION

When in combat, a small, but not insignificant, percentage of soldiers are overwhelmed by their anxiety. They perceive the threat of death as intense, prolonged, and uncontrollable and feel totally vulnerable and powerless. These perceptions mark the psychological breakdown known as combat stress reaction (CSR), also formerly termed as "shell shock," "combat fatigue," and "war neurosis." An acceptable functional definition perceives CSR as a behavior by a soldier under conditions of combat, invariably interpreted by those around him/her as signaling that the combatant has ceased to function as such.

The use of a functional definition rather than a clinical one is due to the multiplicity and variability of CSR's symptoms, both within a single soldier and from casualty to casualty. The psychosomatic symptoms range from loss of bladder and bowel control, trembling and stuttering, to conversion reactions such as blindness and paralysis without organic/biological causes. Cognitive symptoms include confusion and problems in perspective, memory, and judgment. In extreme cases, soldiers may not know who or where they are. The main emotional symptoms are paralyzing anxiety and deep depression, which often alternate. The behavioral symptoms are the manifestations of these emotions: great agitation on one hand and apathy and withdrawal on the other.

With the end of a war, the debilitating effects of combat stress may abate in many cases, either spontaneously or with the help of professional intervention. However, in others, acute stress reaction crystallizes into profound and prolonged psychopathological sequelae in the form of PTSD and other co-occurring diagnoses.

RECOMMENDED READINGS

Solomon, Z. (1993). *Combat stress reaction: The enduring toll of war.* New York: Plenum Press.

Solomon, Z. (2001). The impact of posttraumatic stress disorder in military situations. *Journal of Clinical Psychiatry, 62*(Suppl. 17), 11–15.

Solomon, Z., & Mikulincer, M. (2006). Trajectories of PTSD: A 20-year longitudinal study. *American Journal of Psychiatry, 163,* 659–666.

ZAHAVA SOLOMON
Tel Aviv University

See also: Acute Stress Disorder; Early Intervention; Military Personnel; Psychological First Aid, Adult; Stress; War Trauma

COMMUNITY VIOLENCE

The term *community violence* refers broadly to violence-related experiences within an individual's proximal environment (Shahinfar, Fox, & Leavitt, 2000), and includes criminal violence related to weapons (guns and knives) as well as exposure to gang wars, workplace assaults, riots, terrorist attacks, torture, bombings, wars, and ethnic cleansing. The implications of community violence are inseparable from an understanding of community itself. From the standpoint of social psychology, an individual's relationships within networks of other people and larger systems are integral to psychological health, well-being, social opportunity, and purposeful existence. Community violence can warp, fragment, or even destroy communities, with profound effects on individual members through forces that are understood as acting on higher-order systems. This is important because effective interventions to reduce community violence or mitigate its effects may need to be directed at systems-level problems (e.g., poverty, racism, loss of resources) rather than at individuals (e.g., treatment of violence-related posttraumatic stress disorder [PTSD]).

Community violence affects both the victims and witnesses of these events, as well as persons whose family members, neighbors, friends, or coworkers are harmed or killed (e.g., *see:* **Bereavement; Vicarious Traumatization**). This is especially true for children and adolescents who may be exposed to pervasive violence, such as watching drug deals, hearing gunfire, and witnessing drive-by shootings and murders. For children in communities in which violence is endemic, there is the additional risk that identification with or involvement with perpetrators of violence among adolescents may perpetuate the problem of involvement in or victimization by violent and criminal behavior, since a lifelong pattern of criminal justice problems typically begins in adolescence.

Several aspects of community violence make it different from other types of potentially traumatic experiences. Community violence is similar to many other types of psychological trauma such as abuse, disasters, or life-threatening accidents because it usually happens without warning and within the environment of day-to-day life, perpetuating the fear that the world is unpredictable and dangerous. However, by definition, the scale of community violence is larger and more destructive than traumatic experiences such as abuse or accidents that affect one person or a small group of persons. Additionally, because community violence involves the intentional infliction of harm (unlike disasters or accidents), it may result in an extreme sense of betrayal by others and society and lead to general mistrust of others and of the institutions that purport to preserve order and fairness in society.

Epidemiology

While the risk of exposure to community violence in the United States is greater among poor, nonwhite individuals in urban areas, recent studies have demonstrated that community violence crosses the boundaries of race and socioeconomic status. In a national survey of girls and boys 10 to 16 years old, over one-third reported being the direct victim of violence including aggravated assault, attempted kidnapping, and sexual assault (Boney-McCoy & Finkelhor, 1995). In another study of urban elementary school children living in high-violence and low-violence neighborhoods, exposure to homicide was greater in children living in high-violence neighborhoods in comparison to those living in low-violence neighborhoods (32% versus 9%), but exposure to violent acts such as stabbings, physical assault, and gang violence was similar (Hill & Jones, 1997). Finally, in a study of fifth and sixth grade children living in a moderately violent neighborhood in Washington DC, 59% reported being the victim of violence while 97% reported witnessing violence such as a shooting, mugging, or drug trade (Richters & Martinez, 1993).

One large general population study of more than 4,000 adult women found that 36% of the sample reported exposure to rape, other sexual assault, aggravated assault, or the homicide of someone close to them. More than 12 million women, or 12.7% of the sample, lived through a completed rape (Resnick, Kilpatrick, Dansky, Saunders, & Best, 1993).

Mental Health Consequences of Exposure to Community Violence

Exposure to community violence has been recognized as a major risk factor in the development of psychological and behavioral problems, including depression, anxiety, PTSD, suicidal behavior, and antisocial behavior in children and adolescents. There are characteristics of individuals and their social networks that can diminish the negative consequences of community violence, thus supporting more resilient outcomes. For children, stronger family support can have beneficial (i.e., protective) effects, whereas coping difficulties, violent behavior, and other aspects of impaired family functioning put children at greater risk. Exposure to violence may also disrupt normal development in children. Emotional violence and punitive interactions and rearing practices in the home and community (e.g., schools, peer group) become models for future behavior and place children at risk for developing oppositional and aggressive styles of coping and responding (*see:* **Aggression**).

Research indicates that adolescents are at greatest risk for witnessing or being involved in serious community violence, at a time when they are developing the values, expectations for opportunity, and worldviews that they may retain for the rest of their adult lives. The mental health consequences of community violence on children may be exacerbated further by other risk factors that are embedded in the communities when violence occurs (e.g., low-income, single-parent families, parental unemployment, parental psychopathology, and exposure to other types of traumatic events).

PTSD may be considered one marker of severe mental health consequences after community violence. For example, the prevalence of probable PTSD related to the September 11, 2001, terrorist attacks was as high as 11.2% in the New York City metropolitan 2 months after the attacks, and 4.0% in the rest of the country.

PTSD can affect people of all ages. Symptoms of PTSD in children may differ from those in adults. Children with PTSD (*see:* **Child Development**) may display disorganized or agitated behavior and have nightmares that reflect age-appropriate fears rather than thematically specific content (e.g., being chased by monsters). They may become withdrawn, fearful, or aggressive, have difficulty paying attention, and may regress to earlier behaviors such as thumb-sucking and bed-wetting, and display separation anxiety. They may also compulsively reenact the violence in the ways that they play.

Adolescents (*see:* **Adolescence**) with PTSD also experience nightmares and intrusive thoughts about the trauma. They may be easily startled, become angry, distrustful, fearful, and may feel alienated and betrayed. Many do not feel they have a future, or have no plans for the future, or may even believe that they will not reach adulthood. Other trauma-related reactions can include impaired self-esteem and body image, learning difficulties, and or risk taking behaviors such as running away, drug or alcohol use, suicide attempts, and inappropriate sexual activities. For all persons, the risk of PTSD increases with the severity and proximity of exposure.

Community violence exposure also affects the family in profound ways (*see:* **Family Systems**). A common parental reaction is the development of extreme anxiety concerning the child's health and well-being. Parents may blame themselves for not protecting their child adequately and become overprotective or use punitive discipline in response to their child's acting out behavior. Parents may face the difficult task reassuring their child while trying to cope with their own fears, especially in the setting of chronic community violence exposure. Relationships among family members can become strained; and single-parent families have been shown to be at increased risk for a range of mental health consequences due to community violence.

Adult survivors of community violence may develop PTSD as well, and often struggle with the following issues: rebuilding trust, finding meaning in life apart from the desire for revenge; finding realistic ways to protect themselves and their loved ones from danger; and dealing with feelings of guilt, shame, powerlessness, and doubt. There is also a concern that witnessing violence, whether through identification or modeling, or through development of aggressive coping behaviors, can perpetuate more violent behavior, especially in intimate relationships; although there are no definitive data that establish a causal relationship between community violence and domestic violence.

Intervention and Treatment

From a systems perspective, reducing and preventing community violence depends on its sources and perpetuating factors. Rampant criminal violence linked to collapsed social infrastructure and political corruption, for example, will require very different and complex solutions than preparedness plans to address potential natural disasters. At the microlevel, timely and sensitive care for the affected individuals and families can reduce the burden of mental health problems on victims and thereby reduce the cumulative community effect. Mental-health professionals may direct psychological services within the affected community, and these include *psychoeducation* (*see:* **Psychoeducation**), crisis hotlines, identification of survivors at high risk of developing PTSD, and screening/referral for appropriate continuing treatment (*see:* **Crisis Intervention, Adult; Crisis Intervention, Child; Early Intervention**). Mental-health professionals may also help community leaders develop violence-prevention and victim-assistance programs, and help religious, educational, and health-care leaders and organizations set up relief centers and shelters. They can work with schools to provide education focusing on resilience and coping, and serve as referral resources for affected children.

Some progress has been made in developing violence prevention programs, especially for gang prevention and conflict resolution in high risk youths. These programs appear to be more effective if children are engaged very early, before age 6. After large-scale disaster in the developing world, the complexities of intervention programs can be compounded by cultural and political clashes over the validity of intervention models as well as the timing, consistency, and long-term commitment of those involved.

For individuals who develop PTSD, several *cognitive-behavioral therapies* have been shown to be efficacious: Prolonged Exposure (PE), Cognitive Processing Therapy (CPT), and Stress Inoculation Training (SIT) (*see:* **Anxiety Management Training; Exposure Therapy, Adult; Exposure Therapy, Child**). PE involves repeated imaginal exposure to the traumatic memory (trauma reliving) and repeated *in vivo* exposure to safe situations that are avoided. PE has also been used in combination with antidepressants and anxiolytic (anxiety reducing) medications (*see:* **Pharmacotherapy**). CPT focuses on identifying and challenging trauma-related dysfunctional thoughts and replacing them with more logical and helpful thoughts. SIT (*see:* **Anxiety Management Training**) treatment encompasses anxiety-management training focused on posttraumatic reactions.

Evidence-based treatments for other common mental health problems such as major depressive disorder and substance abuse can be made available and integrated into community violence response programs and strategies. In most communities, such programs must include making effective training available to mental health practitioners to ensure the delivery of quality care.

REFERENCES

Boney-McCoy, S., & Finkelhor, D. (1995). Psychosocial sequelae of violent victimization in a national youth sample. *Journal of Consulting and Clinical Psychology, 63,* 726–736.

Hill, H. M., & Jones, L. P. (1997). Children's and parents' perceptions of children's exposure to violence in urban neighborhoods. *Journal of National Medical Association, 89*(4), 270–276.

Resnick, H. S., Kilpatrick, D. G., Dansky, B. S., Saunders, B. F., & Best, C. L. (1993). Prevalence of civilian trauma and posttraumatic stress disorder in a representative national sample of women. *Journal of Consulting and Clinical Psychology, 61*(6), 984–991.

Richters, J. E., & Martinez, P. (1993). The NIMH Community Violence Project: Pt. I. Children as victims of and witnesses to violence. *Psychiatry, 56,* 7–21.

Shahinfar, A., Fox, N. A., & Leavitt, L. A. (2000). Preschool children's exposure to violence: Relation of behavior problems to parent and child reports. *American Journal of Orthopsychiatry, 70*(1), 115–125.

EUN JUNG SUH
Columbia University

RANDALL D. MARSHALL
Columbia University

See also: Aggression; Criminal Victimization; Domestic Violence; Hate Crimes

COMORBIDITY

There is universal consensus that comorbidity in posttraumatic stress disorder (PTSD) is the rule rather than the exception. In other words, persons suffering with PTSD are very likely to have additional mental disorders as well. According to the National Vietnam Veterans Readjustment Study (NVVRS), almost all veterans with PTSD had at least one comorbid mental disorder. The corresponding comorbidity rate was as high as 88% in the National Comorbidity Survey (NCS). Of the PTSD-diagnosed respondents in the NCS, 44% of women and 59% of men had at least three additional mental disorders. For the most part, those are *lifetime diagnostic* estimates. Comorbid conditions may occur *before* (and, hence, be a risk factor for), *concurrently with,* or *after* development of PTSD.

Comorbid conditions that often occur with PTSD include major depressive disorder (MDD), alcohol and drug abuse, other anxiety disorders, personality disorders, sleep disorders and chronic medical conditions. Few reports also list psychotic, eating, or dissociative disorders. Patients with PTSD and comorbid disorders are more likely to have a chronic course, greater symptom severity, more functional impairment, higher utilization of health services and higher risk of suicide. The fact that PTSD shares multiple symptoms with these comorbid disorders can pose a clinical challenge in differential diagnosis. However, it has been clearly established that increased comorbidity in PTSD is not an artifact of symptom overlap between PTSD and other disorders.

By far, MDD is the most common and most studied comorbid disorder with PTSD (except in veterans, where substance abuse is the most frequent). A very high prevalence of early life trauma was found in chronic, severely depressed patients. In addition, hippocampal volume is reduced and cerebrospinal fluid corticotropin-releasing factor (CRF) concentration is markedly increased in the brains of both MDD and PTSD patients. However, hypothalamic-pituitary-adrenal (HPA) axis functioning is *hypoactive* (with lower cortisol) in PTSD and *hyperactive* (with higher cortisol) in MDD. An earlier observation of unusually low cortisol levels in a subset of MDD patients was later explained by the finding of early childhood trauma.

Individuals with premorbid MDD have a significantly increased risk of exposure to traumatic events and development of PTSD thereafter. Conversely, individuals with PTSD have considerably increased risk of first-onset MDD. In a community study, following trauma exposure, premorbid MDD increased the risk for PTSD threefold, while risk for new onset MDD in PTSD subjects was 2.8 times higher. Those who did not develop PTSD after trauma exposure did not have significantly increased risk for first-onset MDD (Breslau, Davis, Peterson, & Schultz, 2000). In other words, exposure to traumatic events per se does not lead to depression.

These neurobiological and clinical findings led to the hypothesis that PTSD and MDD share more than symptoms, but rather a common, possibly genetic, vulnerability that is uncovered or triggered by the traumatic event. Perhaps it is not the same as depression after all. It could very well be that PTSD and comorbid PTSD/depression are effectively one and the same construct. We could be observing a distinct cohort of individuals whose genetic blueprint makes them more likely to develop a "group of symptoms" when exposed to trauma—symptoms we artificially diagnose as both PTSD and MDD.

The strong association between PTSD and substance use disorders, especially alcohol use, has been well documented—up to 75% in veterans and 43% in civilians with PTSD, mostly in studies of men. Increased nicotine dependence (ND) has been reported as well. Theories explaining this association include: (a) addiction lifestyle increases the risk of trauma exposure, (b) PTSD sufferers use alcohol to relieve PTSD's hyper-arousal symptoms (the widely accepted *self-medication* model), or (c) a shared etiology/vulnerability exists. A growing body of knowledge from epidemiologic samples supports the third model. There seem to be hereditary vulnerability factor(s) that, on exposure to trauma, lead to development of PTSD that is often comorbid with MDD, ND, alcohol and drug abuse.

Being an anxiety disorder, one would expect numerous studies of PTSD comorbid with anxiety disorders. However, compared to depression, much less attention has been given to the relationship between individual anxiety disorders and PTSD. Simple and social phobias are the most common. Reported odds ratios (i.e., in this case, the odds of being diagnosed with another anxiety disorder once diagnosed with PTSD) range from 2.4 to 7.1 for coexisting simple phobia, and 2.4 to 3.3 for social phobia (Kessler, Sonnega, Bromet, Hughes, & Nelson, 1995). The reason behind this association remains theoretical. Originally, some suggested that social phobia develops after PTSD as an outcome of shame, guilt, and homecoming adversity in Vietnam veterans. However, in prospective studies, unlike MDD, phobic disorders primarily *precede,* rather than follow, both trauma and onset of PTSD (i.e., they are risk factors rather than result). While panic attacks are fairly common in PTSD, they are linked to reliving experiences of trauma. Panic disorder is not as common as other anxiety disorders in PTSD patients.

A number of personality *traits* are well known to confer high risk for development of PTSD. Rates of PTSD comorbidity with personality disorders (PD) vary widely, with 45% to 79% of veterans (mostly men) with PTSD having at least one comorbid personality disorder (Bollinger, Riggs, Blake, & Ruzek, 2000; Dunn et al., 2004). Most of the research done in civilian populations has focused on borderline personality disorder (BPD), particularly in women, where the rate of comorbidity also varies; 39% to 68% of PTSD patients have comorbid BPD, while 28% to 61% of BPD patients have PTSD (Hudziak et al., 1996; Yen et al., 2002; Zanarini et al., 1998). Possible reasons for this variability include different populations sampled (veterans versus civilians, outpatients versus inpatients, treatment seeking versus general community), type of trauma (combat, natural disaster, assault, accidents, etc.) and diagnostic and rating methods used (chart review, self-administered questionnaires, unstructured/semi-structured interviews).

Explaining the origin of high comorbidity of PTSD and personality disorders is an area of deep divide and heated debate. Disagreement over BPD is probably the most controversial. On one side is the more traditional view, arguing that given significant symptom overlap, high comorbidity, shared neurobiological features, and high prevalence of early childhood abuse in both, BPD can be placed on the same trauma-related spectrum with PTSD. From this viewpoint, BPD can be considered a form of chronic PTSD, and some even suggest a diagnostic category of "post traumatic personality disorder" (Classen, Pain, Field, & Woods, 2006).

On the other hand, more recent views argue that BPD and PTSD are separate constructs that share a common risk factor (childhood abuse), rather than a common substrate. Accordingly, BPD is not a chronic form of PTSD. Evidence inconsistent with the traditional stress-related theory is growing rapidly. Other personality disorders are also common in PTSD patients. Paranoid personality disorder (PPD) was found to be much more common than BPD in veterans with PTSD.

In a study of civilian outpatients with personality disorders, childhood abuse and early life trauma were common in the group as a whole (not restricted to BPD), and even more common in individuals with PPD. In addition, on path coefficient analysis, there was a significant association for a PTSD diagnosis with history of childhood abuse, rather than with BPD (Golier et al., 2003). Other studies found no significant difference between patients with PTSD plus BPD versus PTSD alone regarding HPA axis changes, severity or frequency of trauma symptoms, and degree of impairment.

Both sides, however, agree that: (a) personality disorders are very common in PTSD patients and (b) chronic PTSD has strong impact on all facets of living and coping of the afflicted individual. As the *DSM-V* is being developed, this strengthens the argument for reconsideration of including a diagnosis similar to the *ICD-10*'s "Enduring personality change due to a catastrophic experience."

Despite the nearly ubiquitous nature of sleep-related symptoms in PTSD, research addressing the presence of comorbid sleep disorders is surprisingly quite limited. The few published studies suggest that sleep disorders (e.g., sleep apnea, restless leg syndrome, and rapid eye movement disorders) are common in trauma survivors with PTSD. Some even suggest that sleep problems in the aftermath of trauma are in fact distinct, intrinsic, diagnosable sleep disorders independent of PTSD. There is limited evidence supporting this proposition, and more studies are needed to examine it.

Further research of sleep disorders in PTSD could have significant impact on patient care. For example, in one study, specific treatment of the comorbid sleep disorder (obstructive sleep apnea) improved PTSD symptoms.

Several questions remain unanswered regarding PTSD's comorbidity: If truly common in PTSD, are these disorders present before the trauma (risk factors)? Can PTSD be a trigger that unmasks their presence, or even has a direct causal relationship? Do those patients have similar biological findings as other noncomorbid PTSD patients? Finally, is there a reliable, quick way for clinicians to screen for other disorders in PTSD patients?

Comorbidity in PTSD is not limited to mental disorders. There is compelling evidence that patients with chronic PTSD have an increased prevalence of a myriad of major chronic illnesses, including cardiovascular (especially coronary artery disease), central nervous system, and respiratory diseases. The risk remains higher than the general population even after controlling for other major risk factors. More recently, compared to those without PTSD, Vietnam veterans with PTSD were more likely to have postwar autoimmune diseases (rheumatoid arthritis, psoriasis, Grave's disease, and insulin-dependent diabetes) with abnormally high T-lymphocyte counts and immunoglobulin-M levels (Boscarino, 2004).

It is not yet known whether these general medical (including mental) illnesses are the *result* of the traumatic incident itself or due to a shared *vulnerability* with PTSD—the same question raised for PTSD's comorbidity

with MDD and alcohol abuse. It is intuitive to assume that effective treatment of PTSD would ameliorate the concurrent medical morbidity. However, there is no empirical data to support that so far.

In reviewing the literature on PTSD comorbidity, clear knowledge gaps and striking observations are evident. First, regarding treatment of comorbid PTSD, a number of "guidelines" have been proposed by experts in the field. All are intuitive and helpful, though lack supporting empirical evidence. In research, however, most medication or psychotherapy treatment trials systematically exclude subjects with comorbid conditions (especially depression and alcohol dependence). In the few studies that did *not* exclude comorbid alcohol dependence, the antidepressant medication, sertraline, was effective for symptoms of both PTSD and alcohol dependence. Only a couple of studies examined treatment of PTSD with comorbid MDD and/or anxiety disorders; again sertraline was effective for both disorders' symptoms. Customized individual and group psychotherapies, mostly based on cognitive behavioral techniques, are emerging. Preliminary results from published pilot studies are promising.

The importance of therapeutic trials (medications or psychotherapy) in PTSD patients with comorbid disorders cannot be overemphasized. Results of such trials will have immediate impact on everyday clinical care as well as clinical research. More can be learned about disorder development and progression if those with comorbid PTSD respond better to certain treatments than others or whether the response varies based on the individual comorbid conditions.

Additionally striking is the observation of the wide variability of comorbidity prevalence estimates, as with personality disorders. In the case of MDD, the most common comorbid disorder with PTSD, lifetime prevalence rates range from 26% (in firefighters), 28% (in Vietnam veterans), 46% (in inner city residents), 49% (in the NCS), 50% (in exposed disaster workers), and 53% (civilian survivors of chemical warfare). Possible reasons for this discrepancy are similar to those mentioned with BPD. This makes it difficult to compare studies or conduct meta-analyses (i.e., quantitative reviews of studies). In fact, there is not a single published meta-analytic report on PTSD's comorbidity.

On that note, two issues in the methodology of comorbidity research deserve more attention: sample selection (epidemiological versus clinical), and the study time frame (cross-sectional versus longitudinal). A major limitation in studies of PTSD's comorbidity is the almost exclusive reliance on *retrospective* self-report of symptoms, with unavoidable recall bias, and upward shift of data due to PTSD-diagnosed individuals being more likely to recall and report symptoms of other disorders. This is especially relevant in cross-sectional studies, but even most longitudinal/prospective studies use trauma exposure as the starting point. Thus, data on *preceding* disorders are also obtained through retrospective recall.

Especially significant are those prospective studies that begin to follow subjects *before* the trauma is made clear. Remarkable findings from the few such studies conducted have challenged time-honored concepts. For example, in a large, inner city, community-based 10-year prospective study, Breslau and colleagues (Breslau, Davis, & Schultz, 2003) found that exposure to trauma did *not* predict new onset alcohol abuse/dependence either in presence or absence of PTSD. On the other hand, risk for ND was higher in subjects exposed to trauma with or without PTSD.

Another astounding example is presented from the same group where a large cohort of children was followed through adulthood. While children with aggressive/disruptive behavior problems were more likely to be *exposed to trauma* as they grew up, they did not have a higher risk for developing PTSD later on. The opposite was true for children with self-reported depressive and anxiety symptoms. This clearly challenges a time-honored principle that higher exposure to trauma in childhood is linked to future development of PTSD.

Again, because of fundamental differences in design, these findings cannot be compared to previous reports. They raise, however, serious questions about which results are indeed valid. What is not disputed or controversial is that much more research is needed to address those outstanding questions, and hopefully help achieve better understanding of the development, course, and effects of PTSD.

REFERENCES

Bollinger, A. R., Riggs, D. S., Blake, D. D., & Ruzek, J. I. (2000). Prevalence of personality disorders among combat veterans with posttraumatic stress disorder. *Journal of Traumatic Stress, 13,* 255–270.

Boscarino, J. A. (2004). Posttraumatic stress disorder and physical illness: Results from clinical and epidemiologic studies. *Annual New York Academy of Sciences, 1032,* 141–153.

Breslau, N., Davis, G. C., Peterson, E. L., & Schultz, L. R. (2000). A second look at comorbidity in victims of trauma: The posttraumatic stress disorder-major depression connection. *Biological Psychiatry, 48,* 902–909.

Breslau, N., Davis, G. C., & Schultz, L. R. (2003). Posttraumatic stress disorder and the incidence of nicotine, alcohol, and other drug disorders in persons who have experienced trauma. *Archives of General Psychiatry 60,* 289–294.

Classen, C. C., Pain, C., Field, N. P., & Woods, P. (2006). Posttraumatic personality disorder: A reformulation of complex posttraumatic stress disorder and borderline personality disorder. *Psychiatric Clinics of North America, 29,* 87–112, viii-ix.

Dunn, N. J., Yanasak, E., Schillaci, J., Simotas, S., Rehm, L. P., Souchek, J., et al. (2004). Personality disorders in veterans with posttraumatic stress disorder and depression. *Journal of Traumatic Stress, 17,* 75–82.

Golier, J. A., Yehuda, R., Bierer, L. M., Mitropoulou, V., New, A. S., Schmeidler, J., et al. (2003). The relationship of borderline personality disorder to posttraumatic stress disorder and traumatic events. *American Journal of Psychiatry, 160,* 2018–2024.

Hudziak, J. J., Boffeli, T. J., Kreisman, J. J., Battaglia, M. M., Stanger, C., & Guze, S. B. (1996). Clinical study of the relation of borderline personality disorder to Briquet's syndrome (hysteria), somatization disorder, antisocial personality disorder, and substance abuse disorders. *American Journal of Psychiatry, 153,* 1598–1606.

Kessler, R. C., Sonnega, A., Bromet, E., Hughes, M., & Nelson, C. B. (1995). Posttraumatic stress disorder in the National Comorbidity Survey. *Archives of General Psychiatry, 52,* 1048–1060.

Yen, S., Shea, M. T., Battle, C. L., Johnson, D. M., Zlotnick, C., Dolan-Sewell, R., et al. (2002). Traumatic exposure and posttraumatic stress disorder in borderline, schizotypal, avoidant, and obsessive-compulsive personality disorders: Findings from the collaborative longitudinal personality disorders study. *Journal of Nervous and Mental Disease, 190*(8), 510–518.

Zanarini, M. C., Frankenburg, F. R., Dubo, E. D., Sickel, A. E., Trikha, A., Levin, A., et al. (1998). Axis I comorbidity of borderline personality disorder. *American Journal of Psychiatry, 155*(12), 1733–1739.

MOATAZ M. RAGHEB
Brown University Alpert Medical School

MARK ZIMMERMAN
Brown University Alpert Medical School

See also: Alcohol Use Disorders; Anxiety Disorders; Depression; Diagnosis of Traumatic Stress Disorders (*DSM & ICD*); Dissociation; Eating Disorders; Insomnia; Medical Illness, Adult; Medical Illness, Child; Personality Disorders; Posttraumatic Stress Disorder, Diagnosis of; Psychosis; Substance Use Disorders

COMPASSION FATIGUE

See: Vicarious Traumatization

COMPENSATION NEUROSIS

See: Diagnosis of Traumatic Stress Disorders (*DSM & ICD*); Forensic Assessment; History of Psychological Trauma; Traumatic Neurosis

COMPLEX POSTTRAUMATIC STRESS DISORDER

Children, adolescents, and adults who experienced "developmentally adverse interpersonal trauma" (DAIT; Ford, 2005) are at risk for not only posttraumatic stress disorder (PTSD) but also for other anxiety, affective, addictive, conduct, eating, psychotic, and personality disorders and for retraumatization. These long-term adverse outcomes reflect disruptions of psychobiological self-regulation that have been labeled "complex" PTSD (Herman, 1992) or "disorders of extreme stress not otherwise specified" (DESNOS; van der Kolk, Roth, Pelcovitz, Sunday, & Spinazzola, 2005).

PTSD involves persistent anxiety, fear, and bodily arousal that can lead to problems with anger, irritability, sleeplessness, and a loss of the ability to feel most emotions. Complex PTSD involves three different fundamental problems: (1) emotion dysregulation, (2) pathological dissociation, and (3) stress-related breakdowns in bodily health.

Emotion dysregulation has three defining features that set it apart from PTSD's problems with anger and emotional numbing. First, when emotions are dysregulated, they shift unpredictably, so the person never knows what he or she will be feeling from moment to moment. Second, dysregulated emotions are extreme in intensity, such as terror, rage, despair, or paralyzing guilt, shame, and self-loathing. Third, when emotions are dysregulated the person cannot get over the distress for prolonged periods, even when attempting to calm down or when other people attempt to provide support or reassurance. Although the origins of emotional dysregulation are not definitely known, it is a state that is very similar to the extreme and inconsolable distress that young children experience if they are unable to form a secure attachment to primary caregivers. Emotion dysregulation also is similar to the distress and confusion that researchers have observed in animals that are severely stressed very early in their lives. Consistent with these findings, people suffering from complex PTSD typically have experienced psychological traumas that caused them to experience intense insecurity and fear in early childhood, such as maltreatment, death of a caregiver, or family violence.

The second feature of complex PTSD is dissociation. Dissociation involves a sudden and involuntary loss of the ability to know who you are, where you, are, and what you are feeling and thinking. When people dissociate, they tend to feel unpleasantly confused and "in a daze," and to be unable to think clearly enough to be in control of their own actions—instead they often feel as if they are "on automatic pilot" and not in control of their own minds or bodies. Temporary dissociation is common when people experience trauma, because traumatic events are shocking and disorienting. However, persistent dissociation is not common even for people who have suffered psychological traumas. Why some people who experience trauma continue to have problems with dissociation and others do not is not fully understood. However, dissociation appears to be a form of biological, emotional, and cognitive "overload" that can become a persistent problem if it begins (like emotion dysregulation) with trauma in early childhood. Dissociation in complex PTSD may involve dissociative identity disorder, but this is an extreme that is not typical (*see:* **Dissociative Identity Disorder**).

The third core feature of complex PTSD is a breakdown in bodily health that cannot be fully explained by physical injuries or medical illness. Individuals with complex PTSD often describe their bodies as "falling apart," or "damaged and broken," or "in constant pain." Children who experience severe adversities such as maltreatment, extreme poverty, or violence in their families or communities are prone to develop medical illnesses. When these physical health problems fail to respond as expected to medical treatment or become a main focus and preoccupation in the person's life, this is a sign of possible complex PTSD. The exact cause of bodily dysregulation in complex PTSD is not known, but it may involve having learned as the result of trauma in early childhood to feel afraid and helpless when experiencing ordinary physical illnesses or discomforts.

As a result of the combination of emotion dysregulation, persistent dissociation, and bodily breakdowns, people suffering complex PTSD tend to have serious problems in self-esteem, relationships, and finding a sense of

meaning in their lives. They tend to feel self-critical or even self-hatred. They often engage in risky behavior such as exposing themselves to physical danger in the form of accidents, fights, or unprotected sex. They have major ups and downs in relationships. And they often feel that life is pointless and hopeless. When past traumas involved being the victim of purposeful assaults, abuse, torture, or war atrocities, complex PTSD also may include "altered perceptions of perpetrators"—beliefs that include chronic hatred, intimidation, or sympathy for those who caused harm.

Complex PTSD was proposed as a separate psychiatric diagnosis from PTSD when the American Psychiatric Association was revising its *Diagnostic and Statistical Manual* for its fourth edition in the early 1990s (van der Kolk et al., 2005). However, complex PTSD was not codified as a separate diagnosis because it was judged to be similar to other diagnoses, especially to borderline personality disorder. Instead, complex PTSD symptoms were included as optional "associated features" of PTSD, so that a diagnosis of PTSD may include complex PTSD symptoms as a way to indicate a severe form of PTSD.

Complex PTSD has been found to occur primarily only in combination with PTSD (van der Kolk et al., 2005), although there is evidence that it may exist distinct from PTSD (Ford, 1999). Complex PTSD also has been found to be a negative prognostic factor for therapy (Ford & Kidd, 1998), meaning that effective treatment for complex PTSD may need to address the core problems of emotional dysregulation, dissociation, and somatization as well as PTSD (Ford, Courtois, van der Hart, Nijenhuis, & Steele, 2005).

A reformulation of complex PTSD specifically for children is under development by the National Child Traumatic Stress Network (van der Kolk, 2005). This syndrome, described as "developmental trauma disorder," is being formulated to enable clinicians and researchers to more effectively treat and study traumatized children who display symptoms similar to—but not precisely the same as—those for severe mental illnesses such as bipolar disorder or major depression, or disruptive behavior disorder diagnoses such as conduct disorder or oppositional-defiant disorder.

REFERENCES

Ford, J. D. (1999). PTSD and disorders of extreme stress following warzone military trauma: Comorbid but distinct syndromes? *Journal of Consulting and Clinical Psychology, 67,* 3–12.

Ford, J. D. (2005). Treatment implications of altered neurobiology, affect regulation and information processing following child maltreatment. *Psychiatric Annals, 35,* 410–419.

Ford, J. D., Courtois, C., van der Hart, O., Nijenhuis, E., & Steele, K. (2005). Treatment of complex posttraumatic self-dysregulation. *Journal of Traumatic Stress, 18,* 467–477.

Ford, J. D., & Kidd, P. (1998). Early childhood trauma and disorders of extreme stress as predictors of treatment outcome with chronic PTSD. *Journal of Traumatic Stress, 11,* 743–761.

Herman, J. L. (1992). *Trauma and recovery.* New York: Basic Books.

van der Kolk, B. A. (2005). Developmental trauma disorder. *Psychiatric Annals, 35,* 401–408.

van der Kolk, B. A., Roth, S., Pelcovitz, D., Sunday, S., & Spinazzola, J. (2005). Disorders of extreme stress: The empirical foundation of a complex adaptation to trauma. *Journal of Traumatic Stress, 18,* 389–399.

Julian D. Ford
University of Connecticut School of Medicine

See also: Abuse, Child Physical; Abuse, Child Sexual; Attachment; Child Maltreatment; Dissociation; Somatic Complaints

COMPLICATED GRIEF

See: Bereavement; Cognitive Behavior Therapy, Childhood Traumatic Grief

CONDITIONED FEAR

While organisms instinctively respond to some stimuli (e.g., loud noises) with fear, most fear responses are conditioned; they occur in reaction to a previously neutral stimulus that the organism has come to associate with an aversive stimulus through a learning experience. The most studied form of conditioned fear occurs as the result of classical conditioning (also called associative or Pavlovian conditioning), a learning phenomenon first demonstrated by Pavlov in 1927.

In the typical classical fear-conditioning paradigm, the subject is presented with an aversive stimulus (the unconditioned stimulus or US) that reliably evokes a fear response without any previous conditioning. The US is paired in temporal proximity with the presentation of a neutral stimulus (the conditioned stimulus or CS). After several pairings of the intrinsically frightening US and the innocuous CS, the subject will exhibit a fearful response to the CS (called the "conditioned response") even when the US is no longer present. For example, if an electric shock (US) is paired repeatedly with the sound of a bell (CS), the subject will eventually express behavioral and physiological fear responses to the bell alone.

Fear conditioning has been demonstrated in animals across species and is considered a highly adaptive process that prepares and motivates organisms to engage in defensive/avoidance behaviors in threatening situations. In mammals, the conditioned fear response may be measured through changes in the autonomic nervous system (e.g., increased heart rate or skin conductance), defensive behavioral maneuvers (e.g., freezing or withdrawal/escape), changes in reflexive behaviors (e.g., fear-potentiation of the startle response), or through a variety of other behaviors and physiological responses.

Properties of Conditioned Fear

Conditioned fear is one of the most extensively studied phenomena in modern psychology, and since Pavlov's pioneering work on the topic numerous studies have been conducted to elucidate the complex properties governing fear conditioning. This research suggests that conditioned fear associations with a variety of stimuli are easily acquired, and that those fear associations can also easily generalize and extend beyond original or direct learning experiences. Fear learning has been demonstrated in response to the pairing of a US both with explicit fear cues (i.e., discrete CSs with constrained physical properties that serve as clear cues for a US, for example, a bell), and with contextual cues (i.e., the situational characteristics of the conditioning environment). Further, the subject need not directly experience the pairing of the US and CS. Studies of vicarious fear conditioning demonstrate that a subject can rapidly acquire a fear association by observing another subject behaving fearfully in the presence of the CS (Cook, Mineka, Wolkenstein, & Laitsch, 1985).

Humans and animals can also come to exhibit fear in response to stimuli similar to but distinct from the original CS through a phenomenon called "stimulus generalization." For example, a chime that is qualitatively similar to the original bell CS may elicit a conditioned fear response, even though that chime was never explicitly paired with the US. Finally, higher-order conditioning can occur when a CS that has been previously paired with a US is subsequently paired with another neutral stimulus. The organism may come to exhibit fear in the presence of this additional stimulus although it has never been explicitly paired with the US.

Research suggests that the speed and strength of conditioned fear associations vary depending on many factors, including the CSs and USs employed, the characteristics of the learning environment, and the learning history and temperament of the subject (see Escobar & Miller, 2004). For example, the salience of the US is directly related to the number of trials needed to produce conditioned fear. In the case of a very intense US, a conditioned fear association can be produced with just a single pairing with the CS. However, if a subject has had experiences with the CS before it was paired with the US, fear conditioning is reduced through "latent inhibition."

Further, there is evidence that conditioned fear of certain objectively dangerous CSs (e.g., snakes) is evolutionarily prepared and acquired very quickly, whereas fear of other objectively nonthreatening stimuli (e.g., flowers) is more difficult to condition (Ohman & Mineka, 2001). Finally, genetic influences and the trait anxiety of the subject may affect subsequent conditioned fear. Some individuals, particularly those who are more anxious or who have had more previous exposure to stressors, may be more easily conditioned than others.

Neuroscience of Conditioned Fear

While the precise neuroanatomy of conditioned fear is unknown, much has been learned in the past 2 decades about some of the key brain regions involved in this type of learning (Fanselow & Poulos, 2005). One particular part of the brain, the amygdala (*see:* **Amygdala**), appears to play a central role in the process of fear conditioning. Information about the CS and US is transmitted to the amygdala, which then controls the expression of fear through output to the various regions responsible for emotional responding, including the brainstem, hypothalamus, and periaqueductal gray. It is not known whether long-term memory for conditioned fear associations is stored in the amygdala or other areas of the brain. Other critical regions are the hippocampus, which is integral to contextual conditioning, and the thalamus and cortex, which have a role in fear conditioning of explicit cues.

Extinction of Conditioned Fear

Although organisms acquire conditioned fear quite easily in experimental preparations, fear can also be easily extinguished (defined as no fear response in the presence of the CS) in the laboratory through a process called *extinction training*. During this process, the CS is repeatedly presented without the US. Outside of a laboratory setting, however, conditioned fear may not be as easily extinguished. This may be related to some features of conditioned fear that operate in uncontrolled settings. For example, Mowrer's two factor theory (1960) proposed that in a naturalistic setting, an organism will reflexively attempt to escape or avoid an aversive conditioned stimulus, thereby interfering with the process of extinction learning.

Also, while extinction is easily demonstrated in experimental settings, there is evidence that even successful extinction does not result in erasure or unlearning of the original fear association. Following extinction training, conditioned fear can often return with the passage of time (spontaneous recovery), a change in context (renewal), or a reexposure to the US or another stressor (reinstatement). Based on these findings, theorists now suggest that extinction is a special form of new learning in which the expression of the conditioned fear response comes under the control of the particular context in which extinction took place (Bouton, 2004). The original learned fear association remains largely intact, but is inhibited if the current context closely resembles the extinction training context. This is a feature of conditioned fear that is particularly relevant for the study of anxiety disorders; conditioned fear associations appear to be unremovable (with some possible exceptions), and are subject to return even after apparently successful treatment.

Conditioned Fear and Trauma

Conditioned fear is an important aspect of behavioral or learning theories of posttraumatic stress disorder (PTSD). Within these theories, the traumatic event, which by definition elicits intense emotion (including fear, terror, or horror), serves as the US. During the course of a traumatic event, a number of explicit and contextual cues, which are not inherently dangerous, are paired with the US and act as CSs. For example, a survivor of a motor vehicle accident may experience the pairing of the car, the roadway, and the act of driving, with the accident. In the future, this individual may demonstrate conditioned fear in response to thoughts of the car, exposure to the road where the accident happened, or other incident. Thus, the strong fear response triggered by exposure to trauma-related cues after a trauma is considered a conditioned version of the original response to the trauma.

Some of the earliest psychological theories of PTSD proposed a fear-conditioning model of the disorder. For example, Keane and colleagues' conditioning model of PTSD (e.g., Keane & Kaloupek, 1982; Keane, Zimering, & Caddell, 1985) described PTSD as resulting from classically conditioned fear that becomes generalized through higher order conditioning and stimulus generalization, and is maintained by avoidance of trauma-related CSs. These early conditioning models were criticized for their limitations in describing the full range of posttraumatic sequelae (e.g., cognitive symptoms, emotional numbing, dissociation) and more recent models appeal to both conditioning and information processing explanations of the development and maintenance of the disorder (e.g., Foa, Huppert, & Cahill, 2006; Keane & Barlow, 2002). However, classical fear conditioning remains one of the most widely accepted aspects of modern cognitive behavioral models of PTSD. The theoretical role of conditioned fear in PTSD forms the rationale for the use of exposure-based therapies that employ principles of extinction learning in the treatment of the disorder.

REFERENCES

Bouton, M. E. (2004). Context and behavioral processes in extinction. *Learning and Memory, 11,* 485–494.

Cook, M., Mineka, S., Wolkenstein, B., & Laitsch, K. (1985). Observational conditioning of snake fear in unrelated rhesus monkeys. *Journal of Abnormal Psychology, 94,* 591–610.

Escobar, M., & Miller, R. R. (2004). A review of the empirical laws of basic learning in Pavlovian conditioning. *International Journal of Comparative Psychology, 17,* 279–303.

Fanselow, M. S., & Poulos, A. M. (2005). The neuroscience of mammalian associative learning. *Annual Review of Psychology, 56,* 207–234.

Foa, E. B., Huppert, J. D., & Cahill, S. P. (2006). Emotional processing theory: An update. In B. O. Rothbaum (Ed.), *Pathological anxiety: Emotional processing in etiology and treatment* (pp. 3–24). New York: Guilford Press.

Keane, T. M., & Barlow, D. H. (2002). Posttraumatic stress disorder. In D. H. Barlow (Ed.), *Anxiety and its disorders* (pp. 418–453). New York: Guilford Press.

Keane, T. M., & Kaloupek, D. G. (1982). Imaginal flooding in the treatment of a posttraumatic stress disorder. *Journal of Consulting and Clinical Psychology, 50,* 138–140.

Keane, T. M., Zimering, R. T., & Caddell, J. M. (1985). A behavioral formulation of posttraumatic stress disorder in Vietnam veterans. *Behavior Therapist, 8,* 9–12.

Mowrer, O. H. (1960). *Learning theory and behavior.* New York: Wiley.

Ohman, A., & Mineka, S. (2001). Fear, phobias, and preparedness: Toward an evolved module of fear and fear learning. *Psychological Review, 108,* 483–522.

Pavlov, I. P. (1927). *Conditioned reflexes.* New York: Dover.

RECOMMENDED READINGS

Ledoux, J. (1996). *The emotional brain: The mysterious underpinnings of emotional life.* New York: Simon & Schuster.

Mineka, S., & Zinbarg, R. (2006). A contemporary learning theory perspective on the etiology of anxiety disorders: It's not what you thought it was. *American Psychologist, 61,* 10–26.

KRISTALYN SALTERS-PEDNEAULT
National Center for Posttraumatic Stress Disorder

TERENCE M. KEANE
National Center for Posttraumatic Stress Disorder

See also: Amygdala; Habituation; Learned Helplessness; Learning Theory

CONDUCT DISORDER

See: Aggression; Antisocial Behavior; Disruptive Behavior Disorders

CONSERVATION OF RESOURCES THEORY

Conservation of resources theory (COR) is a comprehensive motivational stress theory that is built on the premise that people strive to preserve, maintain, and acquire resources that help buffer the effects of stress. COR theory proposes that psychological stress results when there is a threat or an actual loss of resources, or a lack of resource gain following the investment of resources in the person's environment. This process of resource loss is especially apparent in traumatic stress, which can be conceptualized as the process of psychological distress that follows from exposure to severe, life threatening, or horrifying circumstances that produce a rapid loss of key material and psychosocial resources.

Resources can be defined as objects, personal characteristics, conditions or energies that are valued by individuals or serve as a means to acquire other resources. Object resources (e.g., shelter) are valued in and of themselves, but also for the status that is often associated with these resources. Personal characteristics (e.g., self-esteem) can be used to acquire further resources and to enhance people's coping and stress resistance. Conditions (e.g., marriage) are resources in that they foster the acquisition of other resources. Energies (e.g., time) provide resources that can be exchanged for other needed resources from the other categories. Recent biological research on the brain's reactivity to loss indicate that it is a primitive system that sees loss generally, in addition to the higher brain cognitive appraisal of loss that is more detailed and distinguishing. Said another way, on an evolutionary level, because material loss, personal loss, and social loss are all related to survival, there is a generally and powerful reactivity to loss of major resources across domains on biological and psychological levels.

There are two major principles that follow from the basic tenet of COR theory. The first principle is that resource loss is disproportionately more salient in the lives of individuals than resource gain. Research in a variety of areas has supported this claim. Although resource loss impacts individuals more than resource gain, resource gain is important, especially in the face of losses resulting from traumatic stressors. Recent evidence on the trauma associated with terrorism and disaster indicates that psychological distress and disorder following mass casualty is also largely associated with economic loss, a finding that fits COR theory but would be inconsistent with prior trauma theories that focus solely on life threat and perceived horror.

A second principle is that people must invest resources in order to prevent, recover from, and gain resources. When considering the investment of resources to acquire other resources, it is important that there is a match between the resources needed and the resources provided. However, certain variables such as self-esteem and a supportive social network can influence other resources more generally rather than in specific ways. In this regard, research indicates that there are several key resources that have broad positive impact. These include social support, self and collective efficacy, optimism, and self-esteem.

In addition to the two major principles, there are four corollaries of COR theory that allow for predictions as to how resources function over time. The first corollary states that those with greater resources are less vulnerable to resource loss and more capable of resource gain. Conversely, those with fewer resources are more susceptible to resource loss and less capable of resource gain. This is especially pertinent for individuals exposed to traumatic stressors, as the very resources they need to cope are often rapidly depleted. A second corollary is those who lack resources are not only more vulnerable to resource loss, but that initial loss creates future loss. This process can result in a loss spiral, whereby people employ resources to combat initial stress, but in turn, this loss of resources further depletes their resource reservoirs. Again, in the case of traumatic stress, loss cycles may occur rapidly and often with severe consequences. In cases of mass casualty, resource loss may be so widespread that stress contagion effects also occur, whereby the shared stress is powerful enough to affect individuals, families, and even the health systems upon which they might otherwise depend.

The third corollary asserts that people who possess resources are more capable of obtaining further resources. Finally, the fourth corollary states that those who lack resources are likely to adopt a defensive posture to protect their resources. A defensive posture keeps the maximum quantity of resources available in case the person needs to offset potential stressors.

For traumatic stress, the decision to release resource reserves, or to continue to conserve resources, is critical as people often fear follow-up trauma that may occur in the wake of the original trauma. Resources play an important role in the psychological health of individuals and should be especially considered in the aftermath of traumatic events when rapid resource loss often occurs.

COR theory further underscores that personal and social resources are best viewed as aggregates, as they are combined (or fail to be combined) as caravans over people's lifetime. Hence, self-esteem, self-efficacy, optimism, and social support are highly correlated. Those with extended resource caravans tend to be resilient following trauma. Those with weak resource caravans are rather immediately vulnerable. Less obvious, however, is that even those with strong resource reservoirs can become debilitated if facing massive or prolonged trauma as their resources erode over time or due to the severity of the impact. Hence, in a massive disaster such as Hurricane Katrina, those with weak resource reservoirs succumbed quickly, but even those with major resource armamentaria became deeply affected. This also explains why first-responder services, which are trained and well-prepared, also failed in many instances as the rapid taxing of resources overwhelmed their resource reserves.

A potential limitation of COR theory is that anything that is positive could be considered a resource, making the theory tautological. However, COR theory emphasizes key resources that are vital or central to well-being, functioning, or survival. It also cautions that even key resources may actually be vulnerability factors in some situations because resource utility in part depends on situational variables and environmental demands.

COR theory has been criticized for over-emphasizing reality and underemphasizing individuals' appraisal. Recent reanalysis of Vietnam veterans' reports of war zone stress based on objective historical reporting speaks to this key question. Findings indicate that historically verified war zone exposure has greater dose-response relationship than self-report to posttraumatic stress disorder (PTSD), clearly indicating the importance of objective stressors (Dohrenwend et al., 2006). Further, examination of the impact of ongoing terrorism in Israel indicates that psychosocial and economic resource losses are the best predictors of both PTSD and depression. In this way, COR theory suggests that much of what is called people's appraisal is actually largely a product of real occurrences in their lives, rather than individual differences. Further, individual differences that do exist in social support, self-efficacy, optimism, self-esteem, and self-control are themselves largely products of people's lifetime experiences, and these objective experiences do then shape people's appraisals.

COR theory has major clinical implications. It follows from COR theory that therapy should be directed less toward changing people's cognitions and more toward changing their reality. This would place greater emphasis on prevention, but also on increasing people's actual coping skills, their social support, and improving their life circumstances. Following trauma, the theory also suggests that it is critical to (a) interrupt resource loss cycles; (b) restore resources on personal, social, and economic levels; and (c) be attentive to the long-tail of loss that may stretch over years as has been found, for example, following major floods or hurricanes. Many such interventions are on the public mental health level, rather than tasks for individual therapy. Even when trying to change cognitions, such as optimism or self-efficacy, COR theory would direct treatment to increase people's skills and improve their life circumstances so that they have an objective basis to be more optimistic and feel more efficacious. To change cognitions without altering these realities has in fact been found to have little positive impact and is likely to be undermined when actual inability to change life circumstances and resultant life difficulties ensue due to the hollow nature of such change.

REFERENCE

Dohrenwend, B. P., Turner, J. B., Turse, N. A., Adams, B. G., Koenen, K. C., & Marshall, R. (2006, August 18). The psychological risks of Vietnam for U.S. veterans: A revisit with new data and methods. *Science, 313,* 979–982.

RECOMMENDED READINGS

Hobfoll, S. E. (1989). Conservation of resources: A new attempt at conceptualizing stress. *American Psychologist, 44,* 513–524.

Hobfoll, S. E., Canetti-Nisim, D., & Johnson, R. J. (2006). Exposure to terrorism, stress-related mental health symptoms, and defensive coping among Jews and Arabs in Israel. *Journal of Consulting and Clinical Psychology, 74,* 207–218.

Kristen H. Walter
Kent State University

Brian J. Hall
Kent State University

Stevan E. Hobfoll
Kent State University

See also: Coping; Coping Skills Training; Social Cognitive Theory

COPING

Trauma by definition demands maximum coping efforts in order to adapt. Unfortunately, coping has not been well studied in the trauma literature. Coping is a term that is often loosely used within the literature ranging from a description of the overall recovery process associated with trauma to a more specific mechanism through which environmental and intra-individual factors influence trauma psychosocial outcomes. In order to understand the concept of coping, two theoretical frameworks will be described.

Transactional Theory of Stress and Coping

The transactional theory of stress and coping is a theory that provides an elegant framework for understanding the concept of coping within the trauma literature. This theory emphasizes an interactive process between environmental conditions and individual responses to the environment (Lazarus & Folkman, 1984). In explaining the stress and coping response, Lazarus and Folkman (1984) highlight the important role of cognitive appraisals (described next) within the dynamic relationship (i.e., transactions) between environmental demands and the person. This theory distinguishes between two intra-individual cognitive appraisal processes: primary appraisal and secondary appraisal.

Primary appraisal is the evaluation of how important a specific environmental demand is for a person's well-being. Individual judgments fall into three categories: irrelevant, positive, (i.e., the transaction may lead to positive consequences without taxing or exceeding resources), or stressful (i.e., the transaction may lead to positive or negative consequences, but resources need to be engaged). Situations that are appraised as stressful are further evaluated as a potential for harm/loss, threat, or challenge. Clearly, traumatic stress exposure would fall into the stressful category for primary appraisals. It is unknown how many people view trauma recovery as a challenge in some way.

Secondary appraisals (although not necessarily considered to occur after primary appraisals) refer to the evaluation of available resources and perceived ability to utilize those resources (Benight & Bandura, 2004; see: **Coping; Social Cognitive Theory**) in responding to environmental demands. Through these appraisal processes, individuals generate a multitude of coping responses. These responses are often characterized as problem-focused (or active) or emotion-focused (passive) coping. In the trauma literature, avoidant coping is also often assessed due to its linkage with posttraumatic stress response. Problem-focused coping refers to efforts by the individual to change the environmental conditions to make them better. An example of this for a trauma survivor following a hurricane might be seeking out information on housing insurance to rebuild. Emotion-focused coping includes efforts to alleviate emotional distress such as trying not to think about the issue through distraction. Based on this theoretical perspective, coping with a trauma is a *cognitive and behavioral interactional process* that is engaged to manage traumatic recovery demands.

Conservation of Resources Theory

Another theoretical perspective that has also been utilized in understanding coping within a traumatic stress context is conservation of resources theory (COR; *see:* **Conservation of Resources Theory**). Originally proposed by Hobfoll in 1989, the COR theory is built on the premise that coping is the result of human beings' need to retain critical resources when they are threatened or lost. Coping may also be prompted by the lack of gain in resources when extensive resources have already been invested. Resources are defined in COR theory as objects, personal characteristics, conditions, or energies that people value in general or because of what they can provide for them. Hobfoll described 74 such resources and categorized them as objects (e.g., a house), conditions (e.g., marriage), personal characteristics (e.g., social skillfulness), and energies (e.g., credits).

The concept of coping in COR theory is the response generated to regain resources, stop more resources from being lost, or gain critical resources. Hobfoll (1991) applied COR theory to traumatic stress suggesting that trauma is defined by a rapid, often unpredictable, depletion of vital resources (e.g., housing, personal safety). The studies that have been completed within the trauma context utilizing COR theory have typically looked at the extensiveness of resource depletion rather than the cognitive/behavioral aspects of responding to the threat or loss (i.e., coping response). The exception to this is the research that has looked at social support seeking in the context of trauma by Kaniasty and Norris (1993). Several studies support the loss aspect of COR theory in a context of disaster-related trauma.

Frameworks: Summary

COR theory and the transactional theory of stress and coping provide useful frameworks for studying coping within a trauma context. To do so, however, requires clear definitions of constructs, hypothesized relationships, and adequate operationalization of important factors. The current research on trauma and coping has relied almost exclusively on measuring cognitive and behavioral strategies utilized to manage a traumatic situation with little appreciation for the dynamic interplay between environmental conditions and individual adaptations. The findings utilizing the transactional theory of stress and coping are unclear with some studies showing benefits for active coping and negative effects for avoidant coping. However, other studies have shown that all forms of coping are related to increases in distress following trauma. The literature looking at COR theory within a traumatic stress context (primarily following disasters) has found strong support for the importance of resource loss in contributing to psychological outcomes.

Coping Measures

The measures typically utilized to assess coping within traumatic stress situations include: (1) Ways of Coping Checklist—Revised (Vitaliano, Russo, Carr, Maiuro, & Becker, 1985), (2) The COPE (Carver, Scheier, & Weintraub, 1989), (3) the Coping Response Inventory (Moos, 1993), (4) Coping Styles Questionnaire (Roger, Jarvis, & Najarian, 1993), and (5) the Coping Strategies Inventory (Tobin, Holroyd, Reynolds, & Kigal, 1989). Each of these measures lists possible strategies (cognitive and behavioral) that are meant to deal with a stressor. A statistical method known as Factor Analysis has been used to form subsets of coping strategies such as emotion-focused coping, problem-focused coping, active coping, passive coping, detached coping, and so on. The COPE has many different subscales including: active

coping, behavioral disengagement, alcohol and drug use, denial, seeking emotional support, seeking tangible support, and acceptance to name a few. All of these measures have acceptable reliability and validity support, although individual subscales do differ in their internal reliability with some in the questionable range.

Conclusion

The conceptual challenge in understanding coping within the trauma context is to first define the coping process in a more exact way and then determine the predictive and practical utility of the measured constructs (e.g., coping behaviors, cognitive appraisals of coping self-efficacy). It is conceivable that under the extreme stress related to trauma, individuals utilize all coping strategies at their disposal in an attempt to manage the extreme coping demands, leaving previous dichotomizing conceptualizations of coping behaviors less useful in this context. Future studies are needed that more clearly outline the interactive coping process including cognitive appraisal constructs (e.g., coping self-efficacy) as well as cognitive/behavioral coping strategies that are dynamic as environmental conditions unfold.

REFERENCES

Benight, C. C., & Bandura, A. (2004). Social cognitive theory of posttraumatic recovery: The role of perceived self-efficacy. *Behavior Research and Therapy, 42,* 1129–1148.

Carver, C. S., Scheier, M. F., & Weintraub, J. K. (1989). Assessing coping strategies: A theoretically based approach. *Journal of Personality and Social Psychology, 56,* 267–283.

Hobfoll, S. E. (1989). Conservation of resources: A new attempt at conceptualizing stress. *American Psychologist, 44,* 513–524.

Hobfoll, S. E. (1991). Traumatic stress: A theory based on rapid loss of resources. *Anxiety Research, 4,* 187–197.

Kaniasty, K., & Norris, F. (1993). A test of the support deterioration model in the context of natural disaster. *Journal of Personality and Social Psychology, 64,* 395–408.

Lazarus, R. S., & Folkman, S. (1984). *Stress, appraisal, and coping.* New York: Springer.

Moos, R. H. (1993). Coping Responses Inventory. Odessa, FL: Psychological Assessment Resources, Inc.

Roger, D., Jarvis, G., & Najarian, B. (1993). Detachment and coping: The construction and validation of a new scale for measuring coping strategies. *Personality and Individual Differences, 15,* 619–626.

Tobin, D. L., Holroyd, K. A., Reynolds, R. V., & Kigal, J. K. (1989). The hierarchical factor structure of the Coping Strategies Inventory. *Cognitive Therapy Research, 13,* 343–361.

Vitaliano, P. P., Russo, J., Carr, J. E., Maiuro, R. D., & Becker, J. (1985). The Ways of Coping Checklist: Revision and psychometric properties. *Multivariate Behavioral Research, 20,* 3–26.

CHARLES C. BENIGHT
University of Colorado, Colorado Springs

See also: Conservation of Resources Theory; Coping Skills Training; Social Cognitive Theory; Stress

COPING SKILLS TRAINING

The psychotherapies designated as Coping Skills Training (CST), such as Stress Inoculation Training (*see:* **Anxiety Management Training**), are based on the assumptions that if an individual is modestly motivated to change, and is able to learn about and use practical means for managing their symptoms and dealing with typical everyday situations, then symptoms such as those of PTSD may improve or at least will not escalate if the person has to deal with ordinary stressors. The latter point is of particular importance with patients who are especially vulnerable to worsening symptoms or crises, whether because they have several concurrent disorders, such as depression, serious and persistent mental illness, or substance use disorders together with PTSD, or due to other biopsychosocial factors such as poor medical health, having few social supports, or being economically impoverished.

CST approaches are composed of a series of component interventions that build on and reinforce each other. Individual CST component interventions as well as full CST treatment "packages" have been used widely across many disorders, including PTSD, other anxiety disorders, affective and psychotic disorders, and substance use disorders. In PTSD, CST component interventions frequently include the following: psychoeducation; training in relaxation techniques such as deep or diaphragmatic breathing and progressive muscle relaxation; increasing awareness of situations triggering anxiety or distress; techniques for self-monitoring and managing anxiety; and anger awareness and anger management. Cognitive interventions, such as identifying dysfunctional cognitions, use of alternative cognitions, and thought-stopping are also frequently used CST components in treating PTSD. The therapeutic and educational techniques used to teach coping skills include role-playing, guided self-dialogue, and covert modeling. These techniques are also frequently used in many cognitive-behavioral treatments for PTSD and other disorders.

In CST approaches, symptoms or disorders are conceptualized as having cognitive, physical, behavioral (Falsetti, 1997), and emotional elements that result in problems for the person (such as feeling anxious and avoiding important activities) and for the person's relationships (such as conflicts or withdrawal). For example, the symptom of irritability in PTSD may be associated with certain cognitions, such as, "This situation reminds me of how I was victimized and I'm never letting that happen again," or, "This situation makes me feel powerless"; the physical sensation of blood rushing to one's face or through one's body; and the resulting behavior or action of yelling accompanied by the emotion of anger. In order to address PTSD-related irritability and its negative impact, CST techniques identify the skills that are needed to prevent this symptom from becoming or continuing to be a problem. The corrective alternative skills are also conceptualized as having cognitive, physical, and behavioral elements, in order to enable the individual to not just "feel" less irritable but to be able to cope more effectively when feelings of irritability occur.

For example, use of relaxation training can have the emotional effect of inducing calm as an alternative to the tension involved in irritability. A physical effect may include reducing heart rate or making breathing more regular and comfortable, instead of the rapid heart rate and difficulty breathing that tend to accompany irritability. The cognitive effect can involve realizing that is the patient is not vulnerable at the moment, instead of the thought that something terrible and unmanageable is happening. The result of learning and using this type of coping skill is that the patient is likely to feel calmer physically and emotionally, to be able to think more clearly and effectively, and to interact in a less angry, more measured fashion.

CST sessions are used to learn and practice new skills and to examine real-world situations in which these skills may be applied, including problem solving with patients about possible obstacles to applying skills. Patients are then encouraged to practice coping skills outside the therapy session. Subsequent sessions include a review of whether the patient attempted to use a given skill or set of skills, the situations in which the patient tried to use them, the extent to which the skills were used, difficulties the patient encountered when using the skills, and the results in terms of how the patient felt, thought, acted, and got along with other people. This review gives the therapist and patient a basis for fine tuning both the specific coping skills and the way the patient is practicing and using each skill, so that the patient gradually can become proficient in using the coping skills independently in everyday situations. When this is accomplished, the patient is likely to be better able both to handle life challenges and to get along with people. The use of coping skills may not fully relieve or eliminate the patient's symptoms—for example, the patient may still have moments of irritability or anger—but they provide a means for the patient to have some positive control over the symptoms and often to significantly lessen the severity of the symptoms.

Obstacles to skill use can come from multiple sources. The purpose for using the skill or the steps within a skill may not be understood or recalled by the patient. Attempts to use a skill might occur in a too-challenging, too-easy, or in an otherwise inappropriate situation. For example, use of the anger management skill of counting down from 20 before verbalizing or acting on anger may fail if the patient is not in fact angry, or if the patient is faced by a situation with so many anger-inducing stimuli such that the patient feels "too angry" to successfully remember or use the skill.

As with all other therapeutic interventions, the role of underlying psychological and family- or social-system dynamics in a patient's repeated inability to successfully employ a particular skill should also be considered by the therapist. Depending on the nature and goals of the particular therapy, explicit exploration of underlying dynamics with the patient may not be appropriate. For example, in prolonged exposure (PE), an exploration of difficulties in utilizing deep breathing may include an examination of whether deep breathing is a trigger for increased intrusive thoughts, but PE usually does not include an exploration of whether difficulties with deep breathing are a product of oppositional personality traits. In psychodynamic or interpersonal approaches to PTSD therapy, these factors might be explored with the patient in order to assist her or him in being better able to use the coping skill both in therapy and in everyday life.

While CST approaches are largely derived from cognitive-behavioral therapies (CBTs), CST components may be used within a variety of therapeutic approaches. For example, virtually all current CBTs for PTSD include the CST component of psychoeducation and at least one element of relaxation training. At the other end of the spectrum are therapies comprised almost solely of CST interventions. Present-centered therapy (PCT; McDonagh et al., 2005; Schnurr et al., 2003, 2007) features psychoeducation about the impact of trauma and PTSD on how daily living is organized, followed by training in day-to-day problem-solving skills with emphases on recognizing how trauma and PTSD dynamics impact problem solving, and on therapist empathy and warmth. PCT explicitly does not include other CBT or CST techniques for PTSD, such as PE or cognitive restructuring.

Further along the spectrum are those treatments comprised largely of CST interventions, but which also include elements of other treatment approaches. For example, stress inoculation therapy (SIT; Meichenbaum, 1977) includes skills for managing stress reactions in combination with systematic desensitization (SD), which is a form of exposure therapy. In SD, patients generate lists of those situations that cause anxiety, distress or PTSD symptoms. With the guidance of their therapist, patients gradually place themselves in those situations, starting from situations that cause the least distress and ending with the most difficult situations. As they experience each situation, the patient attempts to use coping skills that they have learned in therapy sessions as a way to manage feelings of fear or anxiety. SIT derives its name from the "inoculation" against fear and anxiety (i.e., "stress") that can occur when the coping skills and a gradual exposure to distressing situations enables the patient to feel increasingly less distressed and more confident.

Many more therapies incorporate some elements of CST into a larger treatment approach. For example, in substance dependence PTSD therapy (SDPT; Triffleman, Carroll, & Kellogg, 1999), a two-phase therapeutic approach developed for use in persons with current, active substance dependence and concurrent PTSD. Specifically, coping skills were taught throughout the first or substance-focused, trauma-informed phase of treatment to help patients decrease their substance use while providing preparation for patients to be able to then engage in trauma-focused behavioral treatment such as SD or PE. In addition to the skills noted earlier that are used by CST for PTSD, SDPT includes other skills such as planning and engaging in pleasant activities, assertiveness training, and substance-use specific skills such as those involved in dealing with cravings.

The degree to which a given therapy incorporates CST components is important when examining evidence regarding the effectiveness of CST. Two randomized controlled trials of SIT were conducted with civilian rape victims (Foa et al., 1999; Foa, Olasov Rothbaum, Riggs, & Murdock, 1991). The authors found that simply teaching the SIT stress inoculation skills, without including desensitization, was found to decrease PTSD and depression severity, along with reducing the percentage of those with a PTSD diagnosis at a rate comparable to or greater than prolonged exposure (PE), supportive counseling, and being on a wait-list for treatment. However, PE was more effective than SIT in reducing general anxiety, improving social function, and overall imparting greater benefit. Combining SIT and PE together (SIT-PE) was no more effective than using SIT (or PE) alone, and in fact, appeared to be less effective than the uncombined versions of either SIT or PE.

In a study comparing the combined SIT-PE with eye movement desensitization and reprocessing (EMDR; Lee, Gavriel, Drummond, Richards, & Greenwald, 2002), EMDR was more effective over the course of follow-up, although identical rates of patients in both conditions lost the PTSD diagnosis. EMDR teaches patients to recall a traumatic event in great detail and then to focus on alternate actions or thoughts, such as with saccadic eye movements in which the eyes are moved back and forth from left to right and vice versa. The alternate action or thoughts provide the patient with an easily used coping skill that in some cases is associated with a feeling of more manageable distress by the patient when recalling the traumatic memory. EMDR does not involve teaching the patient to use the alternate action/thoughts to cope with everyday distress, however. In both Lee et al. (2002) and the Foa et al. (1991, 1999) studies, since SIT-PE incorporated interventions from both SIT and PE without increasing the number or length of sessions, it is possible that the combination of the two was somewhat less effective than either individual therapy due to insufficient time for both types of interventions. Thus, CST should not be used indiscriminately in other PTSD psychotherapies, but instead should be used in a way that enables the patient to effectively learn and use the skills within the available therapeutic time frame without attempting to accomplish more than is feasible for patients.

The other CST intervention that has been examined in large-scale randomized controlled trials is PCT, formulated either as an individual treatment for female civilians, veterans, and active-duty personnel with histories of sexual trauma (McDonagh et al., 2005; Schnurr et al., 2007) or as a group treatment for male Vietnam veterans (Schnurr et al., 2003). Mixed results have been found. In examining results from all participants in these three studies, PCT resulted in comparable reductions in PTSD severity, PTSD diagnosis, depression, addiction severity, and quality of life as PE-based treatments, with both conditions resulting in improvement either by treatment's end or during follow-up in comparison with pre-treatment levels. In one study (McDonagh et al., 2005), this meant that neither PCT nor a PE-based treatment resulted in more improvement than occurred among those on a wait-list for treatment. However, when results from only those participants who either completed treatment or received an "adequate dose" of treatment in the three studies are considered, on balance, PCT produced at best comparable and in some cases less positive change than the PE-based treatments.

In all three PCT studies, more persons receiving PCT completed treatment or received an adequate dose. This finding could have different meanings, including the possibility that PCT did not effectively address the needs of those in treatment until the end of treatment, while therapies that included PE and other therapeutic components effectively addressed the participants' needs sooner and/or more completely. Conversely, PE-related treatments may have been more "intense" (given PE's emphasis on repeated, detailed emotional and cognitive processing of the trauma) and therefore were more difficult for some patients to tolerate than PCT.

With the notable exception of the study of PCT in women with child sexual abuse (McDonagh et al., 2005), the conclusions from the PCT and SIT studies taken together are largely consistent with results from many other psychotherapy studies: active treatment, if delivered competently and consistently, tends to result in at least some improvement that is sustained after treatment ends. As of this writing, no studies have been reported in which a given type of patient has been specifically matched to a given treatment in order to further facilitate improvement, in part because there has not been consistent identification of certain types of patients who do better or worse in a given treatment. Nevertheless, although PE-based treatments may yield overall greater improvement, CST approaches result in sufficient sustained improvement to warrant further study and use of CST to improve stress management among patients with PTSD.

REFERENCES

Falsetti, S. A. (1997). The decision-making process of choosing a treatment for patients with civilian trauma-related PTSD. *Cognitive and Behavioral Practice, 4,* 99–121.

Foa, E. B., Dancu, C. V., Hembree, E. A., Jaycox, L. H., Meadows, E. A., & Street, G. P. (1999). A comparison of exposure therapy, stress inoculation training, and their combination for reducing posttraumatic stress disorder in female assault victims. *Journal of Consulting and Clinical Psychology, 67,* 194–200.

Foa, E. B., Olasov Rothbaum, B., Riggs, D. S., & Murdock, T. B. (1991). Treatment of posttraumatic stress disorder in rape victims: A comparison between cognitive-behavioral procedures and counseling. *Journal of Consulting and Clinical Psychology, 59,* 715–723.

Lee, C., Gavriel, H., Drummond, P., Richards, J., & Greenwald, R. (2002). Treatment of PTSD: Stress inoculation training with prolonged exposure compared to EMDR. *Journal of Clinical Psychology, 58,* 1071–1089.

McDonagh, A., Friedman, M., McHugo, G., Ford, J., Sengupta, A., Mueser, K., et al. (2005). Randomized trial of cognitive-behavioral therapy for chronic posttraumatic stress disorder in adult female survivors of childhood sexual abuse. *Journal of Consulting and Clinical Psychology, 73,* 515–524.

Meichenbaum, D. (1977). *Cognitive behavior modification: An integrative approach.* New York: Plenum Press.

Schnurr, P. P., Friedman, M. J., Engel, C. C., Foa, E. B., Shea, M. T., Chow, B. K., et al. (2007). Cognitive behavioral therapy for posttraumatic stress disorder in women: A randomized controlled trial. *Journal of the American Medical Association, 297,* 820–830.

Schnurr, P. P., Friedman, M. J., Foy, D. W., Shea, M. T., Hsieh, F. Y., Lavori, P. W., et al. (2003). Randomized trial of trauma-focused group therapy for posttraumatic stress disorder. *Archives of General Psychiatry, 60,* 481–489.

Triffleman, E., Carroll, K., & Kellogg, S. (1999). Substance dependence-posttraumatic stress disorder treatment: An integrated cognitive-behavioral approach. *Journal of Substance Abuse Treatment, 17,* 3–14.

ELISA TRIFFLEMAN
Private Practice, Port Washington, NY

See also: Anxiety Management Training; Cognitive Behavior Therapy, Adult; Cognitive Behavior Therapy, Child; Exposure Therapy, Adult; Exposure Therapy, Child; Eye Movement Desensitization and Reprocessing

COSTS OF PTSD TREATMENT

See: Health Service Utilization

COUNTERTRANSFERENCE

Countertransference, as it is defined by modern therapists, refers to the therapist's emotional reactions to the patient and/or the patient's situation. The patient's transference (i.e., reactions that the patient "transfers" from other relationships such as with parents to the relationship with the therapist) is "countered," Freud originally argued, by the therapist's objective or conflict-based reaction. Only the latter reactions, those based on the therapists' own conflicts or neuroses, were "countertransference." This definition left the patient-therapist participants in the relationship, as well as the reviewers and critics of a given therapeutic relationship, at odds in defining which emotional reactions should be covered by the term.

Is the therapist's angry reaction to her hostile traumatized patient truly reality-based, or is it influenced by her history with an angry parent-figure (and thus countertransference)? Countertransference researchers now almost universally reject this "particularist" definition, and define countertransference as including all of the therapist's emotional reactions toward the patient regardless of source (the "totalist" position: cf. Dalenberg, 2000; Gabbard, 1995).

The use of the totalist definition allows more reliable measurement of the types of countertransference, since the presence of hostility in the therapist can be identified with greater precision than can the presence of the therapist's internal conflict. Countertransference research has been conducted through vignette studies (Brody & Farber, 1996), laboratory analogues (Hayes & Gelso, 1991), client interviews (Dalenberg, 2000), therapist self-report (Little & Hamby, 1996), or client-therapist transcript ratings (Hayes et al., 1998), enhanced and deepened by the traditional analysis of case studies (e.g., Rustin, 2001). Most recently, the term *countertransference* has also been applied to the therapist's emotional reactions to the event alone (e.g., rape), apart from any details provided by the patient (Danieli, 1994).

The term *countertransference* first appeared in three essays written by Sigmund Freud in the early 1900s—*The Future Prospects of Psychoanalytic Therapy* (1910/1958), *Recommendations to Physicians Practicing Psychoanalysis* (1912/1958), and *Observations on Transference-Love* (1915/1958). These initial observations outline the theoretical basis of one side of the triangle of countertransference theory and research (Dalenberg, 2000)—the view that countertransference is a potential obstacle to neutrality that must be mastered and eradicated by the well-analyzed therapist. Over time, this approach to understanding the role of countertransference has been tempered and augmented by two additional views. First, countertransference can be understood as an inevitable (both positive and negative) outcome of the therapeutic alliance and relationship, and therefore as a sign that the potential therapeutic relationship exists (Kiesler, 2001). Second, countertransference is presented in literature as a powerful source of information about the patient, possibly critical to successful treatment (Kiesler, 2001; Winnicott, 1949). Interestingly, the latter view also traces its origins to Freud, who wrote that the analyst "must turn his unconscious like a receptive organ toward the transmitting unconscious of the patient" (Freud, 1912/1958, p. 116) in order to understand the source underlying conflicts.

The study of countertransference is typically conducted through exposing therapists to vignettes describing certain patients (Brody & Farber, 1996; Lecours, Bouchard, & Normandin, 1995). For example, the therapist might be asked the following:

> John greets you angrily in the waiting room when you are five minutes late beginning his session. He accuses you of not caring about his time and his troubles. How would you respond?

Alternatively, the self-report strategy would ask the therapist to estimate the prevalence of certain behaviors, for instance, the number of times they expressed anger at a client (Pope & Tabachnick, 1993) or acknowledged their sexual attraction openly to a patient (Pope, Tabachnick, & Keith-Spiegel, 1987). Much interesting data has been gathered from these approaches, but social desirability bias is an obvious limitation. Few therapists are likely to respond that they would angrily retaliate, or that they would be deeply hurt and subtly punish the patient. Also, importantly, the original Freudian view of countertransference suggested that many reactions would be unconscious, and therefore unavailable to the reporting therapist (Freud, 1912/1958, 1915/1958). Thus, these mainstay approaches are buttressed by the analysis of transcripts of actual therapy sessions (Dahl, Teller, & Moss, 1978), or analysis of a therapist's views of a specific identified patient (Betan, Heim, Conklin, & Westen, 2005; Hayes et al., 1998). The option of asking the patient about the therapist countertransference (just as we ask the therapist about the patient transference) is also promising (Dalenberg, 2000, 2004).

The literature on countertransference is increasingly seen as important to the treatment of traumatic stress disorders for two interrelated reasons—the intensity and difficulty of the therapeutic material in these cases and the common finding of an unstable alliance that is prone to rupture (cf. Dalenberg, 2000; Davies & Frawley, 1994). Such instability is in part due to difficulties in emotional self-regulation in severely traumatized patients that manifest inside and outside of the therapeutic hour (Ford, 2005), making a contribution to the patient's functional impairment beyond that of PTSD intensity (Cloitre, Miranda, Stovall-McClough, & Han, 2005). This dysregulated and disorganized emotional state is confusing and frustrating for the therapist (Dalenberg, 2000). Yet, the therapist must attempt to "co-regulate" for the client (i.e., serve as a role model and a guide to help the client regain emotional equilibrium) to achieve a therapeutic alliance and assist the client in (re)gaining emotional stability (cf. Solomon & Siegel, 2003). That is, by keeping the client's "mind in mind" (Fonagy, 2002), rather than responding to a traumatic transference with a traumatic countertransference, the mentalizing therapist theoretically gives the traumatized client a prototype for self-regulation (Ford, 2005). For example, if a client becomes extremely angry at the therapist when they are discussing experiences in the client's life that are associated with past psychological trauma, the therapist can best help the client by being aware of her or his own reactions to this misplaced anger (countertransference reactions such as wanting to criticize the client or end the session prematurely) and by regulating her or his own bodily and emotional responses (such as mindfully focusing on breathing and remembering that these are painful topics for the client to discuss).

Traumatic transference tends to be chaotic, manifesting in both withdrawal and extreme dependence, idealization, intense distrust, love, and hate, often in the same individual over short periods of time (Ford, 2005). In the cocreation of the therapeutic relationship, therapists can therefore be pulled into varying reciprocal roles to these intense displays—becoming an unprotective parent to the client's neglected child, abusing perpetrator to the client's wronged survivor of trauma, or idealized rescuer to the client's needy or entitled victim (Davies & Frawley, 1994). The anger and hostility of many traumatic stress disorder clients, often built on a foundation of betrayal by trusted others, is quite common in victims of a variety of forms of psychological trauma (Orth & Wieland, 2006), and has been shown to lead to frequent complications in the countertransference. Intense emotional conflicts, when "transferred" to the therapist in this manner, are stressful for the therapist to experience even if the therapist is highly trained and skilled (Dalenberg, 2004).

Other ways in which therapists may have emotional reactions to their traumatized clients' posttraumatic emotional distress and associated behaviors (e.g., intense emotional outbursts or severe emotional detachment), including "secondary traumatic stress" (defined by symptoms akin to PTSD in the involved therapist: Figley, 1995) or "vicarious traumatization" (defined as a negative transformation in the therapist's inner world due to exposure to the client's trauma: Pearlman & Saakvitne, 1995; *see:* **Vicarious Traumatization**), also are beginning to receive attention among therapists and researchers. These reactions to the intensity of clients' PTSD symptoms are expectable and are not necessarily a problem in therapy so long as the therapist is aware of them and consciously takes steps to maintain (or regain) her or his own and the client's emotional equilibrium. However, when the client's PTSD symptoms include the repeated and intensive transference of emotional needs or conflicts to the relationship with the therapist, the therapist's reactions may manifest as changes in the therapist's sense of safety, power, independence, and capacity to trust.

The issue of boundaries in therapy is of special interest in discussions of treatment of PTSD. The term "boundaries" typically refers to the frame in which therapy operates—meetings in a specific room, with a specific person, at a specific time, with interactions restricted to certain types of behaviors (most often, talk rather than action). Therapy can serve as a container for the intensity of the emotions associated with PTSD, if careful attention is paid to maintaining therapeutic boundaries. Paradoxically,

however, traumatized clients often have difficulty in relationships as a result of being intrusive toward other persons (pushing for boundary shifts) and/or to failing to resist intrusions from other persons on their psychological or bodily boundaries (Somer & Saadon, 1999). Therapists who themselves have been traumatized in their personal lives may have particularly strong reactions to requests for boundary shifts, and may be vulnerable to engaging in actions that involve violations of the client's boundaries (e.g., sexual abuse of the client: Jackson & Nuttall, 2001). The sense of "we-ness" created by sharing deeply personal and often shameful events, and the interaction of the therapist's reaction to idealization and the traumatized patients' need for proof of care, are two of the risk factors for these countertransference enactments (Dalenberg, 2000). Therapists working with traumatized clients should realize that they are dealing with an at-risk group who are likely to elicit countertransference reactions due to their particular vulnerability to boundary violations, their skill in producing them, or both.

The growing research in this area underlines the importance of acknowledgment of common countertransference reactions by therapists to their clients with PTSD. Self-awareness, together with a conceptual understanding of countertransference, appears to predict better countertransference management (Latts & Gelso, 1995). Using the Countertransference Factors Inventory, Gelso, Latts, Gomez, and Fassinger (2002) also found that countertransference management skills predict positive client outcome as rated by supervisors. Although much remains to be studied, particularly in the area of countertransference specific to PTSD clients and their therapists, it is becoming clearer that countertransference management is a critical subarea for future research.

REFERENCES

Betan, E., Heim, A., Conklin, C., & Westen, D. (2005). Countertransference phenomena and personality pathology in clinical practice: An empirical investigation. *American Journal of Psychiatry, 162,* 890–898.

Brody, E., & Farber, B. (1996). The effects of therapist experience and patient diagnosis on countertransference. *Psychotherapy, 33,* 372–380.

Cloitre, M., Miranda, R., Stovall-McClough, K., & Han, H. (2005). Beyond PTSD: Emotion regulation and interpersonal problems as predictors of functional impairment in survivors of childhood abuse. *Behavior Therapy, 36,* 119–124.

Dahl, H., Teller, V., & Moss, D. (1978). Countertransference examples of the syntactic expression of warded-off contents. *Psychoanalytic Quarterly, 47,* 339–363.

Dalenberg, C. (2000). *Countertransference and the treatment of trauma.* Washington, DC: American Psychological Association.

Dalenberg, C. (2004). Maintaining the safe and effective therapeutic relationship in the context of distrust and anger: Countertransference and complex trauma. *Psychotherapy: Theory, Research, Practice, Training, 41,* 438–447.

Danieli, Y. (1994). Countertransference, trauma and training. In J. Wilson & J. Lindy (Eds.), *Countertransference in the treatment of PTSD* (pp. 368–388). New York: Guilford Press.

Davies, J., & Frawley, M. (1994). *Treating the adult survivor of childhood sexual abuse: A psychoanalytic perspective.* New York: Basic Books.

Figley, C. R. (1995). *Compassion fatigue: Coping with secondary traumatic stress disorder in those who treat the traumatized.* New York: Brunner/Mazel.

Fonagy, P. (2002). Understanding of mental states, mother-infant interaction, and the development of the self. In J. M. Maldonado-Durán (Ed.), Infant and toddler mental health: Models of clinical intervention with infants and their families (pp. 57–74). Washington, DC: American Psychiatric Publishing, Inc.

Ford, J. (2005). Treatment implications of altered neurobiology, affect regulation, and information processing following child maltreatment. *Psychiatric Annals, 35,* 410–419.

Freud, S. (1958). The future prospects of psychoanalytic therapy. In J. Stracey (Ed. & Trans.), *The standard edition of the complete psychological works of Sigmund Freud* (Vol. 12, pp. 139–153). London: Hogarth Press. (Original work published 1910)

Freud, S. (1958). Observations on transference-love: Further recommendations on the technique of psychoanalysis. In J. Stracey (Ed. & Trans.), *The standard edition of the complete psychological works of Sigmund Freud* (Vol. 12, pp. 158–171). London: Hogarth Press. (Original work published 1915)

Freud, S. (1958). Recommendations to physicians practicing psychoanalysis. In J. Stracey (Ed. & Trans.), *The standard edition of the complete psychological works of Sigmund Freud* (Vol. 12, pp. 111–120). London: Hogarth Press. (Original work published 1912)

Gabbard, G. O. (1995). Countertransference: The emerging common ground. *International Journal of Psycho-Analysis, 76,* 475–485.

Gelso, C., Latts, M., Gomez, M., & Fassinger, R. (2002). Countertransference management and therapy outcome: An initial evaluation. *Journal of Clinical Psychology, 58,* 861–867.

Hayes, J., & Gelso, C. (1991). Effects of therapist-trainees' anxiety and empathy on countertransference behavior. *Journal of Clinical Psychology, 47,* 284–290.

Hayes, J., McCracken, J., McClanahan, M., Hill, C., Harp, J., & Carrozzoni, P. (1998). Therapist perspectives on countertransference: Qualitative data in search of a theory. *Journal of Counseling Psychology, 45,* 468–482.

Jackson, H., & Nuttall, R. (2001). A relationship between childhood sexual abuse and professional sexual misconduct. *Professional Psychology: Research and Practice, 32,* 200–204.

Kiesler, D. (2001). Therapist countertransference: In search of common themes and empirical referents. *Journal of Clinical Psychology, 57,* 1053–1063.

Latts, M., & Gelso, C. (1995). Countertransference behavior and management with survivors of sexual assault. *Psychotherapy: Theory, Research, Practice, Training, 32,* 405–415.

Lecours, S., Bouchard, M., & Normandin, L. (1995). Countertransference as the therapist's mental activity: Experience and gender differences among psychoanalytically oriented psychologists. *Psychoanalytic Psychology, 12,* 259–279.

Little, L., & Hamby, S. (1996). Impact of a clinician's sexual abuse history gender, and theoretical orientation on treatment issues related to childhood sexual abuse. *Professional Psychology, Research, and Practice, 77,* 617–625.

Orth, U., & Wieland, E. (2006). Anger, hostility and posttraumatic stress disorder in trauma-exposed adults: A meta-analysis. *Journal of Consulting and Clinical Psychology, 74,* 698–706.

Pearlman, L., & Saakvitne, K. (1995). *Trauma and the therapist: Countertransference and vicarious traumatization in psychotherapy with incest.* New York: Norton.

Pope, K., & Tabachnick, B. (1993). Therapists' anger, hate, fear, and sexual feelings: National survey of therapist responses, client characteristics, critical events, formal complaints, and training. *Professional Psychology: Research and Practice, 24,* 142–152.

Pope, K., Tabachnick, B., & Keith-Spiegel, P. (1987). Ethics of practice: The beliefs and behaviors of psychologists as therapists. *American Psychologist, 42,* 993–1006.

Rustin, M. (2001). The therapist with her back against the wall. *Journal of Child Psychotherapy, 27,* 273–284.

Solomon, M., & Siegel, D. (Eds.). (2003). *Healing trauma: Attachment, mind, body, brain.* New York: Norton.

Somer, E., & Saadon, M. (1999). Therapist-client sex: Clients' retrospective reports. *Professional Psychology: Research and Practice, 30,* 504–509.

Winnicott, D. (1949). Hate in the counter-transference. *International Journal of Psycho-Analysis, 30,* 69–74.

RECOMMENDED READINGS

Dalenberg, C. (2000). *Countertransference and the treatment of trauma.* Washington, DC: American Psychological Association.

Figley, C. R. (1995). *Compassion fatigue: Coping with secondary traumatic stress disorder in those who treat the traumatized.* New York: Brunner/Mazel.

Pearlman, L., & Saakvitne, K. (1995). *Trauma and the therapist: Countertransference and vicarious traumatization in psychotherapy with incest.* New York: Norton.

CONSTANCE DALENBERG
Alliant International University

See also: Burnout; Psychodynamic Therapy, Adult; Psychodynamic Therapy, Child; Psychotherapeutic Processes; Therapeutic Relationship; Vicarious Traumatization

CRIMINAL VICTIMIZATION

Criminal victimization includes burglary, assault, aggravated assault (assault with a weapon), rape, sexual assault, homicide, and/or witnessing violence in the home or community. Criminal victimization of children may include physical abuse, sexual abuse, neglect, and/or witnessing violence. A substantial body of literature suggests that the majority of the population in the United States will experience criminal victimization at some point in their lives, and criminal victimization is frequently associated with long-term, deleterious effects. Over the past 25 years, research in the area of criminal victimization has produced a number of landmark studies detailing the prevalence and impact of criminal victimization on the population. The most prominent research domains may be categorically labeled as prevalence, impact, risk factors, assessment, and treatment.

Prevalence

The largest annual assessment of the prevalence of criminal victimization in the United States is the National Crime Victimization Survey (Catalano, 2006), which suggests that of 23 million crimes committed against persons 12 years or older in 2005, 22% were violent crimes. Additionally, for every 1,000 people, there was one victim of rape, one victim of violent assault, and three victims of robbery. Further examination of the literature on adult criminal victimization revealed that 3% of the U.S. population survived a homicide attempt at some point in their lifetime (Amick-McMullan, Kilpatrick, & Resnick, 1991). Moreover, among the 2,000 households participating in the National Family Violence Survey (Gelles & Straus, 1988) approximately 16% had experienced violence within the past year

Investigations in the adult literature reveal gender differences in criminal victimization. For example, Kessler, Sonnega, Bromet, Hughes, and Nelson (1995) surveyed a nationally representative sample of men and women (*n* = 8,098) and found a number of differences in the type of criminal victimization experienced: 11% of men and 7% of women reported a lifetime prevalence of physical assault, 1% of men and 9% of women reported a lifetime prevalence of rape, 19% of men and 7% of women reported a lifetime prevalence of being threatened with a weapon, and 36% of men and 15% of women reported a lifetime prevalence of witnessing violence. Similarly, the National Women's Study (Resnick, Kilpatrick, Dansky, Saunders, & Best, 1993) surveyed a large representative sample of women, 69% of whom reported experiencing at least one form of criminal victimization. More specifically, approximately 13% of women reported being the victim of completed rape, sexual assault, or a survivor of homicide of a family member. While men report higher frequency of criminal victimization overall, and higher frequency of specific types of criminal victimization such as physical assault, witnessing violence, or being threatened with a weapon, women are more likely to experience sexually related offenses.

Taken together, these results suggest that criminal victimization among adults is a significant public health concern, and similarly, large-scale examinations of criminal victimization in children and adolescents reveal equally disturbing results. Specifically, findings from the National Survey of Adolescents (Kilpatrick et al., 2000) revealed that almost half of the adolescents surveyed experienced some form of violent victimization. Also using a nationally representative sample, Finkelhor, Ormrod, Turner, and Hamby (2005) demonstrated similar results. Additionally, they found that approximately 1 in 8 children reported experiencing child maltreatment (including emotional abuse, neglect, or sexual abuse), 1 in 13 children reported experiencing sexual victimization (including rape, sexual assault, or being exposed to child pornography), and 1 in 3 children reported witnessing violence (including witnessing domestic violence, murder, or living in a war zone). Overall, results from various studies by leading researchers in youth mental health introduced a grim reality regarding a large percentage of U.S. children and further evidence suggests that victimized children are at risk for a host of adverse psychological outcomes.

Impact

The consequences of criminal victimization are widespread and varied. Most people who experience criminal victimization report transient difficulties that are not severe enough to require professional treatment and that become mild or nonexistent within a matter of weeks or no longer than several months. However, a substantial minority can be expected to experience chronic problems in mental, physical, social, interpersonal, and occupational areas of functioning. The largest body of research on the impact of criminal victimization has focused on trauma-related symptoms and posttraumatic stress disorder (PTSD). While epidemiological studies find that approximately 9% of trauma-exposed adults and 9% of violence-exposed children will meet criteria for PTSD (Breslau et al., 1998; Kilpatrick et al., 2000), rates vary based on numerous factors including gender, degree of exposure (magnitude or severity of an event), proximity to the event, and the type of event that was experienced. Criminal victimization is generally associated with the highest rates of PTSD, particularly sexual and physical assault. Studies have detected rates of PTSD among victims of rape of around 49%, while the PTSD rate for other forms of sexual assault is about 24%, and the rates of PTSD among persons who were severely physically assaulted was 32% (Breslau, 1998). Kessler and colleagues (1995) found that rape was associated with the highest risk of PTSD for both men and women, and Kilpatrick et al. (2000) reported similar findings for adolescents.

PTSD is only one of many potential difficulties faced by individuals who experience criminal victimization, and other problems may be more numerous and severe when PTSD occurs. Indeed, other features associated with PTSD should be considered during assessment and treatment of people who have experienced criminal victimization. According to the *Diagnostic and Statistical Manual of Mental Disorders* (*DSM-IV-TR;* American Psychiatric Association, 2000), individuals with PTSD may also report difficulties in interpersonal relationships, problems modulating affect, guilt, self-destructive and impulsive behaviors, dissociative symptoms, somatic complaints, feelings of shame, despair, and hopelessness, and social withdrawal. Further, PTSD is associated with higher rates of panic disorder, agoraphobia, obsessive-compulsive disorder, social phobia, specific phobia, major depressive disorder, somatization disorder, and substance-related disorders (Brady, 1997; Kessler et al., 1995). Individuals with PTSD may also report various health problems, such as acute, physical injury, sexually transmitted diseases, irritable bowel syndrome, chronic pain, sleep disruption, and involvement in health risk behaviors.

Experiencing criminal victimization may increase the risk for multiple types of mental health problems. People exposed to criminal victimization are more likely than other people to suffer substance abuse, interpersonal difficulties, aggression, anxiety, dissociation, sexual dysfunction, agoraphobia, obsessive-compulsive disorder, social phobia, eating disorders, sleep disorders, depression, and self-harming behaviors, among others even if they do not develop PTSD.

Risk Factors

Not everyone who is criminally victimized will suffer long-term emotional problems. Several factors have been identified that heightened the risk of a negative response. Most of this research studied people who were exposed to a wide variety of traumatic events, although a few have examined crime victimization specifically. Pre-trauma factors including having mental health difficulties (e.g., depression) and having a history of previous trauma are each associated with worse functioning after being victimized. Certain characteristics of criminal activity itself, such as threat of death or physical injury, actual physical injury, frequency and duration of victimization, number of incidents, relationship to the perpetrator, magnitude of criminal victimization (e.g., completed rape), and extent of actual injury may influence the victim's response and are important to consider. Further, people who reported multiple victimization experiences also reported worse functioning across various domains. Post-trauma factors that are related to worse functioning include acute distress, self-blame, lack of social support, sleep problems, and avoidance coping.

Assessment

Several important factors need to be considered when assessing people who either were or may have been criminally victimized. First, clinicians should assess for exposure to traumatic events other than that which presumably brought a patient into treatment because many people who report a traumatic experience have probably endured more than one type of traumatic event. Numerous instruments are available to assess the type and nature of traumatic events. Gray and Slagle (2006) recently reviewed traumatic event assessment tools for adults. Stover and Berkowitz (2005) reviewed traumatic event assessment tools for children and adolescents. Several measures of potentially traumatic events specific to criminal victimization have also been developed including the Conflict Tactics Scale-2 (Straus, Hamby, Boney-McCoy, & Sugarman, 1996) and the Sexual Experiences Survey (Koss, Gidycz, & Wisniewski, 1987).

A centrally important area of mental health functioning to assess in victims of criminal victimization is PTSD. Numerous standardized self-report and clinician interview measures of PTSD symptoms are frequently used and are covered elsewhere in this volume. Several measures have been developed that broadly assess psychological difficulties or symptoms commonly reported by victims of criminal victimization, including the Trauma Symptom Inventory (Briere, 1995), Modified Personal Beliefs and Reactions Scale (PBRS; Mechanic & Resick, 2000), the Trauma Symptom Checklist for Children (TSCC; Briere, 1996), the Trauma Symptom Checklist for Young Children (TSCYC; Briere et al., 2001), and the Posttraumatic Cognitions Inventory (PCI; Foa, Ehlers, Clark, Tolin, & Orsillo, 1999). Difficulties and disorders that are commonly found in conjunction with trauma and PTSD (i.e., comorbid problems) should also be assessed, in particular, alcohol and other substance use problems, depression, other anxiety disorders, problems with anger and reactive aggression. Given the broad reach of trauma impact, we recommend a comprehensive assessment of the patient's current and recent functioning to inform and guide treatment decisions.

Treatment

Numerous empirically supported treatment options are available for victims of crime, depending on the individual case formulation. Interventions with empirical support for their use with trauma victims include, but are not limited to, prolonged exposure (Foa, Dancu, et al., 1999), cognitive processing therapy (Monson et al., 2006), cognitive behavioral therapy (Devilly & Spence, 1999), and trauma-focused cognitive behavioral therapy (TF-CBT; Cohen, Berliner, & March, 2000). Promising acute interventions targeting trauma difficulties within weeks of a trauma exposure include a brief cognitive behavioral treatment developed by Foa, Hearst-Ikeda, and Perry (1995) and one developed by Bryant and colleagues (1999). Additionally, other treatments with varying levels of empirical support were developed for treating PTSD and comorbid disorders (panic, substance use disorders) or related conditions (nightmares, sleep disturbances).

Conclusion

Criminal victimization and the resulting sequelae are part of a public health crisis with substantial economic and psychosocial repercussions. Indeed, a significant minority of people will experience a crime at some point in their lives and the impact may be wide ranging, including PTSD, anxiety disorders, depression, and substance use. Additionally, victimization may disrupt social, occupational, and interpersonal functioning. Fortunately, a number of efficacious treatments are available for those who seek out assistance and increasingly, early interventions are being developed and studied that may help decrease the development of chronic physical and mental health problems.

REFERENCES

American Psychiatric Association. (2000). *Diagnostic and statistical manual of mental disorders* (4th ed., text rev.). Washington, DC: Author.

Amick-McMullan, A., Kilpatrick, D., & Resnick, H. (1991). Homicide as a risk factor for PTSD among surviving family members. *Behavior Modification, 15,* 545–559.

Brady, K. T. (1997). Posttraumatic stress disorder and comorbidity: Recognizing the many faces of PTSD. *Journal of Clinical Psychiatry, 58*(Suppl. 9), 12–15.

Breslau, N. (1998). Epidemiology of trauma and posttraumatic stress disorder. In R. Yehuda (Ed.), *Psychological trauma* (pp. 1–29). Washington, DC: American Psychiatric Press.

Briere, J. (1995). *Trauma Symptom Inventory Professional Manual.* Odessa, FL: Psychological Assessment Resources.

Briere, J. (1996). *Trauma Symptom Checklist for Children (TSCC): Professional manual.* Odessa, FL: Psychological Assessment Resources.

Briere, J., Johnson, K., Bissada, A., Damon, L., Crouch, J., Gil, E., et al. (2001). Trauma Symptom Checklist for Young Children (TSCYC): Reliability and association with abuse exposure in a multisite study. *Child Abuse and Neglect, 25,* 1001–1014.

Bryant, R., Sackvile, T., Dang, S. T., Moulds, M., & Guthrie, R. (1999). Treating acute stress disorder: An evaluation of cognitive behavior therapy and supportive counseling techniques. *American Journal of Psychiatry, 156,* 1780–1786.

Catalano, S. (2006). Criminal victimization, 2005. *Bureau of Justice Statistics Bulletin,* 1–12.

Cohen, J., Berliner, L., & March, J. (2000). Treatment of children and adolescents. In E. Foa, T. Keane, & M. Friedman (Eds.), *Effective treatments for PTSD* (pp. 106–138). New York: Guilford Press.

Devilly, G. J., & Spence, S. H. (1999). The relative efficacy and treatment distress of EMDR and a cognitive-behavior trauma treatment protocol in the amelioration of posttraumatic stress disorder. *Journal of Anxiety Disorders, 13,* 131–157.

Finkelhor, D., Ormrod, R., Turner, H., & Hamby, S. (2005). The victimization of children and youth: A comprehensive, national survey. *Child Maltreatment, 10,* 5–25.

Foa, E. B., Dancu, C. V., Hembree, E. A., Jaycox, L. H., Meadows, E. A., & Street, G. P. (1999). A comparison of exposure therapy, stress inoculation training, and their combination for reducing posttraumatic stress disorder in female assault victims. *Journal of Consulting and Clinical Psychology, 59,* 715–723.

Foa, E. B., Ehlers, A., Clark, D. M., Tolin, D. F., & Orsillo, S. M. (1999). The Posttraumatic

Cognitions Inventory (PTCI): Development and validation. *Psychological Assessment, 11,* 303–314.

Foa, E. B., Hearst-Ikeda, D., & Perry, K. J. (1995). Evaluation of a brief cognitive-behavioral program for prevention of chronic PTSD in recent assault victims. *Journal of Consulting and Clinical Psychology, 63,* 948–955.

Gelles, R., & Straus, M. (1988). *Intimate violence.* New York: Simon & Schuster.

Gray, M. J., & Slagle, D. M. (2006). Selecting a potentially traumatic event screening measure: Practical and psychometric considerations. *Journal of Trauma Practice, 5,* 1–19.

Kessler, R., Sonnega, A., Bromet, E., Hughes, M., & Nelson, C. (1995). Posttraumatic stress disorder in the National Comorbidity Survey. *Archives of General Psychiatry, 52,* 1048–1060.

Kilpatrick, D., Acierno, R., Saunders, B., Resnick, H., Best, C., & Schnurr, P. (2000). Risk factors for adolescent substance abuse and dependence: Data from a national sample. *Journal of Consulting and Clinical Psychology, 68,* 19–30.

Koss, M. P., Gidycz, C. A., & Wisniewski, N. (1987). The scope of rape: Incidence and prevalence of sexual aggression and victimization in a national sample of higher education students. *Journal of Consulting and Clinical Psychology, 55,* 162–170.

Mechanic, M., & Resick, P. (2000). *The Personal Beliefs and Reactions Scale.* Unpublished manuscript, University of Missouri.

Monson, C. M., Schnurr, P. P., Resick, P. A., Friedman, M. J., Young-Xu, Y., & Stevens, S. P. (2006). Cognitive processing therapy for veterans with military-related posttraumatic stress disorder. *Journal of Consulting and Clinical Psychology, 74,* 898–907.

Resnick, H., Kilpatrick, D., Dansky, B., Saunders, B., & Best, C. (1993). Prevalence of civilian trauma and posttraumatic stress disorder in a representative national sample of women. *Journal of Consulting and Clinical Psychology, 61,* 984–991.

Stover, C. S., & Berkowitz, S. (2005). Assessing violence exposure and trauma symptoms in young children: A critical review of measures. *Journal of Traumatic Stress, 18,* 707–717.

Straus, M. A., Hamby, S. L., Boney-McCoy, S., & Sugarman, D. B. (1996). The revised Conflict Tactics Scales (CTS2): Development and preliminary psychometric data. *Journal of Family Issues, 17,* 283–316.

JOANNE L. DAVIS
University of Tulsa

CAMEO F. BORNTRAGER
University of Hawaii, Manoa

See also: **Abuse, Child Physical; Abuse, Child Sexual; Assessment, Psychometric Adult; Assessment, Psychometric, Child; Child Maltreatment; Cognitive Behavior Therapy, Adult; Community Violence; Domestic Violence; Rape Trauma**

CRISIS INTERVENTION, ADULT

A person is said to be *in crisis* when the emotional, cognitive, and biological effects of a situation are perceived to be so threatening that the resulting stress exceeds the person's coping capacity (Golan, 1969). Being in crisis is understood to indicate a disturbance of a person's psychological equilibrium, thus throwing the person off balance and requiring an extreme compensatory adjustment to regain an adequate level of functioning in one or more areas. While being in crisis is not synonymous with being traumatized, a cardinal characteristic of a crisis is that it is perceived as a threat to one's psychological survival and therefore the conditions for exposure to a traumatic stressor may be achieved (*see:* **Posttraumatic Stress Disorder**). Thus, crises are intensely stressful episodes in people's lives that may include the precursors of traumatic stress reactions.

Crisis intervention is a specialized mental health technique for assisting people who are experiencing a severe disruption of their ability to adapt to stressful circumstances. Crisis intervention is designed first to moderate immediate stress and to facilitate sufficiently effective coping to reduce the risk of deepening the crisis. Subsequently, the focus of crisis intervention shifts to assisting with planning and problem solving, the marshalling of supportive resources, and a progressive improvement in the person's situation. Thus, the primary imperative is to prevent a worsening of the situation and the secondary imperative is to increase the individual and collective capacity for improving the situation and resolving the crisis. In this way and others, crisis intervention is distinct from psychotherapy because of its stronger emphasis on confronting immediate threats to psychosocial functioning and comparatively little emphasis on addressing long-term issues. Moreover, crisis intervention is viewed as less of an end in itself than is psychotherapy and instead focuses on making one or more early referrals to agencies and providers that can serve and support longer term needs and goals.

Background

Crisis intervention developed as a conceptual framework for responding to people exhibiting the aftereffects of extreme shocks, such as fires and natural disasters. Its basic formulation is widely credited to the pioneering work of Erich Lindemann, who studied bereaved survivors of a nightclub fire and concluded that there were prominent predictable sets of reactions to which clinicians could respond effectively and assist survivors through the grieving process (Lindemann, 1944). As crisis intervention techniques were being developed and refined, they were increasingly taught in social work programs, nursing schools, and psychiatry residencies (Caplan, 1964). These early approaches to crisis intervention took hold in settings where crises are most frequently encountered, such as mental health centers, community clinics, psychiatric hospitals, and were incorporated into protocols for suicide prevention hotlines. Along a historical parallel, similar techniques were defined under the rubric of psychological first aid (Reyes, 2006), and these tended to be applied under conditions of major social disruption, such as wars and disasters (see: **Early Intervention; Psychological First Aid, Adult; Psychological First Aid, Child**).

More recently, principles of crisis intervention informed the invention of an extraordinarily popular brief group intervention technique called Critical Incident Stress Debriefing (CISD; Everly, Lating, & Mitchell, 2000), which was later incorporated into a broader intervention model labeled Critical Incident Stress

Management (CISM; see: **Critical Incident Stress Management**). The results from empirical studies of the effectiveness claims of CISD and CISM provoked a heated international debate that expanded into a generalized concern about all forms of psychosocial interventions conducted during or immediately following a crisis (e.g., McNally, Bryant, & Ehlers, 2003; see: **Early Intervention**), especially when claims are made for specific prevention of psychiatric conditions such as posttraumatic stress disorder (PTSD).

The research literature examining the effectiveness of crisis intervention more generally is sparse and riddled with conceptual and methodological flaws, but a meta-analysis of studies examining the effects of crisis intervention does suggest moderate empirical support for this approach limiting the impact of acutely stressful life events (Roberts & Everly, 2006). It is important to conduct further research on crisis intervention in the contexts in which it is most commonly employed, those being emergency settings where people in crisis are most likely to be encountered. Moreover, it is necessary to understand crisis intervention as a tool that may be best applied by mental health professionals, but that is also employed by police and other emergency professionals, and that it is therefore not a brand of psychotherapy to be studied in the same fashion as treatments directed at alleviating psychiatric conditions.

Crisis Situations

The prototypical situation that precipitates a crisis is one in which a person suffers a sudden, shocking, catastrophic loss. Such an incident would be likely to exceed the immediate coping capacity of virtually anyone, regardless of personal characteristics and resources. Prime examples include the death of a child, parent, or spouse, or a disaster that destroys a person's home and belongings, and possibly their workplace and community. Loss is a common element of crises, and not all losses include the loss of lives or of material resources. People who have been victimized by others also experience losses that can be extremely destabilizing.

Examples include brushes with death, being raped or otherwise sexually exploited, being physically attacked and injured, or being bullied, harassed, threatened, or humiliated. Nonviolent and nonlethal disturbances in relationships are also a common precipitant of crises. Examples include divorces and other estrangements, acts of betrayal and violations of trust, infidelity, abandonment, rejection, or separation from attachment figures (especially in regard to children).

Crisis Reactions

When a person perceives a situation to be threatening, the typical base reaction is consistent with the formulation known as the fight-or-flight response. The underlying theory is that evolution prepared animals to survive by either defending themselves (i.e., fight) or by escaping (i.e., flight). A third survival technique involves freezing to elude detection. Regardless of which behavior is enacted, the goal is to survive a threat and the attempt requires substantial psychological and physical resources. The initial reaction involves freezing and an extreme arousal of the sympathetic nervous system, which provides an extraordinary surge of energy and alertness that prepares an animal for the intense muscular activity needed for fighting or fleeing. Physiological changes associated with this response include an increase in cardiovascular activity (i.e., pulse-rate, blood pressure, and respiration), dilation of the blood (i.e., vasodilation) system that serves muscles, constriction of blood flow to the extremities (i.e., vasoconstriction, associated with a temporary paling of the skin), inhibition of the digestive tract, piloerection (i.e., hair standing on end), decreased salivation (i.e., dry-mouth), and profuse perspiration. These reactions are also described as comprising the first stage of the stress response known as the general adaptation syndrome (GAS; Selye, 1956; see: **Stress**), with the understanding that they prepare the organism to resist an acute survival threat and that prolonged resistance will lead to profound fatigue and an eventual collapse into exhaustion.

Psychological reactions to crisis are commonly categorized as emotional, cognitive, somatic (i.e., physical), and behavioral. Emotional reactions often include intense fear or anger, elevated or chronic anxiety, forms of remorse (e.g., shame, guilt, regret), a sense of helplessness and/or hopelessness, and dread in regard to future developments. Conversely, emotional shocks can also be followed by periods of emotional numbness or a flattening of emotional expression. Cognitive reactions to crisis are characterized by perceptual distortions or other difficulties in processing information, such as poor concentration, difficulty with memory retrieval, narrowing of the perceptual range of view (i.e., "tunnel vision"), and a foreshortened sense of time and consequences (i.e., decreased ability to consider long range implications of events). Problem solving capacities may be undermined due to impairments in reasoning, judgment, or decision making. Being in crisis also influences a person's predominant thoughts ("cognitive content"), predisposing those thoughts toward vigilance against further threats to survival (i.e., hypervigilance), with a tendency to persistently ruminate about aspects of the crisis, and some proclivity to engage in unrealistic fantasies directed toward undoing the crisis (i.e., "magical thinking"), which may include fantasies about violent means of exacting revenge. Physical reactions may include shaking, hyperactivity (e.g., pacing, fidgeting), fatigue/exhaustion, headaches, stomachaches, or a generalized sense of physical discomfort (i.e., achiness). Changes in behavior are also common and may include extreme variations on normal appetites, such as excessive eating or loss of appetite, excessive sleeping (hypersomnia) or inadequate sleeping (e.g., insomnia, frequent waking, nightmares), and excessive seeking of social support or alienation from relationships. These reactions, while understandable and at times even useful, generally complicate and impair the person's ability to successfully adapt to a crisis. Thus, crisis reactions can be used gauge the degree and extent of functional impairment while also providing targets for crisis intervention services.

Crisis Intervention Techniques

The objectives and techniques of crisis intervention are in some ways similar to those for psychotherapy and counseling, but the objectives are also more immediate and limited and the techniques tend to be more structured, sequential, and directive than is true for more extensive forms of treatment. As in all forms of psychological intervention, a working relationship with a mutual sense of warmth and trust (i.e., rapport) must first be established. The situational conditions that often characterize a crisis can make it more likely that safety will be a prominent concern, so the crisis worker must build sufficient rapport while also assessing the immediate and imminent safety of the person in crisis. The crisis worker may also be at some risk and must therefore be sensitive to the potential for being harmed in the course of the intervention. Ensuring safety is a primary objective that relies to a great extent on the establishment of sufficient rapport and the skill of the crisis worker at rapidly detecting and assessing risks and threats. An aspect of client safety that must be assessed is often termed "lethality," and refers to the client's dangerousness to self (i.e., suicidality) or to others (e.g., plans to commit violent acts). Crisis workers may be tempted to skip the lethality assessment if there are no blatant signs indicating danger; however, failing to make a lethality assessment is an unadvisable risk given that signs of suicidality or dangerousness to others are often so subtle or hidden that they may go undetected unless properly explored.

Once the preconditions of safety and rapport are met, crisis workers explore the circumstances and problems that are most relevant to the client's reactions. For example, if the client has not already described the immediate situation from her/his perspective, the crisis worker might ask open ended questions such as: "Would you fill me in on what this crisis is about?" or "What is leading you to feel unsafe right now?" Defining the problem opens the door to exploring the client's reactions and the meanings being attributed to the precipitating event. Exploration of the problems and reactions defining the crisis leads to

an examination of the client's coping attempts and a survey of the resources (e.g., social, financial, spiritual) that might be marshaled to improve the situation. The diagramming of the crisis and the related coping options can flow smoothly and concurrently into providing support for the client to express emotions and receive emotional support. Crisis workers can thus explore the crisis with the client while also helping to relieve some of the client's distress, which in turn improves the conditions for a successively deeper exploration of the client's reactions and concerns. A key objective is to reduce the client's high level of arousal to a more manageable level that supports higher levels of cognitive and emotional functioning.

At some point the information about the crisis and the client's reactions and resources should be adequate to allow the crisis worker to ease into a collaborative problem-solving interaction. While problem-solving approaches vary, there is a common progression that includes defining and evaluating a number of alternatives and then selecting the most feasible and promising set of tasks that can be structured into a plan of action. The problem-solving plan needs to be as simple as possible and designed to optimize the chances of success while minimizing the consequences of failures and setbacks. Since the client will be the person who enacts most of the plan and will in turn bear the brunt of the consequences, it is important that the client feels comfortable with the plan and confident in his or her ability to follow through with it (i.e., buy-in). For example, the crisis worker might help the client to think about potential immediate steps that could reduce the degree of distress or danger that the client is feeling, and to develop a plan for taking some of those steps with the help and support of others.

Collaborative problem solving is a form of coping assistance that can prove useful and reassuring to a client who feels too overwhelmed to independently think of or work on some realistic solutions. The collaboration between the crisis worker and the client also helps to serve as a model of a high functioning and empowering relationship, much like that which could prove effective in other settings. This is also a time when the crisis worker can begin to consider some of the services, setting, and providers to whom the client may benefit if a referral is made.

Under crisis conditions, it is predictable that a client will feel less than normally confident and competent to independently carry out a problem-solving plan, so crisis workers often compensate by enacting some of the tasks themselves (e.g., making key telephone calls, especially to other professionals and agencies), supporting a client during the enactment of a task (e.g., being present while the client makes phone calls or completes documents), writing down the elements of the plan with lists of instructions and contact information, and rehearsing the plan and building in contingency responses (i.e., fallback plans) if things do not go as desired. There should also be a component of the plan for a scheduled future contact by the client with the crisis worker or some appropriate alternative person or agency (i.e., follow-up), so that an agreement is in place between the client and crisis worker to exchange communication about the outcome of the plan and the welfare of the client. This component serves multiple functions, including that of a feedback loop on the effectiveness of the intervention, and a safety plan for the client to quickly reengage for support if the situation worsens.

The stages of crisis intervention and the techniques involved are well articulated by a number of authors, but the most prominent example is the Seven-Stage Crisis Intervention Model developed by Albert Roberts (see Roberts & Ottens, 2005, for a thorough description). Roberts defined the stages of his model in the following terms and sequence: (1) plan and conduct the crisis assessment, including the assessment of lethality; (2) establish rapport and the working relationship; (3) identify the precipitating event(s) and the major problems; (4) use active listening and validation to help deal with feelings and emotions; (5) generate and explore alternatives; (6) formulate an action plan; (7) develop a follow-up plan and establish an agreement.

Conclusion

While crisis intervention is not specifically a therapeutic technique for persons who have experienced psychological trauma, it is commonly employed to assist people who are experiencing extreme stressors; thus, the events that precipitate crises frequently qualify as potentially traumatic events. Since the central objectives of crisis intervention include the reduction of risk for further harm (i.e., damage control), the reduction of extreme physiological arousal to support more effective cognitive functioning, emotion regulation, and self-care (e.g., the ability to rest and sleep), the enhancement of resilient coping, and referrals to facilitate access to additional services and resources, it is reasonable to think that crisis intervention may decrease the impact of some traumatic events or decrease the potential for further exacerbation of existing traumatic stressors. Nevertheless, no claims about preventing PTSD or other psychosocial or psychiatric problems can be made for crisis intervention because there is no strong empirical evidence for the mental health benefits of crisis intervention.

REFERENCES

Caplan, G. (1964). *Principles of preventive psychiatry.* New York: Basic Books.

Everly, G. S., Jr., Lating, J. M., & Mitchell, J. T. (2000). Innovations in group crisis intervention: Critical incident stress debriefing (CISD) and critical incident stress management (CISM). In A. R. Roberts (Ed.), *Crisis intervention handbook: Assessment, treatment, and research* (2nd ed., pp. 77–97). New York: Oxford University Press.

Golan, N. (1969). When is a client in crisis? *Social Casework, 50,* 389–394.

Lindemann, E. (1944). Symptomatology and management of acute grief. *American Journal of Psychiatry, 101,* 141–148.

McNally, R. J., Bryant, R. A., & Ehlers, A. (2003). Does early psychological intervention promote recovery from posttraumatic stress? *Psychological Science in the Public Interest, 4*(2), 45–79.

Reyes, G. (2006). Psychological first aid: Principles of community-based psychosocial support. In

G. Reyes & G. A. Jacobs (Eds.), *Handbook of international disaster psychology* (Vol. 2, pp. 1–12). Westport, CT: Praeger.

Roberts, A. R., & Everly, G. S., Jr. (2006). A meta-analysis of 36 crisis intervention studies. *Brief Treatment and Crisis Intervention, 6,* 10–21.

Roberts, A. R., & Ottens, A. J. (2005). The seven-stage intervention model: A road map to goal attainment, problem-solving, and crisis resolution. *Brief Treatment and Crisis Intervention,* 5(4), 329–339.

Selye, H. (1956). *The stress of life.* New York: McGraw-Hill.

GILBERT REYES
Fielding Graduate University

See also: Crisis Intervention, Child; Critical Incident Stress Management; Early Intervention; Prevention, Adult; Prevention, Child; Psychological First Aid, Adult; Psychological First Aid, Child and Adolescent; Stress

CRISIS INTERVENTION, CHILD

Overview of Crisis Interventions

Over the past several decades, a variety of crisis interventions have been developed to assist children after traumatic events such as disasters, injury, war, and community violence. The overarching goal of most of these interventions is to stabilize the child, to teach and enhance the use of positive coping strategies, and to prevent chronic psychopathology. By intervening early, providers can assess children's current reactions, identify children at-risk for more serious disorder or developmental disruptions, make needed referrals for more intensive or specialized services, and plan for appropriate follow-up.

Specific crisis intervention strategies have included: psychoeducation; bereavement support; various forms of psychological debriefing; eye movement desensitization and reprocessing; various cognitive behavioral approaches; discussion of thoughts and feelings; reinforcing adaptive coping, promotion of safety behaviors and use of support systems; structured and unstructured art and play activities; massage;

and pharmacological treatments. Crisis interventions have been delivered using a variety of strategies, including individual, family, group, and classroom sessions, provision of psychoeducational materials, establishment of crisis hotlines, and Internet interventions.

There is a paucity of research evidence regarding the effectiveness of crisis interventions for traumatized children. Indeed, there have been very few randomized controlled research studies, and most other studies have had significant methodological flaws (Steinberg, Brymer, Steinberg, & Pfefferbaum, 2006). The many challenges and obstacles to conducting studies in chaotic crisis situations have contributed to the lack of evidence in this field. (For a review of the current evidence for crisis interventions, see Brymer et al., in press.) Despite these shortcomings, there are several promising crisis and acute intervention approaches that have been employed with traumatized children. These intervention models can be divided into several categories.

Systemic Approaches

Systemic approaches involve working with communities or service systems to deliver crisis interventions. These approaches include a continuum of strategies depending on the type and magnitude of the traumatic event and the specific needs of the individual or community. Services can range from providing training to parents and teachers about common reactions of children after traumatic events, to providing more structured interventions. One such program is the Post-Traumatic Stress Management (PTSM) program, a community-based program employed immediately after a critical incident. The model offers a continuum of services and encourages community members to take the key role in its implementation. One intervention strategy used in PTSM is called classroom/community/camp-based intervention (CBI), a psychosocial intervention that includes a series of highly structured expressive-behavioral activities for children who are facing difficult life circumstances (e.g., living with political conflict, living in refugee camps) or who have been involved in a critical incident. The overall aim of CBI is to identify existing coping resources among these children and to sustain the utilization of those resources over time (Macy et al., 2004).

Another systemic program is the Child Development Community Policing (CD-CP) program, which provides crisis intervention and follow-up services to children exposed to crime and violence. CD-CP includes two types of interventions: (1) the *Domestic Violence Home Visit Initiative,* in which outreach advocates and police officers visit families after an incident of domestic violence, and (2) the *Child and Family Traumatic Stress Intervention,* which is a four-session model to decrease distress symptoms, increase family communication, and facilitate parents' support to potentially traumatized children. Early evaluations of this intervention have shown that children who have received this treatment compare favorably with controls, reporting a significant decrease in severity of PTSD symptoms 4 months post-intervention (Berkowitz, 2007; Marans, Murphy, & Berkowitz, 2002).

For hospitalized injured children, a stepped-care intervention program has been developed that includes a sequence of steps designed to provide continuity of care. The program begins with screening during hospitalization for risk factors or current distress, with subsequent follow-up contacts to monitor recovery, psychoeducation to promote effective coping assistance from parents, specific support for adherence to follow-up medical care; and evidence-based psychological treatment if distress is severe or persistent (Kazak et al., 2006).

School programs have also been developed that adhere to a stepped-care approach after potentially traumatic incidents. Tier 1 includes the provision of psychological first aid to affected students and staff. This may include stabilization of the child or school milieu; addressing immediate health, mental health, and safety concerns; providing practical assistance, enhancing coping strategies, and the use of school and social support resources; providing information on common stress reactions and risk-related behavior; and linkage

with available resources as needed. Tier 2 provides more specialized trauma and grief interventions for those with moderate-to-severe distress and associated impairment. Tier 3 provides specialized psychiatric services for children who require immediate and/or intensive intervention and may include pharmacological treatments or hospitalization (Saltzman, Layne, Steinberg, Arslanagic, & Pynoos, 2003).

Art and Massage Therapies

Various forms of art and massage therapies have been employed separately or in combination with other types of interventions with acutely traumatized children. One randomized controlled study of massage therapy demonstrated greater reduction in depression and anxiety among the group that received massage therapy intervention, but did not evaluate PTSD postintervention (Field, Seligman, Scafidi, & Schanberg, 1996). Additional methodologically sound studies are needed to examine the benefits of this type of therapy, including its potential for the amelioration of PTSD symptoms.

Debriefing

Debriefing strategies typically include reconstruction of the event, identification of thoughts and feelings about the event, psychoeducation and normalization, and information on coping. Over the past decade, research evidence regarding the effectiveness of debriefing strategies, one of the most widely used crisis interventions after a range of traumatic events, has been mixed. The current evidence suggests that debriefing cannot be advocated as effective in preventing the subsequent development of PTSD or other anxiety disorders in traumatized children and adolescents (Stallard et al., 2006).

Cognitive Behavioral Approaches

Many clinicians are familiar with and have utilized cognitive behavioral approaches in acute settings. Cognitive behavioral approaches utilize components summarized by the acronym

PRACTICE, including psychoeducation and parenting skills, relaxation, affective modulation, cognitive coping and processing, trauma narrative, *in vivo* mastery of trauma reminders, conjoint child-parent sessions, and enhancement of future safety and development (Cohen, Mannarino, & Deblinger, 2006). Although these approaches have been shown to be effective in longer-term treatment outcome studies among traumatized children, there have been no child studies in the acute aftermath of exposure to psychological trauma that have formally evaluated outcome. Adult evidence suggests that acute posttraumatic cognitive behavioral interventions hold promise (*see:* **Early Intervention**); however studies need to be conducted to evaluate the effectiveness and optimal timing for children of different developmental stages.

Psychological First Aid

Psychological first aid (PFA) approaches include and synthesize many of the intervention strategies that comprise other crisis intervention protocols for children. PFA allows tailoring of these interventions to meet the specific needs of children and families. In addition, many of the PFA recommendations are supported by a research literature that demonstrates the utility of enhancing coping, social support, and problem solving in the wake of crises and stressful events (*see:* **Coping**), and have been informed by clinicians with extensive experience. While PFA has not yet been systematically studied, one PFA field operations guide has been built on years of experience in providing acute assistance to traumatized children and families and has been found to be acceptable to and well received by children and caregivers who received PFA services (Brymer et al., 2006).

Best Practices

Based on the available literature, there are several components that can be recommended for inclusion in a public mental health approach to providing crisis interventions to

children: (1) Identify children impacted by the event. Crisis interventions should include an information gathering and triage component to allow for an appropriate level of intervention to meet the needs of the affected child population. This triage should not only take into account the child's current distress and functioning, but also include the parent's functioning, available social supports, and ongoing violence or other secondary adversities. (2) Identify available resources to carry out the crisis interventions or to assist the child and their family with further stabilization as they recover. This includes identifying and supporting available child and family service systems and facilitating normal child development activities (e.g., fostering school and family routines, play activities). (3) Map the event. Providers need to have an understanding of what happened during the traumatic event and identify the child's subjective appraisal of the event, in order to clarify any misunderstandings and identify the appropriate intervention strategies. (4) Provide a continuum of services. There is not one type of crisis intervention that will help all children. A continuum of services is needed to ensure that the appropriate level of services is provided for all children impacted by traumatic events. (5) All crisis intervention models should incorporate developmental and cultural perspectives in their strategies. Addressing developmental issues means not only taking into account a child's age and cognitive levels, but also intervening to support the role of parents in a child's recovery and insuring that any developmental disruptions are addressed (Berkowitz, 2003). When conducting crisis interventions in groups or classroom settings, it is important to ensure that groups are homogenous in terms of children's exposure levels, developmental phase, and symptom presentation.

Conclusion

There are currently many different crisis intervention models for traumatized children and adolescents. Psychological first aid is considered a sound initial crisis intervention because it does not assume pathology, assesses current needs, identifies future service requirements, has a cultural and developmental perspective, and identifies the role of parents as a primary source for supporting a child's recovery. For children needing a more specialized intervention, cognitive behavioral approaches appear to be promising. Systemic approaches ensure that crisis interventions are embedded in community resources and oftentimes utilize PFA and cognitive-behavioral approaches in their models. At the time of this writing, there is not sufficient evidence to recommend debriefing in crisis intervention work with children, and more research is needed to further refine and establish the evidence base for early crisis intervention models.

REFERENCES

Berkowitz, S. J. (2003). Children exposed to community violence: The rationale for early intervention. *Clinical Child and Family Psychological Review, 6,* 293–302.

Berkowitz, S. J. (2007, November). *The child and family traumatic stress intervention: A secondary prevention model.* Paper presented at the 23rd International Society for Traumatic Stress Studies annual meeting, Baltimore.

Brymer, M. J., Layne, C., Jacobs, A., Pynoos, R., Ruzek, J., Steinberg, A., et al. (2006). *Psychological first aid field operations guide* (2nd ed.). Los Angeles: National Child Traumatic Stress Network and National Center for PTSD. Available at www.nctsn.org and www.ncptsd.va.gov.

Brymer, M. J., Steinberg, A. M., Vernberg, E. M., Layne, C. M., Watson, P. J., Jacobs, A., et al. (in press). Acute interventions for children and adolescents exposed to trauma. In E. Foa, T. Keane, M. Friedman, & J. Cohen (Eds.), *Effective treatments for PTSD* (2nd ed.). New York: Guilford Press.

Field, T., Seligman, S., Scafidi, F., & Schanberg, S. (1996). Alleviating posttraumatic stress in children following Hurricane Andrew. *Journal of Applied Developmental Psychology, 17,* 37–50.

Kazak, A. E., Kassam-Adams, N., Schneider, S., Zelikovsky, N., Alderfer, M. A., & Rourke, M. (2006). An integrative model of pediatric medical traumatic stress. *Journal of Pediatric Psychology, 31,* 343–355.

Macy, R. D., Behar, L., Paulson, R., Delman, J., Schmid, L., & Smith, S. F. (2004). Community-based, acute posttraumatic stress management: A description and evaluation of a psychosocial-intervention continuum. *Harvard Review of Psychiatry, 12,* 217–228.

Marans, S., Murphy, R., & Berkowitz, S. (2002). Police-mental health responses to children exposed to violence: The child development-community policing program. In M. Lewis (Ed.), *Child and adolescent psychiatry: A comprehensive textbook* (3rd ed., pp. 1406–1416). Baltimore: Lippincott, Williams, & Wilkins.

Saltzman, W. R., Layne, C. M., Steinberg, A. M., Arslanagic, B., & Pynoos, R. S. (2003). Developing a culturally and ecologically sound intervention program for youth exposed to war and terrorism. *Child and Adolescent Psychiatric Clinics of North America, 12,* 319–342.

Stallard, P., Velleman, R., Salter, E., Howse, I., Yule, W., & Taylor, G. (2006). A randomised controlled trial to determine the effectiveness of an early psychological intervention with children involved in road traffic accidents. *Journal of Child Psychology and Psychiatry, and Applied Disciplines, 47,* 127–134.

Steinberg, A. M., Brymer, M. J., Steinberg, J. R., & Pfefferbaum, B. (2006). Conducting research on children and adolescents after mass trauma. In F. Norris, M. Friedman, S. Galea, & P. Watson (Eds.), *Methods for disaster mental health research* (pp. 243–253). New York: Guilford Press.

MELISSA J. BRYMER
National Center for Child Traumatic Stress, UCLA

NANCY KASSAM-ADAMS
Children's Hospital of Philadelphia

See also: Crisis Intervention, Child; Critical Incident Stress Management; Early Intervention; Prevention, Adult; Prevention, Child; Psychological First Aid, Adult; Psychological First Aid, Child and Adolescent; Stress

CRITICAL INCIDENT STRESS DEBRIEFING

See: Critical Incident Stress Management; Early Intervention; Prevention, Adult; Prevention, Child

CRITICAL INCIDENT STRESS MANAGEMENT

Critical incident stress management (CISM) is a collection of crisis intervention and counseling strategies designed to help persons cope with and recover from indirect exposure to crises or traumatic incidents in the immediate aftermath of those events and over time. The conceptual framework for CISM was derived from *crisis intervention theory,* originally developed by Lindemann (1944), following the Coconut Grove nightclub fire in Boston, Massachusetts, in 1944. CISM is a multifaceted intervention, which is an outgrowth of critical incident stress debriefing (CISD), developed by Jeffrey Mitchell in the early 1980s to help emergency medical services personnel cope with occupational exposure to the trauma and suffering of others. CISD remains the core intervention strategy in CISM, and involves helping affected persons to review their stressful and potentially traumatic experiences in a series of steps designed to reduce feelings of helplessness and distress and increase a sense of personal efficacy and social support.

The indirectly exposed populations with whom CISM is applied have expanded to include all types of first-responders, the professionals and volunteers who assist survivors, families, witnesses, and communities affected by disasters or death(s) (including mass casualty incidents). First responders include law enforcement personnel, firefighters, emergency medical technicians, military personnel, and disaster relief workers from organizations such as the Red Cross, as well as employees of schools, hospitals, businesses, and other organizations who have either witnessed a disaster or death(s), known persons who died, were traumatized in a disaster or casualty incident, or provided assistance to these individuals. CISD is the single most commonly used early intervention for psychological trauma worldwide.

CISM consists of various components that are utilized throughout the entire crisis incident, including the pre-crisis, acute-crisis, and post-crisis stages. The pre-crisis stage is the time prior to a crisis's occurrence. The acute crisis stage is the first hours or days after a crisis begins. The post-crisis stage is the time period, ranging from a few weeks to many years, following the crisis incident(s) during which people continue to experience the impact of their experiences in the crisis. A total of seven components comprise the CISM system, each of which is proposed to be necessary for the proper implementation of CISM:

- *Pre-Crisis Preparation*—During this initial stage, stress management education is provided to prepare personnel to work in future crises as first responders.
- *Demobilization*—After a critical incident occurs, emergency personnel who served as first responders complete their work and officially are relieved of further duty. Demobilization may include a formal operational "debriefing" of how the responders handled the crisis incident.
- *Defusing*—This is a three-phase group discussion immediately (i.e., typically within 24 to 72 hours) following a critical incident (or, for first responders, after being demobilized). The discussion includes an *introduction* phase in which the facilitator is introduced and rules of the discussion are reviewed, an *exploration* phase in which the group describes the incident and reactions to it while the facilitator determines the need for further intervention, and an *information* phase in which reactions are normalized and coping skills are suggested.
- *Critical Incident Stress Debriefing (CISD)*—This is a seven-phase group discussion typically occurring within 10 to 14 days of the incident
- *Individual Crisis Intervention*—This is a component of CISM that may be implemented at any time as needed in order to teach participants the fundamentals of, and a specific protocol for, individual crisis intervention and to increase emergency mental health skills.

- *Family Crisis Intervention / Organizational Consultation*—Means of ongoing support are established with family members and organizations. Referrals for social, medical, mental health, or other services are made as needed.
- *Follow-Up*—Offers of additional opportunities for referrals are made as needed.

CISD is by far the most commonly employed and researched component of CISM. It is a single-session semi-structured group intervention that includes both educational and experiential components. It is run by personnel trained in CISD and typically includes at least one facilitator who is a "peer," a member of the target population. For example, a firefighter trained in conducting CISD usually will co-lead a CISD session for firefighters who have recently completed work on a disaster or casualty incident, along with a mental health or human services professional who also is trained to conduct CISD.

The goals of CISD include educating individuals about stress reactions and appropriate coping mechanisms, normalizing stress reactions, providing a venue to promote emotional processing of the incident, and providing information about further intervention if requested by the individual. Attendance is voluntary and open to all members of the target population regardless of the degree of their symptoms or functional impairment. The confidentiality of attendance and all information shared in the discussion is emphasized as a ground rule by the co-leaders, and must be agreed to by all participants. The intervention is presented as a form of discussing each person's experiences and reactions with the assumption that these are expectable given the highly stressful recent experiences and not to be treated as signs of psychological problems unless participants privately request a referral for personal therapy. As such, CISD does not include a formal assessment of mental health problems, nor is it intended to serve as psychotherapy for participants. Instead, the goal is to promote a sense of acceptance by participants of their reactions in order to provide them with a sense of personal closure about their memories of the crisis and their reactions to it.

CISD consists of seven phases that usually are completed within a 2- to 4-hour time period. The phases include: (1) an *introductory phase,* in which the facilitators explains the format of the session and discusses confidentiality; (2) a *fact phase,* in which participants describe the critical incident, each from her or his own perspective; (3) *a thought phase,* in which participants describe the thoughts they had at the time of the incident; (4) a *reaction phase,* in which the participants describe their emotional reactions at the time of the incident and their current reactions and interpretation of the incident; (5) a *symptoms phase,* in which the debriefing team describe typical stress reactions in order to reassure participants that these reactions are expectable and usually manageable; (6) a *teaching phase,* in which the debriefing team discusses stress management strategies with the participants; and (7) a *reentry phase,* in which the facilitators sum up the session and offer information on referrals and follow-up contacts.

Criticisms of Critical Incident Stress Management

No research to date has examined the impact and efficacy of the CISM model. Controlled studies have, however, focused on CISD and similar approaches to assisting first responders and trauma survivors or witnesses to cope with traumatic stress reactions, which have been generically labeled as "debriefing." These research studies have failed to find any significant differences in outcome between persons who received CISD or other forms of debriefing and those who did not, (e.g., Conlon, Fahy, & Conroy, 1999; Rose, Brewin, Andrews, & Kirk, 1999) indicating that receiving debriefing is no more effective in mitigating the emotional effects of psychological trauma exposure than receiving no debriefing. To be fair, these studies did not test CISD as originally prescribed by Mitchell because they involved persons directly exposed to psychological trauma rather than those (such as first responders or witnesses) indirectly exposed. Some of the studies used the full seven-phase CISD process, but many did not.

On the other hand, Everly, Flannery, and Mitchell (2000) have offered evidence in support of CISD and its efficacy. This evidence is based on studies that did not include a control group of persons who did not receive CISD, and therefore we cannot rule out the possibility that the benefits attributed to CISD may instead be due to other factors (such as the natural recovery process, or support from family or friends or clergy). In addition, no well-controlled scientific study has shown CISD (or CISM) to be effective in reducing mental health problems after a potentially traumatic incident.

Other criticisms of CISD have focused on the group format and various complications arising from that format. Some critics note the potential for subtle coercion by employers in order to "force" employees into participating in CISD. Such manipulations could result in counter-therapeutic reactions, such as resentment and anger, as well as inadvertently enhancing feelings of victimization by taking control away from trauma-exposed individuals. Additionally, the CISD format allows the inclusion of peers as co-facilitators in CISD groups. The presence of workplace peers within groups could leave employees feeling unsafe to disclose certain aspects of their traumatic experience or their emotional reactions, fearing such disclosure could place their job-security in jeopardy. Alternatively, group expectations could cause employees to feel pressured into disclosing more than they had intended to, or to feel stigmatized by disclosing details that surpass group expectations. Last, CISD has been described as overly inclusive, because it includes individuals with relatively little trauma exposure (e.g., a first responder who worked near but not right at the disaster site, and who did not know anyone who was seriously hurt or killed) with those who experienced extensive psychological trauma (e.g., a first responder or resident/employee at the disaster site who witnessed gruesome injuries or deaths or was closely involved with someone severely harmed or killed). This could potentially lead to the less exposed individuals feeling horrified and distressed by listening to others' severe experiences of psychological trauma, and to the more severely trauma-exposed individuals feeling unable to fully describe their experiences and reactions for fear of being stigmatized by or harming other participants.

Critics also claim that CISM was developed in direct response to the lack of evidence for the efficacy of CISD. Everly and Mitchell have denied this claim, stressing that CISD was never intended as a stand-alone intervention, and that this misconception can be traced back to the admittedly confusing terminology that was first employed in describing CISM. Prior to coining the term CISM, Everly and Mitchell referred to the program holistically as CISD, and the seven-phase group discussion component as "formal CISD." Questions remain as to whether CISD can be shown to be more effective when contained within the CISM context rather than as a stand-alone treatment.

Of potentially greatest concern are a small number of studies that suggest that debriefing—usually in the form of a single one-to-one session with an individual who very recently survived a life-threatening experience such as a (near) fatal vehicle accident or assault—may lead to greater distress than if no debriefing is done.

Advocates of CISM emphasize that CISM is not psychotherapy but rather a form of psychological first aid, and that none of its individual components were ever intended as stand-alone interventions. Everly and Mitchell (2004) have argued that the negative findings concerning the effectiveness of CISD have not fairly tested CISD as it is conducted in actual practice. Their main critiques of the research studies that find CISD to be of no additional benefit or potentially to have adverse effects on psychological well-being are that these studies:

Use one-on-one debriefing rather than group debriefing;

Use inappropriate measures to evaluate the efficacy of debriefing;

Involve people directly exposed to trauma (primary victims) rather than the emergency service personnel for whom CISD was originally developed;

Depart from the approved CISD protocol; and

Do not test debriefing in the context of a comprehensive CISM program.

Conclusion

Despite criticism about conceptual elements and a lack of empirical support, CISM-based frameworks remain the most widely used approach to assisting first responders in the emergency services, law enforcement, and military systems internationally. CISM has appeal because it has good face-validity and is relatively nondemanding. CISM is also structured favorably for organizations in that its services integrate well within work cultures and are intended to return personnel to work quickly. In addition, CISM can easily be implemented with a large number of individuals and does not require rigorous amounts of training to perform. This point is in contrast with some other forms of intervention shown to be effective in mitigating the effects of psychological trauma exposure, such as cognitive behavioral treatments. Not surprisingly, CISD/CISM is generally well received by managers and workers alike. However, the jury is still out in terms of whether CISD or CISM reduces the risk for chronic mental health problems when first responders or other indirectly affected persons experience psychological trauma. At present, there is little to no scientific evidence to support its use. Evidence-based crisis intervention is critical in order to make efficient use of typically scant professional resources and to ensure that survivors of psychological trauma of any kind get the best possible help.

REFERENCES

Conlon, L., Fahy, T. J., & Conroy, R. (1999). PTSD in ambulant RTA victims: A randomized controlled trial of debriefing. *Journal of Psychosomatic Research, 46,* 37–44.

Everly, G. S., Flannery, R. B., & Mitchell, J. T. (2000). Critical incident stress management (CISM): A review of the literature. *Aggression and Violent Behavior, 5,* 23–40.

Everly, G. S., & Mitchell, J. T. (2004). *A primer on critical incident stress management (CISM).* Retrieved September 20, 2007, from International Critical Incident Stress Foundation, Inc. web site: http://www.icisf.org/about/cismprimer.cfm.

Lindemann, E. (1944). Symptomatology and management of acute grief. *American Journal of Psychiatry, 101,* 141–148.

Rose, S., Brewin, C. R., Andrews, B., & Kirk, M. (1999). A randomized controlled trial of individual psychological debriefing for victims of violent crime. *Psychological Medicine, 29,* 793–799.

RECOMMENDED READINGS

Litz, B. T. (Ed.). (2004). *Early intervention for trauma and traumatic loss.* New York: Guilford Press.

Ritchie, E. C., Watson, P. J., & Friedman, M. J. (Eds.). (2006). *Interventions following mass violence and disasters.* New York: Guilford Press.

LAUREN B. MCSWEENEY
National Center for Posttraumatic Stress Disorder

BEN DICKSTEIN
National Center for Posttraumatic Stress Disorder

BRETT T. LITZ
National Center for Posttraumatic Stress Disorder

See also: Crisis Intervention, Adult; Crisis Intervention, Child; Early Intervention; Prevention, Adult; Prevention, Child; Psychological First Aid, Adult; Psychological First Aid, Child and Adolescent

CULTURE-BOUND SYNDROMES

The fields of medical anthropology and psychiatry have studied the concept of culture-bound syndromes in recognition of the need to account for cultural variations in the manifestation and interpretation of significant mental health conditions. Although all mental disorders are patterned by the cultural context, within which they occur, in culture-bound syndromes culture is both a key element in the understanding and structure of the disorder. Because of the prominence of cultural factors in the etiology of these disorders, they are sometimes referred to as culture-specific syndromes or culture-specific disorders. Fernando (2002) attributes Western observations of other cultures as "being alien and exotic" as contributing to the development of culture-bound syndromes.

Culture-bound syndromes have been debated among anthropologists who argue in favor of the relativistic and culture-specific characteristics of the syndrome, and mental health professionals who view universal and neuropsychological factors as playing a significant role in the etiology and development of the disorder (Belkin, 2003; Levine & Gaw, 1995; Mezzich, Kleinman, Fabrega, & Parron, 1996; Ranjith & Mohan, 2006). Additionally, the mental health field tends to view disorders in the West as the standard against which disorders in other cultures are measured (Bebbington, 1978). Thus, psychopathology in the West is viewed as culturally neutral and unclassifiable psychopathology in non-Western societies as culture bound (Fernando, 2002). Despite a lack of agreement between both disciplines in terms of definition, culture-bound syndromes were included as a type of mental disorder in the fourth edition of the *Diagnostic and Statistical Manual of Mental Disorders* (*DSM-IV;* American Psychiatric Association, 1994) as follows:

> recurrent, locality-specific patterns of aberrant behavior and troubling experience that may or may not be linked to a particular *DSM-IV* diagnostic category. Many of these patterns are indigenously considered to be "illnesses," or at least afflictions, and most have local names. (American Psychiatric Association, 1994, p. 844)

The diagnostic manual also includes a list of the most commonly occurring culture-bound disorders (see *DSM-IV:* Appendix I). Similarly, the *ICD-10* lists culture-specific disorders in its annex (World Health Organization, 1993). In contrast to presentations conforming to other universal *DSM-IV* categories, the particular symptoms, course, and social response of culture-bound syndromes are viewed as primarily influenced by specific cultural factors. Additionally these syndromes are "generally limited to specific societies or culture areas and are localized, folk, diagnostic categories that

frame coherent meanings for certain repetitive, patterned, and troubling sets of experiences and observations" (American Psychiatric Association, 1994, p. 844).

In theory, culture-bound syndromes are folk illnesses in which alterations of behavior and experience are prominent. In practice, culture-bound syndromes are local ways of explaining mishap and misfortunes. Some researchers strongly favor investigating and treating culture-bound syndromes as independent objects of research (Guarnaccia & Rogler, 1999). Fernando (2002) postulates that culture-bound syndromes should be limited to extremes of behavior identified by a particular society as deviant and "not explicable or understandable without an in-depth knowledge of the culture" (p. 43). Incorporating cultural variables in the diagnosis of psychiatric disorders is useful for enhancing cultural sensitivity and increasing the cross-cultural understanding of illness (Wohl & Aponte, 1995).

Culture-bound syndromes can be differentiated across seven broad categories that do not correspond with disorders recognized by Western psychiatry. The first category includes mental illnesses that do not have an identifiable organic cause, are locally recognized as an illness, and do not correspond to an existing Western disorder. The second category includes mental illnesses that do not have an identifiable organic cause, are locally recognized as an illness, and have important local and culture-specific but lacking some symptoms seen as salient in the Western nosology of the disorder. The third category includes distress disorders not yet recognized by Western medicine. The fourth category includes disorders or illnesses that may or may not have an organic cause, and correspond to a subset of Western disorders or with symptoms not recognized as constituting a Western disorder. The fifth category includes culturally acceptable explanations of illness that do not match allopathic mechanisms or Western idioms, and that, in a Western setting, may indicate culturally inappropriate thinking, delusions or hallucinations. The sixth category includes behaviors, including trance or possession states; hearing, seeing, and/or communicating with the dead or spirits; soul loss from grief or fright. These behaviors may or may not be seen as pathological by members within a particular cultural context, but if not recognized as culturally derived could indicate psychosis, delusions, or hallucinations in a Western setting. Finally, the seventh category includes idiosyncratic disorders reported to service providers but having no evidence of existing in a particular culture.

Culture-bound syndromes are conceptually useful for highlighting the salience of cultural, social and contextual factors that may play a formative role in defining an illness, and which may therefore enlighten those trained in dissimilar traditions regarding how to make culturally appropriate diagnoses. A limitation of the concept is that it is not a homogenous category, but instead describes a multitude of seemingly unrelated disorders. This has led to the conclusion that although the term *culture-bound syndrome* has good currency, it is difficult to define the concept clearly since the symptoms tend to differ from one culture to the next; additionally, it is often challenging to distinguish between culture-bound syndromes and other mental (psychotic) disorders (Simons & Hughes, 1985). Moreover, since culture-bound syndromes are often used to describe disorders that do not meet the criteria for mental disorders appearing in the *DSM*, there is a risk that those who may be unfamiliar with the syndrome may minimize their validity as authentic mental disorders. Novel and unusual symptoms may distract the investigator and limit a thorough exploration of the illness.

Perhaps, more than most mental diagnoses, posttraumatic stress disorder (PTSD) represents a complex code of social and contextual values and expectations regarding the ways in which people are likely to be affected by their experiences and how their reactions are commonly expressed. The proposition that the psychological effects of traumatic experiences (especially PTSD) occur similarly in all societies has stimulated much research and debate (e.g., Frey, 2001; Kleber, Figley, & Gersons, 1995; Marsella, Friedman, Gerrity, & Scurfield, 1996a; Wilson & Raphael, 1993).

For example, Chakraborty (1991) indicates that PTSD is a culture bound syndrome that is applicable only to Euro-Americans. In contrast, Marsella, Friedman, Gerrity, and Scurfield (1996b) reviewed a number of Western and non-Western studies and concluded that PTSD could be diagnosed among many ethnocultural cohorts. They also concluded that the prevalence rates of PTSD varied widely from one culture to another (Marsella et al., 1996b). They further proposed that a combination of ethnocultural influences and assessment measures, that were not sufficiently culturally sensitive to detect PTSD accurately across cultures, accounted for this variation. For example, they found that in different ethnocultural groups reexperiencing and arousal symptoms were more easily identified than avoidance and numbing symptoms, a pattern consistent with the idea that PTSD involves both universal and culture-bound dimensions, and a correspondence to biological and cultural influences respectively. Marsella et al. (1996b) went on to suggest that reexperiencing and arousal symptoms may have a greater biological basis while avoidance symptoms appear to have a greater cultural influence. Thus, they concluded that the prevalence of PTSD is highest among cultures in which avoidance and numbing are common methods of dealing with distress.

In their book *The Culture-Bound Syndromes*, Simons and Hughes (1985) list about 200 folk illnesses that may be considered culture-bound syndromes, though Western mental health professions will tend to encounter far fewer than this number. The following are some examples adapted from the *DSM-IV* (American Psychiatric Association, 1994, pp. 844–849) that resemble the conceptual framework of posttraumatic disorders as defined in Western psychiatry, but expressed differently in other cultural contexts:

- *Ataque de nervios:* A distress disorder often reported among Latinos from the Caribbean and many Latin American and Latin Mediterranean groups. The symptoms of the disorder include uncontrollable shouting, fits of crying, trembling, heat in the chest rising to the head, and verbal or physical aggression. *Ataque de nervios* is frequently reported to occur as a result of a stressful family event, the death of a relative, divorce, or a serious disagreement with a family member.

- *Latah:* A disorder described in Malaysia and Indonesia as a distress that develops when people are startled. The jolt of surprise or startle leads to a 30-minute display of screaming, dancing, and hysterical laughter, interspersed with shouting obscenities. Even though the outbursts are experienced as unpleasant for *latahs* (usually middle-aged women), family and friends often find the outbursts entertaining. Sufferers indicate that traumatic events cause the distress (e.g., the death of a child). A similar condition of distress has been described in a number of societies that are historically or culturally unrelated. For example, among the Ainu in Japan, the syndrome is called *imu,* while in a French-Canadian population in Maine, it is called *jumping.*

- *Nervios:* A distress disorder reported to occur in Latin America. It refers to a general state of vulnerability in response to stressful life experiences. The symptoms commonly include emotional distress, headaches, irritability, stomach disturbances, sleep disturbances, nervousness, easy tearfulness, inability to concentrate, tingling sensations, and dizziness. This distress is similar to a disorder called *nevra,* reported to occur in Greece.

- *Susto:* A distress disorder often reported among Latinos in the United States and Latin America. *Susto* is attributed to a frightening event, which causes the soul to leave the body. Soul loss leads to symptoms of unhappiness and sickness. Additionally, the symptoms of *susto* may be variable and sometimes occur months or years after the precipitating event. The disorder is also called *espanto, pasmo, tripa ida, perdida del alma,* and *chibih.*

There are many challenges in diagnosing and treating culture-bound syndromes.

First, because of variations in the disorder, a single diagnostic or therapeutic approach cannot be recommended. Second, for some sufferers, therapy is seldom considered as a viable source of support and behaviors of distress are regarded as eccentricities that do not need treatment. When therapy is likely to be an option, approaches that follow a medical model are preferred. Third, people are responsive to diagnostic labeling and may alter their behavior and self-conceptions in response to classification. Thus, in a cultural setting in which there is a particular folk illness, both the experience and behaviors of the distressed person is shaped by their understanding of an illness.

When working with individuals from another culture presenting with symptoms that may be unfamiliar, it is useful to first find out how they and other concerned individuals conceptualize the disorder. Gaining insight into what authority figures in the community would advise and recommend is valuable. Familiarity with culturally significant beliefs and practices is crucial. In terms of intervention, a therapeutic approach that is culture-specific and inclusive of the sufferer's worldview is likely to be most successful.

REFERENCES

American Psychiatric Association. (1994). *Diagnostic and statistical manual of mental disorders* (4th ed.). Washington, DC: Author.

Bebbington, P. E. (1978). The epidemiology of depressive disorder. *Culture, Medicine and Psychiatry, 2,* 297–341.

Belkin, G. S. (2003). Hard questions in court: Culture and psychiatry on trial. *Culture, Medicine and Psychiatry, 27*(2), 157–161.

Chakraborty, A. (1991). Culture, colonialism, and psychiatry. *Lancet, 337,* 1204–1207.

Fernando, S. (2002). *Mental health, race and culture.* New York: Palgrave.

Frey, C. (2001). Post traumatic stress disorder and culture. In A. T. Yilmaz, M. G. Weiss, & A. Riecher-Rossler (Eds.), *Cultural psychiatry: Euro-international perspectives* (pp. 103–116). Basil, Switzerland: Karger.

Guarnaccia, P. J., & Rogler, L. H. (1999). Research on culture-bound syndromes: New directions. *American Journal of Psychiatry, 156,* 1322–1327.

Kleber, R. J., Figley, C. R., & Gersons, B. P. R. (Eds.). (1995). *Beyond trauma: Cultural and social dynamics.* New York: Plenum Press.

Levine, R. E., & Gaw, A. C. (1995). Culture-bound syndromes. *Psychiatric Clinics of North America, 18*(3), 523–536.

Marsella, A. J., Friedman, M. J., Gerrity, E. T., & Scurfield, R. M. (Eds.). (1996a). *Ethnocultural aspects of posttraumatic stress disorder: Issues, research, and clinical applications.* Washington, DC: American Psychological Association.

Marsella, A. J., Friedman, M. J., Gerrity, E. T., & Scurfield, R. M. (1996b). Ethnocultural aspects of PTSD: Some closing thoughts. In A. J. Marsella, M. J. Friedman, E. T. Gerrity, & R. M. Scurfield (Eds.), *Ethnocultural aspects of posttraumatic stress disorder: Issues, research, and clinical applications* (pp. 529–538). Washington, DC: American Psychological Association.

Mezzich, J. E., Kleinman, A., Fabrega, H., & Parron, D. L. (1996). *Culture and psychiatric diagnosis: A DSM-IV perspective.* Washington, DC: American Psychiatric Press.

Ranjith, G., & Mohan, R. (2006). Dhat syndrome as a functional somatic syndrome: Developing a sociosomatic model. *Psychiatry: Interpersonal and Biological Processes, 69*(2), 142–150.

Simons, R. C., & Hughes, C. C. (Eds.). (1985). *The culture-bound syndromes: Folk illnesses of psychiatric and anthropological interest.* Dordrecht, The Netherlands: Reidel.

Wilson, J. P., & Raphael, B. (Eds.). (1993). *International handbook of traumatic stress syndromes.* New York: Plenum Press.

Wohl, J., & Aponte, J. F. (1995). Common themes and future aspects. In J. F. Aponte, R. Young Rivers, & J. Wohl (Eds.), *Psychological interventions and cultural diversity* (pp. 301–316). Boston: Allyn & Bacon.

World Health Organization. (1993). *The ICD-10 classification of mental and behavioral disorders: Diagnostic criteria for research.* Geneva, Switzerland: Author.

PRISCILLA DASS-BRAILSFORD
Lesley University

See *also:* Anthropological Perspectives; Culture and Trauma; Diagnosis of Traumatic Stress Disorders (*DSM & ICD*); Racial and Ethnic Factors

CULTURE AND TRAUMA

Conceptions of trauma and related stress disorders during the 1960 to 1980 Vietnam War era failed to assign much importance to the possibility of ethnocultural variations in the experience, manifestation, and treatment responsivity. The gradual accumulation of knowledge from international clinical research studies associated with numerous natural (e.g., earthquakes, hurricanes, floods) and human-made disasters (e.g., war, terrorism, accidents), however, have supported a growing acknowledgment of the many cultural influences on the trauma experience and its various clinical parameters. Thus, the number of publications on ethnocultural variations in trauma and related stress disorders is rapidly increasing and clinicians and researchers are now much more inclined to incorporate cultural variables (e.g., concepts of personhood, ethnic identity, religious status, gender status and roles, cultural history, conceptions of health and disorder) in their clinical and research efforts.

While some clinicians may reflexively assume that exposure to a traumatic event elicits similar psychological and physical reactions regardless of cultural, national, or even racial differences, clinical and field experiences indicate that this is false. Indeed, amid the best of intentions that were revealed in response to the December 2004 Indonesian tsunami disaster by Western help providers, it soon became apparent that perceptions and interpretations of the causes and nature of the disaster as well as the conditions necessary for personal and collective recovery and rehabilitation required an understanding of the cultural traditions and lifestyles of the tsunami victims. A similar awareness regarding the importance of culture and racial variations occurred following the responses of leaders, agencies, and help providers to Hurricane Katrina victims in New Orleans and other locations in 2005.

Culture can be defined as a group's shared meanings and beliefs that emerge from socialization efforts to promote adaptation and adjustment with resulting *internal* (e.g., beliefs, values, ways-of-knowing, conceptions of personhood)

and *external* (e.g., artifacts, roles, institutions) referents. In this respect, culture structures our perception and experience of reality and it shapes, often in very profound ways, the perceptual and experiential templates we use to describe, understand, predict, and control the world about us. This is true for both "normal" and "disordered" patterns of behavior (Marsella & Yamada, 2007).

Unfortunately, our understanding of trauma responses and traumatic events is complicated by the problem of *ethnocentricity* in which different groups come to believe that only their construction of reality—their cultural world view—is accurate or true. This has led to some problems, especially among well-intentioned Western help providers. The "power" assigned or assumed by Western mental health sciences and professions because of Western economic, political, and military dominance does not mean that their views are accurate; rather, they are simply a dominant view that can be problematic. Among the mental health sciences and professions, ethnocentric inclinations have led to errors and biases and abuses in the diagnosis, assessment, and treatment by Western personnel working with non-Western or ethnic and racial minority groups of patients. At this time, ethnocentric assumptions about trauma and traumatic events continue to remain a barrier to the accurate understanding of trauma disorders and other forms of psychopathology and maladjustment. However, much progress is occurring in incorporating cultural factors into our understanding of trauma responses.

Within the context of the previous definition of culture and the acknowledged limitations imposed by ethnocentricity, it is now recognized by many scientists and professionals that virtually every aspect of trauma-related mental disorders is shaped by culture (Marsella, Friedman, Gerrity, & Scurfield, 2001; Wilson, 2008; Wilson & Tang, 2007). What, then, is the current state of our knowledge about cultural aspects of trauma-related disorders, traumatic events, and traumatic stress treatments?

- The biopsychological response to stressors associated with traumatic events is universal. This involves the activation of the sympathetic central nervous system response that involves the initiation of the hypothalamic-pituitary-adrenal (HPA) axis changes that prepares the organism for "flight-fight-fright-freeze" responses. There is substantive research that indicates traumatic stress responses can result in both reversible and irreversible CNS changes in the locus coeruleus, amygdala, and hippocampal areas.

- Culture acts as a perceptual and experiential template for responding to traumatic stressors shaping "interpretations" such as the nature, cause, individual-collective experience and interpretation, and various clinical parameters of the response.

- Culture influences the clinical parameters of the diagnostic criteria for PTSD and related stress disorders that may occur in response to "traumatic" events, including:
  —Patterns of onset
  —Idioms of distress
  —Manifestation of symptoms (e.g., guilt, anger, anxiety, somatic)
  —Patterns of reexperience, avoidance, and dissociation symptoms
  —Disabilities and impairments
  —Course, progression, and outcome
  —Patterns of post-trauma culture-bound disorders that may not meet Western diagnostic criteria

- Culture shapes psychosocial aspects of responses to "traumatic" events, including:
  —Meaning of phenomena such as nightmares and visions
  —Role of destiny or fate in the determination of the event and response
  —Disabilities conditions that are independent of symptoms
  —Perception of personal responsibility for the event and response
  —Vulnerabilities to trauma (e.g., social network, social status).

- Cultures have different patterns, rituals, and treatment protocols for dealing with survivors of disaster, trauma, and extreme stress. Depending on the culture, these mechanisms may include what Western medico-psychological experts would classify as nontraditional or alternative modalities of treatment or assistance. Included within this group of "healers" are shamans; medicine "men and women" of non-Western practices; herbal therapies; physical and somatic (bodily) treatments of many varieties; aboriginal dances and incantations, recitations.

- Transcultural lessons from the emerging field of ethnotraumatology clearly show that a global perspective of understanding psychic trauma is critical to many areas of healing care delivery, medical practices, psychotherapy, and other social welfare and social work orientations to care provision (e.g., Kirmayer, Lemelson, & Barad, 2007). The critical question that remains for recovery from significant psychic trauma is: "What forms of care and treatment work best for any given patient at any given time and under what circumstances?" This requires a careful consideration of individual, cultural, and historical variables.

- The interplay between culture, personality, and reactions to stress and trauma is not a new issue in the study of culture and personality. What is perhaps best understood are some specific links between shared belief systems and individual personality traits in terms of how these influence coping across different individuals and cultural groups. These have implications for how people cope with adverse forms of expectable and unexpectable human experiences.

- Last, there is a need to recognize that there are cultures that encounter persistently traumatic circumstances by virtue of their unfortunate daily life contexts. For example, cultures undergoing cultural disintegration, collapse, acculturation, fragmentation, destruction, abuse, and a score of other conditions brought on by oppression, insecurity, war, disaster, and a history of political subjugation and tyranny

exact a harsh toll on their members. Under these circumstances, members are forced to live in conditions of deprivation, fear, hate, anger, and helplessness that leave permanent psychic and physical scars. The cultures, in these circumstances, may foster and sustain trauma. The question must also be asked to what extent places of employment, education, recreation, and residence must also be considered pathological cultures in their nature and consequence for trauma (Marsella, 2005).

These considerations all raise further questions about the interface between culture and traumatic life events. First, while there are numerous studies that document the biopsychological responses to traumatic stressors and their common neuroendocrine pathways in the central nervous system (Wilson & Keane, 2004), there are few cross-cultural comparative magnetic resonance imaging studies (MRI) to determine whether changes in the brain structures (e.g., hippocampus, amygdala) associated with chronic posttraumatic stress disorder (PTSD) are identical in nature.

Second, to what degree do culturally shaped systems of beliefs and expectations filter the perception and definition of traumatic life events and the responses to them? Indeed, what defines trauma for any particular culture? What is the threshold that defines a life event as traumatic as opposed to one located on a continuum of stressful events? This question is of critical importance since the nature of the stress response involving the HPA axis is predicated on the perception of threat to the well-being of the organism which, in turn, triggers the human stress response syndrome and patterns of coping and adaptation.

Third, posttraumatic adaptations fall along a continuum from severely pathological to successful resilience. At the pathological level of the continuum are brief psychoses, depressive disorders, dissociative disorders, PTSD, and chronic anxiety states. In this same regard, there are culturally sanctioned modalities of posttraumatic adaptation as well as culture-specific modalities of treatment and healing from trauma. Therefore, a broad view of the interface between traumatic events and cultural responses to them recognizes that posttraumatic adaptations are person-specific and that there are multiple pathways to recovery and the reestablishment of what a culture defines as normal, acceptable, or healthy behavior. Indeed, sometimes in the face of trauma, people not only recover, but transcend the experience in profound ways that lead them to feel they are better as a result.

Fourth, it must be understood that there is no individual experience of psychological trauma without a cultural history, grounding, or background. Personal identity is rooted and shaped within a cultural context (e.g., Native American, African American, Aboriginal Australian, Hmong people, Eskimo, Mayan). Hence, there is no sense of personal identity without a cultural context. In this way, it may be seen that cultures develop specific forms of posttraumatic recovery, stabilization, and healing for the members of the culture itself.

Fifth, culture also influences clinical diagnosis of posttraumatic adaptation patterns and syndromes. The rationale for what defines a "mental disorder" varies among cultures. For example, among many Native American tribes (e.g., Sioux, Navajo) mental illness, psychic distress, depression, and so on is thought to be the result of a "loss of spirit" (i.e., dispiritedness) caused by a loss of healthy balance between the individual, his or her natural environment, and the world at large. Thus, healing rituals and practices attempt to restore "spirit" and unity in terms of "all relations" to each other.

Sixth, it cannot be assumed a priori that Western-based diagnostic systems (e.g., *DSM-IV-TR*) would necessarily have meaningful applicability in non-Western cultures. Further, by logical extension, one cannot assume that Western psychometric technologies for assessing PTSD and trauma reactions are generalizable to non-Western cultures because of problems with translation and "back translation" of language (Drozdek & Wilson, 2007; Marsella & Yamada, 2007; Wilson & Tang, 2007), among other considerations that must

address the way cultures influence how a person construes reality and, hence, the meaning of understanding of psychological reactions to extreme stress experiences.

Even in the extremes of trauma induced by the physical and psychological torture methods used in such infamous locations as Abu Ghraib, Kandahar, and Guantanamo, reports of those prisoners from various Middle Eastern and South Asian cultures who have been released as well as those who continue to be imprisoned indicate that some collapsed into psychosis and will never recover, some survived with PTSD and other disorders, and some have lived amid their pain and suffering determined to expose the brutality to which they were subjected by various governments. For the latter group, their trauma has served to make them voices for the voiceless and a conscience for the world. This constitutes something more than survival and must be considered nearer to transcendence.

Beyond a doubt, the twenty-first century will see the scientific convergence of globalized knowledge about trauma, culture, and posttraumatic stress disorders. The scientific questions concerning the interface between trauma and culture will provide a center stage for new paradigms of knowledge of that which is universal in nature and that which makes individual characters unique in nature, shaped by the forces of culture, historical events, and an unfolding destiny.

Thus, after initial resistance and hesitancies to include culture in the conceptualization, diagnosis, assessment, and treatment of trauma, there is now a widespread recognition of its importance for understanding trauma responses and traumatic events. Today, virtually all mental health scientists and professionals are sensitive to cultural variations and this is gradually beginning to impact policy development and implementation. While progress may be slower than is necessary, there is nevertheless every reason to believe that cultural factors will be assigned a new level of importance in our forthcoming responses to national and international disasters and related traumatic events.

REFERENCES

Drozdek, B., & Wilson, J. P. (Eds.). (2007). *Voices of trauma: Treating survivors across cultures.* New York: Springer.

Kirmayer, L. J., Lemelson, R., & Barad, M. (2007). *Understanding trauma: Integrating biological, clinical, and cultural perspectives.* New York: Cambridge University Press.

Marsella, A. J. (2005). Culture and conflict: Understanding and negotiating different cultural constructions of reality. *International Journal of Intercultural Relations, 29,* 651–673.

Marsella, A. J., Friedman, M., Gerrity, E., & Scurfield, R. (Eds.). (2001). *Ethnocultural aspects of Posttraumatic stress disorder: Issues, research, and clinical applications.* Washington, DC: American Psychological Association.

Marsella, A. J., & Yamada, A. M. (2007). Culture and psychopathology: Foundations, issues, directions. In S. Kitayama & D. Cohen (Eds.), *Handbook of cultural psychology* (pp. 797–818). New York: Guilford Press.

Wilson, J. P. (2008). Culture, trauma, and the treatment of post-traumatic syndromes: A global perspective. In A. J. Marsella, J. Johnson, P. Watson, & J. Gryczynski (Eds.), *Ethnocultural perspectives on disaster and trauma: Foundations, issues, and applications* (pp. 351–378). New York: Springer.

Wilson, J. P., & Keane, T. (2004). *Assessing psychological trauma and PTSD.* New York: Guilford Press.

Wilson, J. P., & Tang, C. (Eds.). (2007). *Cross-cultural assessment of PTSD and related stress disorders.* New York: Springer.

ANTHONY J. MARSELLA
University of Hawaii, Manoa

JOHN P. WILSON
Cleveland State University

See also: Anthropological Perspectives; Culture-Bound Syndromes; Diagnosis of Traumatic Stress Disorders (*DSM* & *ICD*); International Organizations; Racial and Ethnic Factors

D

DEBRIEFING

See: Crisis Intervention, Adult; Critical Incident Stress Management; Early Intervention; Prevention, Adult; Prevention, Child

DELAYED ONSET

Most people exposed to a traumatic event experience some symptoms of posttraumatic stress in the immediate aftermath. Some develop or continue to have sufficient symptoms and difficulties in functioning for at least 1 month to be diagnosed with posttraumatic stress disorder (PTSD). However, for others, PTSD can take longer to emerge. For example, some soldiers develop PTSD in the first month following traumatic war experiences, but others may not develop PTSD until many months or years later. PTSD with delayed onset is technically defined as beginning *at least* 6 months following traumatic event(s). Once believed to be rare, PTSD with delayed onset has been shown in some populations to occur as often as in over 40% of cases of PTSD (Gray, Bolton, & Litz, 2004). Risk factors for delayed onset PTSD have not been firmly established by research.

When faced with the challenges and losses of aging, some older adults experience a reemergence or exacerbation of trauma-related emotional symptoms, although it is relatively rare for older adults to experience a true first onset of full-blown PTSD decades after a traumatic event (Port, Engdahl, & Frazier, 2001). Research on trauma-related symptoms in later life has been conducted, among others, with aging combat veterans and prisoners of war from World War II, Korea, and Vietnam and with Holocaust survivors. There is also an emerging body of literature concerning aging survivors of sexual abuse, rape, and other interpersonal violence (Somer, 2000). This growing attention to late-life trauma symptoms led to the recent identification of a phenomenon called "late-onset stress symptomatology" (LOSS; Davison et al., 2006). Originally studied in aging combat veterans but now being explored in older sexual trauma survivors, LOSS is postulated as a condition among older adults who were exposed to trauma in their early adult years, who functioned relatively successfully over the course of their lives, but who begin to experience trauma-related reminiscences and/or symptoms in the context of normative late-life events such as retirement, loss of a spouse, or physical illness. LOSS appears to be distinct from delayed onset PTSD in that reminiscence plays a central role, and many do not describe their experience as unduly distressing or disabling. (For a review, see also Andrews, Brewin, Philpott, & Stewart, 2007.)

REFERENCES

Andrews, B., Brewin, C. R., Philpott, R., & Stewart, L. (2007). Delayed-onset posttraumatic stress disorder: A systematic review of the evidence. *American Journal of Psychiatry, 164*, 1319–1326.

Davison, E. H., Pless, A. P., Gugliucci, M. R., King, L. A., King, D. W., Salgado, D. M., et al. (2006). Late-life emergence of early life trauma: The phenomenon of late-onset stress symptomatology among aging combat veterans. *Research on Aging, 28*(1), 84–114.

Gray, M. J., Bolton, E. E., & Litz, B. T. (2004). A longitudinal analysis of PTSD symptom course: Delayed-onset PTSD in Somalia peacekeepers. *Journal of Consulting and Clinical Psychology, 72*(5), 909–913.

Port, C. L., Engdahl, B., & Frazier, P. (2001). A longitudinal and retrospective study of PTSD among older prisoners of war. *American Journal of Psychiatry, 158*(9), 1474–1479.

Somer, E. (2000). Effects of incest in aging survivors: Psychopathology and treatment issues. *Journal of Clinical Geropsychology, 6,* 53–61.

EVE H. DAVISON
Veterans Affairs Boston Healthcare System

See also: Diagnosis of Traumatic Stress Disorders (*DSM & ICD*); Geriatrics; Posttraumatic Stress Disorder; Posttraumatic Stress Disorder, Diagnosis of

DEPRESSION

In addition to traumatic stress, symptoms of depression are common in the acute wake of exposure to psychological trauma, and mood disorders (principally major depressive disorder) are as likely as PTSD to occur over time following exposure to psychological trauma. Survivors of psychological traumas ranging from disaster, terrorism, life-threatening accidents and assaults to war, community, or family violence or abuse, are at risk for major depressive disorder—although the greatest risk is incurred by people who had a history of depression prior to experiencing the psychological trauma (Kessler, Sonnega, Bromet, Hughes, & Nelson, 1995).

Depression and PTSD: Similarities and Differences in Symptoms and Causes

PTSD involves not only persistent anxiety, fear, and bodily arousal but also problems that overlap with classic symptoms of depression and dysthymia, such as anhedonia (loss of the ability to feel most emotions), social detachment, impaired concentration, and sleep disturbances. However, although symptoms of depression and PTSD overlap in these areas, and the fact that both depression and PTSD are more likely to occur if severe or persistent stressors are experienced and if social and psychological resources are depleted, there are several important differences between PTSD and depression. PTSD tends to be particularly associated with life-threatening stressors, while depression is more associated with stressors involving loss or neglect (O'Donnell, Creamer, & Pattison, 2004). Consistent with these findings, the symptoms of PTSD reflect a response to threat (such as heightened bodily arousal, hypervigilance, sensitivity to reminders of past traumatic experiences), while symptoms of depression are more reflective of a response to loss (such as melancholia and fatigue). The sleep disturbances in PTSD often differ from those associated with depression because PTSD often involves trauma-related nightmares that are hypothesized to be associated with the general noradrenergic hyperresponsiveness (Mellman & Hipolito, 2006).

Comorbidity of Depression and PTSD

In light of their overlapping symptoms, it is not surprising that results from analyses of two epidemiological studies of adults (the National Comorbidity Study or NCS) and young adults (the Michigan Study of Young Adults) showed that persons with PTSD were two to eight times as likely to have major depressive disorder as persons who did not have PTSD, and three to eleven times as likely as those who have never experienced psychological trauma (Breslau, Davis, Peterson, & Schultz, 2000). In the NCS, 48% of men and 49% of women who had PTSD also had a major depressive episode (Kessler et al., 1995). Although PTSD is more strongly associated with developing depression than is exposure to psychological trauma alone, there are types of psychological trauma that are strongly associated with depression. Having been kidnapped, raped, or sexually molested, or having a loved one experience psychological trauma were associated with almost a twofold increase in the risk of major depression even among persons who were not experiencing PTSD (Breslau et al., 2000). A recent study also confirmed that PTSD prevalence, comorbidity, and integrity as a diagnostic construct in the general population is not significantly reduced when symptoms of mood disorders (and of other anxiety disorders) are removed from the PTSD symptom criteria (Elhai, Grubaugh, Kashdan, & Frueh, 2008).

Correspondingly, persons with major depressive disorder are twice as likely as those not diagnosed with major depression to experience psychological trauma, and more than three times as likely to develop PTSD as those without major depression (Breslau et al., 2000). Thus, it appears that experiencing psychological trauma may either follow from or lead to major depression, particularly if PTSD occurs soon after a psychological trauma. Neither psychological trauma nor PTSD can be considered the "cause" of depression, nor does depression "cause" people to experience psychological trauma or PTSD—but the three are strongly linked. People who suffer the combination of psychological trauma, PTSD, and depression are likely to experience severe impairment in many areas of functioning, including work, school, relationships, and physical health (O'Donnell et al., 2004; Shalev et al., 1998).

Neurobiology of Depression and PTSD

Similar to their phenomenology, PTSD and depression also share some neurobiological features but differ in critical ways. Prolonged stress has been associated with dysregulation of the hypothalamic-pituitary-adrenal axis with changes in the levels of the stress hormone, cortisol. PTSD and depression both involve alterations in the body's stress response system, but in different ways. Decreased levels of cortisol have been reported in patients with PTSD (Yehuda, Halligan, Gollier, Grossman, & Bierer, 2004), similar to persons with stress-related medical conditions such as chronic fatigue syndrome and fibromyalgia.

Consistent with its low cortisol levels, PTSD is associated with high levels of cortisol receptors and increased sensitivity to dexamethasone in a test used to evaluate HPA axis functioning by administering a synthetic glucocorticoid hormone (the dexamethosone suppression test or DST; Yehuda et al., 2004). In contrast, depression is associated with high cortisol levels and reduced responsiveness to dexamethasone ("nonsuppression" of cortisol

in the DST; Yehuda et al., 2004). Interestingly, PTSD and depression share a similar change (heightened activation) in two body systems that are affected by cortisol, the immune system and the sympathetic nervous system (SNS; Raison & Miller, 2003). Thus, despite their seemingly opposite changes in HPA axis function, both PTSD and depression involve insufficient regulation of stress-related activation of both the SNS (possibly leading to symptoms of hyperarousal and agitation) and the immune system (leading to vulnerability to stress related medical problems; Raison & Miller, 2003).

PTSD and depression also share other neurobiological features, including high levels of neuropeptides (e.g., substance P) and damage to the hippocampus (*see:* **Hippocampus**), a brain structure that is critically involved in HPA axis regulation (Geriacoti et al., 2006; Raison & Miller, 2003). Interestingly, adults who had experienced multiple trauma incidents prior to becoming depressed exhibit low levels of cortisol, similar to findings in patients with PTSD (Yehuda et al., 2004). Similar to depression, PTSD is associated with dysregulation of the monoamine (inserotonin, norepinephrine, dopamine) neurotransmitter systems (Hageman, Andersen, & Jorgensen, 2001). Changes in the noradrenergic system are much more pronounced in patients with PTSD. These include tonically elevated central nervous system (CNS) norepinephrine concentrations, exaggerated CNS responses to noradrenergic activation due to antagonism of the presynpatic α_2 autoreceptor, and noradrenergic hyper-responsiveness to a variety of stimuli including psychological trauma or trauma-related stimuli (Strawn & Geracioti, 2008).

Evidence-Based Psychotherapy for Depression: Applicability to Treating PTSD

Several psychotherapies that have been found to be efficacious in the treatment of depression may have applicability also to PTSD. Cognitive behavior therapy (CBT) for depression has been shown to be comparable in efficacy to pharmacotherapy for acute depressive disorders and to reduce the risk of relapse by 20% to 25% when provided preventively to persons with chronic depressive disorders (Vittengl, Clark, Dunn, & Jarrett, 2007). CBT for depression involves assisting patients in identifying and modifying thoughts associated with anhedonia, dysphoria, and social withdrawal, all of which are cardinal features of PTSD. CBT is widely used for PTSD, but typically with a focus on anxiety-related beliefs rather than thoughts and beliefs associated with depression.

Interpersonal psychotherapy (IPT) for depression has been found to have comparable efficacy in the treatment of acute depression as CBT, particularly for patients experiencing stressful life changes or challenges affecting their social support systems (Parker, Parker, Brotchie, & Stuart, 2007). IPT involves identifying important relationships that are affected by stressors and enhancing those relationships so that they can provide a strong support base to address the alienation and isolation often characterizing depression and PTSD. IPT has recently been pilot tested successfully with adults with PTSD.

Behavioral activation therapy (BAT) has been less extensively researched for depression than CBT or IPT, but appears comparable in efficacy to CBT for the treatment of acute depression (Cuijpers, van Straten, & Warmerdam, 2007). BAT involves scheduling and engaging in activities that provide pleasure and social interaction, and as such is a much less technically complicated treatment than CBT or IPT. Increasing engagement in healthy and pleasurable activities may help to counteract not only the mood problems but also the difficulties with avoidance, anxiety, and hyperarousal that are characteristic of PTSD.

Pharmacotherapies (such as the antidepressant medications) that have been shown to be effective in the treatment of depression also often have been applied to the treatment of PTSD, with generally favorable results obtained in adults (Friedman & Davidson, 2007) and more recently in children. All currently marketed antidepressant drugs are speculated to produce their antidepressant effects through modulatory actions on the monoamine neurotransmitters serotonin (5-HT), norepinephrine (NE), and dopamine (DA), albeit with differing profiles of potency and selectivity. In general, antidepressants show similar efficacy in the treatment of depression with selected differences in side effect profiles (Rush, 2007). They differ in efficacy for selected depression subtypes.

With the exception of bupropion (Wellbutrin), all of the major antidepressant groups have also shown promise in the treatment of PTSD, although with different levels of evidence with respect to their efficacy (Asnis, Kohn, Henderson, & Brown, 2004). The selective serotonin reuptake inhibitors (SSRIs) have been the most studied in PTSD patients and are considered the first-line treatment for PTSD. Sertraline (Zoloft), paroxetine (Paxil), fluoxetine (Prosac), and escitalopram (Lexapro) have all been shown to be efficacious in the treatment of PTSD, and in some studies, their long-term use has been shown to decrease relapse rates. Several agents affecting two or more neurotransmitter systems are considered second-line treatment options for PTSD: serotonin-norepinephrine reuptake inhibitors (SNRIs) such as venlafaxine; and antidepressants with multiple selective pharmacological effects such as mirtazepine and nefazodone. Bupropion, a norepinephrine-dopamine reuptake inhibitor, although an efficacious antidepressant, requires further evaluation as an agent for PTSD. Although the older antidepressant drugs (e.g., the tricyclic antidepressants and the monoamine oxidase inhibitors) have been reported to have efficacy in the treatment of PTSD in more limited studies, they are used sparingly at the present time due to their unfavorable side effect profiles, such as risk of serious cardiovascular complications and safety issues, such as potential lethality with overdose.

Atypical antipsychotics (e.g., aripiprazole, risperidone), when used as an adjunct to antidepressants, have shown promise in the treatment of treatment-refractory depression. In PTSD, some atypical antipsychotic drugs have shown benefit with use as an augmention agent to SSRIs, and they are especially considered when paranoia, flashbacks, or disturbing nightmares are prominent (Asnis et al., 2004). Similar to the antipsychotics, use of selected anticonvulsant agents (e.g., valproic acid) or lithium, is considered in the treatment of treatment-refractory depression as an adjunct to antidepressants. Some anticonvulsant drugs have shown promise as stand-alone treatments for PTSD. Their use is considered when comorbidity of bipolar disorder exists or when anger and impulsivity represents a predominant aspect of PTSD symptomatology (Asnis et al., 2004).

Despite the large number and generally strong evidence of efficacy for PTSD treatment of medications that more typically are used to treat depression, these agents do not represent the full spectrum of pharmacotherapy for PTSD. Medications that reduce noradrenergic hyperactivity in the brain have been found effective in the treatment of hyperarousal and intrusive symptoms of PTSD (Strawn & Geracioti, 2008). These anti-noradrenergic agents include compounds that decrease norepinephrine release (e.g., centrally acting α_2 agonists such as clonidine) and those which block postsynaptic norepinephrine receptors (e.g., centrally acting α_1 or β receptor antagonists such as prazosin or propranolol). Prazosin is the best studied among these agents and has shown to significantly reduce nightmares and improve sleep disturbances associated with PTSD (Dierks, Jordan, & Sheehan, 2007). The use of these medications that have shown promise with PTSD provides additional treatment options for clinicians and researchers working with patients with depression.

Conclusion

Although they are distinct disorders, there are many areas of similarity in the symptoms, causes, and treatment of depression and PTSD, and they often occur together. Although PTSD is currently defined by the American Psychiatric Association as an anxiety disorder, it is important to address its "affective" or mood components (such as anhedonia, the loss of interest in formerly valued activities or relationships, emotional numbing, and irritability) in research, assessment, and treatment. The growing knowledge-base concerning PTSD and its treatment also has provided insights and new options for depression researchers and clinicians.

REFERENCES

Asnis, G., Kohn, S., Henderson, M., & Brown, N. (2004). SSRIs versus non-SSRIs in posttraumatic stress disorder: An update with recommendations. *Drugs, 64,* 383–404.

Breslau, N., Davis, G., Peterson, E., & Schultz, L. (2000). A second look at comorbidity in victims of trauma: The posttraumatic stress disorder–major depression connection. *Biological Psychiatry, 48,* 902–909.

Cuijpers, P., van Straten, A., & Warmerdam, L. (2007). Behavioral activation treatments for depression: A meta-analysis. *Clinical Psychology Review, 27,* 318–326.

Dierks, M., Jordan, J., & Sheehan, A. (2007). Prazosin treatment of nightmares related to posttraumatic stress disorder. *Annals of Pharmacotherapy, 41,* 1013–1017.

Elhai, J. D., Grubaugh, A. L., Kashdan, T. B., & Frueh, B. C. (2008). Empirical examination of a proposed refinement to DSM-IV posttraumatic stress disorder symptom criteria using the National Comorbidity Survey Replication data. *Journal of Clinical Psychiatry, 69,* 597–602.

Friedman, M. J., & Davidson, J. R. T. (2007). Pharmacotherapy for PTSD. In M. Friedman, T. Keane, & P. Resick (Eds.), *Handbook of PTSD* (pp. 376–405). New York: Guilford Press.

Geriacoti, R., Carpenter, L., Owens, M., Baker, D., Ekhator, N., Horn, P., et al. (2006). Elevated cerebrospinal fluid Substance P concentrations in posttraumatic stress disorder and major depression. *American Journal of Psychiatry, 163,* 637–643.

Hageman, I., Andersen, H., & Jorgensen, M. (2001). Posttraumatic stress disorder: A review of psychobiology and pharmacotherapy. *Acta Psychiatrica Scandinavica, 104,* 411–422.

Kessler, R. C., Sonnega, A., Bromet, E., Hughes, M., & Nelson, C. B. (1995). Posttraumatic stress disorder in the national comorbidity survey. *Archives of General Psychiatry, 52,* 1048–1060.

Mellman, T., & Hipolito, M. (2006). Sleep disturbances in the aftermath of trauma and posttraumatic stress disorder. *CNS Spectrums, 11,* 611–615.

O'Donnell, M., Creamer, M., & Pattison, P. (2004). Posttraumatic stress disorder and depression following trauma: Understanding comorbidity. *American Journal of Psychiatry, 161,* 1390–1396.

Parker, G., Parker, I., Brotchie, H., & Stuart, S. (2007). Interpersonal psychotherapy for depression? The need to define its ecological niche. *Journal of Affective Disorders, 95,* 1–11.

Raison, C., & Miller, A. (2003). When not enough is too much: The role of insufficient glucocorticoid signaling in the pathophysiology of stress-related disorders. *American Journal of Psychiatry, 160,* 1554–1565.

Rush, A. (2007). STAR*D: What have we learned? *American Journal of Psychiatry, 164,* 201.

Shalev, A., Freedman, S., Peri, T., Brandes, D., Sahar, T., Orr, S. P., et al. (1998). Prospective study of posttraumatic stress disorder and depression following trauma. *American Journal of Psychiatry, 155,* 631–637.

Strawn, J., & Geracioti, T. (2008). Noradrenergic dysfunction and the psychopharmacology of posttraumatic stress disorder. *Depression and Anxiety, 25,* 260–271.

Vittengl, J. R., Clark, L. A., Dunn, T. W., & Jarrett, R. B. (2007). Reducing relapse and recurrence in unipolar depression. *Journal of Consulting and Clinical Psychology, 75,* 475–488.

Yehuda, R., Halligan, S., Golier, J., Grossman, R., & Bierer, L. (2004). Effects of trauma exposure on the cortisol response to dexamethasone administration in PTSD and major depressive disorder. *Psychoneuroendocrinology, 29,* 389–404.

Julian D. Ford
University of Connecticut School of Medicine

Jayesh Kamath
University of Connecticut School of Medicine

Andrew Winokur
University of Connecticut School of Medicine

See also: Biology, Neurochemistry; Comorbidity; Diagnosis of Traumatic Stress Disorders (*DSM & ICD*); Emotional Numbing; Pharmacotherapy, Adult; Pharmacotherapy, Child; Posttraumatic Stress Disorder; Posttraumatic Stress Disorder, Diagnosis of

DESENSITIZATION

See: Cognitive Behavior Therapy, Adult; Cognitive Behavior Therapy, Child Abuse; Cognitive Behavior Therapy, Childhood Traumatic Grief; Exposure Therapy, Adult; Exposure Therapy, Child

DEVELOPMENTAL ASPECTS

See: Adolescence; Child Development; Geriatrics; Infancy and Early Childhood

DEVELOPMENTAL PSYCHOPATHOLOGY

See: Abuse, Child Physical; Abuse, Child Sexual; Adolescence; Child Development; Child Maltreatment; Infancy and Early Childhood

DIAGNOSIS OF TRAUMATIC STRESS DISORDERS (*DSM & ICD*)

A diagnosis is a technical description of a problem that is designed to present all aspects of the problem with sufficient completeness and clarity to enable a professional with expertise in the relevant field to identify the problem and prevent or fix it. In the health-care fields, a medical diagnosis describes the specific observable symptoms and the extent of discomfort or hazard that constitute a particular illness or injury. Medical diagnoses enable health-care providers to distinguish different illnesses or injuries so that they can utilize specific tests and treatments that have been scientifically shown, respectively, to accurately identify and efficaciously treat (that is, improve or eliminate) or prevent the symptoms of the illness or injury. The best-known system of medical diagnoses is the *International Classification of Diseases* (*ICD*), which has been revised 10 times and was recently updated while an eleventh revision is being developed (World Health Organization, 2005). Each diagnosis in the *ICD* is a distinct physical condition for which there is a numerical code (for example, I21 is the code for a myocardial infarction [heart attack] and C50 is the code for neoplasm of the breast [breast cancer]).

In the mental health field, diagnoses have been defined for mental disorders ranging from conditions primarily beginning in childhood (such as attention deficit hyperactivity disorder or pervasive developmental disorder) to conditions involving problems with impaired reality orientation (such as schizophrenia), mood regulation (such as major depressive episodes or bipolar disorder), eating (such as anorexia or bulimia nervosa), dissociation (such as dissociative identity disorder), substance use (such as alcohol dependence or cocaine abuse), and anxiety (such as phobias or social anxiety disorder). These diagnoses have been codified internationally in the *ICD* and separately in the United States in the American Psychiatric Association's (1952, 1968, 1980, 1987, 1994) *Diagnostic and Statistical Manual,* which was most recently updated in 2000 as a "text revision" of the fourth edition (*DSM-IV-TR;* 2000). Despite many similarities there are important differences between the *ICD* and *DSM* definitions of diagnoses.

The diagnoses most relevant to psychological trauma in both the *ICD* and *DSM* are the traumatic stress disorders. These diagnoses include posttraumatic stress disorder (PTSD; Code 309.89 in the *DSM*; F43.1 in the *ICD*) and acute stress disorder (ASD; *DSM* 308.3) or acute stress reaction (*ICD* F43.0). The *ICD* includes an additional diagnosis of "enduring personality change after catastrophic experience" (F62.0), which is not included in the *DSM*. Two other diagnoses are not directly related to exposure to traumatic stressors but tend to be more often experienced by persons who suffered early childhood psychological trauma that disrupted primary emotional relationships (*see:* **Abuse, Child Physical; Abuse, Child Sexual; Child Maltreatment; Complex Posttraumatic Stress Disorder**). The first are the dissociative disorders, such as Dissociative Identity Disorder (*DSM* 300.14) or "multiple personality disorder" in the *ICD* (F44.8). The second is a personality disorder diagnosis that has been labeled as "borderline personality disorder" in the *DSM* (BPD; 301.83) and *ICD*'s "emotionally unstable personality disorder (F60.3). Each of these diagnoses and their relationship to psychological trauma will be discussed.

Acute Stress Disorder and Posttraumatic Stress Disorder

Before World War II, there was no single accepted diagnosis for the problems experienced by people who were having distress after exposure to an extreme (psychologically traumatic) stressor. Several conditions such as "railway spine" and "soldier's heart" that appear to reflect posttraumatic stress were described in the medical literature in the nineteenth century (*see:* **History of the Concept of Traumatic Stress; Posttraumatic Stress Disorder**). During and after World War II and the Korean War, military personnel who became persistently distressed during or after war experiences were described as having a "war neurosis," "combat stress reaction," or "combat fatigue" (*see:* **History of the Concept of Traumatic Stress; Posttraumatic Stress Disorder**).

At that time, the first version of the *DSM* (1952) was published. Stress disorders resulting from psychological trauma were classified as "Gross Stress Reactions," which were not expected to persist for more than a short time unless the person had prior psychological problems that might lead the stress reactions to become a chronic neurosis (Turnbull, 1998). Fifteen years later, in the *DSM*'s second edition (1968), Gross Stress Reactions was no longer included as a diagnosis. Instead, the diagnosis of "Transient Situational Disturbance" was included in order to explicitly define stress reactions as temporary (transient). This diagnosis clarified that "an overwhelming environmental stressor" was necessary in order to cause clinically significant stress reactions in "otherwise healthy individuals" (American Psychiatric Association, 1968; see Turnbull, 1998). In the 1970s, women who had been sexually assaulted and experienced persistent distress were described as having a "rape trauma syndrome" or "battered woman syndrome" (*see:* **Domestic Violence; Rape Trauma**). In the 1970s, a "post-Vietnam syndrome" was identified among returning soldiers (Lasiuk & Hegadoren, 2006). None of these syndromes ever became codified as official medical or psychiatric diagnoses, but they were crucial forerunners of what now are defined as the diagnoses of acute stress disorder/reaction (ASD) and posttraumatic stress disorder (PTSD).

The diagnosis of PTSD first officially appeared in the third edition of the *DSM* (1980), and was revised to provide a more detailed specification of the diagnostic criteria in the revision of the *DSM* published in 1987 (*DSM-III-R*). PTSD in the *DSM-III-R* included five components that continue to be the basis for the diagnosis (albeit in altered forms) in the most recent version of the *DSM* (the fourth edition text revision, American Psychiatric Association, 2000; *see:* **Posttraumatic Stress Disorder** for a complete description of the current version of the diagnosis). The first component ("Criterion A") of the PTSD diagnosis is the "traumatic stressor," which was defined in the *DSM-III* as exposure to a stressor or set of stressors that are "generally outside the range of usual human experience" (American Psychiatric Association, 1980, p. 236) and that "evoke significant symptoms of distress in almost everyone" (American Psychiatric Association, 1980, p. 238; see Lasiuk, & Hegadoren, 2006). Exposure to a traumatic stressor need not be recent, but may have occurred many years or even decades earlier in the person's life.

The next three components or criteria for the *DSM-III-R* PTSD diagnosis referred to symptoms of distress that the person is experiencing at the time of the diagnosis. These three criteria included a more detailed specification of symptoms than that in *DSM-III*, as well as the deletion of a symptom reflecting memory impairment and a relocating of the avoidance symptoms to include them with emotional numbing. The *DSM-III-R* organization of the symptoms into three domains has remained as the core structure of the PTSD diagnosis for more than two decades (but later discussion for research developments that may lead to revisions of the PTSD diagnosis in *DSM's* fifth edition).

A second component of the *DSM-III-R* PTSD diagnosis ("Criterion B") required the current persistent reexperiencing of the traumatic stressor in at least one of four ways:

B1: memories of the traumatic event(s) that are recurrent (that is, repetitive), intrusive (that is, unwanted and involuntary), and distressing;

B2: repeated distressing dreams of the traumatic event(s);

B3: suddenly acting as if the traumatic event was happening all over again (often in the form of a dissociative episode called a "flashback"), which may occur when intoxicated but also when not under the influence of any substances;

B4: severe distress when reminded of the traumatic event(s): "intense psychological distress at exposure to events that symbolize or resemble an aspect of the traumatic event, including anniversaries."

The third component of the *DSM-III-R* *PTSD* diagnosis ("Criterion C") required that the person is experiencing at least three symptoms involving the avoidance of reminders of the traumatic stressor event(s) and a substantial reduction in the ability to feel emotions such as enjoyment of pleasurable activities, closeness or love in relationships, and optmism about the future (i.e., "emotional numbing"). The symptoms must *not* have been present before the person was exposed to the stressor(s). The symptoms may occur in any combination and need not include all of the symptoms at the same time. The first two "C" symptoms are the avoidance symptoms, and the third through seventh "C" symptoms are the emotional numbing symptoms:

C1: efforts to avoid thoughts or feelings associated with the traumatic event(s)

C2: efforts to avoid activities or situations that evoke memories of the event(s)

C3: inability to recall an important aspect of the event(s) ("psychogenic amnesia")

C4: markedly diminished interest in significant activities ("anhedonia"), which in young children may take the form of regression in previously established developmental skills such as toilet training or receptive or expressive language

C5: feeling emotionally detached or estranged from people ("social detachment")

C6: limited ability or unable to feel most emotions, such as loving feelings ("emotional numbing")

C7: expecting to have one's life cut short, such as not expecting to have or complete a career, family, or long life ("sense of a foreshortened future")

The fourth component of the *DSM-III-R* PTSD diagnosis ("Criterion D") required that the person is experiencing at least two symptoms of persistent excessive physical arousal that were not present before the stressor(s) occurred. As with the avoidance and emotional numbing symptoms, the hyperarousal symptoms may occur in any combination and need not include all of the symptoms at the same time:

D1: difficulty falling or staying asleep

D2: irritability or outbursts of anger

D3: problems with mental concentration

D4: feeling watchful and on guard even when not necessary ("hypervigilance")

D5: easily startled, including an exaggerated physical and behavioral reaction

D6: physically reactive to reminders of the stressor event(s)

The fifth or "duration" criterion ("E") for PTSD in the *DSM-III-R* requires that these symptoms are experienced for a period of at least one month. Not all of the symptoms must be experienced every day during the month (or longer) period. In fact, some of the symptoms may occur as infrequently as once in the month-long period so long as the symptoms cause "disturbance" to the person for that entire duration. The diagnosis may be applicable for periods of time much longer than a month—potentially for many years.

The diagnosis also specifies if the PTSD symptoms had "delayed onset," that is, if they did not begin to occur until at least 6 months after exposure to the stressor. This onset specification is not a requirement to diagnose PTSD, but provides a description of a difference in the development of the disorder that can help the clinician or researcher to distinguish between people who began to suffer PTSD symptoms relatively soon after experiencing psychological trauma versus others who appeared to be relatively symptom free for a long period and then developed PTSD. For example, PTSD has been observed to develop in trauma-exposed individuals who are apparently symptom-free or at most mildly symptomatic and not functionally impaired when changes occur in their lives that subject them to nontraumatic stressors (such as widowhood, retirement, job or residence changes, the birth or developmental transitions of children) or to new incidents of the same or different traumatic stressors (*see:* **Retraumatization**).

The subsequent fourth edition of the *DSM* (*DSM-IV* and *DSM-IV-TR*, American Psychiatric Association, 1994, 2000) retained the basic structure of the *DSM-III-R* PTSD diagnosis, but made significant modifications in the traumatic stressor criterion and some revisions in the specification and placement of symptoms in the B, C, and D criteria. The requirement that traumatic events must be outside the range of usual human experience was deleted, and replaced by a bipartite Criterion A that included both an objective definition of the traumatic stressor (as a life-threatening event or a violation of bodily integrity, Criterion A1) and the initial subjective response (Criterion A2) was specified to involve extreme fear, helplessness or horror. The objective aspect of stressor exposure (Criterion A1 in the *DSM-IV*) was expanded to include events that were witnessed or indirectly experienced as well as events that directly occurred to the person. In addition, the *DSM-IV* added a sixth criterion ("Criterion F"), requiring that the symptoms have an adverse effect on social, occupational, or other areas of functioning. *DSM-IV* also added a specification for the diagnosis's chronicity: "acute" PTSD was defined as a duration of less than 3 months, and "chronic" PTSD as a duration of 3 or more months.

The *DSM-IV* also added acute stress disorder (ASD) as a diagnosis, similar to PTSD but with more focus on dissociative symptoms and with the requirement that it must begin and end within one month of experiencing the traumatic stressor. ASD has an identical Criterion A (traumatic stressor) to PTSD, but differs from "acute" PTSD in several important ways. First, ASD must occur within 4 weeks of exposure to the stressor event(s) and may start as soon as 2 days afterward. Thus, ASD represents a traumatic stress disorder that can be diagnosed almost immediately—although not within the first day after psychological trauma, because most people should not be diagnosed with a traumatic stress disorder when (as is typical) they experience extreme stress reactions in the first hours or day after a traumatic event but go on to recover without developing persistent symptoms or impairment (see **Acute Stress Disorder; Posttraumatic Stress Disorder**). ASD and PTSD were designed to be complementary diagnoses such that PTSD could first be diagnosed almost exactly when ASD no longer can be diagnosed—at the point in time when four weeks or one-month has passed since the traumatic event(s).

Another important difference between ASD and PTSD is that ASD includes an additional symptom criterion (ASD Criterion B) that requires that at least three of five symptoms of pathological dissociation occur either during or after experiencing the stressor event(s). Dissociation (*see:* **Dissociation**) is common during and soon after exposure to psychological trauma—this is called *peritraumatic dissociation* because "peri" signifies that the dissociation is occurring close in time to the stressor event(s). When dissociation involves more than a transient feeling of shock or confusion, but takes the form of feeling emotionally numbed or detached, "in a daze," a sense of unreality (derealization) or being an outside observer of oneself (depersonalization), or unable to recall important aspects of the event(s) (psychogenic

amnesia), Acute Stress Disorder may be occurring and the risk of developing PTSD may be increased (*see:* **Etiology**). It is noteworthy that some of the symptoms of peritraumatic dissociation in the ASD diagnosis are exactly (psychogenic amnesia) or nearly (emotional numbing, social detachment) identical to three of the PTSD Criterion C symptoms. Thus, while dissociation is not formally considered to be a primary symptom of PTSD (see next), the PTSD diagnosis includes symptoms with strong dissociative features. The PTSD intrusive reexperiencing symptom of suddenly feeling as if the traumatic event(s) are happening all over again (e.g., flashbacks, Criterion B3) also may involve dissociation.

ASD's other three symptom criteria directly parallel those for PTSD, including intrusive reexperiencing of the traumatic event(s) (ASD Criterion C), avoidance of reminders of the traumatic event(s) (ASD Criterion D), and hyperarousal/hypervigilance (ASD Criterion E). The intrusive reexperiencing criteria for PTSD (Criterion B) and ASD (Criterion C) are identical. The avoidance criterion for ASD differs from PTSD's avoidance and emotional numbing symptoms (Criterion C) in two ways: the emotional numbing symptoms have been moved to Criterion B in ASD, and any form of avoidance is sufficient to meet the ASD criterion—where in PTSD, three avoidance and numbing symptoms are required, and this requirement permits a diagnosis of PTSD to be made even if *no* avoidance is present, so long as at least three forms of numbing are present. The hyperarousal symptoms in ASD are identical to those in PTSD, but any hyperarousal symptom is sufficient for ASD where at least two types are needed for a PTSD diagnosis. The functional impairment criteria for ASD and PTSD are essentially identical, except that in ASD this Criterion ("F") notes that impairment may include difficulty in getting help after, or telling family members about, the traumatic experience(s).

The *ICD* diagnoses of PTSD and Acute Stress Reactions were established in the most recent (tenth) *ICD* edition, at approximately the same time (1992) that the *DSM-IV* was being finalized (Lasiuk & Hegadoren, 2006b). The *ICD* and *DSM* diagnoses involve very similar but not exactly identical definitions of the stressor criterion, symptom criteria, and duration and functional impairment criteria. Similar to the 1952 *DSM-I* and 1968 *DSM-II* diagnoses that were precursors to PTSD, the ninth edition of the *ICD* (World Health Organization, 1978) defined a diagnosis of "reactions to severe stress" that had similar to the *ICD*-10's PTSD and Acute Stress Reactions diagnoses.

Dissociative and Personality Disorder Diagnoses

Problems with dissociation are not exclusively caused by or associated with exposure to psychological trauma, but children and adults who suffer from pathological forms of dissociation often have histories of severe psychological trauma (*see:* **Abuse, Child Physical; Abuse, Child Sexual; Child Maltreatment, Complex Posttraumatic Stress Disorder; Dissociation**). Dissociative disorder diagnoses in the *DSM* and *ICD* include Dissociative Amnesia (which specifically is noted to "usually" involve memories of events "of a traumatic or stressful nature" in the *DSM*, 300.12; *ICD* F44.0), Fugue (leaving one's usual places of residence or work and being unable to recall one's past; *DSM* 300.13, *ICD* F44.1), Depersonalization (300.14), or DID (experiencing oneself as having two or more distinct identities or personality states that repeatedly take control of one's behavior). The *ICD* has a more nuanced and varied set of dissociative disorder diagnoses than the *DSM,* including dissociative stupor, trance, motor disorders, convulsions, and anesthesia and sensory loss (World Health Organization, 2005, F44.3–F44.6).

The *ICD*-10 also included a diagnosis reflecting enduring personality changes following exposure to psychological trauma (F62.0), which has no counterpart diagnosis in any version of the *DSM*. A study of the feasibility and clinical utility of a similar diagnosis was undertaken in the field trial research studies preceding the *DSM-IV* (van der Kolk, Roth, Pelcovitz, Sunday, & Spinazzola, 2005). The PTSD field trial study results indicated that when people diagnosed with PTSD had experienced interpersonal psychological trauma in early childhood, they often were impaired by other symptoms that did not fit the diagnosis for any other psychiatric disorder. These complex PTSD (*see:* **Complex Posttraumatic Stress Disorder**) symptoms, also known as Disorders of Extreme Stress Not Otherwise Specified or DESNOS (van der Kolk et al., 2005) include dysregulated emotion states, pathological dissociation, physical health problems that cannot be explained or fully treated medically (somatization), and altered beliefs about oneself (e.g., viewing self as fundamentally psychologically damaged), relationships (e.g., expecting to be betrayed and abandoned), and spirituality (e.g., loss of spiritual faith or hope). The latter altered beliefs are primary features of the *ICD* F62.0 "enduring change in personality" diagnosis.

The dissociation symptoms described by the complex PTSD or DESNOS syndrome have been included, along with symptoms of pervasive guilt, as secondary (or associated) features of the *DSM* PTSD diagnosis, which means that they are not considered formally part of the PTSD diagnosis but may occur in complicated cases of PTSD.

The emotion dysregulation symptoms identified in the complex PTSD syndrome are similar to primary symptoms of a personality disorder in the *DSM* (borderline personality disorder, BPD) and one type of a personality disorder in the *ICD* (emotionally unstable personality disorder, borderline type). The *ICD* emotionally unstable personality disorder diagnosis also has a less severe type, the "impulsive type," which is characterized by emotional and behavioral outbursts and impulsivity, but not by the borderline type's self-harm, fundamentally impaired relationships, and chronic feelings of emotional emptiness. Interestingly, these types are consistent with research findings from a U.S. study of patients diagnosed with BPD who were found to be more likely to have severe problems with self-harm, dissociation, dysphoria, and to generally be functionally impaired if they had experienced sexual abuse in childhood, but more likely to have severe problems with emotion dysregulation, impulsivity, and dissociation if they had experienced neglect in childhood (Zanarini et al., 2002). Thus, different types of interpersonal psychological trauma in childhood may be associated with different types of personality pathology in adulthood that can be identified with distinct diagnoses.

PTSD, when chronic over a period of years or decades, also may involve changes in personality (as described in the *ICD* but not the *DSM*), which are consistent with the *ICD* distinction between personality disorders characterized by emotional impulsivity versus chaotic borderline self-dysregulation. Studies of military veterans with PTSD have shown that two personality dimensions, "negative emotionality" and "disconstraint," lead people with chronic PTSD to be more prone to drug and alcohol use disorders (Miller, Vogt, Mozley, Kaloupek, & Keane, 2006). Negative emotionality has features consistent with emotional impulsivity (e.g., unstable, extreme, and predominantly negative or numbed affect), while disconstraint involves features that are similar to those of borderline self-dysregulation (e.g., unstable, distrustful, and alternately over-controlled detachment from or disinhibited over-involvement in primary relationships). These studies and the differences in diagnostic definitions concerning chronic posttraumatic personality problems suggest that research is needed to determine if existing personality disorder diagnoses should be modified to specify types associated with psychological trauma or traumatic stress or supplemented by diagnoses such as complex PTSD.

Future Directions in Psychiatric Diagnoses Associated with Psychological Trauma

As both the *DSM* and *ICD* move toward new editions—the fifth edition of the *DSM* and the eleventh revision of the *ICD* are under development with completion dates of 2011 or 2012—emerging research on traumatic stress disorders is providing valuable hypotheses for refinement of the PTSD and ASD diagnoses.

The *DSM* development process has established several American Psychiatric Association/ National Institutes of Health "research conferences" and work groups (www.dsm5.org) that include one on "Stress-Induced and Fear Circuitry Disorders." Traumatic stress disorders and certain anxiety disorders may be grouped within this domain in the *DSM-V*, while other anxiety disorders may not be included in this domain. For example, separate *DSM-V* research conferences were held on: (a) Generalized Anxiety Disorder and Depression, and (b) Obsessive Compulsive Behavior Spectrum. Whether these domains will be used to reorganize the groupings of diagnoses or the specific diagnoses in the *DSM-V* will be determined by the *DSM-V* governance group of the American Psychiatric Association.

More specific to traumatic stress disorder diagnoses, research suggesting that peri traumatic dissociation symptoms may be prognostic for the development of PTSD primarily when measured after the fact ("retrospectively") but inconsistently when measured at the time of stressor exposure ("prospectively," *see:* **Research Methoodology**), calls into question the need to include dissociative symptoms as a separate criterion for ASD (Breh, & Seidler, 2007; Bryant, 2007). Based on this research evidence, Bryant (2007) calls for a more detailed description of specific types of peritraumatic dissociative symptoms and assessment protocols that do not rely exclusively on self-report (because it is often difficult to accurately report one's own degree of dissociation). Reconsideration of the role of dissociation in ASD also is warranted based on findings that the severity of peritraumatic intrusive reexperiencing, avoidance, and particularly hyperarousal symptoms (including panic reactions; Sinclair, Salmon, & Bryant, 2007) may be better prospective predictors of the risk of developing PTSD and other psychiatric disorders than peritraumatic dissociation symptoms.

With regard to PTSD, research demonstrating distinct subtypes of PTSD (Miller et al., 2006; see previous) and factor analysis studies showing that PTSD symptoms may be most meaningfully organized into different domains than the Criterion B, C, and D groupings in the current PTSD diagnosis suggest a need for further theoretical and empirical reexamination of the organization and specific symptoms included in the PTSD diagnosis (McHugh & Treisman, 2007). Similar to the structure of ASD, the dysphoria and emotional numbing symptoms of PTSD (Criteria C3 through C7) may constitute a separate criterion set. Or, symptoms that overlap with those of depression (i.e., anhedonia, C4; sleep problems, D1; irritability/anger, D2; concentration problems, D3) and dissociative disorders (psychogenic amnesia, C3) might be removed in order to prevent redundancy with mood and dissociative disorders (Spitzer, First, & Wakefield, 2007). When the latter proposal was tested empirically with data from the National Comorbidity Study Replication epidemiological database (*see:* **Epidemiology**), most persons diagnosed with PTSD originally continued to receive the diagnosis; however, the prevalence of PTSD was reduced 0.4% from 6.8% to 6.4%, which may seem like a small difference but could lead to thousands of PTSD cases not receiving the diagnosis if used on a national or international basis. Compared to the original PTSD diagnosis, the revised diagnostic formula did not yield diagnoses that were demonstrably more distinct from related (comorbid) psychiatric (mood anxiety and alcohol use) disorders, nor more internally consistent (*see:* **Assessment, Psychometric, Adult**), nor more strongly associated with functional impairment (Elhai, Grubaugh, Kashdan, & Frueh, 2008). Further, the best model based on confirmatory factor analyses (*see:* **Research Methodology**) was a four-factor model that retained all of the original PTSD items and separated emotional numbing and avoidance symptoms into two distinct subgroups. Thus, a briefer symptom set might be efficient but could lead to large-scale under-diagnosis of PTSD and a lost opportunity to distinguish emotional numbing and avoidance symptoms.

Another future direction for the refinement of the PTSD diagnosis is consideration of the possibility that a less severe variation of the diagnosis may be useful in identifying people who are suffering from posttraumatic stress and need preventive or treatment services. Several approaches to defining a "subthreshold" or "subclinical" or "partial" PTSD diagnosis have been proposed, for example requiring only one symptom from the C and D criterion sets (instead of three and two, respectively) or only requiring that either the C or D criteria are fulfilled but not necessarily both. Studies testing the utility of a partial PTSD diagnosis have demonstrated that adults who do not meet criteria for the full PTSD diagnosis but do meet criteria for partial PTSD tend to have substantial functional impairments (i.e., problems with work, relationships, and physical health; Schnurr et al., 2000; Stein et al., 1997)—albeit less impairment than persons with the full PTSD diagnosis. Thus, early intervention (*see:* **Posttraumatic Stress Disorder**) or prevention (*see:* **Posttraumatic Stress Disorder**) services might be beneficial for people who would be overlooked if only the full diagnosis of PTSD is considered but who are experiencing impairment due to partial PTSD.

These and other potential refinements to the PTSD, ASD/ASR, and other potentially psychological trauma-related dissociative and personality disorders are ongoing and will be a source of a great deal of scientific and clinical scrutiny and debate as the next versions of the *DSM* and *ICD* are finalized and disseminated in the next decade.

REFERENCES

American Psychiatric Association. (1952). *Diagnostic and statistical manual of mental disorders*. Washington, DC: Author.

American Psychiatric Association. (1968). *Diagnostic and statistical manual of mental disorders* (2nd ed.). Washington, DC: Author.

American Psychiatric Association. (1980). *Diagnostic and statistical manual of mental disorders* (3rd ed.). Washington, DC: Author.

American Psychiatric Association. (1987). *Diagnostic and statistical manual of mental disorders* (3rd ed., rev.). Washington, DC: Author.

American Psychiatric Association. (1994). *Diagnostic and statistical manual of mental disorders* (4th ed.). Washington, DC: Author.

American Psychiatric Association. (2000). *Diagnostic and statistical manual of mental disorders* (4th ed., text rev.). Washington, DC: Author.

Breh, D., & Seidler, G. (2007). Is peritraumatic dissociation a risk factor for PTSD? *Journal of Trauma and Dissociation, 8*(1), 53–69.

Bryant, R. (2007). Does dissociation further our understanding of PTSD? *Journal of Anxiety Disorders, 21*, 183–191.

Elhai, J., Grubaugh, F., Kashdan, T., & Frueh, C. (2008). Empirical examination of a proposed refinement to posttraumatic stress disorder symptom criteria using the National Comorbidity Survey Replication data. *Journal of Clinical Psychiatry, 69*, 597–602.

Lasiuk, G., & Hegadoren, K. (2006). Posttraumatic stress disorder part II: Development of the construct within the North American psychiatric taxonomy. *Perspectives in Psychiatric Care, 42*, 72–81.

McHugh, P. R., & Treisman G. (2007). PTSD: A problematic diagnostic category. *Journal of Anxiety Disorders, 21*, 211–222.

Miller, M. W., Vogt, D. S., Mozley, S. L., Kaloupek, D. G., & Keane, T. M. (2006). PTSD and substance-related problems: The mediating roles of disconstraint and negative emotionality. *Journal of Abnormal Psychology, 115,* 367–379.

Schnurr, P., Ford, J.D., Friedman, M., Green, B., Dain, B., & Sengupta, A. (2000). Predictors and outcomes of PTSD in World War II veterans exposed to Mustard Gas. *Journal of Consulting and Clinical Psychology, 68*, 258–268.

Sinclair, E., Salmon, K., & Bryant, R. (2007). The role of panic attacks in acute stress disorder in children. *Journal of Traumatic Stress, 20*, 1069–1073.

Spitzer, R. L, First M. B., Wakefield, J. C. (2007). Saving PTSD from itself in DSM-V. *Journal of Anxiety Disorders, 21*, 233–241.

Stein, M., Walker, J., Hazen, A., & Forde, D. (1997). Full and partial posttraumatic stress disorder: findings from a community survey. *American Journal of Psychiatry, 154*, 1114–1119.

Turnbull, G. (1998). A review of posttraumatic stress disorder (Pt. 1). *Injury, 29*, 87–91.

World Health Organization (1978). *International classification of diseases* (9th rev.). Geneva, Switzerland: Author.

World Health Organization (2005). *International classification of diseases* (2nd ed., 10th rev.). Geneva, Switzerland: Author.

JULIAN D. FORD
University of Connecticut School of Medicine

See also: Acute Stress Disorder; Assessment, Psychometric, Adult; Complex Posttraumatic Stress Disorder; Dissociation; Dissociative Identity Disorder; Personality Disorders; Posttraumatic Stress Disorder; Posttraumatic Stress Disorder, Diagnosis of

DIALECTICAL BEHAVIOR THERAPY

Dialectical behavior therapy (DBT) was originally developed by Linehan (1993a, 1993b) to treat suicidal women with borderline personality disorder (BPD). Given that the majority of individuals with BPD have a history of trauma and many meet criteria for posttraumatic stress disorder (PTSD), the practice of DBT for BPD frequently involves the treatment of PTSD and other complex trauma-related problems. In addition, DBT has been adapted to treat other populations, including substance abusers with BPD, eating disordered individuals, elderly individuals with personality disorders, and forensic populations. To date, nine randomized controlled trials conducted across multiple settings have demonstrated DBT's efficacy in reducing the out-of-control behaviors it aims to treat (e.g., suicidal and nonsuicidal self-injurious behavior, use of crisis services, drug use, binge eating).

DBT is considered a principle-driven treatment (as opposed to protocol-driven; Wagner & Linehan, 2006). At its core, DBT is a behavioral therapy, guided by behavior theory and interventions. DBT is further guided by a biosocial theory of BPD, which proposes that an interaction between a biologically based vulnerability to emotions and an invalidating environment lead to the development of severe emotion dysregulation that is believed to be central to BPD. DBT therefore expands on traditional behavior therapy by including interventions that attend to the role of invalidation in the development of problems, and emotion dysregulation in the maintenance of problems. DBT also utilizes the theory of dialectics, which asserts that reality is comprised of opposing forces, and always changing. The primary dialectic in DBT is between change and acceptance of things as they are now. DBT clients are taught skills for both changing and accepting themselves and their actual lives and relationships.

Based on these theories, DBT is organized hierarchically into stages and targets of treatment that correspond to Linehan's conceptualization of stages of disorder. Stage I is designed to treat severe behavioral dyscontrol; the overarching goal is stabilization, with a focus on achieving safety, behavioral control, and connection to the therapist. The DBT treatment manual and most treatment outcome studies to date have focused on Stage I DBT. Stage II DBT is designed to treat problems with emotional experiencing (including PTSD and other trauma-related behaviors) that remain after behavioral control has been achieved. The overarching goal of Stage II is to increase the capacity to experience emotions without either escalating or suppressing. Linehan (1993a) proposes two additional stages of treatment targeting remaining problems in living (Stage III) and a sense of incompleteness (Stage IV).

Stage I DBT consists of several modes of treatment, each designed to achieve specific functions: individual psychotherapy focuses on increasing client motivation (i.e., identifying specific factors maintaining problem behavior and providing interventions); group skills training teaches basic capabilities (i.e., behavioral skills including distress tolerance, emotion regulation, interpersonal effectiveness, and mindfulness); phone coaching provides the basis for generalization of skills to the natural environment; and the therapist consultation team functions to increase therapist capabilities and motivation. Within individual treatment, problems are prioritized hierarchically, such that behaviors considered life-threatening (e.g., suicidal behaviors) are treated first, followed by those that directly threaten the therapy ("therapy interfering behaviors"), followed by those that significantly interfere with a reasonable quality of life ("quality of life interfering behaviors").

Within this general framework, there are two potential applications of DBT to the treatment of individuals with histories of psychological trauma. First, DBT has been used as a priming intervention prior to initiating formal, typically exposure-based, PTSD treatments (e.g., Harned & Linehan, in press). Trauma experts have long espoused a stage-oriented approach to traumatic stress treatment in which basic safety and stabilization must be achieved before engaging in emotional processing of traumatic memories. As a result, PTSD-diagnosed clients who exhibit unsafe or out-of-control behaviors (e.g., suicidal behaviors, substance dependence, serious comorbid disorders) are often viewed as unsuitable candidates for formal PTSD treatments. Given that the overarching goal of Stage I DBT is to help clients achieve behavioral control, DBT may be an effective treatment for preparing these more complex clients for a formal PTSD treatment. Indeed, DBT has been shown to be effective in reducing many potential contraindications for formal PTSD treatment, including suicidal and nonsuicidal self-injurious behaviors, substance use, and severe depression. Furthermore, the DBT treatment manual (Linehan, 1993a) clearly specifies the treatment strategies to be used to help clients develop a variety of skills (e.g., emotion regulation, distress tolerance) to stop out-of-control behaviors. Thus, DBT is a well-defined and effective treatment that can be used to decrease many of the behaviors believed to interfere with, and improve patient tolerance for, formal PTSD treatments.

A second application of DBT to individuals with trauma histories (particularly those with BPD) involves using the DBT staged approach to treat specific trauma-related problems. Stage II DBT is intended for clients who have attained the behavioral control that is the focus of Stage I, yet remain in a state of "quiet desperation" (i.e., extreme emotional pain in the presence of control of action). The aim of Stage II is to address this extreme and global emotional pain that is often related to histories of severe and chronic trauma. Although this emotional suffering may take the form of PTSD, Stage II is also intended to treat trauma-related problems that extend beyond PTSD to encompass a wide range of disruptions in emotional experiencing. Wagner and Linehan (2006) have proposed the following treatment targets for this stage of treatment: (a) intrusive symptoms (e.g., traumatic memories, nightmares, and flashbacks); (b) avoidance of emotions; (c) avoidance of situations and experiences (including but not limited to trauma-related cues); (d) emotion dysregulation (heightened and/or inhibited emotional experiencing); and (e) self-invalidation (the tendency to judge one's own emotions, thoughts, and actions as wrong or bad).

Stage II DBT incorporates aspects of empirically supported treatments for PTSD, including the use of exposure (both formal and informal) as the primary intervention strategy. Formal exposure refers to a structured protocol for treating a specific disorder (e.g., prolonged exposure for PTSD), whereas informal exposure involves maintaining contact with a relevant emotion-inducing cue as opportunities arise within sessions, and eliciting new, more effective behaviors in the presence of the cue. Exposure-based interventions are used in Stage II to target PTSD symptoms as well as more general avoidance of emotions and situations. Stage II treatment strategies also focus on reducing other complex trauma-related problems, such as dissociation, shame and its associated withdrawal behaviors, and self-invalidation. Often these behaviors pose obstacles to using exposure to treat PTSD (inasmuch as they function as avoidance behaviors that interfere with successful emotional processing of the trauma) and must be addressed in a systematic way in order for progress to be made.

Given the individualized, principle-focused nature of DBT, there is no single Stage II approach to these problems. For example, dissociation in session can be addressed through the use of mindfulness and grounding exercises designed to bring the individual "back" to the present moment. In addition, interventions for reducing the occurrence of dissociation often focus on decreasing reactivity to the prompting event (e.g., an intense emotion or self-invalidating thought). Shame is an emotion that often arises when clients are asked to describe specific traumatic events for which

they feel they are to blame. Shame occurs frequently in instances of childhood abuse (e.g., "I must have done something to cause them to hurt me") as well as adult interpersonal trauma (e.g., "I could have prevented it from occurring if I had done something different"). Using informal exposure and cognitive restructuring to reduce shame in session can allow for discussion of trauma history that is not hampered by withdrawal and avoidance (Rizvi & Linehan, 2005). Finally, self-invalidation is often targeted by having the therapist use validation strategies as a means of demonstrating acceptance of clients as they are, and also to model expressions that encourage generation of self-validating statements. The therapist also typically highlights the presence of self-invalidation when it occurs and works with the client to restructure these comments into more effective and nonjudgmental statements.

In sum, DBT has several potential applications to the treatment of individuals with a history of trauma and its principle-driven approach allows for the individualized use of a variety of behavioral strategies to reduce PTSD and other complex trauma-related problems.

REFERENCES

Harned, M. S., & Linehan, M. M. (in press). Integrating dialectical behavior therapy and prolonged exposure to treat co-occurring borderline personality disorder and PTSD: Two case studies. *Cognitive and Behavioral Practice.*

Linehan, M. M. (1993a). *Cognitive-behavioral treatment of borderline personality disorder.* New York: Guilford Press.

Linehan, M. M. (1993b). *Skills training manual for treating borderline personality disorder.* New York: Guilford Press.

Rizvi, S. L., & Linehan, M. M. (2005). Treatment of maladaptive shame in borderline personality disorder: A pilot study of "opposite action."*Cognitive and Behavioral Practice, 12,* 437–447.

Wagner, A. W., & Linehan, M. M. (2006). Applications of dialectical behavior therapy to PTSD and related problems. In V. M. Follette & J. I. Ruzek (Eds.), *Cognitive-behavioral therapies for trauma* (2nd ed., pp. 117–145). New York: Guilford Press.

RECOMMENDED READINGS

Linehan, M. M. (1993). *Cognitive-behavioral treatment of borderline personality disorder.* New York: Guilford Press.

Wagner, A. W., Rizvi, S. L., & Harned, M. S. (2007). Applications of dialectical behavior therapy to the treatment of complex trauma-related problems: When one case formulation does not fit all. *Journal of Traumatic Stress, 20,* 391–400.

Melanie S. Harned
University of Washington

Shireen L. Rizvi
New School for Social Research

Amy W. Wagner
Portland Veterans Affairs Medical Center

See also: Cognitive Behavior Therapy, Adult; Exposure Therapy, Adult; Personality Disorders; Self-Injurious Behavior

DISABILITY

See: Occupational Disability

DISASTERS

Disasters are potentially traumatic events that are collectively experienced, have acute onset, and are time delimited (McFarlane & Norris, 2006). Disasters usually occur with little or no warning and vary greatly in magnitude. One common indicator of this is their impact ratio, the proportion of the population that is affected directly by the disaster. The prevalence of psychopathology has been minimal after some disasters but substantial after others, with outcomes depending on the extent and severity of loss of life, threat to life, injury, property damage, financial loss, displacement, and social and community disruption (Norris, Friedman, Watson, Byrne, et al., 2002).

Disasters belong to a larger set of potentially traumatic events, a designation that means (a) the person experienced, witnessed, or was confronted with an event or events that involved actual or threatened death or serious injury, or a threat to the physical integrity of self or others, and (b) the person's response involved intense fear, helplessness, or horror (American Psychiatric Association, 1994, pp. 427–428). Not every disaster will cause death or injury to self or others, but all disasters have the potential to do so, and disasters almost always engender fear, helplessness, or horror. Given the high prevalence of trauma exposure among disaster survivors, it is not surprising that the condition most often assessed and observed in disaster mental health research is posttraumatic stress disorder (PTSD; see Galea, Nandi, & Vlahov, 2005, for a review). A common finding is for intrusion (Criterion B for PTSD) and arousal (Criterion D) to be highly prevalent, while avoidance (Criterion C) is less so. Dissociative responses and acute stress disorder also have been observed in the immediate aftermath of disasters.

Types of Disasters

It is common to distinguish between natural disasters, which result from weather or geophysical forces, and human-caused disasters, which result from human negligence and error (technological disasters) or actual intent to harm (mass violence). Natural disasters, such as hurricanes, floods, and earthquakes, have been studied most frequently. The Ash Wednesday bushfires in Australia (1983), Hurricane Andrew in Florida (1992), the Hansin-Awaji earthquake in Japan (1995), the Marmara earthquake in Turkey (1999), and Hurricane Katrina on the U.S. Gulf Coast (2005) are examples of natural disasters that have been studied extensively. Natural disasters are especially likely to engender severe psychological distress when they occur in the developing world. In fact, disaster location (United States, other developed country, developing country) was a stronger predictor of sample-level effects than either disaster type (mass violence, natural, technological) or sample type (child, adult, rescue/recovery) in the empirical review of Norris and colleagues (Norris, Friedman, & Watson, 2002; Norris, Friedman, Watson, Byrne, et al., 2002). Loss of life often numbers in the thousands or tens of thousands when major hurricanes or earthquakes strike poor countries. The Southeast Asian tsunami of December 26, 2004, caused an unfathomable 276,000 deaths, according to a U.S. Geological Survey (retrieved October 21, 2006, from http://www.msnbc.msn.com/id/6948775).

Technological disasters, such as major nuclear, industrial, or transportation accidents, create additional psychological stress by symbolizing the callousness or carelessness of powerful others. The dam collapse in Buffalo Creek, West Virginia (1972), the Three Mile Island nuclear accident (1979), the sinking of the Jupiter Cruise Ship (1988), the *Exxon Valdez* oil spill (1989), and the Lviv air show disaster (2002) are illustrative, well-studied events. Disasters are not always clearly natural or technological in origin. Hurricane Katrina, for example, caused levees in New Orleans to breach, flooding much of the city and resulting in many deaths, harrowing rescues, and prolonged displacement of residents. Technological disasters often have the capacity to divide communities, particularly where one party is seen to represent a sector of privilege and wealth that is exercised with little concern for the welfare of the broader community. The historic 1889 disaster in Johnstown, Pennsylvania, was a dramatic example of this division. This event was historic not only because of the catastrophic losses, but because it was the first major U.S. disaster relief effort handled by the newly formed American Red Cross. Technological disasters are frequently followed by lasting disputes and litigation concerning the allocation of blame. However, the notion that, in general, technological accidents have greater mental health impact than do natural disasters has not withstood empirical test (Rubonis & Bickman, 1991). The natural versus technological distinction is somewhat illusory because the effects of most natural disasters are exacerbated by human elements (e.g., housing quality, building codes, deforestation, resource distribution).

In recent years, disasters of mass violence, such as terrorist attacks and shooting sprees, have received increased attention in the disaster literature. The mass murder of restaurant customers in Kileen, Texas (1991), the bombing of the Murrah Federal Building in Oklahoma City, Oklahoma (1995), and the September 11, 2001, terrorist attacks on the World Trade Center and the Pentagon are prominent examples. When destruction, harm, and death are intentional, they are particularly difficult for survivors to make sense of. The impact of terrorist attacks, in particular, extends past their direct victims (i.e., persons immediately threatened, injured, or bereaved by the incidents) to the community at large. On average, disasters of mass violence have greater impact on mental health than do either natural disasters or technological accidents (Norris, Friedman, Watson, Byrne, et al., 2002), but the differences are not large when there is comparable loss of life.

Most disasters can also be described as centripetal or centrifugal. Centripetal disasters strike an extant community of people, whereas centrifugal disasters strike a group of people congregated temporarily. The former category might describe the prototypical disaster, where members of a geographically circumscribed community are struck by a disaster, such as a hurricane or earthquake. These disasters pose a risk to all those who live and work in these communities and may affect social and community functioning as well as psychological functioning. Centrifugal disasters differ from centripetal disasters in two important ways: (1) they are highly concentrated and localized; and (2) they strike a group who happen to be congregated, often by chance. In these events, very few of the injured or dead may come from the locality of the disaster. Occasionally, these disasters have an international impact, with the survivors or the bereaved coming from many regions. Centrifugal disasters pose particular challenges for research with direct victims, so they have been studied less often than have centripetal disasters. The sinking of the Jupiter Cruise Ship (1988) and the Beverly Hills Supper Club fire (1977) are two examples of centrifugal disasters where survivors were studied.

Timing and Duration of Stress

If the defining characteristics of disasters, relative to other forms of mass trauma, are their acute onset and time-limited threat, it follows that the temporal unfolding of a disaster is extremely important. Most disasters are characterized by an acute threat that is contained, followed by a gradual restoration of order and safety. However, in some disasters, such as the Times Beach contamination disaster (1985) and the Chernobyl nuclear disaster in the Ukraine (1986), the threat persists. Public distrust and fear of misinformation are prevalent in these circumstances. Natural disasters sometimes cause massive relocation of survivors and ongoing hardship and adversities.

Longitudinal research on the psychological consequences of disasters is limited, but the existing research suggests that most individuals and communities do recover over time. Symptoms typically peak in the first few months and decline in severity thereafter. However, the course of recovery is not uniform and may involve some periods of stability in between periods of improvement. There are also important exceptions, showing that extreme disasters have the potential to cause long-lasting psychological problems.

In October 2001, an international panel of experts on trauma and mental health convened to determine best practices in disaster mental health (National Institute of Mental Health, 2002). As part of this effort, the group reached consensus on the differentiation of phases as *preincident, impact* (0 to 48 hours), *rescue* (0 to 1 week), *recovery* (1 to 4 weeks), and *return-to-life* (2 weeks to 2 years), and they identified the primary goals, behaviors, roles of helpers, and roles of mental health professionals that corresponded to each phase. Myers and Wee (2005) also provided an excellent introduction to phased disaster mental health services.

Vulnerability and Resilience

A large body of research has accumulated showing that psychosocial resources, such as hardiness, perceived control, coping self-efficacy, and social support afford critical protection for disaster victims. An important trend in disaster research has been the recognition that these resources are themselves vulnerable to the impact of disasters. Hypotheses derived from Hobfoll's (1988) theory of Conservation of Resources have been supported in several studies showing that post-disaster losses of psychological and social resources are potent predictor of post-disaster distress. Accordingly, the ability of communities to protect, restore, and mobilize resources underlies their resilience to disasters. Community resilience has been emerging as an important theme for public health, mental health, and emergency management policies designed to enhance disaster readiness and the effectiveness of response and recovery efforts (Norris, Stevens, Pfefferbaum, Wyche, & Pfefferbaum, 2008).

REFERENCES

American Psychiatric Association. (1994). *Diagnostic and statistical manual of mental disorders* (4th ed.). Washington, DC: Author.

Galea, S., Nandi, A., & Vlahov, D. (2005). The epidemiology of posttraumatic stress disorder after disasters. *Epidemiologic Reviews, 27,* 78–91.

Hobfoll, S. (1988). *The ecology of stress.* New York: Hemisphere.

McFarlane, A. C., & Norris, F. (2006). Definitions and concepts in disaster research. In F. Norris, S. Galea, M. Friedman, & P. Watson (Eds.), *Methods for disaster mental health research* (pp. 3–19). New York: Guilford Press.

Myers, D., & Wee, D. (2005). *Disaster mental health services: A primer for practitioners.* New York: Brunner-Routledge.

National Institute of Mental Health. (2002). *Mental health and mass violence: Evidence based early psychological intervention for victims/survivors of mass violence—A workshop to reach consensus on best practices* (NIH Publication Office No. 02-5138). Washington, DC: U.S. Government Printing Office. [Note: This report is also available online at www.nimh.nih.gov/research/massviolence.pdf.]

Norris, F., Friedman, M., & Watson, P. (2002). 60,000 disaster victims speak: Pt. II. Summary and implications of the disaster mental health research. *Psychiatry, 65* 240–260.

Norris, F., Friedman, M., Watson, P., Byrne, C., Diaz, E., & Kaniasty, K. (2002). 60,000 disaster victims speak: Pt. I. An empirical review of the empirical literature, 1981–2001. *Psychiatry, 65,* 207–239.

Norris, F., Stevens, S., Pfefferbaum, B., Wyche, K., & Pfefferbaum, R. (2008). Community resilience as a metaphor, theory, set of capacities, and strategy for disaster readiness. *American Journal of Community Psychology, 41,* 127–150.

Rubonis, A., & Bickman, L. (1991). Psychological impairment in the wake of disaster: The disaster-psychopathology relationship. *Psychological Bulletin, 109,* 384–399.

FRAN H. NORRIS
Dartmouth Medical School

See also: Conservation of Resources Theory; Psychological First Aid, Adult; Psychological First Aid, Child and Adolescent; Social Support; Terrorism

DISCLOSURE

For people who have experienced traumatic events, disclosing that fact or the details of the experience to others can be difficult and problematic. Disclosure may be desirable for reasons such as gaining social support, improving other people's understanding of one's condition, or raising public awareness. But there are also risks involved in disclosing information that makes one feel exposed and vulnerable to scrutiny by others and the judgments they might make. This is an important issue for clinicians and researchers, whose efforts to understand and treat victims depend on an adequate degree of disclosure from people for whom the costs and benefits of disclosing are not easy to estimate.

Experimental studies by Pennebaker, Kiecolt-Glaser, and Glaser (1988) have shown that disclosure of traumatic events through writing is related to better health outcomes. Research outside the lab setting, such as studies where participants fill out confidential surveys, suggests that talking to others in the aftermath of traumatic experiences such as sexual assault may be helpful to survivors, depending on various factors. For instance, trauma victims who tell others about their experiences may receive negative reactions from those they tell, such as being blamed or treated differently. When victims do receive negative reactions from others, they may experience more psychological trauma including increased PTSD symptoms. The context, nature, and detail of a trauma disclosure may also affect the outcome for the discloser. For example, research suggests that some support sources (e.g., such as friends) may be more helpful and supportive to victims of rape than others (e.g., police or doctors; Golding, Siegel, Sorenson, Burnam, & Stein, 1989). Volition and control over the disclosure would also seem to be critical factors. Thus, if the person wishes to disclose the trauma, initiates the disclosure, and controls the extent and depth of the disclosure, then according to research on sexual assault victims' disclosures (Ullman, 1999, 2003) the effect may be more positive.

REFERENCES

Golding, J. M., Siegel, J. M., Sorenson, S. B., Burnam, M. A., & Stein, J. A. (1989). Social support sources following sexual assault. *Journal of Community Psychology, 17,* 92–107.

Pennebaker, J. W., Kiecolt-Glaser, J., & Glaser, R. (1988). Disclosure of traumas and immune function: Health implications for psychotherapy. *Journal of Consulting and Clinical Psychology, 56,* 239–245.

Ullman, S. E. (1999). Social support and recovery from sexual assault: A review. *Aggression and Violent Behavior: A Review Journal, 4,* 343–358.

Ullman, S. E. (2003). Social reactions to child sexual abuse disclosures: A critical review. *Journal of Child Sexual Abuse, 12,* 89–121.

RECOMMENDED READINGS

Becker-Blease, K., & Freyd, J. J. (2006). Research participants tell the truth about their lives. *American Psychologist, 61,* 218–226.

Ullman, S. E. (2007). Asking participants about abuse and trauma. *American Psychologist, 62,* 329–330.

SARAH E. ULLMAN
University of Illinois

See also: Therapeutic Writing

DISORGANIZED/DISORIENTED ATTACHMENT

See: Attachment

DISRUPTIVE BEHAVIOR DISORDERS

Disruptive behavior disorders (DBD) such as attention deficit hyperactivity disorder (ADHD), oppositional-defiant disorder (ODD), and conduct disorder (CD) may be associated with trauma exposure and trauma's emotional reactions among children and adolescents in a variety of ways. These associations are just beginning to be explored (Abram et al., 2004; Fletcher, 2003; Ford et al., 2000), but they could have important implications for assessment and treatment of both posttraumatic stress disorder (PTSD) and DBD.

Many of the symptomatic behaviors of children with DBDs may place them at increased risk of exposure to psychological trauma. Impulsiveness and self-regulatory problems experienced by children with DBDs may encourage more risk-taking among these children, at the same time placing them at more risk for accidents, violence, and other extremely stressful events. The hyperactivity of children with ADHD, and the angry, defiant behavior of children with ODD or CD, may increase their risk not only of initiating or engaging in acts of violence but also of being the recipients of interpersonal violence from peers or physical abuse by their elders.

Since PTSD and the DBDs share some symptomatology, caution is required in making an accurate differential diagnosis of these disorders. PTSD's externalizing symptoms of increased arousal—such as irritability or outbursts of anger, hyperactivity, and difficulty concentrating—may be more salient than its internalizing symptoms. Therefore, if a child's psychological trauma history is unknown, a diagnosis of a DBD may be made when the symptoms may be due to PTSD, or to a combination of a DBD and PTSD. On the other hand, these same externalizing symptoms observed in children with preexisting DBDs who have had a potentially traumatic experience may be mistaken for symptoms of PTSD.

DBD and PTSD also share risk factors, such as lower socioeconomic status, parental conflict, and parental psychopathology (Ford et al., 2000). A genetic predisposition to psychophysiologic reactivity appears to play a role in the etiology of PTSD that may be similar to the role temperament plays in the etiology of ADHD. Thus, PTSD may at times codevelop and/or co-occur with ADHD, ODD, or even CD. Histories of child abuse have been found at higher rates among children with ADHD (Wozniak et al., 1999), ODD (Ford et al., 2000), and CD (Abram et al., 2004) than in the general population. Elevated levels of posttraumatic symptomatology and diagnosis have also been found among children with DBDs (Abram et al., 2004; Ford et al., 2000).

Children with DBDs may be unusually sensitive to PTSD symptoms. Children with ADHD, ODD, or a combination of the two have been found to report higher levels of PTSD's intrusive reexperiencing and hyperarousal than children with Adjustment Disorder (Ford et al., 2000). Given such heightened sensitivity to PTSD symptomatology, children diagnosed with a DBD prior to a traumatic experience may risk having their posttraumatic stress responses misattributed to their DBD, leaving any possible PTSD symptomatology unrecognized.

Although tentative and far from conclusive, what little research in this area thus far suggests is that children in treatment for DBDs would benefit from a screening for psychological trauma histories. Those screening positive for traumatic exposure might find some symptom relief from treatment for PTSD.

REFERENCES

Abram, K. M., Teplin, L. A., Charles, D. R., Longworth, S. L., McClelland, G. M., & Dulcan, M. K. (2004). Posttraumatic stress disorder and trauma in juvenile detention. *Archives of General Psychiatry, 61,* 403–410.

Fletcher, K. E. (2003). Childhood posttraumatic stress disorder. In E. J. Mash & R. A. Barkley (Eds.), *Child psychopathology* (2nd ed., pp. 330–371). New York: Guilford Press.

Ford, J. D., Racusin, R., Ellis, C. G., Daviss, W. B., Reiser, J., Fleischer, A., et al. (2000). Child maltreatment, other trauma exposure, and posttraumatic symptomatology among children with oppositional defiant and attention deficit hyperactivity disorders. *Child Maltreatment, 5,* 205–217.

Wozniak, J., Crawford, M., Biederman, J., Faraone, S., Spencer, T., Taylor, A., et al. (1999). Antecedents and complications of trauma in boys with ADHD. *Journal of the American Academy of Child and Adolescent Psychiatry, 38,* 48–55.

KENNETH E. FLETCHER
University of Massachusetts Medical School

See also: Aggression; Anger; Antisocial Behavior

DISSOCIATION

The concept of dissociation as used with regard to mental phenomena and disorders is ill-defined in contemporary literature. For example, *DSM-IV* defines dissociation as "a disruption in the usually integrated functions of consciousness, memory, identity, or perception of the environment" (American Psychiatric Association, 1994, p. 477). Not only are the functions of movements and sensations lacking, this definition remains very imprecise with regard to which psychological phenomena should be regarded as dissociative in nature and which not. Pertaining to a wide variety of psychological phenomena and reflecting different theoretical views, dissociation can denote a process, an intrapsychic structure, a psychological defense, a deficit, and a wide variety of symptoms (e.g., Cardeña, 1994; Nijenhuis, 2004; Van der Hart, Nijenhuis, & Steele, 2006). For example, common alterations of consciousness, such as intense absorption and imaginative involvement, were originally distinguished from dissociative symptoms. However, the domain of dissociative symptoms includes almost any altered state of consciousness in most contemporary publications. The Dissociative Experiences Scale (DES; Bernstein & Putnam, 1986), the most widely used instrument to measure "dissociative" phenomena, is a prime example of this enlargement of the domain of dissociative symptoms. The concept of peritraumatic dissociation—pertaining to symptoms during or directly following traumatic experiences—also includes alterations in consciousness that differ from the original dissociative symptoms. This is exemplified in the Peritraumatic Experiences Questionnaire (PDEQ; Marmar et al., 1994).

Lack of conceptual clarity regarding dissociation, and consequently dissociative symptoms, seriously hinders research and clinical practice. For example, the results of studies into "dissociative" symptoms and their correlates depend on the kind of phenomena that are regarded as dissociative. Thus, various studies have found, but not unequivocally, a relationship between peritraumatic dissociation and subsequent posttraumatic stress disorder (PTSD; Van der Hart, Van Ochten, Van Son, Steele, & Lensvelt-Mulders, in press). Given the lack of clarity regarding the construct of peritraumatic dissociation, it is difficult to know if the correlation exists for the original dissociative symptoms, for the alterations of consciousness that differ from the original dissociative symptoms, or both kinds of symptoms. A highly similar problem exists for correlational studies of trait dissociative symptoms that the DES purports to measure, for example studies exploring the correlation between DES scores, other psychopathological symptoms, and reported exposure to potentially traumatizing events. Therefore this entry provide a brief history of how dissociation has been defined and current approaches to defining dissociation, followed by a description of dissociation's symptoms and the biological correlates of dissociation.

History and Current Definition

Originally, in French nineteenth-century psychiatry, dissociation referred to an undue division or compartmentalization of consciousness or personality—with the latter term indicating that dissociation pertains to more psychobiological phenomena than just consciousness. Some other terms in vogue were: doubling of the personality, double consciousness, psychological disaggregation, and division of the personality (cf., Van der Hart & Dorahy, 2008). Both the earlier and more recent literature used different terms to denote the mutually dissociated subsystems of the personality: identities or personality states (*DSM-IV-TR*), ego states, dissociative or dissociated states, dissociated self-states, dissociative identity states, (alter) personalities or alters, dissociative or dissociated selves, streams of consciousness, Janet's model of systems of thoughts and functions. The generic term favored in this entry is *dissociative parts of the personality* (Van der Hart et al., 2006), given mounting evidence that dissociation entails a biopsychosocial phenomenon stretching much further than a division of consciousness. Dissociation also is defined based on the view that each person has but one personality, however divided into dissociative parts it may be.

Many authors maintain that, whatever terms are used, dissociative parts of the personality include their own idea of self, no matter how rudimentary or developed these parts and their ideas of self may be. Thus, patients with a dissociative disorder have only one personality, but encompass more than one idea of self. Dissociative parts of the personality also include their own ideas of the world and their relation to this world. Like the different ideas of self that are held by dissociative parts of the personality, their ideas of the world and their relation to the world may range from rudimentary forms, involving just one or a very limited number of mental and behavioral states, to complex forms, encompassing many different mental and behavioral states. For example, patients with PTSD have different ideas of self, world, and relation to the world when numbed and avoidant than they do when they are reliving traumatic memories (cf. Wang, Wilson, & Mason, 1996). These differences become ever larger with increasing complexity

of trauma-related disorders (Van der Hart et al., 2006).

Related to this basic understanding of (trauma-related) dissociation is the view that the essence of being traumatized is a lack of psychobiological integration in the face of perceived threat. In its most basic form, this lack involves a division of the personality into two types of dissociative parts. As one dissociative part, the person is focused on daily living and avoiding any reminders or recollections of traumatic memories. When this "apparently normal part" of the personality is dominant, the person tries to act, think, and feel as if life can go on as normal despite having experienced traumatizing events (*see:* **Myers, Charles Samuel**). The other type of posttraumatic dissociative part of the personality is more rudimentary and is fixated on traumatic memories and feelings or cues that are reminders of the traumatic experience(s). This has been called the emotional part. When this part is dominant, the person is fixated in reactivated traumatic memories. As the emotional part, he or she is unable to focus on daily living and instead tends to relive the traumatic experience. These are hallucinatory, solitary, and involuntary experiences that consist of visual images, vehement emotions, sensations, thoughts such as "I am going to die," and physical actions such as measures to protect the body from harm. Although there is nothing abnormal about either of these two perspectives—everyone has times when they are able to act and feel "normal" and other times when are more "emotional"—dissociation differs from those normal fluctuations in mood and state of mind. What sets dissociation apart is that the two types of parts of the personality are insufficiently integrated. That is, because the apparently normal part of the person can engage in particular mental and behavioral actions, that he or she cannot engage in as the emotional part, and vice versa. Thus, posttraumatic dissociation involves a division in the personality. This division into two or more apparently normal and emotional parts of the individual's personality tends to be maladaptive. However, it may to some degree help chronically abused and neglected individuals who are unable to integrate their traumatic experiences to negotiate daily life and to keep their painful emotions at an experiential distance from the apparently normal part(s).

This disassociation of parts of the personality does not imply that the domains of the apparently normal part and the emotional part are totally distinct or split. These different types of parts share an ability to engage in certain mental and behavioral actions in most cases, but they also encompass their separate repertoires of mental and behavioral actions and implied mental contents. For example, the person may be able to walk, talk, remember certain emotionally neutral experiences, and have particular feelings or interests, but each part also includes unshared features.

This two-part division might characterize PTSD. In other words, patients with PTSD do not just suffer from intrusions of traumatic memories. Rather, these memories are associated with a different idea of self, the world, and their relation to this world than what characterizes the individual while being avoidant of these memories and of the dissociative part of the personality that contains them. Clinical observations and empirical data indicate that when psychological trauma and its emotional effect starts early in life and is more chronic, dissociation of the personality becomes more complex, with further division of the emotional parts of the personality that are fixated in the traumatic experiences, and subsequently of the apparently normal parts of the personality that are involved in daily living (which would characterize the most complex dissociative disorder (i.e., dissociative identity disorder or DID; Van der Hart et al., 2006).

The view that dissociation of the personality primarily emerges from an integrative deficiency—that is, from a division of the personality—contrasts with the idea that dissociation involves a psychological defense. Dissociative symptoms such as reexperiencing traumatic memories, receiving commands from other dissociative parts of the personality to mutilate or kill the body, and other aversive intrusive thoughts, feelings, or memories that stem from other dissociative parts of the personality do not constitute a psychological defense at all. In this sense, posttraumatic dissociation is a lack of integration of the personality that is caused by a limitation of the person's integrative capacity (see: **Cognitive Integration, Biopsychosocial**). However, the apparently normal dissociative parts of the personality may function somewhat better in the wake of a traumatic experience when they manage to keep the emotional parts of the personality at a mental distance (e.g., denying or suppressing awareness of distressing emotions). Thus, psychological defenses may be used to cope with traumatic experiences and to maintain dissociative divisions between different parts of the personality, but dissociation per se is not a psychological defense.

A recent extension of the concept of dissociation involves dissociative detachment, defined as an altered state of consciousness characterized by a sense of separation (or detachment) from aspects of everyday experience (Brown, 2006). However, this is not consistent with the original meaning of dissociation because experiences of detachment should be regarded as dissociative only when they are rooted in a dissociation (division) of the personality. For example, many trauma survivors feel detached from their social environment, emotions, and body when engaged in daily living. Emotional detachment is distinct from dissociation because dissociation involves not just a feeling of emotional numbing or detachment but a division in the personality into dissociated parts. Some dissociative parts may seem relatively unemotional (the apparently normal part[s]), but others are overwhelmed or paralyzed by emotion and not actually detached from emotion at all (the emotional part[s]). As a result, posttraumatic dissociation often involves experiencing strong emotions and body feelings, but these feelings tend to be excluded from the person's awareness when she or he is functioning as an apparently normal part of the personality.

Symptoms of Dissociation of the Personality

There are negative and positive dissociative symptoms—although the positive ones are often overlooked in the literature. *Negative dissociative symptoms* constitute losses of functions or other psychobiological phenomena in one part of the personality that are available in another part. For example, in dissociative amnesia, one dissociative part but not another dissociative part remembers some skill, fact, or personal experience. In ordinary forgetfulness, the integrated individual or none of an individual's dissociative parts remembers the lost mental or behavioral content. *Positive dissociative symptoms* constitute intrusion phenomena (i.e., phenomena stemming from one dissociative part of the personality that intrude on another part). Intrusion can pertain to knowledge, emotions, sensations, perceptions, as well as behaviors, and include traumatic memories.

Second, dissociative symptoms—always psychological in nature—manifest as bodily phenomena (i.e., *somatoform dissociative symptoms*) or as mental phenomena (i.e., *psychoform dissociative symptoms*; Nijenhuis, 2004; Van der Hart, Van Dijke, Van Son, & Steele, 2000). Negative psychoform dissociative symptoms include loss of memory (amnesia); loss of affect (emotional numbing); loss of critical function (a cognitive action) resulting in suggestibility and difficulty thinking things through; loss of needs, wishes, and fantasies; and loss of previously existing skills. Negative somatoform dissociative symptoms involve apparent losses of sensory, perceptual, or motor functions, e.g., dissociative anesthesia and sensory loss, and dissociative paralysis.

In the past decade, an instrument measuring somatoform dissociative symptoms (i.e., the Somatoform Dissociation Questionnaire or SDQ-20; Nijenhuis, Spinhoven, Van Dyck, Van der Hart, & Vanderlinden, 1996; Nijenhuis, 2004) has been developed. The severity of somatoform dissociative symptoms distinguishes between patients with and without a dissociative disorder over and above the influence of general psychopathology, and also between more and less complex dissociative disorders (Nijenhuis et al.,

1999). Consistent with theoretical ideas that there is a relationship between major somatoform dissociative symptoms and mammalian defensive reactions (Nijenhuis, 2004; Van der Hart et al., 2006), somatoform dissociation is associated with exposure to potentially traumatizing events in a variety of normal and clinical populations, notably a threat to the integrity of the body, threat to life by another person, and intense pain (e.g., Nähring & Nijenhuis, 2005; Nijenhuis, Spinhoven, Van Dyck, Van der Hart, & Vanderlinden, 1998). Thus, there is a remarkable convergence between major reactions that belong to mammalian defense as an *action system* (*see:* **Cognitive Integration, Biopsychosocial**) and key negative somatoform dissociative symptoms: analgesia (insensitivity or reduced sensitivity for painful stimulation), sensory anesthesia (e.g., insensitivity or reduced sensitivity for touch), and motor inhibitions (being unable or having difficulty to produce vocal sounds or move one or more body parts).

Positive psychoform dissociative symptoms include traumatic memories and nightmares that have affective, cognitive, and somatosensory components. Although, with regard to PTSD, the *DSM-IV* refers to "dissociative flashback episodes," the traumatic stress field is largely unaware of the dissociative nature of this posttraumatic stress symptom. Some symptoms of schizophrenia (which are called "Schneiderian first rank" symptoms)—such as hallucinations, especially hearing voices commenting or arguing internally, and thought insertion and withdrawal—are common in patients with dissociative disorders and are commonly considered to be phenomena related to activities of dissociative parts (Dell, 2006). Positive somatoform dissociative symptoms include intrusions of sensorimotor aspects of traumatic reexperiences, such as pain, uncontrolled behaviors (e.g., tics, sensory distortions, and pseudoseizures). Some symptoms of schizophrenia also are somatoform dissociation symptoms, such as somatic passivity, and "made" bodily feelings, impulses, and motor actions (e.g., feeling the physical urge to drive the car into a bridge; cutting and not being able to stop). Most people who experience these types of positive psychoform and somatoform dissociation symptoms are *not* schizophrenic, but they may be misdiagnosed with schizophrenia if the mental health clinician is not aware that these are primarily dissociative symptoms and only in certain limited special cases, symptoms of schizophrenia.

Psychobiology of Dissociation

The psychobiology of dissociation is mostly studied in the context of trauma-related mental disorders. Whereas few psychobiological studies of dissociative disorders exist, the psychobiology of PTSD is being given increasing attention. Future studies must explore to what degree findings regarding dissociative phenomena in PTSD can be generalized to complex dissociative disorders. The psychobiology of dissociation in acute stress disorder (ASD) patients and hyperaroused mentally healthy individuals are also topics of research.

Peritraumatic dissociation in ASD, as well as in severely stressed, mentally healthy individuals, is linked with hyperarousal (Sterlini & Bryant, 2002), for example with very high heart rates in patients in emergency rooms (Kuhn, Blanchard, Fuse, Hickling, & Broderick, 2006). These results fit findings in PTSD that integrative functions in humans can be hampered by the release of neurochemicals such as norepinephrine and dopamine provoked by severe threat (De Bellis et al., 1999). They support the view originally advanced in the nineteenth century by Pierre Janet that (*see:* **Janet, Pierre**) dissociation is primarily a deficit in the ability to maintain a psychological integration of the personality when exposed to the threat of being harmed. These neurochemicals are concentrated in brain regions involved in psychobiological integration, such as the hippocampus and the prefrontal cortex. Thus, high dopamine and norepinephrine turnover in the prefrontal cortex causes a decrease in metabolism in this brain region, and induces deficits in cognition and working memory. PTSD includes increased noradrenergic

(norepinephrine-related) activity in the brain that impairs the functioning of the prefrontal cortex and strengthens amygdala function (which is involved in fear conditioning and fear memories; Arnsten, 2007). Noradrenergic systems seem to play a role in the creation ("overconsolidation") and reexperiencing of traumatic memories that constitute positive dissociative symptoms. Consistent with this, dissociation severity is positively associated with norepinephrine-related reactivity in the brain under conditions of stress. Related findings are that fearful reexperiencing of traumatic memories that involves altered body states and abnormal behavior—a positive dissociative symptom—is associated with abnormal prefrontal metabolism in PTSD (Shin, Rauch, & Pitman, 2006), borderline personality disorder (BPD; Schmahl, Vermetten, Elzinga, & Bremner, 2004), and DID (Reinders et al., 2006). There is a consistent positive correlation between changes in the "stress" chemicals in the brain, such as glutamate, norepinephrine, epinephrine, glucocorticoids, and endogenous opiates, and the severity of dissociative symptoms. This supports the hypothesis that degree of dissociative symptoms and of exposure to extreme stressors are positively correlated phenomena.

Self-mutilation and substance abuse may temporarily reduce autonomic arousal, intrusions of traumatic memories, and internal command voices (i.e., thoughts that the person experiences as the voices of dissociative parts of the personality that are expressing aggressive feelings and demands). These effects could be related to the release of endogenous opiates in the brain, which also contribute to stress-induced analgesia (in many cases, a negative somatoform dissociative symptom). These dissociative symptoms may at least partially account for the high rate of opiate abuse in trauma survivors with complex traumatic stress disorders.

Structural brain imaging studies suggest that patients with simple and complex dissociative disorders have smaller than normal hippocampal, parahippocampal, and amygdalar volume (Ehling, Nijenhuis, & Krikke, 2007; Vermetten, Schmahl, Lindner, Loewenstein, & Bremner,

2006). Hippocampal volume is negatively correlated with the complexity of the trauma-related disorder. Furthermore, in patients with certain dissociative disorders (including a general type of dissociative disorder categorized in the *DSM-IV* as "Not Otherwise Specified," as well as in DID), hippocampal and parahippocampal volume (*see:* **Hippocampus**) are strongly positively correlated with psychoform and somatoform dissociation, and with reported psychological traumatization.

Patients with DID have abnormal brain wave patterns (EEG), and, like patients with conversion disorder (described in ICD-10 as "dissociative disorders of movement and sensation"), abnormal cerebral flood flow. Irrespective of their different dissociative parts and compared to mentally healthy controls, DID patients have reduced blood flow in the orbitofrontal area of the prefrontal cortex on both sides of the brain (i.e., bilaterally), and increased blood flow in the bilateral frontal and occipital cortex (Sar, Unal, & Ozturk, 2007; *see:* **Frontal Cortex**). Blood flow in the brain is used as a measure of the amount of activity occurring in specific brain areas: thus, increased blood flow indicates more brain activity and decreased blood flow indicates reduced brain activity. Decreased blood flow in orbitofrontal regions also marks BPD. The orbitofrontal area of the prefrontal cortex is thought to be responsible for reducing the intensity of emotional distress. The frontal and occipital cortices are thought to be involved in inhibiting intense impulses and organizing visual information. Thus, increased frontal and occipital cortex brain activity in dissociation may reflect a compensatory response to impulsivity and dissociative intrusions (e.g., reexperiencing traumatic memories) when the orbitofrontal cortex is not sufficiently activated to manage potent trauma-related emotional reactions. Consistent with these findings, dissociation and depersonalization scores in depersonalization disorder are correlated with metabolic activity in the posterior parietal association area and left occipital cortex (Simeon et al., 2000).

Studies have shown that patients with PTSD can have a variety of psychobiological reaction patterns to trauma-reminders (e.g., Osuch et al., 2001). Although few experimental data are available (e.g., Mason et al., 2002), from the core clinical features of the disorder it would be expected that these inter-individual differences might also pertain to intra-individual differences (i.e., to different dissociative parts of the personality). Thus, it is in the very nature of the disorder that the dissociative individual is sometimes *hypo*aroused (emotionally and physically numbed and avoidant) when confronted with trauma-reminders, and at other times *hyper*aroused (as when having flashbacks).

Functional neuroimaging studies of different types of dissociative parts of the personality in DID suggest that their different ideas of self involve different patterns of neural activity, as well as very different subjective, psychophysiological, and neural reactions to consciously perceived threat (Reinders et al., 2003, 2006). Comparing their reactions to neutral and trauma memory scripts, apparently normal parts of the personality have similar heart rate, heart rate variability, and blood pressure. Apparently normal parts also have less intense bodily, behavioral, and emotional reactions to trauma memory scripts than parts fixated in traumatic memories, and more blood flow in prefrontal, frontal, parietal, and occipital cortex. In contrast, emotional parts of the personality that are fixated in traumatic memories and defensive reactions have strong bodily, behavioral, and affective reactions to trauma memory scripts, increased heart rate, decreased heart rate variability, decreased prefrontal and parahippocampal perfusion, and increased blood flow in insular cortex, sensory cortex, and amygdala (*see:* **Amygdala; Hippocampus; Limbic System**). Although further study and replication are needed, these findings do not seem to be intentional: dissociative parts of the personality in DID display psychobiological differences that are generally not reproduced by DID-simulating controls. For example, neither low nor high fantasy prone mentally healthy subjects instructed and motivated to act as if they were dissociated into apparently normal or emotional parts had psychobiological reaction patterns to aversive memory scripts that were similar to the reactions patterns of DID patients (Reinders et al., 2008).

With regard to somatoform dissociation, patients with dissociative paralysis have decreases in frontal and subcortical brain activity (Vuilleumier, 2005). Decreases in somatosensory cortical metabolism are observed in dissociative anesthesia, and dissociative blindness is associated with decreased metabolism in the visual cortex (Vuilleumier, 2005). These changes are commonly not associated with significant changes in early stages of sensory or motor processing. However, changes in later stages of integration have been found, and somatoform dissociative symptoms can be associated with increased activation in limbic regions.

Conclusion

Dissociation is still not a well-understood phenomenon, but advances have been made in its definition and scientific research on its correlates and probable causes. It is often confused with the temporary state of shock that often occurs soon after extremely stressful events or other clinical symptoms or disorders involving emotional dysregulation, other kinds of mental dysregulation, and common alterations of consciousness. Dissociation involves a failure to maintain an adaptive, integrated personality, that is, a division of the personality into at least two parts. Dissociative parts of the personality encompass their own ideas of self, the world and how they relate to the world, although in simple cases of PTSD these differences are far more limited than in complex dissociative disorders such as DID. Dissociative parts can be understood as insufficiently integrated subsystems of the individual's personality that have evolved as a result of exposure to very stressful, potentially traumatizing events, insufficient capacity to integrate the experience, and insufficient social support to synthesize and realize the traumatic experience. This lack of integration of what used to be a relatively integrated whole system (i.e., the individual's personality), or what never was a whole in the first place (as the case of posttraumatic dissociation

from early childhood), is a biopsychosocial phenomenon. Growing scientific evidence suggests that different types of dissociative parts of the personality are associated with distinct biological correlates when they engage in mental and behavioral actions that are specific for these parts. As the biology and psychology of posttraumatic dissociation becomes better understood, treatment will become correspondingly better able to help dissociated patients to regain (or develop for the first time) the capacity to maintain an integrated personality (Van der Hart et al., 2006).

REFERENCES

American Psychiatric Association. (1994). *Diagnostic and statistical manual of mental disorders* (4th ed.). Washington, DC: Author.

Arnsten, A. F. (2007). Catecholamine and second messenger influences on prefrontal cortical networks of "representational knowledge": A rational bridge between genetics and the symptoms of mental illness. *Cerebral Cortex, 17*(Suppl. 1), i6–i15.

Bernstein, E. M., & Putnam, F. W. (1986). Development, reliability, and validity of a dissociation scale. *Journal of Nervous and Mental Disease, 174,* 727–735.

Brown, R. J. (2006). Different types of "dissociation" have different psychological mechanisms. *Journal of Trauma and Dissociation, 7*(4), 7–28.

Cardeña, E. (1994). The domain of dissociation. In S. J. Lynn & J. W. Rhue (Eds.), *Dissociation: Clinical and theoretical perspectives* (pp. 15–31). New York: Guilford Press.

De Bellis, M. D., Baum, A. S., Birmaher, B., Keshavan, M. S., Eccard, C. H., Boring, A. M., et al. (1999). A. E. Bennett Research Award. Developmental traumatology: Pt. I. Biological stress systems. *Biological Psychiatry, 45,* 1259–1270.

Dell, P. F. (2006). A new model of dissociative identity disorder. *Psychiatric Clinics of North America, 29,* 1–26.

Ehling, T., Nijenhuis, E. R. S., & Krikke, A. P. (2007). Volume of discrete brain structures in complex dissociative disorders: Preliminary findings. *Progress in Brain Research, 167,* 307–310.

Kuhn, E., Blanchard, E. B., Fuse, T., Hickling, E. J., & Broderick, J. (2006). Heart rate of motor vehicle accident survivors in the emergency department, peritraumatic psychological reactions, ASD, and PTSD severity: A 6-month prospective study. *Journal of Traumatic Stress, 19*, 735–740.

Marmar, C. R., Weiss, D. S., Schlenger, W. E., Fairbank, J. A., Jordan, K., Kulka, R. A., et al. (1994). Peritraumatic dissociation and posttraumatic stress in male Vietnam theater veterans. *American Journal of Psychiatry, 154*, 173–177.

Mason, J. W., Wang, S., Yehuda, R., Lubin, H., Johnson, D., Bremner, J. D., et al. (2002). Marked lability in urinary cortisol levels in subgroups of combat veterans with posttraumatic stress disorder during an intensive exposure treatment program. *Psychosomatic Medicine, 64*, 238–246.

Nähring, G., & Nijenhuis, E. R. S. (2005). Relationships between self-reported potentially traumatizing events, psychoform and somatoform dissociation, and absorption, in two nonclinical populations. *Australian and New Zealand Journal of Psychiatry, 39*, 982–988.

Nijenhuis, E. R. S. (2004). *Somatoform dissociation: Phenomena, measurement, and theoretical issues.* New York: Norton.

Nijenhuis, E. R. S., Spinhoven, P., Van Dyck, R., Van der Hart, O., & Vanderlinden, J. (1996). The development and psychometric characteristics of the somatoform dissociation questionnaire (SDQ-20). *Journal of Nervous and Mental Disease, 184*, 688–694.

Nijenhuis, E. R. S., Spinhoven, P., Van Dyck, R., Van der Hart, O., & Vanderlinden, J. (1998). Degree of somatoform and psychological dissociation in dissociative disorders is correlated with reported trauma. *Journal of Traumatic Stress, 11*, 711–730.

Nijenhuis, E. R. S., Van Dyck, R., Spinhoven, P., Van der Hart, O., Chatrou, M., Vanderlinden, J., et al. (1999). Somatoform dissociation discriminates between diagnostic categories over and above general psychopathology. *Australian and New Zealand Journal of Psychiatry, 33*, 512–520.

Osuch, E. A., Benson, B., Geraci, M., Podell, D., Herscovitch, P., McCann, U. D., et al. (2001). Regional cerebral blood flow correlated with flashback intensity in patients with posttraumatic stress disorder. *Biological Psychiatry, 50*, 246–253.

Reinders, A. A., Nijenhuis, E. R., Paans, A. M., Korf, J., Willemsen, A. T., & Den Boer, J. A. (2003). One brain, two selves. *Neuroimage, 20*, 2119–2125.

Reinders, A. A., Nijenhuis, E. R., Quak, J., Korf, J., Haaksma, J., Paans, A. M., et al. (2006). Psychobiological characteristics of dissociative identity disorder: A symptom provocation study. *Biological Psychiatry, 60*, 730–740.

Reinders, A. A. T. S., van Eekeren, M. C., Vos, H. P. J., Haaksma, J., Willemsen, A. T. M., Den Boer, J. A., et al. (2008, April). *The dissociative brain: Feature or ruled by fantasy?* Paper presented at the first International Conference of the European Society for Trauma and Dissociation, Amsterdam.

Sar, V., Unal, S. N., & Ozturk, E. (2007). Frontal and occipital perfusion changes in dissociative identity disorder. *Psychiatry Research: Neuroimaging, 156*, 217–223.

Schmahl, C. G., Vermetten, E., Elzinga, B. M., & Bremner, J. D. (2004). A positron emission tomography study of memories of childhood abuse in borderline personality disorder. *Biological Psychiatry, 55*, 759–765.

Shin, L. M., Rauch, S. L., & Pitman, R. K. (2006). Amygdala, medial prefrontal cortex, and hippocampal function in PTSD. *Annals of the New York Academy of Sciences, 1071*, 67–79.

Simeon, D., Guralnik, O., Hazlett, E. A., Spiegel-Cohen, J., Hollander, E., & Buchsbaum, M. S. (2000). Feeling unreal: A PET study of depersonalization disorder. *American Journal of Psychiatry, 157*, 1782–1788.

Sterlini, G. L., & Bryant, R. A. (2002). Hyperarousal and dissociation: A study of novice skydivers. *Behavior Research, and Therapy, 40*, 431–437.

Van der Hart, O., & Dorahy, M. (in press). Dissociation: History of a concept. In P. F. Dell & J. O'Neil (Eds.), *Dissociation and the dissociative disorders: DSM-V and beyond.* New York: Routledge.

Van der Hart, O., Nijenhuis, E. R. S., & Steele, K. (2006). *The haunted self: Structural dissociation and the treatment of chronic traumatization.* New York: Norton.

Van der Hart, O., Van Dijke, A., Van Son, M., & Steele, K. (2000). Somatoform dissociation in traumatized World War I combat soldiers: A neglected clinical heritage. *Journal of Trauma and Dissociation, 1*(4), 33–66.

Van der Hart, O., Van Ochten, J. M., Van Son, M. J. M., Steele, K., & Lensvelt-Mulders, G. (in press). Relations among peritraumatic dissociation and posttraumatic stress. *Journal of Trauma and Dissociation.*

Vermetten, E., Schmahl, C., Lindner, S., Loewenstein, R. J., & Bremner, J. D. (2006). Hippocampal and amygdalar volumes in dissociative identity disorder. *American Journal of Psychiatry, 163,* 630–636.

Vuilleumier, P. (2005). Hysterical conversion and brain function. *Progress in Brain Research, 150,* 309–329.

Wang, S., Wilson, J. P., & Mason, J. W. (1996). Stages of decompensation in combat-related posttraumatic stress disorder: A new conceptual model. *Integrative Physiological and Behavioral Science, 31,* 237–253.

ONNO VAN DER HART
Utrecht University

ELLERT R. S. NIJENHUIS
Mental Health Care Drenthe, Assen, The Netherlands

See also: Cognitive Integration, Biopsychosocial; Complex Posttraumatic Stress Disorder; Dissociative Identity Disorder; Hysteria; Janet, Pierre

DISSOCIATIVE IDENTITY DISORDER

Dissociative identity disorder (DID), previously known as multiple personality disorder (MPD), is a mental health diagnosis defined in the *DSM-IV-TR* as (a) the presence of two or more distinct identities or personality states, each with its own relatively enduring pattern of perceiving, relating to, and thinking about the environment and self; (b) that at least two of these identities recurrently take control of the person's behavior; and (c) the person experiences inability to recall important personal information that is too extensive to be explained by ordinary forgetfulness (i.e., dissociative amnesia). The diagnostic label of multiple personality disorder was used in earlier versions of the *DSM,* and many laypeople continue to use the latter term to describe this diagnosis. The similar term *split-personality* is an outmoded one that has no current medical meaning.

In popular culture, a diagnosis of DID is often, but inaccurately, assumed to be synonymous with that of schizophrenia. Although some symptoms of DID superficially resemble those of schizophrenia (e.g., hearing voices), DID and schizophrenia are unrelated conditions. Schizophrenic patients do not create alter personality states/identities. In general, unlike schizophrenic patients, DID patients do not develop delusions. Also, in contrast to schizophrenics, individuals with DID have a significantly increased capacity for logical and organized thinking and good reality testing, and generally show a much better ability to form relationships with others.

DID can be conceptualized as a childhood onset, posttraumatic developmental disorder in which the trauma-exposed child is unable to complete the normal developmental processes involved in consolidating a core sense of identity. Repeated early trauma disrupts unification of identity through creation of discrete behavioral states associated with mitigating the traumatic experiences and providing reparative experiences for the child. Together with disturbed caretaker-child attachment and parenting, repeated early trauma disrupts the development of normal processes involved in the elaboration and consolidation of a unified sense of self. The child fails to integrate the different experiences of self that normally occur across different contexts, such as with parents, peers, and others (Putnam, 1997).

Formation of the DID "personalities" involves development of multiple centers of information processing in the mind capable of relatively independent thought, emotion, and memory, as well as the capacity to act, such as to take control of the person's behavior. As the child develops into an adult, these alternate identities commonly become more elaborated with different names, personal descriptors (e.g., gender, age, function), and variable ways of presenting themselves to others. In the popular media, much is made of the overt differences between the DID alternate identities. Although psychophysiological variability between alternate identities is of research interest, the elaboration of the characteristics of the self states is not the essential aspect of DID. Rather, this is due to other developmental factors such as the child's intelligence and creativity, exposure to sources of fantasy such as books, TV, or the movies, and contradictory parental expectations, among many others.

From a psychodynamic perspective, DID can be understood as a psychological adaptation to adverse developmental circumstances (Armstrong, 1995). DID defenses provide resilience by preserving important human qualities in the face of trauma exposure. The DID self states are mental constructs, not separate persons inhabiting a body. The "personality" of the DID human being is made up of *all* the self states together, not just one or a few of them. The self states contain important information and may be mobilized for a variety of psychodynamic and adaptive needs. Individuals with DID often experience themselves as a "system" of selves that are variably co-present and that interfere, overlap, and/or are in conflict with one another.

DID has been strongly linked to experiences of severe early childhood trauma, usually maltreatment, in all studies that have systematically examined this question—in both Western and non-Western cultures. Rates of reported severe childhood trauma for both child and adult DID patients range from 85% to 97% of cases across studies (Boon & Draijer, 1993b; Loewenstein & Putnam, 2004; Ross, 1997). Physical and sexual abuse, usually in combination, are the most frequently reported sources of childhood trauma in such clinical research studies, although other kinds of trauma have been reported, such as multiple painful medical and surgical procedures, and wartime trauma.

An alternative etiological model for DID posits that DID is not an authentic condition, but one created through "iatrogenic" factors. Iatrogenic defines disorders or symptoms that arise due to actions of a practitioner (such as a physician, psychologist, or therapist) or the treatment. In the iatrogenesis or sociocognitive model (SCM; Lilienfeld et al., 1999; Spanos, 1996) of the etiology of DID, suggestive influences by therapists who strongly believe in DID and "repressed memories" for trauma are posited to be the iatrogenic factors explaining DID's development in a given patient. This

model posits that DID develops as a learned social role in patients who are suggestible, "fantasy prone," highly hypnotizable, and who may show features of borderline personality disorder (BPD). According to the SCM, naive therapists induce DID behavior in susceptible patients by overtly or covertly cueing the patient to act like someone with multiple personalities (McHugh, 1992). This model is an analogue of the sociocognitive model for hypnosis, which hypothesizes that hypnosis is not caused by an altered state of consciousness, but only by a learned social role (Spanos, 1986).

A major controversy exists among professionals about the validity of these two models. This controversy has spilled over into the media and has been an issue in legal cases in which plaintiffs have sued practitioners alleging "implantation" of false memories of childhood maltreatment and/or iatrogenic creation of DID (see Brown, Sheflin, & Hammond, 1998, for the most complete review of many of these issues).

Despite this controversy, only limited research data support the SCM for DID (Brown, Frischholz, & Scheflin, 1999), and research studies with clinical populations have not attempted to test this model. Proponents of the SCM have raised questions about the validity of DID patients' self-reports of childhood trauma. However, recent studies including large samples of maltreated children with dissociative disorders as well as intensively validated case studies provide independent corroboration of patients' reports of maltreatment (Hornstein & Putnam, 1992; Lewis, Yeager, & Swica, 1997).

Conservative analysis of epidemiologic data from North America, Europe, and Asia suggests a general population prevalence of approximately 1.3% for dissociative identity disorder (Johnson, Cohena, Kasena, & Brook, 2006). Three to 5% of the general population suffers from pathological dissociation consistent with DID and the severe dissociative disorder not otherwise specified (DDNOS; Waller & Ross, 1997). DID has been described in members of multiple family generations; however, there are no data at this time to support a genetic contribution to the development of DID. There is a broad spectrum of DID-diagnosed individuals: from those who are high functioning to those who are chronically and persistently mentally ill. A subgroup abuses their own children. Some inhabit violent, criminal subcultures. Others are chronic substance abusers.

Diagnosis of DID requires assessment of several symptom groups, including process symptoms and chronic complex amnesia experiences. DID process symptoms include switching, depersonalization and derealization, and symptoms of subjective overlap, intrusion, and interference among alternate identities. Switching is defined as relatively sudden, discrete shifts in state of consciousness manifested by changes in state-related variables such as affect, access to memories, sense of self, and cognitive and perceptual style. This may be reflected in alterations in facial expression, speech, motor activity, and interpersonal relatedness. Symptoms of overlap, interference, and intrusion include incursion into awareness of thoughts, feelings, emotions, impulses, or actions (including speech) perceived as "not mine"; repeated episodes of memories, thoughts, feelings, impulses, and/or emotions being removed from the mind; and/or behavior being stopped or inhibited as if by inside forces or presences. DID patients may experience themselves as multiple selves simultaneously, including a simultaneous sense of being more than one age and/or gender at the same time. DID patients frequently report recurrent severe depersonalization (feeling as if one is disconnected from oneself, including out-of-body experiences), and derealization (feeling as if one's surroundings are alien or unreal; Dell, 2006).

Patients diagnosed with DID commonly report hearing voices and/or conversations, primarily within the mind, including voices arguing, commenting on the person's behavior, or discussing neutral topics. There may be supportive voices or voices that seem to be having conversations that the person cannot fully hear. Generally, voices have a personified quality including names, and/or descriptors. Genuine DID patients do not usually have delusional explanations for these experiences, do not have a formal thought disorder (severe thought disorganization characteristic of those with schizophrenia or other psychotic disorders), and are reticent to discuss the experiences for fear of being thought of as "crazy." Unlike psychotic patients, those with DID often describe these experiences in a metaphorical and/or personified way (e.g., "I feel like someone else wants to cry with my eyes").

On standardized assessment, DID patients have the highest hypnotizability of any group (Frischholz, Lipman, Braun, & Sachs, 1992). They naturalistically demonstrate deep trance phenomena including negative hallucinations (not hearing, seeing, perceiving stimuli actually present in the environment), spontaneous age regression (suddenly experiencing oneself as if one is of a younger age or reliving a prior time in their life), spontaneous trances (entering a spontaneous hypnotic state), extreme enthrallment (becoming intensely absorbed in what one is doing), trance logic (tolerance of logical contradiction, characteristic of the hypnotized state), and an eye-roll sign (eyes rolled into the head so only the white sclera are showing—thought to be strongly linked to having high hypnotic capacity) when switching.

Some other experiences commonly reported by DID patients include chronic complex amnesia experiences such as "lost time," blackouts, fugues (finding that one has traveled to another location without recall of how one arrived there), disremembered behavior, unexplained possessions, sudden brief loss of memory for ongoing experience, and marked shifts in access to skills, habits, and knowledge. DID patients may exhibit differing handwriting, handedness, eyeglass prescriptions, musical and artistic abilities, use of and tolerance to drugs and alcohol, and other characteristics over time. DID patients commonly report fragmentary memory and/or dense dissociative amnesia for large parts of their life history. Popular models of DID suggest that only certain patterns of memory loss characterize the disorder, including types of amnesia between alternate identities. In fact, a wide range of amnesia experiences is found in DID, as well as between self states. These vary from dense lack of memory for much of the life history to circumscribed amnesia for particular events or categories of experience.

Standardized self-report questionnaires and semi-structured diagnostic interviews useful in the differential diagnosis of DID include: the Dissociative Experiences Scale (DES), Structured Clinical Interview for *DSM-IV* Dissociative Disorders (SCID-D), Multiaxial Inventory of Dissociation (MID), Dissociative Disorders Interview Schedule (DDIS), Somatoform Dissociation Questionnaire (SDQ), and Multiscale Dissociation Inventory (MDI; see Chu et al., 2005).

DID patients fall within the complex PTSD (CPTSD) spectrum (*see:* **Complex Posttraumatic Stress Disorder**). The latter characterizes individuals with PTSD who report multiple traumatic episodes over several developmental periods, primarily due to childhood maltreatment. CPTSD is characterized by a variety of difficulties with regulation of mood, anxiety and anger; problems with sense of self; lack of trust in others; and multiple forms of self-destructiveness, among others (Courtois, 2004).

In clinical settings, 80% to 100% of DID patients meet diagnostic criteria for PTSD. DID patients commonly exhibit symptoms of somatoform disorders (i.e., physical complaints that have no physiological origin), which may include symptoms of conversion disorder, pain disorder, and somatization disorder (Nijenhuis, 1999). Other common comorbidities include depressive, substance abuse, and obsessive-compulsive symptoms. Suicide attempts, self-mutilation, eating disorders, and risk-taking behaviors are common. Revictimization by rape, domestic violence, and interpersonal exploitation in adulthood are common, as well.

DID may be underdiagnosed. The image derived from classic textbooks of a florid, dramatic disorder with overt switching characterizes about 5% of the DID clinical population. The more typical presentation is of a covert disorder with dissociative symptoms embedded among affective, anxiety, pseudo-psychotic, dyscontrol, and self-destructive symptoms,

among others (Loewenstein, 1991). The typical DID patient averages 6 to 12 years in the mental health system, receiving an average of 3 to 4 prior diagnoses. DID is often found in cases that were labeled as "treatment failures" because the patient did not respond to typical treatments for mood, anxiety, psychotic, somatoform, substance abuse, and eating disorders, among others. Rapid mood shifts (within minutes or hours), impulsivity, self-destructiveness, and/or apparent hallucinations lead to misdiagnosis of cyclic mood disorders (e.g., bipolar disorder) or psychotic disorders (e.g., schizophrenia). Severe posttraumatic grief, shame, or a pronounced inability to experience pleasure (anhedonia) may complicate mood disorder symptoms, leading to misdiagnosis of a melancholic depressive disorder. At the time of correct diagnosis, DID patients may report years of failure to respond, or limited response to psychopharmacological treatments.

Symptoms of severe PTSD and dissociation may resemble the kind of chaotic clinical picture that suggests BPD (Ross, 1997). Compared to BPD patients, DID patients report earlier, and more severe childhood trauma (Boon & Draijer, 1993a). DID patients have significantly more amnesia, identity confusion, and identity alteration on the SCID-D and significantly higher dissociation scores on the DES when compared with BPD patients, as well as more interference, intrusion, overlap symptoms (Boon & Draijer, 1993a; Ross, 1997). Also, compared to BPD patients, DID patients are more psychologically complex, have an enhanced capacity for self-observation, increased overall reality testing (when not traumatically flooded), and greater capacity for interpersonal attachment (Brand, Armstrong, & Loewenstein, 2006).

Neurobiological studies have compared cortisol metabolism and brain morphology in DID patients to those of nondissociative PTSD patients. DID patients differ little from nondissociative PTSD patients in cortisol dynamics, and both show reduced brain hippocampal volumes compared with control subjects. DID patients show reduced amygdalar volume as well (Vermetten, Schmahl, Lindner,

Loewenstein, & Bremner, 2006). Psychometric studies of DID patients show high hypnotizability, low histrionic personality traits, normal interrogatory suggestibility, moderate fantasy-proneness, and introversive traits. Rorschach inkblot test studies show elevated traumatic content responses, elevated self-observation scores, high complexity, hyper-focus and absorption into the ink blots, intact reality testing when not activated by traumatic stimuli, intact relational capacity, and an overall introversive style (Brand et al., 2006). The latter findings are consistent with the conceptualization that DID defenses provide resilience by preserving important human qualities despite trauma exposure.

Treatment of DID is an intensive multimodal psychotherapy usually including psychodynamic and cognitive-behavioral strategies, with adjunctive pharmacotherapy and hypnotherapy. In this form of therapy, the alter self states are worked with directly to facilitate adaptation by creating a more adaptive "system" and promoting internal communication, collaboration, and cooperation. Empirical support for this broad-based model of treatment comes from several case series, as well as cost efficacy studies based on clinical case series (Coons, 1986; Eliason & Ross, 1997; Kluft, 1988; Loewenstein, 1994), but albeit not from randomized clinical trials.

Current best practices, buttressed by a variety of clinical studies, support a tripartite treatment model for complex trauma disorders such as those with DID (Chu, 1998). In the first phase, the focus is on the patient developing safety and stability. After this is achieved, the patient may (optionally) enter a phase of intensive work on traumatic memories. The third phase is one of resolution, in which the DID self states may lose separateness and the patient focuses on building a life in the present, as free as possible from past traumas. These stages are discussed in more detail below.

When presenting for treatment, DID patients commonly are engaging in a variety of self-destructive behaviors that include self-mutilation, suicide attempts, eating disorders, enmeshment in abusive relationships, high-risk behaviors, and substance abuse. At treatment onset, DID patients commonly suffer from dysfunctional switching between self states, resulting in disorganization and life chaos, severe memory problems, and safety problems. Severe PTSD with nightmares, flashbacks, and reexperiencing phenomena are also usually present. Unless these symptoms can be stabilized and the patient achieves safety, progression to later stages of treatment is generally contraindicated (Chu et al., 2005; Kluft & Loewenstein, 2007).

The initial phase of DID treatment is devoted to developing a sense of safety that will allow the patient to engage effectively in treatment (Chu et al., 2005). This includes safety from self-harm, suicide, high-risk behaviors, eating disorders, abuse by others, and substance abuse, as well as safety toward others, particularly, safety toward the DID patient's minor children. Engaging the alter personalities includes accessing them, encouraging inter-alter collaboration and communication, mapping the alter system, developing agreements for safety, and teaching symptom management techniques for self-soothing, grounding, and containment of dissociative and PTSD symptoms.

The second phase of DID treatment is an optional one focusing on detailed processing of memories of overwhelming/traumatic experiences. Some DID patients do not have the psychological or personal resources to engage fully in this stage of therapy. If exposure techniques are employed, they must be modified for the DID population. This includes working directly with the alters around memory processing due to distribution of memory among the alters. Significant titration or "fractionation" of the intensity of affect usually is mandatory. Work at more intense affective levels must be balanced with processing the cognitive, affective, and existential aspects of the patient's history. The therapist remains neutral about the accuracy of memory material since DID patients typically vacillate in their own estimation of how closely their trauma memories conform to historical events. Definitive confirmation or disconfirmation of the patient's memories usually does not occur. Patients may modify their views of their life history as they become less symptomatically dissociative.

In the third phase of treatment, full subjective integration (fusion) of the alters is attempted, although this process begins in prior stages. The subjective self of the patient shifts away from multiplicity toward greater unity, and in many cases full integration occurs. Here, subjective self-division is no longer present when systematically assessed over at least 2 years. Many patients achieve a form of resolution in which some alters persist (rather than fusing), but in a more adaptive configuration. The focus of treatment shifts toward greater emphasis on living well in the present, including mastering new coping skills for life without pathological dissociative defenses, despite everyday stress and even traumatic experiences. Long-term follow-up, rather than formal treatment termination, permits the patient to return as needed after intensive therapy has ended.

DID therapy requires careful attention to therapeutic boundaries, management of traumatic transference themes, cognitive interventions around trauma-based cognitive distortions, management of profound shame, and provision of pacing, mastery, and a sense of control for the patient. The therapist is even-handed with all self states and promotes coordination, cooperation, responsibility for behavior, and internal empathy as an antidote to subjective separation and conflict. The therapist must maintain boundaries, behave responsibly, and remain straightforward and warm.

There is no known pharmacological treatment that specifically targets dissociative symptoms and no studies provide systematic data about psychopharmacology for DID. The standard of care involves providing adjunctive pharmacotherapy designed to improve the management of affective disturbances, PTSD, panic, behavioral dyscontrol, impulsiveness, and self-destructive symptoms, as well as to improve sleep (Loewenstein, 2005). Informed consent involves working with the alters around medications, since some alters are medication phobic and sabotage treatment. Careful delineation of appropriate target symptoms includes ruling out symptoms that are circumscribed within individual alters and/or are related to PTSD-related behaviors that will not respond to medications (e.g., phobic avoidance of sleep due to memories of nocturnal traumas).

Adjunctive hypnotic interventions in the first treatment phases consist of imagery for soothing, calming, containment, safety, and relaxation. Teaching self-hypnosis is effective to help contain symptoms outside of therapy. In the middle phase, hypnotherapy is used to attenuate and fractionate the intensity of traumatic material. In the final stages, hypnotherapy may be used to facilitate fusion of alters and to promote better functioning in the present.

Other adjunctive therapies may include family or couple's therapy with the patient's contemporary family, art therapy, movement therapy, and journaling. However, some of these adjunctive therapies lack empirical evidence for their efficacy. Eye movement desensitization and reprocessing (EMDR) should be used only as an adjunctive technique by therapists already skilled in phasic treatment for DID and who have received supervision in the use of EMDR in this population. Premature or poorly timed use of EMDR usually results in decompensation for the DID patient.

DID patients commonly fall within one of three basic treatment subgroups: a high functioning, treatment-responsive group that usually achieves fusion relatively rapidly; a group with more comorbidities and adaptational pathology that requires longer-term treatment to either integration or resolution; and a severely ill group with more comorbidities, severe characterological pathology, enmeshment in maladaptive relationships/subcultures, and/or narcissistic investment in having DID. The latter may require a long-term supportive treatment focused on stabilization.

Rigorous, controlled psychotherapy outcome studies have not been performed for DID. Existing outcome studies show significant improvement, including full integration, in many patients across numerous symptom dimensions when a phasic DID treatment model is used, as well as good cost-efficacy. Even severely ill state-hospital patients have shown improvement in these studies (Loewenstein, 1994; Loewenstein & Putnam, 2004).

REFERENCES

Armstrong, J. G. (1995). Reflections on multiple personality disorder as a developmentally complex adaptation. *Psychoanalytic Study of the Child, 50,* 349–364.

Boon, S., & Draijer, N. (1993a). The differentiation of patients with MPD or DDNOS from patients with Cluster B personality disorder. *Dissociation, 6,* 126–135.

Boon, S., & Draijer, N. (1993b). *Multiple personality disorder in the Netherlands: A study on reliability and validity of the diagnosis.* Amsterdam: Swets & Zeitlinger.

Brand, B., Armstrong, J. A., & Loewenstein, R. J. (2006). Psychological assessment of patients with dissociative identity disorder. *Psychiatric Clinics of North America, 29,* 145–168.

Brown, D. W., Frischholz, E. J., & Scheflin, A. W. (1999). Iatrogenic dissociative identity disorder: An evaluation of the scientific evidence. *Journal of Psychiatry and Law, 27,* 549–638.

Brown, D. W., Scheflin, A. W., & Hammond, D. C. (1998). *Memory, trauma, treatment, and the law.* New York: Norton.

Chu, J. A. (1998). *Rebuilding shattered lives: The responsible treatment of complex posttraumatic and dissociative disorders.* New York: Wiley.

Chu, J. A., Loewenstein, R. J., Dell, P. F., Barach, P. M., Somer, E., Kluft, R. P., et al. (2005). Guidelines for treating dissociative identity disorder in adults. *Journal of Trauma and Dissociation, 6*(4), 69–149.

Coons, P. M. (1986). Treatment progress in 20 patients with multiple personality disorder. *Journal of Nervous and Mental Disease, 174,* 715–721.

Courtois, C. A. (2004). Complex trauma, complex reactions: Assessment and treatment. *Psychotherapy: Theory, Research, Practice, Training, 41,* 412–425.

Dell, P. F. (2006). A new model of dissociative identity disorder. *Psychiatric Clinics of North America, 29*(1), 1–26.

Eliason, J. W., & Ross, C. A. (1997). Two-year follow up of inpatients with dissociative identity disorder. *American Journal of Psychiatry, 154,* 832–839.

Frischholz, E. J., Lipman, L. S., Braun, B. G., & Sachs, R. G. (1992). Psychopathology, hypnotizability, and dissociation. *American Journal of Psychiatry, 149,* 1521–1525.

Hornstein, N., & Putnam, F. W. (1992). Clinical phenomenology of child and adolescent dissociative disorders. *Journal of the American Academy of Child and Adolescent Psychiatry, 31,* 1077–1085.

Johnson, J. G., Cohena, P., Kasena, K., & Brook, J. S. (2006). Dissociative disorders among adults in the community, impaired functioning, and axis I and II comorbidity. *Journal of Psychiatric Research, 40*(2), 131–140.

Kluft, R. P. (1988). The postunification treatment of multiple personality disorder: First findings. *American Journal of Psychotherapy, 42,* 212–228.

Kluft, R. P., & Loewenstein, R. J. (2007). Dissociative disorders and depersonalization. In G. O. Gabbard (Ed.), *Gabbard's treatment of psychiatric disorders* (4th ed., pp. 547–572). Washington, DC: American Psychiatric Publishing.

Lewis, D. O., Yeager, C. A., & Swica, Y. (1997). Objective documentation of child abuse and dissociation in 12 murderers with dissociative identity disorder. *American Journal of Psychiatry, 154,* 1703–1710.

Lilienfeld, S. O., Kirsch, I., Sarbin, T. R., Lynn, S. J., Chaves, J. F., & Ganaway, G. K. (1999). Dissociative identity disorder and the sociocognitive model: Recalling the lessons of the past. *Psychological Bulletin, 125,* 507–523.

Loewenstein, R. J. (1991). An office mental status examination for chronic complex dissociative symptoms and multiple personality disorder. *Psychiatric Clinics of North America, 14,* 567–604.

Loewenstein, R. J. (1994). Diagnosis, epidemiology, clinical course, treatment, and cost effectiveness of treatment for dissociative disorders and multiple personality disorder: Report submitted to the Clinton administration task force on health care financing reform. *Dissociation, 7*(1), 3–11.

Loewenstein, R. J. (2005). Psychopharmacologic treatments for dissociative identity disorder. *Psychiatric Annals, 35,* 666–673.

Loewenstein, R. J., & Putnam, F. W. (2004). The dissociative disorders. In B. J. Kaplan & V. A. Sadock (Eds.), *Comprehensive textbook of psychiatry* (8th ed., Vol. 1, pp. 1844–1901). Baltimore: Williams & Wilkins.

McHugh, P. R. (1992). Psychiatric misadventures. *American Scholar, 62,* 497–510.

Nijenhuis, E. R. S. (1999). *Somatoform dissociation: Phenomena, measurement, and theoretical issues*. Assen, The Netherlands: Van Gorcum.

Putnam, F. W. (1997). *Dissociation in children and adolescents: A developmental model*. New York: Guilford Press.

Ross, C. A. (1997). *Dissociative identity disorder: Diagnosis, clinical features and treatment of multiple personality*. New York: Wiley.

Spanos, N. P. (1986). Hypnosis, nonvolitional responding, and multiple personality: A social psychological perspective. *Progress in Experimental Personality Research, 14*, 1–62.

Spanos, N. P. (1996). *Multiple identities and false memories: A sociocognitive perspective*. Washington, DC: American Psychological Association.

Vermetten, E., Schmahl, C. G., Lindner, S., Loewenstein, R. J., & Bremner, J. D. (2006). Hippocampal and amygdalar volumes in dissociative identity disorder. *American Journal of Psychiatry, 163*, 630–636.

Waller, N. G., & Ross, C. A. (1997). The prevalence and biometric structure of pathological dissociation in the general population: Taxonmetric and behavioral genetic findings. *Journal of Abnormal Psychology, 106*, 499–510.

RECOMMENDED READINGS

Chu, J. A. (1998). *Rebuilding shattered lives: The responsible treatment of complex posttraumatic and dissociative disorders*. New York: Wiley.

Chu, J. A., Loewenstein, R. J., Dell, P. F., Barach, P. M., Somer, E., Kluft, R. P., et al. (2005). Guidelines for treating dissociative identity disorder in adults. *Journal of Trauma and Dissociation, 6*(4), 69–149.

Loewenstein, R. J., & Putnam, F. W. (2004). The dissociative disorders. In B. J. Kaplan & V. A. Sadock (Eds.), *Comprehensive textbook of psychiatry* (8th ed., Vol. 1, pp. 1844–1901). Baltimore: Williams & Wilkins.

Putnam, F. W. (1989). *Diagnosis and treatment of multiple personality disorder*. New York: Guilford Press.

Vermetten, E., Dorahy, M., & Spiegel, D. (Eds.). (2007). *Traumatic dissociation*. Washington, DC: American Psychiatric Press.

RICHARD J. LOEWENSTEIN
Sheppard Pratt Health Systems

See also: Cognitive Integration, Biopsychosocial; Complex Posttraumatic Stress Disorder; Dissociation; Hysteria; Janet, Pierre

DOMESTIC VIOLENCE

Domestic violence (DV), or intimate partner violence (IPV), is an abusive pattern of physical, sexual, or psychological behaviors, and may include stalking. Its severity can range from mild to extreme life-threatening acts. Although DV may involve a single incident, more commonly there is an ongoing pattern over time. DV occurs in heterosexual and same-sex relationships. In heterosexual relationships, women typically experience more severe injury than do men. The Centers for Disease Control and Prevention developed uniform (Saltzman, Fanslow, McMahon, & Shelley, 1999) definitions:

- *Physical violence* is defined as intentional use of physical force with the potential for causing death, disability, injury, or harm and includes pushing, shoving, slapping, beating, hair pulling, hitting with a fist or object, twisting arms, kicking, strangling, using a weapon, and other acts of physical aggression.

- *Sexual abuse* is defined as intentional touching of the genitalia, anus, groin, breast, inner thigh, or buttocks of any person against his or her will, or of any person who is unable to understand the nature or condition of the act, to decline participation, or to communicate unwillingness to be touched.

- *Sexual violence* is defined as the use of physical force to compel a person to engage in a sexual act against his or her will (e.g., forcible rape). It also includes attempted or completed sex act involving a person who is unable to understand the nature or condition of the act (e.g., because of illness, disability, or the influence of alcohol or other drugs, or due to intimidation or pressure).

- *Threat of physical or sexual violence* involves words, gestures, or weapons to communicate the intent to cause death, disability, injury, physical harm, or to compel a person to engage in sex acts or abusive sexual contact when the person is either unwilling or unable to consent. In addition to direct verbal threats ("I'll kill you"), examples of threats include brandishing a weapon or firing a weapon into the air, gestures, or grabbing for genitalia or breast.

- *Psychological abuse* includes other verbal threats, intimidation, isolation, victim blaming, humiliation, control of daily activities and money, and manipulation of children as a way to abuse the adult partner. These acts are considered psychological abuse when they occur in the context of prior physical or sexual violence.

- *Stalking* is a more recently recognized pattern of behavior that often instills fear and that involves repeated unwanted contacts such as phone calls, letters, or notes. It may include repeatedly showing up at work or outside one's home, often remaining there for long periods. Stalking is not included in the Center for Disease Control's (CDC) taxonomy for DV, but has been well documented as surprisingly common within intimate relationships (Tjaden, Thoennes, & Allison, 2000).

Consequences of Domestic Violence

Many forms of DV are traumatic events, according to the *Diagnostic and Statistical Manual* (*DSM-IV-TR;* American Psychiatric Association, 2000) because they are threats of or actual harm to the self or others and that instill emotions of intense fear, helplessness or horror. DV is unique since violence and abuse are typically repeated and the threat of recurrence often persists for years since the possibility of contact with an abusive partner rarely ends. DV has been associated with a wide-range of mental and physical health problems. Key among these are posttraumatic

stress disorder (PTSD), depression, anxiety, and somatic problems.

Posttraumatic Stress Disorder

A recent meta-analysis of mental health effects of DV has identified prevalence rates of PTSD among battered women ranging from 31% to 84.4% (Golding, 1999; Jones, Hughes, & Unterstaller, 2001). Not all victims exposed to DV develop PTSD. Greater severity and frequency of physical violence (especially that which is life threatening), use of a weapon, greater psychological abuse, and the presence of sexual abuse have been shown to predict greater severity and frequency of PTSD symptoms. PTSD is also reported to a greater extent among women with multiple experiences of victimization throughout both adulthood and childhood, especially those with histories of childhood sexual abuse. Many DV victims have been exposed to other forms of violence—and other traumatic experiences throughout their lifetimes. These additional traumatic experiences can lead to increased risk for PTSD. Other factors, such as social support and positive life events, seem to buffer or protect against developing PTSD.

Depression

Depression has been identified as another common psychological reaction to DV. Among women who develop PTSD following DV, major depressive disorder is the most commonly cited comorbid disorder and occurs in greater than 50% of these women. The factors that predict who is at risk to develop depression are similar to those described above for PTSD. Much less is known about men's risk for depression following exposure to DV. However, one study comparing genders have shown that partner violence victimization increased the odds of depression (OR [Odds Ratio] = 2.41, or increasing odds of depression by 2.41 times), as well as panic (OR = 1.83), eating disorders (OR = 2.50), and suicide attempts or ideation (OR = 2.29) for women compared to no domestic violence victimization, but no association for these mental health problems was found for men (Romito & Grassi, 2007).

Health Problems

Women who have experienced partner violence are more likely than those who have not both to experience higher rates of health problems and perceive their overall health as poor. Common somatic complaints (*see:* **Somatic Complaints**) include headaches, insomnia, chocking sensations, hyperventilation, gastrointestinal symptoms, and chest, back, and pelvic pain. There exists very little research on the physical health problems for men exposed to partner violence. However, one study found an increased risk for self-report "less than good" health (OR = 2.54) among men who reported having experienced domestic violence compared to men who did not report having experienced domestic violence (Romito & Grassi, 2007). Contrary to prior studies; findings, no association between experiencing domestic violence and poor self-reported health was found among women in this study.

Children Witnessing Domestic Violence

Witnessing domestic violence in childhood is associated with a wide range of adverse outcomes. Estimates of the prevalence of having a battered mother from a study of 50,000 men and women in the Adverse Childhood Experiences (ACE) study were 13.7% for women and 11.5% for men (Dube et al., 2001). Children who are exposed to domestic violence experience negative outcomes, including depression, posttraumatic stress disorder, and other forms of anxiety (Jarvis, Gordon, & Novaco, 2005). Adverse consequence associated with exposure to parental violence have even been demonstrated in infants (Bogat, DeJonghe, Levendosky, Davidson, & von Eye, 2006). Adults who as children had a battered mother experienced many other adverse outcomes in adulthood, including alcohol problems, drug abuse, and depression (Anda

et al., 2002; Dube, Anda, Felitti, Edwards, & Williamson, 2002). In a study of Italian university students, investigators found that reported "less than good" physical health was 2.39 and 2.03 times more likely among females and males, respectively, who reported witnessing domestic violence.

Responding to Domestic Violence

Most victims use many different strategies, including formal and informal, personal and public, to respond to acts of DV. Although many of these are ineffective in stopping the violence and abuse—especially in the long-run—many victims are able to escape from the abusive relationship.

Domestic Violence Advocacy

DV advocacy can be found in the civil and criminal courts, in police departments, in social service settings—as well as in programs that have been developed specifically to provide assistance for DV victims (such as hotlines, shelters, respite housing, counseling centers). In the most scientifically rigorous test of the effectiveness of community-based advocacy to date (Sullivan & Bybee, 1999), women who were victims of DV and who worked with advocates were more effective in ending the relationship when they wanted to than were women in the control condition who did not receive advocacy services (96% versus 87% at 24-month follow-up). The study's results also showed that DV advocacy is effective in assisting abused victims to obtain needed resources more easily, to escape physical violence and psychological abuse more effectively, and to experience greater quality of life. Results also showed that working with a DV advocate increased safety even for those women who remained in the abusive relationship.

Safety planning, an intervention commonly used by many DV advocates, is a dynamic process, in which victims assess risks and plan strategies for avoiding or reducing DV risks. Advocates and others working with victims of

DV provide assistance with safety planning in DV programs, health care settings, mental health services, law enforcement crime scenes, courts, social services offices, and almost anywhere that victims are identified.

Many women who experience DV do not get help. A recent study of the female partners of men involved in batterer treatment (Gondolf, 2002) found that only about a third of the women in the study had contact with an advocate other than in the courtroom. Over half of the women reported they felt no need for such services. While it is important to examine the effectiveness of advocacy services for victims who utilize them, an equally important question is how to make such services more accessible—or more relevant—to greater numbers of victims who are striving to keep themselves and their children safe from violence and abuse.

Civil Protection Orders

Civil protection orders (also known as restraining orders) provide a legal avenue for battered victim's efforts to increase their protection from DV and for remedies that address related needs, such as stay-away orders, support for herself and her children, exclusive use of the home, access to transportation, removal of weapons, and temporary custody of children. However, many DV victims do not use protection orders, even among those with police involvement.

Criminal Justice System

The criminal justice system offers another avenue of intervention for DV victims. Most DV-exposed women become involved with the criminal justice system at some point during their abusive relationships (Gondolf, 2002; Tjaden & Thoennes, & Allison, 2000). This involvement can range from a single encounter with the police to many months in criminal prosecution. Although the nature and the extent of victims' contact with the system is often not under their control, there is evidence that women, nonetheless, find ways to shape the system's response to make it more useful to their particular situation, although the extent

of their control is limited. For example, victims who file for and then withdraw a petition for civil protection order or who refuse to testify in a criminal prosecution against an abuser can be understood as shaping the justice system's response within the narrow available options.

Physical and Behavioral Health Care

A small body of research has developed concerning the evaluation of health care interventions for DV victims, including screening for partner violence, which involves a brief series of questions intended to identify those individuals for whom a more in-depth assessment of partner violence victimization and intervention is recommended. However, screening alone has been shown to be inadequate as a gateway for providing services to all the victims who may require it. DV experiences are also associated with higher health-care utilization.

Greater effort is needed focusing on training sensitive and effective health-care providers to respond to DV. While battered women use health-care services at higher rates, they do not commonly utilize mental health or counseling services, although many DV programs now offer mental health services.

Personal Strategies for Responding to DV

Many strategies used by victims for attempting to avoid further violence and to protect their children often go unrecognized. Ending the relationship often has been used as the central measure of whether women are "doing something" in response to DV. It is clear that even when a woman decides to leave, it occurs in the context of many other responses. More information is needed about the strategies victims use on a day-to-day basis while still in an abusive relationship, including safety planning, seeking help of family and friends, and directly resisting or placating the abuser.

REFERENCES

American Psychiatric Association. (2000). *Diagnostic and statistical manual of mental disorders* (4th ed., text rev.). Washington, DC: Author.

Anda, R. F., Whitfield, C. L., Felitti, V. J., Chapman, D., Edwards, V. J., Dube, S. R., et al. (2002). Adverse childhood experiences, alcoholic parents, and later risks of alcoholism and depression. *Psychiatric Services, 53*(8), 1001–1009.

Bogat, G. A., DeJonghe, E., Levendosky, A. A., Davidson, W. S., & von Eye, A. (2006). Trauma symptoms among infants exposed to intimate partner violence. *Child Abuse and Neglect, 30*(2), 109–125.

Dube, S. R., Anda, R. F., Felitti, V. J., Chapman, D. P., Williamson, D. F., & Giles, W. H. (2001). Childhood abuse, household dysfunction, and the risk of attempted suicide throughout the life span: Findings from the adverse childhood experiences study. *Journal of the American Medical Association, 286*(24), 3089–3096.

Dube, S. R., Anda, R. F., Felitti, V. J., Edwards, V. J., & Williamson, D. F. (2002). Exposure to abuse, neglect and household dysfunction among adults who witnessed intimate partner violence as children: Implications for health and social services. *Violence and Victims, 17*(1), 3–18.

Golding, J. M. (1999). Intimate partner violence as a risk factor for mental disorders: A meta-analysis. *Journal of Family Violence, 14,* 99–132.

Gondolf, E. W. (2002). Service barriers for battered women with male partners in batterer programs. *Journal of Interpersonal Violence, 17*(2), 217–227.

Jarvis, K. L., Gordon, E. E., & Novaco, R. W. (2005). Psychological distress of children and mothers in domestic violence emergency shelters. *Journal of Family Violence, 20*(6), 389–402.

Jones, L., Hughes, M., & Unterstaller, U. (2001). Posttraumatic stress disorder (PTSD) in victims of domestic violence: A review of the research. *Trauma Violence and Abuse, 2*(2), 99–119.

Romito, P., & Grassi, M. (2007). Does violence affect one gender more than the other? The mental health impact of violence among male and female university students. *Social Science and Medicine, 65*(6), 1222–1234.

Saltzman, L. E., Fanslow, J. L., McMahon, P. M., & Shelley, G. A. (1999). *Intimate partner violence surveillance: Uniform definitions and recommended data elements, version 1.* Atlanta, GA: Centers for Disease Control, National Center for Injury Prevention and Control, Division of Violence Prevention.

Sullivan, C. M., & Bybee, D. I. (1999). Reducing violence using community-based advocacy for women with abusive partners. *Journal of Consulting and Clinical Psychology, 67*(1), 43–53.

Tjaden, P., Thoennes, N., & Allison, C. J. (2000). Comparing stalking victimization from legal and victim perspectives. *Violence and Victims, 15*(1), 7–22.

MARY ANN DUTTON
Georgetown University Medical Center

See also: Criminal Victimization; Family Systems; Marital Relationships; Substance Use Disorders; Traumatic Bonding; Women and Trauma

DRUG USE

See: Alcohol Use Disorders; Substance Use Disorders

E

EARLY INTERVENTION

Early intervention for psychological trauma survivors is provided in hopes of preventing development of chronic posttraumatic emotional problems (*see:* **Prevention, Adult; Prevention, Child**). The term *early* has no precise accepted definition but usually refers to a time period ranging from within the first hours and days post-event to a few months later. Possible goals of early intervention efforts include the prevention of posttraumatic mental health disorders (e.g., posttraumatic stress disorder [PTSD], major depressive disorder), reduction of posttraumatic problems generally (e.g., alcohol abuse, work or school problems), and reduction of distress. Early interventions can be offered to all survivors of psychological traumas but are more often targeted at the subgroups of survivors who seek help or are considered at-risk for continuing problems, such as those diagnosed with acute stress disorder (ASD; *see:* **Acute Stress Disorder**).

Overview

Although early interventions have been implemented in some settings for many years, approaches developed to date have received little formal evaluation and the field is in an early stage of development in terms of empirical study. Some interventions have been developed for specific groups of psychological trauma survivors. Military organizations commonly send mental health responders with war zone deployed personnel to offer front-line care; such Combat and Operational Stress Control teams seek to maintain combat capacity and to limit the extent of adverse mental health outcomes among personnel exposed to deployment stressors (Jones & Wessely, 2003). For rape or domestic violence survivors, many communities offer immediate support in the hospital environment when assaulted individuals report for care, via sexual assault response teams, battered women's shelters, and other services. In the United States and many other countries, crisis counseling services are established in the immediate aftermath of large-scale disasters by organizations such as the American Red Cross and the Federal Emergency Management Agency (*see:* **Laws, Legislation, and Policy; Nongovernmental Organizations**), to provide education, support, and referrals for specialized mental health or addiction treatment services for those requiring such assistance.

Critical incident stress debriefing (*see:* **Critical Incident Stress Management**) and other psychological debriefing (PD) variants are the most studied of early interventions and are widely used for those employed in high-risk professions (e.g., police, firefighters, disaster workers) and other recently traumatized populations. Usually delivered within 72 hours of the event, PD is a single-session crisis intervention that includes education to help normalize stress reactions, advice about coping, verbal sharing of experiences, encouragement of mutual support, and provision of information about available services. Most debriefing methods start with a focus on factual information and move toward discussion of feelings associated with potentially traumatic experiences. Randomized controlled trials of the efficacy of PD have indicated that it does not prevent development of PTSD or reduce psychological symptoms (Rose, Bisson, Churchill, & Wessely, 2000) and most of those reviewing the evidence have concluded that PD as an intervention should be applied with caution or that it should not be used.

Psychological first aid (PFA; National Child Traumatic Stress Network and National Center for PTSD [NCTSN & NCPTSD], 2005) was developed to assist psychological trauma survivors within hours and days of their experience, in part as an alternative to PD (*see:* **Psychological First Aid, Adult; Psychological First Aid, Child**). Aimed at reducing initial posttraumatic distress and supporting short- and long-term adaptive functioning, it consists of eight "evidence informed" core actions: contact and engagement, safety and comfort, stabilization, information gathering, practical assistance, connection with social supports, information on coping support, and linkage with collaborative services. PFA has not yet been subjected to formal evaluation.

Cognitive Behavioral Early Interventions

While research has not supported the effectiveness of PD and PFA has yet to be evaluated, cognitive-behavioral early interventions (CBEIs) have been evaluated and found to be effective in preventing PTSD (Ehlers & Clark, 2003). To date, CBEIs have been shown to be superior to a number of control conditions (e.g., supportive counseling, Bryant, Harvey, Dang, Sackville, & Basten, 1998; self-help booklet and assessment-only, Ehlers et al., 2003) with its advantage persisting at long-term follow-up (6 months to 4 years). Often adapted from effective treatments for chronic PTSD, CBEIs usually target only those survivors who are experiencing clinically significant distress (e.g., ASD, acute PTSD, or elevated posttraumatic distress) and have to date been applied with adults from 2 weeks to a few months following exposure to traumatic events.

CBEI usually begins with provision of psychoeducation about common posttraumatic psychological reactions to help normalize these reactions and provide survivors with an understanding of how their reactions developed and are maintained. Psychoeducation also provides

the rationale for how the intervention can help and what it will involve. However, while education may be useful in normalizing traumatic stress reactions and helping psychological trauma survivors who are experiencing more than mild transient problems to seek more intensive services, alone it has not been found to prevent PTSD or other posttraumatic problems. Therefore, education can be seen as a necessary but not sufficient component of early intervention for those at higher risk for problems.

Prior to introducing the more challenging aspects of CBEI (e.g., exposure to trauma memories and reminders; see below), clients are typically taught an anxiety management skill that they can immediately put to use. Such skills range from simple paced breathing (e.g., inhaling and exhaling to a count of three) to more elaborate skills, such as progressive muscle relaxation, which requires several sessions and repeated practice to learn. During anxiety management training, clients learn to rate their distress using a rating scale (e.g., subjective units of distress scale; SUDS) so they and their provider can assess the effectiveness of skill. Distress ratings are an integral ingredient in the subsequent exposure exercises (see the following discussion).

The exposure therapy components of CBEI include both imaginal exposure and *in vivo* exposure. In imaginal exposure, clients recount their memories of traumatic events while fully experiencing their attendant emotional and bodily reactions. To optimize access to and processing of trauma memories, clients describe their traumatic experiences and reactions in the present tense, as if they were currently happening. Often the account is audiotaped and listened to as homework (daily or several times a week). Before, during, and after the imaginal exposure, the therapist gauges the client's distress using the distress rating to ensure that the client is experiencing a progressive reduction in distress related to retelling the trauma memories, both within each session and across all of the CBEI sessions.

In vivo exposure entails having clients generate a list of feared or avoided trauma-related situations. Survivors rate their distress for each situation and items are rank-ordered to create a fear hierarchy. Beginning with the lowest fear-level situations, clients are tasked to confront each situation between sessions until their distress lessens. Clients continue to repeatedly tackle each situation on the hierarchy until all situations no longer produce upsetting levels of distress upon exposure. This process is theorized to bring about extinction (*see:* **Conditioned Fear**) of the conditioned associations that were formed at the time of the traumatic events between trauma-related stimuli and neutral stimuli that were also present. For example, a survivor traumatized in a motor vehicle accident may find that exposure to freeways, traffic lights, or other previously neutral driving cues now produces fear reactions, and that repeated exposure to these cues results in reduced fear.

The final core therapeutic element of most CBEIs is cognitive restructuring. Cognitive restructuring begins with identification of maladaptive beliefs related to the traumatic events, which are posited to play an important role in maintaining posttraumatic distress. Such cognitions include negative beliefs about oneself (e.g., "I'm incompetent because I should have done more to prevent it"), the meaning of traumatic reactions (e.g., "I'm going crazy"), and ability to cope ("I can't handle anything anymore"). Survivors are taught ways to challenge their problematic beliefs (e.g., evaluating evidence, testing to see if an expected outcome occurs). Between sessions, individuals monitor their automatic maladaptive thoughts and generate and practice replacing those thoughts with more helpful thoughts.

Early Intervention with Children and Adolescents

Given the vulnerability of children and adolescents to physical/sexual abuse and neglect, domestic, school, and community violence, and separation/loss of parents/caregivers, early intervention is particularly important in this at-risk group (*see:* **Crisis Intervention, Child**).

Children's traumatic stress reactions may take the form of academic, social, and behavioral problems. Training families, teachers, and other community members to detect these signs soon after a potentially traumatic event (such as the death of a family member or friend in a serious accident or a violent incident) can help to initiate supportive services for affected children without delay. PD interventions are commonly used with younger trauma victims, but there is little evidence that they are effective in reducing later difficulties. PFA and CBEI approaches that are developmentally appropriate for children and adolescents can be delivered to families and school groups; resources for evidence-informed early intervention models can be found through the NCTSN web site (www.nctsnet.org; Kazak, Kassam-Adams, & Schneider, 2006; *see:* **Crisis Intervention, Child**).

Conclusion

Although stress reactions are common following traumatic events, rates of help seeking are relatively low. Emotional and behavioral avoidance, hallmark symptoms of posttraumatic stress reactions, may keep trauma survivors from seeking services, and the stigma of mental health problems and services may be an obstacle to help-seeking. In addition, for some time after a psychological trauma, survivors may be focused on recovering from physical injuries, dealing with practical concerns (e.g., return to work, financial demands, childcare), and attempting to "get back to normal." Distress may in fact remit without intervention for a substantial number of trauma survivors. Given that the initial response by mental health response teams is difficult to sustain over time, services may be less available when trauma survivors eventually do seek help.

Early intervention utilization may be facilitated by providing public education about signs of posttraumatic problems and available resources, screening psychological trauma survivors for evidence of these problems and monitoring those considered at risk, embedding early intervention services in community settings that serve recently traumatized individuals (e.g., hospital emergency departments, rape crisis counseling services), and providing multiple opportunities for entry into care (e.g., via initial screening, telephone follow-up to reassess need for treatment, and provision of contact and referral information through victim assistance and health care settings).

REFERENCES

Bryant, R. A., Harvey, A. G., Dang, S. T., Sackville, T., & Basten, C. (1998). Treatment of acute stress disorder: A comparison of cognitive-behavioral therapy and supportive counseling. *Journal of Consulting and Clinical Psychology, 66,* 862–866.

Ehlers, A., & Clark, D. M. (2003). Early psychological interventions for adult survivors of trauma: A review. *Biological Psychiatry, 53,* 817–826.

Ehlers, A., Clark, D. M., Hackmann, A., McManus, F., Fennell, M., Herbert, C., et al. (2003). A randomized controlled trial of cognitive therapy, a self-help booklet, and repeated assessment as early interventions for posttraumatic stress disorder. *Archives of General Psychiatry, 60,* 1024–1032.

Jones, E., & Wessely, S. (2003). "Forward psychiatry" in the military: Its origins and effectiveness. *Journal of Traumatic Stress, 16,* 411–419.

Kazak, A. E., Kassam-Adams, N., & Schneider, S. (2006). An integrative model of pediatric medical traumatic stress. *Journal of Pediatric Psychology, 31,* 343–355.

National Child Traumatic Stress Network and National Center for PTSD. (2005). *Psychological first aid: Field operations guide* (2nd ed.). Available from http://www.ncptsd.va.gov/pfa/PFA.html.

Rose, S., Bisson, J., Churchill, R., & Wessely, S. (2000). Psychological debriefing for preventing post traumatic stress disorder (PTSD). *Cochrane Database of Systematic Reviews, Issue 1.* Art. No: CD000560. DOI: 10.1002/14651858.CD000560.

RECOMMENDED READING

Litz, B. T. (2004). *Early intervention for trauma and traumatic loss.* New York: Guilford Press.

JOSEF I. RUZEK
National Center for Posttraumatic Stress Disorder

ERIC KUHN
Veterans Affairs Palo Alto Health Care System

MATTHEW J. CORDOVA
Veterans Affairs Palo Alto Health Care System

See also: Acute Stress Disorder; Anxiety Management Training; Crisis Intervention, Adult; Crisis Intervention, Child; Critical Incident Stress Management; Prevention, Adult; Prevention, Child; Psychological First Aid, Adult; Psychological First Aid, Child

EATING DISORDERS

Eating disorders, which include anorexia nervosa (AN), bulimia nervosa (BN), binge eating disorder (BED), and eating disorder not otherwise specified (EDNOS), are broadly characterized by disturbed eating behavior, dysfunctional attitudes regarding body weight and shape, and maladaptive efforts to modify body weight. The hallmark of anorexia is refusal to maintain healthy body weight, whereas bulimia is characterized by frequent episodes of binge eating accompanied by maladaptive compensatory behaviors, such as vomiting, laxative misuse, and excessive exercise. The core pathology of these eating disorders includes overvaluation of weight and shape. Binge eating disorder, a variant of EDNOS, consists of binge eating episodes without the compensatory behaviors found with bulimia. EDNOS encompasses other clinically significant disturbances of eating behavior, attitudes, and weight that fall short of the criteria for anorexia or bulimia (e.g., overvaluation of weight and daily vomiting in the absence of binging or significant weight loss). EDNOS often is as severe as other eating disorders and is the most commonly diagnosed eating disorder in clinical practice. Specific diagnostic criteria for subtypes other than BED, however, have yet to be delineated.

Research indicates that traumatic event exposure is a nonspecific risk factor for the development of eating disorders. Trauma has been found to be more closely associated with bulimia than with restricting anorexia. The frequency, but not severity, of traumatic experiences increases the risk of developing an eating disorder. Available data also suggest that having a posttraumatic stress disorder (PTSD) diagnosis is associated with greater risk for onset of eating disorders, particularly bulimia, compared to a history of trauma without a PTSD diagnosis (see Brewerton, 2004, for additional discussion).

To date, treatment research has not determined whether having a trauma history or comorbid diagnosis of PTSD complicates recovery from an eating disorder. Clinically, however, it is generally recognized that patients who present with comorbid diagnoses of PTSD and an eating disorder present a challenge for therapists. Concerns about medical complications associated with eating disorders dissuade some clinicians from embarking on treatment for PTSD. Yet, because an eating disorder often functions as an avoidance coping strategy for managing the emotional sequelae of traumatic events, failure to address PTSD can hinder eating disorder recovery. Clinicians also may find it challenging to chart a consistent course of treatment as eating disorders often worsen during treatment of PTSD and vice versa. One option for managing complicated patients who present with both an eating disorder and PTSD is to adopt a flexible evidence-based case formulation approach to guide treatment (see Zayfert & Becker, 2007).

REFERENCES

Brewerton, T. D. (Ed.). (2004). *Clinical handbook of eating disorders: An integrated approach.* New York: Marcel Dekker.

Zayfert, C., & Becker, C. B. (2007). *Cognitive behavioral therapy for PTSD: A case formulation approach.* New York: Guilford Press.

CAROLYN BLACK BECKER
Trinity University

CLAUDIA ZAYFERT
National Center for Posttraumatic Stress Disorder

See also: Comorbidity

EEG (ELECTROENCEPHALOGRAPHY)

See: Biology, Brain Structure, and Function, Adult; Biology, Brain Structure, and Function, Child

EMERGENCY CARE SYSTEMS

Emergency care systems (ECS) are comprehensive, integrated, multidisciplinary action plan structures designed by federal and local governmental organizations for the purpose of improving the delivery of public and private human services in response to an emergency such as terrorist incidents, natural disaster, or mass casualty accidents. The goal of an ECS is to mitigate the short- and long-term physical and psychological problems (morbidity) caused by emergencies. This includes creating a state of general preparedness and community resilience before emergency events, reducing people's exposure to psychological trauma and physical harm during an emergency event, and facilitating recovery (i.e., the regaining of the level of adjustment that existed before the emergency) of affected communities, organizations, and individual people and families. An ECS also is responsible for making sure that the resources required to respond to an emergency are distributed in an effective and fair manner, so that no individual or institution is forced to bear more than their share of the burden of responding to an emergency.

When effective, emergency care systems help people and communities to be as safe as possible during emergency events and to recover in the aftermath. In a larger sense, an ECS also stabilizes the social matrix, preventing the systemic fragmentation that is otherwise likely to happen during and after traumatic emergencies (Laor, Wiener, Spirman, & Wolmer, 2005).

Use of Resources

No system under severe stress can be selfsufficient, and it must therefore rely on extrinsic human resources and supplies to recover from emergency events. There are two general orientations to the use of outside assistance in ECSs. The classical medical or dependentsupportive model creates an external support structure that provides aid and skilled professionals to communities experiencing upheaval. This paradigm relies, almost exclusively, on human services and resources received from external sources that function within the emergency area. Consequently, the daily presence of this type of ECS, in terms of local emergency preparedness activity, is noticeable only in times of emergency. A prominent example of this model is the deployment of Red Cross or Red Crescent volunteer teams to disaster sites, or disaster medical assistance teams (DMATs), which are self-contained units organized by the U.S. government that include professionals with the necessary training and readily transportable supplies.

On the other hand, the systemic-ecological or empowered-integrating emergency care system creates a meta-organization over a pre-existing infrastructure that provides relief to a population within a familiar econiche. This paradigm takes advantage of the community's care-providers, organizations, and heuristics to deliver services, treatment, and goods. Central to this model is the use of empowered mediators: local nonclinical professionals who, during emergencies, can provide aid under the supervision of specialists (Laor et al., 2005; Pynoos, Goenjian, & Steinberg, 1995). Moreover, these ECSs use a bimodal design that transforms from a *routine mode* to an *emergency mode* as circumstances necessitate. An example of this model was employed after the recent military action in the north of Israel when schools became *social reactivation centers,* sites where individuals received psychological and educational services. This approach can help to facilitate the transition from the pre- to the post-emergency state more effectively by restoring infrastructure organically throughout the process of rebuilding. According to this model, schools are utilized as primary sites for child and adolescent health and psychological screening, treatment, parental education, and for the distribution of water, food, and basic domestic needs (Laor et al., 2005).

These two approaches were created to complement each other and to solve systemic problems with ECSs identified during previous emergencies. These problems include unclear, uncoordinated, conflicting or cumbersome command structures, faulty interorganizational communication, information systems breakdown, unrealistic or unclear planning, poor resource management, lack of foresight for extended recovery needs, poor community motivation, or lack of ability to seek care during and following an event, incorrect or unclear information from internal sources and the media and self-dispatched agencies that are disconnected from the ECS (U.S. House of Representatives, 2006).

A clear although unfortunate example of these post-disaster emergency care system breakdowns occurred in the aftermath of Hurricane Katrina in New Orleans and the Gulf Coast. The dislocation of thousands of families, devastation to the social, economic, and health infrastructure (as well as the thousands of unreclaimed homes and business sites), and the psychological trauma experienced during and following the hurricane, demonstrates the importance of having an effective ECS before and long after emergency events.

Phased Response

The theoretical framework of ECSs describes four distinct phases of emergencies and seeks to identify the most important services to be provided at each point: (1) pre-incident, (2) event, (3) initial response, and (4) resolution (Laor et al., 2005). In the *pre-incident phase,* the main goal of the ECS is to create a state of preparedness in anticipation of an event. This includes the clarification of institutional and individual roles, the creation and teaching of organization specific emergency response procedures, templates, or flowcharts, the administration of continuing educational series for care providers, the implementation of resilience training for the population as a whole, and the maintenance of the response system to ensure quick and seamless execution of the ECS plan if an emergency occurs. For example, in preparation for the second war in Iraq, a Resilience Week was implemented in six neighborhoods in Tel-Aviv, in which citizens learned first aid skills, principles of home protection, family resilience methods, and stress management techniques.

In the *event phase,* the goals of the ECS are to provide emergency services (including medical and psychological evaluations), to reduce actual or risk of exposure (e.g., evacuation, vaccination, quarantine), to partner with internal and external resources (e.g., hospitals, DMATS, schools, law enforcement), to increase a general sense of safety, and to perform initial screening to identify those most affected by the disruption or who are at risk for developing psychopathology due to previous exposures and vulnerability factors (O'Donnell, Bryant, Creamer, & Carty, 2008; Reyes, Miller, Schreiber, & Todd-Bazemore, 2005). For example, minutes after emergency forces clear the scene of a terrorist attack, the Tel-Aviv ECS deploys, as routine protocol, a multidisciplinary site intervention unit (SIU) responsible for screening children and adults living in the vicinity of the emergency event. The screening includes (a) an estimate of an individual's psychological risk and protective factors, (b) an assessment of an individual's initial response and self-identified need for assistance, and (c) a preliminary professional evaluation. An algorithm allows teams to decide whether to refer the victim for psychological assistance, to schedule a follow-up evaluation for the individual over the following week, or to merely provide a brochure with psychoeducational material and information concerning referral.

During the *initial response phase,* the goal of the ECS is to return basic services to those affected by the emergency. This includes the provision of food, water, temporary housing, health care, psychological support, child care, public education about the effects of the exposure (psychological and physical), and ways to minimize harm and maximize recovery, and community-wide reassurance about safety. Interventions for traumatic stress in this phase tend to take the form of brief generalized media messages or educational programs designed to reach as many exposed individuals as possible in an attempt to relieve acute stress and prevent future post-traumatic morbidity. The locus of these interventions can be at the level of DMATs, medical (e.g., emergency departments), mental health, and community centers, as well as local and national media providers and local chains of informal communication.

The *resolution phase* often occupies an extended period of time following the restoration of the community's infrastructure and during which life begins to function more normally. On both the individual and community levels, this stage is punctuated with memories of the recent disruption and can be a time where, after the acute stress of the event diminishes, previously subclinical trauma-induced stress reactions, problematic coping attempts (e.g., increased use of alcohol), and psychopathology may emerge. The goal in this stage is to provide social and psychological support to communities and individuals as they attempt to return to normalcy. This may include follow-up from earlier screening efforts, referral to social or psychological services on a more individual basis for psychological relief, resilience education, and economic support. Whereas the ECS plan in earlier stages focused on the community as a whole, interventions in this phase focus on the needs of individuals who did not improve from earlier, generalized interventions. Longer-term ECS interventions are likely to be delivered through mental health clinics, field stations (e.g., schools), and traumatic stress treatment centers. A successful negotiation of these four stages by the ECS will facilitate a community's recovery to a new preparatory phase with a well-functioning and more resilient population.

Spheres of Authority

Emergency care systems seek to clearly define and maintain roles and hierarchies to decrease confusion, improve efficacy, and increase cost-effectiveness. As such, an ECS identifies several organizational spheres, each with a specific function within the context of an event: (a) federal and local governmental agencies such as the police, fire, public health departments and the military; (b) primary, secondary, and tertiary health-care centers and mental health professionals; (c) schools; (d) social welfare organizations; and (e) the media. Using the temporal model outlined here, each sphere within the ECS must have a clearly defined role at each phase of the event to prevent the conflicting interests of individual groups from impeding the overall improvement of the community. In addition, a clear chain of command must be established to coordinate and regulate each group during the implementation of the ECS plan.

Special Considerations

Different types of emergencies require different ECS responses. For example, unlike the effects of a hurricane, a limited terrorist attack generally leaves a community's social and economic infrastructure intact even though it may still affect a large number of people. Moreover, special groups (e.g., children and elderly, disabled, infirm, and indigent populations) require specifically tailored plans to address their distinctive needs (Reyes et al., 2005). Thus, an ECS needs to actively engage in outreach to these groups and to the larger community in order to ensure that the needs of those affected by an emergency are truly served.

REFERENCES

Laor, N., Wiener, Z., Spirman, S., & Wolmer, L. (2005). Community mental health in emergencies and mass disasters: The Tel Aviv model. In Y. Danieli, D. Brom, & J. Sills (Eds.), *The trauma of terrorism: Sharing knowledge and shared care, an international handbook* (pp. 681–694). New York: Haworth Maltreatment & Trauma Press.

O'Donnell, M. L., Bryant, R. A., Creamer, M., & Carty, J. (2008). Mental health following traumatic injury: Toward a health system model of early psychological intervention. *Clinical Psychology Review, 28* (3), 387–406.

Pynoos, R. S., Goenjian, A. K., & Steinberg, A. M. (1995). Strategies of disaster intervention for children and adolescents. In S. E. Hobfoll & M. W. De Vries (Eds.), *Extreme stress and communities: Impact and intervention* (pp. 445–471). Dordrecht, The Netherlands: Kluwer Academic.

Reyes, G., Miller, T. T., Schreiber, M. D., & Todd-Bazemore, B. (2005). Children's services in disasters and other emergencies. In R. G. Steele & M. C. Roberts (Eds.), *Handbook of mental health services for children, adolescents, and families* (pp. 333–350). New York: Kluwer Academic.

United States House of Representatives. (2006). *A failure of initiative: Final report of the select bipartisan committee to investigate the preparation for and the response to Hurricane Katrina.* Retrieved October 17, 2007, from www.gpoaccess.gov/katrinareport/mainreport.pdf.

NATHANIEL LAOR
Tel Aviv University

LEO WOLMER
Tel Aviv University

BENJAMIN BREGMAN
Tel Aviv University

See also: Crisis Intervention, Adult; Crisis Intervention, Child; Disasters; Emergency Personnel; Public Health; Terrorism

EMERGENCY PERSONNEL

Emergency personnel is a broad and diverse category that may include firefighters, police, paramedics, search and rescue teams, nurses, doctors, and ancillary hospital staff. These personnel are likely to experience a broad range of psychological and physical responses as a result of work-related exposures to both man-made and natural disasters (Benedek, Fullerton, & Ursano, 2007). The adverse emotional consequences experienced by emergency personnel negatively affect their health and may impair their ability to effectively respond during large-scale emergencies.

The range and severity of physical and psychological consequences of traumatic events for emergency personnel are dependent on a multitude of intersecting factors such as the biological and genetic make-up of the individual, the social context of the event, particular characteristics of the event (e.g., the cause, intensity, and duration of exposure), previous traumatic experiences, training, and the psychosocial support available in the aftermath (Benedek et al., 2007). The majority of emergency workers experience transient distress such as sleep and concentration disturbances, increased alcohol and substance use, physical aches and pains, and increased fear, worry, anger or sadness (Institute of Medicine, 2003). Some emergency personnel may experience more persistent symptoms that interfere with interpersonal relations at work, home, and with friends, but that do not constitute a disease or disorder requiring treatment. In addition, a smaller group of emergency personnel may experience episodes of a recurrent or new mental illness such as major depressive disorder, acute stress disorder (ASD) and posttraumatic stress disorder (PTSD), and/or alcohol or other substance use disorders (Institute of Medicine, 2003).

Many studies use a retrospective design to assess psychological distress related to a disaster, asking emergency personnel to recall and describe their experiences and psychological reactions after the fact. However, the results of those studies are limited by the inevitable inaccuracies in respondents' memories. Most of these studies do not include a control group of emergency personnel who did not respond to the disaster, thus further limiting the certainty that results were specifically related to the personnel's traumatic disaster experiences.

A more scientifically rigorous research design was used by Fullerton, Ursano, and Wang (2004), who performed a large-scale longitudinal, prospective study of disaster workers (firefighters, police officers, and EMTs) before and after their response to an airplane crash and explosion that resulted in 112 deaths and 59 injuries. They found that, when compared to nonexposed workers, disaster-exposed workers had a significantly higher rate of ASD in the immediate aftermath, PTSD after 13 months, and depression at both 7 and 13 months following the crash. In addition, the personnel who developed ASD had a 7 times higher likelihood of developing PTSD than disaster-exposed personnel who did not have ASD in the acute aftermath of the disaster. Furthermore, 40% of the exposed disaster workers met criteria for at least one diagnosis (ASD, PTSD, or depression; Fullerton et al., 2004).

Other studies have reported PTSD rates between 7% and 19% in disaster or crisis-exposed police officers and 13% to 18% in disaster exposed firefighters. These estimated incidence levels of PTSD are 5 to 10 times higher than those reported in surveys of recent (e.g., past year) PTSD in general community samples. Thus, although emergency personnel are highly trained and generally very resilient, their exposure to highly traumatic events (e.g., gruesome injuries and deaths, extreme life-threatening danger to themselves, loss of close friends and coworkers) places them at risk for developing serious psychosocial problems in the aftermath of traumatic incidents (ASD) and in the months and years afterward.

All stages of disaster planning must incorporate mental health interventions for emergency personnel in order to address these psychological effects associated with disaster response work. Population-based interventions such as effective public education and preparedness training for emergency personnel may reduce later psychological symptoms (Benedek et al., 2007). Expert panelists have recommended psychological first aid (PFA) as an alternative to the previously widely practiced intervention of critical incident stress debriefing. PFA focuses on establishing a sense of safety, facilitating social connectedness, decreasing arousal by teaching and encouraging relaxation and calming skills, fostering optimism, and restoring a sense of efficacy (Center for the Study of Traumatic Stress, 2005). Critical incident needs assessment teams (CINAT) can implement PFA in the emergency responders' workplace and provide triage, education, support, identification of high risk individuals, grief leadership training and referral for individuals who need further treatment (Hamaoka, Grieger, Benedek, & Ursano, 2007). Further research is required to assess the effectiveness of the newer models of preparedness training, PFA, and CINAT in these highly exposed populations.

REFERENCES

Benedek, D. M., Fullerton, C. S., & Ursano, R. J. (2007). First responders: Mental health consequences of natural and human-made disasters for public health and public safety workers. *Annual Review of Public Health, 28,* 55–68.

Center for the Study of Traumatic Stress. (2005). *Psychological first aid: How you can support well-being in disaster victims.* Retrieved April 22, 2008, from www.centerforthestudyoftraumatic stress.org/downloads/CSTS_Psych1stAid.pdf.

Fullerton, C. S., Ursano, R. J., & Wang L. (2004). Acute stress disorder, posttraumatic stress disorder, and depression in disaster or rescue workers. *American Journal of Psychiatry, 161,* 1370–1376.

Hamaoka, D. A, Grieger, T. A., Benedek, D. M., & Ursano, R. J. (2007). Crisis intervention. In G. Fink (Ed.), *Encyclopedia of stress* (pp. 662–667). Oxford, England: Academic Press.

Institute of Medicine. (2003). *Preparing for the psychological consequences of terrorism: A public health strategy.* Washington, DC: National Academic Press.

HEATHER SHIBLEY
Medical University of South Carolina

DAVID M. BENEDEK
Uniformed Services University of the Health Sciences

ROBERT J. URSANO
Uniformed Services University of the Health Sciences

See also: Disasters; Emergency Care Systems; Psychological First Aid, Adult; Psychological First Aid, Child; Terrorism

EMOTIONAL ABUSE

All forms of childhood maltreatment can be expected to include some degree of emotional impact on the child. Yet in some categories of maltreatment, such as sexual and physical abuse, the reprehensible actions inflicted on the child are so salient that the emotional effects often are seen as secondary to the immoral and often life-threatening or illegal violations inflicted by these abuses. However, inflicting grievous and lasting emotional harm on a child is possible without ever touching the child and without engaging in acts that clearly violate moral principles or legal statutes. Acts of omission or commission that are likely to create lasting emotional and psychological impairment without presenting a physical threat (e.g., verbally abusive behavior) have been categorized by the term *emotional abuse.*

Emotional abuse is less widely accepted as a form of potential psychological trauma than other forms of child abuse (e.g., sexual or physical abuse). Emotional abuse also has been referred to by a multiplicity of names (e.g., emotional maltreatment, psychological abuse, and psychological battering). Disagreement exists among clinicians, researchers, advocacy groups, and legal experts on how emotional abuse should be conceptualized and defined. Parental behaviors toward children such as rejecting, isolating, terrorizing, corrupting, verbally abusing, and over-pressuring have been emphasized as potential forms of emotional abuse by mental health professionals. In contrast, harm and endangerment standards have been espoused as the basis for defining emotional abuse by child advocates (National Clearinghouse on Child Abuse and Neglect Information, 1994). Although a federal definition of emotional abuse is provided by the U.S. Keeping Children and Families Safe Act of 2003 (CAPTA 1974, 2003), the responsibility for defining emotional abuse has fallen on state legislatures (Hamarman, Pope, & Czaja, 2002).

Emotional abuse appears to be a prevalent form of childhood maltreatment. The Third National Incidence Study of Child Abuse and Neglect (Sedlak, Hantman, & Schultz, 1997) found that 3.0 per 1,000 children were identified as being emotionally abused, based on the harm standard definition. This study included not only children who were investigated by child protective service (CPS) agencies, but also children seen by community professionals who were not reported to CPS or who were screened out by CPS without investigation. Yearly incidence data from the 2005 National Child Abuse and Neglect Data System (NCANDS; U.S. Department of Health and Human Services, 2007) indicate that 7.1% of substantiated cases of abuse by state CPS were victims of emotional abuse, which extrapolates to 63,497 children nationwide (U.S. Department of Health and Human Services, 2007). Although rates of emotional abuse appear to vary across states even more so than rates of physical and sexual abuse (Hamarman et al., 2002), the mean number of children exposed to emotional abuse in the United States during federal FY 2005 was 8.7 per 10,000 children. This estimate reflects children identified solely through state CPS and is a conservative one because the NCANDS definition of emotional abuse targets the effects on the child rather than the behaviors of the parents (Hamarman et al., 2002).

The incidence and prevalence of two specific forms of emotional abuse—namely, witnessing domestic violence (DV) and exposure to verbal abuse/aggression (VA)—further illustrate the scope of such abuse on children. Holden and colleagues (Holden et al., 1998) extrapolated that each year more than 17.8 million U.S. children witness physical aggression between their parents. Over 40% of households where DV occurs contain children under 12 years old (Rennison & Welchans, 2000). In addition, 63% of U.S. parents report swearing at or insulting their children (Vissing, Straus, & Gelles, 1991), although the children exposed to frequent verbally abusive acts by their parents were the ones especially prone to exhibit behavior problems such as physical aggression, delinquency, and interpersonal difficulties. Thus, even in the absence of other forms of emotion-related maltreatment (e.g., sibling abuse, bullying in schools, Internet bullying), epidemiological evidence to date suggests that persistent exposure to emotional abuse profoundly affects large numbers of children. Emotional abuse almost always occurs in the context of the ongoing relationship between a primary caregiver and the child rather than demarked by a discrete event or a series of distinct events. Therefore, consensus is emerging that emotional abuse ought to be defined by emphasizing the adverse parenting behaviors, not the psychological consequences experienced by the child. Cultural variations and contextual factors also need to be considered that may influence both the definition and perception of emotional abuse and the adverse effects that emotional abuse has both during childhood and on adults who experienced emotional abuse in childhood (Malley-Morrison, 2004).

Empirical studies provide strong evidence linking emotional abuse to various emotional and behavioral problems as well as psychiatric conditions. Children who are exposed to frequent VA show high rates of physical aggression, delinquency, and interpersonal difficulties (Vissing et al., 1991). Maternal VA during childhood—defined as reports of screaming plus belittling remarks (or multiple threats of physical punishment) in the past month—has been associated with a markedly higher risk for the development of borderline, narcissistic, obsessive-compulsive, and paranoid personality disorders, even after controlling for temperament, physical abuse, sexual abuse, neglect, parental psychopathology, and co-occurring psychiatric disorders (Johnson et al., 2001). Childhood exposure to parental VA is also related to symptoms of dissociation, limbic (emotional) irritability, depression, and anger-hostility among 18- to 22-year-old adults (Teicher, Samson, Polcari, & McGreenery, 2006), as well as to eating disorders in adolescence and adulthood (Mazzeo & Espelage, 2002).

Witnessing DV is associated to similar degrees with internalizing (such as anxiety, depression, and dissociation) and externalizing (such as anger outbursts and impulsivity) problems, as well as social and academic difficulties (Kitzmann, Gaylord, Holt, & Kenny, 2003). Combined exposure to VA and witnessing DV is related to prominent adverse effects, particularly dissociation (Teicher et al., 2006), although witnessing DV plus being physically abused does not seem to lead to worse outcomes compared to witnessing DV alone (Kitzmann et al., 2003). The development of insecure attachment styles, negative beliefs about the self and relationships, viewing oneself as low in competence, poorer social functioning and coping strategies, as well as poor self-esteem have all been linked to a history of childhood emotional abuse (Crittenden, 1992; Toth & Cicchetti, 1996).

The high rates of exposure to multiple types of child abuse as well as community violence complicate studying emotional abuse. The unique, additive, and/or synergistic effects of exposure to multiple types of abuse need to be ascertained (Teicher et al., 2006). Generally, a dose-response relationship exists whereby: (a) a certain minimal number of exposures is necessary for the development of an adverse outcome such as persistent internalizing or externalizing disorders; and (b) the greater the number of forms of abuse experienced, the more severe the subsequent problems and the greater the amount of utilization of mental health care (Caspi et al., 2003; Edwards, Holden, Felitti, & Anda, 2003; Teicher et al., 2006). The potential effects of emotional abuse, by itself and in combination with other forms of abuse, call for paying careful attention to various forms of stressful experiences (traumatic and nontraumatic) that a child might be exposed to at home, school, and community as well as on the Internet.

The need for studies on the neurobiological consequences of exposure to emotional abuse has recently been underscored (Prinz & Feerick, 2003). Children exposed to different types of abuse are likely to have experienced them at different developmental stages as well as disparate periods of brain maturation. Emotional abuse has been hypothesized as a unique stressor that negatively impacts neurodevelopment of certain susceptible brain regions during sensitive "windows of vulnerability" in at-risk individuals, which results in emotional and/or behavioral problems (Teicher et al., 2003). Preliminary evidence of elevated salivary cortisol levels in children exposed to DV provides initial support for this hypothesis (Saltzman, Holden, & Holahan, 2005).

In summary, although the scientific and clinical literature on emotional abuse are less well developed than those on other forms of childhood abuse and other potentially traumatic experiences, emotional abuse appears to be both prevalent and (in its most severe forms) potentially psychologically traumatic. Future research and clinical studies are needed to better define exactly what constitutes emotional abuse, including a better differentiation between stressful or conflictual family relationships and actual emotional abuse. Precisely delineating emotionally abusive behaviors of parents versus their psychological effects on children is paramount to such efforts. In addition, the determination of emotional abuse as a traumatic event needs to be formulated. Although witnessing DV can qualify as a criterion A1 traumatic event necessary for the

DSM-IV-TR diagnosis of PTSD, exposure to VA cannot qualify because this subtype of emotional abuse does not include "an event or events that involve actual or threatened death or serious injury, or a threat to the physical integrity of oneself or others." However, the premise has recently been raised that VA during childhood that constitutes a threat to *mental* integrity and sense of self also may be traumatizing (Teicher et al., 2006). Last, investigations need to be conducted on (a) how emotional abuse negatively impacts neurobehavioral development; (b) the sequelae of abuse in childhood and adulthood that are linked specifically to emotional abuse; and (c) potential distinct or adapted therapies to mitigate the emotional and behavioral outcomes of emotional abuse.

REFERENCES

Caspi, A., Sugden, K., Moffitt, T. E., Taylor, A., Craig, I. W., Harrington, H., et al. (2003). Influence of life stress on depression: Moderation by a polymorphism in the 5-HTT gene. *Science, 301*(5631), 386–389.

Child Abuse Prevention and Treatment Act of 1974, Pub. L. No. 93-247, § 88, Stat 4, codified as amended by Keeping Children and Families Safe Act of 2003, Pub. L. No. 108-36, § 1(a), 117 Stat 800 (2003).

Crittenden, P. M. (1992). Children's strategies for coping with adverse home environments: An interpretation using attachment theory. *Child Abuse and Neglect, 16*(3), 329–343.

Edwards, V. J., Holden, G. W., Felitti, V. J., & Anda, R. F. (2003). Relationship between multiple forms of childhood maltreatment and adult mental health in community respondents: Results from the Adverse Childhood Experiences Study. *American Journal of Psychiatry, 160*(8), 1453–1460.

Hamarman, S., Pope, K. H., & Czaja, S. J. (2002). Emotional abuse in children: Variations in legal definitions and rates across the United States. *Childhood Maltreatment, 7*(4), 303–311.

Holden, G. W., Geffner, R., Jouriles, E. N., (1998). Appraisal and outlook. In G. W. Holden, R. Geffner, & E. N. Jouriles (Eds.), *Children exposed to marital violence: Theory, research, and applied issues* (pp. 409–421). Washington, DC: American Psychological Association.

Johnson, J. G., Cohen, P., Smailes, E. M., Skodol, A. E., Brown, J., & Oldham, J. M. (2001). Childhood verbal abuse and risk for personality disorders during adolescence and early adulthood. *Comprehensive Psychiatry, 42*(1), 16–23.

Kitzmann, K. M., Gaylord, N. K., Holt, A. R., & Kenny, E. D. (2003). Child witnesses to domestic violence: A meta-analytic review. *Journal of Consulting and Clinical Psychology, 71*(2), 339–352.

Malley-Morrison, K. (Ed.). (2004). *International perspectives on family violence and abuse: A cognitive ecological approach.* Mahwah, NJ: Erlbaum.

Mazzeo, S. E., & Espelage, D. L. (2002). Association between childhood physical and emotional abuse and disordered eating behaviors in female undergraduates: An investigation of the mediating role of alexithymia and depression. *Journal of Counseling Psychology, 49*(1), 86–100.

National Clearinghouse on Child Abuse and Neglect Information. (1994). *Treatment for abused and neglected children: Infancy to age 18.* Washington, DC: Administration for Children and Families, U.S. Department of Health and Human Services.

Prinz, R. J., & Feerick, M. M. (2003). Next steps in research on children exposed to domestic violence. *Clinical Child and Family Psychology Review, 6*(3), 215–219.

Rennison, C. M., & Welchans, S. (2000). *Intimate partner violence: Bureau of Justice Statistics special report.* Washington, DC: U.S. Department of Justice.

Saltzman, K. M., Holden, G. W., & Holahan, C. J. (2005). The psychobiology of children exposed to marital violence. *Journal of Clinical Child and Adolescent Psychology, 34*(1), 129–139.

Sedlak, A. J., Hantman, I., & Schultz, D. (1997). *Third National Incidence Study of Child Abuse and Neglect (NIS-3) Public Use Manual.* United States Department of Health and Human Services. Washington, DC.

Teicher, M. H., Andersen, S. L., Polcari, A., Anderson, C. M., Navalta, C. P., & Kim, D. M. (2003). The neurobiological consequences of early stress and childhood maltreatment. *Neuroscience and Biobehavioral Reviews, 27*(1/2), 33–44.

Teicher, M. H., Samson, J. A., Polcari, A., & McGreenery, C. E. (2006). Sticks, stones, and hurtful words: Relative effects of various forms of childhood maltreatment. *American Journal of Psychiatry, 163*(6), 993–1000.

Toth, S. L., & Cicchetti, D. (1996). Patterns of relatedness, depressive symptomatology, and perceived competence in maltreated children. *Journal of Consulting and Clinical Psychology, 64*(1), 32–41.

U.S. Department of Health and Human Services, Administration of Children, Youth and Families. (2007). *Child Maltreatment 2005.* Washington, DC: U.S. Government Printing Office.

Vissing, Y. M., Straus, M. A., & Gelles, R. J. (1991). Verbal aggression by parents and psychosocial problems of children. *Child Abuse and Neglect, 15*(3), 223–238.

RECOMMENDED READINGS

Hart, S. N., Brassard, M. R., & Binggeli, N. J. (2002). Psychological maltreatment. In J. E. B. Myers, L. Berliner, J. Briere, C. T. Hendrix, & C. Jenny (Eds.), *The APSAC handbook on child maltreatment* (2nd ed., pp. 79–103). Thousand Oaks, CA: Sage.

Kaplan, S. J., Pelcovitz, D., & Labruna, V. (1999). Child and adolescent abuse and neglect research: A review of the past 10 years—Pt. I. Physical and emotional abuse and neglect. *Journal of the American Academy of Child and Adolescent Psychiatry, 38*(10), 1214–1222.

CARRYL P. NAVALTA
Harvard Medical School

MAJED ASHY
Harvard Medical School

MARTIN H. TEICHER
Harvard Medical School

See also: Abuse, Child Physical; Abuse, Child Sexual; Child Maltreatment; Domestic Violence

EMOTIONAL NUMBING

Many people with posttraumatic stress disorder (PTSD) report a compromised ability to experience and express emotions, a phenomenon called *emotional numbing* (EN). Formally, a cluster of three sets of disturbances and problems comprise EN in the current nosology for PTSD in *DSM-IV:* (a) markedly diminished interest in significant activities; (b) feelings of detachment or estrangement from others; and (c) restricted range of affect. Although these three symptoms are listed under the Cluster C category in the *DSM-IV* (i.e., "Persistent avoidance of stimuli associated with the trauma and numbing of general responsiveness"), together with two symptoms representing effortful attempts to avoid trauma-related cues and experiences related to the trauma, recent studies suggest that the EN cluster is a unique facet of PTSD. The two remaining symptoms listed under the Cluster C category are "difficulty recalling aspects of the trauma" and "feeling as if one's future will be cut short." These symptoms are sometimes grouped together into the EN cluster in research studies; however, they do not fit well into any conceptual or operational definition of emotional disturbances implicated by exposure to trauma.

Interest in EN has been growing in research, due in part to its impact on functioning and quality of life. Reports of EN are associated with considerable psychosocial functioning problems, including relationship distress, reduced participation in recreational activities, and difficulty meeting work, school, or homemaking responsibilities. Nevertheless, EN is under-researched and remains one of the least understood aspects of PTSD. For example, it is not known whether EN is global, or constrained to specific emotions or domains of emotional responding (i.e., subjective, physiological, behavioral). Further, the *DSM* criteria do not specify whether EN is generalized across contexts or occurs only in response to certain states or situations, or whether the emotional deficits relate to disruption of attention to emotional stimuli or the subsequent experience of emotion.

One issue that has yet to be sufficiently acknowledged or researched is the possibility that the EN construct is not specific to PTSD, but is rather a symptom of comorbid disorders, such as depression or substance abuse. This view is partially confirmed by the high degree of content overlap and correlations between EN symptoms and these disorders.

Another important question is whether the "range of affect" in PTSD is "restricted" as the *DSM-IV* suggests. Without question, people with PTSD often report experiencing more negative affect and less positive affect, which might suggest a restriction in affect *valence;* they also report lower arousal in response to positive cues, although most individuals with depression endorse this pattern, too. Yet, patients with PTSD also endorse a greater intensity of negative affect and *greater arousal* in response to traumatic cues and other unpleasant stimuli. Therefore, on its face, a global restricted affect interpretation is invalid. In addition, there is accumulating empirical evidence that disputes the restricted affect model. Various studies have failed to demonstrate significant differences in self-reported positive affectivity between people with and without PTSD, whereas others have found significant PTSD-related differences in subjective reports of emotional responding only when traumatized individuals are exposed to reminders of their trauma.

Research clarifying the nature of affective deficits will need to contend with the discrepancy between subjective reports of emotional responding in PTSD and levels of emotional numbing measured by other methods. Although individuals with PTSD report alterations in affect and arousal, individuals with and without PTSD have been indistinguishable physiologically. One study of facial expressivity using electromyography (EMG), which can detect physiological impulses below the visually discernible threshold, found diminished zygomatic (i.e., smiling) responses in people with PTSD, but only after they were exposed to cues related to their trauma.

Psychological Models

The conditioning model of EN suggests a link between chronic avoidance of trauma-related cues and trauma-cued emotional experiences on one hand and EN. Effortful strategies for avoiding the situations and cues that trigger trauma-related intrusive thoughts may fail as intrusions become more frequent, making confrontation with stressors inevitable. The conditioning model posits that the affective system needs to "shut down" as a final recourse against experiencing overwhelming distress. A related model views EN as a consequence of the depletion of emotional resources due to chronic hyperarousal. This resource-depletion model derives its support from evidence that trauma-related hyperarousal symptoms strongly predict elevated levels of EN.

Information-processing models characterize EN as a phasic, context-dependent response triggered by intrusive thoughts and emotions related to the trauma. In these models, cues reminiscent of the trauma trigger a network of trauma-related responses. Such responses can include physiological arousal and negative affective states, defensive/avoidance behaviors, and emotions, thoughts, or interpretations related to the traumatic event. While these responses are natural and may be protective during traumatic events themselves, they tend to be maladaptive in normal, nonthreatening situations, because they render brain networks related to healthy responses (e.g., positive emotion, approach behaviors) less available. According to this model, the overall capacity to experience and express emotions is fundamentally unaltered in PTSD; the repertoire of emotional experience and expression becomes narrowed only in trauma-related contexts.

Neurobiology

The neurobiological mechanisms of EN are not well known in part because of the ambiguity of the EN construct. The earliest biological models described EN as comparable to the sequelae of exposure to unpredictable and/or uncontrollable stressors (e.g., electric shock) demonstrated in animal conditioning research. In response to unconditioned aversive stimulation (e.g., electric shock) and in the presence of conditioned fear cues (e.g., a bell that is repeatedly paired with the shock), animals undergo a series of physiological responses, including serotonin depletion and naloxone-reversible opioid brain chemical release, resulting in "stress-induced analgesia," which functions to

minimize pain. Because stress-induced analgesia can be conditioned, several theorists have argued that EN is a result of conditioned fear-based opioid release in response to traumatic conditioning and exposure to conditioned trauma-related cues (i.e., during intrusions of traumatic memories).

The biological substrates of EN have not been rigorously investigated using contemporary methods from the behavioral neurosciences; most of this work has instead focused on the negative emotional hyper-responsivity associated with PTSD. One exception is a small body of electrophysiology research showing that EN severity correlates with diminished activity in the brain's parietal lobe. This suggests that EN may be associated with deficits in attention or the ability to consciously allocate attentional resources, although it may be confounded by a similar relationship between parietal deficits and depression. Another line of research has suggested that affective disturbances in PTSD are the result of unusually strong inhibition of traumatic memory-related emotional arousal, based on evidence of activation in brain regions typically involved in reinterpreting or suppressing thoughts during trauma recall.

Conclusion

There is no doubt that traumatic experiences are profoundly impactful, and that the emotional residue of trauma can last a lifetime. However, it appears that the construct of EN as defined in the nosology fails to capture the unique trauma-linked phenomenology of emotional behavior abnormalities and, not surprisingly, has failed to be confirmed empirically. Although the experience of EN is subjectively significant for individuals with PTSD, more research is needed to clarify its key features and underlying mechanisms. Specifically, future research should clarify the conditions under which emotional deficits occur, which emotions or domains of emotional responding are affected, and the role of neurobiological factors. Ultimately, this research will have value if it impacts early intervention and tertiary care.

Research on treatment outcomes associated with EN is scarce, but there is some indication that severe EN can make it difficult for individuals to benefit from treatments that are currently available. Some researchers have proposed that treatments targeting hyperarousal might indirectly alleviate EN symptoms, while others have called for the development of new treatments specifically targeting EN.

RECOMMENDED READINGS

Flack, W. F., Litz, B. T., Hsieh, F. Y., Kaloupek, D. G., & Keane, T. M. (2000). Predictors of emotional numbing, revisited: A replication and extension. *Journal of Traumatic Stress, 13,* 611–618.

Foa, E. B., Zinbarg, R., & Rothbaum, B. O. (1992). Uncontrollability and unpredictability in post-traumatic stress disorder: An animal model. *Psychological Bulletin, 112,* 218–238.

Frewen, P. A., & Lanius, R. A. (2006). Toward a psychobiology of posttraumatic self-dysregulation: Reexperiencing, hyperarousal, dissociation, and emotional numbing. In R. Yehuda (Ed.), *Psychobiology of posttraumatic stress disorder: A decade of progress* (pp. 110–124). Boston: Annals of the New York Academy of Sciences.

Litz, B. T. (1992). Emotional numbing in combat-related posttraumatic stress disorder: A critical review and reformulation. *Clinical Psychology Review, 12,* 417–432.

Litz, B. T., & Gray, M. J. (2002). Emotional numbing in posttraumatic stress disorder: Current and future research directions. *Australian and New Zealand Journal of Psychiatry, 36,* 198–204.

Vera Vine
National Center for Posttraumatic Stress Disorder

Kristalyn Salters-Pedneault
National Center for Posttraumatic Stress Disorder

Brett T. Litz
National Center for Posttraumatic Stress Disorder

See also: Avoidance; Depression; Diagnosis of Traumatic Stress Disorders (*DSM & ICD*); Posttraumatic Stress Disorder; Posttraumatic Stress Disorder, Diagnosis of

EMPATHY

See: Psychotherapeutic Processes; Therapeutic Relationship

ENDOCRINE FUNCTION

See: Biology, Neurochemistry

EPIDEMIOLOGY

Epidemiology is the study of the distribution and determinants of disease. Epidemiology has two main goals. First, epidemiology aims to estimate the occurrence of a disease or health indicator in a population. Central measures of disease occurrence include incidence, which is a measure of the number of new cases of disease that occur in a population over a particular period of time, and prevalence, the number of cases (both new and existing) of disease in a population over a period of time. Second, epidemiology aims to identify the causes of disease by calculating estimates of the effect of an exposure (e.g., a particular behavior such as smoking, an environmental factor such as automobile pollution, an aspect of the physical or social environment such as the built environment or poverty, or a policy such as the ban on smoking indoors) on a health indicator. In the context of traumatic event exposures, epidemiologic methods can be used to document the prevalence and incidence of traumatic event exposures, of the mental health consequences of such events, and of the variables that influence the distribution of those effects.

The majority of epidemiologic studies of the mental health consequences of traumatic events are focused on posttraumatic stress disorder (PTSD). The aim of many of these studies is to estimate the prevalence of PTSD in a population. Some studies examine the prevalence of PTSD among people who have experienced a particular traumatic event, such as rape victims or victims of a natural disaster, or in a certain segment of the population. Other studies identify risk factors for PTSD following exposure to traumatic events. For example, psychiatric history, history of childhood trauma, and family history of mental disorders have consistently been identified as risk factors for PTSD among persons exposed to traumatic events (Breslau, 2002). Epidemiologists also examine the duration or change in severity of PTSD symptoms, as well as other mental health problems—such as depression, other anxiety disorder, and substance abuse/dependence—that people experience after a traumatic event and often concurrently with PTSD.

Longitudinal Cohort Epidemiologic Studies

Epidemiologic studies can generally be categorized into three main groups, based on their study design. The first, and arguably most useful study design in the examination of the psychological consequences of trauma experience, is the cohort, or longitudinal, study. Participants are divided into two groups of people, the exposed and the unexposed, neither of whom have the disease at the beginning of the study. In this case, the "exposed" group is a group of people who have experienced the traumatic event and the "unexposed" are those who did not experience the event. These two groups are then followed over time (longitudinally) to compare the occurrence of psychological disease between groups. The purpose of the study is to assess whether the group that experienced the trauma has a higher incidence of disease than the group that did not experience the trauma, which would allow us to attribute disease occurrence to experiencing the particular traumatic event.

Longitudinal cohort studies have helped researchers identify the risk factors of psychological disease as well as understand the course of disease. For example, Galea et al. (2008) utilized this type of study to examine predictors of PTSD among adult residents of New York City. This study design allowed the investigators not only to identify factors associated with PTSD incidence, but also to assess how incidence levels of PTSD change over time. Incident stressors and traumas such as family problems and sexual assault, low income, female gender, and Latino ethnicity were all found to be independent predictors of PTSD incidence, after adjusting for both recent and lifetime history of PTSD. The investigators also found that ongoing stressors also increase the risk of developing PTSD.

Although rare in the area of trauma and its psychological consequences, randomized intervention trials build on the longitudinal cohort follow-up design by randomly assigning persons to a particular exposure. The randomization (if carried out correctly) ensures comparability between groups, minimizes confounding, and allows investigators to draw causal inferences about the determination of disease without worrying about temporal ambiguity. In other words, because the population is disease-free before the traumatic event, the investigator can assume that the trauma preceded the mental health outcome. This gives strength to the conclusion that the disease was caused by the event. In the context of trauma-related research, randomizing persons to the receipt of trauma is obviously not a feasible method. However, randomized controlled trials have a place in the evaluation of interventions aimed at mitigating the consequences of traumatic event exposures. Also, a cohort study of the psychological consequences of trauma can be very similar to a randomized intervention trial and can be considered a "natural experiment" if, as in a randomized intervention trial, the trauma is "assigned" to one group randomly, as is the case in a natural disaster such as an earthquake or flood. In this case, an investigator could compare the incidence of disease among those who lived in an area affected by the catastrophe to the incidence of disease among those who live elsewhere.

Though the cohort study has many advantages, it also has limitations. First, conducting these types of studies, which often requires following people over a long period of time and conducting several interviews, can be time-consuming and expensive. Following every study participant over the entire duration of the study can also prove difficult because participants may die, move away, or simply decide they do not want to finish the study. If those people who remain in the study differ in some way from the people who leave the study before its conclusion, the estimate of the effect of the traumatic event on the disease may be under- or overestimated, sometimes leading us to incorrect conclusions.

Case Control Epidemiologic Studies

In a case control study, investigators first identify persons who have the disease and then controls (i.e., persons who do not have the disease). These groups are then compared to assess any difference in exposure to the traumatic experience. To illustrate, imagine that investigators want to see if people who abuse drugs and/or alcohol are more likely to experience PTSD after a sexual assault. Using this type of study design, investigators would identify a group of people who have been sexually assaulted and have been diagnosed with PTSD ("cases") and a group of people who have experienced this type of trauma but do not have PTSD ("controls"). Next, participants from both groups are asked if they abused drugs in the past. Investigators then determine whether or not past drug abuse was more prevalent among those who experienced the trauma and developed PTSD than it was among those who experienced the trauma but did not develop PTSD.

This type of study design, although very useful, is not utilized as much as it could be in mental health epidemiology. Case-control studies can be much more efficient than cohort studies in that they require a smaller sample size and are often less expensive and time-consuming. This study design, however, suffers from its own limitations. First, it is often difficult to be certain that the exposure preceded the traumatic event, which is an important criterion for determining causation. For example, the participants in the study could have abused drugs following the sexual assault, perhaps in an attempt to cope with this trauma. Second, this type of study often relies on participants' recollections of having this exposure in the past, which could be influenced by having the mental health problem, leading to biased effect estimates. Finally, to correctly estimate the effect of an exposure on an outcome, the cases and controls must also be selected from the same source population, which is often a difficult task because the base population (i.e., those who constitute persons at risk of traumatic event exposure) may be hard to define.

Cross-Sectional Epidemiologic Studies

Most of the early studies of PTSD employed a cross-sectional study design. Cross-sectional studies examine a population at a particular time, assessing both exposure to a traumatic event and mental health outcome for each study participant at this time. Often, cross-sectional studies are the only type of study that is feasible after a mass trauma and are useful in calculating prevalence of a disease in a population. This type of study can be completed more quickly and inexpensively than longitudinal studies (which require multiple assessments with participants over several months or years). Cross-sectional studies can provide public health practitioners with information regarding the prevalence and burden of a mental health outcome—such as PTSD—in a population in general, or following a disaster so that appropriate resources can be provided to those who were affected.

Cross-sectional studies of representative community populations such as the National Comorbidity Study (NCS; Kessler, Sonnega, Bromet, Hughes, & Nelson, 1995) and the NCS Replication study (Kessler, Chiu, Demler, & Walters, 2005) have estimated the prevalence of PTSD among adults in the United States and Europe (Perkonigg, Kessler, Storz, & Wittchen, 2000) to be between 2% to 7%, and higher (4% to 15%) in less developed countries (Zlotnick et al., 2006). Higher prevalence estimates are obtained when populations have been exposed to a mass psychological trauma. For example, 12% to 16% prevalence estimates have been obtained in the first year after mass terrorist incidents, although these levels tend to decrease over time (DiMaggio & Galea, 2006). Other studies have found a higher prevalence of other mental health disorders (generalized anxiety disorder, panic disorder, depression, and substance abuse disorder) in persons who developed PTSD after a traumatic event compared to those who were exposed to the event but did not develop PTSD (Breslau, 2002; North et al., 1999). For example, North et al. (1999) reported that among persons who experienced the Oklahoma City bombing, 63%

of persons who developed PTSD also developed other psychiatric disorders, while only 9% of persons who did not develop PTSD developed other psychiatric disorders.

Epidemiologists choose a study design based on what information they are seeking and what resources and data are available. A common goal of these three basic types of studies is to compare groups that have all of the same characteristics except for the traumatic event experience. Achieving this type of comparability is important in that it allows us to attribute adverse outcomes (such as PTSD or associated biopsychosocial problems) to the traumatic event itself, not to some other factor. It is important to note that while some study designs are considered "better" than others, the most informative studies are those that are thoughtfully designed and well executed.

Considerations in Epidemiologic Analyses

Three important issues that influence epidemiologic analyses are confounding, effect modification, and bias. Confounding occurs when the groups being compared differ by a third variable, that is, a factor other than the exposure and disease of interest, which can influence the estimate of association between the exposure and the outcome. It is possible, then, that the difference in outcomes found between groups is due to a difference in that third variable as opposed to a difference in exposure to the traumatic event. Some examples of these variables, called *confounders,* that are frequently seen in epidemiologic studies of psychological and physical health consequences of trauma are neuroticism and risk-taking behavior. These psychological constructs can influence both whether or not a person acquires a psychological disease and whether they are exposed to a traumatic event. Therefore, if these confounders are not accounted for, investigators can incorrectly infer a causal role for the traumatic event exposure and the psychological manifestations, even if the relation between the two is explained by the presence of the third variable—the confounder.

Effect modification occurs when a third variable—a factor other than the exposure and outcome of interest—modifies the relationship between the traumatic event exposure and the psychological or physical health outcome. For example, income status could influence the association between experiencing a traumatic event, such as a natural disaster, and risk of PTSD. A person who does not have the financial resources to help cope with the destruction of property following a hurricane may experience additional stress after the disaster and may be more likely to suffer from PTSD. Other variables that have not been fully considered but may modify the relationship between experiencing a traumatic event and suffering from a mental health problem are gender and ethnicity. We note that effect modification is synonymous with moderation in the terminology frequently used in psychology and described thoroughly by Baron and Kenny (1986).

Because confounding and effect modification can strongly influence a study's conclusions, they should be controlled for in the design or in the analysis of the study. In the design phase of the study, stratification, restriction, and matching are techniques that are used to control for confounders and effect modifiers. Investigators may stratify the group that experienced the traumatic event and the group that did not experience it into additional groups by the confounder, and then estimate the effect of the exposure on the mental health outcome within these groups. They may also restrict the group of participants in the study based on the confounding variable. For example, if they believe that gender might be a confounder, they will choose only women as participants in the study. Finally, the study team might form groups by matching subjects based on a factor that they believe may be a confounder. In the analysis phase of the study, investigators may control for confounders and effect modifications using statistical techniques. If, for example, regression models are used as a statistical analytic tool, potential confounders may be controlled for by inclusion in multivariable models and effect modification may be assessed by using interaction terms. For example, in a study aimed at understanding why Latinos have higher incidence of PTSD after traumatic event exposures than do other ethnic groups, Galea et al. (2004) showed that income may be a confounder of the relation between Latino ethnicity and risk of PTSD but also that level of social support may be an effect modifier of the relation between membership in particular Latino ethnic groups and risk of PTSD.

Bias occurs when there is a systematic error in the design, execution, or analysis of a study. This type of error can result in an association between a traumatic exposure and mental health outcome that does not actually exist, or in the masking of a true association. There are two main types of bias in epidemiologic studies: selection bias and information bias. Selection bias occurs when the exposure or outcome of interest influences how participants are chosen for the study. This type of sampling issue may arise particularly in the study of vulnerable populations. For example, investigators of depression after a sexual assault may chose participants from a list of clients utilizing mental health clinic for help with their depression. If those people who seek out care are less likely to have experienced a sexual assault (because those who experienced this type of trauma feel too ashamed or afraid to seek help), the investigators may underestimate the association between experiencing sexual assault and depression.

Information bias is caused by a misclassification of traumatic exposure or a misclassification of mental health status. Misclassification may result from the difficulty associated with defining or measuring trauma. For example, exposure to a traumatic event is a criterion required in positively diagnosing a person with PTSD. However, it might not always be clear if a certain event qualifies as a true "traumatic exposure," leading investigators to categorize participants as "exposed" or "unexposed" incorrectly, which can lead to under- or overestimated effect estimates (Weathers & Keane, 2007). A systematic error in recalling prior traumatic events is also a type of information bias. For instance, if a person suffers from a mental health problem that is commonly

associated with experiencing this type of event, then they might "recall" having experienced the event when in fact they did not. In other words, the participants may misclassify themselves as having been "exposed" when in truth they were not. This can result in an overestimation of the association between exposure to the traumatic event and the psychological problem of interest. Case-control studies of psychological trauma can suffer most from this type of bias because participants often must recall a past experience.

Conclusion

Epidemiology plays an important role in the study of the psychological consequences of trauma. Epidemiologic methods are used to estimate the burden of psychological disease in populations affected by trauma, determine why certain populations are more likely to develop mental health problems after a traumatic event, and identify determinants of disease. Epidemiology ultimately informs the development and implementation of interventions and policies that may reduce the risk of developing a mental health problem following a traumatic event or lessen the severity of the psychological consequences of traumatic events.

REFERENCES

Baron, R. M., & Kenny, D. A. (1986). The moderator-mediator variable distinction in social psychological research: Conceptual, strategic, and statistical considerations. *Journal of Personality and Social Psychology, 5*(6), 1173–1182.

Breslau, N. (2002). Epidemiologic studies of trauma, posttraumatic stress disorder, and other psychiatric disorders. *Canadian Journal of Psychiatry, 47*(10), 923–929.

DiMaggio, C., & Galea, S. (2006). The behavioral consequences of terrorism: A meta-analysis. *Academic Emergency Medicine, 13*(5), 559–566.

Galea, S., Ahern, J., Tracy, A., Cerda, M., Goldmann, E., & Vlahov, D. (2008). The determinants of posttraumatic stress in a population-based cohort study. *Epidemiology, 19*(1), 47–54.

Galea, S., Vlahov, D., Tracy, M., Hoover, D., Resnick, H., & Kilpatrick, D. G. (2004). Hispanic ethnicity and posttraumatic stress disorder after a disaster: Evidence from a general population survey after September 11. *Annals of Epidemiology, 14*(8), 520–531.

Kessler, R. C., Chiu, W. T., Demler, O., & Walters, E. E. (2005). Prevalence, severity, and comorbidity of 12-month DSM-IV disorders in the National Comorbidity Survey Replication. *Archives of General Psychiatry, 62,* 617–627.

Kessler, R. C., Sonnega, A., Bromet, E., Hughes, M., & Nelson, C. B. (1995). Posttraumatic stress disorder in the National Comorbidity Survey. *Archives of General Psychiatry, 52*(12), 1048–1060.

North, C. S., Nixon, S. J., Shariat, S., Mallonee, S., McMillan, J. C., Spitznagel, E. L., et al. (1999). Psychiatric disorders among survivors of the Oklahoma City bombing. *Journal of the American Medical Association, 282*(8), 755–762.

Perkonigg, A., Kessler, R. C., Storz, S., & Wittchen, H. U. (2000). Traumatic events and posttraumatic stress disorder in the community: Prevalence, risk factors and comorbidity. *Acta Psychiatrica Scandinavica, 101*(1), 46–59.

Weathers, F. W., & Keane, T. M. (2007). The Criterion A problem revisited: Controversies and challenges in defining and measuring psychological trauma. *Journal of Traumatic Stress, 20*(2), 107–121.

Zlotnick, C., Johnson, J., Kohn, R., Vicente, B., Rioseco, P., & Saldivia, S. (2006). Epidemiology of trauma, posttraumatic stress disorder (PTSD) and comorbid disorders in Chile. *Psychological Medicine, 36,* 1523–1533.

RECOMMENDED READINGS

Peleg, T., & Shalev, A. Y. (2006). Longitudinal studies of PTSD: Overview of findings and methods. *CNS Spectrums, 11*(8), 589–602.

Rothman, K. J., & Greenland, S. (1998). *Modern epidemiology.* New York: Lippincott, Williams, & Wilkins.

Susser, E., Schwartz, S., Morabia, A., & Bromet, E. J. (2006). *Psychiatric epidemiology.* New York: Oxford University Press.

Tsuang, M. T., & Tohen, M. (2002). *Textbook in psychiatric epidemiology.* New York: Wiley-Liss.

EMILY GOLDMANN
University of Michigan

SANDRO GALEA
University of Michigan

See also: Public Health; Research Methodology

ETHICS

See: Professional Standards and Ethics

ETHNIC CLEANSING

See: Genocide

ETIOLOGY

Etiology is a term referring to the cause of a disease or some other phenomenon and is derived from the Greek word for cause. The causes of psychological disorders are particularly difficult to identify and are commonly thought to be located in the complex interplay of nature (i.e., genetic endowment) and nurture (i.e., environmental influences). As its name implies, posttraumatic stress disorder (PTSD) is believed to be related to the stress from an antecedent life event of a traumatic nature. Scientists and theoreticians have studied people exposed to extreme stressors and PTSD patients in an effort to ascertain the causal (i.e., etiological) contributions attributable to various environmental and individual characteristics that are known to be associated with the development of this disorder. But establishing the etiology of PTSD is vastly complicated by the fact that a large number of factors can affect how individuals respond to potentially traumatic stressors.

The factors that appear to have causal significance for the development of PTSD include characteristics of individuals (such as genetic or biological tendencies, developmental level and experiences, past trauma exposure, life stress, and gender), varying aspects of high magnitude stressors (such as severity, intentional or accidental nature, and duration), and differences in posttraumatic life experiences and resources (such as social support, availability and use of medical and psychological treatment, and posttraumatic life stress; see Brewin, Andrews, & Valentine, 2000). These factors often operate in combination and may exert their influence over a long period of time. The relative contribution of different factors also varies across individuals. For example, a person who experiences a trauma of relatively low severity may have a strong response as a result of past trauma exposure, current life stress, and low social support, while a person with a very severe trauma (such as one involving death of a loved one) might have just as strong a response despite relatively little life stress, no history of trauma exposure, and high social support.

Since most people do not develop PTSD after exposure to a sudden, high magnitude stressor (Breslau, 2002), it is clear that exposure to such stressors alone does not cause PTSD. Research on a wide range of risk factors has shown that some variables clearly affect responses to extreme stressors, while the impact of others is still ambiguous. Various theoretical formulations about causal mechanisms of psychological trauma's emotional effects have been proposed. Some of the prominent causal theories of PTSD emphasize cognitive-processing concepts such as the predominant processing of sensory as opposed to conceptual information (Ehlers & Clark, 2000), behavioral formulations about the effect of conditioning on the fear network (Foa, Huppert, & Cahill, 2006), psychodynamic conceptualizations about capacity for affect modulation (Herman, 1992), and developmental theories focused on insecure attachment (Fonagy, Gergely, Jurist, & Target, 2002). More recently, new assessment methods have been developed that allow researchers to conduct prospective empirical studies of some of the possible causal mechanisms involved in traumatic stress. To date, however, our information about what causes PTSD comes almost entirely from retrospective studies that show associations between risk factors and outcomes, but provide no information about the direction of causality.

Because it is impossible to experimentally manipulate the various factors thought to cause PTSD, research on the etiology of PTSD will never identify causes of PTSD to an absolute certainty. Even if such manipulation were feasible, it would never be possible to definitively determine causation for an individual person. Studies of groups represent the associations between risk factors and outcomes for the group, but the reasons that any particular individual develops PTSD will be idiosyncratic. All potential causal factors need not be present for PTSD to develop and the relative contributions to the outcome for any particular individual are unlikely to closely match those of any group studied. Still, in the service of prevention and treatment of traumatic stress, trauma experts have long sought to identify factors that appear to play causal roles in the development of PTSD (Horowitz, 1976; van der Kolk, 1987). Studies have examined a wide range of variables in a wide range of populations and identified a large number of risk factors and correlates of PTSD. Some of these may play direct causal roles, but most are likely indirectly causal, which means that they influence the development of PTSD through making individuals more vulnerable to trauma's emotional effects or making recovery more difficult. It is likely that many factors associated with PTSD simply covary with (i.e., occur at the same time as) direct and/or indirect causal factors. Although we discuss only the most likely causal factors here, it should be noted that it is valuable for researchers to identify strong correlates of PTSD because that can lead to understanding of causal factors and because easily assessed correlates are often the most efficient way to identify those most at risk for PTSD following trauma exposure.

Theoretical formulations and an ever-expanding empirical evidence base indicate PTSD is caused by a combination of innate and acquired individual characteristics (such as biological mechanisms of emotion regulation and affective style, developmental level and experiences, and past trauma); characteristics of stressors (such as uncontrollability, suddenness, and negative valence); and individual life experiences (such as trauma exposure, stress at the time of trauma, posttraumatic social support, and posttraumatic social constraints). These factors may influence responses to potentially traumatic stressors by affecting perceptions of the stressful event, the capacity to cope with the event, or both.

Causal Influences of Individual Characteristics

Individual characteristics that may shape responses to stressor exposure include biologically based characteristics (that may be inherited or acquired), developmental level and experiences, and behavioral patterns that are acquired through biological or psychosocial experiences.

Biologically Based Characteristics

Although biological characteristics are often considered to be innate or genetically fixed, they can in fact develop in response to a person's biological environmental during early development or in response to life experiences. It is also possible for an apparent biological correlate of trauma to be a result of some cause largely unrelated to traumatic stress. Misattributions of this sort may arise when conditions that are vulnerability factors for PTSD are mistakenly seen to be the effects of PTSD.

Some studies examining heritability of PTSD have appeared to show a small hereditary component of the disorder (Keane, Marshall, & Taft, 2006). This component appears, in some populations, to share some variance with genetic contributions to trauma exposure (Stein, Jang, Taylor, Vernon, & Livesley, 2002). This means that whatever is inherited that contributes to the development of PTSD also contributes to an increased probability of exposure to trauma. For example, a hereditary deficit in problem-solving capacity may contribute to higher levels of exposure to potentially traumatic stressors and lower levels of resources to promote recovery following exposure. This inherited component is likely to be shaped by many genes, but studies to date that have focused on the most likely relevant

genes have not found consistent associations of any specific genetic markers for PTSD. It appears likely that the same genes associated with depression and other anxiety disorders also are associated with PTSD because the genetic contribution to PTSD seems to share most of its variance with the genetic contribution to depression and to other anxiety disorders (Koenen, 2007). Genetically transmitted biological mechanisms that might be responsible for an increased risk for PTSD include those involved in emotion regulation or affective style (Davidson, 2000) and cognitive abilities (Kremen et al., 2007). Deficits in both of these areas of psychological functioning are associated with specific brain structures and processes, and both could increase the likelihood of exposure to more traumatic stress or reduce the ability of the impaired individual to cope emotionally with stressors once exposed.

A biological characteristic that has been studied extensively in humans and thought to be affected by trauma exposure or PTSD is the functioning of the hypothalamic-pituitary-adrenal (HPA) axis. The HPA axis is a part of the human neuroendocrine system that is involved with stress and fear responses. Most studies of HPA axis functioning related to trauma exposure or PTSD have focused on cortisol, a hormone secreted by the adrenal gland. Typically, stress causes a release of cortisol from the adrenal gland and an increase in cortisol levels in the body. In the early 1990s, studies showing low levels of cortisol in samples of people with PTSD led to a theory proposing that in some people, chronically high distress led to sensitization of the HPA system and inhibition of cortisol release. By the late 1990s, this theory was widely accepted and it was generally believed that cortisol levels were abnormally low in those with PTSD. Further and better-controlled studies after 2000 began to show contradictory findings and a large meta-analysis recently concluded that there were no systematic differences in cortisol levels between people with PTSD and controls (Meewisse, Reitsma, de Vries, Gersons, & Olff, 2007). This entire area of research provides a reminder that it is wise to be cautious about coming to premature conclusions about the roles of biological variables in traumatic stress.

Another biological characteristic that has been the focus of great attention among trauma researchers is the size of the hippocampus (*see:* **Hippocampus**). The hippocampus is a brain region that is thought to play an important role in the consolidation of autobiographical memories, and early studies appeared to show differences in the hippocampi of those with PTSD. At first, findings of a smaller hippocampus in small samples of patients with PTSD led to speculation that trauma exposure or having PTSD might cause atrophy in the hippocampus. But subsequent larger and more rigorously controlled studies did not support the hypothesis that PTSD caused atrophy of the hippocampus (Neumeister, Henry, & Krystal, 2007). In fact, studies of hippocampal volume in twins and of cranial volume and age of first trauma seem to indicate that smaller hippocampi may be a risk factor for PTSD that results from adverse prenatal and early childhood environmental factors (Woodward et al., 2007). In utero and early environmental factors that might impair normal cranial growth include poor nutrition and exposure to toxins or hormones during the early period of brain development.

Environmental and life experiences that occur later in life can also cause relatively permanent biological changes in individuals that may make them more vulnerable to later traumatic stressors. For example, prospective biological studies of sexually abused girls have found evidence that the abuse caused earlier puberty (Putnam & Trickett, 1997). Longitudinal studies of genetics and exposure to adverse experiences have shown that genetic factors can interact with the environment to elevate the risk of negative outcomes. For example, a prospective study from birth to adulthood of a large sample of males in New Zealand (Segman, Shalev, & Gelernter, 2007) found that a particular genetic characteristic interacted with maltreatment experiences such that boys with the characteristic who were maltreated showed more aggressive violence as adults than those who were not maltreated (Caspi et al., 2002; Segman, Shalev, & Gelernter, 2007).

Developmental Level and Experiences

Responses to trauma will be greatly influenced by the level of emotional, social, and cognitive development of the individual at the time of trauma. Children at earlier stages of development are generally more vulnerable to traumatic stress, although, on occasion, lower levels of development may function to protect a child from experiencing an event as traumatic. In terms of emotional development, the nature of the child's attachment or emotional bond with a caretaker is important. For example, a child who has developed a secure attachment would be expected to show a more positive adjustment to trauma than a child who has a disordered attachment style. Similarly, all other factors being equal, adults with more secure attachment styles are likely to cope better with trauma than those with disordered attachment styles. There may also be an interaction between the trauma and attachment style when trauma occurs before or during attachment formation. This can be particularly problematic when the trauma takes the form of abuse inflicted by an attachment figure. Detailed discussions of the relationship between childhood trauma and attachment are available elsewhere (Cloitre, Cohen, & Koenen, 2006). Higher levels of cognitive and social skills in children and adults will increase control over the environment and the ability to obtain social support or other resources. These may also lead to lower anxiety and reduced exposure to later stress and traumatic stress.

Traumatic experiences that occur earlier in development, particularly those that are more severe and chronic, are more likely to have a pervasive impact because symptoms can impede further development and foster dysfunctional interpersonal behaviors. Without intervention, such interpersonal difficulties can become engrained patterns of behaving that essentially constitute personality and manifest as personality disorders. Repeated traumatic experiences in adults appear to have a somewhat cumulative effect, with earlier events increasing the vulnerability to later events (Brewin et al., 2000).

Characteristics of Traumatic Events

The *DSM* diagnostic criteria for PTSD require exposure to an event involving "actual or threatened death or serious injury or a threat to the physical integrity of self or others," which strongly implies a causal process initiated by a precipitating event (American Psychiatric Association, 2000). This criterion implies that the perception of an imminent threat of injury or death plays an essential causal role in the development of PTSD. While there is no doubt that PTSD can and does develop following stressors involving death or injury, there is no reason to believe that imminent injury or death are the only types of experiences that could cause humans to be emotionally overwhelmed. An alternative definition of potentially traumatic stressors is that they are sudden, uncontrollable, and have an extremely negative valence.

The suddenness of an event is an essential part of what makes an experience traumatic. Events that involve imminent threat of harm are more likely to cause overwhelming fear than experiences involving danger that is not imminent. When the amount of time between the person's awareness of a negative, uncontrollable event and the event itself is very brief, there is not enough time for the person to act to either physically protect himself/herself from harm or to psychologically prepare for a negative outcome. Janoff-Bulman (1992) pointed out that some experiences are not traumatizing even if they are negative and frightening because they occur gradually and incrementally. These gradual changes can be adapted to cognitively and emotionally by corresponding changes in one's schemas about oneself and the world. Similarly, actual or threatened psychological pain would not be traumatizing if it occurred gradually rather than suddenly.

The amount of time that is needed to process an event that makes one feel frightened and helpless is likely to be variable, depending on the nature of the event and the individual. Having weeks, months, or years in which to cognitively and emotionally process severe actual or threatened physical or psychological pain would be much less likely to overwhelm a person emotionally than having only minutes, hours, or days. While this aspect of traumatic stressors is implied in the *DSM* criteria for PTSD by the use of the word *imminent*, it is not explicitly stated. Similarly, suddenness is a characteristic of almost all stressors assessed by traumatic stress exposure measures, but has not been explicitly measured or studied to date.

Lack of controllability is a second essential characteristic of events that can cause PTSD. Humans, like other animals, generally try to control their environments to protect themselves from harm and insure their survival. They become distressed when they cannot control what is happening to them, particularly when what is happening is painful (Abramson, Seligman, & Teasdale, 1978; Foa et al., 1989; Mineka & Kilhstrom, 1978), and a perceived lack of controllability of events is widely thought to be a defining element of trauma (Foa, Zinbarg, & Rothbaum, 1992). Trauma survivors often report being particularly troubled by the fact that during the event, they could not exert control over or stop something terrible that was happening, and they frequently report upsetting "if only" and "what if" thoughts.

Individuals subjectively perceive stressful events as having a negative emotional effect when they are physically painful or injurious, emotionally painful, or because they are perceived as likely to cause physical pain or injury, emotional pain, or death. Common types of emotional pain associated with traumatic stressors include emotional loss, horror, and damage to identity in the form of guilt, shame, or lack of autonomy. Physically painful events or events involving threat of injury or death are experienced as negative by most people because the experience of pain from physical injuries and aversion to death are relatively universal. Appraisals of events involving actual or threatened emotional pain vary much more across individuals, because the intensity of emotional pain associated with a particular event depends upon the meaning of the event to the individual. For example, the emotional loss associated with sudden abandonment by a spouse or by losing all of one's possessions in a fire or flood would vary greatly across individuals because their life experiences, emotional dependence on the spouse or possessions, and other factors influence the meaning of the event to the individual.

Perceptions of events as uncontrollable and negative emotional reactions involve both objective and subjective elements, and the threshold for both of these to cause overwhelming emotions is shaped by a person's characteristics, past life experiences, and expectations. These perceptions are not static, but can be altered by situational factors, experiences, and events that occur after the event. Thus a person might perceive a bad car accident as highly uncontrollable and highly negative at the time of the accident, but perceive it as less negative days later if there were no permanent negative consequences. In this way, characteristics of the person, aspects of the stressor, and post-event experiences interact to cause PTSD.

Responses to Traumatic Events

While there is tremendous individual variation in how people respond to sudden, uncontrollable, and negative events, the core or primary responses are cognitive, affective, behavioral, and physiological reexperiencing, and avoidance (van der Kolk, 1987). Reexperiencing symptoms are thought to occur because memories and reminders of the trauma have become associated with anxiety. Cognitive reexperiencing also seems to have the function of processing ideas that do not fit into a person's schemas about herself or the world. For some, traumatic events are distressing, in part because they conflict with peoples' strongly held beliefs and assumptions (Janoff-Bulman, 1992). Avoidance symptoms occur because they afford relief from this trauma-related anxiety. The distinction between reexperiencing and avoidance symptoms can get blurred sometimes because what

appears to be avoidance may be reexperiencing of disconnections felt at the time of trauma.

In addition to these core symptoms, there are at least eight major types of secondary or closely associated response to trauma. Secondary responses are not directly caused by the traumatic experience, but occur later, as a result of problems with reexperiencing and avoidance. They can be considered the "second wave" of symptoms following trauma. Associated responses are those that result from exposure to concomitant elements of the traumatic environment. Associated responses are also not directly related to being emotionally overwhelmed; they are caused or shaped by the social environment, or by other circumstances accompanying or following the traumatic experience. The most prominent secondary and associated responses include depression, aggression, substance abuse, physical illnesses, low self-esteem, identity confusion, difficulties in interpersonal relationships, and guilt or shame (Carlson & Dalenberg, 2000). All of these can be secondary to or associated with trauma, they can be both secondary and associated, and they can also result from other causes. For example, depression can occur as a secondary symptom when core symptoms of reexperiencing and avoidance lead to feelings of loss of control and subsequent feelings of despair. Associated depression may be related to similar feelings of loss of control that are engendered by aspects of the trauma situation. Associated depression is very frequent following traumatic events involving emotional loss, such as losing people or possessions that meet one's emotional needs.

Given the centrality of avoidance and reexperiencing, it is not surprising that some theorists propose that individual differences in cognitive style may make some more likely to develop PTSD. A generally avoidant style of processing, or more specifically, an emotionally avoidant (alexithymic) style, has been shown to be related to PTSD (Bryant & Harvey, 1995). Because evidence is not available about cognitive style before trauma exposure, however, it remains possible that the observed cognitive styles are effects, rather than causes of PTSD.

The Influence of Posttraumatic Experiences

The availability of social, emotional, and financial resources is very important following a traumatic stressor (Hobfoll, 2001). In fact, such resources may make the difference between recovery and development of PTSD for survivors of less extreme stressors. Posttraumatic social support and social constraints are very important influences on responses to trauma. After a traumatic experience, social support can help restore a person's feelings of controllability and can help reduce the negative valence of an experience. Social support might be provided by family, friends, or even by strangers in the form of sympathetic media representations of trauma victims and demonstrations of support for trauma victims. Social constraints, on the other hand, interfere with recovery by increasing the negative valence of an experience, limiting a person's ability to emotionally process distressing events, and by diminishing one's self-esteem. Financial resources can influence recovery because they make it possible for trauma survivors to obtain more support, such as by seeing a mental health professional. They can also result in reduced stress by making it possible for trauma survivors to get needed rest and recovery time without suffering problems such as job loss, inability to pay rent, or inability to afford needed medical care.

Conclusion

Many researchers have commented on the difficulty of PTSD research, given the ethical and practical constraints that prevent manipulation of the purported causal variables. Greater clarity on causality, however, is likely to occur with a number of key shifts in focus for future research. First, more recent research has recognized the importance of psychometric issues—that is, careful and reliable measurement of the symptoms and outcomes—in providing replicable findings. Second, the role of varied designs (longitudinal, retrospective, and small group qualitative) is being explored, so that the same question can be addressed with methodologies with different strengths and weaknesses. Third, more recent research has begun to deal with the complexities of the individual difference variables in PTSD, recognizing that the impact of these differences may vary at differing developmental stages. Finally, overviews of PTSD etiology have begun to acknowledge the interactional nature of the biological, social, and psychological causes of PTSD (rather than simply additive models), opening the door to the study of models including concepts such as the moderation of the biological vulnerability to PTSD by social support or the moderation of trauma severity by cognitive style.

REFERENCES

Abramson, L. Y., Seligman, M. E. P., & Teasdale, J. D. (1978). Learned helplessness in humans: Critique and reformulation. *Journal of Abnormal Psychology, 87,* 49–74.

American Psychiatric Association. (2000). *Diagnostic and statistical manual of mental disorders* (4th ed., text rev.). Washington, DC: Author.

Breslau, N. (2002). Epidemiologic studies of trauma, posttraumatic stress disorder, and other psychiatric disorders. *Canadian Journal of Psychiatry, 47*(10), 923–929.

Brewin, C. R., Andrews, B., & Valentine, J. D. (2000). Meta-analysis of risk factors for posttraumatic stress disorder in trauma-exposed adults. *Journal of Consulting and Clinical Psychology, 68*(5), 748–766.

Bryant, R., & Harvey, A. (1995). Avoidant coping style and post-traumatic stress following motor vehicle accidents. *Behaviour Research and Therapy, 33,* 631–635.

Carlson, E. B., & Dalenberg, C. J. (2000). A conceptual framework for the impact of traumatic experiences. *Trauma, Violence, and Abuse, 1,* 4–28.

Caspi, A., McClay, J., Moffitt, T. E., Mill, J., Martin, J., Craig, I. W., et al. (2002). Role of genotype in the cycle of violence in maltreated children. *Science, 297,* 851–854.

Cloitre, M., Cohen, L. R., & Koenen, K. C. (2006). *Treating survivors of childhood abuse: Psychotherapy for the interrupted life.* New York: Guilford Press.

Davidson, R. J. (2000). Affective style, psychopathology, and resilience: Brain mechanisms and plasticity. *American Psychologist, 55,* 1196–1214.

Ehlers, A., & Clark, D. (2000). A cognitive model of posttraumatic stress disorder. *Behaviour Research and Therapy, 38,* 319–345.

Foa, E. B., Huppert, J. D., & Cahill, S. P. (2006). Emotional processing theory: An update. In B. O. Rothbaum (Ed.), *Pathological anxiety: Emotional processing in etiology and treatment* (pp. 3–24). New York: Guilford Press.

Foa, E. B., Steketee, G., & Rothbaum, B. O. (1989). Behavioral/cognitive conceptualizations of post-traumatic stress disorder. *Behavior Therapy, 20,* 155–176.

Foa, E. B., Zinbarg, R., & Rothbaum, B. O. (1992). Uncontrollability and unpredictability in post-traumatic stress disorder: An animal model. *Psychological Bulletin, 112*(2), 218–238.

Fonagy, P., Gergely, P., Jurist, E., & Target, M. (2002). *Affect regulation, mentalization and the development of self.* New York: Other Press.

Herman, J. (1992). *Trauma and recovery.* New York: Basic Books.

Hobfoll, S. E. (2001). The influence of culture, community, and the nested-self in the stress process: Advancing conservation of resources theory. *Applied Psychology: An International Review, 50,* 337–421.

Horowitz, M. J. (1976). *Stress response syndromes.* Northvale, NJ: Aronson.

Janoff-Bulman, R. (1992). *Shattered assumptions: Toward a new psychology of trauma.* New York: Free Press.

Keane, T. M., Marshall, A. D., & Taft, C. T. (2006). Posttraumatic stress disorders: Etiology, epidemiology, and treatment outcome. *Annual Review of Clinical Psychology, 2,* 161–197.

Koenen, K. (2007). Genetics of posttraumatic stress disorder: Review and recommendations for future studies. *Journal of Traumatic Stress, 20,* 737–750.

Kremen, W. S., Koenen, K. C., Boake, C., Purcell, S., Eisen, S. A., Franz, C. E., et al. (2007). Pretrauma cognitive ability and risk for post-traumatic stress disorder: A twin study. *Archives of General Psychiatry, 64*(3), 361–368.

Meewisse, M., Reitsma, J. B., de Vries, G., Gersons, B., & Olff, M. (2007). Cortisol and post-traumatic stress disorder in adults: Systematic review and meta-analysis. *British Journal of Psychiatry, 191,* 387–392.

Mineka, S., & Kilhstrom, J. F. (1978). Unpredictable and uncontrollable events: A new perspective on experimental neurosis. *Journal of Abnormal Psychology, 87,* 256–271.

Neumeister, A., Henry, S., & Krystal, J. (2007). Neurocircuitry and neuroplasticity in PTSD. In M. Friedman, T. M. Keane, & P. A. Resick (Eds.), *Handbook of PTSD: Science and practice* (pp. 151–165). New York: Guilford Press.

Putnam, F., & Trickett, P. (1997). Psychobiological effects of sexual abuse: A longitudinal study. *Annals of the New York Academy of Sciences, 821,* 150–159.

Segman, R., Shalev, A. Y., & Gelernter, J. (2007). Gene-environment interactions: Twin studies and gene research in the context of PTSD. In M. Friedman, T. M. Keane, & P. A. Resick (Eds.), *Handbook of PTSD: Science and practice* (pp. 190–206). New York: Guilford Press.

Stein, M., Jang, K., Taylor, S., Vernon, P., & Livesley, W. (2002). Genetic and environmental influences on trauma exposure and posttraumatic stress disorder symptoms: A twin study. *American Journal of Psychiatry, 10,* 1675–1681.

van der Kolk, B. (1987). The psychological consequences of overwhelming life experiences. In B. van der Kolk (Ed.), *Psychological trauma* (pp. 1–30). Washington, DC: American Psychiatric Press.

Woodward, S., Kaloupek, D., Streeter, C., Kimble, M., Reiss, A., Eliez, S., et al. (2007). Brain, skull, and cerebrospinal fluid volumes in adult posttraumatic stress disorder. *Journal of Traumatic Stress, 20,* 1–12.

EVE B. CARLSON
National Center for Posttraumatic Stress Disorder

CONSTANCE DALENBERG
Alliant International University

LUMA MUHTADIE
Palo Alto Institute for Research and Education

See also: **Posttraumatic Stress Disorder; Trauma, Definition**

EVENT-RELATED POTENTIAL

See: **Biology, Brain Structure, and Function, Adult; Biology, Brain Structure, and Function, Child; Frontal Cortex**

EVIDENCE-BASED TREATMENT

Evidence-based psychotherapy and pharmaco-therapy for the treatment of traumatic stress-related disorders is, at its very essence, the application of scientific and clinical knowledge toward improving individual patient care. This perspective is consistent with evidence-based care in medicine, as defined by "the conscious, explicit, and judicious use of current best evidence in making decisions about the care of individual patients" (Sackett, Rosenberg, Grey, Haynes, & Richardson, 1996, pp. 71– 72; as cited by the American Psychological Association [APA], 2005).

Across disciplines, terms such as evidence-based practice (Institute of Medicine [IOM], 2001), empirically validated treatments (APA Division of Clinical Psychology, 1995), and empirically supported treatments (ESTs; Kendall, 1998) all denote relatively similar constructs. Of particular note, the APA (2005) definition of evidence-based practice (EBP) makes a shift to include the integration of available findings from scientific research studies with clinical expertise and patient-related factors. Further extending the definition of Sackett and colleagues (1996; as cited by the APA, 2005), EBP has been defined as "the integration of the best available research with clinical expertise in the context of patient characteristics, culture, and preferences" (p. 1; APA, 2005). Thus, according to this definition, both technical and clinical expertise and patient-related factors dramatically influence the interpretation of the "best available research." Evidence-based treatment therefore reflects a combination of the findings of scientific research, the translation of these findings into clinical practice by experienced clinicians, and adaptation of treatment practices to best help patients who have a variety of different backgrounds, problems, needs, and personal characteristics.

An initial step in evidence-based treatment is evaluating a treatment's efficacy; that is, the strength of the evidence establishing that the intervention causes desired changes in the disorder that is being treated (APA, 2002). For example, a psychotherapy or pharmacotherapy would be considered to have evidence of efficacy for the treatment of PTSD if it has been shown to reduce the severity of PTSD symptoms or enable partial or full recovery from PTSD by patients with this disorder. One of the primary means for generating evidence of efficacy is the randomized control trial (RCT), where individuals with specific characteristics such as a disorder of interest are randomly assigned to either active or control treatments. Accordingly, the active treatment must be shown to have a superior outcome (e.g., reduced severity of PTSD symptoms) to the outcome of persons who receive the control treatment.

However, the result of an RCT study in itself does not necessarily constitute good evidence, as clinical trials vary in terms of their quality. Foa and Meadows (1997) highlighted seven "gold standards" that are used to evaluate the quality of RCTs for PTSD. These include clearly defined target symptoms, reliable and valid outcome measures, use of assessors blind to treatment condition to evaluate treatment change, standardized assessor training, manualized and replicable treatment programs, random assignment to treatment conditions, and assessment of treatment adherence.

These quality-control procedures are especially needed in psychotherapy research that is designed to establish evidence-based treatments, as it is easy for therapists to convince themselves of having special insight into the causes and cures for emotional distress, based solely on personal or clinical expertise. Further, patients often seek treatment when they are extremely distressed, unhappy, and motivated to address their problems. It is quite possible then that nontreatment specific factors, such as regression toward the mean (the tendency for very high or low scores to gravitate toward the middle of the range of scores), the placebo effect (the tendency for people to feel better when they believe they are receiving an effective treatment), and self-selection biases (the tendency for people to choose a treatment because they are highly motivated to benefit), may account for therapists perceiving an intervention as successful when improvement had nothing to do with the specific therapy intervention.

Even if a well-designed RCT shows superiority of a treatment, a further factor to consider is whether a treatment yields clinically meaningful change. Specifically, patients receiving a treatment may improve but not be meaningfully recovered. For example, patients in a study might report lower levels of PTSD symptoms on an interview or questionnaire at the conclusion of treatment, and overall the recipients of the therapy in this study might report enough reductions in symptom severity for their scores on the interview or questionnaire to be "statistically significantly" lower. However, some of the recipients of the therapy might still have quite severe PTSD symptoms and thus not have actually "recovered" despite having experienced some benefit. Hence, it is not enough to outperform no treatment or a control treatment, but by the end of the intervention, patients must end up in a range of functioning that renders them comparable to well-functioning individuals (Jacobson, Roberts, Berns, & McGlinchy, 1999). Accordingly, many RCTs report not only statistically significant changes on such things as percent reduction in symptom severity or no longer being diagnosed with the full disorder (such as PTSD), but also more stringent indices of reliable change, good endstate functioning, or clinically significant change itself.

Finally, the demonstration of a particular treatment's effects must be replicable. This means that when the treatment is tested in independent studies, preferably by other researchers in addition to those who developed the treatment, the results of the treatment should continue to be as favorable as in first studies of the treatment. Given that it is common for initial tests of efficacy to be conducted by those who either developed the treatment or believe strongly in it, introducing potential alliance effects, multiple RCTs need to be conducted to assure the stability and replicability of the treatment in question.

In recent years, in an attempt to integrate and quantify the findings from clinical trials, systematic reviews, or treatment guidelines has started to emerge. These reviews seek to integrate current empirical knowledge balancing some of the issues outlined previously. For PTSD, these include systematic reviews from the International Society for Traumatic Stress Studies (Foa, Keane, & Friedman, 2000; Foa, Keane, Friedman, & Cohen, in press), the American Psychiatric Association (2004), the Institute of Medicine (2007), the United Kingdom's National Institute for Health and Clinical Excellence (NICE, 2005), and the Australian Center for Posttraumatic Mental Health (ACPMH, 2007). Given the weight that various reviews place on different levels of evidence, treatment recommendations vary. Of particular note, however, the development of these reviews and the focus on empirically supported treatments (ESTs) in general, has been strongly criticized for neglecting the role of clinical expertise and individual patient characteristics in delivering treatment.

Consistent with these criticisms, the APA's statement on EBP underscores the importance of clinical expertise in promoting positive therapeutic outcomes. This statement implies that ESTs, when skillfully applied by a well-trained experienced clinician, offers the client the most efficacious, efficient, and cost-effective treatment for their distress. However, some argue that treatments evaluated in RCTs cannot address the flexibility required to meet the diverse needs of real-world clinical settings (Westen, 2006) and that ESTs usurp good clinical judgment by replacing professional expertise with strictly prescribed methods (Addis & Cardemil, 2006; Addis, Wade, & Hatgis, 1999; Litz & Salters-Pedneault, 2007). Although treatment packages seldom specify nonspecific therapeutic skills, they are clearly intended to be delivered using good clinical skills and in the context of a strong therapeutic alliance (Addis & Cardemil, 2006; Addis, Hatgis, Soysa, Zaslavsky, & Bourne, 1999). Thus, some amount of flexibility is balanced with a focus on identified key mechanism of change (Rosen & Davison, 2003). Extending this further, many treatment approaches that may provide effective care do not lend themselves to empirical investigation (Marquis & Douthit, 2006;

Stricker, 2006). Although this may be the case, emphasizing clinical expertise may encourage some to underutilize ESTs in favor of their own expert treatment, when only controlled research can identify unsupported, inert (i.e., ineffective), or iatrogenic (i.e., harmful) therapeutic techniques (Marquis & Douthit, 2006).

In regard to integrating "patient characteristics, culture, and preferences" as suggested by the APA definition of EBP, controlled clinical trials are often criticized for their dependence on highly homogenous samples that exclude more complex, comorbid patients (Seligman, 1995; Weston, 2006) and that fail to represent the diversity of patients in clinical settings (e.g., age, ethnicity, socioeconomic status; Marquis & Douthit, 2006; Seligman, 1995; Sue & Zane, 2006; Westen, 2006). Clearly, the process of empirical investigation itself may be restrictive, requiring a level of control unavailable in clinical practice to isolate underlying treatment mechanisms (Chambless & Crits-Cristoph, 2006). Yet, samples used in RCTs, on the whole, may be more representative of clinical practice than critics contend (see Stirman & DeRubeis, 2006, for a review); and thus, ESTs may indeed be informative on the role of individual patient characteristics on treatment outcome (Barlow, Levitt, & Bufka, 1999).

A related criticism is that many targets of psychotherapy (e.g., increased self-understanding, problems of living) cannot be assessed by typical objective outcome measures, thus rendering outcome data limited in its scope (Marquis & Douthit, 2006; Seligman, 1995; Stricker, 2006; Westen, Novotny, & Thompson-Brenner, 2004). Indeed, although outcome data on ESTs focus on specific improvements for a given population (e.g., disorder specific symptom reduction), as part of ascertaining broader treatment effectiveness (e.g., Nathan, Stuart, & Dolan, 2000), many more recent clinical trials not only now include more complex, comorbid samples but also include broader outcome indices such as social functioning, general health, and quality of life.

These criticisms, specifically the neglect of clinical expertise and specific patient characteristics in ESTs, have resulted in a shift by some toward identifying and disseminating empirically supported principles of change (ESPs). Specifically, ESPs refer to principles or techniques that are empirically demonstrated to be contributors to clinical improvement and can be applied in a flexible manner in accordance with a clinician's judgment (e.g., Beutler, Clarkin, & Bongar, 2000; Beutler, Moleiro, & Talebi, 2002; Rosen & Davison, 2003). More specifically, ESPs are defined as "research-informed principles that cut across both different theories of change and variations that exist among different techniques" (p. 1203; Beutler et al., 2002). At present, both trademarked therapy packages and general principles of change can be described as ESTs. However, it is important to distinguish between the mechanism of behavior change (the "principle" that is believed to be responsible for therapeutic change) and the specific treatment package used to deliver the therapy (Borkovec & Castonguay, 1998; Davison, 1998; Rosen & Davison, 2003). "New" treatment packages that rely on the same or similar mechanisms of change as other treatment packages may not represent truly distinct treatment alternatives (Herbert, 2000; Rosen & Davison, 2003).

Notably, the shift in focus from ESTs to ESPs may provide clinicians with research-supported interventions that can be integrated into treatment in a flexible manner that allows for individual variability, diversity of treatment setting, and the application of therapy nonspecifics (Beutler et al., 2002). Emphasizing principles of change rather than trademarked therapy packages may enable clinicians and researchers to focus on the basic mechanisms of treatment and therapeutic change that can guide a variety of treatment interventions (Rosen & Davison, 2003). For example, in the traumatic stress field, helping patients process the emotions that cause distress as a result of traumatic experiences and unwanted memories of those psychological traumas is a potential mechanism of change that is incorporated in different ways in a variety of models of cognitive behavior therapy, interpersonal therapy, psychodynamic therapy, emotion-focused therapy, and marital and family therapy for PTSD.

Scientifically evaluating different approaches to achieving this mechanism of change may enhance the ability of all of these therapies to effectively treat PTSD, and may enable clinicians to select approaches that are most efficacious rather than simply subscribing to a particular theory or trademarked package of PTSD treatment.

However, applying ESPs in practice can be challenging because it assumes that the clinician possesses a high level of proficiency, in both clinical knowledge and in the theory that guides the principles (Beutler et al., 2002); and, at present, little or no evidence exists that flexibly applied ESPs produce comparable outcomes to current ESTs for traumatic stress-related psychopathology. Nevertheless, better understanding and delineating ESPs may be advantageous to both the practicing clinician and diverse patients alike.

In conclusion, evidence-based treatment for traumatic stress-related disorders by the application of interventions is informed by what is known about the efficacy and clinical utility of treatment from well-conducted RCTs. Within this perspective, ESTs corroborated in multiple, well-designed clinical trials ought to be considered first-line interventions, whenever possible, and ought to be viewed as standards of care. That is, a clinician should be aware of and well versed in providing these interventions and should refer patients to other practitioners when they are not. While clinical expertise and individual patient factors ought to be well integrated into treatments, they ought not be used as a rationale for rejecting the use of ESTs. Also within this evidence-based perspective, the choice to use alternative, nonempirically supported treatments should be considered primarily in the face of treatment failure using empirically supported treatments and should still be guided by the use of empirically supported principles. Finally, emphasizing these empirical principles may impart a greater understanding of the theory underlying effective treatment, giving the clinician an adaptable set of tools from which to draw, and may help to bridge the gap between the art and science of psychotherapy.

REFERENCES

Addis, M. E., & Cardemil, E. V. (2006). Psychotherapy manuals can improve outcomes. In J. C. Norcross, L. E. Beutler, & R. F. Levant (Eds.), *Evidenced-based practices in mental health* (pp. 131–140). Washington, DC: American Psychiatric Press.

Addis, M. E., Hatgis, C., Soysa, C., Zaslavsky, I., & Borne, L. S. (1999). The dialectics of manual-based psychotherapy. *Behavior Therapist, 22,* 130–132.

Addis, M. E., Wade, W. A., & Hatgis, C. (1999). Barriers to the dissemination of evidenced-based practices: Addressing practitioners' concerns about manual-based therapies. *Clinical Psychology: Science and Practice, 6,* 430–441.

American Psychiatric Association. (2004). *Practice guideline for the treatment of patients with acute stress disorder and posttraumatic stress disorder.* Washington, DC: Author.

American Psychological Association. (2002). Criteria for evaluating treatment guidelines. *American Psychologist, 57,* 1052–1059.

American Psychological Association. (2005). *APA policy statement on EBPP.* Washington, DC: Author.

American Psychological Association Division of Clinical Psychology. (1995). Training in and dissemination of empirically validated psychological treatments: Report and recommendations. *Clinical Psychologist, 48,* 3–27.

Australian Center for Posttraumatic Mental Health. (2007). *Australian guidelines for the treatment of adults with acute stress disorder and posttraumatic stress disorder.* Melbourne, Australia: Author.

Barlow, D. H., Levitt, J. T., & Bufka, L. F. (1999). The dissemination of empirically supported treatments: A view to the future. *Behavior Research and Therapy, 37,* S147–S162.

Beutler, L. E., Clarkin, J. F., & Bongar, B. (2000). *Guidelines for the systematic treatment of the depressed patient.* New York: Oxford University Press.

Beutler, L. E., Moleiro, C., & Talebi, H. (2002). Resistance in psychotherapy: What conclusions are supported by research? *Journal of Clinical Psychology, 58,* 207–217.

Borkovec, T. D., & Castonguay, L. G. (1998). What is the scientific meaning of empirically supported therapy? *Journal of Consulting and Clinical Psychology, 66,* 136–142.

Chambless, D. L., & Crits-Christoph, P. (2006). The treatment method. In J. C. Norcross, L. E. Beutler,

& R. F. Levant (Eds.), *Evidenced-based practices in mental health* (pp. 191–200). Washington, DC: American Psychiatric Press.

Davidson, G. C. (1998). Being bolder with the Boulder model: The challenge of education and training in empirically supported treatments. *Journal of Consulting and Clinical Psychology, 66,* 163–167.

Foa, E. B., Keane, T. M., & Friedman, M. J. (2000). *Effective treatments for PTSD: Practice guidelines from the International Society for Traumatic Stress Studies.* New York: Guilford Press.

Foa, E. B., Keane, T. M., Friedman, M. J., & Cohen, J. (in press). *Effective treatments for PTSD: Practice guidelines from the International Society for Traumatic Stress Studies* (2nd ed.). New York: Guilford Press.

Foa, E. B., & Meadows, E. A. (1997). Psychosocial treatments for posttraumatic stress disorder: A critical review. *Annual Review of Psychology, 48,* 449–480.

Herbert, J. D. (2000). Defining empirically supported treatments: Pitfalls and possible solutions *Behavior Therapist, 23,* 113–122.

Institute of Medicine. (2001). *Crossing the quality chasm: A new health system for the twenty-first century.* Washington, DC: Author.

Institute of Medicine. (2007). *Treatment of post traumatic stress disorder (PTSD).* Washington, DC: Author.

Jacobson, N. S., Roberts, L. J., Berns, S. B., & McGlinchey, J. B. (1999). Methods for defining and determining the clinical significance of treatment effects: Description, application, and alternatives. *Journal of Consulting and Clinical Psychology, 67*(3), 300–307.

Kendall, P. C. (1998). Empirically supported psychological therapies. *Journal of Consulting and Clinical Psychology, 66,* 3–6.

Litz, B. T., & Salters-Pedneault, K. (2007). The art of evidence-based treatment of trauma survivors. In S. G. Hofmann & J. Weinberger (Eds.), *The art and science of psychotherapy* (pp. 211–230). New York: Routledge/Taylor & Francis Group.

Marquis, A., & Douthit, K. (2006). The hegemony of "empirically supported treatment": Validating or violating? *Constructivism in the Human Sciences, 11,* 108–141.

Nathan, P. E., Stuart, S. P., & Dolan, S. L. (2000). Research on psychotherapy efficacy and effectiveness: Between Scylla and Charybdis? *Psychological Bulletin, 126,* 964–981.

National Institute for Health and Clinical Excellence. (2005). *Clinical guidelines for post-traumatic stress disorder.* London: Author.

Rosen, G. M., & Davison, G. C. (2003). Psychology should list empirically supported principles of change (ESPs) and not credential trademarked therapies or other treatment packages. *Behavior Modification, 27*(3), 300–312.

Seligman, M. E. P. (1995). The effectiveness of psychotherapy: The consumer report study. *American Psychologist, 50,* 965–974.

Stirman, S. W., & DeRubeis, R. J. (2006). Research patients in clinical trials are frequently representative of clinical practice. In J. C. Norcross, L. E. Beutler, & R. F. Levant (Eds.), *Evidenced-based practices in mental health* (pp. 171–179). Washington, DC: American Psychiatric Press.

Stricker, G. (2006). A poor fit between empirically supported treatments and psychotherapy integration. In J. C. Norcross, L. E. Beutler, & R. F. Levant (Eds.), *Evidenced-based practices in mental health* (pp. 275–282). Washington, DC: American Psychiatric Press.

Sue, S., & Zane, N. (2006). Ethnic minority populations have been neglected by evidence-based practices. In J. C. Norcross, L. E. Beutler, & R. F. Levant (Eds.), *Evidenced-based practices in mental health* (pp. 329–337). Washington, DC: American Psychiatric Press.

Westen, D. (2006). Patients and treatments in clinical trials are not adequately representative of clinical practice. In J. C. Norcross, L. E. Beutler, & R. F. Levant (Eds.), *Evidenced-based practices in mental health* (pp. 161–171). Washington, DC: American Psychiatric Press.

Westen, D., Novotny, C. M., & Thompson-Brenner, H. (2004). The empirical status of empirically supported psychotherapies: Assumptions, findings and reporting in controlled clinical trials. *Psychological Bulletin, 130,* 631–663.

Lori A. Zoellner
University of Washington

Michele Bedard-Gilligan
University of Washington

Joyce N. Bittinger
University of Washington

EXPOSURE THERAPY, ADULT

The term *exposure therapy* refers to several behavioral and cognitive behavioral treatment programs that involve safely confronting feared thoughts, images, objects, situations, or activities in order to reduce pathological (unrealistic) fear, anxiety, and related symptoms. In the treatment of PTSD, exposure therapy usually involves prolonged imaginal exposure to the patient's memory of the trauma and *in vivo* (i.e., real life) exposure to various reminders of the trauma.

Exposure therapy, also referred to as flooding, imaginal, *in vivo*, prolonged, or directed exposure, is a well-established treatment for PTSD that assists the patient in vividly focusing on and describing the details of a traumatic experience in a therapeutic manner. Exposure methods share the common feature of confrontation with frightening, yet realistically safe, stimuli that continues until the anxiety is reduced. Although prior trauma experiences were not safe and realistically caused fear at the time, recalling a memory (imaginal exposure) or going to a place or engaging in an activity that is reminiscent of the trauma (*in vivo* exposure) can be safe if done with therapeutic guidance. Exposure therapy is designed to achieve extinction of the conditioned association between the fear (an unconditioned response) that began in the traumatic experience (an unconditioned stimulus) and current memories or reminders of past trauma (the conditioned stimuli) so that the patient no longer feels debilitating anxiety (the conditioned response) in daily life when actually safe. With this reduction in anxiety, the patient is thought to be able to be less avoidant of trauma reminders and therefore better able to engage in and emotionally process (i.e., feel a range of healthy feelings) current life experiences such as work, school, and relationships.

Exposure therapy for PTSD currently is viewed as not just leading to extinction of conditioned fear but also enhancing emotional processing. This expanded theory holds that PTSD emerges due to the development of a fear network in memory that elicits escape and avoidance behavior when the individual recalls or is reminded of a fearful experience. Mental fear structures include stimuli, responses, and meaning elements. Any information associated with the trauma is likely to activate the fear structure. The fear structure in people with PTSD is thought to include a particularly large number of stimuli and therefore is easily accessed. Attempts to avoid the anxiety elicited by trauma reminders and memories result in the avoidance and numbing symptoms of PTSD. Two conditions have been proposed to be required for fear reduction. First, the mental fear structure must be activated, for example by purposefully recalling the fear memory in detail. Second, new information must be provided that includes elements incompatible with the existing fear-evoking elements so that differences between the trauma experience and similar but safe current or future experiences are added to the fear structure to modify it. When exposure therapy is successful, the patient can mentally and emotionally distinguish between past trauma experiences and current or future safe experiences, and thus no longer feel overwhelming fear when reminded of or recalling past trauma.

In addition to promoting extinction and emotional processing of learned fear, several other mechanisms are thought to be involved in exposure therapy's improvement of PTSD (Foa, Steketee, & Rothbaum, 1989):

- Repeated therapeutic recalling of trauma memories or safe revisiting of situations or activities that are reminders of the trauma may promote extinction of the physiological arousal that is a part of fear.

- The process of deliberately experiencing the feared memory blocks the negative reinforcement associated with avoidance of trauma-related thoughts and feelings—in essence, the individual learns that it is not necessary to avoid trauma memories or reminders in order to overcome feelings of fear.

- Reliving of the trauma in a therapeutic, supportive setting incorporates safety information into the trauma memory, thereby helping the patient to realize that remembering the trauma is not dangerous.

- Focusing on the trauma memory for a prolonged period helps the patient to differentiate the trauma event from other nontraumatic events, thereby rendering the trauma as a specific occurrence rather than as a representation of a generally dangerous world and of oneself as a helpless victim.
- The process of imaginal reliving helps change the meaning of PTSD symptoms from a sign of personal incompetence to a sign of mastery and courage.
- Prolonged, repeated reliving of the traumatic event affords the opportunity for focusing on details central to patients' negative evaluations of themselves and modify those evaluations (Foa, Hembree, & Rothbaum, 2007).

Many of these mechanisms also operate *in vivo* exposure. However, the mechanisms most salient during *in vivo* exposure are the correction of erroneous probability estimates of danger and extinction of fearful responses to trauma relevant stimuli.

Prolonged exposure (PE) is a specific exposure therapy program that consists of four components typically administered in 9 to 12 sessions lasting 45 to 90 minutes each: (1) psychoeducation about the symptoms of PTSD and factors that maintain PTSD (e.g., avoidance, cognitive factors) along with a thorough rationale for exposure therapy; (2) training in controlled breathing that patients may use as a stress management skill, although patients are discouraged from using it during exposure exercises (differentiating prolonged exposure from systematic desensitization in which exposures are paired with relaxation); (3) prolonged imaginal exposure to the trauma memory conducted in therapy sessions and repeated as homework; and (4) prolonged *in vivo* exposure implemented as homework. Typically, the imaginal exposure is audiotaped in session and the patient is instructed to listen to the audiotapes daily at home. A hierarchy, or ranked ordered list of avoided or anxiety-provoking situations, is constructed in the beginning sessions and is used to assign *in vivo* homework assignments. Only realistically safe situations are placed on the hierarchy. Detailed instructions for conducting exposure therapy with PTSD patients can be found in Foa et al. (2007). It appears that for an exposure to be "therapeutic," patients must learn new information, so it must be conducted long enough in each session and repeated for enough sessions to enable the patient to experience a reduction in anxiety and should be structured to generalize to other contexts in daily life.

There is substantial evidence that exposure programs are effective in the treatment of PTSD in female sexual assault survivors (5 studies), in male veterans of war (7 studies), in female veterans of war (1 study), in refugees (3 studies), as well as in "mixed" trauma populations (over 10 studies). There is evidence that exposure therapy augments the response to sertraline (an SSRI medication) in patients who have an initial weak response to medication (Rothbaum et al., 2006). There is no compelling evidence that any alternative therapy is more effective than exposure therapy (Cahill, Rothbaum, Resick, & Follette, in press; Rothbaum, Meadows, Resick, & Foy, 2000), and no evidence that adding other components enhances the efficacy of exposure therapy (*see:* **Eye Movement Desensitization and Reprocessing**, for a contrasting view).

REFERENCES

Cahill, S., Rothbaum, B. O., Resick, P., & Follette, V. (in press). Cognitive-behavioral therapy. In E. B. Foa, M. Friedman, & T. Keane (Eds.), *Effective treatments for posttraumatic stress disorder: Practice guidelines from the International Society for Traumatic Stress Studies* (2nd ed.). New York: Guilford Press.

Foa, E. B., Hembree E., & Rothbaum, B. O. (2007). *Prolonged exposure therapy for PTSD: Emotional processing of traumatic experiences (Therapist guide)*. New York: Oxford University Press.

Foa, E. B., Steketee, G., & Rothbaum, B. (1989). Behavioral/cognitive conceptualizations of posttraumatic stress disorder. *Behavior Therapy, 20,* 155–176.

Rothbaum, B. O., Cahill, S., Foa, E. B., Davidson, J. R. T., Compton, J., Connor, K., et al. (2006). Augmentation of sertraline with prolonged exposure in the treatment of PTSD. *Journal of Traumatic Stress, 19,* 625–638.

Rothbaum, B. O., Meadows, E. A., Resick, P., & Foy, D. W. (2000). Cognitive-behavioral therapy. In E. B. Foa, M. Friedman, & T. Keane (Eds.), *Effective treatments for posttraumatic stress disorder: Practice guidelines from the International Society for Traumatic Stress Studies* (pp. 60–83). New York: Guilford Press.

Barbara O. Rothbaum
Emory University School of Medicine

See also: Cognitive Behavior Therapy, Adult; Cognitive Behavior Therapy, Child; Exposure Therapy, Child; Eye Movement Desensitization and Reprocessing

EXPOSURE THERAPY, CHILD

Exposure therapy is the psychotherapeutic treatment that has the strongest scientific evidence base for individuals suffering from posttraumatic stress symptoms. The process of therapeutic exposure is used to help children confront their fears and prevent avoidance of the feared stimulus or cues that are reminders of the stimulus. The rationale behind therapeutic exposure is that anxiety results from the pairing of an unconditional stimulus, such as physical or sexual abuse, which automatically elicits fear, with a previously neutral or even reinforcing stimulus (e.g., a parent, a room, an area of the house, a smell). Because of this association, the previously neutral stimulus acquires the capacity to elicit fear. Thus, when confronted with frightening stimuli, or any reminders of them, the child experiences symptoms of fear and anxiety, even if there is no actual current danger.

One way that children cope with posttraumatic stress symptoms is to avoid any thoughts or reminders of the past traumatic experiences. These avoidance responses may become reinforced by a sense of temporary relief or by the belief on the child's part or by adults or peers that avoidance provides safety from danger or a way to manage intense feelings of fear. Unfortunately, avoidance does not give the child the opportunity to process their traumatic experiences and gain a genuine sense of being safe and able to manage distressing emotions, making it likely that symptoms will intensify or endure longer in the future. Although avoidant coping may produce some short-term relief, it runs the risk of occasioning long-term problems.

Gradual exposure techniques encourage the child to face the fear-producing stimuli safely and in manageable amounts, thereby breaking the association between these negative feelings and the trauma-related cues. The feared-stimuli may be presented in real-life situations, also known as *in vivo* exposure (e.g., safely going to a dark place that has been frightening, visiting a room where traumatic abuse occurred) or in imagination, also known as imaginal exposure.

Therapeutic exposure for children is gradual because the child first begins with stimuli that provoke lower levels of anxiety and then gradually moves on to increasingly distressing stimuli. As treatment progresses, the child is asked to talk about specific sights, sounds, smells, and bodily sensations remembered from the events. Relaxation and anxiety management techniques taught earlier in treatment are used to help the child deal with any symptoms of distress. The exposure sessions are repeated until the memories no longer elicit the fear or avoidance response. The goal of gradual exposure is for the child to be able to discuss and confront trauma experiences in detail without experiencing undue distress, avoidance, numbing or detachment. Clinically, achievement of this goal may serve as a landmark that exposure therapy is approaching a successful conclusion. Again, exposure focuses on gradually discussing and confronting progressively distressing elements of the trauma, and mastering the associated emotions and cognitions at each step. Although this is invariably an emotional process, extreme episodes of emotion (also known as catharsis, abreaction or implosion) are not encouraged within this framework. If affective distress becomes overwhelming, children are encouraged to slow down, master the distress, and process the associated cognitions before proceeding.

When multiple incidents and types of psychological trauma have occurred to a child, it may be difficult for the child to remember specific details or discrete events. The therapist can help the child by providing cues and anchor points to trigger specific events (e.g., the first, last, or worst time). Since the child may be unable to remember specific details about multiple events, it is up to the clinician to decide how many events should be addressed using the exposure procedures. A general rule is to have the child recapitulate any memories that are currently causing the child distress. These memories should be processed until they no longer elicit significant fear symptoms or avoidance.

The basic outline of exposure is similar for children and adults, but multiple refinements are necessary for optimal outcomes and benefits with children. First and foremost, the child's developmental level must be considered throughout the process. The need to attend to developmental level begins with psychoeducation and preparing the child for therapeutic exposure. Awareness of language is imperative as young children require simplistic explanations and vocabulary. Use of analogies is often extremely helpful and can assist in the rapport building process. Additionally, young children should not be expected to remember as many specific details or be able to describe their psychological trauma experiences with as much detail as older children. As a result, of their limited language and memory abilities, young children may be especially susceptible to suggestive comments or repeated questioning by the therapist, and therefore, therapists need to be careful not to push children to recall specifics beyond those that they readily remember.

In order to facilitate the exposure therapy sessions with children, a variety of creative media may be used, such as: (a) reenactment with dolls or puppets; (b) visualization of past events in imagination; (c) recalling sensory details of the abuse/trauma experience; (d) drawing, painting, or writing about thoughts and experiences; and (e) *in vivo* confrontation. The

use of a narrative approach in the form of creating a book that contains drawings, poems, pictures, and written memories of the traumatic experiences often is helpful in maintaining focus and continuity during exposure therapy treatment with young children. The selection of the particular mode of expression will vary, depending on the child's developmental level and preferences. The objective of each medium is to facilitate the child's engagement in the exposure process. It is, therefore, important that the therapeutic goals are not lost in the use of play or other media and that the activity does not become used as avoidance strategies that actually reduce the therapeutic processing of memories of past traumatic events.

Following a therapeutic exposure task, it is important that the therapist reward the child for his or her effort, as confronting anxiety-provoking stimuli is a very difficult task. Positive reinforcement and praise increase the likelihood that the child will engage in exposure in future sessions and serve to increase the child's sense of confidence and competence in mastering the exposure process. Rewards should be consistent with the child's likes, interests, and developmental level. Encouragement and genuine praise are reinforcers to which many children respond positively. Tangible reinforcers should be used sparingly, primarily as a way to share a few moments of quiet comfort following the hard work of recalling traumatic memories (e.g., an enjoyable snack). Reinforcement is not specifically earned as a "payment" for doing exposure therapy, unless this is consistent with the child's social environment in the home or school (e.g., the child can earn points or other forms of reinforcers for positive behaviors in school or at home).

Caregiver involvement is an essential component of the therapeutic exposure process with children. It is necessary that caregivers understand the rationale and exposure process in order to enlist them as advocates during the process, helping them to provide support and encouragement to their children, to respond appropriately to avoidant behaviors, and to troubleshoot around potential obstacles and barriers to treatment. For example, given the initial high rates of anxiety experienced by the child, a child may try to avoid attending treatment. Predicting this response for both the child and caregiver helps to prepare them and increase the likelihood of continued attendance by the child. Additionally, as the child is going through the exposure process, parallel caregiver sessions should be conducted that are focused on the caregiver learning about the child's abuse/trauma experience (e.g., sharing the drawings and writings) and discussing his or her reactions. This sharing exposes the caregiver to the child's traumatic event in order to help the caregiver process their own emotions surrounding the event, help them to better tolerate their own reactions as their child discusses distressing past events, and prepare them for discussing the traumatic event directly with their child.

Given the importance of caregiver involvement and support for children and adolescents, the culmination of the exposure sessions is a conjoint child-parent session in which the child shares the work they have completed (e.g., book, drawings, writings) and information about their traumatic experience(s). The purpose of this session is to help the child feel more comfortable discussing the traumatic experience(s) with their caregiver and to allow the child to address any concerns or questions he or she may have regarding their traumatic experience, such as whether the parent blames them (as opposed to the message of nonblaming parental acceptance of and caring for the child, which is central to exposure therapy).

RECOMMENDED READINGS

Bouchard, S., Mendlewotz, S. L., Coles, M. E., & Franklin, M. (2004). Considerations in the use of exposure with children. *Cognitive and Behavioral Practice, 11,* 56–65.

Cohen, J. A., Mannarino, A. P., & Deblinger, E. (2006). *Treating trauma and traumatic grief in children and adolescents.* New York: Guilford Press.

Deblinger, E., & Heflin, A. H. (1996). *Treating sexually abused children and their nonoffending parents: A cognitive behavioral approach.* Thousand Oaks, CA: Sage.

GENELLE SAWYER
Medical University of South Carolina

ROCHELLE F. HANSON
Medical University of South Carolina

See also: Cognitive Behavior Therapy, Adult; Cognitive Behavior Therapy, Child; Exposure Therapy, Adult

EXTINCTION

See: Biology, Animal Models; Conditioned Fear; Habituation; Learning Theory

EYE MOVEMENT DESENSITIZATION AND REPROCESSING

Eye movement desensitization and reprocessing (EMDR) is a controversial treatment that has been promoted as being effective not only with traumatic stress and fear-based disorders but also with virtually every area of psychopathology. It has been hailed as a breakthrough therapy by some (Shapiro & Forrest, 2004), while being portrayed by others as a pseudoscientific movement that tacks an unnecessary treatment gimmick onto imaginal exposure techniques (Olatunji, Parker, & Lohr, 2005–2006; Rubin, 2003).

Proponents of EMDR describe it as an information processing therapy that alleviates traumatic memories by integrating them with more positive and adaptive information. Its eight-stage process begins with a thorough clinical assessment followed by the targeting of a stressful memory and associated feelings and cognitions with repeated sets of dual attention stimulation (defined next). Each set lasts approximately 25 seconds. After each set, the therapist asks the client to describe the thoughts, feelings, or images they experienced during the stimulation. This process is repeated throughout the treatment session, with each successive set of stimulation typically targeting the thoughts, feelings, or images experienced per set. The ultimate aim is resolve the distress associated with the stressful memory and to restructure related dysfunctional cognitions (Maxfield, Lake, & Hyer, 2004).

The most distinctive treatment component of the eight-stage EMDR process involves the dual attention stimulation, in which the therapist waves her fingers (or uses an alternate device) to stimulate rapid back-and-forth eye movements as the client visualizes a distressful memory while keeping in mind a related feeling and cognition. Alternatively, the therapist might rapidly alternate right and left hand taps or sounds in the right and left ear during the visualization.

Over the years, since the advent of EMDR in the late 1980s, its proponents have changed the label for this distinctive treatment component as well as the speculative explanations for its supposed effectiveness. Once called *bilateral stimulation,* the distinctive component is now called *dual attention stimulation.* Notions as to why it is effective have included ideas drawn from learning theory, emotional and informational processing theory, as well as physiological speculations such as stimulating a part of the brain where traumatic memories remain frozen and unprocessed or helping the rational hemisphere of the brain gain access to and process traumatic memories that are stuck in the opposite hemisphere. None of these speculations have been scientifically tested and confirmed or ruled out, so the mechanisms by which EMDR works are unknown.

Also varying over time have been the criteria used for judging the fidelity of EMDR treatment in outcome studies. For example, after some studies reported results questioning whether EMDR is as effective as its proponents believe it to be, EMDR proponents argued that the EMDR therapists in those studies did not have enough training in EMDR or did not provide enough EMDR sessions. Critics of EMDR disputed that argument, that the "goalposts keep changing" regarding acceptable treatment fidelity criteria (such as by increasing the minimum training requirements or number of sessions), thus enabling EMDR proponents to dispute the fidelity of each outcome study that produces findings that challenge whether EMDR is as effective as they believe it is or

whether its distinctive treatment component is really necessary (Rubin, 2003).

Despite this controversy, a large number of well-controlled outcome studies and some meta-analyses have supported the effectiveness of EMDR in treating adults with noncombat, single-trauma PTSD. The American Psychological Association has deemed EMDR as probably efficacious in treating PTSD, and the International Society for Traumatic Stress Studies has designated EMDR as an effective treatment for PTSD (Davidson & Parker, 2001; Rubin, 2003). Recent meta-analyses of research studies have concluded that EMDR is as efficacious as trauma-focused cognitive behavior therapy (CBT) for PTSD (Seidler & Wagner, 2006) and that both EMDR and trauma-focused CBT are more efficacious for PTSD than stress management or other credible therapies. More research is needed, however, before similar conclusions can be made regarding the effectiveness of EMDR in treating children, military veterans with combat PTSD, or victims of multiple traumas experiencing complex PTSD (Rubin, 2003).

In particular, more research is needed on whether the distinctive dual attention stimulation component of EMDR is really necessary and whether its inclusion has any meaningful effect on clinical symptoms (Davidson & Parker, 2001; Rubin, 2003). Although the findings of some randomized experiments have offered limited support to the notion that the distinctive dual attention stimulation component makes EMDR more effective than alternative forms of trauma treatment (Maxfield et al., 2004), other well-controlled studies have had the opposite findings, leading many to question whether any beneficial effects of EMDR can be attributed exclusively to the imaginal exposure aspects of EMDR treatment (Olatunji et al., 2005–2006; Rubin, 2003).

While waiting for the foregoing controversies to be resolved with future research, evidence-based clinicians can opt to use EMDR or an alternative empirically supported intervention (such as prolonged exposure therapy or trauma-focused CBT) depending on various considerations such as what they've been trained in and the preferences of their clients. They might also consider the claims (supported by some limited findings) that EMDR is more client friendly and requires fewer treatment sessions than prolonged exposure therapy (Maxfield et al., 2004; Rubin, 2003).

REFERENCES

Bisson, J., Ehlers, A., Matthews, R., Pilling, S., Richards, D., & Turner, S. (2007). Psychological treatments for chronic posttraumatic stress disorder: Systematic review and meta-analysis. *British Journal of Psychiatry, 190,* 97–104.

Davidson, P. R., & Parker, K. C. H. (2001). Eye movement desensitization and reprocessing (EMDR): A meta-analysis. *Journal of Consulting and Clinical Psychology, 69,* 305–316.

Maxfield, L., Lake, K., & Hyer, L. (2004). Some answers to unanswered questions about the empirical support for EMDR in the treatment of PTSD. *Traumatology, 10*(2), 73–88.

Olatunji, B. O., Parker, L. M., & Lohr, J. M. (2005–2006). Pseudoscience in contemporary psychology. *Scientific Review of Mental Health Practice, 4*(2), 19–31.

Rubin, A. (2003). Unanswered questions about the empirical support for EMDR in the treatment of PTSD. *Traumatology, 9,* 4–30.

Seidler, G. H., & Wagner, F. E. (2006). Comparing the efficacy of EMDR and trauma-focused cognitive-behavioral therapy in the treatment of PTSD: A meta-analytic study. *Psychological Medicine, 36,* 1515–1522.

Shapiro, F., & Forrest, M. S. (2004). *EMDR: The breakthrough "eye movement" therapy for overcoming anxiety, stress, and trauma.* New York: Basic Books.

RECOMMENDED READING

Shapiro, F. (2001). *Eye movement desensitization and reprocessing: Basic principles, protocols and procedures* (2nd ed.). New York: Guilford Press.

ALLEN RUBIN
University of Texas, Austin

See also: Cognitive Behavior Therapy, Adult; Cognitive Behavior Therapy, Child; Exposure Therapy, Adult; Exposure Therapy, Child

F

FALSE MEMORY SYNDROME

See: Memories of Traumatic Experiences

FAMILY SYSTEMS

Clinicians and researchers have long recognized that the relationship between psychological trauma, recovery, and family dynamics are reciprocal and multidimensional. Beyond direct violence or maltreatment between family members, when one family member is exposed to psychological trauma and experiences traumatic stress, this can affect other family members. The family also can play an exacerbating or ameliorative role in the posttraumatic recovery process.

The family system plays a powerful role in protecting against or aggravating the effects of trauma. When a family is exposed to a traumatic event (e.g., crime or natural disaster), the impact is typically felt by all. However, this can also be the case when a traumatic event is experienced by a single family member. In fact, family functioning is one of the strongest predictors of traumatic stress symptomatology, highlighting the central role of the family in overcoming or worsening the impact of trauma experiences.

Characteristics of the family environment, such as domestic violence and poverty, parental responses to traumatic events, and general parenting practices, influence how children and adults adapt following psychological trauma. Parenting practices—especially the use of consistent and nonharsh discipline, supervision, and monitoring—appear to reduce the development of posttraumatic symptoms as well as depression and anxiety. In addition, research indicates that parents who are able to regulate their own reactions to a child's exposure to psychological trauma reduce their child's risk of developing posttraumatic stress disorder (PTSD) and enhance their child's recovery from PTSD.

Marital relationships also influence trauma-related outcomes. When parents communicate effectively and support one another, the marital relationship typically becomes stronger, which can provide a more cohesive, nurturing, and thoughtful approach to parenting. Conversely, when parents respond to the stress of a traumatic experience with hostility, anger, and conflict, the family environment can exacerbate trauma-related symptoms for family members and for the family system. When a family encounters particularly high levels of stress such as a conflictual divorce or domestic violence, the risk for parenting practices to be negatively influenced by irritability, insensitivity and harshness also is high. Additional factors, such as parental history of psychological trauma or mental health or substance use problems, can exacerbate the impact of psychological trauma experiences on the family by disrupting parenting practices.

Just as family factors can affect an individual's response to psychological trauma, one family member's exposure to trauma can shape family functioning and the family environment. For example, PTSD symptoms of avoidance and withdrawal can result in distancing between family members, and posttraumatic symptoms of arousal can result in irritability, anger, hostility, and aggression among family members.

When child maltreatment or domestic violence involve a parent's aggressive and unpredictable behavior and failure to protect the family, this may have long-lasting negative effects on family members and is likely to affect the sense of security and trust among family members. Children exposed to psychological trauma in their families may develop severe dysregulation of the biological stress response system and disruption of positive parent-child bonding. As a result, these children are at risk for persistent psychological, cognitive, school, peer-group, and health problems, as well as delinquency, substance use, health-risking sexual behavior, and teen pregnancy. In sum, when the effects of psychological trauma within the family are not effectively managed or treated, the associated negative effects can transmit to future generations, typically through parenting practices and the parent-child relationship.

Despite strong empirical support for the central role that parenting and the family play in the posttraumatic recovery process, little research has been conducted to identify effective family centered interventions with traumatized children. The few published studies focus on marital or family systems interventions for the treatment of PTSD, having employed small sample sizes, which limit the conclusions that can be drawn. One exception to this is Trauma-Focused Cognitive Behavioral Therapy (TF-CBT; Cohen, Mannarino, & Deblinger, 2006), a trauma-focused intervention with a family treatment component that has accumulated empirical support.

REFERENCE

Cohen, J. A., Mannarino, A. P., & Deblinger, E. (2006). *Treating trauma and traumatic grief in children and adolescents.* New York: Guilford Press.

READING RECOMMENDATIONS

Kiser, L. J., & Black, M. M. (2005). Family processes in the midst of urban poverty: What does the trauma literature tell us? *Aggression and Violent Behavior, 10,* 715–750.

Smith, D. K., Leve, L. D., & Chamberlain, P. (2006). Adolescent girls' offending and health-risking sexual behavior: The predictive role of trauma. *Child Maltreatment, 11,* 346–353.

DANA K. SMITH
Oregon Social Learning Center

PHILIP A. FISHER
Oregon Social Learning Center

See also: Family Therapy; Marital Relationships

FAMILY THERAPY

The entire family tends to be affected when a family member experiences psychological trauma and develops PTSD or other posttraumatic psychosocial problems (such as difficulties with depression, complicated bereavement, anger and distrust, or addictive behaviors). When a child experiences severe violence, illness, maltreatment, or loss of primary caregiver(s), especially if this occurs within the family (but also when it is the result of incidents with peers or in the broader community or society), the parents and other family members (such as siblings) may experience stress-related problems or disorders as a result of their having witnessed or been unable to protect the child from the resultant harm. When parents experience posttraumatic stress problems, whether as a result of experiencing psychological trauma directly or due to harm to a child, their ability to provide their children with a sense of security, nurturance, and healthy encouragement of growth is compromised despite their best efforts (Cohen, in press). Siblings' and other family members' posttraumatic stress reactions also may affect the whole family.

Therefore, models of psychotherapy that focus on assisting the entire family in the wake of psychological trauma have been developed (Catherall, 1998; Figley, 1989; Saltzman, Babayon, Lester, Beardslee, & Pynoos, in press). Family therapy takes many forms, but there are two common denominators that involve assisting family members in: (1) establishing a functional family system by communicating with one another and solving problems in ways that enhance their actual and perceived sense of safety, respect, caring, trust, and healthy development and (2) accessing social support and resources (e.g., from neighbors and community members, or educational, governmental, or religious organizations or family/parent support programs) (Riggs, 2000). Across a wide variety of psychosocial problems (e.g., family crises, psychiatric disorders, addictions, school failure) family therapy interventions have shown consistent evidence of effectiveness in achieving those goals (Diamond & Josephson, 2005). However, few studies have investigated the efficacy of family therapy with families who have experienced psychological trauma or PTSD (Walsh & Rothbaum, 2007). Although behavioral and cognitive behavioral approaches to marital therapy have shown some promise with couples in which one member has PTSD, only one scientifically rigorous study has been conducted in which participants were randomly assigned to receive family therapy or not. In that study, with adult military veterans with PTSD, most of the cases involved only adult partners in couple's therapy (a small number of cases involved a sibling or a parent), and the addition of family therapy to cognitive behavior therapy for PTSD did not show evidence of incremental benefit (Glynn et al., 1999). A family education and support intervention for families with a terminally ill adult member showed some evidence of benefiting the families' grieving process after 13 months (Kissane et al., 2006).

More promising findings have been reported in family therapy interventions that involve parents and a traumatized young child. Several randomized clinical trial studies from two clinical research groups have demonstrated that Child Parent Psychotherapy (CPP) is more effective than case management and existing supportive services in reducing PTSD symptom severity for both parent and child and in enhancing secure parent-child attachment (Lieberman, Ghosh Ippen, & Van Horn, 2006). In CPP, a therapist guides the parent in playing with her or his child in ways that enable the child and parent to recognize, understand, and manage or overcome traumatic stress reactions. Another parent-child psychotherapy, Parent-Child Interaction Therapy (PCIT), takes a more behavioral approach to teaching parents skills for encouraging positive behaviors (such as active play and compliance with parental rules and requests) and reducing negative behaviors (such as angry defiance or impulsive acts) while they play with their child. PCIT has shown evidence of helping abusive parents to function more effectively in parenting (Timmer, Urquiza, Zebell, & McGrath, 2005), but it does not directly address traumatic stress reactions and it has not been tested with traumatized children in a randomized controlled trial study.

Although school-age children and adolescents often experience psychological trauma and have been shown to benefit from family therapy when they have problems, such as aggressive behavior, depression, and substance use problems (Diamond & Josephson, 2005), no approach to family therapy has been reported for families with traumatized older children or adolescents. The Trauma-Focused Cognitive Behavioral Therapy intervention for abused or bereaved children tends to include separate sessions for parents and sessions with both the child and parent(s), with some preliminary evidence that parental involvement enhances outcomes. An intervention for adolescents who have recovered from cancer and their families, and for children who are newly diagnosed with cancer and their families, has shown evidence of effectiveness in assisting the parents and children in reducing PTSD symptoms (Kazak et al., 2005).

Conclusion

Family therapy is theoretically of importance as an approach to directly helping families when one or several members have experienced psychological trauma and are suffering from traumatic stress or other posttraumatic psychosocial problems. Research is needed to test and refine family therapy approaches for families with adult members who have PTSD, and to further develop the effective and promising family therapy models for families with child members who have experienced psychological trauma, PTSD, or life-threatening illness. Clinical and research testing of models of treatment that coordinate individual psychotherapy for PTSD with family therapy also are warranted in order to determine if this combined treatment can enhance the individual's recovery from PTSD and as well as the family's functioning and ability to support that recovery.

REFERENCES

Catherall, D. R. (1998). Treating traumatized families. In C. R. Figley (Ed.), *Burnout in families: The systemic costs of caring* (pp. 187–215). Boca Raton, FL: CRC Press.

Cohen, E. (in press). Parenting in the throes of traumatic events. In D. Brom, R. Pat-Horenczyk, & J. D. Ford (Eds.), *Treating traumatized children: Risk, resilience, and recovery*. London: Routledge.

Diamond, G., & Josephson, A. (2005). Family-based treatment research: A 10-year update. *Journal of the American Academy of Child and Adolescent Psychiatry, 44,* 872–887.

Figley, C. R. (1989). *Helping traumatized families.* San Francisco: Jossey-Bass.

Glynn, S., Eth, S., Randolph, E., Foy, D. Urbaitis, M., Boxer, L., et al. (1999). A test of behavioral family therapy to augment exposure for combat-related posttraumatic stress disorder. *Journal of Consulting and Clinical Psychology, 67,* 243–251.

Kazak, A. E., Simms, S., Alderfer, M. A., Rourke, M. T., Crump, T., McClure, K., et al. (2005). Feasibility and preliminary outcomes from a pilot study of a brief psychological intervention for families of children newly diagnosed with cancer. *Journal of Pediatric Psychology, 30,* 644–655.

Kissane, D., McKenzie, M., Bloch, S., Moskowitz, C., McKenzie, D., & O'Neill, I. (2006). Family focused grief therapy: A randomized, controlled trial in palliative care and bereavement. *American Journal of Psychiatry, 163,* 1208–1218.

Lieberman, A. F., Ghosh Ippen, C., & Van Horn, P. (2006). Child-parent psychotherapy: Six-month follow-up of a randomized controlled trial. *Journal of the American Academy of Child and Adolescent Psychiatry, 45,* 913–918.

Riggs, D. (2000). Marital and family therapy. In E. B. Foa, T. M. Keane, & M. J. Friedman (Eds.), *Effective treatments for PTSD: Practice guidelines from the International Society for Traumatic Stress Studies* (pp. 280–301). New York: Guilford Press.

Saltzman, W. R., Babayon, T., Lester, P., Beardslee, W., & Pynoos, R. S. (in press). Family-based treatments for child traumatic stress: A review and current innovations. In D. Brom, R. Pat-Horenczyk, & J. D. Ford (Eds.), *Treating traumatized children: Risk, resilience, and recovery.* London: Routledge.

Timmer, S. G., Urquiza, A. J., Zebell, N. M., & McGrath, J. M. (2005). Parent-child interaction therapy: Application to maltreating parent-child dyads. *Child Abuse and Neglect, 29,* 825–842.

Walsh, S., & Rothbaum, B. O. (2007). Emerging treatments for PTSD. In M. Friedman, T. Keane, & P. Resick (Eds.), *Handbook of PTSD: Science and practice* (pp. 469–496). New York: Guilford Press.

Julian D. Ford
University of Connecticut School of Medicine

See also: Family Systems; Marital Relationships; Marital Therapy

FERENCZI, SÁNDOR (1873–1933)

Ferenczi was a Hungarian physician who specialized in neurology and neuropathology, and subsequently became a psychoanalyst. One of Freud's closest friends for 20 years, he was a prolific author, admired speaker, and long-term president of the Hungarian Society of Psychoanalysis and the founder of the International Society of Psychoanalysis. In 1896, Freud repudiated the "seduction theory," which stated too absolutely that patients diagnosed with "hysteria" suffered from symptoms related to childhood sexual abuse. His rejection of any connection between traumatization and clinical hysteria was adhered to by most psychoanalysts. However, Ferenczi maintained that many patients continue to relive traumatic childhood experiences, which is consistent with more recent clinical and research studies demonstrating that actual childhood sexual abuse places the victim at risk of developing PTSD and other mood, anxiety, and disssociative disorders.

During World War I, in the field and then in Budapest as director of a neurological clinic, Ferenczi treated numerous combat soldiers who were suffering from war neuroses. Like Janet, Ferenczi recognized the dissociative nature of traumatic memories and related symptoms in these patients, such as tics: "[A]n unexpectedly powerful trauma can have the result in tic, as in traumatic neurosis, of an over-strong memory-fixation on the attitude of the body at the moment of experiencing the trauma, and that to such a degree as to provoke a perceptual or paroxysmatic reproduction of the attitude" (Ferenczi, 1921/1950, p. 156). This fixation involves dissociation of the personality: "[T]here can be no shock, no fright, without traces of a personality split," as Ferenczi (1949/1984, p. 292) speculated (and perhaps overgeneralized). Ferenczi developed a psychoanalytically informed brief and active form of therapy, which subsequently was criticized by Freud but was a forerunner of the short-term psychodynamic therapies currently used to treat PTSD.

In civilian life, Ferenczi treated patients with a history of childhood maltreatment, including sexual abuse. He observed that the more chronic and severe the abuse, the more complex the dissociation of the patient's personality: "If traumatic events accumulate during the life of the growing person, the number and variety of personality splits increase, and soon it will be rather difficult to maintain contact without confusion with all the fragments, which all act as separate personalities but mostly do not know each other" (Ferenczi, 1949/1984, p. 293). Ferenczi also was first to describe the fear-based phenomenon in abused children of identification with the aggressor, in which one part of the personality imitates the abuser's behavior. He also noticed in some trauma survivors what is now called an observer part of the personality: "It really seems as though, under the stress of imminent danger, a part of the personality splits off in the form of a self-observing psychic instance wanting to give help" (Ferenczi, 1931; as quoted in Leys, 2000, p. 131).

Ferenczi realized that the therapeutic relationship, and in particular trust in the therapist, was an essential factor in the patient's healing. "That trust [i.e., of the therapist] is a certain something that establishes the contrast between the present and the unbearable, traumatogenic past, a contrast therefore which is indispensable to bringing the past to life, no longer as a hallucinatory reproduction, but as an objective memory" (Ferenczi, 1949/1984, p. 287).

Ferenczi's two major works on trauma and dissociation, written at the end of his life, are his article, "Confusion of Tongues between Adults and the Child," a treatise on childhood sexual abuse, and his *Clinical Diary*. Against Freud's wishes, Ferenczi read the treatise at the 1932 International Psycho-Analytic Congress in Wiesbaden, and was subsequently ostracized from the psychoanalytic community. It remains unclear whether this staunch disapproval was directed toward his unorthodox therapeutic techniques or to his emphasis on the traumatic origins, in particular, childhood sexual abuse, of many disorders. The original German version of this paper was published in 1933, but the English version was not published until 1949. Ferenczi wrote his *Clinical Diary* in 1932, but among psychoanalysts it was long considered too revisionistic, and publication was postponed until the 1980s (Ferenczi, 1988). With the rise of awareness that psychological trauma, including childhood sexual abuse, may be a major etiological factor of a variety of mental disorders, interest in his writings on trauma and dissociation has increased.

REFERENCES

Ferenczi, S. (1921). Psychoanalytic observations on tics. *International Journal of Psychoanalysis, 2*, 1–30.

Ferenczi, S. (1949) Confusion of tongues between adults and the child: The language of tenderness and passion. *International Journal of Psychoanalysis, 30*, 225–230.

Ferenczi, S. (1988). *The clinical diary of Sándor Ferenczi* (J. Dupont, Ed.). Cambridge, MA: Harvard University Press.

Leys, R. (2000). *Trauma: A genealogy*. Chicago: University of Chicago Press.

RECOMMENDED READING

Rachman, A. W. (1997). *Sándor Frenczi: The psychotherapist of tenderness and passion*. Northvale, NJ: Aronson.

ONNO VAN DER HART
Utrecht University

See also: Dissociation; Freud, Sigmund; History of Psychological Trauma; Hysteria; Janet, Pierre

FLASHBACKS

The most recent edition of the *Diagnostic and Statistical Manual of Mental Disorders* (*DSM-IV-TR;* American Psychiatric Association, 2000) proposes that flashbacks or "dissociative flashback episodes" are one of the distinguishing symptoms of PTSD. A current scientific puzzle, however, is the precise relationship between flashback memory experiences and ordinary narrative memories of the traumatic event, particularly when patients simultaneously report "amnesia for the details of the event"—another of the *DSM-IV-TR* criteria for PTSD.

At present, there have been few systematic studies of flashbacks and no generally accepted way of measuring them. As generally used in the trauma field, the term refers to a kind of memory experience that most people rarely, if ever, come across. Flashbacks are thought to differ in numerous ways from what we think of as normal memory. For example, they are a form of involuntary memory, triggered automatically by reminders. Flashbacks are usually packed with sensory detail; however, these details are typically disjointed and fragmentary.

During flashbacks individuals may reexperience the pain they had from a traumatic injury and the emotion experienced during the most intense moments of the traumatic event. These emotions commonly consist of fear, helplessness, and horror, but may also involve other emotions such as anger and shame (Hellawell & Brewin, 2004). "Reliving" refers to a distortion of the sense of time so that the events seem to be happening in the present rather than (as in the case of ordinary memories) belonging to the past. Individuals with PTSD often report that the flashbacks are highly repetitive and remain unchanged for months or years, but no empirical data have been collected to support or contradict this claim. The intensity of flashbacks can vary from a transitory, mild reliving to a prolonged dissociative episode in which all awareness of the current environment is lost.

Flashbacks are associated with events involving extreme fear, often including panic attacks (Nixon & Bryant, 2003). Under normal circumstances, attentional processes are needed to bind together individual sensory features to form a stable object, episodic memory, or action sequence (Treisman & DeSchepper, 1996). During traumatic events, such attentional processes operate less efficiently and tend to be restricted to the main source of danger, so that sensory elements from the wider scene may be less effectively bound together. Flashbacks could involve the automatic activation of these memory traces of unattended aspects, resulting in the disorganized and fragmentary reexperiencing of the traumatic scene. There is preliminary evidence that flashbacks are associated with distinct patterns of neural activation in brain areas including the brainstem, and areas associated with motor control, complex visual/spatial cues and memory (Osuch et al., 2001).

Theoretically there is debate centered on the memory mechanisms responsible for flashbacks (Brewin, 2007). It has been suggested that flashbacks are essentially no different from ordinary memories. However, flashbacks have also been hypothesized to be ordinary memories processed in special ways; and additionally they have been speculated to be the product of a special memory system dedicated to encoding low-level sensory, visuospatial, and body state information. The idea that there is a fundamentally distinct type of memory for traumatic events that can be distinguished from ordinary narrative memory dates back at least as far as Pierre Janet (1904), the French neurologist.

Psychological treatments typically involve having the person with PTSD focus for an extended period on the content of the flashback, either drawing it or describing it in words that are written or spoken. Although it is not known why these procedures are effective, it may be that the increased attention recruits different areas of the brain, particularly cortical areas, to process the unattended traumatic material for the first time.

REFERENCES

American Psychiatric Association. (2000). *Diagnostic and statistical manual of mental disorders* (4th ed., text rev.). Washington, DC: Author.

Brewin, C. R. (2007). Autobiographical memory for trauma: Update on four controversies. *Memory, 15,* 227–248.

Hellawell, S. J., & Brewin, C. R. (2004). A comparison of flashbacks and ordinary autobiographical memories of trauma: Content and language. *Behaviour Research and Therapy, 42,* 1–12.

Janet, P. (1904). L'amnésie et la dissociation des souvenirs par l'émotion. *Journal de Psychologie, 1,* 417–453.

Nixon, R. D. V., & Bryant, R. A. (2003). Peritraumatic and persistent panic attacks in acute stress disorder. *Behaviour Research and Therapy, 41,* 1237–1242.

Osuch, E. A., Benson, B., Geraci, M., Odell, D., Herscovitch, P., McCann, U. D., et al. (2001). Regional cerebral blood flow correlated with flashback intensity in patients with posttraumatic stress disorder. *Biological Psychiatry, 50,* 246–253.

Treisman, A., & DeSchepper, B. (1996). Object tokens, attention, and visual memory. In T. Inui & J. L. McClelland (Eds.), *Attention and performance XVI: Information integration in perception and communication* (pp. 15–46). Cambridge, MA: MIT Press.

Steph J. Hellawell
Fleming Nuffield Unit

Chris R. Brewin
University College

See also: Dissociation; Intrusive Reexperiencing; Janet, Pierre; Memory; Posttraumatic Stress Disorder

FORENSIC ASSESSMENT

Clinicians are called on to assess the emotional effects of trauma in both civil and criminal settings. These evaluations may occur to assess psychiatric disability, workers' compensation (in response to a mental disorder caused at one's place of work), emotional damages, mitigation of criminal penalty, and sanity at the time of the offense. Forensic assessments differ significantly from therapeutic assessments because the purpose is to help answer legal questions rather than to guide the treatment of the person being examined.

Agency and Dual Roles

The forensic clinician should first clarify the question of agency, or which party is employing him or her. Because of the differences between the forensic and clinical assessments, it is best to avoid combining the two roles whenever possible.

Clinicians involved in providing treatment are often called on to perform forensic assessments. For example, a patient who has suffered PTSD as a result of a motor vehicle accident may ask his or her treating clinician to serve as an expert witness in a lawsuit. This creates a dual role in which the clinician becomes both a treatment provider and a forensic evaluator. Whenever possible, dual roles should be avoided as they potentially compromise both the treatment and the forensic evaluation. The treatment relationship is likely to be compromised if the clinician reaches conclusions that are unfavorable to the patient/litigant, while the forensic assessment is likely to be compromised by the clinician's role as an advocate for his or her patient.

Referral Issue

Because forensic assessment addresses legal questions, it is critical to obtain the referral question and relevant legal standard in writing before performing the assessment. The referral issue will determine the areas that need to be addressed in the evaluation.

Collateral Information

The forensic evaluator should ideally obtain and review information from relevant collateral sources prior to interviewing the person being evaluated. Potentially useful sources of information include medical and mental health evaluation and treatment records, police reports, and personnel files. It can also be helpful to interview informants such as coworkers, who can often provide insight into the subject's level of functioning. Significant others can corroborate reports of PTSD symptoms such as concentration difficulties, and especially symptoms that are not as readily observable to the forensic evaluator, such as insomnia, and sometimes even nocturnal movement suggestive of nightmares.

Interview

Prior to performing the interview, the clinician must obtain consent from the person to be evaluated. The consent process should include a discussion of the nature and purpose of the evaluation, disclosure of who has retained the expert and to whom information will be released. In addition, the forensic evaluator should explicitly advise the evaluee of the absence of a treatment relationship.

The interview should probe into the personal, medical, and mental health history of the person being evaluated. The mental health history should identify any symptoms and treatments occurring before and after the traumatic event. A careful trauma history including military service, abusive treatment by others, and victimization should be obtained. The evaluator may consider using a standardized measure of traumatic event exposure. If there are multiple traumas, the effect of each should be explored. A detailed account of the litigated traumatic event should be elicited.

The symptoms that followed the trauma should be explored, first in an open-ended fashion and followed by inquiry about each of the *DSM-IV* symptoms of PTSD and other relevant disorders, preferably by using a structured diagnostic interview. Exploration for indications of other mental disorders is important in view of the fact that individuals with PTSD have elevated rates of other psychiatric disorders such as major depressive disorder (MDD; Kessler, Sonnega, Bromet, Hughes, & Nelson, 1995).

After inquiring about the presence of each symptom of PTSD, the evaluator should ask the evaluee to describe each symptom that he or she endorsed, in detail. People who have been coached regarding *DSM-IV* criteria may have difficulty describing symptoms and their effects on life activities in sufficient detail. The evaluator should consider using a standardized instrument to specifically aid in the diagnosis of PTSD, such as the Clinician Administered PTSD Scale. The use of a standardized instrument to augment the clinical interview may increase the reliability and validity of the diagnosis.

Malingering

Malingering is defined in *DSM-IV-TR* as "the intentional production of false or grossly exaggerated physical or psychological symptoms motivated by external incentives" (American Psychiatric Association, 2000). This is an important issue because PTSD is relatively easy to feign since the symptoms are largely subjective and the criteria are widely available. Each malingerer is like an actor playing a role, and the key to detecting malingering is having a detailed understanding of the symptoms that they might fake. Some clues to malingered PTSD include the verbatim recitation of PTSD criteria, an inability to explain how PTSD symptoms affect daily activities, alleging constant or worsening symptoms, and incongruence between reported symptoms and observed signs during the interview (Kleinman & Egan, 2003).

For example, a person under evaluation may report having an exaggerated startle response, yet show no reaction when she hears a passing car backfire. And while nightmares in genuine combat-related PTSD often recur as verbatim reenactments of the combat trauma, malingerers may not know that posttraumatic dreams in civilian PTSD usually vary in content. Thus, a malingerer might allege having persistent dreams precisely reenacting the traumatic event. Further research is required to elucidate the features of malingered PTSD.

Psychological Testing

Psychological testing can be a useful adjunct to the clinical assessment. Psychological testing should be considered when the evaluee is guarded, malingering is suspected, the diagnosis is unclear, or the evaluee's response to the event appears exaggerated (Kleinman & Egan, 2003).

The MMPI-2 is the most widely used psychological test. However, there are two significant limitations to using the MMPI-2 in the assessment of trauma-related psychopathology. First, the MMPI-2 relies entirely on the evaluee's perception of an event as traumatic because it does not require the evaluator to make an objective assessment of whether the trauma meets *DSM-IV-TR* criteria for PTSD. The *DSM-IV-TR* requires that the traumatic event involves "actual or threatened death or serious injury, or a threat to the physical integrity of self or others" (American Psychiatric Association, 2000). Thus, an event that does not meet the *DSM-IV-TR* criterion A for PTSD can erroneously lead to a diagnosis of PTSD if one uses the MMPI-2 in isolation. The second problem is that response patterns specific to malingered PTSD are still under investigation. Thus, the MMPI-2 should be used with caution in the assessment of trauma victims (Resnick, West, & Payne, 2008).

The Structured Interview of Reported Symptoms (SIRS) is specifically designed and validated to detect malingering. However, its ability to reliably detect malingered PTSD is still under investigation.

Communicating the Findings

If an evaluation report is requested, it should address the legal question and avoid technical jargon. The report should list all of the sources of information including clinical interviews, medical records, and legal records reviewed. All opinions should be stated with reasonable medical/psychological certainty. This is a legal term of art that generally means "more likely than not," though the definition varies by jurisdiction. The report should explain the reasoning behind each of the opinions in detail.

REFERENCES

American Psychiatric Association. (2000). *Diagnostic and statistical manual of mental disorders* (4th ed., text rev.). Washington, DC: Author.

Kessler, R. C., Sonnega, A., Bromet, E., Hughes, M., & Nelson, C. B. (1995). Posttraumatic stress disorder in the National Comorbidity Survey. *Archives of General Psychiatry, 52,* 1048–1060.

Kleinman, S. B., & Egan, S. B. (2003). Trauma-induced psychiatric disorders and civil law. In R. Rosner (Ed.), *Principles and practice of forensic psychiatry* (2nd ed., pp. 290–298). London: Arnold.

Resnick, P. J., West, S., & Payne, J. (2008). Malingering of posttraumatic disorders. In R. Rogers (Ed.), *Clinical assessment of malingering and deception* (3rd ed.). New York: Guilford Press.

SHERIF SOLIMAN
Case Western Reserve University

PHILLIP RESNICK
Case Western Reserve University

See also: Assessment, Psychometrics, Adult; Malingering

FREEZING

See: Conditioned Fear

FREUD, SIGMUND

Sigmund Freud (1856–1939), founder of psychoanalysis, pioneered the scientific study of psychological trauma. Freud was introduced to the clinical problem of psychological trauma by his mentors, Josef Breuer and Jean Martin Charcot. His innovation was a psychodynamic perspective. If, as Breuer agreed, "hysterics suffer mainly from reminiscences" (a radical proposition at a time when psychiatric conditions were generally understood as evidence of degenerative brain disease) (Breuer & Freud, 1895/1955), Freud went his own way in holding that the dissociative and conversion symptoms of his patients (discussed elsewhere in this Encyclopedia) were a compromise between an effort to remember and an effort to forget.

Freud hypothesized that forgetting was maintained actively through the psychological defense of repression. At the end of his career, Freud extended this concept by describing the intrusive and avoidant symptoms that arise from past psychological trauma: a perspective that now anchors the diagnostic criteria of posttraumatic stress disorder.

In his earliest writings, Freud held that every case of hysteria began with a childhood seduction. Over time, he realized that many of his patients had never been seduced. Based on this observation, he ultimately saw that psychological distress could also arise from overwhelming conflict between sexual drives and psychological inhibitions. Thus, psychological distress could result from either external (e.g., traumatic events) or internal (e.g., emotional conflicts) stressors (and was often a combination of both).

Freud was drawn back to the study of psychological trauma by his experience with survivors of World War I. The combat nightmares of veterans drove Freud to reassess his theory of dreams as wish fulfillments. While he maintained that normal dreaming fulfilled the function of pursuing pleasure and avoiding what was unpleasurable, he came to see the repetitive, horrific dreams of trauma survivors as evidence of a regressive compulsion to mentally repeat traumatic events. While such repetition might represent a last-ditch effort toward mastery of overwhelming stressors, Freud suggested that it might also represent evidence of a death instinct, which he defined as a basic drive to escape all noxious excitation even if this required the person's own annihilation. These principles, laid out in *Beyond the Pleasure Principle* (Freud, 1920/1955), led to an understanding of psychological trauma as the product of a stressful event having breached the limits of an individual's ability to cope (the so-called "stimulus barrier") resulting in a fundamental alteration of the psyche.

In 1933, Freud and Albert Einstein published *Why War?* a joint effort to advocate against the next wave of traumatic events then looming over the world. To the end of his career, Freud maintained that psychological trauma was a complex, dynamic process with roots in both external events and internal struggles (Gay, 1988). Freud's view of man as imperfectible yet capable of achieving a working balance sufficient to work and to love is in itself an important perspective on the concept of psychological trauma. Traumatic events are not alien to human experience but become pathological when they overthrow that working balance. Psychoanalysis and the psychodynamic psychotherapies that evolved from it are, in large part, an effort to restore balance

through exploration of the past, clarification of the present, and reimagining the future.

REFERENCES

Breuer, J., & Freud, S. (1955). Studies on hysteria. In J. Strachey (Ed. & Trans.), *The standard edition of the complete psychological works of Sigmund Freud* (Vol. 2, pp. 1–335). London: Hogarth Press. (Original work published 1895)

Freud, S. (1955). Beyond the pleasure principle. In J. Strachey (Ed. & Trans.), *The standard edition of the complete psychological works of Sigmund Freud* (Vol. 18, pp. 1–64). London: Hogarth Press. (Original work published 1920)

Gay, P. (1988). *Freud: A life for our time.* New York: Norton.

Harold Kudler
Duke University Medical Center

See also: Ferenczi, Sándor; History of Psychological Trauma; Hysteria; Janet, Pierre; Psychodynamic Therapy, Adult

FRONTAL CORTEX

The human brain's frontal lobe is commonly considered to be the seat of many of the most complex forms of human cognitive, affective, and social information processing. For example, dorsolateral aspects frontal cortex are thought to implement many higher-order cognitive processes involved in working memory and problem solving that facilitate effective coping with stress, whereas more medial and ventrolateral aspects of frontal cortex are thought to mediate our ability to regulate our emotions and self-reflect about our goals. Accordingly, alterations in the structure or the functioning of the frontal cortex have been studied in conjunction with the cognitive, affective, and social effects of traumatic life experiences using neuroimaging technology, most notably magnetic resonance imaging (MRI) and positron emission tomography (PET). Specifically, neuroscientists generally believe that human learning takes place through modifications of brain structure and function, and many traumatologists hypothesize accordingly that traumatic experiences may alter normal brain development in pathological ways. For example, threatening and aversive experiences may sensitize the brain to such stimuli, causing one to be hypervigilant and expect harm even in circumstances where it may be less warranted. In addition, because much of the brain's growth and maturation is thought to require developmentally appropriate learning experiences, psychological trauma experienced in early childhood may express itself at the neural level in a deficiency of learning-related changes occurring within the frontal cortex and related brain areas.

The typical research design of neuroimaging studies has been to compare groups of individuals who have been exposed to psychological trauma (or not) and who have versus have not developed psychiatric disorders as a result of their experiences, most notably PTSD. Unfortunately this strategy makes it difficult to ascertain how much the associated frontal cortex abnormalities that are observed in these studies are directly the result of individuals' traumatic experiences versus other psychopathologic processes that may also be associated with psychiatric disorders. This shortcoming of the current research literature is especially problematic in considering that psychological trauma exposure is only rarely measured in studies of individuals with certain psychiatric disorders where exposure to traumatic events often plays an etiological role (e.g., major depression; Nemeroff et al., 2006). Thus, changes in the frontal lobe of the brain that may seem to be due to the effect of exposure to psychological trauma or PTSD may be due to other factors such as other psychiatric disorders.

Discussion of the human frontal lobe is typically divided in terms of the primary motor and premotor areas, and the more anterior part of the frontal lobe, which is referred to as the prefrontal cortex. The prefrontal cortex in turn is divided into medial and lateral aspects, and each of these broad regions are in turn divided into more specific gyri (outfoldings or ridges identifiable on the surface of the brain, referred to in the singular as *gyrus*) and sulci (infoldings, referred to in the singular as *sulcus*). This entry focuses on a discussion of the effects of psychological trauma on the prefrontal cortex (rather than on the primary motor and premotor cortex) because this is where the majority of research has also focused. The medial (middle) frontal lobe consists of the medial superior frontal gryus, the medial frontal pole, and the medial orbitofrontal gyrus, together housing Brodmann fields 8, 9, 10, 11, and 25 (in the Brodmann system, different areas of the brain have been numbered according to their cytoarchitecture, meaning these regions have been shown to be composed of different types of cells). Anterior (frontal) regions of the limbic system's (*see:* **Limbic System**) cingulate gyrus, encompassing Brodmann fields 32 and 24, are also often included in discussion of the medial frontal cortex. The lateral (side portion of the) frontal lobe is divided running anteriorly and inferiorly (i.e., from front to back) into several gryi: precentral, superior frontal, middle frontal, inferior frontal, orbitofrontal, and frontal pole.

Studies of maltreated boys diagnosed with PTSD determined that total prefrontal cortex volume was approximately 8.6% smaller, and gray matter volume approximately 3.4% smaller in traumatized relative to nontraumatized boys ranging in age from 4 to 17 (De Bellis & Keshavan, 2003; this was measured from the frontal pole to the most anterior part of the corpus callosum, the corpus callosum being the most major connecting region between the brain's left and right hemispheres). Similar differences, however, were not found in girls of the same age range. The same research group had previously demonstrated a lower N-actylaspartylglutamate (NAA) to creatine ratio, considered to be marker of neuronal integrity, within the perigenual region of the anterior cingulate cortex (which is immediately in front of the most anterior part of the corpus callosum; De Bellis, Keshavan, Spencer, & Hall, 2000), although gender differences were not investigated in that study.

The majority of structural imaging studies of adult PTSD have investigated the hippocampus (Nemeroff et al., 2006; *see:* **Hippocampus**). However, studies have also documented reduced gray matter volume (Rauch et al., 2003; Woodward et al., 2006) and/or NAA concentration (Ham et al., 2007) in the perigenual region of the anterior cingulate cortex similar to what was found in children, as well as reduced gray matter volume within specifically the left (Yamasue et al., 2003), right (Corbo, Clément, Armony, Pruessner, & Brunet, 2005), or bilateral (Kitayama, Quinn, & Bremner, 2006; Woodward et al., 2006) dorsal (upper portion of the) ACC. Within the dorsal anterior cingulate cortex, a reduced NAA to creatine ratio was not found in adult women with PTSD due to interpersonal violence, although increased choline and myo-inositol to creatine ratios were found, possibly indicative of white matter abnormalities within this region (Seedat, Videen, Kennedy, & Stein, 2005). Finally, Rauch et al. (2003) observed reduced volume within the subgenual anterior cingulate cortex inclusive of the subcallosal orbitofrontal cortex. Recent studies are also describing altered inhibitory neurotransmitter binding potential within frontal cortical areas, such as for mu-opiod receptors within the anterior cingulate, medial prefrontal, and orbitofrontal cortex (Liberzon et al., 2007) and benzodiazepine receptors within widespread frontal cortical areas (Geuze et al., 2008).

Gray and white matter abnormalities within these medial prefrontal lobe and ACC regions, including reduced volume and neuronal integrity, may be significant in light of many of the cognitive and emotional disturbances commonly accompanying chronic exposure to traumatic stressors (Frewen & Lanius, 2006; Liberzon & Martis, 2006). Specifically, the medial prefrontal lobe and anterior cingulate cortex are involved in many important cognitive and emotional operations, such as generating and modulating emotional arousal and self-referential processing (e.g., "Is this important to me?" "Can I handle this?"). Consistent with this conjecture, reliable differences have been observed with respect to functional responses within the frontal cortex to specific cognitive and emotional tasks. Several studies have investigated how trauma-exposed individuals with versus without PTSD respond to verbally scripted reminders of their traumatic memories (reviewed by Etkin & Wager, 2007). Individuals with PTSD reliably exhibit less response in bilateral anterior cingulate, medial orbitofrontal, and dorsomedial prefrontal cortex. Furthermore, Etkin and Wager (2007)

found that activity within the anterior cingulate cortex negatively correlated with activity in right insular cortex and right amygdala, limbic/paralimbic structures involved in the perception and learning of fearful associations, as well as subjective experience of anxiety and arousal (the insula is found within medial brain generally in the vicinity of where the temporal and parietal cortex meet). The particularly robust finding of reduced response in the perigenual anterior cingulate cortex and medial prefrontal cortex during the experience of trauma reminders in adults with PTSD may relate to the reduced ability of traumatized individuals to regulate their level of emotional arousal, as this region is known to play a role in cognition-emotion interactions and arousal modulation (Critchley, 2005). It is less likely that the findings relate specifically to PTSD's memory reexperiencing phenomena, as a similarly reduced response in individuals with PTSD has been observed when individuals recall negative memories that were not patently traumatic (e.g., sadness and anxiety-inducing memories; Lanius et al., 2003), or view generally aversive pictures (Phan, Britton, Taylor, Fig, & Liberzon, 2006).

Studies have observed poorer performance on certain cognitive tests in traumatized individuals, in particular, on tests of executive functioning including verbal-auditory working memory and set-shifting in individuals with PTSD. Such cognitive tasks are thought to be instrumented by the general cognitive control network, including the dorsolateral prefrontal cortex, anterior cingulate cortex/presupplementary motor area, dorsal premotor cortex, and inferior frontal junction, as well as cortical areas outside of the frontal lobe (the anterior insular cortex and posterior [back portion] of the parietal cortex; see Cole & Schneider, 2007; Vasterling, Proctor, Amoroso, Kane, Gackstetter, et al., 2006; Vasterling, Proctor, Amoroso, Kane, Heeren, et al., 2006). For example, Koso and Hansen (2006) observed that combat veterans with PTSD scored significantly more poorly on tests of verbal working memory, sustained attention and response inhibition, and set-shifting relative to combat veterans without PTSD. These findings are consistent with self-reported general concentration and memory problems in traumatized individuals, particularly those with PTSD, and fMRI studies that have shown altered activity within frontal cortex, including left inferior frontal gyrus, right DLPFC, medial prefrontal cortex, and anterior cingulate cortex (Bryant et al., 2005) and left precentral gyrus and DLPFC (middle frontal gyrus; Clark et al., 2003) during working memory-related tasks in individuals with PTSD. Nevertheless, several large, well-conducted studies have failed to observe robust problems in performance of frontal-lobe related cognitive tests in combat veterans (e.g., Crowell, Kieffer, Siders, & Vanderploeg, 2002; Zalewski, Thompson, & Gottesman, 1994) or individuals exposed to domestic violence (e.g., Stein, Kennedy, & Twamley, 2002) with or without PTSD.

Further research is required to evaluate whether state-dependent problems in emotional processing interact with problems with cognitive processing. For example, it may be that cognitive problems are secondary to current affective disturbance, such that individuals suffering from the effects of psychological trauma need to be in an affectively primed state (e.g., aroused by memory of their trauma) for associated deficits in cognitive processing to be reliably observed. In contrast, it may be that cognitive deficits in adults associated with traumatization vary more as a function of the occurrence of early life trauma than traumas experienced during adulthood. This might be hypothesized to the extent that cognitive processing deficits resulting from exposure to psychological trauma are due to disruption in learning-dependent cognitive development.

REFERENCES

Bryant, R. A., Felmingham, K. L., Kemp, A. H., Barton, M., Peduto, A. S., Rennie, C., et al. (2005). Neural networks of information processing in posttraumatic stress disorder: A functional magnetic resonance imaging study. *Biological Psychiatry, 58,* 111–118.

Clark, C. R., McFarlane, A. C., Morris, P., Weber, D. L., Sonkkilla, C., Shaw, M., et al. (2003). Cerebral function in posttraumatic stress disorder during verbal working memory updating: A positron emission tomography study. *Biological Psychiatry, 53,* 474–481.

Cole, M. W., & Schneider, W. (2007). The cognitive control network: Integrated cortical regions with dissociable functions. *NeuroImage, 37,* 343–360.

Corbo, V., Clément, M.-H., Armony, J. L., Pruessner, J. C., & Brunet, A. (2005). Size versus shape differences: Contrasting voxel-based and volumetric analyses of the anterior cingulate cortex in individuals with acute posttraumatic stress disorder. *Biological Psychiatry, 58,* 119–124.

Critchley, H. D. (2005). Neural mechanisms of autonomic, affective, and cognitive integration. *Journal of Comparative Neurology, 493,* 154–166.

De Bellis, M. D., & Keshavan, M. S. (2003). Sex differences in brain maturation in maltreatment-related pediatric posttraumatic stress disorder. *Neuroscience and Biobehavioral Review, 27,* 103–117.

De Bellis, M. D., Keshavan, M. S., Spencer, S., & Hall, J. (2000). N-Acetylaspartate concentration in the anterior cingulate of maltreated children and adolescents with PTSD. *American Journal of Psychiatry, 157,* 1175–1177.

Etkin, A., & Wager, T. D. (2007). Functional neuroimaging of anxiety: A meta-analysis of emotional processing in PTSD, social anxiety disorder, and specific phobia. *American Journal of Psychiatry, 164,* 1476–1488.

Frewen, P. A., & Lanius, R. A. (2006). Toward a psychobiology of posttraumatic self-dysregulation: Reexperiencing, hyperarousal, dissociation, and emotional numbing. *Annals of the New York Academy of Science, 1071,* 110–124.

Geuze, E., van Berckel, B. N., Lammertsma, A. A., Boellaard, R., de Kloet, C. S., Vermetten, E., et al. (2008). Imaging trauma in vivo: GABA(A) benzodiazepine receptor binding. *Molecular Psychiatry, 13,* 3.

Ham, B.-Y., Chey, J., Yoon, S. J., Sung, Y., Jeong, D.-U., Kim, S. J., et al. (2007). Decreased N-acetyl-aspartate levels in anterior cingulate and hippocampus in subjects with posttraumatic stress disorder: A proton magnetic resonance spectroscopy study. *European Journal of Neuroscience, 25,* 324–329.

Kitayama, N., Quinn, S., & Bremner, J. D. (2006). Smaller volume of anterior cingulate cortex in abuse-related posttraumatic stress disorder. *Journal of Affective Disorders, 90,* 171–174.

Koso, M., & Hansen, S. (2006). Executive function and memory in posttraumatic stress disorder: A study of Bosnian war veterans. *European Psychiatry, 21,* 167–173.

Lanius, R. A., Williamson, P. C., Hopper, J., Densmore, M., Boksman, K., Gupta, M. A., et al. (2003). Recall of emotional states in posttraumatic stress disorder: An fMRI investigation. *Biological Psychiatry, 53,* 204–210.

Liberzon, I., & Martis, B. (2006). Neuroimaging studies of emotional responses in PTSD. *Annals of the New York Academy of Science, 1071,* 87–109.

Liberzon, I., Taylor, S. F., Phan, K. L., Britton, J. C., Fig, L. M., Bueller, J. A., et al. (2007). Altered central Ì-Opioid receptor binding after psychological trauma. *Biological Psychiatry, 61,* 1030–1038.

Nemeroff, C. B., Bremner, J. D., Foa, E. B., Mayberg, H. S., North, C. S., & Stein, M. B. (2006). Posttraumatic stress disorder: A state-of-the-science review. *Journal of Psychiatric Research, 40,* 1–21.

Phan, K. L., Britton, J. C., Taylor, S. F., Fig, L. M., & Liberzon, I. (2006). Corticolimbic blood flow during nontraumatic emotional processing in posttraumatic stress disorder. *Archives of General Psychiatry, 63,* 184–192.

Rauch, S. L., Shin, L. M., Segal, E., Pitman, R. K., Carson, M. A., McMullin, K., et al. (2003). Selectively reduced regional cortical volumes in posttraumatic stress disorder. *NeuroReport, 14,* 913–916.

Seedat, S., Videen, J. S., Kennedy, C. M., & Stein, M. B. (2005). Single voxel proton magnetic resonance spectroscopy in women with and without intimate partner violence-related posttraumatic stress disorder. *Psychiatry Research, 139,* 249–258.

Stein, M. B., Kennedy, C. M., & Twamley, E. W. (2002). Neuropsychological function in female victims of intimate partner violence with and without posttraumatic stress disorder. *Biological Psychiatry, 52,* 1079–1088.

Vasterling, J. J., Proctor, S. P., Amoroso, P., Kane, R., Gackstetter, G., Ryan, M. A., et al. (2006). The Neurocognition Deployment Health Study: A prospective cohort study of army soldiers. *Military Medicine, 171,* 253–260.

Vasterling, J. J., Proctor, S. P., Amoroso, P., Kane, R., Heeren, T., & White, R. F. (2006). Neuropsychological outcomes of army personnel following deployment to the Iraq war. *Journal of the American Medical Association, 296,* 519–529.

Woodward, S. H., Kaloupek, D. G., Streeter, C. C., Martinez, C., Schaer, M., & Ellez, S. (2006). Decreased anterior cingulate volume in combat-related PTSD. *Biological Psychiatry, 59,* 582–587.

Yamasue, H., Kasai, K., Iwanami, A., Ohtani, T., Yamada, H., Abe, O., et al. (2003). Voxel-based analysis of MRI reveals anterior cingulate gray-matter volume reduction in posttraumatic stress disorder due to terrorism. *Proceedings of the National Academy of Sciences, USA, 100,* 9039–9043.

Zalewski, C., Thompson, W., & Gottesman, I. (1994). Comparison of neuropsychological test performance in PTSD, generalized anxiety disorder, and control Vietnam veterans. *Assessment, 1,* 133–142.

Paul A. Frewen
University Of Western Ontario

Ruth A. Lanius
London Health Sciences Center

See also: Anterior Cingulate Cortex; Biology, Brain Structure, and Function, Adult; Biology, Brain Structure, and Function, Child; Biology, Neurochemistry

FUNCTIONING

See: Occupational Disability; Quality of Life

G

GENDER

This entry provides a brief overview of some of the gender issues central to understanding trauma exposure and posttraumatic stress disorder (PTSD). To cover all of the information relevant to this topic would exceed the scope of an encyclopedia entry, but within these limits we examine key conceptual issues, current research findings, and explanations in the field for gender differences in trauma, PTSD prevalence, and PTSD treatment.

Sex and Gender

Sex and gender are terms that refer to different, but related, constructs. Sex denotes the biological fact of being either male or female, while gender describes the interaction between sex and social environment. This conceptualization of gender implies that differences between men and women may vary as a function of culture, social roles, economic characteristics, or other factors. The remainder of this entry further elucidates gender issues that are particularly relevant to traumatic stress.

Trauma Exposure

While more than half of the general population will experience at least one traumatic event over the course of a lifetime, men experience a significantly higher frequency of lifetime trauma exposure when compared with women. There are some distinct gender-related patterns of trauma exposure, with men being more likely to experience physical assault, community and political violence, automobile accidents, combat exposure, being threatened with a weapon or held captive, whereas women experience higher rates of sexual assault, molestation, and child physical abuse. If men experience greater exposure to trauma than women, it might seem natural to conclude that the prevalence of PTSD would also be higher among men than women. This, however, is not the case. The higher prevalence of PTSD among women, despite the fact that men experience greater trauma exposure, is a gender difference that has attracted much attention and deserves further examination (see Kimerling, Ouimette, & Weitlauf, 2007).

Prevalence of PTSD

The prevalence of PTSD in women is approximately twice that of men (see Tolin & Foa, 2006). One factor that appears to at least partially account for this gender difference is that the traumatic events most common to women, such as sexual assault, are associated with a higher conditional risk for PTSD as compared to other events. Though women may tend to experience fewer traumatic events as compared to men, those events may have a more severe impact.

The standard traumatic event inventories used in PTSD research may not reflect the role of trauma severity in women's increased rates of PTSD. For example, a single incident of physical assault by a stranger and prolonged exposure to intimate partner violence would both be categorized as physical assault, yet the more severe and prolonged trauma is more common to women. In fact, when objective trauma severity criteria used in the *DSM-IV* PTSD diagnosis are used to measure trauma exposure, men no longer appear to have higher rates of trauma exposure than women.

While trauma characteristics (type, frequency, severity) may partially explain gender differences in PTSD, gender roles and social context also show some explanatory power, though less research attention has been devoted to these issues. Gender differences in PTSD appear to be more pronounced in traditional cultures or developing countries, and are thought to be exacerbated by traditional gender roles (see Norris, Foster, & Weisshaar, 2002). For example, cultural norms that discourage emotional expression in men may result in underreporting PTSD symptoms in this population. In cultures that establish women as the sole caregiver and where women are dependent on close social networks for their livelihood, trauma may differentially impact the development of PTSD among women more than men. A review of the outcomes associated with natural disaster, often thought to be a "gender neutral" event, revealed gender-specific risk factors for PTSD, such as the social roles of wife or mother (Norris, Friedman, et al., 2002). Additional research in this area is needed to explore the moderating effects of culture, social roles, and other contextual factors on the development of PTSD.

Treatment of PTSD

The quality of treatment for PTSD provided to women is as least as good, if not better, than that provided to men. Two widely used evidence-based treatments for PTSD have been developed with female populations: Prolonged Exposure (PE), and Cognitive Processing Therapy (CPT). Translational research has recently begun to establish the efficacy of these treatments with men. Because the type of traumatic event to which a person is exposed is often intertwined with gender, clinicians are interested in the extent to which treatments need to be tailored when they are applied to new populations. For example, would the same issues arise in translating treatment to populations of males seeking treatment for PTSD related to sexual assault as compared to males seeking treatment for PTSD related to combat exposure? Continued research in this area will help to elucidate gender issues in PTSD treatment.

Gender differences emerge in the pharmacological treatment of PTSD: selective serotonin reuptake inhibitors (SSRIs) show greater efficacy among women as compared to men. Sex differences may play a clear role in the pharmacological treatment of PTSD. Differences in body weight, composition, and hypothalamic-pituitary-gonadotropin hormones can have an effect on choice of medication and optimal dose. Gender differences in comorbid disorders, such as eating disorders or substance abuse are also considered when prescribing medication for PTSD, though less research has addressed this topic.

Conclusion

There are many gender considerations that are relevant to the study and treatment of traumatic stress. Whether in clinical practice or clinical trials, gender is likely to affect the ways in which people respond to traumatic experiences and the effectiveness of the treatments they receive. For these reasons, the authors of this entry propose a dynamic, social-ecological model of gender and trauma (Figure 1). This model is a dynamic one and improves on more static models of gender that emphasize simpler and more direct (i.e., main) effects. The fundamental premise of this perspective is that gender issues are likely to be overlooked or over-simplified when we don't account for these complex interactive effects. The following propositions describe several principles for future directions in this area.

- *Avoid falsely assuming that there is no difference between genders:* Gender issues are often overlooked in clinical trials and other studies. Often examinations in this area are limited to comparing men and women on the outcome of interest. However, research suggests that men and women differ in multiple ways that vary in multiple contexts. When possible, researchers should consider constructing studies so that results can be stratified by gender, so that gender specific effects and risk factors can be elucidated. Even when

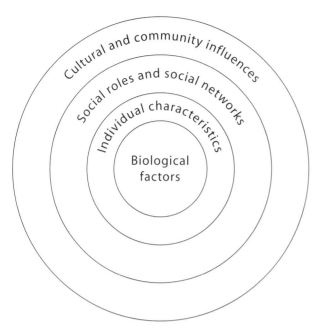

Figure 1. This figure represents a social-ecological approach to examining gender issues in traumatic stress, where gender issues are represented as the interaction of biology with increasingly broad spheres of social influence. Individual characteristics can refer to factors such as demographic characteristics, trauma history, or health status. Social roles and networks refer to in individual's immediate social environment and their function within it, such as wife, mother, or employee. Cultural and community-level influences include broader social and cultural norms, and factors such as gender, racial or socioeconomic disparities.

men and women do not differ in outcomes in a given sample, these may be different mechanisms operating by gender, or magnitude of effects for various predictors may differ by gender. Though women have traditionally been underrepresented in clinical trials, in the field of PTSD we should also attend to the inclusion of men in clinical trials of behavioral treatments, and when possible, construct studies so that effect sizes can be examined separately for men and women. Gender differences in the chronicity or recency of trauma should also be reported. Analyses of process or content factors that may impact men and women differently would also be useful. Subgroup analyses of men and women also permit these issues to be

examined in comprehensive reviews and meta-analyses.

- *Avoid falsely assuming the existence of gender differences:* Traditionally gendered topics in traumatic stress, such as sexual trauma, have falsely assumed gender differences by focusing almost solely on women. Much of what we know about sexual assault has been gleaned from women, and research continues to reveal that there are subpopulations of men in need of treatment for these issues. Similarly, research has also begun to elucidate significant differences in the experience of combat exposure, for example, between men and women, though this event is often solely studied in men. Specific events may be experienced qualitatively differently by men and women, or may be more or less gender-linked in prevalence depending on social context and roles (e.g., querying women about combat exposure is more relevant in veteran samples).

Attention to gender in situations such as these might not only help to elucidate sex differences and the contexts in which they do and do not occur, but could also identify important factors for improving our understanding of trauma exposure and its effects.

REFERENCES

Kimerling, R., Ouimette, P., & Weitlauf, J. (2007). Gender issues in PTSD. In M. J. Friedman, T. M. Keane, & P. A. Resick (Eds.), *Handbook of PTSD: Science and practice* (pp. 207–228). New York: Guilford Press.

Norris, F. H., Foster, J. D., & Weisshaar, D. L. (2002). The epidemiology of sex differences in PTSD across developmental, societal, and research contexts. In R. Kimerling, P. Ouimette, & J. Wolfe (Eds.), *Gender and PTSD* (pp. 3–42). New York: Guilford Press.

Norris, F. H., Friedman, M. J., Watson, P. J., Byrne, C. M., Diaz, E., & Kaniasty, K. (2002). 60,000 disaster victims speak: Pt. I. An empirical review of the empirical literature, 1981–2001. *Psychiatry, 65*(3), 207–239.

Tolin, D. F., & Foa, E. B. (2006). Sex differences in trauma and posttraumatic stress disorder:

A quantitative review of 25 years of research. *Psychological Bulletin, 132* (6), 959–992.

RACHEL KIMERLING
National Center for Posttraumatic Stress Disorder

KATELYN P. MACK
National Center for Posttraumatic Stress Disorder

KATHLEEN KENDRA
National Center for Posttraumatic Stress Disorder

See also: Women and Trauma

GENETICS

The fundamental task of research in genetics and heredity in the behavioral sciences is to determine the extent to which differences in genotype (genetic constitution), account for differences in phenotype (expressed characteristics). Human beings are over 99% genetically identical; therefore research aimed at identifying genes that explain individual differences in the phenotype of Posttraumatic Stress Disorder (PTSD) focuses on the 1% of the deoxyribonucleic acid (DNA) sequences that differ among individuals. Genes, the basic unit of heredity, are segments of DNA composed of four nucleotides (A, T, C, or G); the specific sequences of these nucleotides create alleles, the term for alternate forms of a gene. Almost 90% of human genetic variation is made up of single nucleotide polymorphisms (SNPs), which occur when a nucleotide in the DNA sequence is altered, forming another allele. Concerning trauma and PTSD, genetic research has endeavored to answer two main questions: (1) Is there a genetic basis for trauma exposure? and (2) Is there a genetic basis for PTSD? Answers to these questions come from family studies, twin studies, and candidate gene studies.

If risk for PTSD is partially explained by genetic factors, biological relatives (family members) of individuals with PTSD (called *probands* in genetic studies) should have a higher prevalence of PTSD than nonrelatives. Moreover, among biological relatives of individuals with PTSD, the prevalence of the disorder should be higher in first-degree (parents, siblings) than second-degree (grandparents) or their relatives. Extant research suggests relatives of probands with PTSD are at elevated risk of the disorder as compared to relatives of similarly trauma-exposed controls who did not develop PTSD. However, family studies are limited in that they cannot tell us whether a disorder, such as PTSD, runs in families for genetic or environmental reasons.

Twin studies help to disentangle the role of genetic and environmental factors in risk of developing PTSD. The twin design has been used to calculate the proportion of the variance in a trait or disorder explained by genetic factors; the resulting variance attributed to genetic factors is termed *heritability*. The basic twin method compares the degree of similarity within identical or monozygotic (MZ) twin pairs with the degree of similarity within fraternal or dizygotic (DZ) twin pairs. It is assumed that, whereas MZ twins share 100% of their genes and 100% of the shared environment, DZ twins share approximately 50% of their genes and 100% of the shared environment. If MZ twins are significantly more similar on a characteristic than DZ twins, then this phenotype is interpreted as being genetically influenced.

Twin studies conducted to date further support the heritability of PTSD, yielding three main findings. First, they indicate that genetic factors influence exposure to potentially traumatic events. This is referred to as gene-environment correlation, whereby selection of environment, and subsequently potential for exposure to trauma, is partly determined by genetic factors. A recent review of genetic influences on environmental measures including stressful life events, parenting, and social support, found that heritability estimates fell between 7% and 39% with a weighted heritability estimate for all environmental measures of 27% (Kendler & Baker, 2006).

Second, twin studies suggest that genetic influences explain a substantial proportion of vulnerability to PTSD even after accounting for genetic influences on trauma exposure. Using the Vietnam Era Twin Registry, True and colleagues found that approximately 30% of the variance in reported PTSD symptoms was accounted for by genetic factors (Stein, Jang, Taylor, Vernon, & Livesley, 2002; True et al., 1993).

Third, twin studies have demonstrated that genetic influences on PTSD overlap with those for mental disorders that commonly co-occur in individuals with PTSD. Twin studies have yielded important findings that underscore the existence of a genetic underpinning in PTSD; however, twin studies are limited in that they cannot specify which genes actually increase risk for the disorder. Molecular genetic studies are needed to accomplish this aim.

Molecular genetic studies of PTSD have used the case-control candidate gene association design, which correlates a DNA marker's alleles with an outcome. In comparison to other phenotypes, there have been very few molecular genetic studies of PTSD. As animal and human studies have implicated the dopamine system in PTSD's etiology, nearly half of the association studies of PTSD have focused on the dopamine system genes with inconsistent results. Alternate neurobiological pathways have also been investigated including the serotonin transporter gene (5-HTTLPR), brain derived neurotropic factor (BDNF), Leu7Pro polymorphism in the Neuropeptide Y gene, and two glucocorticoid receptor polymorphisms N363S and BclI (see Koenen, 2007, for a review). Investigators have used gene-environment interaction models (GxE) to afford a more sophisticated approach to examining the interplay of genetic vulnerability and environmental risk factors in the development of PTSD (Moffitt, Caspi, & Rutter, 2005). GxE studies are intended to identify genotypes that may result in vulnerability to phenotypes, such as PTSD, given exposure to environmental stressors, such as traumatic events. Numerous GxE studies that involved the environmental conditions of stress have been conducted for the phenotype of depression. For example, Kaufman and colleagues (Kaufman et al., 2004) found that the s/s genotype for 5-HTTLPR under conditions of maltreatment increased risk of depression in children; however, a positive social support system attenuated this risk. To date, only one GxE predicting PTSD has been undertaken. A recent study of adults exposed to the 2004 Florida hurricanes found that the s/s genotype for 5-HTTLPR conferred increased risk for the development of PTSD under high but not low stress conditions (Kilpatrick et al., in press).

REFERENCES

Kaufman, J., Yank, B., Douglas-Palumberi, H., Houshyar, S., Lipschitz, D., Krystal, J. H., et al. (2004). Social supports and serotonin transporter gene moderate depression in maltreated children. *Proceedings of the National Academy of Sciences, USA, 101,* 17312–17316.

Kendler, K. S., & Baker, J. H. (2006). Genetic influences on measures of the environment: A systematic review. *Psychological Medicine,* 1–12.

Kilpatrick, D. G., Koenen, K. C., Ruggiero, K. J., Acierno, R., Galea, S., Resnick, H. S., et al. (2007). The serotonin transporter genotype and social support and moderation of posttraumatic stress disorder and depression in hurricane-exposed adults. *American Journal of Psychiatry, 164,* 1693–1699.

Koenen, K. C. (2007). Genetics of posttraumatic stress disorder: Review and recommendations for future studies. *Journal of Traumatic Stress, 20,* 737–750.

Moffitt, T. E., Caspi, A., & Rutter, M. (2005). Strategy for investigating interactions between measured genes and measured environments. *Archives of General Psychiatry, 62,* 473–481.

Stein, M. B., Jang, K. J., Taylor, S., Vernon, P. A., & Livesley, W. J. (2002). Genetic and environmental influences on trauma exposure and posttraumatic stress disorder: A twin study. *American Journal of Psychiatry, 159,* 1675–1681.

True, W. J., Rice, J., Eisen, S. A., Heath, A. C., Goldberg, J., Lyons, M. J., et al. (1993). A twin study of genetic and environmental contributions to liability for posttraumatic stress symptoms. *Archives of General Psychiatry, 50,* 257–264.

ANANDA B. AMSTADTER
Medical University of South Carolina

NICOLE R. NUGENT
Kent State University

Karestan C. Koenen
Harvard School of Public Health

See also: Anterior Cingulate Cortex; Biology, Brain Structure, and Function, Adult; Biology, Brain Structure, and Function, Child; Biology, Neurochemistry; Etiology

GENOCIDE

Genocide emerged as a legal term in the 1940s in response to atrocities carried out during the Holocaust. Article II of the Geneva Convention on Genocide defines genocide as:

> any of the following acts committed with intent to destroy, in whole or in part, a national ethnical, racial, or religious group, as such: killing members of the group; causing serious bodily or mental harm to members of the group; deliberately inflicting on the group conditions of life calculated to bring its physical destruction in whole or in part; imposing measures intended to prevent births within the group; forcibly transferring children of the group to another group. (United Nations, 1951)

Genocidal policies typically designate a specific group as harmful to the interests of another group. Rhetoric and other psychological tools are used to justify or rationalize the systematic persecution of the targeted people. These may include seizure of their property, forced resettling as a means to drastically reduce the population, or methodical annihilation. Under such conditions, people are forced to flee their homes, abandon property, scatter their communities, and seek any available refuge. The persistent and pervasive threats to their survival are such that they are likely to experience a deep and abiding terror that can have lasting effects on their psychological, emotional, and spiritual well-being.

Parallels between the definition of genocide and the clinical definition of actions that can precipitate posttraumatic stress disorder (PTSD) are quite striking. For example, both definitions recognize the damage caused by violence to one's body or physical integrity (American Psychiatric Association, 2000). Both definitions address the harm caused by attacks on family members or other close associates or group members. Genocide inevitably involves events that satisfy the criteria for the PTSD diagnosis. Studies of the effects of genocide on victims suggest strongly that survivors suffer from a range of cognitive, emotional, physical, and behavioral effects, not only on an individual level, but also as a group (see Herman, 1992).

In the aftermath of genocide, the world tends to be perceived as a dangerous place by both the perpetrator and the victim (Staub, 2000). Experiencing genocide can precipitate the full range and highest severity of traumatic stress symptoms, such as nightmares, flashbacks, identity building, and difficulty in relating to others. These changes in the group members' worldview is considered to be one crucial change in an environment that may invoke PTSD as it leads to a sense of helplessness and social disruption (Friedman & Marsella, 1996). In describing what she calls "social death," philosopher Claudia Card (2007): "the special evil of genocide lies in its infliction of not just physical death (when it does that) but also social death, producing a consequent meaninglessness of one's life and even of its termination" (p. 21). Moreover, because genocide aims not only to destroy the lives of select individuals, but to systematically eliminate entire peoples and their ways of living, it can profoundly infuse an affected culture and society with traumatic remnants that are not easily extracted (Stamm, Stamm, Hudnall, & Higson-Smith, 2004). Examples of such genocide-related remnants include increased levels of child abuse, increased alcohol and drug abuse, disrupted communal ties, and high rates of poverty.

Research on genocide has focused almost exclusively on the victims or targets, for example, the Tutsi in Rwanda or the Jews in the Holocaust. As noted, the result may be pervasive problems with PTSD that may affect several successive generations even when those future generations are not directly subjected to genocide (Brand, Engel, Candel, & Yehuda, 2006) as well as complex forms of posttraumatic stress reactions (deJong, Komproe, Spinazzola, Van der Kolk, & Van Ommeren, 2005; *see:* **Complex Posttraumatic Stress Disorder**).

However, researchers are beginning to ask questions about characteristics such as prior traumatic events that might predispose groups to develop genocidal motives toward others (e.g., Hatzfeld, 2005). Multigenerational legacies of being victimized are preserved in storytelling, songs, and family patterns, and these serve as precipitants for violence (Lev-Wiesel, 2007). For example, Staub (2000, 2003) has examined the genocide in Bosnia and noted that many of the perpetrators were influenced by shared memories of violence and humiliation from World War II. Research and scholarship of this sort is highly controversial, but the intention is to gain an understanding that could better inform prevention.

Considerable debate exists today regarding the nature of the psychological trauma(s) and the forms of posttraumatic impairment (of the culture and society as well as the individual or family) that result from genocide. These are complex and value-laden constructs representing painful historical events with terribly tragic moral and spiritual implications for those involved and their descendants. Therefore, there is certainly room for legitimate debate and different points of view. But these constructs are meant to reflect serious ongoing social problems, and it is essential to carefully study them if we are to respond to genocide proactively, collectively, and effectively. The consequences of failing to achieve adequate agreement on what constitutes genocide and how to recognize and address the adverse impacts of genocide may include failing to protect and support people at risk of suffering preventable psychological traumas, as well as potentially perpetuating tragic intergenerational cycles of traumatic violence.

REFERENCES

American Psychiatric Association. (2000). *Diagnostic and statistical manual of mental disorders* (4th ed., text rev.). Washington, DC: Author.

Brand, S. R., Engel, S. M., Candel, R. L., & Yehuda, R. (2006). The effect of maternal PTSD following in utero trauma exposure on behavior and temperament in the 9-month-old infant. *Annals of the New York Academy of Sciences, 1071*, 454–458.

Card, C. (2007). Genocide and social death. In C. Card & A. T. Marsoobian (Eds.), *Genocide's aftermath: Responsibility and repair* (pp. 10–23). Oxford, England: Blackwell.

de Jong, J. T. V. M., Komproe, I. H., Spinazzola, J., Van der Kolk, B. A., & Van Ommeren, M. H. (2005). DESNOS in three post conflict settings: Assessing cross-cultural construct equivalence. *Journal of Traumatic Stress, 18*(1), 13–21.

Friedman, M. J., & Marsella, A. J. (1996). Posttraumatic stress disorder: An overview of the concept. In A. J. Marsella, M. J. Friedman, E. T. Gerrity, & R. Scurfield (Eds.), *Ethnocultural aspects of post-traumatic stress disorder: Issues, research, and clinical applications* (pp. 11–32). Washington, DC: American Psychological Association.

Hatzfeld, J. (2005). *Machete season: The killers in Rwanda speak.* New York: Farrar, Straus and Giroux.

Herman, J. L. (1992). *Trauma and recovery: The aftermath of violence-from domestic abuse to political terror.* New York: Basic Books.

Lev-Wiesel, R. (2007). Intergenerational transmission of trauma across three generations: A preliminary study. *Qualitative Social Work, 6*(1), 75–94.

Stamm, B. H., Stamm, H. E., Hudnall, A. C., & Higson-Smith, C. (2004). Considering cultural trauma as a backdrop for the treatment of trauma and PTSD. *Journal of Trauma and Loss, 9*(1), 89–111.

Staub, E. (2000). Genocide and mass killing: Origins, prevention, healing, and reconciliation. *Political Psychology, 21*(2), 367–382.

Staub, E. (2003). *The psychology of good and evil: Why children, adults, and groups help and harm others.* New York: Cambridge University Press.

United Nations. (1951). Convention on the Prevention and Punishment of the Crime of Genocide. *United Nations Treaty Series, 78,* 277.

AMY C. HUDNALL
Appalachian State University

See also: Holocaust, The; Human Rights Violations

GERIATRICS

Much less clinical attention and scientific investigation has been given to traumatic event exposure and PTSD in older (aged 65+)

as opposed to younger adults. In fact, most studies examining the effects of trauma either have not recruited sufficient numbers of older adults to examine age effects or have not included older adults at all. When older adults are included, they are often relegated to a single 60/65+ age category; however, older adulthood encompasses about a 25- to 30-year range in age, therefore potentially obfuscating age-related differences.

The number, proportion, and heterogeneity of older adults are increasing dramatically in industrialized countries and will likely translate to an increased need and range of services for older individuals. This demographic shift demands an increase in research and services to aid older adult trauma survivors. According to lifetime PTSD prevalence rates in adults over 60 years old and projected population estimates, of the 46 million adults over 65 expected to be alive in the United States in 2015, 1.3 million should meet PTSD diagnostic criteria at some point in their lifetime (Harvard School of Medicine, 2005; U.S. Census Bureau, 2007). This percentage becomes substantially higher in groups of older individuals who are known to have suffered severe and prolonged trauma such as the case with Holocaust survivors, former prisoners of war (POWs), and combat veterans.

Knowledge regarding trauma in older adults is mainly derived from two groups: those who experienced trauma earlier in life during military combat/captivity in World War II/Korean War or during the Holocaust; and those who experienced trauma later in life primarily from natural or man-made disaster. There are two fairly comprehensive reviews covering these older adult trauma groups (i.e., Averill & Beck, 2000; Falk, Hersen, & Van Hasselt, 1994). Many studies utilizing clinical samples found that older adult survivors meet diagnostic criteria for PTSD decades after their trauma.

In general, the effects of trauma in older adults often vary in frequency, intensity, presentation, and associated risk factors from those observed in younger populations. Thus a somewhat modified approach to conceptualization, assessment, and intervention is required

between younger and older adult victims. PTSD in older adults is generally less frequent and intense than in younger samples. Older adults may experience different symptoms or exhibit differences in coexisting disorders; for example, dissociation appears to be less persistent over time.

Little is known about the course of PTSD across the life span. Some individuals report being continuously troubled, some experience waxing and waning of symptoms, and others remain symptom-free. One common trajectory of trauma-related symptoms is an immediate and intense surge of symptoms shortly after the trauma, a gradual decline for several decades, and then resurgence later in life (Port, Engdahl, & Frazier, 2001).

A growing interest has been shown in the relationship between history of extreme trauma, PTSD, and cognitive impairment in later life. Indeed, some older individuals exposed to prolonged and severe trauma, such as former POWs or Holocaust survivors, have neurological concomitants, such as impairments in memory, attention, learning and executive functioning, decades after traumatic exposure (Sutker, Vasterling, Brailey, & Allain, 1995).

Older age by itself is not a defining factor in the development or maintenance of trauma-related symptoms. Rather, in an examination of older adult disaster survivors from three different countries, emotional responses were not contingent on age alone, but interacted with social, economic, and cultural variables to predict mental health (Norris, Kaniasty, Conrad, Inman, & Murphy, 2002). Additional vulnerabilities of some older adults have been illuminated by catastrophic events in the United States of the past decade including Hurricane Katrina and the terrorist attacks of September 11, 2001 (i.e., frail or disabled older adults with functional impairments and substantive medical problems). Older adults appear to have contributed to a disproportionate percentage of deaths as a result of Hurricane Katrina because a substantial number could not be evacuated from independent living facilities, particularly nursing homes, and those who were housebound quickly became trapped.

Similarly, after September 11, 2001, many homebound older adults residing in lower Manhattan were left waiting for up to 7 days to receive health services because they were inaccessible to home health care providers, and their meals or medications were not delivered. Emergency disaster preparedness for these subpopulations of older adults is paramount to future response and recovery endeavors.

In addition to the identified vulnerabilities of possible functional impairments and medical problems, the experience, expression, and treatment of trauma-related symptoms in older adults may be confounded by other significant variables. Accessibility to and reimbursement patterns for mental health services may affect whether an older individual seeks or receives adequate treatment. The current older adult cohort may demonstrate trauma-related stress symptoms as somatic complaints causing them to seek medical rather than psychological treatment. The introduction of PTSD into the diagnostic nomenclature in 1980 means that most older adults spent the majority of their adult lives with no clear definition or recognition of their trauma-related symptoms. This group is likely to have quietly suffered, as historically older adults demonstrate a strong ethic of self-reliance. They also often maintain a negative stigma toward psychiatric treatment. These factors may negatively influence the acknowledgment of trauma and its effects to self and others, and have led some investigators to call trauma a "hidden variable" in the lives of older adults.

REFERENCES

Averill, P. M., & Beck, J. G. (2000). Posttraumatic stress disorder in older adults: A conceptual review. *Journal of Anxiety Disorders, 14,* 133–156.

Falk, B., Hersen, M., & Van Hasselt, V. (1994). Assessment of post-traumatic stress disorder in older adults: A critical review. *Clinical Psychology Review, 14,* 383–415.

Harvard School of Medicine. (2005). *National comorbidity survey replication.* Available from www.hcp.med.harvard.edu/ncs/publications. php#date2005.

Norris, F. H., Kaniasty, K. Z., Conrad, M. L., Inman, G. L., & Murphy, A. D. (2002). Placing age differences in cultural context: A comparison of the effects of age on PTSD after disasters in the United States, Mexico, and Poland. *Journal of Clinical Geropsychology, 8,* 153–173.

Port, C. L., Engdahl, B., & Frazier, P. (2001). A longitudinal and retrospective study of PTSD among older POWs. *American Journal of Psychiatry, 158,* 1474–1479.

Sutker, P. B., Vasterling, J. J., Brailey, K., & Allain, A. N., Jr. (1995). Memory, attention, and executive deficits in POW survivors: Contributing biological and psychological factors. *Neuropsychology, 9,* 118–125.

U.S. Census Bureau. (2007). *National population projections.* Available from www.census.gov/population/ www/projections/natsum-T3.html.

RECOMMENDED READINGS

Cook, J. M., & Niederehe, G. (2007). Trauma in older adults. In M. J. Friedman, T. M. Keane, & P. A. Resick (Eds.), *Handbook of PTSD: Science and Practice* (pp. 252–276). New York: Guilford Press.

CASEY O'DONNELL
La Salle University

JOAN M. COOK
Yale University School of Medicine

See also: Delayed Onset

GLUTAMATE

See: Biology, Neurochemistry

GROTESQUE DEATH

Death occurring as a result of natural or technological disaster, war, or terrorism may be considered unnatural, atypical, or *grotesque.* Deaths occurring in natural disasters or severe accidents (e.g., fatal motor vehicle or other transportation accidents, as well as in extreme episodes of family or community violence) may also be particularly gruesome as a result of the physical damage involved or because vulnerable individuals (e.g., young children, disabled persons) have had their lives unexpectedly cut short. Exposure to human remains resulting from grotesque death is a significant psychological stressor, consistent with the American Psychiatric Association's inclusion of "horror" as one of the defining characteristics in the definition of psychological trauma for the diagnoses of posttraumatic stress disorder (PTSD) and acute stress disorder (ASD). Psychological reactions of people exposed to grotesque death are therefore likely to include symptoms of PTSD and ASD, as well as of other frequently comorbid disorders such as major depression and other anxiety disorders. Emergency personnel such as police officers and firefighters often experience transient distress following exposure to gruesome injuries or deaths. This distress often manifests as difficulty with sleep or concentration, somatic complaints, increased substance use, interpersonal difficulties and not infrequently as mental illnesses including depression, ASD, and PTSD (Institute of Medicine, 2003).

Body handlers are the persons most likely to encounter grotesque death close at hand. Body handlers are emergency personnel or mortuary workers who are responsible for placing the remains of human bodies in safe and sanitary containers (often referred to as "body bags") and/or for preparing the remains for autopsy, funeral services, or burial. Some body handlers are specifically trained for this work, but many must take on these potentially traumatic responsibilities without prior training when they are called to respond to a disaster or critical incident involving fatalities. Body handlers may incorporate their experience of death through various senses including sight, touch, and smell, and have been found to have higher rates of traumatic stress symptoms than other disaster workers (McCarroll, Fullerton, Ursano, & Hermsen, 1996). Prior to exposure, body handlers experience stress though anticipation, and feelings of horror, anger, guilt, numbness, disgust, or pity may be experienced during or after handling remains. Children's bodies, natural-looking bodies, and severely damaged bodies were found to be particularly disturbing (Ursano & McCarroll, 1990).

Identification with or emotional involvement with the deceased are risk factors for development of PTSD among body handlers (Ursano & McCarroll, 1990; Ursano, McCarroll, & Fullerton, 2003). Handling the victim's personal effects and the fatigue from working long hours with minimal time to recuperate were also identified as significant stressors (Ursano & McCarroll, 1990). Protective factors include using defense mechanisms such as humor and emotionally distancing from the victim, having a strong support network including spouses and coworkers, and avoiding alcohol use may serve to diminish future psychological distress (Center for the Study of Traumatic Stress, 2005). Further research may identify specific factors related to resiliency after exposure to grotesque death.

Health-care providers may also experience high levels of distress and fatigue when working with those directly exposed to trauma and assisting families who are dealing with nearly unbearable losses. Working long hours and not obtaining adequate rest can further place health care providers at risk for both biological and psychological burn-out, which jeopardizes their ability to care for their patients. Taking regular breaks, optimizing nutrition, and frequently communicating with both colleagues and loved ones increases job performance and may also help minimize later difficulties (Center for the Study of Traumatic Stress, 2005).

REFERENCES

Center for the Study of Traumatic Stress. (2005). *Hurricane Katrina: Sustaining effectiveness in first responders.* Retrieved January 4, 2008, from www.centerforthestudyoftraumaticstress.org/downloads/CSTSSustainingeffectiveness.pdf.

Institute of Medicine. (2003). *Preparing for the psychological consequence of terrorism: A public health strategy.* Washington, DC: National Academic Press.

McCarroll, J. E., Fullerton, C. S., Ursano, R. J., & Hermsen, J. M. (1996). Posttraumatic stress symptoms following forensic dental identification:

Mt. Carmel, Waco, Texas. *American Journal of Psychiatry, 153*(6), 778–782.

Ursano, R. J., & McCarroll, J. E. (1990). The nature of the traumatic stressor: Handling dead bodies. *Journal of Nervous and Mental Disease, 178,* 396–398.

Ursano, R. J., McCarroll, J. E., & Fullerton, C. S. (2003). Traumatic death in terrorism and disasters: The effects on posttraumatic stress and behavior. In R. J. Ursano, C. S. Fullerton, & A. E. Norwood (Eds.), *Terrorism and disaster: Individual and community mental health interventions* (pp. 308–332). Cambridge: Cambridge University Press.

RECOMMENDED READINGS

Center for the Study of Traumatic Stress. (2005). *Information for relief workers on emotional reactions to human bodies in mass death.* Retrieved January 4, 2008, from www.centerforthestudyoftraumaticstress.org/downloads/Info4ReliefWkr.pdf.

Center for the Study of Traumatic Stress. (2005). *Stress management for health care providers.* Retrieved January 4, 2008, from www.centerforthestudyoftraumaticstress.org/downloads/CSTS_SressMgtHCProv.pdf.

HEATHER SHIBLEY
Medical University of South Carolina

DAVID M. BENEDEK
Uniformed Services University of the Health Sciences

ROBERT J. URSANO
Uniformed Services University of the Health Sciences

See also: Mortuary Workers; War Trauma

GROUP THERAPY

Group therapy is one of the most widely used treatments for trauma-related psychological problems. Advantages of a group approach include directly addressing the isolation and alienation common after traumatic experiences by providing a supportive environment that can enhance a sense of connectedness with others and a safe place to share trauma-related emotional responses. It can also be an efficient means of teaching multiple patients simultaneously about frequently occurring posttraumatic reactions and helpful coping skills (Ruzek, Young, & Walser, 2003).

Trauma-related groups vary on multiple dimensions including: length of treatment (time-limited or open-ended), number of members (usually between 5 and 10), and the entry point for members (some groups enroll everyone at once while others enroll on an ongoing basis). Groups for traumatized persons also differ in the degree of focus on traumatic experiences, with some groups emphasizing intensive sharing of traumatic experiences, and others focusing on here-and-now life functioning. Groups for traumatized persons are done from a variety of theoretical approaches and use a variety of therapeutic and educational strategies.

Open-ended, present-focused supportive group therapy is commonly used with persons who have experienced multiple psychological traumas such as childhood sexual abuse and combat. These groups typically involve discussion of members' current life challenges and successes, with a goal of reducing isolation, helping members to recognize and manage trauma-related responses, and providing peer emotional support. One large study with Vietnam veterans found that supportive group therapy, which included education and support for solving problems in living, was associated with modest reductions in PTSD symptoms and improvements in psychological outlook and functioning (Schnurr et al., 2003).

Cognitive behavioral therapy (CBT) groups are often time-limited and teach specific techniques to reduce trauma-related symptoms. For example, Imagery Rehearsal Therapy (IRT) is a CBT technique that requires patients to write down chronic nightmares, then write less aversive versions of these dreams and repeatedly rehearse the new dreams. IRT was studied in a group format with sexual assault survivors, and showed superior reductions in the frequency of nightmares and overall PTSD symptoms compared to wait list controls (Krakow et al., 2001). Other CBT groups have been found to be helpful in reducing PTSD and other psychological symptoms with adults who had experienced diverse traumas including war zone, childhood sexual abuse, and rape.

Psychodynamic group therapy also has been conducted with traumatized persons (Foy, Eriksson, & Trice, 2001). Unfortunately, there has not been enough empirical investigation of this approach to comment about its effectiveness.

Although differing in their approach, both CBT and psychodynamic psychotherapists use trauma-focused groups to seek the integration of traumatic experience at an emotional and cognitive level. CBT may include the repeated detailed description of traumatic memories in order to produce habituation to those memories (exposure therapy). Psychodynamic therapists focus on developing understanding of the unconscious meaning of trauma-related symptoms, how events have affected a person's sense of self, and the relationship between these symptoms and childhood experiences.

A study of group therapy for Vietnam veterans with PTSD found that a trauma-focused CBT group was associated with modest reductions in PTSD symptoms and improvements in psychological outlook and functioning (Schnurr et al., 2003). Group-Based Exposure Therapy (GBET) is a new CBT approach to group therapy that provides a larger dose of exposure therapy than was included in Schnurr and colleagues' (2003) study. A field trial with 102 war veterans diagnosed with PTSD suggested that GBET produced clinically significant and lasting reductions in PTSD symptoms on both therapist-administered and self-report measures for the majority of group members with few dropouts (Ready et al., 2008).

Aside from theoretical model and type of therapeutic strategies, other factors may influence the effectiveness of group therapy with traumatized persons. Group size, length and duration of sessions, gender composition (all one gender versus mixed gender), type of traumatic experiences and posttraumatic problems, and the number and characteristics of group leaders are among the many factors that may affect group therapy outcome. Two studies have examined predictors of outcome in group

therapy with women with histories of childhood sexual abuse. Follette, Alexander, and Follette (1991) found that education attainment, marital status, the specific nature of the sexual abuse, and pretreatment depression and distress were associated with group therapy outcomes. Cloitre and Koenen (2001) found that including a member diagnosed with borderline personality disorder in supportive therapy groups for women who had histories of childhood sexual abuse was associated with poor outcomes for all group members. Beyond these preliminary findings, there is no research evidence to guide group therapists in selecting members or formats to maximize success.

REFERENCES

Cloitre, M., & Koenen, K. (2001). The impact of borderline personality disorder on process group outcome among women with posttraumatic stress disorder related to childhood abuse. *International Journal of Group Psychotherapy, 51,* 379–398.

Follette, V. M., Alexander, P. C., & Follette, W. C. (1991). Individual predicators of outcome in group treatment for incest survivors. *Journal of Consulting and Clinical Psychology, 59,* 150–155.

Foy, D. W., Erikisson, C. B., & Trice, G. A. (2001). Introduction to group for trauma survivors. *Group Dynamics: Theory, Research, and Practice, 5,* 246–251.

Krakow, B., Hollifield, M., Johnston, L., Koss, M., Schrader, R., Warner, T., et al. (2001). Imagery rehearsal therapy for chronic nightmares in sexual assault survivors with posttraumatic stress disorder: A randomized controlled trial. *Journal of the American Medical Association, 286,* 537–545.

Ready, D. J., Thomas, K. R., Worley, V., Backscheider, A. G., Harvey, L. C., Baltzell, D., & Rothbaum, B. O. (2008). A field test of group based exposure therapy with 102 veterans with war-related posttraumatic stress disorder. *Journal of Traumatic Stress, 21,* 150–157.

Ruzek, J. I., Young, B. H., & Walser, R. D. (2003). Group treatment of posttraumatic stress disorder and other trauma-related problems. *Primary Psychiatry, 10,* 53–57.

Schnurr, P. P., Friedman, M. J., Foy, D. W., Shea, M. T., Hsieh, F. Y., Lavori, P. W., et al. (2003). Randomized trial of trauma-focused group therapy for posttraumatic stress disorder: Results from a

Department of Veterans Affairs cooperative study. *Archives of General Psychiatry, 60,* 481–489.

DAVID J. READY
Emory University School of Medicine

M. TRACIE SHEA
Brown University

See also: Cognitive Behavior Therapy, Adult; Psychodynamic Therapy, Adult; Psychotherapeutic Processes

GUILT

Guilt is an emotion that people experience when they recognize that they have behaved in a way that caused harm or that was costly or distressing for others. In its most adaptive form, guilt motivates people to seek ways of repairing the consequences of their harmful behavior or making restitution for their transgressions against others (Orth, Beking, & Burkhardt, 2006). This prosocial form of guilt is adaptive for the person and for relationships because it motivates reparative actions that tend to both reduce the person's sense of distress and enhance trust and responsibility in relationships. However, the guilt associated with psychological trauma tends to be associated with rumination and avoidance of reparative actions. Thus, posttraumatic guilt often leads to increased rather than reduced distress and problems in relationships.

Most psychologically traumatic events contain aspects that could reasonably induce a sense of guilt. This is the case because psychological traumas often involve severe harm or other adverse consequences, and particularly is the case when traumatic events violate people's sense of social obligation to others (e.g., domestic or community violence, abuse). This is not limited to those who perpetrated traumatic actions because people often report feeling a sense of guilt when terrible things happen even if they were not responsible for the actions or the resultant harm. For example, survivors of fatal accidents or war combatants often report feeling guilty because they wish that they could have prevented others from being killed even though they played no part in the deaths. People also report feeling guilty for unintended consequences of their actions and for the perceived consequences of not having taken actions (e.g., feeling guilty for what they did not do to prevent harm or protect someone else). In some cases, people even report feeling guilty for not having done something when it appears that they in fact did not have the capability to have done anything more helpful. Another form of posttraumatic guilt is called "survivor guilt": this is a feeling of guilt for having survived when others died, or for having been less harmed or better able to recover than others who were traumatized.

Although there are numerous references to guilt in the wake of psychological trauma in clinical and research publications in the mental health field and social sciences, there is relatively little empirical evidence regarding the nuances of posttraumatic guilt, how this guilt manifests as a clinical issue, nor how to successfully treat this as a clinical condition.

To avoid confusion and misdirection of effort, it is important to distinguish guilt from shame (Tangney & Dearing, 2002; Tracy & Robins, 2006). While guilt is a painful feeling associated with a negative evaluation of one's behavior or actions, it also reflects awareness of social obligations and directs attention toward what can be done to resolve any resultant consequences. Shame is also an intensely painful feeling state associated with a negative self-evaluation, but it is directed at one's entire being or self and does not readily lend itself to a reparative remedy.

Wilson, Drozdek, and Turkovic (2006) propose that posttraumatic guilt and shame have differential causes and consequences:

> Posttraumatic shame and guilt can be meaningfully compared across eight psychological dimensions: (a) self-attribution processes, (b) emotional states, (c) appraisal and interpretation of action, (d) impact of states of shame and guilt on personal identity, (e) suicidality, (f) defensive patterns, (g) proneness to PTSD, and (h) dimensions of self-structure adversely affected by states of shame and guilt. (p. 124)

Kubany and Watson's (2003) multidimensional model further delineates the features of posttraumatic guilt and distinguish them from shame. Guilt is described as involving five factors: (1) negative affect (e.g., feeling dysphoric, anxious, or angry); (2) perceived responsibility (i.e., a cognitive appraisal of self-blame); (3) insufficient justification (i.e., a cognitive appraisal that one's actions were not justified); (4) violation of one's values (e.g., failing to behave in a way that is honest, honorable, or courageous); and (5) perceived preventability/predictability (i.e., a cognitive appraisal that the results of one's acts could have been prevented or foreseen). Other contextual factors may influence the likelihood or intensity of guilt following psychological trauma include: the extent to which the person was directly involved (as opposed to having been a bystander or witness), whether a loved one was harmed, whether the harm or injury was irreparable, whether the traumatic events were intentionally caused by people (versus accidental or natural disaster traumas), whether there was any choice available to the person that might have prevented or mitigated the harm, whether the outcomes appeared to be arbitrary or unfair, and the extent to which other people blame the person (Kubany & Watson, 2003). Although each of these factors is associated with an increased likelihood of the traumatized person feeling a sense of lasting guilt, it is important to recall that posttraumatic guilt can occur following any traumatic event. This clinical observation suggests a need for research on the characteristics of the person that may be risk factors for developing problems with posttraumatic guilt, such as proneness to rumination or guilt in general, or past experiences of trauma or guilt.

Several specific forms of posttraumatic guilt have been described clinically. Most common is survivor guilt, which is based on self-blame for having survived or been less injured than other people who experienced the same or a similar psychological trauma and died, suffered, or had more severe or lasting physical or psychological injuries. Survivor guilt often does not involve any specific beliefs about one's own misconduct, but instead self-blame for merely having survived when others did not or having been less harmed than others. Survivor guilt is clinically well documented, but not scientifically or theoretically validated (Ayalon, Perry, Arean, & Horowitz, 2007). The relationship of survivor guilt and persistent PTSD, substance abuse, grief, and shame, as well as its prognostic effect on PTSD treatment, remain to be determined.

Other forms of posttraumatic guilt are even less well understood. Victim guilt involves self-blame for having been traumatically victimized, a common reaction among abused children (including when grown up), domestic violence survivors, and persons who suffered torture or genocide. Bystander guilt is a form of self-blame for having not intervened or prevented traumatic harm that happened in one's presence or to someone for whom one feels responsibility (e.g., a nonoffending parent or an older sibling of an abused child; a witness to an assault). Perpetrator or atrocity guilt involve self-blame for having intentionally or unintentionally harmed other person(s) or committed horrific acts.

The most widely used and best psychometrically developed measure is the Trauma-Related Guilt Inventory (TRGI; Kubany et al., 1996). The TGRI is a 32-item self-report questionnaire. It includes three scales that assess: (1) global guilt, (2) distress, and (3) guilt cognitions; and three (cognitive) subscales: (1) hindsight bias/responsibility, (2) wrongdoing, and (3) lack of justification. Another measure that is not specific to traumatic guilt, but which includes subscales for guilt proneness and denial of guilt ("externalization," "detachment/unconcern") is the 16-item self-report questionnaire, the Test of Self-Conscious Affect-3 (TOSCA-3; Tangney & Dearing, 2002). The TOSCA-3 provides specific standard scenarios for the respondent as well as self-rating questions.

Most forms of psychotherapy for PTSD address posttraumatic guilt. There is evidence that several PTSD treatments may reduce guilt, although more specifically guilt-focused treatments may be needed (Kubany, 2004; Stapleton,

Taylor, & Asmundson, 2006). A therapy developed based on extensive personal and clinical experience with Holocaust survivors, Viktor Frankl's logotherapy, has been clinically tested with psychological trauma survivors with severe guilt (Southwick, Gilmartin, McDonough, & Morrissey, 2007) but not yet research tested. Interventions designed to prevent the development of debilitating guilt soon after psychological trauma have not yet been developed but could enhance the armamentarium of early interventions for psychological trauma survivors.

REFERENCES

Ayalon, L., Perry, C., Arean, P., & Horowitz, M. J. (2007). Making sense of the past: Perspectives on resilience among Holocaust survivors. *Journal of Loss and Trauma, 12,* 281–293.

Kubany, E. S. (2004). Cognitive trauma therapy for battered women with PTSD (CTT-BW). *Journal of Consulting and Clinical Psychology, 72,* 3–18.

Kubany, E. S., Abueg, F. R., Brennan, J. M., Haynes, S. N., Manke, F. P., & Stahura, C. (1996). Development and validation of the trauma-related guilt inventory (TRGI). *Psychological Assessment, 8,* 428–444.

Kubany, E. S., & Watson, S. B. (2003). Guilt: Elaboration of a multidimensional model. *Psychological Record, 53,* 51–90.

Orth, U., Berking, M., & Burkhardt, S. (2006). Self-conscious emotions and depression. *Personality and Social Psychology Bulletin, 32,* 1608–1619.

Southwick, S., Gilmartin, R., McDonough, P., & Morrissey, P. (2007). Logotherapy as an adjunctive treatment for chronic combat-related PTSD: A meaning-based intervention. *American Journal of Psychotherapy, 60,* 161–174.

Stapleton, J., Taylor, S., & Asmundson, G. (2006). Effects of three PTSD treatments on anger and guilt. *Journal of Traumatic Stress, 19,* 19–28.

Tangney, J. P., & Dearing, R. L. (2002). *Shame and guilt.* New York: Guilford Press.

Tracy, J. L., & Robins, R. W. (2006). Appraisal antecedents of shame and guilt: Support for a theoretical model. *Personality and Social Psychology Bulletin, 32*(10), 1339–1351.

Wilson, J. P., Drozdek, B., & Turkovic, S. (2006). Posttraumatic shame and guilt. *Trauma, Violence, and Abuse, 7*(2), 122–141.

Deborah Augenbraun
University of Connecticut School of Medicine

Julian D. Ford
University of Connecticut School of Medicine

See also: Perpetration-Induced Trauma; Shame

GULF WAR SYNDROME

Gulf War Syndrome (GWS) first appeared in reports of unexplained physical symptoms affecting military personnel who had taken part in the 1991 war in the Persian Gulf involving Kuwait and Iraq. That war was both short and successful, but in its aftermath service personnel from initially the United States, but then the United Kingdom, Canada, Australia, Denmark, and many other countries, with the possible exception of Saudi Arabia, started to report worsening general health.

At first, GWS was used to describe clusters of unusual medical illnesses occurring in Gulf veterans or their families. Although it is not clear who first coined the term, the initial media reports described either unusual illnesses, such as cancers appearing in previously fit veterans, or birth defects in veterans' children. Soon, however, the term covered virtually any physical or psychological symptom, alone or in combination, occurring in anyone who had served in the region.

The first official response was to set up disease registries linked to comprehensive physical assessments for veterans. Eventually more than 100,000 Gulf veterans were assessed in the United States or the United Kingdom, which would have been sufficient to detect a significant increase in a well-defined disease or a new and hitherto unknown complex of diseases (e.g., as occurred in the homosexual community in San Francisco at the start on the 1980s). Neither was detected, and it is now accepted that, with the possible and still contested exception of a rare neurological disease (motor neuron disease), there is no evidence of an increase in any well-defined physical disorder in Gulf veterans (Gray, Gackstetter, Kang, Graham, & Scott, 2004).

Likewise, it is also now clear that, despite media reports to the contrary, there has been no increase in mortality in Gulf veterans, (Gray & Kang, 2006) other than a small rise in accidental death (United States and United Kingdom) or suicide (United States only). Neither finding is novel in the aftermath of war; both may be linked to an increase in risk-taking behavior that has been observed historically among combatants in the aftermath of war (*see:* **History of Psychological Trauma**).

After some regrettable delays, important information on the nature of GWS began to emerge from a series of large-scale population-based epidemiological studies, commencing with the 1997 Iowa Persian Gulf cohort (Iowa Persian Gulf Study Group, 1997), which clearly documented that Gulf veterans were more likely to report a range of physical and psychological symptoms compared to military personnel who had not deployed to the Gulf. In keeping with the general rise in symptoms, specific symptom-defined conditions such as chronic fatigue syndrome, depression, PTSD,

and others were also elevated in deployed veterans compared to nondeployed personnel.

The first U.K. epidemiological study was undertaken by a research team at King's College London, that studied 4,246 randomly selected U.K. Gulf War veterans, drawn from all three Armed Services, with similar numbers of nondeployed personnel, and with an active duty control group who had served, some years later, in the Bosnian Conflict (Unwin et al., 1999). As in the United States, U.K. Gulf veterans were between two and three times more likely to report each of the 50 somatic symptoms that were inquired about. There was a considerable difference in the subjective perception of health, and to a lesser extent physical function (the latter remains above expected nonmilitary norms). Thus U.K. Gulf veterans experienced more symptoms, endorsed more conditions, felt worse, than either the nondeployed cohort or those deployed to an unpleasant and stressful Bosnian theater of operations despite still physically functioning well.

This finding is illustrated in Figure 1, where each data point represents an individual physical

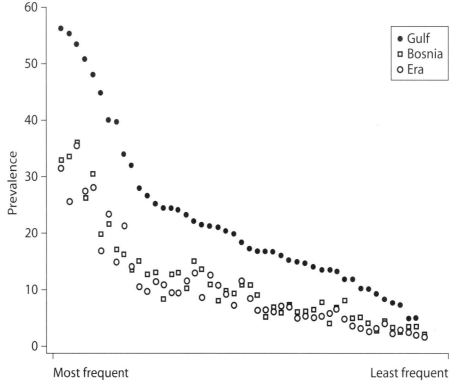

Figure 1. Graphical representation of Gulf health effect.
Source: "Health of UK Servicemen Who Served in the Persian Gulf War," by Unwin et al., 1999, *Lancet, 353,* pp. 169–178.

symptom (Unwin et al., 1999). To the left are common symptoms, such as fatigue or headache; to the right are unusual symptoms, such as a lump in the throat, night sweats, or urinary frequency. It is clear that there is no difference between those deployed to Bosnia and those in the military in 1991, but who had not deployed to the Gulf. However, the Gulf cohort is strikingly different. Of equal interest, is that the shape of the curve between the Gulf and the control groups does not differ, suggesting that no specific symptom is linked with Gulf service. Instead, Gulf veterans report more of every symptom inquired about.

Even without complex statistical analysis, Figure 1 also shows that there is no unique "Gulf War Syndrome"—a constellation of signs and/or symptoms unique to serving in the Gulf. Further studies have replicated this finding, confirming that there is nothing different about the symptoms complained of by Gulf War veterans, either in their nature or associations; they simply report more symptoms than nondeployed controls. "Gulf War Syndrome" turns out to be a misnomer, even if has been adopted by the media and many veterans alike. The only exception comes from the work of U.S. epidemiologist Robert Haley, who claimed to have produced evidence of such a syndrome (Haley, Kurt, & Hom, 1997). However, his claim was based on a study of a single reserve engineering unit, with a poor response rate and no control group.

To date, only two well defined physical conditions have been associated with Gulf War service. Firstly the U.K. research group found an increase in seborrhoeic dermatitis, an unusual if not serious form of dermatitis, which has attracted little scientific or media interest (Higgins et al., 2002). Secondly a large U.S. study reported 40 cases of a rare condition called amyotrophic lateral sclerosis (ALS) also known as Lou Gerhig's disease. Although the U.S. government has declared the disease as service-attributable, there remains good evidence that the excess is due to an ascertainment bias; that is to say that greater efforts were made to find cases in Gulf veterans as opposed to controls, and also, an unusually low rate of ALS in those controls. Given that ALS is regrettably fatal and incurable, the absence of any increase in neurological disease in mortality studies in Gulf veterans is also significant. ALS remains rare in Persian Gulf veterans and cannot explain their overall increase in morbidity.

Given the well-established link between physical and psychiatric symptoms, it is unsurprising that many of the subjects examined in the studies also fulfilled the diagnostic criteria for depression and anxiety disorders and PTSD. Many subjects also fulfilled criteria for chronic fatigue syndrome, multiple chemical sensitivity, and irritable bowel syndrome. However interviews using validated "gold standard" instruments reveal that many did not have formal psychiatric disorders. Although Gulf veterans have about twice the rate of psychiatric disorders as nondeployed controls, the absolute burden of formal psychiatric disorder, remains low. So psychiatric disorders per se cannot wholly account for the Gulf War health effect, although clearly such disorders are still problematic for sufferers and their families.

A significant difficulty with all the GWS epidemiological studies is that they have used self-report measures that tend to be poorly correlated with findings on clinical physical examination. Thus, with some exceptions (Ford et al., 2001), one cannot assume that reporting of symptoms is closely linked with suffering from a diagnosable disease or disorder. Another difficulty for GWS researchers is that of recall and participant bias. It is well established that the recall of military hazards is often patchy and influenced by current psychological health. For example, an attempt to study a group of "prepped but not deployed" veterans, who claimed to have received vaccinations against biological weapons but never deployed, floundered after finding that nearly all had not actually received the vaccinations in question (Greenberg et al., 2003). Recall bias has been a problem in all studies, a process made worse by the delay in mounting systematic studies.

In summation, although there is little evidence supporting a specific Gulf War Syndrome, there is no doubt that the subjective health of between 20% to 30% of those who deployed to the Gulf War has been altered. There is, thus, little to suggest any specific disease process in Gulf veterans, but much to suggest that it is appropriate to talk about Gulf War illness, or even illnesses.

Gulf War Illness: Possible Culprits

The associations of illness in Gulf War veterans are fairly nonspecific. For example, symptoms are not associated with any single service, nor do those in combat show elevated rates of ill health compared to others. Rank though is a consistent marker of ill health—the lower the rank, the greater the burden of symptoms. Although a variety of agents have been alleged to be the "cause" of GWS, most of these claims have not been substantiated. For example, depleted uranium, used in munitions such as tank shells, is often given as a cause of ill health in Gulf personnel. Those most likely to come into contact with depleted uranium would have been personnel working in or around armored vehicles. But, as already discussed, there is no link between the role an individual veteran fulfilled and subsequent development of symptoms. Likewise, those personnel who have been injured by depleted uranium fragments, therefore indisputably exposed, have not suffered adverse health consequences to date. Evidence from the 2003 Iraq War has also failed to link exposure to depleted uranium with health problems in Coalition forces.

Another often mentioned exposure was the use of pyridostigmine bromide (PB) tablets as a prophylactic against the effects of some chemical weapons. However, Canada sent three ships to the Gulf, only two of which used PB prophylaxis, yet the rate of illness was the same in all three ships.

Another putative agent is organophosphate pesticides, which decrease the threat of disease from insect vectors, but if handled incorrectly can cause peripheral nerve damage. Detailed studies of the peripheral nervous system in both U.S. and U.K. subjects failed to

find evidence of neuropathy and a large U.S. epidemiological survey of Gulf veterans and their families came to same conclusion (Davis et al., 2004). Another claim is that ill health has resulted from either accidental or deliberate exposure to organophosphate-based nerve agents, principally sarin, but a series of expert reviews and panels have not been convinced by the evidence supporting such a claim.

On the other hand, there is some epidemiological evidence linking the particular pattern of protective biological warfare vaccinations with subsequent ill health in some. The U.K. group for example reported an association between receiving multiple vaccinations in general, and those against chemical and biological weapons, such as anthrax, in particular, with symptomatic outcomes (Hotopf et al., 2000). However, detailed investigations have failed to confirm that this link is immunologically mediated, and the possibility that problems in record keeping (acknowledged as a major deficiency) and recall bias account for some of this association remains a real one. Other potential causative agents have also been investigated, including fumes from burning oil wells. However, detailed environmental monitoring at the time and subsequent outcome studies have failed to find convincing evidence to support these or other more maverick theories.

Is Gulf War Syndrome Really New?

Although Gulf War Syndrome is often ascribed to what some commentators describe as "the most toxic war in history," in fact similar conditions have been observed before. Interpretable historical records, since the middle of the nineteenth century, show clinical descriptions of ex-servicemen consistent to the Gulf narratives (Hyams, Wignall, & Roswell, 1996). These conditions have received many different labels: Soldier's Heart, later termed Effort Syndrome, Shell shock, neurasthenia, Agent Orange Syndrome, and PTSD (*see:* **History of Psychological Trauma**). Thus taking a historical perspective, the symptoms of GWS show considerable similarities to illnesses that have been reported after all the major conflicts involving the British Armed Forces. The clinical manifestations of service in the 1991 Gulf War may also be influenced by a lack of trust veterans have in government official comments on aspects of the conflict. In this manner, the experiences of Gulf War veterans are similar to those of Vietnam veterans (Scott, 1993).

Conclusion

There is no doubt that many military personnel who served in the 1991 Gulf War report an excess of physical and psychological symptoms, which show no signs of decreasing with the passage of time. It is less clear as to why this is so. There is no compelling evidence implicating either a unique syndrome, or any particular agent or combination of agents in the causation of ill health. The picture is also similar to previous unexplained postconflict syndromes and to similar so called "modern illnesses" or the "contested diagnoses" such as Chronic Fatigue Syndrome and Multiple Chemical Sensitivity, suggesting that cultural factors also play some role.

One final piece of evidence comes from a new generation of studies that have looked at the health outcomes of U.S. and U.K. service personnel who took part in the 2003 invasion of Iraq and subsequent operations. There are numerous similarities between the 1991 and 2003 campaigns—fighting the same enemy on the same terrain. Relevant to the current essay is the fact that some of agents blamed for GWS, such as depleted uranium, pesticides and the anthrax vaccination, were also used in 2003. Other possible risk factors such as psychological stress are, if anything, more prominent in the most recent campaign than in 1991. However, to date there is no evidence to support the emergence of a new Iraq War Syndrome, which adds to the evidence against a prominent role for the above factors in the genesis of the Gulf War health problem (Horn et al., 2006).

The passage of time and the delay in commissioning systematic research (a lesson that was learned before the start of the 2003 invasion of Iraq) means that it is increasingly unlikely that a single cause, or causes, will ever satisfactorily explain the health consequences of the 1991 Gulf War. GWS most likely reflects a combination of events, including the psychological stress induced by the very real threat of chemical and biological weapons in 1991 with possible short-term side effects of a rapidly administered program of protection against these threats, and subsequently social and cultural pressures resulting from both media reporting and political misjudgments.

REFERENCES

Davis, L., Murphy, F., Alpern, R., Parks, B., Blanchard, M., Reda, D., et al. (2004). Clinical and laboratory assessment of distal peripheral nerves in Gulf War veterans and spouses. *Neurology, 63,* 1070–1077.

Ford, J. D., Campbell, K., Storzbach, D., Binder, L., Anger, W. K., & Rohlman, D. (2001). Posttraumatic stress symptomatology is associated with unexplained illness attributed to Persian Gulf War military service. *Psychosomatic Medicine, 63,* 842–849.

Gray, G., Gackstetter, G., Kang, H., Graham, J., & Scott, K. (2004). After more than 10 years of Gulf War veteran medical examinations, what have we learned? *American Journal of Preventive Medicine, 26,* 443–452.

Gray, G., & Kang, H. (2006). Healthcare utilization and mortality among veterans of the Gulf War. *Philosophical Transactions of the Royal Society of London, 361,* 553–569.

Greenberg, N., Iversen, A., Hull, L., Unwin, C., Destrange, M., & Wessely, S. (2003). Vaccination records in Gulf War veterans. *Journal of Occupational and Environmental Medicine, 45,* 219–230.

Haley, R., Kurt, T., & Hom, J. (1997). Is there a Gulf War Syndrome? Searching for syndromes by factor analysis of symptoms. *Journal of the American Medical Association, 277,* 215–222.

Higgins, E. I. K., Kant, K., Harman, K., Mellerio, J., Du Vivier, A., & Wessely, S. (2002). Skin disease in Gulf War Veterans. *Quarterly Journal of Medicine, 95,* 671–676.

Horn, O., Hull, L., Jones, M., Murphy, D., Browne, T., Fear, N., et al. (2006). Is there an "Iraq War Syndrome"? Comparison of the health of UK service personnel after the Gulf and Iraq Wars. *Lancet, 367,* 1742–1746.

Hotopf, M., David, A., Hull, L., Ismail, K., Unwin, C., & Wessely, S. (2000). The role of vaccinations as risk factors for ill-health in veterans of the Persian Gulf War. *British Medical Journal, 320,* 1363–1367.

Hyams, K., Wignall, S., & Roswell, R. (1996). War syndromes and their evaluation: From the U.S. Civil War to the Persian Gulf War. *Annals of Internal Medicine, 125,* 398–405.

Iowa Persian Gulf Study Group. (1997). Self-reported illness and health status among Gulf War veterans: A population-based study. *Journal of the American Medical Association, 277,* 238–245.

Scott, J. (1993). *The politics of readjustment: Vietnam veterans since the war.* New York: Aldine de Gruyter.

Unwin, C., Blatchley, N., Coker, W., Ferry, S., Hotopf, M., Hull, L., et al. (1999). Health of UK Servicemen who served in the Persian Gulf War. *Lancet, 353,* 169–178.

RECOMMENDED READINGS

Institute of Medicine. (2006). *Gulf War and health: Vol. 4. Health effects of serving in the Gulf War.* Washington, DC: National Academy of Sciences.

Vasterling, J., & Bremner, J. D. (2006). The impact of the 1991 Gulf War on the mind and brain: Findings from neuropsychological and neuroimaging research. *Philosophical Transactions of the Royal Society of London, 361,* 593–604.

Wessely, S. (Ed.). (2006). The health of Gulf War Veterans. *Philosophical Transactions of the Royal Society of London, 361,* 531–731.

Wessely, S., Doebbling, G. C., Clauw, B. N., & Reeves, D. J. (2003). Prevalence of symptoms and symptom-based conditions among Gulf War Veterans: Current status of research findings. *Epidemiologic Reviews, 24,* 218–227.

Neil Greenberg
King's College London

Simon Wessely
King's College London

See also: Medical Illness, Adult; Military Personnel; Somatic Complaints; War Trauma

H

HABITUATION

Habituation involves a reduction in an *unconditioned* response (UCR) upon repeated presentation of an unconditioned stimulus (UCS). For example, habituation might involve a decrease in the startle response (UCR) when a loud noise (UCS) is repeated several times. In layman's terms, a person gets used to a loud noise and stops responding as much. Research with animals and humans with phobias has shown that habituation reliably occurs when a UCS is repeated, although the number of repetitions required to achieve a substantial reduction in the UCR will vary depending on when, how, and where the UCS is presented.

In treatment and studies with people with PTSD, the term *habituation* often is used along with *extinction,* which involves a reduction in a *conditioned* response (CR) to a conditioned stimulus (CS). For example, if an individual learns to feel afraid of driving due to being in a motor vehicle accident (UCS), extinction might involve a decrease in fear (CR) after having a number of subsequent safe experiences driving in a car (CS).

Learning theories of PTSD assume that both an unlearned UCR (e.g., fear during an assault) and a CR (anxiety and avoidance of reminders of the assault) are involved in the development and maintenance of PTSD. For example, a woman who was raped and is experiencing PTSD might be hypervigilant and emotionally fearful (CR) when she is in a situation that reminds her of where the assault occurred (CS). Therefore a learning theory account of PTSD assumes that by presenting the nonthreatening stimuli (CS) associated with the trauma (such as memories, situations, and places that triggered memories) over and over, that the fear would decrease. Exposure therapy in humans

is based on the learning principles of habituation and extinction. In exposure therapy for PTSD, the exposure involves having a patient repeatedly imagine a traumatic memory vividly (imaginal exposure) or actually encounter situations that are reminders of the traumatic experience(s) (*in vivo* exposure), but not the actual trauma itself. When the treatment is successful, the result is that the individual can recall the memory or encounter reminders without feeling excessively anxious or fearful (extinction). When people recover from the fear caused by traumatic experiences without developing PTSD, or overcome PTSD through exposure therapy, it is likely that this is due to extinction rather than habituation. This is because a reduction in fear usually does not occur when people repeatedly experience the actual trauma (e.g., to be in an actual vehicle accident over and over—habituation) but instead when they have been able to safely experience reminders of the trauma and this enables them to learn that they need not be afraid of these reminders even though recurrences of the trauma would still evoke fear.

Therefore, during exposure therapy, it is extinction rather than habituation that is occurring. Exposure therapy assists people in learning that they do not need to feel fearful because the trauma actually is no longer happening, rather than simply habituating them to the continued experience of trauma. Extinction occurs both within a single session (as the patient becomes less fearful while the session is proceeding) or between sessions (as the patient experiences less fear from session to session). There is evidence that between-session extinction of fear is more important for a reduction in PTSD symptoms than within-session extinction. In comparing 30- and 60-minute imaginal exposure therapy sessions with patients with PTSD, differences on within-session fear reduction were not related to the amount of improvement in PTSD at the end of treatment, whereas between-session fear reduction was correlated with the improvement in PTSD at the end of treatment (van Minnen & Foa, 2006). It appears for exposure therapy to be therapeutic, it must be long enough and repeated frequently enough to allow extinction, and must be structured to allow the reductions in fear to generalize from the therapy setting to the patient's outside life.

REFERENCE

van Minnen, A., & Foa, E. B. (2006). The effect of imaginal exposure length on outcome of treatment for PTSD. *Journal of Traumatic Stress, 19,* 427–438.

RECOMMENDED READINGS

Foa, E. B., Hembree, E., & Rothbaum, B. O. (2007). *Prolonged exposure therapy for PTSD: Emotional processing of traumatic experiences* [Therapist guide]. New York: Oxford University Press.

McSweeney, F. K., & Swindell, S. (2002). Common processes may contribute to extinction and habituation. *Journal of General Psychology, 129,* 364–400.

Barbara O. Rothbaum
Emory University School of Medicine

See also: Conditioned Fear; Exposure Therapy, Adult; Exposure Therapy, Child; Learning Theory

HALLUCINATIONS

See: Flashbacks; Psychosis

HATE CRIMES

See: Race-Related Stressors

HEALTH IMPLICATIONS/ PHYSICAL HEALTH

See: Medical Illness, Adult; Medical Illness, Child; Somatic Complaints

HEALTH RISK BEHAVIORS

See: Alcohol Use Disorders; HIV; Smoking; Substance Use Disorders

HEALTH SERVICE UTILIZATION

Prior traumatic event exposure and a diagnosis of PTSD appear substantially related to the utilization and costs of mental health and medical services, across large-scale community samples and samples of mental health and medical patients (Elhai, North, & Frueh, 2005; Gavrilovic, Schutzwohl, Fazel, & Priebe, 2005; Walker, Newman, & Koss, 2004). It is not clearly known why people who have experienced psychological trauma and PTSD use more health-care services than other people. It is possible that the physical and emotional stress caused by trauma and PTSD may undermine health by placing a strain on the body and mind. It also is possible that people who have experienced trauma or PTSD may be more anxious about their health and therefore more likely to seek help from expert health-care providers. Research is ongoing to sort out these and other possible explanations for the strong association between trauma and PTSD and high levels of utilization of costly health-care services.

Two comprehensive reviews have been published on personal characteristics related to medical and/or mental health-care use among trauma victims, including survivors of war, disaster, assault, and other crimes, as well as rescue workers and refugees (Elhai et al., 2005; Gavrilovic et al., 2005). The reviews concluded that among trauma victims, increased use of mental health care was related to female gender, the extent and level of prior trauma exposure, and having a PTSD diagnosis or more severe PTSD. Furthermore, people with PTSD also used more medical as well as mental health services. Trauma survivors, especially those with PTSD, tended to more often use health-care services than other persons regardless of other factors such as ethnicity, age, socioeconomic status, severity or type of other illnesses, and having health insurance.

These findings are in contrast to the commonsense view that trauma victims may avoid mental health services because of PTSD avoidance symptoms. In fact, however, few studies demonstrate any relationship between PTSD avoidance symptoms and use of services. Most studies show that people with more severe PTSD avoidance symptoms use *more* healthcare services than people with less severe PTSD symptoms.

PTSD's well-documented mental health and medical comorbidity may not account for its substantial relationship with health-care utilization. People with PTSD often have other psychiatric or medical illnesses (comorbidities), but it appears that it is whether or not a person has PTSD (and not other illnesses) that determines how much medical and mental health treatment they will utilize. For example, after statistically controlling for mental health comorbidity, several studies demonstrate that PTSD's relationship with mental health-care use remained (reviewed in Elhai et al., 2005).

REFERENCES

Elhai, J. D., North, T. C., & Frueh, B. C. (2005). Health service use predictors among trauma survivors: A critical review. *Psychological Services, 2,* 3–19.

Gavrilovic, J. J., Schutzwohl, M., Fazel, M., & Priebe, S. (2005). Who seeks treatment after a traumatic event and who does not? A review of findings on mental health service utilization. *Journal of Traumatic Stress, 18,* 595–605.

Walker, E. A., Newman, E., & Koss, M. P. (2004). Costs and health care utilization associated with traumatic experiences. In P. P. Schnurr & B. L. Green (Eds.), *Trauma and health: Physical health consequences of exposure to extreme stress* (pp. 43–69). Washington, DC: American Psychological Association.

Jon D. Elhai
University of South Dakota

Stefan Priebe
University of London

See also: **Medical Illness, Adult; Somatic Complaints**

HIPPOCAMPUS

The hippocampus, a brain area involved in verbal declarative memory, is very sensitive to the effects of exposure to stressors. Patients with posttraumatic stress disorder (PTSD) show many symptoms that are related to memory disturbance, including intrusive thoughts, flashbacks, nightmares, and changes in memory and concentration, and startle responses. Therefore, it is not surprising that results from a growing number of studies with animals exposed to stressors and humans with PTSD indicate that alterations in the hippocampus, as well as other closely related brain areas that also are involved in memory, including the amygdala and prefrontal cortex, provide a biological basis for these memory-related symptoms of PTSD (Bremner, 2006).

Preclinical (Animal) Studies of Stressors and the Hippocampus

Animals exposed to stressors have been found to have damage to neurons in the hippocampus. Stressors have been shown to cause several biological changes in animals that may explain how the hippocampal neurons are damaged by stressor exposure. These changes include elevations in the stress hormone cortisol, decreased brain derived neurotrophic factor (a brain chemical that promotes nerve growth in the brain), elevated glutamate concentrations (an excitatory amino acid neurotransmitter that can have toxic effects on the brain at high concentrations), and inhibition of new nerve growth (neurogenesis). Evidence for these relationships includes studies showing that antidepressant medications administered to animals block these adverse effects of stress and/or promote neurogenesis in the hippocampus. There is new evidence that neurogenesis is necessary for the behavioral effects of antidepressants although this continues to be a source of debate (Bremner, 2002, 2006).

Clinical Studies of Memory and Cognition in PTSD

Studies with people who are diagnosed with PTSD show changes in cognition that are at least in part mediated by the hippocampus (Bremner, 2006). Multiple studies have demonstrated verbal declarative memory deficits (e.g., memory for facts or lists) in PTSD. Patients with PTSD secondary to combat and childhood abuse were found to have deficits in verbal declarative memory function based on neuropsychological testing. Studies, using a variety of measures (including the Wechsler Memory Scale, the visual and verbal components of the Selective Reminding Test, the Auditory Verbal Learning Test, Paired Associate Recall, the California Verbal New Learning Test, and the Rivermead Behavioral Memory Test), found specific deficits in verbal declarative memory function, with a relative sparing of visual memory and IQ. These studies' findings that PTSD is associated with deficits in verbal declarative memory are consistent with the hypothesis that damage to or deficits in the functioning of the hippocampus may be a contributing factor to the development or maintenance of PTSD. For a more specific link between PTSD and the hippocampus, neuroimaging studies have been done with scans of the brain that focus on the size and the activation of the hippocampus (see the next section).

Neuroimaging Studies of the Hippocampus in PTSD

Multiple structural magnetic resonance imaging (MRI) studies have shown evidence that people with PTSD have smaller hippocampal volumes than similar people who do not have PTSD (see Bremner, 2007, for a detailed description of the studies described in this section). These include studies of combat veterans and adults with childhood abuse related-PTSD, which showed smaller hippocampal volume based on structural imaging with MRI relative to healthy comparison subjects. Other studies in PTSD have found reductions of N-acetyl aspartate (NAA), a marker of neuronal integrity, in the hippocampus using magnetic resonance spectroscopy. Those studies suggest that PTSD may involve both a smaller and poorer functioning hippocampus. One study found smaller hippocampal volume in PTSD subjects compared to trauma exposed non-PTSD subjects, while another study did not. Therefore, it is not clear whether it is exposure to psychological trauma or the presence of PTSD that is associated with a smaller hippocampus. One study indicated that there is a genetic contribution to smaller hippocampal volume in PTSD. Studies in children with PTSD did not find hippocampal volume reduction. In order to attempt to resolve these divergent results, recent meta-analyses pooled data from all of the published studies and found smaller hippocampal volume for both the left and the right hippocampal sides, equally in adult men and women with chronic PTSD, and no change in children (see Bremner, 2007).

Several studies have shown that PTSD patients have deficits in hippocampal activation while performing a verbal declarative memory task or a virtual water maze task. The water maze task is known to specifically activate the hippocampus. Both hippocampal atrophy and hippocampal-based memory deficits have been found to be successfully reversed with treatment with the Selective Serotonergic Reuptake Inhibitor antidepressant medication, paroxetine, which has been shown to promote neurogenesis in the hippocampus in preclinical studies. Phenytoin, an anticonvulsant (seizure) medication also has been shown to increase hippocampal volume in PTSD patients. These studies show that medications that are efficacious in the treatment of PTSD are also associated with an increase in hippocampal volume; interpreted together with the animal studies reviewed previously suggests that medications may act in part through the hippocampus to promote recovery from PTSD.

Results of functional imaging studies measuring brain function with positron emission tomography (PET) and functional magnetic resonance imaging (fMRI) are also consistent with the view that PTSD is associated with dysfunction of the hippocampus. Stimulation of the noradrenergic system with a substance called *yohimbine* resulted in a failure of activation in several frontal lobe regions, as well as decreased function in the hippocampus. Since stressful events are associated with norepinephrine release in the brain, and since high levels of norepinephrine release are associated with decreased brain function, these findings suggest that exaggerated norepinephrine release in PTSD may be associated with decreased hippocampal function during everyday stressors, with associated cognitive impairment. Exposure to traumatic reminders in the form of traumatic scripts of childhood sexual abuse was associated with an increase in PTSD symptoms and decreased blood flow, as measured with PET, in the hippocampus in women with abuse-related PTSD. When women with PTSD due to early childhood abuse were asked to remember emotionally charged words (e.g., rape-mutilate), researchers observed decreases in blood flow in the left hippocampus as well as other brain regions.

Studies have also used declarative memory tasks as specific probes of hippocampal function. Two PET studies showed a failure of hippocampal activation with declarative memory tasks, one using paragraph encoding and the other retrieval of deeply encoded words using a word-stem completion task. An fMRI study found a failure of hippocampal activation using a virtual water maze tasks. In summary, the studies' findings are consistent with altered function and structure of the hippocampus in PTSD.

Neuroimaging of the Hippocampus in Trauma Spectrum Mental Disorders

Several psychiatric disorders share with PTSD a common link to exposure to stressors, including depression associated with early childhood abuse, borderline personality disorder (BPD) associated with early childhood abuse, and dissociative identity disorder (DID) with early abuse. Several studies have found smaller hippocampal volume in BPD. Smaller hippocampal volume has also been shown in studies of patients with depression associated with early childhood abuse, and in women with DID.

REFERENCES

Bremner, J. D. (2002). *Does stress damage the brain? Understanding trauma-related disorders from a mind-body perspective.* New York: Norton.

Bremner, J. D. (2006). Traumatic stress: Effects on the brain. *Dialogues in Clinical Neuroscience, 8,* 445–461.

Bremner, J. D. (2007). Functional neuroimaging in posttraumatic stress disorder. *Expert Reviews in Neurotherapeutics, 7,* 393–405.

J. Douglas Bremner
Emory University School of Medicine

See also: Amygdala; Anterior Cingulate Cortex; Biology, Brain Structure, and Function, Adult; Biology, Brain Structure, and Function, Child; Biology, Neurochemistry; Frontal Cortex; Memory

HISTORY OF PSYCHOLOGICAL TRAUMA

The term *trauma* is derived from the Greek word for wound. The oldest known description of traumatic stress was inscribed on clay tablets 5,000 years ago. The Sumerian *Epic of Gilgamesh* describes a Babylonian king who was terrified and distraught after the death of his closest friend, Enkidu. Gilgamesh's reactions reflect several classic symptoms of posttraumatic stress disorder (PTSD) and traumatic grief (e.g., terrifying memories, inability to sleep, anger, sense of foreshortened future; Birmes, Hatton, Brunet, & Schmitt, 2003). The tenth tablet describes Gilgamesh's ordeal:

> I was terrified by his appearance, I began to fear death, and roam the wilderness. How can I stay silent, how can I be still! My friend whom I love has turned to clay! Am I not like him! Will I lie down never to get up again! That is why I must go on, to see Utanapishtim, "The Faraway." That is why sweet sleep has not mellowed my face, through sleepless striving I am strained, my muscles are filled with pain (www.ancienttexts.org/library/mesopotamian/gilgamesh/).

Two millennia later, famous Greek and Roman storytellers and authors captured the essence of traumatic stress and grief (Birmes et al., 2003). Homer's *Illiad* describes the rageful loss of control of Achilles in the siege of Troy (Shay, 1994), and his *Odyssey* depicts what we now would call chronic PTSD in the inability of Odysseus to emotionally return home after experiencing traumatic betrayal and loss (Shay, 2002). The Greek historian Herodotus and Roman historian Pliny the Younger graphically described acute traumatic shock and dissociation in, respectively, combatants at the battle of Marathon (490 BC) and during the eruption of Mount Vesuvius that destroyed Pompeii and Herculaneum (A.D. 79).

Less common, but equally poignant, are ancient stories of women who suffer traumatic stressors. For example, the Biblical tale of a brother's incestuous rape of a princess (Tamar) in King David's court of Judah, describes her "wisdom, courage, and unrelieved suffering" (Trible, 1984): "Tamar took ashes upon her head and the long robe that was upon her she tore. She put her hand upon her head . . . and she wept. . . . So Tamar dwelt, and she was desolate, in the house of her [other] brother Absalom" (Samuel 13: 19–20). A millennium or more later, in the Renaissance and Reformation periods of the fifteenth to seventeenth centuries, literature and theater produced vivid accounts of psychological trauma and its aftermath. Shakespeare's works portray the traumatic impact of natural disasters (e.g., the *Tempest*), rape (e.g., the *Rape of Lucrece*), war (e.g., *Titus Andronicus; Henry IV; Henry V; Henry VI*), and family violence and murder (e.g., *Romeo and Juliet, Othello, Macbeth,* and *Richard II*).

It was not until the eighteenth century, when medicine became a science-based profession, that traumatic stress first was technically described and treated. Trauma was viewed primarily as a surgical challenge of preventing death due to infection caused by severe physical injury or wounds (Feliciano, Mattox, & Moore, 2004). In the 1860s, physicians began to describe chronic syndromes characterized by fatigue, tremors, pain, anxiety, and depression following life-threatening injuries. John Eric Erichsen's (1866) *On Railway and Other Injuries of the Nervous System* described a condition known as "railway spine" that originally was thought to be the result of physical trauma sustained in railway crashes. A quarter century later, the Jewish German neurologist Hermann Oppenheim reconceptualized the

phenomenon as a "traumatic neurosis" caused by exposure to life-threatening events rather than due to physical injury.

Concurrently, British and American cardiologists Arthur B. R. Myers (1870) and Jacob Mendez DaCosta (1871) nearly simultaneously published of combat soldiers with or without physical injuries who suffered from chronic anxiety and dysphoria, which they attributed to the cardiologic defect of an "irritable soldier's heart." In 1918, at the end of World War I, the syndrome was classified by the U.S. Surgeon General as *neurocirculatory asthenia,* meaning a muscular weakness caused by some combination of neurological and cardiologic/circulatory disease. The 1916 War Congress of the German Association for Psychiatry similarly decided that anxiety and exhaustion among soldiers were due to "hysteria," "feeble-mindedness," and factitious claims made to obtain a disability pension (Lerner, 2003). Seemingly consistent with this view, "neurasthenia" in large military and civilian medical case samples was found to occur not only after war combat, but also among others with mild or no combat exposure and a predisposition to complain of exhaustion and anxiety. Thus, with the exception of Oppenheim's formulation of a traumatic neurosis, early clinical observations of chronic posttraumatic stress were attributed to medical trauma or disease, hysteria, or malingering.

During this period, Freud began to formulate the psychoanalytic approach to the treatment of hysterical neuroses, beginning with discussions with an internal medicine colleague, Josef Breuer (the case of Anna O). The patient was a young woman who suffered from "hysteria"— paralysis, anesthesia, visions, aphasia, dissociative fugue states, and mood swings. Her symptoms subsided when Breuer helped her to reconstruct the events preceding their onset. She (her true name was Bertha Pappenheim) later was an eminent social worker, and creatively described the treatment as "the talking cure" or psychic "chimney sweeping." The case led Breuer and Freud (1893) to publish a psychological theory of hysteria, "On the Psychic Mechanisms of Hysterical Phenomena." Soon afterward, Freud began publishing a series of papers describing "psychoneuroses" such as hysteria as altered "personality structures resulting from defensive attempts to deal with traumatic experiences in childhood predispose the individual to later psychopathology" (Davis, 1994, p. 492). During the next decade, Freud reformulated this "seduction theory" of psychoneuroses, emphasizing the etiologic role of inborn psychic conflicts about sexuality rather than exposure to actual childhood sexual trauma (Davis, 1994). Foreshadowing the contemporary controversy about "false memories" of childhood trauma, Freud noted that "screen memories" of purported sexual abuse might result as a neurotic psychic defense against facing emotional conflicts unrelated to any abuse. Thus, Freud's work both highlighted the potential chronic psychological harm that has since been scientifically and clinically documented to result from childhood abuse and the problem of distinguishing between such complex PTSD and psychiatric or medical disorders that may occur entirely independent of psychological trauma or abuse.

In 1915, during World War I, the British physician Charles Myers advanced a formulation of hysterical neuroses among soldiers as "shell shock." Based on three cases of "loss of memory, vision, smell, and taste" subsequent to exposure to exploding shells, Myers noted that the patients' hearing was intact but other senses and memory were lost or distorted (i.e., a "dissociated complex"), consistent with contemporary descriptions of psychological and somatoform dissociation (Leys, 1994). Another British physician, William Brown, treated more than 3,000 shell-shocked soldiers with Breuer and Freud's approach of encouraging a detailed retelling of the specific events occurring just prior to the hysterical symptoms. In a 1920 presentation to the British Psychological Society, "The revival of emotional memories and its therapeutic value," Brown noted that when vivid, even "hallucinatory," memories were described in detail, the patient's symptoms disappeared due to "a re-synthesis of the mind of the patient [in which] the amnesia

has been abolished" (Leys, 1994, p. 625). Like Freud, Brown viewed *catharsis,* a liberation of repressed emotional distress, as the therapeutic mechanism. Charles Myers and William McDougall provided commentary in which they proposed that the critical factor was that the patient was able to articulate rather than avoid the traumatic memory, and thereby to create a psychologically coherent narrative description of the formerly fragmented and intolerable memory (Leys, 1994). The Myers and McDougall conceptualization is similar to Pierre Janet's 1925 formulation of "presentification," the reconstruction of traumatic memories in a meaningful narrative (Van der Hart & Friedman, 1989)—which Janet developed after earlier attempts to help patients "erase" troubling memories (Leys, 1994). Brown also noted that the treatment was less effective in both eliciting vivid recall and reducing hysterical symptoms if done after the soldier left the war zone and returned home. Thus, Brown's clinical work and the Myers/McDougall and Janet conceptualizations foreshadowed the later development of cognitive-behavioral therapy for acute stress disorder and PTSD, as well as narrative and self-reconstructive therapies for complex PTSD (Herman, 1992).

Additional conceptualizations of traumatic stress and PTSD have been formulated in response to war or major social and political upheavals (Lasiuk & Hegadoren, 2006a). During and after World War II and the Korean War, military psychiatrists such as Abram Kardiner and Herbert Spiegel described "war neurosis," "combat stress reaction," and "combat fatigue," and formulated principles of immediate prevention and treatment that emphasized temporary removal from danger, rest, and maintaining ongoing contact with the combat unit. In fact during World War II, prevention in the U.S. military was conducted by predeployment screening, but this failed because of numerous psychiatric casualities even in light of screening out "at risk" soldiers. With the ascendance of the civil rights, feminist, and human rights movements in the 1960s and 1970s, mental health professionals and advocates put forth the rape trauma syndrome and the battered woman syndrome to describe the traumatic consequences of sexual and domestic violence. In the 1970s, a "post-Vietnam syndrome" was identified among returning soldiers.

The American Psychiatric Association's *Diagnostic and Statistical Manual of Mental Disorders* (*DSM;* 1952) has changed its classification of posttraumatic disorders over time (Turnbull, 1998). In the first version, traumatic stress disorders were classified as Gross Stress Reactions that were expected to be transient unless the person had preexisting psychological problems that predisposed him or her to a chronic neurosis. In the second edition, *DSM-II* (American Psychiatric Association, 1968), this diagnosis was eliminated, but Transient Situational Disturbance appeared as a reaction to an overwhelming environmental stressor among otherwise healthy individuals. The diagnosis of PTSD, developed from these earlier *DSM* diagnoses, first officially appeared in the *DSM-III* (American Psychiatric Association, 1980). PTSD's definition subsequently has been altered, with *DSM-III-R* (American Psychiatric Association, 1987) including more specific definitions of traumatic stressors as events "outside the range of usual human experience" and altered definition and placement of symptoms (such as expanding and relocating avoidance symptoms to include them with emotional numbing, and removal of memory impairment as a symptom). *DSM-IV* (American Psychiatric Association, 1994) removed the requirement that traumatic events must be outside the range of usual human experience and added the possibility that they might be witnessed or indirectly experienced as well as directly occurring to the person, required both an objective definition of the traumatic stressor (as a life-threatening event or a violation of bodily integrity) and an initial subjective response of extreme fear, horror, or helplessness or fear, and imposed a minimum of 1-month duration and an adverse effect on social or vocational functioning. *DSM-IV* also added Acute Stress Disorder as a diagnosis, similar to PTSD but with more focus on dissociative symptoms and with the requirement that it must begin and end within 1 month of experiencing the traumatic stressor.

While the *DSM-III* was being finalized, the major classification system for medical illnesses, the *International Classification of Diseases* (*ICD*) was amended (Lasiuk & Hegadoren, 2006b) to include "reactions to severe stress" as a syndrome in its ninth edition (1978). In the next edition, *ICD-10*, acute stress reactions and PTSD were codified, parallel to the Acute Stress Disorder and PTSD categories in the *DSM-IV*. The *ICD-10* also included categories reflecting enduring personality changes following exposure to psychological trauma, but the *DSM-IV* rejected a proposed parallel diagnosis of complex PTSD (Disorders of Extreme Stress Not Otherwise Specified, DESNOS) and included DESNOS features as optional additional features of PTSD.

As Judith Herman (1992) has noted, advances in raising public and professional awareness about the adverse psychological impact caused by traumatic stressors and the need for effective and empowering prevention and therapeutic interventions to assist in recovery have been more sporadic than continuous—with periods of amnesia in which social and professional attention to traumatic stress has virtually disappeared. The first decade of the twenty-first century has seen the advent of a robust and growing scientific and clinical literature on traumatic stress and PTSD (Rachtman, 2004). For example, a search of PsycInfo in the year 2006 alone identified 778 peer-reviewed published articles on PTSD, almost exactly the number (794) listed in that bibliographic database in the 1980 to 1989 decade. The principal question facing the traumatic stress field at present appears to be how best to fully and accurately account for the range of acute and chronic reactions to the wide variety of traumatic stressors that unfortunately are experienced by more than half of all people according to epidemiologic studies and therefore can *not* be described (as in the original *DSM-III* definition of PTSD) as "outside the range of usual human experience."

REFERENCES

American Psychiatric Association. (1952). *Diagnostic and statistical manual of mental disorders.* Washington, DC: Author.

American Psychiatric Association. (1968). *Diagnostic and statistical manual of mental disorders* (2nd ed.). Washington, DC: Author.

American Psychiatric Association. (1980). *Diagnostic and statistical manual of mental disorders* (3rd ed.). Washington, DC: Author.

American Psychiatric Association. (1987). *Diagnostic and statistical manual of mental disorders* (3rd ed., rev.). Washington, DC: Author.

American Psychiatric Association. (1994). *Diagnostic and statistical manual of mental disorders* (4th ed.). Washington, DC: Author.

Birmes, P., Hatton, L., Brunet, A., & Schmitt, L. (2003). Early historical literature for post-traumatic symptomataology. *Stress and Health, 19,* 17–26.

Breuer, J. & Freud, S. (1893/1957). On the psychical mechanism of hysterical phenomena: Preliminary communication. In J. Breuer & S. Freud, *Studies on Hysteria* (pp. 3–17). New York: Basic Books.

DaCosta, J. M. (1871). On irritable heart; a clinical study of a form of functional cardiac disorder and its consequences. *American Journal of the Medical Sciences, 61,* 17–52.

Davis, D. A. (1994). A theory for the 90s: Freud's seduction theory in historical context. *Psychoanalytic Review, 81,* 627–640.

Erichsen, J. E. (1866). *On railway and other injuries of the nervous system.* London: Walton and Maberly.

Feliciano, D., Mattox, K., & Moore, E. (2004). *Trauma.* New York: McGraw-Hill.

Herman, J. (1992). *Trauma and recovery.* New York: Basic Books.

Janet, P. (1925). *Psychological healing* (2 Vols.). New York: Macmillan.

Lasiuk, G., & Hegadoren, K. (2006a). Posttraumatic stress disorder: Pt. I. Historical development of the concept. *Perspectives in Psychiatric Care, 42,* 13–20.

Lasiuk, G., & Hegadoren, K. (2006b). Posttraumatic stress disorder: Pt. II. Development of the construct within the North American psychiatric taxonomy. *Perspectives in Psychiatric Care, 42,* 72–81.

Lerner, P. (2003). *Hysterical men: War, psychiatry, and the politics of trauma in Germany, 1890–1930.* Ithaca, NY: Cornell University Press.

Leys, R. (1994). Traumatic cures: Shell shock, Janet, and the question of memory. *Critical Inquiry, 20,* 623–662.

Myers, A. B. R. (1870). *On the aetiology and prevalence of disease of the heart among soldiers.* London: Churchill.

Rechtman, R. (2004). The rebirth of PTSD: The rise of a new paradigm in psychiatry. *Social Psychiatry and Psychiatric Epidemiology, 39,* 913–915.

Shay, J. (1994). *Achilles in Vietnam: Combat trauma and the undoing of character.* New York: Atheneum.

Shay, J. (2002). *Odysseus in America: Combat trauma and the trials of homecoming.* New York: Scribner.

Trible, P. (1984). *Texts of terror.* Philadelphia: Fortress Press.

Turnbull, G. (1998). A review of post-traumatic stress disorder: Pt. 1. *Injury, 29,* 87–91.

Van der Hart, O., & Friedman, B. (1989). A reader's guide to Pierre Janet. *Journal of Trauma and Dissociation, 2*(1), 3–16.

World Health Organization (1978). *International classification of diseases* (9th rev.). Geneva, Switzerland: Author.

World Health Organization (1992). *International classification of diseases* (10th rev.). Geneva, Switzerland: Author.

Julian D. Ford
University of Connecticut School of Medicine

See also: Diagnosis of Traumatic Stress Disorders (*DSM & ICD*); Ferenczi, Sándor; Freud, Sigmund; Janet, Pierre; Literary Depictions; Myers, Charles S.; Posttraumatic Stress Disorder; Posttraumatic Stress Disorder, Diagnosis of

HIV (HUMAN IMMUNODEFICIENCY VIRUS)

In addition to having a chronic life-threatening disease, people infected with human immunodeficiency virus (HIV) tend to have high rates of depression and previous trauma (i.e., prior to developing HIV; Orlando et al., 2002). Studies conducted before the advent of highly active antiretroviral therapy (HAART) show that chronic depression, cumulative stressful events and trauma are related to more rapid progression of HIV (e.g., AIDS, mortality; Leserman, 2003). With the advent of more effective treatments, researchers questioned if psychosocial variables would still have an impact on HIV.

Despite HAART, there is continued variability in disease course, and chronic depression and lifetime trauma continue to explain variation in mortality and immunological and clinical decline. For example, a 7.5-year investigation of 1,716 women found that those with chronic depression were more likely to die (13%) than those with few or no depressive symptoms (6%; Cook et al., 2004). Women receiving mental health services were less likely to die from AIDS. Furthermore, Leserman et al. (2007) found that HIV-infected persons with three or more traumatic life events had more than three times the risk of dying than those with fewer events.

These findings underscore the importance of psychological screening, treatment, and referrals to address depression and the psychological sequelae of past trauma as part of standard HIV care. Despite decreasing morbidity and mortality since HAART, we continue to find evidence that chronic depression and trauma are associated with progression of HIV/AIDS.

REFERENCES

Cook, J. A., Grey, D., Burke, J., Cohen, M. H., Gurtman, A. C., Richardson, J. L., et al. (2004). Depressive symptoms and AIDS-related mortality among a multisite cohort of HIV-positive women. *American Journal of Public Health, 94*(7), 1133–1140.

Leserman, J. (2003). HIV disease progression: Depression, stress, and possible mechanisms. *Biological Psychiatry, 54,* 295–306.

Leserman, J., Pence, B. W., Whetten, K., Mugavero, M. J., Thielman, N. M., Swartz, M. S., et al. (2007). Relations of lifetime trauma and depressive symptoms to mortality and HIV. *American Journal of Psychiatry, 164,* 1707–1713.

Orlando, M., Burnam, M. A., Beckman, R., Morton, S. C., London, A. S., Bing, E. G., et al. (2002). Re-estimating the prevalence of psychiatric disorders in a nationally representative sample of persons receiving care for HIV: Results from the HIV Cost and Services Utilization Study. *International Journal of Methods in Psychiatric Research, 11*(2), 75–82.

JANE LESERMAN
University of North Carolina, Chapel Hill

See also: **Medical Illness, Adult; Medical Illness, Child**

HOLOCAUST, THE

The Holocaust (which translates literally to great slaughter or massacre) is a term used to refer to the genocidal persecution and killing of approximately six million European Jews during World War II in an elaborate and systematic process initiated by the National Socialist German Worker's (Nazi) party in Germany. From 1933 through 1945, millions were exiled to ghettos and sent to labor camps and concentration camps. Among the causes of death were maltreatment, exhaustion, disease, starvation, mass shootings, and extermination in gas chambers. Some, including children and twins, were subjected to brutal human experiments—such as testing drugs or measuring the effects of freezing or pressure chamber on them—and then were studied at autopsy.

Those who survived imprisonment or life in the ghetto had witnessed such scenes, been exposed to multiple threatening situations, malnourishment, chronic disease, physical abuse, and assaults on their identity. Those who survived as young children endured separation from their caretakers and may have lived in hiding, in foster care, or orphanages. At the end of the war, survivors were further confronted by the extent of their loss of families, friends, homes, and entire communities. Many took refuge in displaced persons camps. Some left Europe and immigrated to Israel and the United States where they learned new languages and established new families, communities, and means of support; many thrived despite the trauma and chronic stress they endured.

Clinical descriptions and studies of Holocaust survivors have been instrumental in defining the course of the psychological and neuropsychological effects of extreme trauma. The Holocaust's scope, intensity, and enduring effects provided a basis for the development of new concepts regarding individual and collective trauma. The "Concentration Camp Syndrome" was an early description for such effects in the European literature (Krystal & Niederland, 1968). Other names for similar descriptions included the survivor syndrome, persecution syndrome, and traumatogenic anxiety syndrome. Phases of the Concentration Camp Syndrome included an initial predominance of somatic symptoms during convalescence, a period of latency lasting months to years, and the development of personality disturbances and social and occupational impairments. Symptoms included chronic anxiety, depression, insomnia, retrograde amnesia, somatization, survivor guilt, and recurrent trauma-related nightmares. Later phases of the syndrome were viewed as "organic" in nature and characterized by protracted depression, impaired memory, delusional symptoms, dementia, and, in some, neurologic illnesses such as epilepsy or encephalopathy. These symptoms contributed to the idea that premature aging was also an aftereffect of severe trauma and that the effects of such trauma could be progressive (Thygesen, 1980).

The possibility that massive psychic trauma occurring in adulthood could have enduring psychological effects was not an accepted notion in modern psychiatry at the time. Early debates on the etiology of symptoms in Holocaust survivors mirrored those in the subsequent literature on the effects of trauma and the development of PTSD as a psychiatric diagnosis. These included the question of whether symptoms could result from psychological trauma as opposed to physical causes (e.g., head trauma or malnourishment), and if so, whether they were a direct result of the trauma or reflected the uncovering of preexisting personal vulnerabilities (which at the time were described primarily in psychodynamic terms). The extent to which application for reparations impacted the presentation of symptoms was also often debated. It is not

known precisely how many survivors suffered enduring psychological and psychiatric problems. After formal introduction of the diagnosis of PTSD in 1980, a review of one series of Holocaust survivors evaluated by a German compensation board found that 46.8% met *DSM-III-R* (American Psychiatric Association, 1987) criteria for PTSD with the highest rates found among the tattooed death camp survivors (Kuch & Cox, 1992).

Thus, the study of the psychological aftermath of the Holocaust is part of the evolution in psychiatric understanding of the impact of exposure to extreme stress. Early research conducted within a medical-psychiatric framework focused on psychopathology rather than on the influence of coping strategies or the development of specific adaptive mechanisms to contend with a persistently horrific, terrorizing, and dehumanizing context. Subsequent studies have highlighted dynamic variables likely to affect the ongoing well-being of Holocaust survivors (and other survivors of extreme stress). These include the nature and duration of the stress experience, current sociodemographic and economic status, and health and current modes of coping with additional stressors and the survivorship experience itself (Wilson, Harel, & Kahana, 1988).

Those who survived the Holocaust are a heterogeneous group with data indicating that survivors have generally functioned within a broad normal range in terms of personal adjustment, social relationships, and occupational achievement (Krell, Suedfeld, & Soriano, 2004). However, they appeared more inclined to exhibit mild psychological problems such as anxiety or depression (Auerhahn & Prelinger, 1983), or to demonstrate posttraumatic stress reactions. PTSD symptoms, whether diagnosed as the disorder or as evidenced as problems in mood and adjustment, can have serious effects for Holocaust survivors themselves and for their children. In a study of concentration camp survivors (Valent, 2000), many reported a continuing sense of anxiety and fear a full 50 years after they were released. In a 1988 study, Kahana, Harel, and Kahana noted that survivors were found to have lower mental health and morale than a matched comparison group who had not endured such persecution. They also noted the importance of poststress factors and the broader questions of human adaptation and adjustment in the mental health of aging survivors.

The psychological aftermath of the Holocaust also offers insight into societal responses to traumatic events and its effects on survivors. Danieli (1981; Danieli, Dingman, & Zellner, 2005) noted that Holocaust survivors were initially confronted with societal indifference, avoidance, and denial of their experiences that eventually shifted toward increasing recognition of their pain and suffering. Increased social awareness led to collective responses reflected in public memorials that also served to shore up survivors' abilities to "tell their story." Museums dedicated to remembrance of this event catalogue the extent of the emotional damage sustained, and are located in sites where many survivors immigrated or where Holocaust atrocities occurred. Such public testimony and memorials reflect the increased social awareness of the long-term impact of large-scale traumatic events, validate the experience of survivors, their families, and communities, and provide a vehicle for reflection for society at large.

In addition, individual reactions to the Holocaust have contributed to our conceptualization of the needs of those exposed to traumatic stress. As one example, concentration camp survivor and psychiatrist Viktor Frankl developed a therapeutic approach that sought to find meaning in pain, guilt, and death, and was based on personal exposure to the extreme stress of existence in four concentration camps and the loss of his wife, his brother, and his parents (Frankl, 1946). He maintained that humans have the ability to choose how they will respond to extreme adversity, regardless of biological or environmental forces, and that this capacity is crucial to successful trauma resolution. His emphasis on self-direction and meaning-making foreshadowed current trauma treatment trends that emphasize cognitive-behavioral techniques, resilience, and recovery models, and especially those therapies that emphasize the need for restoring meaning,

values, and social involvement to promote well-being (Walser & Westrup, 2007).

In addition to the enduring impact of the Holocaust on psychological health and well-being, recent investigations also underscore its influence on long-term neuropsychological outcomes as well. Empirical data on Holocaust survivors (who were among the youngest survivors at the time of the event) suggest there is an acceleration of some aspects of age-related cognitive decline in Holocaust survivors with PTSD (Golier et al., 2002). Holocaust survivors with PTSD exhibited significant impairments in learning and memory in domains sensitive to the effects of age and stress, as compared to Holocaust survivors without PTSD and healthy demographically similar persons not exposed to the Holocaust. However, survivors with PTSD also preferentially formed new associations to trauma-related material, suggesting an enduring disturbance in associative learning and emotional memory decades after the Holocaust. Over a 5-year period, Holocaust survivors with PTSD compared to those without PTSD showed greater declines in some aspects of memory, compatible with the notion of accelerated aging. However, other aspects of memory improved in tandem with symptom improvement (Yehuda et al., 2006), suggesting that not all of the neuropsychological deficits are fixed, and that they may be amenable to therapeutic intervention.

In addition to the direct impact of the Holocaust on survivors, clinical and empiric observations in children of Holocaust survivors point to possible intergenerational transmission (van Ijzendoorn, Bakerman-Kranenburg, & Sagi-Schwartz, 2003). Terms such as vicarious, empathic, and secondary traumatization have been used to describe this phenomenon. Tauber (1998) held that the Holocaust survivor-parents' experience of deprivation, humiliation, and loss of community, human rights, and family could influence their children so that there would be a reciprocal overprotectiveness and struggles with cultural identity, affect regulation and separation-individuation. There appear to be enduring negative psychological effects of the Holocaust on subsequent generations as expressed in greater anxiety, depression, interpersonal problems, and vulnerability to stress in some adult children of survivors—effects that may be mediated by the biological and psychological sequelae of parental traumatization and PTSD (Yehuda et al., 2007).

REFERENCES

American Psychiatric Association. (1987). *Diagnostic and statistical manual of mental disorders* (3rd ed., rev.). Washington, DC: Author.

Auerhahn, N. C., & Prelinger, E. (1983). Repetition in the concentration camp survivor and her child. *International Review of Psycho-Analysis, 10,* 31–46.

Danieli, Y. (1981). The aging survivor of the Holocaust. *Journal of Geriatric Psychiatry, 14*(2), 191–210.

Danieli, Y., Dingman, R. L., & Zellner, J. (2005). *On the ground after September 11th: Mental health responses and practical knowledge gained.* Binghamton, NY: Haworth Press.

Frankl, V. E. (1946). *Man's search for meaning.* New York: Simon & Schuster.

Golier, J. A., Yehuda, R., Lupien, S. J., Harvey, P. D., Grossman, R., & Elkin, A. (2002). Memory performance in Holocaust survivors with posttraumatic stress disorder. *American Journal of Psychiatry, 159,* 1682–1688.

Krell, R., Suedfeld, P., & Soriano, E. (2004). Child Holocaust survivors as parents: A transgenerational perspective. *American Journal of Orthopsychiatry, 74,* 502–508.

Krystal, H., & Niederland, W. C. (1968). Clinical observations on the survivor syndrome. In H. Krystal (Ed.), *Massive psychic trauma* (pp. 327–348). New York: International Press.

Kuch, K., & Cox, B. J. (1992). Symptoms of PTSD in 124 survivors of the Holocaust. *American Journal of Psychiatry, 149*(3), 337–340.

Tauber, Y. (1998). *In the other chair: Holocaust survivors and the second generation as therapists and clients.* Jerusalem, Israel: Gefen.

Thygesen, P. (1980). The concentration camp syndrome. *Danish Medical Bulletin, 27*(5), 224–228.

Valent, P. (2000). Stress effects of the Holocaust. In G. Fisk (Ed.), *Encyclopedia of stress* (pp. 390–395). San Diego, CA: Academic Press.

van Ijzendoorn, M. H., Bakerman-Kranenburg, M. J., & Sagi-Schwartz, A. (2003). Are children of Holocaust survivors less well-adapted? A meta-analytic investigation of secondary traumatization. *Journal of Traumatic Stress, 16,* 459–469.

Walser, R., & Westrup, D. (2007). *Acceptance and commitment therapy for the treatment of posttraumatic stress disorder: A practitioner's guide to using mindfulness and acceptance strategies.* Oakland, CA: New Harbinger Press.

Wilson, J. P., Harel, Z., & Kahana, B. (1988). *Human adaptation to extreme stress: From the Holocaust to Vietnam* (pp. 171–191). New York: Plenum Press.

Yehuda, R., Teicher, M. H., Seckl, J. R., Grossman, R. A., Morris, A., & Bierer, L. M. (2007). Parental posttraumatic stress disorder as a vulnerability factor for low cortisol trait in offspring of Holocaust survivors. *Archives of General Psychiatry, 64,* 1040–1048.

Yehuda, R., Tischler, L., Golier, J. A., Grossman, R., Brand, S. R., Kaufman, S., et al. (2006). Longitudinal assessment of cognitive performance in Holocaust survivors with and without PTSD. *Biological Psychiatry, 60,* 714–721.

Julia Golier
Mount Sinai School of Medicine

Mary Tramontin
Bronx Veterans Affairs Medical Center

See also: **Genocide; Human Rights Violations**

HOMELESSNESS

Homeless people are among the most disenfranchised and vulnerable subgroups in any society. Marginalized from the community, they live perilously on the streets and in crowded, overburdened shelters. Consisting of single men and women, families, children, and youth, the population is extremely diverse. In Western industrialized nations, such as the United States, members of minority groups are overrepresented among homeless people (Boesky, Toro, & Bukowski, 1997). The causes of homelessness include a lack of affordable housing, inadequate economic and social resources, and exposure to interpersonal violence—especially violence by an adult intimate partner. Exclusion from mainstream resources and services intensifies the stress and magnifies the tragic plight of this group of people.

Pathways onto the street are characterized by danger, abrupt separations, frequent moves, catastrophic illness, violence and victimization, and the fear of impending homelessness. The high levels of exposure to traumatic stress as adults, including homelessness itself, as well as traumatic losses and violent victimization during childhood have been well documented by researchers (e.g., Bassuk et al., 1996). Physical violence and sexual assault, especially during critical developmental years and when perpetrated by a family member or other intimate, carries with it the likelihood of severe effects that last into adulthood. Responses to the cumulative effects of early trauma are exacerbated by the realities of living in shelters and on the streets. Various subgroups, such as homeless women with severe mental illness, are at even higher risk for adverse outcomes. Rates of traumatic stress among these subgroups are high enough (e.g., greater than 90% among homeless women with severe mental illness and among homeless mothers) to be considered normative (Bassuk et al., 1996).

Traumatic events for homeless people are often frequent and ongoing as well as intense and unpredictable. Trauma tends to occur repetitively across a homeless person's lifetime, increasing the likelihood of adverse outcomes. Consistent with complex trauma, the long-term effects can impact every aspect of life, leading to disrupted relationships, inability to work, parenting difficulties, posttrauma responses, severe depression, suicidal behavior, and self-medication with substances (Guarino, Rubin, & Bassuk, 2007). Given the backdrop of oppressive economic conditions, fragmented support networks, and the dangers of living on the streets, it is not surprising that many people experiencing homelessness have high lifetime and current rates of PTSD, often associated with sharply increased risk of comorbidity with anxiety disorders, depression, and substance use.

The service delivery system for homeless people is fragmented, under resourced, and poorly prepared to respond to traumatic stress and its devastating aftermath. Service providers are often overworked, underpaid, and inadequately trained, a situation that results in burnout and high staff turnover. To compound the complexity of service delivery, people experiencing homelessness feel vulnerable and powerless, view the world as dangerous, and may distrust service providers because of past negative experiences with service systems, decreasing the likelihood they will access services in the first place.

With emergence of new research and evaluation chronicling high rates of violent victimization among people experiencing homelessness, the field has begun to examine the inextricable link between homelessness and traumatic stress. This has highlighted the need to create trauma-informed environments to prevent retraumatization and support the integration of specific treatment and services. Most experts now agree that given the extremely high lifetime prevalence of traumatic stress among homeless people, it is imperative that services become trauma-informed—that is, all services must be delivered through the lens of trauma (Moses, Reed, Mazelis, & D'Ambrosio, 2003).

Within systems serving people experiencing homelessness, all program components must be examined to ensure they are sensitive to the needs of traumatized clients. These components include: atmosphere and environment, policies and procedures, treatment and services, and staffing and training. Providers must be educated about the nature of traumatic stress and its devastating impacts, the relationship between prior and current symptoms, systematic strategies for identifying histories of abuse, and ways of responding to posttrauma responses. Most important, the service environment must be made as safe as possible—both physically and emotionally—to dispel the hovering specter of the constant threats and dangers associated with homelessness (Moses et al., 2003). Only then can healing and recovery take place.

REFERENCES

Bassuk, E. L., Weinreb, L., Buckner, J. C., Browne, A., Salomon, A., & Bassuk, S. A. (1996). The characteristics and needs of sheltered homeless and low-income housed mothers. *Journal of the American Medical Association, 276,* 640–647.

Boesky, L. M., Toro, P. A., & Bukowski, P. A. (1997). Differences in psychosocial factors among older and younger homeless adolescents found in youth shelters. *Journal of Prevention and Intervention in the Community, 15*(2), 19–36.

Guarino, K., Rubin, L., & Bassuk, E. (2007). Violence and trauma in the lives of homeless families. In E. Carl (Ed.), *Trauma psychology* (pp. 231–258). Westport, CT: Praeger.

Moses, D. J., Reed, B. G., Mazelis, R., & D'Ambrosio, B. (2003). *Creating trauma services for women with co-occurring disorders: Experiences from the SAMHSA Women with Alcohol, Drug Abuse, and Mental Health Disorders who Have Histories of Violence Study.* Delmar, NY: Policy Research Associates.

Ellen L. Bassuk
National Center on Family Homelessness

HORMONAL STRESS RESPONSE

See: Biology, Neurochemistry

HUMAN RIGHTS VIOLATIONS

The concept of human rights developed across a long historical period with contributions from a variety of cultures and disciplines. The central ideas are that some rights are "naturally" obtained (i.e., they are not conferred by the grace of others) and that these rights are universal (i.e., that they are held by all and not limited to a specified class of people). In the aftermath of the atrocities of World War II, human rights emerged formally with the adoption of the Universal Declaration of Human Rights by the United Nations in 1948. Those who crafted the Declaration were profoundly influenced by the horrifying acts of brutality that had taken place over the preceding decade or more, and the result reflects the types of abuses against humanity that characterized their times. In the decades since

it was first ratified, subsequent human rights instruments have been needed to respond to successive events and to the growing awareness of what is needed to protect the most vulnerable people from being brutalized or exploited.

Among its 30 Articles, the Declaration recognizes a right to security (Article 3). Experiences of physical trauma in general (whether accidental or through intentional injury) may therefore be construed as violations of fundamental human rights because they threaten a person's personal safety and security. However, the bulk of the Declaration deals with violations of human rights that are perpetrated by governments against their citizens. In this regard, the Declaration states that:

"No one shall be subjected to torture or to cruel, inhuman or degrading treatment or punishment" (Article 5),

"No one shall be subjected to arbitrary arrest, detention or exile" (Article 9), and

"Everyone has the right to take part in the government of his [sic] country, directly or through freely chosen representatives" (Article 21).

Despite international developments such as the ratification of numerous human rights treaties and the establishment of watchdog agencies like Amnesty International, human rights abuses that are perpetrated by governments are still being documented in many countries worldwide (Amnesty International, 2006). The information presented next focuses on the psychological effects of organized state violence.

Studies of the psychological effects of political detention, torture, and other politically motivated assaults have sampled survivors still residing in sites of political violence and, more commonly, those who have been displaced from their countries of origin and who are living as refugees or asylum seekers in other countries. Those who continue to reside in sites of political violence face ongoing threats to their physical security and freedom and difficulties in meeting basic needs for food and shelter; while refugees in developed countries must deal with stressors related to ongoing geographic displacement, the process of seeking asylum status and acculturation to a different society. Research on the psychological effects of human rights abuses and the treatment of survivors of such abuses has contributed to the general trauma literature by documenting the experiences of trauma survivors from low-income developing countries and a range of cultural backgrounds, to supplement the majority of trauma research that has been conducted in economically developed countries.

The psychological impact of torture has been more systematically documented than that of other forms of human rights violations. The most commonly reported symptoms across studies with torture survivors include anxiety, depression, memory and attention problems, fatigue, sleep disturbance, sexual dysfunction, irritability and aggression, and social isolation or withdrawal (for a thorough review, see Basoglu, Jaranson, Mollica, & Kastrup, 2001).

With regard to full-blown psychiatric disorders, studies with torture survivors have documented a high occurrence of PTSD (ranging from 30% in some studies to as high as 65% in others) and depression (ranging from 35% to 42% across several studies), with frequent comorbidity of the two (see, e.g., Ramsay, Gorst-Unsworth, & Turner, 1993; van Velsen, Gorst-Unsworth, & Turner, 1996). The weight of evidence from controlled studies indicates that, across different cultures and contexts, torture is associated with higher rates of PTSD than those reported for nontortured political prisoners and for the general population, that risk factors for PTSD in torture survivors include greater subjective severity of torture, family stress in the posttorture environment, and the secondary consequences of war, state repression, and displacement, but that torture remains an independent risk factor for PTSD even when refugee trauma is taken into account (e.g., Basoglu et al., 2001). It remains unclear whether torture survivors are at increased risk for somatization disorders, depression, and anxiety disorders other than PTSD when compared with the general population because research findings from controlled studies have been equivocal.

Although torture is a severe stressor that presents an enormous psychological challenge and results in psychiatric symptoms or full-blown disorders for many torture survivors, research also indicates that many torture survivors do not develop significant psychological symptoms. This may be due to the protection offered by their political belief systems, their psychological preparedness for interrogation and torture, and their social supports in the posttorture context (Basoglu et al., 2001).

Human rights abuses affect not only those who are the direct victims, but also their families. The children of torture survivors often develop a range of psychological difficulties, including depressive and psychosomatic symptoms, learning difficulties and developmental delays, while rates of divorce and family discord are also higher among torture survivors (see review by Campbell, 2007). Among family members of civilians who have disappeared in the context of state-perpetrated violence, mood disorders appear to be elevated (Perez-Sales, Duran-Perez, & Herzfeld, 2000). This may be due to the incomplete bereavement that results from the absence of a body or other proof of death, failure on the part of the perpetrating regime to acknowledge that civilians were deliberately "disappeared," and a pervasive societal silence around the issue of disappearances. The gradual, uncertain bereavement that is brought on by years of waiting to learn about the fate of a disappeared loved one is likely to be qualitatively different from the sudden, unexpected, or violent bereavement that is commonly associated with PTSD in the general population.

Because the psychological effects of human rights abuses are complex, and are often exacerbated by ongoing stressors related to political upheaval or geographic displacement, interventions for survivors of human rights abuses tend to be multidisciplinary, involving psychotherapeutic, social, legal, and medical interventions. Psychological interventions are usually multimodal, including a focus on safety, psychological processing of the trauma experience, empowerment of the survivor, re-integration into the community. Exploration of the meaning of human rights abuses and their aftermath within the survivor's cultural framework is a critical element of all aspects of interventions with survivors of human rights abuses (for a well-integrated review, see Jaranson et al., 2001).

Supportive counseling, exposure therapy, insight-oriented psychodynamic therapy, group therapy, and family therapy have all been used with survivors of human rights abuses such as torture, and case reports and uncontrolled studies indicate that these approaches may be helpful (Jaranson et al., 2001). Probably due to the very challenging social and political circumstances in which such interventions are often conducted, there are very few well-controlled treatment-outcome studies with this population, and existing ones have produced inconclusive results (see review by Campbell, 2007).

There are some forms of psychotherapy that have been developed specifically for survivors of human rights abuses. Testimony therapy was developed as a clinical procedure by mental health professionals working with survivors of state-perpetrated violence, particularly torture, in Chile during the 1970s (Agger & Jensen, 1990). In this form of therapy, the survivor narrates a detailed description of their experience of abuse, with the therapist serving as empathic listener and occasionally asking questions to clarify or to elicit more detail. This testimony is tape-recorded, and later transcribed into written form that can be submitted as legal evidence. Testimony therapy has subsequently been used in a number of countries as an intervention for refugees who have experienced human rights abuses in their country of origin, but outcome studies of testimony therapy remain sparse. While a few uncontrolled studies have indicated significant improvement in PTSD, depression, anxiety, and other symptoms after testimony therapy, the only controlled study to be conducted was not able to establish a clear link between testimony therapy and the amelioration of PTSD. Narrative exposure therapy (NET; Schauer, Neuner, & Elbert, 2005) is a treatment model

that integrates elements of testimony therapy with elements of cognitive behavior therapy. In some controlled studies with refugees and political detainees, NET has been found to be significantly more effective than psychoeducation or supportive counseling in the treatment of PTSD and depression (Schauer et al., 2005), although it has not yet been established whether it offers any additional benefit when compared to exposure therapy alone.

Truth commissions (also known as Truth and Reconciliation Commissions) are an increasingly common phenomenon in those postconflict societies that have been characterized by organized state violence. While the fundamental aim of these commissions has historically been to facilitate reconciliation at a societal level, some truth commissions have also attempted to offer a therapeutic experience for individual survivors of human rights abuses. The South African Truth and Reconciliation Commission was the first to explicitly state that the process of giving testimony about human rights violations to the Commission could provide a therapeutic function for deponents (Truth and Reconciliation Commission of South Africa, 1998, vol. 5), but some subsequent truth commissions have also adopted the aim of personal healing. While some South African survivors of organized state violence have reported positive benefits after giving truth commission testimony, others have reported feeling worse afterward. At present, there is no systematic evidence to support the claim that giving truth commission testimony leads to improved psychological outcomes for survivors of human rights abuses.

REFERENCES

Agger, I., & Jensen, S. B. (1990). Testimony as ritual and evidence in psychotherapy for political refugees. *Journal of Traumatic Stress, 3,* 115–130.

Amnesty International. (2006). *Annual report 2006.* London: Author.

Basoglu, M., Jaranson, J. M., Mollica, R., & Kastrup, M. (2001). Torture and mental health: A research overview. In E. Gerrity, T. M. Keane, & F. Tuma (Eds.), *The mental health consequences of torture* (pp. 35–62). New York: Kluwer Academic.

Campbell, T. A. (2007). Psychological assessment, diagnosis, and treatment of torture survivors: A review. *Clinical Psychology Review, 27,* 628–641.

Jaranson, J. M., Kinzie, J. D., Friedman, M., Ortiz, D., Friedman, M. J., Southwick, S., et al. (2001). Assessment, diagnosis and intervention. In E. Gerrity, T. M. Keane, & F. Tuma (Eds.), *The mental health consequences of torture* (pp. 249–276). New York: Kluwer Academic.

Perez-Sales, P., Duran-Perez, T., & Herzfeld, R. B. (2000). Long-term psychosocial consequences in first-degree relatives of people detained-disappeared or executed for political reasons in Chile: A study of Mapuce and non-Mapuce persons. *Psicothema, 12*(Suppl.), 109–116.

Ramsay, R., Gorst-Unsworth, C., & Turner, S. (1993). Psychiatric morbidity in survivors of organised state violence including torture: A retrospective series. *British Journal of Psychiatry, 162,* 55–59.

Schauer, M., Neuner, F., & Elbert, T. (2005). *Narrative exposure therapy: A short term intervention for traumatic stress disorders after war, terror, or torture.* Cambridge, MA: Hogrefe & Huber.

Truth and Reconciliation Commission. (1998). *Truth and Reconciliation Commission of South Africa Report* (Vol. 5). Cape Town, South Africa: CTP Book Printers.

van Velsen, C., Gorst-Unsworth, C., & Turner, S. (1996). Survivors of torture and organized violence: Demography and diagnosis. *Journal of Traumatic Stress, 9,* 181–193.

Debra Kaminer
University of Cape Town

See also: Human Trafficking; Humanitarian Intervention; Genocide; International Organizations; Laws, Legislation, and Policy; Torture

HUMAN TRAFFICKING

The term *human trafficking* refers to the recruitment (or capture) and transportation of persons within or across boundaries by force, fraud, or deception for the purpose of exploiting them economically. Trafficked people most commonly work in sweatshops, restaurants, on farms, in manufacturing, prostitution, and as private domestic workers. Adults may also be trafficked for the removal of organs. Trafficking of children can also take the form of illicit international adoptions and recruitment of child soldiers.

In general, human trafficking is a demand-driven market facilitated by factors related to both the source country (e.g., poverty, unemployment, country economic and/or political instability, and government corruption) and the destination countries (e.g., growing demand for commercial sex or cheap labor), restrictive immigration policies, existence of "legal" avenues (e.g., domestic work), corruption of government officials, and increase in organized crime. Slavery is the labor or services that are performed or provided by another person and are obtained or maintained through an actor by cause and/or use of threats, physical threats and/or restraints, abuse of the law and/or legal process, withholding of documents, use of blackmail, and/or use of financial control over any person.

According to the 2005 U.S. State Department's annual report, 600,000 to 800,000 people are trafficked across international borders each year, with 14,500 to 17,500 trafficked into the United States. In addition, the U.S. State Department estimated that human trafficking generates up to $9.5 billion per year and, according to some reports, represents the third-largest source of profit for organized crime after drugs and guns.

Effects on Survivors

As with other forms of trauma, trafficking may affect people in a variety ways, including but not limited to emotionally (e.g., feelings of anger, helplessness, hopelessness, stigma, or guilt), physically (e.g., physical assault, food and sleep deprivation), cognitively, somatically (e.g., headache, backache, sleep, or digestive system problems), behaviorally (e.g., self-harm and suicide attempts, risk-taking), relationally (e.g., difficulty in forming trusting relationships) economically, spiritually, and psychologically (e.g., victims of human trafficking may experience PTSD, anxiety, chronic depression, dissociative disorders, low self-esteem, and self-blame; Gajic-Veljanoski & Stewart, 2007; Zimmerman et al., 2003).

Actions of Traffickers

Much of the abuse and harm to victims is intentional. Traffickers use a wide variety of methods to control their victims, including every form of abuse imaginable—physical, sexual, psychological, emotional, and so on. Psychological abuse is usually persistent, extreme, and intended to demolish any and all mental, emotional, and physical defenses. Traffickers use the following methods to control their victims: intimidation and threats; lies and deception; money; unsafe, unpredictable and uncontrollable events; emotional abuse and manipulation; social isolation; forced/intentional drug addiction; identity control; and purposefully impregnating victims (Bales, 2004).

Impact of Trafficking on Society

Trafficking in persons is a human rights violation; it fosters the denial of the person's rights to liberty, integrity, security, and freedom of movement. It also promotes social breakdown and trust. Additionally, the enormous profit of human trafficking fuels organized crime such as drug trafficking, human smuggling, money laundering, and document forgery. Trafficking deprives countries of human capital; more specifically, trafficking individuals negates their opportunity to further their acquisition of human capital in the form of education and occupational skills; this in turn leads to declining workforce productivity. At the societal level, the loss of human potential can inhibit national development. Trafficking undermines Public Health. A specific form of human trafficking, sex trafficking, is believed to be one of the factors influencing the pandemic heterosexual spread of HIV/AIDS around the world. Studies have also found that trafficked women had limited access to health-care and social services, forced and unsafe abortions, and absence of gynecological care and HIV testing (Busza, Castle, & Diarra, 2004).

Gendered and Racialized Aspects of Trafficking

There is a disproportionate trafficking of women and persons from developing countries and, within the United States, of ethnic minorities. In 2006, the majority of trafficked individuals were female, accounting for approximately 80% (Gajic-Veljanoski & Stewart, 2007). According to the 2006 United Nations Population Fund, more than 70% of trafficked women with children are single mothers (Zimmerman et al., 2003). The feminization of poverty in many African and Asian countries results in women being contracted or encouraged by their families to seek economic advancement in more developed countries. These women are often young and poorly educated. Additionally, vulnerability to emotional and mental manipulation is often maximized by traffickers who take advantage of cultural values such as respect for elders and authoritative people, the importance of keeping one's word or honoring contracts (even when they are unfair), and expectations for each person to sacrifice in order to help the larger family that is often facing severe poverty. In addition, research has shown that homeless girls and girls without guardians represent an extremely vulnerable population that is trafficked for prostitution.

Internationally and within the United States, a large number of trafficked persons are of Asian, African, and Latin American ancestry. Additionally, there is a racial/ethnic hierarchy of cost value whereby the cost to purchase a human being of non-Latino European descent is more than the cost of purchasing a human being of African, Latin American, or Asian descent. Some have argued that the lack of responsiveness to the trauma of trafficking is related to the devaluing of women and ethnic minorities.

United Nations Response to Trafficking

The United Nations has created the Global Program against Trafficking in Human Beings, which seeks to address human trafficking in a number of ways. At the national level, the

United Nations program aims to promote awareness (such as public awareness campaigns) of trafficking in human beings and especially strengthen institutional capacity; train law enforcement officers, prosecutors, and judges; advise on drafting and revising relevant legislation; provide advice and assistance on establishing and strengthening anti-trafficking elements; and strengthen victim and witness support.

Psychologists working through the United Nations have a threefold role that includes the provision of education, advocacy, and monitoring. Psychologists seek to educate policy makers and U.N. members about the psychological impact of trafficking and the intervention needs for trafficking victims. Education is needed about the emotional needs of the victim beyond rescue and return because many are faced with shame and rejection by society as a result of having engaged in forced prostitution and other stigmatized activities. Psychologists and trauma experts from other disciplines have sought to address the prevention and intervention needs of trafficking victims at relevant U.N. conferences such as the Commission on the Status of Women; the Permanent Forum on Indigenous People; and the World Conference against Racism, Racial Discrimination, Xenophobia, and Related Intolerance.

Intervention Needs

The intervention needs of trafficking victims include the provision of social services, legal services, training and advocacy, sustainable development, and media intervention and prevention activities. Legal service needs include representation in removal proceedings, securing release from detention, advocacy to protect rights as victim witnesses, preparation for criminal trial, advocacy to obtain continued presence status and a certification letter as a trafficking victim to establish eligibility for refugee benefits, assistance in filing T-Visa, U-Visa, and VAWA applications, and assistance in obtaining child custody and restraining orders.

Training programs are needed for various audiences such as social service providers, faith-based organizations, the community at large, and government agencies on a local, state, and national level. A recommended training philosophy is one that is based on a human rights approach in addressing the issue of slavery and trafficking. Training activities are also needed for social service providers, refugee issuing agencies, and local and federal law enforcement.

Advocacy focus areas include policy advocacy, media advocacy, outreach, public education, and leadership development through community organizing on the local, state, and national levels to raise awareness on trafficking, protecting the rights of trafficking survivors, and improving their access to services. Advocacy is most effective when it is directly informed by the real experiences of survivors and therefore ensures that public policies are victim-centered.

Social Service needs include the provision of comprehensive mental and physical health services tailored to the specific needs of trafficking survivors. It is recommended that clients have access to a broad, diverse, and culturally linguistically appropriate range of services, ranging from traditional talk therapy to the expressive arts. Provision of physically and psychologically safe housing for trafficking survivors is crucial. In addition to temporary housing, more long-term assistance is needed in empowering clients in their efforts to establish independence and self-sufficiency and to build community and expand their own supportive networks.

REFERENCES

Bales, K. (2004). *Disposable people: New slavery in the global economy.* Berkeley: University of California Press.

Busza, J., Castle, S., & Diarra, A. (2004). Trafficking and health. *British Medical Journal, 328,* 1369–1371.

Farr, K. (2004). *Sex trafficking: The global market in women and children.* New York: Worth.

Gajic-Veljanoski, O., & Stewart D. (2007). Women trafficked into prostitution: Determinants, human rights and health needs. *Transcultural Psychiatry, 44,* 338–359.

Orhant, M. (2002). Human trafficking exposed. *Population Today, 30,* 1–4.

Zimmerman, C., Yun, K., Shvab, I., Watts, C., Trappolin, L., Treppete, M., et al. (2003). *The health risks and consequences of trafficking in women and adolescents: Findings from a European Study.* London: London School of Hygiene and Tropical Medicine.

RECOMMENDED READINGS

Bryant-Davis, T. (2005). *Thriving in the wake of trauma: A multicultural guide.* Westport, CT: Praeger Press.

Farley, M. (2004). *Prostitution, trafficking, and traumatic stress.* Binghamton, NY: Haworth Maltreatment and Trauma Press.

Jones, L., Engstrom, D., Hilliard, T., & Diaz, M. (2007). Globalization and human trafficking. *Journal of Sociology and Social Welfare, 34,* 107–122.

Thema Bryant-Davis
Pepperdine University

Shaquita Tillman
Pepperdine University

See also: Humanitarian Intervention; International Organizations; Laws, Legislation, and Policy; Rape Trauma; Torture; Women and Trauma

HUMANITARIAN INTERVENTION

Humanitarian agencies working in armed conflicts and natural disasters increasingly prioritize action to protect and improve psychologically traumatized people's mental health and psychosocial well-being, in order to complement other interventions and services they provide as a means to alleviating suffering, promoting human dignity, and safeguarding human rights. Nevertheless, attempts to address urgent mental health and psychosocial needs in the mass emergencies to which humanitarian agencies respond (such as natural disasters and war) have encountered challenges, not the least of which are the enormous diversity and scale of needs.

Traumatic stress has been recognized as a critical factor in the response of communities and nations to mass emergencies for several reasons (Stein, Seedat, Iverson, & Wessely, 2007). The issues of mental health and psychosocial distress in emergencies are considerably broader than traumatic stress alone. For example, numerous individuals suffer from preexisting problems such as severe mental disorder, neurological problems, or substance abuse. Also, many of the preexisting problems are social, such as political discrimination and oppression. Many emergency-affected people suffer from social effects, including being discriminated against as displaced people, being detained illegally, or being stigmatized as rebels or rape victims. Not uncommonly, inadvertent harm is caused by poorly coordinated humanitarian response (Anderson, 1999). These factors may exacerbate traumatic stress reactions and place people at risk for post-traumatic stress disorder (PTSD) and other mental health and social impairments, therefore requiring a multifaceted, comprehensive response, which should include but go far beyond attention to traumatic stress.

Mental health and psychosocial support (MHPSS) in emergencies has been hampered by a lack of consensus about recommended intervention approaches. Questions have been raised about the appropriateness of many intervention programs, especially when these focus solely on psychological trauma (Boothby, Strang, & Wessells, 2006; Bracken, Giller, & Summerfield, 1995; Stein et al., 2007; van Ommeren, Saxena, & Saraceno, 2005). The lack of consensus owes partly to contrasting ideologies and also to the paucity of hard evidence in this young field. The lack of consensus has enabled the use of questionable approaches, some of which may cause harm. For example, in many emergencies, well-intentioned but often problematic programs have attempted to train inexperienced MHPSS workers how to practice therapeutic counseling as a one-off (i.e., single-session or very brief series of sessions) program. Without adequate training and a functioning supervision system, it is reasonable to believe that some of the counseling provided is harmful. A major gap, then, has been the lack of guidance for the field.

This gap has been filled by the Inter-Agency Standing Committee (IASC) Guidelines on Mental Health and Psychosocial Support in Emergency Settings (IASC, 2007). The product of collaboration among 27 U.N. agencies and international nongovernmental organizations (NGOs), these inter-agency, global Guidelines define minimum responses—the first steps to be taken in mass emergencies, which lay the foundation for subsequent humanitarian services and supports.

The Guidelines emphasize that clinical mental health supports, community psychosocial supports, and self-help are complementary, and they offer specific means of improving inter-agency coordination. In most mass emergencies, two broad approaches emerge. One focuses on clinical assistance in the health sector and the other focuses on community self-help and social support coordinated through work on protection. Too often, these complementary approaches develop into independent domains of activity that compete for funding and influence and have their own separate coordination group that neither coordinates nor communicates with the other. The Guidelines encourage the establishment of a single, overarching coordination group or, where this is challenging, the establishment of subgroups that communicate with each other.

The heart of the Guidelines are 25 Action Sheets that cover topics such as coordination, assessment, social and legal protection, staff care, community self-help, early child development, MHPSS in the provision of health care, care for people with severe mental disorders (including severe presentations of PTSD), harmful substance use, nonformal and formal education, and information dissemination. Overall, the emphasis is on social interventions rather than clinical, individual interventions. A distinctive feature is the view that all sectors have a responsibility to promote MHPSS by virtue of the way in which basic needs are provided for. For example, how the disaster relief shelter is organized for displaced people affects MHPSS because people living in overcrowded facilities or camps may report that lack of privacy is their greatest concern. This view contrasts with an older view that MHPSS is something to be done only after basic needs for survival have been met.

As the Guidelines indicate, six principles guide the delivery of MHPSS services by humanitarian agency workers in mass emergencies:

1. *Human rights and equity.* MHPSS should promote the rights of all affected people regardless of age, gender, religion, ethnicity, or political orientation. It should promote equity among all affected groups and avoid the discrimination that often harms affected people.

2. *Participation.* Humanitarian action should stimulate the participation of affected people and of different subgroups, as participation is a right as indicated in standards such as the U.N. Convention on the Rights of the Child (1989). Also, participation is likely to serve as a means of regaining a sense of control following overwhelming experience. Local people should be involved from the earliest phases of an emergency, helping to assess, design, implement supports, and monitor, and evaluate progress. Participation is widely seen as essential for building the sense of local ownership that contributes to program quality, equity, and sustainability.

3. *Do no harm.* Because work on MHPSS deals with sensitive issues and has the potential to cause harm, agencies and practitioners should take the following steps: work in a self-critical manner; participate in coordination groups; design programs based on sufficient information; be open to scrutiny and external review; develop cultural sensitivity and technical competence in the area one works; stay updated on evidence; avoid privileging particular local groups; and, finally, reflect carefully on universal human rights, power relations between outsiders and emergency-affected people, and the value of participatory approaches.

4. *Building on available resources and capacities.* All affected groups contain

significant social and cultural resources such as social networks, healers, leaders, and rituals that may offer support in an appropriate and sustainable manner. Humanitarians often err by underestimating local people's capacities, resilience, and resources. Where possible, humanitarians should activate support, and build upon local resources and strengthen capacities in both civil society and the government.

5. *Integrated support systems*. In many emergencies, there is a proliferation of stand-alone services such as those dealing only with rape or domestic violence survivors or only with people having a specific diagnosis such as PTSD. This can create a fragmented care system that reaches few people and risks stigmatizing survivors. MHPSS supports should be integrated into wider systems such as existing community support mechanisms, systems of formal and nonformal education, health services, general mental health services, and social services.

6. *Multilayered supports*. In mass emergencies, people are affected in different ways and require different kinds of supports. On the one extreme, there is a small percentage who experience intolerable suffering and may have significant difficulties in basic daily functioning and who need immediate access to psychiatric, or other highly specialized supports. On the other, more positive extreme, there is a large percentage of people who will be able to maintain their mental health and well-being provided that the public well-being is protected through the re-establishment of security, adequate governance, and services that meet basic survival needs. In between these extremes are people who have been affected by disruptions of or separations from key family and community supports and who will benefit from efforts such as family tracing and reunification, communal healing ceremonies, formal and nonformal education, livelihood activities, and the activation of social networks. Humanitarian agencies and practitioners should create a layered system that addresses these diverse needs in an appropriate, proportionate manner that includes effective referrals as well as direct services.

In conclusion, the types of social and psychological problems that people may experience in emergencies are extremely diverse. An exclusive focus on traumatic stress may lead to neglect of many other key mental health and psychosocial issues. The IASC Guidelines aim to provide a balanced approach of recommended minimum actions in the midst of emergencies. The Guidelines include psychological first aid (*see:* **Psychological First Aid, Adult; Psychological First Aid, Child**) for people in acute trauma-induced distress by a variety of humanitarian community workers and care for people with severe mental disorders, including severe depression and PTSD. However, the Guidelines emphasize the importance of social interventions and supports. By following the Guidelines, MHPSS practitioners can implement the first steps that are needed to protect the mental health and psychosocial well-being of people caught in mass emergencies.

REFERENCES

Anderson, M. (1999). *Do no harm*. Boulder, CO: Lynne Rienner.

Boothby, N., Strang, A., & Wessells, M. (Eds.). (2006). *A world turned upside down: Social ecologies of children and war*. Bloomfield, CT: Kumarian Press.

Bracken, P., Giller, J., & Summerfield, D. (1995). Psychological responses to war and atrocity: The limitations of current concepts. *Social Science and Medicine, 40,* 1073–1082.

Inter-Agency Standing Committee. (2007). *IASC guidelines on mental health and psychosocial support in emergency settings*. Geneva, Switzerland: Author.

Stein, D., Seedat, S., Iversen, A., & Wessely, S. (2007). Post-traumatic stress disorder: Medicine and politics. *Lancet, 369,* 139–144.

United Nations Convention on the Rights of the Child (1989). Retrieved from www.ohchr.org/english.law/index.htm.

van Ommeren, M., Saxena, S., & Saraceno, B. (2005). Mental and social health during and after acute emergencies: Emerging consensus? *Bulletin of the World Health Organization, 83,* 71–76.

MICHAEL WESSELLS
Columbia University

MARK VAN OMMEREN
World Health Organization

See also: International Organizations; Laws, Legislation, and Policy; Nongovernmental Organizations; Torture; Women and Trauma

HUMILIATION TRAUMA

Humiliation can be used in three ways: it signifies an action that humiliates, a feeling of having been humiliated, and a process that results in humiliation. In other words, a person or group commits an act that is humiliating to the recipient, the recipient in turn feels humiliated, and the entire process is one of humiliation (Lindner, 2006). Feelings of humiliation can be provoked intentionally or by accident, the experience may be short-lived or enduring, and it is always intensely painful. Humiliation differs from emotions like shame, embarrassment, or guilt, in that it requires the act of impugning or injuring the dignity and honor of individuals or groups. Humiliation may be present when a group or individual believe/s their identity to be misrepresented, withdrawn, or withheld (Lindner, 2006). Internalized outcomes of humiliation can be feelings of loss of significance, loss of dignity, or feelings of worthlessness or inferiority (Lindner, 2007).

Humiliation is a complex phenomenon that is relevant for many fields, such as anthropology, sociology, philosophy, social and clinical psychology, or political science. The "politics of recognition" (Taylor, 2004), or the belief that the human desire for recognition and respect is universal, is key to human dignity and humiliation studies. In regard to the area of trauma studies, humiliation can be an aspect of any discrete part of the traumatizing process or an effect of the entire process. It can impact the victim alone, both the victim and the perpetrator, or the victim, perpetrator, and others. Humiliation is a word that typically is used for the act of humiliation perpetrated by a perpetrator, or a word for the feelings of humiliation felt by a victim. However, the person's intent may be only to help while the recipient ultimately feels humiliated by the help. Thus help may humiliate—a situation where the receiver of help defines a situation as humiliation, not the actor. Finally, neither actor nor actant may define a situation as humiliating, but a third party (e.g., a human rights worker who wants to rescue a battered wife in a male-dominant society).

Much of the work of twentieth-century postmodernist philosophers, for example Michel Foucault's (see 1980, 1982, 1991) analysis of the dynamics of power, formed the foundation for a greater understanding of humiliation's nuanced influence on human interaction. The word *humiliation* did not develop its contemporary etymology—namely as a violation of dignity—until the mid-1700s, when the Western notions of human rights, equality, and natural law took root. Humiliation as an emotion and as a strategy for subjugating others had long been understood, but in the West humiliating acts began to be viewed as socially unacceptable and humiliated groups and individuals began to rebel against perceived injustices. In this historical context, today's theorists of humiliation studies link the rising concern for human rights and the simultaneous decline of rigidly defined hierarchical societies to an increase in violent conflict. Human Dignity and Humiliation Studies was established formally as a discipline by Evelin Lindner through a global consortium of practitioners and academics in 2001 (see www.humiliationstudies.org for fuller information). Drawing on the historical and anthropological theories of William Ury, those working in the area of humiliation studies distinguish humiliation from other concepts like shame, which can be used in pro-social ways. This interdisciplinary group seeks to show how repressed groups, now believing they deserve equal human rights, are subverting the age-old method of humiliation as a controlling mechanism for conformity. For instance, in "honor societies" humiliation is considered an appropriate method of control, as a test of loyalty or for ego deflation (Hartling & Luchetta, 1999). But human rights agendas oppose the use of humiliation, and thus a tension is created between these ideologies and the ways of life they promote.

Unlike the new field of humiliation studies, the somewhat older study of trauma experienced exponential growth and is applicable in contexts from war to natural disasters. Individuals and/or groups can experience a traumatic event in which no humiliation occurs, for example a natural disaster or car accident. On the other hand, humiliation can be a powerful trigger for trauma. An important question is whether trauma always occurs when intense humiliation is felt; humiliation appears to be a key component in situations involving violent, human-driven trauma such as war or spouse abuse. When trauma and humiliation are present, the resilience of the affected individual or collective to overcoming further negative events may be lowered, and the likelihood increased that the victim(s) will experience one or more Criterion A1 events. The role of humiliation in trauma can be better understood by examining survivor accounts of PTSD-diagnosed individuals to determine how humiliation might influence the perception of events as being traumatic and by comparing recovery rates between situations involving humiliation and events where humiliation was not present.

Restoring dignity seems to be the key to healing humiliation (Lindner, 2006). For instance, many survivors of the Rwandan genocide (1994) and the "disappeared" in Guatemala (1960 to 1980s), believe one of the most important aspects of their healing was public recognition of their suffering and the restoration of their dignity.

REFERENCES

Foucault, M. (1980). *Power/knowledge: Selected interviews and other writings, 1972–1977.* New York: Pantheon Books.

Foucault, M. (1982). *The archaeology of knowledge and the discourse on language.* New York: Pantheon Books.

Foucault, M. (1991). *The Foucault reader* (P. Rabinow, Ed.). London: Penguin Books.

Hartling, L., & Luchetta, T. (1999). Humiliation: Assessing the impact of derision, degradation, and debasement. *Journal of Primary Prevention, 19*(5), 259–278.

Lindner, E. G. (2006). *Making enemies: Humiliation and international conflict.* Westport, CT: Praeger.

Lindner, E. G. (2007). In times of globalization and human rights: Does humiliation become the most disruptive force? *Journal of Human Dignity and Humiliation Studies, 1*(1). Retrieved from www.humiliationstudies.upeace.org.

Taylor, C. (2004). Politics of recognition. In C. Farrelly (Ed.), *Contemporary political theory: A reader* (pp. 269–281). London: Sage.

AMY C. HUDNALL
Appalachian State University

See also: Betrayal Trauma; Emotional Abuse; Shame

HYPERAROUSAL

Arousal is a multifaceted term that can denote a state of behavioral excitement or physiological activation, or that can indicate heightened emotionality, including subjective distress. Use of the term is sometimes criticized in scientific contexts for being vague because the intended domain or measurement is not specified. Such lack of specificity can be found in the traumatic stress literature. A well-known principle asserts that optimal behavioral performance occurs when arousal is in the mid-range, neither too low nor too high. Excessively high arousal—*hyper*arousal—is considered a hallmark of posttraumatic stress disorder (PTSD).

There are two well-delineated meanings for hyperarousal in the context of traumatic stress. The most common usage is as a label for the Criterion D cluster of symptoms within the PTSD diagnostic criteria (American Psychiatric Association, 1994). Here, the prefix explicitly signifies excessive persistence of arousal, which is thought to be reflected in disturbed sleep, propensity toward irritability or anger, difficulty with concentration, heightened vigilance, and exaggerated startle reactions.

The second meaning pertains to physiological activation measured either during psychophysiological assessment or in the immediate aftermath of a potentially traumatic experience (e.g., recorded in a hospital emergency department). The prefix *hyper* signifies greater magnitude of arousal in the former context, but may reflect either greater magnitude or greater persistence of arousal in the latter context. Physiological values are usually compared to a normative or reference value to determine their trauma-related meaning. For example, for diagnostic purposes, the increase in heart rate shown by an individual during presentation of a trauma-related cue (reminder) can be compared to norms for individuals with PTSD. Or as a measure of treatment outcome, the cue-elicited reaction of an individual with PTSD prior to treatment can be compared with his or her own reaction to the same cues after treatment.

Two mechanisms are commonly proposed to account for PTSD-related hyperarousal. One mechanism assumes that activation is triggered with greater intensity or more frequently than is typical in the absence of PTSD. In essence, a normal reaction is exaggerated due to heightened sensitivity to trauma-related cues that was established during the traumatic experience. An emotional reaction to these cues may be unusually strong or prolonged, or it may occur unusually often if reminders are encountered frequently in the individual's environment.

The second mechanism involves biological adjustments that occur as a consequence of the emotional activation that characterizes PTSD. For example, receptors for excitatory neurotransmitters may develop increased sensitivity. Such changes may dysregulate processes that normally limit the magnitude of response or that dissipate the response when emotion ends. Physiological reactions that are especially large or slow to recover are potential risk factors for breakdown in biological systems (e.g., development of cardiovascular disorders).

REFERENCE

American Psychiatric Association. (1994). *Diagnostic and statistical manual of mental disorders* (4th ed.). Washington, DC: Author.

RECOMMENDED READINGS

Lindauer, R. J. L., Van Meijel, E. P. M., Jalink, M., Olff, M., Carlier, I. V. E., & Gersons, B. P. R. (2006). Heart rate responsivity to script-driven imagery in posttraumatic stress disorder: Specificity of response and effects of psychotherapy. *Psychosomatic Medicine, 68,* 33–40.

Palmieri, P. A., Weathers, F. W., Difede, J., & King, D. W. (2007). Confirmatory factor analysis of the PTSD Checklist and the Clinician-Administered PTSD Scale in disaster workers exposed to the World Trade Center Ground Zero. *Journal of Abnormal Psychology, 116,* 329–341.

Danny G. Kaloupek
Veterans Affairs Boston Healthcare System

See also: Diagnosis of Traumatic Stress Disorder (*DSM & ICD*); Posttraumatic Stress Disorder; Posttraumatic Stress Disorder, Diagnosis of; Startle Response; Stress Response Syndromes

HYPERVIGILANCE

See: Hyperarousal

HYPNOTHERAPY

Hypnotic techniques have been used successfully for the treatment of posttraumatic conditions (including acute stress disorder [ASD], and posttraumatic stress disorder [PTSD], and related diagnoses used at earlier times: shell shock, combat fatigue, etc.) since at least 1813. Currently, clinicians use hypnotic techniques within the context of a larger therapeutic framework (e.g., psychodynamic or cognitive behavioral), rather than as a stand-alone treatment modality. Hypnosis has been defined as "a procedure during which a health professional or researcher suggests that a client, patient, or subject experience changes in sensations, perceptions, thought, or behavior. The hypnotic context is generally established by an induction procedure" (Kirsch, 1994, p. 143). There are various forms of hypnotic induction, some of which do not include relaxation; features common to all are suggestions to disregard nonrelevant concerns and focus on the hypnotist's communications. Hypnotic procedures can foster a state of attentive focal concentration with a relative decrease of peripheral awareness and heightened sensitivity to suggestions (Spiegel & Cardeña, 1990).

It is useful to distinguish the hypnotic procedure from hypnotic *phenomena* such as behavioral or cognitive alterations that may emerge after, or be enhanced by, a hypnotic procedure. The hypnotic procedure may bring about these changes in some people but not in others because there are important and consistent individual differences regarding the extent to which individuals respond behaviorally and subjectively to hypnotic suggestions (i.e., hypnotizability or hypnotic suggestibility). On the other hand, hypnotic-like phenomena, such as alterations in body image or enhanced suggestibility, may occur spontaneously or following nonhypnotic events such as meditation or traumatic events. For instance, there is evidence of various alterations of consciousness around the time of experiencing psychological trauma including the narrowing and focusing of attention (e.g., Cardeña & Spiegel, 1993).

Various arguments support the use of hypnosis for the treatment of posttraumatic conditions, among them:

- Individuals with ASD or PTSD often exhibit very high hypnotizability, and there is a moderate correlation between this trait and the efficacy of hypnotic treatment (Flammer & Bongartz, 2003).

- Hypnosis can be conceptualized as a form of controlled dissociation (i.e., the lack of integration between psychological processes), and research has shown that posttraumatic conditions are often associated with dissociative symptomatology. Thus, the use of hypnosis can be seen as enhancing the individual's control over states or

processes associated with posttraumatic conditions.

- Hypnotic techniques can be easily integrated into the major therapeutic frameworks, and various meta-analyses have shown that these techniques typically enhance the efficacy of the therapies to which they are an adjunct.

- The dominant models in the treatment of PTSD, cognitive-behavioral and psychodynamic, emphasize the importance of some form of recollection of the traumatic event(s). Hypnotic techniques can help modulate and control these memories and help the individual integrate them in a positive way. There is research showing that similar brain structures are activated during recall of traumatic events and hypnotic responding.

- Various hypnotic strategies may be helpful in treating symptoms associated with posttraumatic conditions such as anxiety, pain, and nightmares.

For uncomplicated conditions following single (or relatively time-limited) traumatic events (e.g., severe accidents, disasters, assaults), many of the hypnotic techniques described below can be tailored to specific symptoms. In the case of chronic or otherwise complicated posttraumatic conditions, a phase-oriented model is recommended (Cardeña, Maldonado, Van der Hart, & Spiegel, in press; Degun-Mather, 2006). The three general phases of treatment include: (1) establishing the therapeutic relationship and frame, providing short-term relief, helping stabilize the patient by making symptoms more controllable, and enhancing coping skills; (2) working-through and integrating the traumatic events into healthier schemas; and (3) furthering psychological integration, anticipating possible difficult situations, and helping the individual have a future perspective with an emphasis on self and relational development. The sequencing of these phases should be flexible (previous stages may be revisited) and tailored individually. For instance, some individuals may need to remain in the first phase for very long periods of time before being able to deal with traumatic memories, if at all.

Some of the hypnotic techniques useful in the first, stabilizing, phase of psychotherapy include teaching relaxation, so that patients can learn to experience a calm and serene state and, through self-hypnosis, maintain this state outside of the consulting room. Especially useful at this stage may be to establish an imaginal "safe place" and use "ego strengthening" hypnotherapy procedures to enhance the person's sense of self-mastery and hope. Other interventions may be used to address specific symptoms associated with posttraumatic conditions that cause instability in patients' lives, including anxiety, physical pain, discomfort, and sleep disturbances.

For the second phase, working-through of traumatic memories, expanding the use of relaxation-focused hypnotherapy to include projective and restructuring techniques, age regression, and imaginal memory containment may be particularly useful (though not necessarily empirically supported). These techniques facilitate manageable processing and restructuring of anxiety-producing memories. For instance, the client may be asked to "project" traumatic images, sensations, and thoughts away from themselves, onto a movie or computer screen, and to also imagine a "remote control" through which he or she may be able to intensify or decrease the image or sound of the retrieved memory. Imaginal and age-regression techniques may help restructure the interpretation of the memory by, for instance, having the person go back in time and provide adult comfort to a victimized earlier version of the self.

In the final therapeutic phase, which focuses on incorporating the benefits of earlier treatment phases into the person's daily life and main areas of functioning, hypnotic techniques may help the person imagine a future, and healthier version of the self, by using "age progression." Other uses of hypnosis include imagining potential stressful situations and mentally rehearsing how to deal with them, which may reinforce healthy coping skills and reduce the likelihood of reverting into avoidant or dissociative processes.

Regarding more specific therapeutic tasks, hypnotic techniques may facilitate therapeutic goals in the treatment of psychological trauma. They include the confrontation of traumatic memories, confession of deeds and feelings that may have been deemed shameful, and professional consolation when dealing with very painful memories. Other therapeutic processes include making fully conscious and integrating aspects of the memory that may have been only partially processed (e.g., remembering the memory as if it had been observed from an external perspective), condensing crucial aspects of the traumatic experience, fostering a person's concentration and control, and enhancing the congruence of memories, and self-images (Spiegel & Cardeña, 1990).

It bears mentioning that hypnotic techniques often accelerate transferential reactions by the patient, which, when managed appropriately and professionally, may help in the recovery process. Naturally, the therapist should be very attentive to the complexities involved in the transferential response of individuals victimized by other human beings. Careful observation of the patient's nonverbal communications and mannerisms when conducting potentially emotionally evocative hypnotherapy interventions, and empathic responses that validate the patient's feelings and help the patient distinguish between past hurt or traumas and the current therapeutic relationship, are essential therapeutic approaches to such reactions.

Up until some years ago, the evidence for the efficacy of hypnosis for posttraumatic conditions consisted mostly of a sizeable series of case studies, many dealing with psychological casualties from the World Wars. Most recently, a controlled study comparing hypnosis with other therapies and a waiting list for PTSD (Brom, Kleber, & Defares, 1989), and another comparing cognitive behavioral therapy (CBT) with CBT + hypnosis for ASD (Bryant, Moulds, Guthrie, & Nixon, 2005) have shown that hypnotic techniques are effective and may accelerate a positive therapeutic outcome. Single case designs and systematic case studies have also supported the efficacy of hypnotic techniques (e.g., Walters & Oakely, 2002). Although most of the research has centered on Caucasian adults from Western European cultures, there is also literature that points out that hypnosis can be effective for children (e.g., Friedrich, 1991) and members of other cultures (e.g., Dobkin de Rios & Friedmann, 1987).

More than 150 years of publications have consistently supported the usefulness of hypnosis for trauma survivors, but as with other techniques, there are circumstances in which hypnosis may be useless or counterproductive, including with the few individuals who are refractory or minimally responsive to hypnotic suggestions, and those who may have strongly negative attitudes toward hypnosis even after a clarification of what it actually entails (e.g., that people do not fall under the control of the hypnotist nor do they become unconscious during hypnosis). For individuals with low blood pressure or proneness to sleep, "active-alert" hypnotic procedures may be preferred.

It is also worth pointing out that hypnosis may be counter-indicated for individuals asking the therapist to use hypnosis to bring forth "repressed" traumatic memories. As considerable literature shows, hypnotic facilitation of recollection may not increase the accuracy of memory recall, but augment instead the level of confidence in what the person may experience as a memory (e.g., Dywan & Bowers, 1983). It is also known that false memories may be induced via hypnotic suggestion, especially more plausible memories. Although research indicates that misleading communication is the most important factor in producing false memories rather than hypnosis per se (e.g., Scoboria, Mazzoni, & Kirsch, 2006), the use of hypnosis to go searching for memories of uncertain validity is contraindicated. The therapist should be careful about using explicit or implicit suggestions in this regard. At this point in time, it is arguable whether hypnosis merits being labeled an "empirically supported" treatment for posttraumatic conditions, but the published evidence points in that direction.

REFERENCES

Brom, D., Kleber, R. J., & Defares, P. B. (1989). Brief psychotherapy for post-traumatic stress disorder. *Journal of Consulting and Clinical Psychology, 57,* 607–612.

Bryant, R. A., Moulds, M. L., Guthrie, R. M., & Nixon, R. D. V. (2005). The additive benefit of hypnosis and cognitive-behavioral therapy in treating acute stress disorder. *Journal of Consulting and Clinical Psychology, 73*(2), 334–340.

Cardeña, E., Maldonado, J., van der Hart, O., & Spiegel, D. (in press). Revised guidelines for the use of hypnosis. In E. Foa, T. Keane, & M. Friedman (Eds.), *Effective treatments for PTSD.* New York: Guilford Press.

Cardeña, E., & Spiegel, D. (1993). Dissociative reactions to the San Francisco Bay Area earthquake of 1989. *American Journal of Psychiatry, 150,* 474–478.

Degun-Mather, M. (2006). *Hypnosis, dissociation and survivors of child abuse.* Chichester, West Sussex, England: Wiley.

Dobkin de Ríos, M., & Friedmann, J. K. (1987). Hypnotherapy with Hispanic burn patients. *International Journal of Clinical and Experimental Psychology, 35,* 87–94.

Dywan, J., & Bowers, K. (1983). The use of hypnosis to enhance recall. *Science, 222,* 184–185.

Flammer, E., & Bongartz, W. (2003). On the efficacy of hypnosis: A meta-analytic study. *Contemporary Hypnosis, 20,* 179–197.

Friedrich, W. N. (1991). Hypnotherapy with traumatized children. *International Journal of Clinical and Experimental Hypnosis, 39,* 67–81.

Kirsch, I. (1994). Defining hypnosis for the public. *Contemporary Hypnosis, 11,* 142–143.

Scoboria, A., Mazzoni, G., & Kirsch, I. (2006). Effects of misleading questions and hypnotic memory suggestion on memory reports: A signal detection analysis. *International Journal of Clinical and Experimental Hypnosis, 54,* 340–359.

Spiegel, D., & Cardeña, E. (1990). New uses of hypnosis in the treatment of posttraumatic stress disorder. *Journal of Clinical Psychiatry, 51,* 39–43.

Walters, V. J., & Oakley, D. A. (2002). Hypnosis in post-abortion distress: An experimental case study. *Contemporary Hypnosis, 19*(2), 85–99.

ETZEL CARDEÑA
Lund University

HYSTERIA

Hysteria had been considered for many centuries a disease of women, stemming from a "wandering uterus" (the Latin meaning of hysteria). The original idea was that extreme anxiety and its physical and mental manifestations affected only women, and the cause was entirely biological: the woman's uterus was detached in her body and subsequently rendered her unable to think clearly or manage stressful life situations in a conventionally acceptable manner.

More objective study of the psychological and biological underpinnings of hysteria was initiated by nineteenth-century French psychiatry. The meticulous observations that emerged remain highly relevant to modern conceptualizations of trauma-related mental disorders. Students of psychological trauma will thus find great value in understanding the phenomenology and theoretical underpinnings of hysteria as a trauma-related dissociative disorder, and its evolution (and periodic abandonment) over the course of the history of modern psychiatry. Such an understanding can help clinicians navigate the often confusing and arbitrary classifications of trauma-related and dissociative mental disorders that have been designated in recent decades, and may help clarify future movement toward a more coherent and scientific understanding of these disorders. Many (if not most) of these apparently disparate disorders, such as posttraumatic stress disorder, some forms of psychosis, borderline personality disorder, conversion disorder, somatization disorder, and dissociative identity disorder (DID) include many features of hysteria and could actually be subsumed under the rubric of hysteria. Indeed, the etiology of hysteria has often been attributed to traumatic experiences, although other factors (such as genetics, severe illness, and physical or mental exhaustion) also contribute to hysteria.

Perhaps the most astute definition of hysteria comes from Pierre Janet. He noted that hysteria is "a form of mental depression characterized by the retraction of the field of consciousness and a tendency to the dissociation and emancipation of the systems of ideas and functions that constitute personality" (1907, p. 332). In Janet's terms, mental depression was not a mood disorder, but rather a low integrative capacity, resulting in an excessive and chronic narrowing of attention (retraction of the field of consciousness) that resulted in a more limited perception than normal of internal and external stimuli, and a concurrent dissociation among psychophysical (sub)systems that comprise the personality of the individual. Retraction of the field of consciousness manifests, for instance, in the patient's inability to do more than one thing at the time or in a certain narrow-mindedness, that is, being able to only have a single perspective or viewpoint on a complex issue. It also involves being absent-minded or forgetful because of lack of adequate attention to one's self and environment. The dissociation among psychophysical subsystems is most obvious in the complex cases of multiple personality disorder (now called dissociative identity disorder), but actually characterize "minor cases," such as what is currently termed "isolation of affect" or "body memories." Janet (1907) described the famous nineteenth-century case of multiple personality, Louis Vivet as having six different "existences." These alternated and involved both dissociation and retraction of the field of consciousness: Each had different memories, personal characteristics, and varying degrees of sensory and movement problems. For example, one was gentle and hard working; another lazy and irritable; another was incoherent with paralysis on the left side; and one had paraplegia (paralysis of the lower body).

Hysteria originally concerned a broad class of disorders characterized by a dissociation of the personality and manifested in a wide range of symptoms. The original prominent symptoms of hysteria included pseudo-epileptic seizures or fits that have no physical cause, now also understood as dissociative in nature (Bowman, 2006), and other types of "attacks" that involved alterations in consciousness and dissociation. Briquet (1859) noted various types of hysterical "attacks," such as doing things without being aware or able to recall them, for example, getting into a fight; being unable to be roused from sleep; appearing unconscious, as if in a coma; extreme lethargy, for example, sitting for hours without being unable to get up; apparently psychotic episodes (known as hysterical psychosis) in which the individual appears completely unaware of present reality, responding to an hallucinated reality (sometimes of a past traumatizing event).

Clinicians influenced by the thinking of Charcot distinguished the major symptoms of hysteria as so-called stigmata (meaning enduring symptoms) and accidents (meaning abrupt, temporary positive symptoms), an original categorization of dissociative symptoms. Mental stigmata, as Janet (1907; cf. Nijenhuis, 2004; Van der Hart, Nijenhuis, & Steele, 2006) called them, were more or less continuous negative dissociative symptoms that reflect functional losses, such as losses of memory (amnesia), sensation (anesthesia), and motor control (e.g., paralysis) in one part of the personality that was present in another part, as in the case of Louis Vivet above.

The mental accidents of hysteria were positive dissociative symptoms that involve acute, often transient experiences such as the pseudoseizures and hysterical attacks mentioned above, as well as other sensations (e.g., pain), movements (e.g., tics), perceptions, and traumatic memories that suddenly intrude into current consciousness without any apparent reason. At the extreme, hysterical mental accidents may take the form of complete switches from one dissociative part of the personality to another part, as occurs in DID.

The transformation of hysteria into a gender neutral and trauma-related disorder began during the late nineteenth century, with the study of men involved in railway accidents, particularly by Charcot. Individuals who were involved in such accidents suffered a wide array of symptoms, both physical and psychological. In many cases symptoms were seen in patients who had no detectable injury or neurological damage, or only minor injuries, and are consistent with what is now seen in posttraumatic stress disorders. They involved both mental accidents and stigmata, that is, transient as well as enduring symptoms. Initially

termed "railway spine," these symptoms were later renamed traumatic neurosis, leading to the present constructs of acute stress disorder and PTSD. They emphasized the necessity of a traumatic event in the onset of the disorder in constitutionally predisposed individuals.

In the first edition of the *DSM* (American Psychiatric Association, 1952), the concept of hysteria was abandoned. Conversion reactions, a major component of hysteria, were separated from dissociative reactions, and were now defined with a distinctly Freudian interpretation that proposed the conversion of psychological conflicts into physical symptoms. Somatofom dissociative symptoms such as anesthesia (physical numbness), paralysis (inability to move), and uncontrollable movements were now classified as symptoms of "conversion disorder," while other diagnoses were created to describe dissociative reactions such as depersonalization, dissociated [multiple] personality, fugue, amnesia, and somnambulism. Thus, ironically, in the first official guidebook to psychiatric diagnoses, the symptoms of hysteria were fragmented into a variety of different disconnected diagnoses.

DSM-II (American Psychiatric Association, 1968) resumed the use of hysteria, proposing an hysterical neurosis classification, which included dissociation and conversion symptoms as separate subtypes. Thus, in *DSM* and *DSM-II*, negative psychoform (mental) and somatoform (physical) manifestations of a dissociation of the personality were separated, as if the different disorders could not include both types of symptoms, and the positive dissociative symptoms of hysteria that Janet and his colleagues had distinguished were mostly ignored.

DSM-III (American Psychiatric Association, 1980) marked a shift toward descriptive diagnoses, in an attempt to become theory-neutral and avoid hypotheses about etiology. The term *hysteria* was eliminated, along with theoretical statements about the unconscious expression of anxiety in dissociative and conversion symptoms. Nevertheless, *DSM-III,* and all subsequent versions, retained the term conversion disorder, a far from theory-neutral classification, and also added another: somatization disorder.

Both disorders continued to be separated from dissociative disorders, as symptoms of hysteria continued to be arbitrarily divided from each other into various classifications. Two other disorders with solid roots in hysteria were added to *DSM-III*, both with a diagnostic criterion that included an etiological factor of exposure to a potentially traumatizing event: acute stress disorder and posttraumatic stress disorder.

Both hysteria and its evolutionary derivations of traumatic neurosis and other trauma-related disorders have remained dogged by persisting myths and pejorative accusations to this day. Beginning with Babinski, hysteria was incorrectly equated with hypnosis, with an emphasis on simulation, especially in "gullible" women, such that suggestibility became confused as the sole cause of the disorder. The etiological role of traumatic events and subsequent psychopathology were summarily dismissed (Babinski & Froment, 1917; cf., Trillat, 1986), though research continues to support a strong relationship between traumatization and dissociation (the modern term for hysteria). Such confusion most recently emerged again in the late twentieth century in regards to women reporting sexual abuse and symptoms of dissociative identity disorder. Clinicians have long been charged with inducing these memories and disorders in fantasy prone women. For male patients, the persisting suspicion has been more on malingering for (military or civilian) compensation following traumatization. Thus, there remain enduring beliefs that characterological flaws are the source of the problem in hysterics who are weak, suggestible, and manipulative, and in their treating clinicians, who are naive, incompetent, or unethical. Clinicians and researchers alike can benefit from understanding the long history of hysteria, recognizing that patients in the present continue to exhibit many of its manifestations described over a century ago. The various symptoms of hysteria now can be better understood as a result of breaches in the psychobiological coherence and cohesiveness of the individual's mental and physical functioning, and the dysregulating effects of traumatization on the inseparable mind, brain, and body.

REFERENCES

American Psychiatric Association. (1952). *Diagnostic and statistical manual of mental disorders.* Washington, DC: Author.

American Psychiatric Association. (1968). *Diagnostic and statistical manual of mental disorders* (2nd ed.). Washington, DC: Author.

American Psychiatric Association. (1980). *Diagnostic and statistical manual of mental disorders* (3rd ed.). Washington, DC: Author.

Babinski, J., & Froment, J. (1918). *Hysteria or pithiatism and reflex nervous disorders in the neurology of war.* London: University of London Press.

Bowman, E. S. (2006). Why conversion seizures should be classified as a dissociative disorder. *Psychiatric Clinics of North America, 29,* 185–211.

Briquet, P. (1859). *Traité clinique de thérapeutique de l'hystérie* [Clinical and therapeutic treatise on hysteria]. Paris: Baillière.

Janet, P. (1907). *The major symptoms of hysteria.* New York: Macmillan.

McDougall, W. (1926). *An outline of abnormal psychology.* London: Methuen.

Nijenhuis, E. R. S. (2004). *Somatoform dissociation: Phenomena, measurement, and theoretical issues.* New York: Norton.

Trillat, E. (1986). *Histoire de l'hystérie.* Paris: Éditions Seghers.

Van der Hart, O., Nijenhuis, E. R. S., & Steele, K. (2006). *The haunted self: Structural dissociation and the treatment of chronic traumatization.* New York: Norton.

RECOMMENDED READING

Ellenberger, H. F. (1970). *The discovery of the unconscious.* New York: Basic Books.

Onno van der Hart
Utrecht University

Kathy Steele
Metropolitan Counseling Services

See also: **Charcot, Jean-Martin; Dissociation; Freud, Sigmund; Janet, Pierre; Memory**

I

IMPACT OF EVENT SCALE—REVISED

Posttraumatic stress disorder (PTSD) was introduced into the world mental health nomenclature in 1978 (World Health Organization, 1978), attesting to the recognition of a near universal symptomatic response to exposure to traumatic life events (e.g., Horowitz, 1976). The characteristic core of the disorder includes the distressing oscillation between intrusion and avoidance. Intrusion is characterized by nightmares, unbidden visual images of the trauma while awake, intrusive thoughts about aspects of the traumatic event, sequelae, or self-conceptions. Avoidance is typified by deliberate efforts to not think or talk about the event and to avoid reminders of the event. In addition to the frank avoidance, Horowitz also described emotional numbing as a not uncommon sequel to exposure to a traumatic life event (Horowitz, 1975; Horowitz & Kaltreider, 1977). Following from this conceptualization, Horowitz and colleagues (Horowitz, Wilner, & Alvarez, 1979) published a simple but powerful self-report measure for assessing the magnitude of intrusive and avoidant symptomatic response in the past 7 days to a specific traumatic life event that was titled the Impact of Event Scale (IES).

With the exception of disturbances in sleep, the scale did not assess the third set of PTSD symptoms, the hyperarousal symptoms presented in the diagnosis's Criterion D according to *DSM-IV* (American Psychiatric Association, 1987). Complete assessment of the response to traumatic events required tracking of response in the domain of hyperarousal symptoms. Beginning with data from a longitudinal study of the response of emergency services personnel to traumatic events, including the Loma Prieta earthquake (e.g., Weiss, Marmar, Metzler, & Ronfeldt, 1995), a set of seven additional items,

with six to tap the domain of hyperarousal, and one to parallel the *DSM-III-R* (American Psychiatric Association, 1987) and now *DSM-IV* (American Psychiatric Association, 1994) diagnostic criteria for PTSD were developed, piloted, then used. These additional seven items were interspersed with the existing seven intrusion and eight avoidance items of the original IES using a table of random numbers to establish placement. The Impact of Event Scale—Revised (IES-R) comprises these 22 items.

An important consideration in the construction of the revised IES was to maintain comparability with the original version of the measure as much as was possible. Consequently, the 1-week time frame to which the instructions refer in measuring symptomatic response was retained. The only modification to the original items that was made was to change the item "I had trouble falling asleep or staying asleep" from its double-barreled status into two separate items. The first is simply "I had trouble staying asleep" and because of a somewhat higher correlation between it and the remaining intrusion items it was assigned to represent the original item in the Intrusion subscale. The second item, "I had trouble falling asleep" was assigned to the new Hyperarousal subscale. The six new items comprising the Hyperarousal subscale targeted the following domains: anger and irritability; jumpiness and exaggerated startle response; trouble concentrating; psychophysiological arousal upon exposure to reminders; and hypervigilance. As mentioned, the one new intrusion item taps the dissociative-like reexperiencing captured in true flashback-like experiences.

Because of the over-weighting of responses of "sometimes" and "often" in the scoring scheme, the IES-R molted into a measure with the following characteristics: (a) the directions were modified so that the respondent is not asked about the frequency of symptoms in the past 7 days but is instead asked to report the *degree of distress* of the symptom in the past 7 days; (b) the response format was modified to a 0 to 4 response format with equal intervals: 0 = Not at all; 1 = A little bit; 2 = Moderately; 3 = Quite a bit; 4 = Extremely (rather than the unequal intervals of the original scale); and (c) the subscale scoring was changed from the sum of the responses to the mean of the responses, allowing the user to immediately identify the degree of symptomatology merely by examining the subscale scores since they are presented in the same metric as the item responses, something the original scale did not. These changes brought the IES-R in parallel format to the SCL-90-R (Derogatis, 1994).

See Weiss (2004) and Creamer, Bell, and Failla (2003) for a summary of the internal consistency of the three subscales, all of which were strong, the pattern of item-total correlations, test-retest stability that was also satisfactory, and communality of the inter-item correlations, and factor structure. Though efforts are made to set cut-offs, the IES-R is not designed to reproduce diagnostic decisions, but rather to give an assessment of the level of symptomatic response.

REFERENCES

American Psychiatric Association. (1987). *Diagnostic and statistical manual of mental disorders* (3rd ed., rev.). Washington, DC: Author.

American Psychiatric Association. (1994). *Diagnostic and statistical manual of mental disorders* (4th ed.). Washington, DC: Author.

Creamer, M., Bell, R., & Failla, S. (2003). Psychometric properties of the Impact of Event Scale—Revised. *Behaviour Research and Therapy, 41,* 1489–1496.

Derogatis, L. R. (1994). *SCL-90-R administration, scoring, and procedures manual* (3rd ed.). Minneapolis, MN: National Computer Systems.

Horowitz, M. J. (1975). Intrusive and repetitive thoughts after experimental stress: A summary. *Archives of General Psychiatry, 32,* 1457–1463.

Horowitz, M. J. (1976). *Stress response syndromes.* New York: Aaronson.

Horowitz, M. J., & Kaltreider, N. B. (1977). The response to stress. *Comprehensive Therapy, 3,* 38–40.

Horowitz, M. J., Wilner, N., & Alvarez, W. (1979). Impact of Event Scale: A measure of subjective stress. *Psychosomatic Medicine, 41,* 209–218.

Weiss, D. S. (2004). The Impact of Event Scale—Revised. In J. P. Wilson & T. M. Keane (Eds.), *Assessing psychological trauma and PTSD: A practitioner's handbook* (2nd ed., pp. 168–189). New York: Guilford Press.

Weiss, D. S., Marmar, C. R., Metzler, T. J., & Ronfeldt, H. (1995). Predicting symptomatic distress in emergency services personnel. *Journal of Consulting and Clinical Psychology, 63,* 361–368.

World Health Organization. (1978). *Clinical modification of the World Health Organization's manual of the international statistical classification of diseases, injuries, and causes of death* (9th rev. ed.). Geneva, Switzerland: Author.

DANIEL S. WEISS
University of California, San Francisco

See also: Assessment, Psychometric, Adult; Stress Response Syndromes

INCARCERATION

There is a popular stereotype of the person with posttraumatic stress disorder (PTSD) who is driven to commit crimes. Indeed, since its inclusion in *DSM-III* (American Psychiatric Association, 1987), the diagnosis of PTSD has been raised in the judicial system to explain a wide range of criminal behaviors. Although epidemiological studies clearly indicate a statistical association between both exposure to traumatic events and PTSD on one hand with subsequent involvement with the criminal justice system, the causal association between PTSD and criminal behavior remains controversial.

Epidemiological studies in both civilian and veteran populations have consistently indicated a relationship between trauma exposure and increased likelihood of history of arrest and convictions. For example, results from the National

Vietnam Veterans Readjustment Study (NVVRS), one of the largest and most comprehensive studies of veterans to date, found increased rates of arrest and incarceration among veterans exposed to high war-zone stress. Furthermore, the NVVRS documented an even stronger association between PTSD and arrest history. Results suggest that almost half of all Vietnam veterans with PTSD have been arrested more than once, compared to less than 12% of those without the disorder. Other epidemiological studies that have attempted to statistically control for childhood factors that are associated with incarceration (e.g., socioeconomic status, race, truancy, family structure, education, prior history of arrests) have also documented a relationship between trauma exposure and increased likelihood of arrests and convictions.

Further, incarcerated populations have high rates of childhood trauma, and compared to the general population, individuals in prison have significantly higher rates of PTSD. Psychiatric disorders, in general, are overrepresented among incarcerated persons, with increased rates of substance use disorders, mood disorders such as depression, and personality disorders including antisocial personality disorder and borderline personality disorder. The identification of high rates of emotional disturbance among incarcerated populations has led many to call for increased treatment of substance abuse and other co-occurring mental disorders in an effort to reduce recidivism/re-offense.

Despite the epidemiological evidence linking trauma and PTSD to increased incarceration, some researchers and legal experts have argued that there is no evidence that criminal behavior leading to imprisonment is a direct consequence of PTSD, such as criminal behavior that occurs during a PTSD-related flashback. There are recurring allegations that the diagnosis of PTSD is frequently abused in the legal system as a basis for a defense of not guilty by reason of insanity. The evidence suggests, however, that PTSD is actually infrequently used as the basis for an insanity defense and when invoked (as is the case with other mental disorders) it is rarely successful.

While the evidence for a direct causal effect of trauma and PTSD on criminal behavior and incarceration remains unclear, the statistical association between trauma and PTSD on one hand and incarceration is well established. Further, PTSD is related to a number of other adjustment problems including increased hostility, family conflict, occupational impairment, increased rates of interpersonal violence, and substance abuse. These related factors may help explain the documented relationship between PTSD and incarceration. Substance abuse, in particular, is highly related to incarceration and may at least partially mediate the relationship between PTSD and arrest history.

REFERENCE

American Psychiatric Association. (1987). *Diagnostic and statistical manual of mental disorders* (3rd ed.). Washington, DC: Author.

RECOMMENDED READINGS

Calhoun, P. S., Malesky, A. L., Jr., Bosworth, H. B., & Beckham, J. C. (2004). Severity of posttraumatic stress disorder and involvement with the criminal justice system. *Journal of Trauma Practice, 3*, 1–16.

Kulka, R. A., Schlenger, W. E., Fairbank, J. A., Hough, R. L., Jordon, B. K., Marmar, C. R., et al. (1990). *Trauma and the Vietnam War generation: Report of findings from the National Vietnam Veterans Readjustment Study*. New York: Brunner/Mazel.

PATRICK S. CALHOUN
Duke University Medical Center

See also: **Aggression; Antisocial Behavior; Substance Abuse**

INFANCY AND EARLY CHILDHOOD

Infancy and early childhood, defined as the period from birth to age five, involve rapid biological, social, emotional, and cognitive development. The brain increases more than threefold in weight (Courchesne et al., 2000), important brain structures like the hippocampus and cerebral cortex continue to develop, and key hormonal stress response systems mature (Watamura, Donzella, Kertes, & Gunnar, 2004). Changes in brain development and biochemistry occur at the same time that the young child attempts to master the key tasks of early development, including the capacity to self-regulate, relate to others, and learn (Shonkoff & Phillips, 2000). These processes unfold in the context of interactions with caregivers and the environment and are profoundly affected by the experience of psychological trauma.

The key features of psychological trauma across the developmental spectrum are unpredictability, horror, and helplessness (Freud, 1926/1959; Pynoos, Steinberg, & Piacentini, 1999). When psychological trauma is part of the environmental context, infants and young children are at particularly high risk of later mental health problems because their abilities to regulate their emotions and use their own coping skills are not fully developed, and they may be overwhelmed by events that older children may not view as "traumatic." Young children cope with stress and psychological trauma by turning to their attachment figures for protection and safety. When traumatic events overwhelm the adults' capacity to respond supportively to the child's bids, the child-caregiver relationship may be severely compromised, with negative consequences for the child's development.

Prevalence of Psychological Trauma Exposure

Violence in the United States has been characterized as a public health epidemic, and studies suggest that many children under age five have experienced violence—as witnesses or direct victims. Although there are few epidemiological studies on the prevalence of young children's exposure to psychological trauma, a number of studies have assessed the rate of exposure in high-risk samples. Together, the epidemiological and high-risk studies reveal consistently high levels of psychological trauma exposure and demonstrate that different types of psychological traumas (e.g., community violence, domestic violence, and child abuse) often co-occur and co-exist with risk factors, such as poverty.

Domestic Violence

A nationally representative study of married or cohabiting couples estimates that in 1 year, 15.5 million (29.4%) American children under age 18 witness domestic violence (McDonald, Jouriles, Ramisetty-Mikler, Caetano, & Green, 2006). Higher rates were found in a randomly selected, community sample of children aged 3 to 7 years old in Suffolk County, New York, where 49% of the families reported interparental physical aggression and 24% reported severe aggression. While these studies did not examine age-related differences in exposure to violence, police reports of domestic violence suggest that children under age five are more likely to be exposed (Fantuzzo & Fusco, 2007). In addition, studies involving high-risk children under age five have found high rates of exposure. The Minnesota Parent-Child Project, a 25-year longitudinal study of mothers and children living in poverty, found that 12% of mothers reported mild partner violence and 25% reported severe partner violence when their children were 18 to 64 months old (Yates, Dodds, Sroufe, & Egeland, 2003). Even infants and toddlers appear to be at risk for domestic violence exposure. Specifically, a study of 1- to 3-year-olds recruited randomly from Yale-New Haven hospital birth records found that 8% had witnessed physical violence toward a family member and 26% had seen family members arguing loudly or fighting (McDonald, Jouriles, Briggs-Gowan, Rosenfield, & Carter, 2007).

Child Maltreatment

Young children are often the direct victims of violence. In 2005, 3.6 million children nationally received a Child Protective Service (CPS) investigation; among these, children aged birth to 3 years old had the highest rates of victimization (U.S. Department of Health and Human Services, 2007). Data gathered from child abuse reports are likely to underestimate the true prevalence of children who experience physical violence. Slep and O'Leary's (2005) study found that in their randomly selected community sample, 87% of children experienced some form of physical aggression and 13%

experienced physical aggression severe enough to meet many definitions of physical abuse, although these episodes were not reported to CPS agencies.

Community Violence

Although data show that adolescents experience the highest rates of victimization, young children are exposed at high rates, with those in urban, low-income, high crime areas at especially high-risk. In interviews with parents and children attending a Head Start program in a high crime area near Washington, DC, 66.5% of parents and 78.1% of children reported that the child had witnessed or been victim to at least one incident of violence (Shahinfar, Fox, & Leavitt, 2000). A study conducted in Boston with a nonreferred pediatric sample of 3- to 5-year-old children recruited because they lived in high crime neighborhoods found that 42% had seen at least one violent event, 21% experienced three or more violent events, and 12% witnessed eight or more such events (Linares et al., 2001). With regards to the severity of exposure, a study involving children ages 1 to 5 years old recruited from the pediatric primary care clinic at Boston City Hospital reported that 10% had witnessed a knifing or shooting and 47% had heard gunshots (Taylor, Zuckerman, Harik, & Groves, 1994).

Consequences of Psychological Trauma Exposure

Over the past 20 years, numerous studies involving diverse populations of young children, different types of psychological traumas, and a variety of research methodologies, including cross-sectional and longitudinal designs, have led to two main conclusions. First, psychological trauma has the potential to disrupt young children's development, interfering with their ability to successfully achieve the key tasks of early development and affecting the long-term course of development. Second, a developmentally informed transactional-ecological framework must be adopted in order to understand how psychological trauma may affect the young

child's developmental trajectory (Pynoos et al., 1999; Sameroff & Fiese, 2000). This perspective involves considering not only the risks conveyed by a single incident, but also the complex transactional or interactive processes among a variety of risk and protective factors. Psychological traumas such as abuse or domestic violence and other stressors such as poverty, isolation, and parental problems with psychiatric or addictive disorders are examples of risk factors because these experiences place the child at risk for problems in development. Caregivers who are responsive to the infant's needs and able to create a positive parent-child relationship represent key protective factors, because these conditions enhance children's ability to grow and develop in a healthy manner.

An understanding of normal development is the foundation for ascertaining the potential pathways through which psychological trauma may affect the young child's emerging developmental capabilities. Young children develop in the context of relationships. The baby's primary caregivers help create the external environment where development unfolds. The way in which caregivers respond to their own and to the baby's experiences shapes the child's beliefs about himself or herself, relationships, and the world. Answers to the most fundamental questions, such as "Am I safe? Am I lovable? Am I capable?" begin to be formed in early childhood through multiple transactional interactions between infant, caregiver, and environment. When psychological trauma—whether experienced directly by the child or indirectly because of parental trauma or historical trauma—is part of the context, it has the potential to negatively affect the child's development. Whether this occurs depends on a number of factors: (a) the magnitude of the psychological trauma, (b) the child's temperament, (c) the child's emerging capacities to regulate emotions, (d) the caregivers' ability to regulate emotions given the magnitude of the psychological trauma and their own history, (e) the caregivers' ability to respond to the child and reestablish safety, and (f) the response of the community and/or cultural group. No one factor can be viewed in isolation because the outcome rests on interactions between them.

Case Example 1

Eva, a 26-year-old Spanish-speaking Nicaraguan immigrant and her two children, Daniel, age three, and Joaquin, age 14 months, were seen 1 year after the children's father died in a car accident. During the initial assessment, Eva reported that she had problems with Joaquin. He had always been a fussy baby but started to cry "all the time" after his father died. Eva felt she could not comfort him and left him to cry by himself. By contrast, Daniel was highly verbal. He told her that he missed his dad, and while Eva found this difficult, she thought she could help him. Although she ignored Joaquin, she was responsive to Daniel. Three months after the initial assessment, Eva found work as a housecleaner. Daniel began to attend a preschool where the majority of the staff spoke English. Joaquin was put in the care of his paternal aunt, who cherished her deceased brother's son and was attentive and affectionate with him. During the following year, the family underwent many changes. Eva had a new boyfriend and felt that she could finally move on after mourning for her dead husband. Joaquin loved Eva's boyfriend and called him "daddy," but Daniel refused to accept him. He frequently talked about his dad and cried when separated from his mother. His teachers noted that he was aggressive with the other children. The problems became worse when Daniel's favorite teacher left and he began hitting the remaining teachers.

This family's history illustrates a number of complex realities. First, children may react in different ways to the same psychological trauma, and these responses may change with new developmental stages and changing family circumstances. Moreover, caregiver responsiveness can vary as a function of the child's reaction. Eva was neither a uniformly responsive mother nor consistently insensitive to the needs of her children. Her ability to nurture her children was influenced by how her children's reactions affected her. Daniel brought up the psychological trauma and loss that she longed to forget. When she could not help him, she was reminded of her own mother's emotional unavailability when she was growing up. Although Eva saw herself initially as incapable of helping her children, she displayed a number of strengths. She recognized that her children were suffering and actively sought help for them. The example also shows the role of context. Extended family members, school, and the larger community all have the potential to influence the family's response to the psychological trauma. The dynamic nature of psychological trauma responses is apparent in every one of these factors. Responses to psychological trauma are not static but are modified by developmental transitions and changes in external circumstances.

This example highlights the uniqueness and complexity of the individual's and family's response to psychological trauma, underscoring the importance of an in-depth multidimensional assessment where the child's functioning is considered in the context of family relationships and the community and culture to which the family belongs (Lieberman & Van Horn, 2004). It is also important to be familiar with the common consequences of psychological trauma exposure. Following psychological trauma exposure, young children may exhibit posttraumatic stress symptoms (e.g., Laor et al., 1997; Scheeringa, Peebles, Cook, & Zeanah, 2001; Stoddard et al., 2006; Terr, 1988), including increased arousal and reexperiencing, shown often through play reenactments. Although studies show that young children can exhibit symptoms of avoidance (e.g., Stoddard et al., 2006), the requirement of at least three avoidance/numbing symptoms required by the *DSM-IV* (American Psychiatric Association, 1994) posttraumatic stress disorder (PTSD) diagnostic algorithm may be inappropriate for children under age seven and may result in under-diagnosis of PTSD (Scheeringa, Wright, Hunt, & Zeanah, 2006).

Exposure to interpersonal violence, in particular, has important consequences for multiple aspects of development. In preschoolers, community violence exposure is associated with worse cognitive performance, more negative social interactions, greater teacher ratings of aggression, and greater behavior problems (Farver, Natera, & Frosch, 1999; Farver, Xu, Eppe, Fernandez, & Schwartz, 2005; Shahinfar et al.,

2000). Domestic violence appears to have especially negative effects for infants and young children. Infants exposed to domestic violence exhibit traumatic stress symptoms (Bogat, DeJohnghe, Levendosky, Davidson, & von Eye, 2006), externalizing behavior problems (Levendosky, Leahy, Bogat, Davidson, & von Eye, 2006), and heightened sensitivity to conflict (DeJonghe, Bogat, Levendosky, von Eye, & Davidson, 2005). Data also suggest that the consequences of violence exposure may be long lasting. Exposure to domestic violence during the preschool years predicts behavior problems at age six (Litrownik, Newton, Hunter, English, & Everson, 2003) and at age 16 (Yates et al., 2003).

While not all children exhibit symptoms following psychological trauma exposure, it is important to differentiate between those who would be classified as resilient and those who may appear "symptom free" despite significant dysfunction. Problems may not be evident for a variety of reasons. First, caregivers may fail to notice the child's symptoms. Parents themselves may be experiencing symptoms, such as PTSD's reexperiencing, avoidance, or hyperarousal symptoms, depression, anxiety, or grief that preclude them from perceiving their child's experience, or they may wish to deny that their child is suffering. Alternately, some behaviors (e.g., avoidance and flat affect) may be difficult to identify, and other problems, such as eating or sleep difficulties, may be overlooked or misinterpreted as normal developmental variations.

Second, because young children's behavior is context dependent, some traumatized children may do well in situations where they feel safe and cared for. The same child's behavior may shift rapidly to become symptomatic in less safe situations or when the child is reminded of the psychological trauma. The following example illustrates this shift.

Case Example 2

Jeremy, 26 months old, was assessed twice, once at the battered women's shelter where he and his mom resided and a second time at the small day-care center he had recently begun to attend. In the shelter, Jeremy was aggressive, and exhibited self-destructive behaviors. He was constantly aroused by the aggressive behavior he witnessed in other children at the shelter. The other children's aggression seemed to trigger his own traumatic responses to the violence he had witnessed between his mother and father. At the day-care center, in contrast, he played well with the other children, followed directions, and was appropriately responsive to the staff.

This example illustrates the importance of changing the context to fit the needs of the child. It also serves as a reminder that in the presence of stressors such as aggressive peers or reminders of traumatic experiences, children who appear to have few symptoms may exhibit behaviors that reveal that their bodies, in particular, remember the psychological trauma they experienced. Although Jeremy cannot provide a verbal description of the violence he witnessed, his body reacts with arousal and distress in the presence of stimuli that remind him of his experience. Dysfunction may be masked by children who realize that their parent is in pain and who try to shield them from their own pain.

Case Example 3

Three-year-old Emma witnessed an episode where her father was shot and slightly wounded by a relative 4 months before her parents brought her to treatment. Emma often woke screaming in the night but otherwise seemed fine and appeared to have a perpetual smile on her face. Her parents did not speak with her about the shooting, but they worried about her persistent night terrors and wanted to help her sleep better. When Emma looked through a book about feelings with her father, she proclaimed cheerfully that everyone was "happy" despite the fact that some animals were clearly drawn as sad or scared. After her father and the therapist openly spoke with her about the shooting, Emma opened up and began to share some of her fears. She told the story of the shooting and showed that she remembered that day, even though neither she nor her parents had been talking about it. Although it is not certain that Emma was hiding her fears in order to prevent her father from feeling upset, she did need to know that he was able to cope with his own feelings before she felt able to share her fears.

Caregiver functioning and the quality of the caregiver-child relationship are important predictors of young children's functioning when the child and/or caregiver has been exposed to psychological trauma (Lieberman, Van Horn, & Ozer, 2005; Scheeringa & Zeanah, 2001). Linares et al. (2001) found that community violence and family violence each were associated with distress felt by a sample of mothers, and that mothers who had experienced violence and were distressed tended to have children with greater internalizing and externalizing symptoms. Bogat et al. (2006) reported that mothers' PTSD symptoms predicted the number of symptoms experienced by their 1-month old infants. Scheeringa et al. (2006) noted that witnessing a threat to a caregiver carries special meaning not only for young children but throughout childhood. These findings echo the clinical wisdom of the field of infant mental health that highlights the importance of the caregiver-child relationship. Infants and young children depend on a secure and nurturing relationship with their primary caregivers to grow and develop, especially if they are faced with a severe threat to their life or well-being as a result of psychological trauma.

Trauma-Focused Treatment

Trauma-focused treatments for this age group should include the caregiver whenever possible because of the salience of the caregiver-child relationship in the early years. In addition, treatment must be tailored to the unique needs of each family due to the complex nature of the child and family's response to the psychological trauma.

Child-parent psychotherapy (*see:* **Psychodynamic Therapy, Child**) is an evidence-based treatment model for psychological trauma exposed children aged 0–6 that involves the caregiver whenever possible and allows for a flexible treatment format (Lieberman, Compton, Van Horn, & Ghosh Ippen, 2003; Lieberman & Van Horn, 2005). The model incorporates a focus on psychological trauma experienced by the caregiver, the child, or both. It examines how the psychological trauma and the caregivers' relational history affect the caregiver-child relationship and the child's developmental trajectory. A central goal is to support and strengthen the caregiver-child relationship as a vehicle for restoring and protecting the child's mental health. Typically, the child and the primary caregiver are seen jointly, and the dyad is the unit of treatment. Treatment also focuses on contextual factors that may affect the caregiver-child relationship (e.g., culture and socioeconomic and immigration related stressors). Targets of the intervention include caregivers' and children's maladaptive representations of themselves and each other and interactions and behaviors that interfere with the child's mental health. Over the course of treatment, caregiver and child are guided to create a joint narrative of the psychological traumatic event, identify and address traumatic triggers that generate dysregulated behaviors and reinforce mutual traumatic expectations, and place the traumatic experience in perspective.

Five randomized controlled trials (RCTs) detailed in seven published studies support the efficacy of CPP with infants, toddlers, and preschoolers (Cicchetti, Rogosch, & Toth, 2006; Cicchetti, Toth, & Rogosch, 1999; Lieberman, Ghosh Ippen, & Van Horn, 2006; Lieberman, Van Horn, & Ghosh Ippen, 2005; Lieberman, Weston, & Pawl, 1991; Toth, Maughan, Manly, Spagnola, & Cicchetti, 2002; Toth, Rogosch, Cicchetti, & Manly, 2006). Of note, four of the RCTs were conducted with predominantly ethnic minorities. Three of these studies were conducted with trauma-exposed children. These studies support the use of CPP with young children with documented histories of maltreatment and exposure to domestic violence. They also suggest that CPP is efficacious for caregivers and children who have experienced multiple, chronic psychological traumas. CPP was found to be efficacious in terms of reducing child and caregiver general symptoms and PTSD symptoms, strengthening the child-caregiver attachment relationship, and improving children's representations of themselves, their caregivers, and their relationships. One study involving a 6-month longitudinal follow-up shows that improvements in child and caregiver symptoms continue after the end of treatment.

Conclusion

Psychological trauma is highly prevalent during the first 5 years of life, especially among high-risk groups, such as children living in poverty. The data suggest that rather than being immune to the effects of such exposure, young children may be especially vulnerable, particularly when the experience negatively affects the caregiver-child relationship. Psychological trauma can alter young children's developmental trajectory leading to difficulties in biological, emotional, cognitive, and/or social functioning. Interventions that address psychological trauma in infancy and early childhood should involve the caregiver whenever possible and focus on the child-caregiver relationship because of the salience of this relationship for this age group and because the literature suggests that the best predictor of the young child's functioning following trauma exposure is the caregiver's functioning and the quality of the caregiver-child relationship.

REFERENCES

American Psychiatric Association. (1994). *Diagnostic and statistical manual of mental disorders* (4th ed.). Washington, DC: Author.

Bogat, G. A., DeJohnghe, E., Levendosky, A. A., Davidson, W. S., & von Eye, A. (2006). Trauma symptoms among infants exposed to intimate partner violence. *Child Abuse and Neglect, 30,* 109–125.

Cicchetti, D., Rogosch, F. A., & Toth, S. L. (2006). Fostering secure attachment in infants in maltreating families through preventive interventions. *Development and Psychopathology, 18,* 623–650.

Cicchetti D., Toth, S. L., & Rogosch, F. A. (1999). The efficacy of toddler-parent psychotherapy to increase attachment security in offspring of depressed mothers. *Attachment and Human Development, 1,* 34–66.

Courchesne, E., Chisum, H. J., Townsend, J., Cowles, A., Covington, J., Egaas, B., et al. (2000). Normal brain development and aging: Quantitative analysis at in vivo MR imaging in healthy volunteer. *Radiology, 216,* 672–682.

DeJonghe, E. S., Bogat, A., Levendosky, A. A., von Eye, A., & Davidson, W. S. (2005). Infant exposure to domestic violence predicts heightened sensitivity to adult verbal conflict. *Infant Mental Health Journal, 26*(3), 268–281.

Fantuzzo, J., & Fusco, R. (2007). Children's direct sensory exposure to substantiated domestic violence crimes. *Violence and Victims, 22*(2), 158–171.

Farver, J., Natera, L. X., & Frosch, D. L. (1999). Effects of community violence on inner-city preschoolers and their families. *Journal of Applied Developmental Psychology, 21*(1), 143–158.

Farver, J., Xu, Y., Eppe, S., Fernandez, A., & Schwartz, D. (2005). Community violence, family conflict, and preschoolers' socioemotional functioning. *Developmental Psychology, 41*(1), 160–170.

Freud, S. (1959). Inhibitions, symptoms and anxiety. In J. Strachey (Ed. & Trans), *The standard edition of the complete psychological works of Sigmund Freud* (Vol. 20, pp. 87–174). London: Hogarth Press. (Original work published 1926)

Laor, N., Wolmer, L., Mayes, L. C., Gershon, A., Weizman, R., & Cohen, D. J. (1997). Israeli preschool children under Scuds: A 30-month follow-up. *Journal of the American Academy of Child and Adolescent Psychiatry, 36*(3), 349–356.

Levendosky, A. A., Leahy, K. L., Bogat, G. A., Davidson, W. S., & von Eye, A. (2006). Domestic violence, maternal parenting, maternal mental health, and infant externalizing behavior. *Journal of Family Psychology, 20*(4), 544–552.

Lieberman, A. F., Compton, N. C., Van Horn, P., & Ghosh Ippen, C. (2003). *Losing a parent to death in the early years: Guidelines for the treatment of traumatic bereavement in infancy and early childhood.* Washington, DC: Zero to Three Press.

Lieberman, A. F., Ghosh Ippen, C., & Van Horn, P. (2006). Child-parent psychotherapy: 6-month follow-up of a randomized controlled trial. *Journal of the American Academy of Child and Adolescent Psychiatry, 45,* 913–918.

Lieberman, A. F., & Van Horn, P. J. (2004). Assessment and treatment of young children exposed to traumatic events. In J. D. Osofsky (Ed.), *Young children and trauma: Intervention and treatment* (pp. 111–138). New York: Guilford Press.

Lieberman, A. F., & Van Horn, P. J. (2005). *Don't hit my mommy: A manual for child parent psychotherapy with young witnesses of family violence.* Washington, DC: Zero to Three Press.

Lieberman, A. F., Van Horn, P. J., & Ghosh Ippen, C. (2005). Toward evidence-based treatment: Child-parent psychotherapy with preschoolers exposed to marital violence. *Journal of the American Academy of Child and Adolescent Psychiatry, 44,* 1241–1248.

Lieberman, A. F., Van Horn, P. J., & Ozer, E. J. (2005). Preschooler witnesses of marital violence: Predictors and mediators of child behavior problems. *Development and Psychopathology, 17,* 385–396.

Lieberman, A. F., Weston, D. R., & Pawl, J. H. (1991). Preventive intervention and outcome with anxiously attached dyads. *Child Development, 62,* 199–209.

Linares, L. O., Heren, T., Bronfman, E., Zuckerman, B., Augustyn, M., & Tronick, E. (2001). A mediational model for the impact of exposure to community violence on early child behavior problems. *Child Development, 72*(2), 639–652.

Litrownik, A. J., Newton, R., Hunter, W. M., English, D., & Everson, M. D. (2003). Exposure to family violence in young at-risk children: A longitudinal look at the effects of victimization and witnessed physical and psychological aggression. *Journal of Family Violence, 18*(1), 59–73.

McDonald, R., Jouriles, E. N., Briggs-Gowan, M. J., Rosenfield, D., & Carter, A. S. (2007). Violence toward a family member, angry adult conflict, and child adjustment difficulties: Relations in families with 1- to 3-year-old children. *Journal of Family Psychology, 21*(2), 176–184.

McDonald, R., Jouriles, E. N., Ramisetty-Mikler, S., Caetano, R., & Green, C. E. (2006). Estimating the number of American children living in partner-violent families. *Journal of Family Psychology, 20*(1), 137–142.

Pynoos, R. S., Steinberg, A. M., & Piacentini, J. C. (1999). A developmental psychopathology model of childhood traumatic stress and intersection with anxiety disorders. *Biological Psychiatry, 46,* 1542–1554.

Sameroff, A. J., & Fiese, B. H. (2000). Transactional regulation: The developmental ecology of early intervention. In J. P. Shonkoff & S. J. Meisels (Eds.), *Handbook of early childhood intervention* (pp. 135–159). Cambridge: Cambridge University Press.

Scheeringa, M. S., Peebles, C. D., Cook, C. A., & Zeanah, C. H. (2001). Towards establishing procedural, criterion, and discriminant validity for PTSD in early childhood. *Journal of the American Academy of Child and Adolescent Psychiatry, 40*(1), 52–60.

Scheeringa, M. S., Wright, M. J., Hunt, J. P., & Zeanah, C. H. (2006). Factors affecting the diagnosis and prediction of PTSD symptomatology in children and adolescents. *American Journal of Psychiatry, 163,* 644–651.

Scheeringa, M., & Zeanah, C. (2001). A relational perspective on PTSD in early childhood. *Journal of Traumatic Stress, 14,* 799–815.

Shahinfar, A., Fox, N. A., & Leavitt, L. A. (2000). Preschool children's exposure to violence: Relation of behavior problems to parent and child reports. *American Journal of Orthopsychiatry, 70*(1), 115–125.

Shonkoff, J. P., & Phillips, D. A. (2000). *From neurons to neighborhoods: The science of early childhood development.* Washington, DC: National Academy Press.

Slep, A. M., & O'Leary, S. G. (2005). Parent and partner violence in families with young children: Rates, patterns, and connections. *Journal of Consulting and Clinical Psychology, 73,* 435–444.

Stoddard, F. J., Saxe, G., Ronfeldt, H., Drake, J. E., Burns, J., Edgren, C., et al. (2006). Acute stress symptoms in young children with burns. *Journal of the American Academy of Child and Adolescent Psychiatry, 45*(1), 87–93.

Taylor, L., Zuckerman, B., Harik, V., & Groves, B. M. (1994). Witnessing violence by young children and their mothers. *Journal of Developmental and Behavioral Pediatrics, 15*(2), 120–123.

Terr, L. (1988). What happens to early memories of trauma? A study of twenty children under age five at the time of documented traumatic events. *Journal of the American Academy of Child and Adolescent Psychiatry, 27*(1), 96–104.

Toth, S. L., Maughan, A., Manly, J. T., Spagnola, M., & Cicchetti, D. (2002). The relative efficacy of two interventions in altering maltreated preschool children's representational models: Implications for attachment theory. *Developmental Psychopathology, 14,* 877–908.

Toth, S. L., Rogosch, F. A., Cicchetti, D., & Manly, J. T. (2006). The efficacy of toddler-parent psychotherapy to reorganize attachment in the young offspring of mothers with major depressive disorder: A randomized preventive trial. *Journal of Consulting and Clinical Psychology, 74*(6), 1006–1016.

U.S. Department of Health and Human Services. (2007). *America's children: Key national indicators of well-being, 2007*. Retrieved July 14, 2007, from www.childstats.gov/americaschildren/famsoc7.asp.

Watamura, S. E., Donzella, B., Kertes, D. A., & Gunnar, M. R. (2004). Developmental changes in baseline cortisol activity in early childhood: Relations with napping and effortful control. *Developmental Psychobiology, 45,* 125–133.

Yates, T. M., Dodds, M. F., Sroufe, L. A., & Egeland, B. (2003). Exposure to partner violence and child behavior problems: A prospective study controlling for child physical abuse and neglect, child cognitive ability, socioeconomic status, and life stress. *Development and Psychopathology, 15,* 199–218.

CHANDRA GHOSH IPPEN
University of California, San Francisco

ALICIA F. LIEBERMAN
University of California, San Francisco

See also: Child Development; Child Maltreatment; Parent-Child Intervention; Psychodynamic Therapy, Child

INFORMATION PROCESSING

Posttraumatic stress disorder (PTSD) is fundamentally a cognitive disorder. A traumatic event results in a memory which, in turn, gives rise to the hallmark symptoms of the illness. Hence, cognition, especially pathogenic memory, constitutes the core of PTSD (McNally, 2003). Unlike most other psychiatric syndromes, PTSD possesses an "inner logic" (Young, 2004, p. 128). PTSD does not merely constitute a laundry list of unrelated signs and symptoms. Rather, the signs and symptoms are causally interconnected. That is, the concept PTSD implies an etiologic process whereby pathogenic memory produces involuntary, distressing recollections in the form of intrusive thoughts, nightmares, flashbacks, and psychophysiologic reactivity to reminders of the traumatic event. These recollections heighten emotional arousal, as reflected in exaggerated startle responses, hypervigilance, and sleep difficulties. The aversive character of these symptoms, in turn, motivates attempts to avoid anything that might trigger recollections of the trauma.

The diagnosis of PTSD depends mainly on introspective self-reports of disturbing recollections. Although introspection is essential for revealing the content of cognition (e.g., what the intrusive recollections are about), it can seldom reveal the mechanisms that mediate the operation of pathogenic memory (McNally, 2001). Accordingly, researchers have increasingly used methods adapted from the information-processing paradigm to elucidate the cognitive abnormalities constitutive of PTSD. The hallmark of this paradigm is the use of objective (e.g., reaction time) measures to make inferences about underlying cognitive processes. This paradigm supplements traditional methods of assessing cognition that rely on introspective self-reports as disclosed on questionnaires and during clinical interviews.

Emotional Stroop Paradigm

Experimental psychopathologists have used the emotional Stroop paradigm to investigate processes mediating intrusive cognition in PTSD. In this paradigm, subjects are asked to view words of varying emotional significance and to name the colors in which the words appear as quickly as possible while ignoring the meanings of the words. If a word's meaning is intrusively accessible, the subject will experience difficulty ignoring it and naming its color. Hence, delays in color-naming (Stroop interference) provide an indirect, quantitative index of intrusive cognition.

Using this method, McNally, Kaspi, Riemann, and Zeitlin (1990) found that Vietnam veterans with PTSD took longer to name the colors of words related to the war (e.g., firefight) than to name the colors of other negative words (e.g., germs), positive words (e.g., friendship), or neutral words (e.g., neutral). Vietnam veterans without PTSD did not differ in their color-naming times as a function of word type.

Delayed color-naming of trauma-related words has occurred in subjects whose PTSD resulted from shipwrecks, rape, automobile accidents, and childhood sexual abuse (CSA). Unlike rape victims with PTSD, rape victims who have recovered from PTSD following treatment do not exhibit delayed color-naming for trauma words. That is, disappearance of the emotional Stroop effect provides an objective marker of reduction in intrusive recollection following recovery from PTSD.

Stroop interference for trauma words in PTSD appears especially marked when words are blocked by type (i.e., all trauma words appear on a single card or one after another on a computer screen) than when trauma words are intermixed with other words. This implies that multiple mechanisms may contribute to delayed color-naming of trauma words. Attentional capture by trauma words, difficulty disengaging attention from these words, and inter-item semantic priming among trauma words all may contribute to difficulty naming their colors quickly.

Researchers have also tested whether PTSD patients exhibit Stroop interference for subliminal trauma words—those presented for very short durations and followed by visual masks. Most studies, however, have failed to reveal evidence of the phenomenon.

Professional actors, taught how PTSD subjects respond in the paradigm, could not simulate the emotional Stroop effect. Instead of being selectively slow at color-naming trauma words, they exhibited slower color-naming across the board. These findings suggest that this test might help to detect individuals attempting to fake (i.e., malingering) PTSD.

Overgeneral Memory

Individuals with PTSD, as well as those who have suffered depression, exhibit difficulty recalling specific personal memories in response to cue words (e.g., *happy*). Unlike healthy control subjects who readily retrieve specific episodes from their past (e.g., "I was happy on the day I got married"), those with PTSD tend to retrieve "overgeneral" memories referring either to a category of event (e.g., "I'm happy when I'm drinking") or to an extended period of time (e.g., "I was happy during the summer after high school"). An overgeneral memory style is associated with poor problem-solving skills, difficulty envisioning one's future, and with difficulty overcoming depression.

Overgeneral memory characterizes individuals with trauma histories, especially those with PTSD (e.g., McNally, Litz, Prassas, Shin, & Weathers, 1994). That is, although these individuals remember their traumatic events all too well, they experience difficulty retrieving other memories from their past when asked to do so in response to cue words.

Although failure to retrieve vivid, specific memories from one's past might function as an emotion-regulation strategy (e.g., cognitive avoidance), recent data indicate that it likely results from deficits in working memory capacity and in attentional control.

Explicit and Implicit Memory Biases

Recall tests tap explicit memory. Explicit memory tasks require conscious recollection of previous experiences (e.g., encountering a word during the experiment's study phase), whereas implicit memory tests reflect previous experiences without requiring conscious recollection of these experiences. If information about trauma is primed in people with PTSD, this may be evident on implicit memory tasks. Therefore, material related to trauma should be highly accessible for people with PTSD and they should recall more trauma words than nontrauma words. Most studies have confirmed that PTSD patients exhibit a recall bias for trauma words (e.g., Paunovic, Lundh, & Åst, 2002).

Amir, McNally, and Wiegartz (1996) tested for implicit memory biases for conceptually complex material. In this experiment, they asked Vietnam veterans with and without PTSD to listen to sentences that were either trauma-relevant (e.g., "The chopper landed in hot LZ [landing zone]") or neutral (e.g., "The shiny red apple sat on the table"). They later listened to these old sentences intermixed with new sentences that were either trauma-relevant or neutral. All of the sentences were embedded in white noise of either low, medium, or high volume. The veterans were asked to rate the volume of the noise accompanying each of these sentences. Implicit memory for old sentences would be revealed if subjects rated the noise accompanying these sentences as less loud than the noise accompanying new sentences, and an implicit memory bias for trauma would be revealed if the difference between volume ratings for new minus old sentences was greater for trauma than for neutral sentences. That is, previous exposure to a sentence should make it easier to hear during a subsequent exposure, thereby making the accompanying noise seem less loud that it otherwise might seem to be. Amir et al. found evidence for this implicit memory bias for trauma sentences in the PTSD group, but only for sentences embedded in the loudest volume of white noise.

Despite some evidence for biases favoring processing of trauma material on conceptual implicit memory paradigms, there is scant evidence for these biases on perceptual implicit memory paradigms (e.g., perceptual identification, word-stem completion). Implicit effects on perceptual tasks are driven by physical (orthographic) features of input, not by its semantic (emotional meaning) aspects.

Directed Forgetting of Trauma-Related Material

Some psychotherapists believe that sexually abused children sometimes acquire an avoidant (or dissociative) encoding style that enables them to disengage attention during abuse episodes. McNally, Metzger, Lasko, Clancy, and Pitman (1998) used a directed forgetting paradigm to test whether adults who had been sexually abused as children are characterized by a heightened ability to disengage attention from trauma cues. They tested three groups of people: women with abuse-related PTSD, women who had experienced CSA but who had no psychiatric illness, and women who had not been sexually abused as children. Subjects viewed a series of trauma (e.g., incest), positive (e.g., celebrate), and neutral (e.g., mailbox) words that appeared on a computer screen. After each word appeared, subjects received instructions

either to forget or to remember the word. After this encoding phase, subjects were asked to recall all words they had seen, irrespective of original instructions. Contrary to the avoidant encoding hypothesis, PTSD-diagnosed subjects exhibited memory impairments for positive and neutral words they were supposed to remember, but they remembered the trauma words very well, including those they were instructed to forget. Rather than exhibiting a superior ability to forget trauma words, the PTSD group experienced relative difficulty disengaging attention from trauma cues and thereby forgetting them. Even subjects who report having once forgotten their CSA do not exhibit superior forgetting abilities for trauma cues in the laboratory.

Cognitive Neuroscience Research

Most information-processing research on PTSD has been confined to elucidating abnormalities at the cognitive level of analysis without regard to how these processes are instantiated in the brain. Experimental psychopathologists, however, are increasingly integrating information-processing methods with those of neuroimaging. For example, in a positron emission tomography study, researchers found that women with CSA-related PTSD, relative to victims without PTSD, had less activation in the anterior cingulate portion of their brains during the emotional Stroop task, but not during the standard Stroop task.

Using functional magnetic resonance imaging, Shin et al. (2001) found that Vietnam veterans with PTSD had diminished rostral anterior cingulate activation when viewing war-related words in the emotional counting Stroop. In this paradigm, subjects viewed displays that contained varying numbers of copies of words of different emotional valence (e.g., firefight, firefight, firefight). For each trial, subjects pushed a key corresponding to the number of copies of the word (e.g., 3). Response latency to indicate the number of copies was delayed to the extent that subjects' attention is captured by the meaning of the word.

Taken together, these studies are consistent with other neuroimaging research suggesting that PTSD is characterized by either a hypoactive medial prefrontal cortex, a hyperresponsive amygdala, or both. Moreover, other findings, such as overgeneral memory difficulties, are likewise consistent with hypoactive prefrontal cortex. Future research on information-processing abnormalities will increasingly incorporate methods from both cognitive psychology and cognitive neuroscience.

REFERENCES

Amir, N., McNally, R. J., & Wiegartz, P. S. (1996). Implicit memory bias for threat in posttraumatic stress disorder. *Cognitive Therapy and Research, 20,* 625–635.

McNally, R. J. (2001). On the scientific status of cognitive appraisal models of anxiety disorder. *Behaviour Research and Therapy, 39,* 513–521.

McNally, R. J. (2003). *Remembering trauma.* Cambridge, MA: Belknap Press/Harvard University Press.

McNally, R. J., Kaspi, S. P., Riemann, B. C., & Zeitlin, S. B. (1990). Selective processing of threat cues in posttraumatic stress disorder. *Journal of Abnormal Psychology, 99,* 398–402.

McNally, R. J., Litz, B. T., Prassas, A., Shin, L. M., & Weathers, F. W. (1994). Emotional priming of autobiographical memory in post-traumatic stress disorder. *Cognition and Emotion, 8,* 351–367.

McNally, R. J., Metzger, L. J., Lasko, N. B., Clancy, S. A., & Pitman, R. K. (1998). Directed forgetting of trauma cues in adult survivors of childhood sexual abuse with and without posttraumatic stress disorder. *Journal of Abnormal Psychology, 107,* 596–601.

Paunovic, N., Lundh, L.-G., & Äst, L.-G. (2002). Attentional and memory bias for emotional information in crime victims with acute posttraumatic stress disorder (PTSD). *Journal of Anxiety Disorders, 16,* 675–692.

Shin, L. M., Whalen, P. J., Pitman, R. K., Bush, G., Macklin, M. L., Lasko, N. B., et al. (2001). An fMRI study of anterior cingulated function in posttraumatic stress disorder. *Biological Psychiatry, 50,* 932–942.

Young, A. (2004). When traumatic memory was a problem: On the historical antecedents of PTSD. In G. M. Rosen (Ed.), *Posttraumatic stress disorder: Issues and controversies* (pp. 127–146). Chichester, West Sussex, England: Wiley.

RECOMMENDED READINGS

Constans, J. I. (2005). Information-processing biases in PTSD. In J. J. Vasterling & C. R. Brewin (Eds.), *Neuropsychology of PTSD: Biological, cognitive, and clinical perspectives* (pp. 105–130). New York: Guilford Press.

McNally, R. J. (2006). Cognitive abnormalities in post-traumatic stress disorder. *Trends in Cognitive Sciences, 10,* 271–277.

RICHARD J. McNALLY
Harvard University

See also: Cognitive Impairments; Cognitive Integration, Biopsychosocial; Frontal Cortex; Memory

INSOMNIA

Individuals with posttraumatic stress disorder (PTSD) experience sleep disruptions. In several different PTSD samples, sleep difficulties were the most prevalent of any PTSD symptom. As compared to normal controls, individuals with PTSD are more likely to report difficulties falling asleep, staying asleep, awakening from nightmares, and experiencing nonrestorative sleep. Most trauma survivors are likely to report more than one of these problems. Patients with PTSD may report having more severe sleep disturbances than is evident by polysomnographic sleep studies. A recent meta-analysis by Kobayashi and colleagues (Kobayashi, Boarts, & Delahanty, 2007) suggests that this may be due to a number of moderating variables not accounted for in research studies.

Posttraumatic insomnia often develops in the context of preexisting and perpetuating influences. Although scant research is available on preexisting sleep disturbances in trauma survivors, a few studies queried patients about their sleep habits prior to a traumatic event exposure and found that as many as 40% of respondents reported insomnia difficulties prior to developing PTSD. Several authors have suggested that insomnia may be a risk factor for the development of PTSD, although prospective research is necessary to test this hypothesis.

Clinical Presentation

Posttraumatic insomnia interacts with PTSD's hyperarousal symptoms. Survivors often maintain hypervigilance at bedtime because they feel vulnerable at night, potentially because this is the time during which traumatic events may have occurred. In response to this vulnerability, they may engage in behaviors that perpetuate anxiety or insomnia. For instance, they may check the locks on their doors multiple times, use substances aimed at inducing relaxation but may instead induce insomnia (e.g., alcohol, coffee, nicotine), or try to fall asleep to the television in order to distract oneself from the anxiety-provoking silence. Intrusion symptoms, such as traumatic memories, nightmares, and flashbacks, exacerbate arousal symptoms and thus promote more sleeplessness. Nightmares also fragment survivors' sleep through periodic or repetitive awakenings, and trauma survivors often report delaying their bedtime to avoid the inevitable disturbing dreams.

This disruptive sleep cycle matches the framework of the following three PTSD symptom clusters defined within the *DSM-IV* (American Psychiatric Association, 1994): intrusion (nightmares) yields hyperarousal (e.g., insomnia) leading to avoidance (actual fear or anxiety about sleeping). From a sleep medicine viewpoint, these precipitants become entrenched to produce maladaptive learned behaviors related to sleep. As the survivor continues to suffer occasional to frequent bad sleep experiences in the bedroom, he or she learns to expect more harmful, unpleasant or dissatisfying sleep experiences.

Moderating and Mediating Variables

In addition to these learned behavioral patterns, insomnia in trauma survivors may also be associated with a number of moderating influences. For instance, younger survivors with posttraumatic insomnia receive less total sleep time as compared to older survivors; whereas, older survivors have less restorative sleep than younger survivors. Also, men with PTSD related to military trauma appear to have more disturbed sleep as compared to other trauma-exposed groups.

Comorbid mental disorders also play a role in posttraumatic insomnia. Preliminary research suggests that the sleep profile of survivors with PTSD and depression differs significantly from the sleep profile of survivors who experience PTSD alone. Trauma survivors experiencing hyperarousal may use alcohol and other sedating substances to facilitate sleep. They may also use caffeine, nicotine, and other alerting substances to maintain vigilance throughout the day or night. Over time, the use of these substances may develop into a comorbid substance abuse or dependence diagnosis.

Medical factors may mediate the development of insomnia in survivors with PTSD. The traumatic event may have had a direct impact on the survivor's body causing physical pain, an extremely common precipitant of unwanted sleeplessness. Trauma survivors are at increased risk for the development of sleep disordered breathing and periodic limb movement disorders. Krakow, Melendrez, Warner, and colleagues (Krakow et al., 2002) suggested that PTSD hypervigilance and sleep disordered breathing symptoms may interact negatively to create increased awareness of nocturnal arousals, increased nightmare recall, and ultimately worse insomnia. Thus, these patients are more likely to experience insomnia than excessive daytime sleepiness.

Finally, traumatic event exposure and social isolation invariably disrupt the survivor's daily routine, creating some degree of disorganization if not outright chaos in lifestyle. The loss of a daily, organized routine that contains regular exposure to light may contribute to circadian dysregulation and trigger insomnia in many survivors.

Conclusion

Trauma survivors have extensive sleep disturbances characterized by subjective reports of poor sleep and difficulties with sleep maintenance. Posttraumatic insomnia is often compounded by hypervigilant and avoidant behaviors. Many trauma survivors report that they experienced insomnia prior to the traumatic event. Insomnia may also occur as a direct physical or mental consequence of traumatic event exposure.

Despite the multiple reasons for the development of insomnia, sustained posttraumatic insomnia is best conceptualized as maladaptive learned behavior related to sleep. However, the pathophysiological interactions between insomnia and other medical sleep conditions such as sleep-breathing or sleep-movement disorders may prove to be critical mediating factors among some as yet undetermined proportion of trauma survivors.

REFERENCES

American Psychiatric Association. (1994). *Diagnostic and statistical manual of mental disorders* (4th ed.). Washington, DC: Author.

Kobayashi, I., Boarts, J. M., & Delahanty, D. L. (2007). Polysomnographically measured sleep abnormalities in PTSD: A meta-analytic review. *Psychophysiology, 44,* 660–669.

Krakow, B. J., Melendrez, D. C., Warner, T. D., Dorin, R., Harper, R., & Hollifield, M. (2002). To breathe, perchance to sleep: Sleep-disordered breathing and chronic insomnia among trauma survivors. *Sleep and Breathing, 6,* 189–198.

RECOMMENDED READINGS

Harvey, A. G., Jones, C., & Schmidt, D. A. (2003). Sleep and posttraumatic stress disorder: A review. *Clinical Psychology Review, 23,* 377–407.

Krakow, B. J., Hollifield, M., Johnston, L., Koss, M., Schrader, R., Warner, T. D., et al. (2001). Imagery rehearsal therapy for chronic nightmares in sexual assault survivors with posttraumatic stress disorder. *Journal of the American Medical Association, 286,* 537–545.

Krakow, B. J., Melendrez, D. C., Johnston, L. G., Clark, J. O., Santana, F. M., Warner, T. D., et al. (2002). Sleep dynamic therapy for Cerro Grande Fire evacuees with posttraumatic stress symptoms: A preliminary report. *Journal of Clinical Psychiatry, 63,* 673–684.

Wittmann, L., Schredl, M., & Kramer, M. (2007). Dreaming in posttraumatic stress disorder: A critical review of phenomenology, psychophysiology and treatment. *Psychotherapy and Psychosomatics, 76,* 25–39.

BARRY KRAKOW
Sleep and Human Health Institute

PATRICIA L. HAYNES
University of Arizona

See also: Hyperarousal; Nightmares

INTERGENERATIONAL EFFECTS

The problems experienced by survivors of psychological traumas may be passed down to their descendents, especially their children and even their grandchildren (Danieli, 1998). These latter groups are referred to as the "second generation" and "third generation" of trauma survivors, respectively. Psychological trauma, especially massive traumas such as genocide, may have long-term effects not only on the victimized generation, but also on the next generations that did not endure the traumatic events directly.

Social scientists and clinicians concerned with the intergenerational consequences of trauma have focused particularly on Holocaust survivors and their offspring. Study of the second generation began with clinical reports by psychiatrists and psychologists starting to treat children of survivors of Nazi concentration camps who sought treatment at a Montreal psychiatric facility. On this basis, clinical researchers proposed that the psychiatric distress of these youth reflected a "survivor syndrome" (Niederland, 1968), transmitted and perpetuated from one generation to the next (Barocas & Barocas, 1973). Researchers set out to study the existence of a "children-of-survivor syndrome," and sought to understand the process whereby parents' Holocaust experiences may have affected the emotional development of their children who were not directly exposed to the massive trauma.

Similarly, based on the treatment of children of Vietnam War veterans whose parents (primarily fathers) were treated for posttraumatic stress disorder (PTSD), clinicians described symptoms and features that these children suffered, such as high levels of anxiety, nightmares, aggressiveness, and preoccupation with specific traumatic events through which the parent actually lived. To indicate the association between the children's and the parent's own PTSD symptoms, this process was labeled "secondary traumatization" (Rosenheck & Nathan, 1985).

Further clinical studies of Holocaust survivors' children who presented for psychotherapy, especially those raised in North America and Israel, portrayed characteristic conflicts and recurrent patterns such as depression, guilt, aggression, problems in interpersonal relationships, separation-individuation conflicts, and identity issues. However, it was suggested that these patterns and symptoms should not be labeled a "syndrome" but rather a "complex" or "profile," since many of the features did not contribute to the formation of psychopathology, and some even constituted expressions of strength. Given that these studies were based on clinical samples of survivors' offspring, researchers set out to test intergenerational effects empirically by studying nonclinical samples and comparing them to control groups without a Holocaust family background (reviewed in Felsen, 1998; Z. Solomon, 1998).

Studies based on nonclinical samples of children of Holocaust survivors did not generally support the bleak picture portrayed in clinical settings. Most studies comparing nonclinical samples of survivors' offspring with control groups reported no significant differences between them and their comparable counterparts on various aspects of personality, family atmosphere, and mental health. This striking discrepancy between clinical case studies and nonclinical controlled studies, and the generally equivocal findings on the second generation have been documented in major reviews of the numerous publications of the past 3 decades (Bar-On et al., 1998). The reviews, conducted mostly in the 1990s, were based on the common qualitative review method, namely counting studies that support and refute intergenerational effects. This reviewing method has been criticized for not taking into account the highly heterogeneous quality and size of samples in the studies.

Meta-analytic procedures, in contrast, facilitate a quantitative analysis (i.e., computing average effect size across studies) that considers the characteristics of each study reviewed. Van

IJzendoorn, Bakermans-Kranenburg, and Sagi-Schwartz (2003) conducted a highly sophisticated meta-analytic investigation (32 samples with 4,418 participants) of the question: "Are children of Holocaust survivors less well-adapted than comparable individuals?" Including only studies of children of survivors and comparison groups, their meta-analysis made important distinctions, taking into account the recruitment and sample characteristics. They showed that only in studies that recruited second-generation participants through convenience samples ("nonselected") rather than through random sampling ("selected") was there evidence of less well-being or poorer psychosocial adaptation than in the comparison group. The distinction between nonclinical and clinical samples, such as survivors' children who themselves were Israeli combat veterans suffering from PTSD after the 1982 Lebanon war (Z. Solomon, Kotler, & Mikulincer, 1988), or breast cancer patients (Baider et al., 2000), led van IJzendoorn and colleagues to conclude that only among offspring who experienced other serious stressors (e.g., combat exposure or breast cancer) did evidence exist of the influence of the parents' traumatic Holocaust experiences on the children's adjustment (more severe posttraumatic stress symptoms). No indication of such effects (i.e., secondary traumatization) was found in the nonclinical samples of offspring of Holocaust survivors.

Despite the sophistication of meta-analytic methodology, given its reliance on quantitative data, it cannot include studies resting on qualitative-narrative methodology, which are also requisite to address such a complex phenomenon as intergenerational effects of trauma (Bar-On et al., 1998).

Studies of survivors' grandchildren consider intergenerational effects on the third generation, who are another generation removed from the survivors' trauma, as they were born to parents (the second generation) who themselves were not exposed directly to the traumatic events. Recently, Sagi-Schwartz, van IJzendoorn, and Bakermans-Kranenburg (2007) reviewed the literature on the adjustment of the third generation of Holocaust survivors. Obviously the number of such studies is much smaller than those on the survivors and their children; still, 23 papers were identified, of which only 13 met the criteria of containing at least one comparison group. A meta-analysis of these 13 samples (involving 1,012 participants) led these researchers to conclude that there was no evidence for "tertiary traumatization" in Holocaust survivor families.

Studies on the third generation within an attachment framework allow consideration of how the parenting that the second generation experienced from their survivor parents may have affected their parenting of their own children, the third generation. Developmental psychology defines intergenerational transmission of parenting as "the process through which purposively or unintendedly an earlier generation psychologically influences parenting attitudes and behavior of the next generation" (van IJzendoorn, 1992, p. 76). Among the mechanisms at work in intergenerational transmission of parenting appear to be the way parents interpret their children's behavior, as well as the way they interpret their own parents' behavior in retrospect, parents' expectations from relationships, and parents' metacognitive functioning.

In a research design with three generations, based on careful matching of Holocaust survivor and comparisons (Sagi-Schwartz et al., 2003), 98 families with grandmother, mother, and infant completed attachment- and trauma-related interviews and questionnaires; the infants and their mothers engaged in Ainsworth's "strange situation" procedure (i.e., a laboratory procedure that involves the parent and a female stranger alternately leaving and returning to the baby) that assesses an infant's attachment security (see J. Solomon & George, 1999). The grandmothers, who were child survivors of the Holocaust, showed more severe signs of traumatic stress than the comparison grandmothers, but they were not impaired in general adaptation. The traumatic effects, however, did not transmit to the mothers (second generation) or to their infants (third generation). Sagi-Schwartz and colleagues (2003, 2007) pointed out the remarkable resilience of traumatized survivors in their

parental roles, even when they themselves were profoundly traumatized.

Another recent study focused on the parenting of second generation mothers and the psychosocial functioning of third generation adolescent grandchildren of Holocaust survivors in the context of the home-leaving transition due to mandatory military service (Scharf, 2007). Two subgroups of this sample of an adolescent third generation were formed: one with both parents, and the other with one parent, being the second generation of Holocaust survivors. Both subgroups were compared with a non-Holocaust background group. Only the both-parent subgroup perceived both mothers and fathers as less accepting and less encouraging of independence; they showed higher levels of ambivalent attachment style, and their peers perceived them as displaying poorer adjustment than their fellow recruits in army basic training in the one-parent subgroup (who were similar to the non-Holocaust group). This study suggests the possibility of the cumulative effects of stress on the third generation when both parents in the family are offspring of survivors, even though, as indicated for the second generation, these are still within the normative range of psychological functioning.

In considering mechanisms of transmission—that is, how traumatic stress experienced by persons of one generation may affect their offspring—an important distinction has been made between two different types of transmission (Schwartz, Dohrenwend, & Levav, 1994). One is "direct-specific" transmission, whereby children learn to behave and think in traumatic stress-related ways similar to those of their parents, resulting in higher rates in the children of the same disorders suffered by the parents who underwent the traumas. The other is "nondirect-general" transmission, whereby the children's difficulties are due to the long-term effects of their parents' extreme traumatization, which cause impairments in the survivor-parents' capacity for parenting that are expected to lead to a variety of psychological problems in the offspring, but not necessarily the ones the parents' suffer. Although it is difficult to test the unique effects of these two types of transmission, there is some evidence to support each type. Yehuda and colleagues (Yehuda, Halligan, & Bierer, 2002) who studied direct effects of the parents' PTSD on PTSD in their offspring, found lowered cortisol excretion (considered a biological marker of risk for PTSD) in a nonselect sample of adult offspring, but only when both parents were reported with PTSD (Yehuda et al., 2002). Some support for nondirect general effects on adult offspring have been found in the area of psychological separation-individuation and interpersonal sensitivities, although within the range of normal psychosocial functioning (reviewed in Felsen, 1998).

According to attachment theory, traumatized parents who are overwhelmed by memories of past abuse or with unresolved losses display frightened or frightening behavior, leading to failure in adequate responsiveness to the child's needs, leaving the child feeling unprotected and frightened (Hess & Main, 1999; Scharf, 2007). Studies on intergenerational patterns in female survivors of childhood sexual abuse (CSA) have begun to explore the long-term interpersonal consequences for parent-child relationships and child adjustment in the succeeding generation (Rumstein-McKean & Hunsley, 2001). The attachment framework may be especially relevant to the case of CSA survivors as in many of these survivors the trauma was inflicted by the attachment figures, causing a breakdown of trust. This is unlike the case of child Holocaust survivors wherein the traumatic events came from an almost anonymous destructive force (Sagi-Schwartz et al., 2003). Future research on second-generation effects of unresolved trauma in nonmaltreating parents, within an attachment framework, will provide further insight into these mechanisms of intergenerational transmission both in relation to individual dispositions and the caregiving environment (see Cassidy & Mohr, 2001).

The familial communication pattern (verbal and nonverbal) about the forbears' traumatic experiences, referred to as the "conspiracy of silence," is considered a key aspect in the intergenerational transmission in families of survivors of various trauma, such as inmates of Japanese American internment camps, Dutch wartime sailors and resistance veterans, Vietnam War veterans, torture victims, and others (Danieli, 1998; Daud, Skoglund, & Rydelius, 2005). An intergenerational communication pattern characterized by nonverbal communication about the Holocaust, coupled with a lack of knowledge of the parents' Holocaust experiences, termed "knowing-not-knowing," was found to be related to higher interpersonal distress in offspring of Holocaust survivors (Wiseman et al., 2002). When the intergenerational consequences of the traumatic events also carry a stigma for the offspring in the form of physical repercussions, as in the case of the survivors of A-bombings of Hiroshima and Nagasaki, disclosure about the psychological traumas may be profoundly silenced (Sawada, Chaitin, & Bar-On, 2004).

According to family theories on multigenerational processes, the "family legacy" of the trauma is passed down to the next generations, especially when the trauma is silenced and closure is absent in the older generation (Chaitin, 2002; Lev-Wiesel, 2007). The wider sociocultural-historical context plays an important role in opening lines of communication and in the working-through process in the family and within society. Cross-cultural studies are needed to further test these multigenerational hypotheses and to examine various variables contributing to both vulnerability and resiliency (Danieli, 1998; Z. Solomon, 1998).

The study of intergenerational effects that began with clinical reports has advanced to complex designs of nonclinical samples and the inclusion of nontrauma-exposed comparison groups. The existence of PTSD in survivors and their offspring has been assessed based on advances in the field of trauma and greater understanding of individual differences and the heterogeneity of adaptation among survivors and across generations. The field would benefit from further carefully designed quantitative studies, including meta-analyses, as well as qualitative-narrative studies that are more sensitive to context and emphasize subjective experiences and the meaning of trauma in the life stories of the survivors and their descendents. Future studies are needed to explore both areas of vulnerability to traumatization across generations, as well as areas of resilience and positive effects.

REFERENCES

Baider, L., Peretz, T., Ever Hadani, P., Perry, S., Avramov, R., & Kaplan De-Nour, A. (2000). Transmission of response to trauma? Second-generation Holocaust survivors' reaction to cancer. *American Journal of Psychiatry, 157,* 904–910.

Barocas, A. H., & Barocas, B. C. (1973). Manifestations of concentration camp effects on the second generation. *American Journal of Psychiatry, 130,* 820–821.

Bar-On, D., Eland, J., Kleber, R. J., Krell, R., Moore, Y., Sagi, A., et al. (1998). Multigenerational perspectives on coping with the holocaust experience: An attachment perspective for understanding the developmental sequelae of trauma across generations. *International Journal of Behavioral Development, 22*(2), 315–338.

Cassidy, J., & Mohr, J. J. (2001). Unsolvable fear, trauma, and psychopathology: Theory, research, and clinical considerations related to disorganized attachment across the life span. *Clinical Psychology: Science and Practice, 8,* 275–298.

Chaitin, J. (2002). Issues and interpersonal values among three generations in families of Holocaust survivors. *Journal of Social and Personal Relationships, 19,* 379–402.

Danieli, Y. (Ed.). (1998). *International handbook of multigenerational legacies of trauma.* New York: Plenum Press.

Daud, A., Skoglund, E., & Rydelius, P. A. (2005). Children in families of torture victims: Transgenerational transmission of parents' traumatic experiences to their children. *International Journal of Social Welfare, 14,* 23–32.

Felsen, I. (1998). Transgenerational transmission of effects of the Holocaust: The North American research perspective. In Y. Danieli (Ed.), *International handbook of multigenerational legacies of trauma* (pp. 43–69). New York: Plenum Press.

Hess, E., & Main, M. (1999). Second-generation effects of unresolved trauma in nonmaltreating parents: Dissociated, frightened, and threatening parental behavior. *Psychoanalytic Inquiry, 19,* 481–540.

Lev-Wiesel, R. (2007). Intergeneration transmission of trauma across three generations: A preliminary study. *Qualitative Social Work, 6,* 75–94.

Niederland, W. (1968). Clinical observations on the survivors syndrome. *International Journal of Psychoanalysis, 49,* 313–319.

Rosenheck, R., & Nathan, P. (1985). Secondary traumatization in children of Vietnam veterans. *Hospital and Community Psychiatry, 36,* 538–539.

Rumstein-McKean, O., & Hunsley, J. (2001). Interpersonal and family functioning of female survivors of childhood sexual abuse. *Clinical Psychology Review, 21,* 471–490.

Sagi-Schwartz, A., van IJzendoorn, M. H., & Bakermans-Kranenburg, M. J. (2007). *Does intergenerational transmission of trauma skip a generation? No meta-analytic evidence for tertiary traumatization with third generation of Holocaust survivors.* Haifa, Israel: University of Haifa, Center for the Study of Child Development.

Sagi-Schwartz, A., van IJzendoorn, M. H., Grossmann, K. E., Joels, T., Grossmann, K., Scharf, M., et al. (2003). Attachment and traumatic stress in female Holocaust child survivors and their daughters. *American Journal of Psychiatry, 160,* 1086–1092.

Sawada, A., Chaitin, J., & Bar-On, D. (2004). Surviving Hiroshima and Nagasaki: Experiences and psychosocial meanings. *Psychiatry, 67,* 43–60.

Scharf, M. (2007). Long-term effects of trauma: Psychological functioning of the second and third generation of Holocaust survivors. *Development and Psychopathology, 19,* 603–622.

Schwartz, S., Dohrenwend, B., & Levav, I. (1994). Nongenetic familial transmission of psychiatric disorders? Evidence from children of holocaust survivors. *Journal of Health and Social Behaviour, 35,* 385–402.

Solomon, J., & George, C. (1999). The measurement of attachment security in infancy and childhood. In J. Cassidy & P. R. Shaver (Eds.), *Handbook of attachment: Theory, research, and clinical applications* (pp. 287–316). New York: Guilford Press.

Solomon, Z. (1998). Transgenerational effects of the Holocaust: The Israeli research perspective. In Y. Danieli (Ed.), *International handbook of multigenerational legacies of trauma* (pp. 69–85). New York: Plenum Press.

Solomon, Z., Kotler, M., & Mikulincer, M. (1988). Combat-related posttraumatic stress disorder among second-generation Holocaust survivors:

Preliminary findings. *American Journal of Psychiatry, 145,* 865–868.

van IJzendoorn, M. H. (1992). Intergenerational transmission of parenting: A review of studies in nonclinical populations. *Developmental Review, 12,* 76–99.

van IJzendoorn, M. H., Bakermans-Kranenburg, M. J., & Sagi-Schwartz, A. (2003). Are children of Holocaust survivors less well-adapted? A meta-analytic investigation of secondary traumatization. *Journal of Traumatic Stress, 16,* 459–469.

Wiseman, H., Barber, J. P., Raz, A., Yam, I., Foltz, C., & Livne-Snir, S. (2002). Parental communication of Holocaust experiences and interpersonal patterns in offspring of Holocaust survivors. *International Journal of Behavioral Development, 26*(4), 371–381.

Yehuda, R., Halligan, S. L., & Bierer, L. M. (2002). Cortisol levels in adult offspring of Holocaust survivors: Relation to PTSD symptom severity in the parent and child. *Psychoneuroendocrinology, 27,* 171–180.

HADAS WISEMAN
University of Haifa

See also: Family Systems; Holocaust, The

INTERNATIONAL ORGANIZATIONS

The impact of psychological trauma on diverse groups of people across multiple regions of the world has led to the formation of organizations that represent the collective interests of people who are affected by traumatic events and those who serve survivors' needs. These organizations have mostly taken the form of member societies, which are associations of individuals who have united voluntarily based on their common aspirations and shared targets of emphasis (e.g., children's welfare, war, disasters, human trafficking). While these organizations clearly pursue a humanitarian set of objectives, they are also meaningfully distinct from international humanitarian organizations (commonly known as nongovernmental organizations or NGOs; *see:* **Nongovernmental Organizations**) because they focus almost

entirely on psychosocial aspects of critical events and even more particularly on traumatic stress and psychological trauma.

Members of these organizations are diverse and often include trauma victims, grassroots activists, chaplains, clinicians, law enforcement personnel, and professionals in the health and human services fields (Bloom, 2000). The diversity of the member profiles reflects the mix of sociopolitical influences that served as a catalyst for the formation of many of these international organizations. These influences, dating back to the 1960s and the 1970s, often reflected the salient issues of those times, such as veterans of the Vietnam War being misdiagnosed and receiving ineffective or inadequate clinical treatment, domestic violence victims receiving increasing recognition with the rise of the feminist movement; and child abuse victims grappling with the presence and devastating consequences of child maltreatment. It is in the midst of such an intense sociopolitical global climate that several regional societies around the world were formed, to bring recognition, diagnostic clarification, and treatment methods to the traumatic experience and related phenomena. Moreover, these organizations have been committed to developing guidelines and standards of practice to promote ethically sound services and treatments.

Strategic Focus

The majority of the regional member societies focused on psychological trauma are housed under an overlapping global umbrella model that aims to foster intersociety collaboration and dialogue (Weisaeth, 1993). However, while many of these international organizations share similar underlying ideologies, strategic nuances in their missions and activities distinguish the activities of some international organizations from others. These strategic nuances can be delineated along four major themes: (1) geographic areas of focus, (2) relative importance of research versus clinical focus, (3) theoretical underpinnings of diagnostic categories related to psychological trauma's effects, and (4) focus on specific victim populations. Each of these four themes, while not necessarily being mutually exclusive, serves to organize the present discussion of the global landscape of organizations focused on psychological trauma.

Geographic Areas of Focus

The International Society for Traumatic Stress Studies (ISTSS) and its member affiliates can be characterized as an interconnected network spanning various geographic regions of the world. The ISTSS was founded in the United States in 1985, with the mission to exchange and advance knowledge on severe stress and trauma, so as to promote prevention, intervention methods, and advocacy initiatives in the field of trauma (Bloom, 2000; International Society for Traumatic Stress Studies, n.d.). Similarly, the European Society of Traumatic Stress Studies (ESTSS) was formed 8 years later, in 1993. The main objective of ESTSS was to create a European network to facilitate the interaction "between academic institutions, treatment centers and individuals with shared interests in the effects of trauma and their resolution" (European Society for Traumatic Stress Studies, n.d.). In addition to the 16 European countries that formed the organization, ESTSS also represented a few non-European countries as well, including Israel, United States, Palestine, South Africa, and Australia (de Loos, 1995). In response to the linguistic diversity of Europe, two member societies—the Association of French Language for the Study of the Stress and Trauma (L'Association de Langue Française pour l'Etude du Stress et du Trauma, or ALFEST) and the German-Language Society for Psychotraumatology (Deutschsprachige Gesellschaft für Psychotraumatologie, or DeGPT)—were created to meet the needs of the French-speaking and German-speaking members, respectively. These organizations remained affiliated to the ESTSS and the ISTSS, reflecting the overlapping collaborative network that connected the various regional and linguistic societies.

The ISTSS and ESTSS also formed a supporting network for several member affiliates in other geographic regions of the world, such as the Canadian Traumatic Stress Network (CTSN), the Australasian Society for Traumatic Stress Studies (ASTSS), the Argentine Society for Psychotrauma (SAPsi), and the African Society for Traumatic Stress Studies (AfSTSS). The CTSN's mission is to organize a network of resources in Canada that are focused on traumatic stress services via enhancing public awareness, professional development and research (Canadian Traumatic Stress Network, n.d.). The Australasian Society for Traumatic Stress Studies (ASTSS) focuses on a similar mission encompassing Australia, New Zealand, and the Pacific Rim (Australian Society for Traumatic Stress Studies, n.d.). In response to a gap in comprehensive coverage of Asia, 2005 saw the formation of the Asian Society for Traumatic Stress Studies (Asian STSS), headquartered in Hong Kong, to bring greater focus to research and clinical initiatives in the Asian region (Asian Society for Traumatic Stress Studies, n.d.).

Research versus Clinical Focus

The creation of the Association of Traumatic Stress Specialists (ATSS) in 1989 signaled a move away from a mission laden with academic and research emphasis, toward relatively more practical clinical considerations, including the exploration of credentialing and training possibilities for professionals working with trauma victims. The key mission of the ATSS as it stands today is to "develop standards of service and education for those who provide critical emotional care to trauma victims and survivors" (Association of Traumatic Stress Specialists, n.d.). ATSS specializes in offering internationally recognized certification for professionals working in the trauma field.

Diagnostic Categorization of Traumatic Stress Disorders

The formation of the International Society for the Study of Dissociation in the mid-1980s, later renamed International Society for the Study of Trauma and Dissociation (ISSTD) in November 2006, marked the recognition of dissociative symptoms associated with traumatic experiences. This characterization stood in contrast to the implicit diagnostic status quo of trauma being strongly associated, first and foremost, with anxiety and stress. ISSTD's mission is to address the clinical relevance and empirical validity of interventions that take into account the importance of dissociation in the presentation of trauma (International Society for the Study of Trauma and Dissociation, n.d.). In addition, ISSTD provided a timely forum in the 1990s to address some of the heated controversies surrounding repressed memories of child abuse, and to build research and clinical bridges between the study of trauma, memory, and child abuse (Freyd, DePrince, & Zurbriggen, 2001). Both ISTSS and ISSTD are actively working to inform the American Psychological Association's development of the next version of the *Diagnostic and Statistical Manual of Mental Disorders* (*DSM-V*) in order to ensure that that widely used guide to diagnosis includes not only PTSD but also complex, psychological trauma-related disorders (*see:* **Complex Posttraumatic Stress Disorder**) and dissociative disorders (*see:* **Dissociation**).

Specific Victim Populations

A notable phenomenon in the 1990s and beyond is the explosion of grassroots, regional, national, and international groups focused on specific victim populations and their unique needs vis-à-vis the trauma experience. Organizations, such as the Global Alliance against Trafficking in Women (GAATF), International Society for Prevention of Child Abuse and Neglect (ISPCAN), World Society of Victimology (WSV), and World Organization against Torture have all begun to traverse the international platform by bringing awareness to the multifaceted needs of specific victim populations. A question that has been posed in the field is whether the sprouting of these organizations marks the next big challenge awaiting the field of psychological trauma—the extent to which the global community can coordinate overarching initiatives in psychological trauma with the unique needs

of specific victim populations. This challenge is succinctly stated in the strategic document of the World Society of Victimology:

> The nature and extent of victimization is not adequately understood across the world. Millions of people throughout the world suffer harm as a result of crime, the abuse of power, terrorism and other stark misfortunes. Their rights and needs as victims of this harm have not been adequately recognized. (World Society of Victimology, 2007)

Accomplishments

International organizations in the field of psychological trauma have contributed to a substantial number of accomplishments over the past 2 decades. By 1993, psycho-historians Wilson and Raphael (1993) noted the presence of newly minted reference books on trauma and related syndromes, standardized psychological assessments, growing knowledge on the biological bases of PTSD, and enhanced understanding of targeted therapeutic techniques. These intertwined organizations were vital in creating an international knowledge-sharing platform that furthered theory and practice in the field. If the first decade (i.e., 1985 to 1995) was characterized by establishing the semantic foundation for the research, policy and clinical practice, the second decade and beyond (i.e., 1995 to present) is striking in several aspects. Contributions of psychological trauma specialists have entered mainstream research and clinical dialogue, with empirically supported interventions and well-established practice guidelines. The development of internationally recognized certification for trauma responders has led to standards and a common language for clinical dialogue. Peer-reviewed journal publications of many of the organizations, such as the *Journal of Traumatic Stress* (through ISSTS), *Journal of Trauma and Dissociation* (through ISSTD), and those from organizations such as the *International Journal of Victimology* (ALFEST), and the *Australasian Journal of Disaster and Trauma Studies* (Massey University, n.d.) have achieved widespread international readership.

A most recent development has been the release of *Guidelines on Mental Health and Psychosocial Support in Emergency Settings* produced by the Inter-Agency Standing Committee (IASC, 2007). The IASC, a forum representing the key agencies of the United Nations (UN) and their non-UN humanitarian partners, was established in 1992 to improve the members' joint capacity for coordination, policy development, and decision making. In recognition of the growing need for a framework that would guide humanitarian organizations in their efforts to relief psychosocial distress and support optimal recovery in the face of disasters and other forms of adversity, a task force was formed that could survey expert opinion and scientific research and derive from their analyses a set of consensus principles of responsible action. Among their goals was to improve the systematic coordination of humanitarian activities intended to enhance psychosocial resilience and to encourage greater accountability among humanitarian organizations for serving these needs. The guidelines themselves stress the importance of bolstering local cultural and community resources rather than displacing them or otherwise competing with or devaluing the very people who could prove most helpful. The broad and inclusive involvement of many highly respected participants from around the globe lent instant credibility to this effort.

Conclusion

Strong sociopolitical influences of a global scale catalyzed the formation of several member societies around the world focused on the impact and ramifications of psychological trauma. A majority of these member societies are arranged in an interconnected international network that fosters collaboration. Strategic nuances in the missions of these organizations distinguish their respective activities. The strategic landscape can be described in terms of geographic areas of focus, research versus clinical focus, diagnostic categorization of trauma, and a focus on specific victim populations. Despite these strategic nuances, the overlapping and affiliative ties between many of the organizations have resulted in collaborative dialogue and an international platform for new

initiatives, thereby fortifying the global organizational response to psychological trauma.

REFERENCES

Asian Society for Traumatic Stress Studies. (n.d.). *What is Asian STSS?* Retrieved January 2, 2008, from www.asianstss.org/whatisasianstss.htm.

Association of Traumatic Stress Specialists. (n.d.). *Mission.* Retrieved January 2, 2008, from www.atss.info.

Australian Society for Traumatic Stress Studies. (n.d.). *Mission of ASTSS.* Retrieved January 2, 2008, from www.astss.org.au/site.

Bloom, S. L. (2000). Our hearts and hopes are turned to peace: Origins of the international society for traumatic stress studies. In A. Y. Shalev, R. Yehuda, & A. C. McFarlane (Eds.), *International handbook of human response to trauma* (pp. 27–50). New York: Kluwer Academic/Plenum Press.

Canadian Traumatic Stress Network. (n.d.). *Mission and goals.* Retrieved January 2, 2008, from www.ctsn-rcst.ca/Mission.html.

de Loos, W. (1995). Regional update: Europe. *Stresspoints, 9*(1), 7.

European Society for Traumatic Stress Studies. (n.d.). *History of the European Society for Traumatic Stress Studies.* Retrieved January 2, 2008, from www.estss.org/info/past.htm.

Freyd, J., DePrince, A., & Zurbriggen, E. (2001). Self-reported memory for abuse depends upon victim-perpetrator relationship. *Journal of Trauma and Dissociation, 2*(3), 5–17.

Inter-Agency Standing Committee. (2007). *IASC Guidelines on mental health and psychosocial support in emergency settings.* Geneva, Switzerland: Author.

International Society for the Study of Trauma and Dissociation. (n.d.). *About the ISSTD.* Retrieved January 2, 2008, from www.isst-d.org/about/about-index.htm.

International Society for Traumatic Stress Studies. (n.d.). *ISTSS mission statement.* Retrieved January 2, 2008, from www.istss.org/what/index.cfm.

Massey University, New Zealand. (n.d.). *Australian Journal of Disaster and Trauma studies.* Retrieved January 2, 2008, from www.massey.ac.nz/~trauma.

Weisaeth, L. (1993). Report from the European region. *Stresspoints, 7*(2), 3.

Wilson, J., & Raphael, B. (1993). *International handbook of traumatic stress syndromes.* New York: Plenum Press.

World Society of Victimology. (2007). *The strategic plan of the World Society of Victimology*. Retrieved January 2, 2008, from www.worldsocietyofvicti mology.org.

APARNA RAO
Fielding Graduate University

GILBERT REYES
Fielding Graduate University

See *also:* Human Rights Violations; Humanitarian Intervention; Nongovernmental Organizations

INTERPERSONAL PSYCHOTHERAPY

Interpersonal psychotherapy (IPT) is a time-limited, diagnosis-targeted, life-event-based manualized treatment originally developed to treat major depressive disorder. By defining the target diagnosis as a treatable illness that is not the patient's fault, IPT relieves self-blame for symptoms. IPT helps patients connect life events with mood and symptoms. Patients develop social skills while addressing an interpersonal crisis such as complicated bereavement, a troubled relationship (role dispute), or major life change (role transition). Patients learn to marshal social supports, which protect against psychopathology. Resolving the current interpersonal crisis also yields symptomatic relief. IPT has demonstrated efficacy for major depression, bulimia, and other disorders in a series of randomized controlled trials (Weissman, Markowitz, & Klerman, 2000).

The life events on which IPT focuses naturally include traumas, and relationship patterns resulting from trauma. Yet, trauma is in the eye of the beholder: an event's subjective meaning matters. IPT focuses on recent life events, the triggers or consequences of the current illness episode, rather than on remote, childhood traumas.

Research has begun to recognize the importance of interpersonal influences as triggers and protective factors in posttraumatic stress disorder (PTSD). Interpersonal traumas have greater impact than impersonal ones. Social supports may protect against developing PTSD in the face of trauma, or aid in recovery from PTSD (Brewin, Andrews, & Valentine, 2000). An open trial ($N = 14$) of IPT, adapted as a nonexposure-based intervention, showed promising results in treating patients with chronic PTSD (Bleiberg & Markowitz, 2005).

REFERENCES

Bleiberg, K. L., & Markowitz, J. C. (2005). Interpersonal psychotherapy for posttraumatic stress disorder. *American Journal of Psychiatry, 162,* 181–183.

Brewin, C. R., Andrews, B., & Valentine, J. D. (2000). Meta-analysis of risk factors for posttraumatic stress disorder in trauma-exposed adults. *Journal of Consulting and Clinical Psychology, 68,* 748–766.

Weissman, M. M., Markowitz, J. C., & Klerman, G. L. (2000). *Comprehensive guide to interpersonal psychotherapy*. New York: Basic Books.

JOHN C. MARKOWITZ
New York State Psychiatric Institute

See *also:* Depression; Social Support

INTRUSIVE REEXPERIENCING

Posttraumatic stress disorder (PTSD) as defined by *DSM-IV* (American Psychiatric Association, 1994) includes (as one of its criteria) intrusive reexperiencing symptoms following exposure to a traumatic event. Intrusive reexperiencing symptoms can consist of repetitive thoughts, images, memories, and impulses related to traumas, and are usually difficult to control and unwanted. Images and memories may include but are not limited to seeing the perpetrator's face in cases of interpersonal violence, seeing the trauma reoccur, or seeing what occurred immediately before or after the traumatic event. Victims who are injured may also have intrusions of being at the hospital and obtaining treatment. Intrusive thoughts may include thoughts that occurred at the time of the traumatic event, such as thoughts of fear of injury or death, thoughts of disgust, and thoughts of escape. Trauma-related intrusions have been linked with a variety of subjective and psychophysiological disturbances (Horowitz, 1969; Rachman, 1981) and are predictive of the development and maintenance of PTSD (Davidson & Baum, 1993; Halligan, Michael, Clark, & Ehlers, 2003).

Intrusive cognitions are a common reaction to trauma exposure. Durham, McCammon, and Allison (1985) found that in a sample of disaster workers (e.g., rescue, fire, and medical personnel and police officers) this was the most frequently reported symptom, with 74% of their sample reporting intrusive thoughts. Intrusive thoughts can be triggered by numerous cues (de Silva & Marks, 1998) including stressful stimuli (e.g., a violent movie can trigger intrusive thoughts about a rape), an internal event such as a related memory, or physiological arousal. Sodium lactate infusion, used in biological panic attack challenge studies to increase respiratory frequency (Jensen et al., 1997; Rainey et al., 1987) and yohimbine, an a2 adrenergic antagonist also used in panic attack challenges (Southwick et al., 1993) have been observed to precipitate flashbacks (a type of intrusive though; *see:* **Flashbacks**). Intrusive thoughts also spontaneously occur with no apparent cue or stimulus. Schreuder, Kleijn, and Rooijmans (2000) reported that 56% of veterans in their sample reported trauma-related nightmares or anxiety dreams more than 40 years after war trauma.

Research on the psychopathology of trauma-related reexperiencing suggests that images are more common than thoughts or purely lexical cognitions (e.g., cognitions consisting of only words; Ehlers et al., 2002; Ehlers & Steil, 1995). Reynolds and Brewin (1999) found that intrusive thoughts typically contain content of personal illness or injury, or personal assault. De Silva and Marks (1998) proposed that individuals also experience intrusive thoughts that are not memories of the traumatic event, but rather questions about the event. These thoughts fall into three broad categories: (1) threat and danger (e.g., "Am I safe?"), (2) negative thoughts about the self (e.g., "Am I a bad person?"), and (3) thoughts about the meaning of the event (e.g., "Why did this happen to me?"). The frequency and distressing nature of these nonrecollection based intrusions are similar to recollection based intrusions (de Silva & Marks, 1998).

Intrusive thoughts may not necessarily reflect traumatic incidents in an accurate way.

Merckelbach, Muris, Horselenberg, and Rassin (1998) found that 22% of those in a nonclinical sample reported that their intrusive thoughts were exaggerated versions of the actual trauma. They suggested that such intrusions might represent "worse case scenarios" of what could have happened. Exaggerated intrusions appeared to be more similar to flashbacks than to nonexaggerated intrusions, and occurred at a higher frequency than realistic intrusions.

Trauma-related intrusions appear to have a strong relationship to the experience of distress following a traumatic event. Davidson and Baum (1993) found that intrusiveness of recalled imagery associated with stressful combat events was an important predictor of long-term symptoms of stress irrespective of intensity of combat exposure. Additionally, the interaction of combat exposure and trauma-related intrusions was significantly related to symptoms of chronic stress. Rothbaum, Foa, Riggs, Murdock, and Walsh (1992) reported similar findings in rape victims, finding that PTSD status 3 months after the assault could be predicted by self-report of early trauma-related intrusions. These data suggest that trauma-related intrusions may reflect an important individual difference variable that could help predict long-term response to trauma.

In an effort to increase understanding of the association between intrusive thoughts and distress, investigators have identified key qualities of intrusions that relate to distress. For example, Dougall, Craig, and Baum (1999) found that characteristics of intrusive memories reflecting the extent to which they were unwanted or uncontrollable were key determinants of distress. Frequency was not found to be a major factor in distress (Dougall et al., 1999). Schooler, Liegey Dougall, and Baum (1999) found that both early uncued thoughts (i.e., thoughts not brought on by trauma related stimuli), and the severity of distress caused by trauma-related intrusions in the month after a trauma were associated with higher frequencies of trauma-related intrusions and avoidance symptoms at 6-, 9-, and 12-month follow-up. Similar to other investigators, Schooler et al. (1999) found that those who experienced uncued trauma-related intrusions were more likely to experience later distress.

Steil and Ehlers (2000) found in a sample of motor vehicle accident victims that whether or not trauma-related intrusions are experienced as distressing depended on their idiosyncratic meaning. Idiosyncratic meanings are found in both the occurrence of the intrusion (e.g., "Having this thought means that I am crazy") and the content of the intrusion, which usually relates to the traumatic event and its sequelae. Negative idiosyncratic meanings were related to distress caused by the trauma-related intrusion, such that intrusive thoughts to which dysfunctional meanings were assigned were related to high levels of trauma-related intrusion distress. When victims assigned meanings such as, "I am going crazy," "I am inferior to other people," "My life is ruined," "It is my fault," or "It will happen again," they were more likely to experience distress than trauma victims who did not assign such meaning. This relationship remained significant when intrusion frequency, trauma severity, and general anxiety-related catastrophic cognitions were statistically partialed out.

In other investigations, various correlates of PTSD trauma-related intrusions have been identified. Resnick (1997) found that initial panic disorder symptoms were predictive of PTSD intrusion symptoms at 3-month follow-up in a sample of women seen at an emergency room following a rape. In a comparing trauma-related intrusions in matched samples of patients with PTSD or major depressive disorder, Reynolds and Brewin (1999) demonstrated that fear was characteristic of trauma-related intrusions in both groups, but high levels of helplessness were uniquely associated with trauma-related intrusions in those with PTSD. Age at the time of the trauma may also be related to severity of trauma-related intrusions, with those who are older reporting more trauma-related intrusions (Hagström, 1995; Yehuda, Schmeidler, Siever, Binder-Brynes, & Elkin, 1997). Hagström (1995) found that individuals who experienced a threat to their lives during the trauma experienced more intrusive thoughts.

Trauma-related intrusions in PTSD have also been associated with memory deficits (Wessel, Merckelbach, & Dekkers, 2002) as well as several stress-related biological outcomes, including resting blood pressure and

hypothalamic-pituitary-adrenal axis (HPA axis) function (Baum, Cohen, & Hall, 1993; Goenjian et al., 1996). Others have found that intrusive thoughts are related to immune function. Ironson and colleagues (Ironson et al., 1997) found that intrusive thoughts were associated with lower natural killer cell cytotoxicity (NKCC). While the implication of lower NKCC is not well understood, lower rates of NKCC have been linked to serious diseases such as cancer (Whiteside & Herberman, 1989).

Conclusion

The research suggests that intrusions can include actual accounts of a traumatic event, thoughts about the meaning of the event, thoughts about the meaning of self, and may also not always be factually accurate, but may be intrusions of a worst case scenario. Research also indicates that trauma-related intrusions are common and can be induced by physiological arousal. Distress following the trauma appears to be an important predictor of trauma-related intrusions and the idiosyncratic meaning given to the occurrence of intrusions may predict how distressing the intrusions themselves are viewed as being to a given individual.

REFERENCES

American Psychiatric Association. (1994). *Diagnostic and statistical manual of mental disorders* (4th ed.). Washington, DC: Author.

Baum, A., Cohen, L., & Hall, M. (1993). Control and intrusive memories as possible determinants of chronic stress. *Psychosomatic Medicine, 55,* 274–286.

Davidson, L., & Baum, A. (1993). Predictors of chronic stress among Vietnam veterans: Stressor exposure and intrusive recall. *Journal of Traumatic Stress, 6,* 195–212.

de Silva, P., & Marks, M. (1998). Intrusive thinking in posttraumatic stress disorder. In W. Yule (Ed.), *Post-traumatic stress disorder: Concepts and therapy* (pp. 161–175). New York: Wiley.

Dougall, A. L., Craig, K. J., & Baum, A. (1999). Assessment of characteristics of intrusive thoughts and their impact on distress among victims of traumatic events. *Psychosomatic Medicine, 61,* 38–48.

Durham, T. W., McCammon, S. L., & Allison, E. J. (1985). The psychological impact of disaster on rescue personnel. *Annals of Emergency Medicine, 14,* 664–668.

Ehlers, A., Hackman, A., Steil, R., Clohessy, S., Wenninger, K., & Winter, H. (2002). The nature of intrusive memories after trauma: The warning signal hypothesis. *Behaviour Research and Therapy, 40,* 995–1002.

Ehlers, A., & Steil, R. (1995). Maintenance of intrusive memories in posttraumatic stress disorder: A cognitive approach. *Behavioural and Cognitive Psychotherapy, 23,* 217–249.

Goenjian, A. K., Yehuda, R., Pynoos, R. S., Steinberg, A. M., Tashjian, M., Yang, R. K., et al. (1996). Basal cortisol, dexamethasone suppression of cortisol, and MHPG in adolescents after the 1988 earthquake in Armenia. *American Journal of Psychiatry, 153,* 929–934.

Hagström, R. (1995). The acute psychological impact on survivors following a train accident. *Journal of Traumatic Stress, 8,* 391–402.

Halligan, S. L., Michael, T., Clark, D. M., & Ehlers, A. (2003). Posttraumatic stress disorder following assault: The role of cognitive processing, trauma memory, and appraisals. *Journal of Consulting and Clinical Psychology, 71,* 419–431.

Horowitz, M. (1969). Psychic trauma: Return of images after a stress film. *Archives of General Psychiatry, 20,* 552–559.

Ironson, G., Wynings, C., Schneiderman, N., Baum, A., Rodriguez, M., Greenwood, D., et al. (1997). Posttraumatic stress symptoms, intrusive thoughts, loss, and immune function after Hurricane Andrew. *Psychsomatic Medicine, 59,* 128–141.

Jensen, C. F., Keller, T. W., Peskind, E. R., McFall, M. M., Veith, R. C., Martin, D., et al. (1997). Behavioral and neuroendocrine responses to sodium lactate infusion in subjects with posttraumatic stress disorder. *American Journal of Psychiatry, 154,* 266–268.

Merckelbach, H., Muris, P., Horselenberg, R., & Rassin, E. (1998). Traumatic intrusions as "worse case scenarios."*Behaviour Research and Therapy, 36,* 1075–1079.

Rachman, S. (1981). Unwanted intrusive cognitions. *Advances in Behaviour Research and Therapy, 13,* 89–99.

Rainey, J. M., Aleem, A., Ortiz, A., Yerigani, V., Pohl, R., & Berchou, R. (1987). A laboratory procedure for the induction of flashbacks. *American Journal of Psychiatry, 144,* 1317–1319.

Resnick, H. S. (1997). Acute panic reactions among rape victims: Implications for prevention of post-rape psychopathology. *National Center for PTSD Clinical Quarterly, 7,* 41–45.

Reynolds, M., & Brewin, C. R. (1999). Intrusive memories in depression and posttraumatic stress disorder. *Behaviour Research and Therapy, 37,* 201–215.

Rothbaum, B. O., Foa, E. B., Riggs, D. S., Murdock, T., & Walsh, W. (1992). A prospective examination of post-traumatic stress disorder in rape victims. *Journal of Traumatic Stress, 5,* 455–475.

Schooler, T. Y., Liegey Dougall, A., & Baum, A. (1999). Cues, frequency, and the disturbing nature of intrusive thoughts: Patterns seen in rescue workers after the crash of flight 427. *Journal of Traumatic Stress, 12,* 571–585.

Schreuder, B. J. N., Kleijn, W. C., & Rooijmans, H. G. M. (2000). Noctornal re-experiencing more than forty years after war trauma. *Journal of Traumatic Stress, 13,* 453–463.

Southwick, S. M., Krystal, J. H., Morgan, C. A., Johnson, D., Nagy, L. M., Nicolaou, A., et al. (1993). Abnormal noradrenergic function in posttraumatic stress disorder. *Archives of General Psychiatry, 50,* 266–274.

Steil, R., & Ehlers, A. (2000). Dysfunctional meaning of posttraumatic intrusions in chronic PTSD. *Behaviour Research and Therapy, 38,* 537–558.

Wessel, I., Merckelbach, H., & Dekkers, T. (2002). Autobiographical memory specificity, intrusive memory, and general memory skills in Dutch-Indonesian survivors of World War II era. *Journal of Traumatic Stress, 15,* 227–234.

Whiteside, T. L., & Herberman, R. B. (1989). The role of natural killer cells in human disease. *Clinical Immunology and Immunopathology, 53,* 1–23.

Yehuda, R., Schmeidler, J., Siever, L. J., Binder-Brynes, K., & Elkin, A. (1997). Individual differences in posttraumatic stress disorder symptom profiles in holocaust survivors in concentration camps or in hiding. *Journal of Traumatic Stress, 10,* 453–463.

SHERRY A. FALSETTI
University of Illinois College of Medicine at Rockford

See also: Flashbacks; Memories of Traumatic Experiences; Posttraumatic Stress Disorder; Posttraumatic Stress Disorder, Diagnosis of; Stress Response Syndromes

J

JANET, PIERRE (1859–1947)

The French philosopher, psychiatrist, and psychologist Pierre Janet is widely recognized as the pioneer of trauma-related dissociation theory. However, it should be noted that this work is only a fraction of the 20,000 printed pages of his complete written works. He observed and treated numerous traumatized patients—describing 257 of them in his first four books—and was one of the first to note the biphasic pattern of avoidance of reminders of traumatic experiences and intrusion/reexperiencing that now is an accepted basis of posttraumatic stress disorder (PTSD).

In the 1880s, Janet began studying dissociation (*see:* **Dissociation**), or psychological *disaggregation,* in patients diagnosed with "hysteria" in the psychiatric hospital of LeHavre, resulting in his doctoral dissertation, *L'automatisme psychologique* (Janet, 1889). Charcot (*see:* **Charcot, Jean-Martin**) invited him to come to the Salpêtrière in Paris, where Janet became head of a psychological laboratory and completed his medical studies. His medical thesis, involving further study of the negative and positive symptoms of hysteria, appeared in 1883 and was published in English in 1901 (Janet, 1901/1977). Janet conceptualized clinical hysteria as "a form of mental depression [i.e., lowered integrative capacity] characterized by the retraction of the field of consciousness and a tendency to the dissociation and emancipation of the systems of ideas and functions that constitute personality" (1907, p. 332). He regarded this dissociation of the personality as an integrative deficit, rather than a psychological defense, and as the core of hysteria, the precursor to modern dissociative disorders. Traumatic experiences, which, by definition, the survivor was unable to integrate, were one of the major

causes of hysteria. Thus, some of these dissociated systems, each with their own sense of self, involved traumatic memories that are experienced in sensorimotor and affective ways. He observed that the patients' dissociated systems dedicated to functioning in daily life had developed a phobia of the traumatic memories and in this way maintained the dissociation of their personality, instead of fostering its integration. By integration, Janet meant those actions that reunite more or less numerous phenomena into a new psychological phenomenon different from its elements. At every moment of life, this activity effectuates new combinations of psychological phenomena that are necessary for adaptive living in changing circumstances (Janet, 1889). Thus, because of the dissociation of their personality, trauma survivors are less adaptive than if their personality was fully integrated.

By concluding that dissociative patients needed to transform traumatic memories into autobiographical narratives and fully realize that the traumatic experience is a thing of the past, Janet also was a pioneer of phase-oriented treatment for PTSD and dissociative disorders. He distinguished three treatment phases: (1) stabilization and symptom reduction, (2) treatment of traumatic memories, and (3) personality (re)integration and rehabilitation (cf., Van der Hart, Brown, & Van der Kolk, 1989). These phases are not linear but rather recursive over time. His two-volume, 1,265-page work *Psychological Healing* presents an extraordinarily interesting history of psychotherapy (Janet, 1919/1925). Perhaps the most relevant chapter is on the study and treatment of traumatic memories. He summarized his approach as follows:

> Strictly speaking, then, one who retains a fixed idea of a happening cannot be said to have a "memory" of the

happening. It is only for convenience that we speak of it as a "traumatic memory." The subject is often incapable of making, with regard to the event, the recital which we speak of as memory; and yet he remains confronted by a difficult situation in which he has not been able to play a satisfactory part, one to which his adaptation had been imperfect, so that he continues to make efforts at adaptation. The repetition of this situation produces an exhaustion which is a considerable factor in his emotions. (p. 663)

Following his early work on hysteria, Janet conducted various other studies of psychopathology, for instance on psychasthenia (i.e., present-day anxiety disorders such as obsessive-compulsive disorders) and paranoid schizophrenia. He also developed a psychology of religious beliefs. In the framework of his *psychology of action,* he combined his psychopathological findings and normal psychology into a unified system. This psychology of action included a hierarchically ordered classification of human activity from simplest to most complex. Traumatized patients often function at a level of reflexive actions: beliefs and related behavioral actions that are reactive in nature and lack reflection. Treatment should help them to at least reach a level of reflective actions, which involve inner and outer discussion, considered reasoning, and taking the position of self and others into consideration. Reflection involves evaluating facts and experiences in the context of the past, the present, and the anticipated future (cf., Van der Hart, Nijenhuis, & Steele, 2006).

Ellenberger (1970) compared Janet's work "to a vast city buried beneath ashes, like Pompeii. It may remain concealed while being plundered by marauders. But it may also perhaps be unearthed some day and brought back to life" (p. 409). The traumatic stress field certainly has discovered the relevance of his studies on hysteria and dissociation for our understanding and treatment of trauma-related disorders. However, many more treasures are waiting in his work for further exploration.

REFERENCES

Ellenberger, H. F. (1970). Pierre Janet and psychological analysis. In H. F. Ellenberger (Ed.), *The discovery of the unconscious* (pp. 331–417). New York: Basic Books.

Janet, P. (1889). *L'automatisme psychologique.* Paris: Félix Alcan. (Reprinted in Paris: Société Pierre Janet, 1973)

Janet, P. (1907). *The major symptoms of hysteria.* New York: Macmillan.

Janet, P. (1925). *Psychological healing.* New York: Macmillan. (Original work published in 1919 as *Les médications psychologiques.* Paris: F. Alcan.)

Janet, P. (1977). *The mental state of hystericals: A study of mental stigmata and mental accidents* (D. N. Robinson, Ed.). Washington, DC: University Publications of America. (Original work published 1901)

Van der Hart, O., Brown, P., & Van der Kolk, B. A. (1989). Pierre Janet's treatment of post-traumatic stress. *Journal of Traumatic Stress, 2,* 379–396.

Van der Hart, O., Nijenhuis, E. R. S., & Steele, K. (2006). *The haunted self: Structural dissociation and the treatment of chronic traumatization.* New York: Norton.

RECOMMENDED READINGS

Ellenberger, H. F. (1970). Pierre Janet and psychological analysis. In H. F. Ellenberger (Ed.), *The discovery of the unconscious* (pp. 331–417). New York: Basic Books.

Van der Hart, O., Nijenhuis, E. R. S., & Steele, K. (2006). *The haunted self: Structural dissociation and the treatment of chronic traumatization.* New York: Norton.

ONNO VAN DER HART
Utrecht University

See also: Dissociation; Freud, Sigmund; History of Psychological Trauma; Hysteria; Psychodynamic Therapy, Adult

JOURNAL OF TRAUMATIC STRESS

The *Journal of Traumatic Stress—JTS—*is the official publication of the International Society for Traumatic Stress Studies (ISTSS). Founded by Charles Figley in 1988, it was the first journal to focus specifically on traumatic stress studies. This unique position has allowed *JTS* to provide a chronicle of the field itself (Schnurr, 2006).

Figley (1988) defined traumatic stress as the "investigation of the immediate and long-term psychosocial consequences of highly stressful events and the factors which affect those consequences" (p. 3). With this broad definition as a guide, *JTS* offers a multidisciplinary forum for publishing peer-reviewed articles on the biopsychosocial aspects of trauma, including epidemiology, assessment, treatment, prevention, etiology, neurobiology, teaching and training, public health, and policy. The target audience is similarly diverse, including clinicians, researchers, students, administrators, and policy makers. *JTS* publishes original studies, theoretical articles, and review papers in both brief and regular formats, as well as case studies and commentaries. Occasionally, the *Journal* devotes a special issue or a special section to a single topic. *JTS* is published six times per year and is distributed in print or electronic format to all ISTSS members as well as individual and institutional subscribers. Information about subscriptions and how to submit an article may be obtained from the ISTSS web site, www.istss.org, or from a recent issue of the journal.

REFERENCES

Figley, C. R. (1988). Toward a field of traumatic stress. *Journal of Traumatic Stress, 1*, 3–16.

Schnurr, P. P. (2006). Toward the future of traumatic stress studies. *Journal of Traumatic Stress, 19*, 1–3.

PAULA P. SCHNURR
National Center for Posttraumatic Stress Disorder

See also: International Organizations

JOURNALISTS, EFFECTS OF TRAUMA ON

Journalists are often first on the scene of traumatic events, where they are exposed to direct danger and bear witness to death, injury, and destruction. In fact, like other first responders, 86% to 100% of journalists report high rates of exposure to potentially traumatic events (e.g., Newman, Simpson, & Handschuh, 2003; Pyevich, Newman, & Daleiden, 2003; Simpson & Boggs, 1999).

Until recently, few studies examined the impact of trauma exposure on journalists' functioning. Although the current studies have methodological limitations, a consistent picture is emerging. Rates of probable PTSD among war correspondents are high (i.e., more than one in four, or as many as 28%), whereas rates of probable PTSD among other groups of journalists range from average to low (between 4% and 13%; Newman et al., 2003; Pyevich et al., 2003; Teegen & Grotwinkel, 2001).

War correspondents report higher levels of depressive symptoms and substance misuse compared to journalists who cover events other than war (Feinstein, Owen, & Blair, 2002). Nevertheless, most journalists exhibit resilience despite repeated exposure to catastrophic events. However, a significant minority of journalists do report high levels of trauma-related symptomatology that may interfere with their lives and may warrant therapeutic assessment and treatment (e.g., McMahon, 2001; Newman et al., 2003; Pyevich et al., 2003; Simpson & Boggs, 1999; Teegen & Grotwinkel, 2001).

Potential risk factors that have been identified for increased risk and level of PTSD symptomatology among journalists include: repeated exposure to both personal and professional traumatic events; less experience as a journalist; low perceived social support/ organizational support; and personality traits of neuroticism, anger, and hostility (e.g., Marais & Stuart, 2005; McMahon, 2001; Newman et al., 2003; Pyevich et al., 2003; Teegen & Grotwinkel, 2001).

Future research is needed to examine the effects of exposure to different types of psychological trauma and traumatic stress symptoms on journalists' occupational functioning, including how they actually cover and report traumatic events such as wars, disasters, or family violence, and occupational problems such as absenteeism and turnover. Further methodological improvements should include the use of samples that are representative of all journalists (or carefully defined subgroups of journalists) rather than self-selected or convenience samples that may not be representative of journalists generally. Research on the impact of psychological trauma on journalists also should look for signs of resiliency in the face of stress by journalists and should measure job performance indices such as dependability and productivity of reporting and awards for quality of reporting. Methods to prepare journalists to be safe and resilient in the face of dangerous or traumatic work assignments also should be developed and evaluated.

REFERENCES

Feinstein, A., Owen, J., & Blair, N. (2002). A hazardous profession: War, journalism, and psychopathology. *American Journal of Psychiatry, 159,* 1570–1576.

Marais, A., & Stuart, A. (2005). The role of temperament in the development of post-traumatic stress disorder amongst journalists. *South African Journal of Psychology, 35,* 89–105.

McMahon, C. (2001). Covering disaster: A pilot study into secondary trauma for print media journalists reporting on disaster. *Australian Journal of Emergency Management, 16,* 52–56.

Newman, E., Simpson, R., & Handschuh, D. (2003). Trauma exposure and post-traumatic stress disorder among photojournalists. *Visual Communication Quarterly, 10,* 4–13.

Pyevich, C., Newman, E., & Daleiden, E. (2003). The relationship among cognitive schemas, job-related traumatic exposure, and post traumatic stress disorder in journalists. *Journal of Traumatic Stress, 16,* 325–328.

Simpson, R., & Boggs, J. (1999, Spring). An exploratory study of traumatic stress among newspaper journalists. *Journalism and Communication Monographs,* 1–24.

Teegen, F., & Grotwinkel, M. (2001). Traumatic exposure and post-traumatic stress disorder of journalists: An Internet-based study. *Psychotherapeut, 46,* 169–175.

Elana Newman
University of Tulsa

See also: **Media Reporting of Trauma; Vicarious Traumatization**

JUDICIAL DECISIONS

See: **Forensic Assessment; Laws, Legislation, and Policy; Public Policy**

KARDINER, ABRAHAM

See: History of Psychological Trauma

KEANE PTSD SCALE OF THE MMPI-2

See: Minnesota Multiphasic Personality Inventory-2 (MMPI-2)

L

LAWS, LEGISLATION, AND POLICY

Although it varies with the nature of the event, the role of the government in addressing traumatic stress is significant. Disasters, war, and crime are all potentially pathogenic areas where the government has an established role. Government research funding, which usually is provided by agencies in the national government that are responsible for health (such as the National Institutes of Health in the United States), education (such as the U.S. Department of Education), civil and criminal justice (such as the U.S. Department of Justice), or military affairs (such as the U.S. Departments of Veterans Affairs and Defense), influences the research agenda for traumatic stress and the development of best practices for traumatic stress treatment and prevention.

Government policies set these agencies' priorities, and government legislation determines the parameters of agency activities and fiscal resources. Professionals concerned with traumatic stress therefore must understand the legislation that is relevant to their research, clinical, and educational activities. This encyclopedia entry outlines some key pieces of legislation in the U.S. federal government, and also outline some key conceptual issues that govern their implementation. Legislation in other nations has a similar impact on the traumatic stress field internationally (*see:* **International Organizations**). Legislation at the state and local level also may impact the practice of traumatic stress clinical providers and programs, but often the local legislation is based upon federal legislation and regulations.

Traumatic Stress Services and Federal Legislation

Since many traumatic stress services are delivered after disasters, support of such services must be understood in the context of federal disaster aid. Federal disaster assistance programs must balance the need to provide assistance when the capacity of state and local resources is temporarily overwhelmed with the need to avoid undermining the integrity of the local system. For example, if after a disaster there is a demand for counseling services that overwhelms the resources of local systems, the federal government may provide additional services through contractors or federal service providers. However, these temporary assets cannot provide long-term care, since extended provision of subsidized services by federal resources might undermine local providers, causing them to leave the community and inhibiting its long-term recovery.

The Stafford Act is the foundation for the United States' national disaster response system, allowing the U.S. president to use national assets to respond to a disaster. This may include services to responders and victims who have mental disorders that are caused, or aggravated, by the disaster, along with essential community services, assistance in health and safety measures, distribution of medicine, and other types of assistance. The Act also allows the Federal Emergency Management Agency (FEMA) to direct the Crisis Counseling Training and Assistance Program (CCP). This program provides funding for victims, using short-term interventions, psychoeducational information about stress and coping, linkage and referral, and supportive listeners as they process and respond to the disaster. FEMA provides technical assistance, consultation, training, grant administration and program oversight through interagency agreements with the Department of Health and Human Services' Substance Abuse and Mental Health Services Administration, also known as SAMHSA (FEMA, 2007). Although CCP grants may assist with the crisis needs of individuals with chronic mental conditions, they may not be used to fund long-term care or psychiatric services, since that is the domain of the local public health system.

The Children's Health Act of 2000 reauthorized SAMHSA's existing programs and added an additional authority to provide aid to local communities experiencing emergencies. Known as SAMHSA Emergency Response Grants (SERG), these funds are awarded in cases where an identifiable emergency event has occurred, local resources are overwhelmed, and no other funding options exist (Substance Abuse and Mental Health Services Administration, 2006). Although this program allows SAMHSA the flexibility to respond in an emergency, it is critical to note that funds for SERG awards arrive by reallocating dollars from other mental health and substance abuse projects. To increase access to information about trauma, SAMHSA also provides technical support through the Disaster Technical Assistance Center (DTAC), a clearinghouse of resources that can be used by states, territories, and local entities to deliver effective behavioral health services during disasters and to find out more about SERG and CCP.

The Pandemic and All-Hazards Preparedness Act (PAHPA) of 2006 codified the role of the Secretary of Health and Human Services (HHS) as the lead for federal responses to public health emergencies. The law includes the creation of the Office of the Assistant Secretary for Preparedness and Response (ASPR) to enhance the federal government's health and human services response to disasters. ASPR also coordinates interagency activities between the agencies of HHS—including the National Institutes of Health (NIH), the Centers for Disease Control and Prevention (CDC) and SAMHSA—and other federal departments, particularly the Department of Defense (DoD), the Veterans Administration (VA) and the Department of Homeland Security (which includes FEMA). Since ASPR's role involves developing plans for preparedness, response, and recovery phases of disasters and public health emergencies, the office may be required to coordinate aspects of the behavioral health response, including deployment of mental health experts, direct service providers, or consultants in support

of local and state entities during a disaster. ASPR also has a mandate to create plans that address "at risk" individuals in the event of a disaster. At-risk individuals are defined in the statute as senior citizens, children, and pregnant women, along with others as determined by the Secretary. This may include groups that are especially vulnerable to the turmoil of a catastrophe, such as people with mental health problems.

HHS controls three types of personnel assets that can be mobilized in a disaster. The first, and the only full-time HHS asset, is the U.S. Public Health Service (PHS). PHS Officers have regular federal positions, but can be rapidly deployed to respond to an emerging public health crisis. PHS currently has five mental health teams that can be deployed for consultation, service to victims, and service to responders. The National Disaster Medical System (NDMS), placed under ASPR by PAHPA, is another deployable asset comprised of intermittent federal employees. NDMS's behavioral health teams currently serve to provide behavioral health services to responders. A third deployable group, the Medical Reserve Corps, consists of civilian health providers, including mental and behavioral health specialists who can be temporarily federalized to respond to a disaster.

Department of Health and Human Services and Trauma Stress Legislation

The legislation that authorized SERG also established the National Child Traumatic Stress Network (NCTSN). The mission of NCTSN is to improve access to care and quality of services for traumatized children and their families through a network including two national centers, additional academic centers, and community-based centers. The 70+ members of the NCTSN address a range of issues including abuse, community violence, terrorism, and disasters. Utilizing its congressional mandate to address mental health and substance abuse issues, SAMHSA established the National Center for Trauma-Informed Care in 2005. This initiative built on prior SAMHSA activities, such as the 5-year multisite Women, Co-occurring Disorders, and Violence Study. Beyond these initiatives at SAMHSA, the U.S. Congress has addressed trauma in children through the Child Abuse Prevention and Treatment Act (CAPTA). As originally enacted, CAPTA defined child abuse and neglect, established basic state grants for prevention and treatment, provided money for prevention and treatment demonstration grants, and established a National Center on Child Abuse and Neglect.

Department of Justice

The 1984 Victims of Crime Act gave the federal government a means to help individuals victimized by crime, by setting up the Crime Victim's Fund. The Fund provides direct aid to individual crime victims, including recovery expenses such as mental health care. The Fund also provided states with money to develop their own victim assistance programs, which may include counseling services (U.S. Department of Justice, Office for Victims of Crime, 2007). While the fund initially helped individual crime victims, recently it has been used to compensate and provide support services for victims of multiple-victim crimes, including victims of the September 11, 2001, terrorist attacks.

Department of Veterans Affairs

PAHPA, in its comprehensive approach to emergency response, directed the Department of Veterans Affairs (VA) to provide medical logistic support to NDMS and to the Secretary of Health and Human Services. This may be important for mental health services because the VA is already the largest federal employer of professional counselors. In 2007, Congress authorized an additional $100,000,000 to enhance mental health services at the VA. The majority of these funds are for research and treatment of veterans. However, during a disaster, PAHPA authorizes the VA to extend its veterans' counseling and services for PTSD to local emergency response providers, active duty military personal and individuals seeking care at department medical centers.

Other Legislative Issues

In addition to the authorizing statutes mentioned, the U.S. Congress can designate funds through the appropriations process. For example, after multiple intense hurricanes in Florida in 2004, Congress appropriated supplemental funds for HHS that provided $11 million to SAMHSA for disaster behavioral health services. After the devastating 2005 hurricane season, Congress appropriated $550 million for the Social Services Block Grant, run by the HHS Administration for Children and Families for Gulf Coast hurricane relief, specifying that the use of funds must include mental health services.

Traumatic Stress Research

Beyond service to victims, the government has a role in supporting research on treatment for traumatic stress. The lead HHS agency for this research is the National Institute of Mental Health (NIMH), part of the NIH. NIMH provides extramural funding for stress-related research ranging from neuroscience to health services delivery. The NIMH web site also provides a link for individuals wishing to participate in clinical trials to treat traumatic stress.

In addition, CDC's National Institute for Occupational Safety and Health (NIOSH) looks at work-based traumatic stress. Under this focus, NIOSH supports research into causes and prevention strategies and interventions for workplace stress, including traumatic stress. It also sponsors a related training program for graduate students.

Because of the link between combat exposure and traumatic stress, both the DoD and VA are mandated to conduct research into the prevention and treatment of traumatic stress disorders. The vast majority of the DoD's role in traumatic stress research is directly related to managing traumatic stress within the context of DoD. However the necessity of developing effective care for veterans and reservists not on active duty has given the DoD a critical role in developing evidence-based practices in both military and civilian settings. According to the statute, "The Secretary of Defense may carry out pilot projects to evaluate the efficacy of various approaches to improving the capability of the military and civilian health care systems to provide early diagnosis and treatment of post traumatic stress disorder (PTSD) and other mental health conditions."

The VA coordinates its research through the National Center for Posttraumatic Stress Disorder (NCPTSD). Created in 1989 in response to a Congressional mandate, the NCPTSD was established to address the needs of veterans with military-related posttraumatic stress disorder. In addition to providing information on ongoing VA studies, the NCPTSD provides validated tools that can be used by non-VA providers to study and treat PTSD in civilian populations. Beyond the work of the NCPTSD, VA researchers use their network of hospitals to conduct research into traumatic stress and its treatment.

Conclusion

Clearly, many statutes have been developed that can address mental health services and research related to trauma. However, each of these statutes is designed to address some specific area of traumatic stress. Agencies therefore must focus on the area designated by their governing statutes. In addition to limitations imposed by the legislation, there are a number of challenges in federal policy on traumatic stress. There is still limited knowledge about what types of interventions will prevent or mitigate traumatic stress. Without such knowledge, it is difficult to determine which interventions the government should fund. Although evidenced-based practices have to come from researchers and providers as the field develops, the federal government can assist this process by supporting research. Nevertheless, federal policy makers must be cognizant of the tension between the need to disseminate best practices, and the need to allow local authorities to tailor responses to local needs.

Many other challenges also exist. Because we do not know who will be a victim of disaster or traumatic event before it happens, it is difficult to take steps to minimize the psychological impact of that event. While researchers and policy makers are looking at ways to mitigate risk factors for pathological traumatic stress and promote effective interventions, there is also recognition that the federal government cannot effect change by itself. In order to promote population resilience and reduce the impact of traumatic stress, collaboration between academic institutions, law enforcement, local practitioners, and policy makers is vital. Only through such collaboration can truly effective solutions be developed.

REFERENCES

Children's Health Act of 2000, Pub. L. No. 106–310.

Federal Emergency Management Agency. (2007). *An overview of the Crisis Counseling Assistance and Training Program.* Retrieved July 28, 2007, from www.fema.gov/txt/media/2006/ccp_over.txt.

Pandemic and All-Hazards Preparedness Act (PAHPA) of 2006, Pub. L. No. 109-417.

Substance Abuse and Mental Health Services Administration. (2006). *Substance Abuse and Mental Health Services Administration emergency response grant.* Retrieved August 2, 2007, from http://mentalhealth.samhsa.gov/dtac/serg.asp.

U.S. Department of Justice, Office for Victims of Crime. (2007). *Grants and funding.* Retrieved August 5, 2007, from www.ojp.usdoj.gov/ovc/fund/welcome.html.

RECOMMENDED READINGS

Centers for Disease Control and Prevention, National Institute for Occupational Safety and Health. (n.d.). *Stress . . . at work.* Retrieved August 2, 2007, from www.cdc.gov/niosh/ohp.html.

U.S. Department of Veterans Affairs. (2007). *HSR&D studies sorted by keywords.* Retrieved August 14, 2007, from www1.va.gov/hsrd/research/keywords.cfm.

DANIEL DODGEN
U.S. Department of Health and Human Services

JESSICA MEED
U.S. Public Health Service

See also: Human Rights Violations; Humanitarian Intervention; Nongovernmental Organizations; Veterans Affairs, U.S. Department of

LEARNED HELPLESSNESS

Learned helplessness refers to profound deficits in motivation and initiative that can result from sustained exposure to severe, aversive stimuli. In his classic study, Seligman (1975) subjected one group of dogs to unavoidable electrical shock. These dogs and nonshocked controls were then introduced to an avoidable shock that could be readily escaped by simply jumping over a barrier. The dogs that were previously exposed to inescapable shock did not attempt to jump over the barrier—that is, they exhibited apparent helplessness. In contrast, the control dogs quickly learned to jump the barrier to escape the shock.

The learned helplessness concept has been invoked to account for deficits in self-agency (free-willed behavior) and problem solving that characterize various forms of psychopathology, and depression in particular. When faced with a series of negative life events, the model proposes that individuals may begin to believe that they lack the ability to have control over the events or outcomes in their lives. In fact, research has suggested that humans develop patterns of helplessness when faced with uncontrollable negative situations. Because not all humans develop helplessness following a series of negative life events, it has been proposed that helplessness is likely to occur only when the individual takes excessive and unwarranted personal responsibility for the event, expects the situation to be of extended duration, and anticipates that it will negatively affect other actions taken by the individual.

In the context of psychological trauma, it has been suggested that learned helplessness may account for battered women remaining in abusive relationships, despite negative consequences of such behavior and despite the obvious benefits of leaving the perpetrator. Although this model is intuitively appealing, empirical support has been fairly limited and inconsistent. Some authors have noted, for instance, that women who are ultimately successful in leaving an abusive relationship often have a history of numerous failed attempts to leave the abusive partner. It is difficult to account for these observations using a learned helplessness model since repeated, failed attempts at leaving should, according to the model, give rise to passivity instead of perseverance. Research has also shown that women who remained with abusive partners were no more helpless than those who successfully terminated the relationship. Further, studies examining battered and nonbattered women have not shown the two groups to express different degrees of perceived helplessness. Many victims of domestic violence choose not to leave abusive partners because of financial dependence, religious beliefs or a whole host of other reasons that may not reflect true learned helplessness.

Finally, it is not clear that the majority of persons faced with repeated, uncontrollable, and unpredictable abuse will experience sustained passivity in other contexts or significant psychological distress. Quite the opposite, the great majority of trauma survivors do not exhibit the severe avolition (lack of motivation) or impairment in mood and self-confidence that would be predicted by the learned helplessness model. According to the reformulated helplessness model (Abramson, Seligman, & Teasdale, 1978), mere exposure to chronic, aversive experiences does not invariably result in learned helplessness among humans. The interpretation and cognitive appraisal of such experiences is critical. Those who attribute causes of abuse to internal, global, and stable causes will be more likely to perceive helplessness and to experience chronic psychopathology as a result of trauma.

Helplessness has been even less thoroughly examined with regards to other (i.e., nondomestic violence) types of psychological trauma. Limited information is available regarding the role of learned helplessness in the development of PTSD symptoms following combat, motor vehicle accidents, or sexual assault. However, the studies that do exist suggest that in many cases helpless attributions are associated with PTSD symptomatology. In an investigation of combat veterans with varying degrees of childhood abuse, early physical abuse was associated with measures of perceived helplessness.

Helplessness was also associated with PTSD following combat exposure (McKeever, McWhirter, & Huff, 2006). Because this study did not test whether helplessness mediated the relationship between childhood trauma and combat-related PTSD, and because the design was cross-sectional in nature, it remains unknown whether childhood trauma increases the likelihood of some form of learned helplessness and whether such deficits exacerbate distress following subsequent traumatic episodes.

Case studies of women who have been sexually assaulted suggest that learned helplessness may play a role in the recovery from sexual assault. These cases indicate that women may attempt to either fully accept responsibility for an uncontrollable event, or alternately, they might espouse helplessness across situations. Within a therapeutic context, it has been suggested that it may be necessary to address helplessness and related attributions in order to prevent excessive perceptions of vulnerability in novel situations (Roth & Newman, 1992).

Learned helplessness connotes that an individual does not recognize viable solutions or perceives outwardly obvious solutions to be inert. It is important to recognize that failure to pursue an apparently viable solution is not necessarily true learned helplessness. The individual might be in a situation where he or she truly lacks compelling alternative options. Inaction may be due to legitimate difficulties of leaving the traumatic situation, rather than his or her perceived inability to act. For example, financial dependence and lack of social support may make the termination of an abusive relationship more difficult than might be apparent to the casual observer.

Conclusion

Learned helplessness is a conceptually appealing model for describing observed deficits in motivation and problem solving among chronically traumatized individuals. At present, however, the evidentiary base is limited. Future studies using longitudinal designs and diverse trauma samples will be required to substantiate the applicability of the learned helplessness model to trauma. Further, researchers need to carefully consider and rule out objective reasons that may exist for failure to act in a seemingly adaptive manner before attributing such a failure to learned helplessness per se.

REFERENCES

Abramson, L. Y., Seligman, M. E. P., & Teasdale, J. D. (1978). Learned helplessness in humans: Critique and reformulation. *Journal of Abnormal Psychology, 87,* 49–74.

McKeever, V. M., McWhirter, B. T., & Huff, M. E. (2006). Relationships between attribution style, child abuse history, and PTSD symptom severity in Vietnam veterans. *Cognitive Therapy and Research, 30,* 123–133.

Roth, S., & Newman, E. (1992). The role of helplessness in the recovery process for sexual trauma survivors. *Canadian Journal of Behavioral Science, 24,* 220–232.

Seligman, M. E. P. (1975). Learned helplessness: Depression, development, and death. New York: Freeman.

RECOMMENDED READING

Flannery, R. B., & Harvey, M. R. (1991). Psychological trauma and learned helplessness: Seligman's paradigm reconsidered. *Psychotherapy: Theory, Research, Practice, Training, 28,* 374–378.

Palker-Corell, A., & Marcus, D. K. (2004). Partner abuse, learned helplessness, and trauma symptoms. *Journal of Social and Clinical Psychology, 23,* 445–462.

Stipek, D. E. P. (1988). *Motivation to learning.* Boston: Allyn & Bacon.

PATRICIA L. METZGER
University of Wyoming

MATT J. GRAY
University of Wyoming

See also: Biology, Animal Models; Conditioned Fear; Learning Theory

LEARNING THEORY

Learning theory describes the complex process by which animals and humans learn and adapt to their environment. Learning-theory models of fear and distress have gained widespread acceptance in the field of psychological trauma and offer clear guidance to researchers and clinicians in the assessment, treatment, and understanding of mental health problems associated with traumatic events. Of particular importance, Mowrer's (1960) two-factor theory accounts for the acquisition and maintenance of fear and distress associated with exposure to a traumatic event. Following a description of terms and definitions, the two-factor theory is described, as well as its application to various forms of psychological trauma.

Definitions

Fear and *distress* are broad terms that refer to behavioral and physiological reactions—which can occur at varying levels of intensity—that are associated with psychological constructs such as posttraumatic stress disorder (PTSD), depression, and anxiety. *Unconditioned stimulus* (US) refers to a stimulus (e.g., object, activity, event, situation) that evokes an innate, evolutionarily programmed (i.e., reflexive) response. US can refer to a traumatic life event, such as a natural or technological disaster, combat exposure, terrorism, sexual assault, physical assault, severe car crash, or other extreme stressor (note that, outside of the field of psychological trauma, US is typically defined more broadly; that is, it does not necessarily refer to a *traumatic* incident). *Conditioned stimuli* (CS) refer to any or all of a "network" of circumstances, cues, triggers, or other stimuli in the environment that have come to be associated with the US and are perceived through one or more sensory systems. These can include sights, sounds, tastes, textures, and smells that were present at the time of the US. An *unconditioned response* (UR) is a natural, reflexive reaction of the animal or person to a US. This can include physiological and/or behavioral discomfort, anxiety, fear, horror, disgust, or other reactions. When these or similar reactions occur in response to a US, they are called URs; when such reactions occur in response to a CS, they are called *conditioned responses* (CR).

Extinction is a process that describes the reduction in frequency and/or intensity of fear and distress over time that occurs as CSs are repeatedly encountered in the absence of the US. Following a period of extinction, *spontaneous recovery, renewal,* or *reinstatement* of fear and distress may occur—this refers to the reemergence (i.e., sudden increase in frequency and/or intensity) of the strength of a CR in response to a CS. This can occur under a variety of circumstances, one of the most common being when a traumatic event (e.g., attack in a dark alley) is encountered in Context A (e.g., direct exposure to cues in a dark alley), extinction training occurs exclusively in Context B (e.g., exposure to cues verbally and imaginally via treatment in a clinic setting), and salient CSs are present when the person subsequently reencounters Context A or a close approximation thereof.

Two-Factor Theory

When understood from a behavioral perspective rooted in Mowrer's (1960) two-factor theory, two types of conditioning—classical and operant—account for the acquisition and maintenance of fear, anxiety, and distress associated with a traumatic event. The two types of conditioning are the two factors in Mowrer's learning theory.

Classical Conditioning (Acquisition) Phase

The person responds behaviorally and physiologically to the experience of a traumatic event, or US, with an immediate and reflexive UR that may involve discomfort, anxiety, fear, horror, disgust, or other reactions. Via classical conditioning, previously neutral stimuli (e.g., sights, sounds, tastes) that are present at the time of the traumatic event can become associated with the US as conditioned stimuli (CS). For example, a physical assault perpetrated by a man with blond hair and a red cap may lead the victim to experience intense fearful reactions when approached in the future by men with blond hair wearing a red cap, particularly if the man happens to be wearing cologne that resembles that used by the perpetrator. In this example, the blond hair, red cap, and cologne (which, prior to the traumatic event, were likely to be neutral in their ability to elicit fearful reactions) all are potential CSs. During a traumatic event, an entire network of conditioned stimuli may be present. The extent to which the CS network is replicated in subsequent situations is likely to be associated with the intensity of the CR. For example, the CR may be more intense as the person encounters a man with blond hair wearing a red cap versus the person being approached by a man with dark hair wearing a red cap, a man with blond hair wearing a brown cap, or a woman with blond hair wearing a red cap. The anxiety and fear that is produced by previously neutral stimuli can take a variety of forms, such as distress, depressive symptoms, and fear reactions, including the reexperiencing, arousal, and avoidance symptoms of PTSD.

Although classical conditioning can account for some of the fear/anxiety symptoms of individuals with traumatic stress reactions, the range of conditioned stimuli to which victims respond is rarely limited to cues present at the time of the traumatic event. Through the processes of higher-order conditioning and generalization, stimuli that are not present at the time of the traumatic event can also come to produce aversive states similar to those first produced by the US. Higher-order conditioning refers to the process by which CSs may come to be associated with other neutral stimuli that then also acquire the ability to produce the CR. Building on the physical assault example above, consider that the victim has a red cap of his or her own that is prominently displayed on a bookshelf next to a baseball. If the red cap on the bookshelf were to acquire the properties of a CS following the assault (i.e., serve as a reminder of the assault), the baseball may eventually also come to serve as a reminder of the assault because it is consistently paired

with the red cap, even though the baseball itself had no direct association with the assault incident. Few studies have been conducted that examine the role of higher-order conditioning in traumatic stress. Stimulus generalization, which has received more research attention, refers to the process by which stimuli similar to those within the original CS network also acquire the ability to elicit fear or distress reactions. For example, a man assaulted with a knife may experience a fearful reaction when he unexpectedly encounters an object that bears some resemblance (e.g., similar shape and color) to the weapon used in the assault.

It is important to note that most individuals are resilient (i.e., do not experience long-term fear and distress) or recover rapidly following a traumatic event. That said, the learned fear reactions described above are fairly common in individuals exposed to traumatic life events. More specifically, whereas few victims of traumatic events go on to develop chronic mental disorders, many victims do experience at least some symptoms for several days or weeks following a traumatic event. Many of these individuals will experience distress or fear reactions in the period of time immediately following a traumatic experience.

Operant Conditioning (Maintenance) Phase

It is through the second phase of Mowrer's (1960) theory, operant conditioning, that the persistence of symptoms in persons who have chronic fear or distress, or who meet *DSM* (American Psychiatric Association, 1952) criteria for PTSD, is explained. Operant conditioning is often described in an A → B ← → C model where *A* refers to an antecedent condition (such as a CS) that sets the occasion for *B* (i.e., a behavior or set of behaviors/reactions), which is followed by *C* (i.e., consequence or set of consequences). Consequences, in turn, have the potential to influence (i.e., decrease or increase) the future likelihood of the behavior in the presence of *A*.

When an individual encounters a stimulus (CS) that has previously been paired with a traumatic event, a natural response is for the person to want to escape/avoid the stimulus. For example, a young adult who is mugged in a dark alley may be inclined to (a) experience fear and distress when encountering dark alleys in the future, and (b) escape or avoid this circumstance when possible. This escape/avoidance behavior is negatively reinforced though termination (i.e., successful escape/avoidance) of the aversive stimuli and therefore is more likely to occur when the aversive stimuli are again encountered in the future. Using the example and A-B-C model, as the young adult encounters a dark alley (A), he or she may evaluate the situation as one that is dangerous and may flee the situation (B). Assuming that the person successfully escapes the situation (C), such escape behavior is reinforced (C → B) and is likely accompanied by a reduction in fear and distress. This escape behavior may even generalize, for example, to alleys that are well lit during the daytime. This process interferes with extinction because, as a CS is continually escaped or avoided, the person is not able to experience the CS in the absence of the US, and therefore is unable to learn that the CS is not inherently dangerous.

Take, for example, a child who is attacked and bitten by a dog and develops a fear of dogs. The child may avoid going near neighborhood households that have dogs. The child may also escape situations when they encounter a dog—such as when a neighbor walks a leashed dog in the street. If the child continues to successfully avoid and escape the presence of dogs (with A = Settings in which dogs are present; B = Escape/avoidance behavior; C = Successful attempts to escape/avoid), the child will have little or no opportunity to learn that most dogs are unlikely to attack him or her. In other words, the child does not exhibit an alternative form of B (e.g., approaching dogs, rather than avoiding/escaping dogs) that can be reinforced. Until such learning occurs, levels of fear and distress probably will not extinguish rapidly when in the presence of dogs.

Behavioral (e.g., exposure-based) treatment for fear and distress associated with traumatic events attempts to aid the process of extinc-tion. That is, it aims to break the pattern of escape and avoidance that treatment-seeking individuals commonly exhibit when confronted with one or more CSs. Rather than encourage the individual to *escape* the feared CSs, he or she is encouraged to *approach* or *confront* the CSs. This involves a set of procedures that allow patients to repeatedly encounter CSs in a controlled context until distress is no longer experienced (i.e., extinguished). Exposure to fear-producing stimuli can be either imaginal (where the patient imagines and verbally describes encountering feared objects or situations—for example, a rape victim would write about or vocally describe the rape to the therapist in vivid detail) or *in vivo* (where the therapist arranges situations in which the patients actually encounter the fear producing stimuli in the absence of danger—for example, the victim of a severe car crash would drive to the location of the crash). Exposure techniques help to reduce the excessive avoidance and escape behaviors that interfere with the extinction of fearful reactions in persons with PTSD. Patients are exposed to CSs in a controlled, realistically nondangerous setting and therefore are able to learn new associations between feared stimuli and other neutral or positive stimuli.

In the context of exposure-based treatment, extinction will often occur when CSs repeatedly are presented in the absence of US. Using the example of the car accident victim, if the victim repeatedly drives his or her car to the location of the crash, his or her fear and distress reactions would be predicted to decrease in severity or intensity over time, assuming they do not experience another accident while doing so! It is important to note that, consistent with the evidence from research on spontaneous recovery and renewal, extinction does not represent an "unlearning" of CS-US associations. The phenomenon of extinction instead represents new (supplementary) learning, which counteracts conditioned fear responses, where associations are made between CSs and nonfear producing stimuli. It is not the passage of time, but the learning that occurs when the CS is presented in the absence of the US, that produces a diminished CR.

Consider the woman in the earlier example. Following an assault, she experienced intense fear when she encountered blonde men in red hats. This woman may, after several non-traumatic (and perhaps positive) encounters with such men, learn new associations between blonde men (perhaps with red caps) and neutral/positive stimuli present at the time of these interactions. These new associations may, over time and with repeated encounters, reduce the salience of the prior CS-US association that initially triggered her pattern of fear reactions.

Case Example

The case of little Albert provides a classic example of how fears can be conditioned. Little Albert, a small child, was given a white rat to touch, to which he showed no fear (*neutral stimulus*). In future trials, as Albert interacted with the rat, the experimenter made a loud sound by striking a hammer upon a suspended steel bar, which Albert naturally responded to fearfully and with distress (e.g., crying). The loud sound was a *US* for fear and distress, the *UR*. Albert learned to associate the rat (now a CS) with the US, and would begin to cry (CR) when he was presented with the rat. Behaviorally, when presented with the rat (Antecedent) in subsequent trials, he would turn away and move away (Behavior) from the rat, which presumably—at least temporarily—successfully enabled him to remove the visual CS out of his field of vision (Consequence).

Little Albert was living in an orphanage at the time of the experiment, and was adopted before any procedures could be performed in which his fear of white rats (which later was found to have generalized to nonwhite rabbits, a furry dog, and other stimuli that visually resembled certain characteristics of the rat) could be extinguished. If Albert had been given *in vivo* exposure-based treatment to address his fear and distress, this probably would involve a clinician gradually introducing stimuli that successively approximated the presence of a white rat. Because these stimuli would not be accompanied by loud noises or other distress-producing circumstances, extinction of fearful responding in the presence of the rat and other CSs would likely occur over time and across several trials. The clinician might begin with a picture of a rat or furry animal, may then progress to introducing a caged rat or animal across the room, and ultimately progress to a situation in which the rat was directly presented to Little Albert, repeatedly and without an accompanying loud sound. Via this process, the association between the rat and the US would weaken over time and new associations would strengthen, thereby likely weakening the frequency and intensity of fearful reactions.

REFERENCES

American Psychiatric Association. (1952). *Diagnostic and statistical manual of mental disorders.* Washington, DC: Author.

Mowrer, O. H. (1960). *Learning theory and behavior.* New York: Wiley.

RECOMMENDED READING

Ayres, J. J. B. (1998). Fear conditioning and avoidance. In W. O'Donohue (Ed.), *Learning and behavior therapy* (pp. 122–145). Boston: Allyn & Bacon.

KENNETH J. RUGGIERO
Medical University of South Carolina

GRACE S. HUBEL
Medical University of South Carolina

See also: Biology, Animal Models; Conditioned Fear; Learned Helplessness

LIMBIC SYSTEM

Basic Anatomy and Function of the Limbic System

More than 125 years ago, Paul Broca made reference to *le grand lobe limbique,* an area of interconnected cortical structures in the brain surrounding the thalamus (Broca, 1878). While

Broca's definition was a purely anatomical one, over the past century, this "great limbic lobe" has been further defined based on both structure and function. In the late 1930s, James Papez (1937) posited that these limbic structures made up a closed circuit, whose function was to process emotional information. Papez identified an area on the medial surface of the brain, the cingulate gyrus, as a key structure in the circuit.

Paul MacLean (1952) later elaborated upon the description of the limbic system both structurally and functionally. Structurally, MacLean acknowledged the additional role of brain areas in the frontal cortex and adjacent areas in the temporal cortex, structures not previously described as part of the limbic system by Papez. Functionally, MacLean posited that the limbic system was an evolutionary development designed to promote preservation in mammals via emotion and its mediation of behaviors such as the fight or flight response, appetite, and sexual activity.

Today, the limbic system refers to a set of interconnected subcortical structures that are involved in the assessment of and response to emotionally relevant stimuli, motivation, and memory. The word 'limbic' means 'border,' and the structures of the limbic system border the cerebral cortex. This set of interconnected structures modulates activity of both the autonomic nervous system as well as the endocrine system (such as the stress-response pathways between the hypothalamus, pituitary gland, and adrenal gland). While many researchers define the limbic system differently, occasionally including structures such as the hypothalamus, fornix, and mammillary bodies as portions of the limbic system, for the purpose of this entry we will discuss the limbic structures most relevant to posttraumatic stress disorder (PTSD): the amygdala, the frontal (anterior) portion of the cingulate, and the hippocampus (see Figures 1 and 2). This entry will begin by giving an overview of the structure and function of these three regions in healthy individuals, followed by an overview of research indicating abnormalities in these regions in PTSD.

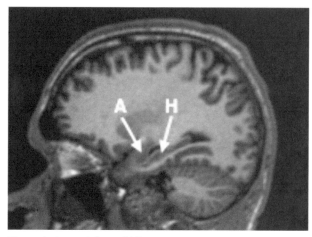

Figure 1. Amygdala and Hippocampus.

Amygdala

The amygdala is located deep within the temporal lobe, directly in front of the hippocampus (see Figure 2). The amygdala is involved in the assessment of potentially threatening and/or ambiguous biologically relevant stimuli and in the process of fear conditioning and emotional memory formation. This structure is also involved in evaluating the emotional significance of facial expressions; as such, the amygdala is particularly likely to activate in response to fearful faces.

Researchers such as Michael Davis (1997) and Joseph LeDoux (1995) have highlighted the amygdala's role in fear conditioning, which

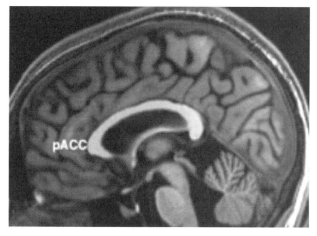

Figure 2. Anterior Cingulate Cortex.

involves learning an association between an aversive stimulus (such as a shock) and a previously neutral stimulus (such as a tone or a light). A number of fear conditioning studies using both auditory and visual stimuli have led to the conclusion that the amygdala is involved in the learning (acquisition) and the behavior involved in the expression of conditioned fear. More specifically, neural receptors activated by a brain chemical known as N-methyl-D-aspartate (NMDA) within the amygdala are believed to be involved in the acquisition of conditioned fear. Other neural receptors in the amygdala that are not activated by NMDA are believed to be involved in the behavioral expression of conditioned fear.

Anterior Cingulate Cortex

The anterior cingulate cortex (ACC) is located just in front of (anterior) and above (dorsal) the corpus callosum (which connects the brain's two hemispheres). In primates, this structure is interconnected with the amygdala (specifically the anterior portion of the ACC that borders the front of the corpus callosum, the perigenual section or pACC), and also sends neural projections to the hippocampus. The pACC (see Figure 2) is involved in the processing of emotional information and emotional response regulation, and lower (ventral) portions of the ACC and surrounding cortex appear to be involved in the process of extinction of fear after fear conditioning and the retention of such extinction (Vogt, in press; Vogt, Berger, & Derbyshire, 2003). Extinction refers to the process of learning that a conditioned stimulus, which previously predicted an aversive event, no longer predicts that event. Ventral portions of ACC and surrounding cortex therefore are involved in learning not to be afraid when an individual is reminded of danger but actually no longer is in danger.

Hippocampus

The hippocampus lies behind (posterior to) the amygdala (see Figure 2). Named for the Greek word for seahorse, this long, curved structure is interconnected with a number of limbic system structures, most notably the amygdala. The main function of the hippocampus is to enable the individual to learn and remember (encode) new memories that can be described in words (explicit, declarative memory). The hippocampus can also be influenced by the amygdala to preferentially encode emotionally arousing material versus neutral material (LaBar & Cabeza, 2006). However, the hippocampus also plays a large role in the more unconscious, nonverbal (implicit) processes of fear conditioning via the encoding of context during fear conditioning (LeDoux, 1995). That is, the hippocampus appears to be necessary for learning that an entire situation, not just a specific cue or portion of the situation, is dangerous even when the individual cannot describe any exact specific threat. It is believed that the hippocampus sends information to the amygdala regarding the context of the conditioning, whereupon the amygdala adds emotional significance to this context.

Limbic System Function in PTSD

As noted previously, all three limbic structures play an important role in the processes of fear conditioning. Thus it comes as no surprise that all three have been implicated in the pathophysiology of PTSD, a disorder of fear regulation. PTSD has been associated with alterations in the structure, function, and interconnectivity of these limbic brain structures.

Amygdala in PTSD

The hyperviligance often demonstrated in PTSD has made the amygdala a prime target in the study of the pathophysiology of PTSD. To date, no conclusive evidence of abnormal amygdala structure has been found in PTSD. However, individuals with PTSD often display abnormalities in amygdalar function. Several studies have reported that the amygdala is hyperresponsive in PTSD, in response to both trauma-related stimuli (such as personalized scripts describing traumatic events or trauma-related sounds or images), and trauma-unrelated stimuli (such as fearful facial expressions). The degree of amygdala responsivity has been positively correlated with PTSD symptom severity such that individuals with relatively high amygdala responses also have relatively high symptom severity. The amygdala also appears to be hyper-responsive when individuals with PTSD undergo fear conditioning. A recent treatment study has shown that greater symptomatic improvements in response to cognitive behavioral therapy were associated with greater decreases in amygdala activation (Felmingham et al., 2007).

Anterior Cingulate Cortex in PTSD

Given the role of the ACC and surrounding cortex in the retention of extinction memories, as well as its numerous interconnections with other limbic structures, it comes as no surprise that abnormalities in both the structure and function of the ACC have been found in individuals with PTSD.

Several magnetic resonance imaging (MRI) studies have reported smaller volumes and differences in shape of the ACC among PTSD patients. Two studies reported a negative correlation between ACC volume and symptom severity. Last, the integrity of pregenual ACC neurons may be impaired in PTSD, as indicated by a diminished ratio of the amounts of two brain chemicals, N-acetyl aspartate (NAA; a brain chemical associated with healthy neurons) and creatine.

On a functional level, while recent research suggests that activation in the top (dorsal) portion of the ACC is normal or exaggerated in those with PTSD, it appears that pACC activation is diminished in this disorder. Several studies have reported diminished pACC activation in persons with PTSD in response both to trauma-related stimuli and to negative stimuli that are unrelated to trauma. In addition, negative correlations have been reported between pACC activation and symptom severity, such that individuals with relatively lower pACC activation display relatively greater PTSD symptom severity. Meanwhile, two treatment studies have reported increased ACC activation with successful symptomatic response to selective serotonin reuptake inhibitor (SSRI) antidepressant medications. Another recent study has shown that greater symptomatic improvements in response to cognitive behavioral therapy were associated with greater increases in pACC activation (Felmingham et al., 2007).

Hippocampus in PTSD

The hippocampus has been implicated in a number of domains relevant to PTSD. As described above, first, this structure is well known to be involved in explicit, declarative memory processes. Second, the hippocampus is specifically involved in the encoding of context during fear conditioning. Last, the hippocampus interacts a great deal with the amygdala during the encoding of emotional information.

On a behavioral level, PTSD is occasionally marked by general memory impairment. Animal models of PTSD have also demonstrated memory impairments in rats exposed to highly stressful laboratory circumstances or tasks. Meanwhile, exposure to psychological trauma and to other extreme stressors has also been associated with neuroanatomical and pathophysiological changes in the hippocampi in both humans and animals. On a structural level, decreased hippocampal volumes have been found in PTSD compared to both trauma-exposed control subjects as well as trauma-unexposed healthy subjects. Negative correlations have also been found between hippocampal volumes and deficits in verbal memory as well as between hippocampal volumes and symptom severity. Additionally, neuronal integrity appears diminished in PTSD, as indicated by decreased amounts of NAA.

Support for the hypothesis that decreased hippocampal volumes may represent a preexisting risk factor for PTSD was found by a study of identical (monozygotic) twins discordant for trauma exposure (i.e., one twin had experienced psychological trauma as a combat soldier but the other had not). The results indicated that co-twins of combat veterans who were diagnosed with PTSD had smaller hippocampal volumes than co-twins of other veterans who were not diagnosed with PTSD (Gilbertson et al., 2002). However, it is important to note that a handful of studies have found no differences in hippocampal volume between persons with PTSD and healthy individuals, indicating that other factors associated with the disorder (e.g., how long PTSD has been suffered and/or other psychiatric or psychosocial problems that co-occur with PTSD) may be responsible for hippocampus volumetric differences. Meanwhile, more recent data have indicated that hippocampal volumes may increase upon successful treatment of PTSD with paroxetine (Vermetten, Vythilingam, Southwick, Charney, & Bremner, 2003).

Only a few studies have examined hippocampal function in PTSD (e.g., Shin, Rauch, & Pitman, 2006). Generally, hippocampal activation during memory tasks appears to be diminished in PTSD. One study, however, raised the possibility that diminished hippocampal activation may be attributable to increased activity in the hippocampus at baseline; that is, persons with PTSD may have higher levels of hippocampal activity in general than people without PTSD. More research is necessary in this area to better characterize hippocampal function in PTSD and to determine whether functional abnormalities in the hippocampus are attributable to volumetric reductions in this disorder.

Limbic System Interactions in PTSD

One neurocircuitry model of PTSD posits that the amygdala is hyperresponsive, the ACC is hyporesponsive, and the ACC and hippocampus fail to inhibit the hyperresponsive amygdala. A small group of studies have specifically examined the functional connectivity of the amygdala and ACC in persons with PTSD. Results have been mixed, with two studies reporting a negative relationship between the two areas and two reporting a positive relationship. Thus, although there appears to be a connection between the two structures, the direction of the relationship is still unclear (and may vary on an individual basis). Additional research is necessary to further examine relationships between all three limbic structures.

Conclusion

A large body of evidence supports the idea that limbic system function is abnormal in PTSD. Independent studies of limbic structures have reported hyperresponsivity of the amygdala, hyporesponsivity of both the ACC and hippocampus, and diminished volume in the latter two structures. People with PTSD also may have different patterns of functional connectivity between the limbic structures than persons who do not suffer from PTSD. These findings are consistent with other research, which has shown that PTSD involves problems with prolonged excessive fear and difficulties in extinguishing fear memories, as well as problems generally with memory, mental concentration, anger and irritability, and emotional numbing.

While most studies are unable to determine whether these abnormalities are the result of PTSD or represent a preexisting risk factor that may make certain people more likely to develop PTSD than others, there is some support for the idea that decreased hippocampal volume represents a preexisting risk factor. More research is necessary in order to examine whether the size of other limbic structures is a risk factor for PTSD. Furthermore, additional research should examine functional connectivity between these structures, as this body of research is still preliminary. More studies are needed to extend the findings of the few recent investigations that have used functional neuroimaging techniques to determine if it is possible to predict who will respond to different types of pharmacotherapy and psychotherapy for PTSD and whether these therapies produce changes in limbic system structures when they successfully reduce PTSD symptoms.

REFERENCES

Broca, P. (1878). Anatomie comparée des circonvolutions cérébrales: Le grand lobe limbique et la scissure limbique dans la serie des mammiferes. *Revue Anthropologique, 2*(1), 385–498.

Davis, M. (1997). Neurobiology of fear responses: The role of the amygdala. *Journal of Neuropsychiatry: Clinical Neuroscience, 9*(3), 382–402.

Felmingham, K., Kemp, A., Williams, L., Das, P., Hughes, G., Peduto, A., et al. (2007). Changes in anterior cingulate and amygdala after cognitive behavior therapy of posttraumatic stress disorder. *Psychological Science, 18,* 127–129.

Gilbertson, M. W., Shenton, M. E., Ciszewski, A., Kasai, K., Lasko, N. B., Orr, S. P., et al. (2002). Smaller hippocampal volume predicts pathologic vulnerability to psychological trauma. *Nature Neuroscience, 5,* 1242–1247.

LaBar, K. S., & Cabeza, R. (2006). Cognitive neuroscience of emotional memory. *Nature Reviews Neuroscience, 7,* 54–64.

LeDoux, J. E. (1995). Emotion: Clues from the brain. *Annual Review of Psychology, 46,* 209–235.

MacLean, P. D. (1952). Some psychiatric implications of physiological studies on frontotemporal portion of limbic system (visceral brain). *Electroencephalography and Clinical Neurophysiology, 4*(Suppl. 4), 407–418.

Papez, J. W. (1937). A proposed mechanism of emotion. *Journal of Neuropsychiatry: Clinical Neuroscience, 7*(1), 103–112.

Shin, L. M., Rauch, S. L., & Pitman, R. K. (2006). Amygdala, medial prefrontal cortex, and hippocampal function in PTSD. *Annals of the New York Academy of Sciences, 1071,* 67–79.

Vermetten, E., Vythilingam, M., Southwick, S. M., Charney, D. S., & Bremner, J. D. (2003). Long-term treatment with paroxetine increases verbal declarative memory and hippocampal volume in posttraumatic stress disorder. *Biological Psychiatry, 54,* 693–702.

Vogt, B. A. (Ed.). (in press). *Cingulate neurobiology and disease: Vol. 1. Infrastructure, diagnosis, and treatment.* New York: Oxford University Press.

Vogt, B. A., Berger, G. R., & Derbyshire, S. W. (2003). Structural and functional dichotomy of human midcingulate cortex. *European Journal of Neuroscience, 18,* 3134–3144.

Kathryn Handwerger
Tufts University

Lisa M. Shin
Tufts University

See also: Amygdala; Anterior Cingulate Cortex; Biology, Brain Structure, and Function, Adult; Biology, Brain Structure, and Function, Child; Biology, Neurochemistry; Conditioned Fear; Frontal Cortex; Hippocampus

LITERARY DEPICTIONS OF PSYCHOLOGICAL TRAUMA

Psychological trauma is at the heart of many, if not most, of both classic and popular literary works depicting people, relationships, and societies facing and attempting to overcome disasters, crises, and both public and private suffering.

Perhaps the first literary depiction of traumatic stress was found inscribed on clay tablets 5,000 years ago. The Sumerian *Epic of Gilgamesh* describes a Babylonian king who was terrified and distraught after the death of his closest friend, Enkidu. Gilgamesh's reactions depict classic symptoms of posttraumatic stress disorder (PTSD) and traumatic grief (e.g., terrifying memories of losing a loved one, inability to sleep; anger; sense of foreshortened future; Birmes, Hatton, Brunet, & Schmitt, 2003). The tenth tablet describes Gilgamesh's ordeal:

> I was terrified by his appearance, I began to fear death, and roam the wilderness. How can I stay silent, how can I be still! My friend whom I love has turned to clay! Am I not like him! Will I lie down never to get up again! That is why I must go on, to see Utanapishtim, "The Faraway." That is why sweet sleep has not mellowed my face, through sleepless striving I am strained, my muscles are filled with pain. (www.ancienttexts.org/library/mesopotamian/Gilgamesh/)

Two millennia later, famous Greek and Roman storytellers and authors captured the essence of traumatic stress and grief (Birmes et al., 2003). Homer's epic tragic poem the *Illiad* describes the rageful loss of control of Achilles in the siege of Troy (Shay, 1994), and his *Odyssey* depicts what we now would call chronic PTSD in the inability of Odysseus to emotionally return home after experiencing traumatic betrayal and loss (Shay, 2002). The Greek playwrights writing in the Golden Age before the fall of Athens in the fourth century BCE, Aeschylus, Sophocoles, and Eurpides, could be said to have created the art form known as the classic Greek tragedy through their theatrical plays. The tragic story of the downfall of the king who led the Greek forces to triumph at Troy (Agamemnon) is chronicled in Aeschylus's trilogy of plays, *The Oresteia.* Agamemnon's son Orestes (whose name means "one who can conquer mountains") and daughter Electra were raised in the countryside. They are absent when their mother, Clytemnestra, murders her husband, on the day he returns to Greece, in order to make her illicit lover king. Eight years later, Orestes and Electra return at the command of the Oracle at Delphi in order to fulfill the gods' command to avenge their father's death by killing their mother and her lover. The themes of traumatic betrayal, loss, and revenge are powerfully evoked in these plays, and in subsequent revisions of the story of Electra written by both Sophocles and Euripedes.

Perhaps the best known of the Greek tragic dramas is the story of *Oedipus Rex,* as memorialized in the play by Sophocles. Oedipus is a king who unknowingly has an incestuous marriage to his mother and kills his father, and as a result of learning of these terrible events he can find no other way cope with the shame he felt than to blind himself. Like many persons with PTSD, Oedipus suffered no physical harm from any other person, but he was sufficiently emotionally overwhelmed by shock and horror that he attempted to expunge this psychic pain by assaulting himself. The manner in which he harmed himself symbolically represented the blindness that permitted he and his parents to commit these atrocities—a symbolic re-enactment and judgment that may be seen in the intrusive memories and episodes of outrage or self-harm that may occur in PTSD. The tragedy of Oedipus continues in two further plays by Sophocles, and in a subsequent play describing the downfall of Oedipus's sons, by Aeschylus, *Seven against Thebes.* Thus, the theme of intergenerational transmission of psychological trauma and PTSD was anticipated through the dramatic writings of these Greek playwrights.

A tragedy written by Eurpides, *Medea* describes the complex forms of PTSD that can follow intimate betrayal. Medea is a woman who has abandoned her father to marry a Corinthian noble, only to have her husband spurn her to marry the daughter of Corinth's ruler. Incensed at the betrayal, Medea poisons his fiancée and then kills her own children:

> In vain, my children, have I brought you up,
> Borne all the cares and pangs of motherhood,
> And the sharp pains of childbirth undergone.
> In you, alas, was treasured many a hope
> Of loving sustentation in my age,
> Of tender laying out when I was dead,
> Such as all men might envy.
> Those sweet thoughts are mine no more, for now bereft of you
> I must wear out a drear and joyless life,
> And you will nevermore your mother see,
> Nor live as ye have done beneath her eye.
> Alas, my sons, why do you gaze on me,
> Why smile upon your mother that last smile?
> Ah me! What shall I do? My purpose melts
> Beneath the bright looks of my little ones.
> I cannot do it. Farewell, my resolve,
> I will bear off my children from this land.
> Why should I seek to wring their father's heart,
> When that same act will doubly wring my own?
> I will not do it. Farewell, my resolve.
> What has come o'er me? Shall I let my foes
> Triumph, that I may let my friends go free?
> I'll brace me to the deed. Base that I was
> To let a thought of wickedness cross my soul.
> Children, go home. Whoso accounts it wrong
> To be attendant at my sacrifice,
> Let him stand off; my purpose is unchanged.
> (www.theatrehistory.com/ancient/bates018.html)

After this graphic depiction of Medea's ambivalence and her ultimate determination to take revenge, she escapes to Athens and the play ends by attributing the terrible events and extreme suffering to forces beyond the control of mortals:

> Manifold are thy shapings, Providence!
> Many a hopeless matter gods arrange.
> What we expected never came to pass,
> What we did not expect the gods brought to bear.

During the subsequent two millennia, until the Renaissance and Reformation periods of the fifteenth to seventeenth centuries, literature and theater were largely dormant. During this period extending from the advent of the Roman empire through the medieval epoch known as the "Dark Ages," literature primarily involved nonfiction texts of religious, historical, and philosophical writings. In these writings there were many vivid accounts of psychological trauma and its aftermath. For example, writings from the Christian church drew on the Bible, which describes many incidents of loss, violence, disaster, and abuse. Saint Augustine of Hippo wrote the classic *Confessions* at the end of the fourth century A.D., chronicling his conversion to Christianity after experiencing the harm caused by greed, corruption, malice, and war. Saint Geoffrey of Tours, in the sixth century A.D., wrote books of miracles about the suffering and transcendence of Christian martyrs, and *Ten Books of Histories*. Virtually concurrently, Saint Isidore of Seville was writing analyses of history, society, language, and religion (such as the *Etymologies*), and a century later the English monk Bede wrote the *Ecclesiastical History of the English People*. These works of religious and historical literature were replete with anecdotes and stories designed to warn of the many evils in the world, with an avowed goal of converting the listener to the Christian church.

At approximately the same time, before and after the rise of Islam in the seventh century, poetry was flourishing in the Arabic world, most notably the "mu'allaqat" or "hanged poems" (because they were hung from the walls of the central shrine at Mecca). These poems predate the Islamic holy book, the Koran (which, like the Christian Bible and Jewish Torah, contains many depictions of psychological trauma). The Arabic poems capture many themes of psychological trauma based on the hardships of the day. For instance, the "Poem of Imru-Ul-Quais" describes traumatic loss and grief:

> Stop, oh my friends, let us pause to weep over the remembrance of my beloved.
> Here was her abode on the edge of the sandy desert between Dakhool and Howmal.
>
> The traces of her encampment are not wholly obliterated even now;
> For when the South wind blows the sand over them the North wind sweeps it away.

> The courtyards and enclosures of the old home have become desolate;
> The dung of the wild deer lies there thick as the seeds of pepper.
>
> On the morning of our separation it was as if I stood in the gardens of our tribe,
> Amid the acacia-shrubs where my eyes were blinded with tears by the smart from the bursting pods of colocynth.
>
> As I lament thus in the place made desolate, my friends stop their camels;
> They cry to me "Do not die of grief; bear this sorrow patiently."
>
> Nay, the cure of my sorrow must come from gushing tears.
> Yet, is there any hope that this desolation can bring me solace?
>
> So, before ever I met Unaizah, did I mourn for two others;
> My fate had been the same with Ummul-Huwairith and her neighbor Ummul-Rahab in Masal.
>
> Fair were they also, diffusing the odor of musk as they moved,
> Like the soft zephyr bringing with it the scent of the clove.
>
> Thus the tears flowed down on my breast, remembering days of love;
> The tears wetted even my sword-belt, so tender was my love.
> (www.fordham.edu/halsall/source/640hangedpoems.html)

Two hundred years later, in the ninth to tenth centuries, a collection of stories known as the *Thousand and One Nights* was compiled by Arabic writers and historians, telling of the adventures relayed by Queen Scheherazade to King Shahryar. These dramatic and comedic tales weave together a fabric of romanticism and life threatening danger with memorable characters such as Aladdin, Ali Baba and the 40 thieves, and Sinbad the sailor.

Toward the end of the medieval period, the Persian poet Omar Khayyam (1048–1123) wrote the classic *Rubiyat* not only as an ode to love but also a warning about danger and the potentially traumatic fate awaiting all people:

> You know how little time we have to stay,
> And once departed, may return no more.

Alike for those who for TO-DAY prepare,
And that after a TO-MORROW stare,
A Muezzin from the Tower of Darkness cries
"Fools! your reward is neither Here nor There!"

Why, all the Saints and Sages who discuss'd
Of the Two Worlds so learnedly, are thrust
Like foolish Prophets forth; their Words to Scorn
Are scatter'd, and their mouths are stopt with Dust.

Oh, come with old Khayyam, and leave the Wise
To talk; one thing is certain, that Life flies;
One thing is certain, and the Rest is Lies;
The Flower that once has blown for ever dies.

Geoffrey Chaucer (1343–1400) wrote of the hopes and sorrows experienced as a result of poverty, war, corruption, and greed by the pilgrims journeying in the *Canterbury Tales.* Chaucer follows the Greek tradition in describing the terrible curse that evil, in particular murder, places upon a person and the family for generations to come: "Mordre wol out, that see we day by day" (*Canterbury Tales, The Nonnes Preestes Tale,* Line 15058). In the Elizabethan period, Shakespeare's works graphically portray the traumatic impact of natural disasters (e.g., the *Tempest*), rape (e.g., the *Rape of Lucrece*), war (e.g., *Titus Andronicus; Henry the IVth/Vth/VIth*), and family violence and murder (e.g., *Romeo and Juliet, Othello, MacBeth, and Richard II*). Shakespeare relied upon classic Greek histories and tragedies for many of his plays plots, and echoed their and Chaucer's theme of the curse of trauma in his classic drama of betrayal and trauma, Hamlet (Act 2, Scene 2): "Murder, though it have no tongue, will speak/ With most miraculous organ."

In the seventeenth and eighteenth centuries, psychological trauma was depicted primarily in an indirect form in comedic and heroic novels and theatrical plays. Classic literary works from this time period include: Miguel Cervantes's *Don Quixote* (a tragic comedy of chivalry and war), Jean Racine's *Andromaque* (a reworking of Eurpides's classic story of the aftermath of the Trojan War), Moliere's *Tartuffe* (a comedy depicting the evil caused by hypocrisy), Nathaniel Hawthorne's *The Scarlet Letter* (on

the tragic outcome of fear and stigma), Sir Walter Scott's *Ivanhoe* (a novel of heroism, loss, and redemption in medieval England and the Crusades), and Alexander Dumas's *The Count of Monte Cristo* (a story of imprisonment, despondency, and escape in the Napoleonic wars).

In the nineteenth century, the satirical commentary was replaced by more direct works of literary social commentary in which the desperate conditions of ordinary people's lives in poverty and war are the focus. Charles Dickens wrote novels about the both obvious and invisible wounds caused when starvation, torture, and death are inflicted intentionally and unwittingly by people upon each other, in novels such as *Oliver Twist, A Tale of Two Cities, Bleak House, Hard Times,* and most graphically, his novel of intergenerational imprisonment, *Little Dorrit.* Victor Hugo wrote *Les Miserables* (subsequently to become a long-running Broadway musical) to memorialize the terror and losses of the French Revolution and the triumph of courage and love. Herman Melville wrote the classic story of obsession and death, *Moby Dick.* Thomas Hardy's novels offer a bleak picture of the alienation and violence experienced and expressed by ordinary people in despair (*The Return of the Native; Tess of the D'Urbervilles*), thus anticipating Fyodor Dostoyevsky's classic depictions of the dehumanizing psychological impact of oppression and violence (*Crime and Punishment, Notes from the Underground*). Bernard Shaw (*Saint Joan; Man and Superman*) and Oscar Wilde (*The Picture of Dorian Gray*) placed scathing criticisms of the harm caused by class oppression and bigotry in their tragicomic classic plays.

Also in the nineteenth century, Edgar Allen Poe (*The Raven*) and Henry James (*The Turn of the Screw*) initiated a genre of novels that bring readers (and contemporary movie viewers) face-to-face with posttraumatic stress in chilling tales of mystery and terror. Mark Twain's *Huckleberry Finn* and Harriet Beecher Stowe's *Uncle Tom's Cabin* George powerfully portrayed the evils of slavery and racism. The American Civil War inspired Stephen Crane's novel, *The Red Badge of Courage,* and obliquely but powerfully in Emily Dickinson's poem, *It Feels a Shame to be Alive:*

It feels a shame to be Alive
When Men so brave—are dead
One envies the Distinguished Dust
Permitted—such a Head

The Stone—that tells defending Whom
This Spartan put away
What little of Him we—possessed
In Pawn for Liberty

The price is great—Sublimely paid—
Do we deserve—a Thing—
That lives—like Dollars—must be piled
Before we may obtain?

Are we that wait—sufficient worth—
That such Enormous Pearl
As life—dissolved be—for Us—
In Battle's—horrid Bowl?

It may be—a Renown to live—
I think the Men who die—
Those unsustained—Saviors—
Present Divinity—

In twentieth century literature, the horrors of war, authoritarianism, and genocide have been chronicled through classic works such as Erich Maria Remarque's *All Quiet on the Western Front* (World War I); Ernest Hemingway's *For Whom the Bell Tolls* (Spanish Civil War); *The Diary of Anne Frank,* Ursula Hegi's *Stones from the River,* William Styron's *Sophie's Choice,* and Giorgio Bassani's autobiographical novel *The Garden of the Finzi-Contini's* (the Jewish Holocaust); Leon Uris's *Exodus* (the founding of modern Israel); James Jones's *From Here to Eternity* and James Heller's *Catch 22* (World War II); Joseph R. Owen's *Colder Than Hell: A Marine Rifle Company at Chosin Reservoir* (Korean War); Tim O'Brien's *The Things They Carry* and *Going after Cacciato,* and Denis Johnson's *Tree of Smoke* (the Vietnam War); Mark Bowden's *Black Hawk Down* (Somalia peacekeeping mission); Anthony Swofford's *Jarhead* (the Persian Gulf War); and Don Delillo's *Falling Man* (the September 11th Terrorist incidents). The subsequent wars in Afghanistan and Iraq

have largely been chronicled in historical and political commentaries to date, such as Wesley Clark's *Winning Modern Wars* and Tom Clancy's *Shadow Warriors.*

The insidious nature of less obviously visible psychological traumas occurring over generations in families and communities (echoing the Greeks and Shakespeare) have been chronicled in such literary dramas of the intersection of family and cultural trauma as Marcel Proust's *The Prisoner* and *The Fugitive,* Albert Camus's *The Stranger* and *The Plague,* James Joyce's *Ulysses* and *Finnegan's Wake,* Eugene O'Neill's *Long Day's Journey into Night,* Henrik Ibsen's *Hedda Gabler,* Ralph Ellison's *Invisible Man,* William Faulkner's *The Sound and the Fury* and *Absalom, Absalom!,* Lorraine Hansberry's *A Raisin in the Sun,* Tennessee Williams's *A Streetcar Named Desire,* Tawfiq al-Hakim's *The People of the Caves,* Arthur Miller's *The Crucible* and *Death of a Salesman,* Yukio Mishima's *The Temple of the Golden Pavilion,* Kenzaburo Oe's *A Personal Matter,* Salman Rushdie's *Midnight's Children,* Mario Vargas Llosa's *Conversation in a Cathedral,* Ruth Prawer Jhabvala's *Heat and Dust,* Gabriel García Márquez's *One Hundred Years of Solitude,* E. L. Doctorow's *Ragtime,* Anthony Burgess's *A Clockwork Orange,* Toni Morrison's *Song of Solomon* and *Beloved,* Maya Angelou's *I Know Why the Caged Bird Sings,* and Alice Walker's *The Color Purple.*

In the past 25 years the interweaving of private and public traumas within different cultures has been featured in such award-winning novels such as Naguib Mahfouz's *The Day the Leader Was Killed,* Margaret Atwood's *The Handmaid's Tale* and *Alias Grace,* Nadine Gordimer's *The Conservationist,* Michael Ondaatje's *The English Patient,* J. M. Coetzee's *Disgrace,* E. L. Mark Helprin's *Refiner's Fire* and *A Soldier of the Great War,* Jane Smiley's *A Thousand Acres,* Charles Johnson's *Middle Passage,* John Irving's *A Prayer for Own Meany* and *Cider House Rules,* Dorothy Allison's *Bastard Out of Carolina,* Peter Hoeg's *Borderliners,* Nicholas Evans's *The Horse Whisperer,* E. Annie Proulx's *The Shipping News,* Chuck Palahniuk's *Fight Club,* Ann Marie MacDonald's *Fall on Your Knees,* Marilynne

Robinson's *Gilead,* Khaled Hosseini's *The Kite Runner* and *A Thousand Splendid Sons,* Cormac McCarthy's *All the Pretty Horses* and *The Road,* Richard Powers's *The Echo Maker,* Kate Grenville's *The Secret River,* and Azar Nafisi's *Reading Lolita in Tehran.*

Extensive commentaries and new writings on topics related to psychological trauma are available contemporaneously in texts such as Tal (1995), the Air Force Academy's literary journal *War, Literature, and Art,* and periodic special articles and issues of journals in the traumatic stress field such as the *Journal of Trauma and Dissociation* (e.g., Gold, 2004; Goldsmith & Satterlee, 2004), *Journal of Psychological Trauma, Trauma, Violence and Abuse,* and *Journal of Aggression, Maltreatment, and Trauma.*

REFERENCES

Birmes, P., Hatton, L., Brunet, A., & Schmitt, L. (2003). Early historical literature for post-traumatic symptomatology. *Stress and Health, 19,* 17–26.

Gold, S. (2004). Fight club: A depiction of contemporary society as dissociogenic. *Journal of Trauma and Dissociation, 5*(2), 13–34.

Goldsmith, R., & Satterlee, M. (2004). Representations of trauma in clinical psychology and fiction. *Journal of Trauma and Dissociation, 5*(2), 35–59.

Shay, J. (1994). *Achilles in Vietnam: Combat trauma and the undoing of character.* New York: Atheneum.

Shay, J. (2002). *Odysseus in America: Combat trauma and the trials of homecoming.* New York: Scribner.

Tal, K. (1995). *Worlds of hurt: Reading the literature of trauma.* Cambridge: Cambridge University Press.

Julian D. Ford
University of Connecticut School of Medicine

See also: Movie Depictions of Psychological Trauma

LOCUS CERULEUS

The locus ceruleus (LC) is a small (needle-sized) bluish nucleus of 25,000 neurons on each side of the dorsorostral pons, an area within the brainstem. These 50,000 neurons are highly elaborated ("arborized") and provide 70% to 90% of the nervous system's norepinephrine (NE). The LC is the noradrenergic component of the fear-response circuitry, and plays a central role, especially in acute and posttraumatic stress. Psychotropic medications that are specifically useful for the treatment and secondary prevention of acute PTSD symptoms, act by blocking activation of neurons in the LC postsynaptically. For example, propranolol, a postsynaptic NE beta receptor antagonist (Beta blocker), administered in the immediate aftermath of motor vehicle accidents has been found to be efficacious for the secondary prevention of PTSD (Pitman et al., 2002; Vaiva et al., 2003).

The LC is the primary location of the neurotransmitter norepinephrine in the brain. The LC transmits neural signals throughout the brain: "this small nucleus innervates a greater variety of brain areas than does any other single nucleus yet described" (Aston-Jones, Valentino, Van Bockstaele, & Meyerson, 1994). The neural pathways from the LC to other brain areas (*Ascending efferents*) can be conceptualized as the main 'alarm siren' of the brain. The most extreme activation of LC efferents occurs during (and in the immediate aftermath of) acute traumatic events in which there is an actual threat to personal survival or to physical integrity. In military veterans with PTSD, LC activity also abruptly increases during the startle response (such as in response to sudden noise and abrupt awakening). Sudden decrease in LC activity has been implicated in the pathophysiology of psychogenic fainting and in a range of other conversion and dissociative symptoms including *La Belle Indifference.* However, LC plays only a minimal role in mood disorders and is unaffected in psychotic disorders.

The LC also is linked to the rest of the body via *"descending efferents,"* which activate the sympathetic arm of the autonomic nervous system (ANS) via projections to preganglionic sympathetic neurons in the spinal cord. Furthermore, the LC simultaneously inhibits the parasympathetic arm of the ANS via projections to the vagus nerve (via the nucleus ambiguus). The resulting abrupt change in sympatho-vagal ratio results in physical symptoms of fear: palpitations, sweaty palms, cold sweat, hyperventilation, dilated pupils, upper abdominal discomfort (gastric vasoconstriction), dry mouth, jaw clenching, decreased vocalization, muscle tensing, tonic immobility, and increased pain threshold.

Neural projections into the LC (*afferents*) emanate primarily from other parts of the brain's fear circuits, and provide highly processed information concerning external survival-relevant stimuli. *Inhibitory afferents* from the anterior cingulate cortex and GABA-ergic afferents from the rostral medulla inhibit LC activity. The LC receives extensive serotoninergic projections from the Raphe nuclei. The therapeutic effects of the antidepressant selective serotonin reuptake inhibitors (SSRIs) in PTSD are due partly to this seratoninergic pathway.

Excitatory afferents into the LC originate in the amygdala and a midbrain area involved in pain and defensive behaviors (the periaquaductal gray). Excitatory (and possibly excitotoxic—causing damage to brain cells) non-NMDA glutamatergic activation of the LC (originating in the ventrolateral-rostral medulla) occurs during extreme stress (Aston-Jones et al., 1994). During more chronic stress, NE synthesis in the LC is increased by corticotropin releasing hormone (CRH).

The LC is the only brain nucleus in which neuron loss has been observed in PTSD. In a postmortem study of the right hemisphere's LC, three WWII veterans with war-related PTSD were found to have about 30% fewer neurons in comparison to four healthy veterans (Bracha, Garcia-Rill, Mrak, & Skinner, 2005). Most of the psychophysiological research in PTSD is consistent with a hyperresponsiveness of the LC target neurons to NE, possibly a compensatory upregulation of LC postsynaptic receptors after trauma-induced loss of LC neurons. This pathophysiological mechanism may be clinically conceptualized as "burning out" or "overuse injury" to the LC in PTSD—similar to the nonpsychiatric example of cartilage loss in the knees of aging professional athletes. Acute and/or subacute tachycardia in an otherwise healthy young individual is a useful clinical marker of LC overactivity. Drugs of abuse that increase the activity (firing) of the LC neurons (e.g., Yohimbe and Cocaine) aggravate PTSD symptoms.

REFERENCES

Aston-Jones, G., Valentino, R. J., Van Bockstaele, E. J., & Meyerson, A. T. (1994). Locus coeruleus, stress, and PTSD: Neurobiological and clinical parallels. In M. M. Murburg (Ed.), *Catecholamine function in posttraumatic stress disorder* (pp. 17–62). Washington, DC: American Psychiatric Press.

Bracha, H. S., Garcia-Rill, E., Mrak, R. E., & Skinner, R. (2005). Postmortem locus coeruleus neuron count in three American veterans with probable or possible war-related PTSD. *Journal of Neuropsychiatry and Clinical Neurosciences, 17,* 503–509.

Pitman, R. K., Sanders, K. M., Zusman, R. M., Healy, A. R., Cheema, F., Lasko, N. B., et al. (2002). Pilot study of secondary prevention of posttraumatic stress disorder with propranolol. *Biological Psychiatry, 51,* 189–192.

Vaiva, G., Ducrocq, F., Jezequel, K., Averland, B., Lestavel, P., Brunet, A., et al. (2003). Immediate treatment with propranolol decreases posttraumatic stress disorder two months after trauma. *Biological Psychiatry, 54,* 947–949.

CAITLIN E. MACY
Hawai'i Pacific University

STACY M. LENZE
Hawai'i Pacific University

JESSICA M. SHELTON
University of Hawai'i

MICHELLE TSANG MUI CHUNG
University of Hawai'i

H. STEFAN BRACHA
National Center for Posttraumatic Stress Disorder

See also: Biology, Brain Structure, and Function, Adult; Biology, Brain Structure, and Function, Child; Biology, Neurochemistry; Conditioned Fear

LONGITUDINAL STUDIES

See: Research Methodology

M

MALINGERING

Malingering is the intentional production of false or grossly exaggerated symptoms, motivated by external incentives. The potential for malingering of posttraumatic stress disorder (PTSD) symptoms has become a growing concern, particularly in health-care and other settings in which the diagnosis is associated with financial incentives such as disability benefits. There are three recognized forms of malingering that are relevant to traumatic stress: (1) *pure malingering*—complete fabrication of symptoms, along with the possible fabrication of traumatic experiences; (2) *partial malingering*—gross exaggeration of existing symptoms or reporting of remitted symptoms as ongoing, along with the possible exaggeration of aversive experiences; and (3) *false imputation*—intentional and false attribution of symptoms to a traumatic event.

There are several reasons why a person might malinger PTSD, the most obvious being financial incentives. For instance, a military veteran might claim to suffer from PTSD to obtain disability benefits. Some people might feign PTSD to deflect blame and justify poor functioning in relationships, occupational pursuits, or when encountering legal problems. In such cases, the person may feign PTSD to "save face" (e.g., "It's not my fault—it's all due to what happened during the war"). A related issue is that some individuals may falsely claim that they were exposed to a traumatic event in the first place (Frueh et al., 2005).

Most of the relevant research has regarded malingering as a monolithic construct, rather than distinguishing among the three forms mentioned. In such studies, PTSD malingering is estimated to occur in at least 20% to 30% of personal injury claimants and at least 20% of compensation-seeking combat veterans (Taylor, Frueh, & Asmundson, 2007). Little is known about prevalence of malingered PTSD specifically among treatment-seeking populations. People malingering PTSD may use clinicians' progress reports from treatment sessions as a means of documenting their psychiatric difficulties.

There are many reported cases in which clinicians have been fooled by patients who were malingering PTSD (Taylor et al., 2007). In the absence of a frank confession or videotaped surveillance indicative of malingering, the detection of malingering must be based on the clinician's estimation of the probability that it has occurred. No single finding from a clinical assessment is sufficient to definitively identify malingering. Each relevant piece of information can be regarded as a "hint" of malingering. As the number of hints increases, so does the odds that the patient is malingering.

The most useful interview measures for detecting malingering include the Structured Interview of Reported Symptoms (SIRS), and Miller-Forensic Assessment of Symptoms Test (M-FAST). Useful questionnaires include the Minnesota Multiphasic Personality Inventory-2 (MMPI-2). Tests such as the SIRS and M-FAST combine a variety of approaches for assessing malingering, such as questions about symptoms that are highly unusual, and symptom combinations that are not typical of mental health patients.

It should be noted, however, that malingered PTSD is especially difficult to detect. Little research has examined malingered PTSD detection beyond using the MMPI-2. Furthermore, even empirical studies using the MMPI-2 demonstrate weaker effects in detecting simulated PTSD than in detecting other simulated mental disorders.

REFERENCES

Frueh, B. C., Elhai, J. D., Grubaugh, A. L., Monnier, J., Kashdan, T. B., Sauvageot, J. A., et al. (2005). Documented combat exposure of U.S. veterans seeking treatment for combat-related posttraumatic stress disorder. *British Journal of Psychiatry, 186,* 467–472.

Taylor, S., Frueh, B. C., & Asmundson, G. J. G. (2007). Detection and management of malingering in people presenting for treatment of posttraumatic stress disorder: Methods, obstacles, and recommendations. *Journal of Anxiety Disorders, 21,* 22–41.

STEVEN TAYLOR
University of British Columbia

See also: Assessment, Psychometric, Adult; Forensic Assessment; Minnesota Multiphasic Personality Inventory-2 (MMPI-2); Projective Personality Measures

MARITAL RELATIONSHIPS

Psychological trauma and posttraumatic stress disorder (PTSD) affect not only the individual but also important relationships in the person's life (*see:* **Family Systems**). The effects of traumatic stress on the family prominently include a destabilization of the trauma-exposed person's marital or couple relationship with a spouse or primary partner. As Shakespeare so aptly said in the Coda to *Romeo and Juliet,* when families experience trauma, "All are punish'd."

Most of what is known about the effects of psychological trauma and PTSD on the marital or couple relationship (MCR) is based on personal accounts of couples told to psychotherapists or couple/family therapists (e.g., Matsakis, 1998). Such personal testimonies are valuable sources of hypotheses for researchers (Walsh & Rothbaum, 2007) and clinicians (Sherman, Zanotti, & Jones, 2005) who are attempting to develop effective treatments to help couples recover from the burden (Calhoun, Beckham, & Bosworth, 2002) of living with PTSD. Scientific research regarding psychological trauma, PTSD, and MCRs is limited to a handful of studies in which one or both members of the couple are interviewed (or less often, actually observed interacting together, although only in laboratory settings) where one spouse or partner is a military veteran with PTSD (Calhoun et al., 2002; Carroll, Rueger, Foy, & Donahoe, 1985; Cook, Riggs, Thompson, Coyne, & Sheikh, 2004; Jordan et al., 1992; Riggs, Byrne, Weathers, & Litz, 1998; Sherman, Sautter, et al., 2005; Solomon, Mikulincer, Fried, & Wosner, 1987). The consistent finding across these studies is that couples in which one partner is a military veteran with PTSD tend to experience (compared to similar couples without PTSD):

- More frequent and severe episodes of verbal conflict (occasionally but not usually escalating to physical conflict or violence) that tend to remain unresolved.
- Less emotional and physical intimacy and more isolation and withdrawal (often initially by the partner with PTSD, but increasingly over time by both partners).

This pattern closely mirrors the marital dynamics that have been shown in studies over 2 decades by Gottman and Levenson (2002) to put couples at high risk for divorce, typically involving the four factors that this research shows to be most likely to lead to escalating conflict and detachment in couple relationships: criticism, contempt, defensiveness, and "stonewalling" (withdrawing or refusing to interact while expressing emotional coldness). Troubled couples tend to have difficulty in "rebounding" from conflictual or hurtful interactions, that is, in regaining a positive attitude toward one another and expressing this "positive sentiment override" (a refocus on what one appreciates and admires about one's partner and values in the relationship) directly and unequivocally to the partner in subsequent interactions (Gottman & Levenson, 2002). PTSD symptoms do not necessarily cause these MCR problems, but they tend to increase the likelihood that a partner will communicate in the actively negative and avoidant ways that are likely to lead his or her partner to feel criticized, held in contempt, blamed, or "stonewalled." PTSD symptoms also can make it very difficult for a person to "override" hurt or angry feelings toward the partner with positive, appreciative, hopeful, friendly, and loving thoughts and communications.

Interview studies concerning MCRs also have been done with women who report a personal history of childhood sexual abuse. College women who disclosed childhood sexual abuse histories described feeling less satisfied and trusting, and having poorer communication in their couple relationships than similar women with no personal history of sexual abuse (DiLillo & Long, 1999). Another study interviewed 240 low-income women and found that those who reported having been sexually abused in childhood (47% of the sample) also reported more episodes of serious physical violence in their couple relationships (including violence toward as well as from their partners) than those with no personal history of childhood sexual abuse (DiLillo, Giuffre, Tremblay, & Peterson, 2001). In qualitative interviews, male partners of women who had experienced childhood sexual abuse described difficulties in their MCR due to their partners' anger, distrust, discomfort with sexuality, and uncertain commitment to the couple relationship as the women engaged in psychotherapy (Bacon & Lein, 1996). These findings, while very preliminary, suggest that experiencing psychological trauma in childhood may lead to an increased risk of conflict and withdrawal by female partners that is similar to that described in studies of couples living with military-related PTSD. The studies with women childhood sexual abuse survivors did not specifically link PTSD symptoms with the couples' difficulties with conflict and withdrawal, but the MCR problems appear to reflect the episodic stress reactivity and chronic and chronic hyperarousal, irritability, avoidance, and emotional numbing of PTSD.

Effects of Psychological Trauma

When a person experiences psychological trauma or posttraumatic stress problems, their ability to engage in an intimate marital/couple relationship with a sense of security, trust, love, compassion, and enjoyment is likely to be compromised despite their best efforts to not let the effects of traumatic stress "spill over" into this vital intimate relationship. Sherman, Zanotti, et al. (2005) describe how PTSD's intrusive reexperiencing symptoms such as nightmares or flashbacks lead the traumatized partner to feel helpless and ashamed, as well as to have problems at work that can adversely affect the couple's financial security. PTSD's avoidance, emotional numbing, and social detachment symptoms may contribute to withdrawal and loss of intimacy (not just sexually, but in all walks of the couple's life). PTSD's hyperarousal symptoms may lead the traumatized partner to be more irritable, critical, and emotionally reactive, as well as to try to prevent danger or problems by hypervigilantly seeking to control the other partner's behavior, beliefs, and emotions. PTSD symptoms tend to have escalating interactive effects: for example, even mild reminders of trauma experiences can elicit physiological arousal and emotional and mental distress that may be expressed in the form of anger, anxious dependency, or emotional disengagement that seems to unpredictably come out of nowhere to both partners. When PTSD symptoms include potentially dangerous behaviors such as substance abuse or suicidality, or extreme forms of intrusive memories (such as blackouts or violent nightmares), emotional disengagement (such as dissociative shifts in identity; *see:* **Dissociation**), or hyperarousal (such as states of rage or panic), both partners tend to feel terrified, helpless, and (if these problems persist) ultimately unable to tolerate living together regardless of the strength of their love for and dedication to one another. In those cases, separation and divorce are common, although some relationships continue unchanged on the surface but emotionally empty in reality.

Effects of Living with a Traumatized Partner

As a result of the severe challenges posed by PTSD symptoms, the partner or spouse of a traumatized person is inevitably affected as well. As a result of the traumatized (i.e., someone who is experiencing traumatic stress reactions) partner's PTSD symptoms, the partner may feel their relationship is like walking through a "mine field" or living with a "time bomb," because apparently minor or ordinary events or stressors seem to evoke an unpredictable and often extremely upsetting or hurtful reaction from the partner. Or the partner may feel as though he or she is being shut out and alone as a result of being unable to penetrate the traumatized partner's barriers of emotional detachment and anger or anxiety. Many partners courageously continue to support and sustain the traumatized partner and their relationship, making adjustments such as assiduously avoiding any conversations or interactions (including those involving other family members or friends) that may trigger PTSD reactions, spending large amounts of time apart from the partner in order to be nonintrusive, sleeping in separate beds or rooms as a result of the partner's posttraumatic nightmares or sleeplessness, and helping the partner to recover emotionally, physically, and interpersonally from episodes of extreme behavior (e.g., intoxication, rage or panic reactions). These adjustments cause an often severe burden on the nontraumatized partner (Calhoun et al., 2002; *see:* **Vicarious Traumatization**), potentially compromising her or his emotional and physical health, relationships with friends and family, and ability to be productive vocationally or academically and to enjoy life.

Assessing and Treating Couples Affected by PTSD

Wilson and Kurtz (1997) provide an overview of the clinical considerations and measures that are relevant to the psychological assessment of couples in which one partner has PTSD. They recommend beginning by educating the couple about PTSD and encouraging the partners to discuss what the traumatic event(s) that one or both of them have experienced mean to each of them and to their relationship, with the therapeutic relationship as a "sanctuary" in which they can explore together how trauma has affected their lives and relationship. Sherman,

Zanotti, et al. (2005) provide a further overview of clinical considerations in conducting psychotherapy with couples in which one partner has PTSD (*see:* **Family Therapy; Marital Therapy**). Both relational/psychodynamic and cognitive behavioral (Monson, Schnurr, Stevens, & Guthrie, 2004) approaches to couples therapy have been developed for MCRs in which one partner has PTSD (Riggs, 2000), with each showing promise in clinical or pilot research studies. Additional clinical studies are needed in order to adapt these couples therapy models to address different types and levels of severity of PTSD with couples from varied socioeconomic and cultural backgrounds, and rigorous scientific studies are needed in order to document their efficacy and effectiveness in both enhancing and preventing breakdowns in the MCR as well as in ameliorating PTSD and related problems.

REFERENCES

Bacon, B., & Lein, L. (1996). Living with a female sexual abuse survivor: Male partners' perspectives. *Journal of Child Sexual Abuse, 5*(2), 1–16.

Calhoun, P. S., Beckham, J. C., & Bosworth, H. B. (2002). Caregiver burden and psychological distress in partners of veterans with chronic posttraumatic stress disorder. *Journal of Traumatic Stress, 15,* 205–212.

Carroll, E. M., Rueger, D. B., Foy, D. W., & Donahoe, C. P. (1985). Vietnam combat veterans with posttraumatic stress disorder: Analysis of marital and cohabiting adjustment. *Journal of Abnormal Psychology, 94,* 329–337.

Cook, J. M., Riggs, D. S., Thompson, R., Coyne, J. C., & Sheikh, J. I. (2004). Posttraumatic stress disorder and current relationship functioning among World War II ex-prisoners of war. *Journal of Family Psychology, 18,* 36–45.

DeLillo, D., Giuffre, D., Tremblay, G., & Peterson, L. (2001). A closer look at the nature of intimate partner violence reported by women with a history of child sexual abuse. *Journal of Interpersonal Violence, 16,* 116–132.

DeLillo, D., & Long, P. (1999). Perceptions of couple functioning among female survivors of child sexual abuse. *Journal of Child Sexual Abuse, 7*(4), 59–76.

Gottman, J. M., & Levenson, R. W. (2002). A two-factor model for predicting when a couple will divorce: Exploratory analyses using 14-year longitudinal data. *Family Process, 41,* 83–96.

Jordan, B. K., Marmar, C. R., Fairbank, J. A., Schlenger, W. E., Kulka, R. A., Hough, R. L., et al. (1992). Problems in families of male Vietnam veterans with posttraumatic stress disorders. *Journal of Consulting and Clinical Psychology, 60,* 916–926.

Matsakis, A. (1998). *Vietnam wives: Facing the challenges of life with veterans suffering posttraumatic stress* (2nd ed.). Towson, MD: Sidran Institute Press.

Monson, C., Schnurr, P., Stevens, S., & Guthrie, K. (2004). Cognitive-behavioral couple's treatment for posttraumatic stress disorder: Initial findings. *Journal of Traumatic Stress, 17,* 341–344.

Riggs, D. (2000). Marital and family therapy. In E. B. Foa, T. M. Keane, & M. J. Friedman (Eds.), *Effective treatments for PTSD: Practice guidelines from the International Society for Traumatic Stress Studies* (pp. 280–301). New York: Guilford Press.

Riggs, D., Byrne, C. A., Weathers, F. W., & Litz, B. T. (1998). The quality of intimate relationships in male Vietnam veterans: The impact of posttraumatic stress disorder. *Journal of Traumatic Stress, 11,* 87–102.

Sherman, M. D., Sautter, F., Lyons, J., Manguno-Mire, G., Han, X., Perry, D., et al. (2005). Mental health treatment needs of cohabiting partners of veterans with combat-related PTSD. *Psychiatric Services, 56,* 1150–1152.

Sherman, M. D., Zanotti, D., & Jones, D. (2005). Key elements in couples therapy with veterans with combat-related posttraumatic stress disorder. *Professional Psychology: Research and Practice, 36,* 626–633.

Solomon, Z., Mikulincer, M., Fried, B., & Wosner, Y. (1987). Family characteristics and posttraumatic stress disorder: A follow-up of Israeli combat stress reaction casualties. *Family Process, 26,* 383–394.

Walsh, S., & Rothbaum, B. O. (2007). Emerging treatments for PTSD. In M. Friedman, T. Keane, & P. Resick (Eds.), *Handbook of PTSD: Science and practice* (pp. 469–496). New York: Guilford Press.

Wilson, J. P., & Kurtz, R. (1997). Assessing PTSD in couples and families. In J. P. Wilson & T. M. Keane (Eds.), *Assessing psychological trauma and PTSD* (pp. 349–373). New York: Guilford Press.

JULIAN D. FORD
University of Connecticut School of Medicine

See also: Domestic Violence; Family Systems; Family Therapy; Marital Therapy; Traumatic Bonding

MARITAL THERAPY

The human brain is relational (Siegel, 1999). When people are in very close contact, as in a marriage relationship, old patterns of interaction that are deeply embedded in the brain become part of the interaction between the partners. Posttraumatic stress disorder (PTSD) involves changes in the brain and body that interfere with the resolution of or recovery from the overwhelming sense of terror, pain, and helplessness in life-threatening or body-violating experiences. Thus, it is not surprising that when one or both partners in an intimate relationship are experiencing PTSD, this may have profound effects on their feelings for and interactions with each other (Solomon & Siegel, 2005).

PTSD can lead either or both partners to be looked to as an island of safety in a frightening, cruel world. There is a yearning to find someone who loves, attunes, and does not re-create the trauma. Often the partner is tested, based on questions such as "Will this relationship provide a safe haven?" Without conscious awareness the partner is on trial. Other questions include: "If I show you the worst in me, the pain, the terror, the rage that I could not let myself feel when I was in the midst of danger, will you be a source of safety, understanding and comfort . . . or will I be hurt again?" If the partner passes one test, a new one takes place so long as PTSD causes a lingering sense of danger.

Unfortunately, the ways that mates select for the familiar, and then interact, may throw each one into reexperiencing or reenacting past traumas. The partner becomes associated with the danger from the past. Each then defends against the pain inflicted by the other. Each feels too vulnerable to express dependency needs from the other (Solomon, 1989).

Therapy with couples who have experienced, and are replaying, psychological trauma is quite different from the work of helping couples who are dealing with nontraumatic issues such as separation and closeness, autonomy and interdependence, or conflictual and unclear communication. Rather than primarily working with the stories that both tell themselves about how the other is causing the problem, the therapist listens for the subtle messages, seen in facial muscles, body position, visceral reactions, and tightened striated muscles, that may signify the intrusion of PTSD into the couple's relationship. The therapist has a number of ways to intervene, providing openings for partners to gain awareness of emotions from past traumas that are being re-created in the moment, while providing safety in the moment-to-moment interaction during the session. The therapist also may give homework assignments in order to maintain continuity of the work between sessions.

By giving a place of safety in the marital counseling sessions, the therapist is modeling new ways of reacting in the present when intense emotion and defense arise as remnants of trauma from the past. Interventions may require slowing down the action, such as by asking: "Let's stop for a moment. Just before you got so angry, your face and eyes looked as though you were holding back intense sadness. Can we go back to that moment for a bit, and talk about how it was for you when your wife said that she is so frightened of you that she thinks of running away with the children?" Or, "I noticed that you stopped breathing when your husband started talking about how you close down when he tries to initiate sex. Can we talk about the sense of numbness that you seem to be experiencing right now?"

Partners are encouraged to resist the impulse to react with fear or rage that is a hallmark of PTSD. They are helped to think while becoming aware of feelings, rather than to act without thinking or feeling. They learn to ask themselves if their perceptions are accurate for the present situation, to take time-outs when emotions are overwhelming, to question whether their behavior is getting them what

they want, and to try out new ways of responding. The goal is to make this relationship the secure environment in which growth beyond PTSD is possible. Although the efficacy of marital therapy for PTSD has not been definitively demonstrated, several promising approaches are building a clinical and empirical evidence base (Johnson, 2004; Riggs, 2000).

REFERENCES

Johnson, S. M. (2004). Facing the dragon together: Emotionally focused couples therapy with trauma survivors. In D. R. Catherall (Ed.), *Handbook of stress, trauma, and the family* (pp. 493–512). New York: Brunner-Routledge.

Riggs, D. S. (2000). Marital and family therapy. In E. B. Foa, T. M. Keane, & M. J. Friedman (Eds.), *Effective treatments for PTSD: Practice guidelines from the International Society for Traumatic Stress Studies* (pp. 280–301). New York: Guilford Press.

Siegel, D. J. (1999). *The developing mind: Toward a neurobiology of interpersonal relationships.* New York: Norton.

Solomon, M. F. (1989). *Narcissism and intimacy.* New York: Norton.

Solomon, M. F., & Siegel, D. J. (2005). *Healing trauma.* New York: Norton.

Marion F. Solomon
Life Span Learning Institute

See also: Family Systems; Family Therapy; Marital Relationships

MEDIA REPORTING OF TRAUMA

From the time that Pheidippides ran 26 miles from Marathon to Athens declaring "Rejoice! We have conquered!" (then collapsing and dying), the reporting of trauma has been dangerous, difficult, and commonplace. But only in the past 15 years have media corporations and schools of journalism paid systematic attention to the subject of trauma and to its toll on those who gather and receive traumatic news.

Accredited American schools of journalism have no standard curricula for teaching traumatic stress, nor for exposing students to the topics of grief, victimization, PTSD, nor for training young reporters on interviewing emotionally vulnerable individuals. In the early 1990s, two schools, Michigan State University and the University of Washington, began courses on these subjects, leading to the first text on journalism and trauma, coauthored by professors from each school (Simpson & Cote, 2006). Other schools of journalism followed suit in Brisbane, Australia; Cardiff, Wales; Oklahoma City; Indianapolis; Boulder; Maryland; and Bournemouth, United Kingdom. Journalism educators share material and methods, often in collaboration with traumatic stress experts and drawing on a common pool of Internet resources that include PTSD curricula prepared expressly for journalists (Dart Center, n.d.-c). A study by the University of Maryland, commissioned in 2007 by the Dart Center for Journalism and Trauma, analyzes the teaching of trauma in American journalism schools.

Awards for excellence in reporting on victims of violence originated in the mid-1990s, with judges drawn from the ranks of working journalists, trauma survivors, and experts in traumatic stress studies. These prize-winning stories, usually in-depth series published on successive days, encompass the spectrum of trauma-related topics: war, crime, abuse, disaster, and the impact of unnatural, unexpected dying on next-of-kin (Dart Center, n.d.-b). Lurid portraits, emphasizing shock and horror attract some readers and offend others. Stories that depict survivors with sensitivity and accuracy, leaving readers sadder and wiser, win awards.

Major media corporations not only competed for these awards, but recognized needs for consultation in preparing reporters and photographers for demanding, traumatic assignments, and in minimizing the risk of physical and emotional damage to these professionals. A senior BBC correspondent who was also a trained trauma psychotherapist launched programs meeting these needs for the BBC (Brayne, n.d.). This approach influenced other large agencies in the United States and Europe. During this era, one large media foundation and one media corporation commissioned a historic study of war journalists, finding an incidence of PTSD, depression, and alcoholism that approached rates for combat veterans (Feinstein, 2003). As media leaders and practitioners came to acknowledge the risk of PTSD and related conditions for their own colleagues, a research agenda emerged, facilitated by a psychologist who was both president of the International Society for Traumatic Stress Studies and director of research for the Dart Center for Journalism and Trauma (Newman, n.d.). Research topics include the impact of trauma reporting on the reporter, media generated vicarious traumatization, comparison of exposure to trauma between reporters and photographers, and evaluation of training techniques.

Media reporting of trauma affects the audience and reporters—often causing emotional distress when drawing attention to human suffering or misconduct. The question facing the modern media is how to perform a time-honored duty with minimal collateral damage and maximal newsworthy information. A growing field of journalism and trauma is addressing that question (Dart Center, n.d.-a).

REFERENCES

Brayne, M. (n.d.). *Staff and personnel: Mark Brayne.* Retrieved from the Dart Center web site: www.dartcenter.org/about/personnel_brayne_m.html.

Dart Center. (n.d.-a). *About the Dart Center.* Retrieved from the Dart Center web site: www.dartcenter.org/about/index.php.

Dart Center. (n.d.-b). *Dart award past winners.* Retrieved from the Dart Center web site: www.dartcenter.org/dartaward/past_winners.html.

Dart Center. (n.d.-c). *Self study.* Retrieved from the Dart Center web site: www.dartcenter.org/training/selfstudy/index.html.

Feinstein, A. (2003). *Dangerous lives: War and the men and women who report it.* Toronto, Ontario, Canada: Thomas Allen.

Feinstein, A. (2006). *Dangerous lives: War and the men and women who report it* (2nd ed.). Toronto, Ontario, Canada: Thomas Allen.

Feinstein, A. (2006). *Journalists under fire: The psychological hazards of covering war.* Baltimore: Johns Hopkins Press.

Newman, E. (n.d.). *Journalism and trauma studies.* Retrieved from the Dart Center web site: www.dartcenter.org/research/index.html.

Simpson, R., & Cote, W. (2006). *Covering violence: A guide to ethical reporting about victims and trauma* (2nd ed.). New York: Columbia University Press.

Frank Ochberg
Dart Center for Journalism and Trauma

See also: Journalists, Effects of Trauma on

MEDICAL ILLNESS, ADULT

Physical health aspects to traumatic events have long been observed in historical accounts of posttraumatic stress disorder (PTSD). For example, "Soldier's Irritable Heart," an early conceptualization (Da Costa, 1871) of PTSD was described as a physiological disturbance caused by the stress of experiencing combat. Physical symptoms were also a prominent component of the "rape trauma syndrome" described by Burgess and Holstrom (1974) based on interviews with women who had endured sexual assault. When the term posttraumatic stress disorder was first introduced in *DSM-III* (American Psychiatric Association, 1980), physical symptoms related to persistently heightened arousal (including exaggerated startle response, irritability, and sleep disturbance) were included in the diagnostic criteria.

In addition to PTSD's physical symptoms, research has sought to determine whether PTSD could influence the development of medical illnesses. This question is of particular importance in light of research indicating that PTSD persists into a chronic condition in approximately one-third of individuals who suffer from it. As a result, any influence of PTSD symptoms on medical illness could accumulate over the course of many years, and might affect not only morbidity (physical health problems) but also mortality (the risk of dying).

Psychological Trauma, PTSD Diagnosis, and Medical Illness

Much of the preliminary evidence for a connection between PTSD and the development of medical illness has been derived from studies using self-reported health ratings or self-reported medical illnesses as the primary outcome measures. These measures impose minimal response burden on participants and provide a numerical continuum (such as a score ranging from 0 to 100) as the outcome variable for studying physical health. Such measures enable researchers to examine subtler differences in physical health than do dichotomous (e.g., sick versus healthy) or categorical (e.g., mildly versus moderately versus severely ill) measures.

Especially in the period preceding the introduction of the term posttraumatic stress disorder, but also in recent studies, many researchers examined relationships between exposure to events likely to be extremely stressful, and therefore potentially traumatic, and later development of medical illness. For example, in New York City residents living in lower Manhattan during the September 11, 2001, terror attacks, higher levels of disaster-related exposure and its aftermath were associated with poorer self-reported physical health 1 year after the event (Adams, Boscarino, & Galea, 2006). A large study of people who were not seeking psychological treatment found that retrospectively recalled childhood sexual or physical abuse was related to poorer self-reported physical health, but PTSD was not assessed (Sachs-Ericsson, Blazer, Plant, & Arnow, 2005).

Similar associations of potential traumatic event/extreme stress exposure with poorer physical health ratings have been observed in people who have experienced combat, sexual assault, and other accidents and disasters. These studies have typically statistically controlled for demographic characteristics that may have been confounded with physical health ratings. Extreme stress exposure has also exhibited associations with functional outcomes related to physical health. For example, veterans surveyed 1 year after returning from deployment in Iraq who were diagnosed with PTSD reported not only poorer physical health ratings but also higher numbers of sick days than similar military veterans who were not diagnosed with PTSD (Hoge, Terhakopian, Castro, Messer, & Engel, 2007).

Studies of self-reported physical health provide valuable information on the correlation of trauma/extreme stress with perceptions of health and somatic symptoms, but they do not address the question of whether it is PTSD in particular, as opposed to extremely stressful or traumatic events in general, that is related to poor physical health. Perhaps more importantly, self-reported physical health could be confounded by response biases such as the ability to recall medical problems or the individual's frame of reference for what constitutes good physical health. Another possibility is that increased rates of medical illness in people with PTSD may also be influenced by the degree of somatization that may characterize severe PTSD. Several authors have noted the possibility that cognitive-related PTSD symptoms (e.g., difficulty concentrating) could complicate the ability of people with this disorder to effectively apprehend and report physical symptoms, including PTSD's physiological symptoms, which may be perceived as medical problems. This could increase patients' focus on and reporting of physical symptoms to physicians as well as influencing self-reported health ratings. While increased focus on somatic symptoms is certainly expected to influence the results of studies utilizing self-reported physical health as the outcome, somatization may also alter physician-diagnosed medical illness by promoting higher utilization of health care. One potential by-product of more frequent interactions with the health-care system is that more assessments will cause more medical illnesses to be detected and diagnosed.

Several studies have documented associations of both traumatic event exposure and traumatic stress reactions with medical illness. In one such study with primary care patients, trauma history was associated with self-reported arthritis and diabetes in men as well as digestive diseases and cancer in women (Norman et al., 2006). The assessment of medical illness by using participant reports on general disease categories may lead to over-

reporting of medical conditions, however. To eliminate bias in subjective health reports and in participant recall of illnesses, physician diagnoses of health conditions have been used in some studies. Not all studies using physician's diagnoses have observed statistically significant differences in physical health status between PTSD participants and non-PTSD participants (Centers for Disease Control, 1988). However, large investigations have noted PTSD's associations with musculoskeletal, respiratory, nervous, digestive, and cardiac illnesses (Boscarino, 2004). In addition, relationships between PTSD diagnosis and medical illnesses have been observed when both patient and physician reports have been used in the same study (Beckham et al., 1998), suggesting a degree of convergence between patient and physician sources of medical information.

In an archival study of U.S. Civil War soldiers, combat exposure characteristics including prisoner-of-war experience, percentage of military company killed, being wounded, and early enlistment age were examined as predictors of disease and mortality. These combat exposure characteristics were related to cardiac and gastrointestinal disease, comorbid nervous and physical disease, and earlier mortality (Pizarro, Silver, & Prause, 2006).

In addition to research on specific chronic illnesses, overall survival following exposure to extreme stressors has been investigated. A large follow-up of Vietnam-era veterans occurring 30 years after discharge from military service found that mortality rates were higher for those serving in Vietnam, as opposed to elsewhere, suggesting a link between combat exposure and risk of death (Boehmer, Flanders, McGeehin, Boyle, & Barrett, 2004).

Schnurr and Green (2004) have proposed a model in which exposure to trauma and extreme stress leads to the development of PTSD, which in turn influences the development of medical illness through biological and psychosocial pathways. Conceptualized in this way, PTSD is termed a mediator of the relationship between trauma/extreme stress and the development of medical illness. An important implication of this model is that the measurement of PTSD is critical to understanding medical effects of trauma. Several studies have reported that PTSD diagnosis and symptoms can mediate this relationship (Lang et al., 2006; Norman et al., 2006).

The existing research generally supports the idea that psychological trauma and extreme stress promote medical illness, but preliminary evidence suggests PTSD contributes more strongly to medical illness outcomes than trauma exposure does. This was reported in an examination of primary care patients, where those with PTSD were found to be at elevated risk for anemia, arthritis, asthma, back pain, diabetes, eczema, kidney disease, lung disease, and ulcer. PTSD was more strongly associated with illness than exposures to trauma (Weisberg et al., 2002).

Studies comparing people who experienced the same trauma/extreme stress are valuable in differentiating effects of the event from effects of having PTSD on physical symptoms and medical illness, and have generally shown those with PTSD to exhibit poorer physical health. For example, in a sample of firefighters following a disaster, those who had developed PTSD were more likely to report cardiovascular, respiratory, musculoskeletal, and neurological symptoms than those who were exposed to the disaster but not diagnosed with PTSD (McFarlane, Atchison, Rafalowicz, & Papay, 1994). Among survivors of an explosion, people with PTSD were more likely to have physician-reported vascular, musculoskeletal, and dermatological problems than people who survived the disaster but did not meet criteria for PTSD. A diagnosis of PTSD was also associated with more self-reported physical symptoms (Dirkzwager, van der Velden, Grievnik, & Yzermans, 2007).

Epidemiological evidence for a link between PTSD and medical illness has come from the Vietnam Experience Study (VES). Participants in this study were 18,581 Vietnam-era veterans, meaning that all veterans served at the time of the Vietnam War but not necessarily in Vietnam, serving between 1965 and 1971. The medical histories of veterans from the VES were examined approximately 20 years after combat exposure, and those with PTSD were reported to have increased rates of physician-diagnosed circulatory, digestive, musculoskeletal, nervous, and respiratory system diseases, as well as increased rates of nonsexually transmitted infectious disease. These results were independent of the influences of a large number of demographic, military, behavioral health, and baseline medical characteristics (Boscarino, 1997). Examination of a larger random sample of veterans from the Vietnam War era found that those diagnosed with PTSD were more than twice as likely to exhibit positive electrocardiogram findings, an indication of pathology for patients at risk for cardiovascular disease (Boscarino & Chang, 1999).

The relative contributions of different types of psychological traumas to health status has received little attention in the research literature, but reports have noted increased risk of medical illness in people who had suffered several types of trauma, including exposure to sexual or physical abuse as children (Cromer & Sachs-Ericsson, 2006), combat (Boscarino, 1997), and accidents/disaster (Dirkzwager et al., 2007). In spite of these findings, extended duration of PTSD may be associated with a greater cumulative effect of the disorder on physical morbidity. Thus again, these findings suggest that even if potential traumatic event exposure increased the risk of medical illness for all who experience it, the development of PTSD contributes substantially to elevations in risk for medical illness.

It is not entirely understood whether PTSD can cause medical illness, however. Most studies investigating this issue are cross-sectional, and thus causality cannot be inferred. For example, the life-threatening hypoglycemic episodes that can occur in people with diabetes are potentially traumatic and could lead to the development of PTSD. This underscores the utility of longitudinal studies that have statistically controlled for baseline medical characteristics and assessments of index traumas in studies attempting to establish an influence of PTSD on medical illness.

PTSD Diagnosis and Mortality

A follow-up of the VES data approximately 30 years after military service revealed increased mortality risk in Vietnam War veterans both overall and for specific causes including cardiovascular disease as well as external events such as suicide, motor vehicle accidents, accidental poisonings, suicides, homicides, injuries of undetermined intent. In addition, veterans who served in Vietnam, as opposed to serving elsewhere, and had PTSD exhibited an increased risk of cancer (Boscarino, 2006). More recent analysis of returning veterans suggests that those with PTSD and internalizing (high negative affect, lower positive affect, depression) and externalizing (high on impulsivity and anger) comorbid psychopathology, compared to those with low comorbid psychopathology, may be particularly vulnerable to early mortality (Flood et al., 2007).

Taken together, these large-scale studies present further compelling evidence, based on large datasets, of a relationship between PTSD and medical illness. However, it should be noted that participants in these studies all served in the military, and a disproportionate number of index traumas were likely combat-related. Further research is needed to investigate the degree to which results on Vietnam-era veterans generalize to people who suffered from other types of index trauma.

Biological Mechanisms

Depression

Research reporting associations between PTSD and medical illness are potentially confounded by the frequent comorbidity of PTSD and major depressive disorder. This is of particular concern in light of research noting a significant association of depression with medical illness (Reynolds, Dew, Lenze, & Whyte, 2007). This confound was investigated in a study of women veterans (Frayne et al., 2004). When all patients with PTSD (including those with comorbid depression) were compared to patients with depression only (but no PTSD), patients with PTSD reported poorer physical health overall and reported higher rates of medical illness than patients with depression alone (Frayne et al., 2004). The influence of

PTSD has similarly been noted to be independent of the effects of depression in women who have experienced a sexual assault (Zoellner, Goodwin, & Foa, 2000). However, it is likely that the presence of depression exacerbates harmful effects of PTSD. This has been supported by research into functional outcomes.

Hypothalamic-Pituitary-Adrenal (HPA) Axis

Human physiological responses to stress appraisals have consistently demonstrated activation of a specific pathway beginning with the brain's hypothalamus, which secretes corticotropin-releasing hormone (CRH). CRH triggers the pituitary gland to secrete adrenocorticotropic hormone (ACTH), leading to stimulation of cortisol secretion by the adrenal cortex (McEwen, 1998). This pathway is referred to as the HPA axis. Cortisol produces metabolic changes, mobilizing energy by promoting the conversion of protein and lipids to usable carbohydrates, providing the organism with the energy resources to confront a stressor (McEwen, 2004) and ideally reduce the intensity of the stressor. The HPA axis is a physiological negative feedback loop, with cortisol actively inhibiting subsequent activation of this system. As a result, of heightened secretion under stress, cortisol presents one means of assessing the effects of psychosocial stress on physiological functioning. Experiencing a traumatic event has been linked with alterations in the HPA axis, including heightened secretion of cortisol when presented with reminders of the traumatic event.

The physiological responses to acute stressors aimed at short-term adaptation have been termed *allostasis,* meaning "the ability to achieve stability through change" (McEwen, 1998, p. 171). Allostasis incorporates responses from several systems in the body, including the HPA axis, the autonomic nervous system, and the cardiovascular, metabolic, and immune systems. Once a stressor is removed, allostatic responses aimed at addressing acute stressors are generally inactivated, returning HPA axis activity to its baseline state.

Although allostatis promotes adaptation, accommodations to stress can exact a toll on the body over time due to chronic underactivation or overactivation of bodily systems influenced by allostasis. The wear and tear on the body associated with repeated stress or insufficient deactivation of allostatic responses has been termed allostatic load (McEwen & Stellar, 1993). Allostatic load can develop due to exposure to frequent and varied stressors, failure to adapt to repeated stressors of the same type, or failure of stress responsive systems to return to baseline following the removal of the stressor (McEwen, 1998). In these instances, chronic overexposure to stress hormones such as cortisol can bring about pathophysiologic consequences. For example, chronic overactivation of the HPA axis can lead to disruption of circadian physiological rhythms, which may be linked with suppressed immune function, sleep disruption, and increased cancer incidence and progression (Sephton & Spiegel, 2003). Continued overactivation of the HPA axis has also been associated with varying conditions including memory impairment, hypertension, osteoporosis, insulin resistance, and cardiovascular disease (Chrousos & Gold, 1998). Changes in the HPA axis may be one mechanism of increased physical health morbidity in PTSD.

Immunity

One implication of HPA axis activation is the potential alteration of immune system processes. End-products of the HPA axis (such as cortisol) inhibit cytotoxicity, the ability of some types of immune cells to destroy target cells. Stress responses can also reduce availability in the body of immune cells such as lymphocytes and affect secretion of cytokines such as interleukin-2 (essential to fighting infection) and interferon-γ, which has anti-tumor properties (Elenkov & Chrousos, 1999). Finally, stress responses to short-term stressors can elevate the immune responses through alterations in cell trafficking, putting body tissues at risk of inflammation and autoimmune disorders, attacks of the immune system on healthy body tissue.

Just as overexposure to stress hormones can be problematic, hypo- (i.e., decreased) responsivity of the HPA axis can also lead to allostatic load. The immune system component of allostasis is typically regulated by glucocorticoids (such as cortisol). When cortisol levels are insufficient for inactivation of the immune response following removal of the stressor, the organism is at increased risk of an immune response against healthy tissue, called an autoimmune response, due to sustained exposure to inflammatory cytokines (McEwen, 1998). Evidence suggests that while healthy individuals tend to have a suppressed immune response to stress, people with PTSD exhibit an increased immune response to stress, leaving them vulnerable to inflammation and autoimmune disease. This pathway is supported by epidemiological evidence from Vietnam-era veterans, where Boscarino (2004) examined PTSD and a number of autoimmune disorders based on self-reported symptoms. PTSD diagnosis was associated with increased risk of autoimmune disorders generally, as well as increased risk of psoriasis and glomerulonephritis (kidney inflammation) specifically. PTSD accompanied by high levels of other self-reported psychopathology was related to increased risk of specific autoimmune disorders including psoriasis, rheumatoid arthritis, diabetes, and hypothyroidism.

The concept of allostasis is particularly interesting as it relates to PTSD because a number of studies have documented altered HPA axis activity in people with PTSD. While the precise nature of these alterations has varied across studies, PTSD generally appears to be related to increased negative feedback inhibition of cortisol secretion. PTSD diagnosis has been associated with lower morning cortisol levels (Boscarino, 1996). This explains the persistently low cortisol levels often observed in those with PTSD. In addition to decreased overall cortisol levels, existing research suggests the hyperarousal symptoms triggered by intrusions related to traumatic events in people with PTSD are accompanied by immediate alterations in HPA activity.

Autonomic Reactivity

PTSD may also influence medical illness through risk factors for cardiovascular disease. PTSD has been associated with alterations in cardiovascular reactivity, a relatively stable individual difference variable measuring cardiovascular changes occurring in response to behavioral stressors (Treiber et al., 2003). Cardiovascular reactivity is hypothesized to be a marker or mechanism in the development of cardiovascular disease (Manuck, 1994), a relationship supported by preliminary research on the topic (Treiber et al., 2003). People with PTSD have exhibited increased levels of catecholamines, a sympathetic nervous system hormone, and higher heart rate in response to stressors related to the trauma. However, catecholamine reactivity to nontrauma stressors has generally been similar to that of people without PTSD. Lower resting heart rates and diastolic blood pressure have also been reported in people with PTSD. This has been conceptualized as stress-induced altered reactivity as potentially changing the structure and functioning of the cardiovascular system (Buckley & Kaloupek, 2001).

PTSD and Behavioral Health

Cigarette Smoking

Cigarette smoking is an important medical and societal problem, as well as being a leading cause of preventable disease. A disproportionately high number of individuals with psychiatric conditions smoke cigarettes. Between 50% and 80% of those suffering from a mental illness smoke, whereas less than 40% of those who have never had mental illness smoke (Lasser et al., 2000).

Evidence suggests that even individuals exposed to traumatic events but who do not develop PTSD are more likely to start smoking following exposure than nontraumatized individuals. However, development of PTSD following trauma appears to substantially increase the risk of becoming a smoker (Breslau, Davis, & Schultz, 2003). Of those with PTSD, an estimated 50% smoke cigarettes, and they tend to smoke more heavily (Beckham, 1999). Furthermore, smokers with PTSD report more craving and negative affect to stress and trauma cues (e.g., taped narration of the individual's

traumatic event) in the laboratory (Beckham et al., 2007) and are more likely to smoke when experiencing a PTSD symptom (Beckham et al., in press).

Nicotine reliably and markedly increases cortisol levels in most humans (Garcia Calzado et al., 1990). Because cortisol feeds back to inhibit subsequent activation of the HPA axis, it is possible that smoking prompts the HPA axis to develop enhanced sensitivity to negative feedback inhibition, causing persistent reductions in cortisol secretion. Increased sensitivity to negative feedback inhibition in smokers is supported by research observing decreased ACTH, a critical component of cortisol secretion, in response to lab stressors, physical activity, a CRH (Kirschbaum, Scherer, & Strasburger, 1994). As discussed previously, blunted HPA axis activity likely promotes increased exposure to immune factors (Altemus, Dhabhar, & Yang, 2006) and is one potential pathway by which elevated smoking in people with PTSD might contribute to the development medical illnesses.

Obesity

Obesity is a risk factor for a number of chronic illnesses and has also been an outcome of interest in PTSD research. One study of veterans with PTSD reported an average body mass index (BMI) in the obese range, with 83% being at least in the overweight range (Vieweg et al., 2006). In light of this finding, it is perhaps not surprising that PTSD diagnosis has been linked with elevations in cholesterol, low density lipoproteins, and triglycerides, as well as lowered high density lipoproteins, factors that increase risk for cardiovascular disease (Kagan, Leskin, Haas, Wilkins, & Foy, 1999). Obesity is also a risk factor for diabetes, and a significant association of PTSD with diabetes has been observed in a large-scale study of adults (Goodwin & Davidson, 2005).

Alcohol Consumption

PTSD may influence the development of medical illness through the increased alcohol consumption sometimes observed in people with PTSD (Kessler, Sonnega, Bromet, Hughes, & Nelson, 1995). Heavy alcohol consumption could contribute to the pathophysiology of chronic illnesses as well as being a risk factor for accidental events causing injury or death. Though the behavioral health outcomes observed in people with PTSD are a promising area of research in explaining pathways linking PTSD and medical illness, existing models suggest that behavioral health accounts for only a portion of the variance in poorer self-reported physical health and medical illness observed in those with PTSD (Asmundson, Stein, & McCreary, 2002; Schnurr & Green, 2004).

Because of the comorbidity of alcohol dependence with PTSD, it is possible that alcohol dependence accounts for associations between PTSD and medical illness. In a study comparing PTSD-diagnosed combat veterans with demographically matched alcohol dependence-diagnosed veterans (without a history of combat or PTSD), veterans with PTSD were found to have an increased chance of having diabetes, osteoarthritis, and heart disease in their medical records. Patients with PTSD also had higher cholesterol, triglyceride, and BMI levels, as well as increased rates of obesity (David, Woodward, Esquenazi, & Mellman, 2004). While exposure to trauma/extreme stress was not controlled in this study, the results suggest that PTSD increases the risk of medical illness more than the risk associated with alcohol dependence.

Conclusion

The evidence suggests that PTSD is associated with increased morbidity and mortality. There is also research to suggest that there are multiple possible contributors to this association, particularly in the areas of biological mechanisms and health behaviors. More research is needed to understand the development of these associations, and which medical conditions are most related to PTSD.

REFERENCES

Adams, R. E., Boscarino, J. A., & Galea, S. (2006). Social and psychological resources and health outcomes after the World Trade Center disaster. *Social Science and Medicine, 62,* 176–188.

Altemus, M., Dhabhar, F. S., & Yang, R. (2006). Immune function in PTSD. *Annals of the New York Academy of Sciences, 1071,* 167–183.

American Psychiatric Association. (1980). *Diagnostic and statistical manual of mental disorders* (3rd ed.). Washington, DC: Author.

Asmundson, G. J. G., Stein, M. B., & McCreary, D. R. (2002). Posttraumatic stress disorder symptom influence health status of deployed peacekeepers and nondeployed military personnel. *Journal of Nervous and Mental Disease, 190,* 807–815.

Beckham, J. C. (1999). Smoking and anxiety in combat veterans with chronic posttraumatic stress disorder: A review. *Journal of Psychoactive Drugs, 31*(2), 103–110.

Beckham, J. C., Feldman, M. E., McClernon, F. J., Mozley, S. L., Collie, C. F., & Vrana, S. R. (2007). Cigarette smoking and script-driven imagery in smokers with and without posttraumatic stress disorder. *Addictive Behaviors, 32,* 2900–2915.

Beckham, J. C., Moore, S. D., Feldman, M. E., Hertzberg, M. A., Kirby, A. C., & Fairbank, J. A. (1998). Health status, somatization, and severity of posttraumatic stress disorder in Vietnam combat veterans with posttraumatic stress disorder. *American Journal of Psychiatry, 155,* 1565–1569.

Beckham, J. C., Wiley, M. T., Miller, S., Wilson, S. M., Dennis, M. F., & Calhoun, P. S. (in press). Ad lib smoking in posttraumatic stress disorder: An electronic diary study. *Nicotine and Tobacco Research.*

Boehmer, T. K., Flanders, W. D., McGeehin, M. A., Boyle, C., & Barrett, D. H. (2004). Postservice mortality in Vietnam veterans. *Archives of Internal Medicine, 164,* 1908–1916.

Boscarino, J. A. (1996). Posttraumatic stress disorder, exposure to combat, and lower plasma cortisol among Vietnam veterans: Findings and clinical implications. *Journal of Consulting and Clinical Psychology, 64,* 191–201.

Boscarino, J. A. (1997). Diseases among men 20 years after exposure to severe stress: Implications for clinical research and medical care. *Psychosomatic Medicine, 59,* 605–614.

Boscarino, J. A. (2004). Posttraumatic stress disorder and physical illness. *Annals of the New York Academy of Sciences, 1032,* 141–153.

Boscarino, J. A. (2006). Posttraumatic stress disorder and mortality among U.S. Army veterans 30 years after military service. *Annals of Epidemiology, 16,* 248–256.

Boscarino, J. A., & Chang, J. (1999). Electrocardiogram abnormalities among men with stress-related psychiatric disorders: Implications for coronary heart disease and clinical research. *Annals of Behavioral Medicine, 21,* 227–234.

Breslau, N., Davis, G. C., & Schultz, L. R. (2003). Posttraumatic stress disorder and the incidence of nicotine, alcohol, and other drug disorders in persons who have experienced trauma. *Archives of General Psychiatry, 60,* 289–294.

Buckley, T. C., & Kaloupek, D. G. (2001). A meta-analytic examination of basal cardiovascular activity in posttraumatic stress disorder. *Psychosomatic Medicine, 63,* 585–594.

Burgess, A. W., & Holstrom, L. L. (1974). Rape trauma syndrome. *American Journal of Psychiatry, 131,* 981–986.

Centers for Disease Control. (1988). Vietnam Experience Study: Health status of Vietnam veterans: Pt. II. Physical health. *Journal of the American Medical Association, 259,* 2708–2714.

Chrousos, G. P., & Gold, P. W. (1998). A healthy body in a healthy mind: And vice versa: The damaging power of "uncontrollable" stress. *Journal of Clinical Endocrinology and Metabolism, 83,* 1842–1845.

Cromer, K. R., & Sachs-Ericsson, N. (2006). The association between childhood abuse, PTSD, and the occurrence of adult health problems: Moderation via current life stress. *Journal of Traumatic Stress, 19,* 967–971.

Da Costa, J. M. (1871). On irritable heart: A clinical study of a form of functional cardiac disorder and its consequences. *American Journal of the Medical Sciences, 61,* 17–52.

David, D., Woodward, C., Esquenazi, J., & Mellman, T. A. (2004). Comparison of comorbid physical illnesses among veterans with PTSD and veterans with alcohol dependence. *Psychiatric Services, 55,* 82–85.

Dirkzwager, A. J., van der Velden, P. G., Grievnik, L., & Yzermans, C. J. (2007). Disaster-related posttraumatic stress disorder and physical health. *Psychosomatic Medicine, 69,* 435–440.

Elenkov, I., & Chrousos, G. (1999). Stress, cytokine patterns and susceptibility to disease. *Bailliere's Clinical Endocrinology and Metabolism, 13,* 583–595.

Flood, A. M., Boyle, S. H., Calhoun, P. S., Dennis, M. F., Moore, S. D., Barefoot, J. C., et al. (2007). *Externalizing and internalizing subtypes of posttraumatic stress disorder and their relationship to mortality and cause of death among Vietnam veterans.* Manuscript submitted for publication.

Frayne, S. M., Seaver, M. R., Loveland, S., Christiansen, C. L., Spiro, A., Parker, V. A., et al. (2004). Burden of medical illness in women with depression and posttraumatic stress disorder. *Archives of Internal Medicine, 164,* 1306–1312.

Garcia Calzado, M. C., Garcia Rojas, J. F., Mangas, R. A., Martinez, I. D., Repetto, M., & Millan, J. (1990). Tobacco and arterial pressure: Pt. I. The hormonal changes in a model of acute nicotine overload. *Anales de Medicina Interna, 7,* 340–344.

Goodwin, R. D., & Davidson, J. R. (2005). Self-reported diabetes and posttraumatic stress disorder among adults in the community. *Preventive Medicine, 40,* 570–574.

Hoge, C. W., Terhakopian, A., Castro, C. A., Messer, S. C., & Engel, C. C. (2007). Association of posttraumatic stress disorder with somatic symptoms, health care visits, and absenteeism among Iraq war veterans. *American Journal of Psychiatry, 164,* 150–153.

Kagan, B. L., Leskin, G., Haas, B., Wilkins, J., & Foy, D. (1999). Elevated lipid levels in Vietnam veterans with chronic posttraumatic stress disorder. *Biological Psychiatry, 45,* 374–377.

Kessler, R. C., Sonnega, A., Bromet, E., Hughes, M., & Nelson, C. B. (1995). Posttraumatic stress disorder in the National Comorbidity Survey. *Archives of General Psychiatry, 52,* 1048–1060.

Kirschbaum, C., Scherer, G., & Strasburger, C. J. (1994). Pituitary and adrenal hormone responses to pharmacological, physical, and psychological stimulation in habitual smokers and nonsmokers. *Clinical Investigation, 72,* 804–810.

Lang, A. J., Laffaye, C., Satz, L. E., McQuaid, J. R., Malcarne, V. L., Dresselhaus, T. R., et al. (2006). Relationships among childhood maltreatment, PTSD, and health in female veterans in primary care. *Child Abuse and Neglect, 30,* 1281–1292.

Lasser, K., Boyd, J. W., Woolhander, S., Himmelstein, D. U., McCormick, D., & Bor, D. H. (2000). Smoking and mental illness: A population-based prevalence study. *Journal of the American Medical Association, 284,* 2606–2610.

Manuck, S. B. (1994). Cardiovascular reactivity in cardiovascular disease: "Once more into the breach." *International Journal of Behavioral Medicine, 1,* 4–31.

McEwen, B. S. (1998). Seminars in medicine of the Beth Israel Deaconess Medical Center: Protective and damaging effects of stress mediators. *New England Journal of Medicine, 338,* 171–179.

McEwen, B. S. (2004). Protection and damage from acute and chronic stress: Allostasis and allostatic overload and relevance to the pathophysiology of psychiatric disorders. *Annals of the New York Academy of Sciences, 1032,* 1–7.

McEwen, B. S., & Stellar, E. (1993). Stress and the individual: Mechanisms leading to disease. *Archives of Internal Medicine, 153,* 2093–2101.

McFarlane, A. C., Atchison, M., Rafalowicz, E., & Papay, P. (1994). Physical symptoms in post-traumatic stress disorder. *Journal of Psychosomatic Research, 38,* 715–726.

Norman, S. B., Means-Christensen, A. J., Craske, M. G., Sherbourne, C. D., Roy-Byrne, P. P., & Stein, M. B. (2006). Associations between psychological trauma and physical illness in primary care. *Journal of Traumatic Stress, 19*(4), 461–470.

Pizarro, J., Silver, R., & Prause, J. (2006). Physical and mental health costs of traumatic war experiences among civil war veterans. *Archives of General Psychiatry, 63,* 193–200.

Reynolds, C. F., Dew, M. A., Lenze, E. J., & Whyte, E. M. (2007). Preventing depression in medical illness: A new lead? *Archives of General Psychiatry, 64,* 884–885.

Sachs-Ericsson, N., Blazer, D., Plant, E. A., & Arnow, B. (2005). Childhood sexual and physical abuse and the 1-year prevalence of medical problems in the national comorbidity survey. *Health Psychology, 24,* 32–40.

Schnurr, P. P., & Green, B. L. (2004). Understanding relationships among trauma, posttraumatic stress disorder, and health outcomes. In P. P. Schnurr & B. L. Green (Eds.), *Physical health consequences of exposure to extreme stress* (pp. 150–159). Washington, DC: American Psychological Association.

Sephton, S., & Spiegel, D. (2003). Circadian disruption in cancer: A neuroendocrine-immune pathway from stress to disease? *Brain, Behavior, and Immunity, 17,* 321–328.

Treiber, F. A., Kamarck, T., Schneiderman, N., Sheffield, D., Kapuku, G., & Taylor, T. (2003). Cardiovascular reactivity and development of preclinical and clinical disease states. *Psychosomatic Medicine, 65,* 46–62.

Vieweg, W. V., Demetrios, A. J., Benesek, J., Satterwhite, L., Fernandez, A., Feuer, S. J., et al. (2006). Posttraumatic stress disorder and body mass index in military veterans: Preliminary findings. *Progress in Neuro-Psychopharmacology and Biological Psychiatry, 30,* 1150–1154.

Weisberg, R. B., Bruce, S. E., Machan, J. T., Kessler, R. C., Culpepper, L., & Keller, M. B. (2002). Nonpsychiatric illness among primary care patients with trauma histories and post-traumatic stress disorder. *Psychiatric Services, 53,* 848–854.

Zoellner, L. A., Goodwin, M. L., & Foa, E. B. (2000). PTSD severity and health perceptions in female victims of sexual assault. *Journal of Traumatic Stress, 13,* 635–649.

Eric Dedert
Durham Veterans Affairs Medical Center

Jean C. Beckham
Duke University Medical Center

See also: Comorbidity; Medical Illness, Child; Primary Care; Somatic Complaints

MEDICAL ILLNESS, CHILD

Medical illness, injury, and associated treatments are increasingly being considered a potentially traumatogenic event—that is, a potential source of psychological trauma—for children and their families. When children are seriously sick or injured, there is real and perceived life threat, pain, and exposure to potentially frightening images or sounds of bodily injury, pain, and death. These events challenge childhood beliefs about the world as a safe place and can remind children and their families about their vulnerability. Children and families can experience intense helplessness in the face of high-tech, complex, and cutting-edge medical treatments. These experiences can result in traumatic stress reactions.

Pediatric medical traumatic stress (PMTS) is a relatively young, but growing field. Literature from the 1970s and 1980s describes stressors experienced by critically ill children and their families in hospital settings, but the posttraumatic stress framework was first applied in the context of pediatric oncology by Nir (1985). A handful of studies documenting the presence and prevalence of PMTS in pediatric populations emerged beginning in 1991, with less than 30 studies from 1991 to 1999. The present decade has seen a substantial increase in the number of studies focusing on traumatic stress in medical settings, with approximately 125 studies published between 2000 and 2007, and also an increase in the range of types of PMTS that research addresses.

Although the empirical base regarding PMTS is expanding, the majority of these studies describe prevalence, predictors, or risk factors associated with pediatric traumatic stress in medical populations; only 10% discuss methods of clinical assessment or intervention for children and families who have experienced PMTS. Although the empirical inquiry into PMTS began with pediatric illness, the research base is now equally divided between injury and illness populations. However, to date, only a handful of studies compare posttraumatic stress *across* both types of potential sources of PMTS—injury and illness.

The majority of studies examine pediatric traumatic stress in cancer populations; and child and adolescent survivors of cancer, in particular, along with their parents, have been well described. The evidence suggests that PTSD incidence or prevalence levels are relatively low in serious pediatric illnesses such as cancer (estimated at 10% to 15% in children; 15% to 25% in parents), when compared to the levels of PTSD incidence or prevalence following abuse or violence. However, these levels are high compared to those for generally healthy children in community or school samples (i.e., typically <5%) or their parents (i.e., typically <10%). Furthermore, moderate to severe posttraumatic stress symptoms are quite common among severely ill children and their families, and can significantly impair treatment adherence, health outcomes, and child and family functioning. In one study, 80% of families of children with cancer had at least one parent with moderate to severe PTSS (Kazak, Boeving, Alderfer, Hwang, & Reilly, 2005). The majority of studies in pediatric illness suggest that parents are more affected by posttraumatic stress than children. This holds true for studies in pediatric oncology, organ transplantation, diabetes, epilepsy, and asthma. Interestingly, one study demonstrated that the risk of PTSD doubled in children with

asthma, as well as their parents, with the occurrence of at least one life-threatening episode (Kean, Kelsay, Wamboldt, & Wamboldt, 2006).

While the diagnosis of a life-threatening illness is not uniformly perceived as traumatogenic, there is some empirical evidence to suggest that the recency of diagnosis can be a potentially traumatic event in medical settings, and worthy of clinical attention. Moderate to severe posttraumatic stress symptoms were identified in 30% of adolescents and young adults as a result of receiving a diagnosis of HIV (Radcliffe et al., 2007). In parents of children newly diagnosed with type 1 diabetes, approximately 25% of mothers and 20% of fathers had PTSD (Landolt et al., 2002). Longitudinal studies suggest that there is some adjustment over time. Over the course of 1 year, PTSD in fathers decreased significantly, while in mothers the decrease was moderate (Landolt, Vollrath, Laimbacher, Gnehm, & Sennhauser, 2005). At the other end of the illness spectrum, posttraumatic stress does not necessarily end with successful medical treatment. Moderate to severe PTSD has been documented in approximately 10% of child and adolescent cancer survivors, 20% in adult survivors of childhood cancer, and in approximately 25% to 33% of parents of survivors (Hobbie et al., 2000; Kazak et al., 2004; Manne, DuHamel, Gallelli, Sorgen, & Redd, 1998; Ozono et al., 2007; Stuber, Christakis, Houskamp, & Kazak, 1996).

Regarding injury populations, the impact of motor vehicle accidents and other unintentional injuries for children has been well described; with full or partial PTSD incidence or prevalence levels estimated to be 12% to 34% in children and adolescents, and 11% to 20% for parents of injured children (Bryant, Mayou, Wiggs, Ehlers, & Stores, 2004; DeVries et al., 1999; Kassam-Adams & Winston, 2004; Landolt et al., 2005; Meiser-Stedman, Yule, Smith, Glucksman, & Dalgleish, 2005; Stallard, Velleman, & Baldwin, 1999). A growing number of studies document that children with acute burns and their parents are at high risk for posttraumatic stress systems (*see:* **Burns**); and a few studies have examined the occurrence of posttraumatic stress in areas such as traumatic brain injury, spinal cord injury, disfiguring injuries, and dog bites.

Special attention has been paid to the relationship between the receipt of medical intensive care unit (ICU) services and posttraumatic stress in children and their parents, because the ICU is where the most invasive procedures occur, where the degree of life threat is high, and where illness and injury overlap. A growing empirical base has documented estimated incidence or prevalence levels of PTSD in intensive care between 12% to 20% for pediatric patients in the ICU, and between 18% to 27% in parents (Balluffi et al., 2004; Colville & Gracey, 2006; Connolly, McClowry, Hayman, Mahony, & Artman, 2004; Elkit, Hartvig, & Christiansen, 2007; Rees, Gledhill, Garralda, & Nadal, 2004; Shears, Nadal, Gledhill, & Garralda, 2005).

As noted earlier, while most studies do not examine posttraumatic stress across pediatric injury and illness populations, it is striking that the majority of studies with both seriously injured and seriously ill children and their families have found risk factors in common. While an increase in posttraumatic stress does not appear to be associated with objective medical factors (e.g., severity of illness or injury, duration of treatment), studies across both pediatric injury and illness populations have identified subjective appraisals, such as perceived life threat, uncertainty regarding outcome, and ongoing medical vulnerability as primary correlates with increased PTSS likelihood severity. Other risk factors for PTSD that have been commonly identified across both pediatric illness and injury populations include: preexisting/premorbid anxiety, social support and other family stressors, and prior trauma. For parents across both injury and illness, functional status of the child is associated with traumatic stress. For children, particularly those in ICU services and those who have been severely injured, invasive medical procedures and disfigurement/disability are associated with increased risk.

Research has elucidated a connection between PMTS and health outcomes. PTSD symptoms have been associated with poorer adherence to medical treatments (Shemesh et al., 2000). Additionally, symptoms are associated with poor health-related quality of life (Holbrook et al., 2005). These findings have raised increased attention to PMTS within the health-care community for the need to address PMTS as part of medical care.

In the past 3 years, there has been a growing research literature base that addresses the role of medical professionals, particularly physicians, in assessing and treating PMTS along the continuum of care. One study surveyed 287 pediatric emergency care providers regarding knowledge of and clinical practices for preventing posttraumatic stress. Strikingly, only 7% of the respondents believed that children were likely to develop PTSD as a result of unintentional injury and/or hospitalization; only 11% were aware of any tools to assess risk for PTSD; only 18% currently provide guidance to children or their parents regarding risk/symptoms of posttraumatic stress (Ziegler, Greenwald, DeGuzman, & Simon, 2005). Another study described the critical role of the primary care provider in assessing posttraumatic stress symptoms in injured children and adolescents and providing intervention and referral for those affected (Spates, Samaraweera, Plaiser, Souza, & Otsui, 2007). Stuber and colleagues (Stuber, Schneider, Kassam-Adams, Kazak, & Saxe, 2006) described a toolkit of materials, guidelines, and patient education handouts for health-care providers to use in providing trauma-informed care for injured and ill children and their families, available from the National Child Traumatic Stress Network, www.nctsn.org/medtoolkit/ (Stuber et al., 2006).

The Medical Traumatic Stress Working Group of the National Child Traumatic Stress Network (www.nctsn.org) developed a definition from their clinical and research expertise in this developing field.

Pediatric medical traumatic stress refers to a set of psychological and physiological responses of children and their families to pain, injury, serious illness, medical procedures, and invasive or frightening treatment experiences. These responses may include symptoms of arousal, reexperiencing, and/or avoidance. They may vary in intensity, are related to subjective experience of the event, and can become disruptive to functioning. The majority of pediatric patients and their families are resilient and do well.

In working with PMTS, clinicians and researchers are interested in not only traumatic stress, but the context of the healthcare system because this affects when and how children with posttraumatic stress symptoms or PTSD are identified and provided with treatment to ameliorate the traumatic stress reactions they and their families experience.

Limited attention has been paid to treatment approaches for children and families who have experienced PMTS. Two models have emerged in the literature, though there has been limited empirical evaluation of either. The medical crisis counseling model is a conceptual framework for the typical themes and fears that behavioral health providers encounter when requested to intervene with pediatric inpatients. The model and the ensuing interventions have been described in some articles with descriptive case examples (Bronfman, Biron Campis, & Koocher, 1998; Meyer, DeMaso, & Koocher, 1996). In the integrative model of pediatric traumatic stress, guidance for trauma-informed practice in pediatric settings, across three time periods in relation to the occurrence of a potentially traumatic event are posited. Several core principles are elucidated as underpinnings of the model (Kazak et al., 2006). Specific interventions for PMTS have been developed for long-term survivors of cancer and their families (Kazak et al., 2004) and for parents of children newly diagnosed with cancer (Kazak, Simms, et al., 2005).

Future work in PMTS will be improved through increased attention to interventions designed to ameliorate the impact of PMTS on health outcomes and child and family function. Such interventions hold the potential for improving health-care outcomes and reducing the psychological distress that can complicate recovery from injury or illness by children and their families.

REFERENCES

Balluffi, A., Kassam-Adams, N., Kazak, A., Tucker, M., Dominguez, T., & Helfaer, M. (2004). Traumatic stress in parents of children admitted to the pediatric intensive care unit. *Pediatric Critical Care Medicine, 5,* 547–553.

Bronfman, E. T., Biron Campis, L., & Koocher, G. P. (1998). Helping children to cope: Clinical issues for acutely injured and medically traumatized children. *Professional Psychology: Research and Practice, 29,* 574–581.

Bryant, B., Mayou, R., Wiggs, L., Ehlers, A., & Stores, G. (2004). Psychological consequences of road traffic accidents for children and their mothers. *Psychological Medicine, 34,* 335–346.

Colville, G. A., & Gracey, D. (2006). Mothers' recollections of the Paediatric Intensive Care Unit: Associations with psychopathology and views on follow up. *Intensive and Critical Care Nursing, 22,* 49–55.

Connolly, D., McClowry, S., Hayman, L., Mahony, L., & Artman, M. (2004). Posttraumatic stress disorder in children after cardiac surgery. *Journal of Pediatrics, 144,* 480–484.

DeVries, A. P. J., Kassam-Adams, N., Cnaan, A., Sherman Slate, E., Gallagher, P., & Winston, F. K. (1999). Looking beyond the physical injury: Posttraumatic stress disorder in children and parents after pediatric traffic injury. *Pediatrics, 104,* 1293–1299.

Elklit, A., Hartvig, T., & Christiansen, M. (2007). Psychological sequelae in parents of extreme low and very low birth weight infants. *Journal of Clinical Psychology in Medical Settings, 14,* 238–247.

Hobbie, W., Stuber, M., Meeske, K., Wissler, K., Rourke, M., Ruccione, K., et al. (2000). Symptoms of posttraumatic stress in young adult survivors of childhood cancer. *Journal of Clinical Oncology, 18,* 4060–4066.

Holbrook, T. L., Hoyt, D. B., Coimbra, R., Potenza, B., Sise, M., & Anderson, J. P. (2005). Long-term posttraumatic stress disorder persists after major trauma in adolescents: New data on risk factors and functional outcome. *Journal of Trauma-Injury Infection and Critical Care, 58,* 764–769.

Kassam-Adams, N., & Winston, F. K. (2004). Predicting child PTSD: The relationship between ASD and PTSD in injured children. *Journal of the American Academy of Child and Adolescent Psychiatry, 43,* 403–411.

Kazak, A., Alderfer, M., Streisand, R., Simms, S., Rourke, M., Barakat, L., et al. (2004). Treatment of posttraumatic stress symptoms in adolescent survivors of childhood cancer and their families: A randomized clinical trial. *Journal of Family Psychology, 18,* 493–504.

Kazak, A., Boeving, A., Alderfer, M., Hwang, W. T., & Reilly, A. (2005). Posttraumatic stress symptoms in parents of pediatric oncology patients during treatment. *Journal of Clinical Oncology, 23,* 7405–7410.

Kazak, A., Kassam-Adams, N., Schneider, S., Zelikovsky, N., Alderfer, M., & Rourke, M. (2006). An integrative model of pediatric medical traumatic stress. *Journal of Pediatric Psychology, 31,* 343–355.

Kazak, A., Simms, S., Alderfer, M., Rourke, M., Crump, T., McClure, K., et al. (2005). Feasibility and preliminary outcomes from a pilot study of a brief psychological intervention for families of children newly diagnosed with cancer. *Journal of Pediatric Psychology, 30,* 644–655.

Kean, E. M., Kelsay, K., Wamboldt, F., & Wamboldt, M. Z. (2006). Posttraumatic stress in adolescents with asthma and their parents. *Journal of the American Academy of Child and Adolescent Psychiatry, 45,* 78–86.

Landolt, M. A., Ribi, K., Laimbacher, J., Vollrath, M., Gnehm, H. E., & Sennhauser, F. H. (2002). Posttraumatic stress disorder in parents of children with newly diagnosed type 1 diabetes. *Journal of Pediatric Psychology, 27,* 647–652.

Landolt, M. A., Vollrath, M., Laimbacher, J., Gnehm, H. E., & Sennhauser, F. H. (2005). Prospective study of posttraumatic stress disorder in parents of children with newly diagnosed type 1 diabetes. *Journal of the American Academy of Child and Adolescent Psychiatry, 44,* 682–689.

Manne, S., DuHamel, K., Gallelli, K., Sorgen, K., & Redd, W. (1998). Posttraumatic stress disorder among mothers of pediatric cancer survivors: Diagnosis, comorbidity, and utility of the PTSD Checklists as a screening instrument. *Journal of Pediatric Psychology, 23,* 357–366.

Meiser-Stedman, R., Yule, W., Smith, P., Glucksman, E., & Dalgleish, T. (2005). Acute stress disorder and posttraumatic stress disorder in children and adolescents involved in assaults or motor vehicle accidents. *American Journal of Psychiatry, 162,* 1381–1383.

Meyer, E. C., DeMaso, D. R., & Koocher, G. P. (1996). Mental health consultation in the pediatric intensive care unit. *Professional Psychology: Research and Practice, 27,* 130–136.

Nir, Y. (1985). Posttraumatic stress disorder in children with cancer. In S. Eth & R. Pynoos (Eds.), *Posttraumatic stress disorder in children* (pp. 121–132). Washington, DC: American Psychiatric Press.

Ozono, S., Saeki, T., Mantani, T., Ogata, A., Okamura, H., & Yamawaki, S. (2007). Factors related to posttraumatic stress in adolescent survivors of childhood cancer and their parents. *Supportive Care in Cancer, 15,* 309–317.

Radcliffe, J., Fleischer, C., Hawkins, L., Tanney, M., Kassam-Adams, N., Ambrose, C., et al. (2007). Posttraumatic stress and trauma history in adolescents and young adults with HIV. *AIDS Patient Care and STDs, 21,* 501–508.

Rees, G., Gledhill, J., Garralda, M. E., & Nadal, S. (2004). Psychiatric outcome following paediatric intensive care unit (PICU) admission: A cohort study. *Intensive Care Medicine, 30,* 1607–1614.

Shears, D., Nadal, S., Gledhill, J., & Garralda, M. E. (2005). Short-term psychiatric adjustment of children and their parents following meningococcal disease. *Pediatric Critical Care Medicine, 6,* 39–43.

Shemesh, E., Lurie, S., Stuber, M., Emre, S., Patel, Y., Vohra, P., et al. (2000). A pilot study of posttraumatic stress and nonadherence in pediatric liver transplant recipients. *Pediatrics, 105,* E29.

Spates, C. R., Samaraweera, N., Plaisier, B., Souza T., & Otsui K. (2007). Psychological impact of trauma on developing children and youth. *Primary Care: Clinics in Office Practice, 34,* 387–405.

Stallard, P., Velleman, R., & Baldwin, S. (1999). Psychological screening of children for posttraumatic stress disorder. *Journal of Child Psychology and Psychiatry, 40,* 1075–1082.

Stuber, M. L., Christakis, D., Houskamp, B., & Kazak, A. E. (1996). Posttrauma symptoms in childhood leukemia survivors and their parents. *Psychosomatics: Journal of Consultation Liaison Psychiatry, 37,* 254–261.

Stuber, M. L., Schneider, S., Kassam-Adams, N., Kazak, A. E., & Saxe, G. (2006). The medical traumatic stress toolkit. *CNS Spectrums, 11,* 137–142.

Ziegler, M. F., Greenwald, M. H., DeGuzman, M. A., & Simon, H. K. (2005). Posttraumatic stress responses in children: Awareness and practice among a sample of pediatric emergency care providers. *Pediatrics, 115,* 1261–1267.

CHIARA BAXT
Children's Hospital of Philadelphia

STEPHANIE SCHNEIDER
Children's Hospital of Philadelphia

See also: **Comorbidity; Medical Illness, Adult; Primary Care; Somatic Complaints**

MEDITATION

Meditation has been practiced for thousands of years in many spiritual and religious traditions. In the last few decades there has been increasing interest in clinical applications of meditation techniques for a variety of mental health conditions, especially substance abuse, anxiety, and depression (Ospina et al., 2007).

Most writers recognize two broad types of meditation: mindfulness and concentrative. Mindfulness techniques are designed to cultivate stable, nonreactive, nonjudgmental, present-moment awareness of one's internal experience (Kabat-Zinn, 2005). Concentrative meditations focus attention on a single point, such as the breath, the repetition of a mantra, or a visualization. In actual practice, these two traditions have considerable overlap. Meditation traditions generally involve detached observation of thoughts, feelings, and sensations. Meditation in the classical yoga tradition emphasizes actively letting go of mental contents as they arise without attempting to engage or avoid them (Waelde, 2004). A recent review identified breath awareness, mantra repetition, relaxation, and self-regulation of attention as main components of meditation practices reported in the scientific literature (Ospina et al., 2007).

In many clinical applications, meditation is combined with related practices, such as mindfulness and *hatha yoga* (physical exercises), or with psychotherapeutic techniques. In addition, clinical applications of meditation do not always include only the silent, seated practice that is usually associated with meditation. For example, mindfulness-based stress reduction (MBSR; Kabat-Zinn, 2005) involves seated mindfulness meditation, mindfulness exercises, hatha yoga, and psychoeducation about stress and coping. Mindfulness-based cognitive therapy (Segal, Williams, & Teasdale, 2002) combines MBSR with cognitive therapy for depression to reduce relapse in recurrent major depressive disorder. Dialectical behavior therapy uses mindfulness exercises designed to improve affect regulation in borderline personality disorder, but does not use seated meditation (Linehan, 1993).

There has been little research about meditation for posttraumatic stress disorder (PTSD). Only one study of meditation for PTSD was identified in a comprehensive review of 813 meditation studies published through September 2005 (Ospina et al., 2007). Brooks and Scarano (1985) conducted a prospective controlled trial of transcendental meditation (TM) versus psychotherapy for Vietnam veterans. Participants in the TM condition reported significant pre/post reductions in PTSD and related symptoms; psychotherapy participants showed no significant improvements. A recent one-sample pilot study of meditation for mental health workers following Hurricane Katrina found that participants' total PTSD, reexperiencing, hyperarousal, and state anxiety symptoms significantly decreased over the 8 weeks of the intervention; these improvements were significantly correlated with the total number of minutes of daily meditation practice. Although the lack of a control group is a serious limitation of this study, the results suggest that meditation is safe and feasible for disaster survivors (Waelde et al., 2008).

Although there has been little research about the efficacy of meditation for psychological trauma's emotional effects, it may be that meditation can directly address the symptoms of hyperarousal, reexperiencing, and avoidance/numbing characteristic of PTSD. Recent findings emphasize the importance of hyperarousal in the development and maintenance of PTSD (Marshall, Schell, Glynn, & Shetty, 2006; Schell, Marshall, & Jaycox, 2004). Hyperarousal may lead to increased distress in the face of trauma-related reminders, which in turn results in attempts to avoid such reminders through dissociation and emotional numbing. Avoidance is also maintained by exaggerated beliefs about danger and vulnerability (for review see Bryant & Harvey, 2000). The meditative practices of relaxation and breath awareness may reduce hyperarousal in PTSD. Taylor and colleagues (Taylor et al., 2003) proposed that relaxation may help PTSD symptoms because it reduces hyperarousal, which in turn reduces reexperiencing distress and the need to avoid distressing trauma reminders. Numerous studies have documented the beneficial effects of meditation for reducing physiological arousal (for review see Ospina et al., 2007).

Other components of meditation may also benefit PTSD symptoms. The practice of letting go of thoughts, feelings, and sensations as they arise may decrease the distress associated with reexperiencing and encourage beneficial cognitive restructuring. For example, through the practice of letting go, practitioners may experience that thoughts, feelings, and sensations are not permanent, but come and go. This observation about the impermanence of mental states may make distressing trauma-related thoughts, feelings, and sensations more tolerable. A study of mediation for dementia family caregivers found that mediation improved caregivers' self-efficacy for dealing with negative caregiving thoughts (Waelde, Thompson, & Gallagher-Thompson, 2004). Baer (2003) reviewed evidence that meditation may be associated with cognitive changes, such as the recognition that thoughts are not always accurate reflections of reality. Thus, meditation may reduce reexperiencing distress and avoidance of trauma reminders. Increased exposure to reminders of the trauma may provide natural opportunities for practitioners to have corrective experiences that will contribute to restructuring erroneous cognitions about their current degree of vulnerability and danger (Nemeroff et al., 2006).

There are promising indications that meditation may be beneficial for PTSD. Mediation and mindfulness interventions have been found to be safe and acceptable in a wide variety of populations. Meditation interventions have been successfully applied in diverse clinical and cultural populations and may avoid the stigma associated with mental health treatment and thus be applicable to a broad range of trauma survivors. Meditation interventions do not usually involve disclosure about the traumatic event, so there is less concern about group participants being overly stressed by others' disclosures. These qualities of meditation may make it especially adaptable to mass trauma, such as disasters and terrorism, where rapid deployment of interventions on a community-wide basis may be desirable (Norris, Friedman, & Watson, 2002). Future research should investigate the efficacy and mechanisms of meditation for PTSD.

REFERENCES

Baer, R. A. (2003). Mindfulness training as a clinical intervention: A conceptual and empirical review. *Clinical Psychology: Science and Practice, 10,* 125–143.

Brooks, J. S., & Scarano, T. (1985). Transcendental meditation in the treatment of post-Vietnam adjustment. *Journal of Counseling and Development, 64,* 212–215.

Bryant, R. A., & Harvey, A. G. (2000). *Acute stress disorder: A handbook of theory, assessment, and treatment.* Washington, DC: American Psychological Association.

Kabat-Zinn, J. (2005). *Full catastrophe living: Using the wisdom of your body and mind to face stress, pain, and illness* (15th anniversary ed.). New York: Delta Trade Paperback/Bantam Dell.

Linehan, M. M. (1993). *Skills training manual for treating borderline personality disorder.* New York: Guilford Press.

Marshall, G. N., Schell, T. L., Glynn, S. M., & Shetty, V. (2006). The role of hyperarousal in the manifestation of posttraumatic psychological distress following injury. *Journal of Abnormal Psychology, 115,* 624–628.

Nemeroff, C. B., Bremner, J. D., Foa, E. B., Mayberg, H. S., North, C. S., & Stein, M. B. (2006). Posttraumatic stress disorder: A state-of-the-science review. *Journal of Psychiatric Research, 40*(1), 1–21.

Norris, F. H., Friedman, M. J., & Watson, P. J. (2002). 60,000 disaster victims speak: Pt. II. Summary and implications of the disaster mental health research.

Psychiatry: Interpersonal and Biological Processes, 65, 240–260.

Ospina, M. B., Bond, T. K., Karkhaneh, M., Tjosvold, L., Vandermeer, B., Liang, Y., et al. (2007, June). Meditation practices for health: State of the research. *Evidence report/technology assessment no. 155* (AHRQ Publication No. 07-E010, prepared by the University of Alberta Evidence-Based Practice Center, Contract No. 290-02-0023). Rockville, MD: Agency for Healthcare Research and Quality.

Schell, T. L., Marshall, G. N., & Jaycox, L. H. (2004). All symptoms are not created equal: The prominent role of hyperarousal in the natural course of posttraumatic psychological distress. *Journal of Abnormal Psychology, 113,* 189–197.

Segal, Z. V., Williams, J. M. G., & Teasdale, J. D. (2002). *Mindfulness-based cognitive therapy for depression: A new approach to preventing relapse.* New York: Guilford Press.

Taylor, S., Thordarson, D. S., Maxfield, L., Fedoroff, I. C., Lovell, K., & Ogrodniczuk, J. (2003). Comparative efficacy, speed, and adverse effects of three PTSD treatments: Exposure therapy, EMDR, and relaxation training. *Journal of Consulting and Clinical Psychology, 71*(2), 330–338.

Waelde, L. C. (2004). Dissociation and meditation. *Journal of Trauma and Dissociation, 5*(2), 147–162.

Waelde, L. C., Thompson, L., & Gallagher-Thompson, D. (2004). A pilot study of a yoga and meditation intervention for dementia caregiver stress. *Journal of Clinical Psychology, 60*(6), 677–687.

Waelde, L. C., Uddo, M., Marquett, R., Ropelato, M., Freightman, S., Pardo, A., et al. "A pilot study of meditation for mental health workers following Hurricane Katrina." *Journal of Traumatic Stress,* in press.

LYNN C. WAELDE
Pacific Graduate School of Psychology

See also: Self-Help

MEMORIES OF TRAUMATIC EXPERIENCES

One of the most enduring controversies in trauma research pertains to whether memory for traumatic events is more likely to be impaired or enhanced. Whereas some people report that every detail of their traumatic experiences is indelibly etched in their memory, contradictory evidence has been found suggesting that traumatic memories may be distorted or difficult to retrieve. Moreover, some researchers assert that repression of trauma-related memories is quite common, whereas others propose that the recall of trauma-related memories is more typical and normal memory decay accounts for failure to recall certain aspects of traumatic events.

Clearly, the difference between the definitions of *repression* and *forgetting* are central to this debate. *Repression* is a defensive mechanism rooted in psychoanalytic theory that represents an inability to consciously access stored memories for events characterized by intense negative emotions. *Forgetting* is an inability to access memories due to processes of encoding, storage, and retrieval that are universal across memories. Trauma-related memory impairment, as documented in the research literature, may be due to repression, forgetting, or some combination of the two. The interpretation of this literature requires both special attention to methodological concerns and a basic understanding of memory derived from cognitive psychology research.

The trauma-related memory debate is complicated by the intrinsic difficulty of measuring trauma memories with accuracy. There are four general methods for measuring trauma memory impairment. Each method is described along with the unique concerns associated with these methods.

The first method examines recall for analogue stressful events observed in the laboratory. For example, a participant may watch a robbery scene on videotape and, following a delay, attempt to recall as many details about the scene as possible. Although this method allows for verification of memory accuracy, researchers disagree on whether data based on memory for such events may be generalized to memory for traumatic events.

The second method asks participants if they have experienced memory impairment for traumatic events. Unfortunately, the extent to which participants are able to reliably report current and past trauma memory impairment is unknown. Additionally, results may vary depending on how trauma memory impairment is defined for participants. For example, if memory impairment is not clearly defined, repression and normal memory decay are conflated.

The third method for measuring trauma memory impairment asks participants to provide written or verbal trauma narratives that may reveal partial memory impairment. One caveat of this method is that the amount of detail that trauma research participants choose to disclose does not necessarily reflect the amount they actually recall. To complicate matters, when participants write or tell their stories of past traumatic experiences, their narratives reflect not only the quality of their memories, but also their verbal skill.

The fourth method compares adult recall of childhood abuse to public records of documented abuse. This method is compromised by the previous concern that one's disclosure may not accurately reflect recall; additionally, the lack of disclosure may not necessarily reflect a lack of recall. Also there is the concern that public documents may be inaccurate or incomplete owing to their own dependence on (earlier) self-report. Given that each method presents unique concerns, conclusions may be best drawn by examining a pattern of results across methods.

In addition to the potential limitations characterizing each method of measuring trauma memory impairment, there are also important considerations for all memory research based on knowledge derived from cognitive psychology research. This body of research suggests that all memories are influenced by multiple factors during encoding, storage, and retrieval. In order to substantiate instances of repression or psychogenic amnesia (i.e., the inability to recall central aspects of the traumatic event), researchers and clinicians must first rule out normative mechanisms that may hinder encoding or recall. For example, peritraumatic (i.e., during the trauma) intoxication or loss of consciousness would likely impair recall of event details and would represent more parsimonious

explanations for memory impairments. Such factors characterize many traumatic events, including motor vehicle accidents and physical or sexual abuse, but are not often assessed in studies of memory for traumatic events.

Even if a memory has been successfully encoded, accurate recall is hardly guaranteed. Natural memory fading and decay compromise memory accuracy for traumatic and nontraumatic events. Thus, adults may have difficulty recalling childhood abuse simply due to the passage of time since the traumatic event. It is also the case that adults are typically unable to consciously recollect events occurring in infancy, referred to as childhood amnesia. In fact, conscious, long-term memory storage for life events is a cognitive developmental milestone. Adults vary in reports of their earliest memories, suggesting that childhood amnesia may influence long-term memory storage up to 5 years of age. As children's cognitive abilities develop, they improve in their ability to form conscious long-term memories for their life experiences. Therefore, childhood amnesia and the natural fading of memories over time are typically viable alternatives to repression as explanations for an inability to recall painful childhood memories.

There is also a need to differentiate false or constructed memories from recovered memories. The veracity of a trauma-related memory may be challenged when the trauma is recalled only after undergoing questionable interview techniques associated with the creation of false memories. In fact, experimental studies have demonstrated that on questioning, children and adults may recall events (traumatic and nontraumatic) or details of an event that never actually occurred (i.e., they may exhibit constructive memory). Cases of false memories may be very difficult to distinguish from cases of repression. Even if multiple parties are interviewed regarding a traumatic event, discordance between reports may be due to retrieval failure or constructive/constructed memory exhibited by either party. Apart from analogue research, it is exceptionally rare to have a means of objectively evaluating the fidelity of the trauma survivors' memory.

Conclusion

Trauma memory research presents unique methodological concerns and it is imperative to assess normative factors that can influence encoding, storage and retrieval. Although a number of studies have documented impoverished recall of traumatic events, most have failed to consider such explanations for observed impairment. It is important to note that memories for nontraumatic events are often spotty, erroneous, or inaccessible. Demonstrating memory impairment for traumatic events is not by itself evidence for repression. In order to document traumatic repression, normal memory decay and other variables impacting encoding and retrieval must be considered. Limited recall of a traumatic event does not necessarily connote psychogenic amnesia.

In terms of the historical and ecological relevance of the trauma memory debate, it should be emphasized that memories of traumatic experiences may reflect what is believed to have occurred (i.e., narrative truth) or what actually occurred (i.e., historical truth). Due to two related trends beginning in the 1980s, academics began to question the historical truth of some memories of traumatic experiences. The first trend reflected an increase in child reports of satanic ritual abuse, while the second trend reflected an increase in adult reports of recovered memories of childhood sexual abuse. Throughout the 1980s, concern for the safety of children increased due to a growing awareness regarding the overall prevalence of childhood sexual abuse as well as publicized cases of young children testifying to bizarre and rather severe instances of abuse perpetrated by their caretakers. The McMartin Preschool case is a prime example of the latter in which several hundred children testified that their teachers had engaged in abuse of a satanic and ritualistic nature. Most of these charges were eventually dropped. A series of investigations suggested the interview techniques used to obtain the children's testimony in the McMartin Preschool case were highly suggestive and social incentives were used to reinforce children for asserting abuse accusations.

The recovered-memory therapy movement began in the late 1980s. A number of factors contributed to the movement, including the publication of *The Courage to Heal* (Bass & Davis, 1988), a book written by nonpsychologists that encouraged adults to attribute a wide array of their current symptoms of distress to repressed memories of child sexual abuse. Some clinicians actively encouraged their clients to focus on recovering memories of these traumatic experiences in order to alleviate symptoms. Due to an increasing number of adults claiming recovered memories of abuse, the statute of limitations for prosecuting childhood sexual abuse was increased in 37 states. However, many of the accused denied the abuse allegations and subsequently joined organizations, such as the False Memory Syndrome Foundation (FMSF), to support other individuals who believe many recovered memories are in fact false memories. Determining whether a memory would be better classified as "recovered" or "false" was often made more difficult by a lack of corroboration for the survivor's memories of abuse. Together, the reports of satanic ritual abuse in day care centers and the recovered-memory therapy movement set the stage for the trauma memory debate. Years later, widespread satanic ritual abuse cases have faded into history, but the debate continues as proponents of repression continue to argue in favor of the legitimacy of recovered memories of abuse.

Several recommendations are warranted based on the previously identified limitations of research in support of trauma-related psychogenic amnesia. In general, clinicians should avoid potentially harmful practices based on theories of psychogenic amnesia. For example, clinicians should not automatically assume psychogenic amnesia to be operating when trauma memories are nonexistent or incomplete. When trauma-related memories are the focus of treatment, clinicians should avoid the use of memory recovery techniques (i.e., hypnosis) often associated with the creation of false memories. Finally, only forensic interviewers with proper training should gather evidence to be used in a court of law.

RECOMMENDED READINGS

Bass, E., & Davis, L. (1988). *The courage to heal: A guide for women survivors of child sexual abuse.* New York: Harper & Row.

Garven, S., Wood, J. M., Malpass, R. S., & Shaw, J. S. (1998). More than suggestion: The effect of interviewing techniques from the McMartin Preschool case. *Journal of Applied Psychology, 83*(3), 347–359.

McNally, R. J. (2004). Is traumatic amnesia nothing but psychiatric folklore? *Cognitive Behaviour Therapy, 33*(2), 97–101.

Shobe, K. K., & Kihlstrom, J. F. (1997). Is traumatic memory special? *Current Directions in Psychological Science, 6,* 70–74.

Katie M. Lindblom
University of Wyoming

Matt J. Gray
University of Wyoming

See also: Exposure Therapy, Adult; Exposure Therapy, Child; Flashbacks; Intrusive Reexperiencing; Memory; Therapeutic Writing

MEMORY

Posttraumatic stress disorder (PTSD) is the most common mental disorder to occur after trauma, and it is characterized by several memory dysfunctions. Most notably, PTSD is marked by intrusive memories of the traumatic event, including flashbacks and nightmares. These memories are distinctive because they are perceived as a reliving of the original event, and typically are accompanied by vivid perceptual detail and strong emotional responses. This pattern highlights that memory patterns are important in stress reactions to trauma.

There is convergent evidence that people with PTSD suffer memory and concentration problems. It is commonly understood that the frequent intrusive memories and the associated distress experienced by people with PTSD can deplete working (i.e., short-term) memory capacity, which results in diminished abilities in attention and memory. There is strong evidence that PTSD is associated with impairments in sustained attention, working memory, and learning; there is also evidence that some of these deficits are correlated with the severity of intrusive memories, which accords with the proposal that reexperiencing symptoms may deplete resources necessary for optimal cognitive functioning.

It should be noted, however, that it is possible that cognitive deficits (such as memory and concentration problems) may actually serve as a *risk factor* for PTSD's development (in addition to serving as a consequence). There is some evidence that higher intelligence is a buffer against PTSD development. There is also some evidence that smaller hippocampal volume may be a risk factor for PTSD development, which may also contribute to cognitive impairment rendering an individual susceptible to PTSD.

Autobiographical Memory

There is also evidence that people with PTSD have a deficit in retrieving specific memories about their personal past. This pattern, which is also seen in depressed patients, results in PTSD-diagnosed individuals retrieving memories about general events (e.g., "I was hurt so often in the past"), which limits their ability to retrieve specific memories of positive or safe experiences that may assist them to adapt after the trauma. This tendency shortly after trauma exposure predicts subsequent PTSD. It also limits the person's ability to problem solve after the trauma because they have difficulty in retrieving specific examples of past events that we require when we solve problems in the present. Possible mechanisms for problems in retrieving specific memories may involve avoidance of specific memories because they evoke distress, or impaired retrieval processes because people with PTSD do not have the requisite cognitive resources to complete the retrieval search as a result of their reexperiencing. Additionally, people with PTSD tend to ruminate and this activity can lead people to focus on more general memories.

Flashback Memories

One of the most dramatic examples of memory dysfunction in PTSD is the flashback phenomenon. These memories reportedly involve a reliving of the traumatic experience, a sense of *being* in the past rather than *recalling* the past, vivid perceptual detail, are involuntarily triggered, and are associated with strong affective states. For example, during a flashback a motor vehicle accident victim may experience the sense of skidding in the car, see the car collide with a pole, feel the windscreen cutting into the face, and smell the fuel.

The most common form of flashback involves visual perceptual memories. Importantly, there is evidence that flashbacks are not necessarily veridical accounts of the traumatic experience because studies demonstrate that the content of flashback memories can change over time, and are influenced by current concerns.

Memory for Trauma

Much controversy has existed over the extent to which memory for traumatic events is enhanced or depleted relative to memories for other events. Much of this debate has focused on the so-called "repressed memory" issue, which involves the proposition that people can suppress traumatic memories for prolonged periods (maybe many years) and then can recall these events later. Also termed *dissociative amnesia,* this phenomenon purportedly occurs when people dissociate memory of a trauma so that it is no longer accessible. Many surveys have been reported concerning trauma survivors' tendency to have amnesia but these are sometimes unreliable sources of information because they often confuse amnesia with normal forgetting, intentional cognitive avoidance, impaired encoding of an event into memory that precludes being able to remember it, and reluctance to report a memory that is retrieved.

Experimental approaches have been applied to adults who have survived childhood sexual abuse. For example, the directed forgetting paradigm is a common cognitive task in which the subject is presented with trauma-related, positive, or neutral words, and after each presentation they are asked to forget or remember the word. Using this paradigm, there is no evidence of superior forgetting in survivors of childhood sexual abuse; in fact, these individuals tend to recall trauma-related information very well. In contrast, there is some evidence that people with acute stress disorder do have a proficiency in forgetting trauma-related information using a directed forgetting paradigm. Notably, these people display dissociative reactions to the trauma and have been affected by the trauma only very recently. There is also evidence that people with PTSD may not retrieve some trauma-related information adequately because their focus on trauma-related memories may lead to automatic inhibition of other trauma information.

Whereas people tend to have good recall of traumatic events, their recall is likely to be as flawed, in terms of its accuracy, as with most memories. Although some theorists have argued that trauma memories are indelibly imprinted in our memories, and that their recollection is an accurate account of exactly what transpired, this is far from the truth. Longitudinal studies that have assessed trauma survivors at different periods after trauma exposure have found that memory for details of the traumatic event is often not accurate. Similarly, memory for earlier stress reactions is not accurately recalled at later times. As with most memory, studies have found that memory for details of the traumatic event, and of one's reactions, is influenced by the emotional state at the time of recall; people with severe PTSD tend to exaggerate how bad their trauma and their reactions were, whereas those who have fewer stress reactions tend to minimize their experience (McNally, 2003).

In summary, our knowledge about how people manage severely distressing trauma memories is limited. At the present time, there is not sound empirical evidence that people do dissociate trauma memories to the extent proposed by dissociative amnesia theories. The general conclusion is that people tend to recall their trauma memories too vividly, although there may be some mechanisms that result in preferential forgetting of other trauma-related information. It is likely that as experimental paradigms are applied to this issue, there will be clearer insights into this complex issue that has often been overly influenced by anecdotal reports rather than by sound research.

Memory Organization

Some theories of PTSD posit that a major reason people have difficulty recovering from the traumatic experience is that their memories of the event are fragmented, and accordingly they are not integrated into one's normal autobiographical memory. It is proposed that by the very shocking nature of trauma, these memories tend to be encoded as fragmented perceptual representations. These memories purportedly intrude into consciousness when triggered by reminders, and in the case of PTSD, the avoidance of these memories preclude them from being placed into the context of a normal narrative of the trauma.

Some theorists argue that successful therapy involves the integration of the trauma memory into a coherent narrative, which assists the survivor to place the experience in a context in which they have survived the experience. Several studies have reported that people with PTSD do display fragmented memories of their traumatic experience, and this fragmentation reduces as they recover; specifically, repeatedly focusing on the memory in the context of therapy usually results in a cohesive narrative of the traumatic experience.

Memory Perspective

There is also evidence that people tend to recall their trauma from an observer's perspective. It has been suggested that people may do this because it reduces the distress that one experiences during the recollection. Several studies have noted this tendency, and there is also evidence that people who do recall trauma from an observer's perspective report less anxiety than individuals who recall their trauma from their own perspective. Consistent with this proposal, people who are more avoidant after trauma tend to adopt the observer perspective more than those who are less avoidant. Taken together, these data suggest that adoption of the observer vantage point is a form of cognitive avoidance that may allow people to cope with trauma memories in a more manageable way.

Conclusion

PTSD appears to be characterized by some paradoxical memory dysfunctions. On the one hand, it is marked by intrusive memories of the trauma and excessive recall of the experience. On the other hand, there are deficits in every day memory and attention, and possibly some strategies that limit one's tendency to retrieve memories that are aversive. It appears that both memory excesses and deficits contribute to the problems experienced by people with PTSD.

REFERENCES

Brewin, C. R. (2003). *Post-traumatic stress disorder: Malady or myth?* New Haven, CT: Yale University Press.

McNally, R. J. (2003). *Remembering trauma.* Cambridge, MA: Harvard University Press.

RICHARD A. BRYANT
University of New South Wales

See also: Amygdala; Biology, Brain Structure, and Function, Adult; Biology, Brain Structure, and Function, Child; Conditioned Fear; Dissociation; Frontal Cortex; Hippocampus; Information Processing; Learning Theory; Therapeutic Writing

MILITARY PERSONNEL

Today's military personnel are both highly exposed to trauma and highly resilient in the face of such exposure. The most common and predictable mental health problem as a result of exposure to war and terrorism is posttraumatic stress disorder (PTSD). Unsurprisingly, as the global war on terrorism has continued, the number of cases of PTSD has increased. Most combat veterans will have some of the symptoms of PTSD for weeks to months after their return to civilian life, and perhaps fleetingly long after. However, many recover from those symptoms without experiencing severe problems in their relationships or work and without requiring treatment. Additionally, PTSD is only one of several deployment-related psychological effects of war. Depression, anxiety, and occasionally suicide also occur, as does abuse of alcohol or other substances. Deployment also causes stress on marriages, families, and other relationships.

The military services recognize the significant impact of war experiences on military personnel and their families and have developed programs that attempt to mitigate that impact and enhance resiliency. Factors shown to increase resiliency include tough realistic individual training, and developing a sense of "esprit de corps" that leads personnel to feel a sense of bonding, cohesion, and morale within their units. In the past 2 decades, a wide range of behavioral health services has been made available to military personnel and to military veterans, including screening for PTSD and appropriate referrals for care.

History

The psychological impact of combat and other operations on military personnel throughout history is well known (Jones, 1995). Emerging patterns in the management of psychiatric casualties (i.e., soldiers who developed mental health problems during combat) can be observed in the programs developed during World War II. These programs were a "rediscovery" of work by British and American psychiatrists during the World War I. In World War I, psychological casualties were initially diagnosed as having "Shell Shock." The term *Shell Shock* developed from the notion that the disorder was due to direct damage to the brain and nervous system from the physical shock of exposure to artillery blasts (Salmon, 1929). In World War II, the official diagnosis was initially "Not Yet Diagnosed, Nervous." This diagnosis

was later changed to "Battle Fatigue." Neither hospital treatment, in World War I, nor psychoanalysis, in World War II, successfully relieved these symptoms (Jones, 1995).

In both wars, many soldiers with mental health symptoms were evacuated out of the combat zone. If evacuated, few returned to the combat environment. Evacuees had to deal with the stigma and shame of evacuation. If, on the other hand, psychological casualties were treated on the front lines with brief supportive therapy and the expectation of return to duty, between 60% to 80% were able to continue as soldiers (Jones, 1995). The term *battle fatigue* was useful, since it implied that military personnel were just exhausted from conflict and would get better with good food and rest, paraphrased as "three hots and a cot."

In the initial months of the Korean War, very high numbers of psychological casualties occurred among American troops, principally among the Army and the Marines, at a rate of 250 per 1,000 (or one in every four soldiers) per year. These numbers, resulting from high-intensity conflict, overwhelmed available resources to manage them at forward locations. Casualties were evacuated to Japan or the United States. Very few returned to duty. The principles of early treatment on the front lines, learned in the previous wars, were then reinstituted. After this, up to 80% of neuropsychiatric casualties were returned to duty (Glass, 1973; Ritchie & Owens, 2004).

Thus, over the course of numerous wars, the military recognized that treating service members close to the front lines leads to a much higher return-to-duty rate. The basic principles, later codified as "Proximity, Immediacy, Expectancy, and Simplicity" (PIES), directed simple but immediate treatment, without evacuation, with the expectation of return to duty (Artiss, 1963; Ritchie, 2002).

In the Vietnam War, the principles of PIES also were followed. Combat stress casualties were relatively few, with about 11% of patients having complaints of a psychological nature. Later on in the war, there emerged a high incidence of alcohol and drug abuse. Substance abuse became associated with a number of incidents of misconduct. The longer-term consequences of exposure to psychological trauma became apparent with the recognition that as many as one in seven combat-deployed personnel in Vietnam suffered PTSD years later.

In the first Gulf War, immediate psychological casualties were few, and mainly related to home front difficulties. However, in subsequent years, veterans exhibited a constellation of physical, psychological, and neuropsychological symptoms that were termed *Gulf War Syndrome*. The extent to which psychological trauma and exposure to chronic stress contributed to these syndromes is not known, but it is thought to be significant (Ritchie & Owens, 2004).

Stresses of the Current Wars

From 1991 to 2003, battlefront casualties attributed to stress were relatively few both in combat and in operations other than war. However, information from the current Afghanistan and Iraq wars and occupation show that as many as one in seven or eight deployed soldiers report psychological symptoms. A seminal article (Hoge et al., 2004) found that 12% to 16% of soldiers reported symptoms of PTSD 3 to 6 months after returning home from deployment.

Given the nature of the conflict (including an initial threat of chemical and biological warfare, suicide bombers and improvised explosive devices [IEDs], civilians killed, wounded and dead American soldiers, kidnappings), both military personnel and civilian employees are at risk for the development of mental health symptoms. Surveys of soldiers deployed during Operation Iraqi Freedom consistently suggest that approximately 15% to 17% will experience PTSD and another 10% will experience other behavioral health problems (Mental Health Advisory Teams; MHATs I-IV). Wounded soldiers and soldiers exposed to frequent firefights are groups that are at increased risk for the development of mental health symptoms (Hoge, Terhakopian, Castro, Messer, & Engel, 2007).

Combat and Operational Stress Control

The military places great emphasis on prevention and early intervention. Primary prevention includes the steps taken to prevent illness or injury from occurring at all. Secondary prevention involves the early identification of individuals who have developed illness or injury. Tertiary prevention is treatment targeted especially toward minimizing development of disability. The military applies prevention at all levels. Basic combat training is central to the transformation of civilians into soldiers, sailors, airmen, and Marines. This education and training is part of primary prevention for all military personnel and is an attempt to inoculate individuals against the adverse effects of exposure to psychological trauma. The effectiveness of these approaches appears mixed. Most military personnel appear to be able to complete their tours of duty successfully (unless severely physically wounded). However, the actual number experiencing PTSD or other psychological symptoms during and after deployment is not yet known, and the estimates of rates of PTSD among these personnel are similar to the rates reported for Vietnam War veterans.

A soldier's first questions after enemy contact will be about the status of his or her buddies, and about the success of the mission. The unit can serve as an extension of individual pride where the soldier's self-esteem becomes linked to the reputation of the unit, providing additional motivation. Unit cohesion is a force that is thought to be protective psychologically as well as militarily for its members.

The purpose of combat and operational stress-control doctrine is to promote personnel and unit readiness by enhancing adaptive stress reactions, preventing maladaptive stress reactions, assisting personnel in recognizing and coping with combat/operational stress reactions, and assisting personnel with treatment when they experience mental disorders. Among other things, stress control is intended to maintain a service member's ability to cope with the potentially damaging effects of combat.

The Wounded

Much has been learned throughout the twentieth century about the medical treatment and mental health care of the wounded. For many wounded soldiers, there is often initially a sense of great relief, almost euphoria: "Thank God, I am alive!" Individuals may initially receive a lot of attention from hospital personnel, their families, the command structure, the media, political figures, and even celebrities. They may see others around them with worse injuries or remember colleagues who were killed in the same action.

This initial relief may give way to a number of negative psychological reactions. Unmanaged pain, recognition of permanent disability or concern regarding degree of disability, and the presence of financial or relationship problems can increase individual vulnerability for the development of mental health symptoms. Survivor guilt, dismay over being separated from one's unit, and depression and problems with alcohol or other substance abuse can occur (Wain, Grammer, Stasinos, & DeBoer, 2006).

For many soldiers, previously fit and healthy, to be bedridden and/or immobilized is a major stressor. Frequently having just obtained independence from their parents, they may now be forced to depend on them for their most basic needs. Addressing the sense of helplessness and demoralization that this can cause, including by providing for adequate pain control, is critical.

Recent advances in state-of-the-art prosthetic devices seem to be delaying, if not altogether preventing, some of the dysphoria, by decreasing disability. Mental health intervention by military specialists focuses on normalizing psychological responses to traumatic experiences and instilling an expectation of an improvement with time in psychological symptoms. Medications may be helpful for symptoms such as anxiety, hyperarousal, intrusive thoughts, nightmares, insomnia, and depression.

Families

Deployment is a major strain on families, including not only spouses and children, but also parents and siblings and the whole extended family. Grandparents and others may have to care for children when parents are gone. The military is increasingly providing support systems for families before, during, and after their loved one's military deployment, including providing them with education, screening, and counseling and support groups.

Separation from family during war deployment is stressful for military personnel as well as for their families. Worries about family finances, the burden of parenting and work that must be shouldered by the nondeployed spouse/parent, and the absence of intimate (emotional as well as otherwise) contact and communication, place a great strain on the deployed soldier or sailor and their family. These stressors are usually not psychologically traumatic, but they may compound the effects of combat trauma and place military personnel at risk for PTSD. When military personnel develop PTSD, this places an additional strain on their family.

Conclusion

Today's U.S. military personnel are well-trained and resilient. Yet, they are currently exposed to an extraordinary level of stress, including firefights, IEDs, suicide bombings, and killed and maimed civilians of all ages. These potentially traumatic stressors will most likely be a part of war for many years to come. The short- and long-term effects of these stressors will need to be carefully monitored. Although military policy and doctrine do not at present make specific reference to "resilience" per se, this is certainly a primary and implied concern of programs and practices that target service members' ability to confront and overcome effects of combat-related stress.

REFERENCES

Artiss, K. L. (1963). Human behavior under stress: From combat to social psychiatry. *Military Medicine, 128*(10), 1011–1015.

Glass, A. J. (1973). Lessons learned. In A. J. Glass (Ed.), *Neuropsychiatry in World War II* (pp. 989–1027).

Washington, DC: Office of the Surgeon General, U.S. Army.

Hoge, C. W., Castro, C. A., Messer, S. C., McGurk, D., Cotting, D. I., & Koffman, R. L. (2004). Combat duty in Iraq and Afghanistan, mental health problems, and barriers to care. *New England Journal of Medicine, 351,* 13–22.

Hoge, C. W., Terhakopian, A., Castro, C. A., Messer, S. C., & Engel, C. C. (2007). Association of posttraumatic stress disorder with somatic symptoms, health care visits, and absenteeism among Iraq War veterans. *American Journal of Psychiatry, 164,* 150–153.

Jones, F. (1995). Psychiatric lessons of war. In F. D. Jones, L. R. Sparacino, V. L. Wilcox, J. M. Rothberg, & J. W. Stokes (Eds.), *War psychiatry* (pp. 1–34). Washington, DC: Office of the Surgeon General, Borden Institute.

Ritchie, E. C. (2002). Psychiatry in the Korean War: Perils, PIES and Prisoners of War. *Military Medicine, 167*(11), 898–903.

Ritchie, E. C., & Owens, M. (2004). Military psychiatry. *Psychiatric Clinics of North America, 27,* 459–471.

Salmon, T. W. (1929). The care and treatment of mental diseases and war neurosis ("shell shock" in the British Army). In P. Bailey, F. E. Williams, P. A. Komora, T. W. Salmon, & N. Fenton (Eds.), *Neuropsychiatry: Vol. 10. The U.S. Medical Department of the United States Army in the World War* (pp. 497–523). Washington, DC: Office of the Surgeon General, U.S. Army.

Wain, H., Grammer, G. G., Stasinos, J., & DeBoer, C. M. (2006). Psychiatric intervention for medical and surgical patients following traumatic injuries. In E. Ritchie, M. Friedman, & P. Watson (Eds.), *Interventions following mass violence and disasters: Strategies for mental health practice* (pp. 278–299). New York: Guilford Press.

ELSPETH CAMERON RITCHIE
Uniformed Services University of the Health Sciences

See also: Combat Stress Reaction; History of Psychological Trauma; Veterans Affairs, U.S. Department of; War Trauma

MINDFULNESS

See: Meditation

MINNESOTA MULTIPHASIC PERSONALITY INVENTORY-2 (MMPI-2)

The MMPI-2 (Butcher et al., 2001) is a 567-item self-report measure of personality and broader psychopathology scored on a true/false basis. Originally developed by Hathaway and McKinley (1943), it is one of the most frequently used and well-researched measures of personality and psychopathology. In addition to its primary 3 validity and 10 clinical scales, the MMPI-2 includes a range of subscales that identify distinct components within the more heterogeneous clinical scales, as well as a series of supplementary and content scales that further identify more specific psychological processes. The MMPI-2 also includes a measure of a five-factor model of personality-based psychopathology, the Personality Psychopathology-5 (Harkness, McNulty, & Ben-Porath, 1995). Scales assessing the *Diagnostic and Statistical Manual of Mental Disorders* (*DSM;* American Psychiatric Association, 1952) personality disorders have also been developed for the MMPI-2 (Morey, Waugh, & Blashfield, 1985). In view of the breadth of its use across clinical settings internationally, its massive research base, and the coverage of personality and psychopathology assessed by its considerable number of items, the MMPI-2 has also been the measure of personality and psychopathology that has been most widely used in the assessment of posttraumatic psychopathology, particularly posttraumatic stress disorder (PTSD).

Work in the area of trauma and PTSD using the MMPI-2 has had three primary foci. First, the measure has been used for the assessment and diagnosis of PTSD. Second, it has been used as a measure of comorbid posttraumatic psychopathology across the clinical spectrum. Finally, there has been considerable research on its validity scales in order to best detect symptom exaggeration or simulation in the context of compensation seeking in PTSD.

Assessment and Diagnosis of PTSD

In this context, a considerable amount of this research has focused on the identification of common mean PTSD profile configurations across the MMPI validity and clinical scales, finding a modal two-point code type (2/8: depression/schizophrenia) and three-point code type (F/2/8: infrequency/depression/schizophrenia; Wilson & Walker, 1990). While the depression scale detects depressive symptoms, it also identifies the "negative" symptoms of PTSD, particularly restricted affect. Rather than frank psychotic phenomena, the schizophrenia scale is likely detecting the "positive" symptoms including the reexperiencing phenomena, particularly intrusions, flashbacks, and concentration disturbance (Wilson & Walker, 1990). Changes to the instrument, introduced in the MMPI-2, resulted in the addition of Scale 7 (psychasthenia) to the mean PTSD clinical scale code type (F/2/7/8; Albrecht et al., 1994). Scale 7 largely reflects generalized anxiety and rumination. Importantly, the majority of this research examining the PTSD codetype has been conducted with veterans with PTSD.

There are also two measures of PTSD included in the supplementary scales, which are the PK scale (Keane, Zimering, & Caddell, 1985) and PS scale (Schlenger & Kulka, 1989), of which the PK is most frequently used. This subscale has demonstrated an improvement in the correct hit classification rate beyond the use of the profile code type, using a cut-off raw score of 30. In adapting to the MMPI-2, the PK recommended cut-off score of 28 was identified for combat samples (Lyons & Keane, 1992).

Identification of Personality and Psychopathology Features Associated with PTSD

The use of the MMPI in assessment also facilitates the identification of broader based or underlying psychopathological processes in traumatized populations. The typical PTSD profile is often associated with elevations across most scales beyond the 2/7/8 high point code type. Possible elevations on other scales include hypochondriasis (scale 1), hysteria (scale 3), psychopathic deviate (scale 4), paranoia (scale 6), hypomania (scale 9) and social introversion (scale 0). While some of these scale elevations may also reflect symptoms of

PTSD and its associated phenomena through somatization (scales 1 and 3), anger (scale 4), mistrust (scale 6), and obsessive rumination of the traumatic event (scale 7), they may also reflect broader psychopathological processes. The MMPI-2 has also been validated as a measure of comorbidity in PTSD (Talbert et al., 1994).

Despite consistent replication of the mean PTSD and broader psychopathology profile across studies, considerable heterogeneity in profiles within these studies has been evident (Forbes, Creamer, & McHugh, 1999; Wise, 1996). One of the most common approaches to the investigation of the heterogeneity of overall profiles involves use of cluster analysis to empirically define subgroups of an identified clinical population on the basis of combinations of underlying personality and psychopathological features. In relation to traumatized populations, the MMPI-2 has been used to assess subgroups in sexual abuse survivors (Elhai, Klotz-Flitter, Gold, & Sellers, 2001; Follette, Naugle, & Follette, 1997) and combat veterans (Forbes et al., 2003; Miller, Kaloupek, Dillon, & Keane, 2004).

Trauma-Specific Developments in the Validity Scales

Another reason the MMPI-2 has been widely used in the assessment of trauma is that it includes a set of validity scales with a substantial supportive literature as to its use in the assessment of exaggerated responses or malingering. Given the substantial prevalence of compensation seeking among trauma populations (Creamer, Morris, Biddle, & Elliott, 1999) and existing literature suggesting the potential for compensation seeking to influence self-reported psychopathology (Franklin & Zimmerman, 2001; Smith & Frueh, 1996), a measure of psychopathology that has features to detect such response sets provides considerable advantages in potentially identifying severely exaggerated or invalid profiles.

Of note in the MMPI-2 PTSD profile is the elevation of the F (infrequency) scale. Elevations of F, and a large differential between

F and K, have traditionally been considered as indications of exaggerated, "fake bad" or, at worst, invalid profiles. However, investigations into the elevation of F in this population demonstrate that these features rarely indicate invalidity, most often reflecting distress and psychiatric comorbidity (and a plea for help) in the context of validated PTSD (Munley, Bains, & Bloem, 1993). The F(p) scale provides some assistance in distinguishing the above factors from profile invalidity. Recent work has also identified the F(p) scale as an effective index of simulation in PTSD samples (Elhai, Gold, Sellers, & Dorfman, 2001). Importantly Elhai, Frueh, and colleagues (Elhai et al., 2002) have also recently developed an F(ptsd) scale that has demonstrated the potential to detect feigned PTSD beyond existing validity scales.

REFERENCES

Albrecht, N. N., Talbert, F. S., Albrecht, J. W., Boudewyns, P. A., Hyer, L. A., Touze, J., et al. (1994). A comparison of MMPI and MMPI-2 in PTSD assessment. *Journal of Clinical Psychology, 50*(4), 578–585.

American Psychiatric Association. (1952). *Diagnostic and statistical manual of mental disorders.* Washington, DC: Author.

Butcher, J. N., Graham, J. R., Ben-Porath, Y. S., Tellegen, A., Dahlstrom, W. G., & Kaemmer, B. (2001). *MMPI-2 (Minnesota Multiphasic Personality Inventory-2): Manual for administration, scoring, and interpretation* (Rev. ed.). Minneapolis: University of Minnesota Press.

Creamer, M., Morris, P., Biddle, D., & Elliott, P. (1999). Treatment outcome in Australian veterans with combat-related posttraumatic stress disorder: A cause for cautious optimism? *Journal of Traumatic Stress, 12*(4), 545–558.

Elhai, J. D., Gold, S. N., Sellers, A. H., & Dorfman, W. I. (2001). The detection of malingered posttraumatic stress disorder with MMPI-2 fake bad indices. *Assessment, 8,* 221–236.

Elhai, J. D., Klotz-Flitter, J. M., Gold, S. N., & Sellers, A. H. (2001). Identifying subtypes of women survivors of childhood sexual abuse: An MMPI-2 cluster analysis. *Journal of Traumatic Stress, 14*(1), 157–176.

Elhai, J. D., Ruggiero, K. J., Frueh, B. C., Beckham, J. C., Gold, P. B., & Feldman, M. E. (2002). The infrequency-posttraumatic stress disorder scale (FPTSD) for the MMPI-2: Development and initial validation with veterans presenting with combat-related PTSD. *Journal of Personality Assessment, 79,* 531–549.

Follette, W. C., Naugle, A. E., & Follette, V. M. (1997). MMPI-2 profiles of adult women with child sexual abuse histories: Cluster-analytic findings. *Journal of Consulting and Clinical Psychology, 65*(5), 858–866.

Forbes, D., Creamer, M., Allen, N., Elliott, P., McHugh, T., Debenham, P., et al. (2003). MMPI-2 based subgroups of veterans with combat-related PTSD: Differential patterns of symptom change after treatment. *Journal of Nervous and Mental Disease, 191*(8), 531–537.

Forbes, D., Creamer, M., & McHugh, T. (1999). MMPI-2 data for Australian Vietnam veterans with combat-related PTSD. *Journal of Traumatic Stress, 12*(2), 371–378.

Franklin, C. L., & Zimmerman, M. (2001). Posttraumatic stress disorder and major depressive disorder: Investigating the role of overlapping symptoms in diagnostic comorbidity. *Journal of Nervous and Mental Disease, 189*(8), 548–551.

Harkness, A. R., McNulty, J. L., & Ben-Porath, Y. S. (1995). The personality psychopathology five (PSY-5): Constructs and MMPI-2 scales. *Psychological Assessment, 7*(1), 104–114.

Hathaway, S. R., & McKinley, J. C. (1943). *Minnesota multiphasic personality schedule.* Minneapolis: University of Minnesota Press.

Keane, T. M., Zimering, R. T., & Caddell, J. M. (1985). A behavioral formulation of posttraumatic stress disorder in Vietnam veterans. *Behavior Therapist, 8*(1), 9–12.

Lyons, J. A., & Keane, T. M. (1992). Keane PTSD Scale: MMPI and MMPI-2 update. *Journal of Traumatic Stress, 5*(1), 111–117.

Miller, M. W., Kaloupek, D. G., Dillon, A. L., & Keane, T. M. (2004). Externalizing and internalizing subtypes of combat-related PTSD: A replication and extension using the PSY-5 scales. *Journal of Abnormal Psychology, 113*(4), 636–645.

Morey, L. C., Waugh, M. H., & Blashfield, R. K. (1985). MMPI scales for DSM-III personality disorders. *Journal of Personality Assessment, 49*(12), 1645–1653.

Munley, P. H., Bains, D. S., & Bloem, W. D. (1993). F scale elevation and PTSD MMPI profiles. *Psychological Reports, 73,* 363–370.

Schlenger, W. E., & Kulka, R. A. (1989). *PTSD scale development for the MMPI-2:* Triangle Park, NC: Research Triangle Institute.

Smith, D. W., & Frueh, B. C. (1996). Compensation seeking, comorbidity and apparent exaggeration of PTSD symptoms among Vietnam combat veterans. *Psychological Assessment, 8*(1), 3–6.

Talbert, F. S., Albrecht, J. W., Boudewyns, P., Hyer, L. A., Touze, J., & Lemmon, C. R. (1994). A comparison of MMPI and MMPI-2 in PTSD assessment. *Journal of Clinical Psychology, 50*(4), 578–585.

Wilson, J. P., & Walker, A. J. (1990). Toward an MMPI trauma profile. *Journal of Traumatic Stress, 3*(1), 151–168.

Wise, E. A. (1996). Diagnosing posttraumatic stress disorder with the MMPI clinical scales: A review of the literature. *Journal of Psychopathology and Behavioral Assessment, 18*(1), 71–82.

DAVID FORBES
University of Melbourne

See also: Assessment, Psychometric, Adult

MISSISSIPPI CIVILIAN SCALE FOR PTSD—REVISED

The Mississippi Civilian Scale for posttraumatic stress disorder (PTSD) was one of the earliest self-report scales for assessing posttraumatic stress. The original 35 items fall into four categories, three that align with criteria B, C, and D for PTSD (intrusion, avoidance/numbing, and arousal, respectively) and a fourth that taps self-persecution (guilt and suicidality). The scale elicits frequency of symptoms "in the past."

Revised to sharpen its focus on traumatic stress, the Revised Civilian Mississippi Scale (RCMS) has 30 items. The first 18 items anchor the symptom to a specific event (e.g., "Since the event, unexpected noises make me jump"); the last 12 items do not ("I am able to get emotionally close to others"). Norris and Perilla (1996) developed equivalent Spanish and English versions of the RCMS, using back translation and centering and pilot research with bilingual

participants who completed the scale in either English or Spanish on the first occasion and in the alternative language 1 week later. The scale was internally consistent (English alpha = .86, Spanish alpha = .88) and stable over the 1-week test-retest period ($r = .73$; $r = .84$ when corrected for attenuation).

In subsequent research in Mexico (Norris, Perilla, & Murphy, 2001), the RCMS showed a four-factor structure (intrusion, avoidance, numbing, arousal) and good agreement with the PTSD module of the Composite International Diagnostic Interview (84% agreement based only on criterion symptoms of the RCMS dichotomized as present/absent). The RCMS was not intended for use in clinical settings or to provide a diagnosis of PTSD, but it performs well as a continuous measure of posttraumatic stress and stands out in terms of its validation for use with Spanish-speaking populations.

REFERENCES

Norris, F., & Perilla, J. (1996). The Revised Civilian Mississippi Scale for PTSD: Reliability, validity, and cross-language stability. *Journal of Traumatic Stress, 9,* 285–298.

Norris, F., Perilla, J., & Murphy, A. (2001). Postdisaster stress in the United States and Mexico: A cross-cultural test of the multi-criterion conceptual model of posttraumatic stress disorder. *Journal of Abnormal Psychology, 110,* 553–563.

FRAN H. NORRIS
Dartmouth Medical School

See also: Assessment, Psychometric, Adult; Mississippi Combat PTSD Scale

MISSISSIPPI COMBAT PTSD SCALE

The Mississippi Combat PTSD Scale, or M-PTSD, is a self-report measure of combat-related PTSD symptoms. It contains 35 Likert-type items reflecting combat-related PTSD experiences. These items, however, are substantially different from the 17 symptoms and criteria that comprise the PTSD diagnosis found in the *DSM-IV* (American Psychiatric

Association, 1994). In the National Vietnam Veterans Readjustment Study (Kulka et al., 1990), the M-PTSD served as a primary indicator of the presence of PTSD and was considered to be the best self-report measure for that purpose. Highly acceptable psychometric properties have been reported for the M-PTSD, with excellent internal consistency (alpha of .94), and test-retest reliability (.97 over a 1-week interval). Using a cutoff score of 107, the M-PTSD was excellent at detecting PTSD that had also been established with a more rigorous structured diagnostic interview (sensitivity = .93), and was adequate for detecting the absence of PTSD (specificity = .89). The overall diagnostic hit rate was a strong .90 (Keane, Caddell, & Taylor, 1988).

REFERENCES

American Psychiatric Association. (1994). *Diagnostic and statistical manual of mental disorders* (4th ed.). Washington, DC: Author.

Keane, T. M., Caddell, J. M., & Taylor, K. L. (1988). Mississippi Scale for Combat-Related Posttraumatic Stress Disorder: Three studies in reliability and validity. *Journal of Consulting and Clinical Psychology, 56,* 85–90.

Kulka, R. A., Schlenger, W. E., Fairbank, J. A., Hough, R. L., Jordan, B. K., Marmar, C. R., et al. (1990). *Trauma and the Vietnam war generation: Report of findings from the National Vietnam Veterans Readjustment Study.* New York: Brunner/Mazel.

Jon D. Elhai
University of South Dakota

See also: Assessment, Psychometric, Adult; Military Personnel; War Trauma

MMPI-2

See: Minnesota Multiphasic Personality Inventory-2 (MMPI-2)

MORTUARY WORKERS

Persons who handle the remains of those who suffered traumatic death are exposed to a complex array of unpleasant and potentially disturbing situations. In mass casualty incidents (such as in war or disasters), medical, human service, and law enforcement personnel, firefighters, morticians, and others may be called on to handle remains. A recent example is in the response to the attacks at the World Trade Center and the Pentagon on September 11, 2001.

In incidents in which there are few deceased, such as traffic accidents and crime, professional workers such as police, emergency workers, and hospital personnel usually are able to respond highly effectively without experiencing more than temporary distress. When mass death occurs, the likelihood that remains handlers will experience persistent psychological disturbance may be increased; however, documentation of such effects is limited and tends to show that posttraumatic symptoms decrease over time. A study of volunteer military remains handlers who assisted with the processing of 47 remains after an explosion aboard a U.S. Navy ship found that intrusive and avoidance symptoms decreased over a 13-month time period (Ursano, Fullerton, Kao, & Bhartiya, 1995).

While no classification of the stressors involved in handling remains in the aftermath of traumatic death will be applicable to all persons and situations, the relative effects of some factors can be anticipated better than others. For instance, handling the remains of children or of persons known to the worker is disturbing to almost anyone, regardless of profession or experience. Individual idiosyncratic responses are also common, but are not readily predictable. Unexpected, novel aspects of the manner of death or the appearance of the body may stimulate such idiosyncratic reactions that are disturbing to one person, but may go virtually unnoticed by others.

The remains handler is bombarded with overwhelming sensory stimuli. Remains may be dismembered, decomposed, mutilated, or badly burned. Each of the senses delivers unique stimuli to the handler, but smell is the most likely to bring back reminders of the moment of exposure at a later time (Engen, 1987). Experienced mortuary workers expect these conditions and are usually not bothered by them. They may prove initially disturbing to the less experienced person, but adaptation (i.e., habituate) usually occurs. Some workers will try to mask offensive odors with other strong scents (such as oil of wintergreen) in a facemask, but this is usually only a temporary measure as olfactory adaptation occurs rapidly. Anecdotal reports are that decomposed and badly burned remains are difficult to mask.

In addition to responses to sensory stimuli, there are many cognitive reactions to the human qualities of remains. Psychological disturbances due to cognitive processes may be called emotional involvement or, in special cases, identification. Emotional involvement can occur when the worker encounters material associated with the life of the decreased. Chief among these are personal effects that facilitate recognition of the life of the deceased such as photographs, letters, rings, and other personal items. Additional personal information, such as hometown, occupation, age, marital status, and age of family members, is also likely to make the life of the deceased vivid to the imagination of the mortuary worker. Identification is said to occur when some aspect of the remains makes the deceased individual seem "like me" or "like someone close to me" (Ursano, Fullerton, Vance, & Kao, 2003). An example is when the mortuary worker has a child of the same age as the children of the deceased or encounters a deceased child. Experienced workers report that handling remains may become a relatively routine process, but they avoid hearing stories about the deceased, meeting the family, or learning personal information about the deceased. Emotional involvement tends to create more disturbing memories than the sensory qualities of the remains and has been anecdotally reported as associated with more posttraumatic symptoms.

Support for mortuary workers in large-scale incidents involving traumatic deaths is imperative. Information, supervision, and appreciation are key elements. A prebriefing should specify the tasks and clearly explain the supervisory and command structures. If inexperienced nonvolunteers are deployed they should be screened, if possible, for prior experience and reactions to death, paired with an experienced worker, and given close supervision. In general, experienced and volunteer workers fare better than those who are inexperienced or nonvolunteers (McCarroll, Ursano, Fullerton, Liu, & Lundy, 2001). During the operation, supervisors should be visible, available, and provide all necessary logistic support. Supervision helps ensure that bodies are handled in a dignified, reverent, and respectful manner. Partitioning areas of the mortuary and ventilation can decrease sensory stimulation. There should be break areas away from the remains with a place to rest, eat, drink, wash, and change clothing. Support also includes access to mental health and spiritual care. Chaplains tend to be the primary resources for personal care although mental health professionals may also be key resources. Both groups should receive specialized training and their own support and supervision when they assist mortuary workers.

In the follow-up phase, there should be an outbriefing for all the remains handlers to provide information about the larger circumstances of the event and to thank them for their efforts and reinforce the importance of their work. Some mortuary workers desire a concluding memorial service. Although the expectation is that workers will make a satisfactory postevent adjustment, resources should be available to them (and to their supervisors) in the event of posttraumatic difficulties (e.g., increased alcohol use, nightmares, family conflict, or other persistent problems).

Responses to mortuary work should not be misconstrued as uniformly traumatic or entirely negative. Workers frequently derive personal benefit from their contribution to the traditions of the nation and perform work that others could not do, work that is vital to surviving family members. Prevention and mitigation of the potentially traumatic impact of handling human remains is possible with proper training, supervision, and support of the personnel involved in this activity.

REFERENCES

Engen, T. (1987). Remembering odors and their names. *American Scientist, 75,* 497–503.

McCarroll, J. E., Ursano, R. J., Fullerton, C. S., Liu, X., & Lundy, A. C. (2001). Effects of exposure to death in a war mortuary on posttraumatic stress disorder symptoms of intrusion and avoidance. *Journal of Nervous and Mental Disease, 189,* 44–48.

Ursano, R. J., Fullerton, C. S., Kao, T., & Bhartiya, V. R. (1995). Longitudinal assessment of posttraumatic stress disorder and depression after exposure to traumatic death. *Journal of Nervous and Mental Disease, 183,* 36–42.

Ursano, R. J., Fullerton, C. S., Vance, K., & Kao, T. C. (2003). Posttraumatic stress disorder and identification in disaster workers. *American Journal of Psychiatry, 156,* 353–359.

RECOMMENDED READINGS

Ursano, R. J., McCarroll, J. E., & Fullerton, C. S. (2003). Traumatic death in terrorism and disasters: The effects on posttraumatic stress and behavior. In R. J. Ursano, C. S. Fullerton, & A. E. Norwood (Eds.), *Terrorism and disaster: Individual and community mental health interventions* (pp. 308–340). Cambridge: Cambridge University Press.

JAMES E. MCCARROLL
Uniformed Services University of the Health Sciences

See also: **Grotesque Death**

MOTOR VEHICLE COLLISIONS

Motor vehicle collisions (MVC) are typically sudden, violent, and unexpected incidents that may threaten the lives of drivers, occupants, and sometime pedestrians. While the majority of MVCs are relatively minor, a significant proportion is severe enough to cause serious injury that includes broken bones, organ damage, disfigurement, and physical disability. The prevalence of MVCs in various parts of the world vary for numerous reasons, but one example is the United States where over 40% of people report experiencing a serious MVC at some stage in their lives. Thus, MVC is one of the greatest causes of posttraumatic psychopathology in that country and to a greater or lesser extent in many others. Most research examining mental health following MVC has been conducted on populations with injuries severe enough to require admission. Little is known about mental health following MVC that do not result in hospitalization.

Prevalence of PTSD

Posttraumatic stress disorder (PTSD) has been the primary focus of research into the psychological consequences of surviving MVC. Although the conditional risk of developing PTSD following MVC is relatively low when compared with interpersonal trauma, the greater frequency with which MVC occurs renders it a leading cause of PTSD. Large epidemiological studies, for example, routinely report that serious accidents account for around one quarter of PTSD cases in community samples. Studies using consecutive or random hospital admissions of MVC survivors have reported PTSD prevalence rates ranging from 2% to 30% at 12 months post injury, with the majority of studies yielding figures between 10% and 20%. The considerable variance in prevalence rates has been attributed to methodological factors such as the use of self report versus structured clinical interview, as well as cultural and environmental factors. It is also important to consider rates of subsyndromal PTSD; research suggests that individuals with partial PTSD may still have comparable levels of impairment to those with a full diagnosis (Amsel & Marshall, 2003).

Other Psychopathology

The prevalence of other posttrauma psychopathology following MVC is less well known. The few studies examining depression following injury provide differing prevalence estimates, but generally indicate that it is one of the most frequent disorders to develop following MVC related injury (see for review, O'Donnell, Creamer, Bryant, Schnyder, & Shalev, 2003).

Although depression may occur independent of PTSD, the two disorders frequently co-occur; between 30% and 50% of MVC survivors with PTSD also have a diagnosis of depression at between 4 and 12 months post injury. The strong relationship between PTSD and depression, and the high prevalence of posttraumatic depression independent of PTSD, highlights the importance of considering depressive symptomatology in the assessment and treatment of psychopathology following MVC. Anxiety disorders other than PTSD appear to be less common than depression in MVC populations, with rates ranging between 4% and 25% at 6 to 18 months post accident. As with depression, other anxiety disorders may appear comorbid with PTSD or develop independently following MVC. Not surprisingly, the development of travel phobia as a consequence of MVC has received increasing attention, with rates ranging from 4% to 29%. Few prospective, longitudinal studies have examined substance use as a sequel to MVC, with most studies being concerned with intoxication as a potential cause of injury rather than a posttraumatic outcome. Given the strong relationship between substance use and injury, however, this is clearly an important line of future inquiry.

Course of Traumatic Stress Symptoms

Immediately following severe MVC, many individuals experience some acute stress symptoms such as shock, anxiety, agitation, and mild dissociative symptoms. While even these mild symptoms can be distressing, they tend to settle relatively quickly in the majority of MVC survivors. The course of more significant psychopathology over time is less clear. Recent research suggests that PTSD symptoms fluctuate over time with people moving in and out of full and subsyndromal PTSD diagnoses. This fluctuation may help to explain the complex issue of delayed onset PTSD. While studies report delayed onset in up to 20% of all PTSD cases in MVC survivors, the majority of those with delayed onset had previous subsyndromal levels of the disorder. Fluctuations in symptom levels may be influenced by the extent of the injury, pain, disability and other stressors that exist following injury, although well-controlled research is required to adequately address this question.

Quality of Life and Disability

There is a complex relationship between severe MVC in which injury occurs, posttraumatic mental health, and subsequent disability and quality of life (Duckworth, Iezzi, & O'Donohue, 2008). Traumatic injury often has a significant adverse impact on long-term disability and quality of life, with psychological factors exerting an important influence on physical recovery following injury. The data suggest, for example, that acute psychological stress symptoms, as well as later PTSD and depression, are independently associated with poor quality of life and functional outcomes.

Vulnerability to Posttrauma Psychopathology

Consistent with other types of trauma exposure, consideration must be given to pre-, peri-, and posttrauma factors in explaining the development and maintenance of PTSD and other posttraumatic psychopathology. In general, meta-analyses exploring vulnerability to PTSD suggest that pretrauma factors have small effect sizes while peritrauma and posttrauma factors have moderate effect sizes. Prior to considering risk for PTSD, however, an important consideration in this population is recidivism: Individuals with prior exposure to a traumatic event are more likely to experience subsequent traumatic events and individuals experiencing traumatic injury are particularly likely to have experienced prior trauma. Such findings have important implications for clinical assessment and intervention.

Few demographic variables have emerged consistently as vulnerability factors in PTSD following MVC although, consistent with the broader PTSD literature, some studies have identified female gender and younger age as risk factors. The role of trauma history, as well as prior psychiatric history, in the development of PTSD in this population is less understood, although they probably play an important indirect role in the development of mental health problems after trauma.

Contrary to expectations, the majority of studies with MVC populations do not find a direct relationship between PTSD and injury severity, although this may be partially explained by the difficulty of defining injury severity. It seems that the consequence of the injury has a far greater impact on mental health than injury severity *per se*. There has been considerable debate about the relationship between PTSD and traumatic brain injury (TBI), with the suggestion that TBI may protect against the development of trauma-related psychopathology by reducing the likelihood that trauma information is encoded and, therefore, recalled. While the evidence for moderate and severely brain injured survivors is lacking, it is clear that individuals with mild TBI are just as likely to develop PTSD and other posttraumatic mental health conditions as those without TBI. As with other trauma types, subjective experience is crucial in the development of posttrauma reactions, with the individuals' appraisal of threat (especially fear for their life) a powerful predictor of PTSD following MVC.

High levels of acute stress are generally predictive of later PTSD, depression, and other mental health problems. Specifically, severity of acute reexperiencing symptoms is predictive of later PTSD development. Importantly, reexperiencing symptoms do not seem to be predictive of general psychopathology, highlighting the unique role played by these phenomena in PTSD. There is increasing evidence supporting the importance of acute hyperarousal symptoms in identifying risk for PTSD. Although peritraumatic dissociation is often found to be a strong predictor of PTSD, there are many issues to consider in the measurement of peritraumatic dissociation in MVC survivors. In particular, the routine use of opiate analgesics in this population, combined with the high rate of mild head injury, indicate the need for great caution when assessing peritraumatic dissociation. High levels of acute depression are predictive of later PTSD and depression. Although

few studies have explored social support following MVC, it has consistently emerged as a strong protective factor against psychopathology in other populations and is likely to be important for injured MVC survivors.

Treatment

Trauma-focused cognitive behavioral therapy has been shown to be the treatment of choice for PTSD in this population. Treatment of injured MVC survivors, however, carries with it several complications. Pain is a common problem that may compound the psychopathology in a mutually reinforcing cycle and will usually need to be addressed in treatment. It can also render the application of traditional approaches (such as 50-minute therapy sessions) impossible in some cases. The complexities of physical recovery, with frequent medical appointments and disruptions to previous life patterns, often make commitment to regular treatment sessions very difficult. Coming to terms with any residual disability may also add another dimension to the psychological treatment process. Finally, clinical assessment and treatments should aim to address the range of psychopathology that develops following injured MVC survivors in addition to PTSD. Research studies are currently focusing on the effectiveness of early intervention treatments in preventing and treating psychopathology following MVC injury. This research enhances our understanding about best practice mental health intervention for injured MVC survivors.

REFERENCES

Amsel, L., & Marshall, R. D. (2003). Clinical management of subsyndromal psychological sequelae of the 9/11 terror attacks (Relational perspectives book series). In S. W. Coates, J. L. Rosenthal, & D. Schechter (Eds.), *September 11: Trauma and human bonds* (pp. 75–97). Hillsdale, NJ: Analytic Press.

Duckworth, M. P., Iezzi, T., & O'Donohue, W. (Eds.). (2008). *Motor vehicle collisions: Medical, psychosocial, and legal consequences.* New York: Elsevier.

O'Donnell, M. L., Creamer, M., Bryant, R. A., Schnyder, U., & Shalev, A. (2003). Posttraumatic disorders following injury: An empirical and methodological review. *Clinical Psychology Review, 23*(4), 587–603.

MEAGHAN O'DONNELL
University of Melbourne

MARK CREAMER
University of Melbourne

See also: Acute Stress Disorder

MOVIE DEPICTIONS OF PSYCHOLOGICAL TRAUMA

Depictions of psychological trauma and related subject matter have been a mainstay in film almost since its inception. Early filmmaker, D. W. Griffith, apparently had an affinity for such topics, depicting the effects of the U.S. Civil War on families in *The Birth of a Nation* (1915), and what are perhaps the earliest film portrayals of child abuse (*Broken Blossoms,* 1919) and of a "mind specialist" (*The Criminal Hypnotist,* 1908).

Movie representations of traumatic events may be historical or fictional, yet they typically concern experiences important to viewers as individuals or as members of a culture, a generation, or a nation, or they employ psychological trauma as a means of story development or central plot twist. In either case, the traumatic event and its psychological effects are often the pivot on which the cinematic story-telling turns.

Depictions of Traumatic Stressors

Filmmakers' creations reflect the concerns of their time, and interest in portrayals of psychological aspects of trauma may be kindled by cultural developments such as public awareness of psychiatric casualties during war or media coverage of child sexual abuse. However, virtually every conceivable type of traumatic event has had its moment on the big screen. Commonly the dramatic action centers on the phenomenology of the experience or its impact on victims. Such portrayals include: military combat (e.g., *The Best Years of Our Lives,* 1946; *Coming Home,* 1978; *Saving Private Ryan,* 1998; *Flags of Our Fathers,* 2006), concentration camp or prisoner of war incarcerations (e.g., *Deer Hunter,* 1978; *Sophie's Choice,* 1982), terrorism (e.g., *Munich,* 2005; *World Trade Center,* 2006), disasters or accidents (e.g., *Ordinary People,* 1980; *Black Rain,* 1989; *Fearless,* 1993), witnessing or suffering violence (e.g., *Suddenly Last Summer,* 1959; *Once Were Warriors,* 1994; *K-Pax,* 2001; *The Secret Life of Words,* 2005), and childhood physical or sexual abuse (e.g., *Dolores Claiborne,* 1995; *Sleepers,* 1996; *Mystic River,* 2003; *Mysterious Skin,* 2004), among many others.

Early traumatic experience also figures prominently in film backstories as the purported wellspring of present mental illness, "wickedness," or obsessional behavior. The *presumption of a traumatic etiology* is common in films that include mentally disturbed persons (Hyler, 1988; Wedding, Boyd, & Niemiec, 2005) or as the motive for characters' actions. For example, rationales for the behavior of villainous protagonists often include child abuse or witnessing a grisly crime as a child (Schneider, 1987), and the frenzied drive with which the scientist in *Twister* (1996) chases tornadoes was apparently motivated by a need to master the early loss of her father to one (Gabbard, 2001).

In addition to films where traumatic events and sequelae are the backdrop for drama or mystery, genres such as horror and disaster films, that (by definition) include traumatic events, seem to have a different purpose. Rather than presenting stories of true or plausible menaces, the traumatic events in these films involve superhuman killers, impossible monsters, or over-the-top disasters. The subject matter appears designed to tap or stimulate, *in the viewer,* the subjective response to traumatic exposure—dread, shock, fear, helplessness, disgust, and horror. The audience's vicarious exposure may also be enhanced by the dissociative suspension of disbelief and reality constraints that movie-viewing induces (Butler & Palesh, 2004). Typically, though, the actions of the film's hero leads to elimination of the threat and the audience's return to safety, thereby reassuring viewers that such challenges (and emotions) can be tolerated and overcome. Films in these genres may flourish because they provide a vehicle through which audiences can struggle with inchoate feelings of anxiety and threat present in the contemporary zeitgeist (such as fears of communism, nuclear attack, terrorism); their abiding success attests to the appeal of such experiences. Notably, the psychological impact of these extraordinary events on the film's characters is typically and unrealistically absent or negligible, unless necessary to enhancing dramatic tension or furthering the plot in the short term.

Depictions of Peritraumatic and Posttraumatic Reactions

Phenomenology of Traumatic Experience

Some movies have portrayed the experience of living through a traumatic event with arresting accuracy and poignancy. For example, several recent films have convincingly portrayed the phenomenology of peritraumatic derealization (Butler & Palesh, 2004); most notably, the sensory alterations captured in the extraordinary images of the brutal, chaotic landing at Normandy in *Saving Private Ryan* (1998) and at the plane crash site in *Fearless* (1993), and the time distortion depicted during the car crash in *Intersection* (1994) and evoked through the protracted rape in *Irreversible* (2002). Other films have used the ostensible interior experience of a character as a plot device. In *Identity* (2003), the audience eventually learns that the murderous elimination of characters during the film actually represents (Hollywood's interpretation of) the phenomenology of a therapeutic integration of a dissociative identity disorder patient's "alters."

PTSD and Dissociative Symptoms as Dramatic Focus or Plot Device

A number of movies have also convincingly depicted characters suffering PTSD, as well as their difficulties in postevent adaptation

(e.g., *Best Years of Our Lives,* 1946; *Coming Home,* 1978; *The Deer Hunter,* 1978; *Ordinary People,* 1980; *Born on the Fourth of July,* 1989; *Mystic River,* 2003; *The Secret Life of Words,* 2005; *Flags of Our Fathers,* 2006). Additionally, some have highlighted specific symptoms of PTSD to enhance the mystery or further the plot, including: intrusive memories, nightmares, and flashbacks (e.g., *Manchurian Candidate,* 1962; *Mysterious Skin,* 2004; *Flags of Our Fathers,* 2006), reactivity to cues reminiscent of the trauma (e.g., *Spellbound,* 1945; *Vertigo,* 1958; *Dead Again,* 1991), amnesia (e.g., *Suddenly Last Summer,* 1959; *Dolores Claiborne,* 1995; *Mysterious Skin,* 2004), numbing and withdrawal (e.g., *Deer Hunter,* 1978; *Coming Home,* 1978; *The Secret Life of Words,* 2005), and insomnia and anger (e.g., *Taxi Driver,* 1976; *Coming Home,* 1978; *Mystic River,* 2003), and associated features, such as event-related guilt and shame (e.g., *Spellbound,* 1945; *Ordinary People,* 1980; *Black Rain,* 1989; *Fearless,* 1993), conversion symptoms (e.g., *Home of the Brave,* 1949; *Color of Night,* 1994), traumatic bonding (*Mysterious Skin,* 2004), alcohol and substance abuse (e.g., *The Best Years of Our Lives,* 1946; *Born of the Fourth of July,* 1989; *Once Were Warriors,* 1994), recklessness or self-injurious behaviors (e.g., *The Deer Hunter,* 1978; *Fearless,* 1993; *Once Were Warriors,* 1994; *Mysterious Skin,* 2004), and traumatic reenactments (e.g., *The Deer Hunter,* 1978; *Dead Again,* 1991), among others.

Another very common posttraumatic diagnosis portrayed in film is of a dissociative identity disturbance (specifically, fugue or dissociative identity disorder). Although a handful of movies provide biographical accounts of actual dissociative patients (e.g., *Three Faces of Eve,* 1957), the majority of films use dissociation-related identity disorders as a central element or device in service of the plot (e.g., *Spellbound,* 1945; *Color of Night,* 1994; *Primal Fear,* 1996; *Fight Club,* 1999; *Nurse Betty,* 2000; *K-Pax,* 2001; *Identity,* 2003). In that capacity "dissociation" has a virtually limitless potential for multifaceted plot twists and exploration of existential concerns and contemporary psychological, social, and cultural issues (see Butler

& Palesh, 2004), but typically the correspondence of these depictions to actual clinical phenomena is strained.

Depictions of Psychotherapy for Trauma-Related Disorders

Because traumatic experiences often figure large in film, psychotherapeutic interventions to address them are also widespread. However, such portrayals generally reflect a lay understanding of psychotherapy, often linking the methods of psychotherapy with criminal detection (Schneider, 1987). Films also routinely perpetuate the misconception that psychotherapy inevitably involves the discovery (often through hypnosis) of a single (long-repressed) traumatic event coupled with a highly emotional abreaction, all aided by an extraordinarily empathic therapist (Gabbard, 2001; Schneider, 1987). These moments may comprise the climax of the film—dramatic and satisfying for viewers, yet frustrating for many trauma professionals because the *cathartic cure* (Gabbard & Gabbard, 1999) does not correspond to current practice and such portrayals may raise unrealistic expectations among mental health consumers about psychotherapy process and outcome (Hyler, 1988; Gabbard & Gabbard, 1999). Although in-office abreactions appear to be less common in recent films, the curative effects of recovering traumatic memories, and the restorative insights that such efforts yield, are still regularly portrayed (e.g., *Ordinary People,* 1980; *Dolores Claiborne,* 1995).

Conclusion

The cinematic depiction of traumatic events, traumatic experience, and their sequelae—like storytelling through the ages—ranges from noteworthy verisimilitude and subtlety to farfetched or simplistic. The experiences for viewers range from insight or catharsis to vicarious excitement or mere diversion. And though films' shortcomings may promote unfortunate distortions, at their best such depictions can be extraordinarily powerful and revealing when they capture the psychological truth of the experience.

REFERENCES

Butler, L. D., & Palesh, O. (2004). "Spellbound: Dissociation in the movies." *Journal of Trauma and Dissociation, 5*(2), 63–88.

Gabbard, G. O. (2001). The impact of psychoanalysis on the American cinema. *Annual of Psychoanalysis, 29,* 237–246.

Gabbard, G. O., & Gabbard, K. (1999). *Psychiatry and the cinema.* Washington, DC: American Psychiatric Press.

Hyler, S. E. (1988). DSM-III at the cinema: Madness in the movies. *Comprehensive Psychiatry, 29*(2), 195–206.

Schneider, I. (1987). The theory and practice of movie psychiatry. *American Journal of Psychiatry, 144*(8), 996–1002.

Wedding, D., Boyd, M. A., & Niemiec, R. M. (2005). *Movies and mental illness: Using films to understand psychopathology.* Cambridge, MA: Hogrefe & Huber.

LISA D. BUTLER
Stanford University School of Medicine

ROBERT W. GARLAN
Stanford University School of Medicine

See also: Literary Depictions

MULTIPLE PERSONALITY DISORDER (MPD)

See: Dissociative Identity Disorder

MYERS, CHARLES SAMUEL (1873–1946)

Charles Samuel Myers, who first coined the term *shell shock* and subsequently regretted it, is considered to be the most important British psychologist of the first half of the twentieth century (Bunn, 2001). He was involved in anthropological fieldwork (together with W. H. R. Rivers), before becoming qualified as a physician in 1902. Subsequently, he was an experimental psychologist at King's College, London, wrote *A Textbook of Experimental Psychology* (Myers, 1909), and held various important positions, including editor of the *British Journal of Psychology.* He set up the Cambridge Laboratory of Experimental Psychology in 1912, largely paid for from his own resources.

Right after the beginning of World War I, Myers decided to join the army—in order work in the field in France. This was no easy feat because he was over the age limit. He began seeing traumatized soldiers in the field in France to offer more immediate treatment and became an innovative pioneer in conceptualizing and treating acute combat trauma. As consulting psychologist to the army, he organized special treatment centers using interventions based on (a) promptness of action, (b) suitable environment, and (c) psychotherapeutic interventions. However, at the end of 1916, the army opted for harsher treatments provided by neurologists with no experience with psychotherapy. Myers, the psychologist, was left in charge of the neurological cases.

In 1915–1916, Myers published a series of important clinical papers in the *Lancet,* containing systematic case descriptions of various trauma-related symptoms (Myers, 1915, 1916a, 1916b, 1916c). As he initially observed only cases in which the precipitating factor was an exploding shell, he coined the term *shell shock* (Myers, 1915). He became soon aware, however, that the three groups of symptoms following shell shock (hysteria, characterized by dissociation; neurasthenia, a mental disorder due to exhaustion; and graver forms of mental disorders) were not only caused by the physical or chemical effects of shell blasts; they also developed in circumstances without shell explosions. "[E]xcessive emotion, for example, sudden horror or fear—indeed any 'psychical trauma' or 'inadjustable experience'—is sufficient" (Myers, 1940, p. 26). Hence, he concluded that shell shock was "a singularly ill-chosen term" (p. 28).

Having seen more than 2,000 acutely traumatized servicemen by mid-1916, Myers observed a specific pattern of alternations of their personality:

[T]he normal personality is in abeyance. Even if it is capable of receiving impressions, it shows no signs of responding to them. The recent emotional [i.e., traumatic] experiences of the individual have the upper hand and determine his conduct: the normal has been replaced by what we may call the "emotional" personality. . . . Gradually or suddenly an "apparently normal" personality usually returns—normal save for the lack of all memory of events directly connected with the shock, normal save for the manifestation of other ("somatic") hysteric disorders indicative of mental dissociation. Now and again there occur alternations of the "emotional" and the "apparently normal" personalities. . . . On its return, the "apparently normal" personality may recall, as in a dream, the distressing experiences revived during the temporary intrusion of the "emotional" personality. The "emotional" personality may also return during sleep, the "functional" disorders of mutism, paralysis, contracture, and so on, being then usually in abeyance. On waking, however, the "apparently normal" personality may have no recollection of the dream state and will at once resume his mutism, paralysis, etc. (Myers, 1940, pp. 66–67)

Even though Myers used the terms "apparently normal" and "emotional" personalities, he was not referring to completely separate personalities, but understood that these were dissociative manifestations of a single individual. Myers referred to what are now called trauma-related psychoform and somatoform dissociative symptoms. These symtoms are manifestations of a dissociation between two different types of psychobiological subsystems of the personality: one dedicated to functioning in daily life and one fixated in traumatic memory. Thus, Myers fundamentally considered posttraumatic stress disorder (PTSD) to be a disorder of dissociation. Treatment, in his view, should be aimed at the (re)integration of both subsystems. When this takes place, trauma-related symptoms disappear. For this purpose, the traumatic memories need to be reactivated and confronted, but without an undue evocation and expression of vehement emotions (Myers, 1920–1921). In modern terms, he emphasized the need for exposure while the patient remains within his or her window of tolerance. Myers' view constitutes a cornerstone of a contemporary view of traumatization, that is, the theory of structural dissociation of the personality (Van der Hart, Nijenhuis, & Steele, 2006), which describes various levels of complexity of this dissociative division.

Myers' humanism and dedication to patients is recognized in an obituary in 2001: "He truly put himself on the line—out in France, doing his best to save soldiers from execution" (Costall, 2001, p. 464). This attitude strongly contrasted to the one that characterized several of his immediate colleagues, including the neurologist who had taken over the treatment of "shell shock" cases (Shepard, 2000). Myers found his own experiences during Word War I personally difficult, some of them perhaps even traumatizing. Following his discharge from the army, he declined invitations to discuss his work, including giving testimony to the War Office Committee on Shell Shock: "The recall of my past five years' work proved too painful" (Myers, 1940, p. 141). While preparing his *Shell Shock in France 1914–1918,* he again expressed that "the revival of these long-repressed memories—particularly those of certain experiences which I have refrained from mentioning—has been extremely unpleasant" (p. 141).

Myers returned from the war with the intention of moving psychology out of the laboratory and applying it more directly to real human problems, particularly in large-scale organizations such as factories. In 1921, he cofounded the National Institute of Industrial Psychology (NIIP). The field of psychotraumatology remains strongly indebted to his clinical insights on acute (war) trauma and its treatment.

REFERENCES

Bunn, G. (2001). Charlie and the chocolate factory. *Psychologist, 14,* 576–579.

Costall, A. (2001). Charles Samuel Myers (1873–1946). *The Psychologist, 14,* 464.

Myers, C. S. (1909). *A textbook of experimental psychology.* Cambridge: Cambridge University Press.

Myers, C. S. (1915, February 13). A contribution to the study of shell shock: Being an account of three cases of loss of memory, vision, smell, and taste. *Lancet,* 316–320.

Myers, C. S. (1916a, January 8). Contributions to the study of shell shock: Pt. II. Being an account of certain cases treated by hypnosis. *Lancet,* 65–69.

Myers, C. S. (1916b, March 18). Contributions to the study of shell shock: Pt. III. Being an account of certain disorders of cutaneous sensibility. *Lancet,* 608–613.

Myers, C. S. (1916c, September 9). Contributions to the study of shell shock: Pt. IV. Being an account of certain disorders of speech, with special reference and their relation to malingering. *Lancet,* 461–467.

Myers, C. S. (1920–1921). The revival of emotional memories and its therapeutic value: Pt. 2. *British Journal of Medical Psychology, 1,* 20–22.

Myers, C. S. (1940). *Shell shock in France 1914–1918.* Cambridge: Cambridge University Press.

Shepard, B. (2000). *A war of nerves: Soldiers and psychiatrists 1914–1994.* London: Jonathan Cape.

Van der Hart, O., Nijenhuis, E. R. S., & Steele, K. (2006). *The haunted self: Structural dissociation and the treatment of chronic traumatization.* New York: Norton.

Van der Hart, O., Van Dijke, A., Van Son, M., & Steele, K. (2000). Somatoform dissociation in traumatized World War I combat soldiers: A neglected clinical heritage. *Journal of Trauma and Dissociation, 1*(4), 33–66.

ONNO VAN DER HART
Utrecht University

See also: Combat Stress Reactions; Dissociation; History of Psychological Trauma; Hysteria; Janet, Pierre; Military Personnel; Traumatic Neurosis; War Trauma

N

NATIONAL CENTER FOR POSTTRAUMATIC STRESS DISORDER (NC-PTSD)

The National Center for Posttraumatic Stress Disorder (NC-PTSD) was created in 1989 within the U.S. Department of Veterans Affairs in response to a Congressional mandate to address the needs of veterans with military-related posttraumatic stress disorder (PTSD). The NC-PTSD was developed toward the ultimate purpose of improving the well-being, status, and understanding of veterans in American society. The mandate called for a center of excellence that would set the agenda for research and education on PTSD without direct responsibility for patient care. Convinced that no single VA site could adequately serve this unique mission, the VA established the NC-PTSD as a consortium of VA academic centers across the United States, located in White River Junction, VT; Boston, MA; West Haven, CT; Palo Alto, CA; and Honolulu, HI.

The mission of the NC-PTSD is to advance the clinical care and social welfare of America's veterans through research, education, and training in the science, diagnosis, and treatment of PTSD and stress-related disorders. The NC-PTSD was designed to provide leadership nationally and internationally as a research and educational center of excellence on PTSD through its extensive research program and by disseminating information synthesized from published scientific research and collective clinical experience to the field.

The NC-PTSD is organized to facilitate rapid translation of science into practice, assuring that the latest research findings inform clinical care; and translation of practice into science and that questions raised by clinical challenges are addressed using rigorous experimental protocols. By drawing on the specific expertise vested at each separate division (e.g., behavioral, neuroscientific), the NC-PTSD provides a unique infrastructure within which to implement multidisciplinary initiatives regarding the etiology, pathophysiology, diagnosis, and treatment of PTSD. These include: development of some of the major assessment

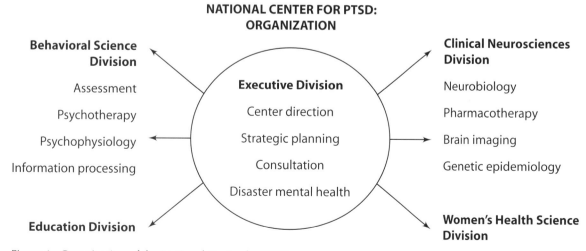

Figure 1. Organization of the National Center for PTSD.

tools for PTSD (e.g., the CAPS and PCL); three large-scale multisite clinical trials (e.g., VA Cooperative Studies) of psychotherapy and pharmacotherapy; and structural and functional brain imaging studies that have advanced our understanding of PTSD.

In the education arena, the NC-PTSD tailors needed information to fit the various needs of a range of audiences including veterans and their families, clinicians, scientists, educators, program directors, and policy makers. Major educational activities include creation and maintenance of a web site on PTSD (www.ncptsd.va.gov) that is visited by over a million unique users per year; development of PILOTS (Published International Literature on Traumatic Stress), the worlds largest computerized bibliographic database; and two projects to disseminate evidence-based cognitive-behavioral therapies (cognitive processing therapy and prolonged exposure) that should train hundreds of clinicians in these techniques.

During the past 18 years, the NC-PTSD staff has obtained approximately $184 million in extramural funding for over 450 peer-reviewed research projects. They have educated over 1,100 mental health practitioners in a week-long Clinical Training Program, and provided clinical training in assessment and treatment of PTSD to over 575 military and civilian clinicians. The NC-PTSD also has provided education to veterans, troops, and family members on war-zone stress, and trained thousands of clinicians in disaster mental health following Hurricane Katrina and other natural disasters.

MATTHEW J. FRIEDMAN
National Center for Posttraumatic Stress Disorder

See also: Laws, Legislation, and Policy; Veterans Affairs, U.S. Department of

NATIONAL CHILD TRAUMATIC STRESS NETWORK

In recognition of the serious impact of trauma on children, their families, and society, Congress authorized the Substance Abuse and Mental Health Services Administration (SAMHSA) to develop a grant program to enhance the provision of evidence-based treatment, trauma-informed services, and access to care for traumatized children and their families across the United States. In 2001, SAMHSA established the National Child Traumatic Stress Network (NCTSN) with the explicit mandate to form a collaborative network of child and adolescent trauma experts from academic and community service settings around the country to work toward achieving this critically important national priority. The NCTSN was designed to address the full range of trauma types and to encompass the spectrum of age ranges from early childhood through late adolescence (Pynoos et al., in press).

The strategic priorities of the NCTSN are to: (1) raise public and professional awareness about the serious impact of child traumatic stress on the safety and healthy development of the nation's children and families; (2) develop and disseminate evidence-based and developmentally and culturally sound assessments, interventions, and treatments; (3) develop and promote the adoption of trauma-informed practices across a wide variety of service settings; (4) contribute to our national disaster and terrorism mental health preparedness and response capacity; (5) conduct policy analyses, develop policy recommendations, and advance public policy; (6) promote cultural competence and youth, family, and consumer engagement in the development and implementation of all Network products and programs; (7) use the most valid and reliable assessment batteries and tools for networkwide clinical data collection, treatment planning, outcome monitoring, and an independent national evaluation; and (8) work toward the sustainability of the Network as a unique and effective transformation system. The Network is comprised of: (a) a joint coordinating National Center for Child Traumatic Stress co-located at UCLA and Duke University; (b) university or large medical center-affiliated Treatment Development and Evaluation Centers primarily responsible for the development, dissemination, adoption, adaptation, and evaluation of evidence-based assessment, intervention, and service delivery models; and (c) Community Treatment and Service Centers primarily engaged in implementing and adapting model treatment protocols and trauma-informed services in community or specialty child service settings. A large and active group of Alumni Centers also contribute to Network products, programs, and partnerships. Each year, the NCTSN serves more than 40,000 children and families and trains an average of 40,000 professionals.

NCTSN members participate in approximately two dozen Network collaborative groups devoted to developing knowledge and improving practice in specific areas of child trauma and across child-serving systems. The NCTSN web site (www.nctsn.org) allows the public to access information regarding child trauma and also provides a platform for distance learning and broad dissemination of NCTSN products, evidence-based treatments, and trauma-informed practices. NCTSN has advanced the use of a quality improvement learning collaborative model as a means of promoting implementation, adoption, and adaptation of interventions and trauma-informed practices.

To improve access and quality of care, NCTSN is developing a growing number of products and tools that cut across a variety of child population groups and multiple service sectors. For example, the NCTSN serves as a national resource in preparedness and response to terrorism and disaster for children and families across the United States in developing the *Psychological First Aid, Field Operations Guide* in collaboration with the National Center for PTSD (Brymer et al., 2006). Since the launch of *Psychological First Aid,* there have been over 30,000 downloads of the field operations guide from the NCTSN and NC-PTSD web sites and over 10,000 copies have been distributed.

Other examples of NCTSN products include the NCTSN Measures Review Database that provides clinicians and researchers with in-depth information about assessment instruments. "Kids, Cops, and Domestic Violence" is a training package to enhance police officer response to children on the scene of domestic violence calls. The "Courage to Remember" material is designed to broaden clinical and public attention to childhood traumatic grief. White papers on complex trauma and refugee mental health address major public mental health issues. The "Promise of Trauma-Focused Therapy for Childhood Sexual Abuse" DVD provides parents, teachers, and health-care professionals with information about trauma-focused cognitive behavioral therapy.

REFERENCES

Brymer, M., Jacobs, A., Layne, C., Pynoos, R., Ruzek, J., Steinberg, A., et al. (2006). *Psychological first aid: Field operations guide* (2nd ed.). Available from www.nctsn.org and www.ncptsd.va.gov.

Pynoos, R. S., Fairbank, J. A., Steinberg, A. M., Amaya-Jackson, L., Gerrity, E., Mount, M., et al. (in press). The National Child Traumatic Stress Network: Collaborating to improve the standard of care. *Professional Psychology: Theory and Practice.*

ROBERT S. PYNOOS
National Center for Child Traumatic Stress at UCLA

JOHN A. FAIRBANK
National Center for Child Traumatic Stress at Duke University

See also: Child Development; Laws, Legislation, and Policy

NEUROBIOLOGY

See: Biology, Brain Structure, and Function, Adult; Biology, Brain Structure, and Function, Child; Biology, Neurochemistry

NEUROIMAGING

See: Biology, Brain Structure, and Function, Adult; Biology, Brain Structure, and Function, Child; Biology, Neurochemistry

NIGHTMARES

Posttraumatic nightmares are a common occurrence in myriad trauma survivors. Conventional formulations of nightmares through nosology or research investigations narrowly describe posttraumatic nightmares as typically awakening the patient from sleep, invoking extremely intense emotions of fear or anxiety, and often involving replays of traumatic experiences. Recent research confers some validity on these views; however, depending on the patient's stage of recovery or stasis, research also shows that many nightmare sufferers report few awakenings from disturbing dreams; a wide array of unpleasant emotions besides fear and anxiety; and dream content that varies across a range of themes from fully symbolic to apparent replays.

Conventional formulations also implicate a psychodynamic or posttraumatic etiology to the onset and maintenance of chronic nightmares, and recent research supports these views. In a sizeable proportion of trauma survivors, however, chronic nightmares may be more usefully explained as learned behavior, which potentially emerges in the wake of a damaged or malfunctioning mental imagery system. Treatment programs utilizing exposure and desensitization models are well established as effective treatments for nightmares. Yet, the most widely tested intervention among trauma survivors with chronic nightmares—Imagery Rehearsal Therapy (IRT)—allegedly deemphasizes exposure therapy. IRT is a cognitive-behavioral approach based on imagery training, conscious revision of nightmare content, and waking rehearsal of the revised content. This methodology supports the theory of a learned "nightmaring" process.

RECOMMENDED READINGS

Krakow, B., Hollifield, M., Johnston, L., Koss, M., Schrader, R., Warner, T. D., et al. (2001). Imagery rehearsal therapy for chronic nightmares in sexual assault survivors with posttraumatic stress disorder. *Journal of the American Medical Association, 286,* 537–545.

Wittmann, L., Schredl, M., & Kramer, M. (2007). Dreaming in posttraumatic stress disorder: A critical review of phenomenology, psychophysiology and treatment. *Psychotherapy and Psychosomatics, 76,* 25–39.

Barry Krakow
Sleep and Human Health Institute

See also: **Insomnia; Intrusive Reexperiencing**

NONGOVERNMENTAL ORGANIZATIONS

Large-scale emergencies can produce traumatic stress for a significant number of people, necessitating resources that exceed traditional mental health services. Beyond government assistance (*see:* **Laws, Legislation, and Policy**), nongovernmental organizations (NGOs) play a critical role supporting and assisting victims. This role often includes providing psychological support through clinical and nonclinical behavioral health services.

While there are many kinds of psychological trauma and disasters, NGOs tend to focus their services on emergencies sufficiently large that local responders require additional assistance. This includes natural disasters (e.g., tornadoes, hurricanes, floods), public health emergencies (e.g., SARS, pandemic influenza), or human-caused incidents (e.g., terrorist attacks, airline crashes, train derailments). NGOs have specifically organized themselves to respond to disasters and are different than the organizations already providing community mental health services and continuing to do so during an emergency. While the traumatic impact of smaller scale and personal emergencies may be significant, NGOs are less likely to become involved in those cases.

A mantra of disaster response is: "All disasters are local." Local responders are invariably first on the scene and frequently remain when the community moves into the recovery phase. When insufficient resources are available, a local community may request help from the country, state, or provincial governments, which in turn may request regional or national assistance from both government and private sectors. For that reason, NGO disaster response agencies, such as the American Red Cross, emphasize the development of local chapters. Just as local police and fire are the first line of defense in an emergency, local chapters of the American Red Cross, United Way, Salvation Army, and other groups are the starting point for many sheltering, feeding, and humanitarian assistance activities, including mental health support. You should remain cognizant of this local system although NGOs generally are organized and respond on a larger scale nationally and internationally.

Authority for the Role of NGOs

Paralleling the roles and responsibilities of government agencies in disasters are those of the private sector, which is represented largely by NGOs and faith-based organizations (FBOs). NGOs and FBOs in the United States communicate and collaborate within the National Response Framework (NRF; Federal Emergency Management Agency [FEMA], n.d.), which guides the nation's all-hazards incident response. The NRF developed from revisions in 2006 and 2007 of the 2004 National Response Plan (NRP). When an incident of national significance occurs, the American Red Cross and the National Voluntary Organizations Active in Disaster (NVOAD, n.d.), signatories to the NRP, have specific responsibilities, which are described in the "Emergency Support Function (ESF) Annexes" (i.e., sections) of the written documents describing the NRP and the NRF. For example, in ESF 6, American Red Cross disaster mental health (DMH) volunteers provide mental health services to shelter populations while the Church of the Brethren provides crisis intervention to young children through their Disaster Child Care (DCC) program.

The 1996 U.S. Aviation Disaster Family Assistance Act gave responsibility to the National Transportation Safety Board (NTSB) for overseeing support services to families and survivors involved in commercial aviation disasters. The NTSB designated the American Red Cross as the nonprofit organization responsible for the victim support tasks defined as Family Care and Mental Health. The American Red Cross staffs Family Assistance Centers (FAC) for disaster-affected communities, provides crisis and grief counseling through its Disaster Mental Health Services staff, and coordinates with the NTSB regarding on-site child care services and interfaith memorial services. NTSB requires sponsoring agencies to train their personnel regarding the range of physical and emotional reactions to psychological trauma, including the long-term effects from posttraumatic stress disorder (PTSD).

Services Provided

Organized in 1970, NVOAD is the umbrella organization coordinating disaster planning efforts of volunteer organizations throughout the United States. At the state and local levels, NVOAD members are known as Voluntary Organizations Active in Disaster (VOAD).

The most widely recognized NGO providing disaster mental health (DMH) services in the United States is the American Red Cross. In 1905, Congress chartered the American Red Cross to "carry on a system of national and international relief in time of peace," to mitigate and prevent suffering caused by national calamities. In 1990, the American Red Cross established a formal DMH Services program and began training licensed and certified mental health professionals to volunteer and alleviate the impact of exposure to trauma. Initially using only licensed psychologists and social workers, the program has since expanded to include other allied disciplines such as psychiatry and master's level counseling professions.

In 2005, the American Red Cross widened its scope of immediate intervention by training all Red Cross volunteers in Psychological First Aid (*see:* **Psychological First Aid, Adult; Psychological First Aid, Child**). The role that American Red Cross plays in training licensed mental health professionals in Psychological First Aid and DMH is a critical one. Even for providers who do not volunteer with the American Red Cross, this training increases the number of providers in any given community who have a basic understanding of disaster response. The American Red Cross provides "just-in-time" training during large-scale events to orient new volunteers.

Supporting the DMH programs of the American Red Cross and other NGOs in the United States is the active participation of the national mental health associations, including the American Psychiatric Association, the American Psychological Association, the National Association of Social Workers, the American

Counseling Association, and the American Association of Marriage and Family Therapy. When a national disaster occurs, the American Red Cross alerts the associations to initiate a call to their membership for recruitment and deployment.

Other NGOs providing some type of psychological support to disaster or trauma-affected populations in the United States include many NVOAD, faith-based, and independent organizations: Catholic Charities United States, Church World Service, Lutheran Disaster Response, National Association of Jewish Chaplains, the National Organization for Victim Assistance (NOVA), Disaster Psychiatry Outreach, and the International Critical Incident Stress Foundation, Inc. (ICISF). Founded in 1989, ICISF membership consists of mental health professionals, emergency responders, clergy, chaplains, and peer support personnel. ICISF provides Critical Incident Stress Management teams to support emergency operations personnel following large and small traumatic events. The National Organization for Victim Assistance (NOVA) has developed and trained NOVA teams that respond to crises of all types and sizes, including disasters.

During 2005 to 2007, the American Red Cross, the Salvation Army, ICISF, and NOVA shared program and training information to develop joint guidelines for early disaster mental health interventions. Without dictating specific practices, the discussions yielded a commitment to improved collaboration and underscored the importance of ongoing dialogue between disaster mental health providers. Two other freestanding programs participating in a DMH response are the Green Cross Assistance Program, which provides trained traumatology specialists and the Association of Traumatic Stress Specialists (ATSS), a membership association for mental health professionals and paraprofessionals responding to victims and survivors of psychological trauma.

A number of U.S. NGOs also work within the international arena to provide psychosocial support and trauma counseling to survivors of disasters and of conflict. Notable for the span of their work abroad are the International Services of the American Red Cross, the United Methodist

Committee on Relief (UMCOR), Church World Services, Green Cross, Action Aid—United States, the American Refugee Committee, and Doctors Without Borders. The Center for Victims of Torture has been instrumental in setting up treatment programs for traumatized survivors and training local community organizations abroad to evaluate their treatment programs. The International Federation of Red Cross and Red Crescent Societies also plays a significant role through national Red Cross organizations serving their own and neighboring countries.

Research

Research into the effects of disaster trauma and interventions for affected persons and communities is undertaken by many different organizations, particularly universities. In 2007, the University of Michigan and Dartmouth Medical School received funding from the National Institutes of Health (NIH) to launch a National Center for Disaster Mental Health Research (NCDMHR) to study the health consequences on victims in disaster and to examine questions related to postdisaster resilience and wellness. The consortium also includes researchers from the University of South Carolina, Yale University, and the University of Oklahoma.

The International Society for Traumatic Stress Studies (ISTSS), founded in 1985, provides a forum for sharing information about the scope and consequences of severe stress and trauma, prevention and treatment. ISTSS publishes a research journal, *Journal of Traumatic Stress,* a quarterly newsletter, *Traumatic Stress Points,* and holds an annual international conference.

A 2006 analysis by Homeland Security Institute found that FBOs and NGOs had a significant beneficial impact during and after Hurricanes Katrina and Rita with mental health and spiritual support among the 10 specific areas noted. The study reported that while FBOs and NGOs faced significant limitations and challenges in providing services, they developed effective practices to deal with them. Mental health and spiritual support was found to be one of the three best-applied special practices, and preserving family unity within shelters had beneficial consequences for mental health and spiritual support.

Case Example

After the September 11, 2001, terrorist attacks in New York, Washington, and Pennsylvania, it was immediately apparent that there would be significant mental health needs. Local mental health providers working in mental health settings mobilized quickly, but needs were expected to surpass local capability. The American Red Cross dispatched DMH providers from local and adjacent communities to provide mental health support and stress reduction assistance. National volunteers recruited from across the country arrived within a few days to augment that mission. Concurrently, ICISF-trained volunteers, some of whom were already part of military mental health systems, also arrived to provide assistance. Other agencies, such as FBOs, also organized support for victims. In Washington, the military was the gatekeeper for volunteers and worked closely with the American Red Cross to coordinate mental health support. In New York, civilian authorities collaborated with the American Red Cross. As family assistance centers were set up to aid grieving families, national DMH volunteers continued providing mental health support. Because the terrorist attacks created a crime scene, access was controlled and NGOs needed official standing to provide assistance.

Incorporating lessons learned from 9/11, a similar event today would be different in several ways: all NGOs and government agencies would organize their response under the National Incident Management System (NIMS) and the NRF, thus creating a more centralized, coordinated response and reducing overlapping or competing activities on the part of NVOADs. Because of ongoing coordination and outreach efforts since 9/11, a greater array of disciplines and specific types of expertise would be available through NGOs. The benefits of these efforts were seen during the responses to Hurricanes Katrina and Rita in 2005.

Conclusion

NGOs play a significant role in responding to the needs of traumatized persons and communities in the wake of disaster. With mental health resources limited in most communities in the best of times, there are an insufficient number of providers available for any large-scale response. NGOs help fill that need by training volunteers, rostering them, and coordinating the deployment of responders who can provide basic mental health assistance during traumatic incidents.

REFERENCES

American Red Cross. (n.d.). *Disaster services*. Retrieved December 19, 2007, from www.redcross.org/services/disaster/.

Federal Emergency Management Agency. (n.d.). *National response framework*. Retrieved December 12, 2007, from www.fema.gov/pdf/emergency/nrf/about_nrf.pdf.

National Voluntary Organizations Active in Disaster. (n.d.). *About NVOAD*. Retrieved December 19, 2007, from www.nvoad.org.

SUSAN HAMILTON
Private Practice, Sterling, VA

DANIEL DODGEN
U.S. Dept of Health and Human Services

See also: Human Rights Violations; Humanitarian Intervention; International Organizations; Laws, Legislation, and Policy

NOSOLOGY

See: Diagnosis of Traumatic Stress Disorders (*DSM & ICD*); Posttraumatic Stress Disorder, Diagnosis of; Typology of Traumatic Stress Disorders

O

OCCUPATIONAL DISABILITY

Occupational disability is one type of functional impairment that can result from exposure to a potentially traumatic event and/or subsequent posttraumatic stress disorder (PTSD) or posttraumatic stress symptoms (Thorp & Stein, 2005). Occupational disability is often associated with the relative seriousness of posttraumatic stress, and was one of the criteria for seriousness of PTSD used in the U.S. National Comorbidity Study (NCS). Functional impairment such as occupational disability may have more weight than diagnosis in legal claims for monetary damages.

Individuals with PTSD appear to be more likely to report interference in recent work or productivity. Individuals who meet criteria for full PTSD report greater occupational impairment and days of work lost compared to both those with partial PTSD (most but not all diagnostic criteria met) and those who had experienced a traumatic event but had not developed full or partial PTSD. The NCS found that PTSD was linked to 3.6 days of missed work per month (Kessler, 2000). Comorbid major depressive disorder (MDD) does not appear to significantly add to impairment among those with PTSD, although survivors of the Oklahoma City bombing with PTSD plus any comorbid psychiatric disorders were more likely to report dissatisfaction with their work performance than survivors with no diagnosis (North et al., 1999).

Vietnam War veterans with PTSD, compared to those without PTSD, have generally been more likely to report work impairment and unemployment, above and beyond the effects of comorbid physical or psychiatric disorders. Assessing occupational disability and overall impairment among veterans may be complicated by the Department of Veterans Affairs (VA) compensation system. The majority of veterans who seek PTSD treatment in the VA system apply for disability related to mental health symptoms, and there is evidence that veterans who seek compensation, compared to noncompensation-seeking veterans: (a) have lower average incomes, (b) report more distress and psychiatric symptoms (despite no difference in PTSD diagnostic status between groups), and (c) are more likely to over-report or exaggerate symptoms (Frueh et al., 2003). These issues may interfere with effective assessment, treatment, and research on treatment outcome.

REFERENCES

Frueh, B. C., Elhai, J. D., Gold, P. B., Monnier, J., Magruder, K. M., Keane, T. M., et al. (2004). Disability compensation seeking among veterans evaluated for posttraumatic stress disorder. *Psychiatric Services, 54*, 84–91.

Kessler, R. C. (2000). Posttraumatic stress disorder: The burden to the individual and to society [Special issue: Focus on posttraumatic stress disorder]. *Journal of Clinical Psychiatry, 61*, 4–14.

North, C. S., Nixon, S. J., Shariat, S., Mallonee, S., McMillen, J. C., Spitznagel, E. L., et al. (1999). Psychiatric disorders among survivors of the Oklahoma City bombing. *Journal of the American Medical Association, 282*, 755–762.

Thorp, S. R., & Stein, M. B. (2005). Posttraumatic stress disorder and functioning. *PTSD Research Quarterly, 16*, 1–7.

STEVEN R. THORP
Veterans Affairs Healthcare System, San Diego

MURRAY B. STEIN
University of California, San Diego

See also: Comorbidity; Epidemiology; Malingering; Veterans Affairs, U.S. Department of

ONSET

See: Diagnosis of Traumatic Stress Disorders (*DSM & ICD*)

OPPENHEIM, HERMANN

Hermann Oppenheim (1858–1919) was one of the leading German neurologists in the late nineteenth and early twentieth century. Having attended the *Gymnasium* in his native town Warburg (Westphalia), Oppenheim studied medicine at the Universities of Goettingen and Bonn. In 1883, he started training in neurology and psychiatry at the Charité Clinic in Berlin and completed his postdoctoral thesis *Habilitation* in 1886. Although Oppenheim enjoyed the respect and support of numerous faculty members, the Prussian Ministry of Culture refused Oppenheim's academic appointment several times. Oppenheim's lasting academic rejection can be explained by the changing political and social landscape of late-nineteenth-century Germany with its growing nationalism and anti-Semitism.

Embittered by the academic establishment, he withdrew from the Charité Clinic and founded a private clinic in Berlin. From the 1890s on, Oppenheim not only became one of the most sought-after nerve specialists in Imperial Germany but continued successfully with his extensive research activities. His neurological textbook *Textbook of Nervous Diseases* became the most influential neurological textbook of his time and went through seven editions and four translations between 1894 and 1923 (Pech, 2007).

Oppenheim became known for introducing the term, *traumatic neurosis,* a much-under-debate diagnostic concept within German psychiatry between the late 1880s and the 1920s, and he made a lasting mark in the history of psychological trauma. Oppenheim had introduced the term in the course of his early research on the significance of shocks for diseases of the nervous system. In 1889, with his book entitled *Traumatic Neuroses,* he published his landmark work on the subject. Based on clinical observations at the Charité Clinic, mainly on working-class men who had been suffering as a result of terrifying accidents in factories or workshops, Oppenheim argued for a direct relationship between traumatic events and the outbreak of nervous symptoms, such as tremors, shaking, stuttering, and disturbances of sight, hearing, and movement. For Oppenheim, a single momentary shock, any burstening event, could cause material, albeit invisible, injuries in the brain or in the nervous system. Therefore, he placed major emphasis on the physical effects of traumatic events rather then the mental effects, which he also considered important (Killen, 2006).

With the traumatic neurosis concept, Oppenheim responded to the swelling controversies over the shocking effects of industrial modernity and its neurological and psychiatric consequences. His views showed some overlapping with other concepts at that time, such as traumatic hysteria advocated by the French neurologist Jean-Martin Charcot. Furthermore, Oppenheim was influenced by neurasthenia, a diagnostic term coined by the American nerve physician George M. Beard, which had astonishing impact in European medical circles. While Oppenheim acknowledged these influences, he emphasized that traumatic neurosis represented a particular pathological condition and independent diagnostic entity.

Oppenheim's contribution to the trauma theory coincided with the advent of state welfare systems and workers compensation legislation in late-nineteenth-century Germany. In 1889, the year when Oppenheim had published his monograph on traumatic neurosis, the Imperial Insurance Office granted post-traumatic neuroses the status of actionable conditions. As a result, workers could receive financial compensation from the state if an accident rendered them nervously or mentally incapable of returning to their work (Lerner, 2003). Though accident compensation based on the traumatic neurosis-diagnosis was quite rare and did not make a difference in real economic terms, Oppenheim came under constant and severe criticism. Many opponents assumed that his trauma theory gave free rein to an artificial epidemic disease of "pension neurosis," with disastrous consequences for the welfare systems of the state and the nation's strength.

The end of the highly politicized diagnosis came in World War I. Facing an ever-growing number of soldiers suffering from the "war neuroses," German war psychiatry gave preference to psychological explanations and rejected traumatic neurosis as a dangerous mistake of the medical profession. Psychoanalysts also took the opportunity to dissociate from Oppenheim's traumatic neurosis concept, but, as Freud's essay "Beyond the Pleasure Principle" (1920) shows, drew some inspiration from it.

REFERENCES

Freud, S. (1920). Beyond the pleasure principle. In J. Strachey (Ed.), *The standard edition of the complete psychological works of Sigmund Freud* (Vol. 18, pp. 1–64). London: Hogarth Press.

Killen, A. (2006). *Berlin electropolis: Shock, nerves, and German modernity.* Berkeley: University of California Press.

Lerner, P. (2003). *Hysterical men: War, psychiatry, and the politics of trauma in Germany, 1890–1930.* Ithaca, NY: Cornell University Press.

Pech, A. (2007). *Hermann Oppenheim (1858–1919): Leben und Werk eines jüdischen Arztes.* Herzogenrath, Germany: Verlag Murken/Altrogge.

HANS-GEORG HOFER
University of Bonn

See also: **History of Psychological Trauma; Traumatic Neurosis**

P

PAIN

See: Medical Illness, Adult; Medical Illness, Child; Somatic Complaints

PARENT-CHILD INTERVENTION

Parents play a crucial role in children's recovery from psychological trauma. The parent's ability to provide safety, reassurance, and guidance is one of the best predictors of a positive outcome when a child experiences psychological trauma. It is not possible for the parent of a trauma-exposed child to be emotionally unaffected. In rare instances, parents may appear to be indifferent or even angry and blaming toward their child in the aftermath of psychological trauma, and this is associated with a high risk of adverse outcomes for the child (e.g., posttraumatic stress disorder [PTSD] or other anxiety disorders, depression, pathological dissociation, externalizing behavior problems such as oppositional-defiant disorder or substance use disorders).

When a child is traumatized, even if they do not actually witness the child's traumatic experiences, the parent(s) often feel a sense of emotional shock and disbelief, fear, helplessness, or horror that may constitute a psychological trauma for them as well as for their child and that can be temporarily incapacitating for the parent(s). When psychological trauma impacts a child, it also impacts the parent-child relationship. Misperceptions and unrealistic expectations may develop on the part of either the child or parent(s). Parents may be at a loss of how they can best help their child. They may inadvertently reinforce problematic feelings (such as despair or fear), beliefs (e.g., about who is to blame and who is responsible), or behaviors (e.g., acting like they are much younger or behaving aggressively) on the part of their child(ren). Even if the child's traumatic experiences and their aftermath are not psychologically traumatic for the parent(s), these experiences are inevitably stressful and require a substantial adaptation by and deliberate efforts by the parent(s) to provide their child(ren) with the sense of security, nurturance, and healthy encouragement of growth that has been shown to be vital in helping the child(ren) to recover (E. Cohen, in press). Without parental involvement in treatment with the child, the outcomes may not be as positive. Parents rarely seek their own treatment after a trauma has touched their family. However, when parents are involved in their child's treatment, they also will learn information and skills that can aid in their own recovery and in their ability to sustain a positive parent-child relationship in the aftermath of traumatic events.

Therefore, models of psychotherapy for psychologically traumatized children typically include the parent(s) in some (although not necessarily all) sessions (*see:* **Family Therapy**). Some psychotherapy models for traumatized children specifically utilize parent-child intervention as the primary, or a central, aspect of treatment, such as child parent psychotherapy (CPP) or parent-child interaction therapy. Other psychotherapies for traumatized children such as trauma-focused cognitive behavior therapy, include parents as integral participants in treatment, with a primary emphasis on helping the child directly through individual therapy and involving parents secondarily to support the child's therapy gains. In the latter case, parents receive education to help them understand their child's posttraumatic symptoms (such as anxiety, depression, or problems with aggressive or impulsive behavior) and to enable them to adapt their parenting to support their child in recovering from the symptoms.

In the immediate aftermath of psychological trauma, children and families are likely to experience many common reactions (*see:* **Child Development; Family Systems**). The first intervention recommended is Psychological First Aid (PFA; *see:* **Crisis Intervention, Child; Early Intervention; Prevention, Child; Psychological First Aid, Child and Adolescent**). PFA is a response to help people who are feeling stress as a result of a disaster situation. Through PFA, a compassionate and caring environment can be provided allowing for an assessment of what the individual may need at the time, offering support, helping the individuals cope, and reducing adverse reactions to the traumatic event. One PFA model, *Listen, Protect, and Connect* (LPC; Schreiber & Gurwitch, 2006) has been designed specifically for parents to help their children after a disaster. As parents may not know what to expect or how to help their children, LPC provides basic information and guidance to parents. This model provides information about common reactions to disaster and traumatic events. It recommends to parents that they be willing to listen and validate what the child has experienced. LPC provides parents with suggestions to help their children including maintaining stability and predictability in their daily routines at home, in the neighborhood, and in school and other activities, with clear expectations, consistent rules, and immediate feedback as well as a return to past routines and activities as soon as the situation and the child's and family's recovery allows. The LPC model stresses the importance of relationship connections and support from adults and peers who are important to the child, especially the parents who may need to be patient and understanding after traumatic event(s), and ensuring that key people "checking in" with the child on a regular basis. LPC encourages parents to help children return to extracurricular and school activities and to recognize and praise their children when they use positive coping strategies. Finally, LPC gives parents information about when and how to seek professional services such as counseling.

Beyond the immediate aftermath of psychological trauma, parent-child interventions for traumatized children have been developed for two age groups: young children (i.e., infants, toddlers, and preschoolers), and school-age children, preadolescents, and adolescents. While there are similarities in interventions across these age cohorts, there are sufficient developmental differences to warrant describing the interventions separately for each of the three age cohorts.

Parent-Child Interventions for Traumatized Young Children

In CPP, a therapist guides the parent in playing with her or his child in ways that enable the child and parent to recognize, understand, and manage or overcome traumatic stress reactions (Van Horn & Lieberman, in press). CPP helps parents recognize developmental milestones and benchmarks (such as language, learning, and self-control skills) that are expectable at different ages for young children, and how they can help their child to overcome barriers or problems in attaining these developmental gains that have resulted from psychological trauma or posttraumatic symptoms. CPP integrates several psychotherapy approaches, including the attachment, psychoanalytic, emotion-focused, and cognitive-behavioral models. Goals of CPP include the encouragement of normal development, emotion regulation, normalizing and gradually modifying posttraumatic symptoms, placing traumatic experience(s) in perspective as harmful events that can nevertheless be recovered from, and building reciprocity in the parent-child relationship. Through spontaneous activities involving play, games, physical contact, and language, the therapist guides, models, and helps parents to understand, feel confident, and participate nurturantly and effectively while interacting with their child. Reenactments by the child of traumatic events are acknowledged and both the child and parent are helped to give voice to their feelings and thoughts about traumatic events without becoming preoccupied with a sense of helplessness, fearfulness, guilt, blame, shame, or anger.

The average length of CPP treatment is 50 sessions, typically conducted on a weekly basis. Through the therapist's guidance as the parent and child naturally interact with each other, the child and parent create (or regain) a sense of mutual trust, liking, and love. The child and parent also are helped to create a narrative—often primarily nonverbally by the child through play or creative arts such as drawing—that expresses their shared understanding of the bad (traumatic) things that have happened to the child and how they together are making life safe, fun, and rewarding again. CPP provides parents with education about child development, PTSD, and individualized parenting skills primarily through informal interactions and guidance by the therapist rather than by having therapists use a preset structured didactic skills curriculum.

Randomized clinical trial studies from two clinical research groups have demonstrated that CPP is more effective than case management or ordinary supportive services in reducing PTSD symptom severity for both parents and children, helping children to modify problematic behaviors, and in enhancing secure parent-child attachment (Lieberman, Ghosh Ippen, & Van Horn, 2006).

Parent-child interaction therapy (PCIT) is a specific form of behavioral parent training. More than 30 randomized clinical trial research studies have evaluated PCIT with a variety of populations of children and families seeking help for socioemotional and behavioral problems. PCIT has been shown to decrease children's conduct problems and oppositional behaviors, improve children's self-esteem, improve other siblings' behavior, improve parental interaction styles with their children, reduce parenting stress and maternal depression (from the clinical to the normal range), and to have positive effects observed in the child's day-care, preschool, and elementary school settings for as long as 6 years after the treatment (Hood & Eyeberg, 2003). In contrast to CPP, PCIT does not directly address psychological trauma memories or PTSD, and PCIT also has not been tested specifically with traumatized children in a randomized controlled clinical trial research study.

Unlike CPP, PCIT takes a structured didactic behavioral approach to teaching parents skills for encouraging positive behavior (such as prosocial behaviors and compliance with parental rules and requests) and reducing negative behaviors (such as defiance, aggression, or impulsivity) during parent-child play sessions and in generalization sessions in which the parent and child practice their new skills at home and in public. Unlike traditional behavioral parent training, caregivers and children meet together with the PCIT therapist in all but two sessions (in which parent[ ] receive education about parenting skills). The behavior management skills are practiced by the parent(s) in sessions with their child, with ongoing coaching by the therapist who observes from behind a one-way mirror and speaks with the parent(s) via a listening device placed in the parent's ear (the "bug-in-the-ear"). Parent-child interactions are observed and scored prior to treatment in order to assess areas most in need as well as to establish a baseline of parent-child interaction patterns. In each PCIT session, parenting skills are scored to help direct the therapist's coaching focus. Families are provided feedback after each session regarding their progress in acquiring targeted skills and homework between sessions; they move through the intervention based on skill acquisition.

In general, PCIT intervention is expected to be completed within 15 weeks. PCIT has been found to be successful with children ages 4 to 12 years old who have been exposed to maltreatment, domestic violence, and prenatal substance exposure (e.g., Chaffin et al., 2004; Timmer, Urquiza, Zebell, & McGrath, 2005), including with parents who have been abusive. An adaptation of PCIT that addresses the relational attunement between parents and their children—a central aspect of CPP—has been developed for maltreated children and is called "parent-child attunement therapy" (Dombrowski, Timmer, Blacker, & Urquiza, 2005).

A third parent-child intervention for young children, "The Incredible Years," was developed by Webster-Stratton (2005) as a combined child, parent, and teacher intervention to prevent oppositional-defiant disorder among 3- to

8-year-old children (and more recently up to age 12, see the National Registry of Evidence-Based Programs and Practices, 2008). Parents attend groups in which they learn and practice behavioral skills for expressing praise, encouragement, and positive emotions to, and serving as a role model for learning, problem solving, and assertive communication for, their child. Parents also learn strategies for working with their child's teacher to reinforce the child's use of prosocial behavior at school and to engage their child in learning activities that support success at school. Teachers and children learn complementary skills in separate groups.

The parent training component of "The Incredible Years" has shown evidence in rigorous randomized clinical trial studies of increasing parents' nurturing behavior and positive emotional communication with their children and decreasing parents' coercive, angry, critical, permissive, or inconsistent behavior with their children. Combined with the teacher component, the program resulted in enhanced parent-child emotional bonding. The children's component was found to be important in improving the child's prosocial, problem solving, and on-task school behavior and reducing aggressive, defiant, disruptive, or withdrawn behavior by the child at home and school. Eight 2-hour sessions of the parent training portion of the curriculum were conducted in a study examining the applicability of the curriculum for parents of abused children ages 3 to 8 years old. The results mirrored those of prior studies with children characterized by defiant or oppositional behavior, including improvement in parents' involvement with their child, and secondarily in parents' ability to provide emotional support and encouragement of autonomy, but no improvement in parents' ability to provide a regular routine and behavioral limits for their children nor in their children's problem behavior at home (Hughes & Gottlieb, 2004). Involving children directly in the intervention as well as parents appears necessary in order to achieve improvements in children's problem behaviors and in parents' ability to effectively and consistently provide positive rules, routines, and limits for their children.

Other parent-child interventions have been clinically developed for troubled young children that have not been specifically adapted for traumatized children and, unlike CPP and PCIT, have not yet been scientifically tested. These parent-child interventions include "Watch, Wait, and Wonder" (N. J. Cohen et al., 1999), "Circle of Security" (Cooper, Hoffman, Powell, & Marvin, 2005), "Interaction Guidance" (McDonough, 2000), "Intervention for Foster Parents" (Dozier, Higley, Albus, & Nutter, 2002), and "Healing after Trauma Skills" (Gurwitch & Messenbaugh, 2004).

Parent-Child Interventions for Traumatized School-Age Children and Adolescents

With the exception of an adaptation of PCIT and the extension of "The Incredible Years" to children as old as 12, no therapy model that primarily focuses on parent-child intervention has been reported and research tested for traumatized school-age children or adolescents (Saxe, MacDonald, & Ellis, 2007; Welch & Rothbaum, 2007). PCIT has been adapted specifically for 7 to 12 years old (middle childhood and preadolescent) children, with a focus on children who have experienced physical abuse in their homes (Timmer et al., 2005). These children and families include persons from two underserved ethnocultural groups: the Native American and Mexican American communities. In addition, a variety of parent-child interventions have been developed and scientifically validated as effective with school age children and adolescents who exhibit socioemotional or behavioral problems that may be related to or exacerbated by psychological trauma and PTSD (Ollendick, King, & Chorpita, 2006).

The "Fast Track" program for school age children with oppositional-defiant and conduct disorders includes education for parents on behavioral management skills (as well as education for teachers and skills groups for children), and has reported reductions in problematic child behavior and increases in prosocial behavior at home and in school (Conduct Problems Prevention Research Group, 2002a, 2002b).

Behavioral parent training is an intervention designed for parents with children diagnosed with oppositional-defiant or attention deficit hyperactivity disorders, teaching parents skills for managing their children's oppositional, inattentive, and hyperactive behaviors. Behavioral parent training has been found to be well accepted and potentially beneficial in terms of reducing these problem behaviors when implemented in a real-world community setting (Tynan, Schuman, & Lampert, 1999).

Multisystemic therapy (MST; Henggeler, Schoenwald, Borduin, Rowland, & Cunningham, 1998) and multidimensional family therapy (MDFT; Liddle, Rodriguez, Dakof, Kanzki, E., & Marvel, 2005) are two intensive in-home parent-child interventions that have been shown to be effective in reducing delinquent behavior and substance abuse by adolescents.

While none of these parent-child interventions, nor other similar interventions that focus on parenting skills and child self-management skills have been specifically designed or tested with parents of traumatized children, the children and adolescents with whom they have been tested and widely disseminated are likely to have experienced psychological trauma and may have behavioral and emotional problems that are due at least in part to undetected and untreated PTSD (Ford, 2002). Integration of models that have shown promise with traumatized children and adolescents with these effective parent-child interventions provides a potential direction for the development and testing of parent-child interventions for school age and adolescent children with PTSD or other posttraumatic problems (Ford & Saltzman, in press).

For traumatized school age and preadolescent children, trauma-focused cognitive behavioral therapy (TF-CBT) for abused or bereaved children (**Cognitive Behavior Therapy, Child Abuse; Cognitive Behavior Therapy, Childhood Traumatic Grief**) includes separate sessions for parents and sessions with both the child and parent(s), as well as conjoint sessions with the child and parent(s). When TF-CBT therapists meet separately with the parent(s) the goal is to teach the parent(s) about psychological trauma and its effects on children (particularly PTSD and depression), and about how the therapy can help their child to learn ways to manage troubling thoughts or memories so that he or she is less troubled by anxiety or depression. TF-CBT parent sessions also are designed to assist the parent(s) with their own stress reactions and stress-related fears or beliefs, and to prepare them for subsequent conjoint sessions in which their child will tell them about her or his traumatic past experience(s). Parents are reassured that their child will be helped to develop a description of traumatic past experiences, which the child can recall without the severe distress of PTSD or depression, and that the parent plays an important role in this process by showing the child that he or she (the parent) is proud of their child.

Although TF-CBT does not primarily focus on parent-child interaction or parenting and behavior management skills, it integrally involves the parent in all phases of treatment (although not directly in the individual therapy sessions with the child) and teaches parents about PTSD and skills they can use to manage their own emotional reactions and to help their child manage traumatic stress and related symptoms (J. A. Cohen, Mannarino, & Deblinger, 2006; *see:* **Cognitive Behavior Therapy, Child Abuse; Cognitive Behavior Therapy, Childhood Traumatic Grief**). There is preliminary research evidence that parental involvement enhances the outcome of TF-CBT, in terms of reduced levels of PTSD and depression symptoms and increased social functioning by the traumatized child (J. A. Cohen et al., 2006). In research studies, TF-CBT is conducted for approximately 12 weekly 60- to 90-minute sessions. In clinical practice, TF-CBT may require additional sessions, usually somewhere between the 15-session PCIT duration and the approximately 50-session CPP duration.

A parent-child intervention for children who are newly diagnosed with cancer and their families, and a variation of that intervention for adolescents who have recovered from cancer and their families, has shown evidence of effectiveness in assisting the parents and children in reducing PTSD symptoms (Kazak et al., 2005).

The program, "Surviving Cancer Competently Intervention Program" (SCCIP), involves a single day with four sessions (both single-family and multifamily group) for the adolescent survivors and their families, and three sessions in a single-family format for parents of newly cancer-diagnosed children. Compared to usual care, SCCIP was associated with reduced parental anxiety and traumatic stress symptoms (Kazak et al., 2005).

Conclusion

Parent-child interventions provide parents with guidance and support have experienced psychological trauma and are suffering from traumatic stress or other posttraumatic psychosocial problems. Research is needed to test and refine family therapy approaches for families with adult members who have PTSD, and to further develop the effective and promising parent training, parent-teacher-child, in-home, and systemic therapy models (Saxe, Ellis, & Kaplow, 2007) for families with child members who have experienced psychological trauma, PTSD, or life-threatening illness. Many of these children may be identified by socioemotional or behavioral problems that are not apparently due to having experienced psychological trauma or PTSD, but when psychological trauma plays a role in children's socioemotional or behavioral problems it is important to address posttraumatic stress in parent-child interventions as well as the more obvious problems. Parents (and other family members, including siblings) may benefit from parent-child interventions for PTSD, as well as the traumatized child. Clinical and research testing continues to be needed to refine the well developed parent-child intervention models for traumatized young children and to develop and evaluate parent-child intervention models for traumatized school-age children and adolescents.

REFERENCES

Chaffin, M., Silovsky, J., Funderburk, B., Valle, L., Brestan, E., Balachova, T., et al. (2004). Parent-child interaction therapy with physically abusive parents: Efficacy for reducing future abuse reports. *Journal of Consulting and Clinical Psychology, 72,* 500–510.

Cohen, E. (in press). Parenting in the throes of traumatic events. In D. Brom, R. Pat-Horenczyk, & J. D. Ford (Eds.), *Treating traumatized children: Risk, resilience, and recovery.* London: Routledge.

Cohen, J. A., Mannarino, A. P., & Deblinger, E. (2006). *Treating trauma and traumatic grief in children and adolescents.* New York: Guilford Press.

Cohen, N. J., Muir, E., Lojkasek, M., Muir, R., Parker, C. J., Barwick, M., et al. (1999). Watch, wait, and wonder: Testing the effectiveness of a new approach to mother-infant psychotherapy. *Infant Mental Health Journal, 20,* 429–451.

Conduct Problems Prevention Research Group. (2002a). Evaluation of the first three years of the Fast Track prevention trial with children at high risk for adolescent conduct problems. *Journal of Abnormal Child Psychology, 30,* 19–35.

Conduct Problems Prevention Research Group. (2002b). The implementation of the Fast Track program: An example of a large-scale prevention science efficacy trial. *Journal of Abnormal Child Psychology, 30,* 1–17.

Cooper, G., Hoffman, K., Powell, B., & Marvin, R. (2005). The circle of security intervention: Differential diagnosis and differential treatment. In L. J. Berlin, Y. Ziv, L. Amaya-Jackson, & M. T. Greenberg (Eds.), *Enhancing early attachments: Theory, research, intervention, and policy* (pp. 127–151). New York: Guilford Press.

Dombrowski, S. C., Timmer, S. G., Blacker, D. M., & Urquiza, A. J. (2005). A positive behavioral intervention for toddlers: Parent-child attunement therapy. *Child Abuse Review, 14,* 132–151.

Dozier, M., Higley, E., Albus, K., & Nutter, A. (2002). Intervening with foster infants' caregivers: Targeting three critical needs. *Infant Mental Health Journal, 23,* 541–554.

Ford, J. D. (2002). Traumatic victimization in childhood and persistent problems with oppositional-defiance. *Journal of Trauma, Maltreatment, and Aggression, 11,* 25–58.

Ford, J. D., & Saltzman, W. (in press). Family therapy approaches to complex traumatic stress disorders. In C. Courtois & J. D. Ford (Eds.), *Complex traumatic stress disorders: An evidence based clinician's guide.* New York: Guilford Press.

Gurwitch, R. H., & Messenbaugh, A. K. (2004). *Healing after trauma skills: A manual for professionals, teachers, and families working with children after trauma/disaster* (2nd ed.). Oklahoma City, OK: Children's Medical Research Foundation.

Henggeler, S. W., Schoenwald, S. K., Borduin, C. M., Rowland, M. D., & Cunningham, P. B. (1998). *Multisystemic treatment of antisocial behavior in children and adolescents.* New York: Guilford Press.

Hood, K., & Eyberg, S. (2003). Outcomes of parent-child interaction therapy: Mothers' reports of maintenance three to six years after treatment. *Journal of Clinical Child and Adolescent Psychology, 32,* 419–429.

Hughes, J., & Gottlieb, L. (2004). The effects of the Webster-Stratton parenting program on maltreating families: Fostering strengths. *Child Abuse and Neglect, 28,* 1081–1097.

Kazak, A. E., Simms, S., Alderfer, M. A., Rourke, M. T., Crump, T., McClure, K., et al. (2005). Feasibility and preliminary outcomes from a pilot study of a brief psychological intervention for families of children newly diagnosed with cancer. *Journal of Pediatric Psychology, 30,* 644–655.

Liddle, H. A., Rodriguez, R. A., Dakof, G. A., Kanzki, E., & Marvel, F. A. (2005). Multi-dimensional family therapy: Science-based treatment for adolescent drug abuse. In J. Lebow (Ed.), *Handbook of clinical family therapy* (pp. 128–163). Hoboken, NJ: Wiley. www.ready.gov/kids/_downloads/PFA_Parents.pdf.

Lieberman, A. F., Ghosh Ippen, C., & Van Horn, P. (2006). Child-parent psychotherapy: Six-month follow-up of a randomized controlled trial. *Journal of the American Academy of Child and Adolescent Psychiatry, 45,* 913–918.

McDonough, S. (2000). Interaction guidance: An approach for difficult-to-engage families. In C. H. Zeanah Jr. (Ed.), *Handbook of infant mental health* (2nd ed., pp. 485–493). New York: Guilford Press.

National Registry of Evidence-Based Programs and Practices. (2008). *The incredible years.* Retrieved February 29, 2008, from www.nrepp.samhsa.gov/programfulldetails.asp?PROGRAM_ID=131#description/.

Ollendick, T. H., King, N. J., & Chorpita, B. (2006). Empirically supported treatments for children and adolescents. In P. C. Kendall (Ed.), *Child and adolescent therapy* (3rd ed., pp. 492–520). New York: Guilford Press.

Saxe, G., Ellis, H., & Kaplow, J. (2007). *Collaborative treatment of traumatized children and teens: The trauma systems therapy approach.* New York: Guilford Press.

Saxe, G., MacDonald, H., & Ellis, H. (2007). Psychosocial approaches for children with PTSD. In M. J. Friedman, T. M. Keane, & P. Resick (Eds.), *Handbook of PTSD: Science and practice* (pp. 359–375). New York: Guilford Press.

Schreiber, M., & Gurwitch, R. (2006). *Listen, protect, and connect: Psychological first aid for children and parents.* Los Angeles: UCLA School of Public Health. Retrieved February 29 2008, from www.ready.gov/kids/_downloads/PFA_Parents.pdf.

Timmer, S. G., Urquiza, A. J., Zebell, N. M., & McGrath, J. M. (2005). Parent-child interaction therapy: Application to maltreating parent-child dyads. *Child Abuse and Neglect, 29,* 825–842.

Tynan, W., Schuman, W., & Lampert, N. (1999). Concurrent parent and child therapy groups for externalizing problems: From the laboratory to the world of managed care. *Cognitive and Behavioral Practice, 6,* 3–9.

Van Horn, P., & Lieberman, A. (in press). Using dyadic therapies to treat traumatized children. In D. Brom, R. Pat-Horenczyk, & J. D. Ford (Eds.), *Treating traumatized children: Risk, resilience, and recovery.* London: Routledge.

Webster-Stratton, C. (2005). The incredible years: A training series for the prevention and treatment of conduct problems in young children. In E. D. Hibbs & P. S. Jensen (Eds.), *Psychosocial treatment research of child and adolescent disorders* (pp. 507–555). Washington, DC: American Psychiatric Association.

Welch, S., & Rothbaum, B. O. (2007). Emerging treatments for PTSD. In M. Friedman, T. Keane, & P. Resick (Eds.), *Handbook of PTSD: Science and practice* (pp. 469–496). New York: Guilford Press.

Julian D. Ford
University of Connecticut School of Medicine

Robin H. Gurwitch
University of Oklahoma Health Sciences Center

See also: Child Development; Cognitive Behavior Therapy, Child Abuse; Cognitive Behavior Therapy, Childhood Traumatic Grief; Crisis Intervention, Child; Early Intervention; Family Systems; Family Therapy; Prevention, Child; Psychodynamic Therapy, Child

PEACEKEEPING

Peacekeeping refers to the deployment of military personnel to a place where armed conflict is occurring on a large scale or likely to occur to attempt to prevent the armed conflict from occurring or worsening. Thus, peacekeeping is an important potential means of reducing the exposure of both civilians and military combatants to psychological trauma. There are some important terms that should be defined before discussing this topic:

- **Peacekeeping:** An impartial military presence established when two parties to a conflict agree to the interposition of a third party to uphold a ceasefire or disengagement.
- **Peace enforcement:** A military presence established to maintain or secure the peace between two parties to a conflict, with or without the agreement of the conflicting parties. Peace enforcement may occur in the absence of a ceasefire agreement.
- **Rules of engagement:** The rules by which peacekeepers or combatants may use force against other parties. In the case of peacekeepers, the rules of engagement are generally limited to self-defense.

Nature of Peacekeeping Missions

The practice of international peacekeeping was formalized in 1948, when the United Nations sent multinational forces to the Middle East to monitor the ceasefire after the Arab-Israeli War. Since that time, 60 peacekeeping missions have been conducted, most of them under the auspices of the U.N. Security Council. However, other multinational organizations (NATO; the European Union) and, in some cases, single nations (the United States in 1981; India in 1987) have also conducted peacekeeping actions. Currently, 16 peacekeeping missions are actively operated by the United Nations.

The scope and duties of peacekeeping missions are varied. The modal duties of a classic peacekeeping mission may include observing withdrawal of combatants, reporting military activity to the Security Council, overseeing firm peace accords, and, by their presence, preventing the resumption of hostilities in situations where a ceasefire exists. In classic peacekeeping missions, forces are lightly armed (for self-defense) and operate under tight rules of engagement, and all parties have agreed to the peacekeeping intervention. Peacekeepers may also police and facilitate elections, oversee refugee resettlement, provide humanitarian aid, and help rebuild war-damaged infrastructure. In recent decades, peacekeeping missions have become more complex, contentious, and fluid; peacekeepers are tasked with creating or enforcing a fragile or even nonexistent peace accord, face much more danger and unpredictability in their roles, and need to be trained and prepared to conduct intense defensive operations.

After the Cold War, perhaps because of a number of successful missions, peacekeeping efforts spread to intrastate conflicts and efforts to intervene in civil wars. In some instances, neither ceasefires nor the consent of all parties involved in the conflict were present. In these instances, the duties of peacekeepers have included disarming and demobilizing combatant troops, clearing landmines, and protecting refugee groups. These missions are more aptly labeled *peace enforcement,* and are sometimes referred to as *peacemaking,* "muscular" peacekeeping, or "peace implementation." Despite the escalation in responsibilities and duties that increasingly put peacekeeping forces in harm's way, the rules of engagement for peacekeepers/peace enforcers still dictate very limited use of force. As a result, peacekeepers are uniquely vulnerable, exposed, and at risk.

Stressors Associated with Peacekeeping

Stressors associated with peacekeeping fall into three categories: noncombat stressors associated with military deployment, stressors associated with combat, and stressors unique to the peacekeeping effort.

Noncombat stressors associated with deployment are shared by all forces that see duty away from home. They include separation from loved ones, crowded living conditions, boredom, lack of privacy, working in harsh climates or harsh terrain, limited supplies or equipment, limited opportunities for recreation, and irregular working and resting hours.

Combat-related stressors may also be associated with peacekeeping, and even though peacekeeping forces are not actually engaged in combat, their duties may be potentially quite dangerous. For example, peacekeepers may be exposed to landmines, they may witness civilian or combatant deaths and atrocities, they may be charged with removing or unearthing bodies from a war zone, and they may be attacked directly. A wealth of research has shown that exposure to the aftermath of death such as grotesque and mangled bodies, especially women and children, is particularly traumatizing and is associated with considerable risk for posttraumatic stress disorder (PTSD).

Unique stressors experienced by peacekeepers may include feelings of helplessness about the inability to reduce civilian suffering or improve civilian safety, and conflict over their restrained yet exposed role as a peacekeeper versus their combat training. Peacekeepers may experience taunting and harassment by civilians or former combatants. They may also be fired upon due to misunderstanding, cross-fire between armed feuding parties, or "firing close," which is an attempt to intimidate peacekeepers into keeping away from certain areas. Peacekeepers may also experience uncertainty about the rules of engagement and the conditions under which offensive action is acceptable. Finally, unlike traditional military forces, peacekeepers are often stationed in close proximity to potentially hostile individuals in order to provide humanitarian assistance and protection. This emphasis on proximity to individuals of unknown intentions may create a constant state of vigilance, hyperarousal, and general anxiety.

Psychological Effects of Peacekeeping

Fewer studies have been conducted on the psychological impact of peacekeeping than on that of traditional warfare. To date, these studies have centered on cataloging various positive and negative experiences associated with a specific peacekeeping mission, and on examining the lasting psychological impact of these experiences.

Despite adversities, demands, stressors, and potentially traumatizing experiences associated with peacekeeping, peacekeepers, not unlike warfighters, can be fulfilled and edified by their experiences. Perceived benefits that peacekeeping personnel have identified include increases in self-confidence, improved ability to cope with stressful situations, pride in the humanitarian services provided, learning about a new culture, developing a better appreciation of their home country, increased political understanding, and enhanced professional qualifications. There is evidence that such rewards associated with peacekeeping service may buffer posttraumatic adaptation difficulties.

For a notable minority of individuals, however, stressful experiences associated with peacekeeping give rise to a number of post-traumatic difficulties. These most frequently include the development of PTSD, depression, substance abuse, and problems pertaining to anger and aggression. Most studies have reported a prevalence of PTSD in the range of 4% to 8% for peacekeepers, somewhat lower than the prevalence of PTSD in combat-exposed forces. However, rates of post-deployment disorders tend to vary depending on the nature of the peacekeeping mission, the amount of life threat typically encountered, and the volatility of the environment in which they are serving. Lower rates of PTSD have been observed among peacekeepers serving in Cambodia (3.7%) and Kosovo (4%), while Litz and colleagues (1997) found that 25% of U.S. peacekeepers deployed to Somalia reported clinically significant psychological distress, and 8% reported clinically significant PTSD. However, many studies have not controlled for pre-deployment levels of mental health or distress. Studies of peacekeepers deployed to Kosovo and Bosnia reported that pre-deployment rates of PTSD symptoms actually exceeded post-deployment rates, perhaps suggesting a negative anticipatory effect among peacekeepers while in the staging phase of their mission. Finally, most studies have been cross-sectional. When examined over time, different trajectories of adaptation emerge, with some peacekeepers experiencing acute difficulties that readily abate over time, while others have a delayed onset after a period of minimal distress.

A number of predictors of PTSD severity have been identified, namely the degree of exposure to war-zone stressors, frustration associated with peacekeeping duties (e.g., restrictive rules of engagement), problems with social adaptation after homecoming, lack of self-disclosure of deployment-related experiences, longer length of deployment and first-time deployment, pre-deployment personality characteristics, and preexisting stress symptoms.

Among those peacekeepers experiencing clinical distress, studies have revealed increased use of mental health-care resources, particularly among those with PTSD and depression. At the same time, however, a number of barriers to mental health care have been highlighted among peacekeepers, such as the personal cost of mental health care. Those most in need of services have also been shown to be those who report the most barriers to care.

Conclusion

Despite the fact that forces returning from peacekeeping deployment report positive experiences and demonstrate lower levels of PTSD than combat forces, the potential for posttraumatic symptoms is still significant. Peacekeepers may experience a wide range of stressors, including a set of potentially traumatic stressors and distinctive rules of engagement that are unique to peacekeeping. Forces engaged in peacekeeping missions, especially peace enforcement, would benefit from secondary prevention interventions to decrease stigma and reduce the risk for chronic mental health difficulties. In addition, treatment providers should be aware of, and sensitive to, the unique stressors encountered by forces assigned to supervise or enforce peace.

REFERENCE

Litz, B. T., Orsillo, S. M., Friedman, M., Ehlich, P., & Batres, A. (1997). Posttraumatic stress disorder associated with peacekeeping duty in Somalia for U.S. military personnel. *American Journal of Psychiatry, 154,* 178–184.

RECOMMENDED READINGS

Dirkzwager, A. J. E., Bramsen, I., & Van der Ploeg, H. M. (2005). Factors associated with post-traumatic stress among peacekeeping soldiers. *Anxiety, Stress, and Coping, 18,* 37–51.

Gray, M. J., Bolton, E. E., & Litz, B. T. (2004). A longitudinal analysis of PTSD symptoms course: Delayed-onset PTSD in Somalia peacekeepers. *Journal of Consulting and Clinical Psychology, 72,* 909–913.

Maguen, S., Litz, B. T., Wang, J. L., & Cook, M. (2004). The stressors and demands of peacekeeping in Kosovo: Predictors of mental health response. *Military Medicine, 169,* 198–206.

Sareen, J., Cox, B. J., Afifi, T. O., Stein, M., Belik, S., Meadows, G., et al. (2007). Combat and peacekeeping operations in relation to prevalence of mental disorders and perceived need for mental health care. *Archives of General Psychiatry, 64,* 843–852.

SHELLEY H. CARSON
Harvard University

MARIA STEENKAMP
Boston University

BRETT T. LITZ
National Center for Posttraumatic Stress Disorder

See also: International Organizations; Military Personnel; War Trauma

PERPETRATION-INDUCED TRAUMA

Perpetration of violence against others is primarily depicted as an immoral and antisocial action with potentially traumatic effects on the victims. Perpetrators are typically painted as people lacking in compassion and with an absence of conscience, from which it follows that they would be impervious to the horrifying aspects of their own behavior. There is, however, evidence indicating that some perpetrators do in fact experience traumatic consequences as a result of committing violent acts (MacNair, 2002; Solomon, Laror, & McFarlane, 1996).

Considerable individual variation exits in reactions to war violence. Grossman (1995) reviewed studies of combat behavior showing reluctance on the part of soldiers to kill despite training and the presence of a dangerous enemy. Dutton (2007) also describes extreme variation in perpetrator reactions to intense combat ranging from exultation to stress reactions. One historical example was provided by Browning's (1998) description of the reactions of "ordinary men" (the Order Police in Nazi Germany) ordered to kill. A minority refused, most experienced revulsion on first killing but subsequently adjusted.

It seems fair to conclude from historical examples that, in situations of extreme violence, the majority of soldiers can be induced to commit atrocities and that a small minority will enjoy doing so. Another small minority declines or experiences extreme psychological distress from the perpetration (see also MacNair, 2002). Of the soldiers who comply and kill, long-term stress disorders are common, typically PTSD, comprised of unwanted recollections or flashbacks, hyperarousal, nightmares, depression, or "psychic numbing"—an automatic defense that serves to blunt threat and anxiety. The latter symptom is often experienced during the killing and hence, is called *peri-traumatic*. Solomon et al. (1996) studied these combat stress reactions in Israeli soldiers, using clinical records of soldiers in the Lebanon War and finding that 48% experienced acute anxiety, 26% fear of death, 21% crying, and 18% psychic numbing. Solomon compared these reactions with other published reports of combat reactions in other soldiers in other wars and found similarity. They concluded that the reactions were universal. Fear reactions are so intense during combat that paralysis of limbs and loss of sphincter control is common. Long-term interpersonal and somatic complaints occur. Less is known about reactions to violence in civilian situations where violence is more frequently voluntary. Some perpetrators describe an initial revulsion to acts of violence (homicide, rape) that decreases with repetition (Dutton, 2007).

REFERENCES

Browning, C. R. (1998). *Ordinary men: Reserve police battalion 101 and the final solution in Poland.* New York: HarperCollins.

Dutton, D. G. (2007). *The psychology of extreme violence: Genocide and massacres.* New York: Praeger.

Grossman, D. (1995). *On killing: The psychological costs of learning to kill in war and society.* Boston: Little, Brown.

MacNair, R. M. (2002). *Perpetration-induced traumatic stress: The psychological consequences of killing.* Westport, CT: Praeger.

Solomon, Z., Laror, N., & McFarlane, A. (1996). Acute posttraumatic reactions in soldiers and civilians. In B. van der Kolk, A. McFarlane, & L. Weisaeth (Eds.), *Traumatic stress: The effects of overwhelming experience on mind, body and society* (pp. 102–116). New York: Guilford Press.

DONALD G. DUTTON
University of British Columbia

See also: Acute Stress Disorder; Aggression; Crime Victimization; Domestic Violence; Military Personnel; Rape Trauma; Traumatic Bonding; War Trauma

PERSONALITY DISORDERS

Personality implies stable and enduring patterns of thinking, feeling, and behaving across time and situation. It is generally accepted that such patterns develop during childhood and adolescence through some combination of biological temperament and learning, and then become relatively stable in adulthood. Perhaps due to some combination of biological vulnerability interacting with negative early experiences, some individuals develop maladaptive personality patterns, or personality disorders (PDs) that are inconsistent with cultural expectations and that cause personal distress or problems in work or relationship functioning. A large body of research showing positive associations between PDs and childhood trauma has led some to propose that PDs develop as a direct consequence of exposure to psychological trauma; however, the true nature of these relationships appears more complicated.

The American Psychiatric Association's (2000) *Diagnostic and Statistical Manual of Mental Disorders* (*DSM-IV-TR*) defines 10 PDs divided into three clusters based on conceptual similarities.

Cluster A PDs are "odd or eccentric" and appear to exist on a continuum with psychotic disorders such as schizophrenia. These include paranoid (unjustified suspiciousness), schizoid (social detachment and emotionally flat), and schizotypal (magical thinking, perceptual distortions, odd behavior, and unremitting social anxiety) PDs.

The "dramatic, emotional, or erratic" Cluster B PDs include antisocial (hedonistic, reckless, aggressive, and prone to violating the rights of others), borderline (emotionally vulnerable and reactive, unstable sense of self and other, and dangerous impulsive behaviors including deliberate self-injury and suicidality), histrionic (attention seeking with rapidly shifting and shallow emotional expression), and narcissistic (e.g., egocentric, exploitative, and lacking in empathy) PDs. The "anxious or fearful" Cluster C PDs include avoidant (socially inhibited due to fears of rejection and feelings of inadequacy), dependant (extreme submissiveness, clinging, and intense need to be cared for), and obsessive-compulsive (controlling and perfectionistic, and extremely preoccupied with order and productivity at the expense of efficiency) PDs. Other problematic personality patterns (e.g., self-defeating, depressive, and passive-aggressive), or personality patterns that are below threshold for the above PDs, are diagnosed as personality disorder, not otherwise specified (PDNOS).

Nearly all of the *DSM-IV-TR* PDs have been associated with childhood maltreatment such as physical, sexual, and verbal abuse, and neglect in prospective longitudinal studies (e.g., Johnson, Cohen, Brown, Mailes, & Bernstein, 1999), suggesting that childhood adversity creates a risk factor for the development of adult PDs. However, the antisocial and borderline PDs have been the most frequently studied in relation to trauma, and role of trauma in the development of borderline PD has been a significant area of controversy.

Antisocial PD and its childhood precursor, conduct disorder, are associated with childhood trauma including witnessing violence, physical abuse, and disrupted attachments. Possible psychological mechanisms explaining these associations include the reduced capacity for empathy due to the inadequate early relational experiences, and the development of externalized "acting out" coping through modeling. An alternative mechanism that could explain the association of antisocial PD and trauma involves gene-environment interactions, discussed next in relation to borderline PD.

Adult antisocial behavior has been extensively investigated in relation to combat-exposure and combat-related posttraumatic stress disorder (PTSD) due to concerns about combat soldiers' reintegration into society and incidents of veterans committing violent acts. Possible reasons for violent behavior in such individuals could include an overall desensitization to violence as well as flashback episodes in which individuals may act out violence as they relive traumatic memories. Research indicates that intense combat exposure, participation in military atrocities, nonsupportive homecoming experiences (i.e., veterans criticized for government policy, particularly distinctive of the Vietnam experience), and subsequent combat-related PTSD increase the risk for engaging in adult antisocial behavior; however, the influence of these combat-related experiences on antisocial behavior is relatively weak as compared to the risk from prewar conduct disorder (Fontana & Rosenheck, 2005).

Childhood trauma is highly prevalent in borderline PD relative to other PDs with reported rates of approximately 90% including physical and sexual abuse, neglect, and emotional withdrawal and invalidation (Zanarini et al., 1997). Retrospective accounts of patients with borderline PD typically include high rates of early, severe, and repeated sexual trauma (particularly in girls) relative to other diagnostic groups. However, there is a discrepancy of opinion on the importance of trauma in the development of borderline PD. Specifically, some describe trauma as central to its development comparable to PTSD (e.g., Herman, Perry, & van der Kolk, 1989) and at least partially supported by biological models (Figueroa & Silk, 1997). Others challenge this assertion given that not all persons with borderline PD report trauma and that the large majority of individuals who experience even severe trauma are resilient from adult psychopathology (Paris, 1997). In addition, many of the traumatic childhood experiences of individuals with borderline (as well as antisocial) PD could be understood as gene-environment interactions. For example, the problematic parenting of children who develop PDs is likely affected by shared and genetically transmitted aggressive/impulsive personality traits in the parents. Further, children who are genetically predisposed to exhibit aggressive or impulsive behaviors are likely to meet parental reactions including extreme efforts to discipline, which might lead to abuse (Paris, 1997).

Studies investigating PDs within PTSD samples have consistently found high rates of overlap of PDs with PTSD. Although the specific PDs observed among PTSD-diagnosed persons have been somewhat inconsistent, possibly varying as a result of the assessment tools used, some of the most frequently cited include avoidant, paranoid, borderline, obsessive-compulsive, and antisocial PDs. Possible explanations for the diagnostic comorbidity observed between PDs and PTSD include: (a) PDs create a vulnerability for the development of PTSD following trauma because of limited coping resources, (b) trauma exposure directly causes the personality changes (as well as the PTSD), and (c) PDs may develop in response to living with the core symptoms of PTSD rather than to exposure to psychological trauma *per se* (Axelrod, Morgan, & Southwick, 2005).

The *DSM-IV-TR* (American Psychiatric Association, 2000) does not recognize maladaptive personality changes following adulthood trauma as a PD, but does recognize such personality change (also called complex PTSD or disorders of extreme stress, NOS) as a potential associated feature of PTSD. However, enduring personality change after catastrophic experience is included as an independent diagnosis within the World Health Organization's (1992) diagnostic manual.

REFERENCES

American Psychiatric Association. (2000). *Diagnostic and statistical manual of mental disorders* (4th ed., text rev.). Washington, DC: Author.

Axelrod, S. R., Morgan, C. A., & Southwick, S. M. (2005). Symptoms of posttraumatic stress disorder and borderline personality disorder features in veterans of Operation Desert Storm. *American Journal of Psychiatry, 162,* 270–275.

Figueroa, E., & Silk, K. (1997). Biological implications of childhood sexual abuse in borderline personality disorder. *Journal of Personality Disorders, 11,* 71–92.

Fontana, A., & Rosenheck, R. (2005). The role of war-zone trauma and PTSD in the etiology of antisocial behavior. *Journal of Nervous and Mental Disease, 193,* 203–209.

Herman, J. L., Perry, J. C., & van der Kolk, B. A. (1989). Childhood trauma in borderline personality disorder. *American Journal of Psychiatry, 146,* 490–495.

Johnson, J. G., Cohen, P., Brown, J., Mailes, E. M., & Bernstein, D. P. (1999). Childhood maltreatment increases risk for personality disorders during early adulthood. *Archives of General Psychiatry, 56,* 600–606.

Paris, J. (1997). Childhood trauma as an etiological factor in the personality disorders. *Journal of Personality Disorders, 11,* 34–49.

World Health Organization. (1992). *International statistical classification of diseases* (10th ed.). Geneva, Switzerland: Author.

Zanarini, M. C., Williams, A. A., Lewis, R. E., Reich, R. B., Vera, S. C., Marino, M. F., et al. (1997). Reported pathological childhood experiences associated with the development of borderline personality disorder. *American Journal of Psychiatry, 154,* 1101–1106.

RECOMMENDED READING

Magnavita, J. J. (Ed.). (2003). *Handbook of personality disorders: Theory and practice*. Hoboken, NJ: Wiley.

SETH R. AXELROD
Yale University School of Medicine

See also: Abuse, Child Physical; Abuse, Child Sexual; Aggression; Child Maltreatment; Comorbidity; Complex Posttraumatic Stress Disorder; Diagnosis of Traumatic Stress Disorders (*DSM & ICD*); Disruptive Behavior Disorders; Emotional Abuse

PHARMACOTHERAPY, ADULT

As summarized by Nagy and Marshall (2002), the selective serotonin reuptake inhibitor (SSRI) sertraline was the first medication to receive approval by the U.S. Food and Drug Authority (FDA) for treatment of PTSD, based on two multicenter randomized controlled trials (RCTs). Subsequently, the SSRI paroxetine was also approved based primarily on a large open trial. While not FDA approved, other SSRIs have also been shown to be effective, for example, fluoxetine and fluvoxamine.

In addition to serotonin, other neurotransmitter systems have become therapeutic targets. Both serotonin and norepinephrine reuptake inhibition suppresses firing of the locus coeruleus (LC). In a multicenter RCT, the combined serotonin-norepinephrine reuptake inhibitor venlafaxine demonstrated efficacy in patients meeting *DSM-IV* criteria for PTSD (Davidson et al., 2006). The alpha-1 antagonist prazosin in placebo-controlled trials has been shown to decrease nightmares and sleep disturbance in combat veterans (Krystal & Davidson, 2007) and general distress in civilians with PTSD (Taylor et al., 2006), possibly by blocking release of the anxiogenic neuropeptide corticotropin releasing factor (CRF). CRF appears to activate two key systems involved in arousal and in the etiology of PTSD: the hypothalamic-pituitary axis (HPA) and the locus coeruleus/norepinephrine (LC/NE) systems.

Alpha-2 agonists, by stimulating presynaptic autoreceptors, suppress release of norepinephrine, and open pharmacological trials with clonidine (Kinzie & Leung, 1989) and guanfacine (Horrigan, 1996) showed benefit, but confirmation of efficacy needs to be demonstrated in RCTs.

In exploring a possible role for antiadrenergic agents in preventing the emergence of PTSD, Pitman et al. (2002) administered propranolol or placebo to accident victims within 6 hours of the acute event and continued treatment for 10 days and found that at 3 months persons who had received propranolol exhibited less psychophysiological reactivity.

For persons with complex PTSD (cPTSD), including persons with serious mental illness and comorbid cPTSD, SSRIs are at best only partially effective. Several mood stabilizers have been found to be effective in treating PTSD, including valproate, topirimate, and lamotrigine. Fesler (1991) reported that valproate was effective in treating arousal and avoidance in 10 of 16 Vietnam veterans, and RCTs have shown efficacy for both topirimate (Akuchekian & Amanat, 2004) and lamotrigine (Hertzberg et al., 1999).

The second generation antipsychotics (SGAs) risperidone, quetiapine, and olanzapine also show promise, and therefore are likely to emerge as first-line treatment for persons with schizophrenia and comorbid PTSD (Muenzenmaier et al., 2005).

Evidence suggests that, when used in combination with psychosocial interventions, pharmacotherapy has an important role in the treatment of PTSD (Foa, Davidson, & Frances, 1999; Opler, Grennan, & Opler, 2006).

REFERENCES

Akuchekian, S., & Amanat, S. (2004). The comparison of topirimate and placebo in the treatment of post-traumatic stress disorder. *Journal of Research in Medical Sciences, 5,* 42–46.

Davidson, J., Baldwin, D., Stein, D. J., Kuper, E., Bermattia, I., Ahmed, S., et al. (2006). Treatment of posttraumatic stress disorder with venlafaxine extended release: A 6-month randomized controlled trial. *Archives of General Psychiatry, 63,* 1158–1165.

Fesler, F. A. (1991). Valproate in combat-related post-traumatic stress disorder. *Journal of Clinical Psychiatry, 52,* 361–364.

Foa, E. B., Davidson, J. R. T., & Frances, A. (1999). The expert consensus guidelines series: Treatment of post-traumatic stress disorder. *Journal of Clinical Psychiatry, 60*(Suppl. 16), 1–76.

Hertzberg, M. A., Butterfield, M. I., Feldman, M. E., Beckham, J. C., Sutherland, S. M., Conner, K. M., et al. (1999). A preliminary study of lamotrigine for the treatment of posttraumatic stress disorder. *Biological Psychiatry, 45,* 1226–1229.

Horrigan, J. P. (1996). Guanfacine for PTSD nightmares. *Journal of the American Academy of Child and Adolescent Psychiatry, 35,* 975–976.

Kinzie, J. D., & Leung, P. (1989). Clonidine in Cambodian patients with posttraumatic stress disorder. *Journal of Nervous and Mental Disease, 177,* 546–550.

Krystal, A. D., & Davidson, J. R. T. (2007). The use of prazosin for the treatment of trauma, nightmares, and sleep disturbance in combat veterans with post-traumatic stress disorder. *Biological Psychiatry, 61,* 925–927.

Muenzenmaier, K. M., Castille, D. M., Shelley, A. M., Jamison, A., Battaglia, J., Opler, L. A., et al. (2005). Comorbid post-traumatic stress disorder and schizophrenia. *Psychiatric Annals, 35,* 2–7.

Nagy, L., & Marshall, R. D. (2002). PTSD psychopharmacology basics for non-physicians and beginning psychiatrists. *National Center for PTSD Clinical Quarterly, 11,* 33–39.

Opler, L. A., Grennan, M. S., & Opler, M. G. (2006). Pharmacotherapy of post-traumatic stress disorder. *Drugs of Today, 42,* 803–809.

Pitman, R. K., Sanders, K. M., Zusman, R. M., Healy, A. R., Cheema, F., Lasko, N. B., et al. (2002). Pilot study of secondary prevention of posttraumatic stress disorder with propranolol. *Biological Psychiatry, 51,* 189–192.

Taylor, F. B., Lowe, K., Thompson, C., McFall, M. M., Peskind, E. R., Canter, E. D., et al. (2006). Daytime prazosin reduces psychological distress to trauma specific cues in civilian trauma post-traumatic stress disorder. *Biological Psychiatry, 59,* 577–581.

LEWIS A. OPLER
Columbia University College of Physicians and Surgeons

MICHELLE S. GRENNAN
Long Island University

See also: **Pharmacotherapy, Child**

PHARMACOTHERAPY, CHILD

Pharmacotherapy providers treat behavioral and emotional symptom clusters associated with posttraumatic stress disorder (PTSD) rather than exposure to psychological trauma itself in children and adolescents. PTSD in children is a heterogeneous disorder with complex symptom presentations and a high prevalence of associated comorbid psychiatric diagnoses. Therefore, a wide variety of medications have been considered for children with PTSD. Currently, there are few randomized controlled trial studies of medication efficacy to guide clinical practice in child psychiatry and there are no FDA approved medications for the treatment of PTSD in children and adolescents.

In one of the few controlled trials available (Robert, Blakeney, Villarreal, Rosenberg, & Meyer, 1999), patients were randomized to either chloral hydrate or the tricyclic antidepressant medication, imipramine (1 mg/kg), for 7 days to treat symptoms of acute distress in pediatric burn victims. Patients randomized to imipramine demonstrated significant improvement in sleep-related flashbacks and insomnia. However, given the risk of heart problems associated with tricyclic agents, these medications are not recommended for use in children with PTSD. In the only other randomized controlled medication trial in pediatric PTSD, sertraline 50 mg to 200 mg/day offered no benefit compared with placebo in patients receiving cognitive behavioral therapy (CBT) for childhood PTSD symptoms. Both groups improved with CBT (Cohen, Mannarino, Perel, & Staron, 2007). All other medication studies for PTSD in children and adolescents are retrospective chart reviews, single case reports, or open case studies. Recent studies of medications in pediatric PTSD are summarized in Table 1.

A wide variety of medications including alpha and beta adrenergic agents, antipsychotics, anticonvulsants, and antidepressants are all reported to have shown some evidence of effectiveness with children with PTSD in studies without control group conditions. Given FDA approval for paroxetine and sertraline in adult PTSD, it is surprising that few SSRI

Table 1. Recent Studies of Medications in Pediatric Posttraumatic Stress Disorder

Study	Drug	Study Type	Number of Subjects	Age Range (years)	Dose (mg/day)	Duration	Outcome
Cohen et al. (2007)	CBT ± sertraline	RCT	24	10–17	50–200	12 weeks	No significant effect for sertraline addition to CBT
Domon & Anderson (2000)	Nefazodone	Open	Not reported	Adolescents	200–600	Not reported	Improvement in hyperarousal, aggression, insomnia
Famularo, Kinscherff, & Fenton (1988)	Propranolol	ABA Open	11	Avg. Age 8.5	0.8 mg/kg/dose given three times per day	4 weeks	Improved hyperarousal and aggression
Harmon & Riggs (1996)	Clonidine	Open	7	3–6	0.05–0.2	4 weeks	Improved hyperarousal and aggression
Horrigan & Barnhill (1999)	Risperidone	Open	18	Child	Average: 1.37	Variable	Improvement in PTSD symptoms in 72%
Kant, Chalansani, Chengappa, & Dieringer (2004)	Clozapine	Open	39	Adolescent	Average: 102	Variable	Effective in 79%
Loof, Grimley, Kuller, Martin, & Shonfield (1995)	Carbamazepine	Open	28	8–17	300–1200; serum levels 10–11.5	2–13 weeks	All patients improved
Perry & Pate (1994)	Clonidine	Open	17	Child	0.1–0.2	Variable	Improved anxiety, hyperarousal, impulsivity
Robert et al. (1999)	Imipramine	RCT	25	2–19	1 mg/kg at bedtime	1 week	80% with improved symptoms
Seedat, Lockhat, Kaminer, Zungu-Dirwayi, & Stein (2001)	Citalopram	Open	24	10–18	20–40	8 weeks	Suggested effectiveness
Stathis, Martin, & McKenna (2005)	Quetiapine	Open	6	Adolescent	50–200	6 weeks	Effective

Note: ABA = Design where treatment and no treatment trials follow each other to establish the effects of treatment versus control; RCT = Randomized controlled trial.

clinical trials in pediatric PTSD have been completed. Despite the lack of data, medication use in children with PTSD has become routine in clinical practice. Since child psychiatrists and pediatric clinicians cannot presently be guided by controlled empirical research, it is clinically important to tailor the decision to use medications to individual patient needs, safety, preferences, and concerns. Medication therapy is considered adjunctive to other psychosocial treatments in childhood PTSD, and has two roles to play in the treatment of pediatric PTSD. These are to: (a) Target disabling PTSD symptoms so that daily impairment is diminished and the child may pursue a healthier developmental and psychosocial trajectory; and (b) Help traumatized children tolerate emotionally painful material in order to participate in rehabilitative psychosocial therapy.

Medication interventions should be considered for pediatric PTSD with the following characteristics: (a) Severe PTSD symptoms that significantly interfere with daily functioning; (b) Moderate PTSD symptoms with a marked physiological component (autonomic nervous system hyperarousal, sleep disturbance, rage attacks, irritability); (c) Disabling PTSD symptoms that do not respond to 6 to 8 weeks of psychosocial intervention with a family component; and (d) PTSD symptoms, which are comorbid with other pharmacologically responsive psychiatric disorders such as attention deficit/hyperactivity disorder, other anxiety disorders, psychotic symptoms, and/or depression.

Ideally, medications should decrease PTSD symptoms of autonomic nervous system hyperarousal, decrease intrusive thoughts and emotions, diminish fear and anxiety, diminish impulsivity and irritability and aggression, improve concentration and sleep, help treat comorbid psychiatric disorders that are known to be medication responsive, and facilitate the child's participation in rehabilitative CBTs. These criteria can serve as a basis for making clinical determinations as to the appropriateness of a trial of psychotropic medication(s) for a child with PTSD and for monitoring the outcome of medication intervention in order to determine if there are sufficient benefits to justify continued use of the medication or to consider therapeutic adjustment of the medication based on successful symptom resolution. On the basis of this brief review, there are insufficient data to support the use of psychiatric medications *alone* for children and adolescents with PTSD. Unless further evidence suggests that certain psychotropic medications can be used alone for pediatric PTSD, medications should always be prescribed for children with PTSD in the presence of an ongoing psychosocial therapy.

REFERENCES

Cohen, J. A., Mannarino, A. P., Perel, J. M., & Staron, V. (2007). A pilot randomized controlled trial of combined trauma-focused CBT and sertraline for childhood PTSD symptoms. *Journal of the American Academy of Child and Adolescent Psychiatry, 46*, 811–819.

Domon, S. E., & Anderson, M. S. (2000). Nefazadone for PTSD. *Journal of the American Academy of Child and Adolescent Psychiatry, 39,* 942–943.

Famularo, R., Kinscherff, R., & Fenton, T. (1988). Propranolol treatment for childhood posttraumatic stress disorder, acute type. *American Journal of Diseases of Children, 142,* 1244–1247.

Harmon, R. J., & Riggs, P. D. (1996). Clonidine for posttraumatic stress disorder in preschool children. *Journal of the American Academy of Child and Adolescent Psychiatry, 35,* 1247–1249.

Horrigan, J. P., & Barnhill, L. J. (1999). Risperidone and PTSD in boys. *Journal of Neuropsychiatry and Clinical Neurosciences, 11,* 126–127.

Kant, R., Chalansani, R., Chengappa, K. N., & Dieringer, M. F. (2004). The off-label use of clozapine in adolescents with bipolar disorder, intermittent explosive disorder, or posttraumatic stress disorder. *Journal of Child and Adolescent Psychopharmacology, 14,* 57–63.

Loof, D., Grimley, P., Kuller, F., Martin, A., & Shonfield, L. (1995). Carbamazepine for PTSD. *Journal of the American Academy of Child and Adolescent Psychiatry, 34,* 703–704.

Perry, B. D., & Pate, J. E. (1994). *Neurodevelopment and the psychobiological roots of post-traumatic stress disorder.* Springfield, IL: Charles C Thomas.

Robert, R., Blakeney, P. E., Villarreal, C., Rosenberg, L., & Meyer III, W. J. (1999). Imipramine treatment in pediatric burn patients with symptoms of acute stress disorder: A pilot study. *Journal of the American Academy of Child and Adolescent Psychiatry, 38*, 873–882.

Seedat, S., Lockhat, R., Kaminer, D., Zungu-Dirwayi, N., & Stein, D. J. (2001). An open trial of citalopram in adolescents with post-traumatic stress disorder. *International Clinical Psychopharmacology, 16*, 21–25.

Stathis, S., Martin, G., & McKenna, J. G. (2005). A preliminary case series on the use of quetiapine for posttraumatic stress disorder in juveniles within a youth detention center. *Journal of Clinical Psychopharmacology, 25*, 539–544.

RECOMMENDED READING

American Academy of Child and Adolescent Psychiatry. (1998). Practice parameters for the assessment and treatment of children and adolescents with posttraumatic stress disorder. *Journal of the American Academy of Child and Adolescent Psychiatry, 37*(Suppl. 10), 4S–26S.

DANIEL F. CONNOR
University of Connecticut School of Medicine

LISA A. FRALEIGH
University of Connecticut School of Medicine

See also: **Adolescence; Child Development; Cognitive Behavior Therapy, Child Abuse; Comorbidity; Disruptive Behavior Disorders; Infancy and Early Childhood; Pharmacotherapy, Adult**

POLITICAL PRISONERS

A political prisoner is a person who has been detained (e.g., under house arrest) or held in prison because a government considers their ideas or image to present a challenge or threat to the authority of the state. The actual reason for the person's imprisonment is often controversial, and the reasons given for the imprisonment may sound plausible to some observers. For instance, the person might be charged with a vaguely defined offense (e.g., sedition, terrorism, conspiracy) that allows for tremendous latitude of interpretation, or the evidence used to implicate the person may not be legitimate. In some instances, the authorities might argue that the person being detained is in protective custody, implying that they are being protected from their real enemies at the benevolence of the state. Thus, it is predictable that nations will argue for the legitimacy of their actions in the face of any accusation of having imprisoned someone for political purposes and resolving such arguments can prove to be a fairly futile exercise.

The definition of political prisoners centers on the person's persecution due to his or her questioning the authority of the state. A first main group of political prisoners are arrested because of their actions or plans to change the political status quo of his or her country (which may include their advocacy of violence). A second main group of political prisoners are arrested because of their belonging to a particular race, religion, color, language, or sexual orientation and is not related to advocacy of violence (e.g., fascist or Nazi regimes like Third Reich Germany). Members of a third main group are in prison without any individual reason due to arbitrary despotism (in regimes based on the principle of terror at random, e.g., Soviet Union under Stalin). The perception of an individual as a political prisoner may depend on subjective political perspective or interpretation of the evidence, and thus there is seldom a broad consensus on who fits this description.

Historically, concentration camp prisoners in Nazi Germany provided a powerful example of how a large group of people may be held as political prisoners and may suffer extreme consequences. The most apparent of these consequences were the massive numbers of people murdered and the physical deprivations and tortures that were perpetrated by their captors. Less obvious, yet profoundly significant, were the social, psychological, political, and spiritual effects on the survivors, their families, and their communities (Schwartz, Dohrenwend, & Levav, 1994). Various scholars, many of whom were themselves holocaust survivors, conducted research or wrote from personal experience regarding the psychological or psychiatric aftermath of political imprisonment (e.g., Niederland, 1968). Commonly observed symptoms associated with political imprisonment include anxiety, depressive symptoms, self-isolation, alienation and other alterations of personality, disturbances of cognition and memory, and somatic conditions.

A systematic study was conducted examining the long-term effects of political imprisonment among former political prisoners from the former communist East German Republic approximately 20 years after their release from prison (Maercker & Schützwohl, 1997). That study revealed PTSD as the most common psychiatric malady with a lifetime prevalence of PTSD of 60%, followed by specific phobia (claustrophobic type; 22%), substance abuse (14%), and social phobia (13%). An importantly related area of research concerns the mental health consequences of *torture* (*see:* **Torture**) because political prisoners are in the majority of cases subject to torture by prison or interrogation personnel (see Basoglu, 1992). It is recommended that psychiatric or psychotherapeutic treatment of prison-related long-term mental health problems be particularly sensitive to cultural and contextual factors.

REFERENCES

Basoglu, M. (Ed.). (1992). *Torture and its consequences: Current treatment approaches.* Cambridge: Cambridge University Press.

Maercker, A., & Schützwohl, M. (1997). Long-term effects of political imprisonment: A group comparison study. *Social Psychiatry and Psychiatric Epidemiology, 32,* 434–442.

Niederland, W. G. (1968). Clinical observations on the survivor syndrome. *International Journal of Psychoanalysis, 49,* 313–315.

Schwartz, S., Dohrenwend, B. P., & Levav, I. (1994). Nongenetic familial transmission of psychiatric disorders? Evidence from children of holocaust survivors. *Journal of Health and Social Behavior, 35,* 385–402.

ANDREAS MAERCKER
University of Zurich

See also: Genocide; Human Rights Violations; Intergenerational Effects; Torture; War Trauma

POSTTRAUMATIC ADAPTATION

The concept of posttraumatic adaptation potentially represents a shift in the paradigm of the traumatic stress field from pathology and distress to resilience, recovery, and even growth (*see:* **Posttraumatic Growth**). Evidence of positive adaptations in the wake of psychological trauma was found initially in reports of some survivors of severe military violence, genocide, family violence, child abuse, and life-threatening accidents, disasters, or illnesses who described having experienced a sense of psychological, emotional, or spiritual growth in themselves or in their relationships as a result of enduring and overcoming these adversities. A classic example is Dr. Viktor Frankl's (1959) observations of his own spiritual and existential rapprochement, and that of other survivors of the Nazi concentration camps in the Holocaust. Clinicians working with survivors of psychological trauma were inspired by similar anecdotal and personal reports of clients who felt they had not just survived but experienced personal growth in the face of psychological trauma, and developed the concept of posttraumatic growth as a way of describing the potential for positive adaptations following exposure to traumatic stressors, and as an alternative to the dominant pathologizing view by the scientific, clinical, and popular communities of psychological trauma as primarily causing damage to the body, mind, and relationships (Joseph & Linley, 2008a; Tedeschi & Calhoun, 2004).

That traumatic stress is a process of adaptation is highlighted by the fact that most people who experience psychological trauma do not develop persistent clinically significant impairment (Charney, 2004), and those who do often report periods of relatively quiescent symptoms on any given day (Frueh, Elhai, & Kaloupek, 2004) and in some cases for periods of weeks, months, or years of remission (Schnurr, Lunney, & Sengupta, 2004). Some trauma survivors describe feeling as if they have been given a second chance and as a result have a keener appreciation of the opportunities that they have in their lives and relationships. Experiences that previously seemed mundane or went unnoticed in the rush to meet deadlines and follow habitual routines might seem to have a new significance. The survivor might feel able, or even inwardly compelled, to "stop and smell the roses"—that is, to mindfully pay attention to and find value in every experience. Some say that they feel a sense of clarity of vision and purpose, or a revised set of priorities, where they had been stagnating or living reflexively before (Salter & Stallard, 2004). From the perspective of "positive psychology," which focuses on the positive attributes and outcomes that characterize psychological development, functioning, and recovery from illness, posttraumatic growth represents an essential counterpoint to the dominant view that psychological trauma must be understood mainly as a damaging experience and that PTSD is the principal outcome (Joseph & Linley, 2008a).

Factor analyses of the data from a number of self-report questionnaires that have been developed to assess the forms of adaptation that has been described as posttraumatic growth (see Joseph & Linley, 2008b for a description of these measures). These studies have yielded a primary ("higher order") factor reflecting a wide range of positive changes following exposure to stressors or psychological trauma, and three secondary ("lower order") factors that represent the positive components of posttraumatic adaptation: (1) enhanced relationships, (2) new beliefs and understanding about oneself, and (3) change in life philosophy (Joseph & Linley, 2008b). Additional analyses of scores from posttraumatic growth self-report measures suggest that the positive adaptations in the wake of psychological trauma may represent a unique dimension of posttraumatic adjustment that is distinct from negative changes such as PTSD symptoms rather than merely the opposite end of a single positive-negative continuum of posttraumatic adaptation (Joseph & Linley, 2008b).

Numerous studies have attempted to measure positive posttraumatic adaptations using posttraumatic growth questionnaires (e.g., 39 studies reviewed by Linley & Joseph, 2004). However, some important limitations in the methodologies of these studies limits the conclusions that can be drawn about using posttraumatic growth as the organizing construct for positive posttraumatic adaptation. Three methodological issues are of particular concern (Ford, Tennen, & Albert, 2008). First, each measure of posttraumatic growth has different questions and response formats and requirements, so it is difficult to compare results across studies. Second, posttraumatic growth almost always is assessed by self-report, which means that what is being studied is the survivor's subjective view rather than more objective evidence of actual personal growth. Third, there are few studies that measure posttraumatic growth at several periods over time ("longitudinal" studies; *see:* **Research Methodology**) and that include measures of the individual's pretraumatic event status in the areas of purported "growth."

Concerning the measurement of posttraumatic growth, most (27/39) of the studies reviewed by Linley and Joseph (2004) did not use well-validated measures of posttraumatic growth. In addition, of the seven published instruments that were used to measure posttraumatic growth in those studies, only two—the Changes in Outlook Questionnaire and the Revised Stress-Related Growth Scale—inquire about negative as well as positive change (Joseph & Linley, 2008b). Thus, respondents may overreport positive changes simply because they are only asked about positive change. On the encouraging side, broadening the field of measurement to include positive as well as the more often assessed negative sequelae of traumatic experiences is an important advance in the traumatic stress field. However, assessment tools for posttraumatic growth should be designed either to include or to be copresented with other measures of negative changes, and to assess threats to validity such as is done with the "validity scales" that are used in many psychological questionnaires (Ford et al., 2008) (*see:* **Assessment, Psychometric, Adult**).

Posttraumatic growth questionnaires also do not differentiate between positive states or outcomes that are an extension or continuation of prior psychological growth or development, versus changes that represent the qualitatively distinct discontinuities in the person's development that are necessary in order to demonstrate that the posttraumatic growth is actually related to experiencing trauma (Ford et al., 2008). Frazier and Kaler (2006) note that retrospective self-report measures of posttraumatic growth are vulnerable to error because of the well-documented difficulty that people have in accurately recalling past states or attributes, making it unlikely that they can accurately compare current states or attributes to past ones when estimating the nature or extent of "growth." Posttraumatic growth measures also do not rule out alternative explanations for outcomes that are putatively the product of exposure to psychological trauma: for example, growth following psychological trauma may be due to survivors receiving unusual amounts of social support from family, friends, community, or professional helpers, or to the opportunity (borne of necessity) to temporarily suspend their usual life routines and responsibilities in the aftermath of psychological trauma (Ford et al., 2008). Thus, growth that seems to be a response to psychological trauma actually may be due to other associated changes that may be at most indirectly related to experiencing trauma per se.

These threats to the psychometric internal and external validity of the construct and the measures of posttraumatic growth are compounded by wishful thinking and denial, particularly in the wake of stressful events (Frazier & Kaler, 2006). McFarland and Alvaro (2000), for instance, found that trauma survivors' reports of positive changes in personal attributes exceeded those of third party observers. Specifically, survivors tended to rate their pre-event functioning less favorably than did other observers, and therefore rated their post-event functioning as more positively changed simply because they viewed themselves in a less favorable light when attempting to recall how they were functioning before a traumatic event. Smith and Cook (2004) suggest that this downplaying of strengths prior to psychological trauma and corresponding increase in estimates of the positive change experienced in the wake of traumatic events, may be an example of the concept of a "positive illusion." Such an illusion—the belief that posttraumatic growth has occurred when

there may be very little actual change—could help survivors cope with the negative impact of psychological trauma. Specifically, altering one's self-perceptions might increase a sense of control following a traumatic event. This could be a positive posttraumatic adaptation, but it might not reflect "growth" and might provide an increase in self-efficacy that could be transient and vulnerable to breaking down if negative posttraumatic changes become pronounced or if further stressors are encountered in the recovery period (Ford et al., 2008).

Frazier and Kaler (2006) cast further doubt on the validity of self-reported posttraumatic growth as a basis for conceptualizing and measuring posttraumatic adaptation, based on the results of three studies. One study found that cancer survivors did not differ from matched controls in well-being. In a second study, college students who reported benefiting from their worst life experience did not actually differ on measures of well-being compared to those who did not report benefiting. They found that a widely used self-report measure of posttraumatic growth (the Perceived Benefit Scales) did not show the hypothesized correlations with measures of other aspects of well-being such as family closeness, spirituality, self-efficacy, and compassion.

Some descriptions of positive outcomes following exposure to psychological trauma may reflect relief at having survived more than actual growth. For instance, Salter and Stallard (2004) interpreted statements by children who had experienced a traumatic accident such that they felt "lucky" to be alive or that, "Anything you want, go for it quicker as you never realize when you are going to go." These statements may reflect an attempt to cope with the heightened realization of mortality that is a hallmark symptom of PTSD (i.e., sense of foreshortened future; Ford et al., 2008). This attitude also may reflect a personality trait that Rabe, Zöllner, Maercker, and Karl (2006) describe as "goal-related approach tendencies" (p. 883). In a study with survivors of life-threatening motor vehicle accidents on average 5 years later, Rabe and colleagues (2006) found that scores on the Posttraumatic Growth

Inventory (PTGI) subscales that represented a tendency to seek control and find meaning were associated with greater degrees of frontal cortical activation in the left (as oppose to the right) hemisphere of the brain. They note that this brain activation pattern is related to enduring tendencies to be goal directed and to cope with adversity by setting goals and seeking personal control and meaning. Thus, Rabe and colleagues' (2006) findings suggest that "growth" may be a preexisting trait and not a situational change—a form of adaptation based primarily on preexisting capacities rather than a response to the experience of psychological trauma per se.

The ultimate evidence of growth following exposure to psychological trauma would come from studies in which people who experience psychological trauma had already been assessed prior to experiencing traumatic events. The optimal scenario would include a series of assessments over a period of months or years prior to trauma exposure, rather than no pre-trauma baseline or only a single static measure of their pre-trauma status. This is an ambitious approach that has not yet been reported in the published research on psychological trauma. It would provide evidence of not only their pre-trauma status at one time-point but whether there already was evidence of "growth" (or stability, or a decline) along potential pathways or trajectories of posttraumatic adaptation that include the many areas of psychological functioning that are assessed following the traumatic event(s). Then it would be possible to test them again using the same or similar measures over a period of time following the traumatic event(s) in order to determine if there is evidence of change (comparing before and after trauma measurements) and if there is an increase in the rate of positive change following the traumatic events compared to their rate of change prior to trauma exposure. No such studies have as yet been reported.

Linley and Joseph (2004) identified three longitudinal studies of posttraumatic growth, but none of them measured pre-event functioning. Two other longitudinal studies have included pre-trauma baseline measures, however. Davis,

Nolen-Hoeksema and Larson (1998) assessed bereaved adults during a hospice program on average 3 months prior to a loved one's death, and then for the next 18 months. Controlling for pre-loss distress levels, they found that making sense of the loss was associated with less distress in the first year post-loss, and reporting benefiting from the experience was associated with less distress more than a year after the loss. However, it is not clear that the pre-loss distress levels were a true baseline because the loss was imminent and the stress of caregiving often already was protracted at the time of the baseline assessment (Ford et al., 2008). It also is not clear that the "benefit" was associated with the loss per se, as opposed to other factors such as social support or their preexisting levels of resilience (Ford et al., 2008).

In the second longitudinal study with a pre-trauma baseline, Ickovics and colleagues (Ickovics et al., 2006) obtained an assessment of psychological distress from inner city adolescent girls who were sexually active (half of whom were pregnant), and re-interviewed them every 6 months for a total of 18 months. Trauma history and posttraumatic growth were assessed at the 12-month assessment, the former by open-ended responses to a question asking about the "hardest thing [they] ever had to deal with" and the latter by the PTGI subscales reflecting a tendency to seek positive experiences in life. Controlling for baseline distress levels, PTGI at 12 months predicted reduced emotional distress 6 months later. However, the traumatic events may have occurred at any point in the girls' lives, so there actually was no pre-trauma baseline. Stability or change in PTGI was not assessed, nor were other factors such as stable personality traits and social support. Thus, the correlation between posttraumatic growth at the 12-month assessment and emotional distress 6 months later may reflect many factors other than posttraumatic growth, and whether the PTGI scores actually reflected growth due to traumatic adversity is unknown.

In addition, much of the research on adaptation following exposure to psychological trauma involved people facing serious illness and other events (Mancini & Bonnano, 2006) that may not actually constitute psychological trauma (i.e., life threatening or a violation of bodily integrity, and eliciting reactions of extreme fear, helplessness or horror; *see:* **Trauma, Definition**). Thus, the specificity of growth or any other form of adaptive change to the occurrence of psychological trauma per se, has not been demonstrated (Ford et al., 2008).

Overall, methodological weaknesses in these studies makes any conclusions premature with regard to whether posttraumatic growth actually occurs, what factors increase or decrease the likelihood of posttraumatic growth, how posttraumatic growth occurs psychologically and neurobiologically, and what temporary or lasting benefits are associated with posttraumatic growth. Nevertheless, posttraumatic growth remains a plausible form of posttraumatic adaptation, given the abundance of testimonials of posttraumatic growth in popular culture and by clinicians who work with psychological trauma survivors, and the many studies attempting to measure posttraumatic growth. As Ford and colleagues (2008) summarize, growth may occur as a result of overcoming adversity, but the evidence is not conclusive as to whether what has been designated as posttraumatic growth in studies of people facing adversity constitutes (a) actual sustained growth; (b) transient changes in mood, expectancies, and lifestyle; (c) adaptive (defensive) re-appraisals to compensate for distress (e.g., positive illusions); (d) the restoration of prior capacities following an adaptive shift from ordinary to survival-based self-regulation (i.e., resilience); or (e) measurement artifact. Options (a) through (e) reflect trajectories of adaptation that extend well beyond either simple pathology or growth (Layne et al., in press). This uncertainty is evident in the relatively guarded conclusion of Linley and Joseph (2004) at the end of their comprehensive view of the literature: "we conclude that greater traumatic experience, dealt with by means of positive reinterpretation and acceptance coping, in people who are optimistic, intrinsically religious, and experience more positive affect, is likely to lead to reports of greater adversarial growth" (p. 17).

Whether positive reinterpretation and acceptance coping are manifestations of actual adaptation, including growth, and not enduring personality traits, and change that has been catalyzed by experiencing traumatic stressors (as opposed to transient attempts to maintain emotional balance and hope in the wake of psychological trauma), remains unknown. The fact that some psychological trauma survivors feel that they have been given a second chance or a new lease on life, and in some cases are able to parlay this sense of relief and renewal into positive adaptations in their lives and relationships, is undeniable and serves as an inspiring reminder of the remarkable resilience that has made possible some of humanity's greatest accomplishments despite—and perhaps in part due to—the adversities of psychological trauma.

REFERENCES

Charney, D. S. (2004). Psychobiological mechanisms of resilience and vulnerability. *American Journal of Psychiatry, 161,* 195–216.

Davis, C., Nolen-Hoeksema, S., & Larson, J. (1998). Making sense of loss and benefiting from the experience. *Journal of Personality and Social Psychology, 75,* 561–574.

Ford, J. D., Tennen, H., & Albert, D. (2008). Posttraumatic growth: A contrarian view. In P. A. Linley & S. Joseph (Eds.), *Trauma, recovery, and growth* (pp. 297–324). Hoboken, NJ: Wiley.

Frankl, V. (1959). *Man's search for meaning.* Boston: Beacon Press.

Frazier, P., & Kaler, M. (2006). Assessing the validity of self-reported stress-related growth. *Journal of Consulting and Clinical Psychology, 74,* 859–869.

Frueh, B. C., Elhai, J., & Kaloupek, D. (2004). Unresolved issues in the assessment of trauma exposure and posttraumatic reactions. In G. Rosen (Ed.), *Posttraumatic stress disorder: Issues and controversies* (pp. 63–84). Hoboken, NJ: Wiley.

Ickovics, J., Meade, C., Kershaw, T., Milan, S., Lewis, J., & Ethier, K. (2006). Urban teens: Trauma, posttraumatic growth, and emotional distress among female adolescents. *Journal of Consulting and Clinical Psychology, 74,* 541–550.

Joseph, S., & Linley, P. A. (2008a). Positive psychological perspectives on posttraumatic stress. In P. A. Linley & S. Joseph (Eds.), *Trauma, recovery, and growth* (pp. 3–20). Hoboken, NJ: Wiley.

Joseph, S., & Linley, P. A. (2008b). Psychological assessment of growth following adversity. In P. A. Linley & S. Joseph (Eds.), *Trauma, recovery, and growth* (pp. 21–36). Hoboken, NJ: Wiley.

Layne, C., Beck, C., Rimmasch, H., Southwick, J., Moreno, M., & Hobfoll, S. (in press). Promoting "resilient" posttraumatic adjustment in childhood and beyond: "Unpacking" life events, adjustment trajectories, resources, and interventions. In D. Brom, R. Pat-Horenczyk, & J. D. Ford (Eds.), *Treating traumatized children: Risk, resilience, and recovery.* London: Routledge.

Linley, P. A., & Joseph, S. (2004). Positive change following trauma and adversity: A review. *Journal of Traumatic Stress, 17,* 11–21.

Mancini, A., & Bonnano, G. (2006). Resilience in the face of potential trauma. *Journal of Clinical Psychology in Session, 62,* 971–985.

McFarland, C., & Alvaro, C. (2000). The impact of motivation on temporal comparisons: Coping with traumatic events by perceiving personal growth. *Journal of Personality and Social Psychology, 79,* 327–343.

Rabe, S., Zöllner, T., Maercker, A., & Karl, A. (2006). Neural correlates of posttraumatic growth after severe motor vehicle accidents. *Journal of Consulting and Clinical Psychology, 74,* 880–886.

Salter, E., & Stallard, P. (2004). Posttraumatic growth in child survivors of a road traffic accident. *Journal of Traumatic Stress, 17,* 335–340.

Schnurr, P. P., Lunney, C., & Sengupta, A. (2004). Risk factors for the development versus maintenance of posttraumatic stress disorder. *Journal of Traumatic Stress, 17,* 85–95.

Smith, S. G., & Cook, S. L. (2004). Are reports of posttraumatic growth positively biased? *Journal of Traumatic Stress, 17,* 353–358.

Tedeschi, R., & Calhoun, L. G. (2004). Posttraumatic growth: Conceptual foundations and empirical evidence. *Psychological Inquiry, 15,* 1–18.

JULIAN D. FORD
University of Connecticut School of Medicine

See also: Attributions; Child Development; Cognitive Integration, Biopsychosocial; Conservation of Resources Theory; Coping; Etiology; Posttraumatic Growth; Social Support; Spirituality; Trauma, Definition

POSTTRAUMATIC COGNITIONS INVENTORY

The Posttraumatic Cognitions Inventory (PTCI) is a 36-item self-report measure designed to assess maladaptive beliefs associated with posttraumatic stress disorder (PTSD). The measure contains three subscales: (1) Negative Cognitions about Self, (2) Negative Cognitions about the World, and (3) Self-Blame. The PTCI's total score and each of its three subscales show adequate inter-rater reliability and acceptable test-retest reliability. The PTCI total score and three subscales correlate strongly with severity of PTSD symptoms (Foa, Ehlers, Clark, Tolin, & Orsillo, 1999).

The three-factor structure of the PTCI was confirmed in a sample of motor vehicle accident survivors (Beck et al., 2004). Unlike the original study, however, the Self-Blame subscale did not correlate strongly with other PTSD measures. One possible explanation for this discrepancy is that self-blame for traumatic events is a more salient feature of PTSD from interpersonal traumas (the Foa et al. study contained a large number of sexual assault survivors) than it is for PTSD from events such as motor vehicle accidents. The Negative Cognitions about the World subscale no longer correlated with PTSD severity when controlling for depression, suggesting that this scale might be sensitive to other forms of negative affect.

The clinical utility of the PTCI was demonstrated in a study of female assault survivors who received cognitive-behavioral therapy for PTSD (Foa & Rauch, 2004). Scores on all three PTCI subscales significantly decreased over the course of treatment, and PTCI score reduction was significantly associated with decreases in PTSD severity (Foa & Rauch, 2004). Thus, the PTCI appears sensitive to treatment effects and is a promising measure of purported cognitive mechanisms of treatment.

Clinically, the PTCI is useful for assessing maladaptive cognitions associated with trauma and PTSD. Cognitive-behavioral therapy in particular aims to modify maladaptive thoughts; identifying such thoughts at baseline may therefore facilitate cognitive restructuring during treatment. In addition, as Foa and Rauch (2004) demonstrated, the PTCI can be used to track patterns of maladaptive beliefs over the course of treatment as a means of examining efficacy. For research purposes, the PTCI may be useful in testing baseline predictors of treatment response, as well as testing hypotheses about whether changes in maladaptive cognitions are necessary for recovery from PTSD.

REFERENCES

Beck, G. J., Coffey, S. F., Palyo, S. A., Gudmundsdottir, B., Miller, L. M., & Colder, C. R. (2004). Psychometric properties of the Posttraumatic Cognitions Inventory (PTCI): A replication with motor vehicle accident survivors. *Psychological Assessment, 16,* 289–298.

Foa, E. B., Ehlers, A., Clark, D. M., Tolin, D. F., & Orsillo, S. M. (1999). The Posttraumatic Cognitions Inventory (PTCI): Development and validation. *Psychological Assessment, 11,* 303–314.

Foa, E. B., & Rauch, S. A. M. (2004). Cognitive changes during prolonged exposure versus prolonged exposure plus cognitive restructuring in female assault survivors with posttraumatic stress disorder. *Journal of Consulting and Clinical Psychology, 72,* 879–884.

MARISA EDELBERG
Institute of Living

DAVID F. TOLIN
Institute of Living

See also: Assessment, Psychometric, Adult; Cognitive Behavior Therapy, Adult; Information Processing

POSTTRAUMATIC GROWTH

Posttraumatic growth refers to the constellation of positive changes that people may experience following exposure to psychological trauma, and has been described as consisting of three broad dimensions. First, people may report that their relationships are enhanced in some way, for example that they now value their friends and family more, and feel an increased compassion and altruism toward others. Second, survivors may develop improved views of themselves in some way. For example, they may report having a greater sense of personal resiliency and strength, which may be coupled with a greater acceptance of their vulnerabilities and limitations. Third, survivors may report positive changes in life philosophy, such as finding a fresh appreciation for each new day, or renegotiating what really matters to them in the full realization that their life is finite.

Posttraumatic growth is the most widely used label for describing such adaptations to traumatic stressors, but other terms are also used including stress-related growth, adversarial growth, positive adaptation, positive changes, positive by-products, benefit finding, perceived benefits, thriving, flourishing, and growth following adversity. Importantly, posttraumatic growth does not require the presence of what is classified in the American Psychiatric Association's *Diagnostic and Statistical Manual of Mental Disorders (DSM-IV-TR;* 2000) as a Criterion A traumatic stressor for the use of the term to be considered appropriate. Psychological growth in response to life events is considered a more normative and dimensional phenomenon than posttraumatic stress disorder, and as such involves types of personal growth that may occur in response to apparently more minor difficulties and stresses and not just major traumatic events.

Theoretical models of posttraumatic growth include the functional-descriptive model (Tedeschi & Calhoun, 2004), the organismic valuing theory (Joseph & Linley, 2005), and the Janus-face two-component model (Zoellner & Maercker, 2006).

Precipitating Events

The events for which posttraumatic growth outcomes have been reported include transportation accidents (shipping disasters, plane crashes, car accidents), natural disasters (hurricanes, earthquakes), interpersonal experiences (combat, rape, sexual assault, child abuse), medical problems occurring to oneself or significant others (cancer, heart attack, brain injury, spinal cord injury, HIV/AIDS, leukemia, rheumatoid arthritis, multiple sclerosis, illness) and more normative life experiences (relationship breakdown, parental divorce, bereavement, immigration). Further, vicarious experiences of posttraumatic growth have been shown in a variety of populations not directly suffering themselves, but exposed to the suffering of others, including counselors, therapists, clinical psychologists, funeral directors, disaster workers, spouses and parents of people with cancer, and even British people who saw the September 11, 2001, terrorist attacks on television.

Correlates of Posttraumatic Growth

Several variables have been found to consistently co-occur with posttraumatic growth (Linley & Joseph, 2004). Posttraumatic growth is more likely to occur to the extent that the person believes that there was a high degree of threat and harm involved in the traumatic event(s), and also at the same time that he or she was able to exert some influence over the events or their outcomes (i.e., controllability). There may, however be a curvilinear relationship between posttraumatic growth and perceptions of threat and harm, such that growth is less likely to occur if the events are perceived as either very low or high in their degree of threat or harm, and most likely to occur if the person views threat or harm as somewhat likely.

The affected person's reported approach to coping also has been found to be correlated with posttraumatic growth, problem-focused, acceptance, and positive reinterpretation coping; optimism; religion; cognitive processing; and positive affect. Studies have shown inconsistent associations between a number of sociodemographic variables (gender, age, education, and income) and psychological distress variables (depression, anxiety, posttraumatic stress disorder), although the evidence suggests that people who report posttraumatic growth and maintain that growth over time are likely to report less subsequent psychological distress.

Assessment of Posttraumatic Growth

The assessment of posttraumatic growth has typically depended on retrospective self-report measures, the most widely used of which are the Posttraumatic Growth Inventory and the Changes in Outlook Questionnaire. The Posttraumatic Growth Inventory measures five dimensions of posttraumatic growth, namely relating to others, personal strength, new possibilities, appreciation of life, and spiritual change. The Changes in Outlook Questionnaire measures both positive changes and negative changes. Other generic self-report measures of positive changes following trauma and adversity include the Stress-Related Growth Scale, the Perceived Benefits Scales, and the Thriving Scale, as well as a number of other measures developed for use with specific trauma populations (e.g., cancer, multiple sclerosis). A number of methodological issues have been raised for research into and assessment of posttraumatic growth.

Clinical Implications

Research into the clinical facilitation of posttraumatic growth among survivors of a variety of events is beginning to flourish, with reports of interventions with war veterans, cancer patients, survivors of sexual abuse, and terrorism, for example, reporting evidence of what could be posttraumatic growth in forms such as increased optimism and sense of closure about past traumatic experiences (see Joseph & Linley, 2007). Among the biggest remaining challenges in studying posttraumatic growth is the need to establish empirical findings on a more rigorous methodological and statistical footing, and to establish therapeutic methods that are supported by empirical evidence.

REFERENCES

American Psychiatric Association. (2000). *Diagnostic and statistical manual of mental disorders* (4th ed., text rev.). Washington, DC: Author.

Calhoun, L. G., & Tedeschi, R. G. (Eds.). (2006). *Handbook of posttraumatic growth: Research and practice.* Mahwah, NJ: Erlbaum.

Joseph, S., & Linley, P. A. (2005). Positive adjustment to threatening events: An organismic valuing theory of growth through adversity. *Review of General Psychology, 9,* 262–280.

Joseph, S., & Linley, P. A. (Eds.). (2007). *Trauma, recovery, and growth: Positive psychological perspectives on posttraumatic stress.* Hoboken, NJ: Wiley.

Linley, P. A., & Joseph, S. (2004). Positive change following trauma and adversity: A review. *Journal of Traumatic Stress, 17,* 11–21.

Tedeschi, R. G., & Calhoun, L. G. (2004). Posttraumatic growth: Conceptual foundations and empirical evidence. *Psychological Inquiry, 15,* 1–18.

Zoellner, T., & Maercker, A. (2006). Posttraumatic growth in clinical psychology: A critical review and introduction of a two-component model. *Clinical Psychology Review, 26,* 626–653.

RECOMMENDED READINGS

Calhoun, L. G., & Tedeschi, R. G. (Eds.). (2006). *Handbook of posttraumatic growth: Research and practice.* Mahwah, NJ: Erlbaum.

Joseph, S., & Linley, P. A. (Eds.). (2007). *Trauma, recovery, and growth: Positive psychological perspectives on posttraumatic stress.* Hoboken, NJ: Wiley.

P. Alex Linley
Centre for Applied Positive Psychology

Stephen Joseph
University of Nottingham

See also: Attributions; Cognitive Integration, Biopsychosocial; Conservation of Resources Theory; Coping; Etiology; Posttraumatic Adaptation; Social Cognitive Theory; Social Support; Spirituality

POSTTRAUMATIC STRESS DISORDER

Posttraumatic stress disorder (PTSD) is a psychological condition that was first defined in 1980 in the *Diagnostic and Statistical Manual of Mental Disorders* (*DSM-III;* American Psychiatric Association, 1980). This definition was based on the evidence that a specific pattern of psychological phenomenology occurs in some individuals who have been exposed to traumatic events. Traumatic events have a different quality than other types of life stresses, being characterized by people's reactions to fear, horror, and helplessness in a setting of severe threat of death or injury.

The importance of PTSD as a diagnosis for the mental health field was that it captured the importance of the external environment as a significant causal factor in the individual's psychological disorder. The acceptance of the causal role of the external traumatic event and its inclusion in the diagnostic criteria separated PTSD from the majority of other disorders in *DSM-III* (and in subsequent versions of the *DSM* including the most recent version, the *DSM-IV-TR;* American Psychiatric Association, 2000). In this system of diagnosis, the general convention is that the definition of a psychiatric disorder is solely based upon a description of the phenomenology of the symptoms to define the boundary of the condition, rather than including presumed etiological (causal) factors (*see:* **Etiology**). Causal factors were only included in the definition of a disorder if the objective evidence was accepted as being sufficiently scientifically robust. PTSD is one of only two psychiatric diagnoses (the other is adjustment disorder)) for which there has been a consensus of experts that there is sufficient scientific evidence to include a causal factor—in the case of PTSD, the experience of psychologically traumatic event(s)—in its definition, in addition to the symptoms of traumatic stress (see discussion that follows).

History

Implicit in the diagnosis of PTSD is that there is a unitary condition manifest following exposure to a range of different traumatic stressors. The underlining assumption is that there is a unitary dimension of psychopathological response to traumatic events, rather than there being specific syndromes arising from different traumas. Historically, terms such as shell shock (war neurosis), rape crisis syndrome, KZ syndrome (describing prisoners of war survivors) and accident neurosis, had been used to diagnose individuals following specific types of traumatic events. However, the hypothesis that there was a unitary disorder characterizing victims of traumatic stress goes back to the use of the term 'traumatic neurosis' coined by Oppenheim (*see:* **Oppenheim, Hermann**) in the late nineteenth century.

Particularly in the setting of World Wars I and II, there were a number of reformulations and descriptions of the symptoms of traumatic neurosis that focused on both the acute reactions such as combat stress reactions and the more chronic outcomes, including neurasthenia (*see:* **History of Psychological Trauma**). Many valuable observations and insights tended to get lost in the postwar environment because of the continued dominance of the psychoanalytic perspective, which emphasized the importance of early childhood conflict as the major determinant of psychopathology rather than severe adversity in adulthood. However, the term *traumatic neurosis* continued to be used and accepted in psychiatric practice. The development of the phrase *posttraumatic stress disorder* emerged in the context where the term *neurosis* was dropped from the *DSM* system of classification in the development of the Third Edition (American Psychiatric Association, 1980), as had similarly occurred with the anxiety and depression neurosis.

The description of PTSD in *DSM-III* provided a major stimulus for systematic clinical observation and research. This body of knowledge has done much to clarify the phenomenology, longitudinal course, and etiology of this condition. PTSD provoked particular interest among stress-related animal researchers (*see:* **Biology, Animal Models**). Furthermore, it is the one psychiatric condition where the date of onset can be relatively well defined as determined by the date of exposure to the traumatic event. As such, it provides a general model for the way that environmental factors modify an individual's neurobiology and in this way can serve as a template for understanding the more general effects of stress and their relevance to mental health.

Recent developments in neuroimaging techniques have also done much to clarify the underlying neurobiology (*see:* **Biology, Neurochemistry**) and circuitry (*see:* **Biology, Brain Structure, and Function, Adult; Biology, Brain Structure, and Function, Child**) involved in PTSD, emphasizing the recruitment of different neural networks in those exposed to traumatic events who develop PTSD, in contrast to those who do not. One of the consequences of the body of research into the effects of traumatic events has been the unexpected finding of the prevalence of traumatic events in epidemiological studies. This has raised questions about the boundary of the disorder and in particular those types of events should be considered as traumatic. In essence, this is a question that requires further research.

Subtypes

The current system of classification differentiates types of PTSD into acute, chronic, and delayed onset. An acute posttraumatic stress disorder is one that emerges in the aftermath of the event if the symptoms have been present for less than 3 months. A chronic PTSD is where the symptoms have been present for 3 or more months. A delayed onset disorder is made when the onset of symptoms is at least 6 months after exposure to the stressor. The acceptance of a delayed onset pattern of disorder has been one of the significant controversies associated with a disorder. The ability to explain the underlying etiology and mechanisms that lead to the late manifestation of symptoms has been a major theoretical challenge that has only more recently been addressed by the field. The notion that an individual could have seemingly coped effectively at the time of their exposure to an extreme stress such as war, only to later develop symptoms as a consequence of the experience, presented a significant challenge to the field. However, careful observation is prospective longitudinal research studies (*see:* **Research Methodology**) has defined and characterized the chronic PTSD pattern of symptoms unequivocally.

Diagnostic Criteria

There are two different diagnostic systems that are outlined in the *Diagnostic and Statistical Manual, Fourth Edition* (*DSM-IV;* American Psychiatric Association, 2000) and second, the *International Classification of Disease (ICD), Edition 10* (World Health Organization, 1992). The diagnostic criteria have been progressively refined as a consequence of major research efforts to characterize individuals' typical responses following major events such as disasters, war, and individual events such as motor vehicle accidents and rape. The evidence from these studies shows that following a variety of traumatic events there is a shared response (diathesis) independent of the type of psychological trauma, rather than an event's specific pattern of symptoms. The critical dimension of PTSD that separates it from other psychiatric disorders is the recognition that extremely traumatic events are able to produce a disorder with a specific pattern of symptomatology in which exposure to those events plays the central etiological role. The stressor criterion—that is, having been exposed to a traumatic stressor—defines the type of events that can lead to the onset of PTSD.

Stressor Criterion

The stressor criterion is the first hurdle or gate to the diagnosis. Its definition has changed since 1980 as a consequence of epidemiological research. Initially, *DSM-III* (American Psychiatric Association, 1980) adopted a definition of a traumatic event as being a stressor that would be *"markedly distressing to anyone."* These stressors included combat, natural disasters, accidental man-made disasters, or deliberate man-made disasters. There was the view that some stressors more frequently produced the disorder, such as torture, in contrast to those where it would occur less frequently, for example a car accident.

The next revision *DSM-III-R* (American Psychiatric Association, 1987) modified this definition as to experience that was *"outside the range of normal human experience."* The frequency of these types of events however, in carefully conducted representative community based epidemiological studies, suggested that this definition did not take account of the high prevalence of these events (*see:* **Epidemiology**). As a consequence, the definition was changed in *DSM-IV* (see Table 1; American Psychiatric Association, 1994). This definition acknowledged the possibility of a personal subjective response to a significantly greater degree than had previously been the case. This was included in an attempt to account for the role of dissociative reactions that were presumed to be one determinant of the outcome. However, the subjective nature of the individual's appraisal has been criticized because of the potential for retrospective "recall bias" and the loss of relative objectivity in the definition of the event. That is, when people are asked to describe their reactions to past stressful experiences, their recollection of their subjective reactions at the time may be unintentionally inaccurate. For example, if a person currently is experiencing distress, they may be more likely to recall their reaction at the time of a stressful experience as one of fear, helplessness, or horror than if they are not currently experiencing distress. Despite concerns about this type of potential recall bias, sufficient scientific evidence has accumulated to suggest that experiencing severe subjective distress during or soon after a stressful experience plays a role in determining the long-term impact of that experience.

DSM-IV-TR (American Psychiatric Association, 2000) describes three main criteria for the diagnosis of PTSD, which includes the causal or etiological prerequisite of having experienced traumatic event(s) (Criterion A) and the phenomenological requirement of experiencing some or all of the symptoms (Criteria B, C, and D) with sufficient duration (i.e., at least 1 month, Criterion E) and clinically significant impairment in life functioning (Criterion F; see Table 1 for a complete description of the PTSD diagnosis and its required criteria).

Table 1. *DSM-IV-TR* Diagnostic Criteria for Posttraumatic Stress Disorder

A. The person has been exposed to a traumatic event in which both of the following were present:
   (1) The person experienced, witnessed, or was confronted with an event or events that involved actual or threatened death or serious injury or a threat to the physical integrity of self or others.
   (2) The person's response involved intense fear, helplessness, or horror. **Note:** In children, this may be expressed instead by disorganized or agitated behavior.

B. The traumatic event is persistently reexperienced in one (or more) of the following ways:
   (1) Recurrent and intrusive distressing recollections of the event, including images, thoughts, or perceptions. **Note:** In young children, repetitive play may occur in which themes or aspects of the trauma are expressed.
   (2) Recurrent distressing dreams of the event. **Note:** In children, there may be frightening dreams without recognizable content.
   (3) Acting or feeling as if the traumatic event were recurring (includes a sense of reliving the experience, illusions, hallucinations, and dissociative flashback episodes, including those that occur on awakening or when intoxicated). **Note:** In young children, trauma-specific reenactment may occur.
   (4) Intense psychological distress at exposure to internal or external cues that symbolize or resemble an aspect of the traumatic event.
   (5) Physiological reactivity on exposure to internal or external cues that symbolize or resemble an aspect of the traumatic event.

C. Persistent avoidance of stimuli associated with the trauma and numbing of general responsiveness (not present before the trauma), as indicated by three (or more) of the following:
   (1) Efforts to avoid thoughts, feelings, or conversations associated with the trauma
   (2) Efforts to avoid activities, places, or people that arouse recollections of the trauma
   (3) Inability to recall an important aspect of the trauma
   (4) Markedly diminished interest or participation in significant activities
   (5) Feeling of detachment or estrangement from others
   (6) Restricted range of affect (e.g., unable to have loving feelings)
   (7) Sense of a foreshortened future (e.g., does not expect to have a career, marriage, children, or a normal life span)

D. Persistent symptoms of increased arousal (not present before the trauma), as indicated by two (or more) of the following:
   (1) Difficulty falling or staying asleep
   (2) Irritability or outbursts of anger
   (3) Difficulty concentrating
   (4) Hypervigilance
   (5) Exaggerated startle response

E. Duration of the disturbance (symptoms in criteria B, C, and D) is more than 1 month.

F. The disturbance causes clinically significant distress or impairment in social, occupational, or other important areas of functioning.

   Specify if:
   Acute: If duration of symptoms is less than 3 months
   Chronic: If duration of symptoms is 3 months or more

   Specify if:
   With Delayed Onset: If onset of symptoms is at least 6 months after the stressor

Source: Diagnostic and Statistical Manual of Mental Disorders, fourth edition, text revision, pp. 467–468, by the American Psychiatric Association, Washington, DC: Author. Reprinted with permission from the American Psychiatric Association.

Phenomenology

There are three main groups of symptoms that constitute the phenomenology of PTSD (i.e., the nature of the disorder). The precise diagnostic algorithm is set down in *DSM-IV* (American Psychiatric Association, 2000) and ICD 10 (World Health Organization, 1992). The first group of symptoms (Criterion B) relates to the repeated reliving of memories of the traumatic experience—also known as "intrusive reexperiencing" symptoms. These symptoms are intrusive because they are unwanted and occur involuntarily in the form of memories that may recur spontaneously or can be triggered by a variety of real and symbolic stimuli. Intrusive reexperiencing symptoms may involve intense sensory and visual memories of past traumatic event(s), which may or may not be accompanied by extreme physiological and psychological distress. They can also occur with a dissociative quality characteristic of "flashbacks" (i.e., the feeling of actually re-living a past event) and also in dreams.

The second pattern of response (Criterion C), which can sometimes dominate the clinical picture, is characterized by avoidance and numbing of emotional experience. Here the individual enters a state of detachment, emotional blunting and being relatively unengaged with his or her surroundings. This pattern of decreased reactivity is associated with an inability to gain the same sense of pleasure out of activities and an avoidance of situations that were reminiscent of the traumatic event(s).

Finally, in the third set of symptoms (Criterion D), the individual demonstrates a pattern of increased arousal, which is indicated by sleep disturbance, difficulties with memory and concentration, hypervigilance, irritability and an exaggerated startle response. In the more chronic forms of PTSD, this pattern of hyperarousal (i.e., excessive arousal) and the avoidance and emotional numbing symptoms tend to be the more predominant clinical features.

The manifestations of PTSD can best be understood as being driven by several simultaneous processes. First, the repetition of traumatic memories is a driven by reminders in the environment, some of which the person will be unaware of. For example, a person who has been in an automobile accident in which someone was killed may be reminded of that traumatic experience not only by subsequently driving in other automobiles, visiting hospitals, or seeing a film in which an automobile crash occurs, but also (unbeknownst to him or her) by being on other forms of transportation (such as a train or a bicycle) or when in places or weather conditions that have even minor similarities to the place or conditions where the accident occurred. The propensity for these memories to be reactivated is probably, in part, because of the continued difficulties that the individual has in processing them and forming a complete representation, particularly in a narrative domain. Research studies suggest that people with PTSD often have difficulty recalling not only portions of traumatic experiences but moreover in developing a clear recollection of the sequence of events in their lives (narrative memory) including positive and other nontraumatic memories as well as traumatic ones (*see:* **Cognitive Impairments; Memory**). The triggering of these memories is also consequent upon fear conditioning (*see:* **Learning Theory**) mechanisms, which are critical to many aspects of human learning. These reminders serve to sustain and kindle (i.e., increase) the hyperarousal that occurs with the passage of time. The avoidance and numbing symptoms represent homeostatic mechanisms, where the individual attempts to modulate and shut down his or her hyperresponsiveness. The disorder arises because of some individuals' inability to progressively quench or shut off the acute stress response, which is ubiquitous at times of exposure to traumatic events.

A consequence of PTSD is that the individuals remain subjectively trapped by an intense traumatic past experience to an unusual degree. This significantly interferes with the person's capacity to maintain involvement in current life activities and relationships.

This happens for two reasons. First, the pattern of emotional numbing and decreased general responsiveness makes it difficult for them to gain the normal rewards from ongoing interactions with their environment. The other issue is that their hyperarousal means that they readily become distressed by what would otherwise be insignificant stimuli, which further encourages their withdrawal. Apart from their detachment, the individual's propensity to experience triggered memories of the past highlights how his or her internal perceptual organization has become excessively centered on the involuntary seeking out of the similarities between the present and the traumatic past. As a consequence, many neutral experiences become reinterpreted as having traumatic associations, and this may perpetuate and amplify intrusive reexperiencing symptoms.

Subsyndromal PTSD

The term *subsyndromal* (also subthreshold, subclinical, or partial) PTSD (*see:* **Diagnosis of Traumatic Stress Disorders [*DSM & ICD*]; Posttraumatic Stress Disorder, Diagnosis of**) has been coined to describe the group of individuals who have a number of symptoms but do not satisfy the full diagnostic criteria for PTSD. A number of studies have highlighted that the avoidance symptoms generally are the set of criteria that determine the threshold barrier for the diagnosis of PTSD. That is, when people have several PTSD symptoms but not enough to meet the diagnostic requirement, they more often have an insufficient number of avoidance and emotional numbing symptoms (Criterion C) than an insufficient number of either intrusive reexperiencing or hyperarousal symptoms. The *ICD* 10 criteria (World Health Organization, 1992) for PTSD do not require the presence of actual avoidance, rather referring to a preference for avoiding rather than encountering of reminders of traumatic experiences. This difference reflects the lack of objective consensus about the optimal threshold for these phenomena: the *ICD* and *DSM* criteria for PTSD are

very similar but also differ at several crucial points, including how "avoidance" is defined.

The impact of subsyndromal PTSD has been examined systematically in several epidemiological studies, which suggest that the degree of disability associated with subsyndromal PTSD is similar to the extent of disability experienced by people who have the full syndrome of PTSD. Furthermore partial PTSD has been associated with an increased risk of binge drinking of alcohol, potentially impeding recovery. Also, the problematic pattern of health care utilization with partial PTSD more closely resembled full PTSD rather than the more positive pattern of health care utilization found with individuals who reported few or no PTSD symptoms. It has been argued that the associated disability warrants partial PTSD being accepted as a subcategory in any revision of the diagnostic criteria; this proposal remains a matter of debate.

Comorbidity

The existence of any psychiatric disorder without the co-occurrence of other disorders in a clinical setting is the exception rather than the rule: most people who are in treatment for psychiatric problems have more than one psychiatric disorder. Large epidemiological studies indicate that a range of other disorders, particularly affective disorders, panic disorder, and alcohol and substance abuse (*see:* **Comorbidity**), frequently emerge in conjunction with PTSD and that this is not isolated to treatment-seeking populations. Patients with comorbid disorders are likely to have a worse long-term outcome than those without comorbidities (i.e., those who have only one disorder), and may require chronic maintenance therapy (i.e., therapy to help them maintain the improvements they have achieved in treatment and to prevent future worsening of their symptoms). Studies also have broadened attention as to the range of psychiatric disorders that may arise as a consequence of traumatic exposure. In some populations, major depressive disorder is a more common outcome of exposure to traumatic event(s) than is PTSD.

It is generally presumed that PTSD is the primary diagnosis if this was the first disorder the person experienced. Often the symptoms of other psychiatric disorders such as depression fluctuate following traumatic events, while the underlying PTSD symptoms remain more constant or persistent.

The question arises as to whether a specific pattern of associated physical symptoms occurs as part of the traumatic stress response. Historically, PTSD was described by a series of names that focused on the physical accompaniments of the response, such as "soldiers' heart" in the American Civil War (*see:* **History of Psychological Trauma**). The controversy about the effects of herbicides (such as Agent Orange) on the physical health of Vietnam War veterans similarly highlights how even in more recent times, the physical symptoms associated with PTSD can be the primary concern of traumatized populations and their search for compensation. The Gulf War syndrome (*see:* **Gulf War Syndrome**) ignited a controversy that again reactivated this debate. The presence of the somatic manifestations of distress (*see:* **Somatic Complaints**) is an important issue in understanding and treating traumatized individuals, including those who were not actually physically injured but who may experience physiological distress as a result of intrusive reexperiencing or of hyperarousal. In the case of a physically injured patient, the significance of PTSD symptoms involving somatic distress or other somatic complaints is particularly likely to be missed or incorrectly attributed to the ongoing sequelae of the physical injury.

Complications and Course

The severity and longitudinal course of PTSD can vary significantly. The course of PTSD over time tends to be more chronic than often presumed, with many individuals having a fluctuating course where intermittent exposure to new stressors (traumatic or nontraumatic) leads to an exacerbation of symptoms. Approximately 40% of persons diagnosed with PTSD will have a disorder that remains for many years. The cognitive decline associated with aging can also

lead to an exacerbation of PTSD symptoms. Substance abuse is a significant complication of PTSD with individuals using drugs and alcohol to self-medicate their distress. While depression has been more typically seen as a major risk factor for suicidality, an increasing body of literature suggests that PTSD appears to be associated with a similar high level of risk of both attempted and completed suicide. PTSD also conveys an increased risk of a decline in the sufferer's physical health (*see:* **Medical Illness, Adult; Medical Illness, Child; Somatic Complaints**) and consumption of general medical services (*see:* **Health Service Utilization**).

Diagnostic Issues

The diagnosis of PTSD is a difficult problem and the challenge this presents to clinicians has been recognized for some time. It is commonly the case that many individuals with psychiatric disorders do not primarily understand themselves to have a psychological illness. In general, individuals have a propensity to primarily present with somatic distress rather than with their psychological symptoms, and to seek help from medical clinics or providers rather than mental health or psychiatric clinics or professionals. Thus, it is frequently by default that a patient gains access to psychological care. In particular, with PTSD, the avoidance of trauma-related or distressing thoughts and feelings means that in a medical consultation these matters are infrequently spoken of or initiated by the patient.

Furthermore, many symptoms are not directly linked to the traumatic exposure in the individual's mind. Symptoms such as emotional numbing, social withdrawal, and interpersonal irritability are also attributed of as having their origins in other people's behavior. In other words, rather than seeing themselves as being unwell and in need of treatment, individuals with PTSD may blame their difficulties on those around them.

Correctly diagnosing PTSD is often a further problem, even if a psychiatric diagnosis is considered and a significant percentage of patients with PTSD go unrecognized by medical practitioners and even trained mental health professionals. Self-report questionnaires and structured clinical interviews detect many cases that are missed by clinicians, but these two methods of detection differ in their accuracy in detecting PTSD (sensitivity) and in distinguishing PTSD from other disorders (specificity; *see:* **Diagnosis of Traumatic Stress Disorders [*DSM & ICD*]**). In research settings, standardized methods of assessment are required because of their great reliability, minimizing the problem of the inter-clinician variability in diagnosis. Some courts also require the use of both clinician interviews and structured diagnostic assessments for a forensic diagnosis of PTSD.

Controversies about the Diagnosis

The validity of PTSD as a diagnostic entity perhaps provokes more controversy than any other disorder in psychiatry. PTSD is a condition that evokes considerable public interest because of its frequent use in medico-legal settings. As a consequence, the science and the validity of observations about traumatized people come under frequent scrutiny outside the profession. Inevitably, in adversarial settings, the arguments about the effect of traumatic events become polarized. It is therefore important that the political and social dimensions of these arguments are separated from the scientific observations that are available to address the questions about the validity of PTSD.

Unlike most psychiatric diagnoses, PTSD has a degree of acceptability among those who have this disorder, particularly war veterans. It removes the primary focus of etiology from the individual vulnerability to the external environment. Psychological trauma victims therefore often see the diagnosis as being less stigmatizing than other psychiatric diagnoses. As a consequence of this sociopolitical dimension, groups such as feminists advocating for rape victims and military veterans' organizations lobbied for the inclusion of PTSD in

DSM-III (American Psychiatric Association, 1980). This political backdrop is sometimes used to question the scientific validity of the condition.

The disorder has also been attacked in other domains because of the argument including that it medicalizes the consequences of political and social events, such as war. In so doing, the diagnosis may be seen as misrepresenting the natural forms of human distress that are inevitable in times of extreme human suffering. However, this argument negates the fact that extreme stress is injurious to people's health, and a precise diagnosis can lead to the instigation of appropriate treatment that is often denied the victims of genocide and civil wars in developing nations.

The reformulation of PTSD being considered in the next version of the *DSM* (the *DSM-V; see:* **Diagnosis of Traumatic Stress Disorders [*DSM & ICD*]; Posttraumatic Stress Disorder, Diagnosis of**) will have to deal with a number of questions that have been raised. First, there is a significant overlap between the diagnostic criteria of PTSD with major depressive disorder and generalized anxiety disorder, conditions that can arise after exposure to traumatic events. Hence, there is a need to clarify the unique elements of PTSD that makes it distinctive from these other disorders. A similar argument has been used to challenge the diagnosis in some individuals who have suffered from a mood or anxiety disorder prior to the traumatic event, where the argument is made that PTSD is simply an exacerbation of these previous disorders. However, it should be emphasized that many issues of a similar nature remain about the separation of bipolar disorder from schizophrenia and the current system of classification of major depressive disorder. A large body of scientific literature now supports the validity of PTSD. A number of the issues raised to challenge the conceptualization of the disorder equally can be leveled in a more general way about the current system of psychiatric diagnosis that does not address issues of dimensionality and the frequent comorbidity that has been described in epidemiological studies with all disorders.

Conclusion

PTSD is a unique psychiatric diagnosis describing the pattern of response in individuals exposed to extreme stressors. At the core of the syndrome, as described originally by Freud, is the imprinting of the traumatic memory of the event that serves to drive the individual's distress and affect dyregulation. These memories serve to reorganize the individuals' cognitive schemas about the world and their primary emotional reactivity to both neutral stimuli as well as those that remind them of the traumatic event. This dimension of PTSD is the primary characteristic that separates it from other psychiatric disorders and emphasizes the interaction between the individual and the stressor to which they have been exposed. While a range of vulnerability factors exist that may predispose some individuals to develop PTSD, these are neither necessary nor sufficient factors to explain the disorder's onset: many persons who are vulnerable to develop PTSD nevertheless do not develop the disorder even after exposure to traumatic events. Importantly, the definition of PTSD has informed the development of a major body of theory and research about treatment where the optimal outcomes are achieved by focusing on the reprocessing of the traumatic memories and the associated cognitions (*see:* **Exposure Therapy, Adult**).

REFERENCES

American Psychiatric Association. (1980). *Diagnostic and statistical manual of mental disorders* (3rd ed.). Washington, DC: Author.

American Psychiatric Association. (1987). *Diagnostic and statistical manual of mental disorders* (3rd ed., rev.). Washington, DC: Author.

American Psychiatric Association. (1994). *Diagnostic and statistical manual of mental disorders* (4th ed.). Washington, DC: Author.

American Psychiatric Association. (2000). *Diagnostic and statistical manual of mental disorders* (4th ed., text rev.). Washington, DC: Author.

World Health Organization. (1992). *The ICD-10 classification of mental and behavioural disorders: Diagnostic criteria for research.* Geneva, Switzerland: Author.

RECOMMENDED READINGS

American Psychiatric Association. (1952). *Diagnostic and statistical manual of mental disorders.* Washington, DC: Author.

American Psychiatric Association. (1968). *Diagnostic and statistical manual of mental disorders* (2nd ed.). Washington, DC: Author.

American Psychiatric Association. (1995). *Diagnostic and statistical manual of mental disorders* (4th ed., rev.). Washington, DC: Author.

Friedman, M. J., Keane, T. M., & Resick, P. A. (Eds.). (2007). *Handbook of PTSD: Science and practice.* New York: Guilford Press.

Shalev, A. Y., Yehuda, R., & McFarlane, A. C. (Eds.). (2000). *International handbook of human response to trauma.* New York: Kluwer Academic/Plenum Press.

Van der Kolk, B. A., McFarlane, A. C., & Weisaeth, L. (Eds.). (1996). *Traumatic stress: The effects of overwhelming experience on the mind, body, and society.* New York: Guilford Press.

ALEXANDER C. MCFARLANE
University of Adelaide

See also: Avoidance; Biology, Animal Models; Biology, Brain Structure, and Function, Adult; Biology, Brain Structure, and Function, Child; Biology, Neurochemistry; Cognitive Impairments; Comorbidity; Diagnosis of Traumatic Stress Disorders (*DSM & ICD*); Emotional Numbing; Epidemiology; Etiology; Health Service Utilization; History of Psychological Trauma; Hyperarousal; Intrusive Reexperiencing; Memory; Posttraumatic Stress Disorder, Diagnosis of; Somatic Complaints; Stress; Stress Response Syndromes; Trauma, Definition; Traumatic Stress; Typology of Traumatic Stress Disorders

POSTTRAUMATIC STRESS DISORDER CHECKLIST

The Posttraumatic Stress Disorder Checklist (PTSD Checklist or PCL; Weathers, Litz, Herman, Huska, & Keane, 1993) is a 17-item self-report measure of posttraumatic stress disorder (PTSD) symptoms. Developed at the National Center for PTSD in 1990, the PCL was originally designed to provide convergent validity evidence as a component of a multitrait-multimethod approach to validating the Clinician-Administered PTSD Scale (CAPS; Blake et al., 1995) in combat veterans. At the time, none of the well-validated PTSD measures, including the Mississippi Combat PTSD Scale (Keane, Caddell, & Taylor, 1988), the Minnesota Multiphasic Personality Inventory's (MMPI) PK scale (Keane, Malloy, & Fairbank, 1984), and the Impact of Event Scale (Horowitz, Wilner, & Alvarez, 1979), corresponded directly with *DSM-III-R* (American Psychiatric Association, 1987) diagnostic criteria for PTSD. Given that the CAPS did correspond directly with *DSM-III-R* (American Psychiatric Association, 1987) PTSD symptom criteria, it was considered essential to include a self-report counterpart as part of its initial validation, and thus the PCL was created to supplement existing measures. The PCL was revised in 1994 to incorporate the changes to the PTSD diagnostic criteria in *DSM-IV* (American Psychiatric Association, 1994). It has become one of the most widely used self-report measures of PTSD (Elhai, Gray, Kashdan, & Franklin, 2005) and has been translated into a number of languages.

The 17 items of the PCL mirror the 17 *DSM-IV* symptoms of PTSD, with each item consisting of a brief phrase describing the key aspects of a given symptom. Respondents indicate how much they were bothered by that symptom over the past month, using a five-point scale ranging from "1 = Not at all" to "5 = Extremely." There are three versions of the PCL, including the original military version (PCL-M), the civilian version (PCL-C), and the specific version (PCL-S). These versions differ only in the description of the index event in the first eight items, that is, the five reexperiencing symptoms, two effortful avoidance symptoms, and amnesia item. The PCL-M, which refers to "a stressful military experience," and the PCL-C, which refers to "a stressful experience from the past," are intended to be administered when a specific stressor has not been identified from which to base PTSD ratings. The PCL-S refers to "the stressful experience," and is intended to be administered when a specific stressor has been identified. On the PCL-S respondents write in the index event and the

date it occurred at the top of the form, then rate items with respect to that event.

The PCL may be scored in two ways. Most often it is used as a continuous measure of PTSD symptom severity. Severity scores may be calculated for each of the three symptom clusters (reexperiencing, avoidance and numbing, and hyperarousal) by summing across the corresponding PCL items. A total PTSD severity score is calculated by summing across all 17 items. The PCL may also be used to create a dichotomous PTSD diagnosis. This is accomplished by considering items rated as "3 = Moderately" or higher as symptoms endorsed, then following the *DSM-IV* diagnostic rule, which requires at least one reexperiencing symptom, at least three avoidance and numbing symptoms, and at least two hyperarousal symptoms.

The PCL has excellent psychometric properties. In the earliest report (Weathers et al., 1993), in a sample of male combat veterans the PCL demonstrated high internal consistency (full-scale alpha = .97) and excellent test-retest reliability (.96) over a 2- to 3-day retest interval. It also demonstrated strong convergent validity with other measures of PTSD and combat exposure, and good diagnostic utility against the Structured Clinical Interview for *DSM*'s (SCID; American Psychiatric Association, 1952) PTSD module (sensitivity = .82, specificity = .83, kappa = .64). In addition, in a sample of victims of a motor vehicle accident or sexual assault (Blanchard, Jones-Alexander, Buckley, & Forneris, 1996), the PCL demonstrated high internal consistency (full-scale alpha = .94), and excellent diagnostic utility against the CAPS (sensitivity = .94, specificity = .86, efficiency = .94). Further, in a sample of college students with a variety of civilian traumas (Ruggiero, Del Ben, Scotti, & Rabalais, 2003) the PCL again demonstrated high internal consistency (full-scale alpha = .94), good test-retest reliability (.68 to .92, depending on the retest interval), and strong convergent validity with self-report measures of PTSD, depression, and anxiety.

The PCL has proven useful for a variety of assessment tasks, including screening for PTSD (e.g., Andrykowski, Cordova, Studts, & Miller,

1998; Dobie et al., 2002), detecting clinical change in treatment outcome studies (e.g., Forbes, Creamer, & Biddle, 2001), and estimating PTSD prevalence in epidemiological studies (e.g., Hoge et al., 2008; Kang, Natelson, Mahan, Lee, & Murphy, 2003). A parent-report version of the PCL has been developed and shown to be psychometrically reliable and valid with pediatric medical (Daviss et al., 2000) and mental health (Ford et al., 2000) populations. The PCL has also been one of the most commonly used measures in factor analytic studies of PTSD (e.g., Asmundson et al., 2000; Palmieri, Weathers, Difede, & King, 2007; Simms, Watson, & Doebbeling, 2002), and thus has been the basis for a growing literature that has challenged the structure of the *DSM-IV* (American Psychiatric Association, 1994) PTSD symptom clusters.

There are several limitations to the PCL and its empirical literature. First, the PCL only assesses the 17 symptoms of PTSD and does not assess trauma exposure or degree of functional impairment. Second, although the three versions of the PCL differ only slightly, it should not be assumed that psychometric properties found for one version necessarily generalize to the other versions. This issue is further complicated by the fact that some studies do not specify the version used. Third, optimal cutoff scores have varied widely across studies, depending on the type of trauma, the setting, and the assessment task (e.g., screening versus differential diagnosis). This means that no single cutoff will be appropriate for all circumstances and careful deliberation is needed in choosing the best cutoff for a given application in a given population.

REFERENCES

American Psychiatric Association. (1952). *Diagnostic and statistical manual of mental disorders*. Washington, DC: Author.

American Psychiatric Association. (1987). *Diagnostic and statistical manual of mental disorders* (3rd ed., rev.). Washington, DC: Author.

American Psychiatric Association. (1994). *Diagnostic and statistical manual of mental disorders* (4th ed.). Washington, DC: Author.

Andrykowski, M. A., Cordova, M. J., Studts, J. L., & Miller, T. W. (1998). Posttraumatic stress disorder after treatment for breast cancer: Prevalence of diagnosis and use of the PTSD Checklist-Civilian version (PCL-C) as a screening instrument. *Journal of Consulting and Clinical Psychology, 66,* 586–590.

Asmundson, G. J. G., Frombach, I., McQuaid, J., Pedrelli, P., Lenox, R., & Stein, M. B. (2000). Dimensionality of posttraumatic stress symptoms: A confirmatory factor analysis of DSM-IV symptom clusters and other symptom models. *Behaviour Research and Therapy, 38,* 203–214.

Blake, D. D., Weathers, F. W., Nagy, L. M., Kaloupek, D. G., Gusman, F. D., Charney, D. S., et al. (1995). The development of a clinician-administered PTSD scale. *Journal of Traumatic Stress, 8,* 75–90.

Blanchard, E. B., Jones-Alexander, J., Buckley, T. C., & Forneris, C. A. (1996). Psychometric properties of the PTSD Checklist (PCL). *Behaviour Research and Therapy, 34,* 669–673.

Daviss, W. B., Mooney, D., Racusin, R., Ford, J. D., Fleischer, A., & McHugo, G. (2000). Predicting post-traumatic stress after hospitalization for pediatric injury. *Journal of the American Academy of Child and Adolescent Psychiatry, 39,* 576–583.

Dobie, D. J., Kivlahan, D. R., Maynard, C., Bush, K. R., McFall, M. E., Epler, A. J., et al. (2002). Screening for post-traumatic stress disorder in female veteran's affairs patients: Validation of the PTSD Checklist. *General Hospital Psychiatry, 24,* 367–374.

Elhai, J. D., Gray, M. J., Kashdan, T. B., & Franklin, C. L. (2005). Which instruments are most commonly used to assess traumatic event exposure and posttraumatic effects? A survey of traumatic stress professionals. *Journal of Traumatic Stress, 18,* 541–545.

Forbes, D., Creamer, M. C., & Biddle, D. (2001). The validity of the PTSD Checklist as a measure of symptomatic change in combat-related PTSD. *Behaviour Research and Therapy, 39,* 977–986.

Ford, J. D., Racusin, R., Ellis, C., Daviss, W. B., Reiser, J., Fleischer, A., & Thomas, J. (2000). Child maltreatment, other trauma exposure, and posttraumatic symptomatology among children with Oppositional Defiant and Attention Deficit Hyperactivity disorders. *Child Maltreatment, 5,* 205–217.

Hoge, C. W., McGurk, D., Thomas, J. L., Cox, A. L., Engel, C. C., & Castro, C. A. (2008). Mild traumatic brain injury in U.S. soldiers returning from Iraq. *New England Journal of Medicine, 358*, 453–463.

Horowitz, M. J., Wilner, N., & Alvarez, W. (1979). Impact of Event Scale: A measure of subjective stress. *Psychosomatic Medicine, 41*, 209–218.

Kang, H. K., Natelson, B. H., Mahan, C. M., Lee, K. Y., & Murphy, F. M. (2003). Post-traumatic stress disorder and chronic fatigue syndrome-like illness among Gulf War veterans: A population-based survey of 30,000 veterans. *American Journal of Epidemiology, 157*, 141–148.

Keane, T. M., Caddell, J. M., & Taylor, K. L. (1988). Mississippi Scale for Combat-Related Posttraumatic Stress Disorder: Three studies in reliability and validity. *Journal of Consulting and Clinical Psychology, 56*, 85–90.

Keane, T. M., Malloy, P. F., & Fairbank, J. A. (1984). Empirical development of an MMPI subscale for the assessment of combat-related posttraumatic stress disorder. *Journal of Consulting and Clinical Psychology, 52*, 888–891.

Palmieri, P. A., Weathers, F. W., Difede, J., & King, D. W. (2007). Confirmatory factor analysis of the PTSD Checklist and the Clinician-Administered PTSD Scale in disaster workers exposed to the World Trade Center Ground Zero. *Journal of Abnormal Psychology, 116*, 329–341.

Ruggiero, K. J., Del Ben, K. S., Scotti, J. R., & Rabalais, A. E. (2003). Psychometric properties of the PTSD Checklist-Civilian version. *Journal of Traumatic Stress, 16*, 495–502.

Simms, L. J., Watson, D., & Doebbeling, B. N. (2002). Confirmatory factor analyses of posttraumatic stress symptoms in deployed and nondeployed veterans of the Gulf War. *Journal of Abnormal Psychology, 111*, 637–647.

Weathers, F. W., Litz, B. T., Herman, D. S., Huska, J. A., & Keane, T. M. (1993, October). *The PTSD Checklist (PCL): Reliability, validity, and diagnostic utility.* Paper presented at the annual meeting of the International Society for Traumatic Stress Studies, San Antonio, TX.

Frank W. Weathers
Auburn University

See also: Assessment, Psychometric, Adult; Assessment, Psychometric, Child

POSTTRAUMATIC STRESS DISORDER, DIAGNOSIS OF

The introduction of posttraumatic stress disorder (PTSD) in *DSM-III* (American Psychiatric Association, 1980) marked the first formal recognition and explication of a characteristic syndrome of psychological trauma conceptualized as distinct from other mental disorders and having a potentially chronic course. Previous versions of *DSM* provided a trauma-related diagnosis only for acute reactions in individuals without apparent premorbid (i.e., prior to the current diagnosis) emotional problems, directing clinicians to change the diagnosis to another mental disorder if symptoms persisted. *DSM-I* (American Psychiatic Association, 1952) included the diagnosis "gross stress reaction," which like PTSD was intended explicitly for pathological reactions to catastrophic life events such as combat and various types of civilian trauma. However, it was categorized under "transient situational personality disorders," distinguished from other disorders by its "reversibility of reaction, and its transient character," and considered "a temporary diagnosis to be used only until a more definitive diagnosis is established" in the event that symptoms did not resolve quickly (p. 40).

For reasons that are unclear, but which may have had to do with a relative lull in military conflict in the years following the release of *DSM-I* (Andreasen, 1980; Bloom, 2000), gross stress reaction was dropped from *DSM-II* (American Psychiatric Association, 1968), leaving the category "transient situational disturbances," with its list of age-based "adjustment reactions," as the only option for diagnosing trauma-related symptoms. This category maintained the emphasis on acute reactions in otherwise normal individuals, again noting that another diagnosis was warranted if symptoms persisted. More importantly, however, in contrast with gross stress reaction it was less explicitly linked to catastrophic events. Although some examples of the various adjustment reactions referred to potentially traumatic events ("fear associated with military combat," "a Ganser syndrome associated with death sentence"), others referred to lower magnitude stressors ("irritability and depression associated with school failure," "feelings of rejection associated with forced retirement") (p. 49).

In this context, therefore, PTSD represented a major conceptual advance that addressed a significant gap in diagnostic coverage for trauma survivors. First, it restored the explicit emphasis on catastrophic life events that was evident in gross stress reaction. Second, it formalized a trauma-related syndrome that was distinct from, albeit potentially comorbid (i.e., co-occurring) with, other disorders. Third, it recognized a chronic course of the syndrome, as well as the possibility of the delayed onset of symptoms. Finally, as with all *DSM-III* categories it contained explicit diagnostic criteria, which articulated the stressor criterion, delineated the symptoms, identified subtypes based on onset and course, and established a diagnostic threshold with respect to the number and pattern of symptoms.

PTSD thus affirmed that trauma has unique deleterious effects that are not sufficiently accounted for by premorbid or comorbid psychopathology, and that these effects may endure long after exposure to the stressor has ended. Further, it is important to note that in the PTSD criteria, as in gross stress reaction, a wide range of stressors, including combat and various types of civilian trauma, was recognized as being capable of producing the disorder. Accordingly, although the political activism of Vietnam combat veterans and their supporters in the psychiatric community played an important role in the creation of the PTSD diagnosis (Scott, 1990), PTSD was not limited to "post-Vietnam syndrome." Rather, it was conceptualized from the outset as a universal disorder that was essentially the same regardless of the trauma that elicited it. As Andreasen (2004), the chair of the *DSM-III* Committee on Reactive Disorders and author of the original PTSD text, explained, "A stress syndrome characterized by reliving, indicators of autonomic hyperarousal, and other such features was simply a

final common pathway with many different sites of entry" (p. 1322).

The diagnostic criteria for PTSD in *DSM-III* consisted of Criterion A, the stressor criterion, defined as an event that would evoke significant distress in most people and was outside the range of common stressful experiences; and 12 symptoms divided into three clusters: a reexperiencing cluster with three symptoms (intrusive thoughts, nightmares, and flashbacks), a numbing cluster with three symptoms (diminished interest, detachment or estrangement, and constricted affect), and an unlabeled cluster with six criteria representing nine miscellaneous symptoms (hyperalertness or exaggerated startle, sleep disturbance, survival guilt and guilt over behavior, memory impairment or trouble concentrating, avoidance of trauma-related activities, intensification of symptoms following exposure to trauma-related events). A diagnosis of PTSD was conferred if an individual had at least one reexperiencing symptom, one numbing symptom, and two symptoms from the third cluster. An acute subtype was given if symptoms started within six months of the index trauma and lasted less than 6 months. A chronic or delayed subtype was given if symptoms lasted more than 6 months or symptoms started at least 6 months after the index trauma.

The diagnostic criteria for PTSD have been revised considerably since *DSM-III*, particularly between *DSM-III* and *DSM-III-R* (Brett, Spitzer, & Williams, 1988). The most significant changes from *DSM-III-R* (American Psychiatric Association, 1987) to *DSM-IV* (American Psychiatric Association, 1994) included (a) modifying Criterion A by incorporating dimensions of trauma such as life threat, and in the text specifying that the characteristic emotional response involves intense fear and helplessness, and introducing the idea that qualifying events might involve indirect exposure, that is, learning about a trauma happening to a loved one, as opposed to directly experiencing or witnessing the event; (b) increasing the number of symptoms from 12 to 17, primarily by breaking out compound symptoms in the *DSM-III* miscellaneous cluster; (c) grouping the 17 symptoms into reexperiencing, avoidance and numbing, and hyperarousal clusters; (d) dropping guilt as a symptom; and (e) adding the requirement that symptoms have lasted at least 1 month.

The most significant additional changes for *DSM-IV* included (a) substantially modifying Criterion A, most notably by creating a two-part definition, with the first part requiring exposure to an event involving death, serious injury, or threat to physical integrity, and the second part requiring an emotional response involving fear, helplessness, or horror (see Weathers & Keane, 2007 for a discussion of the evolution of Criterion A); (b) moving physiological reactivity from the hyperarousal cluster to the reexperiencing cluster; and (c) adding the requirement that symptoms have caused marked subjective distress or functional impairment.

Thus, the current *DSM-IV* criteria PTSD include exposure to a traumatic stressor (Criterion A); the presence of at least one of five reexperiencing symptoms (Criterion B); three of seven avoidance and numbing symptoms (Criterion C); and two of five hyperarousal symptoms (Criterion D); a duration of at least one month (Criterion E); and clinically significant distress or impairment in social or occupational functioning caused by the syndrome (Criterion F). In addition there are three specifiers: acute, if duration is less than three months, versus chronic, if duration is three months or longer; and with delayed onset, if the onset of symptoms occurred six months or longer after the index event. Notably the PTSD criteria do not include the usual exclusion criteria that the syndrome is not due to the physiological effects of a substance or a general medical condition, and is not better accounted for by another disorder.

DSM-IV Diagnosis of PTSD

There are a number of steps involved in making a *DSM-IV* diagnosis of PTSD. In this section, these steps are described and the diagnostic challenges associated with each step are discussed.

Establishing Criterion A

The first step involves determining that an individual has been exposed to an extreme stressor that satisfies both parts of the Criterion A definition of a trauma. Criterion A1 is met if the event involves a close personal experience with actual or threatened death or serious injury, or a threat to physical integrity. Typically this entails directly experiencing or witnessing the event, but it may also include learning about the event happening to someone with whom the individual has a close personal relationship. Criterion A2 is met if the individual responds to the event with an intense emotional response involving fear, horror, or helplessness.

With its explicit emphasis on extreme stressors, where extreme is equated with life-threatening, and its two-part conjunctive requirement, Criterion A in *DSM-IV* could be seen as a more stringent definition of trauma compared to previous versions. However, critics have argued that it represents instead an excessively broad definition that allows too many stressful events to be classified as traumatic, creating what McNally (2003) has referred to as "conceptual bracket creep." Some phrases in the Criterion A language such as "confronted with" and "threat to physical integrity" are in fact ambiguous. They are useful in that they help provide adequate coverage for the full range of potentially traumatic events, but in isolation they could be interpreted too broadly and stretched to include even minor stressors. However, to be interpreted appropriately, these phrases must be considered in the full context of the criterion language and accompanying text, which repeatedly underscores the calamitous nature of qualifying events through specific examples of traumas and phrases such as "extreme traumatic stressor," "extreme trauma," and "extreme (i.e., life-threatening) nature." Doing otherwise would risk distorting the intent of Criterion A and applying it in a manner inconsistent with the original conceptualization of traumas as catastrophic stressors.

Evaluating Symptom Criteria

Once an index trauma has been established, the second step is to evaluate the 17 individual PTSD symptoms. For each symptom the clinician must determine if the respondent's description of a problem fits the criterion phenomenologically and if the problem is severe enough to be clinically significant. There are several challenges involved in this step. First, several of the symptoms, particularly flashbacks, amnesia, and foreshortened future, are inadequately conceptualized and vaguely defined, which contributes to a loss of reliability in information gathering and clinical judgment. Second, there is considerable conceptual and practical overlap of symptoms, both within cluster (e.g., among intrusive thoughts, cued distress, and cued physiological reactivity in the reexperiencing cluster; between the two effortful avoidance items and among diminished interest, detachment or estrangement, and restricted range of affect in the avoidance and numbing cluster) and across clusters (between nightmares and sleep disturbance; between exaggerated startle and cued physiological reactivity). This can lead to "double-coding" in which the same problem is counted under two or more symptom criteria, thereby inflating the symptom tally and making it easier to obtain a PTSD diagnosis. Finally, the avoidance and numbing cluster consists primarily of negative symptoms or behavioral deficits. These are especially difficult to inquire and rate because they involve the absence rather than the presence of a behavior and respondents may be less aware of their impact.

Linking Symptoms to the Index Trauma

The third step, usually carried out simultaneously with the second step, is establishing an explicit link or functional relationship between individual symptoms and the index trauma, as required by the specific phrase in the criterion language "not present before the trauma," and more generally by the conceptualization of PTSD as a trauma-related disorder. This is readily accomplished for the five reexperiencing symptoms, two effortful avoidance symptoms, and amnesia because they all explicitly refer to the index trauma. However, it is more difficult for the remaining nine symptoms, including the emotional numbing and hyperarousal symptoms. These do not refer explicitly to the trauma; some of them are also seen in other disorders, especially major depression, and thus may be attributable to premorbid or comorbid conditions; and respondents may be unaware that they are related to the trauma. Therefore the required link requires at least some degree of inference, and the functional relationship may be difficult to determine.

Establishing a link between PTSD symptoms and the index trauma can be straightforward when the trauma is relatively circumscribed and there is good premorbid functioning, no prior history of trauma exposure, and a sudden, marked decline from a previous level of functioning prior to the trauma. However, the situation is seldom that clear-cut. Many types of trauma, such as combat, childhood physical or sexual abuse, domestic violence, and life-threatening illness, are complex, with manifold stressful elements, and may occur repeatedly over an extended period of time. In such cases the index trauma may of necessity be a summary label for multiple traumatic stressors.

Further, individuals may experience multiple, distinct types of trauma over the lifespan, and the cumulative effects of exposure to multiple traumas can greatly complicate the task of attributing PTSD symptoms to a particular event. As we have discussed elsewhere (Weathers & Keane, 1999), the difficulty of this task can be illustrated by considering the numerous possible outcomes of exposure to even just two distinct traumas: (a) the individual is exposed to the first trauma, resulting in no PTSD, partial PTSD, or full PTSD; (b) over time the individual remains asymptomatic, becomes symptomatic with delayed onset, or if initially symptomatic remains symptomatic, recovers partially, or recovers fully; and (c) the individual is then exposed to the second trauma, which triggers a new PTSD syndrome that would have developed even without the first trauma, triggers a new syndrome potentiated by the first trauma, reactivates a previous syndrome from which the individual has recovered, exacerbates a current partial syndrome into a full one, or exacerbates a current full syndrome into a more severe one. The complexity of this bewildering array of possible outcomes would, of course, increase exponentially with the presence of additional traumas or premorbid or comorbid psychopathology. Therefore, although the PTSD diagnostic criteria require a link between symptoms and stressor, in many cases establishing an unequivocal link is unrealistic, and an inference regarding an incremental functional relationship between symptoms and a given trauma, above and beyond other possible causal factors, may be the best that can be achieved.

Specifying Chronology

The fourth step is to determine the onset and duration of PTSD symptoms. As noted above, Criterion E requires that the syndrome last for at least one month to qualify for a PTSD diagnosis, and the course is specified as acute or chronic. An onset specifier allows for delayed onset, although typically symptoms begin soon after the trauma. All of the complexities involved in linking symptoms to an index trauma obviously also bear on the task of specifying the chronology of the syndrome.

Evaluating Distress and Impairment

The fifth step is to establish that the symptoms cause clinically significant levels of subjective distress or functional impairment, as required by Criterion F. This is a crucial step because it helps determine whether the symptoms are sufficiently severe to warrant a diagnosis of a mental disorder or represent instead normative reactions to extreme stress. The degree of subjective distress typically becomes apparent in the process of evaluating the individual symptom criteria, but a thorough evaluation of functional impairment may necessitate additional

inquiry regarding the impact of the full syndrome on social and occupational functioning.

It is important to consider that currently Criterion F is disjunctive, requiring either distress or impairment, but not both. This means that according to *DSM-IV* individuals can be diagnosed with PTSD if they have clinically significant distress but still manage to work or carry out their daily routine and maintain most aspects of social functioning. This issue has been the focal point of controversy regarding the diagnostic threshold for PTSD and the distinction between pathological versus normative responses to trauma. In a recent reanalysis of the National Vietnam Veterans Readjustment Study (NVVRS), Dohrenwend et al. (2007) found that requiring more than a slight degree of functional impairment was one factor that contributed to a downward adjustment of estimated PTSD prevalence. In response, McNally (2007) argued that this requirement may have been too lenient and that if an appropriately stringent definition of impairment had been used it would have resulted in a substantially greater drop in PTSD prevalence.

In a research context it is informative to examine the impact of different diagnostic decision rules on PTSD prevalence, and from the NVVRS reanalysis it appears that requiring a significant degree of functional impairment would result in diagnosing many fewer individuals with PTSD. Again, however, according to the current diagnostic criteria functional impairment is not an independent criterion, and Criterion F can also be met by clinically significant distress. In a clinical context this issue may be moot because distress and impairment are typically highly correlated, such that individuals who report clinically significant distress also report at least moderate levels of functional impairment.

Establishing Differential Diagnosis

The last step is to establish differential diagnosis, i.e., determining that the symptoms are indicative of PTSD and not another disorder. At the syndromal level the differential diagnosis section of the *DSM-IV* PTSD text alerts clinicians to distinguish PTSD from adjustment disorder and acute stress disorder. A diagnosis of adjustment disorder is appropriate either when an individual is exposed to a stressor that satisfies Criterion A but the symptoms do not meet criteria for PTSD or other specific mental disorder, or when PTSD symptoms occur in response to a stressor that does not satisfy Criterion A. The latter distinction is a crucial one that maintains a stringent threshold of trauma severity for Criterion A and thereby helps reduce the problem of conceptual bracket creep. A diagnosis of acute stress disorder is readily distinguished from PTSD by the time frame involved, in that acute stress disorder is diagnosed only within the first month after the trauma, and the diagnosis is changed to PTSD if symptoms persist beyond a month.

Other differential diagnosis considerations are given for specific symptoms, including the distinction between recurrent intrusive thoughts in PTSD and obsessive-compulsive disorder, and between flashbacks in PTSD and perceptual disturbances in psychosis, delirium, and substance-induced disorders. Further, the *DSM-IV* text notes that avoidance, numbing, and arousal symptoms that are present prior to the trauma should not be counted toward a PTSD diagnosis, and that the symptoms consistent with disorders other than PTSD may be triggered by a traumatic stressor. In either case, other disorders should be considered.

Finally, the *DSM-IV* text states that malingering must be ruled out whenever financial gain or a forensic determination is at stake. Because it is a highly compensable disorder PTSD is particularly vulnerable to attempts at malingering, and a concerted effort must be made to ensure the veracity of self-reports of trauma exposure and PTSD symptoms (Guriel & Fremouw, 2003; Rosen & Taylor, 2007). Because of the widespread availability of information regarding the PTSD syndrome and the relative transparency of most self-report and interview measures of PTSD, it is relatively easy to malinger PTSD on standard clinical assessment tasks. Therefore, strategies designed specifically to detect malingering should be employed routinely in the assessment of PTSD, including (a) corroborating self-report through public records, medical records, and collateral reports; (b) administering multi-scale personality measures with well-validated response validity indicators; and (c) administering specialized assessment instruments designed specifically to assess malingering.

Conclusion

The introduction of PTSD in *DSM-III* was a landmark event in the field of traumatic stress. It provided the first official recognition of a characteristic trauma-related syndrome that could result from a wide variety of catastrophic stressors and have a potentially chronic course. The diagnostic criteria for PTSD have evolved considerably since *DSM-III*, and although they appear to have stabilized, further revisions will no doubt be necessary to incorporate new empirical findings. For example, one potentially influential area of research has to do with factor analytic investigations of the structure of the PTSD criteria. A growing number of confirmatory factor analyses have challenged the organization of the PTSD symptoms into three clusters. Currently, two rival four-factor models have gained support, one of which involves retaining the reexperiencing and hyperarousal clusters but separating effortful avoidance and emotional numbing symptoms into two distinct clusters, and the other of which involves organizing the PTSD symptoms into reexperiencing, avoidance, dysphoria, and hyperarousal clusters (Palmieri, Weathers, Difede, & King, 2007; Simms, Watson, & Doebbeling, 2002). Such investigations may result in revisions of the PTSD symptom structure.

In addition, revisions have been proposed to address some of the more salient criticisms of the PTSD construct. For example, Spitzer, First, and Wakefield (2007) offered several suggestions for improving the PTSD criteria for *DSM-V*. These consisted of tightening the definition of a trauma in Criterion A; increasing the specificity of PTSD symptoms by eliminating symptoms that overlap with the diagnostic criteria for other disorders; emphasizing the need for explicitly assessing and ruling out malingering; deleting acute stress disorder and creating a new V code for acute, nonpathological reactions to stress; and creating more specific guidelines for delayed onset. Although more work clearly remains to be done with respect to refining its diagnostic criteria, PTSD has proven to be an invaluable construct for conceptualizing the impact of psychological trauma and fostering research regarding the phenomenology, etiology, and effective treatment of pathological responses to extreme stress.

REFERENCES

American Psychiatric Association. (1952). *Diagnostic and statistical manual of mental disorders*. Washington, DC: Author.

American Psychiatric Association. (1968). *Diagnostic and statistical manual of mental disorders* (2nd ed.). Washington, DC: Author.

American Psychiatric Association. (1980). *Diagnostic and statistical manual of mental disorders* (3rd ed.). Washington, DC: Author.

American Psychiatric Association. (1987). *Diagnostic and statistical manual of mental disorders* (3rd ed., rev.). Washington, DC: Author.

American Psychiatric Association. (1994). *Diagnostic and statistical manual of mental disorders* (4th ed.). Washington, DC: Author.

Andreasen, N. C. (1980). Posttraumatic stress disorder. In H. I. Kaplan, A. M. Freedman, & B. J. Sadock (Eds.), *Comprehensive textbook of psychiatry* (pp. 458–467). New York: Williams & Wilkins.

Andreasen, N. C. (2004). Acute and delayed posttraumatic stress disorders: A history and some issues. *American Journal of Psychiatry, 161*, 1321–1323.

Bloom, S. L. (2000). Our hearts and hopes are turned to peace: Origins of the International Society for Traumatic Stress Studies. In A.Y. Shalev, R. Yehuda, & A. C. McFarlane (Eds.), *International Handbook of Human Response to Trauma* (pp. 27–50). New York: Springer.

Brett, E. A., Spitzer, R. L., & Williams, J. B. W. (1988). DSM-III-R criteria for posttraumatic stress disorder. *American Journal of Psychiatry, 145*, 1232–1236.

Dohrenwend, B. P., Turner, J. B., Turse, N. A., Adams, B. G., Koenen, K. C., & Marshall, R. (2007). Continuing controversy over the psychological risks for U.S. veterans. *Journal of Traumatic Stress, 20*, 449–465.

Guriel, J. L., & Fremouw, W. (2003). Assessing malingered posttraumatic stress disorder: A critical review. *Clinical Psychology Review, 23*, 881–904.

McNally, R. J. (2003). Progress and controversy in the study of posttraumatic stress disorder. *Annual Review of Psychology, 54*, 229–252.

McNally, R. J. (2007). Revisiting Dohrenwend et al.'s revisit of the National Vietnam Veterans Readjustment Study. *Journal of Traumatic Stress, 20*, 481–486.

Palmieri, P. A., Weathers, F. W., Difede, J., & King, D. W. (2007). Confirmatory factor analysis of the PTSD Checklist and the Clinician-Administered PTSD Scale in disaster workers exposed to the World Trade Center Ground Zero. *Journal of Abnormal Psychology, 116*, 329–341.

Rosen, G. M., & Taylor, S. F. (2007). Pseudo-PTSD. *Journal of Anxiety Disorders, 21*, 201–210.

Scott, W. J. (1990). PTSD in DSM-III: A case in the politics of diagnosis and disease. *Social Problems, 37*, 294–310.

Simms, L. J., Watson, D., & Doebbeling, B. N. (2002). Confirmatory factor analyses of posttraumatic stress symptoms in deployed and nondeployed veterans of the Gulf War. *Journal of Abnormal Psychology, 111*, 637–647.

Spitzer, R. L., First, M. B., & Wakefield, J. C. (2007). Saving PTSD from itself in DSM-V. *Journal of Anxiety Disorders, 21*, 233–241.

Weathers, F. W., & Keane, T. M. (1999). Psychological assessment of traumatized adults. In Philip A. Saigh & J. Douglas Bremner (Eds.) *Posttraumatic stress disorder: A comprehensive approach to research and treatment* (pp. 219–247). New York: Allyn & Bacon.

Weathers, F. W., & Keane, T. M. (2007). The Criterion A problem revisited: Controversies and challenges in defining and measuring psychological trauma. *Journal of Traumatic Stress, 20*, 107–121.

FRANK W. WEATHERS
Auburn University

TERENCE M. KEANE
National Center for Posttraumatic Stress Disorder

See also: Acute Stress Disorder; Assessment, Psychometric, Adult; Comorbidity; Diagnosis of Traumatic Stress Disorders (DSM & ICD); History of Psychological Trauma; Posttraumatic Stress Disorder; Stress Response Syndromes; Trauma, Definition; Traumatic Stress; Typology of Traumatic Stress Disorders

POSTTRAUMATIC STRESS DISORDER SYMPTOM SCALE

The Posttraumatic Stress Disorder (PTSD) Symptom Scale (PSS) is a 17-item PTSD measure, mapping onto *DSM-IV's* (American Psychiatric Association, 1994) 17 PTSD symptoms. It uses a four-point Likert scale and a symptom is considered present if its frequency level is least a "1" or greater, indicating that the symptom has occurred at least once in the past week. There are self-report and interview versions of this instrument.

The reliability of the PSS is considered adequate, with coefficient alpha reported at around 0.70. Large correlations have been reported between scores obtained on the PSS and the results of structured diagnostic interviews for assessing PTSD (e.g., Clinician Administered PTSD Scale; Foa & Tolin, 2000). The diagnostic efficiency of the PSS is estimated to be in the 90% range.

Foa and colleagues adapted the PSS into the Posttraumatic Diagnostic Scale (PDS), by adding the query of traumatic event exposure and additionally assessing PTSD's required 1-month duration and functional impairment (Norris & Hamblen, 2004). Thus, the PDS is preferred if the clinician or researcher is interested in obtaining more PTSD diagnostic information than that afforded by the PSS. Finally, the PSS has been modified to query not just symptom frequency but also symptom intensity, and the resulting Modified PTSD Symptom Scale has performed well psychometrically (Falsetti, Resnick, Resick, & Kilpatrick, 1993).

REFERENCES

American Psychiatric Association. (1994). *Diagnostic and statistical manual of mental disorders* (4th ed.). Washington, DC: Author.

Falsetti, S. A., Resnick, H. S., Resick, P. A., & Kilpatrick, D. G. (1993, June). The Modified PTSD Symptom Scale: A brief self-report measure of posttraumatic stress disorder. *Behavior Therapist, 16,* 161–162.

Foa, E. B., & Tolin, D. F. (2000). Comparison of the PTSD Symptom Scale: Interview Version and the Clinician-Administered PTSD Scale. *Journal of Traumatic Stress, 13*(2), 181–191.

Norris, F. H., & Hamblen, J. L. (2004). Standardized self-report measures of civilian trauma and PTSD. In J. P. Wilson & T. M. Keane (Eds.), *Assessing psychological trauma and PTSD* (2nd ed., pp. 63–102). New York: Guilford Press.

MARY E. LONG
Medical University of South Carolina

JON D. ELHAI
University of South Dakota

See also: Assessment, Psychometric, Adult

PRACTICE GUIDELINES

Clinical practice guidelines are defined as "systematically developed statements to assist practitioner and patient decisions about appropriate health care for specific clinical circumstances." (Field & Lohr, 1990, p. 50). Guidelines have been developed over the past 2 decades in recognition that health-care professionals vary significantly in how they assess and treat medical and psychiatric illnesses, in part, due to the lack of a strong consensus on best practices for managing specific conditions. The Agency for Health Care Policy and Research (AHCPR) was established in December 1989, charged with facilitating the development, review, and updating of clinically relevant guidelines based on the best available research and professional judgment regarding the effectiveness and appropriateness of services and procedures to assist health-care practitioners in the prevention, diagnosis, treatment, and quality assurance in the management of clinical conditions. AHCPR published and disseminated a number of clinical guidelines primarily on medical conditions. The first guideline on a psychiatric disorder was on major depression. It drew general support in the psychiatric and psychological communities but was criticized by psychologists as over relying on pharmacotherapy as the first line of treatment (Munoz, Hollon, McGrath, Rehm, & VandenBos, 1994).

In 1991, the American Psychiatric Association began the development of treatment guidelines on various diagnoses "primarily to assist psychiatrists in their care of patients." Each includes the following introductory statement: "This practice guideline is not intended to be construed or to serve as a standard of medical care. Standards of medical care are determined on the basis of all clinical data available for an individual case and are subject to change as scientific knowledge and technology advance and patterns evolve. These parameters of practice should be considered guidelines only" (American Psychiatric Association, 1995). In 1993, a task force of the Division of Clinical Psychology of the American Psychological Association proposed three categories of psychological treatments based on the level of scientific and clinical evidence supporting their efficacy: well-established treatments, probably efficacious treatments, and experimental treatments—the latter defined as treatments that have not yet been established as at least probably efficacious. In the publication, "Training in and Dissemination of Empirically-Validated Psychological Treatments: Report and Recommendations," 22 well-established treatments were identified for 21 different *Diagnostic and Statistical Manual of Mental Disorders* (*DSM-IV*; American Psychiatric Association, 1994). This document generated spirited discourse within professional psychology. In particular, clinicians expressed their concern that psychotherapy not be reduced to manualized, empirically supported techniques in a way that restricted their knowledge, independence, creativity, and clinical judgment.

These criticisms were buttressed by the proliferation of clinical guidelines being produced by government agencies and commercial organizations such as insurance companies and managed care entities, in addition to those promulgated by professional associations, each seemingly with a different purpose (e.g., government regulation, regulation of access to care, quality standards, "turf considerations" between organizations). Moreover, it became evident that even scientifically based practice guidelines had shortcomings. For example, in 1999, a review article of 279 clinical practice guidelines published in the *Journal of the American Medical Association* (*JAMA;* Shaneyfelt, Mayo-Smith, & Rothwangl, 1999) concluded that the majority did not meet established methodological standards and called for improvement in the identification, evaluation, and synthesis of the scientific literature on which they are based.

The aggregate of various concerns led to the empaneling of a Task Force by the American Psychological Association to develop a Template for Developing Guidelines. The Template required that treatment guidelines be constructed on the basis of two simultaneous dimensions, Treatment Efficacy (the demonstration of an effect in a scientifically controlled setting) and Clinical Utility (the generalization of that effect to a practice setting where control is not readily available) (American Psychological Association, 1995; Stricker et al., 1999). To date, and in contrast to the American Psychiatric Association's strategy (as well as that of the American Psychological Association's Division 12 task force) of developing diagnosis-based treatment guidelines, the American Psychological Association has published evidence-based treatment guidelines on broad-based clinical issues (e.g., custody evaluations; treatment of gay, lesbian, bisexual, and transgendered individuals; culturally sensitive and appropriate treatment; treatment of girls and women) that serve as a general foundation of practice recommendations.

Abrahamson and Saakvitne (2000) offered a critique of therapy guidelines from another perspective. They suggested that a variety of practice resources can be considered as treatment guidelines and that those based only on diagnostic categories are overly narrow in scope. They called for broadening and redefining what constitutes treatment guidelines, emphasizing that many treatments do not rely only on techniques but on a variety of other relational and specialized practice factors that impact the treatment's outcome. In keeping with their suggestions, clinicians treating anxiety and posttraumatic disorders benefit from using treatment guidelines for these conditions as a baseline of their practice and supplementing them with other available resources.

In the past decade, a number of guidelines for the treatment of posttraumatic stress disorder (PTSD) in adults have been produced. Each has made recommendations based on the evaluation of the quality of the aggregate and ever increasing research base and on expert clinical opinion. The initial treatment guideline specifically for PTSD was part of the Expert Consensus Guideline Series of the *Journal of Clinical Psychiatry,* Treatment of Posttraumatic Stress Disorder (Foa, Davidson, & Frances, 1999). Since then, a number of treatment guidelines have been published for PTSD and later for acute stress disorder (ASD) and PTSD, mostly for adults although two have been directed specifically toward the treatment of children, those by the American Academy of Child and Adolescent Psychiatry (AACP, 1998) and those by the International Society for the Study of Dissociation (2000, 2005) on the treatment of dissociative disorders in children and adolescents. A guideline for PTSD in primary care practice was published in the *Journal of the American Academy of Nurse Practitioners* (Miller, 2000). The International Society for the Study of Dissociation has published three sets of guidelines for the treatment of adults with dissociative disorders, most recently in 2005 (ISSD, 1984; 1997; 2005), and two recent sets of guidelines for assessment and treatment of children and adolescents with dissociative symptoms (ISSD, 2004, 2005).

Additional adult treatment guidelines for PTSD that have been published to date include what was regarded as the most definitive, those by the International Society for Traumatic Stress Studies (ISTSS) that were based on reviews assessing the strength of the available evidence for a range of psychological and psychiatric treatments for PTSD (Foa, Friedman, & Keane, 2000)—these guidelines

are currently under revision. Other PTSD treatment guidelines include those by the U.S. Department of Veterans Affairs, 2004; the Clinical Resource Efficiency Support Team (part of the Northern Ireland Health Service [CREST], 2003); the American Psychiatric Association (2004); the British National Institute for Clinical Excellence (for adults and children [NICE]; 2005); the Institute of Medicine of the National Academies of Science (IOM; 2006); and the Australian Center for Posttraumatic Mental Health at the University of Melbourne (ACPMH; 2007). The latter are likely the most comprehensive and definitive at present, having been based on an exhaustive review of available research and clinical writings.

All of these treatment guidelines have been developed based on the criteria for PTSD as available in the *Diagnostic and Statistical Manual of Mental Disorders* (American Psychiatric Association, 1980, 1994, 2000), criteria that do not, by and large, include the symptom constellations and criteria that have been found to be associated with more complex repeated and cumulative interpersonal and attachment-based psychological trauma (Herman, 1992; van der Kolk & Courtois, 2005). Guidelines for the treatment of complex traumatic stress conditions and disorders are under development (Courtois & Ford, in press; Courtois, Ford, & Cloitre, in press; Ford, Courtois, Steele, Van der Hart, & Nijenhuis, 2005).

At the present time, the available PTSD treatment guidelines support the following treatment modalies. The amount and quality of supporting evidence for each varies according to the method and its application and according to whether it is applied to children or to adults (however, modifications of the same techniques have generally been found to be effective when they are applied in age-relevant ways). Several approaches to cognitive behavior therapy have been empirically validated for the treatment of PTSD (*see:* **Cognitive Behavior Therapy, Adult; Cognitive Behavior Therapy, Child; Exposure Therapy, Adult; Exposure Therapy, Child**), principally: (a) exposure therapy (i.e., imaginal [memory recollection] or *in vivo* [confronting actual situations/events related to past psychological traumas]) desensitization (a graduated approach to increasingly trauma-relevant memories/stimuli) or flooding (prolonged immersion in trauma-relevant memories/situations); (b) cognitive restructuring (i.e., challenging generalized fear, anger, or blame focused thoughts or beliefs with specific empowering alternative thoughts or beliefs); (c) stress inoculation training (i.e., anxiety management training); and (d) eye movement desensitization and reprocessing (EMDR; i.e., the imaginal desensitization approach to exposure therapy applied with distracter tasks such as alternating eye movements, plus cognitive restructuring). Additionally, some medications have been empirically supported for treatment of PTSD (*see:* **Pharmacotherapy, Adult**), in particular, the Selective Serotonergic Reuptake Inhibitor (SSRI) class of antidepressants (and especially fluoxetine and paroxetine, two that have specific FDA approval as effective in treating symptoms associated with PTSD).

Some treatment guidelines recommend a combination of psychotherapy and medication immediately upon diagnosis, while others, such as the recently published Australian guidelines and the American Academy of Child and Adolescent Psychiatry guidelines for children recommend psychotherapy first with the addition of medication as needed (or medication if the traumatized individual refuses psychotherapy). It is also generally recommended that assessment precede treatment planning and that treatment be monitored and adjusted as required over its entire course. Although some treatments are quite short-term, it is generally understood that more intensive and extended treatment is required for more complex trauma and developmentally based responses (Ford et al., 2005).

All of the treatment guidelines published to date offer the clinician evidence-based information on best practices derived from the currently available literature and from clinical consensus; however, it should be recognized that PTSD and other traumatic stress conditions and disorders take many forms and involve a range of comorbid disorders and psychosocial problems that cannot be fully covered by any set of guidelines or any recommended treatment(s). Clinical innovation and scientific research on the treatment of disorders associated with psychological trauma also are constantly evolving. A number of hybrid or combination models have been developed and tested and these are constantly being updated (see Courtois & Ford, in press). Thus, it is recommended that formal guidelines and best practices documents be supplemented by consultation of additional treatment information available in professional texts and peer-reviewed publications.

REFERENCES

Abrahamson, D., & Saakvitne, K. W. (2000). Quality management in practice: Re-visioning practice guidelines to improve treatment of anxiety and traumatic stress disorders. In S. Stricker, W. Troy, & S. Shueman (Eds.), *Handbook of quality management in behavioral health* (pp. 217–236). New York: Plenum Press.

American Academy of Child and Adolescent Psychiatry. (1998). Practice parameters for the assessment and treatment of children and adolescents with posttraumatic stress disorders. *Journal of the American Academy of Child and Adolescent Psychiatry, 37*(10 suppl.), 4S–26S.

American Psychiatric Association. (1980). *Diagnostic and statistical manual of mental disorders* (3rd ed.). Washington, DC: Author.

American Psychiatric Association. (1994). *Diagnostic and statistical manual of mental disorders* (4th ed.). Washington, DC: Author.

American Psychiatric Association. (1995). *Practice guideline development process.* Washington, DC: Author.

American Psychiatric Association. (2000). *Diagnostic and statistical manual of mental disorders* (4th ed., text rev.). Washington, DC: Author.

American Psychiatric Association. (2004). *Practice guideline for the treatment of patients with acute stress disorder and posttraumatic stress disorder.* Washington, DC: Author.

American Psychological Association Division 12. (1993). *Report of the task force on promotion and dissemination of psychological procedures.* Washington, DC: Author.

American Psychological Association, Task Force on Psychological Intervention Guidelines. (1995). *Template for developing guidelines: Interventions for mental disorders and psychosocial aspects of physical disorders.* Washington, DC: Author.

Australian Center for Posttraumatic Mental Health. (2007). *Australian guidelines for the treatment of adults with acute stress disorder and posttraumatic stress disorder.* Melbourne, Australia: Author.

Clinical Resource Efficiency Support Team. (2003). *The management of post traumatic stress disorder in adults.* Belfast, Northern Ireland: Author.

Courtois, C. A., & Ford, J. D. (Eds.). (in press). *Complex traumatic stress disorders: An evidence-based clinician's guide.* New York: Guilford Press.

Courtois, C. A., Ford, J. D., & Cloitre, M. (in press). Best practices in the treatment of adults with complex traumatic stress disorders. In C. A. Courtois & J. D. Ford (Eds.), *Complex traumatic stress disorders: An evidence-based clinician's guide.* New York: Guilford Press.

Field, M., & Lohr, K. (Eds.). (1990). *Clinical practice guidelines.* Washington, DC: National Academy Press.

Foa, E. B., Davidson, J. R. T., & Frances, A. (1999). Treatment of posttraumatic stress disorder. *Journal of Clinical Psychiatry, 60*(Suppl. 16).

Foa, E. B., Friedman, M., & Keane, T. (2000). *Effective treatment for PTSD: Guidelines from the International Society of Traumatic Stress Studies.* New York: Guilford Press.

Ford, J. D., Courtois, C. A., Steele, K., Van der Hart, O., & Nijenhuis, E. R. S. (2005). Treatment of complex posttraumatic self-dysregulation. *Journal of Traumatic Stress, 18,* 437–447.

Herman, J. L. (1992). *Trauma and recovery.* New York: Basic Books.

Institute of Medicine of the National Academies. (2006). *Posttraumatic stress disorder: Diagnosis and assessment.* Washington, DC: Author.

International Society for the Study of Dissociation. (2000). Guidelines for the evaluation and treatment of dissociative symptoms in children and adolescents. *Journal of Trauma and Dissociation, 1*(1), 109–134.

International Society for the Study of Dissociation. (2004). Guidelines for the evaluation and treatment of dissociative symptoms in children and adolescents. *Journal of Trauma and Dissociation, 5*(3), 119–150.

International Society for the Study of Dissociation. (2005). Guidelines for treating dissociative identity disorder in adults. *Journal of Trauma and Dissociation, 6*(4), 69–149.

Miller, J. L. (2000). Post-traumatic stress disorder in primary care practice. *Journal of the American Academy of Nurse Practitioners, 12*(11), 475–482.

Munoz, R. F., Hollon, S. D., McGrath, E., Rehm, L. P., & VandenBos, G. R. (1994). On the AHCPR depression in primary care guidelines: Further considerations for practitioners. *American Psychologist, 49,* 41–61.

National Institute for Clinical Excellence. (2005). *Posttraumatic stress disorder (PTSD): The management of PTSD in adults and children in primary and secondary care.* London: Author.

Shaneyfelt, T. M., Mayo-Smith, M. F., & Rothwangl, J. (1999). Are guidelines following guidelines? The methodological quality of clinical practice guidelines in the peer-reviewed medical literature. *Journal of the American Medical Association, 281,* 1900–1905.

Stricker, G., Bologna, N. C., Robinson, E. A., Abrahamson, D. J., Hollon, S. D., & Reed, G. M. (1999). Treatment guidelines: The good, the bad, and the ugly. *Psychotherapy: Theory, Research, and Practice, 36,* 69–79.

U.S. Department of Veterans' Affairs. (2004). *Management of posttraumatic stress.* Washington, DC: Author.

van der Kolk, B. A., & Courtois, C. A. (2005). Editorial comments: Complex developmental trauma. *Journal of Traumatic Stress, 18,* 385–388.

CHRISTINE A. COURTOIS
Private Practice, Washington D.C.

See also: Diagnosis of Traumatic Stress Disorders (*DSM & ICD*); Evidence-Based Treatment; International Organizations; Posttraumatic Stress Disorder, Diagnosis of

PREVENTION, ADULT

There is accumulating evidence that posttraumatic stress disorder (PTSD) symptoms that continue unabated for a period of time after exposure to trauma may become entrenched and resistant to change (Litz, 2004). There are several potential explanations for this: individuals with treatment-resistant symptoms may have been exposed to particularly malicious, grotesque, or sustained trauma; they may have few natural personal and social recovery resources; treatment may not be available or there are various obstacles to care-seeking; they may not get the care they need, they may fail to benefit, or they may drop out prematurely; or too much time has passed before treatment. Regardless of the cause, there is no doubt that chronic PTSD can be pernicious and disabling across the life span and, consequently, it is critically important to develop programs that prevent PTSD from becoming a chronic condition.

Prevention efforts are classified as primary, secondary, and tertiary. Primary prevention efforts are aimed at preventing exposure to, or limiting the impact of, potentially traumatic events. Secondary prevention is designed to reduce the risk for developing PTSD following exposure to potentially traumatic events. Most individuals exposed to potentially traumatic events show distress and impairment very early on, yet recover fully, so secondary prevention interventions should not be provided too early and should only target those who are at the highest risk. Tertiary prevention strategies attempt to reduce the symptom burden and limit the degree of disability among people with chronic PTSD.

Primary Prevention Strategies

Given the unexpected nature of most traumatic events, there are few plausible or realistic means for primary prevention among the public at large. Primary prevention of PTSD has largely targeted high risk professions (e.g., the emergency services and the military), where exposure to potentially traumatic circumstances is an occupational hazard. However, even in these contexts, there can be reluctance to consider primary prevention programs for several reasons: (a) the belief that it is unnecessary (e.g., due to rigorous training and the assumed psychological hardiness and resilience of those who self-select dangerous professions);

(b) the tacit expectation that education about psychological trauma and its impact may encourage litigation or compensation-seeking; and (c) the belief that prevention programs may interfere with critical job training goals. For example, military organizations may view interventions that are designed to prevent soldiers from developing PTSD as an unnecessary or burdensome addition to their existing training procedures, and as encouraging soldiers to believe that they are likely to become psychological casualties and need treatment or disability compensation.

Notwithstanding institutional reluctance, nearly all dangerous occupations incorporate some form of primary prevention. The appeal of the potential upside to primary prevention is undeniable: the cost of training and deploying these personnel is high, and therefore any way of reducing the loss of these personnel as psychological casualties is valuable both economically and in terms of the morale and effectiveness of the organization. Further, there is a body of knowledge about the factors that lead to the development and maintenance of PTSD that can be used to develop interventions, despite the fact that there is little evidence of efficacy of such interventions (Litz, 2004). Most of the research on primary prevention in this arena has been done in the context of helping the military and medical professionals maintain performance in the face of stressful roles, rather than the prevention of mental health problems, per se. The emerging consensus is that primary prevention interventions should at the very least provide preparatory information about roles and accurate expectations about the impact of various adversities, stressors, and potential traumatic events.

Although the empirical literature is sparse, stress inoculation training (SIT; Meichenbaum, 1985), designed to expose individuals to tolerable yet demanding doses of stressors, may help reduce maladaptive responses to traumatic stress. Drawing from the transactional model of stress, the aim of SIT is to provide the individual with resources to ensure that environmental demands do not overwhelm perceived coping resources when the individual is exposed to a future stressful situation. In theory, the individual's resiliency is enhanced by helping them anticipate future demands and adaptive ways of construing stressful events and their reactions to them. Typically, SIT consists of three phases. First, psychoeducation on the nature and impact of stress is provided. Second, specific coping skills, such as relaxation training, problem solving, and cognitive restructuring, are acquired and practiced. Third, techniques such as role play, modeling, and graded *in vivo* (i.e., in daily life events) exposure to nontraumatic stressors that are reminders of past traumatic experiences, are employed to encourage the individual to apply the new coping skills across different intensities of stressors. Although well-designed as a primary prevention, to date, SIT has most often been used as a form of tertiary care for persons who already have PTSD.

Secondary Prevention Strategies

Interest in interventions provided in the acute aftermath of psychological trauma has accelerated greatly in the last decade. Although there are a number of equally valuable early intervention targets and goals (e.g., encouraging healthy coping and self-care, increasing social connectedness, preventing retraumatization), most secondary prevention posttraumatic interventions focus on preventing acute stress disorder (ASD) and chronic PTSD.

ASD is largely a form of early PTSD, that is, posttraumatic symptoms and impairment that occur in the initial month after a trauma. While most psychological trauma survivors who are immediately symptomatic will recover naturally in the months following the trauma, of those individuals who do not recover spontaneously, the overall incidence of ASD is approximately 13% (these rates vary according to trauma type; Bryant & Harvey, 2000). Approximately 80% of people with ASD later develop chronic PTSD. It should be noted that the ASD diagnosis is controversial; however, it is widely used as an indicator that preventive intervention is needed in both clinical and research contexts.

Secondary prevention strategies may be divided into those strategies that are designed for all psychological trauma survivors, and those that target trauma survivors who exhibit greater symptoms of distress and who are consequently at heightened risk of developing PTSD.

Secondary Prevention Strategies for All Trauma Survivors

Psychological Debriefing   Psychological debriefing techniques such as Mitchell's critical incident stress debriefing (CISD) and critical incident stress management (CISM; Everly & Mitchell, 2004; *see:* **Critical Incident Stress Management**) are delivered within hours or days of the trauma and aim to mitigate distress and prevent the emergence of PTSD. Despite the fact that participants tend to describe debriefing as helpful, there is growing consensus that psychological debriefing does not prevent subsequent psychopathology. For example, a meta-analysis of randomized controlled trials of psychological debriefing concluded that there is no evidence that debriefing is useful for preventing PTSD (see McNally, Bryant, & Ehlers, 2003). Although there is limited research evidence supporting its continued use, debriefing continues to be routinely used throughout the world. Neither the U.K.'s National Institute for Clinical Excellence nor the American Psychiatric Association practice guidelines recommend the use of psychological debriefing or single-session techniques, noting that these appear to be largely ineffective in treating individuals with ASD and in preventing PTSD.

Psychological First Aid   The term *psychological first aid* dates back to World War II and has been used to describe a variety of conceptually similar techniques for helping people to cope with acutely stressful situations. A central intention of this approach is to provide innocuous yet beneficial assistance that does not require the involvement of mental health professionals. More recently, psychological first aid (PFA) has been developed into a formally defined and widely disseminated alternative to CISM and other forms of psychological debriefing. PFA is a conversational approach designed to help individuals or groups to reduce excessive, uncontrollable distress, correct negative or unhelpful appraisals, facilitate social connectedness, provide pragmatic resources and information, and help survivors set a plan in motion to recoup resources and recover from the trauma. PFA is an evidence-informed supportive mental health intervention based on consensus recommendations (Ruzek et al., 2007). It is the recommended first-line psychosocial intervention in the wake of mass disaster and terrorism and differs from debriefing in that traumatic events are not reviewed but instead immediate emotional, practical, and informational support is emphasized. PFA is intended to be flexibly delivered to children or adults by any type of care provider. Although PFA is recommended by many experts and organizations, no scientific research studies have been conducted to test its effectiveness to date.

Secondary Prevention for Symptomatic Psychological Trauma Survivors

Although the interventions discussed previously may be broadly applicable to all survivors of psychologically traumatic events and may be delivered by nonprofessionals, more formalized and demanding interventions have been developed for uniquely vulnerable trauma survivors. For example, individuals with early posttraumatic depression and severe hyperarousal, or individuals or groups exposed to psychological trauma that involve human maliciousness, are good candidates for formal professional care. These secondary prevention interventions are more resource-intensive and are less widely available, and are designed to intensively target the trauma survivors who are at highest risk for severe and persistent future problems such as PTSD. Those persons represent a minority of trauma survivors. Targeted secondary prevention interventions require careful assessment to determine appropriateness for each individual recipient.

Cognitive Behavior Therapy Psychological treatments for ASD were mainly adapted from cognitive behavioral therapy (CBT) tertiary care programs. CBT is a brief action-oriented and individualized intervention that is administered collaboratively with a specially trained professional. CBT for ASD usually begins within 4 weeks of the traumatic incident(s). As suggested, if the intervention is provided too early, it is likely that "the net will be cast too widely"—that is, many persons will be provided CBT who do not need this scarce form of expert care. In addition, there is a risk that, if provided too early, the traumatized individual may be preoccupied with addressing other pressing needs such as recovering from injuries, financial difficulties, the loss of home or relationships, and therefore may be unable to successfully engage in and utilize the treatment and its required activities (such as homework).

CBT for recently traumatized individuals varies in the number and length of sessions, but typically includes roughly five 60- to 90-minute sessions. CBT includes psychoeducation on common reactions to traumatic events; anxiety management (e.g., diaphragmatic breathing and progressive muscle relaxation); cognitive restructuring (that provides experiential opportunities for patients to monitor, critically examine, and change the way they think about various trauma-related challenges and to modify beliefs about the meaning and implication of the psychological trauma[s]); imaginal and *in vivo* exposure therapy; and relapse prevention strategies (i.e., education and activities designed to help clients to continue to use and benefit from the skills and knowledge they have gained in the therapy).

The rationale for engaging in exposure therapy soon after a traumatic stressor has occurred is that posttraumatic symptoms may become chronic if the individual does not adequately recall, describe, and emotionally accept the traumatic experience(s). The aim is to allow for the full and sustained activation of traumatic memories so that they can be altered in a therapeutic manner. The person is asked to relive the trauma vividly, in imagination, to counteract avoidance strategies, which help to maintain ASD symptoms. In addition to countering avoidance of trauma-related experiences and allowing for fear habituation/extinction, exposure helps patients to learn that they are able to tolerate and survive focusing on the painful elements of their traumatic experience. Accordingly, trauma memories are discussed in as rich and salient a way as possible: sensations, thoughts, beliefs, and especially feelings that were present during the trauma are repeatedly recalled and disclosed. Cognitive restructuring techniques such as Socratic questioning may also be employed in tandem to help the person to modify unhelpful trauma-related beliefs. Individuals may also be asked to write down a narrative account of the traumatic event, which can be read aloud as homework.

Although fewer studies have been conducted on the efficacy of early intervention strategies for trauma than on interventions for more chronic forms of PTSD, several controlled trials have found CBT to be significantly more effective than supportive counseling (SC) in the treatment of ASD. For example, Bryant and colleagues compared five 90-minute weekly individual sessions of CBT to the same amount of SC in a randomized clinical trial (Bryant, Harvey, & Dang, 1998). Significantly fewer participants receiving CBT (8%) than SC (83%) met criteria for PTSD at post-treatment. This pattern was maintained at 6-month follow-up: 17% of CBT patients met criteria for PTSD compared to 67% of SC patients. Moreover, there were greater clinically and statistically significant reductions in avoidance and intrusive and depressive symptomatology among the CBT participants than among the SC participants.

Comparably favorable results were found by Ehlers and colleagues, who targeted motor vehicle accident survivors approximately 4 months after their accident, comparing 12 sessions and 3 monthly booster sessions of cognitive therapy with repeated assessment (no treatment), and a self-help booklet based on cognitive-behavioral principles (Ehlers, Clark, & Hackmann, 2003). Symptoms of PTSD were assessed via self-report and by independent evaluators at 3- and 9-month follow-up. Cognitive therapy was found to be significantly more effective in reducing symptoms than the self-help booklet or repeated assessments: 11% of CBT participants met criteria for PTSD at follow-up, compared to 61% of the self-help participants.

The effectiveness of CBT in the acute aftermath of psychological trauma appears to vary according to the type of trauma survivor treated. Whereas relatively robust effects are found for CBT among survivors of discrete traumas such as motor vehicle accidents, efficacy data are weaker for traumas involving victimization and interpersonal violence, such as sexual assault. For example, in a recent study, Foa and colleagues provided CBT to female sexual and physical assault survivors within 1 month of the assault (Foa, Zoellner, & Feeny, 2006). CBT did not confer any lasting advantage relative to SC or a monitoring-only condition. It may be that because motor vehicle and industrial accidents are typically circumscribed, CBT is well-equipped to address anxiety and functioning in those contexts, whereas trials that include assault survivors may have less positive results because adaptation to interpersonal violence, especially sexual violence, is more complicated and multifaceted.

In line with these findings, practice guidelines from the U.K. National Institute for Clinical Excellence, the International Society for Traumatic Stress Studies, the American Psychological Association, and the American Psychiatric Association all recommend CBT as the prescriptive secondary prevention intervention for victims of psychological trauma.

Not all treatments for chronic PTSD have been tested in the more acute period soon after the occurrence of psychological trauma. For example, eye movement desensitization and reprocessing (EMDR) has shown some efficacy in treating PTSD, but no clinical trials are available on its use as an early intervention.

Psychopharmacological Interventions

Pharmacological prevention of PTSD has received increasing attention in recent years. In particular, administering propranolol, a beta-adrenergic blocker, in the immediate aftermath of a traumatic event may reduce subsequent PTSD symptoms. In a pilot study, Pitman and colleagues (Pitman, Sanders, & Zusman, 2002) administered a 10-day course of propranolol within an average of 4 hours after participants reported to a hospital emergency room following traumatic events. One month posttrauma, propranolol subjects, as compared to subjects given a placebo, evidenced fewer PTSD symptoms, and also exhibited significantly less physiological reactivity to script-driven trauma images 3 months after the event. However, such studies are still in the experimental phase, and a recent study found that neither propranolol nor an anticonvulsant/mood stabilizer medication (gabapentin), when administered within 48 hours of injury to patients admitted to a medical-surgical trauma center, showed significant benefit compared to a placebo (inactive) medication in reducing posttraumatic stress or depression symptoms 1, 4, or 8 months later (Stein, Kerridge, Dimsdale, & Hoyt, 2007). The American Psychiatric Association has concluded that no specific psychopharmacological agents can be recommended as preventing the developing of ASD or PTSD at this time.

Conclusion

While most individuals exposed to trauma will recover on their own, a salient and often silent minority will go on to develop chronic PTSD. There is some evidence that those exhibiting more distress in the immediate days and weeks following exposure may be at heightened risk for the development of more chronic difficulties, although definitive, accurate, and reliable ways of identifying those trauma survivors least likely to recover on their own remain elusive at this time. Given the heavy lifelong burden associated with PTSD, the importance of developing strategies for primary and secondary prevention has been increasingly recognized. Current strategies focus on prevention at the secondary level (after exposure to trauma) and differ in the amount of empirical support they have received; while both psychological debriefing strategies and CBT have been investigated for their efficacy, only the latter has consistently shown favorable results. Additional promising strategies, like pharmacological treatment, are still in the early phases of testing.

REFERENCES

Bryant, R. A., & Harvey, A. G. (2000). *Acute stress disorder: A handbook of theory, assessment, and treatment.* Washington, DC: American Psychological Association.

Bryant, R. A., Harvey, A. G., & Dang, S. T. (1998). Treatment of acute stress disorder: A comparison of cognitive-behavioral therapy and supportive counseling. *Journal of Consulting and Clinical Psychology, 66,* 862–866.

Ehlers, A., Clark, D. M., & Hackmann, A. (2003). A randomized controlled trial of cognitive therapy, a self-help booklet, and repeated assessments as early interventions for posttraumatic stress disorder. *Archives of General Psychiatry, 60,* 1024–1032.

Everly, G. S., & Mitchell, J. T. (2004). *A primer on critical incident stress management (CISM).* Retrieved September 20, 2007, from International Critical Incident Stress Foundation web site: www.icisf.org/about/cismprimer.cfm.

Foa, E. B., Zoellner, L. A., & Feeny, N. C. (2006). An evaluation of three brief programs for facilitating recovery after assault. *Journal of Traumatic Stress, 19,* 29–43.

Litz, B. T. (Ed.). (2004). *Early intervention for trauma and traumatic loss.* New York: Guilford Press.

McNally, R. J., Bryant, R. A., & Ehlers, A. (2003). Does early psychological intervention promote recovery from posttraumatic stress? *Psychological Science in the Public Interest, 4,* 45–79.

Meichenbaum, D. H. (1985). *Stress inoculation training.* New York: Paradigm.

Pitman, R. K., Sanders, K. M., & Zusman, R. M. (2002). Pilot study of secondary prevention of posttraumatic stress disorder with propranolol. *Biological Psychiatry, 51,* 189–192.

Ruzek, J. I., Brymer, M. J., Jacobs, A. K., Layne, C. M., Vernberg, E. M., & Watson, P. J. (2007). Psychological first aid. *Journal of Mental Health Counseling, 29*(1), 17–49.

Stein, M. B., Kerridge, C., Dimsdale, J. F., & Hoyt, D. B. (2007). Pharmacotherapy to prevent PTSD: Results from a randomized controlled proof-of-concept trial in physically injured patients. *Journal of Traumatic Stress, 20*, 923–932.

MARIA STEENKAMP
Boston University

ANTHONY PAPA
National Center for Posttraumatic Stress Disorder

BRETT LITZ
National Center for Posttraumatic Stress Disorder

See also: Acute Stress Disorder; Anxiety Management Training; Cognitive Behavior Therapy, Adult; Critical Incident Stress Management; Early Intervention; International Organizations; Pharmacotherapy, Adult; Prevention, Child; Psychoeducation; Psychological First Aid, Adult; Rape Trauma

PREVENTION, CHILD

Prevention of posttraumatic stress in children and adolescents encompasses both (a) primary prevention—efforts to prevent or to reduce the frequency of events that can be traumatic for children, and (b) secondary prevention—efforts to reduce the adverse effects, particularly traumatic stress responses, for children and families when an event does occur. Primary prevention often includes education, advocacy, or public policy efforts undertaken in collaboration with experts from other disciplines and sometimes in conjunction with trauma survivors and their families. Examples of primary prevention of child trauma exposure include sexual abuse/assault prevention efforts with school-age children, injury prevention efforts for children or adolescents (e.g., drowning prevention, teen driver safety), and parenting programs aimed at preventing child abuse.

While primary prevention of potentially traumatic events is ideal, it will never be possible to completely eliminate the occurrence of such events in the lives of children and teens. The chief prevention focus of traumatic stress specialists has thus been on the secondary prevention of the adverse effects of experiencing psychological trauma, and the promotion of adaptive responses after trauma exposure has occurred. Secondary prevention of traumatic stress is most often employed in response to specific traumatic events (such as a disaster, a specific exposure to violence, unexpected death of a family member or friend, or a frightening injury) rather than to extended or complex traumatic exposures (such as child abuse or witnessing ongoing family violence). Treatment approaches have been developed for children who are experiencing traumatic stress problems following complex traumatic exposures (*see:* **Cognitive Behavior Therapy, Child; Family Therapy; Psychodynamic Therapy, Child**).

The design and implementation of effective secondary prevention efforts requires careful consideration of logistical and clinical issues such as: Which children and adolescents can benefit from secondary prevention?, Is there anyone who might be harmed by secondary prevention efforts?, When should secondary prevention efforts be initiated and carried out?, Where can such interventions be delivered, and by whom?, What is the optimal delivery format and focus of secondary prevention efforts for trauma-exposed children or adolescents? Current evidence and best practices with regard to each of these issues are summarized here.

Who Can Benefit from Secondary Prevention Efforts?

Long-term distress, impairment, and costs can be substantial for children diagnosed with posttraumatic stress disorder (PTSD). Therefore, it might appear to be prudent to intervene with all children and adolescents exposed to traumatic events in order to prevent the development of PTSD. However, the empirical literature sounds a note of caution regarding universal preventive interventions administered soon after trauma exposure.

Several systematic empirical reviews (National Institute for Clinical Excellence, 2005; Rose, Bisson, Churchill, & Wessely, 2002), mostly concerning interventions with adults, have found that early "debriefing" interventions, applied universally to trauma-exposed individuals (i.e., without regard to degree of distress or risk factors) are ineffective in reducing the psychological sequelae of trauma. Evidence in this regard is more limited for children and adolescents. A recent randomized trial that examined a universal debriefing intervention for injured children was consistent with the bulk of the adult literature in finding no effect, neither benefit nor harm, from a single debriefing session (Stallard et al., 2006).

Instead of universal one-size-fits-all early intervention to prevent later PTSD symptoms, best practice recommendations call for empirically sound screening to identify, among children exposed to psychological trauma, the smaller high-risk group who could benefit from further monitoring or preventive interventions (National Institute for Clinical Excellence, 2005; Rose et al., 2004). This approach has been termed "watchful waiting" or "screen and treat." The approach is consistent with public health prevention models that advise matching the level and type of intervention to the individual's level of need. In such models, interventions are defined as universal (appropriate for all exposed individuals), targeted (appropriate for those with a known increased risk), or indicated (appropriate for those with immediate clinical needs). Most children who are exposed to traumatic events do *not* develop severe lasting psychosocial problems. Therefore, screening as soon as possible after traumatic events is the best practice, in order to identify and provide prevention services to children who are likely to develop posttraumatic problems (i.e., targeted prevention) or who already have serious psychosocial problems (i.e., indicated prevention).

Development of Screening Methods

Screening during the acute aftermath of trauma exposure, to identify a child's risk for future mental health sequelae, presents many challenges. These include practical challenges such as time limitations for the service settings and professionals who may be implementing screening in the midst of other duties, and clinical challenges such as the difficulty of differentiating normative distress reactions from those that presage ongoing distress or impairment. A small but growing empirical literature has prospectively followed children and adolescents exposed to single incident traumatic events, beginning soon after the event, to track the course of traumatic stress reactions and to identify potential early predictors of later PTSD symptoms and impairment. These studies suggest that acute stress reactions help to predict later PTSD, although the full acute stress disorder (ASD) diagnosis does not appear to be an optimal categorical predictor of child PTSD outcome.

There is a clear need to identify evidence-based early markers of risk for mental health problems after trauma exposure, and to translate these into screening methods that can be feasibly implemented in the first days or weeks after a child is exposed to a potentially traumatic event. The metrics by which screening instruments are judged include sensitivity and specificity. In the case of screening to identify children who are likely to later develop PTSD, it is important to maximize sensitivity (the proportion of later PTSD cases that the screening tool correctly identified as "at risk"), while preserving moderate specificity (the proportion of children who will not develop PTSD who are correctly identified as "not at risk"). In the context of secondary prevention, screening is concerned with predicting a child's risk of future or persistent traumatic stress. When examining potential screening tools, it is important to make a distinction between this predictive screening and other purposes for screening—for example, screening for the presence of current psychological distress or PTSD.

Empirical work on predictive screener development has begun in the area of pediatric injury. This work provides an illustration of two overlapping and complementary approaches to screening: (1) focusing on early traumatic stress reactions as predictors of long-term distress and (2) identifying risk indicators from a range of domains, including but not limited to traumatic stress reactions. The Child Trauma Screening Questionnaire (CTSQ; Kenardy, Spence, & Macleod, 2006) is an example of the first approach. This 10-item measure assesses reexperiencing symptoms (5 items) and hyperarousal symptoms (5 items). The CTSQ has demonstrated excellent sensitivity and good specificity in predicting child PTSD symptoms and impairment 6 months post-injury. The Screening Tool for Early Predictors of PTSD (STEPP; Winston, Kassam-Adams, Garcia-España, Ittenbach, & Cnaan, 2003) exemplifies the approach of looking beyond acute stress reactions for other types of risk predictors. This 12-item measure assesses risk indicators for injured children and their parents. The eight items predicting child PTSD risk include prior behavioral problems, separation from parents at the time of the injury, fear and believing death might occur at the time of the trauma, injury or death of others in the same event, child gender (female), presence of an extremity fracture (such as a fractured arm or leg), and high heart rate (assessed in the emergency department). The STEPP has demonstrated excellent sensitivity and moderate specificity in predicting PTSD symptoms and impairment in injured children. Both the CTSQ and the STEPP are promising brief measures that are feasible for implementation in acute health-care settings where injured children are treated, and that are acceptable to children and parents. Further research is needed to establish optimal content and timing for risk screening for injured children, and to develop and evaluate risk screening measures for children and teens exposed to other types of trauma.

What Is the Optimal Format and Focus of Secondary Prevention Efforts?

Most PTSD prevention interventions for children are targeted to children who are at risk or are delivered on an indicated basis to children who are debilitated soon after a traumatic event. Information and education about normative reactions (i.e., typical stress reactions that are expected and are not a cause for concern), signs of traumatic stress that require further evaluation or treatment, and ways that affected children and adults can adjust effectively by adaptively coping after a traumatic event, may be provided universally to trauma-exposed children or adolescents (or their parents, teachers, or other family and community members). This educational information also can be useful for children and adults who are targeted as at risk or identified as having immediate clinical needs based on the results of screening.

When risk factors or problematic early reactions or coping strategies are identified (via screening or ongoing monitoring), targeted preventive interventions may then be implemented to address these factors. A "stepped care" approach is one way to carry out this prevention model. For example, a stepped preventive care model for injured children and teens (now being evaluated) begins with screening for PTSD risk or current distress while the child is still in the hospital, provides follow-up assessment or monitoring over a period of 2 to 6 weeks for those at higher risk, and implements greater levels of care as needed based on these ongoing brief assessments.

When early traumatic stress symptoms cause significant distress or impede the child's use of natural social supports, clinically indicated treatment to ameliorate these symptoms can also serve as secondary prevention of long-lasting distress. This is an area in which crisis intervention overlaps with PTSD prevention (*see:* **Crisis Intervention, Child; Psychological First Aid, Child and Adolescent**). Although cognitive behavioral treatment of adults with acute stress disorder has shown promise in preventing or reducing the development of persistent PTSD, the effectiveness of early treatment for traumatic stress symptoms has not been adequately researched in children and adolescents. Best practice guidelines suggest offering a course of trauma-focused cognitive behavioral treatment to children or adolescents who demonstrate severe traumatic stress symptoms within the first month after a potentially traumatic event (National Institute for Clinical Excellence, 2005).

Informational, self-help, and parent-driven interventions have also been suggested as prevention approaches for traumatized children and families. Informational materials can educate children and parents about normative early reactions and suggest adaptive coping strategies. Well-designed informational materials targeting distress and coping for trauma-exposed children and their parents are rated as helpful by the recipients. It is not yet clear, however, whether such materials actually prevent the development of PTSD. Compelling video presentations of educational information and suggestions for coping with specific reactions such as hyperarousal or new fears have shown promise in reducing later traumatic stress symptoms in adolescent and adult sexual assault survivors (Resnick, Acierno, Holmes, Kilpatrick, & Jager, 1999). In one controlled trial, print informational materials provided after child injury reduced later PTSD symptoms in parents, but had no effect on child PTSD or depression (Kenardy, in press). However, even in the absence of demonstrable symptom reduction, there may be value in the universal provision of information on emotional recovery after trauma exposure: it can provide traumatized young people (and their parents, and other children and adults) with a way to know what to expect and when and how to get help.

The Internet is playing an increasing role in delivering information and psychoeducation after trauma. This is a promising delivery model for secondary preventive interventions for older children, adolescents, and their parents. Web-based resources can incorporate interactive features tailored to the user, can be broadly disseminated in a cost-effective manner, and can be instantly available and provide timely access to information for trauma-exposed children and families. However, like all preventive interventions, web-based interventions will require empirical evaluation of their effectiveness.

When and Where Can Secondary Prevention Efforts Be Implemented?

Potentially traumatic events vary in their frequency of occurrence and in the number of children impacted at any one time or the number impacted across the population as a whole. Each type of event can pose different logistical challenges for screening and secondary prevention efforts. High impact (and high profile) events do not occur every day but can affect large numbers of children or adolescents simultaneously (e.g., natural or man-made disasters, mass violence or terrorism). In contrast, there are many lower profile potentially traumatic events that affect children, adolescents, or families one at a time, out of the public eye, but with such frequency across the general population that the number of children exposed is quite high (e.g., traffic crashes, pediatric injuries, children witnessing violence on the street or in their homes).

There are enormous challenges involved in reaching trauma-exposed children in order to provide risk screening or universal preventive interventions. It makes sense to embed secondary prevention efforts in settings and service systems that already come into contact with children and adolescents soon after traumatic events, that is, during acute medical care (Stuber, Schneider, Kassam-Adams, Kazak, & Saxe, 2006), during police response to family or community violence (Marans, Murphy, & Berkowitz, 2002), and during organized disaster response efforts (National Child Traumatic Stress Network & National Center for PTSD, 2006). Weeks or even months later, screening and monitoring may still be best able to reach children at risk when these activities occur outside traditional mental health service settings. For example, schools and primary care medical settings are well-situated to screen and monitor children exposed to potentially traumatic events (e.g., in New York City after the September 11, 2001, terrorism incidents; in schools in which fatal shootings have occurred), and it may be feasible to set up systems within these settings to identify children at risk for PTSD and initiate appropriate follow-up.

A largely unexplored avenue for systematic secondary prevention efforts is the role of public information or outreach campaigns to prepare parents and caretakers to provide optimal support and coping assistance to their child or teen should a traumatic event occur. Efforts to embed sophisticated parent guidance messages and tips in broadly available formats and popular media have been evaluated in the area of child behavior problems (Sanders, Dadds, & Turner, 2003) and may provide an example for such efforts with regard to preparing parents to assist their children if they are exposed to traumatic events.

Who Can Implement Secondary Prevention Efforts for Trauma-Exposed Children?

Parents and other family members are the single most important resource for a child's or an adolescent's optimal emotional recovery after a traumatic event. Research evidence clearly links parent responses to child outcomes after trauma, and social support is key for both children and adults during the aftermath of trauma. Developmental considerations are also important—parents and caretakers make a difference at every age, but their involvement is essential for the youngest children.

Mental health professionals have a unique role in secondary prevention of PTSD in that they have the training to address severe early traumatic stress symptoms in trauma-exposed children. Professionals other than mental health providers play equally important roles and are more likely to be available close to the time or place where children experience a potentially traumatic event. Training is essential for frontline providers who are involved in screening and providing immediate support for trauma-exposed children. For example, it can be important to overcome misconceptions and to help such providers move beyond common-sense markers of risk (e.g., the objective severity of the event or of a child's injury) that actually are not useful predictors of psychological outcomes such as PTSD.

Health-care providers are involved with children and teens during and immediately after potentially traumatic medical events. Some useful interventions are already part of health-care practice, though they may not have been framed as "PTSD prevention." Actions that reduce the potential for ongoing traumatic stress can also help meet other goals that are valued within the health-care system, for example, optimizing pain management as required by hospital accreditation organizations, or providing family centered care. The Pediatric Medical Traumatic Stress Toolkit provides resources for health-care professionals on providing trauma-informed care for ill and injured children (Stuber et al., 2006).

Police officers, firefighters, and other first responders are on the front lines when children are exposed to potentially traumatic events. These professionals can play an important role in responding to children in ways that promote immediate safety and adaptive coping and can help to prevent long-term traumatic stress. Collaborative efforts such as the Child Development Community Policing (CDCP) model have been successful in bringing law enforcement and mental health providers together to better serve children exposed to violence in their home or community (Marans et al., 2002; National Child Traumatic Stress Network, 2006).

Conclusion

The cutting edge of current research and practice in secondary prevention of child and adolescent PTSD is systematic examination of which interventions work, for whom, during which time period posttrauma, and in which service delivery context(s). Promising models for information provision, screening and stepped care have been developed. Key research questions include the identification of efficacious interventions and the development of practical and effective models for implementation in a wide range of systems that serve children, adolescents, and families.

REFERENCES

Kenardy, J., Spence, S., & Macleod, A. (2006). Screening for posttraumatic stress disorder in children after accidental injury. *Pediatrics, 118,* 1002–1009.

Kenardy, J., Thompson, K., LeBrocque, R., & Olsson, K. (in press). Information provision intervention for children and their parents following pediatric accidental injury. *European Child and Adolescent Psychiatry.*

Marans, S., Murphy, R., & Berkowitz, S. (2002). Police-mental health responses to children exposed to violence: The Child Development-Community Policing Program. In M. Lewis (Ed.), *Child and adolescent psychiatry: A comprehensive textbook* (3rd ed., pp. 1406–1416). Baltimore: Lippincott, Williams, & Wilkins.

National Child Traumatic Stress Network. (2006). *Cops, kids, and domestic violence: Protecting our future.* Retrieved www.nctsn.org/nctsn_assets/acp/dv/NCTSN_DV_rev1.htm. Retrieved November 5, 2007.

National Child Traumatic Stress Network and National Center for PTSD. (2006, July). *Psychological first aid: Field operations guide* (2nd ed.). Available from www.nctsn.org and www.ncptsd.va.gov.

National Institute for Clinical Excellence. (2005). *Post-traumatic stress disorder (PTSD): The management of PTSD in adults and children in primary and secondary care.* London: Royal College of Psychiatrists.

Resnick, H., Acierno, R., Holmes, M., Kilpatrick, D. G., & Jager, N. (1999). Prevention of post-rape psychopathology: Preliminary findings of a controlled acute rape treatment study. *Journal of Anxiety Disorders, 13*(4), 359–370.

Rose, S., Bisson, J., Churchill, R., & Wessely, S. (2004). Psychological debriefing for preventing posttraumatic stress disorder (PTSD; Cochrane review). *Cochrane Library* (Vol. 3). Chichester, West Sussex, England: Wiley.

Sanders, M., Dadds, C., & Turner, K. (2003). *Theoretical, scientific and clinical foundations of the Triple P Positive Parenting Program: A population approach to the promotion of parenting competence.* Brisbane, Australia: University of Queensland, Parenting and Family Support Centre.

Stallard, P., Velleman, R., Salter, E., Howse, I., Yule, W., & Taylor, G. (2006). A randomised controlled trial to determine the effectiveness of an early psychological intervention with children involved in road traffic accidents. *Journal*

of Child Psychology and Psychiatry, 47(2), 127–134.

Stuber, M., Schneider, S., Kassam-Adams, N., Kazak, A., & Saxe, G. (2006). The medical traumatic stress toolkit. *CNS Spectrums, 11,* 137–142.

Winston, F., Kassam-Adams, N., Garcia-España, J. F., Ittenbach, R., & Cnaan, A. (2003). Screening for risk of persistent posttraumatic stress in injured children and their parents. *Journal of the American Medical Association, 290,* 643–649.

NANCY KASSAM-ADAMS
Children's Hospital of Philadelphia

See also: Acute Stress Disorder; Anxiety Management Training; Assessment, Psychometric, Child; Cognitive Behavior Therapy, Child; Critical Incident Stress Management; Early Intervention; Family Therapy; Parent-Child Intervention; Pharmacotherapy, Child; Prevention, Adult; Psychodynamic Therapy, Child; Psychoeducation; Psychological First Aid, Child and Adolescent

PRIMARY CARE

There are at least three reasons why it is important to address posttraumatic stress disorder (PTSD) in primary care medicine. First, it is estimated that 8% to 12% of primary care patients will meet diagnostic criteria for PTSD (Kroenke, Spitzer, Williams, Monahan, & Lowe, 2007; Magruder et al., 2005). This rate is slightly higher than the 7% lifetime prevalence of PTSD in the general population (Kessler et al., 2005; National Comorbidity Survey Replication) and similar to the prevalence of major depression in primary care (Sartorius, Ustun, Lecrubier, & Wittchen, 1996). The increased rate of PTSD in primary care may be due to the robust relationship between medical health problems and PTSD (Schnurr & Green, 2004).

Second, there is a growing literature showing a direct relationship between psychological trauma exposure and increased health-care utilization, morbidity, and self-reported health complaints (Schnurr, Green, & Kaltman, 2007). This relationship appears to be mediated by the diagnosis of PTSD (Schnurr et al., 2007). That is, people who are exposed to psychological trauma are likely to have worse physical health problems than people who have not experienced psychological trauma, but those trauma survivors who develop PTSD have the greatest risk and severity of physical health problems. With over 50% of the population being exposed to at least one psychologically traumatic event (Kessler, Sonnega, Bromet, Hughes, & Nelson, 1995), screening efforts may need to focus on detecting PTSD rather than trauma exposure per se, because it is neither feasible nor necessarily desirable to provide specialized treatment simply because a person has experienced psychological trauma. When the patient is impaired by PTSD, specialized treatment is warranted, and primary care providers can help patients with PTSD to obtain that specialized treatment by providing education and referrals.

Third, up to 50% of primary care patients with PTSD are not receiving any mental health treatment (Magruder et al., 2005). Similar to other mental disorders, primary care providers are often the de facto mental health provider for these patients. That is, patients with psychiatric disorders such as PTSD are more likely to get all of their (mental as well as physical) health care from primary care providers such as internal medicine, family practice, and pediatric physicians and nurses, and unlikely to seek care from mental health providers such as psychiatrists and psychologists. In fact, the general medical health sector is the fastest growing sector from which individuals seek mental health services (Wang et al., 2006).

Screening for a health problem in primary care is warranted when a condition is prevalent, associated with morbidity or impaired quality of life, and treatable (U.S. Preventive Services Task Force, 1996). PTSD appears to meet these conditions. Currently, however, more than half of patients with PTSD are not being detected as having the disorder by primary care providers (Magruder et al., 2005). Education about PTSD screening and treatment are necessary to improve patient care (Schnurr et al., 2007).

Desirable features of a screening instrument for PTSD in primary care include brevity (2 to 4 items), ease of completion (dichotomous scoring), and the demonstrated ability to accurately identify people with and without the disorder (Brewin & Rose, 2003). The Primary Care PTSD Screen (PC-PTSD) is a four-item screen that was validated on a Veterans Affairs Medical Center (VA) primary care sample of male and female veterans (Prins et al., 2004). It has good test-retest reliability (.83) and good operating characteristics in detecting PTSD when a cut-off score of 3 is used (sensitivity = .78; specificity = .87; overall efficiency = .85). The PC-PTSD is not specific to any one traumatic event and assesses PTSD symptoms rather than trauma exposure. The PC-PTSD is in the public domain and reproduced here:

Primary Care PTSD Screen (PC-PTSD)

In your life, have you ever had any experience that was so frightening, horrible, or upsetting that, in the past month, you:

Have had nightmares about it or thought about it when you did not want to?
Yes   No
Tried hard not to think about it or went out of your way to avoid situations that reminded you of it?
Yes   No
Were constantly on guard, watchful, or easily startled?
Yes   No
Felt numb or detached from others, activities, or your surroundings?
Yes   No

Examples of other instruments that have been used in primary care are the longer 17-item Posttraumatic Symptom Checklist (PCL; with empirically derived shorter version; Lang & Stein, 2005) and the SPAN (Brewin, 2005; Yeager, Magruder, Knapp, Nicholas, & Frueh, 2007).

A positive PTSD screen does not mean that a patient definitely has PTSD. Positive screens need to be followed up with additional assessments to confirm the diagnosis. Diagnostic interviews, like the CAPS (Blake et al., 1990), are typically not administered in primary care settings because of resource constraints, but longer self-report instruments, like the PCL, can provide additional symptom information as well as targets for treatment planning and monitoring. Cutoff scores on the PCL appear to vary based on the population being treated. In civilian primary care settings, a cutoff of 30 has been found to be optimal, whereas a cutoff score of 48 was found to be optimal for male and female VA primary care patients (Brewin, 2005; Prins & Ouimette, 2004). Patients scoring above these cutoff scores may need to be referred to specialty mental health services while those scoring below may be appropriate for initial treatment in primary care.

To date, there have been no randomized control trials of specialized treatments in primary care settings for patients with PTSD. Empirically supported treatments for PTSD, such as prolonged exposure, cognitive processing therapy, and eye movement desensitization and reprocessing (EMDR) require a trained mental health professional to administer and have only been delivered and validated in specialty mental health clinics (Resick, Monson, & Gutner, 2007). Primary care providers need to be familiar with these treatments in order to educate patients and to facilitate referrals. Two serotonin specific reuptake inhibitor (SSRI) antidepressant medications have received FDA approval for PTSD, sertraline and paroxetine, and are often used as the first line strategy for the disorder in primary care (Friedman & Davidson, 2007). Based on clinical improvement for primary care patients with depression, (including depression with comorbid PTSD), incorporating care managers for enhancing medication compliance and self-management strategies in primary care services may hold promise for patients with PTSD (Blount, 1998; Green et al., 2006). Such practices may be especially helpful for the 55% to 60% of primary care patients who do not follow-up with mental health referrals and/or for those patients who find mental health problems stigmatizing (Gonzalez, Williams, Noel, & Lee, 2005; Hoge et al., 2004).

REFERENCES

Blake, D. D., Weathers, F. W., Nagy, L. M., Kaloupek, D. G., Klauminzer, G., Charney, D. S., et al. (1990). A clinician rating scale for assessing current and lifetime PTSD: The CAPS-1. *Behavior Therapy, 13,* 187–188.

Blount, A. (1998). Introduction to integrated primary care. In A. Blount (Ed.), *Integrated primary care: The future of medical and mental health collaboration* (pp. 1–43). New York: Norton.

Brewin, C. R. (2005). Systematic review of screening instruments for adults at risk of PTSD. *Journal of Traumatic Stress, 18*(1), 53–62.

Brewin, C. R., & Rose, S. (2003). Screening to identify individuals at risk after exposure to trauma. In R. Ormer & U. Schnyder (Eds.), *Reconstructing early intervention after trauma* (pp. 130–142). New York: Oxford University Press.

Friedman, M. J., & Davidson, J. R. T. (2007). Pharmacotherapy for PTSD. In M. J. Friedman, T. M. Keane, & P. A. Resick. *Handbook of PTSD: Science and practice* (pp. 376–405). New York: Guilford Press.

Gonzalez, J., Williams, J. W., Jr., Noel, P. H., & Lee, S. (2005). Adherence to mental health treatment in a primary care clinic. *Journal of the American Board of Family Practice, 18*(2), 87–96.

Green, B. L., Krupnick, J. L., Chung, J., Siddique, J., Krause, E. D., Revicki, D., et al. (2006). Impact of PTSD comorbidity on one-year outcomes in a depression trial. *Journal of Clinical Psychology, 62*(7), 815–835.

Hoge, C. W., Castro, C. A., Messer, S. C., McGurk, D., Cotting, D. I., & Koffman, R. L. (2004). Combat duty in Iraq and Afghanistan, mental health problems, and barriers to care. *New England Journal of Medicine, 351*(1), 13–22.

Kessler, R. C., Berglund, P., Demler, O., Jin, R., Merikangas, K. R., & Walters, E. E. (2005). Lifetime prevalence and age-of-onset distributions of DSM-IV disorders in the National Comorbidity Survey Replication. *Archives of General Psychiatry, 62*(6), 593–602.

Kessler, R. C., Sonnega, A., Bromet, E., Hughes, M., & Nelson, C. B. (1995). Posttraumatic stress disorder in the National Comorbidity Survey. *Archives of General Psychiatry, 52*(12), 1048–1060.

Kroenke, K., Spitzer, R. L., Williams, J. B., Monahan, P. O., & Lowe, B. (2007). Anxiety disorders in primary care: Prevalence, impairment, comorbidity, and detection. *Annals of Internal Medicine, 146*(5), 317–325.

Lang, A. J., & Stein, M. B. (2005). An abbreviated PTSD checklist for use as a screening instrument in primary care. *Behaviour Research and Therapy, 43,* 585–594.

Magruder, K. M., Frueh, B. C., Knapp, R. G., Davis, L., Hamner, M. B., Martin, R. H., et al. (2005). Prevalence of posttraumatic stress disorder in Veterans Affairs primary care clinics. *General Hospital Psychiatry, 27*(3), 169–179.

Prins, A., & Ouimette, P. (2004). Addendum. *Primary Care Psychiatry, 9,* 151.

Prins, A., Ouimette, P., Kimerling, R., Cameron, R. P., Hugelshofer, D. S., Shaw-Hegwer, J., et al. (2004). The Primary Care PTSD Screen: Development and operating characteristics. *Primary Care Psychiatry, 9,* 9–14.

Resick, P. A., Monson, C. M., & Gutner, C. (2007). Psychosocial treatments for PTSD. In M. J. Friedman, T. M. Keane, & P. A. Resick. *Handbook of PTSD: Science and practice* (pp. 330–358). New York: Guilford Press.

Sartorius, N., Ustun, T. B., Lecrubier, Y., & Wittchen, H. U. (1996). Depression comorbid with anxiety: Results from the WHO study on psychological disorders in primary health care. *British Journal of Psychiatry, 30*(Suppl.), 38–43.

Schnurr, P. P., & Green, B. L. (Eds.). (2004). *Trauma and health: Physical health consequences of exposure to extreme stress.* Washington, DC: American Psychological Association.

Schnurr, P. P., Green, B. L., & Kaltman, S. (2007). Trauma exposure and physical health. In M. J. Friedman, T. M. Keane, & P. A. Resick (Eds.), *Handbook of PTSD: Science and practice* (pp. 406–424). New York: Guilford Press.

U.S. Preventive Services Task Force. (1996). *Guide to clinical preventive services* (2nd ed.). Baltimore: Williams & Wilkins.

Wang, P. S., Demler, O., Olfson, M., Pincus, H. A., Wells, K. B., & Kessler, R. C. (2006). Changing profiles of service sectors used for mental health care in the United States. *American Journal of Psychiatry, 163,* 1187–1198.

Yeager, D. E., Magruder, K. M., Knapp, R. G., Nicholas, J. S., & Frueh, B. C. (2007). Performance characteristics of the posttraumatic stress disorder checklist and SPAN in Veterans Affairs primary care settings. *General Hospital Psychiatry, 29,* 294–301.

ANNABEL PRINS
San Jose State University

See also: Early Intervention; Health Service Utilization; Medical Illness, Adult; Pharmacotherapy, Adult; Prevention, Adult; Somatic Complaints; Veterans Affairs, U.S. Department of

PRISONERS OF WAR

Prisoners of war (POWs) are exposed to some of the most traumatic experiences that are perpetrated by human beings. POW captivity often occurs subsequent to brutal exposure to combat, and typically involves prolonged and repeated exposure to various traumatic experiences (Herman, 1992). Physical and psychological torture, continuous threat to life, systematic humiliation, isolation and deprivation, and being subjected to total control, are only part of the intense trauma exposure. POWs also may lose their identity as active combat soldiers and as a result they may experience a sense of defeat and betrayal along with painful guilt and shame.

Psychological Consequences of War Captivity

A considerable body of research from various wars in different parts of the world consistently found ex-POWs to be at high risk for various and long-lasting psychological sequelae including somatic (Engdahl, Speed, Eberly, & Schwartz, 1991; Neria, Solomon, Ginzburg, et al., 2000; Ohry et al., 1994), cognitive (Sutker, Galina, West, & Allain, 1990; Sutker, Winstead, Galina, & Allain, 1991), and psychosocial adjustment problems (Neria, Solomon, & Dekel, 1998). Among the psychological consequences of being a POW, posttraumatic stress disorder (PTSD) is prominent. Research has consistently documented high prevalence of PTSD among POWs, ranging from 30% (Speed, Engdahl, Schwartz, & Eberly, 1989), and 50% (Goldstein, van Kammen, Shelly, Miller, & van Kammen, 1987; Zeiss & Dickman, 1989), to 70% (Sutker, Allain, & Winstead, 1993) and 76% (Sutker & Allain, 1991) among World War II

POWs; and 88% among returning POWs from the Korean conflict (Sutker & Allain, 1996). However, a study of Israeli war veterans conducted by Neria, Solomon, and colleagues (Neria, Solomon, & Dekel, 2000; Solomon, Neria, Ohry, Waysman, M., & Ginzburg, 1994) found substantially lower rates of PTSD among Israeli war veterans from the Yom Kippur 1973 war (13%, 2 decades after captivity). While the exact reasons are unknown, the differences may be attributed to the relatively shorter duration of captivity, lesser severity of captivity, and a better preparation of the service members beforehand as compared to other populations of POWs.

A large body of research documented a wide range of adverse effects of captivity beyond PTSD, including anxiety and depression (Engdahl, Page, & Miller, 1991; Page, Engdahl, & Eberly, 1991), substance use (Ursano & Rundell, 1990), hysteria and hypochondria (Sutker & Allain, 1991), and problems inhibiting verbal and physical aggression (O'Donnell, Cook, Thompson, Riley, & Neria, 2006). In addition, a range of adjustment problems have been suggested including poor psychosocial adjustment (Cook, Riggs, Thompson, Coyne, & Sheikh, 2004), unemployment (Sutker, Winstead, Goist, Malow, & Allain, 1986), financial difficulties (Van Vranken, 1978), social isolation, suspiciousness and hostility (Sutker & Allain, 1991), sexual dysfunction (Sutker et al., 1986; Ursano, Boydstun, & Wheatley, 1981), family problems (Ursano & Rundell, 1990), and high divorce rates (Nice, McDonald, & McMillian, 1981; Van Vranken, 1978).

Scientifically sound studies that have compared the effects of combat to the effects of POW captivity (e.g., Neria et al., 1998) have shown that war captivity is more pathogenic than combat. While war entails extreme threat to life and limb, most soldiers experience these potentially traumatic threats as a part of a cohesive group with shared goals, structure, and morale. Soldiers also are equipped with weapons and protective devices that enable them to have some control over their safety and a sense of effectiveness as they fight alongside commanders and comrades. The powerful stress-mediating effect of unit cohesion and social support derived from comrades and commanders is well documented as a sustaining force for combatants (e.g., Solomon, Mikulincer, & Hobfoll, 1986). On the other hand, captivity renders the POW totally isolated and deprived of any human compassion and support. The trauma of captivity, which is occurring between the captive and his or her captors, includes concerted efforts to break the individual's will power, to destroy his or her identity and sense of personal control and efficacy as a free person. Having been exposed to continuous isolation and humiliation, the POW is left many times lonely and helpless, and as a result may experience a seriously damaged capacity to trust, feel, and relate to others (Herman, 1992).

Risk Factors

Previous studies identified a number of risk factors for post-captivity emotional problems. The historical and political context of the war (Ursano, Wheatley, Carlson, & Rahe, 1987); the location, duration, harshness of captivity (Crocq, Hein, Duval, & Macher, 1991; Engdahl, Dikel, Eberly, & Blank, 1997); and the degree of the exposure to combat prior to becoming a POW (Neria et al., 1998) were found to be associated with post-captivity problems. In addition a number of factors known as resources were found to be associated with a better post-captivity adjustment, such as high military rank (Sutker, Bugg, & Allain, 1990), high education, and belonging to a privileged ethnic group (Neria et al., 1998). Importantly, social support at homecoming was found to be strongly associated with better outcomes (Hunter, 1993; Neria et al., 1998; Ursano et al., 1996). Indeed, it is expected that after the isolation and the deliberate assault on the individuals' person and integrity, a warm reception at homecoming may crucially serve as a corrective emotional experience that may bolsters the POW's sense of safety, personhood, and belonging.

Few studies have attempted to examine the effect of behaviors in captivity on post-captivity mental health outcomes. For example, an early study suggested that apathy in captivity may be helpful in reducing distress and improve adjustment (Strasman, Thaler, & Schein, 1956) and Neria, Solomon, and Dekel (2000) found that anger against captors and fellow POWs, a sudden development of religious faith in captivity, and feelings described as "loss of emotional control," are strongly associated with post-captivity mental health problems.

Positive Changes Following POW Captivity

Although most studies on the aftermath of war captivity have focused on negative or pathological outcomes, other studies indicated that, along with its pathological and destructive effects, exposure to war captivity may also evoke certain positive changes. Sledge, Boydstun, and Rabe (1980) assessed the consequences of war captivity among air force officers held prisoner during the Vietnam War, and found that 92% of POWs felt that they had benefited from what they had learned and how they had handled their captivity. They saw themselves as more optimistic, believed they had more insight, and felt better able to distinguish between the important and the trivial. They also reported positive changes in the interpersonal realm, claiming that they developed good interpersonal skills, patience, and understanding of others, and an increased awareness of the importance of communicating with others. Similarly, Solomon et al. (1999) found that although POWs suffered from significant post-captivity problems, they also reported increased insight, maturity, enhanced self-esteem, and improved ability to differentiate the important from the trivial. Interestingly, positive changes were more frequently endorsed than negative ones, suggesting that POW survivors do not lose the capacity for maturation and growth even when confronted with prolonged and severe inactivation and torture.

Conclusion

Exposure to war captivity has enabled mental and public health researchers around the globe to examine the effects of exposure to extreme interpersonal traumatization including systematic torture, isolation, and humiliation (Solomon & Dekel, 2005; Ursano, 1981). The evidence suggests that the burden of post-captivity mental health problems among populations exposed to war captivity is substantial. Post-captivity mental health problems, primarily PTSD, occur in many if not most cases. The magnitude of psychopathological effects of exposure to war captivity suggests a critical need for developing treatments for service members released from captivity.

However, specific treatments for POWs are yet to be developed and tested. Given the nature of the POW experience, which is highly interpersonal and involves systematic and brutal exposure to cruelty and deprivation, a treatment approach that can restore safety, a sense of power, control, and self-worth, and trust and belongingness is highly needed among war veterans who undergo POW captivity. Moreover, the chronic nature of mental health problems among POWs likely requires a great focus on rehabilitation of capacities for work and love and social reconnectedness. Treatment also should build upon and strengthen POWs' sense that what they learned from and how they handled POW captivity can be a source of inner strength and personal integrity. Developing such therapeutic methods, standardizing and evaluating their efficacy among populations surviving extensive psychological trauma, such as POWs, constitute a major challenge to both clinicians and researchers.

REFERENCES

Cook, J. M., Riggs, D. S., Thompson, R., Coyne, J. C., & Sheikh, J. I. (2004). Posttraumatic stress disorder and current relationship functioning among World War II ex-prisoners of war. *Journal of Family Psychology, 18,* 36–45.

Crocq, M. A., Hein, K. D., Duval, F., & Macher, J. P. (1991). Severity of the prisoner of war experience and post-traumatic stress disorder. *European Psychiatry, 6,* 39–45.

Engdahl, B. E., Dikel, T. N., Eberly, R., & Blank, A., Jr. (1997). Posttraumatic stress disorder in a community group of former prisoners of war: A normative response to severe trauma. *American Journal of Psychiatry, 154,* 1576–1581.

Engdahl, B. E., Page, W. F., & Miller, T. W. (1991). Age, education, maltreatment, and social support as predictors of chronic depression in former prisoners of war. *Social Psychiatry and Psychiatric Epidemiology, 26,* 63–67.

Engdahl, B. E., Speed, N., Eberly, R. E., & Schwartz, J. (1991). Comorbidity of psychiatric disorders and personality profiles of American World War II prisoners of war. *Journal of Nervous and Mental Disease, 179,* 181–187.

Goldstein, G., van Kammen, W., Shelly, C., Miller, D. J., & van Kammen, D. P. (1987). Survivors of imprisonment in the Pacific theater during World War II. *American Journal of Psychiatry, 144,* 1210–1213.

Herman, J. L. (1992). *Trauma and recovery.* New York: Basic Books.

Hunter, E. J. (1993). The Vietnam prisoner of war experience. In J. P. Wilson & B. Raphael (Eds.), *International handbook of traumatic stress syndromes* (pp. 297–303). New York: Plenum Press.

Neria, Y., Solomon, Z., & Dekel, R. (1998). An eighteen-year follow-up study of Israeli prisoners of war and combat veterans. *Journal of Nervous and Mental Disease, 186,* 174–182.

Neria, Y., Solomon, Z., & Dekel, R. (2000). Adjustment to the stress of war captivity: The role of sociodemographic background, trauma severity and coping in prison in the long-term mental health of Israeli ex-POWs. *Anxiety, Stress, and Coping, 13,* 229–246.

Neria, Y., Solomon, Z., Ginzburg, K., Dekel, R., Enoch, D., & Ohry, A. (2000). Posttraumatic residues of captivity: A follow-up of Israeli ex-prisoners of war. *Journal of Clinical Psychiatry, 61,* 39–46.

Nice, D. S., McDonald, B., & McMillian, T. (1981). The families of U.S. Navy prisoners of war from Vietnam five years after reunion. *Journal of Marriage and the Family, 43,* 431–437.

O'Donnell, C., Cook, J. M., Thompson, R., Riley, K., & Neria, Y. (2006). Verbal and physical aggression in World War II former prisoners of war: Role of posttraumatic stress disorder and depression. *Journal of Traumatic Stress, 19,* 859–866.

Ohry, A., Solomon, Z., Neria, Y., Waysman, M., Bar-On, Z., & Levy, A. (1994). The aftermath of captivity: An 18-year follow-up of Israeli ex-POWs. *Behavioral Medicine, 20,* 27–33.

Page, W. F., Engdahl, B. E., & Eberly, R. E. (1991). Prevalence and correlates of depressive symptoms among former prisoners of war. *Journal of Nervous and Mental Disease, 179,* 670–677.

Sledge, W. H., Boydstun, J. A., & Rabe, A. J. (1980). Self-concept changes related to war captivity. *Archives of General Psychiatry, 37,* 430–443.

Solomon, Z., & Dekel, R. (2005). Posttraumatic stress disorder among Israeli ex-prisoners of war 18 and 30 years after release. *Journal of Clinical Psychiatry, 66,* 1031–1037.

Solomon, Z., Mikulincer, M., & Hobfoll, S. (1986). Effects of social support and battle intensity on loneliness and breakdown during combat. *Journal of Personality and Social Psychology, 51,* 1269–1277.

Solomon, Z., Neria, Y., Ohry, A., Waysman, M., & Ginzburg, K. (1994). PTSD among Israeli former prisoners of war and soldiers with combat stress reaction: A longitudinal study. *American Journal of Psychiatry, 151,* 554–559.

Solomon, Z., Waysman, M., Neria, Y., Ohry, A., Wiener, M., & Schwartzwald, J. (1999). Positive and negative changes in the lives of ex-POWs. *Journal of Social and Clinical Psychology, 18,* 419–435.

Speed, N., Engdahl, B., Schwartz, J., & Eberly, R. (1989). Posttraumatic stress disorder as a consequence of the POW experience. *Journal of Nervous and Mental Disease, 177,* 147–153.

Strassman, A. D., Thaler, M. B., & Schein, E. H. (1956). A prisoner of war syndrome: Apathy as a reaction to severe stress. *American Journal of Psychiatry, 112,* 998–1003.

Sutker, P. B., & Allain, A. N., Jr. (1991). MMPI profiles of veterans of WW II and Korea: Comparisons of former POWs and combat survivors. *Psychological Reports, 68,* 279–284.

Sutker, P. B., & Allain, A. N., Jr. (1996). Assessment of PTSD and other mental disorders in World War II & Korean Conflict POW survivors and combat veterans. *Psychological Assessment, 8,* 18–25.

Sutker, P. B., Allain, A. N., Jr., & Winstead, D. K. (1993). Psychopathology and psychiatric diagnoses of World War II Pacific theater prisoner of war survivors and combat veterans. *American Journal of Psychiatry, 150,* 240–245.

Sutker, P. B., Bugg, F., & Allain, A. N., Jr. (1990). Person and situation correlates of posttraumatic stress disorder among POW survivors. *Psychological Reports, 66,* 912–914.

Sutker, P. B., Galina, Z. H., West, J. A., & Allain, A. N., Jr. (1990). Trauma-induced weight loss and cognitive deficits among former prisoners of war. *Journal of Consulting and Clinical Psychology, 58,* 323–328.

Sutker, P. B., Winstead, D. K., Galina, Z. H., & Allain, A. N. (1991). Cognitive deficits and psychopathology among former prisoners of war and combat veterans of the Korean conflict. *American Journal of Psychiatry, 148,* 67–72.

Sutker, P. B., Winstead, D. K., Goist, K. C., Malow, R. M., & Allain, A. N. (1986). Psychopathology subtypes and symptom correlates among former prisoners of war. *Journal of Psychopathology and Behavioral Assessment, 8,* 89–101.

Ursano, R. J. (1981). The Vietnam era prisoner of war: Precaptivity personality and the development of psychiatric illness. *American Journal of Psychiatry, 138,* 315–318.

Ursano, R. J., Boydstun, J. A., & Wheatley, R. D. (1981). Psychiatric illness in U.S. Air Force Viet Nam prisoners of war: A five-year follow-up. *American Journal of Psychiatry, 138,* 310–314.

Ursano, R. J., & Rundell, J. R. (1990). The prisoner of war. *Military Medicine, 155,* 176–180.

Ursano, R. J., Rundell, J. R., Fragala, M. R., Larson, S. G., Wain, H. J., Brandt, G. T., et al. (1996). The prisoner of war. In R. J. Ursano & A. E. Norwood (Eds.), *Emotional aftermath of the Persian Gulf-War* (pp. 443–476). Washington, DC: American Psychiatric Press.

Ursano, R. J., Wheatley, R. D., Carlson, E. H., & Rahe, A. L. (1987). The prisoner of war: Stress, illness and resiliency. *Psychiatric Annals, 17,* 532–535.

Van Vranken, E. (November, 1978). *Current status and social adjustment of U.S. Army returned prisoners of war.* Paper presented at the 5th annual Joint Medical Meeting Concerning MIA/POW Matters, San Antonio, TX.

Zeiss, R. A., & Dickman, H. R. (1989). PTSD 40 years later: Incidence and person-situation correlates in former POWs. *Journal of Clinical Psychology, 45,* 80–87.

Yuval Neria
Columbia University

See also: Aggression; Coping; Etiology; Human Rights Violations; Medical Illness, Adult; Military Personnel; Political Prisoners; Posttraumatic Adaptation; Posttraumatic Growth; Social Support; Somatic Complaints; Torture; Veterans Affairs, U.S. Department of; War Trauma

PROFESSIONAL STANDARDS AND ETHICS

Professional organizations develop standards and codes of ethics for their members in order to guide conduct, ensure competence, and thus protect consumers of their services. Standards are promulgated in accordance with applicable jurisdictional civil and criminal laws and, as the name implies, set benchmarks and regulations for acceptable practice within the profession as a whole and for subspecialty services (e.g., assessment, psychotherapy, Internet delivery of information or services, custody or other forensic evaluations, and expert witness services). Different organizations hold their members to different standards, some according to their theoretical orientation or their locale. Students and trainees are required to complete coursework and practica in which they are introduced to professional issues along with professional and ethical standards and their application in a practice setting. When trainees are later licensed or certified within a specific profession and jurisdiction and become members of professional organizations, they are expected to know and to abide by their standards and ethical codes or face censure or even loss of license or expulsion from the organization in the case of severe breaches and transgressions.

It is now well recognized (Koocher & Keith-Seigel, 2007; Pope & Vasquez, 1998) that professional standards and a code of ethics do not necessarily provide specific guidance in all cases. Professional standards and codes are dynamic, and subject to revision and updating with the availability of new areas and modes of practice, new legal requirements, and new information and research findings. Pope and Vasquez (1998) stated:

> Ethics codes cannot do our questioning, thinking, feeling, and responding for us. Such codes can never be a substitute for the active process by which the individual therapist or counselor struggles with the sometimes bewildering, always unique constellation of questions, responsibilities, contexts, and competing demands of helping another person. . . . Ethics must be practical. Clinicians confront an almost unimaginable

diversity of situations, each with its own shifting questions, demands, and responsibilities. Every clinician is unique in important ways. Ethics that are out of touch with the practical realities of clinical work, with the diversity and constantly changing nature of the therapeutic venture, are useless. (p. xiii)

Ethics also are not the law and can deviate from what is in the law and even from what practitioners consider to be moral or right according to their personal standards and values. As a result, practitioners must practice "ethical mindfulness" (Steele, 2006) by striving to be knowledgeable about ethical requirements and their evolution and change over time and by maintaining an awareness of their application. Additionally, ethics is not simply following the law since the law can deviate from what is ethical. At times, requirements of ethical standards clash with applicable laws and legal counsel; such a situation can be very confusing and even exasperating for a practitioner who is trying to practice ethically and receives conflicting legal advice or directives.

Practicing ethically requires training on and sensitivity to ethical issues, a practiced method for exploring the ethical aspects of a particular situation or course of action, and a reliance on discussion and dialogue with others when a novel and complex ethical situation is encountered (Steele, 2006). Practicing ethically also requires stability, maturity, and flexibility on the part of the therapist and an ability to be reflective rather than simply reactive. Ideally, one's personal and professional ethics will converge, but, in some situations, that is not possible. Therapists must be mindful of their own personal ethics and values, but also of their professional organizations' ethical standards, decision making, and practice, and never assume that the two are identical.

In clinical practice settings such as private practice psychotherapy or counseling, hospitals or outpatient behavioral health agencies, or school or child guidance clinics, professional standards and ethical codes address issues including the following:

- The treatment frame, which means how professional services are described and delivered to clients, including therapist or evaluator availability, responsibilities, and limitations.
- Professional fees and payment requirements, and use of insurance.
- Confidentiality and informed consent, that is, the client's right to control personal health information and the limitations of privacy (such as legal requirements that helpers report child or elder abuse).
- Therapist qualifications, including professional training, supervised experience, licensure or certification, specialty expertise (such as Board Certification as an expert in certain areas of specialized services).
- Modes of assessment and treatment that are considered "standards of care," that is, the approaches that have scientific and clinical evidence of providing benefit and preventing or minimizing the risk of harm to clients.
- Professional impartiality and fairness, including the prevention or disclosure of dual/multiple or conflicted relationships (such as the general prohibition against providing treatment to family members and against seeking or accepting financial or other benefits from clients beyond the agreed upon fees).
- Professional integrity and boundaries—especially the prohibition of becoming involved in romantic relationships or sexual contact with clients.
- The standard of "first do no harm," which asserts that professionals should not use interventions that are harmful to clients or others.
- Responsibility to provide services in a manner that does not lead to the abandonment of clients and or to abrupt treatment endings.
- Maintaining accurate and complete professional records and documentation.
- Maintaining collegial and respectful relationships with professional colleagues.
- Responsible use of electronic (e.g., Internet, Telemedicine) communications.

All professional standards and ethical codes for practitioners working with clients are oriented toward the protection of the client and the maintenance of his or her well-being. Standards or codes relating to relationships with other professionals indirectly serve the interests of clients of all members of the professional network by increasing the likelihood that standards and ethics of care will be followed by all professionals and supported by their collegial dialogues with one another. The recently added standards concerning Internet and Telemedicine (*see:* **Telemedicine**) delivery of information and services have been developed in acknowledgment of the expanded scope of many professionals' contact with large groups of people who may never formally be clients (e.g., providing descriptions of services or research on an Internet web page) or whom the professional may treat as clients despite not meeting face-to-face except on a "virtual" electronic basis.

Although professional standards and ethics are important in all areas of professional practice, they are particularly important in the treatment of traumatic stress disorders since traumatized persons have already been injured psychologically (and many times also physically), and must be treated in a way that minimizes the possibility of further injury. In fact, the core ethical principle of professional practice "first do no harm" can be modified to "do no *more* harm" in the treatment of persons with traumatic stress disorders.

Psychological trauma and its effects may pose special issues and dilemmas for practitioners, some of which have no clear ethical guidelines. For example, working with psychological trauma survivors may cause practitioners (especially those who are novice, inexperienced, and/or who received little or no training to work with this population; *see:* **Burnout; Vicarious Traumatization**) to overrespond or underrespond to their needs based on countertransference (*see:* **Countertransference**) reactions that are unrecognized or unmanaged and that result in countertransference errors (Wilson & Lindy, 1994). Such problematic responses reduce the competence of the professional to provide services to their client(s). Since competence to treat is an ethical

imperative, practitioners who are in the above-mentioned categories have an obligation to obtain training, consultation, and supervision or to remove themselves from a treatment role until they are able to adhere to professional and ethical standards for competence.

Overresponse can result in "rescuing" of the client that, in turn, can result in a failure to maintain appropriate boundaries and the development of dual relationships. For example, a therapist might meet with the client on a daily basis, have numerous phone calls between appointments, give the client advice on how to handle personal problems, or in more extreme cases provide practical or financial help to the client, arrange meetings outside of the office setting, or in general do a variety of special things for the client that could be as egregious as having sexual contact with the client.

Underresponse can paradoxically be related to overresponse (Dalenberg, 2000). As the practitioner becomes overwhelmed by the demands of the work and the client, he or she might become angry and detach or blame the client as a result. In some cases, this results in hostility toward the client and abrupt and unplanned endings (abandonment) based on these feelings. Underresponse can also be the result of dislike of and stigmatization of the client and his or her psychological trauma history and traumatic stress symptoms. All of these reactions are ethically compromised in that they have the potential to add to the client's distress and to cause further emotional harm.

To summarize, the ethical practitioner who treats traumatized clients must have the training, competence, and emotional competence to treat problems presented by these clients and must also have awareness of and mindfulness about ethical principles. The needs of the client have priority and the mindful, mature therapist is able to respond in flexible and balanced ways that incorporate attention to ethics and other professional standards.

REFERENCES

Dalenberg, C. (2000). *Countertransference and the treatment of trauma.* Washington, DC: American Psychological Association.

Koocher, G. P., & Keith-Spiegel, P. (2007). *Ethics in psychology and the mental health professions: Standards and cases.* New York: Oxford University Press.

Pope, K. S., & Vasquez, M. J. T. (1998). *Ethics in psychotherapy and counseling: A practical guide* (2nd ed.). San Francisco: Jossey-Bass.

Steele, K. (2006). *Towards mindful ethics in psychotherapy: From reflex to reflection.* Atlanta, GA: Metropolitan Counseling Services.

Wilson, J. P., & Lindy, J. D. (Eds.). (1994). *Countertransference in the treatment of PTSD.* New York: Guilford Press.

CHRISTINE A. COURTOIS
Private Practice, Washington, DC

See also: Burnout; Countertransference; Evidence-Based Treatment; International Organizations; Practice Guidelines; Telemedicine; Vicarious Traumatization

PROJECTIVE PERSONALITY MEASURES

Various sources advocate a broad spectrum approach to the assessment of trauma and its effects, rather than relying on a single measure or focused solely on posttraumatic stress disorder (PTSD). Projective assessment techniques may assist in this aim. These techniques have in common their use of ambiguous stimuli or semi-structured tasks from which inferences may be drawn, providing information beyond the capacity of self-report measures. Although their use in clinical practice remains widespread, the use of projective techniques is not without controversy. Common criticisms of projective techniques include complex and time-consuming administration and scoring, subjectivity in scoring and interpretation, poor agreement when more than one person interprets the results (inter-rater reliability), poorly established norms, heavy reliance on psychoanalytic tradition and theory, poorly established validity of such findings, and a lack of usefulness for predicting outcomes (e.g., Hunsley, Lee, & Wood, 2003). Despite this ongoing debate, several projective techniques have been utilized in the study of traumatic stress.

The Rorschach is the most widely studied projective technique among trauma victims, although its utility for assessment of posttraumatic sequelae continues to be debated. A review of the literature by Luxenberg and Levin (2004) noted that "the Rorschach has been found to be very responsive to traumatic experiences" (p. 198), while Wood, Lilienfeld, Garb, and Nezworski (2000) concluded that "there are currently insufficient grounds to conclude that Rorschach scores are related to PTSD" (p. 401). Although the empirical findings have been criticized for being inconsistent across studies (e.g., Wood et al., 2000), some studies have found differences between various traumatized populations and nontraumatized populations, other psychiatric populations, and Exner's normative tables on several Rorschach scores including color, inanimate movement, morbid and aggressive content, form, special scores, shading, and ineffective coping (see reviews, e.g., Briere, 2004; Luxenberg & Levine, 2004). Several trauma-specific scores have been proposed (e.g., Traumatic Content Index, Combat Content Score, and Dramatic Special Score), as well as alternative interpretations of established scores or indices (i.e., SCIZ/Schizophrenia Index). The Rorschach has also shown potential utility in evaluating malingered PTSD (Frueh & Kinder, 1994).

Research with another popular projective technique, the Thematic Apperception Test (TAT), has generally utilized Westen's Social Cognition and Object Relations Scale. Studies have found, for example, abuse to be related to a more malevolent worldview, less capacity for emotional investment in relationships and moral standards, poorer attributions of causality in interactions, greater expression of sexual preoccupation, and guilt (e.g., Ornduff & Kelsey, 1996; Pistole & Ornduff, 1994). Dissociative participants have shown greater interpersonal distance, more trauma and dissociative content, and a lack of positive emotion. Another projective measure, the Roberts Apperception Test, has similarly detected higher rates of some sexual content among children with abuse histories than in children with no history of abuse (Friedrich & Share, 1997).

A more recent approach called the Hand Test utilizes nine drawings of hands in ambiguous positions and a tenth blank card. Two studies using this measure with military veteran samples have indicated higher levels of overall psychopathology, poor coping, and feelings of inadequacy or "damage" among those with PTSD (Hilsenroth, Arsenault, & Sloan, 2005; Walter, Hilsenroth, Arsenault, Sloan, & Harvill, 1998).

Projective drawings (e.g., House-Tree-Person, Kinetic Family Drawings) have a long history of clinical application with trauma. Some aspects of the interpretation of these drawings have not been empirically supported (e.g., the "Tree-Scar-Trauma" hypothesis has met with minimal support; Torem, Gilbertson, & Light, 1990). Some support has emerged for drawings in assessment of abused or neglected children and adult incest survivors (e.g., Waldman, Silber, Holmstrom, & Karp, 1994).

Various other projective techniques have been studied for use with traumatized populations including the sentence completion test, Expectations Test for Children, and the Bar-llan Picture Test for Children. The Angie/Andy Cartoon Trauma Scales are a measure developed specifically to assess complex PTSD among children (Praver, DiGiuseppe, Pelcovitz, Mandel, & Gaines 2000). Clinical use of projective measures with survivors of trauma remains widespread, with some empirical support emerging for their use with specific populations and utilizing specific standardized administration and scoring techniques; however debate over their psychometric properties and utility remains active.

REFERENCES

Briere, J. (2004). *Psychological assessment of adult posttraumatic states: Phenomenology, diagnosis, and measurement.* Washington, DC: American Psychological Association.

Friedrich, W. N., & Share, M. C. (1997). The Roberts Apperception Test for Children: An exploratory study of its use with sexually abused children. *Journal of Child Sexual Abuse, 6*(4), 83–91.

Frueh, B. C., & Kinder, B. N. (1994). The susceptibility of the Rorschach Inkblot Test to malingering of combat-related PTSD. *Journal of Personality Assessment, 62*, 280–298.

Hilsenroth, M., Arsenault, L., & Sloan, P. (2005). Assessment of combat-related stress and physical symptom of Gulf War veterans: Criterion validity of selected Hand Test variables. *Journal of Personality Assessment, 84*, 155–162.

Hunsley, J., Lee, C. M., & Wood, J. M. (2003). Controversial and questionable assessment techniques. In S. O. Lilienfeld, S. J. Lynn, & J. M. Lohr (Eds.), *Science and pseudoscience in clinical psychology* (pp. 39–76). New York: Guilford Press.

Luxenberg, T., & Levin, P. (2004). The role of the Rorschach in the assessment and treatment of trauma. In J. P. Wilson & T. M. Keane (Eds.), *Assessing psychological trauma and PTSD* (2nd ed., pp. 190–225). New York: Guilford Press.

Ornduff, S. R., & Kelsey, R. M. (1996). Object relations of sexually and physically abused female children: A TAT analysis. *Journal of Personality Assessment, 66*, 91–105.

Pistole, D. R., & Ornduff, S. R. (1994). TAT assessment of sexually abused girls: An analysis of manifest content. *Journal of Personality Assessment, 63*, 211–222.

Praver, F., DiGiuseppe, R., Pelcovitz, D., Mandel, F., & Gaines, R. (2000). A preliminary study of a cartoon measure for children's reactions to chronic trauma. *Child Maltreatment, 5*, 273–285.

Torem, M. S., Gilbertson, A., & Light, V. (1990). Indications of physical, sexual, and verbal victimization in projective tree drawings. *Journal of Clinical Psychology, 46*, 900–906.

Waldman, T. L., Silber, D. E., Holmstrom, R. W., & Karp, S. A. (1994). Personality characteristics of incest survivors on the Draw-A-Person Questionnaire. *Journal of Personality Assessment, 63*, 97–104.

Walter, C., Hilsenroth, M., Arsenault, L., Sloan, P., & Harvill, L. (1998). Use of the Hand Test in the assessment of combat-related stress. *Journal of Personality Assessment, 70*, 315–323.

Wood, J. M., Lilienfeld, S. O., Garb, H. N., & Nezworski, M. T. (2000). The Rorschach Test in clinical diagnosis: A critical review, with a backward look at Garfield (1947). *Journal of Clinical Psychology, 56*, 395–430.

RECOMMENDED READING

Briere, J. (2004). *Psychological assessment of adult posttraumatic states: Phenomenology, diagnosis, and measurement.* Washington, DC: American Psychological Association.

EDWARD M. VARRA
Veterans Affairs Puget Sound Health Care System

See also: Assessment, Psychometric, Adult; Assessment, Psychometric, Child; Diagnosis of Traumatic Stress Disorders (*DSM & ICD*); Malingering; Posttraumatic Stress Disorder, Diagnosis of

PROXIMITY/IMMEDIACY/EXPECTANCY/ SIMPLICITY (PIES)

See: Early Intervention; Military Personnel; Psychological First Aid, Adult

PSEUDOEPILEPTIC SEIZURES

See: Dissociation; Hysteria; Somatic Complaints

PSYCHODYNAMIC THERAPY, ADULT

Psychodynamic psychotherapy derives from psychoanalytic concepts and practices first described by Sigmund Freud (1856–1939) and now in their second century of evolution. The term *psychodynamic* expresses the view that mental processes and phenomena represent a balance between psychological, biological, and environmental factors. Freud viewed the dissociative and conversion symptoms (*see:* **Dissociation**) of hysterical patients as symbolic representations of tension between traumatic memory and psychological *defense.* Therefore, in psychoanalysis and in subsequent psychodynamic approaches to psychotherapy, *interpretation* of defense and of what is being defended against (often an unacceptable wish or fear stirred up by a traumatic memory) enables the patient to understand his or her dilemma as a first step toward restoring a stable psychological balance (Kudler, Krupnick, Blank, Herman, & Horowitz, in press).

In a psychodynamic framework, the therapeutic process is complex because the same unconscious defensive process that pushes for repression of memories and their associated thoughts and feelings within the patient also acts as *resistance* against the treatment. Among the most important forms of resistance is *transference.* Transference occurs when, by inappropriately projecting aspects of important past relationships onto the present therapeutic relationship, the patient attempts to avoid awareness of a painful conflict within him/ herself. Transference thus involves a repetition rather than a remembering of past conflicts within the present context of the therapy: a reenactment rather than a *working through* of the problem. Because the patient's transference stems specifically from those past conflicts most closely resembling the present conflict, the psychodynamic psychotherapist is able to enlist transference responses as a means of identifying and isolating repressed unconscious material and bringing it into conscious awareness for therapeutic purposes.

Case Example

Mr. A. entered therapy following a motor vehicle accident in which he escaped serious injury but his wife was killed. He met full diagnostic criteria for posttraumatic stress disorder and had been symptomatic for most of the 8 months since the accident. Mr. A. spoke openly about his memories and symptoms but tended to talk about them in global terms and from a detached, intellectual point of view. He experienced little improvement over the first weeks of treatment. He began to express frustration with himself and frequently wondered out loud if he should simply "give up on therapy." When the therapist gently pointed out the patient's tendency to be self-critical, Mr. A. agreed that he often had such thoughts. He spoke of the high standards he set for himself and pointed out that it was profoundly disappointing to him that he hadn't been able to foresee or avert the accident or find some way to save his wife. He shared a secret fear that the therapist must wonder the same things—that the therapist must think of him as weak and ineffectual or perhaps even cowardly. For some time, he had been thinking of dropping out of therapy because he believed that his therapist must be getting "sick" of him. The therapist pointed out that the response Mr. A feared from his therapist closely resembled the rejection he had feared from his highly successful and rigorously demanding parents. Mr. A agreed with this observation and added that, while his fear of being rejected by his therapist felt quite real to him, he also realized that his therapist had never given him any actual basis for concern. Mr. A added that his therapist's consistently respectful, nonjudgmental response to his criticisms were what made it possible for him to risk bringing his worries out into the open now. Mr. A determined to continue in therapy and confront his persistent self-doubts rather than feel progressively isolated and overwhelmed by them. He subsequently reported a greater sense of competence and efficacy in his activities and relationships as well as progressive improvement in his symptoms.

As this case example demonstrates, the leverage in transference work is considerable. It is relatively easy to deny or minimize memories, thoughts, and feelings about past relationships and situations when they are abstract aspects of a conversation but it is quite another thing to confront them in terms of thoughts and feelings that are alive and active with the therapist in real time. The experience of recognizing, with the help of a sensitive, respectful and facilitating therapist, that the patient is caught up in an inappropriate reenactment of past relationships or past traumatic experiences deepens the patient's self-understanding and strengthens the therapeutic relationship. Over time, the patient becomes more aware of his concerns (conscious and unconscious) and more accepting of him- or herself. Realization that transferential beliefs are not consistent with the reality of the therapist or the therapy helps the patient consider that things are not always what they have seemed and that change may not only be possible but also necessary.

The discovery of transference (and of the therapist's *countertransference*) ensured that psychodynamic psychotherapy would maintain a strong focus on the therapeutic relationship as a key element and driver of change. It

underlies the need for therapeutic *neutrality*. Not to be confused with aloofness (the therapist must always be invested in the patient's well-being and progress), neutrality describes the therapist's consistent effort to avoid siding with either pole of the patient's conflicts (wish versus defense, drive versus morality, reality versus yearning, fact versus fear, etc.). The patient needs to be free to see, consider, and own both sides of the conflict.

There is a broad range of psychodynamic psychotherapies, including formal psychoanalysis (which typically involves four to five sessions per week with the patient lying on a couch, unable to see the therapist), long term psychodynamic psychotherapy (one to two sessions per week of face-to-face meetings over the course of several weeks to years), brief psychodynamic psychotherapy (1 to 2 sessions per week versus 15 to 20 sessions), interpersonal psychotherapy (long or short term and focused primarily on conflicts and misunderstandings in relationships with others), and supportive psychotherapy, among others. These are often described as existing along a continuum between *expressive* psychotherapies (centered on interpretative interventions—especially interpretation of transference) and *supportive* psychotherapies (aimed at restoring or improving a person's capacity to cope without necessarily providing greater insight into underlying issues).

Virtually all psychodynamic psychotherapies combine both expressive and supportive interventions. What unites them as psychodynamic is their shared focus on psychological problems as an expression of conflicts of which the patient is largely unaware and which the patient cannot resolve without gaining greater self-awareness and self-acceptance. This intellectual and emotional growth is facilitated by a skilful therapist and a positive therapeutic relationship.

Psychodynamic work with children also combines expressive and supportive elements (*see:* **Psychodynamic Therapy, Child**). Psychodynamic psychotherapy with adults focuses on statements, insights, and reenactments as they take place within the conversation (and other interactions) between patient and therapist. Psychodynamic work with children generally relies on play as the medium in which ideas and reenactments become available for therapy. The choice to focus on play reflects an appreciation of developmental and social/cultural factors that might otherwise prevent children from directly expressing and working through conflicts and transference with the therapist.

While the term *psychodynamic psychotherapy* often summons up images of two people sharing an intimate conversation, psychodynamic principles are also applied in group and family settings. Psychodynamic principles are also helpful in framing and implementing public health approaches following disaster or war. Survivors, families, and communities each have a role to play in response to psychological trauma—especially communal trauma. From the perspective of psychodynamic psychotherapy, posttraumatic responses may best be understood and addressed within the adaptational, dimensional context of psychodynamic principles rather than the descriptive categorical symptoms that are emphasized in traditional psychiatric formulations and descriptions of PTSD (Herman, 1992; Horowitz, 2003; PDM Task Force, 2006).

A rich clinical literature (beginning with Breuer and Freud's 1955/1895 *Studies on Hysteria*) supports the value of psychodynamic psychotherapy in work with trauma survivors but this literature is primarily composed of case reports, clinical series, and tightly reasoned scholarly works. Randomized studies with documented diagnoses, controlled variables and validated outcome measures are needed to provide additional confirmation of these findings. Randomized clinical trials and other efficacy study methods are difficult to apply to the complex, interactive, and progressive processes involved in psychodynamic psychotherapy but, as Brom, Kleber, and Defares (1989) have demonstrated, such studies can be designed to demonstrate whether clinical outcomes with psychodynamic psychotherapy in patients with PTSD are superior to placebo and equal or superior to those of other established therapies. Effectiveness research (which examines outcomes in real world settings rather than in the laboratory or academic settings) may provide a powerful new lens for psychodynamic studies and new tools for establishing an evidence base for psychodynamic psychotherapy.

In psychodynamic psychotherapy, the meaning of a traumatic event is progressively understood within the context of the survivor's unique history, constitution, and aspirations. This process requires courage, patience, ability to trust, and ability to reflect on one's own experience. It is best approached in a therapeutic relationship that emphasizes safety and honesty. From a psychodynamic perspective, traumatic stress symptoms are not a sign of pathology but rather an effort to cope. Psychodynamic psychotherapy with survivors of psychological trauma is an effort to re-engage normal adaptive processes so that more effective, less painful solutions can be found and a new, more satisfying equilibrium can be achieved.

REFERENCES

Breuer, J., & Freud, S. (1955). Studies on hysteria. In J. Strachey (Ed. & Trans.), *The standard edition of the complete psychological works of Sigmund Freud* (Vol. 2, pp. 1–335). London: Hogarth Press. (Original work published 1895)

Brom, D., Kleber, R. J., & Defares, P. B. (1989). Brief psychotherapy for post-traumatic stress disorders. *Journal of Consulting and Clinical Psychology 57,* 607–612.

Herman, J. (1992). *Trauma and recovery.* New York: Basic Books.

Horowitz, M. J. (2003). *Treatment of stress response syndromes.* Arlington, VA: American Psychiatric Publishing.

Kudler, H. S., Krupnick, J. L., Blank, A. S., Herman, J. L., & Horowitz, M. J. (in press). Psychodynamic therapy. In E. B. Foa, T. M. Keane, & M. J. Friedman (Eds.), *Effective treatments for PTSD: Practice guidelines from the International Society for Traumatic Stress Disorder.* New York: Guilford Press.

PDM Task Force. (2006). *Psychodynamic diagnostic manual.* Silver Spring, MD: Alliance of Psychoanalytic Organizations.

HAROLD KUDLER
Duke University Medical Center

See also: Countertransference; Dissociation; Freud, Sigmund; Hysteria; Psychodynamic Therapy, Child

PSYCHODYNAMIC THERAPY, CHILD

Psychodynamic therapy for traumatized children focuses on enhancing or restoring the child's emotional bond and psychological security in primary caregiving relationships. The importance of caregiving relationships to the healthy development of children cannot be overstated.

Infants internalize the feelings associated with their early experiences as they learn to soothe themselves. It is from the security of their earliest relationships that they learn to explore the world and take on its mental and emotional challenges. If their early relationships provide empathic caring, children learn that the world is a benevolent place in which their needs will be met, that life has meaning, and that the self is worthy. Without caring relationships, or if primary caregiving relationships are compromised or taken away by experiences of psychological trauma, babies and young children cannot learn to calm and regulate their emotions, trust in the benevolence and responsiveness of other human beings, or explore the world and grow psychologically.

Because psychological traumas such as abuse, violence, or losses can be profoundly disruptive of these essential relationships and, therefore, of children's psychosocial development, psychodynamic theorists beginning with Freud (1959/1926) have identified psychological trauma as a central force in human personality development and the etiology of emotional disturbance. The traumatic moment is, at its essence, a confluence of sensory stimuli from outside the person and a cascade of powerful emotional responses within the child that signal unpredictable, uncontrollable, and immediate danger to the life or physical integrity of the individual. These powerful trauma-related stimuli and feelings can overwhelm the child's ability to cope or to seek and trust the emotional support of caregivers or other people, thus and leaving the child feeling terrorized and helpless in the face of danger.

Freud (1959/1926) posited that anxiety serves as a kind of protective shield against overwhelming stimulation, as it signals impending risk, allowing the individual to mobilize defenses and coping strategies to avoid or minimize danger. When children are young, their adult caregivers take on the role of protective shield, appraising risk and taking the necessary action to protect the child from being overwhelmed. If a young child experiences the overwhelming sights, sounds, and internal sensations that make up a traumatic moment, the caregiver has, at least for that moment, failed as a shield and the child's developmentally appropriate expectation of protection from that caregiver is compromised (Bowlby, 1969/1980; Pynoos, Steinberg, & Piacentini, 1999). This does not imply that caregivers have "failed" to care or to do the best they possibly can do to protect and help their children, but simply that their best efforts could not prevent their children from experiencing trauma exposure. Recognizing that the repair of primary caregiving relationships that have been disrupted or, at worst, shattered, by psychological trauma is essential to restoring children to positive developmental trajectories, psychodynamic models of intervention with traumatized children focus on restoring both the child's and the parent's belief that the parent can function as an effective protector for the child. How this is done in psychodynamic therapies for traumatized children will be illustrated using one particular psychodynamic therapy model, child-parent psychotherapy (CPP).

Child-Parent Psychotherapy

CPP emerged from infant-parent psychotherapy (Fraiberg, 1980), a treatment model developed to address situations in which infants or very young children were at risk because their parents' own childhoods were filled with traumatizing "ghosts" that interfered with the parents' capacity for empathic responsiveness to their infants. The parents' reenactment of troubled scenes from their own childhoods inadvertently put their babies and young children at risk. The emphasis of infant-parent psychotherapy is on preventing the intergenerational transmission of psychological trauma and psychopathology. Interventions, directed at the parent-child relationship itself, focus on addressing traumatized parent's distorted and negative beliefs about the child, on helping the parent to understand and respond with nurture to the child's needs and feelings, and on helping the child to experience their parent as motivated by love and caring in order to enable the child to feel loved and trusting in relationship to the caregiver. The goal of infant-parent psychotherapy is to enhance emotional reciprocity in the dyad, that is, to help the parent and child respond to each other in ways that enable their relationship to be healthy and loving despite the parent's difficulties with traumatic stress.

Lieberman and Van Horn (2005) created a manual for CPP that extended infant-parent psychotherapy by applying it to older children (up to the age of six) and embedding it with a distinct focus on addressing the impact of psychological traumas experienced by the child as well as by the parent. Interventions remain based in the parent-child relationship; in CPP, however, the interventions are frequently built around the distorted expectations that the parent and child may have of themselves and each other as a result of the experience of psychological trauma, on helping parents and children recognize and cope with reminders of traumatic experiences, and on supporting them in co-creating a coherent narrative of their lives together that includes a clear and tolerable (although emotionally painful) memory of traumatic experiences.

CPP does not prescribe an order in which interventions must occur or in which treatment goals must be addressed. Rather, interventions are selected according to what the clinician believes will best advance the goal of helping the child and parent interact in ways that will support the child's healthy development. The

manual advises beginning with simple interventions, often based in developmental guidance. Such guidance not only helps parents understand and accept their children's realistic developmental capacities, but also helps them understand the anxieties of early childhood that unfold in a developmentally predictable sequence that progresses from anxieties about being abandoned, to anxieties about losing the parent's love, about being physically harmed, and about doing wrong (Freud, 1959/1926). Establishing safety in the parent-child relationship is also a priority. Most often interventions involve exploring the cognitive or affective meaning behind observed or reported behavior as the therapist helps the parent and child understand one another's motivations and helps the parent understand the child's internal world.

CPP uses a variety of treatment modalities including (a) promoting developmental progress through play, physical contact, and language; (b) offering unstructured, reflective, developmental guidance; (c) modeling appropriate protective behavior; (d) interpreting feelings and actions; (e) providing emotional support; and (f) offering crisis intervention and concrete assistance with problems of daily living. Therapists attend to trauma themes, both in the present and in the parent's past. CPP helps the parent and child to understand the impact of psychological trauma on their experience and expectations of each other, to modulate their emotional responses to traumatic reminders, and place psychological traumas in perspective within the context of their lives. Of particular help in this latter activity is the active quest for memories of positive experiences from the parents' care-receiving pasts that may guide and sustain the parents as they care for their children (Lieberman, Padrón, Van Horn, & Harris, 2004).

Play is often at the center of CPP. Play is often children's preferred modality for creating narratives that help them make meaning of their experience. The therapist's role in CPP is to help the parent and child play together and to support the parent as she witnesses the child's play. If the parent is unable to accept the meaning of the child's play, or cannot tolerate the play because it is too evocative of her own past traumatic experiences, the therapist both creates a space in which the child can tell the story and supports the parent in witnessing the story. As children and parents grow more able to play together, children share their concerns and play provides parents with a vehicle to help children examine distorted expectations created by psychological trauma (such as unrealistic fears or suspicions about other people), to experiment with different outcomes, and to place their memories of psychologically traumatic experiences in perspective as bad things that happened to them that do not have to happen again. As the parent becomes more fully able to engage in the play, the therapist steps aside, allowing the parent and child to create conditions for change.

A central principle of CPP is that children should be told in the first session specifically why they are coming to treatment, including an acknowledgment of both their experience of psychological trauma and of the fact that the parent and the therapist understand that such experiences can be very frightening and distressing. This early statement, coming from both the parent and the therapist, makes it clear to the child that his or her experience can be talked about and need not be hidden. The therapist provides a variety of toys, including toys evocative of the trauma, but generally does not guide the play toward the trauma, allowing trauma-related feelings, beliefs, and expectations to emerge in the child's own time. For some children, a period of organizing play may happen before active play about psychologically traumatic experiences, or traumatic stress reactions may come and go as children work through both their memories of psychological trauma and other developmental concerns that are unrelated to traumatic experiences.

CPP has been demonstrated efficacious with high-risk groups including anxiously attached toddlers of immigrant mothers with trauma histories (Lieberman, Weston, & Pawl, 1991), toddlers of depressed mothers (Cicchetti, Toth, & Rogosh, 1999), children exposed to domestic violence (Lieberman, Ghosh Ippen,

& Van Horn, 2006; Lieberman, Van Horn, & Ghosh Ippen, 2005), and maltreated children (Cicchetti, Rogosch, & Toth, 2006; Toth, Maughm, Manly, Spagnola, & Cicchetti, 2002). These studies used a variety of different outcome measures including problem behaviors, PTSD symptoms in both mothers and children, attachment security, and children's representations of their parents.

Other Psychodynamic Treatment Models

Several other intervention models focus on the dynamics of early attachment relationships with traumatized and at-risk children. These include Circle of Security (Cooper, Hoffman, Powell, & Marvin, 2005), Attachment and Biobehavioral Catch-Up (Dozier, Higley, Albus, & Nutter, 2002), and Watch, Wait, and Wonder (Muir, 1992). These intervention models take various forms, both group and dyadic, but all of them focus on enhancing the quality of attachment between at risk or traumatized children and the adults who care for them, and all of them have established efficacy. In addition to these models, one study has shown that individual psychodynamic therapy, accompanied by intervention with the children's parents, was superior to a psychoeducational group intervention for sexually abused girls aged 6 to 14 years old (Trowell et al., 2002).

Conclusion

All of these psychodynamic therapy models have one thing in common: they acknowledge the centrality of caregiving relationships in children's development and recovery. Many traumatized children and their caregivers will be able to repair the breaches in their relationships without intervention. Parents who can provide sensitive, consistent care to a child following psychological trauma can often restore the child to a positive developmental trajectory. When intervention is needed, however, it should attend to children's relationships and build on their caregivers' capacity to provide the sensitive care and protection that will support healthy development.

REFERENCES

Bowlby, J. (1980). *Attachment and loss: Vol. 1. Attachment.* New York: Basic Books. (Original work published 1969)

Cicchetti, D., Rogosch, F. A., & Toth, S. L. (2006). Fostering secure attachment in infants in maltreating families through preventive interventions. *Development and Psychopathology, 18,* 623–650.

Cicchetti, D., Toth, S. L., & Rogosch, F. A. (1999). The efficacy of toddler-parent psychotherapy to increase attachment security in offspring of depressed mothers. *Attachment and Human Development, 1,* 34–36.

Cooper, G., Hoffman, K., Powell, B., & Marvin, R. (2005). The Circle of Security Intervention: Differential diagnosis and differential treatment. In L. J. Berlin, Y. Ziv, L. Amaya-Jackson, & M. T. Greenberg (Eds.), *Enhancing early attachments: Theory, research, intervention, and policy* (pp. 127–151). New York: Guilford Press.

Dozier, M., Higley, E., Albus, K., & Nutter, A. (2002). Intervening with foster infants' caregivers: Targeting three critical needs. *Infant Mental Health Journal, 23,* 541–554.

Fraiberg, S. (1980). *Clinical studies in infant mental health.* New York: Basic Books.

Freud, S. (1959). Inhibitions, symptoms, and anxiety. In J. Strachey (Ed. & Trans.), *The standard edition of the complete psychological works of Sigmund Freud* (Vol. 20, pp. 77–175). London: Hogarth Press. (Original work published 1926)

Lieberman, A. F., Ghosh Ippen, C., & Van Horn, P. (2006). Child-parent psychotherapy: 6-month follow-up of a randomized controlled trial. *Journal of the American Academy of Child and Adolescent Psychiatry, 45,* 913–918.

Lieberman, A. F., Padrón, E., Van Horn, P., & Harris, W. (2004). Angels in the nursery: The intergenerational transmission of benevolent parental influences. *Infant Mental Health Journal, 26,* 504–520.

Lieberman, A. F., & Van Horn, P. (2005). *"Don't hit my mommy!": A manual for child-parent psychotherapy with young witnesses of family violence.* Washington, DC: Zero to Three Press.

Lieberman, A. F., Van Horn, P., & Ghosh Ippen, C. (2005). Toward evidence-based treatment: Child-parent psychotherapy with preschoolers exposed to marital violence. *Journal of the American Academy of Child and Adolescent Psychiatry, 44,* 1241–1248.

Lieberman, A. F., Weston, D., & Pawl, J. H. (1991). Preventive intervention and outcome with anxiously attached dyads. *Child Development, 62,* 199–209.

Muir, E. (1992). Watching, waiting, and wondering: Applying psychoanalytic principles to mother-infant intervention. *Infant Mental Health Journal, 13,* 319–328.

Pynoos, R. S., Steinberg, A. M., & Piacentini, J. C. (1999). A developmental model of childhood traumatic stress and intersection with anxiety disorders. *Biological Psychiatry, 46,* 1542–1554.

Toth, S. L., Maughan, A., Manly, J. T., Spagnola, M., & Cicchetti, D. (2002). The relative efficacy of two interventions in altering maltreated preschool children's representation models: Implications for attachment theory. *Development and Psychopathology, 14,* 877–908.

Trowell, J., Kolvin, I., Weeramanthri, T., Sadowski, H., Berelowitz, M., Glasser, D., et al. (2002). Psychotherapy for sexually abused girls: Psychopathological outcome findings and patterns. *British Journal of Psychiatry, 180,* 234–247.

PATRICIA VAN HORN
University of California, San Francisco

See also: Countertransference; Dissociation; Family Therapy; Freud, Sigmund; Parent-Child Intervention; Psychodynamic Therapy, Adult

PSYCHOEDUCATION

Taking root as a family intervention for schizophrenia, psychoeducation gradually has been extended to a wider range of psychiatric disorders and general medical conditions, including psychological trauma; yet research on the effectiveness of these extensions is sparse, such that psychoeducation currently qualifies as an evidence-based intervention only for schizophrenia and cancer. Moreover, the term, *psychoeducation,* has been applied to an extremely wide spectrum of interventions, ranging from giving patients brief self-help materials to conducting more elaborate educational groups to engaging in intensive individual counseling. Making a case for uniformity, Lukens and McFarlane (2004) define psychoeducation as "a professionally delivered treatment modality that integrates and synergizes psychotherapeutic and educational interventions" (p. 206). As such, psychoeducation goes beyond merely providing persons with information; it aspires to engage them in collaboration with clinicians, to enhance their competence and resilience and thus, as Lukens and McFarlane aptly put it, "to use the information in a proactive fashion" (p. 206).

Psychoeducational interventions for traumatic stress disorders have been directed primarily to survivors but also may include their family members. Most psychoeducation for traumatic stress disorders is administered in group formats, but cognitive-behavioral approaches routinely incorporate educational interventions into individual treatment. The breadth of psychoeducational content mirrors the breadth of potential traumas, their multifarious effects, and the diversity of available treatments. Thus psychoeducational interventions can be specific to a type of trauma (e.g., disaster, rape trauma, childhood sexual abuse, or domestic violence), a particular disorder (e.g., PTSD), or a treatment modality (e.g., a rationale for exposure therapy). Alternatively, more comprehensive educational curricula encompass the full range of traumatic events, the broader scope of trauma (not only multiple trauma-related psychiatric disorders but also the impact on the self and relationships), and the wide range of treatment approaches (Allen, 2005). Psychoeducation can serve an especially useful function in alerting patients to potential pitfalls of treatment, for example, disabusing them of the illusion of cure through catharsis, alerting them to the risk of generating false memories in uncovering approaches, and emphasizing the need to balance processing of traumatic memories with containment in the form of emotion-regulation strategies and supportive relationships. Some patients and family members also benefit from education about intrinsically puzzling phenomena such as deliberate self-harm and dissociation.

Psychoeducation helps to normalize symptoms and, especially in group formats, counters survivors' feelings of being alone, alienated, and "crazy." Psychoeducation is not a stand-alone treatment for trauma but rather an adjunctive intervention that promotes engagement in treatment and long-range treatment adherence as well as active coping and mastery. Thus, to be effective, clinicians must not only educate patients but also *inspire* them by promoting hope and motivating them to take effective action. Groups help in this regard: patients and family members also can be inspiring—to clinicians as well as to each other.

REFERENCES

Allen, J. G. (2005). *Coping with trauma: Hope through understanding.* Washington, DC: American Psychiatric Press.

Lukens, E. P., & McFarlane, W. R. (2004). Psychoeducation as evidence-based practice: Considerations for practice, research, and policy. *Brief Treatment and Crisis Intervention, 4,* 205–225.

Jon G. Allen
Baylor College of Medicine

See also: Anxiety Management Training; Cognitive Behavior Therapy, Adult; Cognitive Behavior Therapy, Child; Cognitive Integration, Biopsychosocial; Coping; Early Intervention; Evidence-Based Treatment; Group Therapy; Information Processing; Prevention, Adult; Prevention, Child

PSYCHOLOGICAL FIRST AID, ADULT

Psychological first aid (PFA) has been defined as the use of psychosocial interventions delivered during the immediate impact phase (first 4 weeks) following a disaster or other critical incident (such as a life-threatening accident or terrorist incident) to individuals experiencing acute stress reactions or problems in functioning, with the intent of aiding adaptive coping and problem solving (Young, 2006). The term was first coined in the early disaster work of Raphael (1977) and Farberow (1978) with adults, and Pynoos and Nader (1988) with children.

Recently, a team from National Child Traumatic Stress Network (NCTSN) and the National

Center for PTSD (NCPTSD), in consultation with a diverse group of disaster response professionals, has attempted to apply the research literature on disaster mental health toward a systematic, flexible model of psychological first aid. The result is the "Psychological First Aid" (PFA) Field Operations Guide (NCTSN & NCPTSD, 2006). The PFA guide has been designed, as far as possible, to be consistent with research evidence, applicable in field settings, tailored to the full developmental spectrum (from children through older adults), and culturally informed. The guide has been designed to be flexible and targeted at practical assistance and skill-building related to the current concerns and needs identified by survivors of psychological trauma (including victims and other affected persons, such as witnesses or bereaved family members) themselves.

The NCTSN/NCPTSD PFA model includes the following eight core actions:

1. Contact and engagement
   Goal: Respond to contacts initiated by affected persons, or initiate contacts in a nonintrusive, compassionate, and helpful manner.

2. Safety and comfort
   Goal: Enhance immediate and ongoing safety, and provide physical and emotional comfort.

3. Stabilization (if necessary)
   Goal: Calm and orient emotionally overwhelmed/distraught survivors.

4. Information gathering: current needs and concerns
   Goal: Identify immediate needs and concerns, gather additional information, and tailor PFA interventions.

5. Practical assistance
   Goal: Offer practical help to the survivor in addressing immediate needs and concerns.

6. Connection with social supports
   Goal: Reduce distress by helping structure opportunities for brief or ongoing contacts with primary support persons or other sources of support,

including family members, friends, and community helping resources.

7. Information on coping support
   Goal: Provide the individual with information (including education about stress reactions and coping) that may help them deal with the event and its aftermath.

8. Linkage with collaborative services
   Goal: Link survivors with needed services, and inform them about available services that may be needed in the future.

Most PFA contacts will involve providing only a subset of the actions, depending on the context. The choice of actions and the amount of time spent on each will depend on the needs of the survivor and on the context of delivery.

PFA may be delivered by mental health providers from a variety of professions. Beyond the professional training and credentials required for practitioners in those fields, it has been recommended that PFA providers be prepared by specialized training and supervised experience in delivering mental health interventions to survivors of disasters or other critical incidents (Young, 2006).

As a relatively brief, nonstigmatizing, low-cost form of care, PFA's provision of support, practical assistance, and information on positive coping is designed to be tailored to: (a) help survivors better understand a range of posttrauma responses; (b) view their posttrauma reactions as expectable and understandable (not as reactions to be feared, signs of personal failure or weakness, or signs of mental illness); (c) recognize the circumstances under which they should consider seeking further counseling; (d) know how and where to access additional help, including mental health counseling; (e) increase use of social supports and other adaptive ways of coping with the trauma and its effects; (f) decrease use of problematic forms of coping (e.g., excessive alcohol consumption, extreme social isolation); and (g) increase ability to help family members cope (e.g., information about how to talk to children about what happened). Accurate and timely information regarding the nature of the unfolding disaster situation is also an important part of education.

While PFA has not yet been systematically studied, experience in the field suggests that it is acceptable to and well-received by consumers, due to its flexible, tailored approach to helping to solve practical needs, as well as it's voluntary nature. However, it is important to keep in mind that the relative contribution of early and short interventions may be necessarily small because past history, differing exposure, and ongoing stress levels make it difficult to identify which persons are at risk for continued problems. PFA is meant to be embedded in a systemic, multifaceted response involving mental health, public health, medical, and emergency response systems, federal, state, local, and nonprofit agencies.

REFERENCES

Farberow, N. L. (1978). *Field manual for human service workers in major disasters (National Child Traumatic Stress Network and the National Center for PTSD [2006]): The psychological first aid field operations guide* (2nd ed.). Retrieved January 30, 2007, from www.ncptsd.va.gov/pfa/PFA.html.

National Child Traumatic Stress Network and the National Center for PTSD. (2006). *Adult psychological first aid* (DHHS Publication No. ADM 78-537). Rockville, MD: Author.

Pynoos, R. S., & Nader, K. (1988). Psychological first aid and treatment approach to children exposed to community violence: Research implications. *Journal of Traumatic Stress, 1,* 445–473.

Raphael, B. (1977). The Granville train disaster: Psychological needs and their management. *Medical Journal of Australia, 1,* 303–305.

Young, B. (2006). The immediate response to disaster: Psychological first aid. In E. C. Ritchie, P. J. Watson, & M. J. Friedman (Eds.), *Mental health intervention following disasters or mass violence* (pp. 134–154). New York: Guilford Press.

Patricia J. Watson
National Center for Posttraumatic Stress Disorder

See also: Acute Stress Disorder; Anxiety Management Training; Cognitive Behavior Therapy, Adult; Coping; Critical Incident Stress Management; Disasters; Early Intervention; National Center for PTSD; National Child Traumatic Stress Network; Prevention, Adult; Psychoeducation; Psychological First Aid, Child and Adolescent; Social Support

PSYCHOLOGICAL FIRST AID, CHILD AND ADOLESCENT

Principles and procedures for responding to psychological needs of children and adolescents in the first hours and days following disaster have been articulated in the *Psychology First Aid Field Operations Guide,* second edition, developed by the National Child Traumatic Stress Network and National Center for PTSD (2006). PFA comprises eight core actions, each of which can be offered to children and adolescents with appropriate consideration for developmental level and contextual factors. The overriding goal of PFA is to reduce the initial distress caused by traumatic events and to foster adaptive functioning and coping among survivors. The core actions of PFA are practical skills that are consistent with research on risk and resilience following trauma, easily applied in field settings, and appropriate for use across the life span.

In some instances, PFA will be delivered through the parents and other caregivers with little or no direct contact by the professional with the children or adolescents, thereby helping families regain control and reestablish the adult protective shield for youth. In other cases, PFA may be provided directly to children and adolescents. Regardless of the mechanism for delivery, PFA is focused on helping survivors regain control and a sense of safety. The focus is on strengthening families' coping abilities. PFA is designed to support, not supplant, parents and other caregivers in helping their family members cope effectively.

The following excerpts are from the National Child Traumatic Stress Network and National Center for guidelines for disaster responders who provide PFA to children and families. The guidelines are written to help responders use PFA in a helpful and effective manner.

Guidelines

Contact and Engagement

Respond appropriately to contacts initiated by survivors and initiate contacts with at-risk individuals in a nonintrusive way that is both compassionate and helpful. PFA providers should, when possible, obtain caregiver permission before speaking with children and adolescents. When caregivers are not present, inform the caregiver of the PFA contact as soon as possible. Providers should get down physically on the child's level and use language that is easy for children to understand.

Safety and Comfort

Enhance immediate and ongoing safety for survivors as well as take action to provide physical and emotional comfort. For children, this includes ensuring that they are in a safe, supervised environment and protecting them from further trauma exposure (including thought media coverage) as much as possible. Reduce uncertainty by giving children developmentally appropriate factual information about what has happened and what steps are being taken to protect and assist them. Connect children with their caregivers as quickly as possible. Set up a child-friendly space when feasible. For children with a missing, seriously injured or dead family member, give caregivers information on managing children's grief and concerns relating to issues such as death notification, body identification, and participation in funerals or memorial services.

Stabilization

Help calm children who are disoriented or overwhelmed. If possible, enlist and support family members or familiar adults in comforting and orienting highly distressed children. It often helps just to remain calm, quiet, and present for a few minutes. If a child remains extremely agitated, disoriented, or distressed, it may help to refocus attention on the present by asking him or her to listen and look at you, to describe nondistressing features of the current surroundings, and to engage in "grounding" activities (e.g., naming nondistressing sounds or objects in the room, breathe in and out slowly). Consult with medical or mental health professionals if a child remains markedly disoriented or overwhelmed for an extended period.

Information Gathering

Identify children's most immediate needs and concerns. Avoid asking for in-depth descriptions of traumatic experiences, as these may provoke additional distress in the immediate aftermath of the trauma. Instead, focus on identifying current needs and concerns and address these directly using the other components of PFA or referral to additional services if necessary (e.g., if an immediate health need is identified). Caregivers' perspectives on children's immediate needs and concerns should be solicited if possible. Child reports of their current needs and concerns are also valuable, as these may vary from those identified by adults.

Practical Assistance

Help children articulate their immediate needs, develop a realistic plan to meet these, and take action. Children and adolescents may participate in problem solving individually, in groups, or with family members. Adult support is often needed to follow through on plans, so caregivers should be involved when appropriate.

Connection with Social Supports

Reduce children's distress by developing opportunities for contacts with a variety of support systems including family members, friends, and community resources. It may help to bring children of similar ages together for activities that are soothing and familiar, so long as they know where their adult caregivers are. Examples of appropriate activities include art, games, reading, and music. Help children and adolescents decide what types of support they need, who might provide this, how to ask for support, and how to offer it to others. Caregivers should be involved in facilitating access social support if possible.

Information on Coping Support

Offer basic information about stress reactions and coping that may help children and adolescents deal with the psychological impact of disasters. Talk with youth about common physical and emotional reactions to the type of trauma they experienced, using age-appropriate language and examples. Give examples of coping strategies that are helpful and those that may be maladaptive. Relaxation techniques tailored for children and adolescents may be taught. Talk with families about the importance of reestablishing family routines to the extent possible as a way to promote recovery, and give parents information on addressing common posttraumatic reactions in children and adolescents (e.g., sleep problems, anger, guilt or shame).

Linkages with Collaborate Services

Take direct action to link children and adolescents with needed services within their community and provide information about available services that may be helpful in the future. Children and adolescents are unlikely to seek out or follow-through on services without adult support.

REFERENCE

National Child Traumatic Stress Network and the National Center for PTSD (2006). *Adult psychological first aid* (DHHS Publication No. ADM 78-537). Rockville, MD: Author.

ERIC M. VERNBERG
University of Kansas

ANNE K. JACOBS
University of Kansas

See also: Acute Stress Disorder; Child Development; Cognitive Behavior Therapy, Child; Coping; Critical Incident Stress Management; Early Intervention; National Center for PTSD; National Child Traumatic Stress Network; Prevention, Child; Psychoeducation; Psychological First Aid, Adult; Social Support

PSYCHONEUROIMMUNOLOGY

Psychoneuroimmunology is a field of scientific investigation that is concerned with the reciprocal effects of behavior, the central nervous system (i.e., the brain) and various components of the immune system (which is responsible for resistance to infection or other pathology). Research has shown that classical conditioning (e.g., pairing of a novel taste with an immunosuppressive drug such as cyclophosphamide) can cause once neutral stimuli (the taste) to assume characteristics of the effects of immunosuppressive agents administered at the same time. In addition, emotions, exposure to stressors and stress reactions, and syndromes such as depression appear to be linked to changes in the immune system. These relationships are all mediated by the brain and reflect processes that have psychological as well as neuroendocrine (i.e., brain chemicals, particularly those related to stress responses and emotions) elements. Data are also accumulating to suggest that the immune system can have effects on the brain and on how we feel or behave. These findings and others have established the importance of psychoneuroimmunological research in just 40 years of active investigation.

There are several reasons why scientists and clinicians have wondered about the role of psychological trauma on immune system activity and resistance to infection. Clearly, optimally operating immune systems are associated with good health and resistance to pathology. Evidence has also accumulated suggesting that increases in stress reactions or other emotional distress are accompanied by decreases in immune cell function and suppressed healing of wounds. Studies of vulnerability to experimentally applied cold viruses have also shown that stress reactions increase peoples' vulnerability to infection. As an extreme form of stress, it is possible that psychological trauma might be associated with relatively larger changes in immune function than exposure to other stressors. The finding that immune activity can be conditioned provides a second context for relating psychological trauma and immunity, because stress responses to psychological trauma such as the symptoms of posttraumatic stress disorder (PTSD) are at least partly the product of classical conditioning (*see:* **Learning Theory**).

Because of considerable overlap in effects, time frames and measures, it is useful first to briefly consider findings of research on stressor exposure and stress reaction and their relationship to immune function. After that, we turn to studies of disasters or other traumatic events and PTSD, and their relationship to immune system functioning.

Stress and Immunity

There have been many studies of stress and the immune system (e.g., Kiecolt-Glaser & Glaser, 1995). Some studies have focused on the magnitude, duration, and/or consequence of stress-related immune system changes, others have been more concerned with mechanisms such as hormonal activity, and still others have been most concerned with linking stress-related changes in the immune system to disease. Some studies consider short, often laboratory-based stressors such as giving a speech or completing difficult mental arithmetic problems and others focus on more chronic stressors and longer-lasting effects as in the case of stress at work or due to illness (e.g., Bachen et al., 1992; Herbert & Cohen, 1993). Many different measures, theories, and research approaches have characterized this research area but, nevertheless, clear patterns of relationships have emerged. For example, some of the effects of acute exposure to stress are different from those associated with chronic stress. Numbers of some subtypes of immune cells (lymphocytes) increase during acute exposure to laboratory stressors but are lower among people experiencing chronic stressors. Functions of other immune system cells are also altered in different ways. Numbers of natural killer (NK) cells increase but their ability to kill tumor cells is not affected by acute laboratory stress (Delahanty, Dougall, Craig, Jenkins, & Baum, 1997). Numbers of NK cells are generally lower and their ability to kill tumor cells also is suppressed when chronic exposure to stressors occurs. The ability of lymphocytes to proliferate, to make replicates (copies) of themselves when stimulated, appears to be suppressed by both acute and chronic stressor exposure (Bachen et al., 1992; Zakowski, 1995).

Research has also indicated that a wide variety of immune activities that are affected by exposure to stressors. Numbers of different types of immune cells may vary and the activity of several lymphocytes (T cells, B cells), monocytes, cytokines, and NK cells has been linked to stressor exposure. Presumed mediators of these effects include stress hormones (cortisol, norepinephrine, epinephrine; *see:* **Biology, Neurochemistry**) as well as several other hormones or peptides. A number of studies have correlated hormonal activity with stress exposures and responses and with immune function measures, and some studies have been able to eliminate stress-related effects on immunity by eliminating the effects of epinephrine (Bachen et al., 1995; Benschop, Jacobs, et al., 1996; Benschop, Rodriguez-Feuuerhahn, & Schedlowski, 1996).

These studies have demonstrated clear effects of exposure to stressors on the immune system, which is the essential premise of psychoneuroimmunology, that is, that psychological factors (such as stressor exposure or stress reactions) not only affect the body's nervous system (the "neuro" aspect) but that both the psychological and neurological systems also affect the immune system. Psychological interventions to reduce distress in patients also appear to buffer the immune system and minimize effects of stress, and research findings now show that some clinical outcomes (wound healing after injury; resistance to viral infection) are mediated by stressor exposures (Cohen et al., 1998; Kiecolt-Glaser & Glaser, 1995). Debate continues, however, about the magnitude of effects of stressor exposure, particularly transient, brief stressors. Many observed changes are reductions or increases but the immune system levels usually remain in the "normal" range, raising questions about whether observed changes in cell numbers or function translate into stronger or weaker immune defense. The few examples of clinical outcomes that can be traced to stress-immune system relationships are promising but more work is needed.

Stress and Psychological Trauma

There are several ways to approach questions about traumatic stress and immune status. Psychological trauma is not replicable in the laboratory, so investigators must rely on naturalistic traumatic events and the best measures available in often challenging clinical and logistic situations. One approach is to target specific traumatic events, like disasters, motor vehicle accidents, assault, abuse, or other traumatic event and follow survivors from as soon as is possible after the event and into the future. Some of these survivors will develop symptoms of PTSD while others will not, allowing comparisons of these two subgroups of trauma-exposed individuals. In this context, PTSD is a surrogate for greater impact of the traumatic event, and people who were more affected (i.e., who develop PTSD) are compared to those who were less affected (i.e., do not develop PTSD). Alternatively, a control group, matched on some preconceived criteria but who have not experienced a traumatic event can be recruited and compared to participants who did. Samples of PTSD patients can also be assessed and compared to people without traumatic exposure or PTSD, without reference to a specific event. Each of these research approaches has different strengths and weaknesses. For the most part longitudinal designs (in which people are assessed at several points of time after—and preferably also before—exposure to traumatic stressors or the development of PTSD) that include carefully crafted strategies for comparing meaningfully different groups of people and imaginative measurement schemes and rigorous measures have been most productive.

In this context, some research has examined immune system changes that occur during or after psychological trauma. About half report changes or differences in immune cell numbers and/or function as a function of exposure to traumatic events (e.g., Ironson et al., 1997). These studies generally find effects that resemble the acute stressor exposure effects noted earlier, including increased cell numbers and selective suppression of immune system function. Other studies report immune system responses more like those associated with chronic stressor exposure, including lower numbers of some cells and suppression of some immune system functions. Although the evidence seems clear that there is a relationship between psychological trauma and immune status, the nature of this relationship is not yet obvious.

Some studies shed light on this question, studying people during ongoing traumatic events, and reporting that when one measures immunity during psychological trauma exposure, responses look more like acute stress responses than when people are studied at longer periods (e.g., months or years) after psychological trauma has occurred (Sabioncello et al., 2000). Persistent effects that long outlive the direct effects of the traumatic event occur in a substantial minority of people exposed to traumatic events and appear to be similar to changes in immune functions found in chronic stress situations (e.g., DeBellis, Burke, Trickett, & Putnam, 1996; Ironson et al., 1997; Sergerstrom, Solomon, Kemeny, & Fahey, 1998). Because most people recover relatively quickly after most traumatic events, these findings reflect a number of possible differences and factors: those experiencing more persistent effects are also more likely to have PTSD or other psychiatric syndromes and more likely to be in treatment. People recover at different rates for many reasons, some of which may also be immunoreactive. In addition, most studies do not initiate investigation until after the traumatic event has ended and participants have begun to recover. Two studies, one of a horrific air disaster recovery effort and the other of the aftermath of Hurricane Andrew found evidence of immune system effects of disaster-related exposure and both found that these effects were correlated with symptoms of PTSD, underscoring the potential difference between the lesser effects of exposure to traumatic stressors per se on immune system functioning and more severe immune system changes that are associated with the development of chronic posttraumatic stress reactions such as PTSD (Delahanty et al., 1997;

McKinnon, Weisse, Reynolds, Bowles, & Baum, 1989).

There are a handful of studies that examined PTSD in combat veterans years after military service that report mixed results with regard to measures of immune system functioning (e.g., Boscarino & Chang, 1999; Laudenslager et al., 1998). Because of the long (decades in some cases) intervals between traumatic stressor exposure (combat) and immune assessment, it is difficult to interpret these data. A study of immune status among people living near the Three Mile Island nuclear power plant several years after the accident found evidence of lower numbers of some immune cells and less vigorous immune function among those living nearby (McKinnon et al., 1989). In this case, stress reactions associated the experience and a variety of other factors were followed for several years, including the interval between the accident and assessment of immunity. However, the complex nature of the immune system and the often inverse relation among various measures of function make this literature difficult to interpret as well.

Several mechanisms and mediating conditions have been proposed to explain possible links between psychological trauma and immunity. We have known for years that there is extensive innervation (activation) of immune organs by the autonomic immune system and that many immune cells exhibit neuroendocrine receptors that suggest hormonal modulation of function. Sympathetic hormones (i.e., epinephrine, norepinephrine) are related to many stress-immune associations that have been observed, and adrenergic blockade appears to buffer stress-related changes in immune status. In addition, glucocorticoids (primarily cortisol; *see:* **Biology, Neurochemistry**), also produced in the adrenal glands, reduce inflammation and generally suppress immune function and also appear to drive many stress-related immune changes. There are relatively few studies that examined neuroendocrine correlates of traumatic stress. Most find some evidence of mediation by sympathetic hormones after the traumatic stressor has ended. In studies of ongoing stressors, cortisol also has been linked to changes in immunity.

Importance of Psychological Trauma-Related Immune Changes

There are many reasons why studying and understanding the impact of traumatic stressor exposure and traumatic stress reactions on immunity are important. At the top of this list are potential effects on physical health: Evidence suggests that people who experience traumatic events, particularly those who develop PTSD or other mental health problems, are more likely to experience illness or latent viral activity. There is some evidence suggesting that immune system variables are related to vulnerability to illness among psychological trauma victims, but the magnitude of this effect and the likelihood that it is independent of behavioral changes that also occur in the wake of traumatic events are not yet clear. Research findings also suggest possible links between traumatic stressor exposure and traumatic stress reactions and herpes virus reactivation, autoimmune disease, HIV disease progression, and chronic fatigue syndrome (*see:* **HIV**; **Medical Illness, Adult**). These promising leads also need more research attention before definitive conclusions can be drawn.

REFERENCES

Bachen, E. A., Manuck, S. B., Cohen, S., Muldoon, M. F., Raible, R., Herbert, T. B., et al. (1995). Adrenergic blockade ameliorates cellular immune responses to mental stress in humans. *Psychosomatic Medicine, 57,* 366–372.

Bachen, E. A., Manuck, S. B., Marsland, A. L., Cohen, S., Malkoff, S. B., Muldoon, M. F., et al. (1992). Lymphocyte subset and cellular immune response to a brief experimental stressor. *Psychosomatic Medicine, 54,* 673–679.

Benschop, R. J., Jacobs, R., Sommer, B., Shurmeyer, T. H., Raab, J. R., Schmidy, R. E., et al. (1996). Modulation of the immunologic response to acute stress in humans by beta-blockade or benzodiazepines. *FASEB Journal, 10,* 517–524.

Benschop, R. J., Rodriguez-Feuuerhahn, M., & Schedlowski, M. (1996). Catecholamine-induced leukocytosis: Early observations, current research, and future directions. *Brain, Behavior, and Immunity, 10,* 77–91.

Boscarino, J. A., & Chang, J. C. (1999). Higher abnormal leukocyte and lymphocyte counts 20 years after exposure to severe stress: Research and clinical implications. *Psychosomatic Medicine, 61,* 378–386.

Cohen, S., Frank, E., Doyle, W. J., Skoner, D. P., Rabin, B. S., & Gawltney, J. M., Jr. (1998). Types of stressors that increase susceptibility to the common cold in healthy adults. *Health Psychology, 17,* 214–223.

DeBellis, M. D., Burke, L., Trickett, P. K., & Putnam, F. W. (1996). Antinuclear antibodies and thyroid function in sexually abused girls. *Journal of Traumatic Stress, 9,* 369–378.

Delahanty, D. L., Dougall, A. L., Craig, K. J., Jenkins, F. J., & Baum, A. (1997). Chronic stress and natural killer cell activity after exposure to traumatic death. *Psychosomatic Medicine, 59,* 467–476.

Herbert, T. B., & Cohen, S. (1993). Stress and immunity in humans: A meta-analytic review. *Psychosomatic Medicine, 55,* 364–379.

Ironson, G., Wynings, C., Schneiderman, N., Baum, A., Rodriguez, M., Greenwood, D., et al. (1997). Post traumatic stress symptoms, intrusive thoughts, loss and immune function and Hurricane Andrew. *Psychosomatic Medicine, 59,* 128–141.

Kiecolt-Glaser, J. K., & Glaser, R. (1995). Psychoneuroimmunology and health consequences: Data and shared mechanisms. *Psychosomatic Medicine, 57,* 269–274.

Laudenslager, M. L., Aasal, R., Adler, L., Berger, C. L., Montgomery, P. T., Sandberg, E., et al. (1998). Elevated cytotoxicity in combat veterans with long-term post-traumatic stress disorder: Preliminary observations. *Brain, Behavior, and Immunity, 12,* 74–79.

McKinnon, W., Weisse, C. S., Reynolds, C. P., Bowles, C. A., & Baum, A. (1989). Chronic stress, leukocyte subpopulations, and humoral response to latent viruses. *Health Psychology, 8*(4), 389–402.

Sabioncello, A., Kocijan-Hercigonja, D., Rabatic, S., Tomacic, J., Jeren, T., Matijevic, L., et al. (2000). Immune, endocrine, and psychological responses in civilians displaced by war. *Psychosomatic Medicine, 62,* 502–508.

Sergerstrom, S. C., Solomon, G. F., Kemeny, M. E., & Fahey, J. L. (1998). Relationship of worry to immune sequelae of the Northridge earthquake. *Journal of Behavioral Medicine, 21,* 433–450.

Zakowski, S. G. (1995). The effects of stressor predictability on lymphocyte proliferation in humans. *Psychology and Health, 10,* 409–425.

Andrew Baum
University of Pittsburgh

Angela Liegey Dougall
University of Texas, Arlington

See also: Biology, Neurochemistry; HIV; Learning Theory; Medical Illness, Adult; Somatic Complaints; Stress

PSYCHOPHARMACOLOGY, ADULT

See: Pharmacotherapy, Adult

PSYCHOSIS

Psychosis is a general psychiatric term that refers to symptoms that reflect a departure from reality, most notably including hallucinations (i.e., false perceptions) and delusions (i.e., false beliefs not shared by a subculture to which the person belongs), but also including formal thought disorder (i.e., disturbance of the use of language such as neologisms or disordered syntax) and bizarre behavior. Certain mental disorders, most notably schizophrenia, are characterized by persistent vulnerability to psychotic thought processes and behavior. Based on the writings of the neurologist Hughlings Jackson (1931), a common alternative term for psychotic symptoms is *positive symptoms* to describe excesses in normal cognitive, sensory, and behavioral processes. These symptoms are distinguished from *negative symptoms,* which involve a diminution or deficit of such processes (e.g., anhedonia, blunted affective expressiveness).

The interplay between trauma and psychosis has long been a topic of speculation and debate. In this entry, we address four different issues pertaining to the relationships between psychosis and trauma: (a) traumatic life experiences as a precipitant of psychotic symptoms and psychotic disorders (e.g., schizophrenia); (b) psychotic symptoms as a dimension of posttraumatic stress disorder (PTSD) symptomatology; (c) the high rate and impact of trauma exposure and PTSD in persons with psychotic disorders; and (d) psychosis and related treatment experiences as a traumatic event.

Trauma as a Risk Factor or Precipitant of Psychosis

There is abundant evidence from epidemiological surveys in the general population that the experience of traumatic events is predictive of subsequent psychotic symptoms (Janssen et al., 2004; Ross & Joshi, 1992; Shevlin, Dorahy, & Adamson, 2007). Furthermore, this increased risk is present even after statistically controlling for the presence of PTSD (Scott, Chant, Andrews, Martin, & McGrath, 2007). The correlates of trauma do not appear to be limited to psychotic symptoms per se, but also include a broader range of schizotypal personality disorder symptoms such as perceptual aberrations, magical ideation, and peculiarity (Berenbaum, Valera, & Kerns, 2003; Irwin, 1992).

Exposure to traumatic events and other adverse experiences in childhood have also been repeatedly linked to increased rates of psychotic disorders such as schizophrenia (Felitti et al., 1998; Read, van Os, Morrison, & Ross, 2005). In addition, among individuals with severe mental illnesses such as schizophrenia, bipolar disorder, and treatment-refractory major depression, trauma exposure in childhood and adolescence is associated with increased severity of psychotic symptoms (Ellason & Ross, 1997; Goff, Brotman, Kindlon, Waites, & Amico, 1991; Surrey, Swett, Michaels, & Levin, 1990). Thus, traumatic experiences early in life are strongly related to the subsequent development of psychotic symptoms and psychotic disorders.

The etiological or causal significance of trauma to the development of psychosis and disorders such as schizophrenia has been the topic of much debate. For example, the validity of the diagnosis of schizophrenia has been challenged by some who have argued that the characteristic psychotic symptoms are, at least in a subset of cases, the result of neurobiological and psychological effects of early trauma on brain functioning and cognitive processing (Bentall, 2003; Read, Perry, Moskowitz, & Connolly, 2001). Others have suggested that the effects of exposure to traumatic events interact with information processing abnormalities resulting in psychosis (Fowler et al., 2006).

Relatedly, based on the stress-vulnerability model of schizophrenia (Nuechterlein & Dawson, 1984; Zubin & Spring, 1977), it may be argued that early life trauma limits the development of coping skills and the availability of social supports, and serves as a stressor that increases preexisting psychobiological vulnerability to psychosis. These and other hypotheses have spurred increased research efforts aimed at better understanding the relationship between trauma and the later development of psychosis.

Psychosis in Persons with PTSD

Although PTSD is classified as an anxiety disorder, psychotic symptoms such as hallucinations have long been observed in the clinical literature as a response to exposure to traumatic events and bereavement, particularly following exposure to extreme and prolonged trauma (Grimby, 1993; Grinker & Spiegel, 1945; Oruc & Bell, 1995). In recent years, research has focused on the question of whether the presence of psychotic symptoms following trauma exposure is related to the presence and severity of PTSD.

There is now abundant evidence that psychotic symptoms occur in people with PTSD that cannot be explained by other disorders such as schizophrenia of psychotic depression (Butler, Mueser, Sprock, & Braff, 1996; Hamner, Frueh, Ulmer, & Arana, 1999; Mueser & Butler, 1987; Sareen, Cox, Goodwin, & Asmundson, 2005). The most common psychotic symptoms reported include hallucinations, delusions, and bizarre behavior, but not formal thought disorder. Hallucinations are often trauma-related and may be a form of reexperiencing the trauma (e.g., hearing the voices of fallen comrades in combat calling to the individual). Delusions are most often paranoid in nature, may not be systematized, and appear to be an extreme variant of the pervasive distrust that often accompanies interpersonal trauma.

The presence of psychotic symptoms is related to more severe trauma exposure, as well as to more severe PTSD symptoms (Butler et al., 1996; Hamner et al., 1999; Mueser & Butler, 1987). Hispanic ethnicity (Escobar et al., 1983; Wilcox, Briones, & Suess, 1991) also seems to be a risk factor for psychotic symptoms following trauma exposure. Psychotic symptoms do not appear to be simply a by-product of the reexperiencing symptoms of PTSD. In addition, psychotic symptoms in PTSD are not related to family history of psychosis (Sautter, Cornwell, Johnson, Wiley, & Faraone, 2002), suggesting that it does not reflect an underlying psychotic disorder. The findings suggest that psychotic symptoms may be part of the extreme end of the continuum of posttraumatic reactions captured by PTSD.

The treatment implications of psychotic symptoms in PTSD are unclear at this point, mainly because most controlled treatment research has not attempted to evaluate these symptoms. Some case reports indicate the psychotic symptoms in PTSD improve with routine cognitive-behavioral treatment of the disorder (Mueser & Taylor, 1997; Waldfogel & Mueser, 1988). Further research is needed to understand the special needs of this group, as well as risk factors for developing psychotic symptoms in PTSD.

Psychological Trauma and PTSD in Persons with Psychotic Disorders

As awareness of the problem of trauma in the general population has grown, increasing attention has been paid to trauma in vulnerable populations, including people with disabilities (Mueser, Hiday, Goodman, & Valenti-Hein, 2003; Sobsey, 1994). As previously discussed, traumatic events in childhood and adolescence increase the risk of developing psychotic disorders. It is also well established that people with severe mental illness, including those with psychotic disorders, are highly prone to victimization following the onset of their psychiatric disorder (Goodman, Rosenberg, Mueser, & Drake, 1997; Honkonen, Henriksson, Koivisto, Stengård, & Salokangas, 2004).

The high rate of trauma in people with psychotic disorders has spurred interest in examining PTSD in this population. Research on

the evaluation of trauma history and PTSD has shown that reliable and valid assessments can be made in this population (Meyer, Muenzenmaier, Cancienne, & Struening, 1996; Mueser et al., 2001). Furthermore, multiple studies have shown that individuals with psychotic disorders have much higher rates of PTSD than have been found in the general population. The majority of studies report rates of *current* PTSD in persons with psychotic disorders ranging between 28% to 48% (Cascardi, Mueser, DeGiralomo, & Murrin, 1996; Craine, Henson, Colliver, & MacLean, 1988; Mueser et al., 1998; Mueser, Salyers, et al., 2004; Switzer et al., 1999), far exceeding the current (2% to 3%) and lifetime (8% to 12%) rates of PTSD reported in the general population (Breslau, Davis, Andreski, & Peterson, 1991; Kessler, Sonnega, Bromet, Hughes, & Nelson, 1995). In contrast to research in the general population indicating that women are more likely to develop PTSD than men (Breslau & Anthony, 2007), most studies of PTSD in psychotic disorders have failed to reveal gender differences.

The high prevalence of PTSD in persons with psychotic disorders has important clinical implications. PTSD in this population is associated with poorer clinical and psychosocial functioning, including higher levels of distress, poorer social functioning and quality of life, more severe symptoms, greater substance abuse problems, worse health, and higher use of acute psychiatric services such as emergency rooms and hospitals (Mueser, Essock, Haines, Wolfe, & Xie, 2004; Mueser, Salyers, et al., 2004; Resnick, Bond, & Mueser, 2003; Switzer et al., 1999). These associations raise the question of whether PTSD may impact on the course of severe mental illness.

In an effort to understand how PTSD may worsen the course of psychotic disorders, Mueser and colleagues (Mueser, Rosenberg, Goodman, & Trumbetta, 2002) developed a model based on the stress-vulnerability model of schizophrenia (Zubin & Spring, 1977) in which they posited both direct and indirect effects of PTSD on the illness. As illustrated in Figure 1, PTSD is hypothesized to directly worsen psychotic symptoms and functioning

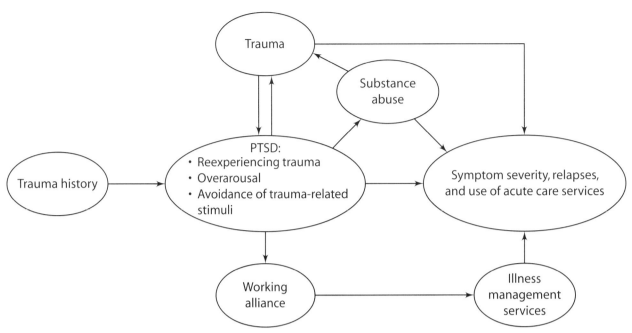

Figure 1. Hypothesized direct and indirect effects of PTSD on psychotic disorders.

through the core PTSD symptoms of reexperiencing the trauma, avoidance of trauma-related stimuli, and overarousal. For example, reexperiencing the trauma (e.g., intrusive memories, flashbacks) may serve as a general stressor, precipitating relapses of psychotic symptoms, whereas avoidance of trauma-related stimuli may lead to social isolation when the traumatic event was interpersonal in nature (e.g., physical or sexual abuse), resulting in lower levels of social support and increased vulnerability to relapses. Hypothesized indirect effects of PTSD include its effects on increasing substance abuse, which can directly precipitate relapses and indirectly result in further exposure to traumatic events, which can in turn lead to relapses. In addition, considering the interpersonal distrust common among trauma survivors, the model suggests that PTSD may impede the development of a good working alliance with the case manager (or other treatment provider), leading to receipt of fewer illness management services (e.g., medication checks, teaching coping strategies), and an increased risk of relapse. The implications of this model are that effective treatment of PTSD could improve the course of psychotic disorders.

Recent efforts have focused on the development of treatment approaches specially designed to address trauma and PTSD in persons with psychotic disorders (Frueh et al., 2004; Harris, 1998; Mueser et al., 2007; Mueser, Rosenberg, Jankowski, Hamblen, & Descamps, 2004). Common among these treatment models is the attempt to address trauma-related problems in an individual or group context that recognizes the high vulnerability of this population to stress, as well as the multitude of other challenges these individuals experience in their lives (e.g., housing instability, substance abuse, cognitive impairment, ongoing trauma exposure). These programs differ with respect to whether they narrowly focus on PTSD or more broadly seek to address a wider range of trauma-related problems that are not necessarily part of the PTSD syndrome (e.g., poor social skills, body image).

Research on different treatment programs for PTSD in persons with severe mental illness is underway. One randomized controlled trial has been completed, which found positive effects at the 6-month follow-up of a 12- to 16-week individual cognitive-behavioral treatment program compared to treatment as usual on PTSD symptoms, depression, other symptoms, trauma-related cognitions, and working alliance with the case manager (Mueser et al., 2008). These findings support the feasibility of treating PTSD in persons with psychotic disorders, and suggest that such treatment could improve the course of psychosis.

Psychosis as a Traumatic Stressor and Its Treatment

Although the *DSM-IV* (American Psychiatric Association, 1994) PTSD's Criterion A1 definition of trauma narrowly focuses on events that pose a grave threat of death or physical injury, the term *trauma* is sometimes more generally used to refer to any sudden life event that is discordant with the individual's view of the world or self, and that presents a challenge in terms of adaptation to that event (Horowitz, 1986). One such more broadly defined traumatic event is the experience of psychosis and related treatment experiences associated with severe psychiatric illness (Shaner & Eth, 1989; Williams-Keeler, Milliken, & Jones, 1994). Individuals who are first developing psychotic symptoms, such as auditory hallucinations or paranoid delusions, often respond with terror to these events, which are outside of their previous life experiences and which certainly may threaten one's sense of integrity and selfhood. In addition, when psychotic symptoms have been controlled, clients may reflect back on their own bizarre behavior (e.g., running around naked) or thinking (e.g., grandiose delusions) with mortification. Aside from psychotic symptoms themselves, elements of the treatment of psychosis may be experienced as "traumatic" when they involve coercive practices such as involuntary hospitalization, forced medication, and use of seclusion or restraints. Finally, individuals who develop a psychosis may be vulnerable to interpersonal trauma that meets *DSM-IV* (American Psychiatric Association, 1994) PTSD's criterion A1 in the psychiatric treatment setting (referred to as sanctuary trauma), including exposure to threats, exploitation, or violence from other patients or staff members (Robins, Sauvageot, Cusack, Suffoletta-Maierle, & Frueh, 2005).

Many of the events described, especially psychological trauma related to psychotic symptoms and treatment, may be experienced and labeled by individuals as "traumatic," but fail to meet the *DSM-IV* (American Psychiatric Association, 1994) PTSD Criterion A1/A2 definition of trauma, either because the events did not pose a genuine physical threat to the person or because the person did not react with negative emotions (e.g., fear, helplessness and horror) at the time of the event. Nevertheless, posttraumatic stress-like symptoms may occur as a result of these experiences. Indeed several studies document rates of PTSD syndrome (not including A1/A2 criteria) ranging 31% to 66% in clients following the onset of a psychotic episode (Frame & Morrison, 2001; McGorry et al., 1991; Morrison, Bowe, Larkin, & Nothard, 2001; Shaw, McFarlane, Bookless, & Air, 2002). It is unclear whether PTSD-like symptoms in these individuals actually reflect PTSD due to the effects of prior exposure to traumatic events meeting A1/A2 criteria, are caused by general high levels of distress, or truly reflect PTSD phenomenology related to psychologically traumatic events that fall outside of the narrow A1/A2 definitions of trauma (*see:* **Diagnosis of Traumatic Stress Disorder [*DSM* & *ICD*]; Posttraumatic Stress Disorder; Posttraumatic Stress Disorder, Diagnosis of; Trauma, Definition**).

The development of PTSD-like symptoms following a psychotic episode could have treatment implications for understanding problems of poor treatment adherence in persons with a first episode of psychosis (Coldham, Addington, & Addington, 2002). Clients may perceive participation in treatment as a trauma-related stimulus (e.g., taking medication, seeing a doctor or case manager), and become nonadherent in order to avoid unpleasant memories and thoughts related to those experiences (Mueser & Rosenberg, 2003). These associations suggest that treating PTSD-like symptoms related to the experience of psychosis and its treatment could improve treatment adherence and outcome in people who have recently developed a psychosis.

Conclusion

Psychotic symptoms are linked to trauma exposure and PTSD in a number of important ways. Psychotic symptoms often occur in severe PTSD, and appear to reflect the extreme end of the continuum of PTSD symptoms. Traumatic experiences in childhood and adolescence also increase the likelihood of individuals developing psychotic disorders such as schizophrenia. After the onset of psychotic disorders, there is ample evidence that subsequent trauma exposure is highly prevalent and is the norm rather than the exception. As would be expected from the high rate of trauma in people with psychotic disorder, high rates of PTSD are also common, and these symptoms appear to interact with and worsen the course of the psychosis. Recent research offers promise for treating PTSD in persons with psychotic disorders. Finally, the experience of a recent onset of psychosis may result in PTSD-like symptoms due to the terrifying nature of psychotic symptoms, and the potentially traumatic effects of coercive treatments such as restraints or involuntary hospitalization. Treatment of PTSD-like symptoms in such persons could overcome fears related to psychosis and its treatment, resulting in improved treatment adherence and better outcomes.

REFERENCES

American Psychiatric Association. (1994). *Diagnostic and statistical manual of mental disorders* (4th ed.). Washington, DC: Author.

Bentall, R. P. (2003). *Madness explained: Psychosis and human nature.* London: Penguin.

Berenbaum, H., Valera, E. M., & Kerns, J. G. (2003). Psychological trauma and schizotypal symptoms. *Schizophrenia Bulletin, 29,* 143–152.

Breslau, N., & Anthony, J. C. (2007). Gender differences in the sensitivity to posttraumatic stress disorder: An epidemiological study of urban young adults. *Journal of Abnormal Psychology, 116,* 607–611.

Breslau, N., Davis, G. C., Andreski, P., & Peterson, E. (1991). Traumatic events and posttraumatic stress disorder in an urban population of young adults. *Archives of General Psychiatry, 48,* 216–222.

Butler, R. W., Mueser, K. T., Sprock, J., & Braff, D. L. (1996). Positive symptoms of psychosis in posttraumatic stress disorder. *Biological Psychiatry, 39,* 839–844.

Cascardi, M., Mueser, K. T., DeGiralomo, J., & Murrin, M. (1996). Physical aggression against psychiatric inpatients by family members and partners: A descriptive study. *Psychiatric Services, 47,* 531–533.

Coldham, E. L., Addington, J., & Addington, D. (2002). Medication adherence of individuals with a first episode of psychosis. *Acta Psychiatrica Scandinavica, 106,* 286–290.

Craine, L. S., Henson, C. E., Colliver, J. A., & MacLean, D. G. (1988). Prevalence of a history of sexual abuse among female psychiatric patients in a state hospital system. *Hospital and Community Psychiatry, 39,* 300–304.

Ellason, J. W., & Ross, C. (1997). Childhood trauma and psychiatric symptoms. *Psychological Reports, 80,* 447–450.

Escobar, J. I., Randolph, E. T., Puente, G., Spiwak, F., Asamen, J. K., Hill, M., et al. (1983). Posttraumatic stress disorder in Hispanic Vietnam veterans: Clinical phenomenology and socio-cultural characteristics. *Journal of Nervous and Mental Disease, 171,* 585–596.

Felitti, V. J., Anda, R. F., Nordenberg, D., Williamson, D. F., Spitz, A. M., Edwards, V., et al. (1998). Relationship of childhood abuse and household dysfunction to many of the leading causes of death in adults: The Adverse Childhood Event (ACE) study. *American Journal of Preventive Medicine, 14,* 245–258.

Fowler, D., Freeman, D., Steel, C., Hardy, A., Smith, B., Hackman, C., et al. (2006). The catastrophic interaction hypothesis: How do stress, trauma, emotion and information processing abnormalities lead to psychosis. In W. Larkin & A. P. Morrison (Eds.), *Trauma and psychosis: New directions for theory and therapy* (pp. 101–124). London: Routledge.

Frame, L., & Morrison, A. P. (2001). Causes of posttraumatic stress disorder in psychotic patients. *Archives of General Psychiatry, 58,* 305–306.

Frueh, B. C., Buckley, T. C., Cusack, K. J., Kimble, M. O., Grubaugh, A. L., Turner, S. M., et al. (2004). Cognitive-behavioral treatment for PTSD among people with severe mental illness: A proposed treatment model. *Journal of Psychiatric Practice, 10,* 26–38.

Goff, D. C., Brotman, A. W., Kindlon, D., Waites, M., & Amico, E. (1991). Self-reports of childhood abuse in chronically psychotic patients. *Psychiatry Research, 37,* 73–80.

Goodman, L. A., Rosenberg, S. D., Mueser, K. T., & Drake, R. E. (1997). Physical and sexual assault history in women with serious mental illness: Prevalence, correlates, treatment, and future research directions. *Schizophrenia Bulletin, 23,* 685–696.

Grimby, A. (1993). Bereavement among elderly people: Grief reactions, post-bereavement hallucinations and quality of life. *Acta Psychiatrica Scandinavica, 87,* 72–80.

Grinker, R., & Spiegel, J. (1945). *Men under stress.* Philadelphia: Blakiston.

Hamner, M. B., Frueh, B. C., Ulmer, H. G., & Arana, G. W. (1999). Psychotic features and illness severity in combat veterans with chronic posttraumatic stress disorder. *Biological Psychiatry, 45,* 846–852.

Harris, M. (1998). *Trauma recovery and empowerment: A clinician's guide for working with women in groups.* New York: Free Press.

Honkonen, T., Henriksson, M., Koivisto, A.M., Stengård, E., & Salokangas, R. K. R. (2004). Violent victimization in schizophrenia. *Social Psychiatry and Psychiatric Epidemiology, 39,* 606–612.

Horowitz, M. J. (1986). *Stress response syndromes* (2nd ed.). New York: Aronson.

Irwin, H. J. (1992). Origins and functions of paranormal belief: The role of childhood trauma and interpersonal control. *Journal of the American Society for Psychical Research, 86,* 199–208.

Jackson, J. H. (1931). *Selected writings.* London: Hodder & Stoughton.

Janssen, I., Krabbendam, L., Bak, M., Hanssen, M., Vollebergh, W., Graaf, R., et al. (2004). Childhood abuse as a risk factor for psychotic experiences. *Acta Psychiatrica Scandinavica, 109,* 38–45.

Kessler, R. C., Sonnega, A., Bromet, E., Hughes, M., & Nelson, C. B. (1995). Posttraumatic stress disorder in the National Comorbidity Survey. *Archives of General Psychiatry, 52,* 1048–1060.

McGorry, P. D., Chanen, A., McCarthy, E., Van Riel, R., McKenzie, D., & Singh, B. S. (1991). Posttraumatic stress disorder following recent-onset psychosis: An unrecognized postpsychotic syndrome. *Journal of Nervous and Mental Disease, 179,* 253–258.

Meyer, I. H., Muenzenmaier, K., Cancienne, J., & Struening, E. L. (1996). Reliability and validity of a measure of sexual and physical abuse histories among women with serious mental illness. *Child Abuse and Neglect, 20,* 213–219.

Morrison, A. P., Bowe, S., Larkin, W., & Nothard, S. (2001). The psychological impact of psychiatric admission: Some preliminary findings. *Journal of Nervous and Mental Disease, 189,* 250–253.

Mueser, K. T., Bolton, E. E., Carty, P. C., Bradley, M. J., Ahlgren, K. F., DiStaso, D. R., et al. (2007). The trauma recovery group: A cognitive-behavioral program for PTSD in persons with severe mental illness. *Community Mental Health Journal, 43,* 281–304.

Mueser, K. T., & Butler, R. W. (1987). Auditory hallucinations in combat-related chronic posttraumatic stress disorder. *American Journal of Psychiatry, 144,* 299–302.

Mueser, K. T., Essock, S. M., Haines, M., Wolfe, R., & Xie, H. (2004). Posttraumatic stress disorder, supported employment, and outcomes in people with severe mental illness. *CNS Spectrums, 9,* 913–925.

Mueser, K. T., Goodman, L. A., Trumbetta, S. L., Rosenberg, S. D., Osher, F. C., Vidaver, R., et al. (1998). Trauma and posttraumatic stress disorder in severe mental illness. *Journal of Consulting and Clinical Psychology, 66,* 493–499.

Mueser, K. T., Hiday, V. A., Goodman, L. A., & Valenti-Hein, D. (2003). People with mental and physical disabilities. In B. L. Green, M. J. Friedman, J. T. V. M. de Jong, S. D. Solomon, T. M. Keane, J. A. Fairbank, et al. (Eds.), *Trauma interventions in war and peace: Prevention, practice, and policy* (pp. 129–154). New York: Kluwer Academic/Plenum Press.

Mueser, K. T., & Rosenberg, S. D. (2003). Treating the trauma of first episode psychosis: A PTSD perspective. *Journal of Mental Health, 12,* 103–108.

Mueser, K. T., Rosenberg, S. D., Goodman, L. A., & Trumbetta, S. L. (2002). Trauma, PTSD, and the course of schizophrenia: An interactive model. *Schizophrenia Research, 53,* 123–143.

Mueser, K. T., Rosenberg, S. D., Jankowski, M. K., Hamblen, J. L., & Descamps, M. (2004). A cognitive-behavioral treatment program for posttraumatic stress disorder in severe mental illness. *American Journal of Psychiatric Rehabilitation, 7,* 107–146.

Mueser, K. T., Rosenberg, S. D., Xie, H., Jankowski, M. K., Bolton, E. E., Lu, W., et al. (2008). A randomized controlled trial of cognitive-behavioral treatment for posttraumatic stress disorder in severe mental illness. *Journal of Consulting and Clinical Psychology, 76,* 259–271.

Mueser, K. T., Salyers, M. P., Rosenberg, S. D., Ford, J. D., Fox, L., & Carty, P. (2001). A psychometric evaluation of trauma and PTSD assessments in persons with severe mental illness. *Psychological Assessment, 13,* 110–117.

Mueser, K. T., Salyers, M. P., Rosenberg, S. D., Goodman, L. A., Essock, S. M., Osher, F. C., et al. (2004). Interpersonal trauma and posttraumatic stress disorder in patients with severe mental illness: Demographic, clinical, and health correlates. *Schizophrenia Bulletin, 30,* 45–57.

Mueser, K. T., & Taylor, K. L. (1997). A cognitive-behavioral approach. In M. Harris & C. L. Landis (Eds.), *Sexual abuse in the lives of women diagnosed with serious mental illness* (pp. 67–90). Amsterdam: Harwood Academic.

Nuechterlein, K. H., & Dawson, M. E. (1984). A heuristic vulnerability/stress model of schizophrenic episodes. *Schizophrenia Bulletin, 10,* 300–312.

Oruc, L., & Bell, P. (1995). Multiple rape trauma followed by delusional parasitosis: A case report from the Bosnian war. *Schizophrenia Research, 16,* 173–174.

Read, J., Perry, B. D., Moskowitz, A., & Connolly, J. (2001). The contribution of early traumatic events to schizophrenia in some patients: A traumagenic neurodevelopmental model. *Psychiatry, 64,* 319–345.

Read, J., van Os, J., Morrison, A. P., & Ross, C. A. (2005). Childhood trauma, psychosis and schizophrenia: A literature review with theoretical and clinical implications. *Acta Psychiatrica Scandinavica, 112,* 330–350.

Resnick, S. G., Bond, G. R., & Mueser, K. T. (2003). Trauma and posttraumatic stress disorder in people with schizophrenia. *Journal of Abnormal Psychology, 112,* 415–423.

Robins, C. S., Sauvageot, J. A., Cusack, K. J., Suffoletta-Maierle, S., & Frueh, B. C. (2005). Consumers' perceptions of negative experiences and "sanctuary harm" in psychiatric settings. *Psychiatric Services, 56,* 1134–1138.

Ross, C. A., & Joshi, S. (1992). Schneiderian symptoms and childhood trauma in the general population. *Comprehensive Psychiatry, 33,* 269–273.

Sareen, J., Cox, B. J., Goodwin, R. D., & Asmundson, G. J. G. (2005). Co-occurrence of posttraumatic stress disorder with positive psychotic symptoms in a nationally representative sample. *Journal of Traumatic Stress, 18,* 313–322.

Sautter, F. J., Cornwell, J., Johnson, J. J., Wiley, J., & Faraone, S. V. (2002). Family history study of posttraumatic stress disorder with secondary psychotic symptoms. *American Journal of Psychiatry, 159,* 1775–1777.

Scott, J., Chant, D., Andrews, G., Martin, G., & McGrath, J. (2007). Association between trauma exposure and delusional experiences in a large community-based sample. *British Journal of Psychiatry, 190,* 339–343.

Shaner, A., & Eth, S. (1989). Can schizophrenia cause posttraumatic stress disorder? *American Journal of Psychotherapy, 43,* 588–597.

Shaw, K., McFarlane, A. C., Bookless, C., & Air, T. (2002). The aetiology of postpsychotic posttraumatic stress disorder following a psychotic episode. *Journal of Traumatic Stress, 15,* 39–47.

Shevlin, M., Dorahy, M. J., & Adamson, G. (2007). Trauma and psychosis: An analysis of the National Comorbidity Survey. *American Journal of Psychiatry, 164,* 166–169.

Sobsey, D. (1994). *Violence and abuse in the lives of people with disabilities.* Baltimore: Paul H. Brookes.

Surrey, J., Swett, C., Jr., Michaels, A., & Levin, S. (1990). Reported history of physical and sexual abuse and severity of symptomatology in women psychiatric outpatients. *American Journal of Orthopsychiatry, 60,* 412–417.

Switzer, G. E., Dew, M. A., Thompson, K., Goycoolea, J. M., Derricott, T., & Mullins, S. D. (1999). Posttraumatic stress disorder and service utilization among urban mental health center clients. *Journal of Traumatic Stress, 12,* 25–39.

Waldfogel, S., & Mueser, K. T. (1988). Another case of chronic PTSD with auditory hallucinations. *American Journal of Psychiatry, 145,* 1314.

Wilcox, J. A., Briones, D. F., & Suess, L. (1991). Auditory hallucinations, posttraumatic stress disorder, and ethnicity. *Comprehensive Psychiatry, 32,* 320–323.

Williams-Keeler, L., Milliken, H., & Jones, B. (1994). Psychosis as precipitating trauma for PTSD: A treatment strategy. *American Journal of Orthopsychiatry, 64*(3), 493–498.

Zubin, J., & Spring, B. (1977). Vulnerability: A new view of schizophrenia. *Journal of Abnormal Psychology, 86,* 103–126.

Kim T. Mueser
Dartmouth Medical School

Stanley D. Rosenberg
Dartmouth Medical School

See also: Cognitive Behavior Therapy, Adult; Cognitive Impairments; Comorbidity; Culture-Bound Syndromes; Diagnosis of Traumatic Stress Disorders (*DSM & ICD*); Epidemiology; Etiology; Flashbacks; Posttraumatic Adaptation; Posttraumatic Stress Disorder; Posttraumatic Stress Disorder, Diagnosis of; Social Skills Training; Substance Use Disorders; Trauma, Definition

PSYCHOTHERAPEUTIC PROCESSES

Psychotherapy for posttraumatic stress disorder (PTSD) involves three phases which are applicable regardless of the specific theoretical and clinical model of treatment (Ford, Courtois, Van der Hart, Nijenhuis, & Steele, 2005; Rauch & Foa, 2006): (a) ensuring safety, developing a working alliance, and acquiring or accessing adaptive life skills and beliefs; (b) working through and gaining closure on trauma-related memories; and (c) rebuilding a productive and satisfying life and relationships. In each phase, PTSD psychotherapy involves several processes designed to achieve these goals that are initiated and guided by the psychotherapist.

The fundamental process involved in PTSD psychotherapy is facilitating the patient's "recognition (rather than avoidance) of posttraumatic self-dysregulation in tolerable ways and amounts, in order to promote proactive self-regulation" (Ford et al., 2005, p. 467). In practice, the PTSD therapist helps the patient to "gain control of overwhelming [emotions], impulsive behavior, and self-destructive thoughts and behaviors by anticipating and replacing them with self-management strategies" (Ford et al., 2005, p. 467). In the first phase of therapy, facilitating self-regulation requires safety planning: identifying and preventing or reducing the danger of behaviors such as self-harm, aggression, suicidality, or addictions, or situations such as domestic or community violence, or recurrent serious accidents or illness. In the second phase, facilitating self-regulation involves assisting the patient in taking control of traumatic memories by proactively choosing when and how to recall these memories (rather than avoiding them) while managing distressing emotions, thoughts, and impulses that are triggered by confronting memories or reminders of past traumas. In the final phase, self-regulation is addressed by extending this proactive approach beyond traumatic memories in order to constructively take charge of one's own life by mindfully choosing how to engage in relationships, work, and recreation without anxiety.

A second psychotherapeutic process is psychoeducation—providing information that enables the patient to be an informed and active participant in all therapeutic activities. In phase one, psychoeducation includes describing the rationale for and the practical steps involved in the treatment approach, to enhance the patient's motivation to engage in treatment. In phase two, psychoeducation involves explaining and actively showing the patient how reminders of past traumas can be safely and helpfully dealt with in treatment, to enable the patient to have the hope and skill to confront these reminders while sustaining positive motivation and expectancies. Psychoeducation in phase three involves coaching rather than teaching: the therapist provides feedback based on observing how the patient handles challenges and opportunities in life, in order to enhance the patient's ability to apply to all walks of life the self-regulated nonavoidant approach he or she has acquired earlier in therapy.

Establishing a working alliance is the third psychotherapeutic process. This means developing a cooperative and collaborative approach to working on therapy goals that enables both the patient and therapist to experience themselves as "allies" in recovery from trauma (Herman, 1992). Therapists contribute to the working alliance with PTSD patients by balancing a knowledgeable and professional manner that conveys expertise and confidence with a flexibility and openness to respect and appreciate the patient's feelings, viewpoints, and preferences that enables the patient to feel understood and valued and the therapy to be best individualized. A working alliance develops over all three therapy phases as the therapist helps the patient to experience an increasing sense of security (Pearlman & Courtois, 2005) in his or her life circumstances and with the therapist (phase one: improved safety and trust), in dealing with trauma reminders (phase two: enhanced personal control), and within her- or himself in important relationships and life pursuits (phase three: enhanced self-esteem and intimacy).

The psychotherapeutic processes of acquiring self-regulation skills, psychoeducation, and forming a working alliance are complementary and mutually reinforcing (but do not necessarily proceed in the sequence mentioned above). As the PTSD therapist provides psychoeducation and engages the patient in developing a working alliance, the therapist's informative and emotionally balanced style provides a model of self-regulation that the patient can directly observe and vicariously experience while dealing with distressing and dysregulated cognitions and emotions. PTSD psychotherapy thus may enable patients not only to better manage and gain closure on memories and reminders of past traumas, but also while doing so to have the experience of co-regulation with the therapist as model and guide that may lead to the development of stronger self-regulation.

A fourth potential psychotherapeutic process in PTSD treatment is the reduction of emotional and physiological distress by repeatedly intentionally recalling traumatic memories. This process has been likened to the fear deconditioning process of "habituation" or the process of learning that reminders of fearful experiences no longer are dangerous (i.e., extinction), and were assumed to require lengthy repetitions of fear memories (e.g., cognitive behavioral prolonged exposure [PE]; Rauch & Foa, 2006). However, positive outcomes achieved with relatively brief (e.g., one or two 60- to 90-minute sessions) periods of traumatic memory recall in eye movement desensitization and reprocessing (EMDR),

and a recent study showing that habituation was not required for positive outcomes in PE (Van Minnen & Foa, 2006), suggest that successful PTSD psychotherapy may not require extended exposure to and habituation of traumatic memories. Extinction learning remains a viable therapeutic process in PTSD treatment because there is ample evidence that recovery from fear or PTSD involves learning that intentionally experiencing memories and being aware of reminders of past traumas reduces distress and enhances a sense of control.

PTSD psychotherapy processes both directly and indirectly address several factors that have been shown to be negative prognostic indicators (Ford et al., 2005; Rauch & Foa, 2006). These include high initial levels of anger, alienation, a sense of mental defeat, extreme emotional lability, and severe dissociation. There are no sure-fire remedies for these potential impediments to PTSD psychotherapy. However, enabling the patient to better self-regulate emotional states and physiological arousal, to become increasingly knowledgeable and skilled in dealing with PTSD symptoms, and to experience trust and security as well as a sense of personal control and self-efficacy as a partner in the therapeutic working alliance, provides a strong psychotherapeutic foundation for recovery from PTSD (Ford et al., 2005).

REFERENCES

Ford, J. D., Courtois, C., van der Hart, O., Nijenhuis, E., & Steele, K. (2005). Treatment of complex post-traumatic self-dysregulation. *Journal of Traumatic Stress, 18,* 467–477.

Herman, J. L. (1992). *Trauma and recovery.* New York: Basic Books.

Pearlman, L. A., & Courtois, C. A. (2005). Clinical applications of the attachment frame-work: Relational treatment of complex trauma. *Journal of Traumatic Stress, 18,* 449–459.

Rauch, S., & Foa, E. B. (2006). Emotional processing theory (EPT) and exposure therapy for PTSD. *Journal of Contemporary Psychotherapy, 32*(2), 61–65.

Van Minnen, A., & Foa, E. B. (2006). The effect of imaginal exposure length on outcome of treatment for PTSD. *Journal of Traumatic Stress, 19,* 427–438.

Julian D. Ford
University of Connecticut School of Medicine

See also: Avoidance; Cognitive Behavior Therapy, Adult; Cognitive Integration, Biopsychosocial; Coping Skills Training; Exposure Therapy, Adult; Eye Movement Desensitization and Reprocessing; Habituation; Memories of Traumatic Experiences; Psychodynamic Therapy, Adult; Psychoeducation; Therapeutic Relationship

PUBLIC HEALTH

Public health is a discipline and practice that monitors and evaluates threats to the health of entire populations and communities, with particular attention to environmental hazards and the social context of disease. The resulting information is used to promote health and prevent disease in communities and populations, in order to improve community health outcomes through education and intervention (Breslow, 2002). Public health systems and agencies from local public health departments, to the U.S. Centers for Disease Control & Prevention (CDC) to the World Health Organization (WHO) have an abiding interest in preserving, promoting, and advocating for mental health (CDC, 2007; Public Health of Seattle and King County, 2007; WHO, 2007).

Public health's roles in these missions stem, in part, from the contribution that positive mental health plays "in one's quality of life" (CDC, 2005c), but also derive from an understanding that poor mental health is linked to an increased prevalence of numerous physical health ailments as well as to an increased risk of accidents and suicide. Mental illness can also adversely affect the prognosis for chronic conditions via links with unhealthy and risky behaviors, suppressed immune function and noncompliance to medical regimens (WHO, 2008).

The primary avenues that public health employs to preserve & promote public mental health are advocacy, policy, and education (American Public Health Association [APHA], 2002). Public health organizations also conduct epidemiologic and other types of research investigations focused on the prevalence of various mental disorders and, more broadly, on community mental health (WHO, 2005).

In the aftermath of the 2001 terrorist attacks on the World Trade Center and the Pentagon, and the contemporaneous anthrax attacks, U.S. public health agencies began to address psychological trauma and trauma-induced mental health issues. This increased emphasis on terrorism-induced trauma has included a greater appreciation for the first responder roles that public health personnel are likely to play in terrorist events involving chemical, biological or radiological exposures (U.S. Department of Homeland Security, 2004). This in turn has led to increased training and the incorporation of posttraumatic mental health awareness into public health disaster preparedness and planning (Beaton, 2006). The psychosocial consequences of the 2001 anthrax attacks included widespread "white powder" events triggered by reports from citizens who became concerned they may have been exposed to anthrax or another bioterrorist agent after encountering white powdery substances that were invariably found to be harmless. These citizen reports were often investigated, hazardous materials teams were deployed, and some samples even underwent laboratory analysis—all draining public health resources. These incidents highlighted one of the potential impacts of terrorist events on public health systems, even when experienced secondhand via the news media (Marshall, Bryant, Amsel, Suh, Cook, & Neria, 2007).

While public health agencies are, with few exceptions, distinct from mental health agencies, they have in recent times made a concerted effort to educate the public, government officials, business leaders, and health professionals regarding the nature and effects of psychological trauma related to disasters and terrorism. For example, the CDC maintains a web site that includes educational information for the general public that addresses the traumatic nature of disasters and terrorist events, describes the symptoms of PTSD, and informs adults about how they can cope with traumatic events and assist children with coping (CDC, 2005b). A companion CDC web site provides related information for health professionals (CDC, 2005a). The CDC web site lists commonly occurring cognitive, emotional, physical, and behavioral trauma symptoms in the immediate aftermath of a traumatic event and provides guidance for health professionals who may interact with patients after a psychologically traumatic event. The web site also lists commonly recognized risk factors for severe and enduing posttraumatic reactions, including existing chronic medical conditions and preexisting psychological disorders. Finally, the web site also suggests that psychoeducation approaches and referrals to mental health professionals are some of the ways for health professionals to treat "traumatized" patients (CDC, 2005a).

In the aftermath of terrorist attacks of 9/11, public health agencies and systems were also challenged to develop risk communication messages consistent with relatively novel chemical, biological, radiologic, nuclear, and explosive threat(s) (CDC, 2005d). At the same time, and especially in the aftermath of Hurricane Katrina, public health systems began to appreciate how posttraumatic reactions could arise in the wake of a natural disaster or other public health emergencies such as a disease pandemic (Beaton et al., 2007). Some public health agencies have responded by developing outreach approaches targeting vulnerable populations that include persons who may be at an increased risk of traumatic stress reactions and PTSD in the aftermath of a disaster or other public health emergency (Public Health of Seattle and King County, 2007).

Public health also has an important role to play in developing community resilience and in trauma prevention (Gurwitch, Pfefferbaum, Montgomery, Klomp, & Reissman, 2007). Public health and its federal, local, and state partners work together to:

- Prepare for and respond to disasters.
- Provide assistance in disaster recovery efforts.
- Prevent infection, epidemics, and deter the spread of communicable diseases.

- Provide timely and credible risk communication messages before, during, and following a disaster or other public health emergency (Breslow, 2002).

Conclusion

Public health systems, agencies, and organizations can and do play significant roles in preventing and ameliorating trauma-induced psychological problems and mental disorders. Acting primarily at the community level, they provide education and training, collaborate with mental health and other agencies, and develop policies to protect and preserve the mental health of all citizens, including assisting emergency responders, health-care providers, and vulnerable and at risk populations who are affected by psychological traumas.

REFERENCES

American Public Health Association. (2002). *American Public Health Association mental health section.* Retrieved January 26, 2008, from http://amh.health.state.hi.us/apha/index.html.

Beaton, R. (2006). *Disaster behavioral health.* Retrieved January 26, 2008, from www.nwcphp.org/training/courses-exercises/courses/disaster-behavioral-health-competencies/searchterm=Disaster%20Behavioral%20Health/.

Beaton, R., Stergachis, A., Thompson, J., Osaki, C., Johnson, C., Charvat, S. J., et al. (2007). Pandemic policy and planning considerations for universities: Findings from a tabletop exercise. *Biosecurity and Bioterrorism: Biodefense Strategy, Practice, and Science, 5,* 327–334.

Breslow, L. (Ed.). (2002). *Encyclopedia of public health.* New York: Macmillan Reference.

Centers for Disease Control. (2005a). *Coping with a traumatic event: Information for health professionals.* Retrieved January 26, 2008, from www.bt.cdc.gov/masscasualties/copingpub.asp.

Centers for Disease Control. (2005b). *Coping with a traumatic event: Information for the public.* Retrieved January 26, 2008, from www.bt.cdc.gov/masscasualties/copingpub.asp.

Centers for Disease Control. (2005c). *Health-related quality of life.* Retrieved January 26, 2008, from www.cdc.gov/hrqol/methods.htm.

Centers for Disease Control. (2005d). *Roundtable on the psychosocial challenges posed by a radiological terrorism event*. Retrieved January 26, 2008, from www.crcpd.org/Reports_on_Mtgs/CDC-RoundtableDec05.pdf.

Centers for Disease Control. (2007). *Mental health workgroup*. Retrieved January 26, 2008, from www.cdc.gov/mentalhealth/.

Gurwitch, R. H., Pfefferbaum, B., Montgomery, J. M., Klomp, R. W., & Reissman, D. B. (2007). *Building community resilience for children and families*. Oklahoma City: University of Oklahoma Health Sciences Center, Terrorism and Disaster Center.

Marshall, R., Bryant, R., Amsel, L., Suh, J., Cook, J., & Neria, Y. (2007). The psychology of ongoing threat relative risk appraisal: The September 11 attacks and terrorism related fears. *American Psychologist, 62*, 304–316.

Public Health of Seattle and King County. (2007). *Vulnerable populations action team* (VPAT). Retrieved January 26, 2008, from www.metrokc.gov/health/VPAT/.

U.S. Department of Homeland Security. (2004). *National response plan*. Retrieved January 26, 2008, from www.dhs.gov/xprepresp/committees/editorial_0566.shtm.

World Health Organization. (2005). *Mental health atlas*. Retrieved January 26, 2008, from www.who.int/mental_health/evidence/atlas/.

World Health Organization. (2007). *Mental health, human rights, and legislation: WHO's framework*. Retrieved January 26, 2008, from www.who.int/mental_health/en/.

World Health Organization. (2008). *Mental health: WHO urges more investments, services for mental health*. Retrieved January 26, 2008, from www.who.int/mental_health/en/.

RANDAL BEATON
University of Washington

See also: Conservation of Resources Theory; Crisis Intervention, Adult; Crisis Intervention, Child; Critical Incident Stress Management; Disasters; Early Intervention; Epidemiology; Health Service Utilization; International Organizations; Laws, Legislation, and Policy; Medical Illness, Adult; Medical Illness, Child; Nongovernmental Organizations; Prevention, Adult; Prevention, Child; Social Cognitive Theory; Terrorism

PUBLIC POLICY

See: International Organizations; Laws, Legislation, and Policy

Q

QUALITY OF LIFE

Quality of life (QoL) has proven to be a difficult construct to define. For instance, Gill and Feinstein's (1994) review of the QoL literature observed that each article offered slightly different expectations and criteria for what constitutes quality of life. They concluded that quality of life is a loosely defined construct, rather than a simple rating of health status or function. According to Gill and Feinstein (1994), quality of life represents a uniquely personal perception, reflecting the way individual patients feel and experience their health, as well as nonmedical aspects of their life. Many scales have been used to measure aspects of quality of life, such as the Child Health Questionnaire (Landgraf, Abetz, & Ware, 1996). Also, later research by O'Donnell, Creamer, Elliott, Atkin, and Kossmann (2005) showed that quality of life can be predicted by both physical and psychological injury after trauma, in particular by acute psychological responses.

A series of investigations established that posttraumatic stress disorder (PTSD) is associated with functional impairments and diminished quality of life (Zatzick, Jurkovich, Gentilello, Wisner, & Rivara, 2002; see Thorpe & Stein, 2005, for a review). For instance, large-scale studies of military combat veterans (Zatzick, Marmar, et al., 1997; Zatzick, Weiss, et al., 1997) have demonstrated this association and revealed that the risks of poorer well-being and functionality in subjects with combat-related PTSD were significantly greater than those of veterans who did not exhibit PTSD. Similarly, a study of civilians (Amaya-Jackson et al., 1999) found that symptoms of posttraumatic stress were associated with several functional impairments including limitations in social, financial, physical function. These studies suggested that both combat veteran and civilian posttraumatic stress symptoms demonstrated significant diminishment in functionality and quality of life.

An investigation that prospectively examined the impact of posttraumatic stress and depressive symptoms in adolescents and found that early high PTSD symptom levels were independently associated with later impairments in role, behavioral, and social functional domains (Zatzick et al., in press). A study of Vietnam veterans concluded that higher PTSD symptoms were associated with poorer psychosocial and physical health-related quality of life. Interventions targeting PTSD symptoms may also have the potential to improve quality of life (Schnurr, Hayes, Lunnery, McFall, & Uddo, 2006).

This body of investigation suggests a strong association across populations between PTSD symptoms and functional impairments and diminished quality of life. Further research, particularly intervention trials, is required to elucidate whether treatments can both relieve PTSD symptoms and improve quality of life.

REFERENCES

Amaya-Jackson, L., Davidson, J. R. T., Hughes, D. D., Swartz, M. S., Reynolds, V., George, L. K., et al. (1999). Functional impairment and utilization of services associated with posttraumatic stress in the community. *Journal of Traumatic Stress, 12,* 709–724.

Gill, T. M., & Feinstein, A. R. (1994). A critical appraisal of the quality of Quality-of-Life measurements. *Journal of the American Medical Association, 272*(8), 619–626.

Landgraf, J. M., Abetz, L., & Ware, J. E. (1996). *The CHQ user's manual* (1st ed.). Boston: Health Institute, New England Medical Center.

O'Donnell, M. L., Creamer, M., Elliott, P., Atkin, C., & Kossmann, T. (2005). Determinants of quality of life and role-related disability after injury: Impact of acute psychological responses. *Journal of Trauma, 59,* 1328–1334.

Schnurr, P. P., Hayes, A. F., Lunnery, C. A., McFall, M., & Uddo, M. (2006). Longitudinal analysis of the relationship between symptoms and quality of life in veterans treated for posttraumatic stress disorder. *Journal of Consulting and Clinical Psychology, 74,* 707–713.

Thorpe, S. R., & Stein, M. B. (2005). Posttraumatic stress disorder and functioning. *PTSD Research Quarterly, 16,* 3.

Zatzick, D. F., Jurkovich, G. J., Fan, M. Y., Grossman, D., Russo, J., Katon, W., et al. (in press). The association between posttraumatic stress and depressive symptoms and functional outcomes in adolescents followed longitudinally after injury hospitalization. *Archives of Pediatrics and Adolescent Medicine.*

Zatzick, D. F., Jurkovich, G. J., Gentilello, L. M., Wisner, D., & Rivara, F. P. (2002). Posttraumatic stress, problem drinking, and functioning after injury. *Archives of Surgery, 137,* 200–205.

Zatzick, D. F., Marmar, C. R., Weiss, D. S., Browner, W. S., Metzler, T. J., Golding, J. M., et al. (1997). Posttraumatic stress disorder and functioning and quality of life outcomes in a nationally representative sample of male Vietnam veterans. *American Journal of Psychiatry, 154,* 1690–1695.

Zatzick, D. F., Weiss, D. S., Marmar, C. R., Metzler, T. J., Wells, K. B., Golding, J. M., et al. (1997). Posttraumatic stress disorder and functioning and quality of life outcomes in female Vietnam veterans. *Military Medicine, 162,* 661–665.

MICHAEL A. NORMAN
University of Washington School of Medicine

DOUGLAS F. ZATZICK
University of Washington School of Medicine

See also: Adolescence; Cognitive Impairments; Coping; Disability, Occupational; Health Service Utilization; Posttraumatic Adaptation; Posttraumatic Growth; Primary Care; Social Support

R

RACE-RELATED STRESSORS

Early psychological literature on race-related traumatic stressors consisted of conceptual models depicting exposure to racism as a stressful life event (Clark, Anderson, Clark, & Williams, 1999). Early research also found that perceived racial discrimination contributed significantly to psychiatric symptoms among African Americans (Klonoff, Landrine, & Ullman, 1999). Clinical case studies were published on ethnic minority Vietnam veterans with posttraumatic stress disorder (PTSD) or other psychiatric symptoms who experienced race-related stressors in the military (see Loo et al., 2001).

The field was significantly advanced by the construction and validation of scales to measure race-related stressors, such as those experienced by Asian American Pacific Islander (AAPI) Vietnam veterans who faced the problem of looking like the enemy and/or identifying with the culture of the host Asian country while identifying oneself as American (Loo et al., 2001). The Race-Related Stressor Scale (RRSS; Loo et al., 2001), for instance, revealed moderately large relationships between exposure to race-related stressors and both PTSD symptoms and general psychiatric symptoms after accounting for combat exposure and military rank (Loo et al., 2001).

In further research with diagnostic implications, it was found that adverse race-related events are associated with PTSD diagnoses (Loo, Fairbank, & Chemtob, 2005), and that PTSD severity increases significantly as a function of frequency of exposure to adverse race-related events. These findings underscore the notion that personal experiences of racism are potent risk factors for PTSD (Loo et al., 2001).

Another advance in the literature has been represented by the development and implementation of forms of treatment for psychological symptoms resulting from race-related stressors experienced by persons who have been racially stigmatized or victimized (see Loo, Ueda, & Morton, 2007). Models that offer a developmental perspective on race-related psychological trauma, along with a model of group treatment, help advance the level of clinically competent health care that can be provided to those victimized on the basis of race.

In the area of hate crimes, there has been some research on the emotional impact of hate crimes on victims, but not all findings demonstrate a distinct class of associated psychic injury (see Perry, 2003). Hate crimes have been distinguished as often sending out a terrorizing message to members of the victim's group in the immediate neighborhood or beyond, or that the hate crime victims are attacked for a specific personal reason—one they are unable to change (e.g., one's race). Research suggests that victims of bias-motivated violence (i.e., hate crimes) report significantly greater levels of negative psychophysiological symptoms than victims of nonbias-motivated violence (see Lawrence, 1999), and Bryant-Davis (2005) delineated the psychological effects of bias-motivated interpersonal trauma. Overall, however, there is less empirical research on the relationship between hate crimes and psychological trauma than there is on race-related stressors and PTSD.

REFERENCES

Bryant-Davis, T. (2005). *Thriving in the wake of trauma: A multicultural guide.* Westport, CT: Greenwood-Praeger.

Clark, R., Anderson, N. B., Clark, V. R., & Williams, D. R. (1999). Racism as a stressor for African

Americans: A biopsychosocial model. *American Psychologist, 54,* 805–816.

Klonoff, E. A., Landrine, H., & Ullman, J. B. (1999). Racial discrimination and psychiatric symptoms among Blacks. *Cultural Diversity and Ethnic Minority Psychology, 5,* 329–339.

Lawrence, F. M. (1999). *Punishing hate: Bias crimes under American law.* Cambridge, MA: Harvard University Press.

Loo, C. M., Fairbank, J. A., & Chemtob, C. M. (2005). Adverse race-related events as a risk factor for posttraumatic stress disorder. *Journal of Nervous and Mental Disease, 193,* 455–463.

Loo, C. M., Fairbank, J. A., Scurfield, R. M., Ruch, L. O., King, D. W., Adams, L., et al. (2001). Measuring exposure to racism: Development and validation of a Race-Related Stressor Scale (RRSS) for Asian American Vietnam veterans. *Psychological Assessment, 13,* 503–520.

Loo, C. M., Ueda, S. S., & Morton, R. K. (2007). Group treatment for race-related stresses among minority Vietnam veterans. *Transcultural Psychiatry, 44,* 115–135.

Perry, B. (Ed.). (2003). *Hate and bias crime: A reader.* New York: Routledge.

Chalsa M. Loo
National Center for Posttraumatic Stress Disorder

See also: Hate Crimes; Racial and Ethnic Factors; Stress; Trauma, Definition

RACIAL AND ETHNIC FACTORS

Social groups strongly influence how people develop in terms of values, beliefs, expectations, identity, and other aspects of relatedness that contribute to individual and collective systems of meaning. Among the most influential characteristics of social groups are complex racial and ethnic qualities that contribute greatly to the context in which members of these groups come to understand and respond to events, including those which could prove to be psychologically traumatic. There is considerable variation in how traumatic events are experienced by individuals and groups, with racial and ethnic distinctions being identified as salient factors before, during, and after trauma exposure (Pole, Gone, & Kulkarni, 2008).

In the United States, race and ethnicity are commonly categorized into five categories with non-Hispanic Caucasian Americans (a.k.a. "Whites") constituting the majority. The four largest ethnoracial minority groups in order of proportion of the U.S. population are: Hispanic Americans (a.k.a. Latinos), African Americans (a.k.a. Blacks), Asian and Pacific Islander Americans (a.k.a. APIAs), and Native Americans (a.k.a. American Indians). There is a great deal of racial, ethnic, cultural, linguistic, geographic, and social diversity within each of these categorical groups that must be taken into account when attempting to describe their members' experiences of and reactions to psychological trauma (Pole et al., 2008).

The following represents a selective review of the relevant findings pertaining to racial and ethnic factors and their importance in understanding the potential for traumatic event exposure and the subsequent impact of psychologically traumatic events in the lives of individuals, families, communities, and groups. Space limitations prevent a full discussion of this subject, but we cannot emphasize enough the immense heterogeneity within these groups and how greatly that limits the generalizations that can be made from group findings to individual group members. In addition, while many forms of psychopathology may be predicated or exacerbated by traumatization (e.g., depression or substance abuse), the focus of this entry is limited to posttraumatic stress disorder (PTSD).

Pre-Trauma Context

Ethnic minority groups disproportionately suffer under chronic stressors that may adversely impact their traumatic stress experiences and responses. Members of these groups commonly report experiencing psychological trauma in a context marked by heightened racial discrimination (e.g., Green, Grace, Lindy, & Leonard, 1990), and such discrimination may exacerbate risk for PTSD (Pole, Best, Metzler, & Marmar, 2005). Furthermore, a study that began by accounting for the effects of psychological trauma exposure found that other race-related stressors accounted for an additional 20% of the variability in PTSD symptoms (Loo et al., 2001). Thus, the impact of psychological trauma on members of different ethnoracial groups is influenced (moderated) for better or worse by circumstances of people's lives prior to the trauma (which are often very different depending on the group's ethnoracial identity). Other contextual factors of note include poverty and acculturative stress that disproportionately affect some minority groups.

Exposure to Psychological Trauma

There are race-related disparities revealed in the likelihood that people are exposed to traumatic stressors. For example, African American, Latino, American Indian, and Native Hawaiian Vietnam veterans reported more combat exposure than did White veterans (e.g., Green et al., 1990). Other examples include the high exposure among many Southeast Asian refugees to war, torture, and murder of family members (Hsu, Davies, & Hansen, 2004), and the multigenerational trauma stemming from generations of genocidal actions against American Indians. On the other hand, Japanese American veterans of the Vietnam War report lesser amounts and degrees of combat exposure than their White counterparts (Friedman, Schnurr, Sengupta, Holmes, & Ashcraft, 2004).

Peritraumatic Responding

Disturbances in emotions and consciousness during or immediately after a traumatic event (i.e., peritraumatic distress and dissociation, respectively) are among the strongest predictors of PTSD (Ozer, Best, Lipsey, & Weiss, 2003). Some studies have revealed that African American and Latino respondents report higher degrees of peritraumatic dissociation than their White counterparts (e.g., Pole et al., 2005). While more research is needed to determine if this finding is consistent across different types of psychological trauma and different specific ethnoracial groups, these findings suggest that dissociation during or soon after experiencing a psychologically traumatic event may be more common and more severe among ethnoracial minority group members, specifically African American and Latinos. Whether there are ethnoracial differences in the extent of distress experienced by people during and soon after a traumatic event, and whether these peritraumatic responses are as strongly associated with the subsequent development of PTSD among ethnoracial minority group members as among Whites, remains unknown and is in need of investigation.

Posttraumatic Coping

Ethnoracial groups also differ in their preferred methods of coping with the aftermath of psychological trauma. For example, African American psychological trauma survivors may be more likely than other survivors to report using religious faith or activities as a way of coping (Torabi & Seo, 2004). Latinos may be more likely than other groups to engage in what has been termed "wishful thinking coping" (e.g., hoping for miracles, faith, or luck to resolve psychological traumas; Pole et al., 2005).

PTSD Symptom Severity and Prevalence of PTSD

On average, ethnoracial minority status is a weak predictor of PTSD (Brewin, Andrews, & Valentine, 2000). However, findings revealing a somewhat stronger relationship between minority status and PTSD suggest that the strength and direction of the relationship may depend on other factors such as the specific ethnoracial group in question. Several studies have found elevated PTSD among Latinos, African Americans, American Indians, and some APIA subgroups when compared to their White counterparts (e.g., Friedman et al., 2004; Kulka et al., 1990; Pole et al., 2001). This result has been especially consistent for Latinos (Pole et al., 2005), but appears to depend on country of ancestral origin and level of acculturation. Caribbean Latinos (e.g., Puerto Ricans) typically show higher PTSD rates than other Latino groups (e.g., Galea et al., 2004). Less acculturated Latinos often report higher PTSD symptom levels than those who are more acculturated (e.g., Perilla, Norris, & Lavizzo, 2002). Among

APIA subgroups, elevated PTSD rates have been observed for Southeast Asian refugees and Native Hawaiian veterans (Friedman et al., 2004; Kinzie et al., 1990). Japanese Americans, on the other hand, have been found to have lower rates of PTSD than both Whites and other APIA subgroups (e.g., Friedman et al., 2004).

Explanations for Ethnic Disparities in PTSD

Elevated PTSD among African American, American Indian, and APIA groups has typically been attributed to greater trauma exposure in these groups (e.g., Kulka et al., 1990). Elevated PTSD among Latinos has not been as easily explained. Sometimes Latinos show elevated PTSD rates despite equal amounts of psychological trauma exposure (Pole et al., 2001). When Latinos have been more highly exposed, controlling for exposure has not fully accounted for PTSD disparities (Kulka et al., 1990). Instead, investigators have cited factors such as elevated peritraumatic dissociation and avoidant coping as explanations for the elevated risk of PTSD among members of ethnoracial minority groups (Pole et al., 2005).

Assessment of PTSD

Explaining findings of ethnic disparities in PTSD presupposes that posttraumatic psychopathology can be adequately assessed and diagnosed in ethnic minority groups. Many common measures of PTSD have been developed using adequate samples of African Americans (Keane, Kaloupek, & Weathers, 1996). However, Latinos, American Indians, and APIAs have been less well represented in psychometric studies of conventional PTSD measures (Loo et al., 2001). One common measure of PTSD, the *Civilian Mississippi Scale,* may overestimate distress in Latinos (Bourque & Shen, 2005) and there is emerging evidence that the relationship between self-reported PTSD and psychophysiology may differ for Latinos (Pole & Kaloupek, 2006).

There are other areas of caution that should be taken into account when assessing PTSD in particular minority groups. African American

patients may mask their emotions during clinical interviews, which may be mistaken for PTSD avoidance/numbing symptoms or display a "healthy paranoia" of White therapists, which may be mistaken for hypervigilance symptoms (Allen, 1996). Latinos may show reporting biases in the direction of underreporting (Pole et al., 2005) or over-reporting distress (Bourque & Shen, 2005; Pole & Kaloupek, 2006). APIAs may comply with cultural prohibitions against public displays of strong emotions (Levenson, Soto, & Pole, 2007) or otherwise under-report distress out of heightened shame and stigma about mental illness thereby leading to under diagnosis of psychopathology and perpetuation of the "model minority" myth (Kulkarni & Pole, in press). Some Native Americans may also be reluctant to disclose distress, especially to people from outside their communities in face-to-face interviews but they may give more valid responses on self-administered questionnaires (Pole et al., 2008).

Service Utilization

Trauma-exposed African Americans, Latinos, and APIAs generally utilize mental health services similarly to their White counterparts (e.g., Boscarino, Galea, Ahern, Resnick, & Vlahov, 2002). However, some research suggests that African American and Mexican American veterans underutilize certain kinds of services (e.g., self-help groups) and that African Americans may be more likely to use formal mental health treatment services inconsistently or end treatment prematurely (e.g., Rosenheck & Fontana, 1994). Moreover, there is evidence that, relative to Whites, American Indians may underutilize standard mental health services in favor of indigenous treatments (e.g., Beals et al., 2005).

Psychotherapy Process

The professional literature is also replete with recommendations for treating ethnic minorities that are based mainly on clinical experience rather than formal research. First, because ethnoracial minority group members have been historically overmedicated, misdiagnosed, and under-referred to psychotherapy, it is especially important for the clinician to strive for accuracy in clinical decision making. Second, because PTSD patients are hyperaware of danger cues, ethnoracial minority group PTSD patients may be especially mistrustful of clinical settings in which other minorities are absent. Thus, clinicians should attempt to provide a culturally welcoming setting (e.g., hire diverse clinic staff and treatment providers, and/or make culture-focused media available in the waiting room). Third, because some minority groups have been treated with indifference, insensitivity, or hostility by the general public, it is especially important that their psychotherapists not act in ways that can be construed as aloof, uncaring, or culturally insensitive. In particular, therapists should maintain an empathically involved stance and avoid neutrality. Finally, therapists should monitor and manage their own discomfort with hearing about race-related daily struggles. Some therapists unwittingly respond to such discomfort by prescribing medications or by becoming overly active, interpretive, or didactic (Allen, 1996). Before altering your standard practices, however, it is important to assess the patient's ethnic identity development and/or acculturation level to determine whether such alterations are warranted.

Psychotherapy Outcome

Some evidence suggests that African Americans and Whites achieve comparable outcomes in psychotherapy for PTSD (Zoellner, Feeny, Fitzgibbons, & Foa, 1999). Unfortunately, there are no well-designed studies in the literature focusing on differential psychotherapy outcome for other ethnic minority groups with PTSD.

REFERENCES

Allen, I. M. (1996). PTSD among African Americans. In A. J. Marsella, M. J. Friedman, E. T. Gerrity, & R. M. Scurfield (Eds.), *Ethnocultural aspects of posttraumatic stress disorder: Issues research, and clinical applications* (pp. 209–238). Washington, DC: American Psychological Association.

Beals, J., Manson, S. M., Whitesell, N. R., Spicer, P., Novins, D. K., Mitchell, C. M., for the AI-SUPERPFP Team. (2005). Prevalence of DSM-IV disorders and attendant help-seeking in two American Indian reservation populations. *Archives of General Psychiatry, 62,* 99–108.

Boscarino, J. A., Galea, S., Ahern, J., Resnick, H., & Vlahov, D. (2002). Utilization of mental health services following the September 11th terrorist attacks in Manhattan, New York City. *International Journal of Emergency Mental Health, 4,* 143–155.

Bourque, L. B., & Shen, H. (2005). Psychometric characteristics of Spanish and English versions of the Civilian Mississippi Scale. *Journal of Traumatic Stress, 18,* 719–728.

Brewin, C. R., Andrews, B., & Valentine, J. D. (2000). Meta-analysis of risk factors for posttraumatic stress disorder in trauma-exposed adults. *Journal of Consulting and Clinical Psychology, 68,* 748–766.

Friedman, M. J., Schnurr, P. P., Sengupta, A., Holmes, T., & Ashcraft, M. (2004). The Hawaii Vietnam Veterans Project: Is minority status a risk factor for posttraumatic stress disorder? *Journal of Nervous and Mental Disease, 192,* 45–50.

Galea, S., Vlahov, D., Tracy, M., Hoover, D. R., Resnick, H., & Kilpatrick, D. (2004). Hispanic ethnicity and post-traumatic stress disorder after a disaster: Evidence from a general population survey after September 11, 2001. *Annals of Epidemiology, 14,* 520–531.

Green, B. L., Grace, M. C., Lindy, J. D., & Leonard, A. C. (1990). Race differences in response to combat stress. *Journal of Traumatic Stress, 3,* 379–393.

Hsu, E., Davies, C. A., & Hansen, D. J. (2004). Understanding mental health needs of Southeast Asian refugees: Historical, cultural, and contextual challenges. *Clinical Psychology Review, 24,* 193–213.

Keane, T. M., Kaloupek, D. G., & Weathers, F. W. (1996). Ethnocultural considerations in the assessment of PTSD. In A. J. Marsella, M. J. Friedman, E. Gerrity, & R. Scurfield (Eds.), *Ethnocultural aspects of posttraumatic stress disorder: Issues, research and clinical applications* (pp. 183–205). Washington, DC: American Psychological Association.

Kinzie, J., Boehnlein, J. K., Leung, P. K., Moore, L. J., Riley, C., & Smith, D. (1990). The prevalence of posttraumatic stress disorder and its clinical significance among Southeast Asian refugees. *American Journal of Psychiatry, 147,* 913–917.

Kulka, R. A., Schlesenger, W. E., Fairbank, J. A., Hough, R. L., Jordan, B. K., Marmar, C. R., et al. (1990). *Trauma and the Vietnam War generation: Report of findings from the National Vietnam Veterans Readjustment Study*. New York: Brunner/Mazel.

Kulkarni, M., & Pole, N. (in press). Psychiatric distress among Asian Americans following the Northridge earthquake. *Journal of Nervous and Mental Disease*.

Levenson, R. W., Soto, J. A., & Pole, N. (2007). Emotion, biology, and culture. In S. Kitayama & D. Cohen (Eds.), *Handbook of cultural psychology* (pp. 780–796). New York: Guilford Press.

Loo, C. M., Fairbank, J. A., Scurfield, R. M., Ruch, L. O., King, D. W., Adams, L. J., et al. (2001). Measuring exposure to racism: Development and validation of a Race-Related Stressor Scale (RRSS) for Asian American Vietnam veterans. *Psychological Assessment, 13*, 503–520.

Ozer, E. J., Best, S. R., Lipsey, T. L., & Weiss, D. S. (2003). Predictors of posttraumatic stress disorder and symptoms in adults: A meta-analysis. *Psychological Bulletin, 129*, 52–73.

Perilla, J. L., Norris, F. H., & Lavizzo, E. A. (2002). Ethnicity, culture, and disaster response: Identifying and explaining ethnic differences in PTSD six months after Hurricane Andrew. *Journal of Social and Clinical Psychology, 21*, 20–45.

Pole, N., Best, S. R., Metzler, T., & Marmar, C. R. (2005). Why are Hispanics at greater risk for PTSD? *Cultural Diversity and Ethnic Minority Psychology, 11*, 144–161.

Pole, N., Best, S. R., Weiss, D. S., Metzler, T., Liberman, A. M., Fagan, J., et al. (2001). Effects of gender and ethnicity on duty-related posttraumatic stress symptoms among urban police. *Journal of Nervous and Mental Disease, 189*, 442–448.

Pole, N., Gone, J., & Kulkarni, M. (2008). Posttraumatic stress disorder among ethnoracial minorities in the United States. *Clinical Psychology: Science and Practice, 15*, 35–61.

Pole, N., & Kaloupek, D. G. (2006, November). *Do Hispanic veterans with PTSD show exaggerated physiological reactivity?* Paper presented at the International Society for Traumatic Stress Studies, Hollywood, CA.

Rosenheck, R., & Fontana, A. (1994). Utilization of mental health services by minority veterans of the Vietnam era. *Journal of Nervous and Mental Disease, 182*, 685–691.

Torabi, M. R., & Seo, D. (2004). National study of behavioral and life changes since September 11. *Health Education and Behavior, 31*, 179–192.

Zoellner, L. A., Feeny, N. C., Fitzgibbons, L. A., & Foa, E. B. (1999). Response of African American and Caucasian women to cognitive behavioral therapy for PTSD. *Behavior Therapy, 30*, 581–595.

Nnamdi Pole
University of Michigan

Elisa Triffleman
Private Practice, Port Washington, NY

See also: Culture and Trauma; Culture-Bound Syndromes; Epidemiology; Etiology; Health Service Utilization; Race-Related Stressors

RACISM

See: Genocide; Hate Crimes; Racial and Ethnic Factors; Race-Related Stressors

RAPE TRAUMA

Survivors of rape often show a distinct set of symptoms similar to responses of survivors of other types of potentially traumatic experiences. The term *rape trauma syndrome* began to appear in the literature in the early 1970s, concurrent with the growing feminist movement in the United States. It was within this climate that Burgess and Holmstrom published their landmark study of women's responses to rape in an effort to describe the symptoms and problems that commonly follow sexual assault and to inform the clinical management of rape trauma. Burgess and Holmstrom (1974) described rape trauma syndrome as "the acute phase and long-term reorganization process that occurs as a result of forcible rape or attempted forcible rape," and further noted that "this syndrome of behavioral, somatic, and psychological reactions is an acute stress reaction to a life-threatening situation" (p. 982). Because their work is seminal to this topic, we begin by describing their study of a large sample of women who presented to the emergency room of a large city hospital with the complaint of rape.

Burgess and Holmstrom Study

Burgess and Holmstrom (1974) investigated the immediate and long-term effects of rape (as reported by victims) by designing a study in which they interviewed all people who sought treatment for rape in the emergency department of Boston City Hospital in a one-year period. The final sample of 92 women were aged 17 to 73 and were heterogeneous with respect to ethnicity, socioeconomic level, employment status, and marital status. The interviewers (A. Burgess and L. Holmstrom) were called when a rape victim presented to the emergency room; one of them arrived to see the victim within 30 minutes. They conducted detailed interviews not just in that setting but also through follow-up visits and phone contacts. The authors also provided support to the rape victims, including accompanying them to rape-related court proceedings, where they recorded the women's responses to these events.

Characteristics of Rape Trauma Syndrome

On the basis of their observations and interviews, Burgess and Holmstrom (1974) characterized rape trauma syndrome as a two-phase reaction. The initial, acute phase was distinguished by a high degree of disorganization in lifestyle, with prominent physical symptoms, a subjective state of fear or terror, and overwhelming fear of being killed. During the first several weeks after a rape, victims reported numerous physical problems, including soreness, bruising, tension headaches, sleep disturbances, stomach pains, and gynecological symptoms. In addition, many victims felt fear, humiliation, embarrassment, anger, and had thoughts of revenge and self-blame. The second phase typically began about 2 to 3 weeks after the rape and reflected the survivor's beginning to reorganize her life. During this long-term process of reorganization, an increase in physical activity was common, and many of the women studied changed residences. In addition, the authors found that the women in the study routinely expressed fear of situations that reminded them of their rape. Finally, many women experienced sexual dysfunction and described nightmares related their traumatic experiences.

Burgess and Holmstrom were among the first investigators to describe and normalize the kind of psychological and physical symptoms that often follow rape, and to describe a pattern of strong reactions followed by reorganization and return to prior functioning. They stressed that the majority of rape survivors were able to reorganize their lives successfully after the acute phase, even though many continued to view the world differently (specifically, as a traumatic environment or more dangerous place) after the rape. They also stressed that while some rape victims were vulnerable to regression to prior levels of impaired functioning a month or two post-assault, none of the women in their study showed severe disintegration or bizarre behavior in the acute aftermath of rape. However, they did observe two patterns of response that seemed more complex and tended to be associated with slower recovery.

The *compounded reaction* was sometimes evident in rape victims with a preexisting (past and/or current) history of other significant psychiatric or social problems. Burgess and Holmstrom noted that this group tended to develop additional problems in the reorganization phase including depression, psychotic or psychosomatic symptoms, or suicidal behavior and self-destructive use of alcohol or drugs. Women with this compounded reaction were seen as needing more comprehensive psychological intervention than that provided in crisis counseling (described next). They recommended that a rape crisis counselor providing support to a woman with such a reaction coordinate with the primary provider of mental health services (psychotherapist, psychiatrist).

Silent rape reaction was the term Burgess and Holmstrom (1974) used to describe a pattern of response in someone who has "not told anyone about the rape, who has not settled her feelings and reactions on the issue, and who is carrying a tremendous psychological burden" (p. 985). They saw this pattern primarily in women with a history of prior trauma (rape or sexual abuse in childhood or at some point in earlier life), and observed that the recent rape reactivated their reaction to prior traumatic experiences. The authors offered guidelines regarding when to suspect that silent reaction might be associated with a history of exposure to traumatically stressful experiences.

Importantly, Burgess and Holmstrom (1974) also offered recommendations for the clinical management of rape trauma syndrome. They emphasized crisis intervention as the first line of intervention that was appropriate for most survivors. Crisis intervention remains today the most common form of intervention offered to rape victims in community settings, especially in the early aftermath of the assault.

Long-Term Recovery from Rape Trauma

Burgess and Holmstrom also published a series of papers detailing the coping responses and recovery patterns observed in the aftermath of rape among women in their sample. In one of these, Burgess and Holmstrom (1979) described long-term follow-up results for 88% of the women assessed in their original sample. Eighty-one of the original 92 participants were interviewed 4 to 6 years after the rape about their coping methods, patterns of adaptation, and length of recovery. Approximately 74% of these women described themselves as recovered at the time of follow-up; the remaining 26% did not feel recovered. Of the recovered group, about half reported that they felt they had recovered within months of the assault, and the other half reported that it took years to recover. While other factors are known to be associated with recovery from rape trauma (e.g., prior trauma history, characteristics of the assault itself, degree of physical injury, social support network), Burgess and Holmstrom were among the first to describe the impact that rape has on how the survivor thinks about herself and the world, and how recovery from the psychological trauma of rape sets in motion an evaluative process that affects the survivor's views as well as her recovery.

Burgess and Holmstrom (1979) noted that the tremendous anxiety suffered by victims in the aftermath of rape ensues from the impact of a life-threatening or highly stressful experience. They categorized the survivors' responses in the aftermath of rape as adaptive or maladaptive and examined them with regard to extent and rate of recovery. Categories included self-esteem and associated self-assessment, defense mechanisms, actions, and maladaptive responses. Rape survivors who recovered

more quickly and fully tended to: (a) make positive statements about their self worth (i.e., had higher self-esteem); (b) use conscious cognitive strategies or defense mechanisms (e.g., explanation, minimization, suppression); and (c) show increased action in the aftermath of the assault (e.g., changed residences, traveled away from the area, moved in temporarily with friends or family members, read or wrote about rape) as opposed to decreased action (withdrawing from social interaction or life events, staying in bed most of the time). A minority of rape victims responded in ways Burgess and Holmstrom categorized as maladaptive (e.g., increased use of drugs or alcohol, making a suicide attempt). These latter responses were clearly associated with impeded recovery. Finally, Burgess and Holmstrom also examined quality of life after rape, and found that: (a) recovery was associated with resumption of social roles or tasks, and (b) women reporting more stability in their romantic relationships had more rapid recovery. Overall, Burgess and Holmstrom's follow-up data suggested that the way that survivors cope and resume involvement in important social roles and relationships following the psychological trauma of rape influences the rate and quality of their recovery.

Rape Trauma and Posttraumatic Stress Disorder

In 1974, when Burgess and Holmstrom published their first observations of rape trauma, the *Diagnostic and Statistical Manual of the American Psychiatric Association* (*DSM-II*; American Psychiatric Association, 1968) classified trauma-related pathology as "transient situational disturbances." Such disturbances were described as "more or less transient disorders of any severity (including those of psychotic proportions) that occur in individuals without any apparent underlying mental disorders and that represent an acute reaction to overwhelming environmental stress" (p. 49). It was also noted in the *DSM-II* that in patients with good adaptive capacity, the symptoms typically diminish as the stressor event(s) end or become less severe. Military combat was specifically mentioned as an event sufficiently stressful to lead to such a reaction, but there was no reference to rape or sexual assault. Nonetheless, the *DSM-II* depiction is consistent with Burgess and Holmstrom's description of rape trauma syndrome.

The third version of the *DSM* (*DSM-III;* American Psychiatric Association, 1980) introduced posttraumatic stress disorder (PTSD; *see:* **Posttraumatic Stress Disorder**) as an anxiety disorder, and listed rape among the traumatically stressful experiences that could lead to the development of the disorder. Burgess (1983) offered an in-depth discussion of the relationship between rape trauma syndrome and the individual diagnostic criteria for PTSD, finding the early conceptualizations of rape response to be highly consistent with PTSD. Perhaps even more interesting is the consistency of Burgess and Holmstrom's 1974 description of rape responses and recovery to the findings of subsequent investigations of the development of PTSD in survivors of rape. Two large prospective studies of women's recovery from rape and nonsexual violent assault have yielded results that are quite comparable to those described by Burgess and Holmstrom. Rothbaum, Foa, Riggs, Murdock, and Walsh (1992) followed 95 female survivors of rape and nonsexual assault and found that while the vast majority of rape victims had high levels of PTSD symptoms soon after the assault, PTSD symptom severity and diagnosis systematically declined in the following months. Cahill, Street, Jayawickreme, and Foa (2008) assessed 134 female rape victims up to 6 times in the year following the assault. At the initial assessment (less than 1 month post-assault), nearly 90% of the women met symptomatic criteria for PTSD. At the 3-month assessment, when PTSD may be coded as chronic, 50% of rape victims met PTSD diagnosis. By the 1-year postevent assessment, PTSD diagnosis declined to one-fourth of the rape victims, which is the same percentage of women who described themselves as not yet recovered in Burgess and Holmstrom's (1979) follow-up study.

While these results show that many women recover from the effects of rape, epidemiological research has indicated that rape is associated with higher rates of PTSD than other types of trauma such as accidents, natural disasters, and nonsexual assault (Kessler, Sonnega, Bromet, Hughes, & Nelson, 1995). Faravelli, Giugni, Salvatori, and Ricca (2004) compared the psychiatric symptoms reported by 40 adult women who were victims of rape during the previous 9 months with the symptoms of 32 women who were victims of other types of recent trauma (i.e., nonsexual, life-threatening events such as car accidents, physical attacks, or robberies). PTSD and also sexual, eating, and mood disorders were found significantly more prevalent in the rape survivor group. Notably, in this study, none of the rape survivors had history of previous sexual abuse during childhood or adolescence.

Beyond Rape Trauma Syndrome

Burgess and Holmstrom's pioneering work on rape trauma syndrome and recovery from the psychological trauma of rape was vitally important in many ways. Prior to their investigation, little was known about the physical and psychologically traumatic effects of rape, and there was almost no literature on psychological interventions for victims. The conceptualization of rape trauma syndrome offered a way to understand and normalize victims' reactions and led to recommendations for early support and crisis intervention rather than ignoring (or worse, blaming) the victim. This not only brought rape and its impact out of the darkness, but also was the foundation for subsequent investigations of the psychological trauma of rape and how it might be treated. Burgess and Holmstrom strongly advocated that rape to be seen as a societal concern, and that professionals educate themselves about rape trauma and be prepared to help survivors. Their work had far-reaching effects. Subsequent research has focused on a range of topics: identification of risk factors for developing PTSD following sexual assault, patterns of recovery, the role of factors such as the characteristics of the assault, prior trauma history, psychiatric comorbidity, social support, and the survivor's coping behavior in facilitating (or impeding) recovery, and the prevention and treatment of long-term psychopathology following rape.

The literature on the effects of rape on women and how to best treat women with rape-related traumatic stress has grown tremendously in the past 30 years. However, literature on the effects of rape on men is quite sparse. Studies consistently show that women and girls experience sexual assault and childhood sexual abuse at much higher rates than do men or boys (see Tolin & Foa, 2006, for a detailed examination of sex-related differences in trauma and PTSD), but men may be more likely than women to not report sexual assault. The empirical findings to date, although few, suggest that men may be even more severely affected by the trauma of rape. For example, Elliott, Mok, and Briere (2004) included both men and women in a study of prevalence and impact of adult sexual assault. In their survey sample of 941 adults, 22% of women and 3.8% of men reported a history of sexual assault. A history of childhood sexual abuse was especially common among sexually assaulted men and women (61% and 59%, respectively). Men who had been sexually assaulted reported greater trauma related symptoms than women with history of sexual assault. Walker, Archer, and Davies (2005) compared the psychological functioning of 40 male rape survivors with a matched control group of men (i.e., men who were similar demographically but had not experienced rape). The investigators found that the men with a history of rape reported high levels of intrusive thoughts and avoidance in relation to the assault and also had much poorer psychological functioning than the controls including lower self-worth and lower self-esteem.

Burgess and Holmstrom's findings regarding coping responses and recovery from rape have been replicated and extended. For example, Ullman, Filipas, Townsend, and Starzynski (2007) examined the effects of psychosocial factors on current PTSD symptoms of a large group of sexual assault survivors. They found that greater PTSD symptom severity was associated with history of prior trauma, perceived life threat during the assault, post-assault self-blame, avoidance coping, and negative social reactions from others. Rape survivors' perception of greater control over their recovery process was associated with fewer PTSD symptoms. Ullman, Filipas, Townsend, and Starzynski (2006) reported that women who were attacked by strangers reported greater perceived life threat and more severe sexual assaults. This group also reported more negative social reactions from others as compared to victims of acquaintances or romantic partners. In a similar vein, being assaulted by strangers and relatives was associated with greater PTSD symptoms as compared to being assaulted by acquaintances and romantic partners.

Interventions for Rape Trauma

Crisis Intervention

As noted above, Burgess and Holmstrom (1974) recommended crisis intervention in the early or acute phase of rape trauma. The basic assumptions of the crisis intervention model are as follows. First, the rape represents a crisis in which the victim's life is abruptly and severely disrupted. Second, the rape victim is a person who was functioning adequately or normally prior to rape, and whose extreme symptoms and behaviors in response to the rape may be seen as normal reactions to an abnormal event. Third, crisis intervention counseling is present-focused and has the goal of returning victim to her pre-assault level of functioning as quickly as possible. It is to be distinguished from psychotherapy in that it does not delve into prior or ongoing problems or life difficulties, but is focused on rape-related issues and disturbances. Finally, crisis counseling is actively initiated by the counselors rather than waiting for rape survivor to seek services. For example, crisis counselors often see a rape victim in the hospital emergency department as Burgess and Holmstrom did, and might do home visits when necessary.

This model became the primary form of acute psychological aid for rape survivors. The idea that rape crisis counselors should go to the hospital and offer support and help to victims immediately, should remain in supportive roles during reorganization and integration, and offer support and advocacy services to the rape victim in court appearances during criminal proceedings became well established in rape crisis centers around the United States. These interventions are still the most common forms of assistance used in community settings for survivors of rape.

Over the past 2 decades, as researchers have developed and studied treatments for PTSD, victims of rape and crime comprised one of the groups that have been extensively studied. Most of what is known now about effective interventions for the psychological trauma of rape has come from studies of rape-related PTSD. These interventions for individuals who suffer significant symptoms related to rape (e.g., PTSD, depression, anxiety, and extensive avoidance) are generally quite effective. Some research has evaluated early intervention as a means of facilitating the recovery process and preventing the development of PTSD and related psychopathology. Other studies have focused on treatments designed to ameliorate the symptoms of chronic and long-term PTSD.

Early Intervention

Given the consistent finding of systematic decline in symptoms over time, the benefit of an early intervention should exceed the decrease in symptoms that comes about via natural recovery processes in order to be useful or worthwhile. A number of early intervention programs for assault survivors have been studied. Foa, Hearst-Ikeda, and Perry (1995) compared a brief (4-session) cognitive behavioral therapy (CBT) program to a control condition consisting of repeated assessment of symptoms with 20 female survivors of recent assault. The CBT program included *in vivo* and imaginal exposure (*see:* **Exposure Therapy, Adult**), cognitive therapy, education, and relaxation. The CBT program was more effective than the assessment condition at reducing PTSD severity and diagnosis immediately after intervention. However, these differences disappeared by 5-months posttrauma as the participants in assessment condition continued to improve.

Foa, Zoellner, and Feeny (2006) studied this same CBT prevention program in a larger group of 90 female recent assault survivors. The brief CBT intervention was compared to an assess-

ment condition and to supportive counseling; each condition was administered in four sessions. Assault survivors reported decreases in PTSD symptoms, depression, and anxiety over time in all conditions. Immediately following the intervention phase, those in the CBT program reported greater decreases in self-reported PTSD severity and a trend toward lower anxiety than those in supportive counseling. By the last follow-up assessment (about 9 months post-assault), women in all three conditions were generally similar in outcome. While these findings show that a trauma-focused intervention after an assault can accelerate recovery, they also provide another example of how many assault survivors tend to continue to recover in the year following the trauma even if not receiving trauma-focused treatment.

In another example of early intervention, Resnick et al. (2007) evaluated the efficacy of a video intervention to reduce PTSD and other rape-related symptoms. The video intervention was implemented prior to the forensic medical examination that was conducted within 72 hours of the sexual assault. Results of an assessment conducted 6 weeks later showed that the video intervention was associated with less severe PTSD and depression symptoms among women with a history of prior rape compared to the scores of women with a prior rape who did not view the video. Follow-up assessment at 6 months showed lower depression scores among those with a prior rape history who were in the video condition compared to those who did not see it (i.e., standard care condition).

Interventions for Chronic PTSD

Cognitive behavior therapy (CBT) has the most empirical support for adults with PTSD related to sexual assault. CBT treatments are generally aimed at helping the rape survivor to face the memory of the trauma, her thoughts and feelings about it, and situations or activities that are safe or low risk yet avoided because of their association with the rape. The goal is to help her return to former level of functioning by processing and integrating the traumatic event and reducing avoidance behavior, which allows the survivor to attain a realistic perspective on the rape.

Treatment studies have been conducted using exposure therapy, cognitive therapy, anxiety management approaches such as stress inoculation training (SIT), and eye movement desensitization and reprocessing (EMDR). In general, adults (primarily women, in studies of treatment for rape survivors) treated with all of these interventions achieve comparable and highly significant reductions in trauma related symptoms including PTSD, depression, and anxiety.

Conclusion

The work of Burgess and Holmstrom greatly increased awareness of rape as a psychologically, as well as physically, traumatic experience. They identified and documented a reliable pattern of intense symptoms that are triggered by rape and that begin to subside as the survivor integrates the event and reorganizes her life. This pattern is quite consistent with current views of PTSD, and many of their findings have been repeatedly replicated.

A vast body of literature has accumulated in the three decades since Burgess and Holmstrom published their observations. Numerous studies have increased our understanding of capacity for natural recovery as well as individual differences in patterns of response and vulnerability to the development of chronic traumatic stress disorders. Theories regarding the mechanisms responsible for natural processing of traumatic events have informed the development of treatments that are designed to facilitate recovery when those natural mechanisms have failed or been overwhelmed. Cognitive behavioral interventions, built on these theories, have been found especially efficacious. One important direction for current and future research involves the dissemination of these treatments to nonacademic settings such as rape crisis centers and other community clinics.

REFERENCES

American Psychiatric Association. (1968). *Diagnostic and statistical manual of mental disorders* (2nd ed.). Washington, DC: Author.

American Psychiatric Association. (1980). *Diagnostic and statistical manual of mental disorders* (3rd ed.). Washington, DC: Author.

Burgess, A. W. (1983). Rape trauma syndrome. *Behavioral Sciences and the Law, 1*(3), 97–113.

Burgess, A. W., & Holmstrom, L. L. (1974). Rape trauma syndrome. *American Journal of Psychiatry, 131*, 981–986.

Burgess, A. W., & Holmstrom, L. L. (1979). Adaptive strategies and recovery from rape. *American Journal of Psychiatry, 136*, 1278–1282.

Cahill, S. P., Street, G. P., Jayawickreme, N., & Foa, E. B. (2008). *Predictors of initial severity and recovery from post-trauma psychopathology: A prospective study.* Manuscript in preparation.

Elliott, D. M., Mok, D. S., & Briere, J. N. (2004). Adult sexual assault: Prevalence, symptomatology, and sex differences in the general population. *Journal of Traumatic Stress, 17*(3), 203–211.

Faravelli, C., Giugni, A., Salvatori, S., & Ricca, V. (2004). Psychopathology after rape. *American Journal of Psychiatry, 161*, 1483–1485.

Foa, E. B., Hearst-Ikeda, D., & Perry, K. (1995). Evaluation of a brief cognitive-behavioral program for the prevention of chronic PTSD in recent assault victims. *Journal of Consulting and Clinical Psychology, 63*, 948–955.

Foa, E. B., Zoellner, L. A., & Feeny, N. C. (2006). An evaluation of three brief programs for facilitating recovery after assault. *Journal of Traumatic Stress, 19*, 29–43.

Kessler, R. C., Sonnega, A., Bromet, E., Hughes, M., & Nelson, C. B. (1995). Posttraumatic stress disorder in the National Comorbidity Survey. *Archives of General Psychiatry, 52*, 1048–1060.

Resnick, H., Acierno, R., Waldrop, A. E., King, L., King, D., Danielson, C., et al. (2007). Randomized controlled evaluation of an early intervention to prevent post-rape psychopathology. *Behaviour Research and Therapy, 45*(10), 2432–2447.

Rothbaum, B. O., Foa, E. B., Riggs, D. S., Murdock, X., & Walsh, W. (1992). A prospective examination of posttraumatic stress disorder in rape victims. *Journal of Traumatic Stress, 5*, 455–475.

Tolin, D. F., & Foa, E. B. (2006). Sex differences in trauma and posttraumatic stress disorder: A quantitative review of 25 years of research. *Psychological Bulletin, 132*, 959–992.

Ullman, S. E., Filipas, H. H., Townsend, S. M., & Starzynski, L. L. (2006). The role of victim-offender relationship in women's sexual assault experiences. *Journal of Interpersonal Violence, 21*(6), 798–819.

Ullman, S. E., Filipas, H. H., Townsend, S. M., & Starzynski, L. L. (2007). Psychosocial correlates of PTSD symptom severity in sexual assault survivors. *Journal of Traumatic Stress, 20*, 821–831.

Walker, J., Archer, J., & Davies, M. (2005). Effects of male rape on psychological functioning. *British Journal of Clinical Psychology, 44*, 445–451.

ELIZABETH A. HEMBREE
University of Pennsylvania School of Medicine

SARA B. COHEN
University of Pennsylvania School of Medicine

See also: Anxiety Management Training; Betrayal Trauma; Cognitive Behavior Therapy, Adult; Criminal Victimization; Diagnosis of Traumatic Stress Disorders (*DSM & ID*); Domestic Violence; Early Intervention; History of Psychological Trauma; Posttraumatic Stress Disorder, Diagnosis of; Retraumatization; Shame; Women and Trauma

REFUGEES

According to Article 1 of the 1951 UN Convention Relating to the Status of Refugees, a refugee is a person who, "owing to well-founded fear of being persecuted for reasons of race, religion, nationality, membership of a particular social group or political opinion, is outside the country of his nationality and is unable or, owing to such fear, is unwilling to avail himself of the protection of that country; or who, not having a nationality and being outside the country of his former habitual residence as a result of such events, is unable or, owing to such fear, is unwilling to return to it" (UN High Commissioner for Refugees, 1951, p. 16).

These characteristics make refugees distinct from illegal immigrants, economic migrants, environmental migrants, labor migrants, and immigrants. Refugees are forced to flee their homes, communities and loved ones without knowing where they will end up. Prior to or during flight they very often endure extreme traumatic experiences including siege, combat, torture, atrocities, rape, witnessing violence, fear for their lives, hunger, lack of adequate shelter, separation from loved ones, and destruction and loss of property.

Not all persons who have been displaced as a consequence of political violence are counted as refugees. The reported number of refugees does not include millions of internally displaced persons, stateless persons, and asylum seekers. Thus, the actual number of persons who experience the psychological traumas associated with being displaced by political violence may be substantially greater than the estimates provided by the United Nations High Commissioner for Refugees.

Today's Refugees

In 2006, the Office of the UN High Commissioner for Refugees (UNHCR) estimated that there were then more than 10 million refugees and that over one million of those had become refugees in the past year. Women and children accounted for 75% of these refugees, with 65% of all refugees being from Africa and 60% being Muslim. The top five countries of origin for refugees were Afghanistan, Palestine, Iraq, Myanmar, and Sudan. The top five countries of resettlement were Pakistan, Iran, the United States, Syria, and Germany.

The United States has admitted 2 million refugees since 1980. After a decline in refugee admissions following September 11, 2001, the United States admitted 54,000 in 2005 and 41,000 in 2006. Refugees enter the United States either as part of legally approved refugee programs, or with some legal migration documents (e.g., student visas), or undocumented. Refugee program admissions are authorized by the U.S. Refugee Act of 1980. Refugees are provided with an initial package of benefits that includes housing, financial assistance, job placement, English language instruction, school placement, and health and mental health services.

The experience of resettlement for refugees in the United States presents both new challenges and opportunities. Refugees resettled in cities, like other urban populations, experience increased economic pressures from poverty and low-wage work, and live in communities strained by crime, gangs, drugs, AIDS, and troubled schools. Increasingly, refugees are also being resettled in suburban and rural areas. For many refugees, the site of resettlement is not a solitary point, but one node on a global system of transnational families and Diasporic communities. A refugees' life under these conditions is like to involve prolonged separations from loved ones, family contact through telecommunications, money transfer, air travel, and perhaps someday, return.

Psychological Traumas Experienced by Refugees

Refugee trauma is a concept used by mental health and human rights professionals to explain the psychologically traumatic impact of the refugee experience on individual, family, and community mental health. The earliest descriptions of refugee trauma in the mental health literature were in reference to Holocaust survivors, and were sometimes named "concentration camp syndrome" (Eitinger, 1961). With the advent of the posttraumatic stress disorder (PTSD) diagnosis in the *Diagnostic and Statistical Manual of Mental Disorders,* (*DSM-III;* American Psychiatric Association, 1980), refugee trauma was viewed primarily through the lens of traumatic stress theory. There was a burgeoning of scientific literature that documented traumatic stress symptoms and the PTSD diagnosis in multiple refugee populations displaced through the Vietnam War and the killing fields of Pol Pot in Cambodia. This was part of a larger movement in the mental health field that involved the proliferation of the concept of psychological trauma and the use of PTSD diagnosis, not only in refugees.

Refugees are exposed to many risks for PTSD and other mental health problems—first and foremost, directly experiencing or witnessing traumatic events. Research evidence indicates that pre-departure risk factors also play a role in poorer mental health outcomes, including older age, higher socioeconomic status, higher education, and female sex. Post-flight, poorer mental health outcomes may be associated with such factors as unstable living arrangements, lack of economic opportunity in the new living situation, and repatriation.

Refugee children present a unique set of needs and challenges (Henderson, 2008). They may exhibit PTSD, but are also likely to have subsyndromal traumatic stress symptoms, behavioral disturbances, developmental delays, or learning problems. It is also important to recognize that children are known to exhibit resilience to refugee trauma, and are often a key source of hope for their families in resettlement.

Refugee women have been found to have higher rates of PTSD and other mental health problems than other women. They may have also been subject to sexual assault in war or in transit, and also may be subject to domestic violence in the resettlement context. Some refugee women may be drawn into doing sex work (*see:* **Human Trafficking**) or may be vulnerable to exploitation by the human trafficking industry.

Treating Refugee Trauma

Although PTSD has received the most attention in the psychiatric literature and mass media, many professionals agree that refugee mental health services cannot be focused only on the clinical treatment of PTSD. Services must be concerned with treating and preventing a range of possible mental health and behavioral problems, including other mental disorders, substance abuse disorders, negative behavioral outcomes (e.g., domestic violence), and HIV/AIDS risk behaviors.

Mental health care for refugees may also be provided by nongovernmental organizations conducting humanitarian interventions during complex emergencies. In these instances, the desire to help may not necessarily be matched by the results from the field. Mental health care for refugees cannot be expected to succeed without adequate attention to basic public health needs and ordinarily present psychiatric disorders such as schizophrenia.

In resettlement settings, clinical treatment for refugee trauma is typically organized through refugee mental health clinics or specialized torture victim treatment centers.

Services include crisis intervention, psychopharmacology, individual psychotherapy, group psychotherapy, and self-help groups. To deliver culturally appropriate services, some programs have utilized traditional healers, socialization groups, multifamily groups, and cultural activities. Services are typically provided by bicultural workers from the refugee ethnic community in collaboration with psychiatrists and psychologists.

Even when mental health services are available free of charge and in the refugees' home language, refugees face multiple obstacles toward seeking mental health care. These include lack of familiarity with mental health treatment and stigma regarding mental illness and psychiatric care. Because many refugees who suffer from emotional distress do not seek mental health services, some programs have developed outreach and education activities.

There are at present few if any formal preventive mental health services for refugees. But through a prevention approach, services may be able to enhance protective resources so as to stop, lessen, or delay possible mental health and behavioral sequelae in refugees.

Researching Refugee Trauma

Research has consistently demonstrated that refugee adults and children have high rates of psychological trauma exposure and mental health sequelae, including high rates of PTSD and depression. Several longitudinal studies have shown high rates of PTSD and depressive symptoms (e.g., 50% in Cambodians) that generally diminish over time.

PTSD focused studies of refugee populations have been important in establishing the existence of mental health problems. However, many of these studies are methodologically limited by small sample sizes, clinical populations, lack of standardized instruments, and lack of cross-cultural adaptation of instruments. Conceptually, psychological studies of refugee trauma have come under criticism for overemphasizing the negative individual mental health consequences of the refugee experience and underemphasizing other priority

dimensions such as family, school, community, and religion.

Resilience in refugees is not well studied. There are no known large-scale epidemiological studies or prospective studies of refugees concerning resilience. There are a number of small and mostly cross-sectional quantitative studies, and these have identified possible protective resources, such as family and social support, connection to the large community, connections to the culture of origin, ideological commitment, collective self-esteem, and affirmation through shared experience.

Future studies are called for that focus on: (a) the underlying processes of risk and protection for refugee trauma; (b) the roles of ecological factors related to family, community, and culture; (c) specific subgroups and their problems, such as refugee children with learning disorders; (d) interventions and service experiences, including access; and (e) longitudinal outcomes, such as how people cope with and recover from the psychological traumas associated with being refugees over time.

Questions, Dilemmas, and Challenges

The concept of refugee trauma grew further during the 1990s with the genocides and wars in the Balkans, Rwanda, and Liberia, leading to the development of more programs to treat refugee trauma in complex emergencies, post conflict countries, and in resettlement countries. This in turn led to a backlash from some professionals advocating broader approaches addressing a range of psychosocial problems and overall public health needs. The figure of the Western-based trauma expert, who would go to a refugee setting and provide consultation and training to local professionals and paraprofessionals based on individually and cognitively focused approaches to refuge trauma, came under criticism (Weine, 2006).

Because refugees come from varying cultural and social backgrounds, understanding and helping with psychological trauma is necessarily complicated by many contextual variables that the mental health field has struggled to understand. The issue of culture is central to mental health work with refugees. It calls for attention to cross-cultural assessment of symptoms and diagnoses, cross-cultural translation and adaptation of interventions, cultural systems of meeting, and the processes and of cultural adjustment.

Family is also a key issue in thinking about both refugees and refugee trauma. Most but not all refugees come as families in some configuration. They carry with them family beliefs, rituals, and histories, and live within established patterns of family structure and functioning, all of which have profound implications for their experiences as refugees and their coping with refugee trauma. Loss and separation from family members is known to worsen mental health problems. Family resiliency is often cited as an important variable, but is in need of greater study.

The focus on PTSD has lead to concerns of overemphasis on disorder. Is diagnosing trauma and refugees an unnecessary medicalization of suffering and injustice? Is the focus of refugee trauma too slanted toward the experiences of war and not enough toward the experiences of poverty, low-wage work, discrimination, inadequate school opportunities, or other family and social problems? Does it take into account their resiliency and strengths?

Alternatively to traumatic stress theory, refugee trauma has been conceptualized from several different points of view (Weine et al., 2002). These include the concepts of cultural bereavement, cultural trauma, family consequences of refugee trauma, community trauma, and social suffering. These concerns have led some to pursue innovative interventions including health education, community building, testimony therapy, family interventions, and art therapies. Policy changes are also important because efforts to improve mental health consequences of refugee trauma cannot expect to succeed if not accompanied by efforts to improve the life situation of refugees.

Refugees may have several opportunities to receive mental health services, either in the context of a refugee camp or after resettlement, but for various reasons not all will take advantage of these. For instance, while they may be aware of their suffering, they may also be hopeful that as their daily circumstances improve they will begin to feel better. The system of refugee resettlement is based in part on that kind of hope. The practice and study of psychological trauma as applied to refugees is still learning how to best identify and help with refugees' psychological vulnerabilities, while also acknowledging and facilitating their hopes and strengths, which in so many instances, are no less impressive than their hardships.

REFERENCES

American Psychiatric Association. (1980). *Diagnostic and statistical manual of mental disorders* (3rd ed.). Washington, DC: Author.

Eitinger, L. (1961). Pathology of the concentration camp syndrome. *Archives of General Psychiatry, 5,* 79–87.

Henderson, S. (Ed.). (2008). Child and adolescent refugee mental health. *Child and Adolescent Psychiatry Clinics of North America.* New York: Elsevier.

U.N. High Commissioner for Refugees. (1951). *Convention and protocol relating to the status of refugees.* New York: Office of the United Nations High Commissioner for Refugees. Retrieved on April 18, 2008 from http://www.unhcr.org/protect/PROTECTION/3b66c2aa10.pdf.

U.N. High Commissioner for Refugees. (2006). *UNHCR statistical yearbook 2006.* New York: Office of the United Nations High Commissioner for Refugees. Retrieved on April 18, 2008 from http://www.unhcr.org/statistics/STATISTICS/478cda572.html.

Weine, S. M. (2006). *Testimony after catastrophe: Narrating the traumas of political violence.* Evanston, IL: Northwestern University Press.

Weine, S. M., Danieli, Y., Silove, D., van Ommeren, M., Fairbank, J., & Saul, J. (2002). Guidelines for international training in mental health and psychosocial interventions for trauma exposed populations in clinical and community settings. *Psychiatry, 65*(2), 156–164.

STEVAN M. WEINE
University of Illinois College of Medicine

See also: Asylum Seekers; Community Violence; Culture and Trauma; Family Systems; Genocide; HIV; Human Rights Violations; Human Trafficking; Humanitarian Interventions; Nongovernmental Organizations; Posttraumatic Adaptation; Social Support; Trauma, Definition; War Trauma

RESEARCH ETHICS

See: Professional Standards and Ethics; Research Methodology

RESEARCH METHODOLOGY

There has been a continuous expansion of research addressing traumatic life events, their consequences, and strategies for intervention to prevent or alleviate distress. The research literature has grown from a handful of studies 50 years ago to more than 10 thousand published articles and books today (see the National Center for PTSD bibliographic database, the Published International Literature on Traumatic Stress, PILOTS, www.ncptsd.va.gov). As this body of literature has increased, the research methods used to answer important questions about psychological trauma and its aftermath have likewise expanded and matured.

Research methods in all sciences are designed to test whether independent variables (such as life experiences, personality or biological characteristics, or treatments) are associated with dependent variables (such as emotional well-being or dysfunction and medical or psychological health or illness). In the field of research on psychological trauma and traumatic stress, independent variables have included the amount and type of traumatic events to which people are exposed, psychological, biological, and interpersonal characteristics of trauma victims, and educational and therapeutic interventions designed to prevent or ameliorate distressful consequences of exposure. Dependent variables in the traumatic stress research field include the type and severity of posttraumatic stress disorder (PTSD) that people suffer following exposure to psychological trauma, other psychiatric or medical disorders, and indicators of psychological, medical, social, and vocational well-being and adjustment.

Much early research work centered on postwar readjustment of U.S. veterans of the Vietnam War, with simple dichotomous comparisons of this group to others, usually veterans who did not serve in Vietnam or peers who never entered the military. For example, Enzie, Sawyer, and Montgomery (1973) noted higher levels of manifest anxiety among Vietnam veterans as compared to civilian controls; and Boscarino (1979) documented that Vietnam veterans reported more substance abuse than other military personnel who had no war-zone experience.

As the field of psychological trauma research advanced—again bolstered by a focus on combat veterans, but increasingly applied to other trauma populations (such as persons who experienced childhood abuse, domestic violence, assault, natural or human-caused disasters, or life-threatening accidents)—the way researchers viewed the "constructs" or variables of interest in the study of trauma became increasingly sophisticated. On the independent variable side, the study of trauma exposure has varied from its consideration as a dichotomy (e.g., exposure to combat or not; exposure to abuse or not) to the operationalization of exposure to psychological trauma as a continuum (e.g., Keane, Caddell, & Taylor's, 1988, Combat Exposure Scale; Straus's, 1979, Conflict Tactics Scale for intimate partner violence). In addition, researchers have noted that trauma exposure has both objective and subjective aspects (e.g., Solomon, Mikulincer, & Hobfoll, 1987): that is, psychological trauma involves both actual danger, harm, or death, as well as emotional responses such as extreme fear or a sense of helplessness or horror. Exposure to psychological trauma also is likely a multidimensional experience (e.g., D. W. King, King, Gudanowski, & Vreven, 1995), which means that there are several features of a traumatic event that may each uniquely contribute to the response to that event. For example, if one experiences a serious automobile accident, there may be a variety of trauma elements that come into play such as actual physical injuries, fear of death, whether others were injured or killed, and a sense of culpability or guilt.

Regarding dependent variables, or consequences of exposure to psychological trauma, PTSD officially entered the professional and scientific nomenclature in 1980 (American

Psychiatric Association, 1980). PTSD in and of itself has generated considerable research aimed at understanding its underlying structure, its causes, covariates (other variables related to PTSD development or severity), and consequences, its proper assessment, and its amenability to various treatment protocols. In addition, there is strong emphasis on understanding other conditions that follow highly stressful events and circumstances and are frequently comorbid with (occur in combination with) PTSD: depression, substance abuse, problems in work and relationships, and violent behavior, among others. In more recent years, the dependent variables of psychological trauma research have included aspects of physical health, social and work adjustment, as well as posttraumatic growth (i.e., positive changes experienced by persons who have been exposed to psychological trauma).

As a part of this elaboration and refinement of important trauma-related constructs or variables, there has been a search for other variables that might be implicated in posttrauma dysfunction. Demographic characteristics, such as gender, age, education, and socioeconomic status, have been convincingly related to the development and severity of PTSD and a variety of other posttraumatic outcomes. Additionally, the psychological trauma victim's prior exposure to abuse, assault, or other highly stressful life events, history of mental distress, and dissociation, panic attacks, or other reactions during or soon after exposure to psychological trauma have been associated with PTSD and other posttrauma sequelae (changes that occur following exposure to psychological trauma). A number of intrapersonal or individual characteristics also have been identified as associated with adverse or positive short- and long-term sequelae of exposure to psychological trauma. These include hardiness, self-esteem, and coping style. Finally, a broad body of existing research points to the power of social support as an interpersonal variable ameliorative of the detrimental results of trauma exposure.

The key research questions surrounding these variables and their interrelationships have focused on what factors might mediate the linkage between stressor and outcome, or moderate or work jointly with a stressor to mitigate or exacerbate its effect. An example of a mediating variable might be the individual's opportunity to disclose feelings and share fears about the traumatic experience, such that it serves as an intervening factor between the traumatic event and mental distress that can "filter" the effect of the traumatic event on emotional response. An example of a moderating variable might be the individual's history of exposure to earlier-life traumatic stressors, wherein for those who have such a history the effect of the current traumatic event on emotional distress is stronger than for individuals who lack such a history. It is important to keep in mind that these two research concepts, mediation and moderation, are not mutually exclusive phenomena; it is possible for a moderating variable to also serve as a mediator. Baron and Kenny (1986), Aiken and West (1991), and Jaccard (1991) provide further details on the definition and statistical techniques used in research studies to test hypotheses related to moderation and mediation.

Psychological trauma research has been highly enriched by the identification and testing of mediator or moderator variables that may serve as risk and resilience factors. This research can help us better understand who is most vulnerable to PTSD and other posttraumatic outcomes and what personal resources are most predictive of recovery or chronic problems (see meta-analyses by Brewin, Andrews, & Valentine, 2000; Ozer, Best, Lipsey, & Weiss, 2003; and methodological reviews by D. W. King & King, 1991; D. W. King, Vogt, & King, 2004; Vogt, King, & King, 2007).

Accompanying these advances in conceptualizing and understanding the antecedents and consequences of psychological trauma, there has been concomitant growth and refinement in the research designs and statistical methods used to answer critical questions. What follows is a summary of four overlapping methodological trends that reflect positively on the quality of inquiry into psychological trauma and its effects: (1) greater reliance on longitudinal designs, (2) growing use of a latent variable framework to explain observed behaviors, (3) rethinking posttraumatic change in terms of an individual's unique trajectory of symptoms over time, and (4) applying contemporary solutions to the challenge of missing data.

Greater Reliance on Longitudinal Designs

The ultimate goal of any scientific endeavor is to unambiguously demonstrate a cause-effect relationship between an independent variable and a dependent variable. It is generally accepted that three conditions must be obtained to establish such causality: (1) covariation (that an independent variable, or variations in it, is accompanied by changes in a dependent variable); (2) temporal precedence (the putative cause must precede the outcome in time); and (3) the elimination of any alternative explanations (also known as *third variables*) that could explain the association between cause and effect (such as other independent variables or covariates).

With the exception of treatment outcome research, the majority of psychological trauma research has been observational and cross-sectional (i.e., based on data collected at a single point in time), with after-the-fact (retrospective) reports of events and circumstances before, during, and after the occurrence of psychological trauma. While such designs can demonstrate a covariation between psychological trauma or other independent variables and posttraumatic outcomes, establishing temporal precedence and eliminating alternative explanations are serious problems for these types of research methodologies. Indeed, with regard to temporal precedence, ambiguity about the direction of cause and effect frequently has surfaced as a challenge to research findings. For example, D. W. King and King (1991) discussed how faulty recollections and possibly reconstructed memories combined with current mental health problems may lead research participants who are suffering from PTSD or other mental health problems to unintentionally describe themselves as having more or worse past experiences of psychological trauma than others who are not suffering from those problems. In that case, the correct research finding would not be that actual exposure to psychological trauma might cause PTSD or mental health problems. Psychological trauma might, in fact, cause PTSD or mental health problems, but the research design simply does not allow the scientist to rule out the alternative possibility that memories of trauma might be "caused" to be worse (although not necessarily to occur) by suffering from PTSD or other mental health problems.

Largely to overcome the concerns about direction of causality, and thus enhance the validity of research findings, researchers have turned more and more to longitudinal designs (conducted over time), both in PTSD treatment outcome research studies that track changes after intervention, and naturalistically in field research to track the course of recovery or dysfunction following exposure to psychological trauma. In the former, participants are randomly assigned to treatment or control conditions, and the design has the potential to yield causal statements regarding the impact of treatment on PTSD and other posttraumatic problems or positive outcomes. In naturalistic studies of the course of problems and recovery following exposure to psychological trauma, the temporal order of events and the precedence of independent variables before dependent variables may be more clearly identified, although the third-variable problem remains because many other factors may affect the dependent variable in addition to the independent variable of psychological trauma.

There are many current programs of exceptional longitudinal trauma research. To cite just a few: Shalev et al. (1998) studied victims of various psychological traumas for a year or more after first assessing them in a hospital emergency department, monitoring a broad array of psychosocial and biological outcome measures. Saxe et al. (2001) studied seriously injured children, also starting at the point of hospital emergency admission, with repeated assessments of child and family characteristics, health, and adjustment. Resnick et al. (2007) incorporated a longitudinal approach to evaluate the impact of a cognitively based video intervention for female victims of sexual assault, with measures of PTSD, depression, and psychosocial adjustment outcomes assessed over time. For these and many other research endeavors, the goal is to understand how people are affected and how they cope at several time points following exposure to psychological trauma.

Longitudinal research designs are potentially informative, but, by recruiting participants who have already have experienced psychological trauma, these studies rely on retrospective accounts of pre-trauma factors, resulting in ambiguity about the direction of causality for associations involving these factors. Ideally, longitudinal research should assess potential psychological trauma victims prior to the occurrence of the traumatic event. This obviously is a difficult task, but it has been accomplished by chance or an unexpected opportunity (e.g., Silver, Holman, McIntosh, Poulin, & Gil-Rivas, 2002, in the context of the September 11, 2001, terrorist incidents) or by design given a population expected to face extremely stressful and challenging events (e.g., Vasterling et al., in press, in the context of pre-deployment testing of U.S. army personnel under orders to the Iraq War).

There are some cautions to observe when planning and conducting longitudinal trauma research. Perhaps the most important caution is to be sure that the schedule of repeated assessments is controlled by the researcher and not by study participants. In the latter case, a third variable (e.g., participants avoiding assessment when they are feeling particularly healthy or ill, or participants with the least resources tending to delay or cancel appointments) interferes with the ability to achieve valid inference (D. W. King et al., 2006). In addition, it is wise to target more frequent assessments at critical points of expected change and fewer assessments during periods of expected relative stability in the characteristics being monitored. Moreover, it goes without saying that longitudinal research should use the same assessment devices and measures at every time point. If changes in measures are deemed necessary (as might be the case in studying traumatic stress in children and then into adolescence and young adulthood), measures must be checked statistically to ensure they are comparable, such as by using item response theory (IRT) methods (Embretson & Riese, 2000). Finally, for research efficiency and in order to prevent participants from being unduly burdened, longitudinal traumatic stress studies can utilize methods that allow some participants to be exempted at some time points, using "planned missingness" designs (Graham, Taylor, Olchowski, & Cumsille, 2006). In such designs, the researcher purposefully assigns subgroups of participants to provide data at targeted subsets of assessment occasions (no single person is assessed on all occasions). Statistical procedures are then used to deal with the incomplete data and still derive conclusions based on the full sample of participants.

Growing Use of a Latent Variable Framework to Explain Observed Behaviors

In 1904, Spearman introduced factor analysis, a statistical method to evaluate the convergence of indicators as evidence for abstract entities responsible for observed behaviors (such as personality traits or intellectual abilities). Later, Cronbach and Meehl (1955) emphasized the importance of such factors, which are called "hypothetical constructs" or "latent variables" because they are believed to represent phenomena that are not evident by simple observation alone. Cronbach and Meehl proposed a process of "construct validation," whereby support for a postulated organization of associations among unobserved or latent variables, the "nomological network," serves as the basis for understanding observed behavior. This type of thinking was codified by Joreskog (1970) with the introduction what he called the "analysis of covariance structures" (the discovery of relationship patterns that underlie associations among observed variables). This approach was later dubbed linear structural relations (LISREL), which evolved to be more generically called structural equation modeling (SEM) today.

SEM is comprised of two components: a *measurement component* and a *structural component*. The measurement component involves what is called "confirmatory factor analysis," a method for identifying and quantifying the unobserved sources or latent variables underlying associations among observed scores on measured variables (which may be called "manifest indicators"). The structural component is aimed at documenting relations among the latent variables themselves. In SEM, both components are incorporated in a collection of simultaneously solved regression equations.

For example, assume that we are interested in the relationships among three hypothetical constructs or latent variables. The first variable is perceived threat, defined as the one's sense of fear of bodily harm in the presence of a traumatic event. Perceived threat is measured by responses to a scale containing 5 item statements (e.g., "I was afraid I would die."). The second variable is social support, defined as the individual's belief that he or she can count on family or close friends to be concerned and emotionally helpful in a crisis, such as a traumatic experience. This social support variable is also measured by a scale with 5-item statements (e.g., "My family and friends are there for me when I need them."). The third variable is posttraumatic depression as assessed by a 8-item measure of the person's degree of sadness and withdrawal (e.g., "I feel as though I can't go on."). In the SEM analysis of data supplied by trauma victims on these assessment scales, one would use statistical methods (a confirmatory factor analysis) to examine how well the sets of 5 perceived threat items, 5 social support items, and 8 depression items map onto the latent variables that they are purportedly measuring. With support for the three latent variables and their manifest indicators (the items) in the measurement model, the question of how the latent variables are associated with one another is resolved in the structural component. This can be in the form of simple nondirectional associations among the latent variables, or in some set of hypothesized directional associations (e.g., perceived threat leads to depression, social support intervenes in, or mediates, this association to prevent excessive depression, or, perhaps, both perceived threat and social support simultaneously predict level of depression).

The SEM approach has become an increasingly useful and powerful tool in the psychological trauma research enterprise. It is a highly flexible method that can concurrently accommodate large numbers of variables, thus enabling the researcher to contemplate complex multivariate explanations for the consequences of psychological trauma exposure. There are a number of other advantages to using SEM that allow the researcher to be more confident in the strength and direction of documented associations among latent variables. Finally, SEM yields indices of overall "model-data fit," which, in conjunction with other information provided in the model, inform the researcher about the adequacy of the theoretical representation and offer the ability to appraise competing models.

One area of specialized inquiry within the larger SEM domain is the nature of PTSD as revealed by its latent structure. As summarized by L. A. King, King, Orazem, and Palmieri (2006), the preponderance of findings from confirmatory factor analyses of PTSD data suggests that the PTSD construct is multidimensional and likely consists of four correlated factors. A current debate exists as to whether the best four-factor framework is one that coincides relatively closely to the *Diagnostic and Statistical Manual of Mental Disorders* PTSD (*DSM-IV;* American Psychiatric Association, 1994) conceptualization (reexperiencing, avoidance, numbing, and hyperarousal; D. W. King, Leskin, King, & Weathers, 1998) or one that attempts to reconcile PTSD's placement within a larger context of mood and anxiety disorders (reexperiencing, avoidance, hyperarousal, and dysphoria; Simms, Watson, & Doebbeling, 2002). Interestingly, both solutions call for the disaggregation of the *DSM-IV* PTSD criterion C cluster into separate effortful avoidance (Items C1 and C2) and emotional numbing (Items C3–C7) factors. The debate essentially hinges on the placement of three items: D1 (sleep disturbance), D2 (irritability), and D3 (difficulty concentrating). In the D. W. King et al. (1998) model, these three items remain with their *DSM-IV*-assigned hyperarousal cluster; in the alternative model, they are shifted to the numbing cluster to produce what Simms et al. (2002) label "dysphoria." There will continue to be serious interest in documenting the structure of PTSD well into the future, across different trauma groups, genders, cultures, age cohorts, and so on. From a methodological and substantive perspective, demonstration of the invariance or equivalence of factor solutions (McArdle & Cattell, 1994) over groups and over time within groups is important to the validity of PTSD as a useful construct.

Another method that incorporates the notion of a latent variable construct is IRT (item response theory; Embretson & Riese, 2000), a contemporary approach to test development and evaluation. As with factor analysis, IRT assumes that one's status on a hypothetical construct or latent variable determines how one will respond to an item on a psychometric instrument. One advantage of IRT over more traditional strategies is that estimates of item characteristics (statistical indices of how well the item is performing) are not dependent on the sample on which they are computed (such as clinical patients versus healthy community members). Also, an estimate of a person's standing on an attribute (e.g., score on a PTSD or depression continuum) does not depend on what specific sets of items are employed, thus allowing for flexibility in the composition of item sets and in making comparisons between individuals assessed with different instruments. IRT is prominent in the larger arena of psychological measurement, especially the assessment of cognitive constructs. At present, IRT studies of trauma-related measures are sparse (see D. W. King, King, Fairbank, Schlenger, & Surface, 1993; Orlando & Marshall, 2002, for exceptions), but they hold promise for future work where test equating is required, such as cross-cultural/cross-language trauma studies or longitudinal research that tracks childhood psychological trauma victims into adulthood.

Unique Trajectories of Posttraumatic Symptoms over Time

Over the past decade, statistical treatment of longitudinal data has shifted from an emphasis on averaging the results of many individuals in group data, via the repeated measures analysis of variance, to change as characteristic of the individual person. In this newer approach, each study participant provides data from which is calculated one or more indices of unique change for that person, that then can be incorporated into subsequent analyses. In this section, we briefly present three methods of operationalizing and analyzing change as an individual differences characteristic.

Perhaps the simplest method of documenting change in scores on a variable from occasion to occasion is to calculate a simple difference score for each study participant: a person's score at an earlier occasion subtracted from that person's score at a subsequent occasion. While it has been suggested that such direct difference scores lack reliability and should be avoided (e.g., Cronbach & Furby, 1970), a strong case has been made that such an assertion does not take into consideration all of the factors contributing to difference score reliability. In particular, those asserting unacceptable reliability of difference scores assume that the dispersion or "spread" of the distributions of scores will be the same over both assessments. Many (e.g., Nesselroade & Cable, 1974) have demonstrated that such an assumption may be incorrect; hence, the threat of difference score unreliability is likely overstated, and simple computation of direct difference scores should not be altogether dismissed (see L. A. King, King, McArdle, Saxe, et al., 2006, for further details).

On the other hand, if a researcher is still concerned about the reliability of difference scores—perhaps because the scores from which the difference is calculated themselves have questionable reliability—the reliability of the difference score can be bolstered through the use of latent difference scores. Latent difference scores are difference scores calculated from perfectly reliable component scores using an SEM algorithm to model measurement error. Such models have been developed by McArdle and his associates (e.g., McArdle & Hamagami, 2001) and demonstrated in the context of traumatic stress data by L. A. King, King, McArdle, Grimm, et al. (2006).

Finally, inter-individual differences in intra-individual change are also represented in what are called latent growth curve models in the SEM tradition and as multilevel regression models in the random coefficients regression tradition. In the simplest case, the relationship between an individual's score on a variable of interest on a particular occasion and the time since trauma exposure for that assessment is considered, generating an intercept and a slope (statistical concepts) that define the trajectory of change for each study participant. While the slope describes individual change, the intercept is an estimate of the individual's score at some designated occasion, usually the initial assessment. These individual differences characteristics, in turn, are used in further analyses, perhaps as outcomes in SEM or possibly as predictors of other dependent variables in SEM (to determine if variations in trajectory influence other outcomes). A few examples of such analyses (e.g., Orcutt, Erickson, & Wolfe, 2004; Resnick et al., 2007) have appeared in the psychological trauma literature. As an example, with a sample of sexual assault victims, Resnick et al. showed that, on average, the greatest decrease in PTSD symptom severity occurred in the initial days and weeks after the assault, followed by subsequent "leveling off" of symptoms weeks and months later, but there was a great deal of variation in individual change trajectories. While the majority of victims improved over time (hence, the average trend toward wellness), there were a number of study participants for whom change did not occur and still others whose symptom severity increased over time. Obviously, an understanding of these trajectories of individual change

give information that can help locate the best points for intervention and also identify the types of persons who do not follow a trend toward recovery.

Applying Contemporary Solutions to the Challenge of Missing Data

The problem of missing or incomplete data historically has been viewed as, at best, an annoyance, and at worst, a grave impediment to valid research inferences. However, innovative statistical work has prompted an exciting reconceptualization of the problem of incomplete data and provided new methods to overcome earlier concerns. The newer approaches are based on statistical techniques called "maximum likelihood" methods and are of two general types. The first, called "full information maximum likelihood," uses all of the available information in the data to arrive at parameter estimates that would most likely have produced the existing data, given the proposed model. The emphasis is on direct parameter estimation and not on "filling in" data "blanks" (e.g., Arbuckle, 1996; McArdle & Bell, 2000). The second approach to the treatment of missing data is "multiple imputation." Here, the goal is to generate values for missing information and then use these imputed values to calculate desired parameter estimates. Recognizing that there are two sources of error in the imputed values, error attributable to sampling variability and inaccuracy in the imputed values themselves, multiple imputations are performed that result in numerous new complete data sets. For each imputed data set, parameter estimates are derived using the desired analytic procedure, and then averaged to yield unbiased parameter estimates. Special formulas (Rubin, 1987) are available to calculate standard errors and degrees of freedom (two concepts in statistical analysis). Schafer and Graham (2002) is an excellent source for further information on contemporary missing data techniques, especially for the assumptions that underlie the use of these procedures. As psychological trauma research continues to mature, these techniques will become more and more mandated, and purposeful incomplete data designs to conserve resources and alleviate participant burden will become increasingly popular (see Graham et al., 2006, for details).

Conclusion

In the years since the initiation of the formal study of psychological trauma and its consequences, the research methods within this realm have become more and more sophisticated. In turn, the improved precision, quality, and yield of these methods has allowed us to answer questions and achieve research goals that may not have been possible before. In this entry, we set forth four trends that have made an impact on the field, all of which rely on highly intensive modern numerical algorithms for their solutions. Indeed, like other areas of study, research on psychological trauma has benefited dramatically from the development and use of high-speed computers. The ultimate objectives of research on psychological trauma are to better understand the complex process by which exposure to a traumatic event impacts its victims and develop informed treatments to alleviate suffering and promote well-being. Attention to research methods is an important component to achieving these objectives. Research methodology is a dynamic process. By constantly striving to refine research strategies, adapt techniques from other disciplines, and create new methods, the study of psychological trauma will continue to advance toward the attainment of these objectives.

REFERENCES

Aiken, L. S., & West, S. G. (1991). *Multiple regression: Testing and interpreting interactions.* Newbury Park, CA: Sage.

American Psychiatric Association. (1980). *Diagnostic and statistical manual of mental disorders* (3rd ed.). Washington, DC: Author.

American Psychiatric Association. (1994). *Diagnostic and statistical manual of mental disorders* (4th ed.). Washington, DC: Author.

Arbuckle, J. L. (1996). Full information estimation in the presence of incomplete data. In G. A. Maroulides & R. E. Schumacker (Eds.), *Advanced structural equation modeling* (pp. 243–277). Mahwah, NJ: Erlbaum.

Baron, R. M., & Kenny, D. A. (1986). The moderator-mediator variable distinction in social psychological research: Conceptual, strategic, and statistical considerations. *Journal of Personality and Social Psychology, 51,* 1173–1182.

Boscarino, J. (1979). Current drug involvement among Vietnam and non-Vietnam veterans. *American Journal of Drug and Alcohol Abuse, 6,* 301–312.

Brewin, C. R., Andrews, B., & Valentine, J. D. (2000). Meta-analysis of risk factors for posttraumatic stress disorder in trauma-exposed adults. *Journal of Consulting and Clinical Psychology, 68,* 748–766.

Cronbach, L. J., & Furby, L. (1970). How we should measure change: Or should we? *Psychological Bulletin, 74,* 68–80.

Cronbach, L. J., & Meehl, P. E. (1955). Construct validity in psychological tests. *Psychological Bulletin, 52,* 281–302.

Embretson, S. E., & Riese, S. P. (2000). *Item response theory for psychologists.* Mahwah, NJ: Erlbaum.

Enzie, R. F., Sawyer, R. N., & Montgomery, F. A. (1973). Manifest anxiety of Vietnam returnees and undergraduates. *Psychological Reports, 33,* 446.

Graham, J. W., Taylor, B. J., Olchowski, A. E., & Cumsille, P. E. (2006). Planned missing data designs in psychological research. *Psychological Methods, 11,* 323–343.

Jaccard, J. J. (1991). *Interaction effects in multiple regression.* Newbury Park, CA: Sage.

Joreskog, K. G. (1970). A general method for analysis of covariance structures. *Biometrika, 57,* 239–251.

Keane, T. M., Caddell, J. M., & Taylor, K. L. (1988). Mississippi Scale for Combat-Related Posttraumatic Stress Disorder: Three studies in reliability and validity. *Journal of Consulting and Clinical Psychology, 56,* 85–90.

King, D. W., & King, L. A. (1991). Validity issues in research on Vietnam veteran adjustment. *Psychological Bulletin, 109,* 107–124.

King, D. W., King, L. A., Fairbank, J. A., Schlenger, W. E., & Surface, C. R. (1993). Enhancing the precision of the Mississippi Scale for Combat-Related Posttraumatic Stress Disorder: An application of item response theory. *Psychological Assessment, 5,* 457–471.

King, D. W., King, L. A., Gudanowski, D. M., & Vreven, D. L. (1995). Alternative representations of war zone stressors: Relationships to posttraumatic stress disorder in male and female Vietnam veterans. *Journal of Abnormal Psychology, 104,* 184–196.

King, D. W., King, L. A., McArdle, J. J., Grimm, K., Jones, R. T., & Ollendick, T. H. (2006). Characterizing time in longitudinal trauma research. *Journal of Traumatic Stress, 19,* 205–215.

King, D. W., Leskin, G. A., King, L. A., & Weathers, F. W. (1998). Confirmatory factor analysis of the Clinician-Administered PTSD Scale: Evidence for the dimensionality of posttraumatic stress disorder. *Psychological Assessment, 10,* 90–96.

King, D. W., Vogt, D. S., & King, L. A. (2004). Risk and resilience factors in the etiology of chronic PTSD. In B. T. Litz (Ed.), *Early interventions for trauma and traumatic loss in children and adults: Evidence-based directions* (pp. 34–64). New York: Guilford Press.

King, L. A., King, D. W., McArdle, J. J., Saxe, G. N., Doron-LaMarca, S., & Orazem, R. J. (2006). Latent difference score approach to longitudinal trauma research. *Journal of Traumatic Stress, 19,* 771–785.

King, L. A., King, D. W., Orazem, R. J., & Palmieri, P. A. (2006). Research on the latent structure of PTSD. *PTSD Research Quarterly, 17,* 1–7.

McArdle, J. J., & Bell, R. W. (2000). An introduction to latent growth models for developmental data analysis. In T. D. Little, K. U. Schnabel, & J. Baumert (Eds.), *Modeling longitudinal and multi-level data: Practical issues, applied approaches, and specific examples* (pp. 69–107). Mahwah, NJ: Erlbaum.

McArdle, J. J., & Cattell, R. B. (1994). Structural equation models of factorial invariance in parallel proportional profiles and oblique confactor problems. *Multivariate Behavioral Research, 29,* 63–113.

McArdle J. J., & Hamagami, F. (2001). Latent difference score structural models for linear dynamic analyses with incomplete longitudinal data. In L. M. Collins & A. G. Sayer (Eds.), *New methods for the analysis of change* (pp. 139–175). Washington, DC: American Psychological Association.

Nesselroade, J. R., & Cable, D. G. (1974). "Sometimes it's okay to factor difference scores": The separation of state and trait anxiety. *Multivariate Behavioral Research, 9,* 273–284.

Orcutt, H. K., Erickson, D. J., & Wolfe J. (2004). The course of PTSD symptoms among Gulf War veterans: A growth mixture modeling approach. *Journal of Traumatic Stress, 17,* 195–202.

Orlando, M., & Marshall, G. N. (2002). Differential item functioning in a Spanish Translation of the PTSD Checklist: Detection and evaluation of impact. *Psychological Assessment, 14,* 50–59.

Ozer, E., Best, S., Lipsey T., & Weiss, D. (2003). Predictors of posttraumatic stress disorder and symptoms in adults: A meta analysis. *Psychological Bulletin, 129,* 52–73.

Resnick, H., Acierno, R., Waldrop, A., King, L., King, D., Danielson, C., et al. (2007). Randomized controlled evaluation of an early intervention to prevent post-rape psychopathology. *Behavior Research and Therapy, 45,* 2432–2447.

Rubin, D. B. (1987). *Multiple imputations for no response in surveys.* New York: Wiley.

Saxe, G. N., Stoddard, F., Sheridan, R., Courtney, D., Cunningham, K., King, L. A., et al. (2001). Relationship between acute morphine and courses of PTSD in children with burns. *Journal of the American Academy of Child and Adolescent Psychiatry, 40,* 915–921.

Schafer, J. L., & Graham, J. W. (2002). Missing data: Our view of the state of the art. *Psychological Methods, 7,* 147–177.

Shalev, A. Y., Freedman, S., Peri, T., Brandes, D., Sahar, T., Orr, S. P., et al. (1998). Prospective study of posttraumatic stress disorder and depression following trauma. *American Journal of Psychiatry, 155,* 630–637.

Silver, R. C., Holman, E. A., McIntosh, D. N., Poulin, M., & Gil-Rivas, V. (2002). Nationwide longitudinal study of psychological responses to September 11. *Journal of the American Medical Association, 288,* 1235–1244.

Simms, L. J., Watson, D., & Doebbeling, B. N. (2002). Confirmatory factor analysis of posttraumatic stress symptoms in deployed and nondeployed veterans of the Gulf War. *Journal of Abnormal Psychology, 111,* 637–647.

Solomon, Z., Mikulincer, M., & Hobfoll, S. E. (1987). Objective versus subjective measurement of stress and social support: Combat-related reactions. *Journal of Consulting and Clinical Psychology, 55,* 577–583.

Spearman, C. (1904). "General intelligence," objectively determined and measured. *American Journal of Psychology, 15,* 201–292.

Straus, M. A. (1979). Measuring intrafamily conflict and violence: The Conflicts Tactics (CT) Scales. *Journal of Marriage and the Family, 41,* 75–88.

Vasterling, J. J., Schumm, J., Proctor, S. P., Gentry, E., King, D. W., & King, L. A. (2008). Posttraumatic Stress Disorder and health functioning in a non-treatment seeking sample of Iraq War veterans: A prospective analysis. *Journal of Rehabilitation Research and Development, 45*, 347–358.

Vogt, D. S., King, D. W., & King, L. A. (2007). Risk pathways for PTSD: Making sense of the literature. In M. J. Friedman, T. M. Keane, & P. A. Resick (Eds.), *Handbook of PTSD: Science and practice* (pp. 99–115). New York: Guilford Press.

DANIEL W. KING
Veterans Affairs Boston Healthcare System

LYNDA A. KING
Veterans Affairs Boston Healthcare System

See also: Assessment, Psychometric, Adult; Etiology; Posttraumatic Adaptation; Posttraumatic Stress Disorder; Trauma, Definition

RESILIENCE

During the course of their lives, most people experience at least one potentially traumatic event (PTE), such as the death of a close relation or a violent or life-threatening situation. Until recently, it was widely assumed that healthy functioning following exposure to such PTEs was rare and occurred only in people of exceptional emotional strength. However, research now demonstrates that *most* people maintain relatively stable, healthy levels of psychological and physical functioning as well as the capacity for generative experiences and positive emotions after being exposed to a PTE (Bonanno, 2004). This capacity is now widely seen as reflecting *resilience* to the deleterious effects of even the most aversive human experiences. For example, following bereavement, serious illness, or terrorist attack, almost 50% of exposed persons have been found to display healthy levels of functioning or resilience (Bonanno, 2004).

There are measurable and important individual differences in how people respond to PTEs, and most of the variability can be cap-

tured by four prototypical trajectories: chronic dysfunction, recovery, resilience, and delayed reactions (Bonanno, 2004). Historically, trauma researchers and theorists have tended to discount the prevalence of the resilience trajectory, even regarding it as a form of denial or hidden psychopathology. However, evidence now shows that resilience is neither a pathological state nor the result of exceptional strength. For example, among the prototypical outcome trajectories, resilience appears to be the most common response to a wide variety of PTEs (Bonanno, 2004). Furthermore, resilience can be empirically distinguished from the recovery trajectory by the degree and duration of symptoms following a PTE (Bonanno, 2004; Deshields, Tibbs, Fan, & Taylor, 2006).

A key point is that even resilient individuals may experience some transient difficulties. However, these reactions are usually mild to moderate, relatively short-term, and do not significantly interfere with functioning (Bonanno et al., 2002). For example, resilient individuals may have difficulty sleeping, or experience intrusive thoughts or memories of the event for several days or even weeks, but still manage to perform the everyday tasks of their life or career.

Why are some people more or less likely to be resilient following a specific PTE? Initial pioneering research on children suggested that multiple protective factors buffer against adversity, including person-centered variables (e.g., temperament of the child) and socio-contextual factors (e.g., supportive relations, community resources). Research on resilience among adults exposed to isolated PTEs suggests a similar conclusion: A variety of independent risk and protective factors may each contribute or subtract from the overall likelihood of a resilient outcome.

Researchers have grouped person-centered factors associated with resilience into two broad categories: pragmatic coping and flexible adaptation (Bonanno, 2005; Mancini & Bonanno, 2006). Because PTEs are by definition outside the range of normal human experience, they often pose unique coping demands. Successfully meeting these demands suggests the need for a highly *pragmatic* approach that is single-minded and goal-directed. For example, people who are narcissistic and habitually utilize self-serving biases tend to evoke negative reactions in others but also cope extremely well with isolated PTEs, such as war and terrorist attack. Another group of individuals, known as repressive copers, tend to avoid unpleasant emotional experiences and are possibly susceptible to health deficits. Yet, repressive copers have also been found to cope extremely well with adversity.

A more genuinely healthy personality dimension is suggested by the concept of *adaptive flexibility*. A core aspect of flexibility is the capacity to shape and modify one's behavior to meet the demands of a given stressor event. This capacity for adaptive flexibility helps bolster resilience to aversive events, such as childhood maltreatment, but may also be enhanced or reduced by developmental experiences. Preliminary research suggests that adaptive flexibility becomes stable in adulthood and predicts resilience to PTEs.

Theorists have also delineated a crucial role for social and personal resources. For example, available financial and social resources are associated with resilience following PTEs, as is maintaining full-time employment and social support (Bonanno, Galea, Bucciarelli, & Vlahov, 2007). Not surprisingly, the relative absence of current and prior life stress is also associated with resilience.

A number of demographic characteristics, such as male gender, older age, and greater education, have been shown to predict resilience to PTEs. Racial or ethnic minority status is often considered a risk factor for PTSD but is also confounded with socioeconomic status. When statistical methods are used to control for socioeconomic status, the effects of racial or ethnic minority status usually disappear. A recent exception, however, was a finding that among New Yorkers, ethnic Chinese were considerably more likely to be resilient following the September 11, 2001, attack (Bonanno et al., 2007). Additionally, people with children were less likely to be resilient after hospitalization for SARS (Bonanno et al., in press).

The burgeoning literature on resilience has highlighted the role of intrinsic recovery processes in adaptation to PTEs. This perspective offers a sharp contrast to historical assumptions regarding the usefulness of psychotherapeutic intervention for all exposed persons. Rather, for most people exposed to a PTE, intrinsic recovery processes will restore equilibrium relatively soon after exposure and thus treatment is neither necessary nor desirable except in cases of genuine dysfunction.

REFERENCES

Bonanno, G. A. (2004). Loss, trauma, and human resilience: Have we underestimated the human capacity to thrive after extremely aversive events? *American Psychologist, 59,* 20–28.

Bonanno, G. A. (2005). Resilience in the face of potential trauma. *Current Directions in Psychological Science, 14,* 135–138.

Bonanno, G. A., Galea, S., Bucciarelli, A., & Vlahov, D. (2007). What predicts psychological resilience after disaster? The role of demographics, resources, and life stress. *Journal of Consulting and Clinical Psychology, 75,* 671–682.

Bonanno, G. A., Ho, S. M. Y., Chan, J., Kwong, R. S. Y., Cheung, C. K. Y., Wong, C. P. Y., et al. (in press). Psychological resilience and dysfunction following SARS: The mental health of hospitalized survivors after the 2003 epidemic in Hong Kong. *Health Psychology.*

Bonanno, G. A., Wortman, C. B., Lehman, D. R., Tweed, R. G., Haring, M., Sonnega, J., et al. (2002). Resilience to loss and chronic grief: A prospective study from preloss to 18-months postloss. *Journal of Personality and Social Psychology, 83,* 1150–1164.

Deshields, T., Tibbs, T., Fan, M. Y., & Taylor, M. (2006). Differences in patterns of depression after treatment for breast cancer. *Psychooncology, 15,* 398–406.

Mancini, A. D., & Bonanno, G. A. (2006). Resilience in the face of potential trauma: Clinical practices and illustrations. *Journal of Clinical Psychology, 62,* 971–985.

RECOMMENDED READING

Masten, A. S. (2001). Ordinary magic: Resilience processes in development. *American Psychologist, 56,* 227–238.

ANTHONY D. MANCINI
Columbia University

GEORGE A. BONANNO
Columbia University

See also: Bereavement; Depression; Medical Illness, Adult; Posttraumatic Adaptation; Posttraumatic Growth; Trauma, Definition

RETRAUMATIZATION

Exposure to a potentially traumatic event puts individuals at risk for developing a variety of psychological disorders, including posttraumatic stress disorder (PTSD). Some individuals who have already developed a traumatic reaction following exposure to such an event are later exposed to another traumatically stressful event, and under such conditions the person may be "retraumatized." Thus, retraumatization has been defined as exposure to one or more potentially traumatic events subsequent to an initial exposure to psychological trauma, with the subsequent trauma exposure serving as a reminder of a past psychological trauma and exacerbating the distress that is related to the prior traumatic experiences (Layne et al., 2006). Retraumatization includes both the exposure to additional psychological traumas and the process that takes place when a second traumatic event occurs and the preexisting posttraumatic stress symptomatology is intensified.

At present, while retraumatization is a phenomenon that has been of increased interest in the trauma literature, it remains a poorly defined construct. There is no specified period of time or context in which the subsequent exposure to additional psychological trauma(s) must occur in order for retraumatization to have occurred. Once the initial, or "index," psychological trauma has occurred, any subsequent exposure to traumatic stressors may result in retraumatization. Retraumatization can occur regardless of whether the environmental or contextual factors of the first traumatic exposure are different at the time of the later traumatic exposures or remain consistent. Therefore, if the first traumatic experience is sexual abuse experienced as a child, retraumatization can occur through exposure to very different types of traumatic stressors, such as a natural disaster or combat experience.

In some cases, the term *retraumatization* also has been used to describe acute exacerbations of trauma-related distress by cues (reminders) that resemble aspects of past psychological traumas. For example, there is evidence to suggest that involvement in the judicial system can prove retraumatizing to crime victims when they are forced to recount their experience or are mandated to testify in trials. In such cases, the person is not exposed to additional psychological trauma, but experiences increased posttraumatic distress as a result of encountering reminders of the past trauma. It is important to distinguish between this usage of the term retraumatization from the other usage (i.e., actual exposure to additional traumatic stressors) because, while the results may be similar (i.e., increased distress), the second case does *not* actually involve exposure to traumatic stressors. If this difference is not carefully noted, experiences or events that are stressful but not actually traumatic may be misconstrued as being traumatic stressors. In the example above, such confusion could lead to the false conclusion that stressful experiences such as judicial proceedings are inevitably forms of psychological trauma.

There is a growing empirical literature on the impact of repeated exposures to traumatic events. Multiple exposures to psychological trauma are associated with increases in PTSD or related trauma symptomatology, especially in comparison to a single exposure to a traumatic event (Follette, Bechtle, Polusny, & Naugle, 1996; Kaysen, Resick, & Wise, 2003). Thus, retraumatization provides an important reminder that, in addition to the adverse effect that the "dose" (i.e., duration, frequency, and intensity) of exposure to a single type of traumatic event has on posttraumatic stress reactions, when a person is exposed to additional psychological traumas this too increases the likelihood that posttraumatic reactions will be distressing and potentially debilitating.

Interpersonal Violence: Revictimization as a Special Case of Retraumatization

Interpersonal violence refers to forms of violence that are perpetrated by one individual upon another, with the intent to cause harm or injury. It includes physical or sexual abuse to children, partner violence, rape (acquaintance and stranger), as well as other forms of physical assault. Some investigators have included emotional abuse as yet another form of interpersonal violence.

Revictimization is a related construct to retraumatization, and primarily refers to repeated forms of interpersonal violence such as physical or sexual abuse/assault. Revictimization and retraumatization have been used interchangeably to refer to the same construct, and while there is some conceptual overlap, there are some distinctions between the two and usage of these terms should be precise. Traumatization and retraumatization are broad categories describing the effects of exposure to any form of traumatic stressor, while victimization and revictimization are a subset of traumas that specifically involve interpersonal violence. It is true that a person who experiences any form of psychological trauma may be considered a "victim," but it is helpful to reserve the term "victimization" to specify acts interpersonal violence. Revictimization therefore would require an initial experience of interpersonal violence which may be followed either by another experience of interpersonal violence, by a different form of psychological trauma, or by a nontraumatic stressor that reactivates or intensifies the person's distress related to the initial experience of victimization.

While the risk of revictimization has been associated with all forms of interpersonal violence, survivors of sexual trauma have been a particular focus of research. Additionally, individuals with a history of childhood sexual abuse are at particular risk for severe and lasting posttraumatic problems. While reports vary, studies suggest that one out of eight women is sexually victimized at some point during her life (Cloitre & Rosenberg, 2006). In the United States, the range of women reporting a history of child sexual abuse (CSA) is 15% to 32%. Over the course of a lifetime, 67% of women who have been victimized will report at least one additional incident of victimization (Cloitre, Cohen, & Koenen, 2006). The factors associated with increased risk for sexual revictimization/retraumatization include having a history of child or adolescent sexual abuse and the characteristics of previous victimization (the severity and frequency of those abuses, the age at which the abuse began, the nature of the abusive sexual contact, the victim's relationship with the abuser, the duration and number of exposures to victimization). A history of CSA is one of the most robust risk factors for sexual victimization as an adult; women with a history of CSA are 1.8 times more likely to be assaulted in adulthood and men with a CSA history are 5.5 times more likely to be assaulted as an adult (Classen, Palesh, & Aggarwal, 2005).

Combat

Participation in combat is a risk factor for the development of PTSD and other psychological disorders (Brewin, Andrews, & Valentine, 2000). Data suggests that trauma severity, including duration of exposure, is a significant variable in the development of PTSD and related psychological disorders. The duration of exposure to combat has been measured as the length of time in military service or in a combat zone. Higher rates of exposure to combat situations, high levels of perceived danger (e.g., living in a combat zone, roadside bombs) or distressing events (e.g., waiting for combat, handling dead bodies or witnessing the death of friends) are associated with higher levels of traumatic stress symptoms. In addition to the substantial traumatic impact of any single combat event, combat involves multiple events over time and therefore potentially involves retraumatization. Thus, military combatants with higher rates of combat exposure are also associated with a greater risk of retraumatization.

The risk for retraumatization in military veterans is elevated by the current international sociopolitical context, according to data from military personnel serving in conflict zones. Changes in military policy and procedure regarding deployment, as well as changes in the manner in which warfare is conducted, have consequently exacerbated exposures to potentially traumatic events. The length and number of deployments has been extended and there is frequently not a clearly identifiable front line or enemy. These factors serve to increase perceived stress and danger in combat zones, and subsequently impact the likelihood of exposure to actual psychological traumas and the development of posttraumatic psychological difficulties. It has been suggested that the risk for retraumatization has greatly increased due to extended deployments and due to the inaccessibility of necessary mental health resources to military personnel during their tour or on their return.

Natural Disasters

Disasters such as earthquakes, fires, floods, hurricanes, and tornadoes have psychological effects for a significant number of people. The psychological symptoms associated with natural disasters include PTSD, depression, anxiety, anger, dissociation, aggression and antisocial behavior, somatic complaints, and substance abuse problems. An important distinction in relation to the traumatic stress associated with natural disasters is that they are frequently associated with significant resource loss such as loss of a loved one, property damage or loss, loss of employment and social structures. Hurricane Katrina, which affected the southeast region of the United States in 2005, provides an example of a natural disaster that resulted in extensive property loss with far reaching consequences for both individuals and the community. Thus, in addition to the more apparent traumatic impacts of being exposed to a life-threatening disaster, many disaster survivors experience retraumatization as a result of the stressful reminders of the disaster that are caused for many months or years afterward by the loss of key resources. In the example of Hurricane Katrina, survivors reported that they were retraumatized from coping with the loss of loved ones, leaving or losing their homes, and inadequate access to necessary resources. Those postdisaster stressors were generally not traumatic in and of themselves, but they reactivated the survivors' traumatic stress reactions by serving as ongoing reminders of the disaster.

Risk Factors for Retraumatization

Among the factors that may affect the risk of retraumatization are prior psychological trauma exposure, attachment styles, and early developmental history. It may seem obvious that retraumatization can occur only if a psychological trauma has occurred, but the additional important research finding is that, when an individual experiences a single traumatic event, it increases the chances of experiencing subsequent psychological trauma(s) or developing other psychological or medical disorders. While the specific mechanisms that increase this risk for revictimization remain under investigation, it is hypothesized that responses to traumatic events can impact the way an individual responds to subsequent traumatic events, thus further increasing the risk of future traumatization. Intrapersonal variables, which include psychological disorders, substance use, and sexual practices, can also put an individual at risk for retraumatization by affecting the ways they are able to respond to subsequent stressful events (Banyard, Williams, & Siegel, 2002). For example, an individual who utilizes dissociation as a form of coping with posttraumatic stress problems is at significantly greater risk to experience another traumatic event. Although individual risk factors are an important consideration this should not be misinterpreted as "blaming the victim." In most such cases, the traumatized individual does not intentionally cause the occurrence of additional traumas, but she or he may be less careful or more prone to taking risks as a result of experiencing posttraumatic distress or dissociation—or the person may simply live in circumstances that are unavoidably dangerous (such as violent communities or families).

Attachment history and developmental history also may have an impact on the risk of retraumatization. Attachment is a potential risk or protective factor depending on individual history. A secure attachment enables individuals to experience healthy and developmentally appropriate relationships, which allows them to learn effective interpersonal skills and healthy emotion regulation strategies. Children or adolescents who do not develop secure attachments with caregivers tend to have developmental trajectories that are impeded by irregular, unhealthy or dangerous experiences, and are therefore at risk for experiencing multiple traumatic events. Children in developmentally inappropriate environments also may not learn effective interpersonal skills and are not always able to distinguish between what is healthy and unhealthy and safe or unsafe. This inability to make these crucial discriminations increases the risk of retraumatization.

Environmental or contextual factors also seem to increase risk of retraumatization as well. Factors such as poverty or neglect can increase the likelihood of a person being exposed to multiple potentially traumatic events, including childhood abuse and family and community violence. Poverty may also be a risk factor for retraumatization among people exposed to disasters because they are more likely than more affluent people to lose (or simply not have access to) vital resources that facilitate postdisaster recovery.

Thus, retraumatization may occur when individuals are exposed to multiple traumatic events or to cues that evoke the reminders of past psychological traumas. Sexual retraumatization, combat, and natural disasters are areas where this phenomenon is commonly seen, and it is possible for someone to be retraumatized by experiencing events in any of these domains or any other type of traumatic experience (e.g., physical abuse, family or community violence, traumatic accidents). There are multiple factors including exposure to multiple traumas, individual factors, attachment style, developmental trajectory and environmental factors that can serve to increase the risk of retraumatization.

REFERENCES

Banyard, V. L., Williams, L. A., & Siegel, J. A. (2002). Retraumatization among adult women sexually abused in childhood: Exploratory analyses in a prospective study. *Journal of Child Sexual Abuse, 11*(3), 19–48.

Brewin, C. R., Andrews, B., & Valentine, J. D. (2000). Meta-analysis of risk factors for posttraumatic stress disorder in trauma-exposed adults. *Journal of Consulting and Clinical Psychology, 68,* 748–766.

Classen, C. C., Palesh, O. G., & Aggarwal, R. (2005). Sexual revictimization: A review of the empirical literature. *Trauma, Violence, and Abuse, 6,* 103–129.

Cloitre, M., Cohen, L. R., & Koenen, K. C. (2006). *Treating survivors of childhood abuse: Psychotherapy for the interrupted life.* New York: Guilford Press.

Cloitre, M., & Rosenberg, A. (2006). Sexual revictimization: Risk factors and prevention. In V. M. Follette & J. I. Ruzek (Eds.), *Cognitive-behavioral therapies for trauma* (pp. 321–361). New York: Guilford Press.

Follette, V. M., Polusny, M. A., Bechtle, A. E., & Naugle, A. E. (1996). Cumulative trauma: The impact of child sexual abuse, adult sexual assault and spouse abuse. *Journal of Traumatic Stress, 9,* 25–35.

Kaysen, D., Resick, P. A., & Wise, D. (2003). Living in danger: The impact of chronic traumatization and the traumatic context on posttraumatic stress disorder. *Trauma, Violence, and Abuse, 4,* 247–264.

Layne, C. M., Warren, J. S., Saltzman, W. R., Fulton, J. B., Steinberg, A. M., & Pynoos, R. S. (2006). Contextual influences on posttraumatic adjustment: Retraumatization and the roles of revictimization, posttraumatic adversities and distressing reminders. In L. A. Schein, H. I. Spitz, G. M. Burlingame, P. R. Muskin, & S. Vargo (Eds.), *Psychological effects of catastrophic disasters: Group approaches to treatment* (pp. 235–286). New York: Haworth Press.

Victoria M. Follette
University of Nevada

Aditi Vijay
University of Nevada

See *also:* Abuse, Child Physical; Abuse, Child Sexual; Child Maltreatment; Community Violence; Complex Posttraumatic Stress Disorder; Criminal Victimization; Disaster; Domestic Violence; Etiology; Military Personnel; Rape Trauma; War Trauma

REVICTIMIZATION

See: Retraumatization

RISK FACTORS

See: Etiology; Research Methodology; Resilience

RITUAL ABUSE

See: Abuse, Child Sexual; Child Maltreatment

S

SECONDARY TRAUMA

See: Vicarious Traumatization

SELF-HELP

What Are Self-Help Programs?

There are two general meanings attached to the term *self-help*. The first meaning refers to self-help groups—typically, people who have a problem and who join organizations or less formal groups, where the purpose is to come together to be helped and to help others with similar problems. The second meaning of self-help refers to the use of materials—books, pamphlets, audio/visual tapes, CDs, DVDs, or computer-delivered programs, where specific information or more complex forms of treatment are offered within these various media venues. It is this second meaning of the term self-help that is addressed in this entry.

The content of these programs vary, but typically includes several different components that together are designed to help the individual deal effectively with the identified problem. These include: (a) assessment tools designed to help individuals better understand whether or not they have the type of problem being addressed by the SH program. These assessment tools may also include forms that help the individual track progress on dimensions germane to the identified problem. (b) Information about the problem itself, including what defines it, how it may have developed, and ways to treat it. (c) Examples of people who have had and successfully dealt with the problem. (d) Specific strategies for dealing with the problem;

and (e) A systematic ordering of these strategies to produce the best result. When self-help programs are evaluated in formal research studies, assessments of all participants are conducted by a professional who is an expert on the disorder/problem. Access to such experts during the time participants are engaged in the program sometimes is provided in self-help interventions, both to maintain the participant's motivation to complete the program and to provide each participant with individualized guidance about how best to proceed as they utilize the program.

Self-help programs for Posttraumatic Stress Disorder (PTSD) or for subclinical forms of this disorder have been developed and tested for effectiveness. To date these programs have been limited to self-help books and self-administered Internet-based programs, with only the latter being formally evaluated in scientifically controlled treatment outcome studies.

Basis of Self-Help Treatment Programs

Self-help treatment programs for PTSD or other traumatic stress problems have been adapted from the psychological treatment literature that has evaluated therapist-administered treatment programs. Such studies, for the most part, have employed strategies based on cognitive-behavioral therapy (CBT) approaches for traumatic stress disorders. Such approaches are based on coping models and/or exposure models (*see:* **Coping; Exposure Therapy, Adult**) or combinations of the two. An example of the coping model approach is provided by the Stress Inoculation Training program developed by Kilpatrick and Amick (1985). In this model clients are taught a variety of coping skills that are individually tailored to their problems. The first phase of this approach involves an informational component to help the individual understand the nature and causes of PTSD as well as their personal responses to the traumatic event they have experienced. Six coping skills are then taught, with instructions designed to enable the learner to become proficient in at least two of them. The six skills include muscle relaxation, breathing control, covert modeling (practicing the skills in imagination), role playing (practicing skills with others), thought stopping, and guided self dialogue. These skills are practiced in hierarchical fashion, proceeding from how to use these strategies to deal with mild, everyday stressors to dealing with more complex and difficult situations.

Prolonged exposure techniques have also served as a model for the development of self-help approaches. In these approaches individuals are asked to recall their traumatic event(s) for extended periods, and to imagine or actually place themselves in feared situations associated with their past traumatic experiences. Exposures typically progress from imagined to real-life situations or to carefully guided partial reenactments of the original traumatic event(s) in a safe manner that does not involve any further actual psychological trauma. In another approach, developed for rape victims, exposure has been broadened within an individually administered treatment format to include homework assignments in which traumatized individuals are asked to write about their traumatic event. In this instance writing exposure typically proceeds from writing about the event itself, to writing about one's emotional and cognitive responses to the event, and to writing about one's world view and attitudes that have been changed by experiencing the event.

To date, self-directed interventions for dealing with PTSD have included both books and Internet-based treatments. They have also, for the most part, included elements of both coping and exposure. Formal research evaluations of self-directed treatment programs, however, have focused entirely on Internet-based interventions.

Content of Self-Help Programs for PTSD

Few programs exist for delivering self-help interventions for psychological trauma sequelae. Most of these programs are Internet-based with the majority of those formally evaluated being developed in European countries. One Internet-based program developed in the United States—The Self-Help Therapy for Trauma consequences (SHTC; Hirai & Clum, 2005) targeted individuals who had experienced a variety of traumatic events and who had nonclinical levels of PTSD. This program consists of a mastery approach delivered within the context of four treatment modules: (1) information about the nature, causes, and treatment of PTSD; (2) information about and prescribed practice with three different relaxation techniques; (3) information about and prescribed practice in cognitive strategies designed to challenge erroneous beliefs about their traumatic event; and (4) writing exposure about the event and the individual's response to it. The mastery experience utilized a controlled access approach, in which the four modules were hierarchically organized so that individuals could access more challenging modules only after they had demonstrated competence with the easier coping skills. Thus, individuals accessed the information module first, followed by the relaxation skills, cognitive skills, and exposure skills modules thereafter.

One of the few online treatment programs that has been extensively evaluated was developed by Lange and colleagues (Lange et al., 2003; Lange, van de Ven, Schrieken, & Emmelkamp, 2001) in the Netherlands. This program—Interapy—consists of three distinct phases. In the first phase trauma victims were instructed to write about their traumatic events on 10 separate occasions for 45-minute periods and to employ positive cognitive reappraisal of the events. Individuals who used the program were asked to write about the factual details of their traumatic event in the first person and in the present tense. They were also asked to write their intimate fears and thoughts concerning the event. Therapist feedback was provided frequently during the five-week treatment period, making this treatment a therapist-assisted SH program. Feedback was provided in written form of no more than 450 words and typically included instructions to confront an aspect of the trauma event that the therapist thought was being avoided. In the second phase of this treatment participants received information about the principles of cognitive reappraisal. Participants were to identify and practice new ways of thinking about the traumatic event through the mechanism of providing advice to a friend who had undergone a similar event. In the third and last phase participants were asked to share what they had learned with someone else who had also experienced a traumatic event.

Each of these programs share common elements, including information about traumatic events and their effects and an explanation of why the approach being offered was expected to be effective. Additionally, individuals treated were required to undergo exposure to the event in the form of writing about it and then taught skills regarding how to reappraise the event. It is unknown which of these elements are essential and which, if any, are not. Another Internet treatment program, offered in Great Britain, that was not effective, did not include the writing exposure element. These comparisons suggest that some form of exposure to the traumatic event might be an essential element when treatment is offered in a self-administered form. Additional support for the importance of exposure comes from the Interapy studies that found greater levels of improvement in individuals who had not previously shared the details of their traumatic event with others compared to participants who had previously disclosed their traumatic experiences to other persons. This finding indicates that the exposure element had the biggest effect for individuals who had not yet recalled and disclosed the event in the detail that is required when one tells others what happened.

The Role of Assessment

Assessment plays an important role in the deployment and evaluation of self-help treatment programs in general. Two types of

assessment are requisite: (1) assessment of the problem being addressed by the self-help program; and (2) assessment of change during the self-help program. The importance of the first type of assessment comes from the necessity of treating only those individuals who have the problem for which the treatment was devised. Such assessment can come from an expert who formally interviews each potential participant or from self-report questionnaires that evaluate individuals' personal assessment of whether they possess the requisite characteristics for the treatment offered. This latter type of assessment suffers from the potential risk that nonexperts may misunderstand a question or symptom that is being described. The problems associated with assessment are reduced when self-help treatments are evaluated in the context of a formal study. They are most acute when individuals access existing programs where no formal evaluations take place.

The second type of assessment is intended to track changes in each participant's functioning as a result of engaging in the self-help intervention. This type of assessment is grounded in self-regulation theory, which conceptualizes self change as partially a function of goal setting and feedback about success approaching the goal. If the goal is learning and executing new coping skills or the reduction of symptoms then assessment of progress on these dimensions will enhance treatment outcome. Demonstrations of the contribution of such assessments have been documented by Febbraro and Clum (1998).

Effectiveness of Self-Help Treatments for PTSD

Very few treatment outcome studies have evaluated the effectiveness of self-help treatments for PTSD and other traumatic stress problems. Accordingly, only tentative conclusions can be reached at this point in time. To date the evidence suggests that Internet treatments are better than no treatment at all, a conclusion that is elaborated later in this entry. Further, the Interapy approach offered in the Netherlands was found to produce stable improvements over a 6-week follow-up period. No information is available on whether self-directed interventions are as effective as therapist-directed interventions or pharmacologic interventions, or whether self-directed interventions are helpful over more lengthy follow-up periods. Similarly, no information is available on what treatment components are the most helpful or how they are best delivered. Two research studies have evaluated the Interapy program for trauma victims (Lange et al., 2001, 2003) and one study (Hirai & Clum, 2005) has evaluated the SHTC program.

Treatment for PTSD and related problems, including self-help approaches, can be evaluated by assessing impact on primary symptoms of the disorder and on secondary symptoms associated with the disorder. Primary symptoms of PTSD include reexperiencing symptoms, avoidance and emotional numbing symptoms and hyperarousal symptoms. Secondary symptoms include such things as depression, general anxiety, sleep problems and somatic symptoms. Further, in addition to evaluating whether individuals improve on these dimensions, an assessment is also made of the number of people who are "significantly clinically improved" after participating in the treatment. Significant clinical improvement may be defined in several ways, including a sufficiently large reduction in symptoms to constitute a meaningful improvement or to achieve a relatively normal level of symptom severity, or sufficient improvement in important areas of life functioning (such as school, work, or family) to no longer require treatment.

All three of the studies reviewed found that individuals treated with the self-help programs described above were successful when compared to individuals in wait-list conditions. Findings support the conclusion that both primary and secondary symptoms were improved by the self-help programs. Moreover, while individuals in the wait-list control conditions experienced little or no change, a large percentage of those in the treatment groups experienced clinically significant change. In the Interapy program, there was no loss of treatment effect in the six weeks after the conclusion of treatment.

Another question that arises is whether learning specific skills occurs as a result of program participation and whether learning those skills is related to improvement on PTSD symptoms. These questions were addressed in the Hirai and Clum study, which evaluated whether individuals who were in the program learned coping skills that were taught in the program. Evidence from this study indicated that treated individuals improved on targeted skills and in their confidence that they could use such skills to deal with their symptoms. Moreover, individuals who learned these skills were the ones whose symptoms improved the most. Taken together these findings provide encouraging support for the effectiveness of Internet-based, self-help treatment programs for individuals who have suffered significant trauma events and subsequent trauma-related symptoms.

Very little information is available on who profits from such self-help interventions and who does not. On a commonsense basis, only individuals with eighth-grade reading skills and with basic computer skills can participate successfully in bibliotherapy (written texts) or Internet-based treatment programs. Individuals without such skills would have to access audio/visual tapes, CDs or DVDs to gain access to such programs. Unfortunately, self-help programs for PTSD that have been tested for effectiveness do not yet exist in these forms. Also, individuals in remote geographical areas or with limited access to professional or financial resources might be ideally suited for self-help interventions (*see:* **Telemedicine**), though fitting this description does not ensure that such individuals will profit from these programs. A number of experts have recommended the exclusion of some types of individuals from self-help treatments, based largely on commonsense criteria. These have included individuals who are suicidal, individuals who are psychotic, and individuals who have major cognitive deficits that lead them to be easily severely confused. The recommendation to exclude suicidal individuals stems from a concern that exposure treatments can exacerbate symptoms and that the self-help process precludes careful monitoring of suicidal thoughts and behavior. The recommendation to exclude psychotic or cognitively impaired individuals stems from the possibility that such individuals may misinterpret important aspects of the treatment program and that a therapist would not be present to recognize such misinterpretations.

While inclusion and exclusion criteria have been recommended, no systematic review exists that summarizes factors that are empirically related to either improvement or deterioration secondary to participation in self-help interventions.

Where to from Here?

The development and evaluation of self-help treatment programs for PTSD is in its infancy. To date, all evaluated programs have required contact with study professionals, thus basically altering the self-help nature of the programs. Future research studies will be required to determine whether pure self-help programs, in which evaluations are done completely by computer, and in which all later contact is automated, are similarly effective. Also needed are studies that evaluate the effectiveness of self-help programs for particular types of psychological trauma or traumatic stress symptoms, for example interpersonal traumas such as rape and physical assault or natural disasters such as fires and hurricanes, and secondary symptoms (such as depression or somatic symptoms) as well as different levels of severity of PTSD symptoms. Comparisons of self-help treatments with other venues for providing treatment are needed, as are studies that identify characteristics that predict response to self-help treatments.

REFERENCES

Febbraro, G. A. R., & Clum, G. A. (1998). Meta-analytic investigation of the effectiveness of self-regulatory components in the treatment of adult problem behaviors. *Clinical Psychology Review, 18,* 143–161.

Hirai, M., & Clum, G. (2005). An Internet-based self-change program for traumatic event related fear, distress, and maladaptive coping. *Journal of Traumatic Stress, 18,* 631–636.

Kilpatrick, D. G., & Amick, A. E. (1985). Rape trauma. In M. Hersen & C. Last (Eds.), *Behavior therapy casebook* (pp. 86–103). New York: Springer.

Lange, A., Rietdijk, D., Hudcovicova, M., van den Ven, J. P., Schrieken, B., & Emmelkamp, P. M. G. (2003). Interapy: A controlled randomized trial of the standardized treatment of posttraumatic stress through the Internet. *Journal of Consulting and Clinical Psychology, 71,* 901–909.

Lange, A., van de Ven, J. P., Schrieken, B., & Emmelkamp, P. M. G. (2001). Interapy: Treatment of posttraumatic stress through the Internet—A controlled trial. *Journal of Behavior Therapy and Experimental Psychiatry, 32,* 73–90.

GEORGE A. CLUM
Virginia Tech University

See also: Anxiety Disorders; Anxiety Management Training; Cognitive Behavior Therapy, Adult; Coping; Coping Skills Training; Criminal Victimization; Depression; Disasters; Psychoeducation; Rape Trauma; Social Skills Training; Somatic Complaints; Telemedicine

SELF-INJURIOUS BEHAVIOR

Self-injurious behavior (SIB) refers to any behavior that involves the intentional self-infliction of tissue damage. Most commonly, researchers have used the term SIB to describe self-injury among persons with developmental impairments/disabilities or children (see Carr, 1977, for a review). Although the term technically could include any behavior that involves intentional self-injury, typically SIB includes the deliberate, direct destruction or alteration of bodily tissue without suicidal intent (Chapman, Gratz, & Brown, 2006). Other terms used to describe SIB include nonsuicidal self-injury, deliberate self-harm, self-mutilation, self-harm, and self-injury.

Different forms of SIB are often observed among different types of individuals. Among psychiatric outpatients, the most common forms of SIB tend to be cutting, burning, self-hitting, excoriating wounds, biting, and scratching. Among persons with psychotic disorders or severe developmental or genetic disorders, more severe forms of SIB sometimes occur, such as self-immolation (setting fire to oneself), self-castration, and self-injury to the genitals or facial regions.

The prevalence of SIB in the general population is approximately 4%, and the onset of SIB is typically in adolescence or early adulthood. Some studies have reported prevalence estimates that are similar for women (4%) and men (3%) (Briere & Gil, 1998). Certain populations have demonstrated a high prevalence of SIB, particularly psychiatric patients (inpatients and outpatients), incarcerated men and women, and college students. In terms of clinical populations, prevalence rates of SIB are particularly high among persons with borderline personality disorder, posttraumatic stress disorder (PTSD), dissociative disorders, and depressive disorders. Although sometimes not life-threatening itself, SIB is one of the best predictors of future suicide attempts and completed suicide; thus, SIB constitutes a serious public health problem.

Several theoretical explanations for SIB have been proposed. Across theories, the most striking commonality is a focus on the escape or avoidance of aversive experiences, such as unwanted or unpleasant thoughts, emotions, or situations. For cognitively normal, no psychotic adults, findings from research studies suggest that escape or avoidance of emotions may negatively reinforce SIB in many cases (for a review, see Chapman, Gratz, & Brown, 2006). SIB is often found at elevated prevalence rates among clinical groups characterized by avoidance behaviors. As an example, the lifetime prevalence of SIB among individuals with PTSD is approximately 50% (Cloitre, Koenen, Cohen, & Han, 2002).

The avoidance of trauma-related cues and memories, and thoughts and emotions related to traumatic events is a prominent symptom of PTSD that predicts poor outcomes among individuals with this disorder. SIB may often function to help individuals with PTSD escape or avoid unwanted emotions or thoughts related to past trauma. For other samples, such as children and individuals with certain developmental disabilities, positive reinforcement (i.e., social attention), negative reinforcement (e.g., reduction in

demands from the environment; reduction in emotional arousal), or sensory stimulation may maintain SIB.

Findings from research on SIB suggest that people engage in SIB for several key reasons: (a) to escape from unpleasant emotional states, (b) to self-punish for some perceived transgression or for an undesirable characteristic of the self, (c) to generate feelings or alleviate feelings of boredom, numbness, or dissociation, or (d) to communicate something to other people. Some research has indicated that emotional escape is a common reason for both SIB and suicide attempts, but that there are two key differences in the reasons for these behaviors: People are more likely to report engaging in SIB in order to self-punish or generate feelings (i.e., alleviate boredom, dissociation or numbness). In contrast, people are more likely to report engaging in suicide attempts in order to relieve a burden on other people.

Although the correlates and risk factors for SIB and suicidal behaviors are similar, this research does underscore the importance of distinguishing between suicidal and nonsuicidal forms of self-inflicted injury for the purposes of treatment. If SIB functions differently from suicidal behaviors, treatment of SIB might focus on different areas, such as helping the individual learn to generate feelings or reduce numbness or dissociation without engaging in SIB, or helping the individual learn to reduce self-punishing behaviors or self-deprecatory thinking. In contrast, treatment of suicidal behavior would focus more strongly on reducing hopelessness and challenging beliefs that persons in the patient's social network would be better off if the patient were to commit suicide.

Most of the treatment outcome studies on SIB have focused largely on individuals with borderline personality disorder (BPD). There is evidence that Dialectical Behavior Therapy (DBT; Linehan, 1993) is efficacious in treating SIB among suicidal and self-injurious women with BPD (Linehan et al., 2006). DBT includes individual psychotherapy as well as a therapy group that involves teaching behavioral skills in the areas of regulating emotions, being mindful of the present moment, managing interpersonal situations, and tolerating distress. Future research might examine the efficacy of DBT and other treatment programs for people who engage in SIB who do not have BPD or who are not suicidal.

REFERENCES

Briere, J., & Gil, E. (1998). Self-mutilation in clinical and general population samples: Prevalence, correlates, and functions. *American Journal of Orthopsychiatry, 68,* 609–620.

Carr, E. G. (1977). The motivation of self-injurious behavior: A review of some hypotheses. *Psychological Bulletin, 84,* 800–816.

Chapman, A. L., Gratz, K. L., & Brown, M. (2006). Solving the puzzle of deliberate self-harm: The experiential avoidance model. *Behaviour Research and Therapy, 44,* 371–394.

Cloitre, M., Koenen, K. C., Cohen, L. R., & Han, H. (2002). Skills training in affective and interpersonal regulation followed by exposure: A phase-based treatment for PTSD related to childhood abuse. *Journal of Consulting and Clinical Psychology, 70,* 1067–1074.

Linehan, M. M. (1993). *Cognitive behavioral treatment of borderline personality disorder.* New York: Guilford Press.

Linehan, M. M., Comtois, K. A., Murray, A. M., Brown, M. Z., Gallop, R. J., Heard, H. L., et al. (2006). Two-year randomized controlled trial and follow up of dialectical behavior therapy vs. therapy by experts for suicidal behaviors and borderline personality disorder. *Archives of General Psychiatry, 63,* 757–766.

ALEXANDER L. CHAPMAN
Simon Fraser University

See also: Comorbidity; Depression; Dialectical Behavior Therapy; Dissociation; Emotional Numbing; Personality Disorders; Suicide

SENSORIMOTOR PSYCHOTHERAPY

Developed in the 1980s by Pat Ogden, PhD, as a body-centered talking therapy, Sensorimotor Psychotherapy (Ogden, Minton, & Pain, 2006) directly addresses the bodily symptoms that so often complicate the treatment of traumatic stress disorders. Traumatic experiences result in a bewildering array of cognitive, emotional and physical symptoms: emotions of fear, shame, and rage; numbing of feelings and body sensation; loss of physical energy; and painful, negative beliefs about the self that often intensify the distressing feelings and bodily responses. Most challenging for many survivors of trauma are the effects of these experiences on the nervous system and on the ability to take adaptive action.

In the wake of psychological trauma, individuals typically experience alterations in their autonomic nervous system responses to daily life stress, especially to any subtle or obvious reminders of the traumatic event. Without a nervous system that easily recovers from either heightened states of emotion or states of depression and numbing, survivors often report difficulty tolerating emotional arousal without becoming overwhelmed, maintaining states of calm, and recovering from experiences of intense activation or depression. The body becomes either frozen, collapsed, or driven: action becomes impossible or impulsive.

Sensorimotor Psychotherapy addresses each of these symptom-clusters by first guiding clients in learning to simply track and observe in a mindful way the interplay of thoughts, feelings, and body experience related to the traumatic past, rather than be overwhelmed by the symptoms. Mindful observation often takes practice: clients are asked to try just observing and naming any thoughts, feelings, body sensations, and movement impulses that occur in the moment as they are sitting with the therapist. As they observe and describe what is noticed, clients typically begin to notice how easily a trauma-related body sensation leads to a thought that evokes an emotional response, or a feeling evokes body responses that leads to negative thoughts, resulting in increased overwhelm. Through the practice of mindful observation under the guidance of the therapist, they develop greater ability to become aware of these inner experiences without becoming overwhelmed and to choose which sources of information to entertain and which to put aside for the time being. Both of these forms of mindful internal awareness tend to increase feelings of confidence and mastery.

In addition to increasing internal awareness, the sensorimotor therapist also teaches the use of somatic skills that increase the nervous system's ability to recover from traumatic reminders, prevent overwhelm, and restore states of calm. Clients learn to decipher the body's signals: to notice impulses to move, to slow down, to take self-protective action. When these impulses are noticed, the therapist helps the client to engage in conscious, intentional movement that increase the experience of the body as a resource, a body that can set a healthy boundary, stand its ground, or effectively fight and flee. Mastery and choice are taught through the use of "mindful experiments," in which the client first learns to notice habitual reactions and then to practice alternative responses that are studied and evaluated, and then either repeated or discarded in favor of yet another experiment.

Utilizing interventions that "uncouple" traumatic memories from their intense emotional and somatic responses, clients are helped to experience a sense of safety in the body even when faced with reminders of past psychological trauma. The "uncoupling" process involves learning to shift focus from the details of a memory to the way in which the body is responding during the remembering. For example, as a client recalls being beaten by his father as a child, what is his internal experience of that event? Does the recall trigger body sensations? Or a thought or belief? Some feelings or emotions? Or impulses to move in some way? With the guidance of the therapist, the client is asked to notice, "What is happening right here, right now?" If one of the characteristics of trauma-related disorders is the loss of present time orientation, Sensorimotor Psychotherapy addresses that issue by helping clients to differentiate past and present: "When you remember that experience *then,* what happens here and *now* inside you?"

Sensorimotor Psychotherapy incorporates techniques from psychodynamic psychotherapy, gestalt therapy, cognitive-behavioral treatments, and the Hakomi method of body psychotherapy (Kurtz, 1972). Although similar in some ways to the sensorimotor therapy or sensorimotor integration therapy modalities used in occupational and physical rehabilitation for chronic or childhood physical impairments, it is a completely distinct *psycho*therapeutic model. Its theoretical principles draw heavily on the work of Pierre Janet, Bessel van der Kolk, Allan Schore, Steven Porges, Onno van der Hart, and Ellert Nijenhuis, emphasizing attention to therapeutic attunement and collaboration, modulation of autonomic arousal, and reinstatement of adaptive defensive responses (Van der Kolk, McFarlane, & Weisaeth, 1996). Because all psychological trauma involves some loss of interpersonal support and disconnection from those around us, the restoration of a sense of support and collaboration is key to trauma recovery. In Sensorimotor Psychotherapy, the therapist functions much like an adult might with a young child, experimenting to find just the right combination of voice tone, pace of speech, energy versus calm, and amount of information versus comfort and reassurance, until the client experiences a sense of greater equilibrium and support.

The effects of psychological trauma on the nervous system must also be addressed: if clients experience current daily life as unbearably overwhelming or dull and meaningless, then past and present are confused and conflated. Learning how to regulate autonomic responses to traumatic triggers or memories helps clients to experience some sense of control over their current experience. Last but not least, psychological trauma often leaves individuals feeling overpowered, helpless, hopeless, or chronically angry and hypervigilant, prepared to flee or fight. Restoration of the ability to move and to feel a greater sense of control over the environment is a prerequisite for being able to resolve traumatic stress. Many traumatized clients report increased feelings of control and mastery when they are encouraged to respond to movement impulses: for example, when the hands come up in a defensive posture or they rise from their chairs and begin to move toward and away from some disturbing stimulus.

In Sensorimotor Psychotherapy, the body is utilized both as a source of information about the effects of psychological trauma and as an avenue for treatment intervention and therapeutic change. Rather than asking the client to talk about "what happened" in narrative detail, we guide the client in bringing up "slivers" of memory so that we can first attend to how the body has "remembered" the trauma. As therapist and client engage verbally, just as they would in any psychotherapy setting, the client is asked to mindfully observe and describe the thoughts, feelings, inner body sensations, and movements that arise in the moment when something from the past is remembered. When autonomic nervous system arousal becomes dysregulated, emotions overwhelming, or cognitions punitive, the therapist encourages experimentation with changes in posture, movement, sensation, gesture or cognition until some transformation occurs in these intense reactions. Rather than reactivating PTSD symptoms, Sensorimotor Psychotherapy capitalizes on the resources of the body to challenge the helplessness, shame, and terror connected to traumatic memories. Unlike many other treatment approaches, Sensorimotor Psychotherapy can be utilized throughout all three stages of a phase-oriented treatment: it is equally applicable to stabilizing the symptoms, processing traumatic memories, and integrating past, present, and future experience.

Currently, there is no formal research validating the efficacy of Sensorimotor Psychotherapy in the treatment of traumatic stress disorders, though a multisite research study is underway. Based on single case studies, however, clients report satisfaction with its effectiveness in resolving their symptoms and increasing mastery and well-being when used either as a "stand-alone" treatment or incorporated into psychodynamic or cognitive-behavioral work. The elements of Sensorimotor Psychotherapy reported most helpful by clients include: its emphasis on mindfulness and therapeutic attunement, inhibition of negative cognitive schemas, practice of dual awareness, attention to action and arousal, and facilitation of new somatic and emotional experience. Therapists and clients interested in this work may refer to the web site of the Sensorimotor Psychotherapy Institute (www.sensorimotor.org) for more information.

REFERENCES

Kurtz, R. (1972). *Body-centered psychotherapy: The Hakomi method.* Mendocino, CA: LifeRhythm.

Ogden, P., Minton, K., & Pain, C. (2006). *Trauma and the body.* New York: Norton.

Van der Kolk, B. A., McFarlane, A. C., & Weisaeth, L. (Eds.). (1996). *Traumatic stress: The effects of overwhelming experience on mind, body, and society.* New York: Guilford Press.

JANINA FISHER
Sensorimotor Psychotherapy Institute

See also: Biology, Neurochemistry; Biology, Physiology; Complex Posttraumatic Stress Disorder; Dissociation; Janet, Pierre; Meditation; Psychotherapeutic Processes; Somatic Complaints

SERVICE UTILIZATION

See: Health Service Utilization

SEXUAL MOLESTATION

See: Abuse, Child Sexual; Child Maltreatment; Rape Trauma

SEXUALITY

Traumatic experiences can impact an individual's sexuality to varying degrees. As with other consequences of trauma, the nature and extent of the sexual consequences vary based on the type and severity of the trauma. Most of the research that addresses the consequences of trauma on sexuality has focused on the impact of sexual trauma—specifically, adult sexual assault (ASA) and childhood sexual abuse (CSA).

ASA and CSA can include a variety of nonconsensual sexual experiences ranging from noncontact sexual abuse (e.g., exhibitionism) to forcible rape. Not all nonconsensual sexual acts are potentially traumatic, in inducing adverse mental health consequences. Whether a particular nonconsensual sexual act is traumatic for a particular individual will depend on many factors, including the type of sexual act, the relationship between the victim and the perpetrator, the level of force or violence involved, and the victims' attributions about the experience. Although both ASA and CSA can have negative consequences for a person's sexuality, sexual trauma in childhood tends to have a more severe and longer lasting impact on sexual functioning than does sexual trauma in adulthood.

On average, individuals who have experienced ASA and CSA are more likely to suffer from sexual dysfunction than nonsexually victimized individuals are. Common sexual problems following sexual trauma include a lack of satisfaction with sex, infrequent sex, low levels of sexual desire, and lack of sexual arousal. Greater severity of sexual trauma is associated with a greater likelihood of sexual dysfunction.

Sexual trauma also is associated with sexual risk-taking (i.e., engaging in sexual behaviors that place one at risk for undesirable outcomes including unwanted pregnancy and HIV and other sexually transmitted diseases). On average, individuals with a history of sexual trauma are more likely than individuals without sexual trauma to engage in sex (a) at a younger age, (b) with a larger number of partners, and (c) without protection. These findings seem at odds with the aforementioned association between sexual trauma and infrequent sexual activity. It is unclear why some individuals seem to respond to sexual trauma by refraining from sex while other individuals seem to respond by engaging in more risky sex. It is possible that, for some victims, traumatic sexual experiences result in a cognitive disconnection between sex and respectful relationships. Some sexual trauma victims may respond by avoiding sexual relationships altogether; whereas, other victims may repeatedly seek new sexual relationships without knowing how to identify safe and respectful relationships.

Sexual trauma also places individuals at risk for sexual "revictimization." Once an individual has experienced one instance of sexual trauma, data suggest that she or he is more likely than other individuals to be sexually mistreated again in the future (e.g., see Koenig, Doll, O'Leary, & Pequegnat, 2004). Researchers have suggested many factors that may contribute to this phenomenon. For example, low self-esteem, dissociative symptoms, and substance use among victims of sexual trauma may interfere with their ability to detect danger and may provide an opportunity for sexual perpetrators to take advantage of them.

There is limited research on the effects of nonsexual trauma (e.g., combat trauma, trauma following natural disasters, trauma associated with auto accidents) on sexuality. However, it is well established that feelings of interpersonal and emotional detachment are common reactions to traumatic experiences of all types. Given these barriers to intimacy among many trauma victims, it seems likely that nonsexual trauma also may impact sexual functioning and the capacity to maintain stable sexual relationships.

Psychological treatment of sexual problems following trauma typically involves combining elements of traditional sex therapy (including sensate focus exercises and guided masturbation) with common elements of trauma-related treatment (including cognitive restructuring to address feelings of guilt and shame, especially as they apply to sex). Additionally, because traumatized individuals commonly experience discomfort with or avoidance of intimacy, couple's therapy (alone or in combination with individual therapy) is often valuable.

REFERENCE

Koenig, L. J., Doll, L. S., O'Leary, A., & Pequegnat, W. (Eds.). (2004). *From child sexual abuse to adult sexual risk: Trauma, revictimization, and intervention.* Washington, DC: American Psychological Association.

RECOMMENDED READINGS

Leonard, L. M., & Follette, V. M. (2002). Sexual functioning in women reporting a history of child sexual abuse: Review of the empirical literature and clinical implications. *Annual Review of Sex Research, 13,* 346–388.

van Berlo, W., & Ensink, B. (2000). Problems with sexuality after sexual assault. *Annual Review of Sex Research, 11,* 235–257.

ZOË D. PETERSON
University of Missouri

JULIA R. HEIMAN
The Kinsey Institute for Research in Sex, Gender and Reproduction

See also: Abuse, Child Sexual; Cognitive Behavior Therapy, Adult; Criminal Victimization; Domestic Violence; Marital Relationships; Marital Therapy; Rape Trauma; Retraumatization; Women and Trauma

SHAME

Shame is a self-evaluative emotion in which the self is experienced as defective. The experience of psychological trauma can precipitate feeling shame in individuals who believe that what has happened to them is the result of a personal failure (Tangney & Dearing, 2002). Guilt, often confused with shame, is typically a less debilitating emotion because the object of condemnation is a specific behavior rather than the entire self. Guilt motivates the desire to approach other people for the purpose of making amends and repairing the damaging consequences of one's actions. In contrast, the experience of shame motivates a desire to hide, disappear, or die in order to avoid the exposure of a self perceived as irreparably defective and socially unacceptable.

Shame is associated with the collapse of bodily posture (shrinking of the self), the disruption of ongoing behavior, confusion in thought, and an inability to speak about traumatic events. While individuals may not spontaneously volunteer feelings of shame, this emotion can readily be inferred from an individual's use of language (e.g., describing the self as permanently damaged by the trauma, as believing defects in or damage to the self are evident to others even if they have not been told), reluctance to disclose having experienced traumatic events and traumatic stress symptoms, and nonverbal behaviors

(e.g., avoidance of eye contact, covering the face, hiding the body). Assessing the likelihood of trauma-specific shame from these multiple indicators must include consideration of cultural customs and expectations. Shame may predate or occur independently of exposure to psychological trauma. Therefore, it is also important to assess the individual's life history and other relevant life events before concluding that shame is the result of having experienced psychological trauma or posttraumatic stress symptoms.

Shame is not elicited by specific situations but by an individual's interpretation of an event. It typically occurs when a person believes that they have failed to live up to important self-relevant standards or are responsible for negative events (Tangney & Dearing, 2002). The key cognitive process related to shame is self-blame, defined by attributing negative events to internal (something about the self) and global (the whole self) causes. For example, shame can occur when a child attributes sexual abuse to her not being smart enough to avoid the perpetrator, when a soldier attributes a friend's death to his cowardice, or when a crime victim attributes a robbery to his being too weak to stop it. Family, friends, and professionals may inadvertently reinforce feelings of shame by avoiding discussions of the trauma (as if to say that what happened is so shameful it can not be discussed) and by directly or indirectly attributing the cause of the traumatic events or their adverse consequences to a defect or characteristic of the victim (Deblinger & Runyon, 2005).

In efforts to regulate shame, individuals may avoid disclosing their experiences of psychological trauma or traumatic stress symptoms to others, avoid thinking about or attempting to repair the harm caused by traumatic experiences, or become angry at others who are perceived witnesses of their humiliation. Such efforts at controlling shame may be unsuccessful and can contribute to posttraumatic stress, depression, and externalizing behavior (such as problems with anger or impulsivity). Recent research on psychological trauma has implicated shame in the development of PTSD symptoms for victims of various traumatic events (Andrews, Brewin, Rose, & Kirk, 2000; Feiring,

Taska, & Lewis, 2002; Leskela, Dieperink, & Thuras, 2002; Street & Arias, 2001).

Although many accounts of PTSD have emphasized the centrality of intense fear as the emotional experience, shame has recently become a target for intervention as well (Deblinger & Runyon, 2005; Feiring & Taska, 2005). While therapeutic approaches differ, clinical work suggests that successful treatment does not allow the individual to avoid elements of the traumatic experience that elicit shame, instead helping the client to process, organize, and make meaning of the entire traumatic experience. Cognitive behavioral therapy approaches, for example, use gradual exposure across sessions to confront increasingly distressing elements of the trauma, and cognitive restructuring to challenge dysfunctional beliefs. Both of these techniques can be used to target shame-provoking aspects of the trauma experience. Rigorous research on victims of childhood sexual abuse has compared trauma-focused cognitive behavioral therapy (TF-CBT) to supportive or child-centered therapy using random assignment to well defined manualized treatments. TF-CBT was more effective in reducing symptoms of abuse-specific shame, distorted attributions, and PTSD (Cohen, Deblinger, Mannarino, & Steer, 2004). During treatment it is crucial that therapists pay careful attention to their own discomfort or possible feelings of shame (Gilbert, 1997). The verbal or nonverbal expression of these feelings by the therapist could have the effect of inadvertently reinforcing the client's feelings of shame or, in fact, inducing new shame.

REFERENCES

Andrews, B., Brewin, C. R., Rose, S., & Kirk, M. (2000). Predicting PTSD symptoms in victims of violent crime: The role of shame, anger and childhood abuse. *Journal of Abnormal Psychology, 109,* 69–73.

Cohen, J. A., Deblinger, E., Mannarino, A. P., & Steer, R. (2004). A multisite, randomized controlled trial for children with sexual-abuse related PTSD symptoms. *Journal of the American Academy of Child and Adolescent Psychiatry, 43,* 393–402.

Deblinger, E., & Runyon, M. (2005). Understanding and treating feelings of shame in children who have been maltreated. *Child Maltreatment, 10,* 364–376.

Feiring, C., & Taska, L. (2005). The persistence of shame following sexual abuse: A longitudinal look at risk and recovery. *Child Maltreatment, 10,* 337–349.

Feiring, C., Taska, L. S., & Lewis, M. (2002). Adjustment following sexual abuse discovery: The role of shame and attributional style. *Developmental Psychology, 38,* 79–92.

Gilbert, P. (1997). The evolution of social attractiveness and its role in shame, humiliation, guilt and therapy. *British Journal of Medical Psychology, 70,* 113–147.

Leskela, J., Dieperink, M., & Thuras, P. (2002). Shame and posttraumatic stress disorder. *Journal of Traumatic Stress, 15,* 223–226.

Street, A., & Arias, I. (2001). Psychological abuse and posttraumatic stress disorder in battered women: Examining the roles of shame and guilt. *Violence and Victims, 16,* 65–78.

Tangney, J. P., & Dearing, R. L. (2002). *Shame and guilt.* New York: Guilford Press.

CANDICE FEIRING
College of New Jersey

LYNN S. TASKA
Center for Family Resources

See also: Abuse, Child Sexual; Attributions; Betrayal Trauma; Child Maltreatment; Cognitive Behavior Therapy, Child; Crime Victimization; Emotional Abuse; Guilt; Humiliation Trauma; Posttraumatic Adaptation

SLEEP DISORDERS

See: Insomnia; Nightmares

SMOKING

Individuals with trauma exposure are more likely than nonexposed persons to begin smoking, and individuals who develop posttraumatic stress disorder (PTSD) are at even greater risk for smoking (Breslau, Davis, & Schultz, 2003).

PTSD is also associated with heavier consumption of cigarettes and lower rates of quitting smoking (Cook, McFall, Calhoun, & Beckham, in press). The specific reasons for the relationship between PTSD and smoking are not fully known.

In an examination of the causal relationship between nicotine dependence and PTSD using a twin study methodology, three hypotheses were each supported (PTSD leads to increased risk of nicotine dependence; nicotine dependence leads to increased risk of PTSD; and nicotine is used to self-regulate PTSD symptoms; Koenen et al., 2005). Rasmusson has hypothesized that elevations of corticosterone (a hormone found in the body) induced by various factors in those with PTSD (e.g., stress, nicotine, conditioned contextual cues) enhances both tolerance and sensitization to various effects of nicotine, and may help account for increased smoking in those with PTSD (Rasmusson, Picciotto, & Krishnan-Sarin, 2006).

Individuals with PTSD are also more likely to misuse a range of substances other than tobacco so treatment of comorbid substance misuse complicates cessation treatment efforts. People with PTSD are often diagnosed with other psychiatric disorders as well, and it is unknown how much these additional conditions may contribute to the association between smoking and PTSD (Feldner, Babson, & Zvolensky, 2007; Morissette, Tull, Gulliver, Kamholz, & Zimering, 2007). Smokers with PTSD are more likely to smoke when they experience a PTSD symptom or negative emotion states (Beckham et al., 2005, in press), and smoking a cigarette helps reduce smoking craving and negative emotion states (Beckham et al., 2007).

Little research regarding smoking cessation treatment in those PTSD has been conducted (Fu et al., in press). However, integrated smoking cessation treatment from mental health providers may improve rates of quitting smoking in smokers with PTSD (McFall et al., 2005).

REFERENCES

Beckham, J. C., Feldman, M. E., McClernon, F. J., Mozley, S. L., Collie, C. F., & Vrana, S. R. (2007). Cigarette smoking and script-driven imagery in smokers with and without posttraumatic stress disorder. *Addictive Behaviors, 32,* 2900–2915.

Beckham, J. C., Feldman, M. E., Vrana, S. R., Mozley, S. L., Erkanli, A., Clancy, C. P., et al. (2005). Immediate antecedents of cigarette smoking in smokers with and without posttraumatic stress disorder. *Journal of Experimental and Clinical Psychopharmacology, 13,* 218–228.

Beckham, J. C., Wiley, M. T., Miller, S., Wilson, S. M., Calhoun, P. S., & Dennis, M. F. (in press). Ad lib smoking in posttraumatic stress disorder: An electronic diary study. *Nicotine and Tobacco Research.*

Breslau, N., Davis, G. C., & Schultz, L. R. (2003). Posttraumatic stress disorder and the incidence of nicotine, alcohol and other drug disorders in persons who have experienced trauma. *Archives of General Psychiatry, 60,* 289–294.

Cook, J. W., McFall, M., Calhoun, P. S., & Beckham, J. C. (2007). Posttraumatic stress disorder and relapse to cigarette smoking: A theoretical model. *Journal of Traumatic Stress, 20,* 989–998.

Feldner, M. T., Babson, K. A., & Zvolensky, M. J. (2007). Smoking, traumatic event exposure, and posttraumatic stress: A critical review of the empirical literature. *Clinical Psychology Review, 27,* 14–45.

Fu, S., McFall, M., Saxon, A. J., Beckham, J. C., Carmody, T. P., Baker, D. G., et al. (2007). Posttraumatic stress disorder and smoking: A systematic review. *Nicotine and Tobacco Research, 9,* 1071–1084.

Koenen, K. C., Hitsman, B., Lyons, M. J., Niaura, R., McCaffery, J., Goldberg, J., et al. (2005). A twin registry study of the relationship between posttraumatic stress disorder and nicotine dependence in men. *Archives of General Psychiatry, 62,* 1258–1265.

McFall, M., Saxon, A. J., Thompson, C., Yoshimoto, D., Malter, C., Straits-Troster, K., et al. (2005). Improving the rates of quitting smoking for veterans with posttraumatic stress disorder. *American Journal of Psychiatry, 162,* 1311–1319.

Morissette, S. B., Tull, M., Gulliver, S. B., Kamholz, B. W., & Zimering, R. T. (2007). Anxiety, anxiety disorders, tobacco use and nicotine: A critical review of interrelationships. *Psychological Bulletin, 133,* 245–272.

Rasmusson, A. M., Picciotto, M. R., & Krishnan-Sarin, S. (2006). Smoking as a complex, but critical covariate in neurobiological studies of posttraumatic stress disorders: A review. *Journal of Psychopharmacology, 20,* 693–707.

JEAN C. BECKHAM
Duke University Medical Center

ANNE M. RAKIP
Durham Veterans Affairs Medical Center

See also: Comorbidity; Medical Illness, Adult; Substance Use Disorders

SOCIAL COGNITIVE THEORY

Social Cognitive Theory (SCT) is a comprehensive theory of human behavior (Bandura, 1997). As an extension of Bandura's earlier work on social learning theory, SCT outlines a theoretical framework demonstrating how people are agents in their environments acting intentionally to bring about desired outcomes and not simply reacting to environmental stimuli (Bandura, 1997).

The unique human attribute of self-reflective thought gives humans the ability to self-regulate through the use of forethought to guide and regulate behavior. A part of self-reflection is self-evaluation. The ability to evaluate past behavior is used to determine possible courses of action and predict future success or failure. In turn, people set goals and act intentionally to achieve desired outcomes based on the self-regulatory process. Self-agency operates through a concept called triadic reciprocal determinism—a dynamic process that involves the bidirectional influence of three primary determinants of human behavior: environmental factors, personal variables, and behavior. The interplay of these three factors determines human behavior. The predictive power of environmental conditions versus person-related factors is dependent upon the intensity of environmental demands (e.g., extreme conditions such as drowning create strong environmental demands dominating the chosen course of action: swim or die). Whereas, when situations are more ambiguous (e.g., generating meaning following a traumatic event) personal factors play a more dominant role in the self-regulatory process (e.g., the self-reflective/self-evaluative process). A key self-evaluative personal factor that is highly predictive of motivational, affective, physiological, and behavioral outcomes is perceived self-efficacy.

Self-efficacy beliefs are a person's perceived ability to organize and execute courses of action to generate desired outcomes (Bandura, 1997). Self-reflection of past successes and failures combined with environmental conditions and one's behavioral skill level give rise to an individual's perception of capability to enact specific behaviors or set of behaviors (i.e., self-efficacy beliefs). Self-efficacy is a strong predictor of human behavior and is considered an integral component of the self-evaluation process (Bandura, 1997). People engage in self-referential thought to judge how capable they are to perform a task. Cognitive, motivational, and emotional processes influence how an individual judges his or her abilities and turns them into action. For example, previous competence beliefs of a required skill, specific goals, and anxiety related to the desired goal all influence self-efficacy perceptions that then translate into behavioral activation or inhibition. For example, self-efficacy perceptions for mathematics are generated through one's actual math skill, goals related to doing math, and anxiety about doing math. The higher one's self-efficacy for a particular context results in enhanced motivation, improved ability to manage setbacks, more effective goal setting, and more positive emotional states.

A person's perceived ability to cope after a trauma (i.e., trauma-related coping self-efficacy) is predictive of posttraumatic outcomes (Benight & Bandura, 2004). Coping self-efficacy is the perceived capability to deal with stressful environmental demands. Within a traumatic stress context this implies that the demands will be related to recovery from a traumatic stressor. For example, following a motor vehicle accident, individuals must cope with a myriad of high stress demands related to recovery including dealing with insurance companies, finding transportation, dealing with possible injuries, as well as managing the traumatic aspects of the accident itself. Theoretically, individuals with high coping self-efficacy will display less distress than individuals with lower perceived coping self-efficacy. Research on coping self-efficacy has shown that it is predictive of mental health outcomes following a wide range of traumatic stress contexts. Following major natural disasters (hurricanes, wild fires, earthquakes, and floods) coping self-efficacy was found to be a strong predictor even after statistically controlling for a host of other critical environmental, individual, and social variables (Benight & Harper, 2002; Benight, Ironson, & Durham, 1999; Benight, Swift, Sanger, Smith, & Zeppelin, 1999; Sumer, Karanci, Berument, & Gunes, 2005). Coping self-efficacy also predicted distress outcomes (longitudinally) following a terrorist bombing again after controlling for other relevant constructs (e.g., threat of death; Benight et al., 2000). Coping self-efficacy has shown to be important in understanding reactions to interpersonal trauma as well, such as losing one's spouse to cancer (Benight, Flores, & Tashiro, 2001). Coping self-efficacy perceptions in relation to dealing with military combat has also been shown to be an important predictor of psychological outcomes (Solomon, Benbenishty, & Mikulincer, 1991). Thus, the perception of one's ability to manage posttraumatic recovery demands provides an important contribution to understanding the psychological outcomes following a major trauma. These perceptions have also been found to mediate (or serve as an intermediate variable in explaining) the relationships between other critical factors and psychological outcomes.

Coping self-efficacy has mediated between important posttraumatic recovery factors—including peri-traumatic distress, social support, lost resources, and optimism—and mental health outcomes following a traumatic event. These findings underscore the interplay between environmental and intrapsychic variables and how self-perceptions of efficacy serve as a conduit through which these other variables translate their effects on psychological recovery.

SCT also includes an extension of the individual perception of coping self-efficacy by looking at a group's belief in the collective ability to respond to environmental demands (i.e., collective efficacy; Bandura, 1997). Collective efficacy (the perceived capability for a group, or community, to organize, set goals, and perform the necessary courses of action to respond to a future disaster) has been assessed in a variety of contexts including athletics, school systems, and political environments. More recently, collective efficacy has been looked at following mass traumas (Benight, 2004). Natural disasters are a type of traumatic event that can be catastrophic for entire communities. Collective efficacy may serve as a buffer between the effects of the disaster and subsequent psychological distress (Benight, 2004).

Conclusion

SCT provides a very useful theoretical framework, with decades of empirical support, documenting the critical role of self-efficacy beliefs at the individual and community level in human adaptation. Available research supports the extension of SCT in helping to understand the coping process required for adaptation following trauma. Understanding this process of recovery requires a deeper understanding of the key mechanisms of adaptation across time that includes environmental, cognitive, and behavioral factors. The self-evaluative process outlined in SCT is instrumental to understanding human's ability to cope under extreme stress.

REFERENCES

Bandura, A. (1997). *Self-efficacy: The exercise of control.* New York: Freeman.

Benight, C. C. (2004). Collective efficacy following a series of natural disasters. *Anxiety Stress and Coping, 17,* 401–420.

Benight, C. C., & Bandura, A. (2004). Social cognitive theory of posttraumatic recovery: The role of perceived self-efficacy. *Behaviour Research and Therapy, 42,* 1129–1148.

Benight, C. C., Flores, J., & Tashiro, T. (2001). Bereavement coping self-efficacy in cancer widows. *Death Studies, 25,* 97–125.

Benight, C. C., Freyaldenhoven, R., Hughes, J., Ruiz, J. M., Zoesche, T. A., & Lovallo, W. (2000).

Coping self-efficacy and psychological distress following the Oklahoma City bombing: A longitudinal analysis. *Journal of Applied Social Psychology, 30,* 1331–1344.

Benight, C. C., & Harper, M. (2002). Coping self-efficacy as a mediator for distress following multiple natural disasters. *Journal of Traumatic Stress, 15,* 177–186.

Benight, C. C., Ironson, G., & Durham, R. L. (1999). Psychometric properties of a hurricane coping self-efficacy measure. *Journal of Traumatic Stress, 12,* 379–386.

Benight, C. C., Swift, E., Sanger, J., Smith, A., & Zeppelin, D. (1999). Coping self-efficacy as a prime mediator of distress following a natural disaster. *Journal of Applied Social Psychology, 29,* 2443–2464.

Solomon, Z., Benbenishty, R., & Mikulincer, M. (1991). The contribution of wartime, pre-war and post-war factors on self-efficacy: A longitudinal study of combat stress reaction. *Journal of Traumatic Stress, 4,* 345–361.

Sumer, N., Karanci, A. N., Berument, S. K., & Gunes, H. (2005). Personal resources, coping self-efficacy, and quake exposure as predictors of psychological distress following the 1999 earthquake in Turkey. *Journal of Traumatic Stress, 18,* 331–342.

EDDIE WALDREP
University of Colorado, Colorado Springs

CHARLES C. BENIGHT
University of Colorado, Colorado Springs

See also: Attributions; Conservation of Resources; Coping; Disasters; Information Processing; Social Support; Terrorism; War Trauma

SOCIAL SKILLS TRAINING

Social skills training (SST) typically involves teaching patients the requisite skills that are needed to have rewarding and successful social interactions. Usually the focus is on increasing a patient's ability to attend and respond to social cues, improving communication and assertiveness skills, and providing patients with the necessary tools to effectively initiate and maintain rewarding social relationships.

Other less common applications of SST might include efforts to target specific skills, such as those needed for successful independent living and employment. With regard to the most common application of SST (i.e., improving a patient's general repertoire of skills), treatment usually includes a combination of instruction, appropriate modeling, rehearsal (e.g., role plays), corrective feedback, encouragement, and practice (within and outside of sessions).

SST has been found to be effective in a number of controlled trials, most notably for the treatment of schizophrenia or other forms of severe mental illness (Dilk & Bond, 1996; meta-analysis). These studies demonstrate that patients are able to learn new social skills, maintain these skills over time, and improve the quantity and quality of their social interactions. However, SST typically demonstrates modest and/or mixed results with regard to psychiatric symptom reduction and relapse prevention.

Although the efficacy of SST has not been specifically tested or established for the treatment of posttraumatic stress disorder (PTSD), social skills and interpersonal difficulties (i.e., social anxiety and avoidance, feelings of social alienation, difficulties with assertiveness, irritability, hostility, anger) are core or associated symptoms of the disorder. To date, a few studies specifically including SST components have yielded promising results with regard to clinical symptoms and social functioning (Cloitre, Koenen, Cohen, & Han, 2002; Foa, Keane, & Friedman, 2000). However, SST in these studies was examined as part of a larger treatment program, and thus, causal conclusions about SST on PTSD related outcomes cannot be made.

Although only a few studies specifically mention SST as part of a comprehensive treatment package, the majority of PTSD interventions likely include informal elements of SST; and when tailored appropriately, SST techniques can likely serve as an effective adjunct component to frontline interventions for this disorder. For example, if a clinician and patient recognize that symptoms of PTSD (such as avoidance of reminders or past traumatic experiences or difficulties with anger or hyperarousal) are interfering with the patient's ability to socialize with others and form new friendships, some combination of cognitive restructuring, exposure, and SST techniques would likely be used. The degree to which SST is emphasized during the course of treatment would be influenced by the severity and nature of the patient's social avoidance.

REFERENCES

Cloitre, M., Koenen, K. C., Cohen, L. R., & Han, H. (2002). Skills training in affective and interpersonal regulation followed by exposure: A phase-based treatment for PTSD related to childhood abuse. *Journal of Consulting and Clinical Psychology, 70,* 1067–1074.

Dilk, M. N., & Bond, G. R. (1996). Meta-analytic evaluation of skills training research for individuals with severe mental illness. *Journal of Consulting and Clinical Psychology, 64,* 1337–1346.

Foa, E. B., Keane, T. M., & Friedman, M. J. (2000). *Effective treatments for PTSD: Practice guidelines from the International Society for Traumatic Stress Studies.* New York: Guilford Press.

ANOUK L. GRUBAUGH
Medical University of South Carolina

See also: Anxiety Management Training; Cognitive Behavior Therapy, Adult; Cognitive Behavior Therapy, Child; Coping Skills Training; Psychoeducation; Psychosis; Social Support

SOCIAL SUPPORT

Coping with traumatically stressful events is seldom a solitary task and typically requires considerable amounts of assistance and support from other people. Social support refers to those social interactions that provide people with *actual assistance* and *embed them* into a web of social relationships *perceived to be* loving, caring, and readily available in times of need. This definition, endorsed by many researchers (e.g., Cohen, Underwood, & Gottlieb, 2000), eloquently encompasses major aspects of social support because it points out that this cherished resource may be: *believed, actual,* and *embedded.* Thus, it is necessary to differentiate among the three most prominent manifestations of support: *perceived social support, received social support, and social embeddedness.*

Perceived social support is defined as a cognitive appraisal of being reliably connected to others. These assessments represent not only concurrent relational experiences and characteristics of contemporaneous social environments, but may also reflect early developmental attachments, interpersonal schemas, and influences of people's personalities. Questionnaires for measuring perceived support attempt to assess an individual's confidence that adequate support would be available if needed or to characterize the extent to which potential sources of support are helpful and cohesive.

Received social support pertains to factual instances of helpful behaviors. Instruments measuring received support assess specific behaviors that are involved in the expression of support or actions that people perform when rendering assistance. Various types of perceived and received social support are cataloged in the literature, but most frequently investigated are *emotional support, informational support,* and *tangible support.* Each of these types of support may be linked to specific sources, such as kin relations (spouse, family, relatives), nonkin informal networks (friends, neighbors, coworkers), and people outside the immediate support circles (charitable organizations, professional service providers).

The third category of social support, called *social embeddedness,* represents structural aspect of social networks and refers to the number of connections individuals have with significant others in their environments. The existence of social ties based on marital status, number of friends and neighbors, or frequency of participation in community activities are examples of broad indicators of embeddedness. In summary, perceived support is helping behavior that might happen, received support is helping behavior that did happen, and social embeddedness represents a network of people who might provide or did provide these supportive acts.

There are a variety of ways in which social support may benefit psychological well-being and physical health. For example, people who care for us may prevent the occurrence of stress or reduce its severity. Social support networks can facilitate more accurate appraisal of ambiguous stressful encounters and assist in the reappraisal of ongoing stressors. Social support most routinely serves directly to meet demands caused by consequences of the stressor, such as when people provide material aid and other necessities to disaster survivors. Physical presence of other people may hasten a return to physiological equilibrium (e.g., closely embracing a victim of terror). Concerned helpers may also suggest coping options, such as persuading a victim of crime to seek professional help. These expressions of support may help to sustain self-efficacy, self-esteem, optimism, and other psychological resources severely threatened by exposure to stress. Thoughtful supporters may validate emotional reactions and help with cognitive processing of stressful experiences. Family and friends facilitate recovery of emotional equilibrium through continuous expressions of caring as well as by simply creating opportunities for diversions.

Although social support operates through many different pathways, two theoretical models depicting its influence on well-being have dominated research in the past three decades: *the stress buffer model* and *the main effect model* (Cohen & Wills, 1985; Cutrona & Russell, 1990). The buffering model suggests that social support benefits individuals in crisis by protecting them from the negative consequences of stressful conditions. The most commonly discussed form of this model refers to social support as *moderating* the effects of stress (e.g., traumatic event), meaning that the adverse consequences of stress (e.g., PTSD) are less severe for those survivors who have higher levels of social support as compared to equally traumatized survivors who have lower levels of social support. One of the first studies in the area of traumatic stress that addressed the buffering function of social support compared a group of people living near the Three Mile Island (TMI) nuclear power plant with demographically similar group of people living outside the areas affected by the incident. Fleming, Baum, Gisriel, and Gatchel (1982)

documented that perceived social support was reliably and beneficially related to a variety of emotional and behavioral symptoms of distress (main effects of support, more support less symptoms). Most importantly, the level of perceived social support statistically interacted with the accident exposure (i.e., the stressor), such that the TMI residents with lower levels of perceived support exhibited more symptoms of global distress, depression, alienation, and anxiety than respondents from all other groups.

Similar patterns of classic stress-buffering interactions have been documented in the context of coping with various traumatic events, yet not all studies show such pure and unqualified buffering effects of social support. It appears that the stress-buffering properties of social support are limited to specific sources of support, subgroups of participants, or types of support. A study examining the effects of exposure to community violence on children from urban middle schools (Ozer & Weinstein, 2004) demonstrated that perceived helpfulness of support from mothers, fathers, and siblings reduced (i.e., buffered) the effect of violence exposure on PTSD and depression. That study did not find evidence, however, that perceived support from friends shielded children (i.e., buffered) against psychological effects of exposure to community violence. Another study suggested that the impact of traumatic experiences on PTSD of police officers (Stephens & Long, 1999) was attenuated only for those who reported greater perceived social support from their coworkers. Social support from supervisors and family/friends did not show the stress moderating effects. A study of coping with disaster (Solomon, Smith, Robins, & Fischbach, 1987) documented that the advantage of having social support was present only for victims with moderate, but not high, levels of perceived support. A study of Kuwaiti children (Llabre & Hadi, 1997) showed that perceived social support lessened the impact of war trauma on PTSD and depression for girls, but not for boys, suggesting that gender differences are also important for understanding the complexities of social support. Higher levels of perceived kin support protected Euro-American residents of areas affected by the *Exxon Valdez* oil spill, but not native Alaskans (Palinkas, Russell, Downs, & Petterson, 1992).

Some studies have produced results that are contrary to conventional notions regarding the stress buffering benefits of social support. For example, victims of traumatic events who reported higher levels of perceived support exhibited more symptoms of distress (e.g., Hammack, Richards, Luo, Edlynn, & Roy, 2004; Kaspersen, Matthiesen, & Götestam, 2003). These at times perplexing findings revealed by research on coping with extreme stress must be taken into account to avoid oversimplifying the benefits of social support. Nevertheless, the majority of investigations examining social support and traumatic events have routinely documented a directly beneficial effect of perceived social support on the psychological well-being of victims. Such findings are consistent with the direct (or main) effect model that states that social support has an equivalent impact on well-being regardless of whether the stress is low or high. This view gained recognition when it became clear that many examinations found no evidence of a buffer effect, showing instead a direct effect of social support on physical and mental health. All-in-all, research suggests that direct effects and interactive (buffering) effects of social support do occur, and the presence of either, or both, is determined by the ecological context of stressful encounters and the type of social support assessed. Broadly speaking, it is unusual not to observe some beneficial effects of social support on physical and psychological symptomatology in the context of coping with traumatic stress (Brewin, Andrews, & Valentine, 2000; Guay, Billette, & Marchand, 2006; Ozer, Best, Lipsey, & Weiss, 2003).

Interestingly, and somewhat ironically, the often heralded beneficial effects of social support on psychological health are primarily the domain of perceived social support, which is hypothetical, cognitive, and evaluative. Findings of studies that assessed social support as actual receipt of help are less consistent in showing the benefits of social support than those of the studies that examined support as perceptions or expectations. There are not as many trauma studies that documented stress-buffering functions of received social support, and measures of social support receiving are not frequently used in traumatic stress research (for one notable exception see the Crisis Support Scale; Joseph, 1999). In general, received social support seems to be neglected by the stress and coping research, most likely because many investigations reveled no effects, or worse, reported positive correlations between receiving help and psychological distress. The more social support was received by a trauma survivor, the more symptoms of distress she or he exhibited.

Fortunately, there are various ways that can explain this seemingly paradoxical finding. Most obviously, it could be the other way around such that people experiencing more psychological symptoms simply receive more help. Notwithstanding this parsimonious alternative interpretation, we must recognize that providing and receiving help in crisis is a difficult and sensitive process, and the list of factors undermining the helpfulness of assistance is as long as the list of ways making assistance helpful. People have typically high expectations concerning the how much help they should receive (i.e., perceived support) and the amount of support actually received may not meet these expectations. This can be particularly true when the stressor affects many people at the same time (e.g., disasters, community trauma) and the potential support providers are victims themselves. Helping resources may be depleted overtime. The merit of help received depends on who provides it. Its type may not be appropriately matched with the practical requirements posed by a specific stressful encounter. Even best intentioned help may be delivered ineptly and that in turn may implicate the person in need as a coping failure or burden to others. In fact, there is a strong branch of social support literature investigating "negative responses of support providers" that shows how unintentionally or deliberately misguided, insensitive, judgmental, or dismissive interactions, with even the closest people, may impede recovery from all traumas (e.g., Maercker & Müller, 2004; Ullman & Filipas,

2001). All these potential liabilities of actual exchanges of social support should serve as a warning that helping others, while laudable, is not simple and that not all forms of help prove equally helpful. This list of "things that could go wrong" with received support also helps explain why the superiority of perceived support over received support has been so readily accepted by stress researchers—because between the two facets of social support, it is the perceived support that more reliably promotes and protects psychological health.

These complexities of social support exchanges also expose a major conceptual problem of both the buffering and direct effect models, illustrating how social support influences well-being. The principal assumption of both formulations is that stress and social support are unrelated to one another. However, the results of most trauma studies reveal that trauma exposure is often negatively associated with perceived support (i.e., more trauma experienced, less support perceived) and positively associated with received support (i.e., more trauma experienced, more support received). These linkages are consequential and must not be ignored as they point to different mechanisms by which social support operates in the process of coping with traumatic events.

The *social support deterioration model* describes a mechanism whereby traumatic experiences instigate declines in social support that in turn contribute to the detrimental impact of stress on psychological health. Kaniasty and Norris (1993), in testing the mediating role of erosion of social support, found that declines in the availability of perceived support and social embeddedness following a disaster partially accounted for (i.e., mediated) the immediate and delayed impact of disaster on symptoms of distress. Thus, one of the reasons why traumatic events exert deleterious effects on mental health is because extreme stress tends to undermine the sense of being reliably connected with others.

In recent years, studies investigating a variety of potentially traumatic events, such as interpersonal violence, child abuse, or war combat exposure, presented evidence congruent with the social support deterioration model and showed how declines in social support (especially perceived support), fully or partially explained the translation of trauma exposure into symptoms of enduring distress (e.g., Taft, Stern, King, & King, 1999; Thompson et al., 2000; Vranceanu, Hobfoll, & Johnson, 2007; Yap & Devilly, 2004). In trauma research, the social support deterioration model represents a viable alternative to the *stress buffering* and the *main effect* models.

It is well established that most victims of traumatic events receive a considerable degree of support from informal and formal sources and frequently experience post-crisis benevolence and solidarity (Elklit, Pedersen, & Jind, 2001; Kaniasty & Norris, 2004). Thus important questions remain. What is happening with received social support when perceived social support deteriorates as a result of traumatic experience? Can these two seemingly contradictory facets of social support processes, the instantaneous mobilization of received support and subsequent deterioration of perceived support, be combined into one comprehensive explanatory model? Norris and Kaniasty (1996) proposed a *"social support deterioration deterrence model,"* and showed that victims of hurricanes who received greater levels of help after the impact experienced a subsequent erosion of perceived support to a lesser extent. In other words, it is possible that the impact of help actually received by trauma survivors does not have to exert its influence on their mental health directly. Received social support may act indirectly on psychological well-being through preservation and protection of perceived social support.

Social support is a critical resource for helping people to cope with traumatic stress. It is composed of a complex set of facets and functions, and is not a generic or a proxy variable for "good social relationships." Its remarkable effects should not be taken for granted, it should instead be respectfully appreciated and cultivated to improve people's general well-being and their resilience in the face of adversity.

REFERENCES

Brewin, C., Andrews, B., & Valentine, J. (2000). Meta-analysis of risk factors for posttraumatic stress disorder in trauma-exposed adults. *Journal of Consulting and Clinical Psychology, 68,* 748–766.

Cohen, S., Underwood, L., & Gottlieb, B. (Eds.). (2000). *Social support measurement and interventions: A guide for health and social scientists.* New York: Oxford University Press.

Cohen, S., & Wills, T. A. (1985). Stress, social support, and the buffering hypothesis. *Psychological Bulletin, 98,* 310–357.

Cutrona, C., & Russell, D. (1990). Type of social support and specific stress: Toward a theory of optimal matching. In B. R. Sarason, I. G. Sarason, & G. R. Pierce (Eds.), *Social support: An interactional view* (pp. 319–366). New York: Wiley.

Elklit, A., Pedersen, S. S., & Jind, L. (2001). The crisis support scale: Psychometric qualities and further validation. *Personality and Individual Differences, 31,* 1291–1302.

Fleming, R., Baum, A., Gisriel, M., & Gatchel, R. (1982). Mediating influences of social support on stress at Three Mile Island. *Journal of Human Stress, 8,* 14–22.

Guay, S., Billette, V., & Marchand, A. (2006). Exploring the links between posttraumatic stress disorder and social support: Processes and potential research avenues. *Journal of Traumatic Stress, 19,* 327–338.

Hammack, P., Richards, M., Luo, Z., Edlynn, E., & Roy, K. (2004). Social support factors as moderators of community violence exposure among inner-city African American young adolescents. *Journal of Clinical Child and Adolescent Psychology, 33,* 450–462.

Joseph, S. (1999). Social support and mental health following trauma. In W. Yule (Ed.), *Post-traumatic stress disorders: Concepts and therapy* (pp. 71–91). Chichester, West Sussex, England: Wiley.

Kaniasty, K., & Norris, F. H. (1993). A test of the support deterioration model in the context of natural disaster. *Journal of Personality and Social Psychology, 64,* 395–408.

Kaniasty, K., & Norris, F. H. (2004). Social support in the aftermath of disasters, catastrophes, and acts of terrorism: Altruistic, overwhelmed, uncertain, antagonistic, and patriotic communities. In R. Ursano, A. Norwood, & C. Fullerton (Eds.), *Bioterrorism: Psychological and public health interventions* (pp. 200–229). Cambridge: Cambridge University Press.

Kaspersen, M., Matthiesen, S. B., & Götestam, K. G. (2003). Social network as a moderator in the relation between trauma exposure and trauma reaction: A survey among UN soldiers and relief workers. *Scandinavian Journal of Psychology, 44,* 415–423.

Llabre, M., & Hadi, F. (1997). Social support and psychological distress in Kuwaiti boys and girls exposed to the Gulf crisis. *Journal of Clinical Child Psychology, 26,* 247–255.

Maercker, A., & Müller, J. (2004). Social acknowledgment as a victim or survivor: A scale to measure a recovery factor of PTSD. *Journal of Traumatic Stress, 17,* 345–351.

Norris, F. H., & Kaniasty, K. (1996). Received and perceived social support in times of stress: A test of the social support deterioration deterrence model. *Journal of Personality and Social Psychology, 71,* 498–511.

Ozer, E., Best, S., Lipsey, T., & Weiss, D. (2003). Predictors of posttraumatic stress disorder and symptoms in adults: A meta-analysis. *Psychological Bulletin, 129,* 52–73.

Ozer, E., & Weinstein, R. (2004). Urban adolescents' exposure to community violence: The role of support, school safety, and social constraints in a school-based sample of boys and girls. *Journal of Clinical Child and Adolescent Psychology, 3,* 463–476.

Palinkas, L. A., Russell, J., Downs, M. A., & Petterson, J. S. (1992). Ethnic differences in stress, coping, and depressive symptoms after the *Exxon Valdez* oil spill. *Journal of Nervous and Mental Disease, 180,* 287–295.

Solomon, S. D., Smith, E., Robins, L., & Fischbach, R. (1987). Social involvement as a mediator of disaster-induced stress. *Applied Journal of Social Psychology, 17,* 1092–1112.

Stephens, C., & Long, N. (1999). Posttraumatic stress disorder in the New Zealand police: The moderating role of social support following traumatic stress. *Anxiety, Stress, and Coping: An International Journal, 12,* 247–264.

Taft, C., Stern, A., King, L., & King, D. (1999). Modeling physical health and functional health status: The role of combat exposure, posttraumatic stress disorder and personal resource attributes. *Journal of Traumatic Stress, 12,* 3–23.

Thompson, M., Kaslow, N., Kingree, J., Rashid, A., Puett, R., Jacobs, D., et al. (2000). Partner violence, social support, and distress among inner-city African American women. *American Journal of Community Psychology, 28,* 127–143.

Ullman, S., & Filipas, H. (2001). Predictors of PTSD symptom severity and social reactions in sexual assault victims. *Journal of Traumatic Stress, 14,* 369–389.

Vranceanu, A., Hobfoll, S., & Johnson, R. (2007). Child multi-type maltreatment and associated depression and PTSD symptoms: The role of social support and stress. *Child Abuse and Neglect, 31,* 71–84.

Yap, M., & Devilly, G. (2004). The role of perceived social support in crime victimization. *Clinical Psychology Review, 24,* 11–14.

Krzysztof Kaniasty
Indiana University of Pennsylvania

See *also:* Anthropological Perspectives; Culture and Trauma; Coping; Criminal Victimization; Disasters; Etiology; Family Systems; Interpersonal Psychotherapy; Marital Relationships; Medical Illness, Adult; Medical Illness, Child; Somatic Complaints

SOMATIC COMPLAINTS

Individuals who are exposed to psychological trauma often report problems with physical health and associated pain and functional limitations (such as problems with mobility or work), particularly if they develop and chronically suffer from posttraumatic stress disorder (PTSD). Clinicians and researchers tend to refer to self-reported physical health problems as "somatic complaints" because these are problems with the body's functioning ("soma" is the Greek and Latin word for "body") that the person reports ("complains of"). When somatic complaints occur more often or are more severe following exposure to psychological trauma or the development of PTSD, they are considered to be "psychosomatic"—that is, bodily problems that are caused or contributed to by psychological factors. Psychosomatic factors after psychological trauma exposure can be cardinal emotional difficulties in PTSD: anxiety, dysphoria (depressed mood), anger and irritability, sadness, guilt, and emotional numbing (a sense of having limited or muted or absent emotions that feels like being numb).

Although psychological factors may play a role in the somatic complaints associated with

PTSD, this does *not* mean that these bodily problems are actually (or are the result of) "mental" problems such as excessive worry, self-doubt, guilt, low self-esteem, emotional conflicts, or excessive or suppressed/repressed anger. Research suggests that somatic complaints associated with exposure to psychological trauma or PTSD may result from any of five different sources, separately or in combination: (1) medically diagnosable illnesses or injury-related conditions; (2) stress-related or stress-exacerbated medical conditions that appear to have biological causes but are not included in current medical diagnoses; (3) stress-related behaviors that place the person at risk for medical illness ("behavioral risk factors"); (4) conversion of unexpressed or unconscious psychological distress into physical symptoms; or (5) dissociative splits of the personality that are expressed in part as problematic altered bodily states or functioning. Each of these potential sources of trauma- or PTSD-related somatic complaints will be described in this entry.

Psychological Trauma, PTSD, and Medical Illness

People are at heightened risk for diagnosed medical illnesses if they have experienced psychological trauma, particularly if this occurred in developmentally adverse interpersonal experiences in childhood (Ford, 2005), and when PTSD (Schnurr & Green, 2004; *see:* **Medical Illness, Adult**) or complex PTSD (*see:* **Complex Posttraumatic Stress Disorder**) develop following traumatic exposure(s). Prospective longitudinal studies have not yet been done but are needed in order to determine, beginning in childhood and continuing through adolescence and adulthood with the same representative sample of persons (*see:* **Research Methodology**), how exposure to psychological trauma and the development of PTSD (Fairbank, Putnam, & Harris, 2007) precede, follow, or co-occur with changes and problems in physical health and serious medical illnesses. Until such a study is done, it is not clear whether experiencing psychological trauma and PTSD actually can cause or contribute to the development of medically diagnosed illnesses; or whether medical illness or genetic or environmental factors that lead people to be vulnerable to medical illness precede and contribute to (or simply co-occur with) exposure to psychological trauma and PTSD (*see:* **Research Methodology**).

The largest study with a relatively representative sample of adults (all of whom were patients in the Kaiser Health Maintenance Organization) whose medical health and illness status was known based on medical examinations, tests, and diagnoses, is the "Adverse Childhood Experiences Study" (ACES; Felitti et al., 1998). The ACES and large scale epidemiologic research studies (Chartier, Walker, & Naimark, 2007) concluded that adults who report having either or both socioeconomic adversities (such as living in poverty) or psychological traumas in childhood have between two and more than sixteen times greater risk than other adults of having obesity, sexually transmitted disease, cancer, stroke, ischemic heart disease, diabetes, or chronic bronchitis or emphysema. These findings suggest that, even when other risk factors such as age, ethnicity, gender, and health risk behaviors (see below) are taken into account, experiencing adversity—particularly multiple forms of potentially traumatic adversity—in childhood leads to a heightened risk of not just somatic complaints but serious medical illness in adulthood (*see:* **Medical Illness, Adult**).

Traumatic Stress-Related Medical Conditions

Findings of the ACES and similar studies have led clinicians and researchers to question how psychological trauma and PTSD could cause, or more likely contribute to, the development of serious medical illnesses. These clearly are not just "complaints" but potentially life altering or threatening disruptions in the body's self-regulation and physiological and neurochemical functioning. Friedman and McEwen (2004) have surveyed the research on the biological changes that occur as a result of psychological trauma and PTSD (Neumeister, Henry, & Krystal, 2007; Southwick et al., 2007), and showed that they share a common factor which

McEwen has described as "allostatic load." They identify a number of stress-related medical illnesses that include not only several of the serious illnesses described above as potential risks following childhood psychological trauma, but also several other stress-related biological abnormalities.

- Disorders involving dysregulation of the hypothalamus-pituitary-adrenal (HPA) Axis, including hypercortisolism, Cushings Syndrome, reproductive abnormalities and inflammatory/autoimmune disorders (see below).
- Disorders involving dysregulation of the sympathetic branch of the autonomic nervous system, the brain's adrenergic systems, and the cardiovascular system (including myocardial infarction, stroke, atherosclerosis, hypertension, and cardiac arrhythmias)
- Disorders involving dysregulation of the opioid systems, including chronic pain and headaches
- Disorders of the endocrine and metabolic systems, including hyperthyroidism, dyslipidemia, Type II diabetes, and osteopenia/osteoporosis
- Disorders of the immune system, including immunosuppression (insufficient immune response) and inflammatory and autoimmune diseases such as irritable bowel syndrome (IBS), chronic fatigue syndrome, fibromyalgia, Type I diabetes, multiple chemical sensitivity, and rheumatoid arthritis

Each of the biological systems involved in these stress-related medical conditions has been found to be dysregulated among adults with PTSD as a result of the chronic state of physiological reactivity (e.g., hyperarousal, irritability, sleeplessness involved in PTSD). While Friedman and McEwen (2004) do not claim that PTSD causes these medical conditions, they demonstrate that PTSD's chronic physiological arousal may contribute to the dysregulation of the underlying biological systems and may therefore increase the risk of developing biological abnormalities that could lead to a variety of somatic complaints. To the extent that somatic complaints associated with PTSD such as fatigue, pain, and tension are related to the biological adaptation necessitated by chronic states of stress (allostasis; Friedman & McEwen, 2004), these complaints reflect real medical problems and not simply mental distress or anxiety (*see:* **Medical Illness, Adult**).

Psychological Trauma, PTSD, and Health Risk Behaviors

Somatic complaints related to exposure to psychological trauma and the development of PTSD could be the result of biological alterations that result from engaging in behaviors that are known to increase the risk of illness. These health risk behaviors prominently include smoking and excess alcohol consumption, as well as poor diet (e.g., excess or insufficient consumption, foods with high levels of red meats, transfats, and simple carbohydrates), lack of exercise, risky sexual behavior, insufficient sleep, and limited or conflictual social support systems. Exposure to psychological trauma, particularly to violence, and PTSD have been found to be associated with each of these health risk behavior patterns (Haglund, Cooper, Southwick, & Charney, 2007; Kendall-Tackett, 2007) (*see:* **Medical Illness, Adult**). Therefore, somatic complaints associated with psychological trauma exposure or PTSD may be, in part, the result of chronic behavior patterns that increase the allostatic load (Friedman & McEwen, 2004) on the body and predispose the person to biologically based medical problems.

Health risk behavior patterns may begin long before an individual is exposed to psychological trauma, and may increase in frequency or amount as a result of traumatic stress reactions or PTSD—but they also may develop in reaction to exposure to psychological trauma. For example, increased alcohol consumption was found to occur among a small subgroup of adults living near New York City within the first three months following the September 11, 2001 terrorist attacks. Those individuals also tended to report higher levels of emotional distress immediately after the incidents and to more often seek support in the following year than other adults in that community sample (Ford, Adams, & Dailey, 2006). Thus, somatic complaints may emerge following psychological trauma as a result of continued, increased, or newly developed patterns of behavior that reflect attempts to cope with traumatic stress reactions (such as anxiety, irritability, or hypervigilance) but that also place the person's physical health at risk.

Psychological Trauma, PTSD, and Medically Unexplained Physical Symptoms

Somatic complaints related to exposure to psychological trauma and the development of PTSD also may be due to physical symptoms that cannot be explained by medical examination, testing, and diagnosis. Roelofs and Spinhoven (2007) review the scientific research and clinical theories that have been developed in an attempt to explain the origins of medically unexplained physical symptoms. These physical symptoms include physical health problems and limitations related to chronic pelvic pain, IBS, and "conversion" or somatization disorders (historically referred to as hysterical disorders; *see:* **History of Psychological Trauma**). A subspecialty within the medical profession, psychosomatic medicine, developed largely based on a need to understand and treat medical patients who reported ("complained of") pain (often in the pelvic area, but also in the form of migraine or tension headaches) and discomfort (often due to gastrointestinal conditions such as IBS), or strange changes in their body's capabilities (such as paralysis or pain that move from place to place in the body without any neurological basis). The symptoms are considered to be a "conversion" of emotional distress into physical disability or pain, and thus as a way of indirectly expressing emotions via the body ("somatic" expressions of the psychological distress, hence the term "psychosomatic"). Research on these conditions has demonstrated that women who report chronic pelvic pain, IBS, or conversion symptoms are more often survivors of childhood sexual, physical, and emotional abuse than women who do not report those psychosomatic problems (Roelofs & Spinhoven, 2007). Sexual abuse, but not physical abuse, appears to be particularly associated with these conditions rather than with other types of pain including medically/neurologically explained pain disorders. A tendency to express emotional distress in bodily symptoms (or somatization), was found to be involved in IBS and in conversion disorders, but only in two studies, which require replication.

Research or clinical reports describing medically unexplained physical symptoms among men is scarce, and primarily has been done with military personnel or veterans. A study was done with military veterans who had been deployed in Operation Desert Storm (Persian Gulf War, 1990 to 1991) and were tested between five and seven years later, 85% of whom were men, found that those who reported medically documented but unexplained chronic fatigue syndrome symptoms or neurological, gastrointestinal, orthopedic, or dermatologic symptoms (Ford et al., 2001). In addition to somatization, symptoms of PTSD or depression and having experienced potentially traumatic combat duties, were associated with the presence of these medically unexplained physical health problems (compared to a matched healthy control group). Thus, not only childhood abuse trauma but also war trauma and associated PTSD or depression, may be a factor in the development or persistence of medically unexplained symptoms, at least for men.

Somatic complaints associated with exposure to psychological trauma may be difficult to explain medically if they are expressions of traumatic stress reactions that are the product of a particular culture or of the individual's personality. Concerning culture, cross-cultural studies of psychological trauma and its aftermath have documented a number of culture-specific terms for expressing posttraumatic emotional and biological reactions—often involving the description of changes in the body rather than mental or emotional distress. For example, Mexican survivors of an earthquake were found to frequently describe problematic reactions as "ataques de nervios"—as has been found to be the case in other studies of Spanish-speaking populations

in the wake of disaster (Norris et al., 2001). Cultural effects are not limited to specific language communities or nations, but may also differ substantially within those groups based upon the era in which people were born and raised. For example, World War II military veterans have been found to be less likely to express traumatic stress difficulties in terms of the psychological distress symptoms of PTSD and more likely to endorse physical health problems, compared to Vietnam War veterans. The differences may be related to the type of war trauma (*see:* **War Trauma**) experienced by military personnel in those different eras, or to other factors such as exposure to toxic chemicals (which is associated with largely undiagnosed PTSD among World War II veterans; Ford et al., 2004), but they also may be the product of different cultural norms in these two age cohorts.

With regard to personality, the trait of "anxiety sensitivity" or "neuroticism" has been shown to be associated with an increased tendency to express somatic complaints that cannot be medically explained among adults with PTSD (Jakupcak et al., 2006). Thus, somatic complaints expressed by survivors of psychological trauma and persons with PTSD may be related to cultural norms or personality traits that lead people to express traumatic stress reactions and emotional distress in terms of bodily symptoms.

Psychological Trauma, PTSD, and Somatoform Dissociation

When psychological trauma occurs at developmentally sensitive periods in a person's life (particularly in early childhood; *see:* **Biology, Brain Structure, and Function, Child; Child Development**) and compromises or prevents the development of a secure attachment relationship with primary adult caregivers such as parents (*see:* **Attachment**), a cascade of biological changes may occur that disrupt or block the development of the two key psychological capabilities that enable children to develop a healthy and durable sense of self, that is, the abilities to: (1) regulate physical arousal and emotions; and (2) use attention, working and long-term memory, verbal/declarative and narrative/autobiographical memory, and executive problem-solving and decision-making skills to think clearly when stressed (Ford, 2005). When infants, toddlers, or preschool-age children develop a secure attachment bond with their primary caregivers, they learn the core emotion regulation and information processing skills by practicing ways to feel good (physically and emotionally) and think clearly while they play and interact with caregivers who model the same skills and nonverbally guide the child in using them. The result is that the child becomes able to recognize and utilize bodily reactions (feelings of energy, hunger, or fatigue) while experiencing her/himself as an effective agent in her/his own life. This is the beginning of achieving a sense of psychological integration (see: **Cognitive Integration, Biopsychosocial**). However, when psychological trauma leads to, or occurs along with, an undependable or unresponsive (or at worst, a neglectful or abusive) relationship with primary caregiver(s), the child may not develop this integration of mind/emotions and body, and may instead be unable to not only regulate emotions and think clearly but also to tolerate and manage bodily reactions.

In these adverse circumstances, children often develop a range of minor and serious health problems that may persist into adulthood and take the form of serious medical illnesses (as discussed above) and that are either more severe or chronic than can be medically explained (i.e., somatization; see Haugaard, 2004; Waldinger, Schulz, Barsky, & Ahern, 2006). These somatic complaints are the physiological counterpart to psychological dissociation, because they are the result of a fragmentation (rather than integration) of the child's self and personality (see: **Dissociation**) but in the form of a breakdown of the child's ability to mentally organize and regulate bodily reactions. This form of dissociation is called somatoform dissociation (Nijenhuis, 2004) and it is particularly associated with both childhood abuse and adult somatization (Brown, Schrag, & Trimble, 2005). Somatoform dissociation includes symptoms reflecting bodily states of disorganization such as tics, pseudoseizures (seizure-like states that do not involve abnormal brain wave activity), medically unexplainable pain, anesthesia, or paralysis, intense physical impulses to act without regard to safety, and distorted auditory, visual, tactile, and gustatory (taste) sensory experiences (for example, bodily feelings that are extremely intense, opposite to those expected in the current environment, rapidly changing, or entirely absent). Somatoform dissociation tends to persist and become progressively more severe as children grow into adolescence and adulthood, and lead to somatic complaints that are very difficult to treat unless their link to developmental trauma and attachment failures are addressed (Nijenhuis, 2004).

Somatic Complaints and Medical Illness as Precipitants for PTSD

Although experiencing and expressing somatic complaints often is highly stressful, especially if the symptoms and associated distress and discomfort are persistent and medically unexplained (and therefore more difficult for the medical provider to treat and for the patient to develop an internal sense of control, efficacy, and optimism), they are not psychologically traumatic per se unless they are actually (or perceived to be) life threatening. Not surprisingly, therefore, even an illness such as cancer is not necessarily psychologically traumatic and may not lead to the development of PTSD for most children who experience it, but often their parents are psychologically traumatized (that is, experience traumatic stress reactions) and these parents are more likely to develop PTSD than parents of other less severely medically ill or healthy children (see: **Medical Illness, Child**). Older children and adolescents who have recovered from cancer are thought to be more in need of (or better able to benefit from) treatment for posttraumatic stress than younger pediatric cancer patients or those of any age who are recently diagnosed with cancer and still in the early or intensive phases of medical treatment for the illness (Kazak et al., 2005).

However, serious medical illness—particularly when this is discovered in a manner that is emotionally shocking to the person and their support system (e.g., Ford et al., 2004)—may be a psychologically traumatic stressor that can lead to PTSD. Patients with cardiovascular/coronary heart disease who have experienced a myocardial infarction (heart attack) or cardiac surgery, are somewhat more likely than patients with less severe somatic complaints or healthy individuals to develop PTSD, although the severity of the illness per se does not predict the likelihood of developing PTSD (Tedstone & Tarrier, 2003). The best predictor of PTSD among adult medical patients was receiving intensive care unit (ICU) treatment and human immunovirus (HIV) infection (Tedstone & Tarrier, 2003), regardless of specific medical illnesses. At the time that the studies reviewed by Tedstone and Tarrier were conducted (i.e., 1980s to 1990s), HIV+ status was considered a relatively virulent infection that almost inevitably led to an untreatable and lethal disease state (AIDS). Thus, the lethality of the condition, and the low likelihood of being able to prevent or control its adverse progression, made HIV/AIDS a highly life-threatening stressor. With the advent of more effective approaches to managing HIV infection and preventing AIDS, it will be important to determine whether this condition remains as strongly associated with PTSD as in these earlier studies.

ICU treatment is required when illness is acute and therefore likely to be dangerous, painful, and disorienting, all of which can lead to a sense of life threat and the subjective reactions of intense fear, helplessness, or horror that are the cardinal features of psychological trauma. ICU treatment also exposes the patient to a chaotic and overwhelming multiplicity of often frantic and fragmented sights, sounds, smells, and bodily sensations (e.g., hearing other patients screaming or moaning, seeing one's own or other patients' severe bodily damage and profuse bleeding, hearing and seeing medical personnel working under conditions of high stress, and invasive and painful medical procedures). Thus, the relationship between ICU care and psychological trauma or PTSD is likely to be more an association between traumatic events and traumatic stress reactions than a traumatic reaction to medical illness per se.

Somatic Complaints and Health-care Utilization

Extensive research literature have documented a strong relationship between high (often excessive) levels of utilization of primary care and specialty health-care services with the severity of medically unexplained physical symptoms (Roelofs & Spinhoven, 2007) and also with anxiety (including posttraumatic stress) and depression (Ford, Tennen, Trestman, & Allen, 2005). A study with Vietnam War military veterans found that combat exposure and PTSD were associated with the extent of use of mental health services by men, but not with their use of medical services—nor was the extent of men's somatic complaints related to their use of medical services (Maguen et al., 2007). Among women veterans, those who reported potentially traumatic war-zone experiences (including witnessing horrific wounds and deaths in medical triage and nursing roles, as well as in combat duty) were more likely than other women veterans to report physical health problems and to more extensively use medical (but not mental health) services (Maguen et al., 2007).

While it is premature to draw more than conclusions, these findings and a large body of research on medically unexplained physical symptoms (Roelofs & Spinhoven, 2007), suggest that traumatized women are more likely than other women to report somatic complaints and to utilize amounts of medical care that are consistent with the extent of these somatic complaints. When somatic problems can be medically explained and treated, this is advantageous because it provides the woman and her medical providers with opportunities to prevent severe or chronic illnesses with timely early medical intervention. However, when the somatic complaints cannot be medically explained, the patient may require psychological treatment for anxiety or depression secondary to a history of childhood or war trauma in order to recovery medically. For men, although there appears to be a relationship between exposure to war trauma and both exacerbated toxin-related illness (Ford et al., 2004) and medically unexplained physical symptoms (Ford et al., 2001), neither a history of war trauma nor somatic complaints appear to be related to acquiring more medical services. This may lead to an underutilization of medical care by traumatized and physically symptomatic men, which could lead them to overutilize mental health services (Maguen et al., 2007) and place them at risk for developing more severe and chronic medical illness (Ford et al., 2004). More research is needed to more definitively test these hypothesized relationships between gender, psychological trauma, PTSD, somatic complaints, and health-care utilization (*see:* **Health Service Utilization**).

Conclusion

Somatic complaints—expressions of discomfort, pain, or disability related to bodily health—are commonly expressed by persons who have recently experienced psychological trauma, and particularly by those who develop PTSD. Somatic complaints may be the product of genuine medical illnesses or physical injuries, particularly stress-related illnesses and physical health problems that are in part the result of risky behaviors or lifestyles (such as obesity and cardiovascular or lung diseases). Somatic complaints also may reflect physical health problems that cannot be medically explained, potentially resulting from the psychosomatic expression of emotional distress or somatoform dissociation. Physical health problems, whether medically explainable or not, also may be a source of traumatic stress or PTSD, particularly when shocking and life-threatening. When people with PTSD seek medical care for somatic complaints, they may utilize large amounts of services, which is costly to them and to society. Although these health-care services may be necessary due to the often complicated and chronic medical illnesses and somatic complaints that may occur among people with PTSD, further research and clinical

innovation is needed in order to determine if addressing the biological hyperarousal and the emotional distress associated with PTSD can improve the outcomes and reduce the amount and costs of health-care services for people with PTSD (Zatzick & Roy-Byrne, 2006).

REFERENCES

Brown, R., Schrag, A., & Trimble, M. (2005). Dissociation, childhood interpersonal trauma, and family functioning in patients with somatization disorder. *American Journal of Psychiatry, 162,* 899–905.

Chartier, J., Walker, M., & Naimark, B. (2007). Childhood abuse, adult health, and healthcare utilization. *American Journal of Epidemiology, 165,* 1031–1038.

Fairbank, J., Putnam, F., & Harris, W. (2007). The prevalence and impact of child traumatic stress. In M. J. Friedman, T. M. Keane, & P. A. Resick (Eds.), *Handbook of PTSD: Science and practice* (pp. 229–251). New York: Guilford Press.

Felitti, V., Anda, R., Nordenberg, D., Williamson, D., Spitz, A., Edwards, V., et al. (1998). Relationship of childhood abuse and household dysfunction to many of the leading causes of death in adults. *American Journal of Preventive Medicine, 14,* 245–258.

Ford, J. D. (2005). Treatment implications of altered neurobiology, affect regulation and information processing following child maltreatment: *Psychiatric Annals, 35,* 410–419.

Ford, J. D., Adams, M., & Dailey, W. (2006). Prevalence and risk factors for psychological problems and patterns of receipt of help by Connecticut adults 5–15 months after the September 11th terrorist incidents. *Social Psychiatry and Psychiatric Epidemiology, 40,* 1–10.

Ford, J. D., Campbell, K., Storzbach, D., Binder, L., Anger, W. K., & Rohlman, D. (2001). Posttraumatic stress symptomatology is associated with unexplained illness attributed to Persian Gulf War military service. *Psychosomatic Medicine, 63,* 842–849.

Ford, J. D., Schnurr, P., Friedman, M., Green, B., Adams, G., & Jex, S. (2004). Posttraumatic stress disorder symptoms and physical health outcomes fifty years after exposure to toxic gas. *Journal of Traumatic Stress, 17,* 185–194.

Ford, J. D., Tennen, H., Trestman, R. L., & Allen, S. (2005). Relationship of anxiety, depression, and alcohol use disorders to persistent high utilization and potentially problematic under-utilization of primary medical care. *Social Science and Medicine, 61,* 1618–1625.

Friedman, M. J., & McEwen, B. (2004). Posttraumatic stress disorder, allostatic load, and medical illness. In P. P. Schnurr & B. L. Green (Eds.), *Physical health consequences of exposure to extreme stress* (pp. 157–188). Washington, DC: American Psychological Association.

Haglund, M., Cooper, N., Southwick, S., & Charney, D. (2007). 6 keys to resilience for PTSD and everyday stress: Teach patients protective attitudes and behaviors. *Current Psychiatry, 6,* 23–24, 27–30.

Haugaard, J. (2004). Recognizing and treating uncommon behavioral and emotional disorders in children and adolescents who have been severely maltreated: Somatization and other somatoform disorders. *Child Maltreatment, 9,* 169–176.

Jakupcak, M., Osborne, T., Michael, S., Cook, J., Albrizio, P., & McFall, M. (2006). Anxiety sensitivity and depression: Mechanisms for understanding somatic complaints in veterans with posttraumatic stress disorder. *Journal of Traumatic Stress, 19,* 471–479.

Kazak, A. E., Simms, S., Alderfer, M. A., Rourke, M. T., Crump, T., McClure, K., et al. (2005). Feasibility and preliminary outcomes from a pilot study of a brief psychological intervention for families of children newly diagnosed with cancer. *Journal of Pediatric Psychology, 30,* 644–655.

Kendall-Tackett, K. (2007). Inflammation, cardiovascular disease, and metabolic syndrome as sequelae of violence against women: The role of depression, hostility, and sleep disturbance. *Trauma, Violence, and Abuse, 8,* 117–126.

Maguen, S., Schumm, J., Norris, R., Taft, C., King, L., King, D., et al. (2007). Predictors of mental and physical health service utilization among Vietnam veterans. *Psychological Services, 4,* 168–180.

Neumeister, A., Henry, S., & Krystal, J. (2007). Neurocircuitry and neuroplasticity in PTSD. In M. J. Friedman, T. M. Keane, & P. A. Resick (Eds.), *Handbook of PTSD: Science and practice* (pp. 151–165). New York: Guilford Press.

Nijenhuis, E. R. S. (2004). *Somatoform dissociation: Phenomena, measurement, and theoretical issues.* New York: Norton.

Norris, F. H., Weisshaar, D., Conrad, M., Diaz, E., Murphy, A., & Ibañez, G. (2001). A qualitative analysis of posttraumatic stress among Mexican victims of disaster. *Journal of Traumatic Stress, 14,* 741–756.

Roelofs, K., & Spinhoven, P. (2007). Trauma and medically unexplained symptoms: Towards an integration of cognitive and neuro-biological accounts. *Clinical Psychology Review, 27,* 798–820.

Schnurr, P. P., & Green, B. L. (2004). Understanding relationships among trauma, posttraumatic stress disorder, and health outcomes. In P. P. Schnurr & B. L. Green (Eds.), *Physical health consequences of exposure to extreme stress* (pp. 247–275). Washington, DC: American Psychological Association.

Southwick, S., Davis, L., Aikins, D., Rasmusson, A., Barron, J., & Morgan III, C. A. (2007). Neuro-biological alterations associated with PTSD. In M. J. Friedman, T. M. Keane, & P. A. Resick (Eds.), *Handbook of PTSD: Science and practice* (pp. 166–189). New York: Guilford Press.

Tedstone, J., & Tarrier, N. (2003). Posttraumatic stress disorder following medical illness and treatment. *Clinical Psychology Review, 23,* 409–448.

Waldinger, R., Schulz, M., Barsky, A., & Ahern, D. (2006). Mapping the road from childhood trauma to adult somatization: The role of attachment. *Psychosomatic Medicine, 68,* 129–135.

Zatzick, D., & Roy-Byrne, P. (2006). From bedside to bench: How the epidemiology of clinical practice can inform the secondary prevention of PTSD. *Psychiatric Services, 57,* 1726–1730.

Julian D. Ford
University of Connecticut School of Medicine

See also: Abuse, Child Physical; Abuse, Child Sexual; Biology, Brain Structure, and Function, Child; Biology, Neurochemistry; Biology, Physiology; Complex Posttraumatic Stress Disorder; Culture-Bound Syndromes; Dissociation; Gulf War Syndrome; Health Service Utilization; HIV; Hysteria; Janet, Pierre; Medical Illness, Adult; Medical Illness, Child; Psychoneuroimmunology

SPIRITUALITY

Considering spirituality in the context of psychological trauma denotes the existential nature of traumatic distress. This entry first describes the intersection between spirituality and religious variables, and then presents a rationale for including spiritual issues in the discussion of trauma. The literature suggests that there are key themes for understanding how spirituality and religion can both help and hinder recovery from psychological trauma. Finally, clinical issues are identified in planning how spiritual resources and beliefs may be part of traumatic stress treatment.

Spirituality and Religion

A working definition of spirituality is "an individual's understanding of, experience with, and connection to that which transcends the self" (Drescher et al., 2004, p. 330). What is beyond oneself may be a higher power, nature, a universal energy, or God. One way to understand the complex interplay between spirituality and religion is that spirituality is an individual experience, and religion is communal. Thus, while an individual's spirituality can be understood to rely mainly upon an internal awareness, religion is characterized by a shared set of beliefs, rituals, values, and practices that are rooted in community and history.

Most cultures in the world hold a perspective that reality is not only based in the material world. For many nonwestern cultures, the idea of sorting one's experience into material and spiritual is quite strange, as spirituality is deeply embedded into daily life. Even within the United States, where the two are more often dichotomized, opinion surveys consistently report that most people ascribe to spiritual beliefs. For example, in a recent Gallup poll 91% of Americans reported a belief in God or a greater "force" or "spirit," and only 2% indicated they did not believe in a God or "spirit" (Gallup International Association, 1999). The Fetzer Institute developed a framework of twelve dimensions of religion and spirituality that have been demonstrated to contribute to physical and mental health: daily spiritual experiences, meaning, values, beliefs, forgiveness, private religious practices, religious/spiritual coping, religious support, religious or spiritual history, commitment, organizational religiousness, and religious preference (Fetzer Institute, 1999). For many individuals, spirituality or religious faith is a critical source of comfort and direction in

life, particularly following exposure to psychological trauma and in recovery from traumatic stress.

Each client's spiritual and religious history and current affiliation provide critical information about her or his potential resources and challenges in recovery from traumatic stress. Pargament (2002) has identified the complexity of costs and benefits of religiousness:

> Well-being has been linked positively to a religion that is internalized, intrinsically motivated, and based on a secure relationship with God and negatively to a religion that is imposed, unexamined, and reflective of a tenuous relationship with God and the world. (p. 168)

Therefore, the nature of the beliefs, the level of personal commitment, the motivation for practice, and the extent to which this is integrated with other aspects of the person's life create the framework for religion and spirituality as aspects of how most people adapt in the face of adversity. Therefore, religion and spirituality have implications for personal resilience or risk when individuals face psychological trauma and experience traumatic stress.

Research on Spirituality in Relation to Psychological Trauma

The literature examining spiritual and religious factors in relation to traumatic stress has focused on event traumas, including prominent examples such as child and adult sexual abuse, military combat, natural disasters, and more recently medical traumas such as life-threatening illness. It is difficult to find consistent results among studies, which may be due to differences in trauma type studied and varied operational definitions of religious and spiritual variables. For example, as compared to other women, survivors of childhood sexual abuse indicate higher levels of anger at God (Kane, Cheston, & Greer, 1993) and report lower religious participation (Hall, 1995), but those who regularly attend services demonstrate less emotional distress (Elliot, 1994).

Despite this complexity, research findings may be organized around four key themes:

(1) spirituality and religion can buffer the negative effects of psychological trauma; (2) spiritual well-being is positively associated with quality of life; (3) spirituality can be an aspect of growth following a traumatic experience; and (4) traumatic experiences may negatively impact spirituality and/or religious beliefs (Drescher et al., 2004).

Buffering the Negative Effects of Psychological Trauma

Spiritual and religious activities can provide practical, relational, and emotional buffering against the impact of traumatic events. Survivors who are active in a religious or spiritual group may find that there are caring individuals who are open to provide emotional support and instrumental support through acts of service and/or financial aid. Research has particularly noted the benefits of coping behaviors that are based on a relationship with a trustworthy, benevolent, divine presence. Positive religious coping has been associated with lower psychosomatic distress and greater stress-related growth in survivors of a variety of traumatic events (Pargament, Smith, Koenig, & Perez, 1998).

Spiritual Well-Being

Spiritual well-being emphasizes the internal or existential aspects of spirituality such as meaning or purpose. Research has demonstrated the importance of spiritual well-being in the overall well-being and quality of life of medical patients. For example, when compared to severely ill or healthy adults, a group of terminally ill patients demonstrated greater spiritual perspective and well-being (Reed, 1987). A study of breast cancer patients found positive correlations between spiritual well-being, quality of life, and psychological adjustment (Cotton, Levine, Fitzpatrick, Dold, & Targ, 1999).

Adversarial Growth

Some individuals experience enhanced spiritual well-being and report feeling closer to God even in the aftermath of severe traumas such as disaster or sexual assault (Linley & Joseph, 2004). Falsetti and colleagues (Falsetti, Resick, & Davis, 2003) discovered higher levels of internalized religiousness among individuals who experienced more than one trauma. Even in the context of the death of a child to sudden infant death syndrome, religious participation was positively related to discovering meaning in the loss and feeling greater support (McIntosh, Silver, & Wortman, 1993).

Negative Impact

For some, trauma can lead to a loss of faith, or reduced participation in religious or spiritual activities. Research with combat veterans has shown that exposure to severe combat trauma is associated with a weakening of religious faith (Fontana & Rosenheck, 2004), and that military veterans score lower than the normative sample on a measure of religious orientation (Drescher & Foy, 1995). In addition, religious coping strategies that focus on doubt, spiritual restlessness, or a perspective of God as punitive (termed negative religious coping) have been associated with poorer mental health, such as increased PTSD symptoms in survivors of a terrorist attack (Pargament et al., 1998) and military combat veterans (Witvliet, Phipps, Feldman, & Beckham, 2004). Witvliet and colleagues also identified that a lack of forgiveness toward self and others was associated with increased PTSD and depression.

Limitations of the Spirituality and Religion Research

The complex nature of religious and spiritual constructs, the interaction between personal, environmental, and spiritual factors, and the restrictions of cross-sectional research create a number of limitations in the research reported. For example, it is not clear that having experienced childhood sexual abuse is the determinant of differences in religious beliefs or practices, as there are many other potential factors that may be related to both spiritual beliefs and behavior (such as exposure to other psychological traumas, or involvement in family and social support systems). It is also not yet known whether the findings on adversarial growth and religious coping reflect a general quality of resilience on the part of people who report less distress and more growth after psychological trauma, or a specific benefit of religious beliefs. Similarly, additional research is required to investigate whether resilience and growth in the aftermath of psychological trauma is due to social support in general, as opposed to a specific benefit of involvement in a religious community. More research is also needed to identify whether a positive sense of meaning and purpose is the result of general psychological health, an explicitly spiritual process, or a more complex interaction of personal and spiritual factors.

Spiritual and Religious Issues in Traumatic Stress Disorder Treatment

Themes of Spiritual Distress

In addition to spiritual and religious experiences that have been the focus of empirical research, other themes have been identified in theoretical and clinical contexts. Janoff-Bulman's construct of "shattered assumptions" suggests that experiencing traumatic events can confront an individual's core beliefs about the meaning of life, self-worth, and safety in the world (Janoff-Bulman, 1992). An individual who fixes her/his core beliefs on religious or spiritual constructs may find those beliefs fundamentally shaken. Often called "the problem of evil," the philosophical dilemma of "theodicy" poses the question: If God is both all-powerful and all-good, how does She/He allow evil to exist in the world? Historically, philosophers have created answers to this question that either diminish the qualities of God (i.e., God is not real, or is not all-powerful, or is not all-good), lessen the evil (i.e., God will use it to create a greater good, or God is punishing an individual or community for sin), or focus on the action of the participants (i.e., God has given humans free will). However, for trauma survivors, "theodicy" is not simply an intellectual exercise; these questions often are experienced within a context of personal turmoil. This may limit the recovery of a religious person by creating guilt about a "loss of faith," isolation from a religious community, and cognitive dissonance related to anger or distrust of the divine.

Another key spiritual theme in trauma recovery is moral questioning. There are traumatic situations (e.g., war, gang violence) where a person can be both a victim and a perpetrator of violence. A soldier in combat could witness the injury or death of others, be wounded him/herself, and participate in killing the enemy. These experiences can create a tension between core elements of that individual's worldview (e.g., patriotism and faith), leading to uncertainty regarding the best, most moral choice. The resultant long-lasting questions and internal moral dilemmas are associated with alienation from others and God ("how could anyone understand?"), guilt and self-blame, and even a loss of faith.

Spiritual and Religious Resources in Intervention for Traumatic Stress

Spiritual and religious beliefs, actions, and rituals may be incorporated in a number of ways throughout treatment. As mentioned earlier, assessment of an individual's religious and spiritual history helps to identify ways that practices and beliefs have been a resource or vulnerability in the past. Current involvement in religious communities may provide a context for supportive relationships, practical resources, and spiritual direction or teaching. Religious values that influence healthy lifestyle choices can be useful in moderating unhealthy coping such as substance abuse, sexual acting out, or other addictive behaviors. In addition, trauma survivors may recover a sense of meaning and perspective outside of their own pain through acts of humanitarian service that many religious communities encourage. Beyond these natural ways that participation in religious communities may help to alleviate traumatic stress symptoms, specific methods can also be used in the context of treatment to introduce themes of forgiveness, theodicy, meaning, and spiritual practices, as long as they are congruent with the client's worldview (Drescher et al., 2004).

Finally, certain posttraumatic stress symptoms may be addressed directly in the context of spiritual or religious resources. Social isolation and withdrawal may be reduced by joining supportive communities, such as 12-step groups or religious congregations. Spiritual practices such as prayer, contemplation, mindfulness meditation, or yoga can be useful for the reduction of arousal and anxiety symptoms. Trust in relationships and one's sense of safety in the world can be significantly impacted by allowing survivors to verbalize the "broken trust" in the struggle of theodicy: "Can I trust that God intends good, when something so horrible has happened?" Working through these trust questions combats isolation and withdrawal. Anger, rage, and the desire for revenge may be understood (and not devalued) as a desire for justice, yet the spiritual practices of "letting go" or considering the possibility of forgiveness of others can address the hostility that hurts the survivor and limits ongoing relationships. Self-forgiveness and beliefs about the inherent value of self can also challenge a survivor's self-blame, guilt, or shame. In the context of the PTSD symptom of expecting a foreshortened future, it may be quite difficult for trauma survivors to have hope that it is possible to recover before their lives are ended. Sometimes a mental health provider acts in a spiritual manner by simply holding out the hope that something "new" or "different" can happen to transcend the current circumstances.

Involvement of Community Religious Professionals and Spiritual Leaders

A discussion of religion and spiritual response to trauma survivors would not be complete without acknowledgment of the role of community religious professionals. Some mental health practitioners may be uncomfortable with incorporating the discussion of spiritual issues in treatment. Knowledge of one's competency, accurate cultural understanding, and humility are a part of this practice. Mental health practitioners can access the support and knowledge of community clergy members or spiritual leaders either through consultation on specific cases in the religious community (with a signed release of information), or in general consultation regarding a set of beliefs or religious rituals that may be helpful or harmful to a trauma survivor. The community religious professional could also act as a supportive resource as the survivor navigates relationships in the religious community. The trained trauma therapist can also assist clergy in understanding the dynamics of trauma disclosure, the intensity of relationships with individuals who have complex trauma histories, and the reality of secondary exposure to vicarious trauma. A mutually respectful relationship between mental health workers and community religious professionals ultimately serves the purpose of creating a structure of care for trauma survivors.

Conclusion

The interaction between spirituality and psychological trauma is complex. Understanding the nature of spiritual or religious beliefs, the individual's integration of these beliefs in personal practice and involvement in spiritual or religious communities, and the spiritual meaning or context of traumatic experiences all contribute to the mental health practitioners' ability to incorporate spirituality into effective intervention. Collaboration and consultation by mental health practitioners with community religious professionals and spiritual teachers augment this network of care.

REFERENCES

Cotton, S. P., Levine, E. G., Fitzpatrick, C. M., Dold, K. H., & Targ, E. (1999). Exploring the relationships among spiritual well-being, quality of life, and psychological adjustment in women with breast cancer. *Psycho-Oncology, 8,* 429–438.

Drescher, K. D., & Foy, D. W. (1995). Spirituality and trauma treatment: Suggestions for including spirituality as a coping resource. *National Center for PTSD Clinical Quarterly, 5*(1), 4–5.

Drescher, K. D., Ramirez, G., Leoni, J. J., Romesser, J. M., Sornborger, J., & Foy, D. W. (2004). Spirituality and trauma: Development of a group therapy module. *Group, 28,* 323–338.

Elliott, D. M. (1994). The impact of Christian faith on the prevalence and sequelae of sexual abuse. *Journal of Interpersonal Violence, 9*(1), 95–108.

Falsetti, S. A., Resick, P. A., & Davis, J. L. (2003). Changes in religious beliefs following trauma. *Journal of Traumatic Stress, 16*(4), 391–398.

Fetzer Institute. (1999). *Multidimensional measurement of religiousness/spirituality for use in health research: A report of the Fetzer Institute/National Institute on Aging Working Group.* Retrieved October 18, 2007, from www.fetzer.org/PDF/Total_Fetzer_Book.pdf.

Fontana, A., & Rosenheck, R. (2004). Trauma, change in strength of religious faith, and mental health service use among veterans treated for PTSD. *Journal of Nervous and Mental Disease, 192*(9), 579–584.

Gallup International Association. (1999). *Gallup international millennium survey.* Retrieved October 18, 2007, from www.gallup-international.com.

Hall, T. A. (1995). Spiritual effects of childhood sexual abuse in adult Christian women. *Journal of Psychology and Theology, 23*(2), 129–134.

Janoff-Bulman, R. (1992). *Shattered assumptions: Towards a new psychology of trauma.* New York: Free Press.

Kane, D., Cheston, S. E., & Greer, J. (1993). Perceptions of God by survivors of childhood sexual abuse: An exploratory study in an underresearched area. *Journal of Psychology and Theology, 21*(3), 228–237.

Linley, P. A., & Joseph, S. (2004). Positive change following trauma and adversity: A review. *Journal of Traumatic Stress, 17*(1), 11–21.

McIntosh, D. N., Silver, R. C., & Wortman, C. B. (1993). Religion's role in adjustment to a negative life event: Coping with the loss of a child. *Journal of Personality and Social Psychology, 65,* 812–821.

Pargament, K. I. (2002). The bitter and the sweet: An evaluation of the costs and benefits of religiousness. *Psychological Inquiry, 13,* 168–181.

Pargament, K. I., Smith, B. W., Koenig, H. G., & Perez, L. (1998). Patterns of positive and negative religious coping with major life stressors. *Journal for the Scientific Study of Religion, 37,* 710–724.

Reed, P. G. (1987). Spirituality and well-being in terminally ill hospitalized adults. *Research in Nursing and Health, 10,* 335–344.

Witvliet, C., Phipps, K., Feldman, M., & Beckham, J. (2004). Posttraumatic mental and physical health correlates of forgiveness and religious coping in military veterans. *Journal of Traumatic Stress, 17*(3), 269–273.

CYNTHIA B. ERIKSSON
Fuller Theological Seminary

KENT D. DRESCHER
National Center for Posttraumatic Stress Disorder

KATHARINE M. PUTMAN
Fuller Theological Seminary

DAVID W. FOY
Pepperdine University

See also: Abuse, Child Physical; Abuse, Child Sexual; Betrayal Trauma; Complex Posttraumatic Stress Disorder; Coping; Culture-Bound Syndromes; Disasters; Guilt; Posttraumatic Adaptation; Posttraumatic Growth; Prevention, Adult; Shame; Social Support

STARTLE RESPONSE

Exaggerated startle responding has been recognized as a symptom of posttraumatic stress disorder (PTSD) since the earliest descriptions of combat soldiers suffering adverse effects of exposure to the stress of combat. Many individuals with PTSD report extreme reactions to startling events in the environment. For example, some report flinching or recoiling in response to an unexpected touch. Others spring awake in response to an unexpected noise in the night and are unable to fall back to sleep, Combat veterans describe "hitting the dirt" or "ducking for cover" at the sound of a car backfiring. In each instance, the initial startle response may be followed by a cascade of anxious arousal symptoms that may that may take minutes to hours to recover from.

Studies have found this to be one of the most commonly self-reported symptoms of the disorder (Davidson, Hughes, Blazer, & George, 1991; Pynoos et al., 1993) and among the symptoms that best differentiate individuals with and without PTSD (Meltzer-Brody, Churchill, & Davidson, 1999). Elevated startle may also be one of the first symptoms to emerge following trauma exposure. For example, among survivors of an industrial disaster, Weisaeth (1989) found that intense startle was the most commonly reported PTSD symptom within one week of the trauma and endorsed by 80% and 86% of participants with moderate and high levels of exposure to the accident, respectively. Similarly, Southwick et al. (1993, 1995) reported that exaggerated startle was among the top three most frequently endorsed PTSD symptoms in Gulf War veterans assessed one month, six months, and two years after the war.

In contrast with the foregoing self-report based studies, clinical laboratory research has yielded more equivocal findings regarding the validity of exaggerated startle as a symptom of PTSD. From a psychophysiological perspective, the startle response is a constellation of reflexive motor movements, phasic (changing) autonomic responses, and voluntary orienting responses that occur in response to any sudden, intense change in stimulus intensity. The reflexive component of the reaction begins with an eyeblink between 20 and 50 milliseconds after the onset of a startle-eliciting stimulus (e.g., car backfiring) and spreads distally throughout the body. In humans it is measured via electromyography (EMG) recordings of the contraction of the orbicularis oculi muscle that closes the eyelid. Startle-eliciting stimuli are typically loud noises presented over headphones and the magnitude of the muscle contraction is the primary measure of interest. Secondary, longer latency autonomic responses include heart rate acceleration and skin conductance increases. These begin within a second after the onset of a startling stimulus and typically peak several seconds later.

Pole (2007) recently conducted a meta-analysis of 20 studies that compared samples of individuals with and without PTSD on measures of startle and found that the effect size for the eyeblink reflex, weighted to control for sample size differences, was modest. Of those 20 studies, only approximately half showed significant group differences in eyeblink startle amplitude. However, a subset of the studies that Pole reviewed also examined heart rate responses to the startling stimuli and meta-analysis showed

that the size of the group effect for this measure of startle was significantly larger than for the eyeblink component.

These findings implicate autonomic hyperreactivity to startle stimuli in the pathophysiology of PTSD and they relate to other research suggesting a link between PTSD and elevated heart rate (Buckley & Kaloupek, 2001; Orr, Metzger, Miller, & Kaloupek, 2004). However, it remains unclear to what extent this is an acquired versus constitutional characteristic. One prospective study that addressed this question found that elevated heart rate responses to startle stimuli were evident in individuals who developed PTSD at one month, but not one week, following trauma exposure suggesting that it is an acquired characteristic and manifestation of the development of the disorder (Shalev et al., 2000). Similarly, Orr et al. (2003) compared the startle responses of Vietnam combat veterans to their noncombat-exposed monozygotic twins and found that veterans with PTSD showed larger heart rate responses to startling sounds compared to (a) their noncombat-exposed identical twin brothers, (b) non-PTSD combat veterans, and (c) the noncombat-exposed twin brothers of those without PTSD. Again, the implication is that greater heart rate reactivity in individuals with PTSD is a consequence of the development of PTSD, as opposed to an inherited trait or product of shared familial environment.

On the other hand, there is also evidence suggesting that exaggerated startle represents a pre-trauma vulnerability factor for PTSD. For example, Guthrie and Bryant (2005) conducted a prospective study of recently hired firefighters and found that the magnitude of pre-trauma skin conductance responses to startling stimuli was a prospective predictor of the development posttraumatic stress symptoms following exposure to trauma on the job.

Of course, the acquired versus constitutional hypotheses are not mutually exclusive. It is conceivable that exaggerated startle is both a marker of vulnerability for the development of PTSD and a characteristic that is augmented or accentuated as a function of the development of the disorder. Additional prospective studies with startle assessments administered pre-trauma exposure and/or behavioral genetics designs are needed to clarify these possibilities.

Research on animal models of exaggerated startle can also help answer these questions. Exaggerated startle is unique among the PTSD symptoms in terms of the degree of correspondence between the clinical symptom that occurs in humans and the behavioral analogue that can studied with animal models. Perhaps because of this, more is known about the neurocircuitry and neuromodulators of exaggerated startle than for any other symptom of the disorder. Two primary systems in the brain have been implicated as possible mechanisms for the symptom of exaggerated startle in PTSD: the locus coeruleus/norepinephrine system and the hypothalamic/corticotropin-releasing hormone (CRH) system. Evidence for these links includes studies showing that lesions of the locus coeruleus and drugs that inhibit its activity decrease startle reactivity, whereas drugs that increase locus coeruleus activity have the opposite effect (Davis, Redmond, & Baraban, 1979). Likewise, CRH administration produces a pronounced, dose-dependent enhancement of startle that can be blocked by pretreatment with a CRH receptor antagonist (e.g., Swerdlow, Britton, & Koob, 1989). These findings show the startle response to be a potentially fruitful target for future trans- and inter-disciplinary research on the etiology, mechanisms and treatment of PTSD.

REFERENCES

Buckley, T. C., & Kaloupek, D. G. (2001). A meta-analytic examination of basal cardiovascular activity in posttraumatic stress disorder. *Psychosomatic Medicine, 63,* 585–594.

Davidson, J. R. T., Hughes, D., Blazer, D. G., & George, L. K. (1991). Posttraumatic stress in the community: An epidemiological study. *Psychological Medicine, 21,* 713–721.

Davis, M., Redmond, D. E., Jr., & Baraban, J. M. (1979). Noradrenergic agonists and antagonists: Effects on conditioned fear as measured by the potentiated startle paradigm. *Psychopharmacology, 65,* 111–118.

Guthrie, R. M., & Bryant, R. A. (2005). Auditory startle response in firefighters before and after trauma exposure. *American Journal of Psychiatry, 162,* 283–290.

Meltzer-Brody, S., Chruchill, E., & Davidson, J. R. T. (1999). Derivation of the SPAN, a brief diagnostic screening test for post-traumatic stress disorder. *Psychiatry Research, 88,* 63–70.

Orr, S. P., Metzger, L. J., Lasko, N. B., Macklin, M. L., Hu, F. B., Shalev, A. Y., et al. (2003). Harvard/Veterans Affairs Post-Traumatic Stress Disorder Twin Study investigators: Physiologic responses to sudden, loud tones in monozygotic twins discordant for combat exposure—Association with posttraumatic stress disorder. *Archives of General Psychiatry, 60,* 283–288.

Orr, S. P., Metzger, L. J., Miller, M. W., & Kaloupek, D. G. (2004). Psychophysiological assessment of posttraumatic stress disorder. In J. P. Wilson & T. M. Keane (Eds.), *Assessing psychological trauma and PTSD* (2nd ed., pp. 289–343). New York: Guilford.

Pole, N. (2007). The psychophysiology of posttraumatic stress disorder: A meta-analysis. *Psychological Bulletin, 133,* 725–746.

Pynoos, R. S., Goenjiam, A., Tashjian, M., Karakashian, M., Manjikian, R., Manoukian, G., et al. (1993). Post-traumatic stress reactions in children after the 1988 Armenian earthquake. *British Journal of Psychiatry, 163,* 239–247.

Shalev, A. Y., Peri, T., Brandes, D., Freedman, S., Orr, S. P., & Pitman, R. K. (2000). Auditory startle response in trauma survivors with post-traumatic stress disorder: A prospective study. *American Journal of Psychiatry, 157,* 255–261.

Southwick, S. M., Morgan, C. A., Darnell, A., Bremner, D., Nicolaou, A. L., Nagy, L. M., et al. (1995). Trauma-related symptoms in veterans of Operation Desert Storm: A 2-year follow-up. *American Journal of Psychiatry, 152,* 1150–1155.

Southwick, S. M., Morgan, C. A., Nagy, L. M., Bremner, D., Nicolaou, A. L., Johnson, D. R., et al. (1993). Trauma-related symptoms in veterans of Operation Desert Storm: A preliminary report. *American Journal of Psychiatry, 150,* 1524–1528.

Swerdlow, N. R., Britton, K. T., & Koob, G. F. (1989). Potentiation of acoustic startle by corticotropin-releasing factor (CRH) and by fear are both reversed by a-helical CRH(9–41). *Neuropsychopharmacology, 2,* 285–292.

Weisaeth, L. (1989). The stressors and the post-traumatic stress syndrome after an industrial disaster. *Acta Psychiatrica Scandanavica, 80*(Suppl. 355), 25–37.

MARK W. MILLER
National Center for Posttraumatic Stress Disorder

See also: Acute Stress Disorder; Biology, Neurochemistry; Biology, Physiology; Conditioned Fear; Genetics; Hyperarousal; Learning Theory; Posttraumatic Stress Disorder; Posttraumatic Stress Disorder, Diagnosis of; Stress Response Syndromes

STRESS

Stress is a negative emotional experience or physiological response that is produced following exposure to life circumstances that are threatening or represent harm or loss to the individual or those things valued by the individual. These events are commonly referred to as stressors. Stressors exist on a continuum and may come from a variety of sources. They may take the form of daily hassles, such as running out of gasoline, forgetting to pay a bill, or arguments with spouses or friends. Stressors may also be more moderate in nature and include events such as a family member's injury or medical diagnosis. Severe stressors, also termed "potentially traumatic" are exemplified by events such as motor vehicle accidents, rape or sexual assault, or exposure to terrorism. Stress may also come from environmental sources such as living in areas with high noise levels, crowding and traffic jams. Stress also can arise from work in the form of job-related stress owing to work overload and eventually, work burnout.

Holmes and Rahe (1967) suggested that stressful life events cause the most distress when they require a person to make substantial changes to adapt to their environment. For example, they rated the death of a spouse as the most significant stressful life event given that it can cause the greatest degree of change in the surviving spouse's life. At the lower end of the stress continuum are minor and moderate stressful life events, which are stressors that can be disruptive to a person's functioning. In contrast to minor to moderate stressful life events, exposure to potentially traumatic events can lead to the development of post-traumatic stress disorder (PTSD). PTSD is a psychological disorder marked by intrusive recollections of a traumatic event, avoidance of reminders of a traumatic event, numbing of feelings, and hyperarousal marked by difficulties with sleeping, anger, and vigilance toward environmental threats (discussed in detail elsewhere in this Encyclopedia).

People respond to stress in a variety of ways. The fight-or-flight response—originally proffered by Walter Cannon (1932)—involves a person either fighting or fleeing from an event or stimulus that is perceived as stressful and threatening. In addition to actually becoming physically aggressive, fighting can take the form of becoming verbally aggressive or hostile after a stressful provocation; and rather than running from a stressful event, fleeing can also be conceived of as social withdrawal or alcohol and drug use.

Hans Selye (1956) outlined the first stress model: the general adaptation syndrome. When a person is confronted with a stressor, he or she mobilizes into action. This reaction is the same, regardless of the stressor. In time, after repeated exposures to stress, the system begins to develop wear and tear. There are three phases of response to stress: alarm, resistance, and exhaustion. In the alarm phase, the person will ready itself to respond to the stressor. The resistance phase includes the organism's attempt to cope. The exhaustion phase concludes the stress response cycle, and occurs when the organism is overwhelmed, and unable to effectively cope, having already depleted required resources. Research has supported the link between continued stress and its debilitating effects on people, as stress has demonstrated an association with cardiovascular disease, arthritis, and hypertension.

Although Selye supported a general adaptation to stress, Lazarus and Folkman (1984) stressed the importance of appraisal in the stress process. According to their theory, when people confront new or changing environments, they determine the meaning of the event through the process of primary appraisal. Events are interpreted as positive, neutral or negative. Negative events are further evaluated regarding the level of harm, threat or challenge. Harm pertains to the assessment of negative consequences that have already occurred as a result of the event. Threat is related to the assessment of negative consequences that have yet to occur, that resulted from the event. Challenge appraisals involve a person's ability to view the event in terms of their ability to overcome, or even profit from the event. Secondary appraisals are initiated at the same time as primary appraisals, and involve the assessment of the skills and resources a person has to cope with the harm, threat, and challenge of an event. So, according to this model, stress is a result of primary and secondary appraisals. First, people appraise their situation, while also appraising their ability to cope. In situations that are perceived as threatening, and when a person believes their coping to be lacking, he or she will experience the greatest degree of subjective stress.

In addition to appraisal-based stress conceptualizations, the diathesis-stress model is another important model for understanding the stress process. According to the model, two continuously interacting factors combine to determine a person's susceptibility to stress: predisposing factors (i.e., genetic and biologic factors), and precipitating factors that are environmental in nature (e.g., death of a spouse, loss of a job). This model accounts for individual differences with respect to stress reactivity. That is, some people are highly reactive to stressful events and, thus, more prone to develop stress-related illnesses.

In contrast with an appraisal-based theory of stress, conservation of resources theory (COR)—a comprehensive motivational stress theory—is built on the basic tenet that people strive to create, preserve, foster, and protect that which they value: their critical resources. COR theory posits that psychological stress follows circumstances that result in a threat of losing resources, experiencing actual loss of resources or not gaining resources following the investment of resources (*see:* **Conservation of Resources Theory**). Evidence suggests that, especially where the nature of the stressor is major, chronic and/or unambiguous (i.e., clear threat or harm outcome), the objective nature of events is the foremost predictor of psychological and health outcomes. Hence, research is increasingly detailing the nature of people's stress exposure *and,* secondarily, their appraisals and coping resources.

Another model has recently emerged that accounts for the variability in gender responses to stress. Taylor and colleagues (2000) posited a different theory for females she coined the "tend-and-befriend." This theory focuses on the interpersonal, affiliative process in people. According to her theory, women are more likely to respond to stress with social and nurturant behaviors. She links historical female roles of nurturing and caring for offspring, compared with male roles of hunting and gathering, supporting the notion that women may be especially inclined to seek social affiliation during stress. She also links the hormone oxytocin—a stress hormone more often expressed in females—to this befriending process. Oxytocin has been linked to affiliative behaviors, especially mothering.

Overall, the more details we know about the history of people's stress exposure, how this exposure influenced them, their family and greater environment, and their coping resources, the better we can predict their mental and physical health outcomes. People's developmental history of exposure to stressful circumstances has a major impact on their well-being, their interpersonal relationships, and their physical health.

REFERENCES

Cannon, W. B. (1932). *The wisdom of the body.* New York: Norton.

Holmes, T. H., & Rahe, R. H. (1967). Holmes-Rahe Life Changes Scale. *Journal of Psychosomatic Research, 11,* 213–218.

Lazarus, R. S., & Folkman, S. (1984). *Stress, appraisal, and coping.* New York: Springer.

Selye, H. (1956). *The stress of life.* New York: McGraw-Hill.

Taylor, S. E., Klein, L. C., Lewis, B. P., Gruenewald, T. L., Gurung, R. A. R., & Updegraff, J. A. (2000). Biobehavioral responses to stress in females: Tend-and-befriend, not fight-or-flight. *Psychological Review, 107,* 411–429.

RECOMMENDED READINGS

Hobfoll, S. E. (1988). *The ecology of stress.* New York: Hemisphere.

BRIAN J. HALL
Kent State University

KRISTEN H. WALTER
Kent State University

STEVAN E. HOBFOLL
Kent State University

See also: Aggression; Attributions; Avoidance; Biology, Neurochemistry; Biology, Physiology; Conservation of Resources Theory; Habituation; Learning Theory; Social Support; Stress Response Syndromes; Trauma, Definition

STRESS INOCULATION TRAINING

See: Anxiety Management Training; Coping Skills Training

STRESS RESPONSE SYNDROMES

Stress response syndromes are deflections from usual experiences that are instigated by precipitating events or changes in circumstances. They are caused in part by changes in life events or in the person (e.g., news of development of a serious disease). Existing diagnoses that might be included in stress response syndromes are acute stress disorder, posttraumatic stress disorder or PTSD, and adjustment disorders. Other unofficial diagnoses might include pathological and prolonged grief disorders.

These are stress response syndromes because they are change-induced crises that disrupt the dynamic psychobiological equilibrium of an individual within his or her environment, and can overwhelm the individual's capacity to adapt. While each disorder might have different criteria, the stress response syndromes share some general characteristics, including increased levels of intrusive or unbidden thoughts, and pangs of emotion ("intrusion"), and increased levels of avoidance, denial, and numbing ("avoidance").

Positive life changes as well as losses or traumas can create stress. Response to stress depends on both the magnitude of the stressful event, and the individual's psychophysiology. Within the wide individual variability of stress responses, a generalized tendency has been observed toward the opposing extremes of intrusive reexperiencing and denial of the stressful event.

Nature of Stressful Events

Life events of varying severity have potential to produce a form of stress response syndrome. Generally, the more severe the stressor, the greater will be the likelihood for the person to develop a symptomatic stress response syndrome (reviewed by Horowitz, 2001). Even seemingly minor events or those that are commonly part of human experience can precipitate a stress reaction, especially when the event is subjectively significant to the person and discordant with the person's view of the world and own response capabilities. Divorce, economic problems, difficulties with child rearing, retirement, and bereavement are some examples of events that are potentially stressful, but not necessarily traumatic.

Some events are so potent at evoking stress response syndromes that they are called "traumatic." Traumas may involve experiencing or witnessing a serious threat to physical or psychological integrity of self or others. Examples include combat, rape, natural disasters, and motor vehicle accidents. The stressor may set in motion a cascading series of associated events, such as economic hardship and displacement following a natural disaster. Such events can have enormous implications for self-organization, attachments, and meaning structures, and may in turn alter internal models of how one relates to others and the world.

Individuals differ in their level of stress tolerance. Persons with lower stress tolerance will "break down" at lesser levels of stress than persons with higher stress tolerance. Lower stress tolerance was more often found in persons with latent neurotic (i.e., anxious) conflicts or those predisposed to particular stress triggers and alarm reactions. However, virtually anyone exposed to enough stress may develop a symptomatic stress reaction (Hocking, 1970; Horowitz, 2001).

Stress Response

Normal and Pathological Responses

An individual's response to stress involves a mixture of elements from earlier unresolved conflicts, as well as recent experience. Cardinal symptoms include distressingly intense pangs of emotion and intrusive phenomena, as well as emotional numbness and maladaptive avoidances or denial. The two response tendencies may occur following all types of stressful events studied to date and, to varying degrees, across the entire range of stress response syndromes. Different stressors may cause additional symptoms, and sufferers vary in resiliency, areas of vulnerability and accessible supports, contributing to differences among individual reactions.

At least after major stressors, the intrusion and denial/avoidance elements have been observed to occur in a succession of phases in time. Horowitz (2001) abstracted the following general cognitive-emotional sequence from a wide range of variation in individuals and types of stressors: (a) initial realization that a stressful event transpired, usually associated with an emotional outcry; (b) suppression or denial of the threatening news, and emotional numbing (e.g., having difficulty experiencing one's positive or negative emotions); (c) alternating periods of suppression and intrusive reexperiencing of the event in cognitive, emotional or behavioral domains (e.g., avoiding discussion of the stressor, while experiencing intrusive thoughts about it); (d) further cognitive and emotional processing or working through, leading to acceptance and adaptation, or stable defensive distortion.

Pathological stress response syndromes result from intensifications and/or deflections from the normal stress response. The initial realization, if overwhelming, could be associated with a state of panic, exhaustion, dissociation (discussed elsewhere in this Encyclopedia), or reactive psychosis. The denial phase might lead to maladaptive avoidance (e.g., in form of suicide, substance abuse, counterphobic acts); or to a delayed stress reaction or depression. Excessively prolonged or intense intrusion states may turn into a prolonged posttraumatic reaction (e.g., PTSD). If the working-through phase is blocked before reaching completion, the individual may develop psychosomatic reactions (i.e., emotional problems experienced through physical symptoms) or maladaptive behavioral patterns; over time, these become consolidated into a personality disorder or a constriction with compromised ability to act or love.

Diagnostic Categories Pertaining to Stress Response Syndromes

The most frequently cited mental disorder related to stress response syndromes is PTSD (Horowitz, 2001). The criteria used for diagnosing PTSD begin with having first experienced a traumatic event to which the person responded with fear, horror, or helplessness, which was then followed for at least one month by some combination of persistently reexperiencing sensory aspects of the event, avoiding reminders of the event, and exhibiting an elevated level of physiological arousal (i.e., hyperarousal; *DSM-IV-TR*; American Psychiatric Association, 2000).

There are several other diagnoses for which stress is considered to be a contributing factor. Acute stress disorder is based on criteria similar to PTSD, but has a more immediate onset and the duration of the disturbance is limited to one month following the trauma. Adjustment disorder, in comparison to PTSD, contains a lesser degree of intrusions and avoidance, and occur in response to psychosocial stressors of lesser severity. Complicated grief/bereavement is diagnosed in a person whose symptoms of intrusions, avoidance, and failure to adapt persist for more than a year after the loss, and interfere with daily functioning (Horowitz et al., 1997). Mood and anxiety disorders can also be precipitated or exacerbated by stress. Brief reactive psychoses, characterized by intrusions and emotional turmoil along with one or more profoundly psychotic symptom (such as a delusion, or major signs of thought disorder), may appear suddenly and unexpected within two weeks of a powerfully stressful event. Thus, it is conceivable that future diagnostic systems will classify these disorders under a single etiologic category of stress response syndromes.

Psychological stress response syndromes may occur alone or in combination with biological ones. An organic brain syndrome should be considered in any trauma involving sharp bodily impact (e.g., car accidents) or extended physiological disruption (e.g., food or water deprivation). Additionally, persons trying to avoid involuntary reexperiencing of trauma-related content may turn to alcohol, drugs, food or other maladaptive habits in attempt to regulate or numb the intense emotion. These complicating conditions should be diagnosed in addition to, rather than instead of PTSD.

Biological Underpinnings of Response to Stress

The principal effectors of stress response and resilience on biological level are hypothalamic-pituitary-adrenocortical (HPA) axis and locus coeruleus-norepinephrine-sympathetic systems (LC-NE). Resilience has been associated with the ability to regulate the HPA and LC-NE systems within an optimal range during exposure to stress and terminate their activation once the stressor is no longer present. Dysregulation of these systems has been implicated in development of PTSD (Charney, 2004). With chronic stress, resultant prolonged activation of HPA and noradrenergic systems may lead to serious adverse effects such as immunosuppression, cardiovascular, and metabolic problems including hypertension, dyslipidemias, coronary heart disease, and osteoporosis.

Psychological Factors

Several themes have been observed in people who are working through stressful life events (which may occur as intrusive, deliberately contemplated, or warded-off ideas). These include fear of repetition of the event. Repetitions can occur by provocative actions or real life-induced recurrence. Repetitions may also be feared as internal, vivid experiences, including dreams. And repetitions can be feared, as activation of emotions related to the trauma in other circumstances.

Stress response syndromes may also be colored by fear of identification or merger with victims, shame over being helpless in the face of the event, rage at the source of the event with ensuing guilt over this rage, rage at those exempted, survivor guilt, fear of loss of control of alarm emotions such as fear, shame, despair, and rage involved in these themes, and sadness over losses. These may appear to be deliberately contemplated thoughts or as intrusive and involuntary reactions; they may also be interpreted as "warded-off" wishes.

The traumatic event may activate latent intra-personal (psychological) or interpersonal conflicts, or exacerbate existing problems. Stressful events are always interpreted according to the meaning structure of the individual who experiences them and this may include a range from realistic to fantastic or dysfunctional interpretations. Differentiating reality from fantasy is an important psychological aspect of ameliorating stress response syndromes.

In addition, many persons prone to anxiety, separation distress, or depressive disorders, may have stressful life events as one factor in the exacerbation of a cyclic illness pattern, or in the first episodic occurrence of these disorders. The incipient stage of the development of some disorders may lead some persons to expose themselves to increased risks and hazards (e.g., substance use), and therefore careful formulation should encompass an understanding of the pre-event history and life problems of the patient.

Psychological working through of traumatic life events must eventually change inner models of how one articulates with the world. The cognitive processes required for integrating change are often slow, and therefore extended time to review the implications of stressful news may be necessary. The mind continues to process the new information until reality and inner cognitive maps are brought into agreement; this processing is mainly unconscious. The tendency to persist in information processing until new external conditions match with inner mental models has been called "the completion tendency" (Horowitz, 2001).

Stress response syndromes, especially PTSD, can in some cases persist for months and years because the amount of information requiring changes in schemas (i.e., one's cognitive map of viewing the world) is usually so great that complete processing and integration are impossible in a short time. This relates to biological changes likely to occur at synaptic junctions and in large networks of interconnected brain cells. At the psychological level, it is important to note that the emotional implications may be at times overwhelming. Efforts to assimilate stressful news may be regulated slowly (i.e., inhibited) to allow the information to be integrated gradually, dose by dose. Excessive inhibitory controls may interrupt the assimilation and accommodation process.

A high level of control relative to the tendency of active memory toward repeated representation leads to the denial and numbing phases of stress response syndromes. Insufficient inhibitory controls lead to prolongation of outcry, as in protracted panic-stricken states, or to other intrusive states. Optimally adaptive controls reduce ideational and emotional processing to tolerable levels. Therapeutic efforts often aim to reduce excessive or strengthen deficient controls. By improving self-regulation the therapist bolsters the patient's own natural stress response of seeking optimal levels of coping and defense. These efforts enhance the sense of self competency and allow the patient to take advantage of available social supports.

Social Factors

Social factors join with biological and psychological factors to moderate or exacerbate the effects of stressful events on individuals. The conditions in a community may either promote resilience among its members or increase the likelihood of PTSD after a trauma/disaster. High levels of social support appear to protect against development of PTSD, whereas low social supports have been associated with heightened stress reactivity. Good leadership, high group affiliation, and strong, unambivalent ideologies are among the factors suggested to increase endurance. Weak social coherence will increase the rate of non-resolution of stress responses. The Vietnam War and its aftermath exemplify a situation of failed social support during times of high stress and trauma. Johnson et al. (1997) reported homecoming stress as the strongest predictor of current PTSD symptomatology in a cohort of Vietnam veterans in treatment for PTSD.

Treatment

There are a variety of psychological, biological, and social approaches to treatment of stress response syndromes. The first challenge is helping the person gain a sense of control over their moods and states of mind. Then the usual goal of treatment is to help the person achieve an adaptive emotional equilibrium, process the meanings of the stressor events, and re-schematize/re-characterize his or her identity and relationships (Horowitz, 2003).

Proper treatment deals both with regulatory controls and information processing that is regulated. As mentioned, the initial aim is to assist the patient so that he or she is neither emotionally blunted nor emotionally flooded. In general, therapists attempt to help people reach a restored sense of safety—a state in which they can use optimum skills in decision making, engage in adaptive coping, and be able to make rational preparations for the future. The focus includes efforts to restore a realistic concept of the self as stable coherent, competent, and worthwhile, with a sense of competence in work, community, family, and personal functions. While many losses cannot be compensated, stress response syndromes are treatable and can be an opportunity for personal growth.

REFERENCES

American Psychiatric Association. (2000). *Diagnostic and statistical manual of mental disorders* (4th ed., text rev.). Washington, DC: Author.

Charney, D. S. (2004). Psychobiological mechanisms of resilience and vulnerability: Implications for successful adaptation to extreme stress. *American Journal of Psychiatry, 161,* 195–216.

Hocking, F. (1970). Extreme environmental stress and its significance for psychopathology. *American Journal of Psychotherapy, 24,* 4–26.

Horowitz, M. J. (2001). *Stress response syndromes* (4th ed.). New York: Aronson.

Horowitz, M. J. (2003). *Treatment of stress response syndromes.* Washington, DC: American Psychiatric Publishing.

Horowitz, M. J., Siegel, B., Holen A., Bonanno, G. A., Milbrath, C., & Stinson, C. H. (1997). Diagnostic criteria for complicated grief disorder. *American Journal of Psychiatry, 154,* 904–910.

Johnson, D. R., Lubin, H., Rosenheck, R., Fontana, A., Southwick, S., & Charney, D. (1997). The impact of homecoming reception on the development of posttraumatic stress disorder: The West Haven Homecoming Stress Scale (WHHSS). *Journal of Traumatic Stress, 10,* 259–277.

MARDI HOROWITZ
University of California, San Francisco

MARTINA SMIT
University of California, San Francisco

See also: Acute Stress Disorder; Attributions; Avoidance; Biology, Neurochemistry; Biology, Physiology; Diagnosis of Traumatic Stress Disorders (*DSM & ICD*); Hyperarousal; Intrusive Reexperiencing; Learning Theory; Memory; Posttraumatic Stress Disorder; Stress; Trauma, Definition; Typology of Traumatic Stress Disorders

STRUCTURED CLINICAL INTERVIEW FOR *DSM-IV*—DISSOCIATIVE DISORDERS (SCID-D)

See: Dissociation; Dissociative Identity Disorder

STRUCTURED CLINICAL INTERVIEW FOR *DSM-IV*—POSTTRAUMATIC STRESS DISORDER MODULE

The Structured Clinical Interview for *DSM-IV* (SCID; First, Spitzer, Gibbon, & Williams, 1996) is a comprehensive structured interview designed to diagnose the major *DSM-IV* disorders. There are several versions of the SCID, including research and clinical versions for assessing Axis I (clinical) disorders and a version for assessing Axis II (personality) disorders. A SCID module for assessing posttraumatic stress disorder (PTSD) was created for use in the National Vietnam Veterans Readjustment Study (NVVRS; Kulka et al., 1990) and subsequently has become one of the most widely used PTSD interviews. The SCID PTSD module may be administered as part of a full administration of the SCID, but typically is administered as a stand-alone measure or is supplemented with a few other SCID modules to assess only the most common of PTSD's comorbid disorders such as depression, other anxiety disorders, and substance use disorder.

As with all SCID modules, the PTSD module corresponds directly to its respective *DSM-IV* diagnostic criteria. The module begins with a single question to screen for potentially traumatic events, that is, events that meet PTSD's Criterion A1. If the respondent identifies at least one such event, the module continues with two questions that screen for possible reexperiencing symptoms. If the respondent acknowledges reexperiencing at least one event, the module continues with two questions that determine the worst event (if there are multiple events) and whether that event elicited an intense emotional response, that is, meeting Criterion A2. Once an index event has been identified, the module continues with the assessment of the three symptom clusters, Criterion B (reexperiencing), Criterion C (avoidance and numbing), and Criterion D (hyperarousal). A single standard prompt is provided for each of the 17 symptoms, although interviewers are encouraged to clarify ambiguous responses or ask additional questions ad lib in order to obtain sufficient information to make an accurate rating.

The module continues with a question to determine if the syndrome lasted at least one month, and thus satisfies PTSD's Criterion E. Next, the interviewer rates Criterion F, that is, whether the syndrome is associated with clinically significant distress or functional impairment. The module concludes with several questions to establish age of onset, course, current and lifetime diagnostic status (rated as currently meets criteria, in partial remission, in full remission, and prior history), and current severity of the syndrome (rated as mild, moderate, or severe). Individual symptoms and other criteria are rated as "? = inadequate information," "1 = Absent or false," "2 = Subthreshold," or "3 = Threshold or true." A diagnosis of PTSD is assigned if all criteria are met, including exposure to a traumatic event; at least one reexperiencing symptom, three avoidance and numbing symptoms, and two hyperarousal symptoms rated as a 3; duration of symptoms of at least one month; and clinically significant functional impairment associated with the syndrome.

The SCID PTSD module appears to have good reliability and validity. Reliability estimates have varied, but generally have been strong, with inter-rater reliability (based on a single interview) typically higher than test-retest reliability (based on repeated interviews). The earliest studies were conducted with male combat veterans. In the NVVRS a kappa of .93 was found for inter-rater reliability, based on a design in which audiotaped interviews were independently scored by a second clinician (Schlenger et al., 1992). In a similar design, Keane et al. (1998) found good inter-rater reliability for PTSD ratings of current, never, and lifetime, with a weighted kappa of .68. They also found good test-retest reliability, with a weighted kappa of .66. Similar results have been reported in populations other than male combat veterans. For example, Zanarini et al. (2000) found kappas of .88 for inter-rater reliability and .78 for test-retest reliability. Further, Zanarini and Frankenburg (2001) found kappas of 1.0 for both inter-rater and test-retest, indicating perfect reliability. In addition, Franklin, Sheeran, and Zimmerman (2002) found excellent inter-rater reliability using the joint-interview method, with a kappa of .91. Regarding validity evidence, in the NVVRS the SCID PTSD module correlated moderately with self-report measures of PTSD, including the Mississippi PTSD Scale (kappa = .53) and the Minnesota Multiphasic Personality Inventory's (MMPI) Keane

PTSD Scale (PK) (kappa = .48), and had excellent diagnostic utility (sensitivity = .81, specificity = .98, kappa = .82) against a composite PTSD diagnosis (Schlenger et al., 1992).

The SCID PTSD module has several advantages. It is relatively brief, it corresponds directly to the *DSM-IV* criteria for PTSD, and it incorporates the other well-established features of the SCID. However, it also has several disadvantages. First, exposure to potentially traumatic events is assessed with a single prompt, which may not be sufficiently sensitive for some applications (Elhai, Franklin, & Gray, in press). Second, it provides only a single prompt for each symptom, leaving it up to the interviewer to generate appropriate follow-up prompts. This reduces standardization, potentially increasing information variance and decreasing reliability. Third, and perhaps most important, it yields essentially dichotomous ratings for individual symptoms and for the diagnosis. Because it does not yield continuous severity scores it cannot be used as a dimensional measure of PTSD, nor can it be used to detect changes in symptom severity.

REFERENCES

Elhai, J. D., Franklin, C. L., & Gray, M. J. (in press). The SCID PTSD module's trauma screen: Validity with two samples in detecting trauma history. *Depression and Anxiety*.

First, M. B., Spitzer, R. L., Gibbon M., & Williams, J. B. W. (1996). *Structured Clinical Interview for DSM-IV Axis I disorders—Clinician version (SCID-CV)*. Washington, DC: American Psychiatric Press.

Franklin, C. L., Sheeran, T., & Zimmerman, M. (2002). Screening for trauma histories, posttraumatic stress disorder (PTSD), and subthreshold PTSD in psychiatric outpatients. *Psychological Assessment, 14*, 467–471.

Keane, T. M., Kolb, L. C., Kaloupek, D. G., Orr, S. P., Blanchard, E. B., Thomas, R. G., et al. (1998). Utility of psychophysiological measurement in the diagnosis of posttraumatic stress disorder: Results from a Department of Veterans Affairs Cooperative Study. *Journal of Consulting and Clinical Psychology, 66*, 914–923.

Lisa M. Najavits
National Center for Posttraumatic Stress Disorder

See also: Alcohol Use Disorders; Comorbidity; HIV; Smoking

SUICIDE

There is extensive evidence that traumatic events can be related to the risk for suicidal ideation, behavior, and completed suicide. This entry is organized along two lines. First, it summarizes the literature on this relationship in children and adolescents, and then the association among adults. Secondly, all traumatic events are not created equal, so this entry explores some specific types of trauma, by age group, which may be particularly highly associated with suicide, or may be unique to the age group.

Trauma and Suicide in Children and Adolescents

Traumatic events that happen in the lives of children and adolescents are well known to increase the likelihood of reactions that may be either directly suicidal or that in turn increase the risk for suicidal behavior. The most common traumatic events explored in the literature include physical and sexual child abuse, the loss of a parent to death, and natural disasters or serious life-threatening accidents, particularly ones that involve injury. All of these events are not particularly unique to childhood; however, the psychological reactions of children to such events can very well be quite different from reactions to similar events in adults. There are also other events, such as experiencing bullying and witnessing violence done to a loved one (e.g., domestic violence), that may elicit a more acute response in children than in adults, or that may be events relatively unique to children.

Due to both immature neurological development as well as incomplete personality development in those younger than their mid-twenties, reactions to these events may be more likely to be severe and prolonged. Such reactions include reactive depression and/or anxiety, which in children can be exhibited by more traditional 'sadness' symptoms but may also be expressed as hostility, irritability, or violence, withdrawal, or severe anxiety and worry; as well as immature or dangerous coping mechanisms such as reckless behavior, deliberate risk taking, or deliberate self-harm (which is not considered suicidal behavior). Some of these reactions (such as sadness or anxiety) may at first be considered normal responses to a traumatic event, however, if unrecognized may develop into more severe depressive symptoms, including suicidal behavior. In addition, some of these reactive behaviors may be interpreted as disruptive or delinquent (e.g., irritability, hostility, aggression) due to their disruptive or irritating nature to parents and teachers, or their dangerousness/criminal aspects (e.g., reckless/illegal behavior, violence). However, there is evidence that letting such symptoms go unrecognized, or worse punished as bad behavior, may increase the likelihood of worse outcomes over time, including suicidal behavior.

Serious suicide attempts are often, though not always, impulsive (as opposed to premeditated) acts of aggression toward self. In adolescents and young adults, the ability to control impulses and to understand the full consequences of an action is not yet fully developed. This may place children and young adults who have experienced a particularly upsetting event at greater risk for suicidal behavior and attempts. In addition, if other mental health problems and/or alcohol or substance use are also present, the risk of suicide can increase dramatically.

Trauma and Suicide in Adults

The Role of PTSD

There is a large body of literature that links trauma to suicide in adults. However, the mechanisms of this link are not necessarily clear. Much of the research has shown that the link between trauma and suicide is mediated by posttraumatic stress disorder (PTSD). That is, experiencing a trauma causes the onset of PTSD, and it is the PTSD that increases the risk of suicide. Research has indicated that in people diagnosed with PTSD, high levels of intrusive memories and arousal symptoms increase the risk for suicide. It is possible that these symptoms of PTSD are less amenable to medication treatment in some individuals, or may engender more psychic pain than other symptoms, and thus increase the likelihood that suicide would be perceived by a patient as the only solution to such pain. However, there is little rigorous research to date that explores these hypotheses.

While it is probable that PTSD has a direct relationship to the risk of suicide, this risk may also be moderated by the presence of other mental disorders, including (but not limited to) major depressive disorder and alcohol or substance abuse/dependence. Major depression is commonly comorbid with PTSD, and though only a small proportion of people with depression commit suicide, the majority of people who commit suicide have depressive symptoms, if not a diagnosable major depressive episode. Thus, whether PTSD increases the risk of suicide may be different in people with and without a comorbid depressive episode. Similarly, the use of alcohol and/or drugs is a common problem in people with PTSD. It may be a precursor to PTSD (e.g., alcohol abuse may put people at higher risk of developing PTSD given a traumatic event) or may be the result of self-medicating for symptoms of PTSD. However, substance abuse/dependence increases the risk of suicide specifically through impaired impulse control. Thus it may moderate the risk associated with PTSD by adding an additional level of impulsivity while under the influence of drugs and alcohol.

The Role of Psychological Trauma Independent of PTSD

While there is much evidence that PTSD mediates the association between trauma and suicide, traumatic events may have a direct association with suicide, independent of PTSD. For example, there is some evidence that traumatic grief reactions, which are differentiated from PTSD as intense responses to the loss of a loved one, may occur as a result of a traumatic event to a loved one such as a homicide, accident, or disaster, and may increase the risk of suicide. This is a situation where a "normal" grief reaction to a loss persists and develops over time into a longer-term syndrome of grief that includes intense affective symptoms as well as comorbid psychiatric distress, higher risk for substance abuse, increases in physical pain, including experiences of pain that mirror those experienced by the deceased, and worsening of preexisting physical health conditions.

There is evidence that people who experience multiple traumas, either at once (e.g., being in a disaster where loved ones are killed) or over a lifetime (e.g., being raped or abused multiple separate times) can have an additive effect on the risk of many poor mental health outcomes, including suicide. One unique example of such a multiplicative effect may be seen in the effects of combat. Sustained exposure to life-threatening experiences, seeing friends killed, and participating, even willingly, in the killing of others, is known to increase the risk of PTSD based on the severity of exposure, and thus to increase the risk of suicide. Research with combat veterans has also demonstrated that those who have sustained serious injuries, as well as those who have high levels of combat-related guilt about their involvement, are at higher risk for suicide. Similar to nonveterans who have experienced trauma, highly intrusive and recurring thoughts regarding the combat experience appear to place veterans at particularly high risk for suicide, though it is unclear exactly why, particularly in those who are in treatment. It is clear that the presence of firearms in the home (or otherwise easily accessible), whether in a veteran or civilian, is a known and strong risk factor for suicide.

Combat may be one experience that involves sustained and repeated traumatic events, but it is certainly not the only one. There are many people in the world who experience sustained experiences of abuse, poverty, discrimination, deprivation, and helplessness in the face of horror. There is much evidence in the literature that such experiences are directly associated with suicide risk, independent of any other symptoms or mediating factors.

There is some, though limited, evidence that the type of psychological trauma may affect the likelihood of PTSD and suicidal behavior. In particular, it appears that traumas not of an interpersonal nature (e.g., a hurricane, tornado, burglary without direct confrontation with the burglar, or epidemic) may have a lower risk of suicide risk than more interpersonal traumas such as abuse, combat, or sexual assault. This hypothesis has some, but relatively little, empirical evidence, to support it. However, further research is needed to understand the role that types of traumas play in the risk for PTSD, and the risk for suicidal behavior.

Two types of trauma that are relatively unexplored in terms of their relation to suicide risk are (1) the trauma of a dramatic psychiatric event (e.g., a psychotic break, an involuntary psychiatric hospitalization); and (2) the trauma of previous suicide attempts (that is, a suicide attempt being experienced as a traumatic event in itself). Not much research has focused on these types of traumas. However, to those directly experiencing them, they are often seminal, and traumatic, life events. A first psychotic break or a first panic attack when a person though they were dying, could be a very distressing event, and could even potentially meet PTSD's traumatic event stressor criterion. Being hospitalized in a psychiatric institution may also be distressing, particularly if it was involuntary, which may have involved police or other law enforcement personnel; such experiences often also include traumatic events (e.g., physical or sexual harm perpetrated by patients or staff).

An unsuccessful suicide attempt(s) may also engender trauma, in a way that is often counter-intuitive. Many people consider a suicide attempt to be a deliberate choice to self-annihilate. However, those who have unsuccessfully attempted suicide sometimes describe the event as traumatic, in the sense that they had a feeling of helplessness and horror before, during, or in the aftermath of the attempt.

Conclusion

Psychological trauma, PTSD, and suicide are strongly related, though mediated, and mod-

erated, by many different factors. Clinically, a traumatic event should be considered an important event in determining suicide risk, regardless of the presence of any other symptoms or disorders. In addition, much research is still needed on the real risk posed by traumatic events and PTSD and their connection to suicidal behavior.

RECOMMENDED READINGS

Ferrada-Noli, M., Asberg, M., Ormstad, K., Lundin, T., & Sundbom, E. (1988). Suicidal behavior after severe trauma: Pt. I. PTSD diagnoses, psychiatric comorbidity, and assessments of suicidal behavior. *Journal of Traumatic Stress, 11,* 102–112.

Jamison, K. R. (1999). *Night falls fast: Understanding suicide.* New York: Random House.

Maris, R. W., Berman, A. L., & Silverman, M. M. (Eds.). (2000). *Comprehensive textbook of suicidology.* New York: Guilford Press.

Marshall, R. D., Olfson, M., Hellman, F., Blanco, C., Guardino, M., & Struening, F. L. (2001). Comorbidity, impairment, and suicidality in subthreshold PTSD. *American Journal of Psychiatry, 158,* 1467–1473.

Schneidman, E. S. (2001). *Comprehending suicide: Landmarks in 20th century suicidology.* Washington, DC: American Psychological Association.

Tarrier, N., & Gregg, L. (2004). Suicide risk in civilian patients: Predictors of suicidal ideation, planning and attempts. *Social Psychiatry and Psychiatric Epidemiology, 39,* 655–661.

RANI A. DESAI
Yale University School of Medicine

See also: Alcohol Use Disorders; Alienation and Trauma; Bereavement; Comorbidity; Depression; Guilt; Intrusive Reexperiencing; Self-Injurious Behavior; Substance Use Disorders

SUPERVISION AND TRAINING

Although extensive documentation exists suggesting that the psychological trauma-related difficulties comprise a major sector of general clinical practice (Gold, 2004), it is the general consensus that structured supervision and training in this area is rare (Courtois, 2002). It is therefore not surprising that it has been repeatedly observed that mental health professionals, first responders, and lay volunteers all frequently lack adequate training to effectively help people with psychological trauma-related difficulties (see, e.g., Martin, Young, Billings, & Bross, 2007; Russell, Silver, Rogers, & Darnell, 2007; Suite, Rollin, Bowman, & La Bril, 2007). In many graduate programs there is no formal coverage of psychological trauma in the didactic curriculum. Supervision in trauma work in graduate training often is left to chance, depending on where the trainee is placed and whether the supervisor happens to be knowledgeable about and experienced in psychological trauma-related treatment. Organized training in the supervision of trauma-related practice is even more uncommon (Wells, Trad, & Alves, 2003).

The literature suggests that thorough training in trauma-related practice is a multi-pronged enterprise. Unquestionably, specialized knowledge and skills pertaining to trauma is one of the requisite elements. Those whose emotional difficulties result from or are associated with exposure to traumatic incidents present with unique problems that require clinicians to be well versed in psychological trauma and its impact. Understanding the nature of psychological trauma, its common short and long term psychobiological consequences, the diverse syndromes that can stem from psychological traumatization, the unique challenges to forming a resilient therapeutic relationship with traumatized clients, and specialized treatment strategies for trauma survivors, are among the areas with which trainees must become familiar. Without mastery of this material, clinicians may inadvertently conduct psychotherapy in a way that exacerbates rather than ameliorates psychological trauma survivors' difficulties.

Lansen and Haans (2004), for example, note that supervision specifically designed for therapists new to psychological trauma treatment reduces the likelihood of common errors such as steering away from trauma-relevant material, responding to clients with countertransference reactions that intensify clients' distress and difficulties, and engaging in boundary violations. Such harmful boundary violations in the therapeutic relationship with a trauma survivor could involve adopting the stance of a friend instead of maintaining an appropriate therapeutic role or "boundary," or adopting a "rescuer" posture instead of one that assists the client in developing effective problem solving.

Beyond an understanding of psychological trauma in general, it is essential that trainees be made aware of the divergent needs of major subgroups of trauma survivors. Differential skills sets are needed for working with clients whose difficulties are related to (a) past or historical psychological trauma, (b) current ongoing psychological trauma, and (c) catastrophic or disaster-related psychological trauma (e.g., terrorist attacks, natural disasters). Working with historical trauma, such as childhood abuse, often requires therapists to be able to help clients confront disturbing material and come to terms with its debilitating consequences. Therapy for clients who are currently faced with traumatic circumstances, such as the persistent threat of domestic violence, calls for practitioners trained in assisting clients to recognize the potential danger they face and in facilitating the development of strategies that will maximize their current safety. In the immediate aftermath of a disaster, survivors need mental health professionals who have been prepared to respond to their urgent physical and interpersonal needs (e.g., adequate food and water, shelter, medical care, cell phone contact with loved ones from whom they have been separated during the catastrophe) rather than encouraging intensive discussion of the overwhelming experiences they have just endured.

As important as specialized knowledge and skills are, a basic principle of trauma-related treatment is that it is grounded in core generalist mental health best practices. Adhering to basic principles such as maintaining appropriate professional boundaries and supporting self-sufficiency rather than making excessive accommodations because of the exceptional circumstances of the traumatized client is indispensable. Since psychological trauma may contribute to or exacerbate a wide range of emotional difficulties beyond posttraumatic stress disorder (PTSD)—such as depression, anxiety disorders other than PTSD, eating disorders, substance abuse, dissociative disorders, and even personality disorders and psychotic reactions (Gold, 2004)—a firm foundation in the fundamental knowledge base in mental health is required for skilled trauma practice.

Although often overlooked, knowledge of life span development is another area in which trauma-informed practitioners should be trained (Chard & Hansel, 2006). Psychological trauma can have an extensive disruptive influence on the successful negotiation of developmental tasks. Obviously, this impact can differ markedly depending on when in the life cycle psychological trauma is encountered, and when in the developmental sequence intervention occurs. Only with an understanding of the normal course of development across the life span can trainees be primed to orient intervention to clients' developmental needs.

Another key but underidentified area relevant to effective trauma practice is cross-cultural competency (Brown, 2008). Perceptions of trauma and how to respond to it are inevitably filtered through culturally based perceptions and assumptions. Individuals and groups are often targeted for trauma via interpersonal violence on the basis of race, class, gender, sexuality, and culture. Moreover, culture-specific forms of social support can be a powerful buffer against traumatic stress. For all these reasons, cross-cultural competency needs to be included in training for trauma practitioners.

In addition to knowledge and skills, training and supervision in trauma treatment must address certain personal qualities of the therapist. Due to the centrality of empathic understanding of extraordinary experiences in psychotherapy for traumatic stress-related disorders, and the risk that clinicians' own unresolved traumatic experiences can interfere with their ability to help others come to terms with trauma, training and supervision must assist trainees in developing not only technical skills but also self-awareness (Wells, Trad, & Alves, 2003).

Additionally, in the course of bearing witness to the horrific experiences trauma survivors have endured, helping professionals are vulnerable to becoming debilitated themselves. Therefore, an extensive literature on "vicarious traumatization" (Sommer & Cox, 2005) or "compassion fatigue" (Gentry, Baggerly, & Baranowsky, 2004), which highlights the role of self-care in trauma work, is a vital resource in training and supervision of therapists who work with survivors of psychological trauma. Training in recognizing vicarious traumatization or compassion fatigue, and in steps to ensure self-care, include the teaching of strategies for recognizing, attenuating and coping with the stressors inherent in the treatment of persons with trauma-related disorders. In orienting trainees to be aware of and responsive to their emotional needs, it is often appropriate for supervisors to schedule regular meetings dedicated to providing supervisees with a forum for acknowledging the stressors inherent in treating psychological trauma survivors and receiving validation and social support (see, e.g., Gold, 1997).

A related and pervasive theme is the role of interpersonal connection, social support and collaboration in both the training of trauma-focused psychotherapists and in trauma practice (Miller, 2003; Pardees, 2005; Wells, Trad, & Alves, 2004). Exposure to psychological trauma is often isolating and stigmatizing. Psychological trauma taxes individual coping resources and frequently leads to feeling damaged, powerless, shameful, and different from others. Via vicarious traumatization, working with trauma survivors can elicit analogous experiences in the clinician. Trainees need to learn both how to cope with such feelings and how to form a resilient working alliance with trauma survivor clients who are struggling with these alienating experiences. As the field of trauma training and supervision evolves, means of drawing on interpersonal resources to promote practitioner resiliency, establish habit patterns of drawing on collegial support and collaboration as a routine aspect of trauma practice, and provide clinicians with a first-hand experience of how to foster a collaborative working relationship with trauma survivor clients will need continued development. Due to the centrality of these forces in trauma practice, group supervision is a particularly valuable component of preparing trainees and professionals to work in this arena.

REFERENCES

Brown, L. S. (2008). *Cultural competence in trauma therapy: Beyond the flashback.* Washington, DC: American Psychological Association.

Chard, K. M., & Hansel, J. E. (2006). Supervising therapists working with traumatized children. In T. K. Neill (Ed.), *Helping others help children: Clinical supervision of child psychotherapy* (pp. 193–207). Washington, DC: American Psychological Association.

Courtois, C. A. (2002). Traumatic stress studies: The need for curricula inclusion. *Journal of Trauma Practice, 1*(1), 33–57.

Gentry, J. E., Baggerly, J., & Baranowsky, A. (2004). Training-as-treatment: Effectiveness of the certified compassion fatigue specialist training. *Journal of Social Work Education, 40*(2), 305–317.

Gold, S. N. (1997). Training professional psychologists to treat survivors of childhood sexual abuse. *Psychotherapy: Theory, Research, Practice, Training, 34*(4), 365–374.

Gold, S. N. (2004). The relevance of trauma to general clinical practice. *Psychotherapy: Theory, Research, Practice, Training, 41*(4), 363–373.

Lansen, J., & Haans, T. (2004). Clinical supervision for trauma therapist. In J. P. Wilson & B. Drozdek (Eds.), *Broken spirits: The treatment of traumatized asylum seekers, refugees, war, and torture victims* (pp. 317–353). New York: Brunner-Routledge.

Martin, S. L., Young, S. K., Billings, D. L., & Bross, C. C. (2007). Health care-based interventions for women who have experienced sexual violence: A review of the literature. *Trauma, Violence, and Abuse, 8*(1), 3–18.

Miller, M. (2003). Working in the midst of unfolding trauma and traumatic loss: Training as a collective process of support. *Psychoanalytic Social Work, 10*(1), 7–25.

Pardess, E. (2005). Training and mobilizing volunteers for emergency response and long-term support. *Journal of Aggression, Maltreatment and Trauma, 10*(1/2), 609–620.

Russell, M. C., Silver, S. M., Rogers, S., & Darnell, J. (2007). Responding to an identified need: A joint department of defense/department of veterans affairs training program in eye movement desensitization and reprocessing (EMDR) for clinicians providing trauma services. *International Journal of Traumatic Stress Management, 14*(1), 61–71.

Sommer, C. A., & Cox, J. A. (2005). Elements of supervision in sexual violence counselors' narratives: A qualitative analysis. *Counselor Education and Supervision, 45*(2), 119–134.

Suite, D. H., Rollin, S. A., Bowman, J. C., & La Bril, R. D. (2007). From fear to faith: Efficacy of trauma assessment training for New York-based Southern Baptist church groups. *Research in social work practice, 17*(2), 258–263.

Wells, M., Trad, A., & Alves, M. (2003). Training beginning supervisors working with new trauma therapists: A relational model of supervision. *Journal of College Student Psychotherapy, 17*(3), 19–39.

STEVEN N. GOLD
Nova Southeastern University

See also: Countertransference; Practice Guidelines; Professional Standards and Ethics; Psychotherapeutic Processes; Therapeutic Relationship; Trauma-Informed Services; Vicarious Traumatization

SUPPORT GROUPS

See: Group Psychotherapy; Self-Help

SYSTEMATIC DESENSITIZATION

See: Cognitive Behavior Therapy, Adult; Cognitive Behavior Therapy, Child Abuse; Exposure Therapy, Adult; Exposure Therapy, Child

T

TELEMEDICINE

Telemedicine, or telehealth, involves remote video-conferencing technology for the provision of health services. Telemedicine is important because, although general medical care is widely available in the United States, specialty health care is often lacking, such as in geographically remote rural locations, and in institutionalized settings such as jails and prisons. In particular, mental health services are not uniformly widely available throughout the United States, especially lacking in rural settings (New Freedom Commission on Mental Health, 2004). Therefore, approaches have been developed to deliver medical or mental health treatment to the recipient's home or community, rather than requiring the recipients to come to a distant clinic or hospital site. Although home visits or community outreach are one possible method of bringing treatment to recipients, in many cases, it is not feasible or cost-effective to send treatment providers to the recipient. Telemedicine offers a practical alternative in those cases.

Little attention in the mental health literature has been paid to treating psychological trauma survivors or posttraumatic stress disorder (PTSD) patients using telemedicine. For example, two case studies of patients without local access to mental health care have been published. These studies demonstrated telemedicine's efficacy in treating psychological trauma survivors' mental health symptoms (Shore & Manson, 2004; Todder, Matar, & Kaplan, 2007). Additionally, a randomized controlled trial of 17 military veterans with PTSD found equivalent levels of patient satisfaction and session attendance across telehealth and in-person PTSD coping skills groups (Morland, Pierce, & Wong, 2004).

More recently, Frueh, Monnier, Yim, et al. (2007) randomized 38 veterans diagnosed with PTSD to either telemedicine or in-person treatment conditions, receiving Social and Emotional Rehabilitation treatment, a standardized treatment protocol. They found no significant treatment condition effects on clinical outcomes over time for depression, PTSD or general emotional distress. Furthermore, in a separate report from that study, the authors found comparable ratings of therapist competence and adherence for telemedicine and in-person treatment (Frueh, Monnier, Grubaugh, et al., 2007).

Clearly more studies are needed to test telemedicine treatments for PTSD, as only three reports from randomized trials have been published. At this point, it would be important to test exposure-based PTSD psychotherapies for their effectiveness in a telemedicine delivery format, given the consistent empirical support for in-person exposure therapy. It is unclear whether the emotional processing of psychological trauma (as done in exposure treatments) can be successfully implemented remotely via telemedicine, and thus this question should be empirically tested.

Several procedural considerations require attention when telemedicine is used, in general and for PTSD. For adequate picture and sound quality, telemedicine requires a personal computer and broadband Internet connection, and can use a sophisticated videoconferencing unit (e.g., with zoom and picture-in-picture advanced features), or a more economical "webcam" (a camera that is attached to a computer) available in most computer stores. Through this technology, a health professional in one location (e.g., an urban city's hospital) can treat a patient in another location (e.g., a rural health clinic or community center, or patient's home). Thus, telemedicine has been raised as an alternative for individuals who lack access to traditional in-person care. Despite earlier reports of technical problems with telemedicine, more recent equipment has resulted in picture and sound quality that is virtually live, with no audio/video delays (Hilty, Marks, Urness, Yellowlees, & Nesbitt, 2004).

Regarding *telemental* health care, a volume of literature has demonstrated that patients tend to be quite satisfied with this mode of treatment (for reviews, see Frueh et al., 2000; Frueh, Monnier, Elhai, Grubaugh, & Knapp, 2004; Hilty et al., 2004; Monnier, Knapp, & Frueh, 2003). Furthermore, one study found that approximately three-quarters of rural primary care patients reported that they would use telemental health care if it saved them from having to make a 1 to 2 hour drive to get in-person care (Grubaugh, Cain, Elhai, Patrick, & Frueh, 2008).

Much of the outcome research on telemental health care, however, involves case reports and program descriptions, with little attention to treatment efficacy. Furthermore, much of this literature has evaluated psychiatrist-delivered services, with little attention to psychotherapy trials. Few studies have implemented randomized, controlled clinical trials of telehealth's efficacy for mental health problems, by randomly assigning patients to telemental health and in-person treatment conditions. These few studies have generally all found that telemental health had comparable benefits to in-person mental health treatment.

Two notable limitations are apparent across this body of telemental health randomized clinical trials. First, almost none of these studies appeared to use a standardized treatment manual to ensure adherence to a standardized intervention protocol. Because it is impossible for the therapist to be unaware of the research condition in telehealth studies for obvious reasons, using a nonstandardized treatment protocol can influence how the treatment is delivered across conditions. Second, most of these studies included patients with a diverse set of mental disorders, resulting in limited conclusions about telehealth's efficacy for a particular mental disorder (e.g., PTSD).

REFERENCES

Frueh, B. C., Deitsch, S. E., Santos, A. B., Gold, P. B., Johnson, M. R., Meisler, N., et al. (2000). Procedural and methodological issues in telepsychiatry research and program development. *Psychiatric Services, 51,* 1522–1527.

Frueh, B. C., Monnier, J., Elhai, J. D., Grubaugh, A., & Knapp, R. G. (2004). Telepsychiatry treatment outcome research methodology: Efficacy versus effectiveness. *Telemedicine Journal and E-Health, 10,* 455–458.

Frueh, B. C., Monnier, J., Grubaugh, A. L., Elhai, J. D., Yim, E., & Knapp, R. (2007). Therapist adherence and competence with manualized cognitive-behavioral therapy for PTSD delivered via videoconferencing technology. *Behavior Modification, 31,* 856–866.

Frueh, B. C., Monnier, J., Yim, E., Grubaugh, A. L., Hamner, M. B., & Knapp, R. G. (2007). A randomized trial of telepsychiatry for post-traumatic stress disorder. *Journal of Telemedicine and Telecare, 13,* 142–147.

Grubaugh, A. L., Cain, G. D., Elhai, J. D., Patrick, S. L., & Frueh, B. C. (2008). Attitudes toward medical and mental health care delivered via telehealth applications among rural and urban primary care patients. *Journal of Nervous and Mental Disease, 196,* 166–170.

Hilty, D. M., Marks, S. L., Urness, D., Yellowlees, P. M., & Nesbitt, T. S. (2004). Clinical and education telepsychiatry applications: A review. *Canadian Journal of Psychiatry, 49,* 12–23.

Monnier, J., Knapp, R. G., & Frueh, B. C. (2003). Recent advances in telepsychiatry: An updated review. *Psychiatric Services, 54,* 1604–1609.

Morland, L. A., Pierce, K., & Wong, M. Y. (2004). Telemedicine and coping skills groups for Pacific Island veterans with post-traumatic stress disorder: A pilot study. *Journal of Telemedicine and Telecare, 10,* 286–289.

New Freedom Commission on Mental Health. (2004). *Subcommittee on rural issues: Background paper* (No. SMA-04–3890). Rockville, MD: Department of Health and Human Services.

Shore, J. H., & Manson, S. M. (2004). The American Indian veteran and posttraumatic stress disorder: A telehealth assessment and formulation. *Culture, Medicine, and Psychiatry, 28,* 231–243.

Todder, D., Matar, M., & Kaplan, Z. (2007). Acute-phase trauma intervention using a videoconference link circumvents compromised access to expert trauma care. *Telemedicine Journal and E-Health, 13,* 65–67.

JON D. ELHAI
University of South Dakota

See also: **Health Service Utilization; Primary Care**

TERMINAL ILLNESS

The impact of severe medical illness on psychosocial functioning may include traumatic effects consistent with posttraumatic stress disorder (PTSD). Terminal illness, referring to a health condition that is likely to eventuate in the patient's death, can prove to be a particularly potent traumatic stressor and clearly satisfies PTSD's diagnostic criterion for experiencing of a life-threatening event (APA, 2000). Like other traumatic experiences, being diagnosed with a severe or terminal illness can involve a sudden loss of control, physical threat, uncertainty, and intense feelings of fear and helplessness.

A number of studies have documented the traumatic impact that severe and terminal illnesses may have (for reviews see Green, Epstein, Krupnick, & Rowland, 1997; Kangas, Henry, & Bryant, 2002; Mundy & Baum, 2004). Some questions persist however, regarding whether a life-threatening illness can be directly compared to traumatic experiences such as rape, physical assault, natural disaster, accidents, or combat. For example, the content of the intrusive thoughts about the illness may be more anticipatory than reflective (e.g., worrying more about disease progression or death than about what has already transpired). Also, such illnesses are not discrete events, and individuals with these illnesses are unlikely to ever achieve a "posttraumatic" condition. Further, some symptoms attributed to PTSD may actually reflect symptoms of the illness or side effects of treatment (e.g., sleep disruption, concentration problems).

Nonetheless, traumatic stress reactions have been documented in persons facing a number of life-threatening conditions, including cancer (Kangas et al., 2002), HIV/AIDS (Delahanty, Bogart, & Figler, 2004), multiple sclerosis (Chalfant, Bryant, & Fulcher, 2004), myocardial infarction (Spindler & Pedersen, 2005), brain hemorrhage (Powell, Kitchen, Heslin, & Greenwood, 2004), and others. Traumatic stress reactions have also been found among family members of those with life-threatening illness, including parents (Stuber & Shemesh, 2006), spouses (Butler et al., 2005), children (Boyer et al., 2002), and siblings (Alderfer, Labay, & Kazak, 2003).

Most research on illness-related PTSD has focused on individuals with cancer. The shock and fear associated with diagnosis and the physical invasiveness of treatment are experienced as traumatic for many facing malignant disease. Prevalence estimates of cancer-related PTSD range from 5% to 35% (Kangas et al., 2002), and cancer survivors commonly report subclinical levels of intrusive ideation and avoidance. Greater cancer-related PTSD symptomatology has been linked to younger age, lower education and income, greater past trauma, more concurrent life stressors, poorer social support, certain personality traits (e.g., neuroticism), history of psychiatric problems, less knowledge of disease stage, dissociative symptoms at the time of diagnosis, fear of disease recurrence, shorter time since diagnosis or treatment completion, greater disease severity, and recurrent or metastatic disease (Kangas et al., 2002). Greater cancer-related PTSD has also been associated with greater emotional distress (e.g., mood disturbance, depression) and poorer overall quality of life (Gurevich, Devins, & Rodin, 2002; Kangas et al., 2002).

As is true with many traumatic experiences, those facing cancer commonly report positive life changes and personal growth due to their experiences and it appears that these reactions may be independent of traumatic stress reactions (for review, see Stanton, Bower, & Low, 2006). Examples of these posttraumatic growth responses may include increases in one's appreciation of life, spirituality, closeness with others, and a greater sense of personal strength (*see:* **Posttraumatic Growth**). This positive aspect of the otherwise dire health condition may result from actively engaging in and processing the illness experience.

Although effective clinical interventions for illness-related PTSD are yet to be established, cognitive-behavioral stress management (Antoni et al., 2001), supportive-expressive (Classen et al., 2001), and problem-solving (Nezu, Nezu, Felgoise, McClure, & Houts, 2003) therapies have been shown to be useful in reducing distress in those facing life-threatening illness.

REFERENCES

Alderfer, M. A., Labay, L. E., & Kazak, A. E. (2003). Brief report: Does posttraumatic stress apply to siblings of childhood cancer survivors? *Journal of Pediatric Psychology, 28,* 281–286.

American Psychiatric Association. (2000). *Diagnostic and statistical manual of mental disorders* (4th ed., text rev.). Washington, DC: Author.

Antoni, M. H., Lehman, J. M., Kilbourn, K. M., Boyes, A. E., Culver, J. L., Alferi, S. M., et al. (2001). Cognitive-behavioral stress-management intervention decreases the prevalence of depression and enhances benefit-finding among women under treatment for early-stage breast cancer. *Health Psychology, 20,* 20–32.

Boyer, B. A., Bubel, D., Jacobs, S. R., Knolls, M. L., Harwell, V. D., Goscicka, M., et al. (2002). Posttraumatic stress in women with breast cancer and their daughters. *American Journal of Family Therapy, 30,* 323–338.

Butler, L. D., Field, N. P., Busch, A. L., Seplaki, J. E., Hastings, T. A., & Spiegel, D. (2005). Anticipating loss and other temporal stressors predict traumatic stress symptoms among partners of metastatic/recurrent breast cancer patients. *Psycho-Oncology, 14,* 492–502.

Chalfant, A. M., Bryant, R. A., & Fulcher, G. (2004). Posttraumatic stress disorder following diagnosis of multiple sclerosis. *Journal of Traumatic Stress, 17,* 423–428.

Classen, C., Butler, L. D., Koopman, C., Miller, E., Dimiceli, S., Giese-Davis, J., et al. (2001). Supportive-expressive group therapy and distress in patients with metastatic breast cancer: A randomized clinical intervention trial. *Archives of General Psychiatry, 58,* 494–501.

Delahanty, D. L., Bogart, L. M., & Figler, J. L. (2004). Posttraumatic stress disorder symptoms, salivary cortisol, medication adherence, and CD4 levels in HIV-positive individuals. *AIDS Care, 16,* 247–260.

Green, B. L., Epstein, S. A., Krupnick, J. L., & Rowland, J. H. (1997). Trauma and medical illness: Assessing trauma-related disorders in medical settings. In J. P. Wilson & T. M. Keane (Eds.), *Assessing psychological trauma and PTSD* (pp. 160–191). New York: Guilford Press.

Gurevich, M., Devins, G. M., & Rodin, G. M. (2002). Stress response syndromes and cancer: Conceptual and assessment issues. *Psychosomatics, 43,* 259–281.

Kangas, M., Henry, J. L., & Bryant, R. A. (2002). Posttraumatic stress disorder following cancer: A conceptual and empirical review. *Clinical Psychology Review, 22,* 499–524.

Mundy, E., & Baum, A. (2004). Medical disorders as a cause of psychological trauma and post-traumatic stress disorder. *Current Opinion in Psychiatry, 17,* 123–127.

Nezu, A. M., Nezu, C. M., Felgoise, S. H., McClure, K. S., & Houts, P. S. (2003). Project Genesis: Assessing the efficacy and problem-solving therapy for distressed adult cancer patients. *Journal of Consulting and Clinical Psychology, 71,* 1036–1048.

Powell, J., Kitchen, N., Heslin, J., & Greenwood, R. (2004). Psychosocial outcomes at 18 months after good neurological recovery from aneurysmal subarachnoid haemorrhage. *Journal of Neurology, Neurosurgery, and Psychiatry, 75,* 119–124.

Spindler, H., & Pedersen, S. S. (2005). Posttraumatic stress disorder in the wake of heart disease: Prevalence, risk factors, and future research directions. *Psychosomatic Medicine, 67,* 715–723.

Stanton, A. L., Bower, J. E., & Low, C. A. (2006). Posttraumatic growth after cancer. In L. G. Calhoun & R. G. Tedeschi (Eds.), *Handbook of posttraumatic growth: Research and practice* (pp. 138–175). Mahwah, NJ: Erlbaum.

Stuber, M. L., & Shemesh, E. (2006). Post-traumatic stress response to life-threatening illnesses in children and their parents. *Child and Adolescent Psychiatric Clinics of North America, 15,* 597–609.

RECOMMENDED READINGS

Kangas, M., Henry, J. L., & Bryant, R. A. (2002). Posttraumatic stress disorder following cancer: A conceptual and empirical review. *Clinical Psychology Review, 22,* 499–524.

Stanton, A. L., Bower, J. E., & Low, C. A. (2006). Posttraumatic growth after cancer. In L. G. Calhoun & R. G. Tedeschi (Eds.), *Handbook of posttraumatic growth: Research and practice* (pp. 138–175). Mahwah, NJ: Erlbaum.

MATTHEW CORDOVA
Pacific Graduate School of Psychology

See also: Bereavement; Family Systems; HIV; Medical Illness, Adult; Medical Illness, Child; Posttraumatic Growth

TERRORISM

Terrorism is a special type of disaster, one caused by human malevolence that usually produces higher rates of psychiatric casualties than do natural disasters or technological accidents (North, 1995). Terrorism refers to a threat or action that creates terror or horror and is undertaken to achieve a political, ideological, or theological goal. Terrorism disrupts society by creating intense fear and disorganization and can be distinguished from other natural and human-made disasters by its primary goal of propagating terror in large populations. Terrorist attacks result in extensive fear, loss of confidence in institutions, feelings of unpredictability of the future, and a pervasive experience of loss of safety. Terrorism violates the basic underpinnings of daily life by attacking where one lives, works, and plays thereby shattering our usual routines, their predictability, our beliefs in a just world, and our sense of personal and community safety. Whether the perpetrators of terrorist acts represent powerful nations attempting to exert social control or small revolutionary religious or political groups attempting to impose their will on their opponents, the purpose of most terrorists is to change the behavior of others by frightening or terrifying them and to kill those whose beliefs or objectives are viewed as antagonistic to those of the terrorist. How the psychological response to a terrorist attack is managed may be the defining factor in the ability of a community to recover (Holloway, Norwood, Fullerton, Engel, & Ursano, 1997).

The primary goal of terrorism is to create terror. This simple but often forgotten element means that the targets of terrorism include not only those who are killed, injured, or even directly affected, but also entire nations. Thus, there are three populations of concern for mental health professionals: (1) those directly exposed, who may suffer from posttraumatic stress disorder (PTSD), depression, and alcohol use; (2) those who were vulnerable before the event and now must manage their lives with fewer resources (e.g., the loss of child care or a much longer commute)—such losses of social supports may tip the vulnerable over the edge of illness; and (3) the potentially millions who experience an altered sense of safety and hypervigilance. All three of these populations require care but the tools for reaching the different groups and their needs are different. Because the ultimate goal of terrorism is to

disrupt the social cohesion, values, and social capital of a society, protecting and repairing mental health is an important aspect of community preparedness and response planning.

Terrorists have used bombings, contamination, and weapons of mass destruction including chemical and biological agents. Terrorist events such as the World Trade Center attack on September 11, 2001, the Tokyo subway gas attack, the bomb that exploded on a busy shopping street in Omagh, Northern Ireland, the 1998 embassy bombing in Nairobi, Kenya, the Oklahoma City bombing, and the ongoing suicide attacks in the Middle East vividly demonstrate the strong psychological and social responses engendered by terrorism and their impact on our beliefs and values.

Weapons of Mass Destruction

Weapons of mass destruction (WMD), including biological, chemical, radiological, or nuclear agents, are particularly potent instruments of terrorist. The use of WMD by terrorists gained international attention after the Japanese cult Aum Shinrikyo released sarin gas in the Tokyo subway system in 1995. Concern was heightened when it was learned that the group had also (unsuccessfully) released anthrax and had attempted to obtain the Ebola virus. In the United States, the letters containing anthrax spores that were mailed to media outlets and government officials in October 2001 shattered Americans' belief that they were immune from such events. Although the actual destruction involved in a WMD attack is likely to be limited, the psychological impact can be more extensive as the altered sense of safety and the future resonates to distant sites. While it is common for terror attacks to overwhelm local resources and threaten the function and safety of the community, attacks that employ WMD pose particular challenges to communities and health-care systems. Chemical and biological weapons are particularly insidious because they may be undetectable to the human senses, can have prolonged incubation periods, carry the ruthless potential for causing high numbers and wide dispersion of casualties with a grotesque disease presentation. Exposure symptoms may appear innocuously common (e.g., flu-like) or be unrecognizable, thus heightening uncertainties, fears of contagion, and suspicion of others. Anxiety symptoms may be misidentified as signs of infection and the public may engage in fear driven evacuations or self-quarantines. Available treatments may be limited or without clear efficacy and a hoarding of medications may occur. Factors such as these will lead both casualties and the worried well to seek evaluation and medical treatment, overwhelming health-care resources, and creating competition for available resources. Further terror threats and hoaxes will exacerbate existing fears.

The release of toxic biological agents instills terror in communities (Ursano, Norwood, & Fullerton, 2004). An outbreak in one spot or in multiple spots can simultaneously spread disease, illness, distress, and community disruption for days to weeks to months to years. Social propagation of the resulting fear and distress can spread disruption throughout community groups and the social infrastructure. The sarin nerve gas release in Tokyo and the anthrax attacks in the United States demonstrated the particular ability of chemical and biological weapons to create fear and social disruption. In addition to injuries and killing victims, the anthrax attack also forced the desertion of commercial and public buildings, disrupted the distribution of mail, occasioned social conflict, and evoked considerable fear and concern despite the fact that these attacks produced fewer causalities than car accidents and probably no greater economic loss.

Health Consequences of Terrorism

The deliberate infliction of pain and suffering, as occurs in a terrorist attack, is a particularly potent psychological stressor. The behavioral and psychological responses to terrorism are not random and frequently have predictable structure and time course. Initial psychological distress responses include fear, helplessness, horror, disbelief, emotional numbing, dissociation, hyperarousal, anxiety, and grief. Distress is moderated by exposure characteristics (e.g., proximity and intensity of exposure to event, degree of personal harm, and role in response and recovery) event characteristics (e.g., event magnitude, complexity, lethality, duration, and cost), and perception of community threat or safety. For example, following the 2001 terrorist attack on the U.S. Pentagon, 4% of employees reported psychological distress before the attack while 34% reported acute psychological distress after the attack (Grieger, Fullerton, & Ursano, 2003, 2004). In New York City after the September 11 terrorist attacks, 7.5% of southern Manhattan had probable PTSD (Galea et al., 2002). Nearly one-third of people with the highest levels of exposure (e.g., 37% of those in the building or 30% of the injured) had PTSD. Rates of PTSD decreased to 0.6% 6 months later.

Posttraumatic stress disorder is not uncommon after terrorist events. Acute stress disorder and early PTSD may be more like the common cold—experienced at some time in life by nearly all. If they persist, they can be debilitating and require psychotherapeutic and pharmacological intervention. However, PTSD is neither the only trauma-related disorder nor even perhaps the most common. People exposed to terrorism are at increased risk for developing depression, generalized anxiety disorder, panic disorder, and increased substance use. After a terrorist event, the contribution of the psychological factors to medical illness can also be pervasive. Important is that injured survivors often have psychological factors affecting their physical condition.

Community Response to Terrorism

Terrorism's primary goal is to destabilize trust in public institutions. The effects of terrorism can echo through a nation. Disruption of the community and workplace increases distress, health risk behaviors, and risk of posttraumatic stress disorders. In a longitudinal national study of reactions to September 11, 64.6% of people outside of New York City reported fears of future terrorism at 2 months and 37.5% at 6 months (Silver, Holman, McIntosh, Poulin, & Gil-Rivas, 2002). In addition, 59.5% reported fear of harm to family at 2 months and 40.6% at 6 months. In the weeks following the bombings in London, 31% of Londoners reported substantial stress and 32% reported that they intended to travel less (Rubin, Brewin, Greenberg, Simpson, & Wessely, 2005). Those reporting greater stress were 3.8 times more likely to have thought they could have been injured or killed and 1.7 times more likely to report having difficulty contacting friends or family by mobile phone. Findings following the Madrid March 11 train bombings in 2004, again indicate that the magnitude of a terrorist attack is one of the primary determinants of the prevalence of PTSD (Miguel-Tobal et al., 2006). Those who are indirectly exposed to ongoing threats of terrorism may experience significant symptoms (Shalev, Tuval, Frenkiel-Fishman, Hadar, & Eth, 2006).

In addition to the psychological toll, terrorism may also lead to negative economic and social changes such as disrupted communication, mail, energy, and transportation lines; altered financial and insurance markets; reduced work attendance and productivity; and damaged or destroyed commercial and public facilities. Concerns about safety may alter food consumption or travel plans, and major purchases and life changes may be postponed.

In the immediate aftermath of a terrorist attack, individuals and communities may respond in adaptive, effective ways or they may make fear-based decisions, resulting in unhelpful behaviors. Psychiatric disease and psychological function including the subthreshold distress of individuals is dependent on the rapid, effective, and sustained mobilization of health-care resources as well as community level responses and resources. Knowledge of an individual's and community's resilience and vulnerability before a terrorist event as well as understanding the psychiatric and psychological responses to such an event, may enable leaders and medical experts to communicate more effectively with the public in order to promote healthy behaviors, sustain the social fabric of the community, and facilitate recovery (IOM, 2003).

The adaptive resources and capacities of individuals and groups within a community are variable and need to be understood before a crisis in order to target needs effectively after disaster (see Ursano, Fullerton, Raphael, & Weisaeth, 2007, for an extensive reference). For example, community embeddedness (i.e., the degree to which one belongs to and is connected in one's neighborhood and community) may be both a risk factor and a protective factor after community level disasters. Community and workplaces also serve as important physical and emotional support systems. A coordinated systems approach across the medical care system, public health system and emergency response system is necessary to meet the mental health-care needs in planning and responding to terrorist events (Ursano, Fullerton, & Norwood, 2003).

REFERENCES

Galea, S., Ahern, J., Resnick, H., Kilpatrick, D., Bucuvalas, M., Gold, J., et al. (2002). Psychological sequelae of the September 11 terrorist attacks in New York City. *New England Journal of Medicine, 346*(13), 982–987.

Grieger, T. A., Fullerton, C. S., & Ursano, R. J. (2003). Posttraumatic stress disorder, alcohol use, and perceived safety after the terrorist attack on the pentagon. *Psychiatric Services, 54*(10), 1380–1382.

Grieger, T. A., Fullerton, C. S., & Ursano, R. J. (2004). Posttraumatic stress disorder, depression, and perceived safety 13 months after September 11. *Psychiatric Services, 55*(9), 1061–1063.

Holloway, H. C., Norwood, A. E., Fullerton, C. S., Engel, C. C., & Ursano, R. J. (1997). The threat of biological weapons: Prophylaxis and mitigation of psychological and social consequences. *Journal of the American Medical Association, 278*, 425–427.

Institute of Medicine. (2003). *Preparing for the psychological consequences of terrorism: A public health strategy.* Washington, DC: National Academies Press, National Academies of Science.

Miguel-Tobal, J. J., Cano-Vindel, A., Gonzalez-Ordi, H., Iruarrizaga, I., Rudenstine, S., Vlahov, D., et al. (2006). PTSD and depression after the Madrid March 11 train bombings. *Journal of Traumatic Stress, 19*(1), 69–80.

North, C. S. (1995). Human response to violent trauma. *Clinical Psychiatry, 1*, 225–245.

Rubin, G. J., Brewin, C. R., Greenberg, N., Simpson, J., & Wessely, S. (2005). Psychological and behavioural reactions to the bombings in London on 7 July 2005: Cross sectional survey of a representative sample of Londoners. *British Medical Journal, 331*(7517), 606.

Shalev, A., Tuval, R., Frenkiel-Fishman, S., Hadar, H., & Eth, S. (2006). Psychological responses to continuous terror: A study of two communities in Israel. *American Journal of Psychiatry, 163*, 667–673.

Silver, R. C., Holman, E. A., McIntosh, D. N., Poulin, M., & Gil-Rivas, V. (2002). Nationwide longitudinal study of psychological responses to September 11. *Journal of the American Medical Association, 288*, 1235–1244.

Ursano, R. J., Fullerton, C. S., & Norwood, A. E. (Eds.). (2003). *Terrorism and disaster: Individual and community mental health interventions.* Cambridge: Cambridge University Press.

Ursano, R. J., Fullerton, C. S., Raphael, B., & Weisaeth, L. (Eds.). (2007). *Textbook of disaster psychiatry.* Cambridge: Cambridge University Press.

Ursano, R. J., Norwood, A. E., & Fullerton, C. S. (Eds.). (2004). *Bioterrorism: Psychological and public health interventions.* Cambridge: Cambridge University Press.

CAROL S. FULLERTON
Uniformed Services University of the Health Sciences

ROBERT J. URSANO
Uniformed Services University of the Health Sciences

QUINN M. BIGGS
Uniformed Services University of the Health Sciences

See also: Community Violence; Disaster; Early Intervention; Emotional Numbing; Etiology; Health Service Utilization; Prevention, Adult; Prevention, Child

THERAPEUTIC RELATIONSHIP

The therapeutic relationship, perhaps the most important of the so-called "nonspecific elements" in treatments for mental disorders, plays a significant role across therapeutic modalities, including pharmacotherapy as well as psychotherapy (Krupnick et al., 1996). As noted in Horowitz and colleagues (1984), the effectiveness of any psychological intervention depends, at least in part, on whether a safe relationship can be established between therapist and patient.

It is only within the context of this safe relationship that patients can gradually develop a sense of trust in the therapist and in themselves that allows them to reappraise traumatic life events and the meanings associated with these experiences. When implementing any psychotherapeutic approach, the patient must feel this sense of safety and trust in order to engage in the specific processes that constitute the technical elements of these interventions.

While the therapeutic relationship is essential to the conduct of treatment for any type of disorder, this bond is of particular salience and presents particular challenges when treating patients for posttraumatic stress disorder (PTSD). Due to the very nature of the psychological trauma to which the individual has been exposed, often including interpersonal violence or relationship violations, establishing a sense of trust and safety may be more difficult than would be the case with patients who have not experienced psychological trauma or are seeking help for other types of problems than PTSD.

In describing the optimal therapeutic stance for the treatment of adult survivors of incest, for example, Courtois (1988) observes that it is important for the therapist to maintain a position of openness to and acceptance of the patient. She recommends that the therapist maintain neutrality while simultaneously being active in engaging the patient. Neutrality involves the therapist communicating a nonjudgmental attitude to the patient verbally and nonverbally, and maintaining appropriate therapeutic boundaries. Boundaries include not telling the patient what to think, feel, or do (while providing guidance that the patient may accept or reject), and not disclosing information from the therapist's personal life that might lead the patient to be more concerned with the therapist's life and concerns than with her or his own needs and goals.

The risk in appearing nonresponsive is that the traumatized patient may perceive the therapist as judgmental and unavailable, a perception that precludes the patient's feeling safe enough to disclose sensitive material and engage in self-exploration. On the other hand, therapeutic neutrality also is important in order to prevent patients from feeling caught in the bind of feeling responsible for helping or winning the approval of the therapist. Patients who have experienced childhood psychological trauma, particularly if this involved abuse, neglect, or violation by a trusted adult or family member, may experience nonneutral therapists as replicating the failure of caregiver protection and support that they experienced during or after these incidents of trauma.

The aim of the therapeutic relationship in the treatment of PTSD (as well as the treatment of other disorders) is the establishment of an atmosphere in which the patient feels free to reflect on and express ideas and feelings more openly than would be customary in social circumstances. Of particular importance in working with psychological trauma survivors is remaining aware that the experience of psychological trauma and its aftermath may have resulted in certain types of relationship conflicts or issues. Since trauma survivors may have encountered significant others who were exploitive, manipulative, or unhelpful, it becomes particularly vital for the therapist to communicate that he or she will be receptive, understanding, and available.

The patient also may test the therapist in various ways to determine whether the therapist can tolerate hearing about his or her painful experiences and the distress associated with the memory of those experiences. Traumatized patients may be particularly sensitive to issues of power since their experiences may have left them feeling helpless and alone. By contrast with authoritarian or unavailable others in the patient's time of need, the therapist ideally remains respectful of the patient's autonomy, yet sufficiently supportive to enable the patient to experience and express the cognitive and emotional themes that may be too overwhelming to process alone.

While a positive therapeutic relationship is likely to be beneficial in all forms of therapy for PTSD, some approaches to PTSD psychotherapy provide specific guidance for therapists concerning the development and maintenance of a therapeutic alliance. Relational psychotherapy approaches to PTSD treatment utilize the research and theory on attachment—the emotional bonding between persons in intimate relationships, and the evolution of cognitive models of trust, cooperation, and caring—as a framework for assisting therapists in helping patients overcome the sense of emotional numbing, social detachment, and helplessness that is integral to PTSD by interacting with patients in ways that simultaneously foster the patient's autonomy and realistic reliance on the therapist as one (but not the only) trusted source of emotional support (Pearlman & Courtois, 2005). Although there has been very little research on the nature of the therapeutic relationship in PTSD psychotherapy or its role as a contributor to treatment outcomes, one study of an intervention designed specifically to facilitate a positive therapeutic relationship early in treatment found that patients who experience a positive therapeutic alliance early in treatment had the best outcomes in a subsequent prolonged exposure phase of PTSD psychotherapy. Further research and theoretical models describing the specific elements in and outcomes of the therapeutic relationship in the treatment of PTSD are needed.

REFERENCES

Courtois, C. A. (1988). *Healing the incest wound: Adult survivors in therapy.* New York: Norton.

Horowitz, M., Marmar, C., Krupnick, J., Wilner, N., Kaltreider, N., & Wallerstein, R. (1984). *Personality styles and brief psychotherapy.* New York: Basic Books.

Krupnick, J. L., Sotsky, S. M., Simmens, S., Moyer, J., Elkin, I., Watkins, J., et al. (1996). The role of the therapeutic alliance in psychotherapy and pharmacotherapy outcome: Findings in the national institute of mental health treatment of depression collaborative research program. *Journal of Consulting and Clinical Psychology, 64*(3), 532–539.

Pearlman, L. A., & Courtois, C. A. (2005). Clinical applications of the attachment framework: Relational treatment of complex trauma. *Journal of Traumatic Stress, 18,* 449–459.

RECOMMENDED READINGS

Cloitre, M., Koenen, K., Cohen, L., & Han, H. (2002). Skills training in affective and interpersonal regulation followed by exposure: A phase-based treatment for PTSD related to childhood abuse. *Journal of Consulting and Clinical Psychology, 70,* 1067–1074.

Janice L. Krupnick
Georgetown University School of Medicine

See also: Attachment; Countertransference; Psychodynamic Therapy, Adult; Psychotherapeutic Processes

THERAPEUTIC WRITING

Following a traumatic experience, it is common for a person to react to the shock through avoidance of anything resembling the trauma, with hyperarousal to trauma reminders, and with recurring intrusive thoughts of the event. Increased psychosomatic complaints and depressive symptoms are common sequelae as well. It is widely accepted that recovery from traumatic stress is facilitated by therapeutic confrontation of the traumatic memories in a safe environment so that conditioned fear and anxiety responses diminish, and fear- or anxiety-based cognitions are tempered. Typically, this takes place within the supportive context of the therapist-client relationship where the patient can be guided through the process and encouraged to develop new coping skills.

The notion that clients will benefit from discussing painful or threatening thoughts and emotions can be traced back to Freud and Breuer (1895), who recognized the impact of inhibition on "hysterical" clients. They reported dramatic results by encouraging clients to talk about traumatic memories and express themselves. Current trauma psychotherapies, such as prolonged exposure and other variants of trauma-focused cognitive behavioral therapy (CBT), focus more on diminishing anxiety and the development of coping skills, but the importance of a trusting interpersonal relationship between the client and the therapist is still deemed to be essential.

Recently, the requirement that such trauma memory confrontation and processing must occur in the presence of a therapist has been called into question. Instead, it may be possible for some individuals to overcome posttraumatic stress reactions by privately writing about their memories. This is called *written disclosure* because the person is disclosing what they remember in the form of writing rather than by speaking with a therapist. The idea behind written disclosure is that inhibited emotion is the main source of sustained posttraumatic symptomatology, and therefore once emotions are expressed, the client will experience less anxiety or other forms of emotional distress. Some have suggested that repeated recounting of the traumatic event promotes narrative clarity and integration of previously fragmented trauma memories, and that these changes are required for reductions in distress to occur. Regardless, what sets written disclosure apart from other therapies is the implicit assumption that a therapist's involvement is not needed for benefits to accrue. Instead, a client can work through memories and emotions on their own with only a quiet place to write, an interval of uninterrupted time, and instructions to guide the writing. The simplicity of this method makes written disclosure an appealing alternative in situations where therapy sessions may not be possible for a number of reasons, such as inability to pay for professional services, remote client location, and so forth.

Much of the research testing the viability of purely written disclosure has been conducted with comparatively healthy college student participants. This is problematic because the subjects of the psychological "trauma" writings in these studies often involve experiences such as disagreements with a significant other or family member, upset over being away from home, or difficulties with school—not technically traumatic stressors but rather mild to moderate sources of conflict or distress. Only a small percentage write about genuinely traumatic events such as physical or sexual abuse. Whether this is due to the participants not actually experiencing major psychological traumas or a result of choosing not to confront major traumas is unknown, but the results, considered typically positive, make it difficult to generalize to a clinical population. When clinical samples have been studied, the focus or the investigation or observed benefits have largely pertained to physical health outcomes. To date, there is little evidence from well-controlled studies that written disclosure by itself can substantively reduce trauma-related distress in clinical samples. Rather than calling into question the efficacy of written disclosure as a stand-alone intervention, the limited evidentiary base may instead reflect the practical and ethical barriers to conducting such studies with vulnerable clinical samples.

The typical disclosure study examines two randomly assigned groups of participants—those who are asked to write about a traumatic event they have experienced, investing as much emotion into the writing as possible, versus a control group of participants who are asked to write about a mundane subject such as the layout of their closet with as much objectivity as possible. Both groups write for 2 to 4 sessions of 20 to 30 minutes in duration each. Most early studies measured various levels of affect, the number of recent visits to a health-care center, and other health measurements (saliva cortisol or blood immunities, for example), as researchers in this were focused largely on physical health as opposed to mental health outcomes.

Nearly all published studies of this nature have found that those in the trauma-writing group experience a rise in emotional upset during or immediately after the writing exercise (Sloan & Marx, 2004). However, these studies have also found a correlation between emotional upset during the writing, and improvement of mood at the follow-up period. Some researchers assert that fully experiencing the trauma-generated emotion allows the person to then process the memory fully and integrate it into a cohesive life narrative. Several studies have found that those who typically have the greatest difficulty expressing themselves (e.g., those prone to rumination and those with low self-awareness) experience the greatest benefits.

Although therapeutic writing exercises appear to hold promise, it is presently unclear whether such interventions, by themselves, are capable of effectively ameliorating trauma-related difficulties in more severely distressed samples. Further, the magnitude of change that can reasonably be expected in clinical samples given the limited scope and duration of the intervention is certainly a concern. Finally, the mechanisms behind its apparent successes are still being debated. The questions raised are: Is the act of inhibition a stressful process that taxes the body and suppresses the immune system? Does writing allow for the processing of deep emotions? Does writing help prevent the storing away of traumatic memories by organizing a jumble of feelings into a structured narrative of the events? Does writing allow the person to reevaluate the events from a removed perspective so that they may adjust their perceptions—either of the traumatic event (situational meaning) or their environment (global meaning)? Does writing about the traumatic event encourage the person to develop ways of coping with their experience? Does writing somehow provide a sense of control and mastery over the traumatic event? Future research efforts will need to grapple with these questions and will need to operationalize and test possible mechanisms of action.

What is known, based on predictors of change in therapeutic writing protocols, is that disclosers need to invest emotionally in the task and also need to form a clear narrative through the process in order to experience benefits. While studies have shown that this is possible with a healthy, nonclinical population, it is presently unclear whether such an approach will be efficacious with clinical samples. By way of example, one study found that participants were often too inhibited to spontaneously cope with the subject of their writing and in fact experienced higher rates of somatic pain and frequented their doctors more often following the study (Gidron, Peri, Connolly, & Shalev, 1996). This suggests that in at least some clinical contexts where support and guidance are clearly needed, written disclosure may prove most beneficial as an adjunct to psychotherapy.

REFERENCES

Gidron, Y., Peri, T., Connolly, J., & Shalev, A. (1996). Written disclosure in posttraumatic stress disorder: Is it beneficial for the patient? *Journal of Nervous and Mental Disease, 8,* 505–507.

Sloan, D. M., & Marx, B. P. (2004). Taking pen to hand: Evaluating theories underlying the written disclosure paradigm. *Clinical Psychology: Science and Practice, 11,* 121–137.

JEREMY S. JOSEPH
University of Wyoming

MATT J. GRAY
University of Wyoming

See also: Cognitive Behavior Therapy, Adult; Disclosure; Exposure Therapy, Adult; Freud, Sigmund; Memories of Traumatic Experiences

TORTURE

The infliction of torture is performed with malicious intent and a total disregard for the recipient's dignity and humanity. Thus, torture is among the most egregious violations of a person's fundamental right to personal integrity and a pathological form of human interaction. The United Nations (UN) Convention against Torture and Other Cruel, Inhuman or Degrading Treatment or Punishment (CAT), adopted in 1984, defines torture as:

> For the purpose of this Convention, the term "torture" means any act by which severe pain or suffering, whether physical or mental, is intentionally inflicted on a person for such purpose as obtaining from him or a third person information or a confession, punishing him for an act he or a third person has committed, or is suspected of having committed, or intimidating or coercing him or a third person, or for any reason based on discrimination of any kind, when such pain or suffering is inflicted by, or at the instigation of, or with the consent or acquiescence of, a public official or other person acting in an official capacity. It does not include pain or suffering arising only from, inherent in, or incidental to lawful sanctions. (United Nations, 1995, pp. 294–300)

This definition is accepted by the 210 countries that have ratified this Convention. In summary, torture is defined as a political act inflicted by a public official, with the intent and purpose of extracting a confession or information, punishment, intimidation, coercion, or discrimination. Although the severity of pain and suffering may affect the severity of the posttraumatic distress and impairment of torture survivors, the most important criteria in the definition of torture are the intention and purpose. In addition, torture occurs during detention when the prisoner is powerless and under the control of authorities. The use of force and the infliction of pain under these circumstances violate the principle of proportionality, forbidden by international law (Nowak, 2006). This principle is the UN code of conduct for law enforcement officials, authorizing the use of force as is reasonably necessary under the circumstances for the prevention of a crime or in the lawful arrest of offenders. Torture has been defined by other organizations, such as the World Medical Association, and by individual countries in their national laws, but the UN definition is the most applicable and widely accepted among governments (Quiroga & Jaranson, 2005).

Amnesty International, in a worldwide survey in 2000, found that 75% of countries practice torture systematically, despite the absolute prohibition of torture and cruel and inhuman treatment under international law, even though these countries have signed the CAT (Amnesty International, 2000). Most countries criminalize torture in their domestic laws, but do not prohibit cruel, inhuman or degrading treatment (CIDT) or punishment. Countries intent on practicing torture may use an extremely restrictive definition of torture and make the severity of the inflicted pain the most important criterion of the definition. For instance, a memo written in December 2004 and circulated by the Executive Branch of the U.S. government (U.S. Department of Justice, Office of Legal Council, 2004) argued for a threshold of pain severity just short of organ failure before it would deem the act to be torture. Such a sharp deviation from how torture is conventionally and historically defined can be used to allow the practice of torture while officially denying its use.

Countries have developed a number of other methods to circumvent the absolute prohibition to practicing torture or CIDT. People have been forcefully abducted and detained in secret detention centers around the world. Torture methods are practiced in these places, but disguised by euphemisms such as "enhanced interrogation techniques." Detainees have been transported for interrogation aboard secret flights to other countries that are more willing to use torture. All of these practices are illegal under international law. International human rights laws and humanitarian principles absolutely prohibit the practice of torture and all other forms of CIDT. No exceptions are permitted under any circumstance, not even in an emergency.

Biopsychosocial Effects of Torture on Survivors

Assessment of torture survivors has only recently been systematized by the Istanbul Protocol, a manual on the effective investigation and documentation of torture and other cruel, inhuman, or degrading treatment or punishment. It includes modules for medical, psychological, and legal professionals. The Protocol was approved as an international instrument by the General Assembly of the UN resolution 55/89 on December 4, 2000 (OHCHR, 2001).

The mental health consequences of torture to the individual are usually more persistent and protracted than the physical aftereffects. The psychological problems most often reported are emotional symptoms (anxiety, depression, irritability/aggressiveness, emotional liability, self isolation, withdrawal); cognitive symptoms (confusion/disorientation; memory and concentration impairments); and neurovegetative symptoms (lack of energy, insomnia, nightmares, sexual dysfunction) (Quiroga & Jaranson, 2005). The most frequent psychiatric diagnoses are posttraumatic stress disorder (PTSD) and major depression, either of which may be found either discretely or concurrently. Other anxiety disorders besides PTSD, such as panic disorder and generalized anxiety disorder, are also frequently diagnosed among torture survivors, and in some instances substance abuse may

also be a problem. Longer-term effects include changes in personality or worldview, which at present are not adequately described in the diagnostic nomenclature. Complex PTSD and related concepts have been proposed to identify some of these responses (Quiroga & Jaranson, 2005). It must also be noted that the sociopolitical context of torture and the culture of those tortured can also affect the way in which survivors respond to the experience.

Studies show that perceived distress and controllability of torture stressors, not just exposure to them, is associated with greater likelihood of PTSD and depression. Higher resilience levels, meaning greater ability to maintain a sense of personal control, efficacy, and hope while enduring torture, is associated with less perceived distress during torture and less prevalent PTSD subsequently (Basoglu, Livanou, & Crnobaric, 2007; Basoglu & Paker, 1995).

Basoglu et al. (2007), in a sample from the Balkan War (1991 to 2001) studied from 2000 to 2002, showed that the division of torture methods into physical and nonphysical (psychological) methods is artificial because, from the point of view of the psychological impact, both produce similar levels of PTSD and depression. The division between torture and CIDT is also artificial because both methods produce similar psychological consequences (Basoglu et al., 2007).

The most important physical consequence of torture is chronic, long-lasting pain experienced in multiple areas of the body. Olsen (2006) showed that 10 years after physical and nonphysical torture pain is still highly prevalent. Survivors also experience diverse psychophysiologic symptoms. All torture victims who have been physically abused show some acute injuries, sometimes temporary, such as bruises, hematomas, lacerations, cuts, burns, and fractures of teeth or bones, if examined soon after the torture episode. Permanent lesions, such as skin scars on different parts of the body, have been found in 40% to 70% of torture victims. Complex lesions with temporary or permanent disability have rarely been documented (Quiroga & Jaranson, 2005).

A few medical consequences of torture have been clearly identified and well documented.

Falanga, beating the sole of the feet with a wooden or metallic baton, has been studied extensively. Survivors complain of chronic pain, a burning sensation. Visualization of the structure of feet with magnetic resonance imaging (MRI) showed a thickness of the membranes (plantar aponeurosis) that support the arch of the foot (Skylv, 1995). Acute renal failure secondary to rhabdomyolysis, or destruction of skeletal muscle, is a possible consequence of severe beating involving damage to muscle tissue. This condition can be fatal without hemodialysis (Malik, Reshi, Najar, Ahmad, & Massood, 1995).

A severe traumatic brain injury that is caused by a blow or jolt to the head or a penetrating head injury may disrupt the function of the brain by causing a fracture of the skull, brain hemorrhage, brain edema, seizures, and dementia. The effects of less severe brain injury have not been well studied. Damage to peripheral nerves has been documented in cases where victims have been suspended by their arms or tightly handcuffed (Moreno & Grodin, 2002).

Treatment for Torture Survivors

Treatment for torture survivors ideally requires a multidisciplinary approach, since the sequelae of torture are both acute and chronic, and may include physical, psychological, cognitive, and sociopolitical problems. Treatment also requires a long-term approach. Many treatment approaches have been developed, but little consensus exists concerning the standard of practice, and treatment effectiveness has not been scientifically validated by treatment outcome studies (Quiroga & Jaranson, 2005).

A generic treatment approach for severely traumatized patients also applies to torture survivors. The basic principles are: (a) do no harm; (b) focus treatment on the individual's unique treatment needs; (c) have a single professional act as a case manager; (d) provide pharmacotherapy for PTSD symptoms of impaired sleep, nightmares, hyperarousal, startle reactions, and irritability; (e) provide supportive psychotherapy; (f) support the physical, social, and medical needs of survivors; (g) do not refocus on memories of the trauma until the PTSD symptoms

are decreased to a level that the individual considers manageable; (h) do not encourage or discourage political activities or public activism until survivors are ready; (i) use groups for socializing and supportive activities to reestablish a sense of family and cultural values; and (j) support the traditional religious beliefs of the victim (Jaranson et al., 2001).

The medical, psychiatric, and social needs of torture survivors may be multiple and persistent or easily exacerbated. Specific physical treatment modalities include physiotherapy and medical care for specific conditions. Individual psychotherapeutic approaches include psychotherapy and pharmacotherapy. Of the psychotherapies, cognitive behavioral therapy (CBT) is well documented as effective. Psychotropic medications, most frequently antidepressants, may facilitate psychotherapy by reducing symptoms. Psychosocial interventions are community-based rather than individually based. Most of these programs take a development approach to empower and rebuild a community. Some strategies include socioeducational, social action, self-help groups, and training members to be leaders of their communities (Quiroga & Jaranson, 2005).

The sociopolitical movement advocating for the rehabilitation of torture survivors began at the end of the 1970s in Latin America. By the early 1980s, a handful of centers operated in Europe and North America. Today, nearly 250 centers or programs have been identified in the world, 134 of them accredited as members of the international network known as the International Rehabilitation Council of Torture Victims (IRCT), which has its secretariat in Copenhagen (IRCT, 2006). Since torture adversely affects not only survivors, but also their families and societies, many centers treat not only the individual but confront larger social issues related to torture, such as reparation, impunity, and the ultimate goal of preventing torture.

REFERENCES

Amnesty International. (2000). *Torture worldwide: An affront to human dignity*. Washington, DC: Author.

Basoglu, M., Livanou, M., & Crnobaric, C. (2007). Torture vs. other cruel, inhuman, and degrading treatment: Is the distinction real or apparent? *Archives of General Psychiatry, 64,* 277–285.

Basoglu, M., & Paker, M. (1995). Severity of trauma as predictor of long term psychological status in survivors of torture. *Journal of Anxiety Disorders, 9,* 339–350.

International Rehabilitation Council for Torture Victims. (2006). *Centres and programmes in the global IRCT network: An overview.* Copenhagen, Denmark: Author. Available from www.irct.org.

Jaranson, J. M., Kinzie, J. D., Friedman, M., Ortiz, D., Friedman, M. J., Southwick, S., et al. (2001). Assessment, diagnosis, and intervention. In E. Gerrity, T. M. Keane, & F. Tuma (Eds.), *The mental health consequences of torture* (pp. 249–275). New York: Kluwer Academic/Plenum Press.

Malik, G. H., Reshi, A. R., Najar, M. S., Ahmad, A., & Massood, T. (1995). Further observation on acute renal failure following physical torture. *Nephrology Dialysis Transplantation, 10,* 198–202.

Moreno, A., & Grodin, M. A. (2002). Torture and its neurological sequelae. *Spinal Cord, 40,* 213–223.

Nowak, M. (2006). What practices constitute torture?: US and UN standards. *Human Rights Quarterly, 28,* 809–841.

Office of the High Commissioner for Human Rights. (2001). *Istanbul protocol: Manual on the effective investigation and documentation of torture and other cruel, inhuman, or degrading treatment or punishment* (Professional training series No. 8). Geneva, Switzerland: United Nations. Available from www.phrusa.org.

Olsen, D. R. (2006). *Prevalent pain in refugees previously exposed to torture.* Unpublished doctoral dissertation, University of Aarhus, Denmark.

Quiroga, J., & Jaranson, J. (2005). Politically-motivated torture and its survivors: A desk study review of the literature. *Torture, 13*(2/3), 1–111. Available from www.irct.org.

Skylv, G. (1995). Falanga: Diagnosis and treatment of late sequelae. In K. Prip, L. Tived, & N. Holten (Eds.), *Physiotherapy for torture survivors: A basic introduction* (pp. 58–72). Copenhagen, Denmark: International Rehabilitation Council for Torture Victims.

United Nations. (1995). Convention against torture and other cruel, inhuman, or degrading treatment or punishment. In *Human Rights 1945–1995* (Blue Book Series, Vol. VII: Documents, pp. 294–300). Geneva, Switzerland: Author.

U.S. Department of Justice, Office of Legal Council. (2004, December 30). *Memorandum for Jamey P. Comey, Deputy Attorney General.* Retrieved April 18, 2008, from http://fl1.findlaw.com/news.findlaw.com/hdocs/docs/terrorism/dojtorture123004mem.pdf.

RECOMMENDED READINGS

Gerrity, E., Keane, T. M., & Tuma, F. (Eds.). (2001). *The mental health consequences of torture.* New York: Kluwer Academic/Plenum Press.

Jaranson, J. M., & Popkin, M. K. (Eds.). (1998). *Caring for victims of torture.* Washington, DC: American Psychiatric Press.

JOSE QUIROGA
Program for Torture Victims, Los Angeles

JAMES JARANSON
International Rehabilitation Council for Torture Victims

See also: **Asylum Seekers; Complex Posttraumatic Stress Disorder; Human Rights Violations; Political Prisoners; Prisoners of War; Refugees; War Trauma**

TRANSFERENCE

See: **Countertransference; Psychodynamic Therapy, Adult; Psychodynamic Therapy, Child**

TRAUMA, DEFINITION

Trauma is a fundamental concept in the field of traumatic stress, but is difficult to define and has been the source of much confusion and controversy. As distinct from the medical concept of physical trauma—the shock and transient or permanent damage caused to the body by severe injury or illness—psychological trauma is the focus of the present entry. Trauma in this context refers to exposure to catastrophic life events such as combat, sexual assault, and natural disasters. Traumatic stressors may include physical and psychological elements, as, for example, in the case of military personnel who experience psychological shock as well as a traumatic brain injury when wounded in combat. Traumatic stressors that involve no actual physical injury may nevertheless have profound effects on the victim's body (*see:* **Medical Illness, Adult; Medical Illness,**

Child; Somatic Complaints) as a result of their psychological impact.

A further complication is introduced by the fact that, like the more general concept of stress, psychological trauma is used variously to refer to three overlapping but theoretically distinct domains, namely, the objective aspects of the stressor, an individual's subjective appraisal of the stressor, and an individual's acute and chronic distress in response to the stressor. Currently there is no clear consensus on what trauma denotes, and this inconsistency in usage creates considerable ambiguity. Until such a consensus is reached, it is essential to recognize that there is no single definition of trauma, that the term is used in diverse ways, and that the meaning of trauma in a given context should not be assumed, unless the intended usage has been made explicit.

The official definition of trauma is provided in Criterion A of the *Diagnostic and Statistical Manual of Mental Disorders,* fourth edition, text revision (*DSM-IV-TR*) criteria for post-traumatic stress disorder (PTSD; American Psychiatric Association, 2000) and explicated by the accompanying text. The following discussion refers to both the specific criterion language and the text. Criterion A has evolved substantially since PTSD was first introduced as a diagnostic category in the third edition of the *DSM* (*DSM-III,* American Psychiatric Association, 1980; for a full discussion see Weathers & Keane, 2007). The original Criterion A in *DSM-III* defined trauma as a stressor that "is generally outside the range of usual human experience" and that "would evoke significant symptoms of distress in most people." In addition, the text illustrated this definition by providing examples of traumatic stressors (rape, combat, floods, car accidents, death camps) and contrasting them with examples of nontraumatic stressors (simple bereavement, chronic illness, business losses, marital conflict).

The *DSM-III* definition of trauma has several limitations. First, traumatic events have been found to occur more frequently than previously thought, and thus may not be "outside the range of usual human experience." Second, this definition confounds objective aspects of the event

with subjective response. Third, it provides little guidance for determining which events are in fact outside the range of usual experience and would be markedly distressing to everyone (Davidson & Foa, 1991). Finally, it relies on a categorical approach to identifying traumatic stressors rather than delineating the underlying dimensions of such events.

The *DSM-III-R* revision of Criterion A (American Psychiatric Association, 1987) built on the *DSM-III* version, maintaining continuity while adding several new elements. First, the two key aspects of the *DSM-III* definition were retained and incorporated into the criterion language with the phrases "outside the range of usual human experience" and "would be markedly distressing to almost anyone." Second, in an effort to specify the dimensions most traumatic events have in common (Green, 1993), a new list of qualifying events emphasizing life threat, serious injury, and threat to physical integrity was added. Third, witnessing and learning about a traumatic event were explicitly identified as other possible forms of trauma exposure in addition to directly experiencing an event. Finally, the nature of the distress was more specifically characterized as involving "intense fear, terror, and helplessness."

Although the *DSM-IV* revision of Criterion A (American Psychiatric Association, 1994) built on *DSM-III* and *DSM-III-R,* in several respects it represented a substantial departure from previous versions. First, a two-part definition was created, with the first part (A1) specifying the type of exposure ("experienced, witnessed, confronted with") and core aspects of the stressor ("actual or threatened death or serious injury, or a threat to the physical integrity of self or others"), and the second part (A2) requiring an emotional response involving "intense fear, helplessness, or horror." Events satisfying the A1 criterion are referred to in the traumatic stress literature as potentially traumatic events (PTEs), and events satisfying both criteria A1 and A2 are referred to as traumatic events (TEs). All of the elements of Criteria A1 and A2 appear in recognizable form in *DSM-III-R,* but in *DSM-IV* they were moved to the more specific criterion language and incorporated in the new two-part requirement.

Second, the phrase "outside the range of usual human experience" was dropped altogether in the *DSM-IV* definition of trauma. Third, although a distress response was retained in Criterion A2, the emphasis was changed from a normative standard based on how most people would respond to an idiosyncratic standard based on each individual's subjective response. Finally, a more comprehensive list of PTEs was provided that incorporated a number of stressors not explicitly identified in *DSM-III* or *DSM-III-R,* including "being diagnosed with a life-threatening illness"; "developmentally inappropriate sexual experiences without threatened or actual violence or injury"; "learning about the sudden, unexpected death of a family member or a close friend"; and "learning that one's child has a life-threatening disease."

The *DSM-IV* version of Criterion A could be seen as a narrower definition of trauma, given the explicit focus on life threat and serious injury, the conjunctive requirement of Criteria A1 and A2, and the emphasis throughout the text that the event must be extreme ["extreme traumatic stressor," "the stressor must be of an extreme (i.e., life-threatening) nature"]. However, critics have argued instead that it represents an excessively broad definition that has promoted what McNally (2004) referred to as "conceptual bracket creep," or a trend toward classifying low-magnitude or even trivial stressors as traumatic events. As McNally argued, an overly broad definition of trauma poses a significant problem for the field of traumatic stress. First, it could increase heterogeneity of research participants, thereby making it more difficult to identify etiological factors in PTSD. Second, it dilutes the meaning of trauma and could lead to misuse of the concept in forensic applications (*see:* **Forensic Assessment**).

The *DSM-IV* version of Criterion A does in fact include several ambiguous elements that if taken out of context and misconstrued could be used to justify an excessively broad definition of trauma. Notable examples include the phrases "confronted with," which allows for indirect exposure; "threat to physical integrity," which is ill-defined and, as with the use of "threat" elsewhere in the criterion language and text, allows for the nonoccurrence of an event; and "developmentally inappropriate sexual experiences without threatened or actual violence or injury," which seems at odds with the emphasis on life threat and serious injury.

However, these elements should not be evaluated or utilized in isolation; appropriate use of Criterion A requires that its constituent elements be considered in the full context of the criterion language and text, which together articulate the current conceptualization of psychological trauma. The *DSM-IV* version of Criterion A is not rigidly prescriptive nor does it attempt to provide an exhaustive list of possible PTEs. Rather, it provides a set of flexible guidelines that outline the nature of trauma and the parameters for distinguishing traumatic events from ordinary stressors. In this sense, these ambiguous elements are an asset because they provide sufficient coverage for the full range of PTEs and allow for the use of clinical judgment in classifying an event as traumatic.

Conclusion

Psychological trauma is an important concept, but difficult to define. The official definition, provided in Criterion A of the PTSD diagnostic criteria, has evolved considerably since PTSD was first introduced in *DSM-III.* The current version of Criterion A has been criticized as being overly broad, but is actually a viable, clinically useful definition. Any risk of conceptual bracket creep due to the more ambiguous aspects of Criterion A can be attenuated by adequate consideration of its overall characterization of traumatic events as extreme, life-threatening stressors. Criterion A plays a crucial role in the diagnosis of PTSD, serving as a gatekeeper by setting a threshold of stressor severity that must be met before symptoms can be assessed, and providing the basis for the differential diagnosis between PTSD and adjustment disorder. Therefore, it is essential to continue to clarify the definition of psychological trauma and eventually achieve a practicable consensus for the field of traumatic stress.

REFERENCES

American Psychiatric Association. (1980). *Diagnostic and statistical manual of mental disorders* (3rd ed.). Washington, DC: Author.

American Psychiatric Association. (1987). *Diagnostic and statistical manual of mental disorders* (3rd ed., rev.). Washington, DC: Author.

American Psychiatric Association. (1994). *Diagnostic and statistical manual of mental disorders* (4th ed.). Washington, DC: Author.

American Psychiatric Association. (2000). *Diagnostic and statistical manual of mental disorders* (4th ed., text rev.). Washington, DC: Author.

Davidson, J. R. T., & Foa, E. B. (1991). Diagnostic issues in posttraumatic stress disorder: Considerations for the DSM-IV. *Journal of Abnormal Psychology, 100,* 346–355.

Green, B. L. (1993). Identifying survivors at risk: Trauma and stressors across events. In J. P. Wilson & B. Raphael (Eds.), *International handbook of traumatic stress syndromes* (pp. 135–144). New York: Plenum Press.

McNally, R. J. (2004). Conceptual problems with the DSM-IV criteria for posttraumatic stress disorder. In G. M. Rosen (Ed.), *Posttraumatic stress disorder: Issues and controversies* (pp. 1–14). Hoboken, NJ: Wiley.

Weathers, F. W., & Keane, T. M. (2007). The Criterion A problem revisited: Controversies and challenges in defining and measuring psychological trauma. *Journal of Traumatic Stress, 20,* 107–121.

Frank W. Weathers
Auburn University

Terence M. Keane
National Center for Posttraumatic Stress Disorder

See also: Diagnosis of Traumatic Stress Disorders (*DSM & ICD*); Etiology; Exposure Therapy, Child; Posttraumatic Stress Disorder, Diagnosis of; Stress; Stress Response Syndromes

TRAUMA-FOCUSED COGNITIVE BEHAVIOR THERAPY

See: Cognitive Behavior Therapy, Child Abuse; Cognitive Behavior Therapy, Childhood Traumatic Grief

TRAUMA-INFORMED SERVICES

Trauma-informed human services are services that have been modified to incorporate knowledge about psychological trauma into all facets of service delivery. Specifically, in trauma-informed human services, an understanding of the prevalence and consequences of psychological trauma and of the factors that facilitate recovery from traumatic stress shapes the activities, physical settings, and relationships involved in providing help to people in need. For example, because trauma disrupts a person's core belief that the world is a safe and secure place, trauma survivors are acutely sensitive to issues of safety and security. Consequently, trauma-informed human services, whether they are delivered in a psychological, medical, or even a criminal justice service system, should be provided in a physically safe setting and delivered by staff who are trained to maintain appropriate emotional and physical boundaries.

Trauma-informed approaches are generally contrasted with *trauma-specific* services (Harris & Fallot, 2001). The primary tasks of the latter are to address directly the impact of trauma and to facilitate healing and recovery; therapeutic interventions focusing on PTSD or other trauma sequelae are, in this sense, trauma-specific. In contrast, *any* service or program can be trauma-informed, regardless of its primary goal or its size and complexity. Individual or group interventions can be trauma-informed by taking an understanding of trauma into account in their structure or content. Substance abuse groups, for example, may address connections between trauma and addictions. Most commonly, though, the trauma-informed approach applies to larger programs, agencies, or systems of care. These service *contexts,* characterized by a special awareness of the particular strengths, challenges, and vulnerabilities of trauma survivors, arrange their settings and activities to be safe, welcoming, and engaging for service recipients.

A unique aspect of trauma-informed services, whether at the level of the individual practitioner or the human service program is the effort to minimize the possibility of reenacting trauma-related dynamics and thus causing retraumatization. Trauma-related dynamics refer to the interpersonal patterns that characterize relationships in which psychological trauma occurs (such as abusive or violent families) or that have been adversely impacted by psychological trauma (such as families whose members have experienced war, disaster, or community violence). Finkelhor (1987) describes four "traumagenic dynamics" that arise from sexual abuse, which are relational dilemmas that survivors struggle to overcome and that services must not replicate: stigma, powerlessness, betrayal, and sexualization. For example, a typical abuse dynamic occurs when the victim of abuse is forced to do things against his or her will, potentially replicating the traumagenic dynamic of powerlessness. In such an instance, the person has no say in making decisions nor in preventing the abuse and consequently may feel frightened and threatened rather than safe and able to regain healthy functioning.

Any human service system that replicates traumagenic dynamics such as disempowerment is inadvertently causing the individual to feel revictimized in the service/care relationship. A trauma-informed knowledge of this dynamic might result in providers paying special attention to giving consumers an active voice in the services they receive and to providing consumers a standard mechanism whereby they might appeal decisions they did not like without fear of reprisal. Thus, trauma informed services do not have to specifically provide treatment for traumatic stress disorders, but they recognize the impact that traumatic stress has had on the consumers of their services and develop approaches to delivering their services that enhance trauma survivors' sense of safety, trust, and empowerment.

Though professional consensus has begun to emerge around this basic definition of trauma-informed services, there are many paths to implementing trauma-informed approaches. Most share the conviction that becoming trauma-informed involves a fundamental paradigm shift that moves trauma from the periphery to the center of a program's understanding and practice. Conceptualizations of psychological trauma and its impact, of the consumer-survivor, of the services offered, and of the relationship between staff and consumer are reformulated in a trauma-sensitive way (Harris & Fallot, 2001). In this model, psychological trauma is viewed as a core event (or series of events) around which the person's subsequent life experiences are shaped. A trauma survivor's "symptoms" tend to be seen as extensions of understandable attempts to cope with traumatic events rather than as an illness or other deficit. Survivors' skills and strengths are assessed, affirmed, and enhanced. Collaborative rather than hierarchical service relationships are valued, built around recovery goals and a time line comfortable for the consumer. Consumer-survivors therefore play a central role in planning, implementing, and evaluating trauma-informed services. Based on the experiences and priorities of trauma survivors, trauma-informed programs adopt guiding principles that offer consistent alternatives to potentially harmful traumagenic-dynamics (Finkelhor, 1987): safety, trustworthiness, choice, collaboration, and empowerment.

Trauma-informed approaches attend to all aspects of programmatic culture: informal activities and the physical environment as well as formal policies and procedures; support staff as well as direct service staff; and direct services as well as systems-level processes. Universal screening for psychological trauma and traumatic stress is expected in trauma-informed services. Providers then, as appropriate, may discuss with individuals their particular history of trauma exposure and their specific responses to trauma in a more extensive assessment as well as ensuring that service planning takes into account this history and the strengths and vulnerabilities that each survivor has as a result of having experienced psychological trauma. In trauma-informed settings, training and supervision support staff in making referrals for trauma-specific treatments when indicated.

In terms of staff education, training in trauma-informed principles and practices is offered for *all* staff (including administrators). The primary goal of such general training is to enhance all staff members' understanding of traumatic stress so that they may respond more positively to trauma survivors in their own work roles. For example, reception and other support staff may focus on becoming more hospitable and engaging with consumers and on handling difficult situations in ways that minimize the possibility of escalation and inadvertent retraumatization. Residential staff learn about the potential "triggers" for trauma-related responses that are part of many living arrangements (such as limited privacy, shared spaces, staff access to bedrooms) Administrators actively support trauma-informed changes in organizational policies and in the physical and interpersonal setting. Where the human service agency is also a mental health service provider, administrators provide the capacity to deliver effective, accessible, trauma-specific interventions. Human resource practices also prioritize sensitivity to the experience of psychological trauma. Interviews of prospective staff include questions about their knowledge of psychological trauma. Orientation for all new staff may present basic information about trauma and emphasize the centrality of trauma-informed approaches in the agency's mission. Employee performance evaluation and promotion policies also may give weight to continuing education in the field of psychological trauma or to on-the-job accomplishments that enhance the program's ability to deliver trauma-informed services. Finally, and very importantly, trauma-informed agencies emphasize the necessity of staff support and care in order to help providers and other staff members identify and deal with their own work-related stress in serving trauma survivors.

Research examining the effectiveness of trauma-informed approaches is in the early stages. The Women, Co-Occurring Disorders, and Violence Study, a multisite project funded by the federal Substance Abuse and Mental Health Services Administration, has provided preliminary evidence in support of the enhanced effectiveness of trauma-informed services, in a quasi-experimental comparison to usual services (Morrissey et al., 2005). Ongoing work focuses on the further operational specification of the concept of trauma-informed services and the effects of implementing such services in a wide variety of settings.

REFERENCES

Finkelhor, D. (1987). The trauma of child sexual abuse: Two models. *Journal of Interpersonal Violence, 2,* 348–366.

Harris, M., & Fallot, R. D. (Eds.). (2001). *Using trauma theory to design service systems: New directions for mental health services series.* San Francisco: Jossey-Bass.

Morrissey, J., Jackson, E., Ellis, A., Amaro, H., Brown, V., & Najavits, L. (2005). Twelve-month outcomes of trauma-informed interventions for women with co-occurring disorders. *Psychiatric Services, 56,* 1213–1222.

Roger D. Fallot
Community Connections

Maxine Harris
Community Connections

See also: Cultural and Trauma; Practice Guidelines; Professional Standards and Ethics; Psychoeducation; Supervision and Training

TRAUMA SYMPTOM CHECKLIST FOR CHILDREN

The Trauma Symptom Checklist for Children (TSCC; Briere, 1996) is a standardized, 54-item self-report measure of posttraumatic symptomatology in children ages 8 to 16 years old. It contains two validity scales (Underresponse and Hyperresponse), measuring potential under- and overreporting of symptoms, and six clinical scales (Anxiety, Depression, Posttraumatic Stress, Sexual Concerns, Dissociation, and Anger), tapping a range of symptom clusters commonly seen in traumatized children. Two TSCC scales have subscales (Sexual Concerns contains Sexual Preoccupation and Sexual Distress, Dissociation contains Fantasy and Overt Dissociation). The frequency of each symptom item is rated on a scale ranging from 0 ("never") to 3 ("almost all of the time"). Symptoms are not anchored to a specific trauma, but, rather, reflect the overall level of trauma-related distress reported by the child. As a result, the TSCC does not render a diagnosis of posttraumatic stress disorder (PTSD).

The TSCC typically requires approximately 10 to 20 minutes to complete. A 44-item alternate version of the TSCC (the TSCC-A) does not contain Sexual Concerns items, for use in circumstances where sexual item content must be avoided. There is also a parent-report instrument version that parallels the TSCC at the scale level (the Trauma Symptom Checklist for Young Children or TSCYC; Briere, 2005), used for children 3 to 12 years of age.

Based on a large ($N > 3,000$) sample of urban, suburban, and inner city children, separate norms are available for males and females and for two age groups (8 to 12 and 13 to 16). Seventeen-year-olds also can be evaluated on the TSCC, using normative adjustments described in the TSCC manual. Various reviews of the TSCC suggest that it is internally consistent and has various indices of validity in clinical, nonclinical, and juvenile justice contexts (e.g., Crouch, Smith, Ezzell, & Saunders, 1999; Nader, 2004; Wolpaw, Ford, Newman, Davis, & Briere, 2005). As is generally true when interpreting psychological tests, data from the TSCC should be considered in the context of other psychological instruments and at least one clinical interview. Because children and their parents often disagree, to some extent, on the child's psychological distress, it is often helpful to administer both a child-report (e.g., the TSCC) and a caretaker-report of child symptoms (Friedrich, 2002; Lanktree et al., in press).

REFERENCES

Briere, J. (1996). *Trauma Symptom Checklist for Children (TSCC)*. Odessa, FL: Psychological Assessment Resources.

Briere, J. (2005). *Trauma Symptom Checklist for Young Children (TSCYC)*. Odessa, FL: Psychological Assessment Resources.

Crouch, J. L., Smith, D. W., Ezzell, C. E., & Saunders, B. E. (1999). Measuring reactions to sexual trauma among children: Comparing the Children's Impact of Events Scale and the Trauma Symptom Checklist for Children. *Child Maltreatment, 4,* 255–263.

Friedrich, W. N. (2002). *Psychological assessment of sexually abused children and their families*. Thousand Oaks, CA: Sage.

Lanktree, C. B., Gilbert, A. M., Briere, J., Taylor, N., Chen, K., Maida, C. A., et al. (in press). Multi-informant assessment of maltreated children: Convergent and discriminant validity of the TSC-C and TSC-YC. *Child Abuse and Neglect*.

Nader, K. O. (2004). Assessing traumatic experiences in children and adolescents: Self-reports of DSM PTSD criteria B-D symptoms. In J. P. Wilson & T. M. Keane (Eds.), *Assessing psychological trauma and PTSD* (2nd ed., pp. 513–537). New York: Guilford Press.

Wolpaw, J. M., Ford, J. D., Newman, E., Davis, J. L., & Briere, J. (2005). Trauma Symptom Checklist for Children. In T. Grisso, G. Vincent, & D. Seagrave (Eds.), *Handbook of mental health screening and assessment for juvenile justice* (pp. 152–165). New York: Guilford Press.

JOHN BRIERE
University of Southern California

See also: Abuse, Child Sexual; Assessment, Psychometric, Child; Child Maltreatment

TRAUMA SYMPTOM INVENTORY

The Trauma Symptom Inventory (TSI; Briere, 1995) is a self-report survey measure that can be used to assess a wide range of symptoms potentially arising from trauma exposure. It evaluates not only classic symptoms of posttraumatic stress (i.e., symptoms such as flashbacks, numbing, avoidance behaviors, and jumpiness), but also more complex issues and behaviors associated with chronic and/or early trauma, such as dissociation, identity disturbance, self-injury, interpersonal problems, aggression, and sexually dysfunctional behaviors. The TSI related to posttraumatic stress in adults. It is composed of 100 symptom—items that are rated on a 0 ("never") to 3 ("often") scale according to how often each has occurred in the prior 6 months . . . standardized, 100-item psychometric review measure of posttraumatic symptoms in adults. It is appropriate for adults aged 18 or older, and requires a fifth to seventh grade reading level. It does not generate *DSM-IV* diagnoses; instead, it is intended to evaluate the relative level of various forms of posttraumatic distress.

The TSI contains 10 "clinical" scales for assessing categorically distinct types of symptoms and three "validity" scales to help determine whether the respondent is underreporting symptoms, reporting symptoms that are unlikely to be true or that reflect psychosis, or reporting symptoms in an inconsistent manner ensure that the responses provided reflect the respondent's actual experience. The clinical scales are labeled Anxious Arousal, Depression, Anger/Irritability, Intrusive Experiences, Defensive Avoidance, Dissociation, Sexual Concerns, Dysfunctional Sexual Behavior, Impaired Self-reference, and Tension Reduction Behavior. The validity scales are labeled (Response Level, Atypical Response, and Inconsistent Response.), 10 clinical scales (Anxious Arousal, Depression, Anger/Irritability, Intrusive Experiences, Defensive Avoidance, Dissociation, Sexual Concerns, Dysfunctional Sexual Behavior, Impaired Self-reference, and Tension Reduction Behavior), and TSI also contains 12 critical items that indicate symptoms or behaviors that may require immediate attention (e.g., suicidal thoughts or behaviors, danger to others, significant substance abuse). There is an 86-item alternate version (the TSI-A) that does not contain the Sexual Concerns or Dysfunctional Sexual Behavior scales that is also available.

The TSI was normed and standardized on a random sample of 828 individuals from the general population. For comparison to one's gender and/or age group, norms are available for males and females, ages 18 to 54 or 54 or older than age 54. The TSI's clinical scales of the TSI are demonstrate strong internally consistency across a variety of groups, including the general population, clinical samples, university students, and military personnel (mean alphas of .86, .87, .84, and .84 in standardization, clinical, university, and military samples, respectively; Briere, 1995). It has also exhibited reasonable convergent, discriminant predictive, and incremental validity in a variety of studies (e.g., Briere, 1995; Green et al., 2000; McDevitt-Murphy, Weathers, & Adkins, 2005).

A computer program is available that scores the TSI and produces a profile on the TSI validity and clinical scales. The program also yields three additional, summary scores (Trauma, Self, and Dysphoria) derived from statistical data reduction techniques (Briere, 1995; based on confirmatory factor analysis).

REFERENCES

Briere, J. (1995). *Trauma symptom inventory professional manual.* Odessa, FL: Psychological Assessment Resources.

Green, B. L., Goodman, L. A., Krupnick, J. L., Corcoran, C. B., Petty, R. M., Stockton, P., et al. (2000). Outcome of single versus multiple trauma exposure in a screening sample. *Journal of Traumatic Stress, 13,* 271–286.

McDevitt-Murphy, M. E., Weathers, F. W., & Adkins, J. W. (2005). Use of the Trauma Symptom Inventory in the assessment of PTSD symptoms. *Journal of Traumatic Stress, 18,* 63–67.

JOHN BRIERE
University of Southern California

See also: **Assessment, Psychometric, Adult**

TRAUMATIC BONDING

Traumatic bonding is the development of strong emotional ties between two persons where one person intermittently harasses, beats, threatens, abuses, or intimidates the other (Dutton & Painter, 1981, 1993). It was originally reported in reference to women victims of spouse assault but has been reported in a variety of studies, both experimental and observational, with both human and animal subjects. For example, people taken hostage may subsequently show positive regard for their captors, abused children have been found to have strong attachments to their abusing parents, and cult members are sometimes amazingly loyal to malevolent cult leaders.

There are two common features of social structure in such apparently diverse relationships as battered spouse/battering spouse, hostage/captor, abused child/abusing parent, cult follower/leader, and prisoner/guard. The first feature is the existence of a power imbalance wherein the maltreated person perceives him- or herself to be subjugated to or dominated by the other. The second is the discontinuous, unpredictable or intermittent nature of the abuse.

Power Imbalance

Attachment to a person or group larger or stronger than the self increases feelings of personal power. Social psychologists have found that unequal power relationships can become increasingly unbalanced over time to the point where the power dynamic itself produces pathology in individuals. Features of the group structure itself can contribute to Anna Freud's concept of "identification with the aggressor" (Freud, 1942). Recast from its psychoanalytic mode, this concept would predict that in situations of extreme power imbalance where a person of high power is occasionally punitive, persons of low power would adopt the aggressor's assumed worldview and internalize or redirect it toward others similar to themselves.

As the power imbalance increases, the person of low power feels more negative in their self-appraisal, less capable of fending for themselves, and thus more in need of the high-power person—whether or not high dependency existed in the low-power person prior to the imbalanced relationship. These feelings of dependency and lowered self-esteem through repetition eventually create a strong affective bond to the high-power person.

Periodicity of Abuse

The second feature of traumatic bonding situations is the fact that abuse occurs from time to time, in bouts. During bouts of abuse, the dominant party maltreats the submissive party by threats and verbal or physical abuse. Between bouts of abuse occur intervals of more normal and acceptable social behavior. As a result, the victim is subject to an alternation of periods of aversive or negative arousal and periods of relief and release. The situation of alternating aversive and pleasant conditions is an experimental paradigm within learning theory known as partial or intermittent reinforcement, which is highly effective in producing persistent patterns

of behavior that are difficult to extinguish or terminate. Such intermittent maltreatment patterns have been found to produce strong emotional bonding effects in both animals and humans.

Intermittent Reinforcement and Traumatic Bonding

There is considerable evidence from both naturalistic and laboratory-based studies with animals that severe arousal, even when caused by an attachment object and especially when it is repeatedly increased and reduced, provides a basis for strong emotional attachment. In reviewing the literature on maltreatment effects, Rajecki, Lamb, and Obsmacher (1978) found conclusive evidence for enhanced infant attachment under conditions of intermittent maltreatment in birds, dogs, and monkeys. Harlow and Harlow (1971) reviewed the research they carried out with infant monkeys, in which "evil surrogate mothers" were used as potential attachment objects. These surrogates would exude noxious air blasts, extrude brass spikes, hurl the infant to the floor, or vibrate so violently as to make the infant's teeth chatter. None of these behaviors disrupted the bonding behavior of the infant monkeys. The authors concluded that "instead of producing experimental neurosis we have achieved a technique for enhancing maternal attachment" (p. 196).

Therapy

Since, by definition, traumatic bonding is a powerful process that occurs outside awareness, the therapist can only bring it to the client's awareness and make the client mindful of the thoughts and cues that signal the onset of the "undertow" or pull back to the perpetrator.

REFERENCES

Dutton, D. G., & Painter, S. L. (1981). Traumatic bonding: The development of emotional bonds in relationships of intermittent abuse. *Victimology: An International Journal, 6*(1/4), 139–155.

Dutton, D. G., & Painter, S. L. (1993). The battered woman syndrome: Effects of severity and intermittency of abuse. *American Journal of Orthopsychiatry, 63*(4), 614–622.

Freud, A. (1942). *The ego and the mechanisms of defense.* New York: International University Press.

Harlow, H. F., & Harlow, M. (1971). Psychopathology in monkeys. In H. D. Kinnel (Ed.), *Experimental psychopathology* (pp. 171–198). New York: Academic Press.

Rajecki, P., Lamb, M., & Obmascher, P. (1978). Toward a general theory of infantile attachment: A comparative review of aspects of the social bond. *Behavioral and Brain Sciences, 3,* 417–464.

DONALD G. DUTTON
University of British Columbia

See also: Attachment; Child Maltreatment; Domestic Violence; Emotional Abuse; Family Systems; Marital Relationships; Women and Trauma

TRAUMATIC GRIEF

See: Bereavement

TRAUMATIC NEUROSIS

Although the term, *traumatic neurosis,* is officially obsolete in psychiatry and does not appear in recent editions of the *Diagnostic and Statistical Manual of Mental Disorders* (*DSM IV-TR;* American Psychiatric Association, 2000), it continues to have considerable historical and conceptual value. Neurosis derives from "neuron" and suggests a malfunction of the nervous system. Hence, the ordinary meaning of neurosis is to be unusually anxious or "nervous." From the late nineteenth century to the mid-twentieth century, medical professionals defined neurosis as a functional disorder for which no related physical cause could be demonstrated. Neuroses were primarily classified by their precipitating causes. The traumatic neuroses were those thought to have been instigated by overwhelming dangerous experiences such as accidents, attacks, or disasters.

Over the past 150 years, several types of specific traumatic neuroses have been identified (including war neuroses and military neuroses), but medical opinion eventually concluded that these were all of one nature: an extremely stressful event leading to a functional disorder. Further, war neuroses were no different than those of peacetime. The traumatic neuroses fit well within the broader medical rubric of *hysteria* on the basis of their common dissociative and conversion symptoms (*see:* **Dissociation; Hysteria**).

Modern mental health professionals are accustomed to closely delineated definitions of mental disorders with strictly ordered criteria. Traumatic neuroses, on the other hand, have myriad expressions. These can include aphonia (functional inability to speak) or stuttering, blindness, paralysis, tremor, anesthesia (functional loss of sensation), amnesia, excitation or excessive fatigue/depression, morbid fears, intrusive images, changes in perception or experience of time and space, of reality (derealization), and/or of self (depersonalization) among others. Kardiner (1941) described his work with over a thousand such patients after World War I, and Grinker and Spiegel's *Men Under Stress* (1945) summarized the experience of military psychiatrists during World War II. The dramatic success of abreactive treatments (methods to discharge overwhelming yet repressed emotions) employing hypnosis or sodium amytal for the war neuroses (as suggested by psychoanalytic principles and described by Grinker and Spiegel) helped spur the growth of psychoanalysis and departments of psychiatry across the United States in the years following World War II.

Acute stress disorder (ASD) and posttraumatic stress disorder (PTSD) could be considered the traumatic neuroses of modern psychiatry. ASD is defined by the *DSM-IV-TR* to include dissociative phenomena such as derealization, depersonalization, dissociative amnesia or a reduction in awareness of surroundings. These encompass many of the classic elements of the traumatic neuroses. The World Health Organization (WHO, 1992) defines an additional diagnostic entity, Acute Stress Reaction (ASR), which can begin within minutes of an overwhelming event and that usually subsides within a few days. ASR can involve dissociative symptoms, depression or excitation, and/or physiologic hyperarousal. In military settings, such responses are of paramount practical importance in terms of the safety of the individual, of those who depend on him or her, and of tactical priorities.

In order to better conceptualize and respond to acute stress responses in military settings, the framers of the joint U.S. Department of Veterans Affairs, Department of Defense Clinical Practice Guidelines on the Management of Posttraumatic Stress (2003) defined a separate entity: Combat and Operational Stress Reaction (COSR) during ongoing military operations. COSR may begin with a single traumatic stressor but may also result from the cumulative stress of combat operations including a broad array of stressors such as severe fatigue, hunger, and/or extended exposure to the elements. The onset and symptoms of COSR closely resemble those of ASR but specifically include exhaustion/burnout, somatic complaints involving virtually any organ system, guilt/hopelessness, conversion symptoms (including aphonias, blindness, paralysis, etc.), behavioral changes, emotional dysregulation, anger/irritability, and/or brief, manageable "psychotic symptoms" (e.g., hallucination due to sleep deprivation and mild "paranoia").

ASD and PTSD have, by definition, an onset of 4 days and 30 days, respectively, after the traumatic stressor. ASR and COSR can begin immediately after the traumatic event and are expected to subside within a few days. While these different diagnostic entities, taken together, cover the entire time line of posttraumatic responses, it is important to emphasize that these disorders do not necessarily represent a single continuum or a simple progression of stress response. Not everyone who develops ASR or COSR will develop ASD just as not every person with ASD will go on to develop PTSD. In addition, many trauma survivors who develop PTSD never met criteria for ASR, COSR, or ASD (Bryant, 2003). On the other hand, it is very common for survivors of traumatic events to have one or more acute or chronic posttraumatic symptoms even if they never go on to meet criteria for any *DSM* or *ICD* diagnosis. These are the real-world clinical conditions that were once organized under the heading of traumatic neurosis. Despite attempts to define the traumatic neuroses out of existence, these familiar human responses to severe stress are still very much with us. A significant amount of research and thought will be required before the universe of psychological responses to trauma can be more succinctly or more accurately described.

REFERENCES

American Psychiatric Association. (2000). *Diagnostic and statistical manual of mental disorders* (4th ed., text rev.). Washington, DC: Author.

Bryant, R. A. (2003). Early predictors of posttraumatic stress disorder. *Biological Psychiatry, 53,* 789–795.

Grinker, R., & Spiegel, J. (1945). *Men under stress.* New York: McGraw-Hill.

Kardiner, A. (1941). *The traumatic neuroses of war.* New York: Hoeber.

U.S. Department of Veterans Affairs, Department of Defense Clinical Practice Guideline Working Group. (2003). *Management of post-traumatic stress* (Publication No. 10Q-CPG/PTSD-04). Washington, DC: Office of Quality and Performance. Available from www.oqp.med.va.gov/cpg/PTSD/PTSD_Base.htm.

World Health Organization. (1992). *The ICD-10 classification of mental and behavioural disorders: F43.0 acute stress reaction.* Geneva, Switzerland: Author.

HAROLD KUDLER
Duke University Medical Center

See also: Acute Stress Disorder; Combat Stress Reaction; Dissociation; Etiology; Freud, Sigmund; History of Psychological Trauma; Hysteria; Oppenheim, Hermann; Posttraumatic Stress Disorder; Stress; Stress Response Syndromes

TRAUMATIC STRESS

Traumatic stress is a phrase that refers to psychological and physiological reactions to stressors that threaten the person's life or bodily integrity (or witnessing this happen to another person) and that involves the subjective experience of extreme fear, helplessness, or horror due to being beyond the person's ordinary capacity to cope. Traumatic stress is the product of: (a) shocking and threatening changes in the person's life (a major shift in incoming information from the expectable events in daily life to conditions of significant danger), (b) a sense of being unable to rely on familiar ways of solving problems and coping with stressors (a major discrepancy between the appraisal of that incoming information and existing contingency plans within the person's mind), and (c) emotionally charged and unfamiliar memories (a major set of memories that are "raw" in the sense of being associated with intense emotions and experiences that are inconsistent with the person's prior "life story").

Traumatic stress requires substantial time and effort for the person to assimilate and accommodate. Traumatic stress results from an extreme mismatch between new circumstances and the person's existing schemas for interpreting the world and organizing self-concepts. This mismatch evokes strong emotional responses that have physiological as well as psychological qualities. Traumatic stress in the psychological sense is not primarily the result of a physical injury. Thus, a bone fracture from being struck by the fender of a car, which is a "traumatic stress fracture" may or may not also involve psychological "traumatic stress." The metaphor of traumatic stress applies to both cases, however: something has "fractured" the person's existing adjustment to the world, and that something includes psychological meanings such as "I don't know if I can stand the pain," "This could kill me," or "Everything I value has been swept away."

In traumatic stress states, the inner psychological experience can extend far longer than the external inciting events. That is because there is a kind of mental metabolism of the experience and a process of learning a new picture of world and self. Along this emotional passage there may be extremes of affective response.

Traumatic stress is characterized by the presence of two emotional extremes, including: (1) the sense of numbness that may be present when denial symptoms are prominent; and (2) its opposite, pangs of strong emotion that accompany intrusive reexperiencing symptoms, such as a piercing recollection of traumatic images. In addition, a third element in traumatic stress reactions is hyperarousal, that is, states of high levels of physiological arousal characterized by tension that is associated with difficulty with anger, sleep, and mental concentration, and a psychological sense of being threatened (hypervigilance). These are the core traumatic stress symptoms in posttraumatic stress disorder (PTSD), as well as key symptoms of acute stress disorder (ASD).

Posttraumatic emotional numbness is not simply an absence of emotions; it is a felt sense of being remote, muffled, or stifled. The individual may actually feel surrounded by a layer of insulation. Emotional blunting may alter patterns of interaction with support systems that can affect family life, friendship, and work relations. Members of the support network may be offended by this alteration in the nature of their relationship and withdraw. Actions of withdrawal associated with emotional numbing tend to reduce social supports just when this support often is most needed by the person with a traumatic stress reaction.

Intrusive emotional states contain reenactments of traumatic events, and may also include fantasized responses. For example, unwanted memories of having been assaulted may include recollections that are like a replay (hence, the term reenactment) of what led up to and followed the assault, as well as certain aspects of the assault and the victim's attempts to flee or fight back that are particularly physically or emotionally painful or significant. Intrusive trauma memories also may include thoughts or even an imagined scenario of what the victim wishes she or he had been able to do or would want to do should a similar event ever happen again (the "fantasized responses"). These compulsive repetitions may be behavioral and/or in memory. A behavioral reenactment might take the form of engaging in risky behavior that leads to or provokes a physical altercation similar to the assault. Such a repetition can range from a minor fragment of the traumatic experience (such as replaying a single crucial moment in the assault) or a larger complex (such as recalling the entire experience from start to finish), to a complete reliving of the event as if in real time (i.e., a flashback).

One emotional aspect of intrusive states stems from the process of associating "alarm" emotions such as fear, anger, or grief with topics other than, but still in some way associated with traumatic events. Through such overgeneralizations, situations that are usually calm may be infused with one or several of these alarm emotions. In normal reactions to stressor events, one expects to see a diminution of such reactions. This is due to a combination of factors that include "habituation," "extinction learning," and "desensitization." In abnormal reactions, a persistent or intermittent highly alarmed reaction occurs in response to nontraumatic stressors: in such cases, the person is experiencing posttraumatic stress disorder (PTSD).

Denial or disavowal of aspects of traumatic experiences can be used to attenuate states of emotion that threaten otherwise to be too disorganizing. This can include misappraisal or avoidance of the meanings of the event (e.g., "It wasn't such a terrible experience"), constriction of associational width (e.g., "It doesn't really affect the rest of my life"), and avoidance of trauma-related places, memories, or activities (e.g., "I just don't go around that place or that sort of person any more"). Sometimes a contrived continuation of "life as usual" contains an altered subjective quality; the person continues thinking about the same topics in the same way as before the stressor event, in a way that can now strike others as bizarrely inappropriate (e.g., "It's really no big deal that my family was killed, that's what happens in war, so I just have to put that all behind me"). The person, however, may also feel like an automaton, one who is carrying out habitual patterns that may now be inappropriate.

The most common traumatic stress response is intrusive review of the traumatic experience(s). This is not necessarily bad: it can be a natural way of enabling the person to emotionally and cognitively process the experience and its meaning, and this can lead to a sense of successful mastery of the experience. Nonetheless, if progress is not made to do so, the intrusive reviewing of traumatic memories become symptoms (i.e., interfere with functioning), and are included in such diagnoses as PTSD.

RECOMMENDED READINGS

Horowitz, M. (2002). *Stress response syndromes* (4th ed.). New York: Littlefield and Rowman.

Horowitz, M. (2005). *Treatment of stress response syndromes.* Washington, DC: American Psychiatric Publishing.

MARDI HOROWITZ
University of California, San Francisco

See also: Acute Stress Disorder; Diagnosis of Traumatic Stress Disorders (*DSM & ICD*); Emotional Numbing; Hyperarousal; Intrusive Reexperiencing; Posttraumatic Stress Disorder, Diagnosis of; Stress; Stress Response Syndromes; Trauma, Definition

TYPOLOGY OF TRAUMATIC STRESS DISORDERS

Typology is the systematic classification or study of types that have characteristics or traits in common. Any given "type" of things will need to have a sufficient degree of similarity (homogeneity) so that the category is meaningful and yet will also contain some variability (heterogeneity). Psychiatric typologies traditionally account for heterogeneity within a diagnostic category by identifying homogeneous subtypes that differ from each other with respect to the manifestation of symptoms of the overarching parent disorder. For example, in attention-deficit/ hyperactivity disorder, 18 symptoms are listed under two broad classes: inattention (A1) and hyperactivity-impulsivity (A2). The "predominantly inattentive" subtype is defined by the presence of A1 without A2, the "predominantly hyperactive" subtype by A2 without A1. Other subtypes listed in *DSM-IV* include bipolar I versus bipolar II, and the various forms of schizophrenia.

DSM-IV defines posttraumatic stress disorder (PTSD) with a list of 17 symptoms subsumed under three higher-order criteria (reexperiencing, avoidance/numbing, hyperarousal). Each criterion has a different number of requisite symptoms for diagnosis, yielding a vast number of mathematically possible combinations within this single diagnosis. Thus, considerable heterogeneity in symptomatology may exist within any sample of individuals with the disorder. Studies attempting to identify clinically meaningful subtypes on the basis of differences in the manifestation of these core symptoms have generally found subgroups differing in the severity of disturbance (i.e., showing *quantitative* as opposed to *qualitative* differences between them). Investigators have yet to identify a clinically meaningful and/or replicable typology based on qualitative differences in the core symptoms of the disorder. (The *DSM-IV* acute, chronic, and delayed onset specifiers for PTSD do not constitute a typology per se because they refer to variability in temporal characteristics of the disorder as opposed to the manifestation of its symptoms.)

There is, however, growing support for a typology of traumatic stress disorders based on diagnostic comorbidity, symptom complexity, and other clinical features associated with the disorder. In the "Associated Features and Disorders" section of the diagnosis, *DSM-IV* (American Psychiatric Association, 1994, p. 424) lists an array of symptoms that fall outside the 17 core symptoms that have become known as Complex PTSD. Herman (1992) originally conceptualized the syndrome as involving (a) symptoms that are more complicated, diffuse, and persistent than what is captured by the symptom criteria for "simple" PTSD; (b) marked personality disturbance; and (c) heightened vulnerability to repeated harm. Although controversial, a number of empirical studies have supported the validity of at least the first two elements

of the construct and its distinction from "simple" PTSD. Advocates assert that the construct is clinically useful because it captures the severe and diverse psychiatric sequelae manifested by some survivors of trauma that are not adequately represented by the simple diagnosis. On the other hand, critics have argued that its value is limited by an overly broad spectrum of symptoms and traits and fuzzy boundaries with comorbid diagnoses (especially borderline personality disorder). Others have suggested that complex PTSD could be redefined using the existing nomenclature, as PTSD accompanied by personality disturbance and extensive diagnostic comorbidity (Miller & Resick, 2007).

Support for this reconceptualization and a new *internalizing/externalizing typology of posttraumatic psychopathology,* has been reported in several recent studies of trauma survivors (e.g., Miller, Greif, & Smith, 2003; Miller, Kaloupek, Dillon, & Keane, 2004; Miller & Resick, 2007). Specifically, in each of these studies, cluster analyses of personality profiles of individuals with PTSD yielded evidence for a three-group typology. The first type was a lower pathology or "simple PTSD" cluster comprised of individuals with PTSD diagnoses but low levels of comorbidity and normal-range personality profiles. The other two were more pathological, or "complex" clusters that differed on variables related to externalizing versus internalizing comorbidity (cf., Krueger, Caspi, Moffitt, & Silva, 1998). (The internalizing/externalizing model of comorbidity, rooted in over 30 years of research in the area of childhood behavior disorders, has recently come to the fore in adult psychopathology research as the result of a series of influential factor-analytic studies of the latent structure of adult mental illness conducted, most notably, by Krueger and colleagues.) Similar patterns that might now be interpreted as simple, internalizing, and externalizing subtypes were described in earlier studies of veterans with PTSD (e.g., Hyer, Davis, Albrecht, Boudewyns, & Woods, 1994).

Across these studies, "externalizers" were characterized by the tendency to express posttraumatic distress outwardly through antagonistic interactions with others and behavior that conflicts with societal norms and values. Individuals in this subgroup endorsed elevated levels of anger and aggression, substance-related disorders, *DSM-IV* Cluster B personality disorder features, and their personality profiles were defined by high disconstraint (i.e., impulsivity) coupled with negative emotionality. In contrast, internalizers were characterized by tendencies to direct their posttraumatic distress inwardly through shame, self-defeating/deprecating and anxious processes, avoidance, depression, and withdrawal. Individuals of this type were characterized by high rates of comorbid major depressive disorder and panic disorder, schizoid and avoidant personality disorder features, and personality profiles defined by high negative emotionality combined with low positive emotionality.

The internalizing/externalizing typology has potential utility for the search for PTSD's biological markers where one of the major challenges is the problem of psychiatric comorbidity. Because of the high rates of comorbidity in samples of individuals with the disorder, multiple overlapping psychiatric phenotypes (i.e., describing physical appearance) may be present in any PTSD sample that can obscure the search for markers that can reliably distinguish cases from controls. The typology offers a useful framework for parsing samples into subgroups that would be expected to show greater homogeneity in their biologic profiles.

With respect to clinical utility, converging lines of evidence predict poorer treatment outcomes for externalizers. Research linking externalizing disorders with emotional hyporeactivity to fear and punishment cues predict poor outcomes in interventions based on exposure and extinction of pathological fear responses. Pretreatment anger (a primary correlate of externalizing) has been shown to be a predictor of poor outcome and deficits in impulse control. And the ability to sustain attention would be expected to interfere with treatments predicated on learning to modulate cognition and behavior according to changing environmental cues.

One caveat regarding this typology is that it is not unique to posttraumatic psychopathology. To the contrary, there is a close correspondence between the subtypes identified in this work and three major personality "types" identified by developmental psychologists (cf., Asendorpf & van Aken, 1999). Moreover, these subtypes are conceptualized as the consequence of traumatic stress operating on individual difference propensities toward the development of internalizing versus externalizing psychopathology. Strengths of the model are that it is consonant with contemporary theories of personality and psychopathology that posit a fundamental structure of individual differences spanning the domains of normal and abnormal behavior, and that it links the structure of posttraumatic psychopathology to the organization of common mental disorders more broadly.

REFERENCES

American Psychiatric Association. (1994). *Diagnostic and statistical manual of mental disorders* (4th ed.). Washington, DC: Author.

Asendorpf, J. B., & van Aken, M. A. G. (1999). Resilient, overcontrolled and undercontrolled personality prototypes in childhood: Replicability, predictive power, and the trait-type issue. *Journal of Personality and Social Psychology, 77*, 815–832.

Herman, J. L. (1992). Complex PTSD: A syndrome in survivors of prolonged and repeated trauma. *Journal of Traumatic Stress, 5*, 377–391.

Hyer, L., Davis, H., Albrecht, W., Boudewyns, P., & Woods, G. (1994). Cluster analysis of MCMI and MCMI-II on chronic PTSD victims. *Journal of Clinical Psychology, 50*, 502–515.

Krueger, R. F., Caspi, A., Moffitt, T. E., & Silva, P. A. (1998). The structure and stability of common mental disorders (DSM-III-R): A longitudinal-epidemiological study. *Journal of Abnormal Psychology, 107*, 216–227.

Miller, M. W., Greif, J. L., & Smith, A. A. (2003). Multidimensional Personality Questionnaire profiles of veterans with traumatic combat exposure: Internalizing and externalizing subtypes. *Psychological Assessment, 15*, 205–215.

Miller, M. W., Kaloupek, D. G., Dillon, A. L., & Keane, T. M. (2004). Externalizing and internalizing subtypes of combat-related PTSD: A replication and extension using the PSY-5 Scales. *Journal of Abnormal Psychology, 113,* 636–645.

Miller, M. W., & Resick, P. A. (2007). Internalizing and externalizing subtypes in female sexual assault survivors: Implications for the understanding of complex PTSD. *Behavior Therapy, 38,* 58–71.

Mark W. Miller
National Center for Posttraumatic Stress Disorder

Annemarie F. Reardon
National Center for Posttraumatic Stress Disorder

See also: Acute Stress Disorder; Comorbidity; Complex Posttraumatic Stress Disorder; Diagnosis of Traumatic Stress Disorders (*DSM & ICD*); Posttraumatic Stress Disorder; Posttraumatic Stress Disorder, Diagnosis of; Stress Response Syndromes; Trauma, Definition; Traumatic Stress

U

UCLA PTSD REACTION INDEX

Over the past 2 decades, the UCLA Posttraumatic Stress Disorder Reaction Index (Steinberg, Brymer, Decker, & Pynoos, 2004) has been a widely used self-report instrument for the assessment of posttraumatic stress reactions among traumatized children and adolescents. The Reaction Index has been used across a variety of trauma types, age ranges, settings, and cultures. It has been broadly used around the world after major disasters and catastrophic violence and has been translated into many languages.

The Reaction Index was designed for use with youth from 7 to 18 years of age. As diagnostic criteria for PTSD have evolved, the Reaction Index, which was first developed in 1985, has gone through a number of revisions. The current version assesses *DSM-IV* (American Psychiatric Association, 1994) diagnostic criteria for PTSD. This version has a child, adolescent, and parent form. Abbreviated versions of the Reaction Index are also available for efficiently conducting needs assessment and screening.

The Reaction Index is a three-part paper-and-pencil instrument for the assessment of trauma exposure and posttraumatic stress symptoms among children and adolescents. Time for completion varies with age, reading ability of the child, and with method of administration, but typically can be completed in 20 to 30 minutes. It is designed to be administered by a licensed mental health professional or graduate level student under the supervision of a licensed clinician. Part I constitutes a brief lifetime trauma screen, permitting categorization of traumatic experiences, including exposure to such experiences as community and interpersonal violence, natural disaster,

medical trauma, and abuse. Part II allows for a systematic evaluation of objective and subjective features of the traumatic experience. Part III provides for an evaluation of the frequency of occurrence of posttraumatic stress reactions (scored 0 to 4) during the past month. These items map onto the *DSM-IV* PTSD criteria B (Intrusion), C (Avoidance), and D (Arousal). Twenty items assess the B, C, and D criteria symptoms, while two additional items assess associated features, including fear of recurrence of the trauma and trauma-related guilt. The instrument is accompanied by a frequency rating sheet to visually assist children in providing accurate responses about how often the reaction has occurred over the past month. To score the Reaction Index, only 17 items (across symptom criteria B, C, and D) make up the total score in Part III. Three of the symptoms have two alternative items, with the highest frequency score of the two items used to calculate the score for each.

Successive versions of the Reaction Index have been psychometrically studied. Validity across all versions is suggested by numerous studies that have consistently found higher Reaction Index scores among traumatized samples as compared with controls, and a clear "dose of exposure" relationship of Reaction Index scores across exposure groups (i.e., with higher scores found in more severely exposed groups). The *DSM-IV* version has good convergent validity, correlating .70 with the PTSD Module of the Kiddie Schedule for Affective Disorders and Schizophrenia-Epidemiological Version (K-SADS-E); it correlates .82 with the Clinician-Administered PTSD Scale for Children and Adolescents (CAPS-CA), with a cutoff of 38 having sensitivity of .93 in detecting PTSD and specificity of .87 in ruling out the disorder.

In terms of internal consistency, several reports have found Chronbach's alpha coefficient to fall in the range of .90, and test-retest reliability of .84 or higher (Steinberg et al., 2004). In regard to the seven-item and nine-item abbreviated UCLA PTSD Reaction Index scales, Cronbach's alpha was .85 for the seven-item version, and .87 for the nine-item version. Receiver operating curve (ROC) results indicated that corresponding cutoffs to the full scale are 16 for the seven-item version, and 20 for the nine-item version.

Overall, the Reaction Index has proven to be an extremely useful part of an assessment battery, (along with specific exposure questions, questions about postevent stresses and adversities, and measures of comorbid depression, grief, and anxiety), that has been used effectively to conduct needs assessment, surveillance, screening, clinical evaluation and treatment outcome evaluation after traumatic events (Balaban et al., 2005). The Reaction Index is currently being employed by the National Child Traumatic Stress Network to gather Network-wide data on treatment outcome.

REFERENCES

American Psychiatric Association. (1994). *Diagnostic and statistical manual of mental disorders* (4th ed.). Washington, DC: Author.

Balaban, V. F., Steinberg, A. M., Brymer, M. J., Layne, C. M., Jones, R. T., & Fairbank, J. A. (2005). Screening and assessment for children's psychosocial needs following war and terrorism. In M. J. Friedman & A. Mikus-Kos (Eds.), *Promoting the psychosocial well-being of children following war and terrorism* (pp. 121–161). The Netherlands: IOM Press.

Steinberg, A. M., Brymer, M. J., Decker, K. B., & Pynoos, R. S. (2004). The University of California at Los Angeles Posttraumatic Stress Disorder Reaction Index. *Current Psychiatry Reports, 6*(2), 96–100.

ALAN M. STEINBERG
National Center for Child Traumatic Stress at UCLA

MELISSA J. BRYMER
National Center for Child Traumatic Stress at UCLA

See also: Assessment, Psychometric, Child

V

VETERANS AFFAIRS, U.S. DEPARTMENT OF

The U.S. Department of Veterans Affairs (VA) is, perhaps, the largest provider of health services for people with posttraumatic stress disorder (PTSD) in the world. The VA has played a leading role in providing services, as well as in research and education, concerning the long-term psychological effects of military service, and especially war zone service. In 2006, the VA provided services to almost 350,000 veterans who received a clinical diagnosis of PTSD, and almost 90% of these veterans received services from mental health specialty inpatient, residential, and outpatient programs (Fontana, Rosenheck, Spencer, & Grey, 2006). The majority of these veterans (66%) reported military service during the Vietnam War era. But the next largest group (14%) reported service during the Gulf War era, defined as the period since the first U.S. troops went to the Middle East in response to the invasion of Kuwait in August 1991. Another 8% served during World War II or the Korean conflict and about 10% served in other war and peace times. The steepest increase in the numbers of a veterans seeking treatment for PTSD from VA is not surprisingly those who served during the Gulf War era, with a 63% annualized increase in veterans treated from 2003 to 2006. Even as this younger generation of war veterans begins to seek help for PTSD from VA, the numbers of veterans of other eras who seek VA services still continues to increase. Between 2003 and 2006, the number of Vietnam War era veterans seeking help for PTSD from mental health programs also increased—at an annualized rate of 9% per year, a rate of increase that has been consistently documented back to 1997, the first year that diagnostic data were included in VA administrative databases. Awareness of PTSD among veterans continues to increase year by year.

While VA and its predecessor agencies have provided health-care services to veterans with what is now known as PTSD since well before the Civil War, the current array of programs was developed largely in response to the needs of Vietnam Veterans. In the late 1970s even before PTSD was formally identified as a psychiatric diagnosis, several VA medical centers established Specialized Inpatient PTSD Units (SIPUs). By current standards, these were long-term inpatient programs with structured lengths of stay of 90 days. SIPUs were extraordinarily popular among veterans and developed extensive waiting lists. Substantial emphasis was placed on sharing of traumatic war experiences, building of veteran support networks, and rehabilitation, with some use of formal behavioral therapies.

In 1979, as a result of extensive advocacy by Vietnam veterans themselves, the VA Readjustment Counseling program, or Vet Centers were established to offer community, store-front services, largely provided by Vietnam veterans. The Vet Center program was designed to offer "help without hassles" from fellow soldiers who had also experienced the reality of Vietnam service under scrupulously confidential conditions. The program has continued and expanded to serve veterans of other conflicts including the first Gulf War and the recent conflict in Afghanistan and Iraq. Currently, Vet Centers number 207 and operate in every state.

In 1988, the VA-sponsored National Vietnam Veterans Readjustment Survey was released showing that, 15 to 20 years after the war ended, over 15% of Vietnam era veterans who served in Vietnam met criteria for a current diagnosis of PTSD. In response to this evidence, VA made a strong commitment to developing specialized mental health programs for the treatment of war-related PTSD. In addition to the well-established SIPUs, over 100 specialized PTSD outpatient programs have been established, some specializing in the treatment of veterans with comorbid substance abuse and others in the treatment of PTSD among female veterans. A number of short-term inpatient and residential rehabilitation models were also developed and evaluated (Fontana & Rosenheck, 1997). These programs turned out to be as effective and far less costly than the original SIPUs and eventually replaced them, as the VA shifted more generally toward being an outpatient and community-based system of care. Continuous monitoring of the outcomes of specialized intensive PTSD programs has shown that the systemwide shift to more efficient models of care has not resulted in any loss of effectiveness (Rosenheck & Fontana, 2001).

In 2006, the VA funded a series of over 40 Returning Veterans Outreach and Education Clinics (RVOECs) designed to facilitate access of recently discharged veterans to VA mental health and other services. Staffed by over 100 professionals, the program provided clinical services to over 11,000 veterans in its first year of operation, two-thirds of whom served in Iraq and Afghanistan. Outreach is a specific focus of this program and VA staff have made contact with veterans at military bases as well as at schools and other community organizations.

The idea of post-Vietnam syndrome was little more than a rumor in 1973. Now, with soldiers returning everyday from combat experience in Iraq, Afghanistan, and elsewhere, an experienced national network of VA specialists, informed by research that extends from genes to generations, offers a well-defined array of evidence-based services. Much remains to be learned and much progress in treatment effectiveness remains to be made, but current VA services for PTSD, shaped as much by veterans themselves as by professionals, could not possibly have been imagined when the last U.S. solider was airlifted out of Saigon.

REFERENCES

Fontana, A., & Rosenheck, R. A. (1997). Effectiveness and cost of inpatient treatment of posttraumatic stress disorder. *American Journal of Psychiatry, 154,* 758–765.

Fontana, A., Rosenheck, R., Spencer, H., & Grey, S. (2006). *Long journey home XIV: Treatment of posttraumatic stress disorder in the Department of Veterans Affairs: Fiscal year 2005 service delivery and performance.* West Haven, CT: Northeast Program Evaluation Center.

Rosenheck, R. A., & Fontana, A. (2001). Impact of efforts to reduce inpatient costs on clinical effectiveness: Treatment of posttraumatic stress disorder in the Department of Veterans Affairs. *Medical Care, 39,* 168–180.

ROBERT ROSENHECK
Veterans Affairs Northeast Program Evaluation Center

ALAN FONTANA
Veterans Affairs Northeast Program Evaluation Center

See also: Health Service Utilization; Laws, Legislation, and Policy; Military Personnel; National Center for Posttraumatic Stress Disorder (NC-PTSD); War Trauma

VICARIOUS TRAUMATIZATION

As the field of traumatic stress studies has developed over the course of the past 30 years, it has become increasingly evident that the effects of psychological trauma extend beyond the primary victim(s). Others in relationship with victims (such as family members or friends), those who intervene or assist victims on site (such as emergency medical technicians, police officers, fire personnel, combat medics, disaster and aid workers), or those to whom victims turn to in order to share their traumatic experiences and get support for dealing with traumatic stress reactions (such as therapists or health-care providers), can begin to develop reactions that mimic those of the victim and that are similar to the symptoms of posttraumatic stress disorder (PTSD). Changes in the therapist's self-image and disruptions in identity, memory, and belief systems also may occur. A variety of terms and definitions have been coined to describe this process: *secondary traumatization, compassion fatigue, burnout,* and *vicarious traumatization.* These terms are used rather interchangeably in the field; however, here we focus on vicarious traumatization (VT) as originally defined by McCann and Pearlman (1990), the authors who coined the term.

VT refers to "the enduring psychological consequences for therapists of exposure to the traumatic experience of victim clients. Persons who work with victims may experience profound psychological effects, effects that can be disruptive and painful for the helper and persist for months or years after work with traumatized persons" (McCann & Pearlman, 1990, p. 135). VT also has been defined as the "transformation of the therapist's or helper's inner experience as a result of empathic engagement with survivor clients and their trauma material" (Saakvitne & Pearlman, 2000, p. 25). VT is seen as an occupational hazard for those who provide treatment for the traumatized since the very mechanism of their ability to relate to and understand the client, namely empathy, leaves them vulnerable to be impacted by the client and his or her story and current suffering. Repeated exposure to traumatized persons' memories and distress can have profound and often negative effects on the therapist/helper's core beliefs about the world. The specific form and impact of VT is determined by the unique circumstances of each therapist/helper and client's interaction and therapeutic relationship, and by the personal characteristics of the therapist/helper. Although VT is believed to affect all who help traumatized persons, those who are especially at risk for a more severe impact from VT include:

- Those who treat or are exposed to a large number of traumatized clients over a long period of time (especially those without an adequate professional support system, knowledge base, or mechanisms for self-care)
- Those whose exposure is especially horrific or graphic in nature

- Those with a personal history of trauma or family disruption (especially if it is unresolved or closely matches the client's experience in some significant way)
- Those with major current life stressors
- Those whose own health is compromised by personal or professional stressors or a limited support system
- Those whose organizational or societal cultures require them to "keep things to themselves" and discourages discussion or debriefing after traumatic exposure (societal or organizational cultures may also convey that therapists/helpers are weak if they have any negative or adverse reaction to their work or if it "gets to them in any way")
- Those who underutilize supervision/consultation and/or who work in isolation and who have little or no experience with personal psychotherapy,
- Novice therapists and other helpers who are not prepared by experience for these reactions, and who may become overidentified and overinvolved with their clients and whose supervisors do not teach them about VT nor adequately monitor them in their work or in its aftermath,
- Helpers or therapists who attempt to "debrief" in a sporadic or primarily cathartic ("venting") manner, which has been shown to be associated with poorer outcomes for both psychological trauma victims and helpers (*see:* **Critical Incident Stress Management; Early Intervention**)

VT may occur more often when the psychological trauma involves interpersonal violence that is profoundly disquieting to the therapist/helper and is upsetting to his or her belief in the goodness of other humans and sense of interpersonal safety in the world.

VT should not be construed as an unhealthy breakdown or as a form of PTSD, but rather as a normal reaction that is also a cost associated with being exposed to those who have been traumatized and an unavoidable consequence of empathic engagement. Nor should VT be construed as something that the traumatized client *intentionally does to the therapist.* Even clients who cannot seem to contain their fervent expressions of emotional distress or graphic retellings of horrific experiences usually do not consciously intend to cause the therapist to become distressed. VT is also differentiated from countertransference reactions (*see:* **Countertransference**) since it is not specific to one client or therapeutic relationship but rather takes place over time and across a number of client relationships. VT is less focused on symptoms than on alterations in the meanings or beliefs, and the personal and professional adaptations, of the therapist/helper (Pearlman & Saakvitne, 1995).

McCann and Pearlman developed an interactive model and a theory (constructivist self-development theory; CSDT) to account for traumatic stress responses pertaining to the self of the victim and to the reactions to others. They identified seven schema about self and others that are often altered in the aftermath of traumatization, including: (1) the individual's personal frame of reference about self and others in the world, including identity, spirituality, self-capacities, and ego resources; (2) safety; (3) dependency and trust; (4) power; (5) esteem; (6) independence; and (7) intimacy. In parallel process to the trauma victims they treat, therapists and other helpers may have their schema about self and others transformed and their life circumstances shaken—this is vicarious traumatization.

Some common signs by which a helper might identify VT include: traumatic nightmares and daytime fears or intrusive recollections of a client's trauma (frame of reference and safety); shutting down emotionally, isolation, mistrust of others, distancing from family, difficulty with intimacy and sexuality (intimacy, trust, and safety); irritability and feeling exhausted, emotionally numb, cynical, overwhelmed, and hopeless (frame of reference, power, safety); use of substances to numb out memories and feelings (frame of reference, power, safety, trust) and hypervigilance with regard to, and overprotection of, children due to knowledge of danger in the world. All of these VT reactions represent a fundamental shift in frame of reference in personal and professional life, and in core beliefs about safety, dependence/independence, and trust.

If left unaddressed, VT can result in serious mental health consequences to the therapist/helper, including the development of persistent secondary traumatic stress reactions and ultimately symptoms and psychosocial problems similar to PTSD. VT also may lead to boundary slippage and boundary violations with clients (*see:* **Countertransference; Practice Guidelines**), professional burnout (*see:* **Burnout**), and inability to continue in one's field or work, as well as severe disruptions in the therapist's personal relationships. While these severe problems are not inevitable consequences of VT, they are of sufficient concern for helpers and therapists to be alert to signs of VT and to address VT in an ongoing way. Addressing VT is also an ethical imperative. In order to maintain hope (an essential element of the work) and to remain effective in work with traumatized clients, therapist/helpers must maintain their own heath and capacity through ongoing self-care and mindfulness (Wicks, 2008). VT is modifiable and preventive, and proactive strategies on the part of professionals and organizations can make an enormous difference.

With these considerations in mind, it is helpful to include information about VT in the training of all professional caregivers, to normalize VT, and, importantly, to help them to expect it as a reaction to their work and to understand it and address it when it occurs. Additionally, therapist/helpers can be encouraged to engage in ongoing self-care and self-monitoring in anticipation of these responses in order to support their ongoing ability to engage in work with the traumatized. Ongoing sources of professional support and mechanisms for personal renewal away from the work setting are also recommended strategies for dealing effectively with VT.

Since the introduction of the term in 1990, VT has been widely discussed and researched. Numerous books and articles are available on VT and on therapist self-care and the maintenance of boundaries between one's personal life and professional responsibilities. Additional strategies for organizational and personal support can be found in Norcross and Guy (2007); Pearlman and Saakvitne (1995); Rothschild and Rand (2006); Saakvitne, Gamble, Pearlman, and Lev (2000); Saakvitne and Pearlman (2000); Seigel (2007); Stamm (1995); and Wicks (2008).

REFERENCES

McCann, I. L., & Pearlman, L. A. (1990). Vicarious traumatization: A framework for understanding the psychological effects of working with victims. *Journal of Traumatic Stress, 3,* 131–149.

Norcross, J. C., & Guy, J. D. (2007). *Leaving it at the office: A guide to psychotherapist self-care.* New York: Guilford Press.

Pearlman, L. A., & Saakvitne, K. (1995). *Trauma and the therapist: Countertransference and vicarious traumatization in psychotherapy with incest survivors.* New York: Norton.

Rothschild, B., & Rand, M. (2006). *Help for the helper: The psychophysiology of compassion fatigue and vicarious trauma.* New York: Norton.

Saakvitne, K. W., Gamble, S. G., Pearlman, L. A., & Lev, B. (2000). *Risking connection: A training curriculum for working with survivors of childhood abuse.* Lutherville, MD: Sidran Foundation Press.

Saakvitne, K. W., & Pearlman, L. A. (2000). *Transforming the pain: A workbook on vicarious traumatization.* New York: Norton.

Siegel, D. J. (2007). *The mindful brain: Reflection and attunement in the cultivation of well-being.* New York: Norton.

Stamm, B. H. (1995). *Secondary traumatic stress: Self-care issues for clinicians, researchers, and educators.* Lutherville, MD: Sidran Foundation Press.

Wicks, R. J. (2008). *The resilient clinician.* New York: Oxford University Press.

CHRISTINE A. COURTOIS
Private Practice, Washington, DC

See also: Burnout; Countertransference; Professional and Ethical Standards; Psychotherapeutic Processes; Supervision and Training

VIRTUAL REALITY EXPOSURE THERAPY

Virtual reality (VR) describes a human-computer interaction that is a multimedia interactive display in which the user experiences a sense of presence or immersion in the virtual environment that changes in real time with head and body movements. In virtual reality exposure (VRE) therapy for PTSD, the patient describes the traumatic experience and the therapist attempts to match in the virtual environment what the patient is describing. VRE increases the intensity of exposure over that provided in imaginal exposure by providing the sights, sounds, smells, and movements in addition to the memory and the emotions. VR has been used to treat Vietnam veterans with PTSD using a virtual Huey helicopter that can fly over different terrain including jungle, rice paddies, or follow a river and lands in a virtual clearing. It is being used more recently to treat Iraq veterans with PTSD using a virtual Humvee driving down a desert highway or an Iraq city scene. It is being used to treat World Trade Center survivors using a virtual World Trade Center. Other applications include a virtual bus bombing in Israel, virtual Angola, and virtual earthquake scenes.

RECOMMENDED READINGS

Difede, J., Cukor, J., Jayasinghe, N., Patt, I., Jedel, S., Spielman, L., et al. (2007). Virtual reality exposure therapy for the treatment of posttraumatic stress disorder following September 11, 2001. *Journal of Clinical Psychiatry, 68,* 1639–1647.

Rothbaum, B. O., Hodges, L., Ready, D., Graap, K., & Alarcon, R. (2001). Virtual reality exposure therapy for Vietnam veterans with posttraumatic stress disorder. *Journal of Clinical Psychiatry, 62,* 617–622.

BARBARA O. ROTHBAUM
Emory University School of Medicine

See also: Exposure Therapy, Adult

W

WAR TRAUMA

War can be psychologically traumatic in many ways for civilians and military personnel behind the front lines as well as for combatants. All war-exposed persons experience a threat to their lives, whether this is direct and immediate (such as being attacked in hand-to-hand combat, by weapons at close or long range, by artillery or airplane bombardment, or with toxic agents such as poison gas, chemicals, or biological agents) or indirect and unpredictable (such as being held hostage or as a prisoner of war for unknown periods of time and subjected to starvation, isolation, and torture, or having one's home, community, support system, and means of livelihood lost or destroyed as "collateral damage" in warfare).

The traumatic effects of war include many forms of extreme danger and privation during, and often for prolonged periods after, active warfare. For example, the immediate and long-term consequences of war have included the death of millions of people due to starvation, disease, exposure to harsh weather, unsanitary conditions, long-term environmental contamination (e.g., in the aftermath of nuclear or chemical warfare), and accidental injury or death (e.g., unexploded landmines left behind by combatants). War also inevitably causes traumatic losses for the families and friends both of combatants and civilians who were lost, imprisoned, assaulted, tortured, or killed in the war and its aftermath. War affects children at least a harshly as it does adults, potentially creating lifelong posttraumatic psychological scars similar to those caused by abuse and neglect or family and community violence. Accidental injuries and deaths also are common in the chaos of war and its aftermath. Thus, war can be a source of virtually every form of psychological trauma, and its traumatic impacts are highly varied for each affected individual whether they are adult combatants (Ford, Fisher, & Larson, 1997; Ford et al., 2001, 2004) or civilian adults (Begic & McDonald, 2006) or children (Kinzie, Cheng, Tsai, & Riley, 2006).

Studies of war trauma almost always focus either on psychological trauma among military combatants or on refugees and other war-exposed civilian populations. This is reflected in the fact that questionnaires and interviews used to assess war trauma are designed for use either with civilian or military respondents, or have alternate forms for military or civilian respondents. The effects of war trauma on children also have been investigated (Laor, Wolmer, & Cohen, 2001).

War traumas experienced by military personnel have been documented since the earliest historical accounts of warfare (*see:* **History of Psychological Trauma; Military Personnel**). In modern times, the focus of scientific and clinical studies of war trauma and its effects on military personnel focused initially on the threat and shock of combat (e.g., "shell shock," "combat fatigue"). The first comprehensive and psychometrically reliable and validated measure of war trauma exposure by military personnel was the seven-item Combat Exposure Scale (CES; Keane et al., 1989). The CES asks about the number of times that military personnel were on combat duty (including perimeter guard duty, helicopter assaults, riverboat patrols, truck convoys, and combat patrols), under enemy fire, surrounded by the enemy, fired on the enemy, saw other combatants wounded by enemy weapons or artillery, or were in life-threatening situations (including being ambushed, trapped, or overrun), and the number of other personnel known to have been killed or wounded in action. Expanded versions of the CES have been developed in order to include war zone incidents and dangers beyond those from the Vietnam War cohort for which the CES was developed, such as the CES-R created for Operation Desert Storm Persian Gulf War personnel (Ford et al., 2001). Based on scientific and anecdotal evidence that military personnel are exposed to a wider variety of potentially stressful or traumatic incidents than combat per se, King, King, Vogt, Knight, and Samper (2006) developed and psychometrically validated and refined the Deployment Risk and Resilience Inventory, which assesses self-reported exposure to 14 types of war-related stressors with 201 items: pre-deployment stressors (e.g., prior military operations, community or domestic violence, sexual or physical assault) and childhood family environment; deployment preparation (e.g., combat and rescue training), discomforts or deprivations (e.g., noxious climate, food or water shortages, inadequate equipment), home front worries (e.g., job loss, relationship separations and conflicts), harassment by leaders or co-combatants (emotional, work, and sexual), specific threats of death or severe harm, specific dangerous combat activities, and exposure to nuclear, biological, or chemical (NBC) hazards; and post-deployment stressors (e.g., homecoming, reintegration into military unit, resuming civilian job).

An omnibus questionnaire measuring self-reported exposure to war trauma, the Comprehensive Trauma Inventory-104 (CTI-104), has been shown to be psychometrically reliable and valid with civilian Kurdish and Vietnamese war refugees by Hollifield and colleagues (2006). Respondents reported having experienced an average of 32 (of the 104 possible) types of war trauma. The war traumas surveyed included 12 types of psychological trauma: psychological injury (e.g., human rights abuses); physical injury, detention, and intentional abuse (e.g., torture); sexual trauma, witnessing abuse or injury or death; hearing about injury or death; deprivation and discrimination; betrayal (e.g., being turned in to military authorities by a fellow citizen); domestic violence; displacement (e.g., forcible eviction and exile); separation and isolation; and danger or

hardships during migration. A briefer (17-item) reliable and validated self-report measure of refugee war trauma exposure, the Harvard Trauma Questionnaire (Mollica et al., 1992), also measures posttraumatic stress symptoms and has been found to produce similar (although less detailed) reports of refugee war trauma exposure compared to the CTI-104.

The variety of potentially psychologically traumatic stressors to which both combatants and noncombatant military personnel and civilians are exposed before, during, and after war is extensive. Research is just beginning to determine how different types and combinations of these exposures to war-related psychological stressors and traumas impacts the mental and physical health, emotional well-being, quality of life, and family, interpersonal, and vocational/school functioning of war-affected individuals—children and adults—and their communities (King et al., 2006). However, it is clear that war trauma—although fortunately experienced by a relatively small proportion of the population in most places in the world (with the exception of locales and countries that experience pervasive ongoing or episodic wars or ethnic and national tensions that make war always a threat)—places combatants (Milliken, Auchtelonie, & Hoge, 2007) and civilians (Kessler, Sonnega, Bromet, Hughes, & Nelson, 1995) at very high risk for posttraumatic stress disorder (PTSD). Research findings suggest that 15% to 25% of people exposed to war develop PTSD, which is significantly higher than the 5% to 10% prevalence of PTSD in the general population.

Moreover, while the focus of this entry is on psychological trauma and PTSD, it should still be noted that a variety of other psychological, behavioral, vocational, and interpersonal problems are also associated with exposure to war. While not all persons exposed to war exhibit evidence of clinically significant psychological disturbances, all indications point to war as a potent psychological risk factor for the development of psychological distress and, for individuals who are particularly vulnerable due to extreme or prolonged traumatic exposure (before, during, or after the war) or background factors (e.g., prior psychological or psychiatric problems, limited social support networks), to potentially chronic psychological and behavioral disorders.

REFERENCES

Begic, S., & McDonald, T. (2006). The psychological effects of exposure to wartime trauma in Bosnian residents and refugees: Implications for treatment and service provision. *International Journal of Mental Health and Addiction, 4,* 319–329.

Ford, J. D., Campbell, K., Storzbach, D., Binder, L., Anger, W. K., & Rohlman, D. (2001). Posttraumatic stress symptomatology is associated with unexplained illness attributed to Persian Gulf War military service. *Psychosmoatic Medicine, 63,* 842–849.

Ford, J. D., Fisher, P., & Larson, L. (1997). Object relations as a predictor of treatment outcome with chronic PTSD. *Journal of Consulting and Clinical Psychology, 65,* 547–559.

Ford, J. D., Schnurr, P., Friedman, M., Green, B., Adams, G., & Jex, S. (2004). Posttraumatic stress disorder symptoms and physical health outcomes fifty years after exposure to toxic gas. *Journal of Traumatic Stress, 17,* 185–194.

Hollifield, M., Warner, T., Jenkins, J., Sinclair-Lian, N., Krakow, B., Eckert, V., et al. (2006). Assessing war trauma in refugees: Properties of the Comprehensive Trauma Inventory-104. *Journal of Traumatic Stress, 19,* 527–540.

Keane, T., Fairbank, J., Caddell, J., Zimering, R., Taylor, K., & Mora, C. (1989). Clinical evaluation of a measure to assess combat exposure. *Psychological Assessment, 1,* 53–55.

Kessler, R. C., Sonnega, A., Bromet, E., Hughes, M., & Nelson, C. B. (1995). Posttraumatic stress disorder in the National Comorbidity Survey. *Archives of General Psychiatry, 52,* 1048–1060.

King, L., King, D., Vogt, D., Knight, J., & Samper, R. (2006). Deployment Risk and Resilience Inventory: A collection of measures for studying deployment-related experiences of military personnel and veterans. *Military Medicine, 18,* 89–120.

Kinzie, D., Cheng, K., Tsai, J., & Riley, C. (2006). Traumatized refugee children: The case for individualized diagnosis and treatment. *Journal of Nervous and Mental Disease, 194,* 534–537.

Laor, N., Wolmer, L., & Cohen, D. (2001). Mothers' functioning and children's symptoms 5 years after a SCUD missile attack. *American Journal of Psychiatry, 158,* 1020–1026.

Milliken, C., Auchterlonie, J., & Hoge, C. (2007). Longitudinal assessment of mental health problems among active and reserve component soldiers returning from the Iraq War. *Journal of the American Medical Association, 298,* 2141–2148.

Mollica, R. F., Caspi-Yavin, Y., Bollini, P., Truong, T., Tor, S., & Lavelle, J. (1992). The Harvard Trauma Questionnaire: Validating a cross-cultural instrument for measuring torture, trauma, and posttraumatic stress disorder in Indochinese refugees. *Journal of Nervous and Mental Disease, 180,* 111–116.

Julian D. Ford
University of Connecticut School of Medicine

See also: Community Violence; Gulf War Syndrome; History of Psychological Trauma; Human Rights Violations; Military Personnel; Refugees; Torture; Trauma, Definition; Veterans Affairs, U.S. Department of

WITNESSING TRAUMATIC EVENTS

See: Domestic Violence; Trauma, Definition

WOMEN AND TRAUMA

In general population studies, women report lower rates of trauma exposure than men overall, but higher rates of exposure to certain types of traumatic events. The National Comorbidity Study (NCS; Kessler, Sonnega, Bromet, Hughes, & Nelson, 1995) found that 60.7% of men and 51.2% of women reported lifetime exposure to at least one traumatic event. A significantly higher proportion of women than men reported having experienced rape, sexual molestation, childhood physical abuse, and parental neglect. The National Violence Against Women (NVAW) Survey (Thoennes & Tjaden, 1998), based on a random sample of 16,000 men and women, found that 17.6% of women reported attempted or completed rape and 51.9% reported physical assault over the course of their lifetime.

A consistent finding throughout the epidemiological literature is that women develop posttraumatic stress disorder (PTSD) at approximately twice the rate of men. In the NCS, 10.4% of women versus 5.0% of men met criteria for lifetime PTSD. There is also some evidence of increased PTSD chronicity among women (Breslau & Davis, 1992). While a number of factors may contribute to gender differences in PTSD prevalence (Gavranidou & Rosner, 2003; Saxe & Wolfe, 1999), there are major differences in the nature and characteristics of traumatic stressors experienced by men and women, and the importance of these differences should not be underestimated. Women have significantly greater exposure to traumas associated with a high conditional risk of PTSD, such as rape and sexual abuse (Kessler et al., 1995). Women are also much more likely to be victimized by a known perpetrator. The NVAW Survey found that 76% of adult women who were raped and/or physically assaulted were victimized by an intimate partner, as compared with 17.9% of men. Conversely, 60% of men were assaulted by a stranger, as compared with only 14.1% of women. These differences may help to explain the finding that women develop PTSD at significantly higher rates than men following physical assault (Breslau, Chilcoat, Kessler, Peterson, & Lucia, 1999; Seedat & Stein, 2000). Given the closeness of their relationship to the perpetrator, women are at greater risk of experiencing traumas with a high social betrayal component (DePrince & Freyd, 2002). The types of trauma most frequently experienced by girls and women, such as childhood abuse and domestic violence, are also likely to be repeated over a prolonged period of time, in contrast to single incidents of violence perpetrated by strangers. Finally, many of these traumas occur at a young age, and may thus impact subsequent development. In the National Women's Study, a large epidemiological study of adult women in the United States, Acierno, Resnick, Kilpatrick, Saunders, and Best (1999) found that almost one-third of rape cases occurred before age 11, and approximately two-thirds occurred before age 18.

Dimensions of social identity that may impact women's experience of trauma include race, class, culture, and sexual orientation. These factors may affect women's risk of exposure to trauma and their access to ameliorating resources. The relatively sparse literature on trauma among ethnic and racial minority populations in the United States suggests that stress related to minority status, such as racial prejudice, may increase risk for developing PTSD, and that women of color are often at particular disadvantage with respect to safety and securing access to care (Tummala-Narra, 2007). Socioeconomic status has also received very little attention in the trauma literature; however, there is ample evidence that poor women are at high risk for adverse mental health outcomes in general (Belle, 1990). The limited data on trauma among lesbian and bisexual women suggests that they experience childhood abuse, domestic violence, and sexual assault at rates similar to if not higher than heterosexual women; however, these experiences occur in the context of social homophobia, which may include exposure to hate crimes (Balsam, 2003). In regard to culture, it has been reported that women's risk for developing PTSD appears to be more pronounced in societies that emphasize traditional sex roles (Norris, Foster, & Weisshaar, 2002).

Although PTSD remains the most frequently investigated consequence of trauma exposure, women who have experienced chronic interpersonal trauma are also vulnerable to a wide range of other problems, including generalized anxiety, major depression, dissociation, somatization, eating disorders, sexual and interpersonal difficulties, substance abuse, suicidality and self-injury, and increased risk of revictimization (Briere & Jordan, 2004; Herman, 1992; van der Kolk et al., 1996). This complex clinical presentation often requires a multimodal approach to treatment that can be adapted to the needs of individual survivors, and that can evolve over the course of recovery. Community interventions, advocacy, and social activism also play an important role in women's recovery from the violent and traumatic events in their lives.

REFERENCES

Acierno, R., Resnick, H., Kilpatrick, D. G., Saunders, B., & Best, C. L. (1999). Risk factors for rape, physical assault, and post-traumatic stress disorder in women: Examination of differential multivariate relationships. *Journal of Anxiety Disorders, 13,* 541–563.

Balsam, K. F. (2003). Traumatic victimization in the lives of lesbian and bisexual women: A contextual approach. *Journal of Lesbian Studies, 7,* 1–14.

Belle, D. (1990). Poverty and women's mental health. *American Psychologist, 45,* 385–389.

Breslau, N., Chilcoat, H. D., Kessler, R. C., Peterson, E. L., & Lucia, V. C. (1999). Vulnerability to assaultive violence: Further specification of the sex difference in post-traumatic stress disorder. *Psychological Medicine, 29,* 813–821.

Breslau, N., & Davis, G. C. (1992). Posttraumatic stress disorder in an urban population of young adults: Risk factors for chronicity. *American Journal of Psychiatry, 149,* 671–675.

Briere, J., & Jordan, C. E. (2004). Violence against women: Outcome complexity and implications for assessment and treatment. *Journal of Interpersonal Violence, 19,* 1252–1256.

DePrince, A. P., & Freyd, J. J. (2002). The intersection of gender and betrayal in trauma. In R. Kimerling, P. Ouimette, & J. Wolfe (Eds.), *Gender and PTSD* (pp. 98–113). New York: Guilford Press.

Gavranidou, M., & Rosner, R. (2003). The weaker sex? Gender and posttraumatic stress disorder. *Depression and Anxiety, 17,* 130–139.

Herman, J. L. (1992). Complex PTSD: A syndrome in survivors of prolonged and repeated trauma. *Journal of Traumatic Stress, 3,* 377–391.

Kessler, R. C., Sonnega, A., Bromet, E., Hughes, M., & Nelson, C. B. (1995). Posttraumatic stress disorder in the National Comorbidity Study. *Archives of General Psychiatry, 52,* 1048–1060.

Norris, F. H., Foster, J. D., & Weisshaar, D. L. (2002). The epidemiological of sex differences across developmental, societal, and research contexts. In R. Kimerling, P. Ouimette, & J. Wolfe (Eds.), *Gender and PTSD* (pp. 3–42). New York: Guilford Press.

Saxe, G., & Wolfe, J. (1999). Gender and posttraumatic stress disorder. In P. A. Saigh & J. D. Bremner (Eds.), *Posttraumatic stress disorder: A comprehensive text* (pp. 160–179). Boston: Allyn & Bacon.

Seedat, S., & Stein, D. J. (2000). Trauma and posttraumatic stress disorder in women: A review. *International Clinical Psychopharmacology, 15,* S25–S33.

Thoennes, N., & Tjaden, P. (1998). *Prevalence, incidence, and consequences of violence against women: Findings from the National Violence against Women Survey, Research in Brief* (NCJ 172837). Washington, DC: National Institute of Justice.

Tummala-Narra, P. (2007). Conceptualizing trauma and resilience across diverse contexts: A multicultural perspective. *Journal of Aggression, Maltreatment, and Trauma, 14,* 33–53.

van der Kolk, B. A., Pelcovitz, D., Roth, S., Mandel, F., McFarlane, A., & Herman, J. L. (1996). Dissociation, affect dysregulation and somatization: The complexity of adaptation to trauma. *American Journal of Psychiatry, 153*(Festschrift Suppl.), 83–93.

MICHAELA MENDELSOHN
Cambridge Health Alliance

JUDITH L. HERMAN
Harvard Medical School

See also; **Betrayal Trauma; Complex Posttraumatic Stress Disorder; Gender; Rape Trauma; Retraumatization**

WORKPLACE VIOLENCE

Workplace violence is a specific type of aggression consisting of behaviors in the workplace that are physical or physically threatening and may cause physical harm. The most serious form of physical violence is homicide, which is very rare and mostly occurs during armed robberies or other types of crime. A much more frequent form of violence is nonfatal physical violence or threats of violence, which is primarily a problem in jobs where employees are likely to have unpleasant interactions with the public (e.g., patients, clients, customers, prisoners, students).

Risk of Violence

Being subjected to workplace violence involves a complex set of conditions that may include individual, situational, and structural risk factors. Among individual factors are age, gender, education, and training, and also occupational and organizational experience. Especially young employees seem to be at risk and, apart from age, this may also reflect less formal education and/or training and less working experience. More women than men are exposed to violence at work, and most workplace violence is found in jobs dominated by female employees (e.g., nursing, social work, teaching). Prior exposure to violence at work is a potent risk factor that substantially raises the risk of subsequent exposure.

Situational risk factors refer to conditions or circumstances in a working environment and context, such as interpersonal conflicts, having to use force toward a client/patient/prisoner, having close physical contact with people who are impulsive or emotionally unstable, and working with people who are under the influence of alcohol or drugs. Some common structural risk factors for workplace violence include shift-work, working in the evening or at late at night, and working during mealtimes. Research does not reveal a very consistent picture of what may lead to workplace violence due to the complex interplay of both common and atypical risk factors that are often involved.

Consequences

Exposure to violence and threats of violence may have serious acute and long-term consequences for the health and well-being of the exposed employees. The symptoms may be cognitive, such as having difficulties understanding what happened and trouble with concentration, or emotional, such as anger, distress, fatigue, anxiety, fear. Symptoms of PTSD have also been found in victims of workplace violence (Fisher & Jacoby, 1992; Ryan & Poster, 1989; Wykes & Whittington, 1998).

The more frequently an employee is exposed to violence or threats of violence at work, the higher is the risk of long-lasting effects. There also seem to be variations in the way employees react to violence that could be related to the severity of the assault or to subsequently continuing to work in a high-risk environment. Individual differences in how employees perceive and cope with workplace violence may partly explain why some employees develop severe stress symptoms following exposure while others seem to be relatively unaffected. And a threat may very likely be perceived as more severe if the employee has to work with the perpetrator soon after an aggressive, intimidating, or violent interaction.

REFERENCES

Fisher, N., & Jacoby, R. (1992). Psychiatric morbidity in bus crews following violent assault: A follow-up study. *Psychological Medicine, 22*, 685–693.

Ryan, J. A., & Poster, E. C. (1989). The assaulted nurse: Short-term and long-term responses. *Archives of Psychiatric Nursing, 3*, 323–331.

Wykes, T., & Whittington, R. (1998). Prevalence and predictors of early traumatic stress reactions in assaulted psychiatric nurses. *Journal of Forensic Psychiatry, 9*(3), 643–658.

RECOMMENDED READINGS

Hogh, A., & Viitasara, E. (2005). A systematic review of longitudinal studies of nonfatal workplace violence. *European Journal of Work and Organizational Psychology, 14*, 291–313.

Leather, P., Brady, C., Lawrence, C., Beale, D., & Cox, T. (Eds.). (1999). *Work-related violence: Assessment and intervention.* New York: Routledge.

ANNIE HOGH
National Research Center for the Working Environment

See also: Aggression; Occupational Disability

AUTHOR INDEX

Note: * indicates the author of an entry(ies) in this volume.

SUBJECT INDEX